Milwaukee, Wisconsin, USA
March 10–13, 2010

Association for
Computing Machinery

Advancing Computing as a Science & Profession

SIGCSE 2010

SIGCSE'10

Proceedings of the 41st ACM Technical Symposium on Computer Science Education

Sponsored by:

ACM SIGCSE

Edited by:

Gary Lewandowski, Xavier University
Steven Wolfman, University of British Columbia
Thomas J. Cortina, Carnegie Mellon University
Ellen L. Walker, Hiram College
David R. Musicant, Carleton College

Association for Computing Machinery

Advancing Computing as a Science & Profession

The Association for Computing Machinery
2 Penn Plaza, Suite 701
New York, New York 10121-0701

Notice to Past Authors of ACM-Published Articles

ACM intends to create a complete electronic archive of all articles and/or other material previously published by ACM. If you have written a work that has been previously published by ACM in any journal or conference proceedings prior to 1978, or any SIG Newsletter at any time, and you do NOT want this work to appear in the ACM Digital Library, please inform permissions@acm.org, stating the title of the work, the author(s), and where and when published.

ISBN: 978-1-60558-885-8

Additional copies may be ordered prepaid from:

ACM Order Department
PO Box 30777
New York, NY 10087-0777, USA

Phone: 1-800-342-6626 (US and Canada)
+1-212-626-0500 (Global)
Fax: +1-212-944-1318
E-mail: acmhelp@acm.org
Hours of Operation: 8:30 am – 4:30 pm ET

ACM Order Number 457100

Printed in the USA

Cover and Title Page Photo courtesy of Greater Milwaukee Convention & Visitors Bureau.

Message from the Symposium and Program Chairs

Welcome to the proceedings of the 41st ACM Technical Symposium on Computer Science Education, or SIGCSE 2010. Contained within you will find the archival record of over one hundred papers as well as multiple other session formats that change Computer Science education by bringing together researchers, educators, students, tool creators, textbook authors and publishers, and the many other groups that improve learning in our field. SIGCSE 2010 celebrates and encourages the connections we make as we discuss the challenges and excitement of computer science education, which is why this is SIGCSE's thematic year for "Making Contact". We hope the theme also applies as we all return to our everyday activities: maintain contact with the community you create at SIGCSE and make contact with the students whose learning is the heart and end goal of our efforts!

We are pleased to announce the winners of the two annual SIGCSE awards. Sally Fincher of the University of Kent will receive the SIGCSE award for Outstanding Contribution to CS Education, and will provide the opening keynote. Distinguished Professor Peter Denning of the Naval Postgraduate School, Monterey will accept the SIGCSE Award for Lifetime Service to the CS Education Community and speak at our First Timer's Lunch. In addition, we've invited two keynote speakers to discuss the future of pedagogy and technology: Carl E. Wieman—Director of the Carl Wieman Science Education Initiative and Professor of Physics at the University of British Columbia and Director of the Science Education Initiative and Distinguished Professor of Physics at the University of Colorado at Boulder—will give Friday's address on "*Science Education for the 21st Century: Using the Insights of Science to Teach/Learn Science.*" Michael Wrinn—Manager of Innovative Software Education at Intel Corporation—will address Saturday's concluding luncheon on "*Suddenly, All Computing Is Parallel: Seizing Opportunity Amid the Clamor.*"

Symposium statistics are presented below. Many thanks to the authors, reviewers, and Program Committee members whose enormous and vital service generated this program! Special thanks to Tzu-Yi Chen, Birds-of-a-Feather Chair, for creating the new round of "Lightning" BoFs to address compelling, late-breaking topics at the Symposium!

Proposal type	*Accepted*	*Received*	*Acceptance Rate*
Paper	103	303	34 %
Panel/Special Session	24	47	51 %
Workshop	39	86	45 %
Poster	48	88	55 %
Birds of a Feather (pre-Lightning round)	31	42	74 %
Video	11	14	79 %

This year's program includes the usual wide selection of events, including the First-Timer's Lunch and Evening Reception on Thursday and the SIGCSE luncheon on Saturday. We have an immense exhibit hall with even more exhibits than last year! On Wednesday, we have a range of pre-symposium events. We are particularly excited to welcome the AccessComputing Alliance's Deaf and Hard of Hearing Community of Practice to SIGCSE and, with their leadership, to increase accessibility at SIGCSE 2010 for the deaf and hard of hearing. We are also excited about our other pre-symposium (and one post-symposium!) events on AlgoViz, Cloud Computing by Microsoft, Commonsense Computing, the CSTA Source Web Repository, Department Chairs' Issues, Humanitarian Free and Open Source Software, Introducing Computing with Personal Robots, Media Computation, New Educators' Issues, Qualitative Research Methods, and the Software Engineering Disciplinary Commons. During Friday lunch, the UPE will present their annual Abacus Award, with a speech by the awardee. On Saturday, top undergraduate and graduate students will present their work at the ACM SIGCSE Student Research Competition, managed by Ann Sobel.

Our sincere thanks go out to the people who made this Symposium extraordinary. First, the rest of our team: Carl Alphonce, Ruth Anderson, Dennis Bouvier, Dennis Brylow, Tzu-Yi Chen, Lynn Degler, John Dooley, Mohsen Dorodchi, Steve Edwards, Mark Guzdial, Michael Helmick, Lisa Kaczmarczyk, Cary Laxer, Lester McCann, Scott McElfresh, Larry Merkle, Brianna Morrison, Dave Musicant, Kristine Nagel, Jill Pala, Stuart Reges, Susan Rodger, Ingrid Russell, Beth Simon, Laurie Smith King, RoxAnn Stalvey, Lynda Thomas, Kimberly Voll, Henry Walker, and Ursula Wolz. Special thanks to Andrew Kuemmel for filling a new role as "Accessibility Coordinator" on short notice. Lisa Tolles of Sheridan Printing brought all materials together.

In difficult economic times, we extend a *very* grateful thank you to our supporters, vendors, and exhibitors whose participation literally made the symposium possible. Special thanks go to our Supporter/Exhibitor Liaison Susan Rodger (who crafted her own onerous volunteer position) and Dorothea Heck of D. Lawrence Planners for coordinating this massive endeavor.

We reserve a huge thank you for our amazing Platinum Plus supporter, Microsoft!

We also especially thank our Platinum supporters Intel and Google!

Finally, we welcome IBM this year as a Gold supporter!

We received support and guidance from SIGCSE Symposium Site Coordinators Bob Beck and Scott Grissom, SIGCSE President Barbara Boucher Owens, and the entire SIGCSE Board, as well as from Brooke Hardy and Ashley Cozzi of ACM. The City of Milwaukee gave us help at every turn through their excellent Convention and Visitor's Bureau, especially Robert Moore and Kim Brunzelle. We were supported at the Midwest Airlines Center by Shannon Harring and Samantha Catena, at the Hyatt by Aaron Kraemer, and at the Hilton by Gregory Roettgers and Bill Bull.

Special thanks to our home institutions for providing needed resources: the University of British Columbia, Xavier University, Carnegie Mellon University, and Hiram College. We genuinely hope you enjoy the Symposium and find these Proceedings of use for your work now and your future projects and activities.

Symposium Chairs
Gary Lewandowski, *Xavier University*
Steven Wolfman, *University of British Columbia*

Program Chairs
Ellen L. Walker, *Hiram College*
Thomas J. Cortina, *Carnegie Mellon University*

Message from the SIGCSE Chair

Welcome to Milwaukee and the 41st SIGCSE Technical Symposium on Computer Science Education! I am particularly excited by the symposium theme, Making Contact, since SIGCSE is all about building a network of supportive teacher/scholars.

I am delighted at the wealth of pre-symposium activities this year including two SIGCSE Board sponsored roundtables – the full-day roundtable for department chairs and the half-day symposium to mentor recently-hired teaching faculty. There are at least seven other pre-symposium events covering a wide range of topics.

But it is the symposium itself around which the excitement is built. This year's program, with its papers, panels, special sessions, student research competition, supporter sessions, and fantastic speakers, is fabulous. The offerings range from the award presentations, this year to Sally Fincher from Kent University in the UK as outstanding educator and Peter Denning for his lifetime of service, to our guest keynote speakers, to our annual first-timer's luncheon and all the other inspirational activities.

Special thanks to the symposium co-chairs, Gary Lewandowski and Steven Wolfman, and the program co-chairs, Tom Cortina and Ellen Walker, and their excellent committee. Without all the volunteers, folks who submit papers, those who review them and those who make everything come together, we could not have this Symposium. We truly appreciate the contributions of our exhibitors and especially our Platinum Plus supporter Microsoft, our Platinum supporters Google and Intel, and our Gold supporter IBM. Thank you, thank you, thank you.

A word to first-timers – SIGCSE represents a "family" of scholars devoted passionately to the effective teaching and mentoring of computing students. We welcome you to this family and hope that you find ways to become involved for the long-term with us.

Keep in mind our upcoming conferences that include the 15th Conference on Innovation and Technology in Computer Science Education (ITiCSE) that will be in Bilkent, Turkey — June 26-30, 2010. Also, keep in mind the Sixth International Computing Education Research Workshop (ICER) coming up August 9th and 10th in Aarhus, Denmark.

Additional information about SIGCSE can be found on our website at http://sigcse.org.

Barbara Boucher Owens
SIGCSE Chair

Table of Contents

Session 3: Computation and The Sciences

Session Chair: Crystal Peng *(Southwestern College)*

Session 4: Curriculum Design

Session Chair: Yu Cai *(Michigan Technological University)*

Session 5: Panel

Session Chair: Reynold Bailey *(Rochester Institute of Technology)*

Session 6: Panel

Session Chair: Valerie Barr *(Union College)*

Session 7: Special Session

Session Chair: Mark Guzdial *(Georgia Institute of Technology)*

Session 8: Capstones and Professional Development

Session Chair: Peter Froehlich *(Johns Hopkins University)*

Session 9: Upper-Level Courses

Session Chair: Stefan Andrei *(Lamar University)*

Session 10: Concept Inventories

Session Chair: Keith Shomper *(Cedarville University)*

Session 11: Spamming, Hacking, and Social Networks: Themes for Educating the Next Generation

Session Chair: Wayne Summers *(Columbus State University)*

Session 12: Panel

Session Chair: Michael Goldweber *(Xavier University)*

Session 13: Special Session

Session Chair: Scott Grissom *(National Science Foundation)*

Session 14: Special Session

Session Chair: Billy L. Lim *(Illinois State University)*

Session 15: Networks and Security

Session Chair: Dennis Brylow *(Marquette University)*

Session 16: Course Design

Session Chair: Chenglie Hu *(Carroll University)*

Session 17: Coaching and Mentoring

Session Chair: Jan Vahrenhold *(Technische Universität Dortmund)*

Session 18: Tools

Session Chair: William Birmingham *(Grove City College)*

Session 19: Panel

Session Chair: Sally Fincher *(University of Kent)*

Session 20: Panel

Session Chair: Joel C. Adams *(Calvin College)*

Session 21: Special Session

Session Chair: David G. Kay *(University of California, Irvine)*

Keynote Address

Session Chairs: Thomas J. Cortina *(Carnegie Mellon University)*, Ellen L. Walker *(Hiram College)*

Session 22: Philosophy

Session Chair: Valerie Barr *(Union College)*

Session 23: Concurrency

Session Chair: Robert Walker *(Kent State University)*

Session 24: Middle School Issues

Session Chair: Barbara Ericson *(Georgia Tech)*

Session 25: Pairs and Partners

Session Chair: Suzanne Buchele *(Southwestern University)*

Session 26: Panel

Session Chair: Mark Guzdial *(Georgia Institute of Technology)*

Recipients of the SIGCSE Award for Outstanding Contributions to Computer Science Education

1981 **William F. Atchison**, *University of Maryland*

1982 **Alan Perlis**, *Yale University*

1983 **Karl V. Karlstrom**, *Prentice-Hall*

1985 **Elliot I. Organick**, *University of Utah*

1986 **Donald Knuth**, *Stanford University*

1987 **Niklaus Wirth**, *ETH, Zurich*

1988 **Grace Murray Hopper**, *Rear Admiral, USN, Digital Equipment Corp.*

1989 **Edsger W. Dijkstra**, *The University of Texas at Austin*

1990 **Curriculum '68 Committee**: William F. Atchison, Samuel D. Conte, John Hamblen, Thomas E. Hull, Thomas A. Keenan, William B. Kehl, Edward J. McClusey, Silvio O. Navarro, Werner Rheinboldt, Earl J. Schweppe, William Viavant, David M. Young, Jr.

1991 **David Gries**, *Cornell University*

1992 **Daniel D. McCraken**, *City College, City University of New York*

1993 **Alan C. Kay**, *Apple Computer*

1994 **Norman E. Gibbs**, *Software Engineering Institute*

1995 **Robert M. Aiken**, *Temple University*

1996 **Nell B. Dale**, *The University of Texas at Austin*

1997 **Andrew Tannenbaum**, *Vrije University*

1998 **William A. Wulf**, *University of Virginia and National Academy of Engineering*

1999 **Peter J. Denning**, *George Mason University*

2000 **Andries Van Dam**, *Brown University*

2001 **Allen B. Tucker**, *Bowdoin College*

2002 **Elliot Soloway**, *University of Michigan*

2003 **Eric Roberts**, *Stanford University*

2004 **Mordechai Ben-Ari**, *Weizmann Institute of Science*

2005 **Kim Bruce**, *Williams College*

2006 **Richard Pattis**, *Carnegie Mellon University*

2007 **Judith Gal-Ezer,** *Open University of Israel* and **John Hughes**, *University of Technology, Sydney*

2008 **Randy Pausch,** *Carnegie Mellon University*

2009 **Elliot B. Koffman,** *Temple University*

2010 **Sally Fincher,** *University of Kent, Canterbury*

Recipients of the SIGCSE Lifetime Service Award

1997 **Richard Austing**, *University of Maryland*

1998 **Della Bonnette**, *University of Southwestern Louisiana*

1999 **Robert Aiken**, *Temple University*

2000 **James E. Miller**, *University of Southern Mississippi*

2001 **Lillian N. (Boots) Cassel**, *Villanova University*

2002 **Joe Turner**, *Clemson University and Zayed University*

2003 **Harriet Taylor**, *National Science Foundation and Louisiana State University*

2004 **Bruce Klein**, *Grand Valley State University*

2005 **Andrew McGettrick**, *University of Strathclyde*

2006 **Joyce Currie Little**, *Towson State University*

2007 **John Impagliazzo**, *Hofstra University*

2008 **Dennis Frailey**, *Raytheon Corporation*

2009 **Michael J. Clancy**, *University of California, Berkeley*

2010 **Peter Denning**, *Naval Postgraduate School*

SIGCSE 2010 Symposium Committee

Gary Lewandowski, Symposium Co-Chair
Xavier University

Thomas J. Cortina, Program Co-Chair
Carnegie Mellon University

Steve Edwards, Associate Program Chair
Virginia Polytechnic Institute and State University

Stuart Reges, Associate Program Chair
University of Washington

Beth Simon, Associate Program Chair
University of California, San Diego

Laurie Smith King, Panels and Special Sessions
College of the Holy Cross

Ruth E. Anderson, Workshops
University of Washington

Tzu-Yi Chen, Birds-of-a-Feather
Pomona College

Scott McElfresh, Treasurer
Carnegie Mellon University

RoxAnn Stalvey, Student Volunteers and Activities
College of Charleston

Cary Laxer, Registration
Rose-Hulman Institute of Technology

Lynn Degler, Registration
Rose-Hulman Institute of Technology

Henry Walker, Database Administrator
Grinnell College

Lynda Thomas, International Liaison
Aberystwyth University

Susan Rodger, Supporter/Exhibitor Liaison
Duke University

Kristine Nagel, Kid's Camp Coordinator
Georgia Gwinnett College

Dennis Brylow, Local Arrangements
Marquette University

Andrew Kuemmel, Accessibility Coordinator
Madison West High School

Ann Sobel, Student Research Competition
Miami University (Ohio)

Steven Wolfman, Symposium Co-Chair
University of British Columbia

Ellen L. Walker, Program Co-Chair
Hiram College

Mark Guzdial, Associate Program Chair
Georgia Institute of Technology

Ingrid Russell, Associate Program Chair
University of Hartford

Ursula Wolz, Associate Program Chair
The College of New Jersey

Carl Alphonce, Posters
The University at Buffalo

Lisa Kaczmarczyk, Workshops
University of California, San Diego

Dennis Bouvier, Videos
Southern Illinois University - Edwardsville

David R. Musicant, Publications
Carleton College

Brianna Morrison, Student Volunteers and Activities
Southern Polytechnic State University

Larry Merkle, Registration
Wright State University

Michael T. Helmick, Webmaster
Amazon.com, Amazon Web Services

John Dooley, Database Administrator
Knox College

Jill Pala, K-12 Liaison
Girls Preparatory School

Lester I. McCann, Evaluations
The University of Arizona

Kimberly Voll, Kid's Camp Coordinator
University of British Columbia

Mohsen M. Dorodchi, Local Arrangements
Cardinal Stritch University

SIGCSE 2010

SIGCSE 2010 logo designed by Cortny Helmick (cortny.helmick@gmail.com)

CALL FOR PARTICIPATION

SIGCSE 2011: Reaching Out
The 42nd ACM Technical Symposium on Computer Science Education

March 9-12, 2011, Dallas, Texas, USA

http://www.sigcse.org/sigcse2011

SIGCSE 2011 continues our long tradition of bringing together colleagues from around the world to present papers, panels, posters, special sessions, and workshops, and to discuss computer science education in birds-of-a-feather sessions and informal settings at breaks and meals. The SIGCSE Technical Symposium addresses problems common among educators working to develop, implement and/or evaluate computing programs, curricula, and courses. The symposium provides a forum for sharing new ideas for syllabi, laboratories, and other elements of teaching and pedagogy, at all levels of instruction.

We encourage participation that addresses our theme, "reaching out". We need to reach out to colleagues in other fields, to develop interdisciplinary courses and research projects that integrate computer science and other fields, which enriches both. We need to reach out to create programs that attract and educate the next generation of computer scientists, especially currently underserved populations. We need to reach out to policy makers, educating them on the importance and promise of our discipline. Finally, we need to reach out to each other, as always sharing our best ideas and experiences with the SIGCSE community. We invite those interested in computer science education and computer science education research to contribute to SIGCSE 2011.

PAPERS

Papers describe a classroom experience, teaching technique, curricular initiative, or educational research project. Two versions of a submission are required: a full version having author names and affiliations and an anonymous version for use in reviewing. Papers will undergo a blind reviewing process and must not exceed six pages. Authors will have approximately 25 minutes for their presentations, including questions and answers. At least one author of each accepted paper must register and attend the conference to present.

PANELS

Panels present multiple perspectives on a specific topic. To allow each panelist sufficient time to present his or her perspective and still enable audience participation, a panel will normally have at most four panelists, including one moderator. Panel submissions should include a list of the panelists, their affiliations, and a description of the topic, with brief position statements from panelists. Proposals with more than four panelists must provide a statement connecting the extra panelist to the effectiveness of the panel and must convincingly show that each panelist will be able to speak, and the audience able to respond, within the session time. Panel abstracts must not exceed two pages. A panel session is approximately 75 minutes long.

SPECIAL SESSIONS

Special sessions are your opportunity to customize and experiment with the SIGCSE conference format. Possible special sessions include a seminar on a new topic, a committee report, or a forum on curriculum issues. More generally, they must be 75 minutes in length, held in standard conference spaces, and justifiably distinct from the panel, paper, and poster tracks. Within those constraints, the form is yours to design. Special session abstracts must not exceed two pages.

WORKSHOPS

Workshops provide introductory and advanced topics to help make participants more effective teachers and scholars. Workshop proposals (including abstract) must not exceed two pages. Submissions must specify equipment needs (e.g., participant laptops or projector required) and any limitation on the number of participants. Workshops are scheduled for a three-hour session and are offered separately from the technical track session times.

BIRDS OF A FEATHER SESSIONS

Birds of a Feather (BOF) sessions provide an environment for colleagues with similar interests to meet for informal discussions. A maximum one-page description (including abstract) is requested to describe the informal discussion topic. A/V equipment will not be provided for these sessions. Approximately 45 minutes are allocated to each BOF topic.

POSTERS

Posters describe computer science education materials or research, particularly works in progress. Proposals (including abstract) are limited to two pages. Poster demonstrations are scheduled to permit one-on-one discussion with conference attendees, typically during session breaks. Prepared handouts are encouraged in order to share your work.

VIDEO EXHIBITION

Video submissions for the Video Exhibition should demonstrate real or dramatized pedagogical situations or challenges for computer science education. Video submissions that address the theme of the symposium are particularly desired.

IMPORTANT DUE DATES

Friday, September 10, 2010: *Paper, Panel, Special Session, and Workshop submissions*
Monday, November 1, 2010: *Birds of a Feather, Poster, and Video submissions*

PROGRAM COMMITTEE

Association for Computing Machinery
Advancing Computing as a Science & Profession

SIGCSE
ACM Special Interest Group on Computer Science Education

SIGCSE 2010 Board-Sponsored Pre-Symposium Events

New Educators Roundtable

Julie Zelenski, *Stanford University*; Dave Reed, *Creighton University*

The New Educators Roundtable is a half-day workshop designed to mentor college and university faculty who are new to teaching. Participants include tenure-track faculty at institutions where teaching is central, teaching-track faculty and lecturers, and graduate students who currently teach or are looking forward to an academic career. These new educators are brought together with experienced colleagues in a small-group setting to discuss strategies and tactics for successful teaching. Topics include organizing a coherent course, delivering engaging lectures, designing worthwhile assignments, managing course logistics, working well with students, juggling priorities, and more.

Department Chairs' Pre-Symposium Workshop

Sandra J. DeLoatch, *Norfolk State University*; Joyce Currie Little, *Towson University*; Frank Friedman, *Temple University*; C. Dianne Martin, *George Washington University*

The Pre-Symposium Workshop for Department Chairs is an opportunity for all department chairs (experienced and inexperienced) to improve their understanding of their duties and their ability to perform them. Participants also include those interested in becoming department chairs. Four experienced former department chairs serve as resources for the group as the participants review and discuss the duties of the department chair and explore ways that chairs can do their jobs efficiently and effectively. Some specific discussion topics include leadership styles, time management, legal issues, academic program assessment, and faculty promotion and tenure.

Upcoming Events

ITiCSE 2010

Bilkent University
Bilkent, Ankara, Turkey
June 26-30, 2010
http://sigcse.org/ITiCSE2010
Conference Co-Chairs
Reyyan Ayfer, *Bilkent University*
John Impagliazzo, *Qatar University*

ICER 2010
& SIGCSE Doctoral Consortium

Aarhus, Denmark
August 8-10, 2010
http://sigcse.org/icer/2010
General Chair
Michael E. Caspersen, *Aarhus University*

SIGCSE 2011

Dallas, Texas, USA
March 9-12, 2011
http://sigcse.org/sigcse2011/
Symposium Co-Chairs
Thomas J. Cortina, *Carnegie Mellon University*
Ellen L. Walker, *Hiram College*

SIGCSE 2010 Reviewers

Adel Abunawass, *University of West Georgia*
Ernest Ackermann, *University of Mary Washington*
Donald Acton, *University of British Columbia*
Victor Adamchik, *Carnegie Mellon University*
Elizabeth S. Adams, *James Madison University*
Evans Adams, *Fort Lewis College*
Robert Adams, *Grand Valley State University*
Paul Addison, *Ivy Tech Community College*
Iwan Adhicandra, *University of Pisa*
Raul Antonio Aguilar Vera, *Universidad Autonoma de Yucatan*
Shakil Akhtar, *Clayton State University*
Paul Albee, *Central Michigan University*
Vicki Almstrum, *University of Texas at Austin*
Carl Alphonce, *University at Buffalo, The State University of New York*
Jamal Alsabbagh, *Grand Valley State University*
Stefan Andrei, *Lamar University*
Danner Andrew, *Swarthmore College*
Peter Andrews, *Eastern Illinois University*
Steven K. Andrianoff, *St. Bonaventure University*
Karen Anewalt, *University of Mary Washington*
Barbara Anthony, *Southwestern University*
Florence Appel, *Saint Xavier University*
Antonio Araujo, *Faculdade de Engenharia da Universidade do Porto*
Michal Armoni, *Weizmann Institute of Science*
David Arnow, *Brooklyn College*
Charles Ashbacher, *Charles Ashbacher Technologies*
Owen Astrachan, *Duke University*
Pavel Azalov, *Pennsylvania State University*
Mark Bailey, *Hamilton College*
Laura Baker, *St. Edward's University*
Doug Baldwin, *SUNY Geneseo*
Jie Bao, *University of Minnesota*
Catherine Bareiss, *Olivet Nazarene University*
Ian Barland, *Radford University*
David Barnes, *Department of Computer Science, University of Kent*
Tiffany Barnes, *University of North Carolina at Charlotte*
Lewis Barnett, *University of Richmond*
N. Dwight Barnette, *Virginia Polytechnic Institute and State University (Virginia Tech)*
John Barr, *Ithaca College*
Valerie Barr, *Union College*
Joao Barros, *Instituto Politecnico de Beja - ESTIG*
Phillip Barry, *University of Minnesota*
Rebecca Bates, *Minnesota State University Mankato*
Michael Bauer, *University of Hawaii - Leeward Community College*
Jessica Bayliss, *Rochester Institute of Technology*
Robert Beck, *Villanova University*
Byron Weber Becker, *University of Waterloo*
Andrew Begel, *Microsoft Research*
John Beidler, *University of Scranton*
Mordechai Ben-Ari, *Weizmann Institute of Science*
Jens Bennedsen, *Engineering College Aarhus*
Chris Bennett, *University of Maine Farmington*
Joseph Bergin, *Pace University*
Susan Bergin, *National University of Ireland, Maynooth*
Seth Bergmann, *Rowan University*
Mikael Berndtsson, *School of Humanities and Informatics, University of Skovde*
Gian Mario Besana, *CTI DePaul University*
Giovanni M. Bianco, *University of Verona*
Robert Biddle, *Carleton University*
Cathy Bishop-Clark, *Miami University*
M. Brian Blake, *Georgetown University*
Michael Blumenstein, *Griffith University*
Esmail Bonakdarian, *Franklin University*
Chutima Boonthum, *Hampton University*
William Booth, *Baylor University*
Jurgen Borstler, *Umea University*
Matthew Boutell, *Rose-Hulman Institute of Technology*
Dennis Bouvier, *Southern Illinois University-Edwardsville*
Roger Boyle, *School of Computing, University of Leeds*
Stefan Brandle, *Taylor University*
Anna Bretscher, *University of Toronto at Scarborough*
Josef Breutzmann, *Wartburg College*
Monica Brockmeyer, *Wayne State University*
Kim Bruce, *Pomona College*
Renee Bryce, *Utah State University*
Joel Brynielsson, *Royal Institute of Technology*
Suzanne Buchele, *Southwestern University*
Everett Bull, *Pomona College*
David Bunde, *Knox College*
Barry Burd, *Drew University*
Darci Burdge, *Nassau Community College*
Kevin Burger, *Arizona State University*
Debra Burhans, *Canisius College*
Vicky Bush, *University of Gloucestershire*
Greg Butler, *Fort Lewis College*
Anne Cable, *Eastern New Mexico University*
Caldeira Caldeira, *University of Evora*
Mary Elaine Califf, *Illinois State University*
Andre Paul Calitz, *University of Port Elizabeth*
Debra Calliss, *Arizona State University*
Johan Calu, *KHBO*
Mario Camilleri, *University of Malta*
Alistair Campbell, *Hamilton College*
Daniel Canas, *Wake Forest University*
Angela Carbone, *Monash University*
Joao Cardoso, *FEUP/Universidade do Porto*
James Caristi, *Valparaiso University*
Stephen Carl, *Sewanee: The University of the South*
Martin Carlisle, *US Air Force Academy*
Janet Carter, *University of Kent at Canterbury*
Lori Case, *University of Waterloo*
Michael E. Caspersen, *University of Aarhus*
Lillian N. Cassel, *Villanova University*
Tim Chamillard, *University of Colorado at Colorado Springs*
Tat Chan, *Methodist College*
Maiga Chang, *Athabasca University*
Mahesh Chaudhari, *Arizona State University*
Ranjan Chaudhuri, *Eastern Michigan University*
Tom Cheatham, *Middle Tennessee State University*
Hang Chen, *Johnson C. Smith University*
Jimmy Chen, *Salt Lake Community College*

Peng-Wen Chen, *Oriental Institute of Technology*

Tzu-Yi Chen, *Pomona College*

Wei Kian Chen, *Ohio Northern University*

Li-hsiang Cheo, *William Paterson University of New Jersey*

Aswani Kumar Cherukuri, *VIT University*

Chia-Chu Chiang, *University of Arkansas at Little Rock*

Archana Chidanandan, *Rose-Hulman Institute of Technology*

Donald Chinn, *University of Washington, Tacoma*

Mohamed Chouchane, *Columbus State University*

Vincent Cicirello, *Richard Stockton College*

John Cigas, *Park University*

Dawn Cizmar, *University of Texas at Austin*

Michael Clancy, *University of California, Berkeley*

Misti Clark, *Ouachita Baptist University*

Peter Clarke, *Florida International University*

Tony Clear, *Auckland University of Technology*

Daniel Cliburn, *University of the Pacific*

Curt Clifton, *Rose-Hulman Inst. of Technology*

Joe Clifton, *University of Wisconsin, Platteville*

Osvaldo Clua, *Universidad de Buenos Aires*

Porter Coggins, *University of Great Falls*

Avi Cohen, *Ministry of Education*

Ben Coleman, *Moravian College*

Constantinos Constantinides, *Concordia University*

Robert Cook, *Georgia Southern University*

Peter Cooper, *Sam Houston State University*

Stephen Cooper, *Saint Joseph's University*

Jean f. Coppola, *Pace University*

David Cordes, *University of Alabama*

Jose L. Cordova, *University of Louisiana at Monroe*

Marc Corliss, *Hobart and William Smith Colleges*

Lee Cornell, *Minnesota State University, Mankato*

Jill Courte, *Miami University Hamilton Campus*

Mary Courtney, *Pace University*

Michelle Craig, *University of Toronto*

Al Cripps, *Middle Tennessee State University*

James Cross, *Auburn University*

Joyce Blair Crowell, *Belmont University*

Daniela da Cruz, *Universidade do Minho*

Diana Cukierman, *Simon Fraser University*

Jose Cunha, *New University of Lisbon*

Steve Cunningham, *Brown Cunningham Associates*

Edwin P. Curran, *University of Ulster*

Jorge Filipe Custodio, *Faculdade de Ciencias e Tecnologia-Universidade Nova Lisboa*

Robert Cutler, *Tutor Crossing*

Quintin Cutts, *University of Glasgow*

Mohammad Dadfar, *Bowling Green State University*

Roy Daigle, *University of South Alabama*

Nell Dale, *University of Texas at Austin*

Andrew Dalton, *Western Carolina University*

Mats Daniels, *Uppsala University*

Douglas Dankel, *University of Florida*

Wanda Dann, *Ithaca College*

Lawrence D'Antonio, *Ramapo College of New Jersey*

Stephen Davies, *University of Mary Washington*

Janet Davis, *Grinnell College*

Renzo Davoli, *University of Bologna*

Armando De Giusti, *Universidad Nacional de La Plata - CONICET*

Susan Dean, *University of Maryland University College - Europe*

Adrienne Decker, *University at Buffalo SUNY*

Katherine Deibel, *University of Washington-Seattle*

Nicholas DeLillo, *Manhattan College*

Stavros Demetriadis, *Aristotle University of Thessaloniki*

William Denny, *McNeese State University*

Peter DePasquale, *The College of New Jersey*

Dorothy Deremer, *Montclair State University*

Molisa Derk, *Dickinson State University*

Yogesh Deshpande, *University of Western Sydney*

Richard Detmer, *Middle Tennessee State University*

Lucia Dettori, *DePaul University - College of Computing & Digital Media*

Kamyar Dezhgosha, *University of Illinois at Springfield*

Paloma Diaz, *Universidad Carlos III de Madrid*

Martin Dick, *RMIT University*

Suzanne W. Dietrich, *Arizona State University*

Wei Ding, *University of Massachusetts-Boston*

Adair Dingle, *Seattle University*

Zachary Dodds, *Harvey Mudd College*

Ada Dong, *Oakland University*

John Dooley, *Knox College*

Michael V. Doran, *University of South Alabama*

Brian Dorn, *Georgia Institute of Technology*

John Dougherty, *Haverford College*

Maureen Doyle, *Northern Kentucky University*

Peter Drexel, *Plymouth State University*

Robert Duvall, *Duke University*

James Early, *State University of New York at Oswego*

J. Philip East, *University of Northern Iowa*

Jeffrey Edgington, *University of Denver*

Stephen Edwards, *Virginia Polytechnic Institute and State University (Virginia Tech)*

Mary Anne Egan, *Siena College*

Roger Eggen, *University of North Florida*

Kurt Eiselt, *University of British Columbia*

Joseph Ekstrom, *Brigham Young University*

Hala ElAarag, *Stetson University*

Heidi J. C. Ellis, *Western New England College*

Stephanie Elzer, *Millersville University*

Richard Enbody, *Michigan State University*

Alec Engebretson, *Doane College*

Gerald Engel, *University of Connecticut, Stamford*

Eileen B. Entin, *Aptima, Inc.*

Ed C. Epp, *Intel Corp.*

Daniel Ernst, *The University of Wisconsin - Eau Claire*

John Estell, *Ohio Northern University*

Henry Etlinger, *Rochester Institute of Technology*

Sergio F. Lopes, *University of Minho*

Barry Fagin, *US Air Force Academy*

Homma Farian, *State University of New York at Geneseo*

Dave Feinberg, *Carnegie Mellon University*

Alan Fekete, *University of Sydney*

Maria Feldgen, *Universidad de Buenos Aires*

John Fendrich, *Bradley University*

Ernest Ferguson, *Northwest Missouri State University*

Roger Ferguson, *Grand Valley State University*

Joao Miguel Fernandes, *Universidade do Minho*

Francesc J. Ferri, *Universitat de Valencia*
Sue Fitzgerald, *Metropolitan State University*
Robin Flatland, *Siena College*
Rudolf Fleischer, *Fudan University, Shanghai*
Jeffrey Forbes, *Duke University*
Abbe Forman, *Temple University*
Timothy Fossum, *State University of New York at Potsdam*
Kent Foster, *Winthrop University*
Edward Fox, *Virginia Polytechnic Institute and State University (Virginia Tech)*
Susan Fox, *Macalester College*
Charles Frank, *Northern Kentucky University*
Robert Franks, *Central College*
Karen Fraser, *University of Ulster*
Andre Freire, *University of York*
Bill Freitas, *The Lawrenceville School*
Ines Friss de Kereki, *ORT Uruguay University*
S. Jane Fritz, *St. Joseph's College*
Sherri Frizell, *Prairie View A&M University*
Daniel Frost, *University of California, Irvine*
Stephen Fyfe, *Central College*
Angel Garcia-Beltran, *Universidad Politecnica de Madrid*
Alessio Gaspar, *University of South Florida*
Dick Gayler, *Kennesaw State University*
Edward Gehringer, *North Carolina State University*
Edward M. Gellenbeck, *Central Washington University*
Carlisle E. George, *Middlesex University, London*
Jill Gerhardt, *Richard Stockton College of New Jersey*
Judith Gersting, *Indiana University Purdue University at Indianapolis*
Ahmad Ghafarian, *North Georgia College & State University*
Lila Ghemri, *Texas Southern University*
J Paul Gibson, *T&M Sud Paris*
Don Goelman, *Villanova University*
Michael Goldwasser, *Saint Louis University*
Michael Goldweber, *Xavier University*
Evan Golub, *University of Maryland*
Mercedes Gomez-Albarran, *Dep. Ingenieria del Software e Inteligencia Artificial*
Marco Antonio Gomez-Martin, *Universidad Complutense de Madrid*
Pedro Pablo Gomez-Martin, *Universidad Complutense*
Annegret Goold, *Deakin University*
Aaron Gordon, *Fort Lewis College*
Kinnis Gosha, *Auburn University*
Mary Granger, *George Washington University*
Cary Gray, *Wheaton College*
Simon Gray, *College of Wooster*
Jean Greyling, *University of Port Elizabeth*
Larry Griffith, *Westfield State College*
Mario Guimaraes, *Zayed University*
Jiang Guo, *California State University, Los Angeles*
Mark Guzdial, *Georgia Institute of Technology*
Bruria Haberman, *Holon Institute of Technology & The Weizmann Institute of Science*
Hisham Haddad, *Kennesaw State University*
Max Hailperin, *Gustavus Adolphus College*
Susan Haller, *SUNY Potsdam*
Ranette Halverson, *Midwestern State University*
Denis Hamelin, *Ryerson University*
John Hamer, *University of Auckland*
Nadeem Hamid, *Berry College*
Judy Hankins, *Middle Tennessee State University*
William Hankley, *Kansas State University*
Brian Hanks, *Fort Lewis College*
Stuart Hansen, *University of Wisconsin - Parkside*
Charles Hardnett, *Spelman College*
Ronald Harkins, *Miami University*
Mindy Hart, *Purdue University*
Jessen Havill, *Denison University*
Christopher Haynes, *Indiana University*
Carol Hazlewood, *Texas State University*
Orit Hazzan, *Technion – Israel Institute of Technology*
Sarah Heckman, *North Carolina State University*
Phillip Heeler, *Northwest Missouri State University*
Cecily Heiner, *University of Utah*
Rachelle Heller, *George Washington University*
Michael Helmick, *Amazon.com*
David Hemmendinger, *Union College*
Peter Henderson, *Butler University*
Dean Hendrix, *Auburn University*
Tyson Henry, *California State University, Chico*
Matthew Hertz, *Canisius College*
Gregory Hislop, *Drexel University*
Lewis Hitchner, *California Polytechnic State University, San Luis Obispo*
William Hochstettler, *Franklin University*
Mark A. Holliday, *Western Carolina University*
Joe Hollingsworth, *Indiana University*
Ralph Hollingsworth, *Muskingum University*
Geoffrey Holmes, *University of Waikato*
Charles Hoot, *Oklahoma City University*
Cay Horstmann, *San Jose State University*
Hoda Hosny, *The American University in Cairo*
Mahmood Hossain, *Fairmont State University*
Shahadat Hossain, *University of Lethbridge*
Dwight House, *Fayetteville State University*
David Hovemeyer, *York College of Pennsylvania*
Brian Howard, *DePauw University*
James Howatt, *Luther College*
Trudy Howles, *Rochester Institute of Technology*
Michelle Hribar, *Oregon Health & Science University*
Wen-Jung Hsin, *Park University*
Chenglie Hu, *Carroll University*
Meriel Huggard, *Trinity College, Dublin*
James Huggins, *Kettering University*
Janet Hughes, *University of Dundee*
Richard Hull, *Lenoir-Rhyne University*
Dalton R. Hunkins, *St. Bonaventure University*
Frances Hunt, *Educational Testing Service*
Kenny Hunt, *University of Wisconsin - La Crosse*
Steven Huss-Lederman, *Beloit College*
Michelle Hutton, *The Girls' Middle School/CSTA*
Deborah Hwang, *University of Evansville*
Jorge Eduardo Ibarra-Esquer, *Universidad Autonoma de Baja California*
Pourang Irani, *University of Manitoba*
Lubomir Ivanov, *Iona College*
Sridhar Iyer, *Indian Institute of Technology, Bombay*
Jana Jackova, *University of Zilina*
Mark Jaeger, *Baker College*
Richard James, *Rollins College*
David Janzen, *California Polytechnic State University, San Luis Obispo*
Giti Javidi, *Virginia State University*
Carver Jeff, *University of Alabama*
Jam Jenkins, *Georgia Gwinnett College*
Kuodi Jian, *Metropolitan State University*
Mike Jipping, *Hope College*

David John, *Wake Forest University*
Colin Johnson, *University of Kent at Canterbury*
Julie Johnson, *Vanderbilt University*
Kenneth Johnson, *Grand Valley State University*
Bruce W. Johnston, *University of Wisconsin-Stout*
Edward Jones, *Florida A&M University*
Lawrence G. Jones, *Software Engineering Institute, Carnegie Mellon University*
Anthony Joseph, *Pace University*
Mike Joy, *University of Warwick*
Daniel Joyce, *Villanova University*
Maria Jump, *King's College*
Edward Jung, *Rutgers, The State University of New Jersey*
Jorma Kajava, *University of Oulu*
Pankaj Kamthan, *Concordia University*
Debbie Kaneko, *Old Dominion University*
Evangelos Kanidis, *University of Athens / Ministry of Education*
Ville Karavirta, *Helsinki University of Technology*
Elizabeth Katz, *Millersville University*
David Kauchak, *Pomona College*
Amogh Kavimandan, *The MathWorks Inc.*
Amogh Kavimandan, *The MathWorks Inc.*
David G. Kay, *University of California, Irvine*
Jennifer Kay, *Rowan University*
Charles Kelemen, *Swarthmore College*
Thomas Kelliher, *Goucher College*
Andreas Kerren, *Vaxjo University*
Mark Kerstetter, *Western Michigan University*
Sami Khuri, *San Jose State University*
K. N. King, *Georgia State University*
Nancy Kinnersley, *University of Kansas*
David Klappholz, *Stevens Institute of Technology*
Myungsook Klassen, *California Lutheran University*
Frank Klassner, *Villanova University*
Carsten Kleiner, *University of Applied Sciences&Arts Hannover*
Allen Klinger, *University of California, Los Angeles*
Peter J. Knoke, *University of Alaska Fairbanks*
Jane Kochanov, *Pennsylvania State University - Capital College*
Elliot Koffman, *Temple University*
James Kolasa, *Bluegrass Community and Technical College*
Michael Kolling, *University of Kent*
Ari Korhonen, *Helsinki University of Technology*
Yana Kortsarts, *Widener University, Chester*
Janet Kourik, *Webster University*
Nicholas Kraft, *The University of Alabama*
Ray Kresman, *Bowling Green State University*
Joan Krone, *Denison University*
Jan Kruger, *Unisa School for Business Leadership*
Marja Kuittinen, *University of Joensuu*
Amruth Kumar, *Ramapo College of New Jersey*
Deepak Kumar, *Bryn Mawr College*
Durgesh Kumar, *DRDO*
Benjamin Kuperman, *Oberlin College*
Stan Kurkovsky, *Central Connecticut State University*
Zachary Kurmas, *Grand Valley State University*
Reggie Kwan, *Caritas Francis Hsu College*
Brian Ladd, *State University of New York at Potsdam*
Thomas Lancaster, *University of Central England*
H. Chad Lane, *University of Southern California*
Joan Langdon, *Bowie State University*
Yedidyah Langsam, *Brooklyn College of City University of New York*
Mick Lantis, *Purdue University North Central*
Eric Larson, *Seattle University*
Mary Last, *self-employed*
Deirdre Lawless, *Dublin Institute of Technology*
Cary Laxer, *Rose-Hulman Institute of Technology*
Lucas Layman, *Fraunhofer USA*
Alina Lazar, *Youngstown State University*
Christopher League, *Long Island University*
Cathie LeBlanc, *Plymouth State College*
Mark LeBlanc, *Wheaton College*
Arthur Lee, *Claremont McKenna College*
Byong Lee, *Bennett College*
Tony Lee, *Boeing-Integrated Defense Systems*
Noel LeJeune, *Metropolitan State College of Denver*
Chuck Leska, *Randolph-Macon College*
Scott Leutenegger, *University of Denver*
David Levine, *St. Bonaventure University*
Anany Levitin, *Villanova University*
Roy Levow, *Florida Atlantic University*
Scott Lewandowski, *Marietta College*
John Lewis, *Virginia Polytechnic Institute and State University (Virginia Tech)*
Weidong Liao, *Shepherd University*
Billy Lim, *Illinois State University*
Hong Lin, *University of Houston-Downtown*
Janne Lindqvist, *Helsinki University of Technology*
Raymond Lister, *University of British Columbia*
Joyce Currie Little, *Towson University*
Jiang-Jiang Liu, *Lamar University*
Jigang Liu, *Metropolitan State University*
Mei-Ling Liu, *California Polytechnic State University, San Luis Obispo*
Peter Liu, *Seneca College*
Hunter Lloyd, *Montana State University*
William S. Lloyd, *University of West Georgia*
Kate Lockwood, *California State University, Monterey Bay*
Antonio M. Lopez Jr, *Retired*
Amparo Lopez-Gaona, *Professor at Universidad Nacional Autonoma de Mexico*
Salvador Lopez-Mendoza, *Universidad Nacional Autonoma de Mexico*
Joao Lourenco, *Dep. Informatica – FCT / Universidade Nova de Lisboa*
Susan Loveland, *Adams State College*
Joan Lucas, *State University of New York, College at Brockport*
Stephanie Ludi, *Rochester Institute of Technology*
Chris Lueer, *Ball State University*
Geoffrey Lund, *University of Abertay Dundee*
Andrew Luxton-Reilly, *The University of Auckland*
William Lyle, *Murray State University*
Ian Macdonald, *Victoria University*
Peter Macpherson, *Rogers State University*
Joaquim Madeira, *University of Aveiro*
Michael Main, *University of Colorado at Boulder*
David Malan, *Harvard University*
Bill Manaris, *College of Charleston*
Chad Mano, *Utah State University*
Yannis Manolopoulos, *Aristotle University of Thessaloniki, Greece*
Bill Marion, *Valparaiso University*
Kenneth Martin, *University of North Florida*
Manuel Martins Barata, *Instituto Superior de Engenharia de Lisboa*

Bruce R. Maxim, *University of Michigan-Dearborn*
Bruce Maxwell, *Colby College*
Lester McCann, *The University of Arizona*
Robert McCloskey, *University of Scranton*
O. William McClung, *Nebraska Wesleyan University*
Jeffrey McConnell, *Canisius College*
Frank McCown, *Harding University*
W. Michael McCracken, *Georgia Institute of Technology*
Sean McCulloch, *Ohio Wesleyan University*
Chris McDonald, *The University of Western Australia*
Charlie McDowell, *University of California, Santa Cruz*
Scott McElfresh, *Carnegie Mellon University*
Ryan McFall, *Hope College*
James McGuffee, *St. Edward's University*
Hugh McGuire, *Grand Valley State University*
Tim McGuire, *Sam Houston State University*
Dawn McKinney, *University of South Alabama*
Michael McMillan, *Pulaski Technical College*
Bonita McVey, *St. Norbert College*
Pedro Medeiros, *Universidade Nova de Lisboa*
Dee Medley, *Augusta State University*
Lisa Meeden, *Swarthmore College*
Sahami Mehran, *Stanford University*
Gloria Melara, *California State University, Northridge*
Antonio Jose Mendes, *University of Coimbra*
Susan Mengel, *Texas Tech University*
Suzanne Menzel, *Indiana University*
Laurence Merkle, *Wright State University*
Jose Metrolho, *Polytechnic Institute of Castelo Branco*
Timothy Meyer, *Edinboro University of Pennsylvania*
Gail Miles, *Lenoir-Rhyne College*
Bradley Miller, *Luther College*
James Miller, *Bradley University*
James Miller, *University of Alberta*
Keith Miller, *University of Illinois at Springfield*
Joe Miro, *Universitat de les Illes Balears*
Susan Mitchell, *University of Maryland, Baltimore County*
Sriram Mohan, *Rose-Hulman Institute of Technology*
Sara Miner More, *McDaniel College*
Nelma Moreira, *University of Porto*
Ralph Morelli, *Trinity College*
Patricia Morreale, *Kean University*
Briana Morrison, *Southern Polytechnic State University*
Joline Morrison, *University of Wisconsin - Eau Claire*
Judy Mullins, *University of Missouri-Kansas City*
Laurie Murphy, *Pacific Lutheran University*
Michael Murphy, *Southern Polytechnic State University*
Keitha Murray, *Iona College*
Krish Narayanan, *Eastern Michigan University*
Pavol Navrat, *Slovak University of Technology*
Rance Necaise, *Washington and Lee University*
Robert Neufeld, *McPherson College*
Tia Newhall, *Swarthmore College*
Dung Nguyen, *Rice University*
Lijun Ni, *Georgia Institute of Technology*
Delmer Nicholson, *University of Cincinnati*
Jaime Nino, *University of New Orleans*
Daniel Nohl, *Benedictine University*
Robert Noonan, *College of William and Mary*
Cindy Norris, *Appalachian State University*
Linda Null, *Penn State University*
William Oblitey, *Indiana University of Pennsylvania*
Rainer Oechsle, *University of Applied Sciences, Trier*
Chris Okasaki, *United States Military Academy*
Amos Olagunju, *St. Cloud State University*
Joseph Oldham, *Centre College*
Cristovao Oliveira, *Faculdade de Ciencias e Tecnologia / UNL*
Richard Ord, *University of California, San Diego*
Mary Jo Orzech, *The College at Brockport*
Lawrence Osborne, *Lamar University*
Youwen Ouyang, *California State University at San Marcos*
Cherry Owen, *The University of Texas of the Permian Basin*
Barbara Owens, *Southwestern University*
Jill Pala, *Girls Preparatory School*
Greta Pangborn, *Saint Michael's College*
Iraklis Paraskakis, *City College, Intern. Faculty of the University of Sheffield*
Abelardo Pardo, *Carlos III University of Madrid*
Young Park, *Bradley University*
Brenda C. Parker, *Middle Tennessee State University*
David Parker, *Salisbury University*
Jim Parker, *University of Calgary*
June Parsons, *MediaTechnics*
James Paterson, *Glasgow Caledonian University*
Marta Patino, *Technical University of Madrid*
Laurie Patterson, *University of North Carolina Wilmington*
Richard E. Pattis, *University of California, Irvine*
Anand Paul, *National Cheng Kung University*
Thaddeus Pawlicki, *University of Rochester Computer Science*
Ramanee Peiris, *University of Dundee*
Manuel A. Perez-Quinones, *Virginia Polytechnic Institute and State University (Virginia Tech)*
Teresa Peterman, *Grand Valley State University*
Andrew Petersen, *University of Toronto Mississauga*
Chrisila C. Pettey, *Middle Tennessee State University*
Vreda Pieterse, *University of Pretoria*
Paul Piwowarski, *University of Kentucky*
Jennifer Polack-Wahl, *University of Mary Washington*
Shannon Pollard, *Elon University*
Wayne Pollock, *Hillsborough Community College*
Irene Polycarpou, *Colorado School of Mines*
Jeffrey Popyack, *Drexel University*
Lori Postner, *Nassau Community College*
George J. Pothering, *College of Charleston*
John-Paul Pretti, *University of Waterloo*
Roger Priebe, *Texas State University - San Marcos*
Reid Priedhorsky, *University of Minnesota*
Philip Prins, *Seattle Pacific University*
William Pugh, *University of Maryland*
Sarah Monisha Pulimood, *The College of New Jersey*
Tarsem Purewal, *University of Tennessee at Chattanooga*
Atanas Radenski, *Chapman University*
John Rager, *Amherst College*
Noa Ragonis, *Beit Berl Colleg, Technion*
Rajendra Raj, *Rochester Institute of Technology*
Muthu Ramachandran, *Leeds Metropolitan University*

Sita Ramakrishnan, *Monash University*
Bina Ramamurthy, *University at Buffalo, State University of New York*
Eliseo Reategui, *Universidade Federal do Rio Grande do Sul*
Samuel Rebelsky, *Grinnell College*
Michael Redmond, *La Salle University*
David Reed, *Creighton University*
Donna Reese, *Mississippi State University*
Stuart Reges, *University of Washington*
Karen Reid, *University of Toronto*
Margaret Reid-Miller, *Carnegie Mellon University*
Dan Resler, *Virginia Commonwealth University*
Eugene K. Ressler, *United States Military Academy*
Loren Rhodes, *Juniata College*
Catherine Ricardo, *Iona College*
Brad Richards, *University of Puget Sound*
Charles Riedesel, *University of Nebraska - Lincoln*
Suzanne Rivoire, *Sonoma State University*
Steven Robbins, *University of Texas at San Antonio*
Christian Roberson, *Plymouth State University*
Eric Roberts, *Stanford University*
Stefan Robila, *Montclair State University*
Paolo Rocchi, *IBM*
Timothy Roden, *Angelo State University*
Susan H. Rodger, *Duke University*
Ken Rodham, *Brigham Young University*
Guido Roessling, *Technische Universitaet Darmstadt*
John Ross, *Indiana University Kokomo*
Jerry Roth, *Vanderbilt University*
Constantine Roussos, *Lynchburg College*
Martin Ruckert, *Munich University of Applied Sciences*
Anthony Ruocco, *Roger Williams University*
Ingrid Russell, *University of Hartford*
Adrian Rusu, *Rowan University*
Amalia Rusu, *Fairfield University*
Rebecca Rutherfoord, *Southern Polytechnic State University*
Roberta Evans Sabin, *Loyola College*
Shazia Sadiq, *The University of Queensland*
Richard Salter, *Oberlin College*
Samuel Sambasivam, *Azusa Pacific University*
Dean Sanders, *Northwest Missouri State University*
Ian Sanders, *University of the Witwatersrand*
William Sanders, *University of Hartford*
Donald Sanderson, *East Tennessee State University*
Pete Sanderson, *Otterbein College*
Vijayalakshmi Saravanan, *VIT University, Vellore*
Amit Sawant, *NetApp*
Christelle Scharff, *Pace University*
Stephen Schaub, *Bob Jones University*
Diane Schwartz, *California State University Northridge*
Leslie Schwartzman, *University of Illinois Springfield*
Dino Schweitzer, *United States Air Force Academy*
Otto Seppala, *Helsinki University of Technology*
Behrooz Seyed-Abbassi, *University of North Florida*
Christine Shannon, *Centre College*
Stephen Sheel, *Coastal Carolina University*
Victor R.L. Shen, *National Taipei University*
Ching-Kuang Shene, *Michigan Technological University*
Linda B. Sherrell, *University of Memphis*
Angela B. Shiflet, *Wofford College*
Yasuto Shirai, *Shizuoka University*
Scott Sigman, *Drury University*
Gavin Sim, *University of Central Lancashire*
Maria Simi, *Universita di Pisa*
Beth Simon, *University of California, San Diego*
Menaka Sivakumar, *VIT University*
Oberta Slotterbeck, *Hiram College*
William Slough, *Eastern Illinois University*
Peter Smith, *California State University - Channel Islands*
Robert Snapp, *University of Vermont*
Leen-Kiat Soh, *University of Nebraska*
Joel Sommers, *Colgate University*
Sara Sood, *Pomona College*
Raja Sooriamurthi, *Carnegie Mellon University*
Vijayasree Sooriamurthi, *Carnegie Mellon University*
Jonathan Sorenson, *Butler University*
Barry Soroka, *California State Polytechnic University, Pomona*
Jaime Spacco, *Colgate University*
Greg Speegle, *Baylor University*
David Spooner, *Rensselaer Polytechnic Institute*
Carol Spradling, *Northwest Missouri State University*
Denbigh Starkey, *Montana State University*
Lynn Stauffer, *California State University, Sonoma*
Mark Stehlik, *Carnegie Mellon University*
Lynn Andrea Stein, *Franklin W. Olin College of Engineering*
Josh Steinhurst, *Bucknell University*
Daniel Stevenson, *University of Wisconsin - Eau Claire*
Khadija Stewart, *DePauw University*
Evelyn Stiller, *Plymouth State University*
Vojislav Stojkovic, *Morgan State University*
Christopher Stone, *Harvey Mudd College*
Jeffrey Stone, *Pennsylvania State University*
Fred Strickland, *South University*
Catherine Stringfellow, *Midwestern State University*
Lena Stromback, *Linköping University*
Deborah Sturm, *College of Staten Island, City University of New York*
Fred Sullivan, *Wilkes University*
Ken Surendran, *Southeast Missouri State University*
Jerry Talton, *Stanford University*
Joo Tan, *Kutztown University*
Yonglei Tao, *Grand Valley State University*
Michael Tashbook, *State University of New York at Stony Brook*
Blair Taylor, *Towson University*
Carol Taylor, *Eastern Washington University*
James Teresco, *Clickshare Service Corp.*
Allison Elliott Tew, *Georgia Institute of Technology*
William Thacker, *Winthrop University*
Soe Than, *Virginia Military Institute*
Lynda Thomas, *Aberystwyth University*
Megan Thomas, *California State University Stanislaus*
Rebecca Thomas, *Bard College*
Stan Thomas, *Wake Forest University*
Alfred Thompson, *Microsoft*
John Thompson, *Buffalo State College*
Jodi Tims, *Baldwin-Wallace College*
Fergus Toolan, *University College Dublin*
Massood Towhidnejad, *Embry-Riddle Aeronautical University*
Gloria Childress Townsend, *DePauw University*
Quocnam Tran, *Lamar Texas State University*
Christian Trefftz, *Grand Valley State University*
Deborah Trytten, *University of Oklahoma*
George Tsiknis, *University of British Columbia*

David S. Tucker, *Midwestern State Univ.*
Douglas Turnbull, *Swarthmore College*
William Turner, *Wabash College*
Guenter Tusch, *Grand Valley State University*
Sharon M. Tuttle, *Humboldt State University*
Paul Tymann, *Rochester Institute of Technology*
Suleyman Uludag, *The University of Michigan - Flint*
Susan D. Urban, *Texas Tech University*
Timothy Urness, *Drake University*
Jaime Urquiza-Fuentes, *Rey Juan Carlos University*
Ian Utting, *University of Kent at Canterbury*
Ignatios Vakalis, *California Polytechnic and State University*
David Valentine, *Slippery Rock University*
Robert Van Camp, *Marietta College*
Ian van der Linde, *Anglia Ruskin University*
Tammy VanDeGrift, *University of Portland*
Jorge Vasconcelos, *Johns Hopkins University*
Troy Vasiga, *University of Waterloo*
Kam Vat, *University of Macau, Macau*
Steven Vegdahl, *University of Portland*
J. Angel Velazquez-Iturbide, *Universidad Rey Juan Carlos*
Tamar Vilner, *The Open University of Israel*
Vivian Vimarlund, *Linköping University*
Ken Vollmar, *Missouri State University*
David Voorhees, *Le Moyne College*
Paul Wagner, *University of Wisconsin - Eau Claire*
James Walden, *Northern Kentucky University*
Henry Walker, *Grinnell College*
Xinli Wang, *Michigan Technological University*
Yi Wang, *City University of Hong Kong*
Stan Warford, *Pepperdine University*
Richard Wasniowski, *California State University Dominguez Hills*
Thomas Way, *Villanova University*
Scott Weiss, *Mt. St. Mary's University*
Stephen Weiss, *University of North Carolina at Chapel Hill*
Emily Wenk, *Penn State York*
Linda Werner, *University of California, Santa Cruz*
Roger West, *University of Illinois at Springfield*
Curt White, *DePaul University*
Elizabeth White, *George Mason University*
Laurie White, *Mercer University*
Howard Whitston, *University of South Alabama*
Richard Wicentowski, *Swarthmore College*
Michael Wick, *University of Wisconsin - Eau Claire*
Paul Wiedemeier, *The University of Louisiana at Monroe*
Sheila Wiggins, *Morgan State University*
Linda Wilkens, *Providence College*
Judith Williams, *William Penn University*
Linda Wilson, *Texas Lutheran University*
Charles Winton, *University of North Florida*
Michael Wirth, *University of Guelph*
Lee Wittenberg, *GW Software*
Marty Wolf, *Bemidji State University*
Walter Wolf, *Rochester Institute of Technology*
Rosalee Wolfe, *DePaul University*
David Wolff, *Pacific Lutheran University*
Greg Wolffe, *Grand Valley State University*
Ursula Wolz, *The College of New Jersey*
David Wonnacott, *Haverford College*
Karl Wurst, *Worcester State College*
T. Andrew Yang, *University of Houston - Clear Lake*
Arthur Yanushka, *Christian Brothers University*
Sarita Yardi, *Georgia Institute of Technology*
Ken Yasuhara, *University of Washington*
Dowming Yeh, *National Kaohsiung Normal University*
Juang Yih-Ruey, *Jinwen University of Science & Technology*
Duane Yoder, *University of West Georgia*
Benjamin Yu, *University of British Columbia*
Kwok-Bun Yue, *University of Houston-Clear Lake*
Timothy Yuen, *University of Texas at San Antonio*
Marsha Zaidman, *University of Mary Washington*
Carol Zander, *University of Washington, Bothell*
Alan Zaring, *Ohio Wesleyan University*
Julie Zelenski, *Stanford University*
Dean Zeller, *Kent State University*
Uta Ziegler, *Western Kentucky University*
Guy Zimmerman, *Bowling Green State University*
Jill Zimmerman, *Goucher College*
Daniel Zingaro, *University of Toronto*
Fani Zlatarova, *Elizabethtown College*

Keynote Talk

Useful Sharing

Sally Fincher
School of Computing
University of Kent
S.A.Fincher@kent.ac.uk

Abstract

In this talk, I'll explore some of the ways educators share details of their practice and of how they find out "what works" from others. This exploration will include examining some barriers and inhibitors to successful exchange and some thoughts on the importance of representations of practice; that is how we represent our teaching to ourselves, to each other and for posterity.

As part of this exploration, I will present a model of sharing I have devised with Josh Tenenberg, called the Disciplinary Commons: further details of this can be seen at: http://www.disciplinarycommons.org.

Categories & Subject Descriptors: K.3.2 [Computers and Education]: Computer and Information Science Education – computer science education

General Terms: Human Factors

Bio

Sally Fincher is Professor of Computing Education in the School of Computing at the University of Kent where she leads the Computing Education Research Group. Her work is centrally concerned with the teaching and learning of Computing, with particular emphasis on teachers and teaching practices. She has worked on several major computing education projects, such as the Bootstrapping Research in Computer Science Education series, and currently manages the UK "sharing practice" project: http://www.sharingpractice.ac.uk. She is Editor-in-Chief of the Journal *Computer Science Education* (jointly with Laurie Murphy), a UK National Teaching Fellow, a Senior Fellow of the UK Higher Education Academy, a Fellow of the Royal Society of Arts and a Distinguished Scientist of the ACM.

SIGCSE'10, March 10–13, 2010, Milwaukee, Wisconsin, USA.
ACM 978-1-60558-885-8/10/03.

Building Server-Side Web Language Processors

Ariel Ortiz
Information Technology Department
Tecnológico de Monterrey, Campus Estado de México
Atizapán de Zaragoza, Estado de México, Mexico. 52926
ariel.ortiz@itesm.mx

ABSTRACT

This paper discusses some useful insights for instructors who might want to consider using a web approach in courses involving language design and implementation. The basic idea is to have students build a language processor that actually runs on the web, instead of a processor that just runs on a command-line shell. The author documents the advantages and possible shortcomings of this approach, as well as his class experiences.

Categories and Subject Descriptors

K.3.2 [**Computers & Education**]: Computer & Information Science Education—*Computer Science Education*; D.3.4 [**Programming Languages**]: Processors—*Code Generation, Compilers, Interpreters*; C.2.4 [**Computer-communication Networks**]: Distributed Systems—*Client/server*.

General Terms

Design, Languages.

Keywords

Programming Languages, Compilers, Interpreters, Web Development, Web Frameworks.

1. INTRODUCTION

Compiler design courses have been a relevant part of the computer science undergraduate curricula at many universities around the world. Generally, students build a fully functional, yet relatively small, compiler during one semester. This compiler project commonly requires the translation of a subset of a conventional procedural language like C or Pascal. Using specialized tools, such as scanner and parser generators, students develop their translator going through all the well known compiler phases: lexical/syntax analysis, semantic analysis, intermediate code generation, code optimization, and object code generation. At the end, they have a standalone compiler that in general works just like the typical standalone compilers they have used in the past to build typical standalone applications.

In recent years, the software development efforts of many individuals and organizations have shifted from building standalone programs to building web-based applications. An important number of CS courses have been adapted to conform to this shift. For example, a CS1 course might have its students learn the Java programming language by building applets and running them in a web browser. Similar examples can be found in courses such as Operating Systems, Databases, Human-Computer Interactions, Computer Graphics and Software Development. Courses that deal with language design and implementation can also have a web orientation. In this case, students build a language processor that runs on the web.

This paper is a summary of the author's experience on teaching undergraduate students how to build interpreters and compilers that can be integrated into a web environment.

1.1 Why use a web-based approach?

Implementing a web language is not a trivial task. Here are two important reasons that justify this approach:

- **Curriculum organizing principles.**

  In the original CC2001 Computer Science Volume [2] Section 8.2, a number of principles for organizing the curriculum beyond the introductory courses was defined. Two specific approaches are worth mentioning here. To quote:

  > *A compressed approach:* For institutions that need to reduce the number of intermediate courses, the most straightforward approach is to combine individual topics into thematic courses that integrate material from related areas of computer science. ...this strategy also begins to address the problem of classes that focus too narrowly on "software artifacts" ...
  >
  > *A web-based approach:* This model has grown out of a grass-root demand for curricular structures that focus more attention on the Internet and the World-Wide-Web, using these domains to serve as a common foundation for the curriculum as a whole.

  Thus, incorporating web technology and language implementation into a single course could be part of a hy-

SIGCSE'10, March 10–13, 2010, Milwaukee, Wisconsin, USA.

brid curriculum, as described is Section 8.3 of CC2001, that may also meet more effectively the needs of a particular institution.

- **It is relevant and appealing to our students.**

  We can't ignore the fact that many of our CS students will become professional web developers once they graduate. Showing them how the web works from the perspective of a web language implementer gives them a deeper insight of many important technical issues.

  Additionally, as pointed out in [7]: "web programming promotes diversity in computer science because the programs are more motivating to a diverse audience". The author has witnessed that students have a much more engaging learning experience when they develop a web language than when they just build a conventional language translator. This is probably because it is more exciting to see a program running on a web browser than on a command-line shell.

1.2 General Concepts

1.2.1 Language Processors

A *programming language processor* is "... any system that manipulates programs expressed in some particular programming language. Language processors allow us to run programs, or prepare them to be run" [12]. For this discussion, a language processor can be a compiler or an interpreter, or even a combination of both known as an *interpretive compiler*, like those used in most Java implementations.

1.2.2 Runs on the Web

The World-Wide Web is a *client-server* architecture. This means that there are two different physical locations in which a web language processor can run:

Client-side language processors: These run within a user-agent, most commonly a web browser. Possible implementation technologies include: ECMAScript (JavaScript), Java applets, Flash, Silverlight, JavaFX, and plugins for specific browsers.

Server-side language processors: These run on the server computer and somehow interact with a web server. Almost any modern programming environment can be used to develop these types of processors. Section 3 covers three possible implementations.

The remainder of this paper will only focus on server-side technologies.

2. DESIGN CONSIDERATIONS

What specific characteristics must a web language have? Actually, it can be similar to any conventional programming language. However, it is probably best to design a web language so that it has at least a few "scripting" features (for example: compact syntax, dynamic types, garbage collection, and direct support for high level collections such as strings, lists and dictionaries) if one wishes to make it more like the current languages used for web development (for example: JavaScript, PHP, Perl, Ruby or Python). Anyhow, all web specific features can be made available to almost any kind of language through runtime library functions.

The next subsections point out some of the issues worth considering during the design of a web language.

2.1 Overall Syntax

The purpose of a web language is to do some computations and then produce an output in the form of an HTML web page (or XML document, plain text, etc.). This means that a resulting page is built from two types of elements: *dynamically generated elements* and *static content elements*. The overall syntax of the web language should reflect this. There are two possible ways in which these elements can be combined within one source program:

- The presentation code (static elements) can be embedded inside the web language code (dynamic elements), for example:

  ```
  print "<html><body><ul>"
  for i in 0..10 do
    print "<li>" + (2 ** i) + "</li>"
  end
  print "</ul></body></html>"
  ```

  In this example, the `print` statement is used to generate the desired output.

- The web language code can be embedded inside the presentation code. This is known as a *Template View* [6] and it is the preferred notation because of its similarity with the desired output. An example:

  ```
  <html><body><ul>
      {% for i in 0..10 do %}
        <li> {{ (2 ** i) }} </li>
      {% end %}
  </ul></body></html>
  ```

  The delimiters `{{ ... }}` indicate that the surrounded expression should be evaluated and its result displayed as part of the output. The other delimiters `{% ... %}` represent statements that are to be executed for their effect, and don't produce any output by themselves. Everything outside these delimiters is static content, so it is part of the output.

For implementations purposes, the language processor might receive a program like the one in the second example, transform it to something like the first example, and then proceed to execute it. This is actually how JavaServer Pages (JSP) [3] work.

2.2 Hypertext Transfer Protocol

A general understanding of the Hypertext Transfer Protocol (HTTP) [8] is fundamental when designing and implementing a web language. HTTP is a request/response standard between a client and a server. An HTTP client initiates a request by establishing a Transmission Control Protocol (TCP) connection to a particular port on a host computer. An HTTP server listening on that port waits for the client to send a request message. Upon receiving the request, the server sends back a response. This response can be the contents of a static file (like an image or an HTML page), or it can be a dynamically generated resource produced by a web language processor.

2.3 Names and Scoping Rules

Web language applications should have all the request headers and parameters readily available. One option is to provide a library of functions, like `get_header("name")`. Another option is to use a special naming convention. So, for example, if a variable has a dollar symbol prefix, it can represent a request parameter, an exclamation mark prefix could represent a header, and so on. Dealing with the response can follow similar approaches.

It is also important to give some thought on how scoping rules should work. A name with *local scope* can only be used within the procedure that defines it. Alternatively, a name can have a *page scope* (visible in the whole web page or document), *request scope* (visible through several pages chained by the same request), *session scope* (visible throughout the user session), or *application scope* (visible to all the application users). Library functions or naming conventions can also be used to manage names in different scopes.

2.4 Security Issues

A web language should provide a simple mechanism for filtering special characters before sending them as output. If a user input contains the characters `&`, `<`, or `>`, these should be probably replaced by `&`, `<`, or `>` when sending them back as output to HTML and XML documents. Not doing so makes a web applications susceptible to HTML Injection and Cross-Site Scripting (XSS) exploits [11]. Emphasizing these kinds of issues helps promoting security awareness among our students.

A special function can be used when the result of an expression should be filtered within a web program, for example: `{{ filter("some <output>") }}`. Better yet, the default behavior of the pair of braces `{{ ...}}` could automatically do any necessary filtering, while a different pair of delimiters `{! ... !}` could be used when no filtering should be done.

3. IMPLEMENTATION STRATEGIES

To keep things as simple as possible, most of the development and testing of any web language processor should be carried out on a command-line shell, using stubs if required. The integration with a web technology should be attempted only when the main functionality of the language processor is already in place.

For the sake of keeping the following discussions short, the implementation details will assume that the web language processor being developed is actually an interpreter instead of a compiler. Hopefully, the knowledgeable reader should not have any major problem extrapolating the information presented here in order to use it in the context of a compiler or an interpretive compiler.

3.1 Using the Common Gateway Interface

The Common Gateway Interface (CGI) is a simple interface for running external programs under a web server in a platform-independent manner [9]. When a client sends a request, the web server determines if the requested resource is a file stored on disk or an executable program. In the former case, the web server takes the file, pre-appends it with the status line and headers, and sends that as the response to the client. In the later case, the web server runs the executable program as a new process, and whatever output it produces is sent to the client as the response.

Popular scanner and parser generator tools (like *lex* and *yacc*) can be used to build a CGI-based language processor which can be invoked by a web server, such as the Apache HTTP server [1].

Any programming language can be used as an implementation language for a CGI-based web language processor, as long as it is able to:

1. Write to the standard output (to generate the response).
2. Read from the standard input (to read the body of the request).
3. Read OS environment variables (to read the request headers).

The response headers and body are generated by writing the desired information to the standard output. The web server completes the response message by adding the status line and some server specific headers to the start of the CGI output, and sends the entire result to the client.

CGI was the first technique available for generating dynamic content in the World-Wide-Web, dating back to 1993. Its main drawback is that the web server has to create a new process for every request involving a CGI. Process creation is an expensive operation in most operating systems, thus the server performance can be severely affected if many requests arrive during a short time period. This could be a common scenario in a production environment, but in a student project this is probably never the case.

CGI seems an old and low-tech approach, especially when compared to the web development technologies available today. It is important to consider this, because students already familiar with other web tools and techniques might be reluctant to use CGIs. Yet the approach is straightforward, and it allows using all the language construction tools we are all familiar with. CGIs are at least worth considering.

3.2 Building Over an Existing Web Technology

When developing a web language processor, why not use all the infrastructure already available from some existing web technology? For example, JavaServer Pages allow defining custom tags [3]. The body of a custom tag can be any text, including the source code for an arbitrary programming language. Thus, it is possible to have a JSP source file like this one:

```
<%@ taglib prefix="lispish"
           uri="LispishCodeTagLibrary" %>
<html><body>
  <lispish:stm>
    (define fact
      (lambda (n)
        (if (= n 0) 1 (* n (fact (- n 1))))))
  </lispish:stm>
  Factorial of 5 is
  <lispish:exp> (fact 5) </lispish:exp>
</body></html>
```

In the previous example, the `taglib` directive allows importing a tag library referred as `LispishCodeTagLibrary`. All the tags for this library will use "`lispish`" as their prefix.

The `<lispish:stm>` tag executes its body for its side-effects only, while the `<lispish:exp>` tag evaluates its body and writes the result to the output.

These are the general steps to write a JSP custom tag:

1. A Tag Library Descriptor (TLD) file must be created. This is an XML file that contains information about the library as a whole and about each tag contained in the library. The tag declaration inside the TLD file must specify that its body content is `tagdependent` so that the web container (for example Apache Tomcat) treats the tag's body as plain text with no special meaning.

2. A Java class has to be defined, and it must extend the `javax.servlet.jsp.tagext.SimpleTagSupport` class. The class must also contain an overridden `doTag()` method. This method is called automatically by the web container when the tag is to be processed at request time. Inside this method it is possible to obtain the body contents of the tag. At this point, the web language processor can be called to carry out its duty.

The main advantage of using an approach like this one is that the web language processor has access to the all the facilities provided by the hosting environment. Things like session tracking, cookie management, request parameter parsing, header processing, and response generation are typically just a library method call away. On the other hand, the main downside is that you might end up having less options when selecting tools to build a language processor due to the restrictions imposed by the hosting environment. This means that if you want to build a language processor that is available as a JSP custom tag, you can only use tools available for the Java platform.

3.3 Programming Your Own Web Server

This implementation strategy consists of programming a web server from scratch. The web server should be able to serve static resources, but its main function is to host a language processor that allows generating dynamic content.

The server component can be implemented using any language supporting TCP sockets. The language processor should most likely be implemented using that same language.

The following general outline describes how a simple web server with an embedded language processor could work. Assume *SS* is a server socket. Repeat the following steps indefinitely:

1. Listen for a connection to be made to *SS* and accept it. Let *S* be the new connection socket.

2. Serve the request received through *S* using an available or newly created thread:

   (a) If the resource requested is a static resource *Q*, map the file extension of *Q* to its corresponding MIME type so that the correct `Content-Type` header is reported. Add also to the response message the contents of *Q* plus a 200 status code and send it back through *S*.

   (b) If the resource requested refers to a source program *P*, execute *P* using the corresponding language processor and let *O* be its output. Build the response message with *O* plus a 200 status code and send it back through *S*. If *P* produces a runtime error, the response should instead be: `500 Internal Server Error`; send it back through *S*.

   (c) If the resource requested does not exist, the response should be: `404 Not Found`; send it back through *S*.

The main disadvantage of this approach is that practically everything in the HTTP protocol has to be explicitly dealt with: headers have to be parsed, request parameters have to be decoded, errors have to be detected and reported, and so on. On the bright side, implementing a web server gives a tremendous insight on the low-level details of web development.

Having students write a web server from scratch can be deemed as too complex and/or time consuming. A simple way to alleviate this chore is to give students the source code for a simple web server kernel and allow them to extend it in order to incorporate new functionality. Some languages might even have a standard (or third party) API offering some support for building web servers. For example, Python includes the module `SimpleHTTPServer` that provides a basic HTTP request handler mechanism [10].

4. CLASS EXPERIENCE

Since 1998, the author has been sporadically using the described implementation strategies of Section 3 to teach three different courses at the Tecnológico de Monterrey, Campus Estado de México. These courses are part of a nine semester Computer Systems Engineering undergraduate program, which basically blends together computer science with software engineering. The following subsections briefly describe representative project examples for each of these courses.

4.1 Programming Languages

Programming Languages is a 5th semester course focused mainly on teaching different programming styles (functional, logic, concurrent, etc.). It concludes with a brief introduction to language translators. Course prerequisites include Data Structures and Theory of Computation.

Students were once required to write an infix expression evaluator using *flex* and *bison* with C. The evaluator was available through a CGI as described in subsection 3.1. A user interface was provided as an HTML web form containing a text field where the expressions could be typed. When the form got submitted, the CGI was called, and the result was displayed in a new HTML page.

This project was developed in teams of two people, with a time requirement of about two weeks. Almost all of the projects worked flawlessly.

4.2 Language Translators

This is a conventional Compiler Construction course, offered during the 8th semester. It has Programming Languages as its prerequisite.

In one particular semester, the project consisted in writing a compiler that was available as a JSP tag, just like the one explained in subsection 3.2. The compiler was written in Java using the JavaCC scanner and parser generator. It produced Java Virtual Machine (JVM) assembly language code, which was immediately assembled into byte-code. The byte-code was then dynamically loaded and executed by the

JVM, which was also running the web container. All this process was actually orchestrated during a single client request.

This project was developed during a whole semester. Students were allowed to work individually or in teams of two people. The code generation phase as well as the integration into the web container proved to be quite challenging to an important number of students. At the end, about two thirds of the projects worked as expected.

4.3 Software Development Project

This is a 6th semester course that focuses on the integration of the knowledge and skills acquired during the second third of the program through the development of a software-based application. Its prerequisites are: Analysis and Modeling of Software Systems, and Web Applications Development. The project developed during the course can have two orientations: as a computer-science related project (software systems with a specific goal such as translating, searching engines, machine controlling, etc.) or as a Business Information System. The course was introduced into the Computer Systems Engineering program in 2008. At the same time, the Language Translators course was removed.

On one occasion, students were required to develop an MVC (Model-View-Controller) web framework using the Erlang programming language [5]. The view component was developed using *yecc* (an Erlang parser generator) and it was basically a template system inspired by the Django framework [4]. The support for the controller and model components was implemented directly in Erlang. Students also developed their own web server as explained in Section 3.3, taking advantage of the concurrency facilities available in Erlang.

For this full semester project, students worked in teams of three or four members using the Extreme Programming (XP) development methodology. Iterations lasted one week and were closely supervised by the instructor.

All the projects were successfully concluded. Students' feedback was extremely positive. Here are some quotes taken from student surveys:

> In this course I learned how programming languages and compilers work, just like those I've been using since my first semester. It was a good experience as a future Computer Systems Engineer, specially because my program's curricula does no longer have a Compilers course. ...I also learned something vital: the inner workings of the MVC architecture, which is employed in many applications. There's no doubt that I learned a lot thanks to this project.

Another student wrote:

> What I most liked about this project in particular (an MVC framework) was that I was finally able to blend together the things I had learned previously in college. We built an application that allowed us to build other applications! ...

And a last quote:

> ...Definitely, this course exceeded my expectations. It was a course in which I was able to relieve my passion for software development.

5. CONCLUSIONS

It is possible to incorporate successfully a web-based approach into courses involving language design and implementation. For the author, the best results were obtained in the Software Development Project, but it is important to note that other factors, such as the use of XP, also influenced the outcome.

When using a web-based approach in more traditional courses, such as Programming Languages and Compiler Construction, the main drawback experienced by the author is that additional material needs to be presented to students. This material can be lectured in as little as one or two weeks out of a 16 week semester. It is more work for the students and the instructor, but the results are very rewarding.

Complete source code examples for the implementation strategies of Section 3 are freely available for any one to use and modify at: `http://weblang.arielortiz.com/`

6. REFERENCES

[1] The Apache Software Foundation. *The Apache HTTP Server Project.* http://httpd.apache.org/ Accessed November 7, 2009.

[2] CC2001. *Computing Curricula 2001: Computer Science Volume.* ACM/IEEE Joint Task Force on Computing Curricula, 2001.

[3] K. Chung and J. Luehe. *JSR 245: JavaServer Pages Specification, Version 2.1.* Sun Microsystems, 2009. http://jcp.org/en/jsr/detail?id=245 Accessed November 7, 2009.

[4] Django Software Foundation. *The Django Framework.* http://www.djangoproject.com/ Accessed November 7, 2009.

[5] Ericsson AB. *Open Source Erlang.* http://www.erlang.org/ Accessed November 7, 2009.

[6] M. Fowler, D. Rice, M. Foemmel, E. Hieatt, R. Mee, and R. Stafford. *Patterns of Enterprise Application Architecture.* Addison-Wesley Professional, 2002.

[7] J. Miller. (jessica.k.miller@gmail.com) (March 26, 2009). *SIGCSE 2009 Web Programming Recap and Welcome to New Mailing List Members.* Email to: Webdev mailing list (webdev@cs.washington.edu).

[8] Network Working Group. *RFC 2616: Hypertext Transfer Protocol – HTTP/1.1,* 1999. http://tools.ietf.org/html/rfc2616 Accessed November 7, 2009.

[9] Network Working Group. *RFC 3875: The Common Gateway Interface (CGI) Version 1.1,* 2004. http://tools.ietf.org/html/rfc3875 Accessed November 7, 2009.

[10] Python Software Foundation. *Simple HTTP request handler,* 2009. http://docs.python.org/library/simplehttpserver.html Accessed November 7, 2009.

[11] J. Rafail. *Cross-Site Scripting Vulnerabilities.* CERT Coordination Center, Carnegie Mellon University, 2001.

[12] D. Watt and D. Brown. *Programming Language Processors in Java: Compilers and Interpreters.* Prentice Hall, Harlow, England, 2000.

MieruCompiler: Integrated Visualization Tool with "Horizontal Slicing" for Educational Compilers

Katsuhiko Gondow
Tokyo Institute of Technology
gondow@cs.titech.ac.jp

Naoki Fukuyasu
Wakayama University
fukuyasu@sys.wakayama-u.ac.jp

Yoshitaka Arahori
Tokyo Institute of Technology
arahori@sde.cs.titech.ac.jp

ABSTRACT

This paper proposes a novel visualization tool for educational compilers, called MieruCompiler. Educational compilers that generate native assembly code like i386 have many practical and pedagogical advantages, but they also have a disadvantage that the undergraduate students need to acquire a wide range of knowledge on native machine instructions, assembly directives, application binary interface (ABI), and so on. To reduce this learning cost, MieruCompiler provides various visualizations as a rich internet application (RIA) including: (1) highlighting all related slices (called "horizontal slicing" after [13], but not implemented in [13]) among the source code, abstract syntax tree, assembly code, symbol table, stack layout and compiler code, when the user hovers the mouse pointer over a piece of them, (2) displaying tooltips for machine instructions, assembly directives, etc., and (3) visualizing stack layouts which are very likely to be implicit. As a preliminary evaluation, MieruCompiler was used in two universities, which produced promising results.

Categories and Subject Descriptors

K.3 [**Computers and Information Science Education**]: Computer Science Education.

General Terms

Design, Languages

Keywords

Compiler course, Code Generation, Visualization, Program Understanding, Rich Internet Application (RIA)

1. INTRODUCTION

For computer science undergraduate students (students for short), compiler courses are common and important at most universities [1, 2]. In the compiler courses, educational compilers are often used to provide hands-on experience through compiler construction. PL/0 compiler [14] is a popular classical educational compiler, and many other educational compilers have been proposed so far [15–18].

SIGCSE'10, March 10–13, 2010, Milwaukee, Wisconsin, USA.

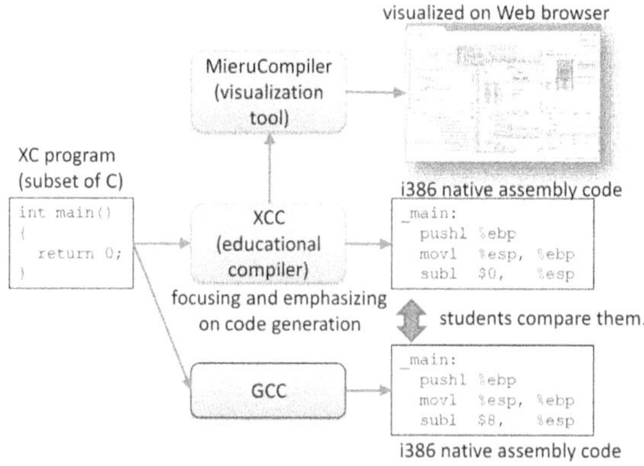

Figure 1: Overview of our approach

They are classified into two types according to the generated code. One is a *native compiler* that generates native machine code or native assembly code, and the other one is a *non-native compiler* that generates virtual machine code (or bytecode). Although both types have their own advantages and disadvantages, we argue that native compilers are more pedagogically effective than non-native compilers (see Section 2.1 for details).

Although there are many important advantages in native educational compilers, the most difficult problem in the native compiler approach is that the learning cost is greatly increased. To solve this problem, we took the following approach depicted in Fig. 1 (Section 2.2).

- We carefully defined a source language (called XC) of our own educational compiler (called XCC) as a strict syntactic *subset* of the C programming language [22].
- We emphasize and focus on *code generation*, but not on parsing and optimization.
- We provide a *visualization* tool (called MieruCompiler) for better understanding of the educational compiler and knowledge on i386 instructions, etc.

XC is a compact language while preserving the high expressive power (Section 3.1). XCC is our educational compiler, which translates an XC program into i386 or MIPS assembly code (Section 3.2). Since XC is a subset of C, real-world C compilers like GCC can compile any XC program. This means the students can compare the two versions of native assembly code; one is generated by XCC, and the other by GCC. This has a great benefit in compiler courses, since the students practically know what code should be generated and what alternatives there are.

Here by "code generation" we mean the direct translation from source code to native assembly code (`.s` file) without using intermediate code. Fig. 2 shows an example of our "code generation."

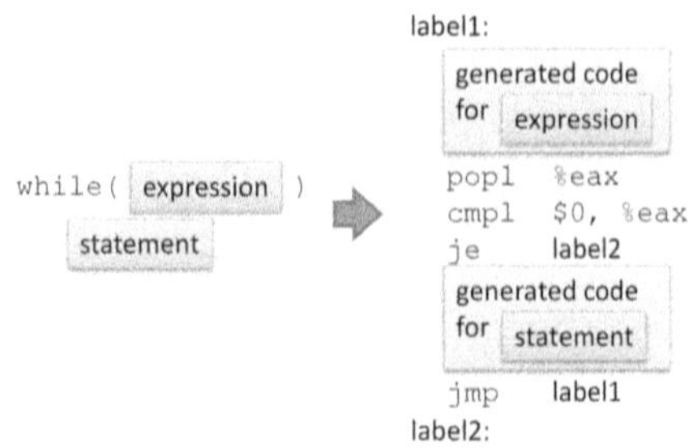

Figure 2: Example of code generation (i386 assembly code for `while` statement)

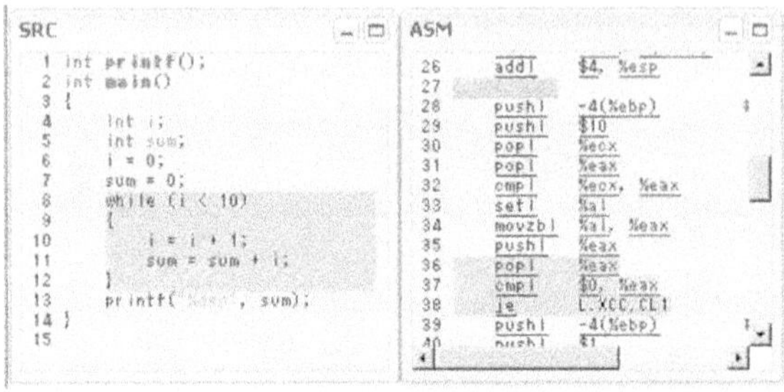

Figure 3: Example of "horizontal slicing" (a `while` statement and its corresponding assembly code are highlighted)

Thus our term "code generation" corresponds to "intermediate-code generation" in compiler textbooks [4]. A `.s` file generated by our educational compiler XCC can be assembled and linked into `a.out` file, for example, by GCC.

MieruCompiler[1] is our integrated visualization tool with "horizontal slicing." MieruCompiler statically visualizes the source code, assembly code, abstract syntax tree (AST), compiler code[2], symbol table and stack layout in XCC. By "horizontal slicing" [13], we mean highlighting all related slices from any selected piece. As shown in Fig. 3, for example, the corresponding assembly code (Fig. 3, right) is highlighted when selecting a `while` statement (Fig. 3, left). "Horizontal slicing" is bidirectional; not only what are generated from the selected piece, but also what generated the selected piece are highlighted. For example, when selecting a `cmpl` instruction in the assembly code, the corresponding `while` statement in the source code will be highlighted.

Our major contribution in this paper is two fold:

- We have proposed and implemented a novel visualization tool called MieruCompiler for our educational compiler XCC. MieruCompiler is integrated and has a feature of "horizontal slicing." As mentioned in Section 5, [13] introduced the term "horizontal slicing", but did not implemented it in [13]. The source code of XCC and MieruCompiler is freely available on `http://www.sde.cs.titech.ac.jp/~gondow/MieruCompiler/`.
- We show valuable educational experiences obtained through the projects where 15 students in two universities developed (a part of) code generator in XCC using MieruCompiler.

The rest of this paper is organized as follows. Section 2 discusses the native compiler approach. Section 3 describes our XC, XCC and MieruCompiler. Section 4 gives a preliminary evaluation. Section 5 describes related work. Finally, Section 6 gives the conclusion.

[1] *Mieru* means "visible" in Japanese.

[2] The compiler code in MieruCompiler can be hidden by option for educational purpose.

2. NATIVE COMPILER APPROACH

2.1 Why native compiler approach is better

We argue that native compilers are more pedagogically effective than non-native compilers because of the following reasons:

- Generating native (i.e., real) assembly code motivates students to learn whatsoever are required in developing educational compilers, which results in a high learning effect. The reasons for this tendency are (probably) because:
  - Knowledge and experiences obtained from real assembly code will be widely applicable for many other areas including embedded systems, computer architectures, and operating systems. Also they are extensible in the sense that further learning leads students to more advanced topics like real compilers (eg., GCC) and techniques on JIT compilers or optimizers.
  - Real assembly code is complex as a result of satisfying real-world constraints and requirements, so learning real assembly code is simply interesting and challenging for students; it is just a kind of happy hacking.
  - In some senses, virtual machines are *imitations*, which demotivates students to learn them. For example, most native machines are register-based, while most virtual machines are stack-based. There are many differences and gaps in design decisions on real CPU instruction sets and virtual ones. Furthermore, real CPU instruction sets cannot be modified, while most virtual ones can be easily modified. A mission of real-world compiler is to generate low-level code using a *fixed* instruction set, but this does not often hold true for non-native compilers.
- By comparing the two versions of native assembly code: one generated by *real-world* compilers (eg., GCC) and the other generated by the *educational* compiler, students practically know what code should be generated and what alternatives there are. Even if the technique mentioned in [12] is used, it is still quite difficult for students to understand the internal data structures of real-world compilers. On the other hand, it is not so difficult for students to understand the assembly code generated by GCC.

  For this purpose, it is desirable that a source language of the educational compiler is a strict syntactic subset of the existing programming language (eg., C), to make it possible to compare different results for the same source program. This is the reason why XC is a subset of C.
- There are many high quality documents (eg., [20, 23]) and tools (eg., GCC and GNU Binutils) for real machines, while not for most virtual machines[3].
- Library functions (eg., `printf` in the C standard library) can be directly called from the source program, if the educational compiler conforms to the application binary interface (ABI). This is the case for XCC.

  This widens the application area written in the source code of the educational compiler, and gives another reality to the students.

[3] The only exception that we know is Java Virtual Machine (JVM).

2.2 Problems in native compiler approach and our solutions

As mentioned in Section 2.1, there are many important advantages in native educational compilers. Unfortunately, however, the most difficult problem in the native compiler approach is that the learning cost is greatly increased, since students need to acquire a wide range of knowledge on native machine instructions, assembly directives, application binary interface (ABI), and so on. Moreover, data structures for AST, symbol table, and type representation are difficult for students to understand and implement.

To solve these problems while preserving the good essence of the native compiler approach, we took the following three ways:

- We carefully defined the source language of our own educational compiler as a strict syntactic subset of the C programming language, which has the following benefits:

    - This saves the time spent in teaching the syntax and semantics of the source language, since the instructors only have to explain the syntactic difference from C.
    - This helps students more deeply understand the C semantics, for example, about "left-to-right evaluation" [22] in `&&` and `||` operators, pointer arithmetic in `+` and `-` operators, the difference between "call by value" and "call by reference", and the lifetime of automatic variables. This is required to preserve the meaning of the source program being compiled, which is a very basic compiler's mission.

    Note that PL/0 [14], for example, is not a syntactic subset of Pascal, even though PL/0 is a simplified version of Pascal. For example, no type is specified in PL/0 (`var i;`), while a type is always specified in Pascal (`var i:  integer`). This implies Pascal compilers cannot compile PL/0 programs, while C compilers can always compile any XC program without modification.

- We emphasize and focus on code generation, but not on parsing and optimization.

    For example, we would like to put more emphasis on how to translate a `while` statement into i386 assembly code in Fig. 2 than on parsing and optimization. This is because in our opinion the most important thing is, for example, to teach a `while` statement can be implemented by combining a conditional branch (`je` in Fig. 2) and an unconditional branch (`jmp` in Fig. 2).

    Parsing techniques are often emphasized in compiler courses, since LALR parser generator is regarded as a great victory in computer science (eg., in [19]). Unfortunately, LALR parser generator is not the best solution. The grammar and action rules by GNU Bison (an LALR parser generator) are often complicated, since some *kludges* using "Actions in Mid-Rules", etc. are required to handle context dependencies [21]. As a result, the parsers in GCC-3.4 and later are changed to hand-written recursive descent one, while the parser in old GCC was implemented by GNU Bison.

    In order to avoid the tedious kludges and to maximize the time for the students to concentrate on code generation, we decided to use the strategy of providing to the students the source code of the XCC front-end (scanner, parser and semantic analyzer) and course materials that explain how to access the AST, symbol table, etc. in the XCC front-end.

    Optimization plays a great important role in compiler systems. For a first course in compiler construction, however, optimization is too complicated for the students to understand and implement. For this reason, our educational compiler XCC only uses a very naive register allocation method where general-purpose registers are used as a part of stack frame. This keeps XCC very compact.

- We provide a visualization tool for better understanding.

    As mentioned before, in native compiler approach, the students need to understand native machine instructions, assembly directives, and internal data structures in the educational compiler itself. The cost of learning and understanding them is very high. There is a limit to reduce the cost by enriching the course materials, or by improving the source code using software engineering techniques (eg., modularization and refactoring). Using a debugger (eg., GDB), students can examine the internal data structures, but they often get lost in the AST with hundreds of nodes. Also, technical documents tend to be large (eg., [20] has about 3,000 pages), so students often get lost in those large documents.

    Therefore, we provide a visualization tool to solve this problem, which includes:

    - (1) Highlighting "horizontal slices", that is, all related slices among the source code, assembly code, AST, symbol table, stack layout and compiler code.
    - (2) Interactive tooltips[4] that explain machine instruction mnemonics, assembly directives, fundamental architecture components like registers, etc.
    - (3) Visualization of the AST, symbol table and stack layout.

    This visualization tool is implemented as a rich internet application (RIA), which implies that students do not have to install it.

3. XCC AND MieruCompiler DETAILED

3.1 XC

XC is a very compact language while preserving the high expressive power. XC has only 57 grammar rules in GNU Bison, while C has about 200 ones. XC has most features of C including types (eg., `int`, `char`, `void`, function types, pointer types), operators (eg., `=`, `||`, `&`, `*`, `+`), control structures (eg., `if-else`, `while`, `goto`, `return`), and function (calls) with parameters.

In XC, we eliminated most features that have alternative ways to write. For example, XC does not have the array operator (`[]`), but as a substitute for it, we can use `malloc` and pointer arithmetic in XC. For `int a[10]; a[3]=5;` in C, we can write `int *a; a=malloc(40); *(a+3)=5;` in XC.

3.2 XCC

XCC is the educational compiler we developed; XCC translates an XC program into native assembly code (i386 and MIPS assembly code for now[5]). To keep XCC simple, XCC does not have intermediate code nor optimizers. The code size of XCC for i386 is about 2,100 lines in C, GNU Bison and GNU Flex. So far, the projects using XCC have been conducted in Japan Advanced Institute of Science and Technology (JAIST) in 2000, in Tokyo Institute of Technology from 2003 through 2009, and in Wakayama University in 2009.

3.3 MieruCompiler

MieruCompiler is our integrated visualization tool with "horizontal slicing." MieruCompiler statically visualizes the source code (XC), assembly code (i386 and MIPS), AST, compiler code (optional), symbol table and stack layout in XCC.

[4]Tooltip is a small message window appearing when the user hovers the mouse pointer over an item, without clicking it.

[5]XCC was originally developed to generate SPARC assembly code, but SPARC is not supported in the current XCC.

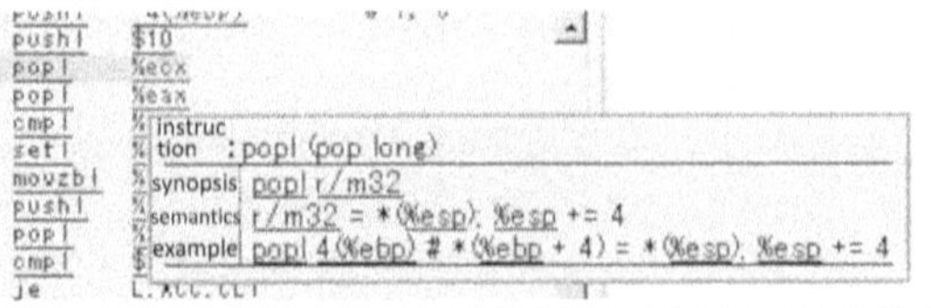

Figure 4: Example of tooltips in MieruCompiler (a tooltip for `popl` instruction appearing [6])

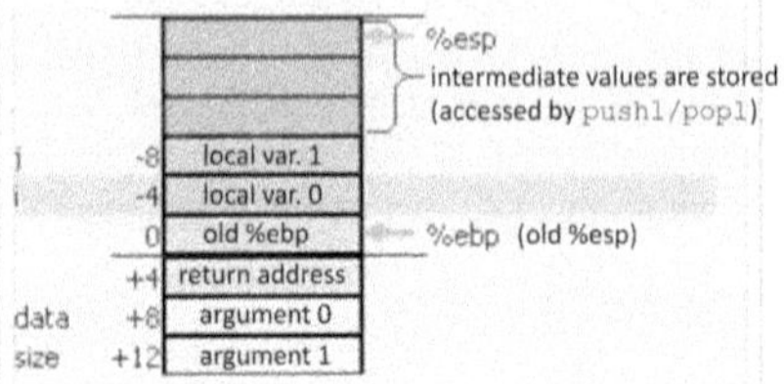

Figure 5: Example of stack layouts in MieruCompiler (local variable `i` is highlighted)

3.3.1 Visualization in MieruCompiler

As mentioned in Section 1, MieruCompiler provides a mechanism of "horizontal slicing." As an example of "horizontal slicing", in Fig. 3, the corresponding assembly code is highlighted when selecting a `while` statement. Note that all the other related slices in the AST, compiler code, symbol table and stack layout are also highlighted in MieruCompiler, but they are not shown in Fig. 3 for the lack of space.

Fig. 4 shows an example of tooltips in MieruCompiler, which shows a compact description about i386 `popl` instruction (its format, semantics and usage example). In MieruCompiler, a tooltip will appear when the user hovers the mouse pointer over machine instructions, assembly directives (eg., `.text`), register names (eg., `%esp`) and any form of addressing mode (eg., `4(%ebp)` and `r/m32`) in assembly code and other tooltips. Note that MieruCompiler tooltips can be nested; the first tooltip contains many items which show a second tooltip. Thus the user can see two or more tooltips simultaneously by hovering the mouse pointer over several items successively.

Fig. 5 shows an example of the stack layout visualized in MieruCompiler, which shows that, from the bottom to the top, the stack consists of two arguments (`size` and `data`), a return address, an old value of `%ebp` pointed by `%ebp`, two local variables (`i` and `j`), and other intermediate values unknown at compile-time; and the stack top is pointed by `%esp`. This graphical information about the stack layouts is quite important to help the students to map a local variable or function argument to its corresponding location on the stack relative to the base pointer (`%ebp` for i386). This is necessary because application binary interface (ABI), including calling convention, alignment constraints and stack layouts, is often implicit and not clear, and thus ABI should be explicitly and compactly (i.e., graphically) provided.

3.3.2 Design and Implementation

The code size of MieruCompiler is about 6,500 lines in C, GNU Flex and JavaScript (including JSON data files). JSON data files have all the data required by the MieruCompiler tooltips. As a GUI toolkit for Web browsers, we use ExtJS 2.2.

MieruCompiler is implemented as a rich internet application (RIA), which implies no installation procedure is required. Moreover, MieruCompiler is easy for the students to use, since it runs on Web browsers like Firefox and Google Chrome.

[6]Slightly modified for presentation purpose. Some descriptions in MieruCompiler are localized (i.e., Japanese is used) considering that most our undergraduate students are not good at English.

```
static void emit_code (struct AST *ast, char *fmt, ...) {
    va_list  argp;
    va_start (argp, fmt);
    vfprintf (fp, fmt, argp); /* fp is a global variable. */
    va_end   (argp);
}
```

```
#define emit_code(ast, fmt, ...)                              \
      emit_code(ast, "%s_%d,%s,%d," fmt, ast->ast_type,      \
      ast->ast_nth, __FILE__ , __LINE__, ##__VA_ARGS__)
```

Figure 6: The macro `emit_code` for minimal modification

We needed to modify XCC so that MieruCompiler can obtain data being visualized from XCC. One important design policy is to minimize this modification to XCC, which is required because it becomes much difficult for the students to understand the XCC source code if XCC is heavily modified.

Although we cannot go into detail for the lack of space, we achieved this goal; only 5 manual source code instrumentations to XCC were required, whose total code size is only 15 lines. One way we took is to define a macro `emit_code` (Fig. 6, bottom) to transparently override the original function `emit_code` (Fig. 6, top). The function `emit_code` is just a wrapper function of `printf` with an extra parameter `ast` for debugging purpose. The macro `emit_code` is recursively defined, but this works well since the C standard guarantees to expand a recursive macro only once (6.10.3.4 in [22]).

4. PRELIMINARY EVALUATION

In this section, we discuss our experience using XCC and MieruCompiler in Tokyo Institute of Technology and Wakayama University. 15 students tried to implement (a part of) code generator for i386 architecture using XCC and MieruCompiler. The student skills vary widely from a student with no experience on compiler to a student with experience on developing PL/0 compiler. At the beginning of the projects, we gave the source code of XCC front-end to the students. XCC and MieruCompiler were well received by most our students.

4.1 Experience on XCC

The following are comments from the students.

- XCC is suitable for learning a foundation of i386 assembly language programming.
- It is good that after the projects XCC gives other advanced exercises for eager students like implementing optimizers (register allocation in particular) and their own front-end.
- XCC gave me a new point of view for programming through understanding XCC's AST and compilation mechanism.
- It is not clear for me to what extent XCC's semantic analysis is done in the given front-end. (eg., in XCC, a type analysis is done, but no analysis on L-value and R-value is done.)
- XCC is difficult for less experienced students. Simpler compiler projects might be better for them using a simpler source language with basic operators, control structures (eg., `if` and `while`) and no functions; and a simpler virtual machine code like P-code.

4.2 Experience on MieruCompiler

The following are comments from the students.

- "Horizontal slicing" in MieruCompiler enables me to quickly understand the corresponding i386 assembly code when pointing at a code fragment of XCC, and thus it is quite useful. Stack layouts shown in MieruCompiler are also useful.

- Tooltips are popped up in MieruCompiler when pointing at a code fragment of i386 assembly code. This immediately reminds me of its meaning. Thus the tooltips are quite useful since the i386 addressing mode is complex in particular.

- I did not use the visualization mechanism at all. (Note: he is a relatively experienced student.)

- More detailed information should be provided in MieruCompiler, for example, about all members in AST (`struct AST`) and types (`struct Type`).

- I want MieruCompiler to provide a comprehensive tutorial and reference for i386 assembly language programming, since tooltips are not enough for less experienced students to learn i386 from the scratch.

5. RELATED WORK

To our knowledge, there are no ones available on the Internet that have the same concept as XCC and MieruCompiler, although many educational compilers/visualizers have been proposed so far.

5.1 Educational compilers

Unexpectedly, there are few educational compilers that have all the following features, (1) which generate native code, (2) whose source language is a strict syntactic subset of real-world procedural programming languages like C, (3) which have an integrated visualization tool with "horizontal slicing."

PL/0 [14] do not generate native code, and the source language is not a subset of real-world procedural languages. [15] generate native code, but their source languages are not a subset of real-world procedural languages. Conversely, [16]'s source language are a subset of real-world procedural languages, but they do not generate native code.

MiniJava [3], Cool [15] and Bantam Java [17] are educational compilers whose source languages are object-oriented. Although the features in object-oriented languages like information hiding or inheritance are very important, but we believe that they are too difficult for undergraduate students to learn in a first compiler course.

All the above do not have an integrated visualization tool with "horizontal slicing."

5.2 Visualization tools for compilers

Many visualization tools have been proposed so far, but most of them are point solutions and thus not integrated. For example, many tools have a specific feature like visualizing only parsing [5]ĄC AST [6]ĄC assembly code [7]ĄC symbol tables [8]ĄC optimizers [9]ĄC compiler behaviors [10, 11]ĄD

Only the UW illustrated compiler [13] provides an integrated visualization for the scanner, parser, PL/0 source code, generated P-code, AST, the runtime stack, etc. [13] mentioned that "horizontal slicing" is important, but it is not implemented due to the following reason:

> *There is nothing intrinsically difficult about implementing this slicing but maintaining the maps between IRs, including the graphical display of the IRs, was too complex for our implementation.*

To our knowledge, there are no visualization tools that provide "horizontal slicing" even at present, while MieruCompiler provides an integrated visualization with "horizontal slicing."

6. CONCLUSION

This paper proposes a novel visualization tool called MieruCompiler and an educational compiler called XCC for undergraduate students. To reduce the learning cost of XCC, MieruCompiler provides visualizations for (1) "horizontal slicing", (2) tooltips for native machine instructions, etc., (3) stack layouts, etc. XCC and MieruCompiler support native code generation for students in a first compiler course without sacrificing their learning experience. As a preliminary evaluation, MieruCompiler was used in two universities, which produced promising results.

7. REFERENCES

[1] Association for Computing Machinery and IEEE Computer Society, Computer Science Curriculum Update 2008, `http://www.acm.org/education/curricula/ComputerScience2008.pdf`, 2008.

[2] Saumya Debray, Making compiler design relevant for students who will (most likely) never design a compiler, Proc. 33rd SIGCSE tech. sympo. on Computer science education, pp.220–223, 2002.

[3] Andrew W. Appel and Jens Palsberg, Modern Compiler Implementation in Java (2nd ed.), ISBN: 052182060X, 2002ĄD

[4] Alfred V. Aho, Ravi Sethi and Jeffrey D. Ullman, Compilers: Principles, Techniques, and Tools, ISBN: 0321428900, Addison-Wesley, 2006.

[5] Alan Kaplan and Denise Shoup, CUPV—a visualization tool for generated parsers, SIGCSE'00: Proc. 31st SIGCSE tech. sympo. on Computer science education, pp.11–15, 2000.

[6] Steven R. Vegdahl, Using visualization tools to teach compiler design, Journal of Comput. Sci. in Colleges, 16(2), pp.72–83, 2001.

[7] Joshua C. Estep and Christopher A. Healy, A flexible tool for visualizing assembly code, Journal of Comput. Sci. in Colleges, pp.55–67, 2005.

[8] Jaime Urquiza-Fuentes and Micael Gallego-Carrillo and Francisco Gortázar-Bellas and J. Ángel Velázquez-Iturbide, Visualizing the symbol table, ITICSE '06: Proc. 11th annual SIGCSE conf. on Innovation and technology in computer science education, Poster session, pp. 341–341, 2006.

[9] Boyd, M. and Whalley, D., Graphical visualization of compiler optimizations, Journal of Prog. Lang., 3(2), pp.69–94, 1995.

[10] R. Daniel Resler, VisiCLANG—a visible compiler for CLANG, SIGPLAN Not., 25(8), pp.120–123, 1990.

[11] M. Eduard Tudoreanu, Designing Effective Program Visualization Tools for Reducing User's Cognitive Effort, ACM Sympo. on Software Visualization, pp.105–114, 2003.

[12] Elizabeth White, Ranjan Sen and Nina Stewart, Hide and show: using real compiler code for teaching, Proc. 36th SIGCSE tech. sympo. on Computer Science Education, pp.12–16, 2005.

[13] K. Andrews and R. R. Henry and W. K. Yamamoto, Design and implementation of the UW illustrated compiler, SIGPLAN Not., 23(7), pp.105–114, 1988.

[14] Niklaus Wirth, Algorithms + Data Structures = Programs, ISBN-10: 0130224189, Prentice Hall, 1976.

[15] Alexander Aiken, Cool: A portable project for teaching compiler construction, ACM SIGPLAN Notices, 31(7), pp.19–26, 1996.

[16] Evgeny A. Eremin, Educational Pascal compiler into MMIX code, Proc. 6th Baltic Sea Conf. on Computing education research, Koli Calling, Poster Session, pp.143–144, 2006.

[17] Marc L. Corliss and E. Christopher Lewis, Bantam: a customizable, Java-based, classroom compiler, ACM SIGCSE Bulletin, 40(1), pp.38–42, 2008.

[18] Martin Ruckert, Teaching compiler construction and language design: making the case for unusual compiler projects with postscript as the target language, Proc. 38th SIGCSE tech. sympo. on Computer science education, pp. 435–439, 2007.

[19] John S. Mallozzi, Thoughts on and tools for teaching compiler design, Journal of Comput. Sci. in Colleges, 21(2), pp.177–184, 2005.

[20] Intel, Intel 64 and IA-32 Architectures Software Developer's Manuals, `http://www.intel.com/products/processor/manuals/`.

[21] GNU Project, Bison Manual — The Yacc-compatible Parser Generator, `http://www.gnu.org/software/bison/`.

[22] Programming languages–C: ISO/IEC 9899:1999.

[23] System V Application Binary Interface, Intel386 Architecture Processor Supplement 4th Ed., `http://www.caldera.com/developers/devspecs/abi386-4.pdf`, 1997.

Frances: A Tool For Understanding Code Generation

Tyler Sondag
Dept. of Computer Science
Iowa State University
226 Atanasoff Hall
Ames, IA 50014
sondag@cs.iastate.edu

Kian L. Pokorny
Division of Computing
McKendree University
701 College Road
Lebanon, IL 62254
klpokorny@mckendree.edu

Hridesh Rajan
Dept. of Computer Science
Iowa State University
226 Atanasoff Hall
Ames, IA 50014
hridesh@cs.iastate.edu

ABSTRACT

Compiler and programming language implementation courses are integral parts of many computer science curricula. However, the range of topics necessary to teach in such a course are difficult for students to understand and time consuming to cover. In particular, code generation is a confusing topic for students unfamiliar with low level target languages. We present Frances, a tool for helping students understand code generation and low level languages. The key idea is to graphically illustrate the relationships between high level language constructs and low level (assembly) language code. By illustrating these relationships, we take advantage of the students existing understanding of some high level language. We have used Frances in a compiler design course and received highly positive feedback. Students conveyed to us that Frances significantly helped them to understand the concepts necessary to implement code generation in a compiler project.

Categories and Subject Descriptors

K.3.0 [**Computers and Education**]: General; K.3.2 [**Computers and Education**]: Computer and Information Science Education—*computer science education, curriculum*; D.3.4 [**Programming Languages**]: Processors—*compilers*

General Terms

Languages

Keywords

Frances, Code Generation, Compilers, Visualization

1. INTRODUCTION

A compiler is a software system designed to translate programs written in a source language (usually a high level language), to another target language (frequently machine code) [12]. Developing a compiler is a difficult but rewarding experience for students since it requires a wide range of knowledge and techniques [8]. Compiler and language implementation has always been listed in the ACM Computing Curricula (CC) as a main curriculum topic [16]. The latest revision of CC '01 also states the importance of these topics: "...good compiler writers are often seen as desirable; they tend to be good software engineers [2, pp.11]."

Unfortunately, the complexity of compilers makes it difficult to sufficiently cover the necessary concepts and construct a compiler in a single semester [8]. One problem is that students must have a thorough understanding of the high level (source) language and the target language [8]. Most students at this point in their education have learned at least one, if not several, high level languages (Java, C++, etc). However, many students have not learned assembly like languages commonly used as compiler target languages. In recent years assembly language courses have been supplanted by other topics in many undergraduate curricula [11]. This significantly complicates the task of writing the compiler, specifically, the portions dealing with code generation and optimizations.

Our contribution is a tool called *Frances*[1] which has the primary use of assisting in the learning of code generation [3]. The main intuition of our approach is to take advantage of the students existing knowledge of some high level language. We allow students to enter source code in a language of their choice, then show a graphical representation of the corresponding target code. This graphical representation is shown in a way that allows users to quickly identify how different types of high level language features are represented in a lower level language. Our representation makes use of several techniques to improve understanding, most importantly we,

- maintain actual target code **ordering**,
- show different types of possible run-time **paths**, and
- **color code** types of instruction blocks.

Frances provides a simple graphical interface that helps to reduce the burden of learning to use the tool.

The key benefits of Frances is that it helps students

- understand **code generation**, and
- gain familiarity with **assembly language** .

This tool helps students understand code generation and assembly language by showing how high level language source code translates to assembly language. Additionally, Frances generates graphs which clearly illustrate the purpose of code segments. This greatly improves the understanding of the target code. Naps *et al.* claim

[1]We named the tool Frances in honor of Frances E. Allen . She received the Turning award for pioneering contributions to the theory and practice of optimizing compiler techniques that laid the foundation for modern optimizing compilers and automatic parallel execution.

that in computer science education, visualization techniques are more beneficial when they engage students [15]. Our approach is not only visual, but allows students to experiment with program code in a variety of high level languages. A small example is shown in Figure 1 where the assembly language equivalent of a small loop in the high level language C is graphically illustrated in Frances.

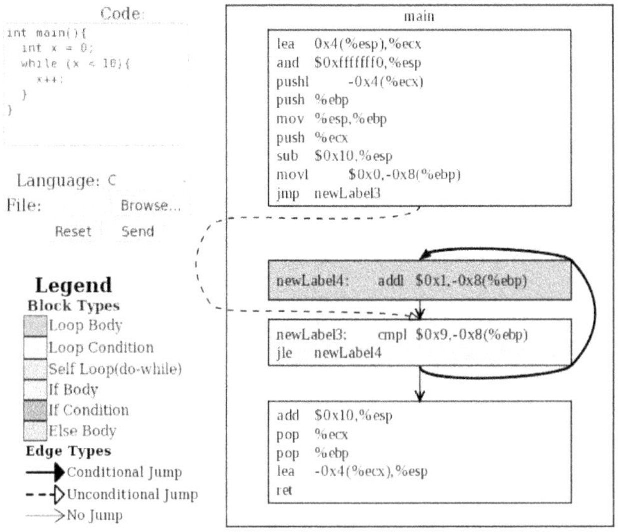

Figure 1: A simple C while loop

We have used this tool in an undergraduate compiler design course with encouraging results. The students in this course were given the opportunity to use Frances when learning the topics of code generation. These students communicated that the tool was very useful for understanding concepts necessary for code generation. Based on this experience, Frances is becoming a more integral part of future offerings of this course.

The rest of this paper is organized as follows. Section 2 gives a brief overview of related work. Then, Section 3 outlines the goals of Frances. Next, in Section 4, we describe the Frances tool. Section 5 discusses our experiences and observations from using the Frances tool as part of a compiler design course. Finally, Section 6 concludes and discusses future work.

2. RELATED WORK

Since developing a compiler is difficult, especially within a single semester course, a large body of work has been done to improve this process. Aiken presented Cool, a language and compiler designed for course projects to reduce the overhead for the instructor and keep assignments modular [5]. Similarly, Corliss *et al.* developed Bantam which is a Java compiler project for courses [8]. Modularity is also achieved in Bantam since components of the compiler can use the provided modules, or be swapped out with custom versions. Rather than developing a new infrastructure, our technique is complementary to these existing techniques in order to help understand specific portions of compiler implementation.

Resler *et al.* propose a visualization tool, VCOCO, for understanding compilers [13]. VCOCO provides several view panes which show source code, language grammar, compiler, parser, and scanner. Each pane is updated throughout the compilation process. We also propose a visual approach, however, we are interested specifically with code generation and present a graphical approach.

Bredlau *et al.* suggest using the Java Virtual Machine (JVM) for teaching assembly [7]. The idea is to let the java compiler create JVM code which is compared to the source code. We take a similar approach but with assembly language and we provide a simple graphical comparison to aid in this process.

3. GOALS FOR FRANCES

In this section, we discuss the goals we had in mind when developing the Frances tool as well as details for accomplishing these goals. Briefly, these goals include making code generation easy to understand by clearly and quickly showing how familiar high level language constructs translate to low level language code. Additionally, the tool is made as easy as possible, making the learning curve for the tool minimal.

3.1 Understanding Code Generation

The first and most important goal, was to help students understand the concepts behind code generation.

We have observed that for many students, code generation can be the most difficult challenge when writing a compiler for the first time. This is largely because of the differences in already familiar high level languages and unfamiliar low level languages. This includes differences in syntax as well as the ordering of statements related to the various programming constructs. For example, in Figure 1 the order of the loop condition and loop body are opposite in the two representations. With this tool, we intend to ease this challenge by clearly showing how familiar high-level language code and constructs map to target, low-level assembly code. The idea is that students already understand at least one high level language. By understanding how the high level and low level languages relate to each other, students can quickly understand how to translate from one language to the other. Then when students write their own compiler they can use Frances as a guide for dealing with various high level constructs including memory management and code order.

A simple way to do this is to have students compare source code with equivalent assembly code (for example, gcc can generate assembly from source). The benefit of this is that it allows students to see what types of instructions their code is mapped to as well as ordering of instructions. This is a helpful process, however, we felt that more could be done to improve this process especially for larger programs. To improve this process, we show the source to target language mapping and improve upon this mapping in two ways. First, we represent target code as a graph that shows execution paths that may be taken at run-time. Second, we color code this graph to quickly show how control structures are represented in the target language. Most students are familiar with high level languages constructs. Thus, being able to quickly identify how language constructs in familiar high level languages map to assembly code significantly eases this comparison process. The details of these features and how they work are described in Section 4.

3.2 Ease of Use

We felt it was important for the tool to be as easy to use as possible. If not, the cost of learning how to use the tool could easily overshadow the benefits it provides. Therefore, we take several steps to make the tool easy to use: make it easy to run on a wide variety of platforms, provide a simple interface, and support a variety of high level or source languages.

First, to avoid issues with different operating systems, hardware platforms, software versions etc., we make the tool available via the web. Thus, we eliminate the need for users to build Frances on their machine. This removes any problems that may arise when building a software package from source and allows any user to make use of Frances as long as they have a web browser.

Second, to make the tool easy to use, we provide a simple graphical interface. Many compiler tools operate from the command line and require the users to learn complicated syntax. While powerful and flexible, learning how to use such a tool if you are only planning on using it for a short period of time is undesirable. We believe our interface is simple enough for users to immediately begin using it and understanding the output.

Third, it is required that users are familiar with some high level language. Restricting the tool to a single language would clearly not be useful for users not familiar with this language. Therefore, we provide support for several common high level languages (C, C++, and Fortran).

4. FRANCES

We now discuss the details of the Frances tool. This includes what facilities the tool provides to students as well as how it provides these facilities. Additionally, we give detailed explanations of why certain approaches are taken. A general discussion of why these facilities are provided is included in Section 3.

The core of Frances is a framework built for another research project. This framework makes use of the GNU Binutils [9] for converting an executable to an object oriented representation that we can analyze, modify, and output as a new executable. This framework is not yet publicly available, but will be released as an open source project in the future. Until then, the tool is made available as a web service.

Frances generates a simple graphical representation of the target code corresponding to the source code. For example, in Figure 1, this simple while loop is shown graphically as four blocks of code. Furthermore, the edges or *paths* between these blocks that can be taken at run-time are shown. To generate the graphical program representation, we make use of `dot` which is part of the GraphViz [10] graph visualization software. We now describe the major components of Frances including how blocks and edges are drawn as well as a brief discussion about the interface.

4.1 Blocks

Basic blocks of instructions are generated by Frances. A basic block is a sequence of instructions with a single entry point and single exit point with no jumps between [6]. For simple control structures (non-nested structures) basic blocks capture the main components of the structures. For example, in Figure 1, the sample while loop can be divided into two parts which have a different purpose: the *loop body*, and the *loop condition*. Therefore, the graphical version of the target code illustrates these two components of the loop in two separate blocks. Additionally, the blocks before and after the loop are also shown separately.

A major difference between previous tools and our tool is the way in which we lay out blocks. Similar tools [1, 4, 14] represent blocks as a flow chart. Since our major goal was to help students understand code generation, we make this graphical representation as close as possible to real generated code. We do this by maintaining the instruction ordering of the actual target code. This includes the ordering of the blocks. To make this ordering clear, we represent blocks in a linear fashion in the same way that programs are represented in target code.

For example, in Figure 1, the layout of blocks is not done in a way that is immediately obvious from the source code. Consider the loop condition. In the source code, this is before the loop body whereas in the target code, it is after the loop body. This is not immediately clear; however, this is how target code is generated by the compiler. Thus, understanding this ordering is necessary for understanding code generation. Therefore, our tool exposes students to such orderings. Given that this ordering is confusing, we take steps to help clarify this ordering.

4.2 Color Coding

Following that students are already familiar with a high level language, we aim to quickly and clearly illustrate how control structures in a high level language are represented in the target language. We show this by coloring the graph to highlight the different parts of the various control structures. Our tool performs simple control flow analyses [12] on the code to determine the different parts of the control structures. Then, the tool colors blocks based on which part of the control structure they make up (loop condition, loop body, etc). For example, in Figure 1 a while loop is shown in both forms. Both the loop condition and the loop body are colored differently to make it easy to distinguish between the two. As mentioned previously, the ordering of these two blocks is confusing at first since it differs from the source code ordering. This coloring quickly points out this ordering by showing that for this high level language while loop, the loop condition goes after the loop body.

For simple control structures, that is, non-nested control structures, we shade the background of the blocks to corresponding colors for each part of control structures. This includes structures such as loops (loop body and loop condition are colored differently), *if/else* blocks, etc. As discussed previously, Figure 1 shows this for a simple while loop.

For nested control structures, the coloring must be done differently. We start by shading the blocks in the innermost structures as described previously. Then, all other structures are surrounded with boxes. These boxes are then shaded to show what kind of structure the member blocks are a part. Furthermore, this helps to show how the different structures interact. For example, consider the nested loop in Figure 2. The inner loop is composed of two blocks, the loop condition and the loop body. These two blocks are shaded in the figure. We can see that both of these blocks (the entire inner loop) are contained within another structure since they are contained in a larger shaded box. This structure is the loop body of the outer loop which is shown clearly by the shading.

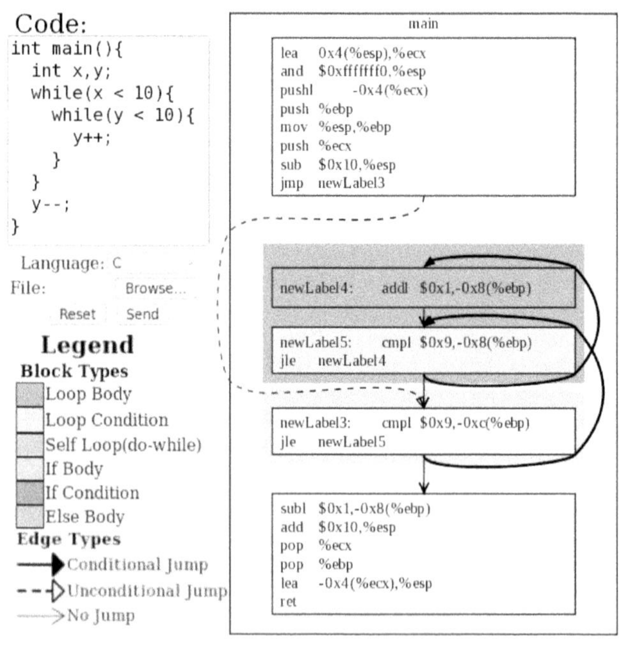

Figure 2: A simple nested while loop

This drawing of blocks shows how target code is laid out. Then the coloring helps to quickly show how components in familiar high level code are represented in the target code. Furthermore, by breaking this representation down, we can focus on a smaller subset of the code. Next, we describe how edges are illustrated.

4.3 Paths

The edges between blocks represent the *paths* that can be taken at run-time. A jump in the target code can have up to two possible next instructions. The paths show what these possible next instructions are. For example, in Figure 1, we see that the loop condition (shown in green) has two outgoing paths: one edge leading to the loop body if the condition is true and one edge leading to the next block after the loop (exiting the loop) if the condition is false.

In combination with blocks, edges help the user see how different structures are represented. For example, consider the first block in Figure 1. This figure illustrates how, in the target code, you first jump past the loop body to the loop condition for this type of loop. This illustrate a key difference between `while` and `do-while` loops since `do-while` loops are not organized this way.

As mentioned previously, the instruction (and block) ordering in the target code can be confusing to students because it is frequently different than the source code ordering. Our graphical representation of blocks helps by highlighting the components of the different control structures. Illustrating the ordering of control structures is helpful, however, we still need to show execution flows between these structures. Figure 2 shows an example of a nested loop where paths help to illustrate the initially confusing code layout. In this figure, we see that the edge corresponding to entering the inner loop actually goes to the second block in the inner loop. This is slightly confusing at first since the path does not go to the beginning of the inner loop code. This example shows that it is important to understand how execution enters and exits loops. Furthermore, understanding how execution flows through others structures such as `if /else` blocks is also important. Thus, we take steps to help contrast the differences between edges.

4.4 Edge Types

There are multiple types of edges. We illustrate the different types by using different styles of lines and arrowheads for drawing the edges. For example, in Figure 1, we see all three different types of edges. We now give a brief description of each edge type.

- First, we have *"unconditional jumps"*. In the figure, this jump is illustrated with a dashed line and an empty triangular arrowhead. In Figure 1, the first block ends with the instruction `jmp newLabel3`. With this type of jump, the path is taken no matter what when the instruction is executed.

- Next, we have *"fall through"* or *"branch not taken"* edges. This edge type is illustrated with a thin edge and a "wedge shaped" arrowhead. This edge type refers to when we simply go to the next sequential instruction when either the current instruction is not a jump or a condition is false. For example, the edge going from the loop body to the loop condition in the figure. In this case, since the block does not end with a jump, the next instruction is just the next sequential block. Another example of this type of edge is the edge from the loop condition to the last block in Figure 1. This edge is taken when the condition on the jump, in this case `$0x9 >= -0x8(%ebp)`, is false. This may seem trivial since the *"branch not taken"* edge is always the edge to the next sequential block, however, for students just learning this concept may not be immediately obvious.

- Finally, we have *"branch taken"* edges. These edges are drawn with a thick solid line and a solid triangular arrowhead. These edges are those which are taken when a jump condition is true. For example, in Figure 1, we have an edge from the loop condition block to the loop body block. This edge is taken whenever the loop condition on the loop is true. Another example is shown in Figure 3. In this example we can see a branch taken edge from the *if condition* block to the *else body* block. This edge is taken whenever the condition is true, however, in the source version, we have that this edge is taken whenever the if condition is false. This is another interesting difference between source and target code which is nicely illustrated in Frances.

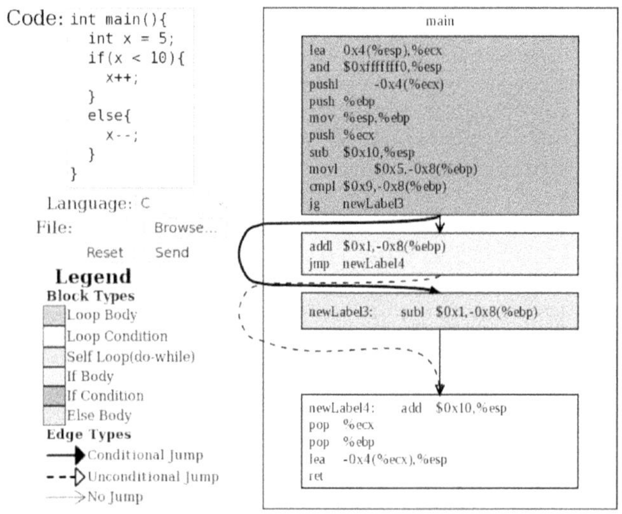

Figure 3: if-else block

This edge drawing helps illustrate the finer details of the target code. This includes how individual instructions such as jumps are created and how complex control structure components interact such as nested loops. Together with our block drawing and coloring, Frances generates informative and easy to understand figures which illustrate how code generation is performed.

4.5 Interface

To make Frances as easy to use as possible, we make it available via a web interface. Since we make it available through a web interface, it does not require installation and thus avoids compatibility problems. This simple and easy to use interface is available at http://www.cs.iastate.edu/˜sapha/tools/frances/.

Since we can not be sure what high level languages each user is familiar with, we give users the option of writing code in a variety of high level languages. The language is selected in a simple drop down list. Figure 1 shows an example where the C language is selected.

To enter code, users can type into a text box as part of the web interface of Frances. Since a user may not want to enter all the code for each example in the web interface, users have the option to upload a file. The input code is shown side-by-side with the graphical representation generated by Frances. Because of space restrictions the figures in this paper show a trimmed version of this interface.

By not requiring installation, interfacing with a wide variety of high level languages, and giving users options for inputting code, we have a tool which is easily accessible to a wide range of users.

Summary of Representation: We believe that Frances' block layout and coloring in combination with the edge drawing greatly helps to teach the instruction layout of low level language code. Furthermore, we believe that when viewed alongside familiar source code, this representation makes the process of understanding translating between the two languages significantly easier. With its simple and easy to use interface we believe Frances is easy to use in a course, will help students understand these difficult concepts, and save valuable course time for other topics.

5. EXPERIENCES AND DISCUSSION

Our first uses of Frances in an undergraduate compilers course gave very positive results. Initially, Frances introduced students to fundamental assembly language concepts through demonstration. The demonstration consisted of a simple program with only variable declaration and a single if-statement. This simple program demonstrated the initialization of registers, memory allocation and a few simple assembly instructions. Prior to this most students had little or no exposure to actual assembly language code.

As stated previously, the order of instructions in high level languages contrasted with the generated low level language is foreign to most students. Often, students that only have exposure to high-level languages have difficulty understanding the relationship between the source and target code. The graphical features of Frances help to close this gap in understanding by providing a side by side comparison with color coded identification of control structure components. The visualization techniques used in Frances allow students to quickly assimilate how the assembly is accomplishing the implementation of the source code.

Several course exercises, available on the Frances website, have been developed that allow students to experiment with Frances. The exercises are developed to demonstrate each basic control structure. Additionally, the nesting of structures provides a deeper understanding of why it is important for the assembly code to be generated in the given order. Other course materials demonstrate more concepts. Memory allocation for variables, including arrays, provides the student insights into how space requirements of a program are utilized. Additionally, materials have been created to demonstrate details of transferring control to functions.

As part of the curriculum of the compiler course, students are required to build a compiler for a language they create. The compiler is written directly in Java or C++. The use of Frances allows students to gain an understanding of how and why to generate code for given control structures and function calls. This has allowed the pace of the course to significantly increase. Students questioning how to program the code generation for a particular construct simply go to Frances and get a direct demonstration.

6. CONCLUSION AND FUTURE WORK

Compiler design courses are an integral component to most Computer Science curricula [2]. Prior to this course, in much of today's curriculum, students have limited exposure to low level languages. This makes the code generation components of these compiler design courses particularly challenging. In this paper, we presented Frances, a tool to aid in the understanding of code generation and compiler construction. The main goal of this tool is to help students understand the relation between familiar high level languages and not so familiar low level target languages. This is accomplished by giving a side by side comparison with graphical cues of the target language. The graphical representation includes color coded target code to highlight control structures and execution paths. This representation also maintains the actual order of instructions of the compiled version of the program. Frances has shown to be highly useful in practice by significantly easing the process of teaching code generation concepts.

As part of future work we plan to extend the tool in the direction of illustrating and understanding program analysis techniques and automatic compiler optimizations. We plan to have the option in Frances to illustrate a variety program analysis techniques (control flow, data flow, etc). This will help illustrate where optimizations are applicable and how optimizations are performed. For optimizations, the plan is to have the ability to illustrate common optimizations step by step using similar figures as those used to illustrate code generation techniques shown in this paper. We plan to implement a wide range of common optimizations as well as a hot-spot finder to illustrate which portions of the program are in most need of optimization. Along with making common techniques available, we also plan to allow users to write their own analysis and optimization routines. Frances is a powerful tool for a basic compilers course and we believe these enhancements will extend its use to advanced undergraduate and graduate level compiler and programming language courses.

Acknowledgments

The authors would like to thank the students who tested the tool as well as the anonymous reviewers for their comments and suggestions. Sondag and Rajan are supported in part by the US National Science Foundation under grants 06-27354 and 08-08913.

7. REFERENCES

[1] *aiSee - Graph Visualization*. http://www.absint.com/aisee/.

[2] Computing curricula 2008: An interim revision of cs 2001. http://www.acm.org/education/curricula/ComputerScience2008.pdf.

[3] *Frances: Control FLow Graph Generator*. http://www.cs.iastate.edu/~sapha/tools/frances/.

[4] *ICD-C Compiler Framework*. http://www.icd.de/es/icd-c/.

[5] A. Aiken. Cool: a portable project for teaching compiler construction. *SIGPLAN Not.*, 31(7):19–24, 1996.

[6] F. E. Allen. Control flow analysis. In *Symposium on Compiler optimization*, pages 1–19, 1970.

[7] C. Bredlau and D. Deremer. Assembly language through the java virtual machine. In *SIGCSE*, 2001.

[8] M. L. Corliss and E. C. Lewis. Bantam: a customizable, java-based, classroom compiler. In *SIGCSE*, 2008.

[9] Free Software Foundation. Gnu binutils: a collection of binary tools, 2009. http://www.gnu.org/software/binutils/.

[10] J. Ellson *et al.* Graphviz - open source graph drawing tools. *Graph Drawing*, 2001.

[11] M. C. Loui. The case for assembly language programming. *IEEE Transactions on Education*, E-31(3):160–164, 1988.

[12] S. S. Muchnick. *Advanced Compiler Design & Implementation*. Academic Press, 1997.

[13] R. D. Resler and D. M. Deaver. Vcoco: a visualisation tool for teaching compilers. *SIGCSE Bull.*, 30(3):199–202, 1998.

[14] B. Titzer, D. Lee, and J. Palsberg. Avrora: Scalable sensor network simulation with precise timing. In *Information Processing in Sensor Networks (IPSN)*, 2005.

[15] T.L. Naps *et al.* Exploring the role of visualization and engage- ment in computer science education. In *ITiCSE-WGR*, 2002.

[16] L. Xu. Language engineering in the context of a popular, inexpensive robot platform. In *SIGCSE*, 2008.

Do Roadshows Work? Examining the Effectiveness of Just Be

Joseph A. Cottam, Samantha S. Foley, and Suzanne Menzel
Indiana University - School of Informatics and Computing
Bloomington, IN 47405
{jcottam, ssfoley, menzel}@cs.indiana.edu

ABSTRACT

Outreach programs communicating the importance and diversity of computing to K-12 students are essential to improving attitudes toward computing. However, the effectiveness of outreach programs, and roadshows in particular, has only recently come under study. *Just Be* is an outreach roadshow program at Indiana University. It directly addresses stereotypical attitudes towards computing. This paper demonstrates, through statistical analysis of surveys given to college students who participated in a *Just Be* presentation prepared for high school students, that the *Just Be* roadshow effectively shifts attitudes for the better.

Categories and Subject Descriptors

K.3.2 [**Computer and Information Science Education**]: Computer science education

General Terms

Human Factors

Keywords

K-12, Outreach, Roadshow, Changing Attitudes, Stereotypes, Broadening Participation, Gender, Diversity

1. INTRODUCTION

The effectiveness of outreach programs is largely unknown, even for programs that have run for several years. *Just Be* is an interactive K-12 outreach program developed and managed by Indiana University's Women in Informatics and Computing (WIC) group over the past five years [6]. It is based on the roadshow model pioneered at Carnegie Mellon University [8]. *Just Be* attempts to expand interest in computing-related fields and dispel myths about computing professionals. This paper presents evidence for the effectiveness of *Just Be* in changing attitudes towards computing.

SIGCSE'10, March 10–13, 2010, Milwaukee, Wisconsin, USA.

Figure 1: Middle-school girls run toy cars through a sorting network during a *Just Be* activity.

At the CSTA Roadshow Workshop in May 2008, Lecia Barker questioned the practice of roadshows directly addressing myths, under-representation, and job security [1]. Barker strongly encouraged programs to regularly assess the effectiveness of their efforts and update content based on recipient feedback. This paper presents such an assessment with respect to the *Just Be* program. Particularly, Barker warned that talking about misconceptions can actually reinforce them; a result that was demonstrated for older adults about commercial product claims over short periods of time in [5]. Significantly, the *Just Be* program directly addresses common misconceptions and thus is an important test to see if the lessons learned in marketing transfer to outreach activities.

To assess the impact on attitudes about stereotypes, educational requirements, and job prospects, we administered surveys to college students before and after they participated in a *Just Be* presentation (using college students to assess a K-12 program is discussed in Section 3.2). These surveys included open-ended and Likert-scale delimited questions. This paper gives an overview of the *Just Be* program (Section 2 and the results of the Likert-scaled questions (Section 3).

2. JUST BE PROGRAM

Just Be is an outreach program started by the WIC group at Indiana University. WIC is an organization for students,

Figure 2: Elementary students work out a 4x4 Sudoku puzzle during a *Just Be* presentation.

faculty, staff, and professionals who wish to create a better environment for women in computing at Indiana University and beyond. The *Just Be* roadshow is one way we are working towards a more inclusive, friendly, and productive computing field.

Just Be was inspired by roadshow presentations done at Carnegie Mellon University and described in Unlocking the Clubhouse [3]. Over five years of activity, the *Just Be* presentation has been given to 46 groups, covering more than 3000 different students aged 10 to 25 (primarily middle and high school students). Since this effort relies heavily on volunteers, we only serve schools within 50 miles of the Bloomington campus of Indiana University. This includes Indianapolis schools, many rural areas, and the city of Bloomington itself.

While the *Just Be* program has been geographically constrained, we have participated in broader education activities encouraging other groups to develop outreach programs. Central to this effort are the *Bring IT On!* workshops held in 2006 and 2007 (with a follow-up in 2008), where many undergraduate students and educators were trained on roadshow creation [4]. Additionally, *Just Be* was featured in the Computer Science Teacher's Association (CSTA) Roadshow Workshop at Google in 2008, SIGCSE workshops in 2007 and 2009, and contributed to the upcoming National Center for Women and Information Technology (NCWIT) Roadshow-in-a-box.

2.1 Goals

The *Just Be* program is constantly evolving, but we have remained focused on these desired outcomes:

- Increase awareness of the true nature of computing: An exciting, diverse, cooperative, and interdisciplinary field that benefits from the involvement of people with different interests, backgrounds, and experiences.
- Contradict prevailing negative stereotypes about people in computing and their work by providing real-life examples.
- Engage students by employing interactive demonstrations, and providing information about next steps at their school.

Our presenters, undergraduate and graduate students at IU, also gain confidence and experience creating presentation materials, practicing public speaking, and taking on leadership roles.

2.2 Format

The *Just Be* presentation is an interactive experience that integrates a slideshow with a personal response system and physical props to facilitate discussion and engage students. The content of the presentation is customized for each visit based on the age-group and time allotted. Two presenters typically take turns presenting the content. This provides different points of view for the students. Most presentations follow this outline:

Introduction: The presenters introduce themselves and the program. They typically describe (verbally and in pictures) an activity that they enjoyed when they were at the same age level as the audience participants, how they first became interested in computing, what they are doing now in computing, and what they like to do for fun. The idea is to demonstrate that there are many paths to a career in computing and that the presenters are well-rounded individuals.

Stereotypes examined: Computing stereotypes are elicited from the audience by asking how they imagine computing professionals look and work. Descriptions of geeks in basements are offered freely, indicating that such images firmly entrenched. After a good laugh at the stereotypes, we all decide they are not always true.

Real people in computing: The students are asked to identify the occupations of various people based on their pictures using a classroom voting system. It quickly becomes clear that this is an unreasonable request and people should not be judged based on appearance. After each question is answered, we go over what the people in the pictures actually do.

Fields of computing: This section is dedicated to interesting and practical applications of computing. We focus on occupations that employ computing, rather than on the computing techniques. After asking the students what they think computing is used for, we show them a variety computing research projects. We emphasize the collaborations, diversity and required skills in the projects. We include grade-appropriate activities students can do now to prepare for similar projects. Our examples illustrate the ubiquity of computing and its applicability to a variety of fields.

Computing skills: To give students a sense of the thought processes of computing professionals, we conduct a number of interactive group activities (e.g., logic games and algebraic word-problems using slides or props, see Figure 2). The presenters facilitate the activities so that all students are encouraged to share opinions and explain why they think they are correct. Throughout these activities, we emphasize that a variety of viewpoints are important in complex problem-solving as the first suggestion is rarely the correct one. Tim Bell's "Magic Parity Board" is an activity that we use [2].

Career information: We often take time to discuss the practical issues of job security and salary with high

Keyword	Statement	Pre-survey	Post-survey	p
Diverse	Computing is a sufficiently diverse field	57%	84%	< .0001
Life-long	Understanding computing is an important life-long skill	84	93	<.0001
Programming	Computing is mostly about writing programs	24	17	<.0001
Employable	Taking 2+ computing classes will make me more employable	73	83	<.0001
Limiting	A degree in computing will limit the places I could work	11	8	<.0001
Exciting	Computing is full of exciting opportunities	55	81	<.0001
White&Male	Only white males do computing jobs	7	5	<.0049
Geeks	Computing professionals are geeks	25	16	<.0001
No People	Most computing jobs do not involve working with people	22	12	<.0001
High School	Students who do not take computing in high school are ill-equipped to major in computing in college	25	15	<.0001

Table 1: The ten Likert-coded questions, the pre- and post- percent agreement and t-test change significance (N = 520). The Keyword column shows how the question is referred to in other tables.

school students. During this section, we typically discuss how computing can be used in conjunction with skills typically associated with other professions.

Conclusion: The presentation concludes with contact information for the presenters and an open question and answer session.

Hands-on tasks: Acting on feedback from students, presenters, and teachers, we have developed a library of hands-on activities (e.g., Scratch-based [7], adaptations of Computer Science Unplugged [2] lessons, controlling scribbler robots; see Figure 1). We deploy these activities at science fairs, residential summer camps and in school visits when time permits.

3. STUDY

To evaluate the effectiveness of the *Just Be* program, we measured the attitudes of college students before and after a *Just Be* presentation. A pre-survey was made available to students one week before the presentation was scheduled. The same survey (minus demographic information) was made available for one week after the presentation. The survey includes ten questions (see Table 1) regarding the student's personal attitude towards computing. We used a 5-point Likert scale to measure degree of agreement with a given statement in the survey. In the analysis, the top two values (Strongly Agree, Agree) and bottom two (Disagree, Strongly Disagree) are grouped.

The surveys were administered in multiple sections of two courses over six semesters. A110 is an introduction to computer concepts and applications course; it is typically taken by non-majors to fulfill general education requirements. The other course is our CS1 course and is comprised primarily of freshman and sophomores, about half of which are considering computer science as a major or minor. The majority of responses are from A110 because it has substantially larger class sizes; however, the results of both courses are combined except where indicated.

The surveys were conducted online; students could participate anytime during the week before (for the pre-survey) or after (for the post-survey) the presentation. Responses tended to spike very close to the closing times of each survey.

3.1 Methods

We are interested in the shift of attitudes experienced by the populations between their pre- and post-survey. To accomplish this, we used a paired t-test. For each question, students who did not respond to both the pre- and post-survey for that question were eliminated. A significant t-test result indicates that the null hypothesis, that there was no shift in attitudes, should be rejected. In addition to t-test values, the mean, standard error of the difference, and p-value of the t-test were calculated and examined. We further examine the results that had p-values less than .05, a common cutoff for high significance.

3.2 Limitations

Evaluation forms were obtained from 666 students over three years, however only the 613 that returned both a pre- and post-survey are considered in this study. Additionally, if a student did not answer a particular question in either the pre- or post-survey, the data from that question was omitted from both surveys results. The data collected on individuals who only returned one survey may be useful to discover prevailing attitudes, but our analysis is concerned with the change in attitudes over time. Non-responses for a single item occurred from 12% to 25%. Such omissions may introduce bias in the same way that any convenient sample does.

This analysis indicates changes in beliefs for the responding students. However, as the students were not randomly selected, generalizing to other groups of students should be done with caution. Further, the pre- and post-surveys were administered within a short time period, immediately before and after the *Just Be* activities. It is not known if the changes in beliefs measured in this study will be sustained over time. A further potential cause of bias is in the presentation method itself. Each section of each course was given the presentation separately, often by different people in subsequent semesters. We make no attempt to account for or measure this effect, but the presentation method is consistent with how *Just Be* is conducted in the K-12 arena.

A major limitation of this study is that K-12 students were not directly studied. The *Just Be* program is delivered in various forms across the K-12 age range, but we studied its effect on college students. To minimize the difference, the presentation given during the study was identical to a presentation given to high school students. To help gauge shifts that occur with age, we separately analyzed college

Gender and Course	A110	CS1	Total
Female	349	11	360
Male	205	38	243
Total	554	59	613

Table 2: Gender/course breakdown. Totals include only students who responded to both surveys.

freshman, typically only one year older than our target population (see Table 5). Given the small difference between college freshman and high school seniors and the size of the shifts that occurred between college freshman and the rest of the study group, we believe that these results can be applied to presentations given in high schools. However, a study using participants in the target age ranges would provide greater confidence.

3.3 Results

Analysis of survey responses have been divided into a number of significant comparisons which are analyzed separately in this section. The overall results and question text can be found in Table 1.

Demographics of the respondents are found in Table 2. Consistent with other observations, women are significantly under-represented in CS1 while the general education course (A110) is similar to the gender division in the university at large (females are slightly over-represented). Freshman represent 39% of respondents, sophomores 30%, juniors 15% and seniors 15%. Interestingly, one-third of the respondents are first generation college students, (meaning that neither parent had completed a four year degree or they grew up in foster care).

Our demographics questions included questions about prior and planned computing related education. Overall, 1 in 10 students said they were considering an undergraduate degree in Computer Science or Informatics. Following current norms, males were 5 times more likely to say this than females (4% females vs. 20% males). Ten percent of respondents said they were taking or had taken other classes in the School of Informatics and Computing (SoIC), 8% of females and 12% of males. This result corresponds well for females indicating interest in a computing related field (7%), but is substantially less than the number of males considering a computing related field (25%). Even before participating in the *Just Be* program, many students were planning on future computing related courses (15% of females and 39% of males). The higher numbers of students planning on computing courses vs. planning on computing-related degrees is interesting, but its cause is unknown.

3.3.1 Statements

All of the questions analyzed showed a significant change between pre- and post-survey at the .005 significance level (see Table 1). Increases in percent agreement were encouraging. The statements that showed the largest increase in percent agreeing were:

- Computing is a sufficiently diverse field (57% in the pre-survey to 84% in the post-survey)
- Computing is full of exciting possibilities (55% to 81%).

Similarly, the statements that showed the largest decrease in agreement are also indicative of successfully communicating the desired ideas. The statements that showed the largest decrease in percent agreeing were (1) "Most computing jobs do not involve working with people" (22% agreed in the pre-survey compared to 12% in the post-survey) and (2) "Students who do not take CS in high school are ill-equipped to major in CS in college" (25% agreed in the pre-survey compared to 15% in the post-survey).

Table 3 shows the percent of students agreeing with the ten statements in the pre- and post-survey by gender. Notable results indicate that females in the pre-survey generally had a lower of opinion of the social aspects of computing careers, but those impressions improved on the post-survey. Examples of this include:

- In the pre-survey, males were more likely than females to agree that "Computing is full of exciting opportunities" (49% of females and 66% of males). In the post-survey, 79% of females and 84% of males agreed with this statement.
- The gap between males and females narrowed from the pre-survey to the post-survey for the statement "Computing jobs do not involve working with people." In the pre-survey, females were twice as likely as males to agree with this statement (26% females; 13% males). However, in the post-survey 14% of females agreed compared to 11% of males.

Table 4 shows the percent of students agreeing with the ten statements in the pre- and post-survey by course. Due to the content matter of the courses and their intended

	Females (N=313)			Males (N=201)		
Keyword	Pre-	Post-	p	Pre-	Post-	p
Diverse	53%	84%	<.0001	64%	84%	<.0001
Life-long	85	94	<.0001	83	92	=.0007
Programming	24	16	<.0001	23	19	=.0018
Employable	73	81	<.0001	75	86	<.0001
Limiting	10	8	=.0008	11	8	=.0136
Exciting	49	79	<.0001	66	84	<.0001
White&Male	7	4	=.0060	7	6	=.2933
Geeks	25	15	<.0001	25	17	=.0019
No People	26	13	<.0001	14	11	=.0097
High School	27	13	<.0001	23	17	=.0123

Table 3: Results split by gender.

	A110 (N=469)			CS1 (N=49)		
Keyword	Pre-	Post-	p	Pre-	Post-	p
Diverse	57%	84%	< .0001	63%	84%	=.0036
Life-long	83	92	< .0001	96	96	——
Programming	23	16	< .0001	33	33	——
Employable	72	82	< .0001	83	92	=.0569
Limiting	11	8	< .0001	8	10	=.5983
Exciting	53	81	< .0001	82	88	=.2611
White&Male	8	5	=.0025	4	6	=.8113
Geeks	23	14	< .0001	44	31	=.2017
No People	23	13	< .0001	10	2	=.0484
High School	25	15	< .0001	20	16	=.3511

Table 4: Results split by course. A110 is a general-education course with sections covering office applications and basic HTML.

	Freshmen (N=234)			Others (N=431)		
Keyword	Pre-	Post-	p	Pre-	Post-	p
Diverse	58%	88%	< .0001	57%	81%	< .0001
Life-long	86	96	< .0001	83	91	< .0001
Programming	24	18	=.0006	24	17	< .0001
Employable	74	86	< .0001	73	81	< .0001
Limiting	12	7	< .0001	10	9	< .0001
Exciting	55	83	< .0001	56	80	< .0001
White&Male	7	3	=.0192	7	6	< .0001
Geeks	24	12	< .0001	25	18	< .0001
No People	20	10	< .0001	23	14	< .0001
High School	25	16	< .0001	25	14	< .0001

Table 5: Results split by class year.

audience, this split is a reasonable approximation for differences in attitudes between computer science majors and non-majors.

- More than half of majors and non-majors agreed with the statement "Computing is a sufficiently diverse field" (63% of majors compared to 57% of non-majors). After the *Just Be* program 84% of both groups agreed with this statement.
- Between the pre- and post-surveys, non-majors dropped from 23% to 16% agreeing with the statement, "Computing is mostly about writing programs". Among majors, 33% agreed with this statement in both the pre- and post-surveys.
- In the pre-survey, majors were nearly twice as likely as non-majors to agree with the statement "Computer professionals are geeks" (44% majors and 23% non-majors). After the *Just Be* program, majors were still twice as likely as non-majors to agree with this statement (31% majors and 14% non-majors).

Analysis was also conducted comparing freshmen to all other class levels. Though attitude change values were significant in both class levels, they were not significantly different between class levels (Table 5).

4. FUTURE WORK

The analysis presented here represents a small fraction of the data collected. We have reported all significant quantitative findings, but we have yet to analyze the qualitative questions: (1) What sort of work do you think a typical computer scientist performs? (2) Please describe what you think a typical computer scientist looks like. (3) Please describe how you think a typical computer scientist performs his or her work. Coding the responses to these short answer questions is the next logical step.

As noted in Section 3, our survey was conducted with college students, primarily freshman. This was done to simplify study administration, particularly acquiring informed consent. Though college freshman are a suitable model for high school juniors and seniors, they are less satisfactory as a model for the younger children who represent a large part of our target population. Developing a close partnership with a local school to facilitate information gathering in this important population is a clear next step for the evaluation of *Just Be* and similar roadshows.

The roadshow technique is a straightforward, low-cost, easily replicable method of conducting outreach activities. An interesting evaluation challenge is to compare the effectiveness of a roadshow to other programs (e.g., computer clubs, competitions, weekend workshops), with attention to the time and financial investments required by each.

5. CONCLUSION

Just Be is an exemplar roadshow outreach program. It directly confronts stereotypical attitudes towards computing. Our study provides evidence that countering stereotypes with vibrant images of real people doing real work results in a more positive attitude toward computing-related fields, persisting up to a week later. How long the effect continues thereafter is an open question.

6. ACKNOWLEDGMENTS

We thank Janet Greenblatt and Maureen Biggers for their contributions to the data analysis. *Just Be* is made possible by generous support from the IU School of Informatics and Computing, and the Open Systems Laboratory; the hours donated by the volunteers who schedule, prepare, and conduct presentations; and the Indiana school children and their teachers who invite us into their classrooms. We greatly appreciate the teachers who gave us access to their students, especially Charles Pope for his constant support through this evaluation.

7. REFERENCES

[1] L. Barker. What Research Tells Us. `http://csta.acm.org/Communications/sub/Videos.html`, May 2008.

[2] T. Bell, I. H. Witten, and M. Fellows. Computer Science Unplugged. `http://csunplugged.org/`, 2002.

[3] A. Fisher and J. Margolis. *Unlocking the Clubhouse: Women in Computing*, volume 34. MIT Press, 2002.

[4] K. A. Siek, K. Connelly, S. Menzel, and L. Hopkins. Propagating Diversity through Active Dissemination. *IEEE Computer*, Feb 2007.

[5] I. Skurnik, C. Yoon, D. Park, and N. Schwarz. How Warnings About False Claims Become Recommendations. *Journal of Consumer Research*, 31, 2005.

[6] WIC@IU. Women in Informatics and Computing. `http://wic.informatics.indiana.edu`.

[7] U. Wolz, J. Maloney, and S. M. Pulimood. 'Scratch' Your Way to Introductory CS. In *SIGCSE '08*, pages 298–299. ACM, 2008.

[8] Women@SCS. `http://women.cs.cmu.edu`.

Connecting K-16 Curriculum & Policy: Making Computer Science Engaging, Accessible, and Hospitable for Underrepresented Students

Joanna Goode
Education Studies
University of Oregon
Eugene, OR 97403-5277
goodej@uoregon.edu

ABSTRACT

In this paper, a K-16 computer science reform effort is described as an effort that depends on curriculum development, professional development, and collaborative policy strategies.

Categories and Subject Descriptors

K.3.2 [**Computers and Education**]: Computer and Information Science Education – *computer science education, curriculum.*

General Terms

Human Factors

Keywords

Gender & Ethnicity, Wider Access, Pedagogy, CS Reform, CS Policy, Curriculum

1. INTRODUCTION

While there has been much research about the need to transform K-16 computer science education and broaden participation in computing, we have very few examples of large-scale K-12 computing programs that have successfully reached considerable numbers of girls and students of color. A university-district alliance is showing promising results for designing a joint curricular and policy approach for reforming computer science education.

This paper will highlight the parallel nature of curriculum development and policy strategy in providing an accessible and hospitable introduction to the dynamic nature of computing. The discussion will begin with a description of the development process of *Exploring Computer Science* - a curriculum designed to provide an innovative and engaging introduction to computing for students. The accompanying professional development emphasizes a student-centered instructional approach which reflects contemporary knowledge about how students learn. The results from a one-year pilot study suggest that this foundational course has a positive impact on motivation and interest in computing for diverse groups of high school students. However, without a policy framework to create the space for computing in the curriculum, opportunities for students to study computing will remain limited. Offering this course as a college-preparatory course in Los Angeles high schools requires endorsement from the state university system, school district, and high school principals. Navigating this complex system has only been possible due to the district-university collaboration which is driving this reform effort.

2. THE COMPUTER SCIENCE EQUITY ALLIANCE

The Computer Science Equity Alliance first began reforming computer science education in Los Angeles Unified School District (LAUSD) in 2004. Charged with the results of a three-year qualitative research study which highlighted instructional and structural barriers to computer science education for girls and students of color [1-2], this alliance includes educational researchers, university computer scientists, K-12 school district officials, and leadership from the Computer Science Teachers Association (CSTA). Each summer from 2004-2007, the alliance offered a week-long professional development in the form of a Summer Institute for Advanced Placement Computer Science (APCS) teachers. An AP Readiness Program was launched so teachers can bring their students to the UCLA campus once a month for supplemental instruction and embedded professional development. These monthly meetings became a place for APCS teachers to continue to collaborate and build a teaching community. This approach of providing instructional and pedagogical resources and structural support to teachers led to staggering results – the number of students studying APCS in LAUSD tripled – girls quadrupled, Latinos quintupled, African Americans doubled [3].

However, formative and summative research identified a significant tension between the Alliance's goals of accessibility and the goals of the APCS course. Teacher interviews revealed that as a first course in computer science, the learning curve was too steep for the students to learn APCS content in time for the May exam. Teachers also reported that the course's focus on program methodologies in Java failed to attract the interest of students who were not already enamored with computing. It was clear from conversations with district officials and school administrators that the APCS enrollment increases were successful largely due to the college preparatory status of the course for college-bound students. This status is an important indicator of academic rigor, but also, students' course schedules are so impacted by graduation and college-preparatory requirements that they are often not able to take any non college-preparatory electives. It seemed that the success of the computing reform efforts were due to the academic status of the APCS course, not the particular content. University computer scientists joined this conversation and offered a host of computing topics that were more likely to tap into the interests of students. It became clear that in order to reform computing in Los Angeles, a new college preparatory course must be offered that introduces students to exciting introductory topics in computer science within an instructional framework informed by educational learning theories.

3. EXPLORING COMPUTER SCIENCE

Designing a curriculum for a new foundational content-area course requires deep knowledge in content, learning theory, and the communities from which students draw their informal knowledge about the world [4]. The resulting curricular materials reflect a selection of computing topics that are accessible and related to the academic interests of urban high school students.

3.1 Curricular Development Process

The development cycle for *Exploring Computer Science* sought to integrate these three types of knowledge into a curriculum designed for Los Angeles high school students. It was important to draw from many forms of local and national expertise in computer science education to inform the course content.

3.1.1 Instructional Framework

The instructional framework of the course was developed as a collaboration of university education researchers and LAUSD. Drawing from social constructivism [5] and sociocultural learning theories [6], this framework encourages a student-centered approach which draws from the informal knowledge students bring into each course. The course adopts an inquiry-based learning environment which requires students to engage in complex computing projects. Ongoing opportunities for collaboration, communication, and multiple ways of knowing are embedded into the design of the course.

3.1.2 Course Topics

The list of course topics for this curriculum was initially framed in an informal conversation at SIGCSE 2007 with leading K-12 and university computer science curriculum experts. With a general agreement of course topics and the sequence of these topics, educational researchers shared this list with LAUSD mathematics and science leaders and UCLA computer scientists who work closely with local computer science teachers and students. The scope and sequence outline was further revised after this additional input.

3.1.3 Developing Content

Five teachers, including two LAUSD teachers, contributed to the writing of curricular units in the course. Each of these teacher developers was provided the scope and sequence of the entire course, the instructional framework, and a list of objectives for their particular unit. The teacher writers drew from their own knowledge and teaching experiences to contribute towards a particular computing topic. The authors of the curriculum integrated these ideas into a cohesive, six-unit curriculum designed to take place over a two-semester school year. Daily teacher instructional plans and supplementary resources are included in this curriculum.

3.1.4 Training for Pilot Teachers

Six teachers came together for a pilot professional development session in 2008. These teachers were later joined by 25 prospective teachers twice during the school year for continued professional development. The professional development opportunities were carefully designed to highlight the instructional strategies and the content of *Exploring Computer Science while* providing a format for feedback about the curricular materials.

3.1.5 Piloting of course

A total of seven teachers piloted the course during 2008-2009. Almost 300 students enrolled in the pilot courses across these seven comprehensive high schools. Females accounted for 42% of course enrollment and African American and Latino students made up 92% of course enrollment. Semi-structured teacher interviews, teacher surveys, student surveys, and observations informed specific and general revisions that were needed in the curriculum and a major overhaul took place in 2009. The pilot study revealed promising findings about the effectiveness of *Exploring Computer Science* for students. Using pre- and post-survey instruments, research showed that participation in the course resulted in:

- changed students' perceptions of the usefulness of computer science in a positive direction ($p<.05$);
- changed students' beliefs about the appeal of computer science in a positive direction ($p<.01$);
- increased students' perceptions of computer science as enjoyable and stimulating ($p<01$);
- increased students' motivation to stick with a difficult problem ($p<.001$);
- students' willingness to have the answer given to them instead of working it out decreased ($p<.05$);

Further, students reported that they were more likely to take computer science courses after high school and pursue computer science as an academic major after enrolling in the course. These results point to the impact of *Exploring Computer Science* in shaping urban students' understanding and appreciation of this discipline.

3.1.6 Distribution of Materials for Course

The release of *Exploring Computer Science* took place prior to the summer professional development in 2009. An early release of this curriculum allowed an exploration of the materials before the 2009-10 school year embarked. The curricular materials have been released to the computer science education community through the CSTA website [7].

3.1.7 School District Expansion of Course

The final step of this curricular process was the buy-in of the school district to offer this course. Armed with the university support to offer professional development and ongoing instructional support in addition to free curricular materials, the Los Angeles Unified School District utilized its policy influence and professional networks to bring the course content to classrooms across Los Angeles.

3.2 Content of *Exploring Computer Science*

The resulting course is composed of six instructional units: 1) Human Computer Interaction; 2) Problem Solving; 3) Web Design; 4) Introduction to Programming; 5) Robotics; 6) Computing Applications. The course reflects topics and objectives drawn from Levels II and III of the ACM's K-12 curricular framework [8]. Each unit begins with a discussion of the final project so students have an appreciation of the problem they are working towards solving while learning the necessary skills required to solve the problem. Assignments and instructional strategies weave through the six units, conceptually linking the topics together. The curricular materials include original assignments as well as lessons drawn from other computing education materials, including Scratch [9] assignments, Lego Mindstorms robotics challenges, and Computer Science Unplugged [10] activities.

3.3 Professional Development for Course

The professional development designed to accompany the curriculum is an essential companion to the *Exploring Computer Science* course. In order to offer the course at a school site, principals must send a teacher to the ECS Summer Institute and weekend workshops. Participating teachers receive a stipend for their participation in the professional development events.

In 2008, six teachers attended the ECS Summer Institute in preparation for teaching the pilot course in 2008-09. In 2009, 23 teachers from 20 schools participated in the Summer Institute. These culturally diverse teachers represent the geographical diversity of the Los Angeles basin. As the first year of district-wide *Exploring Computer Science* formally launches in 20 Los Angeles public high schools in 2009-10, teacher reflections of the preceding ECS Summer Institute radiate a sense of passion and justice for providing accessible computer science education to students of color attending large, public schools. Teachers report a shared sense of community amongst one another and an awareness of explicit pedagogical approaches that create places of academic hospitality.

The goals of the professional development programs include but reach far beyond the learning the computing content included in the instructional materials and extend building instructional strategies that support learning in a computing community of practice. Such goals, however, require ongoing professional development opportunities.

3.3.1 Modeling Engaging Pedagogy

Given the instructional design of the curriculum, it is important to explicitly model the inquiry-based design of the course in teacher workshops. To this end, several instructors take turns facilitating the professional development activities and publicly reflecting on their own teaching. As a result, teacher participants report that their deepened understanding of how computer science content can be taught through role playing, jig sawing activities, pair and small-group collaboration, structured tinkering, multiple solutions, utilizing manipulatives, simulations, English language learner modifications, journal reflections, and interdisciplinary connections. Rather than providing the answers, the instructors facilitated participant discussions of problems and drew from the rich and varied expertise in the classroom.

3.3.2 Computing Community of Practice

A unique feature of the professional development is the distributed nature of expertise about teaching, computing knowledge, and the culture of Los Angeles high school students. No one participant or instructor in the professional developments has the singular solution for broadening participation in computing; rather, the professional development becomes a space where conversations about teaching wisdom and innovative computing topics intersect. Teachers, some who have been teaching APCS for years, join other teachers who have powerful pedagogical ideas but need to build their computing content knowledge. University computer science educators and veteran practitioners facilitate the conversation and continue to learn from the classroom teachers who connect with students daily. Important professional relationships have been built amongst co-learners and a computing community of practice has been cultivated and continues to grow with each subsequent workshop. Evaluations of teacher participants point to the desire to bring this academic accessibility and hospitality to their own classroom community.

3.3.3 Ongoing Professional Development

Since the ECS Summer Institute is only a week-long, three follow up Saturday sessions are held during the school year to focus on the last two and a half units of the curriculum. This ongoing model of professional development provides teachers a chance to come together and reflect on their classroom teaching experiences while learning new curricular material.

Newly hired computer science coaches, provided through additional NSF support, have begun following and supporting these teachers into their classrooms to provide content tutorials, co-teaching opportunities, collaborative planning sessions, and instructional support as needed.

4. POLICY STRATEGY

Though the development of the *Exploring Computer Science* course underwent a rigorous design process, the accompanying policy strategy was essential for ensuring the integration of this course in the school curriculum. New courses require the support and buy-in of school and district administrators. Though each school system is unique, the process of building an accessible program of computer science education in Los Angeles high schools provides lessons and considerations for other school systems interested in reforming computer science education. Due to the inter-connected and bureaucratic nature of state, district, and school policies, these efforts require a strategic multi-tiered approach to integrate this curriculum into the classroom setting so it is accessible to all students.

4.1 State University Level Policy

In 2008, California released a call for the development of new college-preparatory courses which merge the topics of traditionally academic courses with the applied nature of Career Technical Education (CTE). University education researchers collaborated with district officials to submit an application to the University of California Office of the President to deem *Exploring Computer Science* a college preparatory elective course. The first year there was a question about prerequisites for the course and the district was encouraged to resubmit the application with a preparatory course in place – a full year later. The resubmitted application reflected Algebra I as the pre-requisite for this course. The University of California Office of the President has approved this college-preparatory application with glowing reviews, noting that this course is "a very strong course submission" that they would like "to use it as a model CTE course". This means that the course satisfies multiple purposes for students on various pathways towards college, careers, or other directions.

4.2 District Level Procedures

The administrative structure of the school district relies on official, school board-approved memorandums to superintendents and principals in order to formally provide any notices in the district. To publicize this course and gain principal approval, school district Equity Alliance partners work internally to navigate this process and develop informative memorandums about the course and accompanying professional development opportunities. Without this insider status, maneuvering within this complex system would be difficult given the tight resources and multiple demands of school districts.

4.3 School Level Implementation

These official district memorandums were followed up with individual meetings and conference calls with high school principals. Principals who express a signed commitment to offering *Exploring Computer Science* were asked to identify a dynamic teacher able to attend the extensive accompanying professional development. Importantly, one of the Computer Science Equity Alliance's leaders is the former LAUSD Director of Secondary Science and current school principal of one of the largest LAUSD high schools (which serves the largest number of African Americans in the district), and another Alliance member is now the secondary science director for LAUSD; together they are able to draw on an extensive professional network to offer ECS to principals and place *Exploring Computer Science* in a growing number of schools.

Once connected with the CSEA community, teachers are provided support and resources (counselor information forms, student recruitment forms, parent information, posters, etc.) to further advocate for computing courses at their school site. Teachers are in an important position for working with counseling offices and other educators to advocate for the steering of traditionally underrepresented students towards *Exploring Computer Science.*

5. A CASE OF LOCAL REFORM

Though the particular details of reforming computer science education outlined in this paper are unique to Los Angeles schools, a select set of the procedures and strategic choices made to broaden participation in computing in this diverse city might serve as a model for other collaborative reform efforts.

5.1 Policy Work is Collaborative

Securing bureaucratic approval for a new course in the second largest school district, and in the largest state, requires a careful navigation of school system demands and opportunities. Each policy move was a result of collaborative decision making of district officials, educational researchers, university computer scientists, professional organizations, and lead teachers. The Computer Science Teachers Association advises this project and situates it within a national context of computer science education. University computer science educators were instrumental in providing content guidance while educational researchers brought in a framework for curricular reform. In addition to the value of multiple perspectives on policy decisions, several of the endorsement applications require district-university partnerships. The strength and successes of the Equity Alliance are a testimony of the power of collaboration. However, there are limitations to shaping only district and state stances on computing. National policy which incorporates computing into education legislation is a necessary step in encouraging state and district leaders to support computing education and intensify the impact and sustainability of local reform efforts [11].

5.2 Example of Dynamic Foundation Course

As the College Board reconsiders the APCS programs, there has been much discussion about a sequence of courses in computing. The decision to offer a survey course of major computing topics as a high school computing course was based on a desire to introduce students to the broad field of computing through an exploration of engaging and accessible topics. The curricular materials offer structured activities and projects which allow students to dabble in the computational thinking practices championed by computer scientists [12]. It is anticipated that some students will use this course as a launching pad to a soon-to-be revised APCS program.

Though curricular development is most effective when created as part of a local effort, many districts and states do not have the capacity to design their own curricular materials. Though developed with the particular needs of Los Angeles students in mind, these curricular materials could certainly be adapted nationwide to supplement other instructional materials. Apart from the cost of robots, this course does not rely on expensive computers, a particular platform, proprietary software, or costly textbooks – making it an attractive option for schools, districts, and states struggling to provide accessibility with scarce resources.

The organization of the *Exploring Computer Science* curricular materials makes each unit amenable to dynamic substitutions or modifications as engaging new computing topics are brought into the curriculum. For example, a Computing Applications unit currently draws from seismic data provided by UCLA's Center for Embedded Network Sensing (CENS), a member of the Computer Science Equity Alliance. As the CENS data evolves, or large-scale application projects are developed elsewhere, these changes will be added or interchanged in the curriculum. This structure allows more local connections to be included or emphasized based on the needs of students. Importantly, this dynamic design is necessary for students and teachers to keep up with the rapid pace of computing innovations.

5.3 Teachers are Key

The close link of the curriculum to professional development is a necessary coupling for introducing a new course in high schools. In this model of reform, the effectiveness of the course is limited if not accompanied by high quality professional development which focuses on content and instructional strategies. Though research has shown that the ECS Summer Institutes and weekend workshops are helpful in supporting *Exploring Computer Science* teachers, the data also shows a need for more personalized mentoring. The new computing coaching program will seek to answer that need.

Working with teachers is critical because the implementation of reforming computer science education ultimately takes place in the classroom setting. Observations from this project have captured powerful teachable moments when skilled computing teachers link students' knowledge and interests with computing topics – such as JavaScript and MySpace page design. Many of the Los Angeles teachers in computer science share a common vision of inspiring youth. In addition to focusing their passion, beauty, joy, and awe on the computing *content*, these teachers focus their passion, beauty, joy, and awe towards the enormous *potential* of their computing students. This subtle shift in perspective – from *teaching content* to *teaching students through content* – emphasizes a critical distinction in purpose.

5.4 Measuring Success

Sharing a goal of broadening participation in computing, the Computer Science Equity Alliance will continue to work to improve the engagement, accessibility, and hospitality in computer science education. Collecting quantitative and qualitative data to measure students' engagement with computer science is integral to evaluate the effectiveness of this model of reform. However, the Equity Alliance resists the call to make the longitudinal impact of this course on college major patterns as the primary evaluation criteria. The measurement for success differs: For students to have access and understanding of computing as a result of this course is considered a successful effort by the Equity Alliance regardless of students' future academic ventures. It is opportunities, not just a narrow end goal that the Equity Alliance seeks to provide.

6. ACKNOWLEDGMENTS

This work would not be possible without all the contributions from the members of the Computer Science Equity Alliance. This work is supported by the National Science Foundation. I would also like to express appreciation to Ruwan Jayasinge, a passionate Los Angeles computing teacher, who coined the term "academic hospitality" to describe a Summer Institute experience.

7. REFERENCES

[1] Margolis, J., Estrella, R., Goode, J., Holme, J. J. and Nao, K. *Stuck in the shallow end: Education, race, and computing*. MIT Press, Cambridge, MA, 2008.

[2] Goode, J., Estrella, R. and Margolis, J. *Lost in translation: Gender and high school computer science*. MIT Press, Cambridge, MA, 2006.

[3] Goode, J. If you build teachers, will students come? The role of teachers in broadening computer science learning for urban youth. *Journal of Educational Computing Research*, 36, 1 (2007), 65-88.

[4] Bransford, J., Brown, A. L. and Cocking, R. R. *How people learn: Brain, mind, experience, and school*. National Academy Press, Washington, D.C., 1999.

[5] Vygotsky, L. *Mind in society: Development of higher psychological processes*. Harvard University Press, Cambridge, MA, 1978.

[6] Wenger, E. *Communities of practice: Learning, meaning, and identity*. Cambridge University Press, Cambridge, UK, 1998.

[7] Goode, J. and Chapman, G. *Exploring computer science*. Computer Science Equity Alliance, Los Angeles, 2009.

[8] Tucker, A., Deek, F., Jones, J., McCowan, D., Stephenson, C. and Verno, A. *A model curriculum for K-12 computer science: Final report of the ACM K-12 task force curriculum*. Association for Computing Machinery, Computer Science Teachers Association, New York, NY, 2003.

[9] Maloney, J. H., Peppler, K., Kafai, Y., Resnick, M. and Rusk, N. Programming by choice: Urban youth learning programming with scratch. In *Proceedings of the Proceedings of the 39th SIGCSE technical symposium on Computer science education* (Portland, OR, USA, 2008).

[10] Bell, T., Fellows, M. and Witten, I. *Computer science unplugged!* , City, 2009.

[11] Wilson, C. and Harsha, P. The long road to computer science education reform. *Communications of the ACM*, 52, 9 (Sep 2009), 33-35.

[12] Wing, J. M. Computational Thinking. *Communications of the ACM*, 49, 3 (March 2006), 33-35.

Integrating Evaluation into Program Development: Benefits of Baselining a NSF-BPC Alliance

W. Richards Adrion
Renee Fall
CAITE□/CS Department
University of Massachusetts Amherst
Amherst MA 01003
413-577-4431
{adrion,rfall}@cs.umass.edu

Manuel Matos
Alan R. Peterfreund
SageFox Associates
30 Boltwood Walk
Amherst MA 01002
413-256-6169
{mmatos,apeterfreund}@sagefoxgroup.com

ABSTRACT

The Commonwealth Alliance for Information Technology Education (CAITE) is one of 11 National Science Foundation Broadening Participation in Computing (BPC) alliances aimed at increasing the participation and success of underrepresented groups in information technology (IT). From the beginning, CAITE partners worked to integrate a detailed and comprehensive evaluation strategy to provide a quantitative assessment of the effectiveness of CAITE action plans on its main objectives. We collected large institutional data sets for the seven academic years prior to the project inception from each of the nine original partners, the six additional partners and several other institutions. These data serve as a baseline for assessing the efficacy of CAITE interventions and make it possible to examine trends in student participation and success across each CAITE partner and the alliance as whole. Importantly, these data provide valuable insight into each of the institutions that has allowed CAITE to tailor its inventions to reflect local conditions at each institution and within each region. From the evaluation data, it became clear that we needed to adjust action plans to better meet CAITE objectives. We describe specific aspects that warranted data-driven adjustments, and highlight lessons learned from these revelations.

Categories and Subject Descriptors

K.3.2 [**Computing Milieux**] Computer and Information Science Education

General Terms

Management, Measurement, Human Factors

Keywords

Broadening participation, community colleges, information technology education and workforce

1. INTRODUCTION

The Commonwealth Alliance for Information Technology Education (CAITE) [1-2] is an initiative funded by the National Science Foundation's (NSF) Broadening Participation in Computing (BPC) program [3-5]. CAITE (pronounced "Kate") hopes to increase the participation and success of underrepresented groups in information technology (IT) through a regional strategy that includes all four, non-medical campuses of the University of Massachusetts (UMass), two state colleges (Bridgewater and Worcester) and nine community colleges (Bristol, Bunker Hill, Cape Cod, Greenfield, Holyoke, Middlesex, Northern Essex, Roxbury and Springfield Technical). CAITE takes a broad view of IT, that ranges from "IT across the curriculum" [6] to traditional computer science, computer engineering, information systems, and information technology.

The CAITE program was originally developed out of growing concern over the declining numbers of women and underrepresented minorities majoring in IT while, concurrently, there was and continues to be a demand for IT professionals throughout the spectrum of industry. Since community colleges serve as a gateway for students in economically underserved regions and attract large numbers of students to career and technical (CTE) IT programs, CAITE places a special emphasis on community-college-4-year-college pathways and hopes to reach out to community college students and to support their transfer and retention in 4-year programs. Our objectives and plans of action were based on the available literature and best practices [7-9] that suggest reasons for the low percentage of underrepresented ethnic minorities and women enrolled in IT programs and interventions that we might try in Massachusetts two- and four-year institutions.

From the beginning, the CAITE partners and its evaluators, SageFox Associates, worked to integrate a detailed and comprehensive evaluation strategy to the CAITE initiative. The primary goal of the evaluation process is to provide a quantitative assessment of the effectiveness of CAITE interventions. To establish a baseline, we needed to address two main questions: who are the students currently participating in IT programs and what is the status of their academic performance, including retention and degree completion? We were able to collect large sets of institutional data for the seven academic years prior to the CAITE formation in 2007. We are in the process of gathering a second round of data covering the first few years of CAITE activities. These data allow us to examine trends in student participation and success across each CAITE partner and the alliance as whole, and importantly characterize the challenges and issues at each institution so we can tailor our interventions.

SIGCSE'10, March 10–13, 2010, Milwaukee, Wisconsin, USA.

Data requests included enrollment information, demographics, test scores, transfer information, course performance and other academic outcomes (degrees, GPA, etc.). Data were collected for all students enrolled in an IT major or taking at least one IT course. Our evaluation plans also include surveys of CAITE event attendees, interviews with partner institutions, and a continuing assessment of the project management and the alliance as a whole.

Once the first evaluation reports detailing baseline information of student demographics, program offerings, event expectations and feedback were processed, it became clear that there were opportunities to adjust CAITE plans of actions to better meet the project objectives. We also identified a number of difficulties in collecting, validating and analyzing data from 15 CAITE institutions and several other "control" (from the CAITE perspective) institutions. These led to some revisions in the data collection rubrics and methods that have been corrected in our current second phase.

school students, parents, teachers and counselors. CAITE seeks to facilitate pathways that provide multiple points of entry and a variety of opportunities for IT degrees and careers.

2.1 Action Plan

The CAITE approach to accomplishing its core goals (Figure 1) is bifocal: focusing on outreach and creating and supporting novel and existing pathways to degree completion. The outreach component includes a variety of career fairs, seminars, workshops and contests aimed at invigorating student (and their parents', teachers' and counselors') interest in and knowledge of IT fields. Institutions have an opportunity to showcase their diverse IT programs and associated career opportunities. Often these efforts are coordinated among community colleges and 4-year campuses within a region. In one region, for example, the university hosted a "Mind the Gap! – A Career Summit for Women & Technology" where fifty percent of the participants were university students and the rest were from three community colleges within the region. Events are often co-sponsored with other initiatives such as the Boston Area Technical

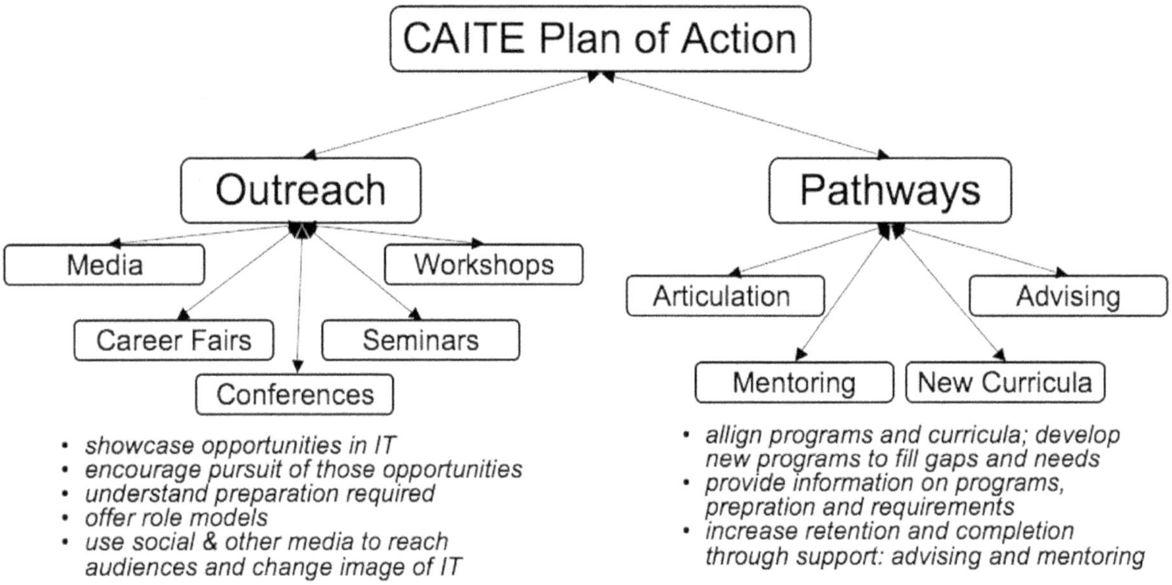

Figure 1. CAITE Plan of Action

Integrating evaluation and baselining can be used to continually reassess and revise project plans. We will share examples of baselining, describe specific aspects of our plans that warrant data-driven adjustments, and highlight lessons learned. We will also highlight the importance of community colleges in the efforts to impact diversity in IT fields. The ongoing assessments indicate that increasing the diversity of students enrolling and completing 4-year degrees may be achieved through better understanding the diversity of the programs and students at community colleges.

2. CAITE PROGRAM DESCRIPTION

Now in its third year and recently in receipt of an extension award from NSF that will carry the project at least through five years, the CAITE alliance expanded from three to four University of Massachusetts campuses, added two state colleges, and grew from six to nine community colleges. The CAITE mission is multi-dimensional: reaching out not only to community college, and four-year college/university students, but also to middle school and high

Connections (BATEC), the Urban Massachusetts and New England Louis Stokes Alliances for Minority Participation, and various CAITE partnerships (Empowering Leadership, the CRAW/CDC Alliance, Georgia Computes!, AccessComputing, etc.). In addition to events, CAITE also has an extensive media program including websites (project reporting, collaboration and student recruiting), printed materials in Spanish and English, newsletters and so on.

The second component of the plan of action is the implementation and support of novel and existing pathways towards degree completion. Two core goals drive this plan: facilitating recruiting for, enrollment in and transfer to degree programs and supporting and retaining students through successful program completion.

The CAITE plan for achieving these goals include:

- "Transfer pathways" to facilitate student enrollment in IT degree programs – both traditional articulated programs and transfer from Career and Technical Education (CTE) programs;

- Mentoring structures including supplemental peer-mentoring and facilitated study groups:
- Professional development efforts across the alliance with special focus on community college and high school faculty, advisors and guidance counselors;
- Collaboration with TechPrep and others to use assessment tools and other methods (e.g., Accuplacer) for assessing college readiness early enough for appropriate intervention;
- "Dual enrollment" programs on site (HS and CC), on-line and/or with technology support; and
- Formal and informal middle and high school programs.

Working in tandem with the state's "Mass Transfer" program, our pathways effort focuses on both student-centered and institution-centered reform. Student-centered initiatives aim to provide students with access to a wealth of education resources. A

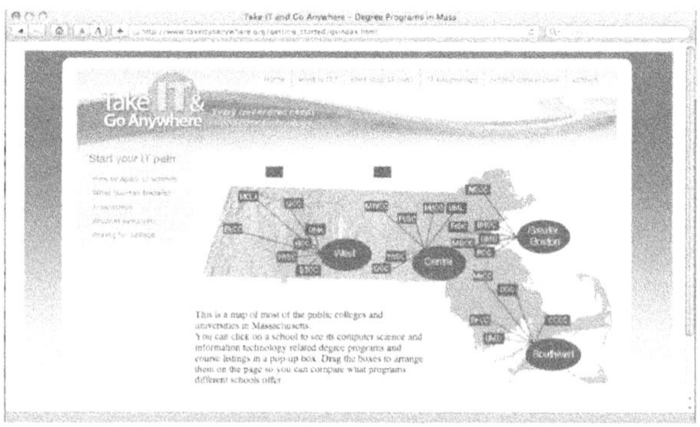

Figure 2. Student Website

website (Figure 2) connects interested middle school, high school, and college students with information regarding IT careers, education opportunities, and networking events. The website includes sections that address frequent misconceptions and gaps of knowledge that are known to deter interest in IT. In addition, the website includes links to IT programs and events by geographic region. We are adding information on course equivalency and transfer credit information that reflect standing academic policies shared by participating institutions.

Institution-centered initiatives include: development of articulation agreements between community colleges and universities and professional development. CAITE sponsored several articulation "summits" to gather course information, create a map of course equivalents between institutions, identify common links to program and degree requirements, and to determine potential common courses and curricula.

Improving student retention and degree completion involves an integrative approach between mentoring and academic advising. CAITE, with assistance from Mt. Holyoke College Professor Becky Packard (a national leader in peer mentoring research), is piloting a peer-mentoring strategy in six institutions each semester over the next few years. Typically, three 4-year schools and three community colleges participate. The primary mechanism of the peer-mentoring program is a supplemental instruction style intervention where step-ahead peers provide students with guidance on course materials in selected "gateway" courses. Once evaluations are completed, best practices will be disseminated to remaining campuses. Articulation agreements, which involve university and community college faculty and admissions office staff, improve academic advising by providing clearer understanding of program offerings and course requirements.

3. EVALUATION STRATEGY

CAITE evaluation provides constant feedback to event and outreach coordinators, and also provides the means by which to determine the overall efficacy of both outreach and pathway interventions in quantitative terms. Baseline data that describe the target-points prior to a proposed intervention is a fundamental component of successful longitudinal assessment. It is precisely the effort of analyzing baseline data that has led to very important

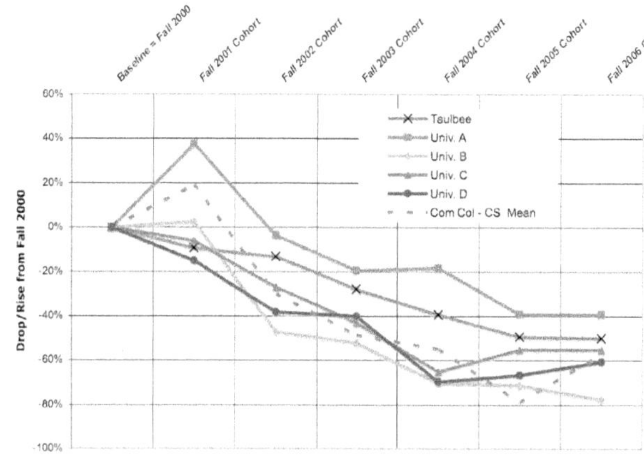

Figure 3 – Trend of Students Matriculating as CS Majors.

adjustments to the CAITE initiative and strategy.

CAITE evaluators gather extensive data on outreach activities using surveys, questionnaires, interviews and focus groups. This allows us to identify participant demographics, attitudes and awareness of IT careers. Resources and human subject constraints do not allow us to "track" individuals from outreach events through enrollment in a program, however analysis of institutional data will allow us to identify any changes in the number, makeup and origin of the students enrolling, succeeding and/or transferring on a yearly basis. These data allow us to infer a relation between events or activities given at student origins and changes in enrollment, retention, etc.

Baseline evaluation provides large amounts of institutional data. Institutional research offices at participating institutions provide us with baseline data on cohorts of students beginning or switching into IT majors (CS, CIS, CE, SE, M/IS, IT, etc.) as well as those who take IT courses without eventually becoming IT majors. We collected data for consecutive years dating back to the 2000 – 2001 academic year.

Figure 3[1] displays trends in enrollment of students matriculating as computer science majors at 4 university campuses and an average over the community colleges for each of the seven years prior to beginning of CAITE. These data are compared with national data, such as the CRA Taulbee data ("x" marker in Figure 3). Our pre-CAITE data tracks rather closely with the Taulbee data, which should allow us to see if our interventions

[1] Institution names are not used to avoid unnecessary "comparisons."

result in outcomes that differ from national trends at the next round of data collection.

The institutional data allows us to determine trends in the participation of women and minorities (Figure 4) and compare it with national data sources when available. Again our data is consistent with the Taulbee data on women entering degree programs. These two charts do highlight some real differences between institutions. The percentage of URM at community colleges is much higher than at the university campuses with one clear exception, the urban university campus. For women, the enrollment at the predominately research campuses is somewhat lower than for the primarily undergraduate campuses. While our most recent data shows significant increases for both women and URM across CAITE, these data aid us in designing interventions.

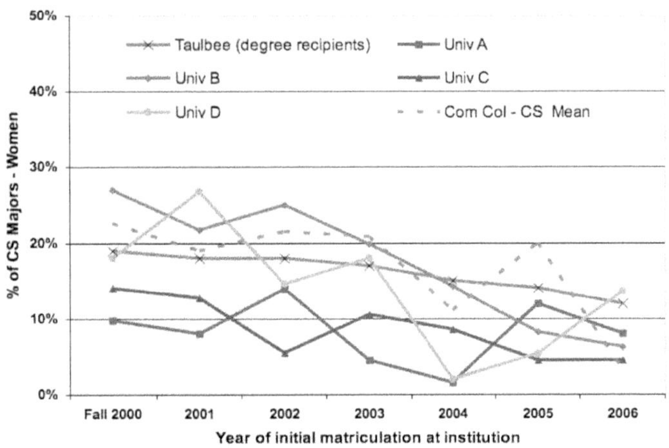

(a) Women

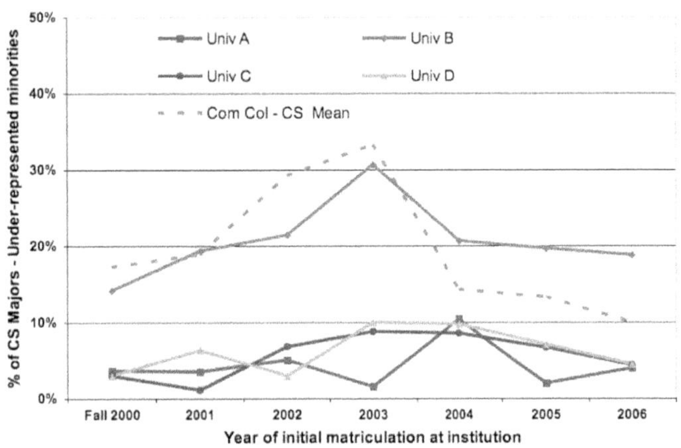

(b) Underrepresented Minorities

Figure 4 – Proportion of total students matriculating as computer science majors who are Women or URM.

Other relevant factors such as the age of matriculating students, the proportion and source of transfer students, time to degree, numbers of IT courses taken, course grades, and GPA etc. are useful in identifying trends throughout the alliance and also allow us to delineate the differences and similarities within institutions, between institutions, by type of institution and ultimately for the alliance as a whole.

A particularly useful tool is the ability to identify the proportion of students transferring from other schools. Given that the alliance is organized by geographic region, where community colleges work together with the neighboring university and 4-year college campuses, we track student enrollment from "feeder" schools (Table 1). Clearly "Univ. B" draws significant numbers of transfers from many sources, a characteristic of the mission of the school. The strategy for this campus has to be different than for the other two. Similar data on high schools helps aid outreach targeting, where we can focus on schools that send significant numbers of graduates to a specific college.

Table 1. Distribution of Matriculating Computer Science Transfer Students From Feeder Schools.

4 Year Partner	*Univ A*		*Univ B*		*Univ C*	
Total Transfers	73		468		75	
Feeder School	CC 1	CC2	CC 3	CC 4	CC 5	CC 6
Feeder Transfers	2	16	4	10	20	8
% From Feeder CC	25%		3%		37%	

3.1 Data-driven Adjustments

3.1.1 "Outreach" Adjustments

The various surveys and questionnaires used for outreach events provide insight into the barriers and positive impacts of these efforts. The data indicate that while there is excellent attendance at inaugural events, attendance often drops when the event is repeated but not when it is replicated elsewhere. Except for urban College Fairs, large events are not very successful in attracting student participation. College Fairs tend to be more successful if they are targeted and encourage student interaction with panelists and leaders in workshops and seminars; students prefer learning about funding, application processes, college selection and career paths rather than the more traditional booth-style format with admissions officers. Demographic data indicate that all day events are a poor match with student schedules and time commitments. As a result, CAITE has focused on shorter durations, more targeted events, events held locally, and replication. Moreover, we identified a need to survey incoming students in order to link outreach interventions with enrollment and are beginning that process with the AY09-10 cohorts.

3.1.2 "Pathways" Adjustments

Our baseline evaluation for the pathway interventions produces striking student age distribution data. We find, as we would expect, that student populations skew younger at university campuses than at feeder community colleges. In the three regions of Table 2, there are more community college students in the 24+ age groups than university students, reflecting that community colleges attract older students (often holding degrees) to technical and career programs in response to career changes and market skill demands. Recognizing the breadth of community college IT offerings allows for more appropriate interventions. The articulation summits have provided a clearer picture of just how complex this task will be. Computer information systems programs and, particularly CTE programs, align poorly with traditional computer science programs. While CTE students transfer to 4-year programs in numbers similar to articulated-transfer-program students, it may take 3 or more years for a transferring CTE student to make up for the lack of transferable coursework applying to degree programs. In response, CAITE is developing new degree programs that allow transfer students to complete the requirements for a bachelor's degree more quickly.

Understanding the diversity of program offerings and student populations at community colleges alerts administrators and program developers to the reality that, in a variety of aspects, universities and 4-year colleges often do not have the infrastructure to support incoming community college students, who may be older, have family responsibilities and must hold down full- or part-time jobs. In Region B, the age distribution of the university and community college students are similar, which may suggest that this university campus is more "friendly" to older student populations.

Table 2. Age Distribution of Paired Institutions in Regions

	Region A		*Region B*		*Region C*	
Age Groups	Univ	CC	Univ	CC	Univ C	CC
≤ 19 yrs.	82%	49%	30%	27%	73%	50%
20-23 yrs.	15%	22%	38%	36%	18%	18%
24-39 yrs.	3%	22%	30%	33%	8%	20%
≥ 40 yrs.	0%	8%	2%	5%	1%	11%

Recently, community colleges have seen a dramatic rise in enrollment, particularly in developmental courses. With more students entering college without necessary mathematics and language skills, CAITE increased emphasis on early identification (at the middle school and high school level) of college preparation deficiencies. We are piloting "IT academies" for high school students to provide support through the HS-CC-4-year-college pathway. CAITE also is working with school officials to expand high school dual enrollment courses offered by community colleges and 4-year institutions at high schools, on college campuses and through blended and distance education.

Our advising and mentoring strategy was also modified. CAITE began with university advisors offering services at community colleges. Evaluation demonstrated that coordinating time for student advising, inherent differences in program offerings, and institutional cultures made it difficult to offer effective academic advising at the community college level. To address this, CAITE is piloting peer-mentoring programs and strengthening the emphasis on student-driven information resources.

4. Conclusions

CAITE, working with its evaluators and institutional research offices, collected baseline data covering 15 institutions and seven entering cohorts of IT majors, students who entered or left IT majors after initial matriculation, and students who enrolled in IT courses but did not become majors. A biennial series of collection and analyses will allow us to provide quantitative evidence of the efficacy of CAITE interventions. We will reference our analysis against national and local data, and we have a strategy for linking quantitative analysis with the qualitative evaluation.

The important lesson here, however, is in how integrated evaluation and assessment has allowed us to better understand the similarities and differences among institutions in our alliance and the characteristics of the students who enroll in them. As a result, we have already tailored our interventions to address the issues revealed by our baseline analysis and introduced new interventions where gaps were identified. This baseline data collection is critical for planning, implementation, evaluation and the success of the project – a process we strongly encourage other programs adapt.

5. ACKNOWLEDGMENTS

The authors thank the NSF CISE Broadening Participation in Computing Program for support under awards CNS- 0634412 and CNS-0837739. All opinions reflected in this paper are those of the authors and not necessarily those of the National Science Foundation.

6. REFERENCES

[1] Adrion, W. R. and Fall, R. 2009. Broadening participation: a community college strategy. In the Fifth Richard Tapia Celebration of Diversity in Computing Conference: intellect, initiatives, insight, and innovations (Portland, Oregon, April 01 - 04, 2009). TAPIA '09. ACM Press, New York, NY, 46-51. DOI= http://doi.acm.org/10.1145/1565799.1565811

[2] Adrion, W.R., Biskup, S., Boisvert, D., Clarke, L., Fountain, J., Grocer, P., Mackler, S., Peterfreund, A.R., Rath, K.A., Smith, A., Snyder, D.D., and Wiens, A. 2008. Broadening participation in computing: K12-community-college-university-graduate pathways. In Proceedings of the 38th Annual Frontiers in Education Conference (Saratoga Springs NY, October 22-25, 2008) FIE 2008. S4F-15-S4F-20.

[3] Cuny, J. and Aspray, W. 2002. Recruitment and retention of women graduate students in computer science and engineering: results of a workshop organized by the computing research association. *SIGCSE Bull.* 34, 2 (June 2002), 168-174. DOI= http://doi.acm.org/10.1145/543812.543852

[4] Peckham, J., Harlow, L. L., Stuart, D. A., Silver, B., Mederer, H., and Stephenson, P. D. 2007. Broadening participation in computing: issues and challenges. In *Proceedings of the 12th Annual SIGCSE Conference on innovation and Technology in Computer Science Education* (Dundee, Scotland, June 25 - 27, 2007). ITiCSE '07. ACM Press, New York, NY, 9-13. DOI= http://doi.acm.org/10.1145/1268784.1268790

[5] Gilbert, J. E., 2006. Making a case for BPC [Broadening Participation in Computing]. Computer, vol.39, no.3, pp. 83-86 (March 2006)

[6] Israel, Bill. 2003. Information Technology Across the Curriculum. In Proceedings of the Learning Conference 2003, (London, July 15-18, 2003) Institute of Education, University of London.

[7] Cohoon, J. M. and Aspray, W. 2006 Women and Information Technology: Research on Underrepresentation. The MIT Press.

[8] Gürer, D. and Camp, T. 2002. An ACM-W literature review on women in computing. SIGCSE Bull. 34, 2 (Jun. 2002), 121-127. DOI= http://doi.acm.org/10.1145/543812.543844

[9] Blum, L., FriezeHafkin, N. J. and Huyer, S. 2008. Women and gender in ICT statistics and indicators for development. *Inf. Technol. Int. Dev.* 4, 2 (Jan. 2008), 25-41. DOI= http://dx.doi.org/10.1162/itid.2008.00006

Use of Satellite Imagery in Multidisciplinary Projects

Ali Erkan*
aerkan@ithaca.edu
Ithaca College
401B Williams Hall
Ithaca, NY 14850, U.S.A.

Jason Hamilton†
jhamilton@ithaca.edu
Ithaca College
252 Cntr. Nat. Sci.
Ithaca, NY 14850, U.S.A.

Tom Pfaff‡
tpfaff@ithaca.edu
Ithaca College
311A Williams Hall
Ithaca, NY 14850, U.S.A.

Michael Rogers§
mrogers@ithaca.edu
Ithaca College
265 Cntr. Nat. Sci.
Ithaca, NY 14850, U.S.A.

ABSTRACT

The most important problems of our century require collaborative work. Therefore, as educators, we must be producing individuals who understand how to communicate and work with professionals from other fields. In this paper, we outline our ongoing efforts in addressing this need, without compromising discipline specific qualities or goals. Specifically, we present a number of programming projects that fulfill curricular requirements as well as making students aware of the Science Technology Engineering and Math (STEM) context of their work.

Categories and Subject Descriptors

K.3.2 [**Computers and Education**]: Computer and Information Science Education—*Computer science education*; J.2 [**Physical Sciences And Engineering**]: Earth and atmospheric sciences; E.1 [**Data Structures**]: Arrays

General Terms

Algorithms, Measurement, Experimentation

Keywords

Scientific computing, active learning, satellite imagery

*Assistant Professor of Computer Science.

†Associate Professor of Biology.

‡Associate Professor of Mathematics.

§Associate Professor of Physics.

1. INTRODUCTION

College education has always had the responsibility to produce individuals who are well on their way to becoming experts in their field of interest. But as society faces ever more complex problems that require systems thinking, we witness the growing importance of producing professionals with the skills to collaborate across disciplinary boundaries [11, 7]. Unfortunately, despite individual efforts and contributions (such as [6] and [14] in the context of CS), STEM education in general has not been evolving sufficiently fast in this regard [1] and it should thus be getting additional attention to address the deficit [12]. We speculate that this educational challenge can be addressed in one of two ways:

- Through an **interdisciplinary** approach, ideas and concepts from different disciplines can be integrated to generate new ways of thinking. This approach assumes that participants must become fluent in the participating disciplines, creating new concepts and theories.
- Through a **multidisciplinary** approach, the distinct perspectives and concepts of each discipline can be used to tackle particular *portions* of a complex problem; fluency in *all* of the participating disciplines, however, is no longer emphasized. The important thing is for each participant to understand the multi-faceted nature of the problem and to have the necessary skills to communicate with others to produce a collaborative solution through a common scientific perspective[1].

Although numerous significant scientific challenges may require an *interdisciplinary* arrangement, we believe that a *multidisciplinary* approach to scientific education has tremendous value. First, a strictly interdisciplinary approach needs to restructure the boundaries between disciplines and can thus require serious financial and administrative support. A multidisciplinary approach, however, works well with the existing systems we see in today's institutes of higher education. Second, we believe that a multidisciplinary emphasis

[1]"Multidisciplinary" overlaps with "transdisciplinary" but since we are yet to find an authoritative definition of the subtle difference between the two, we go with the one that makes more intuitive sense to us.

is a prerequisite for producing individuals who may later become interdisciplinary problem solvers.

Four faculty members of our institute (representing Computer Science, Mathematics, Biology, and Physics) are currently working on the creation of an NSF supported framework for incorporating multidisciplinary projects in scientific education. Specifically, these faculty members are focusing on the rich set of problems encountered in sustainability and formulating how they can be addressed by students from different disciplines working collectively and iteratively over a set of online tools for exchanging data, code, reports, and expertise. This is to be contrasted with other approaches for exposing students to STEM disciplines [13, 15, 3] and computational sciences [10] that hinge on the creation of new courses and/or degrees.

The goal of this paper is to provide a description of the computer science footprint of our endeavor. Specifically, we outline a few representative projects for processing satellite images and drawing conclusions about ongoing climate changes. Despite the presence of the underlying theme of collaboration, we intentionally keep our focus on the computing value of what we cover to make it apparent that integration with other departments/disciplines is not a prerequisite for engagement (i.e. these projects are usable even within existing silos). In fact, since image processing provides an effective way to teach array processing in CS1/CS2 [2, 8] as well as ray tracing, depth/breadth first search, and recursion in data structures [9, 4], these projects belong to a pattern that has already been recognized and utilized in computer science education.

Section 2 outlines our planned mode of operation with respect to the exchange of data, questions, and answers between computer science and other STEM courses. Section 3 describes a set of programming projects to draw climate related information from a repository of satellite images. Section 4 illustrates an optimization problem that emerges from what we cover in section 3. Finally, section 5 reports student responses from our "Introduction To Computation with Matlab" course where we have tested some of our smaller scale projects.

2. MULTIDISCIPLINARY OPERATION

The key idea of our multidisciplinary approach is to allow students of different courses to take turns addressing different aspects of large scale problems that are too broad to be categorized within one discipline. Therefore, the best possible illustration is to outline the first educational module we are building to interconnect our Ecology, Thermodynamics, Calculus, and "computing" courses. We say "computing" in place of a conventional course name because the exercises outlined in sections 3 and 4 can be used in CS1, CS2, Data Structures, and any flavor of an "Introduction to Scientific Computation" course. What we subsequently refer to as "the repository" is some type of content management system for the communication between the participating courses and for the storage of questions, answers, data files, and reports.

We start by assuming that Calculus students bootstrap our example by curve fitting average global temperature data to create a simple model[2]. They then use this model to predict future changes by extrapolating the curve and by studying the tangent line at particular points of interest. In order to justify their predictions, they also consult with thermodynamics and ecology students to learn more about the driving forces behind the expected changes and the ramifications of the associated warming. Specifically, they find out that changes in Carbon emissions (information from ecology) and the reflective properties of the planet (information from thermodynamics) are yet to render their long term effects. They also send several satellite images of the Arctic to the computing class to get an estimate of the extent of changes in ice coverage. The computer science students perform the required computations in the context of a lab focusing on array processing. They also (subsequently) produce a more detailed report based on the color histograms of the images, conceivably of importance for thermodynamics since this directly relates to the estimation of the reflective properties of the planet. At the end, students from all classes draw their discipline specific conclusions.

There are, of course, many issues to be resolved, such as the timing of the outlined communications, which hinge on the paces of the individual courses[3]. However, the advantage of the ideal arrangement is apparent: with a real-world context for the problems they address, students engage in deeper learning [5]. In fact, if this pattern is exercised consistently throughout their college years (with progressively more complex problems), it is reasonable to assume that students will feel more integrated with many 21st century problems that need to be addressed by tomorrow's scientists.

3. PROCESSING CRYOSPHERE IMAGES

Provided that the above approach increases multidisciplinary problem solving skills, how does it influence the discipline specific development of students?

Teamwork leads to synergy only when members contribute as experts of their field. Therefore, an important responsibility of educators going in a multidisciplinary direction is to make sure that their students acquire discipline specific knowledge just as much as their counterparts did in prior (and more "compartmentalized") years. As we try to illustrate in this section, we think this an achievable goal through carefully selected projects.

Cryosphere Today[4] is a web site that provides satellite images of the north pole for any date between 1979 and the present. By browsing these images, it is easy to see the gloomy trend that has already been noted for many years: we are losing the Arctic. This observation, which has dire consequences for the ecological and thermodynamic character of the planet, also leads to a particular question for computer science students to address: what is the rate at which the Arctic is disappearing?

As outlined in figure 1, a functional decomposition of the problem leads to a number of distinct computational stages, each requiring a different level of programming sophistication (for clarity, the A, B, C, D, and E labels we use below in identifying these stages are also depicted in figure 1a):

(A) The original images from Cryosphere Today use a multi-color scale, with the color sequence blue $\rightarrow$ green $\rightarrow$

[2]This is one of many real world data sets utilized in the third author's calculus class. For more information, please visit `http://www.ithaca.edu/tpfaff/sustainability.htm`.

[3]We are also exploring an "asynchronous" mode of operation to simulate the communication when the participating courses are taught at different semesters.

[4]`http://arctic.atmos.uiuc.edu/cryosphere`

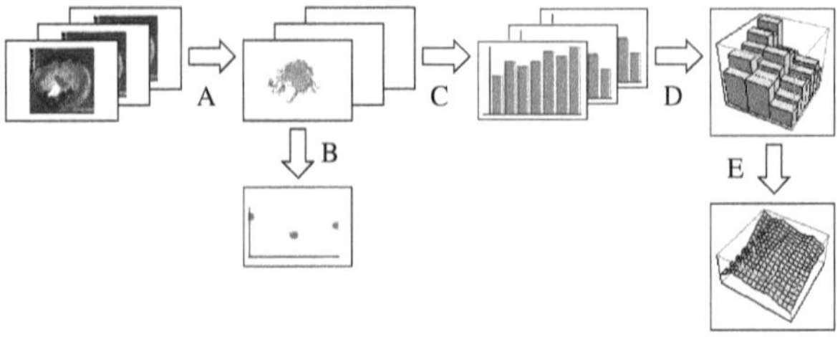

(a) *Five stages of computation A through E*

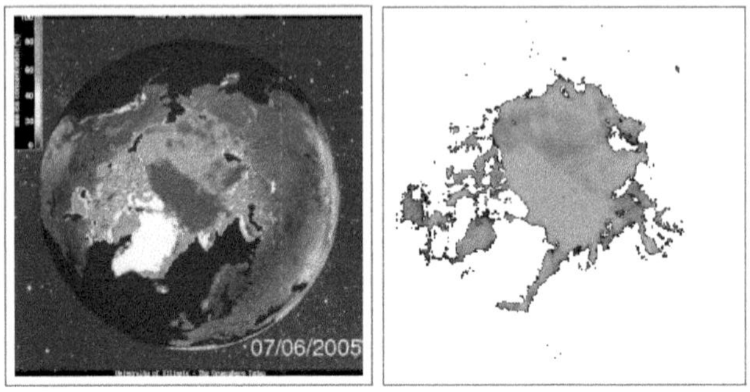

(b) *Multi- vs uni-color representation of ice concentrations*

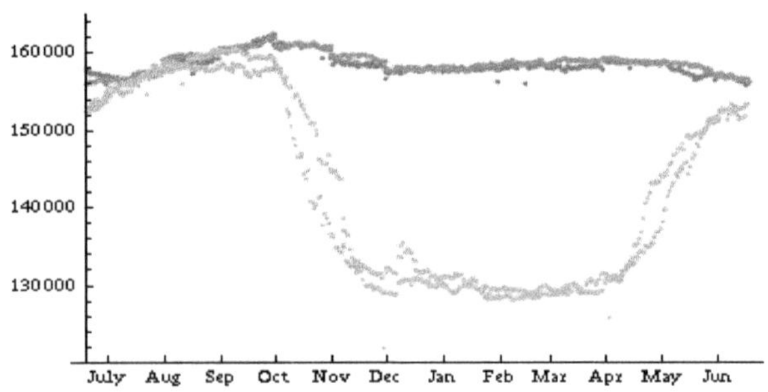

(c) *1996 and 2001 (flat) vs 2006 and 2007 (sagging)*

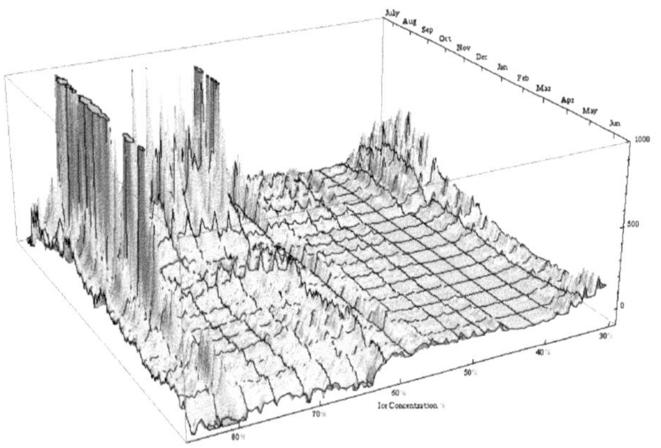

(d) *Changes in ice concentrations between 2001 and 2007*

Figure 1: *A summary of the computations performed on the satellite images received from Cryosphere Today as well as a few of the obtained results. In figure 1c, the horizontal axis has 365 steps (one for each day of an Arctic year), while the vertical axis counts the number of red pixels in each uni-color satellite image. In figure 1d, the second horizontal axis represents ice concentration levels from 30% to 85% while the vertical axis indicates ice concentration changes from 2001 to 2007, with a value above the 0 plane representing a loss from 2001 to 2007.*

yellow → orange → red → magenta progressively indicating increased concentrations of ice (left image in figure 1b). Although ideal for human perception, this scheme is inconvenient for computer processing and thus the images are first converted to a uni-color scheme (right image in figure 1b).

(B) By counting the number of colored pixels in each uni-color image, a whole year is turned into a plot of 365 points, profiling the changes in the size of the Arctic (in figure 1a, this is symbolically represented with three images leading to three plot points).

(C,D) Since the conversion of an entire image into a single point loses too much information, each image is also turned into a color intensity histogram (C). These histograms are then layered (as 3d bar charts) to create a surface plot of the changes throughout a year (D).

(E) The satellite images for two consecutive days typically (and unfortunately) differ more than one would expect[5] and, consequently, the surface plots produced by (D) are almost always too noisy. Therefore, before one can look for trends, these surface plots are smoothed with a moving average based on the recurrence relation

$$H(n) = \alpha H(n-1) + (1-\alpha)h(n)$$

which states that the nth **average histogram** $H(n)$ is based on the previous average $H(n-1)$ as well as the nth specific histogram $h(n)$, with the $0 \rightarrow 1$ range α value determining how aggressive the averaging should be (greater α values put more weight on the previous average and lead to smoother results).

Figure 1c is an actual product of stage B, revealing the profiles of four year-long intervals, each properly containing a winter season: **1996** (July 1996 to June 1997), **2001** (July 2001 to June 2002), **2006** (July 2006 to June 2007), and **2007** (July 2007 to June 2008). Despite the crudeness of the underlying computation (where an entire satellite image is mapped to a single data point), we can still see some of the dramatic changes that have taken place within the first few years of the new millennium: the dip between the October to May period for 2006 and 2007 is absent in 1996 and 2001.

Figure 1d, on the other hand, is based on the surface plots produced by stage E. Specifically, what we see is the subtraction of the surface plot for 2007 from that of 2001, allowing us to focus on the *changes* between the concentration levels of the two chosen years rather than their *absolute* levels. Since most of the values are above the 0 plane, we conclude that the Arctic has also been suffering loss in its ice concentrations, in addition to its shrinking size. Once identified and quantified, the consequences of these changes on the wild life habitats and the heat transfer equations of the planet are interpreted by our peers from ecology and thermodynamics, respectively.

Is this relevant to computer science education? We think the answer is yes since more than 90% of the computations are done with the fundamental constructs (array processing, loops, lists, look-up tables, etc) and concepts (functional decomposition, recurrence relations, etc) we expect our students to master within the first few courses in our discipline. Even the code to issue Mathematica commands to produce the plots in figure 1 are generated by '`toString()`' methods.

[5]This probably has to do with the instrumentation/software used to capture/process the images at Cryosphere Today.

4. SEQUENCING SATELLITE IMAGES

In the previous section, it was stated that Cryosphere Today releases a new image of the Arctic each day. Other providers of satellite imagery are similarly periodic; for example, Accuweather[6] releases two satellite images every hour for various types of measures (storm clouds, humidity, pollen counts, etc) and thus a new image is expected from them every 30 minutes. Yet, many consecutive image pairs turn out to be not so uniformly spaced in time. Furthermore, numerous images are repetitions of earlier ones or corrupted; as shown in figure 2a, the elimination[7] of such unusable ones exacerbates the spacing problem.

When temporal regularity is more important than making use of all the available images, it is possible to focus only on a subset of these images where the time difference between any consecutive pair is more or less the same. For example, if we have a set of nine images from the 14th, 15th, 17th, 20th, 22th, 25th, 26th, 28th, and 30th of a month, then by focusing only on the ones from the 15th, 20th, 25th, and 30th, we can attain a fixed gap of five days.

As a second illustration of how sustainability driven multidisciplinary efforts lead to problems that are of significance to computer science, we now formulate an algorithm to solve a relatively simple version of this problem. In order to avoid ambiguity, we refer to the entire (usable) image set as $\{I_i\}$ and the selected subset as $\{F_i\}$. The $\{F_i\}$ images are also named as **frames** since their uniform spacing makes it possible to construct video streams (an exercise not discussed in this paper). The time value of an image (which indicates when the image was taken) is expressed as $t(I_i)$ or $t(F_i)$. Figure 2 is an overview of the process.

Given the desired time s of the first frame (which was "the 15th" in the above example) and the desired gap g between consecutive pairs (which was "5 days" in the previous example), the algorithm registers in a hash map $s, s+g, s+2g, s+3g, \ldots$ as the time values of the ideal frame set; we use a hash map for the bookkeeping since two look-ups will subsequently occur for each member of $\{I_i\}$. As shown in figure 2b, each I_i falls somewhere within the time-line established by the frame times (some close, some not). By iterating through $\{I_i\}$, each I_i is then associated with frames F_a and F_b where $t(F_a)$ is the highest time value less than $t(I_i)$ and $t(F_b)$ is the smallest time value greater than $t(I_i)$. We also enqueue two elements into a minimizing priority queue, the first relating F_a to I_i with key=abs($t(F_a) - t(I_i)$) and the second relating F_b to I_i with key=abs($t(F_b) - t(I_i)$) (figure 2c). Finally, by dequeuing as many elements as there are frames, we determine those images that come closest to the given start time and gap constraints (figure 2d).

When the above frame set is generated, its "goodness" can be quantified by the average abs($t(T_i) - t(F_i)$) value for all member frames (the smaller, the better) and the ratio of the size of $\{F_i\}$ to that of $\{I_i\}$ (the higher, the better). And once the goodness of a frame set is known, a sufficiently good one can be found by experimenting with different start times and gap values. Figure 2e shows the average abs($t(T_i) - t(F_i)$) value for three different starting times (leading to three plot

[6]http://www.accuweather.com

[7]Typically, this is done by hand, but our planned CMS will make available only the usable images so that other users are not burdened by such a non-algorithmic task. In fact, the image set will most likely be also available off of our project portal at 'http://www.ithaca.edu/mse'.

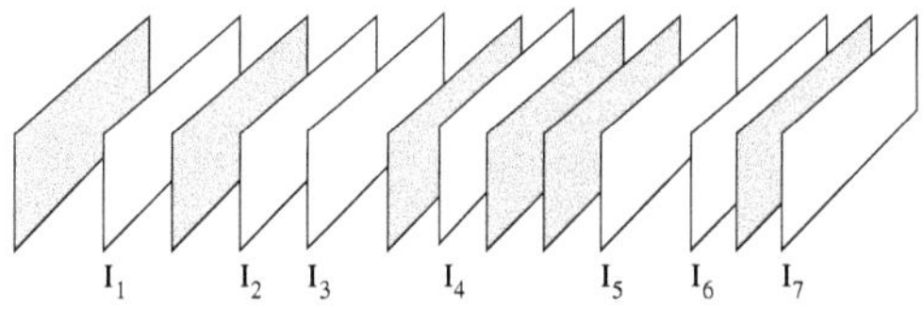

(a) *Unevenly spaced usable images:* $\{I_i\}$

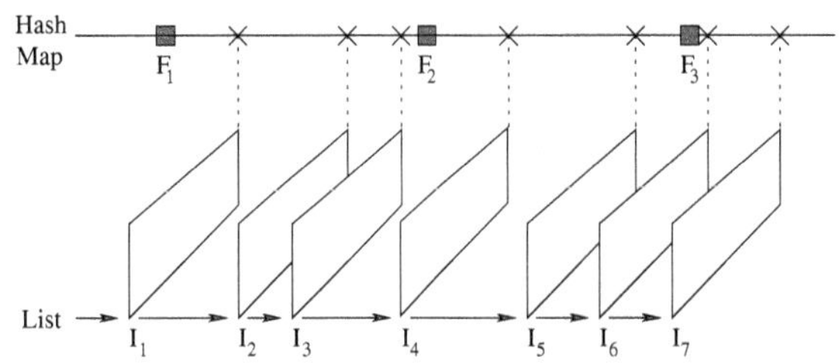

(b) *Frame times vs available image times*

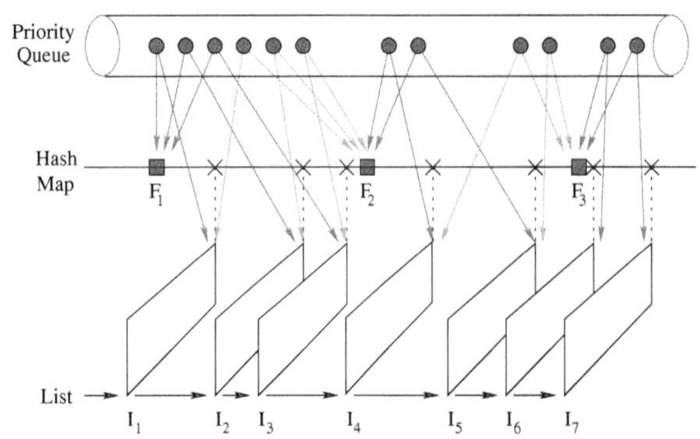

(c) *Use of a priority queue for frame-image association*

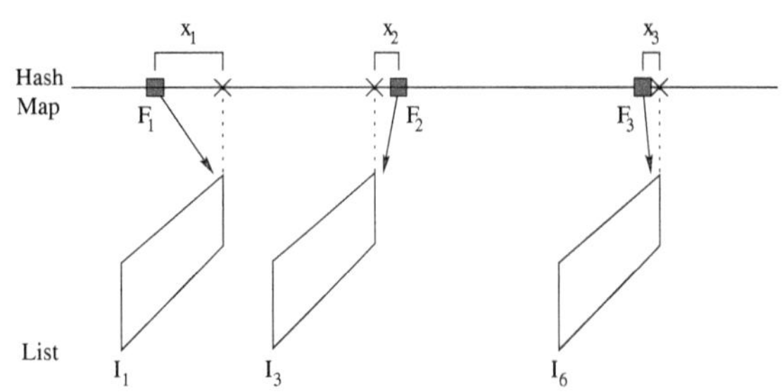

(d) *Original frames and associated (closest) images*

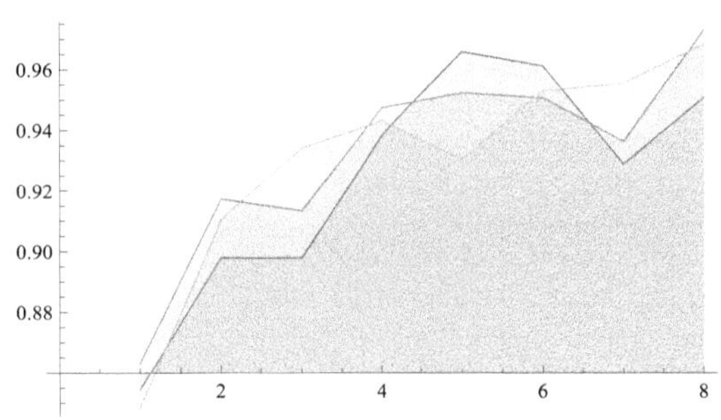

(e) *Images to frames goodness*

Figure 2: *Selection of a subset of images* $\{F_i\}$ *(AKA "frames") from the set of usable images* $\{I_i\}$.

PROJECT TYPE	RATING
Image manipulations	5.35/6 = 89.22%
Cellular automaton	5.12/6 = 85.29%
Statistical computations	5.00/6 = 83.33%
Simple DNA searches	4.94/6 = 82.35%
Markovian systems	4.71/6 = 78.43%

Figure 3: *Student ratings of the exercises conducted in our "Instruction to Computation with Matlab" course. The possible responses (with assigned numeric values) were "Unacceptable" (0), "Poor" (1), "Below average" (2), "Average" (3), "Above average" (4), "Good" (5), and "Excellent" (6).*

lines) and various different gaps expressed as multiples of a particular atomic value (shown on the x axis). Perhaps in a slightly counter intuitive way, we see higher gap values (corresponding to throwing away too many usable images for the sake of regularity in the selected frames) do not necessarily maximize the goodness of the frame set. This constitutes an optimization problem, connecting the above lists/hashmaps/priority-queues project to one that could be addressed in an Algorithms class.

5. ASSESSMENT AND CONCLUSION

Since we are at the beginning stages of our grant work, we are yet to produce results that establish the advantage of connecting STEM courses in the mode outlined in section 2. However, some of the computer science portions of the above projects have been used in isolation in some of our programming oriented courses. In this section, we provide some assessment information to establish the effectiveness of the projects and the significance of the scientific backdrop.

During the second trial version of our "Introduction to Computation" course which had a group of 17 students (9 physics, 8 life sciences and chemistry), we used a wide range of exercises, each targeted to particular problems rooted in the majors of the enrolled students. At the end of the course, we gathered these exercises into five groups and asked the students to rate their effectiveness in learning the presented material. The responses were provided over a seven level scale (assigned numeric values in parentheses): unacceptable (0), poor (1), below average (2), average (3), above average (4), good (5), excellent (6).

The computed averages for the student responses are presented in figure 3. As we can see, "image manipulations" which are based mostly on stages 'B' and 'C' of figure 1a received the highest rating, ranked even higher than cellular automaton which has always been one of the most popular exercises in our programming classes.

For the four faculty members who are working on developing the multidisciplinary modules and creating the operational model outlined in section 2, the real assessment will be a more complex and longitudinal process. However, our professional experiences as well as anecdotal evidence indicate that showing the multidimensional nature of worthy problems by actively tying several STEM courses will allow our students to see connections early on.

6. ACKNOWLEDGEMENTS

This work is supported by the NSF DUE #0837721 grant. The portal for our work is `http://www.ithaca.edu/mse`.

7. REFERENCES

[1] N. R. C. Board on Sustainable Development, Policy Division. *Our Common Journey: a transition toward sustainability.* National Academies Press, 1999.

[2] J. W. Chastine and J. A. Preston. Teaching 2d arrays using real-time video filters. In *SIGITE '05: Proceedings of the 6th conference on Information technology education*, pages 133–137, New York, NY, USA, 2005. ACM.

[3] D. Deremer and K. G. Herbert. An interdisciplinary undergraduate science informatics degree in a liberal arts context. *SIGCSE Bull.*, 38(1):179–183, 2006.

[4] A. Erkan and D. Gochev. An image background detection project for a visual exploration of dfs and bfs. In *SIGCSE '08: Proceedings of the 39th SIGCSE technical symposium on Computer science education*, pages 483–487, New York, NY, USA, 2008. ACM.

[5] M. Guzdial and E. Soloway. Teaching the nintendo generation to program. *Commun. ACM*, 45(4):17–21, 2002.

[6] D. T. Kaplan. *Introduction To Scientific Computation and Programming.* CL-Engineering, 2003.

[7] J. Lubchenco. Entering the century of the environment: A new social contract for science. *Science*, 279:491–497, 1998.

[8] S. Matzko and T. Davis. Using graphics research to teach freshman computer science. In *SIGGRAPH '06: ACM SIGGRAPH 2006 Educators program*, page 9, New York, NY, USA, 2006. ACM.

[9] S. Matzko and T. A. Davis. A graphics-based approach to data structures. In *ITiCSE '08: Proceedings of the 13th annual conference on Innovation and technology in computer science education*, pages 109–113, New York, NY, USA, 2008. ACM.

[10] J. L. Noyes. A first course in computational science: (why a math book isn't enough). In *SIGCSE '02: Proceedings of the 33rd SIGCSE technical symposium on Computer science education*, pages 18–22, New York, NY, USA, 2002. ACM.

[11] M. A. e. A. Palmer. Ecological science and sustainability for the 21st century. *Frontiers in Ecology and the Environment*, 3(4-11), 2005.

[12] M. R.A., R. DeHaan, and J. Schuck, editors. *Improving Undergraduate Instruction in Science, Technology, Engineering, and Mathematics: Report of a Workshop.* 2003. Steering Committee on Criteria and Benchmarks for Increased Learning from Undergraduate STEM Instruction, Committee on Undergraduate Science Education, National Research Council.

[13] G. M. Schneider. Computational science as an interdisciplinary bridge. *SIGCSE Bull.*, 31(1):141–145, 1999.

[14] R. Sedgewick and K. Wayne. *Introduction to Programming in Java: An Interdisciplinary Approach.* Addison-Wesley, 2008.

[15] A. B. Shiflet. Computer science with the sciences: an emphasis in computational science. *SIGCSE Bull.*, 34(4):40–43, 2002.

MPCT – Media Propelled Computational Thinking

Eric Freudenthal, Mary K. Roy, Alexandria Ogrey, and Tanja Magoc
University of Texas at El Paso
500 W. University Ave
El Paso, Texas, 79968
915-747-6954
{efreudenthal, mkroy, tmagoc}@utep.edu, anogrey@miners.utep.edu

Alan Siegel
New York University
251 Mercer Street
New York, NY, 10012
212-998-3122
siegel@cs.nyu.edu

ABSTRACT

Media-Propelled Computational Thinking (MPCT – pronounced *impact*) is a course designed to introduce programming in the context of engaging problems in media computation, math, and physics. Programming concepts are introduced as incremental steps needed to solve pragmatic problems students already understand. The problems, graphical API, and hands-on program features are intended to expose fundamental concepts in mathematics and quantitative science.

MPCT is offered in an entering students program for freshmen who plan to specialize in a variety of STEM (science, technology, engineering and math) and non-STEM subjects. The curriculum is intended to strengthen student intuition and interest in mathematical modeling and programming by engaging students in the direct manipulation of simple mathematical systems that model and display familiar physical phenomena. MPCT uses programs as concrete and manipulatable examples of fundamental concepts to engage a diverse range of students including women and underrepresented minorities.

Variants of MPCT are being developed for high schools, and as a means to introduce computational science to upper division undergraduates studying non-computational STEM disciplines. This paper provides an overview of MPCT and representative problem studies including models of ballistics and resonant systems. The evaluation plan is described and very preliminary results are presented.

Categories and Subject Descriptors

K.3.2 Computer and Information Science Education – *curriculum, computer science education*

General Terms

Algorithms, Design.

Keywords

First year programs, computational thinking, CS-Zero

1. Introduction

At the University of Texas at El Paso (UTEP), many entering students must spend two-to-three semesters in remedial math courses prior to becoming calculus ready and able to enroll in their first computer science course (CS-1). The attrition rate in these remedial courses is high. Even after this preparation, only half of the students remaining in the program pass CS-1 on their first attempt.

In the Fall of 2007, MPCT was introduced in an effort to reduce attrition among students who lack the prerequisites for CS-1, and to maintain student interest in the subject. The first version was based on Mark Guzdial's Media Programming [1] because it had documented success in engaging students with weak math skills [2]. However, Media Programming is designed for students in Liberal Arts programs, and focuses on aesthetic -- rather than engineering -- creativity. Our course reviews were consistent with observations by Guzdial at other institutions [3]: students enrolled in pre-engineering and other pre-professional programs (e.g. nursing) enjoyed learning how programs worked, but were generally not engaged by the aesthetically focused projects that dominate the Media Programming curriculum [4].

Consequently, we were forced to rethink our course objectives. Following Guzdial's lead, we realized that programming should not be taught for its own sake. In response, we designed a curriculum where students construct simple graphical programs in Python that simulate familiar physical phenomena. Through these hands on projects and guided class discussions, students discover the mathematical principles that relate their program's iterative execution with the continuous processes that are being modeled.

MPCT now principally uses image manipulation to strengthen mathematical intuition at the pre-calculus level, and to illustrate the modeling of physical processes. Furthermore, we discovered that it is easier for students to focus on problem-solving and algorithm development using a minimal and mostly-imperative graphical library than Java's object-oriented AWT framework.

MPCT has been incorporated into selected sections of a required first-semester "University Studies" program designed to strengthen academic skills and to provide career guidance. These sections offer an accessible introduction to programming and pre-calculus via Python-based modeling. The content includes some closed-form calculations for basic concepts such as slopes, accelerations, summations and parabolas. MPCT supports the course's career guidance components by providing experiences representative of actual work in STEM disciplines.

Programming techniques in early courses should be chosen to minimize cognitive load while maximizing pedagogical value. The redirection of MPCT to introductory computation included a significant reevaluation of the programming interfaces used to support coursework. The original programming interface used the rich object oriented (OO) Java AWT toolbox. With this approach, even the design of extremely simple algorithms requires fairly complex access code before anything can be programmed. Consequently, the *conceptual* content embedded within our introductory programming lessons were often overwhelmed by the mainly *clerical* task of managing the access and manipulation abstractions for pixels in Java.

We developed the alternative shallow Raster class described in the upper row of Table 1. All pixel accesses explicitly specify row-column addresses. Thus, a pixel location is just a (row ,column) pair of integers, and a pixel color is just a red-green-blue triple. Algorithms that visit all pixels in a rectangular region can be programmed by a pair of nested loops. As reported in [5], students have little trouble understanding nested iteration in this context.

The course begins with by presenting simple code that draws dots and lines. Students adapt it to draw rectangles, triangles, trapezoids and parallelograms by the end of the second class. The lower row of Table 1 presents a program examined within the first two weeks of class that dramatically modifies a familiar cartoon image. The example was selected to illustrate low-overhead programming – *the code does not even require a function definition.*

In order to facilitate projects that plot mathematical functions and leverage students' incoming knowledge, `Raster`'s origin is located in the lower-left corner, and thus column-row addressing directly mimics x-y coordinates within the first quadrant of a Cartesian plane.

In short, the simplifications in the necessary code allow the class to focus on the logic and the algorithms rather than object-oriented hierarchies that provide abstractions ill suited to the problem being addressed. Later projects require the plotting of functions with negative range that are (deliberately) inconvenient to be represented with Raster's origin, which is located in the image's lower-left corner. MPCT pragmatically utilizes this inconvenience to motivate the introduction of a `PosNegGraph` class that extends `Raster`. Both `Raster` and `PosNegGraph` are referenced by examples in this paper.

The next section summarizes the curriculum, including example problems in the newly developed modules on mechanical resonance and coupling, and planned extensions of MPCT's pedagogical approach to other courses. Finally, we report on our in-progress course evaluation and adaptations to the evaluation plan in response to MPCT's evolved focus.

2. Topic Sequence

Table 3 indicates the sequencing and approximate duration of each of MPCT's major educational themes. After familiarizing students with iteration through generation of geometric shapes, MPCT proceeds to introduce if-statements and Boolean expressions in the context of modifying images. Follow-up projects draw ensembles of lines and curves. For students intending to study a STEM discipline, the course also includes the construction of simple programs that model ballistic and resonant systems. Exercises mimic the familiar phenomenon of ball bounce and spring resonance, which are frequently poorly understood, even by students who have completed a semester of college physics [6].

Table 1.
Random-access Raster class

Public interface of `Raster`	Constructors • `Raster((numCols, numRows))` • `Raster((filename))` Accessors *Origin is in lower-left corner* *Parameters & return values are tuples* • `r, g, b = getRGB((col, row))` • `setRGB((col, row), (r, g, b))` Controls • `autoRepaint` *true: redraw on every access* • `ignoreOutOfRange` *true: silently ignore out-of-range accesses* Actions • `write(filename)` *save to file* • `repaint()` *redraw now*

Program presented in early session that dramatically recolors a familiar cartoon image.	`url = "http:….jpg"`
	`p = Raster(url)`
	`green = (0, 255, 0)`
	`cols,rows = p.widthHeight()`
	`for col in range (cols):`
	`  for row in range (rows):`
	`    r,g,b = p.getRGB((x,y))`
	`    if r<40 and g<40 and b<40:`
	`      p.setRGB((col,row), green)`

Table 2.
PosNegGraph

Public interface of PosNegGraph	Constructor • `PosNegGraph((numCols, range))` The y axis extends from +range to –range
Extends Raster	Public interface *Same as Raster* *only* `setRGB` *and* `getRGB` *are overloaded*

To ensure that students are not intimidated by unfamiliar mathematical abstractions, we prefer to first introduce evolving processes using the simplest-possible generators, and then to guide students into discovering algebraic simplifications they are fully prepared to understand.

The topics sequence through increasingly complex computational themes where all of the physical modeling is based on rates of change or summations (as opposed to integration). Table 4 presents a characteristic exercise associated with each theme.

For problems in mathematics and physics, we endeavor to minimize the level of outside knowledge required, and prefer show how processes evolve at an intuitive level and where incremental changes in the process state can be explained in physical and computational terms -- much like [7].

Math-centric programming projects generally begin with an exploration of the effects of rates-of-change. Afterwards, students are guided to reduce the already familiar summation problems (implicitly a recursive formulation) to closed form.

Theme A: Introduction to (graphical) programming. In a manner analogous to an immersive language course, students begin to 'converse' in Jython using only three statements to draw a multitude of geometric objects:

- `Raster(size)` – Used to "construct" a computer image:
- `setRGB(pos, color)` – Used to draw a dot:
- `for loops` – Used for iteration.

Table 3.
Course modules, themes, outcomes, and schedule

Theme & Wk	Major Course Module	Outcomes
A 1-2	**First week / teaser** • **"Conversational" introduction to programming** ○ **Login, start IDE** ○ **Use looping to draw lines, boxes, triangles, parallelograms, etc**	• Can login to computer • Knows what a program is • Can run a program • Familiarity with variables, expressions, looping, drawing w/ Raster class • Ability to draw rectangles and other simple geometric forms
B 2-3	**If-statements, relational, and Boolean operators** • **Conditional re-coloring of images**	• RGB encoded as tuples • Familiarity w/ if-statements and Boolean expressions
C 4-8	**Generating lines w/ summation and object extension** • **Horiz, vert, slope, y-intercept** • **Relate summation to closed form (y=mx+b)** • **Examine translation, negative ranges and PosNegGraph object**	• Intuition that slope is a "rate of change." • Functions and objects – to reduce complexity • Intuition re. multiplication • Greater proficiency at programming
D 9	**Touch of OO: (classes)** • **Define & use PosNegGraph** • **Plot lines w/ neg range**	• Familiar w/ objects • Can plot fns w/ negative range
E 10-11	**Generating curves (parabolas)** • **Using summation** • **Relate to closed form**	• Intuition that curves have 'slope that changes' • Knowledge: parabolas' slope changes linearly. • Familiarity w/ linear sums ○ Including geometric proofs
F 12	**Ballistic motion (in vacuum)** • **Acceleration as change-of-rate** • **Gravity as constant acceleration** • **Program that simulates bounce** • **Relationship to parabola**	• Intuition: physics models familiar phenomena • Familiarity: ○ Velocity as rate ○ Acceleration as rate of velocity change ○ Gravity as constant accel ○ Relationship to parabola
G 13-14	**Resonance** • **Idealized (linear) spring** • **Construct and run simulation** ○ **Plot position & velocity** ○ **Coupled resonance**	• Knowledge: ○ Generated by linear acceleration ○ Rate-of-change is sinusoidal ○ Frequency independent of amplitude

Together, these commands allow students to:

- Draw lines as a sequence of dots stacked in a row.
- Draw boxes as a sequence of lines stacked in a column
- Draw triangles, parallelograms, and trapezoids by deriving the inner loop's range from the outer loop's iteration variable.

Table 4.
Characteristic projects for each theme

```
# Theme A - geometric shapes
nCols, nRows = 100,100
p = Raster((nCols, nRows))
for row in range(0, 30):
 for col in range (0, row):
  p.setRGB((row+20, col+20), white)
```

```
# Themes C-D
def drawLine(row=45, step=-1):
  nCols, range = 100,50
  i = PosNegRaster((nCols, range))
...
  row = 45          # y-intercept
  step = -2         # slope
  for col in range(numCols):
    i.setRGB((col, row), white)
    i.setRGB((col, slope), green)
    row += step
```

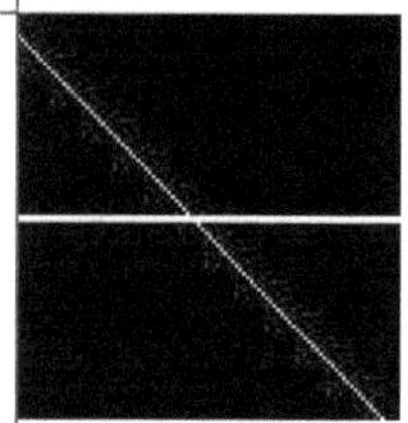

```
def parabola():            # Theme E
  ...
  row=45; slope=0 # initial params
  rate = -.1      # acceleration
  for col in range(numCols):
    i.setRGB((col, row), white)
    i.setRGB((col, slope), green)
    row += slope
    slope += rate
```

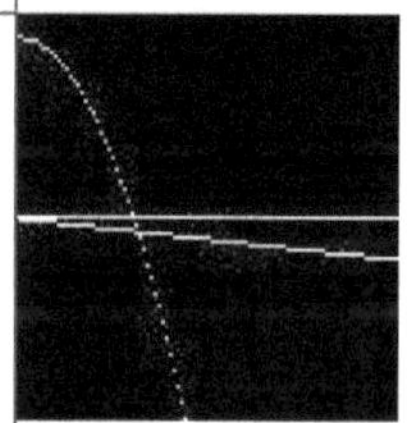

```
def bounce():              # Theme  F
  ...
  row=45; slope=0; rate = -0.2
  decay = .8      # bounce
  for col in range(numCols):
    i.setRGB((col, row), green)
    i.setRGB((col, slope), blue)
    if (row <= 0 and slope < 0):
      slope *= -decay # bounce!
    row += slope
    slope += rate
```

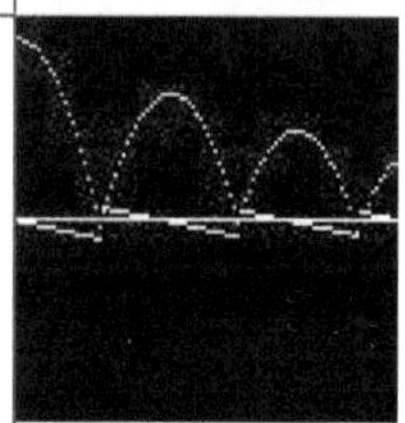

```
                           # Theme G
def harmonic(pos = 45, speed=0):
 i = PostNegGraph()
 springConst = 0.01
 interval = 0.1; mass = 0.01
 for x in range(i.width):
   i.setRGB((x, pos), green)
   i.setRGB((x, speed), blue)
   force = -pos * springConst
   accel = force / mass
   speed += accel * interval
   position += speed * interval
```

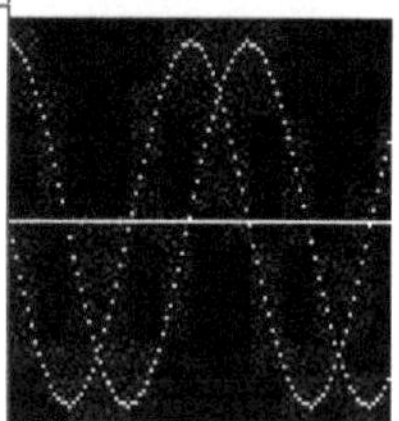

Initial programming exercises are sufficiently short to be conveniently typed directly to the interpreter. The first exercises contain no explicit arithmetic operations, which are gradually introduced to implement increasingly sophisticated computation. The difficulty of reliably typing more advanced programs motivates their storage within files.

The overall program is designed to foster experimentation and to encourage students to review fundamental concepts in algebra and geometry in a way where motivated understanding leads to successful program-generated displays.

Theme B: Control flow and Boolean expressions: The program presented at the bottom of Table 1, which is adapted from Guzdial's Media Programming course, introduces RGB encoding, relational operators, Boolean expressions, and if-statements in the context of re-coloring images. Students are very engaged by this project and enjoy manipulating images taken by their camera or discovered on the web.

Theme C: Drawing lines. Once students are familiar with Python's syntax and semantics, follow-up projects examine various approaches to drawing lines. Early projects utilize only progressive generators such as drawLine. Even this project is intended to review (or revitalize) such basic mathematical concepts as slope and y-intercept in a hands-on visceral way that is difficult to match with pencil and paper or a graphing calculator.

Theme D Functions and Objects: Projects in this theme will plot multiple graphs with both positive and negative ranges. The equivalence of progressive and standard "closed form" equations of lines are also discussed in class and reinforced with short programming assignments that draw parallel lines and manipulate the dynamic range of grayscale images. User-defined functions and the PosNegGraph class are introduced as an approach to simplify the task of programming through modularization.

Theme E: Examination and generation of curves. The main study concerns curves whose slope changes linearly as shown in the parabola in Table 3. Projects in Theme E examine the effect of various initial conditions and rates of change including examples where the slope and rate have different and same signs. These are intended to provide students with intuitive understandings necessary to examine ballistic motion in Theme F. Finally, the relationship between parabolas and quadratic functions are made concrete through geometric proofs such as depicted in Figure 1.

Theme F: Ballistics. In ballistic problems, objects are accelerated only by gravity. Their trajectory is parabolic. The slope of their trajectory with respect to time corresponds to velocity. The slope of their velocity with respect to time corresponds to acceleration. The mapping of trajectories to parabolas is straightforward: slope corresponds to velocity, and the slope's constant rate of change maps to acceleration. Students first simulate a single "toss," and then are challenged to simulate a bounce as a simplified inelastic collision with the ground, where at each bounce, velocity is reduced by 20%. This leads to an exponential decay in the maximum height achieved after each bounce. The `parabola` program's overlaid plot of position and velocity illustrates both continuous and discontinuous evolution of physical parameters.

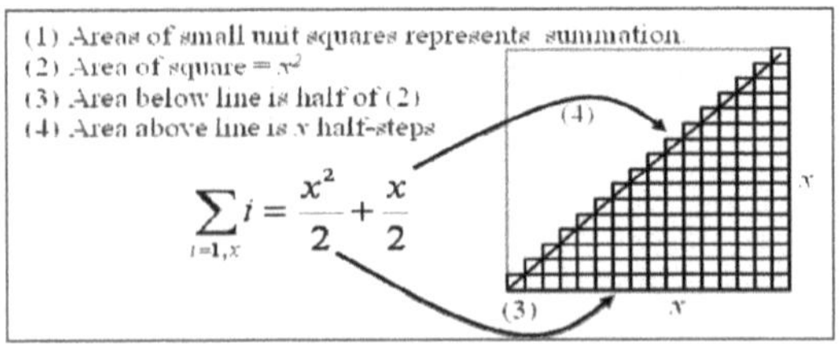

Figure 1.
Graphical depiction of linear sums in closed form as a quadratic function

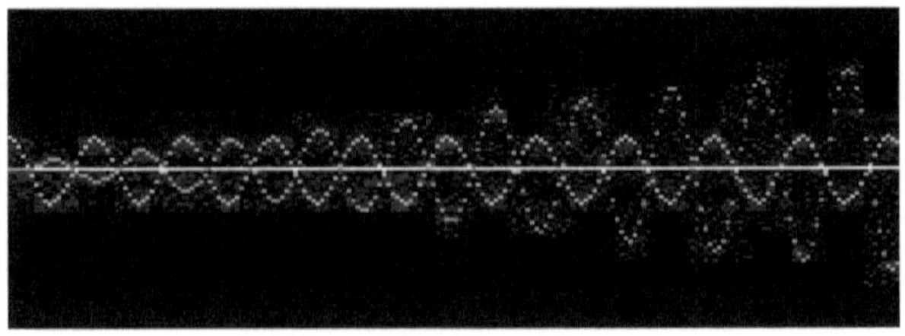

Figure 2
Simulation of Coupled Resonance

Theme G: Resonance. MPCT completes with a simplified example of coupled resonance illustrating the principle underlying an opera singers' wine-glass shattering trick and the catastrophic failure of the Tacoma Narrows bridge (see Figure 3) in 1940 and the crashes of several Lockheed Electras around 1960.

Figure 2 illustrates the result of an advanced project that examines coupling when both the oscillator and resonator are tuned to the same frequency. Like the catastrophic failures enumerated above, this resonator quickly accumulates energy from the oscillator.

3. Extensions to other courses

A new introductory course in computational science intended for upper-division students of STEM disciplines that traditionally do not include computation such as biology, geology, finance, and math is planned for the Spring of 2010. This course will introduce programming using examples from MPCT, and then will proceed to implement simulations modeling more dynamic systems in which a sudden action could change the "normal" or expected behavior such as production-consumer markets, investment valuation, predator-prey models, and biological processes.

We are also adapting this approach of motivating math from concrete problems to the teaching of algorithms. There, the objective is to use specific problems as a vehicle for teaching algorithms as general methods that can be adapted to solve related problems of interest. We find that by teaching algorithmic schemas to solve "purified" problems, students can follow the reasoning far more easily and can sometimes develop the computational idea themselves. As in MPCT, the layered elaborations are introduced step-by-step to solve increasingly complex problems as described in [9].

Figure 3
The Tacoma Narrows Bridge

4. Evaluation

More than half of the students entering UTEP intending to study CS are not "calculus ready," as required for CS1. First-attempt pass rates for CS-1 range from 50 to 70%, which surely contributes both to student time-to-graduation and attrition. Thus the need for intervention is clear. During the development of MPCT, several variants of Media Programming were offered at UTEP. In all versions, almost all students demonstrated proficiency at basic programming concepts and passed.

UTEP is a member of the Computing Alliance of Hispanic Institutions (CAHSI), which is evaluating various CS-zero courses offered at multiple institutions serving predominantly Hispanic populations of students. These evaluations include intermittent classroom observations and both pre- and post-course surveys examining preparation, social context, student engagement with the course, interest in further study of computation, and success in subsequent coursework.

In their 2008 report, the CAHSI evaluator measured high levels of both interest and confidence [10] among entering students prior to attending the course, though less than 20% had previously programmed. Post-course surveys of students attending the precursor courses indicate that 25% of the students were not motivated to continue studies related to computer science. This is likely a positive result if the course helped students correct unrealistic expectations about computer science early in their academic careers.

Students who attended a variety of CS-0s (including Media Programming at UTEP and Alice at other institutions) had similar passing rates that were similar to the general population. The mathematically-oriented revisions to MPCT have required several semesters of development and have only recently been implemented – hence no longitudinal data is available yet.

During the Spring 2009 term, the evaluation was broadened to include instruments that examine changes in interest, self-efficacy and competence related to mathematics. Several open-ended essay questions were included in order to guide the selection of relevant questions for the intended Fall evaluation.

Our longitudinal evaluation will be broadened to also compare the academic success of students in subsequent math courses with the academic success of students who do not attend MPCT.

Entering STEM students attended MPCT during the Fall semester of 2008, and non-STEM students attended distinct sections during both the Fall and Spring semesters. The mathematics included in the section was first offered Spring 2009, and therefore was only attended by non-STEM students. A post-course survey of the Spring 2009 non-STEM cohort examined changes in (1) perceptions of knowledge and understandings of key concepts, (2) perceptions of mathematics' relevance to 'real life' scenarios, and (3) attitudes toward learning math concepts in the context of programming.

As described in [11], the preliminary findings from the non-STEM section are encouraging. Although the sample size was too small to draw reliable conclusions, they reflect the instructors' observations of student motivation and engagement. Survey results indicate shifts from low level to higher levels of understanding math concepts introduced in MPCT, positive attitude toward MPCT structure and its intended objectives, and highly favorable perceptions of MPCT's relevance to real-life applications. We expect statistically reliable results from the Fall 2009 cohort, which is much larger, containing more than sixty pre-STEM and twenty non-STEM students.

5. Conclusion

Continuing evaluation of introductory programming offerings at UTEP targeting pre-STEM students have motivated evolutions in curriculum, course objectives, and evaluation strategies. Interestingly, the resulting course, MPCT, which engages students in a "computational reasoning," integrates both programming and mathematics, is engaging to both pre-STEM and non-STEM students with weak math skills. Results from early evaluation efforts are encouraging and have lead to refinements in evaluation strategy that mirror the course's evolution.

6. Acknowledgement

This report is based on work supported by the National Science Foundation through grants CNS-0540592, IIS-0829683, and DUE-0717877 and by gifts from Texas Instruments Inc. and Calculex Inc. Any opinions, findings, and conclusions or recommendations expressed in the paper are those of the authors and do not necessarily reflect the views of the NSF or other sponsors.

7. References

[1] Guzdial, *Computing and Programming with Python, a Multimedia* Approach, Prentice Hall, 2006.

[2] Guzdial, *Design Process for a Non-Majors Computing* Course, Proc.36th ACM Technical Symposium on Computer Science Education (SIGCSE), ACM, 2005.

[3] Guzdial, *Narrating Data Structures: The Role of Context in CS2*, The Journal of Educational Resources in Computing (JERIC), ACM, 2008.

[4] Freudenthal,, Roy, Ogrey, Terrell, Kosheleva, Gonzalez, and Gates, *Work in progress – Initial evaluation of an introductory course in programming that assists in career choices*, Proc. FIE, 2008.

[5] Freudenthal, Roy, Ogrey, Gates, *A Creatively Engaging Introductory Course in Computer Science that Gently Motivates Exploration of Mathematical Concepts,* Proc. ASEE, 2009

[6] Hestenes, Wells, and Swackhamer, *Force Concept Inventory*, The Physics Teacher, Vol. 30, March 1992, pp 141-158.

[7] Kalman, *Elementary Mathematical Models*, Mathematical Association of America (Press), 1997.

[8] Ed Elliott (1940) The Camera Shop.

[9] Siegel and Freudenthal, *Experiments in teaching an engaging and* demystifying introduction to algorithms: Installment 1: Huffman Codes, UTEP Computer Science Technical Report UTEP-CS-09-12, April 2009.

[10] Thiry, Barker, and Hug, CAHSI Evaluation Progress Report, The Computing Alliance for Hispanic Serving Institutions, 2009, http://cahsi.cs.utep.edu/Portals/0/2008InterimEvaluationReport.pdf

[11] Suskavcevic, Kosheleva, Gates, and Freudenthal, Preliminary Assessment of Attitudes towards Mathematics for a Non-STEM Section of Computational Computer Science Zero, UTEP CS Technical Report UTEP-CS-09-13, May 2009.

Computational Thinking for the Sciences

A Three Day Workshop For High School Science Teachers

Sheikh Iqbal Ahamed, Dennis Brylow, Rong Ge, Praveen Madiraju, Stephen J. Merrill, Craig A. Struble
Department of Mathematics, Statistics, and Computer Science
Marquette University
Milwaukee, WI, USA
firstname.lastname@marquette.edu

James P. Early
Department of Computer Sciences
SUNY Oswego
Oswego, NY, USA
earlyjp@cs.oswego.edu

ABSTRACT

This paper describes "Computational Thinking for the Sciences", a 3-day summer workshop for high school science and mathematics teachers. Our workshop emphasizes the deep connections between the natural sciences, mathematics and computer science through activities and simulation development appropriate for scientific explorations. Teachers were exposed to simulation development in VPython, a visual extension to the popular Python programming language. By broadening exposure of computational thinking to the natural sciences and developing activities specifically for science domains, we hope to attract new students into computer science and better prepare natural science students to employ the computational tools they will utilize in the future.

Categories and Subject Descriptors

K.3.2 [**Computer and Info Science Education**]: Computer science education

General Terms

Algorithms

Keywords

Computational thinking, K-12 outreach, high school science, high school mathematics

1. INTRODUCTION

In recent years, computer science has seen decreasing enrollments and growing gaps in participation by women and minorities. Yet, the need for trained computer scientists and training in computational thinking is growing. This is particularly true in the sciences, where the rate of data collection and generation outpaces our ability to interpret it.

In this paper, we describe "Computational Thinking for the Sciences" summer workshop, a 3-day workshop for 9-12 grade high school science and mathematics teachers sponsored by the Way Klingler College of Arts and Sciences and the Department of Mathematics, Statistics, and Computer Science at Marquette University. This workshop builds on the experiences from the "Linking Mathematics and Computer Science" workshop developed at Purdue University [6] and has the same overarching goals:

- Supporting K-12 teachers in their educational mission,
- Inspiring K-12 students in their studies,
- Increasing the pipeline of underrepresented populations into our undergraduate programs,
- Creating awareness of and interest in computer science as a discipline in the K-12 environment.

We had several reasons for expanding the workshop audience to include science teachers:

- Computational thinking is increasingly important in college and university science and mathematics training,
- Incorporating the sciences broadens the student pool exposed to computational concepts,
- Relatively few resources exist that integrate computational thinking directly into science contexts,
- Computation in the sciences demonstrates the team-oriented, interdisciplinary potential of computer science as a career.

Several initiatives already exist for disseminating knowledge about computer science to K-12 teachers and students. We briefly describe two that have gained significant attention. Computer Science Unplugged [1] is a freely available resource containing computer science activities without requiring a computer. The CS4HS [2] effort is an outreach program with workshops around the United Status exposing K-12 teachers to computer science concepts. These initiatives provide outstanding resources for foundational computer science concepts and communicate these concepts to K-12 teachers. We leveraged some of these resources in our workshop.

Many initiatives, however, are largely divorced from direct applications in the sciences and have not emphasized the development of lesson plans for computation in the sciences. It was critical for our workshop to place computation in the context of addressing scientific questions. It was also important to have teachers leave with lesson plans using computational techniques that directly impact their courses in the upcoming year.

The SECANT project at Purdue University [5] has focused on embedding computational concepts directy into scientific disciplines at the college and university level. In SECANT, Python [9] and VPython [8] are used to develop simulations appropriate for different scientific disciplines. We used SECANT as a model for our workshop, but changed the structure and activities to be appropriate for high-school teachers. The emphasis, however, remained on developing and using simulations to augment scientific instruction. We saw tremendous opportunities for interactions between computer science and the natural sciences through simulations.

The remainder of this article provides workshop details. We begin with the logistics of running the workshop in Section 2, including a discussion of costs for others planning similar workshops. The indiviual sessions are described in Section 3, with brief overviews of activities and simulations that were developed. Evaluation of the workshop is presented in Section 4. This article concludes with a discussion of the outcomes and future work in Section 5.

2. WORKSHOP LOGISTICS

Our target audience for the workshop was area science teachers working with grades 9–12. We also accepted several teachers who taught courses in mathematics or computer science – some in a blended load with other science courses, and some who taught purely in those fields. We recruited participants through direct mail to area schools, postings on computing- and science-related e-mail lists for secondary school teachers, and our workshop website.

The structure of our workshop is based on Purdue's summer workshop series linking secondary school mathematics with post-secondary computer science topics [6]. The schedule of the workshop is shown in Figure 1. The content of our workshop is novel, developed to appeal to the needs of American high school science teachers. In addition to modules addressing physics, biology, chemistry, and mathematics, we also designed modules for common areas of overlap, including probability, simulations, and computational thinking. These modules are described further in Section 3.

We chose VPython [8] as a tool to enhance our discussions and demonstrations of bringing computation into the high school science classroom. The tutorials included in the workshop schedule were designed not to equip our participants to teach VPython to their students, but rather to enable them to use VPython examples in their teaching. The participants demonstrated not only that they were capable of running a wide variety of simulations and demonstrations appropriate to their courses, but also that they could make adjustments to existing demonstrations and create new content.

As has become routine practice, we introduced teachers to Computer Science Unplugged [1], usually during breaks or topic transitions, as tools for use in their classrooms.

A secondary goal of our workshop was to be cost effective so other smaller and medium sized universities can hold similar workshops. The total cost for the workshop was

Day 1	
8:30am	Breakfast, Registration, Pre-Survey
9:00am	Introductions
9:30am	Session 1: Computational Thinking and Science
10:45am	Session 2: Simulations
12:00pm	Lunch
12:45pm	Session 3: Probability
2:30pm	Session 4: Python and VPython
4:45pm	Daily Evaluation
Day 2	
8:30am	Breakfast
9:00am	Session 5: Mathematics
10:45am	Session 6: Physics
12:00pm	Lunch
12:45pm	Session 7: Biology
2:30pm	Session 8: More VPython
3:30pm	Lesson Planning
5:00pm	Daily Evaluation
5:30pm	Dinner
Day 3	
8:30am	Breakfast
9:00am	Careers in Computational Sciences
10:45am	Session 9: Chemistry
12:00pm	Lunch
12:45pm	Lesson Planning
2:30pm	Sharing of Lesson Plans and Projects
4:30pm	Daily Evaluation, Post-Survey

Figure 1: Workshop schedule

\$6236.59, or about \$173 per participant. The budget covered catering, a stipend of \$300 for each teacher and guest speaker, parking (relevant for venues in cities), and note taking materials.

We did not provide lodging for participants because we limited our recruiting effort to schools within convenient driving distance of the metropolitan area. This differs from prior work where participants traveled significant distances as in [2]. The trade-off is that evenings were not available for instructional or laboratory time.

Involved faculty donated their time for planning and carrying out the workshop. Half a dozen meetings were held for planning prior to the workshop. Individual faculty took responsibility for key areas like advertising, catering, registration and scheduling. In addition to planning meetings, each faculty member prepared for approximately two weeks to research school science standards, learn VPython, and develop materials.

3. SESSION OVERVIEWS

Our workshop consisted of nine technical sessions, a session on careers in computational sciences, and additional sessions for teachers to prepare lesson plans with assistance from the workshop organizers. The first four technical sessions emphasized foundational material in computational thinking, simulations, probability, and VPython. The remaining technical sessions illustrated computational thinking concepts in scientific domain contexts through a combination of hands-on activities and simulation development. Simulation development was often done interactively with the participants, with the session leader guiding the simulation structure. Brief descriptions of each session follow. When appropriate, related Wisconsin Model Academic Standards [11] from the Wisconsin Department of Public Instruction (WDPI) are listed at the end of each description. Similar standards apply in other states.

3.1 Computational Thinking

This session introduced participants to the workshop by describing our goals and the motivation behind those goals. We highlighted current concerns in computer science and general STEM education, including: low enrollments, lack of diversity, and lack of preparedness for STEM majors. Teachers were shown the "Pathways in Computer Science & Engineering" video developed at the University of Washington [3], to convey career possibilities that apply computational thinking in the natural sciences.

This session also discussed Jeannette Wing's article on computational thinking [10] and emphasized the concepts of abstraction, algorithms, and simulation and their application to the sciences. The session ended with participants developing algorithms for some common tasks, such as making a peanut butter and jelly sandwich and sorting by middle names. Sample puzzles were also provided to illustrate computational thinking concepts.

This session is relevant to WDPI Technology Education Standard, C12.1.

3.2 Simulations

In the sciences, simulations play an important role in understanding and exploring ideas that would otherwise be infeasible due to cost or impracticality. Participants were introduced to the wide variety of simulations that might exist, and key concepts such as *deterministic* and *stochastic* simulations. The core of a simulation is a *computational model*, which is frequently expressed in mathematical forms.

We used Microsoft Excel 2007 to illustrate the development and application of simulations. We chose Excel since it is a commonly available tool and to demonstrate that simulations can be done without the need for traditional programming. One of the simulations investigated **Newton's Law of Cooling**, which allowed participants to explore different cooling rates and ambient temperatures, to plot those explorations, and draw conclusions. Other simulation concepts covered including generating measurement noise, model fitting (using linear models), and extrapolation.

This activity is relevant to WDPI Mathematics Performance Standards A12.3, E12.1 and E12.2.

3.3 Probability

While probability is not strictly a high school science topic, it underlies ideas explored in physics, biology and chemistry, and is at the core of many computational simulations. In the workshop, we introduced probability with a simple version of the Monty Hall game, based on the television game show "Let's Make a Deal." This was used to illustrate interactive and non-interactive simulations and randomness.

A second round of workshop material on probability demonstrated simulated percolation, in which a fluid propogates through a grid of spaces randomly blocked or unblocked according to some probability, ρ. While an abstract implementation of this simulation is not difficult, this conceptual framework is applicable to scientific simulations in hydrogeology, semiconductor structure, and forest fire propagation.

Taking this another step, we constructed a VPython simulation that runs many random percolations with successive values of the blocking probability, ρ, to demonstrate a macro property "tipping point" of the problem that could not be predicted via closed-form equations.

This activity is relevant to WDPI Mathematics Performance Standards, E12.1, E12.2 and E12.5.

3.4 Python and VPython

The goal of this session was to provide teachers with tools they can use to inspire students to explore problems using computational thinking. Several lecture and lab exercises focused on VPython [8]. We chose VPython because its syntax is easy to learn, and users can produce complex animations with just a few lines of code.

None of the participants had experience with VPython (or Python), and only a few had any programming experience. So, our challenge was to present the material such that the participants could grasp key elements quickly. We prepared small lectures with corresponding lab exercises highlighting each of the following topics: i) objects, attributes, and methods; ii) conditional and iterative statements; iii) and graphing capabilities.

In Lab 1, participants created instances of sphere objects and manipulated various attributes (e.g., color, position in the scene). Through this exercise, they observed how changes to attributes cause the VPython interpreter to change the object rendering. Lab 2 introduced conditional and iterative statements with exercises built on ideas from Lab 1. For example, participants animated the Earth's rotation about the Sun using two sphere objects. Producing a trace of the Earth's rotation (using an `arc` object) was a bonus challenge.

In the final lab, teachers were given exercises highlighting graphing capabilities in VPython. They were shown the `gcurve`, `gvbars`, and `gvhistogram` objects, used to plot continuous curves, curves formed by vertical bars, and histograms respectively. They then produced a variety of plots in 2D using the `arange` object to generate data.

3.5 Mathematics

The mathematics session of the workshop illustrated concepts behind cryptographic protocols and public key encryption using CS Unplugged [1]. The teachers formed groups with 2–4 teachers in each group. The idea was to have 1–2 teachers in each group play as "Amy", another teacher play as "Bill", and one other teacher play as intruder. Bill gives his public key in the form of a map to Amy. Amy encrypts the message and sends the encrypted message (map) to Bill. The intruder is also given the encrypted message, but cannot decrypt the message without the private key (map) which only Bill has. The interactive and simple examples from CS Unplugged conveys the important points about encryption.

This activity is relevant to WDPI Mathematics Performance Standard B.8.6.

3.6 Physics

We used two representative problems that both directly address existing high school standards and showcase the usefulness of computational simulations in the classroom.

The *Inclined Plane* is a ubiquitous physics problem. A rectangular block sits on a flat surface inclined at a particular angle. Gravitational force acts to accelerate the block down the incline, and frictional force acts to slow the downward acceleration. In the simplest, static phrasing of the problem, concepts explored include Newton's Second Law ($F = ma$), gravity, and trigonometry for calculating the perpendicular and parallel components of gravity.

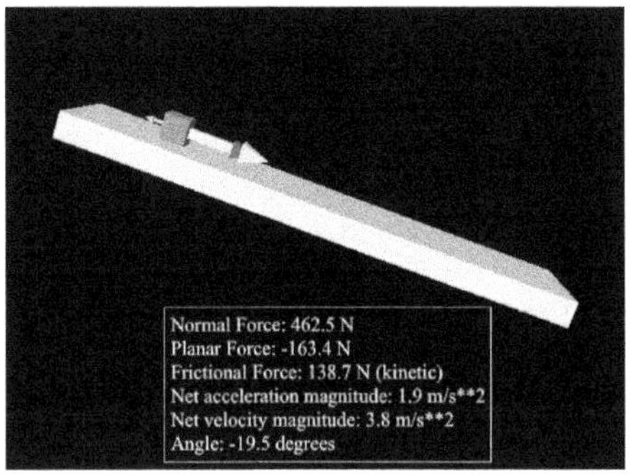

Figure 2: Friction on an inclined plane.

The VPython simulation constructed during the workshop allows teachers to visually demonstrate the problem. Students can also "play" to develop a greater intuition for the forces at work by trying various angles of incline, and checking simulation results against their calculations. Visible vectors are included to show the forces and velocities at work.

The deluxe formulation of the inclined plane introduces more advanced concepts, like static and kinetic friction, normal force, frictional coefficients, and summation of forces. The full featured simulation includes a slide control that changes the angle of incline in real time, allowing users to slide the block back and forth on the plane.

The inclined plane simulation is directly relevant to WDPI Physical Science Performance Standards D.12.7 and D.12.8.

3.7 Biology

Mendelian genetics is often taught with a combination of mathematics and actual *in vivo* experiments with kits such as Fast Plants [4]. Students compare the behavior of breeding with the expected theoretical results, but frequently the small plant sample does not match theoretical expectations.

A genetics simulation was developed in VPython, which simulated mating of a population consisting of dominant and recessive alleles (e.g., green vs. yellow peas). Simulation parameters include population size, number of generations, and selection probability of dominant alleles. Teachers and students can explore small populations, where Mendelian theory breaks down, and larger populations where it holds.

The second activity covered the Needleman-Wunsch sequence alignment algorithm to align two DNA sequences [7]. This activity is an ideal example of the concepts of *recursion* and *dynamic programming*. Participants were arranged in a grid representing the dynamic programming table. Each participant was responsible for looking at neighboring locations, adding appropriate penalties and alignment scores, and then choosing the best of three scores to place in their grid location. The overall grid was recorded on a blackboard.

The genetics simulation is directly relevant to WDPI Life and Environmental Science Performance Standards F.12.3, F.12.5, and F.12.6. The sequence alignment activity is directly relevant to F.12.5 and F.12.6.

3.8 Chemistry

The motivating application presented for computation in chemistry was virtual screening in drug design, where small molecules are computationally *docked* or placed into medically important protein structures. Conceptually, docking is similar to putting puzzle pieces together. Docking is accomplished by *minimizing* the energy that occurs after bond formation between the atoms in the molecule and those in the protein. A key component of computational docking models is the Lennard Jones potential formula to model van der Waals forces, $V(r) = 4\epsilon \left[\left(\frac{\sigma}{r}\right)^{12} - \left(\frac{\sigma}{r}\right)^{6} \right]$, where ϵ is the minimum energy potential, σ is the distance where the energy potential is 0, and r is the distance between atoms.

Teachers and the session leader developed an interactive simulation to calculate the van der Waals forces between two hydrogen atoms. In the simulation, dragging one of the two hydrogen atoms plots the current energy potential with a persistent trail to show the shape of the energy potential function. Using this, one can discover the ideal distance between two hydrogen atoms, which is where the energy potential reaches its minimum.

Protein docking and the van der Waals simulation are directly related to WDPI Physical Science Performance Standards D.12.8, D.12.11 and D.12.12.

3.9 Careers in Computational Sciences

The goal of the careers session was to bring awareness to high school educators regarding the possible careers for a Computer Science/Computational major. The broad ranges of topics covered in the session are: (i) career roles/titles, (ii) career outlook, (iii) salary outlook, and (iv) women/under represented minorities. Additional videos from the University of Washington [3] were used to inform the teachers that computer science is not just about programming and sitting in front of a computer. Several discussions with additional resources, such as information from the Bureau of Labor Statistics, dispelled the myths about the impact of outsourcing and the future of technology jobs. The teachers communicated that this information was very useful and that many negative stereotypes and perceptions of technology careers are still propogated in their schools.

3.10 Lesson Plans

At the conclusion of the workshop, each participant presented lesson plans illustrating how they plan to incorporate computational thinking in their classroom. Most participants used VPython simulations as part of their lesson plan. Examples of simulations included conservation of momentum, the genetics simulation described in Section 3.7, an isotope abundance estimator, cell volume vs. surface area, and a derivation of the formula for the volume of a sphere using increasing numbers of pyramids. One pair of participants used Excel to develop an analytical spreadsheet for a seed germination laboratory, which explored model fitting, interpolation, and extrapolation concepts.

4. EVALUATION

The effectiveness of our workshop was evaluated using a 14 statement anonymous survey given before and at the conclusion of the workshop (shown in Table 1). Participants were asked to rate how strongly they believed a statement

Q	Statement
1	I can define computational thinking.
2	Computational thinking is important in the courses I teach.
3	Computational thinking is important in my field.
4	Computational thinking is too complex to use at the level of my classes.
5	I incorporate computational thinking in my classroom.
6	I am familiar with some computational tools.
7	I use computational tools in my classes.
8	I routinely look for computational tools to enhance my teaching.
9	I routinely update my lesson plan to incorporate computational tools.
10	I am familiar with general software applications such as MS Word and Excel.
11	I know a high level programming language such as C#, Java, C/C++, etc.
12	I believe my students can benefit from seeing or using computational tools in their science and math courses.
13	I am familiar with Python OR VPython.
14	I believe that incorporating computational thinking activities into my teaching could increase student interest in science and technology.

Table 1: Statements used in our evaluation survey.

on a 5 point Likert scale: strongly disagree (SD), disagree (D), neutral (N), agree (A), and strongly agree (SA).

All twelve (12) participants completed the before-workshop survey, but only eleven (11) completed the after-workshop survey. Mean results are presented as (Q# before/after). We saw substantial improvements in participants' understanding of computational thinking (Q1 2.92/4.91), and importance to their fields (Q2 3.67/4.73, Q3 3.83/4.91). There is no change, however, in the perception of how complex it is to teach computational thinking (Q4 2.08/2.00). We also saw improvements in teaching computational thinking in their classrooms (Q5 2.58/3.91) and use of computational tools (Q6 3.33/4.08, Q7 3.08/3.72). We saw slight gains in perceptions of the role of computational tools and computational thinking in their classes (Q12 4.42/4.64, Q14 4.33/4.91). Interestingly, there is essentially no change in participants perception of knowing a high level language (Q11 2.25/2.00), yet all participants responded with A or SA to being familiar with VPython (Q13 1.08/4.27).

5. CONCLUSIONS AND FUTURE WORK

This workshop is the initial step toward our ultimate goal for increasing high school students' interest in the careers in STEM, and computer science in particular. We chose to introduce computational thinking to high school teachers to change long-term perceptions about computer science and its relationship with other disciplines. We are considering new workshops for high school students. Direct interaction with students expands the opportunities for activities, which will not have to conform to state curricular standards. The challenge, however, is having the necessary experience to make the topics interesting and content levels appropriate for high school students. We hope that parternships with teachers attending the workshop can guide development of materials for the students.

Overall, the workshop met our designed goals for high school teachers. We measured improvements in defining computational thinking, understanding its role in the natural sciences, and in developing and using simulations in their classes. Work remains on making the material easier to incorporate into the high school curriculum, so that teachers have the confidence needed to include computational thinking concepts in their lessons. We will be sending a follow-up survey to the teachers after a full semester to see if the workshop had longer-term effects.

Python and VPython were very successful in this workshop. All teachers were engaged in the lab assignments and successfully completed the exercises, to different degrees of complexity. Given that most of the teachers had limited programming experience, it was encouraging to see that the skills to develop simple simulations including randomness, conditional logic, functions, and graphics could be taught in a very short period of time. We hope to hear that the teachers pass along Python and VPython to their students.

6. ACKNOWLEDGEMENTS

The authors thank the Helen Way Klingler College of Arts and Sciences at Marquette University for providing funding. We also thank Mindy Hart from the Purdue University Computer Science Department for her work on the Linking Mathematics and Computer Science workshop, which formed the foundation of our workshop. Finally, the authors deeply appreciate the participation of the high school teachers, who made the workshop enjoyable and an incredible success.

7. REFERENCES

[1] T. Bell, I. Witten, and M. Fellows. Computer Science Unplugged, `http://csunplugged.org`.

[2] L. Blum and T. J. Cortina. CS4HS: an outreach program for high school cs teachers. In *SIGCSE '07*, pages 19–23.

[3] Department of Computer Science and Engineering, University of Washington. Why Choose CSE?, `http://www.cs.washington.edu/WhyCSE`.

[4] Fast Plants. `http://www.fastplants.org/`.

[5] S. Hambrusch, *et al.* SECANT : Science Education in Computational Thinking, `http://secant.cs.purdue.edu/`.

[6] M. Hart, J. P. Early, and D. Brylow. A novel approach to k-12 cs education: linking mathematics and computer science. In *SIGCSE '08*, pages 286–290.

[7] S. B. Needleman and C. D. Wunsch. A general method applicable to the search for similarities in the amino acid sequence of two proteins. *J Mol Biol*, 48(3):443–453, Mar 1970.

[8] D. Scherer and B. Sherwood. VPython, `http://vpython.org`.

[9] G. van Rossum. Python, `http://www.python.org`.

[10] J. M. Wing. Computational thinking. *Commun. ACM*, 49(3):33–35, 2006.

[11] Wisconsin Department of Public Instruction. Model Academic Standards `http://dpi.wi.gov/standards/`.

Expanding the Frontiers of Computer Science: Designing a Curriculum to Reflect a Diverse Field

Mehran Sahami
Computer Science Department
Stanford University
Stanford, CA 94305, USA
sahami@cs.stanford.edu

Alex Aiken
Computer Science Department
Stanford University
Stanford, CA 94305, USA
aiken@cs.stanford.edu

Julie Zelenski
Computer Science Department
Stanford University
Stanford, CA 94305, USA
zelenski@cs.stanford.edu

ABSTRACT

While the discipline of computing has evolved significantly in the past 30 years, Computer Science curricula have not as readily adapted to these changes. In response, we have recently completely redesigned the undergraduate CS curriculum at Stanford University, both modernizing the program as well as highlighting new directions in the field and its multi-disciplinary nature. As we explain in this paper, our restructured major features a streamlined core of foundation courses followed by a depth concentration in a track area as well as additional elective courses. Since its deployment this past year, the new program has proven to be very attractive to students, contributing to an increase of over 40% in the number of CS major declarations. We analyze feedback we received on the program from students, as well as commentary from industrial affiliates and other universities, providing further evidence of the promise this new curriculum holds.

Categories and Subject Descriptors

K.3.2 [**Computers and Education**]: Computer and Information Science Education – *Computer science education, Curriculum.*

General Terms

Design, Documentation, Experimentation, Management.

Keywords

Curriculum, Concentrations, Tracks, Multi-disciplinary.

1. INTRODUCTION AND GOALS

While the discipline of computing has evolved significantly in the past 30 years, Computer Science curricula have been much slower to adapt to these changes. In particular, CS has relatively recently spawned a number of sub-fields that have rapidly grown in both intellectual and practical importance but are under-represented in the typical CS undergraduate curriculum. Furthermore, CS is having a pervasive impact on a wide range of other disciplines, a phenomenon that is likely to continue for many years, but opportunities for undergraduates to study these advances at the boundaries between disciplines remain relatively rare. At Stanford University, we undertook to bring the Computer Science curriculum in line with what is happening in the field, completely redesigning the undergraduate CS major to explicitly show the diversity of topics in Computer Science and provide greater opportunities for inter-disciplinary work. Although not the primary motivation, recent declines in CS program enrollments [12] added impetus to our desire to capture student interest by increasing awareness of the great diversity and intellectual challenge that computing presents.

At Stanford, between 2001 and 2006, we witnessed a drop in CS enrollments generally in-line with national trends, as the number of annual CS major declarations dropped from over 150 to approximately 80. While enrollment stabilized and even began to grow modestly in 2007, the strong correlation between student enrollments and the health of the high-tech economy cannot be denied [10]. More recently, the media portrayal of "a supposedly horrific loss of [computer programming] jobs" due to off-shoring [9] has deterred potential students from CS. While recent analysis has found that job off-shoring has not resulted in a net loss of IT jobs in the US [1], it is instructive to see that students' decision making is significantly affected by *perceptions* of job prospects. More subtly, students choosing to not major in CS because of their belief that programming jobs are being off-shored indicates that students are equating majoring in CS with being a programmer as the eventual (perhaps, only) career outcome. A similar phenomenon has been cited in other work looking at enrollment declines [7] and has also been used as the basis of curricular revision which stresses the importance of *context* for computing [4]. In a similar vein, we believe that explicitly broadening the "footprint" of Computer Science to show its many intellectually challenging subfields and strong multi-disciplinary ties can cast a wider net in piquing student interest to pursue CS. Thus, the primary goals of our curriculum revision are aimed at:

- providing students greater awareness of the breadth of options in CS and opportunities to pursue these areas in depth,
- incorporating relatively new, but already mature, sub-fields of CS on par with more traditional topics within the curriculum,
- highlighting and promoting multi-disciplinary connections,
- establishing a structure with sufficient flexibility to allow for lightweight revision in response to the evolution of the field.

These goals (especially the first three) are in-line with recommendations on engineering education from the National Academy of Engineering [8] as well as a recent NSF workshop on Integrative Computing Education and Research [5].

Interestingly, while increasing enrollments was not a direct goal of our curriculum revision efforts, we were happy to see a significant increase in CS major declarations in the year since our new program was launched. A detailed analysis of the reasons for this increase is presented in Section 4.

2. CURRICULAR STRUCTURE

Immediately prior to our new curriculum, our program structure consisted of a large core of required classes (CS1, CS2, advanced programming, discrete math, automata/computability, algorithms, AI, and computer architecture), a few restricted choices (operating systems or compilers), and roughly three restricted CS electives. In the past two decades, this curriculum saw only minor revisions in adjusting a few particular course requirements—the essential structure remained untouched. During that same period, new frontiers had emerged in CS and multi-disciplinary ties to other fields had been established, but the large and inflexible major requirements limited the ability of students to take advantage of courses in those areas.

In alignment with our goals, we pursued a *track-based* model for our new curriculum, with the following general structure:

- *Core*: a common set of courses all CS majors are required to take to establish a shared intellectual foundation.
- *Track*: a chosen topical concentration area (selected from a menu), aimed at giving students greater depth in the area(s) of CS they find the most interesting.
- *Electives*: additional course options allowing students to pursue greater breadth, depth, multi-disciplinary ties, or combinations thereof.
- *Senior Project*: a capstone course with either a software development or research emphasis.

Being homed in the School of Engineering, general requirements such as mathematics and science still exist in the new curriculum, but we discuss them only in relation to the requirements above. We describe the Core, Tracks, and Electives presently.

2.1 The Core

The Core curriculum focuses on providing a common intellectual experience in CS, setting a foundation for use across a variety of depth areas. This raises the opportunity—indeed, the necessity—to have the Core include only essential elements common to the many directions in which CS has evolved. Given our program's historical context, agreeing to have a Core was not contentious. Rather, the challenge was to keep the Core as streamlined as possible. We gathered input from a number of faculty detailing their "must-haves" for any computer science student and modeled the Core based on the *intersection* of those lists rather than the *union*. Our Core is composed of six courses: three in "Theory" and three in "Systems", detailed below.

> *Systems I: Programming Abstractions*—a classic CS2 course emphasizing common data abstractions and structures as well as recursion.

While this is a CS2 course, it does not have our CS1 as a strict prerequisite (our CS1 course is in Java, whereas CS2 is in C++, lessening the mechanical dependency between the two courses). An analysis revealed that roughly half of our CS majors did not take CS1 (due to AP credit or prior programming experience), providing evidence that a reasonable number of students can begin the Systems Core immediately. Of course, we do not expect all students to do so, and offer an accessible CS1 course taken by a large percentage of the entire undergraduate student population that is meant to "funnel" students into the CS program. Our CS1 and CS2 courses were unchanged as a result of the curriculum revision. We note that the selection of Core topics is somewhat orthogonal to the detailed contents (e.g., programming language) of CS1, making such a structure more readily adoptable by others.

> *Systems II: Computer Organization and Systems*—a course with the theme of taking students "from the hardware up to the source code". Topics include machine architecture, memory models, data representation, and elements of compilation and concurrency.

Systems II is meant to provide students with a unified introduction to the lower levels of the machine. We feel that it is essential for students in any subfield of computing to understand the fundamental abilities and limitations of real computing systems. Even students with a theoretical focus benefit from seeing such material as applications of automata theory or program analysis/verification. This course is not a replacement for a full course in either compilers or machine architecture, but since it contains the foundational material we believe all students need in this area, it allows for streamlining the curriculum to no longer require a full course in either of these topics.

> *Systems III: Principles of Computer Systems*—the theme of this course is "modern computer systems and networks". Topics include processes and concurrency mechanics, file systems, virtualization, networking and distributed systems.

This course explains the facilities and paradigms that modern operating systems, networks and distributed systems provide. The need for this course is reflected in the fact that computing has and will continue to move toward a much more distributed paradigm (both multicore chips as well as large scale data centers and the web), and all students must be facile with such workings. Across such diverse areas such as HCI (where practitioners consider how distributed systems affect end-user interaction through issues such as latency or information consistency) or Computational Biology and Artificial Intelligence (where researchers develop algorithms for parallel, distributed systems), the direction in which computing is moving in the 21st century makes such a class important to all Computer Scientists.

Again, we stress that this course is not a replacement for a course focused on implementing an operating system or designing and implementing network protocols. The course is meant to be a foundation relevant to all students—it will be a reasonable endpoint for some, while providing a stepping stone for those who choose to pursue further work in systems design and implementation. As a result, we eliminated the requirement for all students to take a full course on operating system implementation.

> *Theory I: Mathematical Foundations of Computing*—this is a course on discrete math and automata. Topics include logic, induction, proof techniques, sets, functions, relations, and an introduction to automata and NP-completeness.

The goal of Theory I is to give students the mathematical language of computing, the ability to present cogent arguments (i.e., proofs), and an understanding of what is possible to compute. The material is motivated *in situ* through real world applications, while also presenting topics, such as finite automata, which will be built upon in Systems II and III, reflecting the importance of theory to systems and vice versa.

Theory II: Probability Theory for Computer Scientists—an introductory course meant to provide students with tools for probabilistic analysis and modeling in computing. The course also provides an introduction to Machine Learning.

Theory II is perhaps the most significant departure from a "standard" CS curriculum [6], but it is a reflection of where we believe the field is headed. Indeed, probabilistic analysis has become widespread as a tool in analyzing systems, constructing algorithms, and modeling uncertainty in user interactions. It forms the basis for many well known applications including Google's PageRank algorithm, modern email spam filters, and the analysis of biological and social networks. While many CS curricula (including our previous program) require a course in Probability, such courses are generally not taught in CS departments and are much more focused on theoretical results and proofs. They are generally devoid of any discussion of the real use of these models in computing and provide no examples of real-world software systems based on their use. For these reasons (among others), we chose to develop our own probability class in-house, allowing us to specifically target the use of probability in computing. Moreover, we also use the course as a vehicle to teach elements of Machine Learning and AI, showing applications both within computing as well as their use in other disciplines. Such applications can help students better understand the potential impact and social context of their work.

Theory III: Data Structures and Algorithms—an advanced course in the design and analysis of algorithms, presenting various data models (e.g., algorithms for trees and graphs) and a range of algorithmic techniques (e.g. greedy and randomized algorithms, dynamic programming).

The focus of Theory III is to provide the algorithmic tools that we believe a facile computer scientist needs to know to think *computationally* in a variety of contexts. Such a course is common in many computing curricula, and we are in agreement with many of our peer institutions that this material is foundational and necessary for all computer scientists.

The prerequisite structure for the Core courses is shown in Fig. 1. We include our current CS1 (and potential future alternatives) in the diagram to show the variety of entry points into the Core.

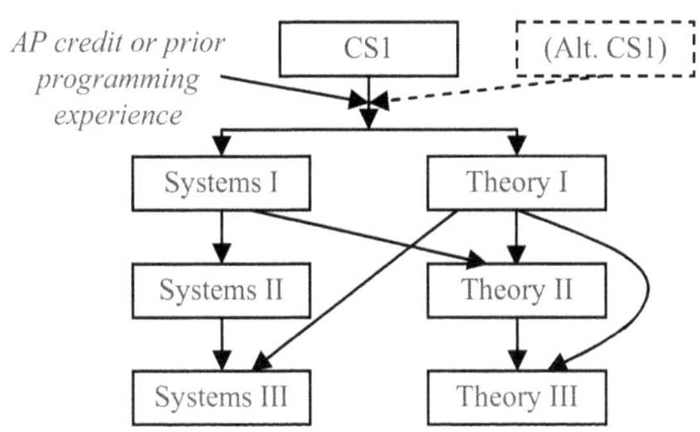

Figure 1. Prerequisite structure for Core courses.

Since our regular academic year is composed of three quarters, it is possible for students to complete the Core material in a single year, but we expect most students to space this material out during the course of their Freshman and Sophomore years.

While others have argued that a common core in a computing curriculum can be avoided [4], we have found that providing such a core offers several advantages. First, it provides a general foundation that students can use to pursue many areas in CS *after* they graduate. Indeed, the field of computing grows so quickly that it is simply not realistic to expect the education students receive as undergraduates to be sufficient for their whole careers, or that their interests will even remain in one subfield of the discipline. Thus, the Core aims to provide a foundation on which continued work in a variety of areas within CS may be pursued. Equally importantly, however, is that the Core provides students with a common *social* experience—the "bonding" that takes place as students undertake common challenges and have shared experiences. But perhaps most importantly, having a designated Core allows students to defer the selection of a concentration area (i.e., track) in CS until they have more exposure to the field. This is especially important given the findings that most students in high school do not know what CS is about [2]. The idea of a Core has been well-received by our students. As we show later in this paper, a recent survey of our CS undergraduates found 51% of respondents indicated that a streamlined set of core courses was one of the most appealing aspects of the new curriculum, while only 3% viewed it negatively.

2.2 Tracks

All CS students are required to complete the requirements for one track in our program. This provides the opportunity for students to better align their program with their interests in the field, and also pursue multi-disciplinary work related to that area. In its initial roll-out, our curriculum offers nine track choices:

- Artificial Intelligence
- Theoretical Computer Science
- Systems
- Human-Computer Interaction
- Graphics
- Information (management and application of data)
- Biocomputation
- Unspecialized
- Individually Designed

A track is generally composed of 4-5 courses, with requirements structured as follows:

a.) one or two designated *gateway* courses

b.) selection of one or two courses from a menu of courses highly related to the track area

c.) selection of additional courses from (b) and/or from a list of more broadly related courses to the track area

For example the Artificial Intelligence track looks as follows (shown with a much abbreviated sample of course offerings):

a.) Required: *Principles of Artificial Intelligence*

b.) Two courses from: *Intro. Robotics*, *Computer Vision*, *Agent Systems*, *Natural Language Processing*, *Machine Learning*

c.) One additional course from (b) or from: *Speech Synthesis*, *Advanced Robotics*, *Computation Genomics*, *Web Search*, *Decision Analysis*, *Stochastic Control*, *Information Theory*, *Modern Applied Statistics*

The designated "gateway" course(s) are the foundational course(s) in the track area (for example, "Principles of Artificial Intelligence" in AI or "Introduction to Human-Computer Interaction" in HCI). These courses provide a more in-depth introduction to the area, assuming students have already taken some portion (but not necessarily all) of the Core courses. The gateway courses serve two purposes. First, they provide a clear mechanism for students to sample a particular track area to decide if they wish to pursue it further (and such sampling can be done prior to the completion of the entire core, so students can generally take gateway courses as early as their Sophomore year). Second, all gateway courses are also designated as general CS *electives* (described in more detail later). This allows students who sample a gateway course and decide not to pursue that respective track to incur no programmatic penalty as the gateway course can simply be counted as one of their in-major electives.

We make special note of the last three tracks listed above, as their requirements are somewhat different from the other six. The *Biocomputation* track requires additional science courses (specifically, a year of Chemistry and two quarters of Biology) beyond the standard CS requirements (in Physics). To offset these additional requirements, students take fewer courses in other categories. Importantly, the track contains many requirements for a collegiate pre-medical program, allowing pre-med students an option to major in CS without significant undue burden.

The *Unspecialized* track is essentially composed of each of the gateway courses of the other tracks, with a few additional breadth options. This track serves two purposes. First, it provides a "breadth" track option for students who choose not to pursue one area in particular depth. Indeed, students who sample several gateway courses and cannot decide on a particular track can simply graduate under the Unspecialized track as they will have satisfied its requirements by taking five gateway courses from other tracks. Second, the Unspecialized track mimics the requirements of our previous curriculum. In this way, the new curriculum is largely a superset of our previous program requirements, allowing in-flight students to graduate under the new requirements without significant adjustment.

The *Individually Designed* "track" is simply a set of guidelines allowing students to propose their own coherent set of track requirements (requiring faculty approval). It provides an added level of flexibility to address individual needs or fast-emerging areas without the need for university-level program approval.

More generally, the designation of tracks allows students to explicitly see the diversity of options available to undergraduates in CS. Since our CS program no longer has one monolithic set of requirements, but rather explicitly lists a number of subfields, the program itself serves as an advertisement for the diversity of the field. Furthermore, by allowing students to pursue greater depth in the area of CS they find most appealing, we increase the frontier of the field that is accessible to undergraduates. This makes the overall "footprint" of our curriculum larger and casts a wider net to attract student interest.

Finally, an explicit goal of our curriculum redesign was to make future updates to the curriculum easier. Modularizing our program into the track-based structure accomplishes this goal, as it is now possible to add or remove tracks without affecting other tracks or the set of Core courses.

2.3 Electives

Beyond the Core and Track requirements, students complete their CS depth requirements by selecting from a set of elective courses. Students are required to take a minimum of seven courses, including their track requirements and electives. The electives come from two sources. First, a set of *General CS Electives* is available to choose from for students pursuing *any* track area. This list includes most of the undergraduate courses in the CS department. Each track then designates a set of *Track-specific Electives*—additional courses that are available as electives for students pursuing that track area. The track-specific electives are intentionally selected to include appropriate multi-disciplinary courses (including such diverse areas as economics, engineering management, linguistics, statistics, studio art, psychology, and philosophy, as well as other engineering disciplines) as well as advanced graduate courses in the track area. For example, the *Graphics* track provides electives such as *Design* and *Photography* from the Art department, *Introduction to Perception* from Psychology, and *Game Studies* from the program in Science, Technology and Society. Thus, the program can serve students interested in computational media, perceptual issues in digital art, and/or game development all within the same track.

Electives allow students to pursue additional breadth (by taking general CS elective courses), further depth (by pursing graduate courses), multi-disciplinary ties (by taking appropriate non-CS courses), or some combination thereof. This flexibility helps address a variety of student interests/career paths as well as highlights the growing multi-disciplinary nature of CS. Indeed, if we were to use AP Exams as a leading indicator of student interest, we would find that while CS numbers are stagnant, there are growing numbers of students interested in areas related to CS (e.g., Biology and Statistics, which had over 7 times and 5 times as many exam takers as CS, respectively, in 2008 [3]) who could be well served by a CS program that combines computing with other areas of interest (e.g., Biocomputation for Biology students, AI/Machine Learning for Statistics students, etc.).

3. PROCESS

The need for substantial curricular reinvigoration was widely recognized in our department (composed of roughly 50 faculty members), and our curriculum revision process was driven, unsurprisingly, by an 11-member departmental Curriculum Committee. Initially, we focused on determining a high-level structure for the curriculum, reaching consensus on the model of a Core, Tracks, and Electives before filling in the details. This provided a general framework—which was at times revisited—to determine the detailed program requirements. Importantly, this concrete initial proposal was put before the full faculty before moving on to the detailed work. Gaining unanimous departmental faculty support provided early buy-in that a curricular change was needed and gave the committee a mandate for significant reform.

The next task was defining the Core courses and their content. Two factors made this often contentious process successful. First, rather than having open-ended discussions about "what every computer scientist should know," we always maintained a concrete working document defining the latest revision of the Core courses and their detailed contents. This allowed for much more directed committee discussions and detailed analysis of the trade-offs in including or removing certain topics. More importantly, however, at least one of the likely instructors for each of the new Core courses was intimately involved in the discussion of the course topics. As a result, there was a realistic assessment of the amount of material that could be covered in each course as well as a potentially willing instructor for it—a critical factor for eventually translating curriculum documents into real courses.

Once the Core was defined, additional committees were formed to develop each track (and track-specific electives) separately. The track committees were composed of a subset of members of the Curriculum Committee as well as additional faculty in the track area (in some cases including faculty from other departments). Again, a concrete proposal for the requirements for each track was always maintained to drive the discussion. The critical aspect of this process was that a large portion (well over half) of the entire CS faculty became involved in the curriculum development process. This cemented wide support for the new curriculum. When the requirements for each track were finalized, the result was reviewed by the Curriculum Committee for coherence and level-setting across all tracks. When the entire curriculum was defined, it was unanimously adopted by the CS department faculty and then approved by our School of Engineering. The curriculum was rolled-out in its entirety during the 2008-09 academic year.

4. ASSESSMENT AND CONCLUSIONS

To assess our new curriculum, we examined enrollment statistics in CS, surveyed student attitudes toward the program and actively sought feedback from industrial affiliates. Most notably, after the deployment of the new curriculum this past year, we witnessed a surge of over 40% in undergraduate CS major declarations (from 87 in 2007-08 to 123 in 2008-09). While CS enrollment increases have been reported recently at other universities, the magnitude of our increase is well above the numbers we have seen from peer institutions, and survey data suggests our new curriculum is the cause. A voluntary on-line survey (primarily multiple choice questions) of our students who declared CS as their major this past year (N = 58) shows that over 36% of respondents indicated that the new CS curriculum influenced their choice of major, with 7% stating explicitly that they would have majored in something other than CS if not for the new curriculum. Statistical extrapolation from survey respondents (47% of the population) to the entire population of students declaring CS in the past year reveals that between 9 to 44 *incremental* students declared CS as their major as a result of the curricular changes. Given that the total incremental increase in CS declarations we saw in 2008-09 was 36 students, it appears that a solid majority of the incremental increase is due to the revised curriculum. We also assessed the aspects of the new curriculum students (N = 96) found most/least appealing, shown in Fig. 2. Note that students could select multiple options so the percentages across categories do not sum to 100%. With regard to *most* appealing aspects, students could choose "Flexibility in requirements", whereas the analogous question for *least* appealing aspects was "New required courses" they would have to take. As can be seen in Fig. 2, students overwhelmingly found the new curriculum to be appealing, with the ability to focus on a particular track being the most compelling aspect of the program (77% positive response).

We also reviewed the curricular changes with many members our of industrial affiliates program and received uniformly positive responses from them. Discussion of our new curriculum has been

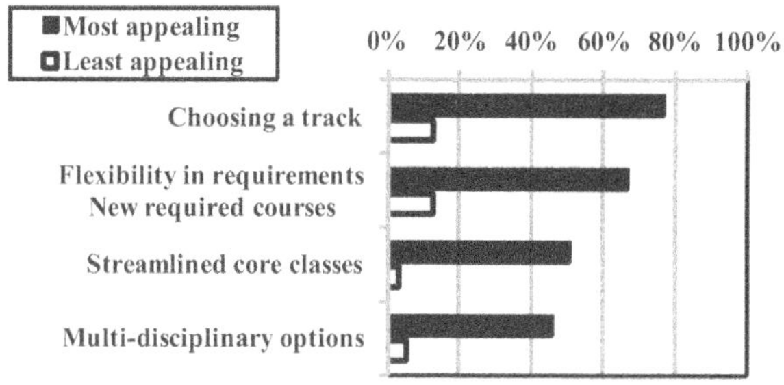

Figure 2. Aspects of curriculum most/least appealing (N=96).

taken up in several leading CS departments both nationally and internationally, giving us useful feedback on the program, including invitations to help two other universities restructure their CS curricula. While most feedback we have received has been positive, we have also received one important criticism: the lack of functional programming in our Core courses [11]. While our prior curriculum also lacked much functional programming, we now plan to use the functional statistical language R in a lab adjunct to our Theory Core II course to help address this point.

In conclusion, we believe our new curriculum helps capture student interest by explicitly reflecting the broadening frontiers of the discipline and allowing students to better align their academic programs with their interests. We would encourage others to consider a similar model, playing to strengths of their individual departments. For small departments, we recognize that having an extensive list of tracks may not be possible and we would encourage partnering with non-CS departments to provide more multi-disciplinary tracks as a means of highlighting the increasingly broad influence of computing in other areas. Smaller CS departments also have the potential to attract more students by targeting the larger departments at their institutions to work with in creating multi-disciplinary tracks. Indeed, in discussions with small CS departments, we have seen such opportunities arise, for example, in partnering with media studies programs.

5. ACKNOWLEDGMENTS

We are grateful to members of our Curriculum Committee and the many other faculty involved in our curriculum revision process.

6. REFERENCES

[1] Aspray, W., Mayadas, F., and Vardi, M. Y. (Eds). 2006. Globalization and Offshoring of Software: A Report of the ACM Job Migration Task Force.

[2] Carter, L. 2006. Why Students with an Apparent Aptitude for Computer Science Don't Choose to Major in Computer Science. In *Proc. of SIGCSE '06*.

[3] College Board. 2008. AP Program Size and Increments 1984–2008.

[4] Furst, M., Isbell, C., and Guzdial, M. 2007. Threads™: How to Restructure a Computer Science Curriculum for a Flat World. In *Proc. of SIGCSE '07*.

[5] Integrative Computing Education and Research (ICER). 2006. Final Report of the Northwest Regional Meeting.

[6] Joint Task Force on Computing Curricula. 2001. ACM/IEEE Computing Curricula 2001 Final Report. http://www.acm.org/sigcse/cc2001.

[7] Morris, J. H. and Lee, P. 2004. The Incredibly Shrinking Pipeline is Not Just for Women Anymore. *Computing Research News*, 16(3), May 2004.

[8] National Academy of Engineering. 2005. Educating the Engineer of 2020: Adapting Engineering Education to the New Century. Nat'l Academies Press.

[9] Reynolds, A. 2004. Offshoring Which Jobs? *Washington Times*, June 6, 2004.

[10] Sahami, M. 2007. The Google Education Summit. http://research.google.com/university/relations/eduSummit2007/MehranSahami.pdf

[11] SIGPLAN Proposal on Functional Programming. 2008. http://wiki.acm.org/cs2001/index.php?title=SIGPLAN_Proposal

[12] Vegso, J. 2008. Enrollments and Degree Production at US CS Departments Drop Further in 2006-07. *Computing Research News*, 20(2), March 2008.

Connecting Across Campus

Mark D. LeBlanc, Tom Armstrong, Michael B. Gousie
Computer Science
Wheaton College
Norton, MA 02766
508.286.3970
{mleblanc, armstrong_tom, mgousie}@wheatoncollege.edu

ABSTRACT
Computer science holds a unique position to craft multidisciplinary curricula for the new generation of faculty and students across the academy who increasingly rely on computing for their scholarship. We propose that computer science programs cease curricula models that begin with a two-course sequence that emulates the natural sciences and mathematics. We report on an aggressive strategy to work with faculty from across the disciplines of arts, humanities, and the social and life sciences to help design and deliver sets of multidisciplinary, applied, and "connected" pairs of introductory courses. Preliminary results at our small liberal arts college include an increase in the percentage of women enrolling in our connected courses, more students taking an additional course in computing, a faculty energized with sharing their research early on, and new interdisciplinary research opportunities for computer science faculty and students.

Categories and Subject Descriptors
K.3.2 [**Computer and Information Science Education**] *Computer science education, Curriculum*

General Terms
Design, Experimentation

Keywords
Applied computer science, arts, bioinformatics, curricula, humanities, intelligent systems, interdisciplinary, multidisciplinary, pipeline, recruitment, retention, social sciences, web programming, women in computing

1. INTRODUCTION
Computer Science curricula at small colleges suffers from a unique dilemma: other than our own majors, few programs require their students to take a course in computer science. When compared to other science and mathematics programs, very few, if any, require their majors to enroll in a computer science course. On the contrary, biology and environmental science programs require their majors to take at least a year of chemistry, calculus, and possibly statistics. Pre-medical students are similar but have the additional requirement of a year of physics. Chemistry students often take a year of mathematics and biology. Physics majors require their students to take a strong complement of courses in mathematics.

So why should this matter? In a word: recruitment. As an academic program, the absence of students in computer science (CS) courses who are exploring possible majors removes the opportunity for students, especially those early in their college years, to experience the joys of computational thinking. Missing from many computer science programs are opportunities for professors to look the undecided student in the eye and say, "You are good at this. You should consider taking another course." A counter case in point: our mathematics colleagues recruit many of their majors during the introductory calculus courses. Many of these students, taking calculus to satisfy a requirement in another potential major, find they enjoy problem solving and working in the symbolic world. Coupled with praise from a professor, calculus becomes the "math farm". Assuming that computer science has "no farm", we argue here for hosting our own farm, a CS "co-op" where students with interests in other disciplines are exposed to computing applied to their area of strength.

Historically, the CS1-CS2 sequence has attempted to emulate the introductory two-course sequence of the science and mathematics majors: Physics I and II, Chemistry I and II, Biology I and II, and Calculus I and II. The difference, of course, being that each of these programs relied on the others to offer enriched, focused content. Not true for computer science, despite the increasing reliance on and use of computational thinking in math and the sciences. Nationally and locally, we labored for and successfully established computer science as its own discipline, unique and independent of math and the sciences. Through these early decades, we relentlessly modified our content, language, and/or pedagogy in the initial two computer science courses.

On our own small liberal arts campus, we reached out to the science and math programs, offering to modify our introductory course syllabi to help prepare their students for computing within their respective disciplines. After a decade of lobbying, the results are barely minimal. Within our course catalog, only two places mention computer science courses other than in the computer science section: mathematics allows CS1 to count as an elective and physics recommends CS1. Once our computer science

SIGCSE'10, March 10–13, 2010, Milwaukee, Wisconsin, USA.

program was built, we hoped "they would come". Yet beyond those few students who know they are interested in computing from the start, technologically savvy students from across campus do not find themselves electing or required to take computer science. This is especially true in the liberal arts setting where very few students intend to major in computer science from the start. In fact, like many institutions, a significant majority of our incoming first year students come to campus "undecided".

At this point, we restrain ourselves from a critique of the mistakes computer science may have made in its early history to dissuade programs from requiring our courses. Rather, we share a suite of introductory courses that taps into a larger multidisciplinary model to "enlarge the funnel" [10] that leads students to additional courses in computing. Clearly, today's undergraduates constitute a wired, communicating, computationally-dependent generation. Embedded and assumed, computers are no longer "cool" for their own sake; students' comments of their experience in computing courses concur [7]. Yet, we submit that student scholars from all disciplines, the arts, humanities, and life and social sciences, are eager to know how to apply computational thinking and tools to their areas of scholarship.

In the sections to follow, we introduce the idea of "course connections" and provide four examples of new introductory courses that not only reach out to faculty across campus but rely on their multidisciplinary collaboration for successful execution, some of which have spawned new research directions for participating faculty. We close with preliminary data that offers encouraging support and a proposal that computer science should cease attempts to emulate the I-II course sequence inherited from traditional natural science and mathematics by offering connected courses as an introductory but vital beginning to the major.

2. CONNECTIONS

In December of 2001, the Wheaton College faculty adopted an innovative new curriculum centered on "Connections," pairs of linked courses that connected significantly different disciplines. In short, the faculty voted to "teach together" in various combinations. This unique alternative to a list of requirements provides an exciting way to explore different areas of knowledge and different approaches to problems. Courses are linked across any two of six academic areas: creative arts, humanities, history, math and computer science, natural sciences, and social sciences. Pairs of connected courses may be taken in either order and do not need to be taken in consecutive semesters, although departmental planning across campus attempts to offer each course of a connection within a year of the other.

In response to this institutional curriculum change, computer science has established a strong suite of six connected courses, four of which are presented here: "Computing for Poets" connected with the humanities, "Web Programming, Graphics, and Design" with the arts, "DNA" with both the life sciences and philosophy, and "Intelligent Systems" with the social sciences. Unlike models that rely on "courses outside of computer science" [3], connected courses involve multidisciplinary faculty in the design and execution of the computer science courses.

Our "computing connections" offer a number of novel features, especially for programs on small liberal arts campuses. Creating a "funnel" of introductory courses is one recommendation for small institutions [10]. Similar models are in progress for IT [1] and CIS [8] programs, used at large universities [3], and employed for reaching multiple sub-disciplines in computing [2, 7]. Collectively, our connected courses have forged new relationships across campus, with both faculty and students from a range of majors. Because students are required to take two pairs of connections, students have an incentive to consider completing a connection while taking the first course in a pair. For example, humanities students, typically from the highly-enrolled English program who are taking either "Anglo-Saxon Literature" or "Tolkien" courses are encouraged to consider completing a connection by subsequently enrolling in "Computing for Poets". Professors from each side of the connection highlight the interdisciplinary connection as often as possible in each course. Participating faculty guest lecture in the other's course. Our experience supports the recent recommendation that faculty from other departments take an active role in course development and delivery [5].

In computer science, the faculty have additionally and strategically agreed that each of our connected courses satisfy the College's Quantitative Analysis ("math") requirement so that each connected course (i) satisfies one-half of a connection and (ii) and satisfies a core curriculum requirement. With limited faculty resources, a common constraint for most small programs in computer science, the decision to exceed a minimum level of "logical and algorithmic thinking" has led each course to share a common thread, often realized via an exposure to scripting in some language [2]. By doing so, we reject a "softer introduction to computer programming" [9] and promote our introductory suite of courses with a campus-wide standard for rigor.

In a concerted effort, we have designed these introductory, applied, interdisciplinary courses *around* the research agendas of the faculty involved. This is an important element of our plan that we see as positively impacting the longevity and robustness of the model. Rather than "taking turns" teaching a common course that covers a wide spectrum of topics in computing (*cf.* the many examples of breadth courses), we present four courses that stem from faculty research. Although outside the scope of this particular paper, our decision to support a teaching model that intersects with our individual research programs should not be missed. Not only do these introductory courses allow an opportunity for faculty to share their scholarship *while* teaching at the introductory level, the courses introduced below have the added advantage of acquainting students early in their college careers with faculty's research areas.

2.1 Connecting with the Arts

Students are naturally interested in building Web pages, and many courses exist that teach how to use various tools to do just that. While we do teach how to use tools such as Dreamweaver and Fireworks in the course entitled "Web Programming, Graphics, and Design" (COMP 161), we reach much further: we teach basic graphic design principles, delve into graphics issues, such as choosing between GIF and JPEG formats, and devote about half of the semester to cover Flash movie creation. The latter includes significant programming in ActionScript, which enables students to incorporate non-trivial interactivity and custom computations to their Web site projects [4, 11].

The course is formally connected with "Graphic Design I" in the Arts, the idea being that students would first learn about design and then enroll in our course where they would implement their ideas. Students can be flexible in the order they take their courses, so we cannot assume they will take this path. Therefore, the first portion of the course focuses on design issues. Indeed, this portion was devised with the help of an Arts instructor, who also gives guest lectures in aspects of design. The course then morphs from an artistic and design focus to implementing Web pages with Flash components to, ultimately, programming as a major element of student projects. This offers non-majors a blend of creative and computational thinking that affords plenty of opportunity for rigor within a familiar domain. Another aspect of the course is that it is also open to computer science students as a non-major elective. The department gains breadth for majors, a perennial problem at small institutions, while students have used what they learned in this course in later courses. For example, one group of majors who took the course later applied their knowledge to further research involving an information visualization problem of a faculty member in Sociology.

2.2 Connecting with the Humanities

"Computing for Poets" (COMP 131) is connected with two courses in English: "Anglo-Saxon Literature" and "J.R.R Tolkien". For example, in the connection with Anglo-Saxon Literature, the relationship between Old English poems has been a vexed question for nearly 150 years. Most of the poetry is anonymous and exists only as tenth-century copies in manuscripts (some of it is assumed to be much earlier). We have only three named authors of poetry in the Anglo-Saxon period (Cædmon, Cynewulf and King Alfred), and there are various problems with linking these names (much less their biographies) with more than a very few specific poems. Although a few prose texts are by known authors (particularly the homilists Ælfric and Wulfstan), even the majority of the prose is anonymous. Thus for years scholars of Old English have struggled to divine relationships between texts based on vocabulary, meter, and style. These results have been at best contentious and at worst completely unsuccessful. Starting with a new completely digitized Old English corpus, the computer science course focuses on algorithmic thinking and experimental design while the Anglo-Saxon course provides an in-depth review of the poems and prose in the corpus. Because students may take the courses in either order, both English and Computer Science faculty participate in syllabus design and make several guest lectures in the other course to help reinforce the connection between the disciplines.

For students majoring in the humanities and taking the computer science course, an exposure to the application of computers to manage the storage and retrieval of written texts shows by example the many new opportunities for scholars of ancient and other written works. In particular, the "Poets" course teaches computer programming as a vehicle to personalize the exploration of vast collections of poems and corpora now available online, including stylometry and authorship attribution. Course work includes a rich exposure to pattern matching with regular expressions, parsing large collections of XML files (e.g., corpora marked up according to the Text Encoding Initiative (TEI) schema), building a concordance, examining the top-N words in your own writing, and elementary statistical methods for authorship attribution [11]. Final projects ask students to design and implement an experiment to search for relationships among texts across the entire Anglo-Saxon or Tolkien corpus.

2.3 Connecting with the Social Sciences

Intelligent Systems (COMP 198) is a new non-major course we plan to connect with a number of offerings from the Psychology department (e.g., Learning and Memory - PSY 211; Cognition - PSY 222; Comparative Animal Behavior - PSY 226). To assist in planning the connection, faculty from Computer Science and Psychology have met to discuss curricular overlap for the last year. Additionally, one Psychology faculty member is attending and participating in discussions during our current offering. Through these interactions we have identified existing content that links the two disciplines. For example, Valentino Braitenberg's book *Vehicles: Experiments in Synthetic Psychology* details excellent thought experiment examples (e.g., vehicles behaving cowardly or aggressively) and motivates the connection for perspective students.

The course provides an introduction to robotics and a survey of selected topics from artificial intelligence. Unlike the Artificial Intelligence-area courses we offer for majors, this course is available to students with no programming experience. Without an explicit computational thinking requirement in the College's curriculum, we are still able to include those concepts in this non-CS1 course to non-majors. We equip students with the technical know-how to program a modern robotics platform, iRobot's Create robot, using both Alice and Python. Programming exercise topics range from mimicking simple animal behaviors (e.g., wall following) to discovering the emergence of swarm behaviors. On the theoretical side, students critically analyze seminal articles in AI to ultimately address Alan Turing's question, "can machines think?" In addition to students from Psychology, the course has attracted majors from Linguistics to Economics. These students bring to bear perspectives and other literatures that further inform class discussions on sentience, consciousness, and self-awareness.

2.4 Connecting with Science and Philosophy

An amazing blend of science, computing, mathematics, and ethics emerges when considering the molecule "Deoxyribonucleic Acid" (DNA). DNA is the blueprint of life for all organisms on Earth and throughout evolutionary time and is at the center of future personalized medical profiles. Fully sequenced genomes including the human genome and hundreds of microbial genomes have become the starting point for attempts to answer a wide range of biological and quantitative questions.

In this connection, two courses in Philosophy "Ethics" (PHIL 111) and "Medical Ethics" (PHIL 242) are paired with the computer science – biology team-taught, cross-listed course called "DNA" (COMP/BIO 242). The "DNA" course teaches computer programming as an introductory means of data mining genomic data [6, 11]. Building off a "DNA as text" metaphor, students apply a heavy dose of regular expressions in assignments for finding genes (e.g., olfactory seven trans-membrane proteins) and upstream regulatory motifs in microbial genomes. Emulating the instructors' ongoing research, final projects pair life science and computer science students in interdisciplinary teams to apply authorship attribution and genomic signature techniques for identifying and/or clustering like-genomes based on motif frequencies. Programming topics include processing large numbers of input files, professional documentation, the data structures of arrays and hash tables, and designing *in silico* experimental methods. While satisfying an elective in both the biology and computer science majors and attracting a rich diversity of students from the computational and life sciences, students in the DNA course are also exposed to the ethical aspects of living in a post-genomic world. In both the ethics and computing courses, particular attention is paid to the increasing use and challenges of sequenced genomes as applied to personalized medicine. A series of assignments and events with students in ethics classes include: a showing of the movie GATTACA and follow-up discussion, talks and discussions with both a genetic counselor and professor of bioethics, and student-produced, one-minute YouTube "commercials" of companies (e.g. 23andME, deCODEme) currently promoting and selling medical profiles based on individual genomes. The commercials are framed from one of two points of view: (i) from the point of view of the company or (ii) from a consumer advocacy point of view.

2.5 Teaching Leads to Research

From the outset, it was clear that teaching together in connected courses would be good for our students. What was not so clear was how good it would be for the faculty's professional development and research output. Years before the connections curriculum, computer science was actively engaged in interdisciplinary teaching which in turn led to new research agendas. An NSF-funded model for our campus centered around bioinformatics and the "linking" of biology's "Genetics" and computer science's "Algorithms" courses. We define "linked" courses as two independently run courses that share bioinformatics as a common thread in their respective syllabi and that share time in the form of guest lectures, some common lab sessions (e.g., 4 out of 12 labs over the semester), collaborative programming assignments outside of lab time, and/or final interdisciplinary team projects and presentations. This early work led to the previously mentioned CS-bio-ethics connection, an introductory scripting text for biologists [6], and an active faculty and student research group focusing on new techniques for detecting horizontal transfer in microbial genomes.

Intrigued and encouraged by the process of how teaching influenced research and how the research fueled new ideas for teaching, faculty applied bioinformatics techniques that distinguish microbial genomes to differentiate multiple authors in Old English manuscripts. This led to the previously mentioned connection between English and Computer Science. A successful experience with getting undergraduates to ask computational questions across an entire corpus led to another active research group and current funding from the National Endowment for the Humanities (NEH). New, exciting experimental techniques and results on the Anglo-Saxon corpus will be integrated into the next iteration of the connected courses. As a direct result of connecting our teaching, new research was spawned where faculty bring their research into the classroom so that undergraduates can ask novel questions across digitized corpora of their choice.

3. TAKING ADDITIONAL CS COURSES

Our current recruitment strategy includes an increase in the number of connected courses offered and early enrollment data is providing encouraging support. Table 1 shows that each of our new connected courses (Poets, Web Programming, Intelligent Systems, and DNA) encourage a larger percentage of students to take at least one more of these introductory courses than our traditional CS0. (Note that CS2 is not included in these data.)

Course	Percentage of students taking this course and then at least +1 more
FYS	31
CS0	8
CS1	23
Poets*	12
Web*	14
IntellSystems*	33
DNA*	12

Table 1. Percentage of students who initially took each course and then proceeded to take at least one more of the courses in this list. An asterik (*) denotes a new connected course.

In addition, we are pleased with the success of our recent First Year Seminar (FYS) entitled "Storytelling through Computer Animation". As a complement to our connected courses, participating in the seminar program continues to be a wise and worthwhile effort.

While we originally assumed that students would follow a path from a connected course to CS1, we are pleased to see that 23% of students who start in CS1 are subsequently enrolling in a connected course. We of course recognize that "connections" are part of the general requirements and that students' course preferences are so influenced. However, connecting widely across campus and consistently offering our connections is a strategic effort on our part. If students take connections, then let them take them with us.

This raises one additional and important rationale for connections beyond enrollment numbers and recruitment strategies for the computer science program and that is our commitment to providing relevant experiences in computing for students across the academy. The reality is that most students in our connected courses will only take but one computer science course. We are convinced that an increasing number of students in our connected courses will sample applications of computing in the arts, humanities, social or life sciences and for the first time experience the relevance and benefit of computing in their academic and professional lives.

4. ATTRACTING WOMEN TO CS

Our enrollment data reveals a strong increase in the number of female students in our connected courses relative to our traditional CS0, CS1, and CS2 offerings. As shown in Figure 1, since 2000 the percentage of women in our traditional CS0 continues to decline (note that CS0 was not taught in 2004 and 2006). On the other hand, the percentage of women in our set of connected courses outpaces the traditional CS0 and CS1 entry-level courses in all but one semester.

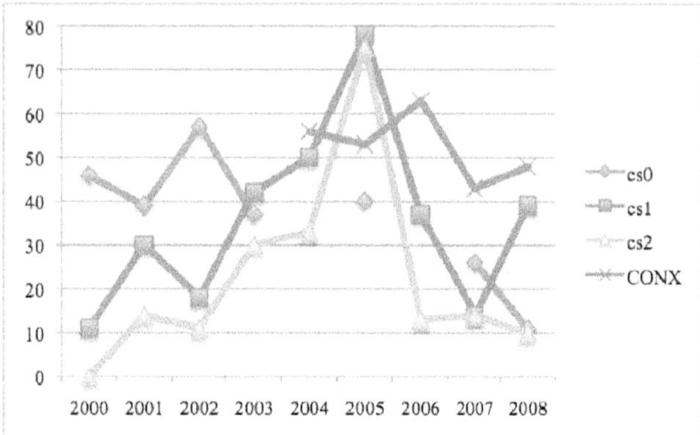

Figure 1. The percentages of female students in the traditional CS0, CS1, CS2, and new set of connected (CONX) courses. (Note that CS0 was not taught in 2004 and 2006).

5. THE END OF CS1 AS WE KNOW IT?

In our small liberal arts college setting, the model of offering non-majors courses in parallel with an introductory two-course sequence for majors is not attracting a healthy number of majors. While we are pleased with the rigor in our program (e.g., a full year of discrete math) and the success of our graduates to find jobs and get accepted in graduate programs, the tightening of academic budgets, decrease in computer science enrollments, and heightened administrative scrutiny of the number of students served is a call for creative change. We submit that computer science programs, especially those at small colleges, seriously consider (i) a more multidisciplinary approach to the "funnel model" of introductory courses, one that actively involves faculty from other programs in not only the design but also the delivery of the course(s) and (ii) eliminating the traditional CS1 course and replacing the starting curricula pipeline with a funnel from interdisciplinary, connected courses. The challenge is for each new "connected" course to equip students for further study, specifically to be ready for a course focused on data structures. We fully appreciate the scheduling constraints on small programs, and thus we assume that these new courses will replace the traditional CS1. In short, we reject the notion that by replacing CS1 with interdisciplinary courses that "something else in the curriculum must go." Rather, our proposal is an endorsement of and encouragement for the creativity of computer science faculty to craft curriculum that leverages the strengths of their local academy. No recommended two-course sequence should constrain our attempts to reach a new generation of scholars who desire to experience the relevance of computational thinking.

For decades, computer science has followed the I-II introductory model used in the natural sciences and mathematics, except these other curriculums send their students to the other programs. For various reasons, some beyond our control, computer science is not in this mix. What is increasingly clear to us and apparently to the new generation of faculty and students across campus who are confronted with and rely on computing in their scholarship, computer science has a unique opportunity to change our curriculum, flex our interdisciplinary strengths, and connect our courses to those across campus.

6. REFERENCES

[1] Besana, G.M., Dettori, L., and Steinbach, T.A. 2006. An Invitation to IT: Redesigning the First Year. *Journal of Computing Sciences in Colleges* 21, 6 (Jun. 2006), 130-139.

[2] Bills, D.P. and Canosa, R.L. 2007. Sharing Introductory Programming Curriculum across Disciplines. *SIGITE '07* (Oct. 2007), 99-106.

[3] Furst, M., Isbell, C., and Guzdial, M. 2007. Threads™: How to restructure a computer science curriculum for a flat world. Proceedings of 38th SIGCSE symposium on Computer science education. Covington, KT (Mar. 2007), 420-424.

[4] Gousie, M.B. 2006. A robust web programming and graphics course for non-majors. Proceedings of the 37th SIGCSE technical symposium on Computer science education. Houston, TX (Mar. 2006), 72-76.

[5] Guzdial, M. 2009. Teaching Computing to Everyone. *Communications of the ACM*, 52, 5 (May 2009), p31-33.

[6] LeBlanc, M.D. and Dyer, B.D. 2007. *Perl for Exploring DNA*. Oxford University Press.

[7] Margolis, J. and Fisher, A. 2001. *Unlocking the Clubhouse: Women in Computing*. MIT Press.

[8] Pearce, J. and Nakazawa, M. 2008. The Funnel that Grew Our CIS major in the CS Desert. Proceedings of the 39th SIGCSE technical symposium on Computer science education. Portland, OR (Mar. 2008), 503-507.

[9] Pokorny, K.L. 2009. Introduction to Computing: A Fresh Breadth of Disciplines. *Journal of Computing Sciences in Colleges* 24, 5 (May 2009), 166-172.

[10] The Joint Task Force for Computing Curricula 2005. The Computing Curricula 2005: The Overview Report. (Sept. 2005). Retrieved from http://www.acm.org/education/curric_vols/CC2005-March06Final.pdf in Dec 2005.

[11] Computer science course URLs involved in connections:

with Art:

http://cs.wheatoncollege.edu/~mgousie/comp161.html

with Biology and Philosophy:

http://cs.wheatoncollege.edu/~mleblanc/dna/

with English:

http://cs.wheatoncollege.edu/~mleblanc/131/syllabus.pdf

with Psychology:

http://cs.wheatoncollege.edu/~tarmstro/IS-fall2009

Women in CS: An Evaluation of Three Promising Practices

Christine Alvarado
Harvey Mudd College
alvarado@cs.hmc.edu

Zachary Dodds
Harvey Mudd College
dodds@cs.hmc.edu

ABSTRACT

Historically, Harvey Mudd College (HMC) has had very little success attracting women to the study of computer science: women have chosen CS less than any other field of study. In 2006 HMC began three practices in order to increase the number of women studying and majoring in CS; these practices have now been in place for 3 years. With this paper we describe these practices and present a thorough evaluation of the quantitative and qualitative differences that have accompanied them. In sum, these efforts have rebalanced our department by significantly increasing women's participation in our computer science program.

Categories and Subject Descriptors

K.3.2 [**Computers and Education**]: Computer and Information Science Education—*Computer Science Education, Curriculum*

General Terms

Human Factors, Design, Measurement

Keywords

gender, women in CS, CS1, promising practices

1. INTRODUCTION

The gender imbalance in computer science is no secret. For years researchers and practitioners have worked to increase the representation of women in CS. Numerous research studies have uncovered reasons women have not chosen CS: an unattractive/hostile culture, misperceptions of the discipline, lack of role models and/or mentoring support, and lack of experience and confidence [4, 7, 1, 9, 11].

To address women's lack of pre-college experience, many recent programs target girls in middle and high school. Languages such as Alice [10] and Scratch [12] are aimed at underrepresented populations such as girls and inner-city youth in this age group. Other programs have used robots as a platform to attract girls to CS [8]. These projects have shown great success, but the fact remains that a large number of beginning college students, especially women, still have little or no computer science experience.

At the college level, initiatives to recruit and retain women in CS range from new introductory curricula, to more active outreach, to increased mentoring support. Media-themed CS1 courses have improved women's interest and success in CS1 [15]. Others themes include AI, robotics and music [6, 17, 13]. Also, targeted recruiting, mentoring and community building has greatly increased the number of women in CS at several schools, most notably Carnegie Mellon University [2].

Harvey Mudd College (HMC), a science and engineering-focused liberal arts college with approximately 740 undergraduate students, struggled for years with few women joining CS. Although over one third of the members of our student body are women, the percentage of women CS majors was less than 10%. In 2006, we sought to increase this percentage. Many of the reasons for the under-representation of women applied to us, but we also perceived an important but less-studied factor: Women did not really understand what CS is and thus were not interested. We hypothesized that by giving students this fundamental understanding we could increase the number of women CS majors and dramatically improve the CS experience for all of our students.

We implemented three practices focused on first-year students and designed to reveal to our students the true nature of CS. First, our CS1 course became a breadth-first view of the discipline. We believed its breadth would pique the interests of the women who disproportionately arrived with less CS experience. Second, we began offering trips for first-year women to the Grace Hopper Celebration of Women in Computing (GHC). Rather than use GHC as a retention mechanism, as has proven effective, we use it as a *recruiting* tool. Third, we provided research opportunities for women after their freshman year, even if (in fact, especially if) they have taken only one CS course. These research projects offer students an engaging invitation into real CS problems.

Through enrollment and survey data, we find that these three practices have succeeded in increasing the number of women in computer science at HMC. Here we detail these practices and results here with the hope that other institutions will also find them effective and beneficial.

2. PRACTICES OVERVIEW

A central goal of each practice is to expose students to the true nature of CS as early in their college career as possible.

SIGCSE'10, March 10–13, 2010, Milwaukee, Wisconsin, USA.

2.1 An engaging view: Broad CS1

In 2006, we replaced our traditional, Java-based CS1 course with a Python-based, breadth-first CS1 course [6]. This new CS1 is presented and evaluated in more detail elsewhere [6].

The course comprises five modules over a 14-week semester. The initial module provides students with a small set of tools to write interesting and useful programs *within the first week of the course*, principally lists, numbers, conditional statements, and recursion. The other four modules in our existing course are (2) three weeks on computer organization, (3) a three-week module on imperative programming ideas, (4) a two-week module on object-oriented concepts and (5) a two-week module on the theory of computing. Collectively, these modules provide students with an understanding of the breadth of modern computational thought, its connections with other disciplines, and skills and tools for writing their own substantial programs.

CS1 also benefitted from two key structural changes. First, we split students into a standard track for those without experience and an enrichment track for those with prior CS background. We offer two sections of the standard track and one section of the enrichment track, each with about 60 students. This separation keeps the latter students challenged without intimidating students new to CS. Second, we implemented optional, but incentivized, faculty-staffed closed lab sessions each week. Students can attend a weekly two-hour lab and receive full-credit for one of the three or four weekly homework problems, regardless of whether they finish the problem or not. This arrangement lessens the workload for inexperienced students and, even more importantly, allows them to get early help with difficult concepts. These structural changes have slightly increased the faculty load dedicated to CS1, from 0.8FTEs to 1.2FTEs in the fall semester (the only semester it is offered).

HMC has the advantage that all first-year students take CS1. The new CS1 course has also boosted enrollment of students from sibling institutions. We note that the majority of these cross-registrations are women.

2.2 True CS community: Recruiting via GHC

Even as this new introductory course exposes students to a compelling cross-section of real CS, it does not expose them to *actual computer scientists* beyond the instructors. To engage our students in CS's vibrant community, we organized our first trip to GHC in 2006. We specifically targeted first-year students, using GHC for recruiting, rather than retention. We believed that interactions with the professionals at GHC would reinforce *experientially* the opportunities we sought to present in the curriculum.

The number of students we have taken to the conference has grown steadily over the years: they are mostly first-year women with a few upper-class women CS majors as mentors. In 2006, the trip was open to all first-year students, regardless of gender. We took 12 students, including 8 first-year women, 2 first-year men and 2 upper-class women. In subsequent years we restricted the trip to women due to expanding interest. In 2007, 14 students (12 first year women and 2 upper-class women) attended the conference in Orlando, FL. In 2008, 28 women students (22 first-year students and 6 upper-class students) attended the conference in Keystone, CO. In 2009 32 women students (26 first-year and 6 upper-class) will attend the conference in Tuscon, AZ.

The trip to GHC is fully funded by our institution and outside sources and costs between $15K and $20K each year; it is organized and attended by CS faculty and staff. Because GHC falls midterm, we have found success by contacting incoming students during the summer *before* they arrive on campus. Organizing the trip over the summer has the additional advantage of having students commit to the trip before the semester's workload overwhelms them! Thus far we have been able to take all interested women students. However, if we had to select a subset we would aim for a balance of curiosity and experience with CS.

2.3 Building confidence: Research experiences for first-year women

The new CS1 gives students a broad introduction to what CS actually is, and GHC exposes them to what computer scientists actually do. The only thing missing for incoming women was the confidence to feel that they too could do real-world computer science. To this end, we organized research experiences for rising sophomores.

Undergraduate research experience has been shown to be a key factor in retaining students in computer science, particularly in the undergraduate to graduate school transition [14, 5]. Unfortunately, however, research opportunities are not usually available until students have completed several undergraduate computer science classes. In other disciplines this is not the case. Students in physical sciences can often get jobs in research labs doing tasks supportive of a larger research project with little or no advanced training.

We sought to provide this type of hands-on opportunity to involve students in computer science research before they have had much formal training in CS. In the summer of 2007 we hired 10 students to work on ongoing projects in artificial intelligence, robotics, games and filesystems. In the summers of 2008 and 2009, we continued to hire first-year women to work on projects in similar areas. Although these students had very little experience (one or two semesters of CS) they made concrete progress on real research problems.

Experiences were crafted to ensure maximal success. Projects usually involved tools students had learned in their one or two computer science classes (e.g., Python). Students working on more advanced projects were paired with upperclass mentors selected for their knowledge and teaching skills. Students also worked closely with a faculty member, meeting with their mentor several times a week if not daily.

3. TRACKING PARTICIPATION

Though not the only goal, increasing women's interest and involvement in CS was the primary motivator for Section 2's programmatic changes.

The first statistics we have followed are the number and percentage of women choosing CS as a major. We focus on incoming classes since 2003: three years before and three years after the three new practices. Figure 1 suggests that, indeed, the balance between women and men choosing CS as a major changed. 2006 seems the fulcrum of this change: the percentage of women majors almost doubled to 20%. Subsequent years have seen an even more dramatic shift in demographics.

Although these numbers are encouraging, they are also deceptive because they hide large changes in our student body's demographic balance. We address the rebalancing of CS relative to our whole student body next.

In addition to seeking a better balance within the CS

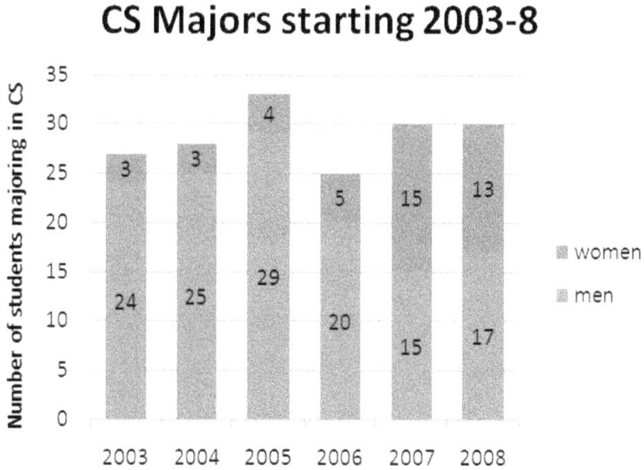

Figure 1: Numbers of women and men majoring in CS, in the *entering-year* classes of 2003-2008. The 2008 majors numbers may still rise.

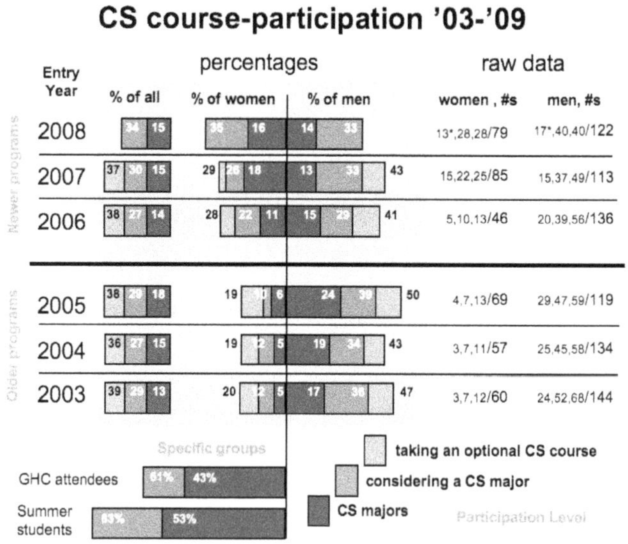

Figure 2: Percentages of students, of women, and of men participating in CS at three levels of involvement: majors, considering the major, and CS-interested (see text). The vertical axis represents students' *entry* year. Raw data appear at right; GHC and summer-project cohorts (all women) appear below. *Major and CS-interested numbers in entry-year 2008 may still increase.

community, we have sought to highlight the importance and value of computer science to students *outside the CS major.* To this end we have measured trends among our whole student body and their computer science course choices across three levels of involvement. Figure 2 summarizes these trends.

The backbone of Figure 2 illustrates how CS1, which is required for all students, has yielded CS majors. In contrast to Figure 1, Figure 2's reported percentages of men and women are measured *relative to our whole student body.* We report percentages within the female and male student populations, respectively, in order to accommodate the high variance in the yearly raw numbers at our small institution. The raw data at right show those variations.

We have identified two levels of student engagement with CS beyond choosing a CS major. The first is students "seriously considering" CS as a major, a superset of the majors themselves. These are students who take an additional, optional CS course early enough to become majors. The second group is "CS-interested" students who take an additional, optional CS course at *any* time in their college career. Thus, the three groups – majors, major-considerers, and CS-interested – are each a subset of the next. Enveloping the CS majors (dark bars) in Figure 2 are the major-considerers and CS-interested. Numbers are provided as percentages of all students (left), women (middle), and men (right). For example, in the incoming class of 2007 37% of all students (i.e. 25 women + 49 men of 85 total women and 113 total men) took another CS class after CS1. 30% took a second class early enough to have completed a CS major (22 women + 37 men) while 15% of the incoming class of 2007 has actually declared CS as a major (15 women + 15 men).

A bird's-eye observation from Figure 2 is that CS course participation has not changed dramatically at any of the three levels among all students, but that the gender balance has increased across all three. Though certainly not independent samples, numbers from GHC attendees and summer-project participants (lower left) suggest that those programs contribute to this rebalancing.

In the next section we present survey data that suggest potential causes for theses shifts. Here we report on Figure 2's correlations. We ran a gamut of Pearson's chi-squared tests for independence on Figure 2's data in order to measure the significance of the apparent shifts. To assess the shift in women's, men's, and all students' participation in CS as majors, major-considerers or CS-interested, we created nine 2x2 tables contrasting actual and expected participation pre- and post-2006. Figure 3 shows one of those nine: the significant change in the number of women CS majors.

Figure 4 summarizes the results of our nine statistical comparisons. It shows shifts in different populations and underscores the significance of the shift in *who* makes up our CS community, even as overall participation has, for the most part, held steady.

4. ROOT CAUSES: SURVEY RESULTS

The enrollment numbers detailed in the previous section suggest that our practices have had a positive effect on

women	post-2006	pre-2006	totals
CS major	33	10	43
other major	177	176	353
totals	210	186	396
CS expected	22.8	20.2	43
other exp.	187.2	165.8	353
totals	210	186	396

Figure 3: (top) The 2x2 contingency table of women choosing to major in CS or another field both pre- and post-2006. (bottom) The table of expectations, based on the null hypothesis of the independence of major choice (rows) and era (columns) from the top table. This table yields Figure 4's seventh row.

Δ women interested	$X^2(1, N = 396) = 7.52, \mathbf{p < .05}$
Δ men interested	$X^2(1, N = 768) = 4.42, \mathbf{p < .05}$
Δ all interested	$X^2(1, N = 1164) = 0.32, p > .05$
Δ women considering	$X^2(1, N = 396) = 18.1, \mathbf{p < .05}$
Δ men considering	$X^2(1, N = 768) = 2.15, p > .05$
Δ all considering	$X^2(1, N = 1164) = 0.56, p > .05$
Δ women CS majors	$X^2(1, N = 396) = 10.9, \mathbf{p < .05}$
Δ men CS majors	$X^2(1, N = 768) = 4.32, p > .05$
Δ all CS majors	$X^2(1, N = 1164) = 0.82, p > .05$

Figure 4: Significance results from the nine cohorts summarized in Figure 2.

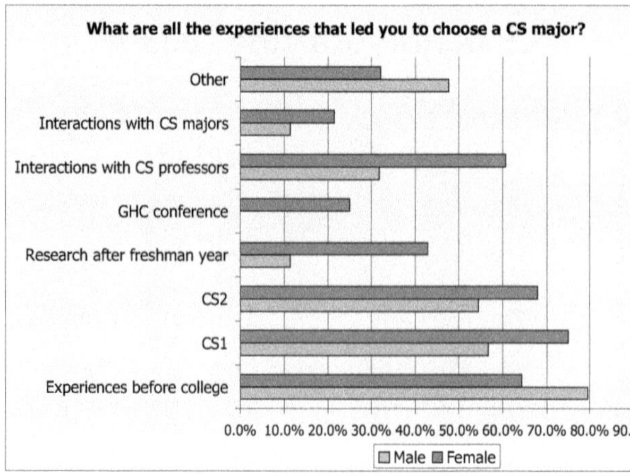

Figure 5: Percentage of students who cited each experience as important in choosing a CS major.

women in CS. But enrollment numbers never tell the whole story. A recent study found that enrollment numbers can be too variable to reveal stable trends [16]. Second, enrollment numbers cannot provide insight into the specific aspects of the practices that affect women's experience in CS.

With these thoughts in mind, we conducted two student surveys to get a better understanding of how our initiatives impacted our students: a single broad student survey aimed at all of our students (the "CS Experience Survey") and a smaller annual survey aimed at GHC attendees.

The CS Experience Survey asked students about each of the practices we described above, as well as about their main reasons for choosing their current major. Space prohibits us from including all of the questions in the survey. We include the most relevant questions as we discuss our results.

We designed and administered the CS Experience Survey in the summer of 2009. Through email we invited 784 students and alumni including all current and just-graduated students (classes of 2009-2012) as well as all CS major alums through the class of 2007 to take our survey. 449 students completed the electronic survey (57% response rate). This response rate includes a representative spectrum of respondents: The response rate of CS majors (58%) was approximately equal to the overall response rate, and the gender and race demographics of the respondents approximately match the gender and race demographics of the whole student body.

Our survey revealed that all three practices had a positive impact on students, both women and, where applicable, men. 75.4% (n=227) of students who took the new CS1 reported that it changed the way they thought about CS, compared to 46.5% (n=40) who took the old version of CS1. This difference is statistically significant (chi-square, p<0.001). Qualitative responses to how it changed their perception reveal that for most students, it gave them a more accurate and more positive view of the discipline. Many students made comments such as, "I had no idea how many different aspects of CS there were. I also was pleasantly surprised by how much fun it is to program.". Perhaps more importantly, 21% of respondents specifically mentioned that CS was "fun". This result is particularly encouraging as Carter found in 2006 that "fun" was a major motivating factor in choosing a CS major [3].

Indeed, the new CS1 was cited as one of the major influencing factors for why students chose a CS major, particularly for women. We asked the CS majors to select all of the experiences that led them to choose a CS major. Figure 5 shows the results of this question for students in incoming classes since 2006 (i.e. since we implemented our new practices) in percentage of students who selected each experience. The results clearly show that the new CS1 was very influential for both genders, but that it had an even bigger impact, proportionally, on the women. The reason for this larger influence is partly because a higher proportion of men place out of CS1, so a higher proportion of women take the course. However, even when we limit our attention to the respondents who took the new CS1, we still find that a slightly higher percentage of women than men list it as an important experience: 84% (n=21) of women vs. 81% (n=25) of men, though this difference is not statistically significant. In addition, we also asked students to choose the single most important experience in their choice of a CS major, and almost a third of CS majors chose the new CS1: making it the most popular single experience. This percentage again was slightly higher for women (36%) than it was for men (29%), though not statistically significant.

Figure 5 also shows that summer research after freshman year was an important factor in women students' decisions to become CS majors. Narrowing our focus to only those students who participated in summer research after their first year, we find that 67% (n=10) of women students listed this research experience as an influence in choosing a CS major, while only 25% (n=3) of men did. This difference is statistically significant (χ^2, p<0.05). Furthermore 2 women students listed this research experience as the single most important experience in their choice of major, while no men cited research as the most important experience.

59% of women and 44% of men reported that their research experience after their first year changed their perception of computer science. Although this difference is not statistically significant, we notice that women's responses to the question of *how* their perceptions changed were qualitatively different from men's responses. For women, their experiences not only helped them understand the discipline better, but also built their confidence in their own skills. Representative responses include: "I didn't realize how much I could accomplish just through one frosh level CS class!" and, "Doing research made me much more confident about my skills and knowledge in CS."

Both this survey and the annual post-trip surveys reflect the impact attending the GHC conference has on women students and suggest that it is an important factor in influ-

	2007 (out of 5)	2008 (out of 7)
Attending GHC was a positive experience	**5.0**	**6.54**
Attending GHC gave me a better understanding of CS	**4.11**	**5.83**
Attending GHC changed my perception of the culture of CS	**4.22**	**5.59**
Attending GHC increased my desire to take another CS class	**4.13**	**4.82**
Attending GHC increased my desire to major in CS	3.56	4.54

Figure 6: Student responses to GHC surveys. In 2007 1=strongly disagree, 5=strongly agree; in 2008 1=very strongly disagree, 7=very strongly agree. Bold numbers indicate statistical significance above neutral (Wilcoxon signed-rank, 2-tail, p<0.05).

encing students to take more CS classes and to decide to major in CS. In 2007 9 students completed our post-conference survey, and in 2008 22 students completed the survey. Figure 6 shows student responses to a number of the survey questions. The survey confirms that GHC is the successful recruiting tool we intended it to be: students reported that attending GHC increased their desire to take another computer science class. The survey results did not show a statistically significant average increase in their desire to major in CS. However, it did inspire several individuals to consider a CS major: in 2007 3 out of 9 students responded positively (4-5) to this statement (the other 6 were neutral) and and in 2008 10 out of 22 students responded positively (5-7). Our CS Experience Survey revealed that GHC was an important factor in students choosing a CS major: 47% (n=7) of CS majors who attended GHC listed it as one of the experiences that led them to choose a CS major.

Our CS Experience survey also revealed some surprises beyond this work's focus practices. For example, our computer science culture negatively affects men and women equally. When we asked non-CS majors who had *considered* majoring in CS to list important factors in their *not* choosing a CS major, 28% of women and 31% of men listed "I didn't feel like I fit in as a CS major/I didn't feel comfortable with the culture" as an important factor. In addition, we find that more women (26%) than men (14%) choose a different major in part because CS was "too hard." This result indicates that although our CS1 class has improved the experience for our women students, it has not entirely solved the problem.

5. PERSPECTIVE

This paper's practices have not only increased women's participation in CS, but they have improved the department's tenor and experience for women (and men) both inside and outside of the CS major. The changes to CS1 have re-energized our core curriculum, GHC has engaged our students in CS's large and active community, and research opportunities for first-year students have deepened their hands-on participation in compelling, open projects.

We look forward to investigating the transfer of these successful practices. We recognize that direct large-scale implementation of these practices may be difficult due to their high costs. To this end, we note that the research opportunities have a large impact on each student who participates, so including even a very small number of students still could be quite beneficial. We also believe that regional women in CS celebrations could serve the same purpose as GHC at a lower cost. Finally, even if the specifics are unattainable, the fundamentals underlying these three practices may succeed broadly: (1) recruiting even before students arrive on campus and actively through the first semester and year, (2) hands-on programs that challenge and stretch students, and (3) a top-down curricular focus that emphasizes the reality - not the stereotype - of CS. We are thus hopeful that the enrollment and survey changes seen at HMC will be borne out at many others, as well.

6. REFERENCES

[1] S. Beyer, K. Rynes, J. Perrault, K. Hay, and S. Haller. Gender differences in computer science students. In *Proc. SIGCSE '03*, pages 49–53, 2003.

[2] L. Blum. Women in computer science: The Carnegie Mellon experience. http://www-2.cs.cmu.edu/ lblum/PAPERS/women_in_computer_science.pdf.

[3] L. Carter. Why students with an apparent aptitude for computer science don't choose to major in computer science. In *Proc. SIGCSE '06*, 2006.

[4] J. M. Cohoon. Toward improving female retention in the computer science major. *CACM*, 44(5):108–114, 2001.

[5] J. Cuny and W. Aspray. Recruitment and retention of women graduate students in computer science and engineering: results of a workshop organized by the computing research association. *SIGCSE Bull.*, 34(2):168–174, 2002.

[6] Z. Dodds, R. Libeskind-Hadas, C. Alvarado, and G. Kuenning. Evaluating a breadth-first CS 1 for scientists. In *Proc. SIGCSE '08*, pages 266–270, 2008.

[7] A. Fisher and J. Margolis. Unlocking the clubhouse: the Carnegie Mellon experience. *SIGCSE Bull.*, 34(2):79–83, 2002.

[8] M. Gupta, M. N. Muhammad, and S. Prashad. Robots byte in: An exploration of computer science education in middle schools. CREU Final Report: http://www.roboteducation.org/files/CREU_Final_Report.pdf.

[9] S. Katz, D. Allbritton, J. Aronis, C. Wilson, and M. L. Soffa. Gender, achievement, and persistence in an undergraduate computer science program. *SIGMIS Database*, 37(4):42–57, 2006.

[10] C. Kelleher, R. Pausch, and S. Kiesler. Storytelling alice motivates middle school girls to learn computer programming. In *Proc. CHI '07*, pages 1455–1464, 2007.

[11] M. Klawe, T. Whitney, and C. Simard. Women in computing—take 2. *Commun. ACM*, 52(2):68–76, 2009.

[12] J. H. Maloney, K. Peppler, Y. Kafai, M. Resnick, and N. Rusk. Programming by choice: urban youth learning programming with scratch. In *Proc. SIGCSE*, 2008.

[13] A. Misra, D. Blank, and D. Kumar. A music context for teaching introductory computing. In *Proc. ITiCSE '09*, pages 248–252, 2009.

[14] J. Peckham, P. Stephenson, J.-Y. Hervé, R. Hutt, and M. Encarnaç ao. Increasing student retention in computer science through research programs for undergraduates. *SIGCSE Bull.*, 39(1):124–128, 2007.

[15] L. Rich, H. Perry, and M. Guzdial. A CS1 course designed to address interests of women. *SIGCSE Bull.*, 36(1):190–194, 2004.

[16] B. Richards. Representation of women in cs: how do we measure a program's success? In *Proc. SIGCSE*, 2009.

[17] J. Summet, D. Kumar, K. O'Hara, D. Walker, L. Ni, D. Blank, and T. Balch. Personalizing cs1 with robots. In *Proc. SIGCSE '09*, pages 433–437, 2009.

Relevant Real-World Undergraduate Research Problems: Lessons from the NSF-REU Trenches

Reynold Bailey
(Moderator)
Rochester Institute of Technology
Rochester, NY 14623
rjb@cs.rit.edu

Guy-Alain Amoussou
Humboldt State University
Arcata, CA 95521
amoussou@humboldt.edu

Tiffany Barnes
University of North Carolina at Charlotte
Charlotte, NC 28223
Tiffany.Barnes@uncc.edu

Hans-Peter Bischof
Rochester Institute of Technology
Rochester, NY 14623
hpb@cs.rit.edu

Thomas Naps
University of Wisconsin - Oshkosh
Oshkosh, WI 54901
naps@uwosh.edu

SUMMARY

Projects funded by the National Science Foundation (NSF) Research Experiences for Undergraduates (REU) program aim to (a) enhance participation of students who otherwise might not have research opportunities, and (b) increase the number of students interested in graduate programs, thus expanding the pool of a well-trained scientific workforce. To provide meaningful experiences for these students, REU projects make use of a set of interesting, appropriate research problems that can be tackled in 8 to 10 weeks in summer.

The panelists have all served as PIs or Co-PIs on NSF REU projects in computing. They will present their REU research problems, highlight challenges they encountered, and present their results. They will also discuss what they have done, or what can be done, to incorporate such research problems within the regular computing curriculum, for example, in capstone courses or senior projects. A significant amount of time will be set aside for audience participation and discussion.

Categories and Subject Descriptors

K.3.2 [**Computer and Information Science Education**]: Computer science education

General Terms

Design

Keywords

Undergraduate research, computing problems

1. BACKGROUND

The inclusion of meaningful research experiences for undergraduates has received increased attention in recent years at computing conferences including SIGCSE for a variety of reasons. Such experiences foster recruitment of undergraduate students, who otherwise might not have research opportunities including the underrepresented, into graduate programs via early research exposure [3]. Additionally, it has been shown that students benefit from exposure to highly interdisciplinary research problems [1, 8]. REU-style research problems can address the needs of many undergraduate computer science curricula that require some form of senior project or capstone experience [9]. Involvement in undegraduate research also helps with faculty professional development [6] and there is evidence that the early involvement in research helps with student retention [5, 7].

Attributes of successful undergraduate research projects have been previously discussed [2]. At SIGCSE 2006, a related panel focused on the benefits and challenges of providing research experience for undergraduates, and how faculty can fund and develop their own undergraduate research programs [4].

This panel focuses instead on specific REU research problems. The panelists are PIs or Co-PIs on NSF REU projects in computing. The NSF REU program provides support for undergraduate research through various channels including the establishment of summer research programs at academic institutions around the country. The students involved in these programs typically work on specific research problems for 8-10 weeks.

To provide meaningful research experience for students involved in these programs, the assigned research problems must be interesting and significant enough in scope to cover the duration of the program. The panelists will focus on how they developed relevant real-world research problems, what was achieved, and how these problems can be generalized in other undergraduate contexts. The focus on specific research problems makes this substantially different than previous SIGCSE panels. Finally, a higher number of panelists is justified for this session to ensure that a wider variety of research problems is presented.

2. THE PANELISTS

Dr. Reynold Bailey serves as a mentor for an REU site in computer science at Rochester Institute of Technology. He

SIGCSE'10, March 10–13, 2010, Milwaukee, Wisconsin, USA.
ACM 978-1-60558-885-8/10/03.

has also been involved in efforts to broaden participation in computing programs among underrepresented communities. He will function as the moderator for this panel.

Dr. Guy-Alain Amoussou has served as PI of two consecutive REU sites at Humboldt State University, a California State University campus. Since 2005, his REU programs have trained forty four students in an interdisciplinary environment including computer science, math modeling, geographic information systems and engineering. The overarching theme is related to the science of design (SoD) with a focus on creativity, design activities, and methodology for thinking about and solving problems. Examples of projects students investigated include: robotic systems for visual placement, study of fusion energy, design of multi-platform real-time collaborative sketching infrastructures, and computational coastal management.

Dr. Tiffany Barnes serves as co-PI of the Socially Relevant Computing REU Site at the University of North Carolina at Charlotte, where four labs have engaged students in 60 research experiences that advance technology to empower people to solve problems of personal interest, as well as problems that are important to society at large. Specific problems include developing: games to teach computing concepts, visualization tools and algorithms to help people develop mental maps for improved navigation, digital humans for more effective computer-based education of children, and sensor network protocols and systems to monitor environments for preserving historical and artistic artifacts.

Dr. Hans-Peter Bischof serves as PI of an REU site in computer science at Rochester Institute of Technology, where students work on different aspects of an interdisciplinary project to analyze and visualize the simulation of galactic events such as the formation of galactic nuclei and supermassive black hole mergers. Specific problems include the development of high performance distributed file systems based on commodity hardware, addition of sound to visualizations of galactic events using data-driven audio synthesis, and improved visualization of gravity waves and black hole mergers using various rendering techniques.

Dr. Thomas Naps serves as PI of an REU site in computer science at the University of Wisconsin Oshkosh, where students work on open source algorithm visualization projects. These projects are carried out using the JHAVÉ algorithm visualization environment (http://jhave.org), a large open source platform for staging instructional algorithm visualizations. JHAVÉ offers students the opportunity to be involved in all the components that contribute to successful algorithm visualization, including graphics, automated assessment strategies, and accompanying hypertextbooks. Student projects focus on developing a complete visualization-based instructional module on a topic of their choice.

3. SESSION OUTLINE

The moderator will provide the panel background and motivation, and introduce the other panelists. Panelists will speak for 10 minutes and discuss the research projects tackled by students at their REU sites. Each panelist will:

- Describe how their REU site is structured and the expectations of the students involved.
- Present an overview of the research problems including relevant background, challenges, and possible applications.
- Discuss the actual progress of student projects, focusing on student background, learning, and final achievements.
- Discuss the lessons learned and how their work can be generalized to other undergraduate contexts such as capstone courses or senior projects.

Finally, at least 30 minutes of the session are reserved for audience participation and discussion.

Acknowledgments

The student research described by the panelists was supported by the National Science Foundation under grant Nos. 0851743, 0851569, 0851745, 0755582, and 0453491.

4. REFERENCES

[1] J. Beck, B. Buckner, and O. Nikolova. Using interdisciplinary bioinformatics undergraduate research to recruit and retain computer science students. In *SIGCSE '07: Proceedings of the 38th SIGCSE technical symposium on Computer science education*, 2007.

[2] Bhagyavati, B. Latka, G.-A. Amoussou, and S. Mishra. Attributes of successful undergraduate research projects. *J. Comput. Small Coll.*, 21(5), 2006.

[3] T. Dahlberg, T. Barnes, A. Rorrer, E. Powell, and L. Cairco. Improving retention and graduate recruitment through immersive research experiences for undergraduates. In *SIGCSE '08: Proceedings of the 39th SIGCSE technical symposium on Computer science education*, 2008.

[4] M. J. Granger, G.-A. Amoussou, M. A. Labrador, S. Perry, and K. M. Van Busum. Research experience for undergraduates: successes and challenges. In *SIGCSE '06: Proceedings of the 37th SIGCSE technical symposium on Computer science education*, 2006.

[5] G. W. Hislop, H. J. Ellis, A. B. Tucker, and S. Dexter. Using open source software to engage students in computer science education. In *SIGCSE '09: Proceedings of the 40th ACM technical symposium on Computer science education*, 2009.

[6] D. L. Knox, P. J. DePasquale, and S. M. Pulimood. A model for summer undergraduate research experiences in emerging technologies. *SIGCSE Bull.*, 38(1), 2006.

[7] J. Peckham, P. Stephenson, J.-Y. Hervé, R. Hutt, and M. Encarnaç ao. Increasing student retention in computer science through research programs for undergraduates. In *SIGCSE '07: Proceedings of the 38th SIGCSE technical symposium on Computer science education*, 2007.

[8] D. S. Raicu and J. D. Furst. Enhancing undergraduate education: a reu model for interdisciplinary research. In *SIGCSE '09: Proceedings of the 40th ACM technical symposium on Computer science education*, 2009.

[9] E. L. Walker and O. A. Slotterbeck. Integrated research components: a practical and effective alternative to senior projects. *J. Comput. Small Coll.*, 22(1), 2006.

Building Bridges to Other Departments: Three Strategies

Valerie Barr (Moderator)
Union College
807 Union Street
Schenectady, NY 12308
barrv@union.edu

Chun Wai Liew
Lafayette College
Easton, PA 18042
liew@cs.lafayette.edu

Rich Salter
Oberlin College
10 N. Professor Street
Oberlin, OH 44074
rms@cs.oberlin.edu

1. SUMMARY

With the declining interest among incoming college students and the nationwide drop in computer science (CS) enrollments ([2, 1]), many CS departments would like to broaden participation in computing by reaching out to other departments on their campuses. One tactic is to encourage interdisciplinary work that has computing as a significant component. These efforts may result in more CS majors, increased enrollments in certain CS courses, and a student population that is better equipped to utilize computing within the contexts of their disciplines.

This panel presents three approaches to building bridges to other departments and disciplines. Rich Salter, Oberlin College, will discuss the involvement of CS in the Oberlin Center for Computation and Modeling. Chun Wai Liew, Lafayette College, will discuss ways in which the CS department has built tools specifically to assist faculty in other departments, facilitating student exposure to and understanding of computation. Valerie Barr, Union College, will focus on the infusion of computation into course curricula outside CS, in many cases coupling the use of existing tools with discussion of the underlying models and computational issues.

Categories and Subject Descriptors

K.3.2 [**Computer and Information Science Education**]: Miscellaneous

General Terms

Human Factors

Keywords

Computational Science, Non-majors, Outreach

2. OBERLIN

With the widespread availability of powerful personal computers and software systems, many intractable and/or experimentally unfeasible scientific problems can now be addressed, even by undergraduates, through models and simulations. An opportunity exists for CS departments to play a leadership role in helping institutions transition to a science curriculum that incorporates computational thinking. CS curricula need to be innovative, going beyond traditional topics, to tap into the real power of computation, namely simulations and model building. This foundation, in turn, invites exploration, hypothesis building, experimentation, critical thinking, and engaged/deep problem solving capacity for the scientists of the future.

The Oberlin Center for Computation and Modeling (OCCaM) was established by interested faculty from across the natural and social sciences. The goal was to develop a unified approach to introducing computation and modeling into the curriculum. An underlying consensus was the need to define an independent and self-contained approach to computation and modeling that could be generally applied across subject areas, and would meet the needs of those varying disciplines. We have introduced several courses that present modeling as a methodology based on a well-defined structure. We used software tools in place of rigorous mathematical analysis, thereby making it accessible to students with a range of mathematical backgrounds. The courses include:

- A team-taught course by faculty members from CS, Economics, Neuroscience, Physics, Psychology, and Environmental Studies, presenting modeling as it is used in those fields.
- A projects-oriented CS course in dynamic system and agent-based modeling using the modeling software tools STELLA and NetLogo.
- Discipline-specific courses in Physics (climate modeling, computational physics) and Environmental Studies (ecological systems).

Students have successfully built on this training to participate in student-faculty research collaborations. We were fortunate that our early efforts were recognized as significant and supported by grants from the Booth-Ferris Foundation and NSF. Oberlin College has just received an NSF CPATH-2 grant to add a modeling component to introductory courses throughout the social and natural science divisions. This will expose large numbers of students to a modeling experience.

In my presentation I will describe the courses on computation and modeling that have already been introduced at Oberlin, and discuss the planned activities of our CPATH project to further infuse modeling throughout the social and natural science curriculum.

3. LAFAYETTE

Over the past two years, the CS department at Lafayette has put together several collaborative projects with faculty from other departments specifically to develop tools that

SIGCSE'10 March 10–13,2010, Milwaukee, Wisconsin, USA.
ACM 978-1-60558-885-8/10/03.

assist them in research and teaching. The goal of these projects is to expose both faculty and students in the classroom to computation and for them to develop an understanding of how computation can help them in their discipline.

On our campus, many students (and faculty) find computation (and mathematics) intimidating and generally avoid taking (1) courses in those disciplines, (2) courses that are quantitatively oriented. The new tools will help the students and faculty to see the utility of computational tools in both the classroom and in research. We anticipate that as faculty become more comfortable with computation, they will incorporate more computation into their courses and perhaps, even develop courses that have computation or math and statistics as pre-requisites. When several faculty within a department are interested in computation, they can lead efforts to change the curriculum for that discipline to incorporate computation.

Some of the tools that we have developed are:

- *Art:* We have developed a tool that uses Lindenmeier systems (L-systems) to generate recurring visual images. Artists have used the tool to generate a series of complex images and animations that will be displayed at an art exhibition in October 2009. The tool is being used in two art classes - *Introduction to Painting* and *Intermediate Painting*.

- *Engineering & Public Policy*: We have developed a module that allows students to specify land use policies that will then be simulated and the results are then displayed visually, including the results of some simple economic analyses. This tool will be used in a course in the fall (2009) and the department is considering requiring computation in the curriculum.

- *Social Science*: We have developed a user-friendly front end to clustering and statistical analysis packages. The tool will be used by political scientists to analyze economic data from several NGO's.

The panel presentation will describe the ways in which we established connections with individual faculty in other disciplines and developed research and teaching modules. We will also discuss the impact of our efforts after two years of NSF support through a CPATH grant.

4. UNION

The CS department at Union, with NSF CPATH support, has worked with thirteen faculty-student pairs from 10 departments, supporting efforts to incorporate the use of computation into other disciplines. We have supported projects across the campus, including humanities, social science, natural science, and engineering departments. These efforts dovetail with our recent development of a computational methods minor. We can prepare students from non-CS fields to better carry out computationally oriented discipline specific work, while at the same time exposing CS majors to the wide range of computing applications.

In each case the faculty-student pair has developed some form of curricular component (lab, module, or complete course) that infuses computation into the study of their own discipline. Some examples are:

- Biology: One supported project uses the DayCent bio-geo-chemical model to introduce students to modeling ecosystem implications of biofuel production.

- Classics: The supported project will lead to a module for upper level Greek classes. Students will use a new front end for the *Thesaurus Linguae Graecae* [4] in order to search for echoes and other interesting related phrases in Greek texts. This serves the dual purposes of exposing students to a use of computation while at the same time enabling them to explore more texts than they would be able to read completely in a single term.

- Engineering: One engineering project added a programming component (based on robotics) to the introductory engineering course. Another project added a computational module to an upper level course on speech acoustics which makes it possible for students to analyze speech files using Praat [3].

- Economics: One project led to the development of a computational component for the course *Contemporary Issues in Macroeconomics*, while another led to the development of a completely new course on dynamic models in economics.

Other supported efforts were in astronomy, physics, political science, film studies, and chemistry. We expect that exposure to the utility of computation in their own field will encourage students to enroll in additional CS courses and complete the computational methods minor. In general, the faculty in non-CS departments have been very enthusiastic about adding a computational component to their courses.

The panel presentation will include discussion of how we have established connections to other faculty and departments, and how CS supports their efforts when the new curricular modules are rolled out. We will also discuss factors effecting the sustainability of the curricular infusions.

5. PANEL FORMAT

Each panelist will give a 10 minute overview, following which there will be 45 minutes of Q&A and discussion.

6. REFERENCES

[1] Freshmen interest in cs and degree production trends. CRA Bulletin, http://www.cra.org/wp/index.php?cat=34, October 2007. Last accessed on 09/05/2009.

[2] Higher Education Research Institute, university of California at Los Angeles. http://www.gseis.ucla.edu/heri/cirpoverview.php. Last accessed on 09/05/2009.

[3] Praat: doing Phonetics by Computers. http://www.fon.hum.uva.nl/praat.

[4] Thesaurus Linguae Graecae. http://www.tlg.uci.edu.

Variations on a Theme: Role of Media in Motivating Computing Education

Mark Guzdial (Moderator)
School of Interactive Computing, Georgia Tech
85 5th Street NW
Atlanta, GA 30332-0760
+1-404-894-5618
guzdial@ cc.gatech.edu

David Ranum, Brad Miller
Luther College
Computer Science
700 College Drive
Decorah, IA 52101
+1-901-GONORSE
{ranum,bmiller}@luther.edu

Beth Simon
University of California, San Diego
Computer Science & Engineering Dept.
La Jolla, California 92093-0404
+1-858-534-5419
bsimon@cs.ucsd.edu

Samuel A. Rebelsky, Janet Davis
Grinnell College
Department of Computer Science
Grinnell, IA 50112
+1-641-4410
{rebelsky, davisjan}@grinnell.edu

Barbara Ericson
College of Computing, Georgia Tech
801 Atlanta Drive
Atlanta, GA 30332
+1-404-385-2108
ericson@cc.gatech.edu

Deepak Kumar, Doug Blank
Bryn Mawr College
Department of Computer Science
Bryn Mawr, PA 19010
+1-610-526-7485
{dkumar,dblank}@brynmawr.edu

Categories and Subject Descriptors
K.3.2 [**Computing Milieux**]: Computers and Education – *Computer and Information Science Education*

General Terms
Design, Experimentation

Keywords
Multimedia, Education, Motivation, Media Computation

SUMMARY
The SIGCSE community has been exploring the role of multimedia to enhance computing education since the earliest algorithm visualization systems and studies [1]. We have been exploring for years how images, sounds, and video might improve how students learn computer science. Media Computation is a shift in focus [2]. Where algorithm visualization presents information to the student to facilitate their understanding, media computation is about having students manipulate media as the data for their programming, i.e., as the focus of the course activities. Students in media computation produce *new* images, sounds, and video. The reason for the media is to increase student engagement and motivation. We aim to show that computer science is about more than numbers and strings. Computer science is also about creative expression.

The original media computation work focused on using media to motivate non-computing majors [3]. The role of media in motivating student learning for computing education has broadened. Inventive teachers are using media computation for lots of different kinds of students, at different kinds of institutions, with a range of languages and toolkits.

This special session is a mixture of "Five Minute Madness," science fair, and art gallery. Each participant will present how he or she is using media to motivate student learning, and some student work will be available for audience inspection. To be specific, each participant (or participant group) will have five minutes (with an ironhand on the stopwatch):

- To describe *why* the participant is using media in his or her class. What's the advantage? What does it buy you and your students? Do you plan to keep using media as an introductory context?
- To describe in detail *one* assignment that your students really work on, at your institutional setting.
- To show *two* different student artifacts, with at least one being an output from that assignment.

The rest of the time will be left for Q&A with the audience. Participants are asked to provide a poster with an example of an assignment definition and some student work, to be displayed in the room. Participants may reference their poster in their session or in response to questions. Audience members are invited to peruse the student art gallery before and after the session.

SIGCSE'10, March 10–13, 2010, Milwaukee, Wisconsin, USA.
ACM 978-1-60558-885-8/10/03.

1. PARTICIPANTS
David Ranum and Brad Miller, *Luther College.*

In the Introduction to Computer Science I course at Luther College, we use image processing as an example of basic object-oriented programming. Digital images are treated as objects made up of a grid of RGB pixels, each of which is also an object. Students use methods such as `getWidth`, `getHeight`, `getPixel`, `setPixel`, `getRed`, and `setRed` to manipulate the images. Two interesting projects are image enlargement and edge detection. Enlarging an image requires students to find mapping patterns to copy pixel values from the smaller image to the larger. This also leads to a need for image smoothing to remove the "blockiness" that occurs. Edge detection requires students to compute gradients that surround a pixel. To do this we introduce the concept of a weighting mask and a convolution pattern. Pixels found to exist on a large gradient are considered to be edge pixels and are colored accordingly.

Beth Simon, *University of California—San Diego.*

UCSD is a large research-intensive university which adopted media computation in Java during the 2008-2009 academic year. The traditional introductory 10-week course for students with "no prior programming experience" which targets approximately 2/3 of the incoming majors used this approach. The goal of the change was to address a large attrition rate in majors -- by the beginning of the second year 32% of incoming majors are no longer taking computing courses. Additionally, since the major was only recently re-opened to allow students to change into the computing major (having been locked down to incoming freshman only during the dot.com boom), we sought an approach that was likely to appeal to students "giving computer science a try" – while still providing them an authentic programming experience and keeping them on track to continue in major sequence courses. Response so far has been overwhelmingly positive.

Barbara Ericson, *Georgia Institute of Technology (and Lakeside High School).*

I am co-teaching an Advanced Placement Computer Science A high school course using Alice and Media Computation. We will be using the new book "*Exploring Wonderland: Java Programming with Alice and Media Computation*" [2]. We will be using Alice to introduce new computing concepts and then facilitating the transfer of those concepts to Java using Media Computation. You can think of Media Computation as the special effects studio for Alice movies. It is how we will create sound clips so that we don't violate copyright by using a complete song in an Alice movie. We can also merge live action and Alice movies using chromakey.

Sam Rebelsky and Janet Davis, *Grinnell College.*

In the MediaScripting approach to media computation that we use at Grinnell, students write Scheme scripts to create and manipulate images within the GIMP, an open-source raster graphics application. Because they script within the GIMP, students are able to use a mixed-mode approach to image creation and manipulation: Sometimes they write scripts, sometimes they do things "by hand", with the tools of the application. This mixed-mode approach helps motivate programming problems; often, students will find that they want to write scripts to replace what they do by hand - to ensure precision, to encode a sequence of actions so that they can do it again, and even to experiment. We believe that this approach encourages students to think about how the ability to program can help them in a variety of contexts. Scheme allows us to have students think about images in multiple ways, for example, not only do they use an imperative approach to scripting the tools, they also model images as functions from positions to colors.

Deepak Kumar and Doug Blank, *Bryn-Mawr College.*

In the introductory computing course developed by IPRE (Institute for Personal Robots in Education), students learn computing by exploring the context of programming robot behaviors [4]. Each student's personal robot includes a camera, a gamepad controller, speech and sound/music synthesis. This allows for a rich set of experiences for students. They learn to capture, and manipulate camera images for many applications including robot navigation, object tracking, as well as creating creative image transformations. Several aspects of media manipulation find a natural place in this context. The Python-based Myro toolkit used in this course was designed to cater to such pedagogical goals. In another introductory course we are experimenting with media and creative computing aspects in using the Processing programming language.

2. REFERENCES

[1] Brown, Marc H. and Robert Sedgewick. 1984. A System for Algorithm Animation. *Proceedings of the 11th Annual ACM Conference on Computer Graphics and Interactive Techniques.* 177-186.

[2] Dann, Wanda P., Stephen Cooper, and Barbara Ericson. 2009. *Exploring Wonderland: Java Programming with Alcie and Media Computation.* Prentice-Hall.

[3] Guzdial, Mark. 2003. A Media Computation Course for Non-Majors. *ACM SIGCSE Bulletin*, 35(3), 104-108.

[4] Kumar, Deepak (editor), Learning Computing With Robots, IPRE, 2009.

Using the Imagine Cup SDI as the Foundation for Computer Science Capstone Projects

James Parrish, Jr., Ph. D.
University of Arkansas
at Little Rock
Little Rock, AR, USA
1-501-569-3293
jlparrish@ualr.edu

Janet Bailey, Ph. D.
University of Arkansas
at Little Rock
Little Rock, AR, USA
1-501-569-3293
jlbailey@ualr.edu

Bradley Jensen, Ph. D.
Microsoft Corp.
Dallas, TX, USA
1-214-674-3630
bjensen@microsoft.com

ABSTRACT
This paper describes the use of the Microsoft Imagine Cup Software Design Invitational (SDI) as a way to overcome some of the issues related to traditional or "closed" style capstone projects. Problematic issues with traditional capstone projects, as identified by literature, are discussed in conjunction with how the SDI addresses them. The main premise is participation in the Imagine Cup SDI can address the issues faculty wrestle with as they attempt to provide students with the best possible learning experience. Additionally, the authors present some of the advantages and challenges that they have noted from personal experiences using SDI as a part of a capstone course.

Categories and Subject Descriptors
K.3.2 [**Computers and Education**]: Computer and Information Science Education – *Computer Science Education*

General Terms
Design

Keywords
Education, Capstone course, Software engineering, Computer science, Imagine Cup

1. INTRODUCTION
One of the biggest challenges to educators teaching computer science (CS) and software engineering (SE) capstone courses is developing a relevant, interesting curriculum that incorporates learning from all prerequisite coursework [2]. While capstone curriculum may take many forms, a common approach is to offer a pre-defined, traditional, "closed" project that lacks applicability outside the classroom, but allows the educator more control over the educational experience [1]. "Closed" projects are those projects that, while potentially complex, appear in a textbook and require no interaction with outside organizations. These type of projects also commonly come with a complete list of predefined specifications for the project. Many researchers have noted that closed projects present problematic issues. This paper focuses on three of the major issues and discusses how incorporating participation in Microsoft Imagine Cup Software Design Invitational (SDI) can overcome each. First, closed projects are problematic because students tend to spend the majority of their time focusing on grading criteria rather than developing valuable experience in determining actual client requirements leading to a techno-centric view of the project. Techno-centric means students consider the problem in terms of the technology or code needed to implement a solution prior to considering the client requirements or situation [1]. To combat this issue, many researchers have turned to projects that rely on partnerships with real-world organizations [1, 2, 3].

Second, closed projects do not necessarily teach the managerial and interpersonal skills graduates will require in the workplace. Some address this issue by integrating management skills such as quality assurance, project management, and the use of cross-functional teams into the capstone course [2, 3].

Last, traditional closed projects promote a lack of attachment or interest in student capstone courses in CS [1]. To counteract the student apathy, faculty have implemented some innovative approaches to the capstone course curriculum. For example, some have turned to integrating computer game projects [5, 8]. Others have students develop projects relevant to society, such as providing assistance to the disabled [1].

While each approach partially addresses the listed issues associated with traditional capstone projects, none addressed them all. This being the case, a need for a truly integrative capstone project framework in the CS curriculum still exists. The purpose of this paper is to offer the Imagine Cup SDI as a possible solution. The remainder of this paper contains the following components:

- A discussion of the structure and purpose of the Imagine Cup competition.
- An introduction to the SDI portion of the Imagine Cup competition.
- An analysis on how student participation in the SDI can overcome the issues with traditional CS capstone projects.
- Final closing remarks.

2. IMAGINE CUP

The Imagine Cup, as stated on its website (www.imaginecup.com), "... encourages young people to apply their imagination, their passion and their creativity to technology innovations that can make a difference in the world – today. Now in its eighth year, the Imagine Cup has grown to be a truly global competition focused on finding solutions to real world issues [7]." The theme for the 2010 Imagine Cup is "Solve the World's Toughest Problems," and focuses on providing innovative technological artifacts that address the United Nations eight Millennium Goals, presented in Table 1.

Table 1. United Nations Millennium Goals [7]

1.	End and Hunger
2.	Universal Education
3.	Gender Poverty Equality
4.	Child Health
5.	Maternal Health
6.	Combat HIV/AIDS
7.	Environmental Sustainability
8.	Global Partnership

The competition invites participants to submit their work related to the above themes in different competition categories. These categories for the 2010 competition include the ones described in Table 2.

Table 2. The Imagine Cup Competitions [8]

Competition	Description
Software Design (SDI)	Involves creation of software applications and services including mobile apps using Microsoft technology to address UN goals.
Embedded Devices	Embedded devices meeting the UN theme are created using the Windows Embedded client environment.
Game Development	Games are produced using XNA to meet the theme of the competition.
Robotics and Algorithm	Students compete with their creations to solve increasingly difficult puzzles in a virtual environment.
Web Design	Working websites are developed related to the theme of the competition.
Digital Media	Competitor's shoot, edit, and share what they hope are web-video hits related to the theme.
IT Challenge	Not related to the UN Goals, students compete to demonstrate their capability to develop, deploy, and maintain efficient, functional, robust, and secure IT systems.

While the other areas are also applicable to CS coursework, this paper will focus on the SDI competition portion of the Imagine Cup. The SDI challenges students to leverage their creativity to produce an innovative software application addressing, at a minimum, one of the UN Millennial Goals (although some applications may cross boundaries between more than one goal). Students form and compete in teams of up to four members in order to design and implement their applications. Student teams also have the opportunity to choose a mentor who can provide the team with guidance and insight during the competition. The mentor may be a faculty member, someone from practice, or in some cases a team may choose to have both a faculty and industry mentor.

3. THE SOFTWARE DESIGN INVITATIONAL

The SDI portion of the competition is divided into multiple rounds with various deliverables associated with each. The United States holds three rounds culminating with the National Finals. The first place team advances to compete in the World Cup competition – in 2010 this competition will be held in Poland. The first round is a qualifying round and requires students come up with an idea that addresses one of the millennium goals, form a team, and submit the deliverables for that round. The deliverables consist of a preliminary business plan – a wireframe or prototype is optional. Teams that submit the deliverables by the deadline are automatically entered into the national semi-final round.

For the national semi-final round, students must develop and refine their idea into a product viable in the global marketplace. They do so by further developing the initial business plan submitted in the qualifying round to include a detailed description of the solution, an explanation of how the solution addresses a specific UN Millennial goal, an analysis of the competitive marketplace, feedback from potential users, preliminary information about the application's acceptance in the market, and financial analysis of start-up costs. They must also develop an alpha prototype with minimal functionality. The final submission for the national semi-final round includes a 3-5 minute video that introduces the team, describes why the application is important, how the application is relevant to the competition theme, and provides an overview of the alpha application.

At this point, the semi-final round submissions are reviewed by a panel of judges at Microsoft Corporation. The top 10 submissions (five each from the Fall and Spring semester rounds) are then invited to present their solutions as well as more functional "beta" (at least 80% functional) versions of their solutions to a group of judges consisting of Executives from Microsoft and other public and private sector organizations. From the 10 competitors, three national finalists are chosen and they will make a final presentation to a panel of judges and an audience of invited guests. The first place team will then go on to represent the United States in the SDI global competition. The intellectual property associated with the solutions is retained by the submitting teams. All teams submitting applications are encouraged to consider making their solutions viable commercial products (either non-profit or for profit). During the national round, investors are invited to review the applications and talk with the teams. This gives students a sense of whether their application is addressing a problem where a solution is needed, quality feedback regarding the marketplace viability of their application, and an outstanding opportunity to interact with corporate executives in a very real and unparalleled fashion. .

3.1 How the SDI Addresses Issues with Traditional Projects

This paper argues that the SDI addresses all of the traditional CS capstone project issues mentioned earlier. The SDI addresses the issue of students viewing the projects from a techno-centric perspective by structuring the problem as a social problem-solving competition. This allows students to focus more on the problem they have selected and the design appropriate to the application, rather than just focusing on what coding elements need to be included to achieve the grade they desire. During the process, students must plan, analyze, and design the specification for their application rather than taking specs provided by someone else. In addition, the focus must be on an application that has a global impact not just local. Students can be encouraged to link up with local non-profit organizations to create an application that will benefit the local community since they will ultimately need local support for proof of concept. The richness of the learning process from focusing on how to use technology to make a difference in the lives of others is much greater than that of simply figuring out how to simply code for a grade.

The lack of the managerial and interpersonal skill development in the traditional project method is also addressed by the SDI. Managerial skills are developed as students work to create a full entrepreneurial business plan for their solutions. To stay on track with the intensity of the project and the deadlines imposed by Microsoft, they must also develop and maintain a project schedule. The intense group work required to create their solution, the interactions they have with their faculty and/or industry mentors, and the presentation skills that they develop as a result of the project all serve to help develop their interpersonal skills.

Finally, allowing students to select a societal issue they are passionate about increases interest and excitement in the project. This passion can translate into increased involvement because not only are they being allowed to leverage their creativity to generate a solution to a problem they believe is important, they are also providing real world solutions that help others. So now, instead of the results of their project helping some fictitious company or some problem that will never leave a lab, they have the real potential to make a difference in the world.

4. IMPLEMENTING THE SDI IN THE CLASSROOM

Implementing the SDI in the classroom has advantages to instructors as well as providing some challenges. The primary advantage is the SDI provides structure to the capstone course. The SDI guidelines/competition requirements provide standards for deliverables in the course. The result of this is that the instructor does not have to focus so much time and effort on designing the course and they have a standardized manner in which to manage the diversity of projects generated by their students.

Despite the benefits to students and instructors, the SDI does come with some challenges. One challenge is that the SDI competition is a time-intensive endeavor. This can prove to be rather problematic when a single faculty member is managing multiple teams with projects that are vastly different. One way to overcome this challenge is to enlist the aid of professionals in industry to become secondary or even primary mentors to the project teams. The authors obtained mentors through referrals from Microsoft and by contacting professionals in the local business community. As far as soliciting help from local business, contacting members of the departmental advisory board is an excellent place to begin. Another source for soliciting help is area non-profits. Contacting the non-profits that have information relating to the type of project student teams want to pursue and those that might be able to benefit from a joint venture is the best place to start. For example, if a team wants to do a project related to the health of diabetic mothers, contact the local American Diabetes Foundation.

Another challenge is the variety of directions student projects can take from a technical perspective. While students will likely use the technologies they have been taught in prior coursework, many times they may also need to use technologies that were not part of their curriculum in order to deliver their solution. This serves as an excellent learning opportunity for the students since they will have to learn to use unfamiliar technology when entering industry. However, it also requires the faculty mentors have the time and ability to "gear-up" on these technologies rather quickly to assist the student project teams. Again, the authors found one way this can be accomplished is by bringing in industry professionals familiar with the technology to provide tutorial sessions to students and faculty or to serve as project team mentors. Microsoft also provides online learning modules to project teams and their mentors on various technologies.

A common concern is what happens if the team does not make it to the national finals? One option is to require students to continue with their project as though they had been selected and have them present their solution to the members of the local advisory board or to local industry professionals. This will allow them to get experience speaking in a business forum, provide a critical evaluation of their project, and provide them feedback on how they can improve the solution. If a sufficient number of teams are submitting at the local level, a campus (or campuses) might consider holding a local competition of their own complete with prizes.

Assessing project deliverables can be challenging. Depending on how a course is structured, students may receive both individual and team grades for the project deliverables. If the group's project is chosen as a national finalist, the grade decision is easy – the group receives an "A" – after all, top executives have judged the product and determined it is among the best in the country. If they are not selected, then the group project will need to be evaluated by the instructor and possibly industry professionals for a grade assignment. Individual assessment can be accomplished in multiple ways. One way is to have the students claim responsibility for certain portions of the overall project, grade those deliverables separately, and assign a grade to the individual responsible. Another way to assess individual performance is to allow the group members to assess the contributions of their group mates and then assign each student a percentage of the group score based on the average of the ratings they received. For example, if a student had an average rating of 9 or 10 on a scale of 1 to 10 with 10 representing a superior effort, they would receive all of the points for the group's effort. However, if a student received an average score of an 8, then they may only receive 95% of the group score. The scale would continue with lower average peer scores resulting in the student being awarded a lower percentage of the points earned by the entire group.

The advantages and challenges reported here are based on the experiences of the authors from their first year of participation. Continued participation in SDI will produce additional data from which actual research findings may be analyzed and reported. While the authors believe the advantages of the SDI will be common to most programs, those who choose to implement the SDI may have similar challenges or entirely new ones. Additionally, the reported methods for overcoming these challenges may not be effective in all cases. They are only provided here as a possible solution for those who wish to use the SDI as a part of their course.

5. CONCLUSION

This paper advocates the use of the Imagine Cup SDI in the capstone course for CS and SE majors. The primary reason for so doing is that it addresses issues previously identified with traditional "closed" capstone projects, or at least the issues identified in this paper. It overcomes the techno-centricity of some traditional projects by allowing students to focus on solving a problem rather than simply meeting grading criteria. Creating the SDI deliverables helps to build the managerial and interpersonal skills needed in the workplace, something not addressed in most CS or SE projects. Finally, it increases student interest in the project because the problem is relevant to the real-world, the solution has the potential to impact human lives, and it is one the students have selected because they feel passionately about it.

Implementing this type of project in the capstone course can be challenging. It requires a good deal of time and energy on the part of the instructor to manage the projects and to become quickly knowledgeable on various technologies. Despite these challenges, the benefits competing in the Imagine Cup SDI provides to students makes its inclusion as a part of the capstone curriculum worthwhile.

6. REFERENCES

[1] Buckley, M., et al. Benefits of Using Socially-Relevant Projects in Computer Science and Engineering Education. In *SIGCSE '04*, 482-486.

[2] Chambillard, A.T. and Braun, K. The Software Engineering Capstone: Structure and Tradeoffs. In *SIGCSE '02*, 227-231.

[3] Fornaro, R., Heil, M. and Jones, V. Cross-Functional Teams Used in Computer Science Senior Design Capstone Courses. In *30th ASEE/IEEE Frontiers in Education Conference*.

[4] Information, U.N.D.o.P. United Nations Millennium Development Goals. (January 20, 2009); http://www.un.org/millenniumgoals/.

[5] Jones, R. Design and Implementation of Computer Games: A Capstone Course for Undergraduate Computer Science Education. In *SIGCSE 2000*, 260-264.

[6] Microsoft. Imagine Cup Student Competition - Competition Overview. (January 20, 2009); http://imaginecup.com/Competition/Overview.aspx.

[7] Microsoft. Imagine Cup Student Competition - What is the Imagine Cup? (January 20, 2009); http://imaginecup.com/About/Whatis.aspx.

[8] Parberry, I., Roden, T. and Kazemzadeh, M. Experience with an Industry-Driven Capstone Course on Game Programming. In *SIGCSE '05*.

Industry Fellows

Bringing Professional Practice into the Classroom

Josh Tenenberg
Computing and Software Systems
Institute of Technology
1900 Commerce Street
University of Washington, Tacoma
Tacoma, Washington, USA
jtenenbg@u.washington.edu

ABSTRACT

The *Industry Fellows* project involves a practicing college or university faculty member and practicing industry professional (the *industry fellow*) in the joint curriculum review, planning and delivery of a course related to the professional's domain of expertise. *Working together exploits what each does best.* The faculty member brings a broad, theory-based understanding to the discipline, while the industry fellow brings knowledge gained from professional practice. The faculty member retains full responsibility for all academic aspects of the course: planning and writing the syllabus, developing the assignments and examinations, and assigning grades. The professional joins the faculty member in the classroom on a regular basis as a co-lecturer, interacts directly with the students, and evaluates a sample of the student work on an advisory basis. This model was successfully run in winter 2009, with the project leader collaborating with an interaction designer from Google on teaching a Human Computer Interaction course at the University of Washington, Tacoma (UWT). This paper describes the *Industry Fellows* model, its instantiation at UWT, and an evaluation of this instantiation.

Categories and Subject Descriptors

K.3.2 [**Computer and Information Science Education**]: Computer science education; K.3.2 [**Computer and Information Science Education**]: Information systems education; K.7.0 [**Occupations**]: General

General Terms

Human Factors

Keywords

Professional practice, industry/academic collaboration

1. THE ACADEMIA-INDUSTRY GAP

A recent study on Engineering Education from the Carnegie Foundation for the Advancement of Teaching concludes that "[I]f students are to be prepared to enter new-century engineering, the center of engineering education should be professional practice, integrating technical knowledge and skills of practice" [13]. But because of the fast pace at which technological change occurs and the practice-based nature of the software and information technology professions, teachers in these fields can become remote from the technologies, practices, and pragmatics associated with professional work as it is currently practiced in industry. Faculty may thus be limited to the extent to which they are able to teach their students the practices that students will use as professionals once they have completed their degree studies. Practicing computing professionals, on the other hand, have up-to-date technical knowledge of specific areas of software development, but their time commitments to their employer and lack of knowledge of teaching, classroom management, and curriculum development hinder their ability to be effective as teachers. As the authors of *How People Learn* state "[e]xpertise in a particular domain does not guarantee that one is good at helping others learn it" [1]. These differences in expertise between teachers and practitioners often result in gaps between the academic studies of computing students and the required practices that they will employ in professional settings. As one student remarks "A lot of the time in courses, I find myself asking 'how much of this stuff am I actually going to use[1].'"

2. SHRINKING THE GAP: THE *INDUSTRY FELLOWS MODEL*

The *Industry Fellows* model involves a community college or university faculty member and a practicing industry professional (the *industry fellow*) in the joint curriculum review, planning and delivery of a course related to the professional's domain of expertise. *Working together exploits what each does best.* The faculty member brings a broad, theory-based understanding to the discipline, while the industry fellow brings knowledge gained from professional practice. The faculty member retains full responsibility for all academic

[1]This student quote and the others given in this proposal were obtained from a survey of students as part of the pilot evaluation described later in this paper.

aspects of the course: planning and writing the syllabus, developing the assignments and examinations, and assigning grades. The professional aids the faculty member in reviewing the course curriculum, joins the faculty member in the classroom on a regular basis as a co-lecturer, interacts directly with the students, and evaluates a sample of the student work on an advisory basis. Targeted courses–whether from the community college or university–are those tied closely to professional practice using tangible representations of work, such as prototypes, storyboards, UML diagrams, and flow diagrams. These tangible representations serve both as externalizations of student thinking about the disciplinary knowledge in computing and information technology, and also to mediate the interaction between students, the teacher, and the practicing professional.

The *Industry Fellows* model is designed to satisfy three objectives:

1. Increase student learning of course material, motivation to attend classes, and engagement in the coursework.
2. Increase the knowledge of participating faculty members from community colleges and universities in current practice in disciplinary areas of computing and information technology.
3. Increase the knowledge of teaching-related skills (such as goal setting, managing work groups, and communicating ideas effectively) for participating professionals from the computing and information technology industry.

This paper is organized as follows. The next section provides an example of how the *Industry Fellows* model is enacted by describing a pilot running of it undertaken by the author in winter, 2009, includng an evaluation of its impact on students. A brief summary of the theoretical underpinnings of this project is presented, grounded in research on how people learn. The paper concludes with a summary of the model.

3. THE PILOT INSTANTIATION

The *Industry Fellows* model as just described was run as a pilot during the 10-week winter term, 2009[2]. The author, a professor at the University of Washington, Tacoma (UWT) paired with an Interaction Designer at Google to teach the Human-Computer Interaction course at UWT. The course involved a design project carried out by student teams using a human-centered design process. Students were engaged directly in user inquiry, ideation, brainstorming, sketching, prototyping, interface design, and user evaluation. Students delivered three project milestones, with the final milestone-a prototype, "envisionment video" demonstrating their prototype in use, and the results of usability tests-presented to an external panel of industry practitioners from Microsoft and Google.

The faculty/industry fellow pair met for three 3-hour planning sessions during summer 2008 and delivered the course January-March 2009. The faculty member handled generation of all of the documents and course materials, including writing the syllabus, assignments, project outline, and project documentation requirements. The course met twice weekly in sessions of two hours each, with the industry fellow attending one class session weekly. Approximately half of each class session attended by the industry fellow focused on critiques of student work for their term-length group projects, with the other half of each session devoted to presentations by the industry fellow and discussion with students of case studies and artifacts derived from his past professional work. The industry fellow also arranged the external industry panel for the final presentations through his professional network. On the class sessions when the industry fellow did not attend class, the sessions were devoted to discussions of the course readings, monitoring groupwork, and practicing the methods that would be used on the project, such as contextual inquiry, observations, prototyping, and design brainstorming.

As an example, week 6 of the course was centered on design representations such as wireframes and storyboards, and the basics of interface design. During the first class session of the week (without the industry fellow), students carried out a heuristic analysis of student-chosen websites in small groups, based on the interface design principles discussed in their associated readings. There was also discussion on the requirements for the second project milestone (due in one week), and how design is fundamentally concerned with wicked problems [10]. In the second session of the week two days later, the industry fellow discussed example wireframes and storyboards that he had used in previous projects. In addition, students demonstrated current versions of their prototypes to get early feedback from one another, the instructor, and the industry fellow.

3.1 Evaluation of the Pilot

The industry fellow reported two distinct benefits of participation. The first was in the realization of his goal for participating in the partnership: to directly influence the education of future software developers, to "make it better" in his words. In addition, he commented on his deeper appreciation of the complexity and demands of being a teacher in the university setting, particularly the number of interlocking decisions that need to be made about task setting, the management of student groups, and instructional design. As a result of working with the industry fellow, the participating faculty member reported significant learning gains in the subject area. In addition, by attending to the kinds of comments that the industry fellow made in critiquing student work, the faculty member also learned more about how to apprentice students into the key practices associated with HCI. Additional discussion from the faculty member's perspective can be found in [15].

The author also undertook an evaluation of the impact of the industry fellow on the student experience in the HCI course using a survey with both constrained-choice and short answer questions. The survey was administered electronically and was completed the last day of the academic term. Ten of the twelve enrolled students in the course completed the survey. On a 5-level Likert scale (strongly positive, positive, neutral, negative, strongly negative), students were asked to indicate how the participation of the industry fellow impacted several aspects of the course. No students indicated negative impact on any items. 9 of 10 indicated positive or strongly positive impact on *motivation to do coursework*, 8 of 10 indicated positive or strongly positive impact

[2]See `http://faculty.washington.edu/jtenenbg/courses/452/w09/` for course materials

on *motivation to attend class session*, 7 of 10 indicated positive or strongly positive impact on *engagement in the course activities*, and all 10 students indicated a positive or strongly positive impact on *learning the course material*.

Two short-response questions were also asked: "Compared to other courses in the Institute of Technology at UW Tacoma, what difference did it make having the industry fellow as part of the teaching team?" and "How has interaction with the industry fellow affected the design and execution of your final project?" All ten students made some response to each of these questions. A few themes predominated: *legitimization of the course material*, *connecting the classroom to the "real world"*, *a higher standard of performance was required as well as enabled*, and *students value both academic knowledge and practical knowledge*. Each is described in turn.

Legitimization of the course material

The presence of the industry fellow conveyed the sense to students that what they were working on was not simply an academic exercise. "[The industry fellow's] presence helped us to think of our project as serious work rather than a practice exercise that simply simulated the real work. I think this encouraged us to think more deeply about the problems we faced rather than simply grasping at 'good enough' answers." "The biggest thing he did for the course was to validate how important HCI is for the technology community." "Having an industry fellow in the classroom provided validation that what was being taught could actually be used in the industry that we plan to (or already) work in. In turn, I think this increased the level of attention in class to everything that was being discussed."

Connecting the classroom to the "real world"

Students indicated that they often fail to see the connection between what they study in the classroom and how to apply it in practice, or even if they will ever user it in a professional setting. Students also commented on the increased sense of authenticity of the work that they were carrying out. "A lot of the time in courses, I find myself asking 'how much of this stuff am I actually going to use,' and come with an answer myself. Having and [sic] industry fellow present to clear up any ambiguity to this question helps a lot." "The industry fellow gave the design and execution of our project a real 'professional' feeling. It made the project feel like a REAL project, instead of just another assignment. It helped tie in some of the key concepts that we would need to learn and be conscious of for work outside of an academic setting."

A higher standard of performance was required as well as enabled

Students perceived that having a practicing professional in the room increased the level of scrutiny of their work as well as the level of performance expected, which increased their motivation to meet these expectations. But they also felt that his feedback and instruction increased the quality of what they were producing. "The feedback he was able to give us on our milestones was well-grounded, and the fact that he didn't hold his punches made us more determined to work hard." "He also pointed out some key design choices that we never would have thought about. If anything, [the industry fellow] was like a model of doing things right. Although we would probably never really meet his high expectations at this point, I know that our group was better off having seen a pro in action!" "I think that the input received from the industry fellow improved the quality of our final project." "I feel that since we were going to be presenting our project to an industry professional, we wanted to increase the quality of the project." "The industry fellow really added to the standards of the class. I personally had the feeling that without him it would have just been another difficult class. But because this person had a large amount of experience and offered up his knowledge, I felt that the demands and expectations for the class was much higher. I personally felt that knowing that he was going to work hard for us made me work harder for him and the class."

Students value both academic knowledge and practical knowledge

Students commented that the course combined types of knowledge, symbolized by having both a professor and an practitioner in the classroom. Having the industry perspective did not negate the academic knowledge, but helped contextualize and integrate it within a body of practical knowledge. "Having a representative from the industry provides a much needed alternate perspective. We have been able to get both the research and experimentation view alongside the practical hands on perspective." "There's an academic side to things and a practical, product-driven side. Normally, a professor is either an academic who has written many research papers or, and more rarely, and [sic] industry professional. In this class we got both. It really helped to have both broad readings and instruction as well as real-life examples." "Having [the industry fellow] around ... provided an alternate perspective on a lot of issues, including some unexpected areas like the ethics [of] Interaction Design work."

In university-administered end of course evaluations, students in aggregate ranked the course in the 90-100th percentile ("among the best") of all courses that they have taken both in the department and at the university. They frequently mentioned the industry fellow in associated comments.

These results provide evidence that there is considerable value in the *Industry Fellows* program, but dissemination of this model will benefit from running it again and having additional expertise and externality on its evaluation. In addition, the replication of this model needs to be undertaken in different institutional contexts, in different subject matter, with different participants, in order to understand those factors which influence the success or failure of this intervention.

4. RESEARCH GROUNDING

The design of this model is informed by research on how people learn, particularly in technical disciplines. This research is clustered in the following three areas: learning as participation in communities of practice, the nature of expertise, and the transfer of professional practice into the classroom. Each is discussed in turn, along with implications for the project design.

4.1 Communities of Practice

Recent work in educational psychology and anthropology has shed light on the importance of cultural participation in human development and learning. Rogoff [11] summarizes this view by stating "people develop as participants in cultural communities. Their development can be understood only in light of the cultural practices and circumstances of their communities." Lave and Wenger [7] provide an elaboration of these concepts by arguing that much of learning occurs when people participate in communities of practitioners in specific settings. Newcomers to these communities start at the periphery, observing and making low-risk contributions, with expertise increasing with further participation and engagement. Hutchins [5] provides a similar account of the development of expertise onboard Navy ships, detailing the way in which novice shipmen are slowly incorporated into increasingly complex tasks and responsibilities through participation in coordinated activities with those more experienced. As he states "human cognition differs from the cognition of all other animals primarily because it is intrinsically a cultural phenomenon."

The implications of this perspective for the *Industry Fellows* project are twofold. First, it is important to recognize that computing faculty participate primarily in communities of practitioners in which the key practices relate to teaching and, at the university level, to undertaking research within an area of disciplinary specialization. Given the commitment of time and energy required to become proficient within these communities, college and university faculty are not (with the rare exception) also participants in a community of professional software developers and information technologists. This is not to denigrate the expertise that faculty develop, only to underscore that college and university faculty may be limited to the extent to which they are able to teach and socialize their students into the practices that students will use as professionals once they have completed their degree studies. But this is exactly the kind of teaching and socialization that the industry fellow can provide, since he or she will be a member of one or more professional communities in the computing and information technology fields.

4.2 The Nature of Expertise

There has been considerable research over the last two decades in cognitive science, education, and the sociology of science into the nature of expertise that provides insight into the different kinds of knowledge that faculty members and industry practitioners might have. In an important volume on expert reasoning [2], the authors provide evidence that experts in a variety of domains are able to build complex cognitive structures in which to encode knowledge about their domain so that it is accessible for skilled action. Experts also have *adaptive expertise*, the ability to be flexible and adaptive in new situations [1]. And, when "[c]onfronted with complex problems, experts can assess the complexity in ways that enable them to bring their knowledge and experience to bear quickly and efficiently" [13].

Schön's [12] studies of professional practitioners in the design professions indicates that much of this expert knowledge is tacit. That is, expert skill is often embodied in practice within specific settings, yet the practitioner may have little explicit access to their expertise in a form that is amenable to linguistic analysis or transfer. Schön calls this *knowing-in-action*: "I shall use knowing-in-action to refer to the sorts of know-how we reveal in our intelligent action ... We reveal it by our spontaneous, skillful execution of the performance; and we are characteristically unable to make it verbally explicit." Collins [3] also emphasizes that a considerable amount of technical knowledge and skill is tacit, and can only be learned through direct face-to-face contact. The *Industry Fellows* model ensures this face-to-face contact between students and the industry fellow directly in the classroom. The industry professional's tacit knowledge is made visible through presentation and discussion of representations drawn from their own professional practice. And this tacit knowledge is learned by students through the industry fellow's critique of student-generated representations of domain knowledge, a hallmark of studio-based learning models [9, 6]. This mode of interaction is supported by research on learning. As Sheppard et al. [13] state "[t]he best learning happens as experts model performance in such a way that learners can imitate the performance. And this process is greatly facilitated if the experts provide feedback to learners about their performance."

The kinds of knowledge that comprise teaching expertise have received study during the last decades. Shulman [14] discusses content knowledge about the domain as being a key component of expertise, which is increasingly recognized as a necessary aspect to teaching within a domain [1]. And this is the area of teaching to which industry fellows will significantly contribute, since their content knowledge is quite deep. But teachers also possess considerable *pedagogical content knowledge* about the courses that they teach, which Shulman describes as "the most useful forms of representation of those ideas, the most powerful analogies, illustrations, examples, explanations, and demonstrations-in a word, the ways of representing and formulating the subject that make it comprehensible to others." And finally, teachers develop considerable "local" knowledge [4] about the context in which they teach, about such things as the resources available within their universities and classrooms, the frequency and duration of class sessions, the topics that must be covered in particular courses, the level preparation of the students, the availability of labs, tutors, and peer mentors for the students, to name just a few. So although industry practitioners have considerable content knowledge, often far exceeding that of their faculty counterparts, they lack the pedagogical content knowledge and the local knowledge to ensure success were they to teach alone in the classroom.

Because of skilled yet tacit performance by both teachers and industry fellows, it is crucial that they both be in the classroom together, interacting directly with students and the artifacts that students create. Both will contribute content knowledge, with specialized knowledge coming from the industry fellow. But the pedagogical content knowledge and local knowledge of the faculty member will be critical to ensure that the industry fellow's content knowledge can be leveraged. By working face-to-face, each will learn some of the deep tacit knowledge possessed by the other, exactly as was observed between the faculty member and the industry fellow in the pilot instantiation of this project.

4.3 Professional Practice in the Classroom

It has become clear to policy setting and advisory bodies that faculty and professional practitioners need to cooperate more closely in educating the next generation. Both the National Research Council, in their report *How People Learn* and the Carnegie Foundation's *Preparation for the Professions Program* "stress the need for ... teachers to work with practicing professionals as they create robust strategies for teaching and learning in the various professional disciplines" [8], with similar sentiments echoed by the National

Academy of Engineering [8]. A recent large scale study of 11 mechanical and electrical engineering programs at 6 engineering schools was undertaken under the sponsorship of the Carnegie Foundation for the Advancement of Teaching [13]. Their key result is that in order to educate the engineer of the 21st century, *education must be centered on professional practice.* As such "faculty need to make clear what expert practice looks like, modeling or otherwise making visible both thinking and doing." One important avenue for doing so is for "engineering educators [to] engage practitioners from business, industry, and government. Practitioners can ... also work with faculty to help bring approximations of professional practice into the classroom." With its direct interaction between students and practicing professionals, the *Industry Fellows* begins to realize these research-based recommendations.

The *Industry Fellows* model is novel, drawing inspiration from but also distinct from past attempts to link practitioners and academics. Industry advisory boards can provide important input into curricula, yet are divorced from the classroom, most commonly operating at a programmatic level. Guest speakers from industry provide students a window into the world of work; yet speakers have no opportunity to provide feedback to students on their work, and they rarely understand the context of specific academic settings. Industry professionals moonlighting as part-time teachers can be an important addition to an academic department. They have deep content knowledge and a keen awareness of one or more specific work settings. Yet, as discussed above, they do not have the pedagogical content knowledge that only comes from experience in teaching. Without significant contact with skilled teaching faculty, part-time teachers will improve as teachers only very slowly through their own trial and error. The *Industry Fellows* program thus complements all of these efforts to bring the classroom and professional practice into closer alignment, while at the same time having the potential to be extended to other STEM disciplines and diverse settings.

5. CONCLUSION

The *Industry Fellows* model is a novel approach to bridging the gap between academic coursework and professional practice. It is different from but complementary to guest speakers, industry advisory boards, and part-time teaching by industry professionals. Its power arises from leveraging the separate and overlapping expertise of professional teachers and computing professionals by placing them together in the classroom. Having a clear division of responsibilities exploits what each does best. The project is grounded in research on how people learn, and implements recent proposals to connect professional practitioners with educators in the engineering professions. It is directed toward changing students' conceptions and perceptions of the value of coursework and its link to professional practice, faculty learning disciplinary practices and skills from industry professionals, and the learning of transferable skills in teaching by industry professionals that they can apply to training and mentoring in the workplace. The model has been instantiated in an HCI course at UW Tacoma with an industry fellow from Google. An evaluation of this course indicates a positive impact of the industry fellow's participation on student learning and motivation.

This model begins to fulfill one of the key aspirations stated by the National Academy of Engineering in their recent report *The Engineer of 2020: Visions of Engineering in the New Century* [8]: "It is our aspiration that engineering educators and practicing engineers together undertake a proactive effort to prepare engineering education to address the technology and societal challenges and opportunities of the future."

6. ACKNOWLEDGMENTS

I am grateful to Beth Simon for a critical reading of an earlier draft of this paper. Jessica Yellin also provided a critical reading, along with several important references to the literature, for which I am grateful. Thanks as well to Yi Chen for help with the evaluation. Thanks to Adam Barker of Google for his participation as the first industry fellow. And many thanks to the students in the HCI course at the Institute of Technology for their engagement during the quarter in which Adam and I worked together on this course.

7. REFERENCES

[1] J. Bransford, A. Brown, and R. Cocking, editors. *How people learn.* National Academy Press, 2000.

[2] M. Chi, M. Farr, and R. Glaser. *The nature of expertise.* Lawrence Erlbaum Associates, 1988.

[3] H. Collins. Tacit knowledge, trust and the Q of sapphire. *Social studies of science*, 31:71–85, 2001.

[4] C. Geertz. *Local knowledge: further essays in interpretive anthropology.* Basic Books, 2nd edition, 1983.

[5] E. Hutchins. *Cognition in the wild.* MIT Press, 1995.

[6] S. Kuhn. Learning from the architecture studio: implications for project-based pedagogy. *International Journal of Engineering Education*, 17:349–352, 2001.

[7] J. Lave and E. Wenger. *Situated learning: legitimate peripheral participation.* Cambridge University Press, 1991.

[8] National Academy of Engineering. *The engineer of 2020: visions of engineering in the new century.* National Academies Press, 2003.

[9] Y. Reimer and S. Douglas. Teaching hci design with the studio approach. *Computer Science Education*, 13:191–205, 2003.

[10] H. Rittel and M. Webber. Dilemmas in a general theory of planning. *Policy Sciences*, 4:155–169, 1973.

[11] B. Rogoff. *The cultural nature of human development.* Oxford University Press, 2003.

[12] D. Schön. *Educating the reflective practitioner: toward a new design for teaching and learning in the professions.* Jossey-Bass, 1987.

[13] S. Sheppard, K. Macatangay, A. Colby, and W. Sullivan. *Educating engineers: designing for the future of the field.* Jossey-Bass, 2009.

[14] L. Shulman. Those who understand: knowledge growth in teaching. *Educational Researcher*, 15(2):4–14, 1986.

[15] J. Tenenberg. The ultimate guest speaker: a model for educator/practitioner collaboration. In *Proceedings of the Eleventh Annual Northwestern Regional Conference of the Consortium for Computing Sciences in Colleges*, 2009.

Teaching Communication, Leadership, and the Social Context of Computing Via a Consulting Course

Joseph Mertz
H. John Heinz III College
Carnegie Mellon University
Pittsburgh, PA 15213
+1.412.268.2540
JoeMertz@cmu.edu

Scott McElfresh
Computer Science Department
Carnegie Mellon University
Pittsburgh, PA 15213
+1.412.268.4859
scottm@cs.cmu.edu

ABSTRACT

This paper describes a course at Carnegie Mellon University that engages students as consultants working with non-profit organizations. Different from most "service learning" courses, students in the Technology Consulting in the Community course focus on building capacity within organizations to sustain IT solutions without ongoing assistance. They do not merely provide IT support, nor do they focus on system development. Rather they focus on solving organizational problems using IT solutions. In doing so, they may develop a system, or adapt open source or commercial tools as appropriate to the situation. Computing systems do not exist in isolation, but in the context of people, organizations, and their policies. We want to train leaders in our community who can not only develop new technologies, but can solve organizational and societal problems. The course has as its learning goals to build inquiry, communication and leadership skills, in addition to engaging students in project development. At the same time it provides a valuable service in the community.

Categories and Subject Descriptors

K.3.2 **[Computers and Education]:** Computer and Information Science Education — *Computer Science Education*

General Terms

Management, Documentation, Design, Human Factors.

Keywords

Leadership, professional skills, consulting, service-learning, project course, capstone course.

1. INTRODUCTION

Computer science and related disciplines have always had a need to include communication skills as part of training students. [1] Furthermore, students need to be exposed to the applications of computer science and its impact on people and society in order to attract certain segments of the population to the field. [1] Computer technology does not live in a vacuum, but in the context of people, organizations, and their policies that surround us. We want to be training leaders in our community who can solve problems by developing new technologies.

"Service Learning" in computer science curricula is not new, and many schools have students engaged in the community using their IT skill, typically working with segments of the community that are on the other side of the digital divide. Some have included a service learning component to existing courses, such as CS0 or CS1 [2, 3], while other schools have developed extracurricular activities for students to engage in helping the community [4, 5]. Carnegie Mellon has project courses in which teams are engaged in the community, as well as campus groups that engage students in providing IT support or training to the community. We have created a course that engages students in these types of situations in a unified manner within an academically rigorous course.

The course is titled Technology Consulting in the Community (TCinC). Each student is placed individually in the role of a Technology Consultant for a community organization. Students are led through a consulting process developed to enhance their organization's ability to use technology effectively in order to better meet its mission. Going beyond IT support, the course aims to provide a sustained ability for the organization to use technology effectively, without returning to us for support at the moment of any glitch. In this process, students visit the organization and meet with staff members to learn about all aspects of the organization and their mission. The non-technical aspects of the organization are just as important as the technical environment. Students report their findings and negotiate a scope of work with the organization. The leader of the organization is most often from a non-technical background, but is an equal partner in the work, and thus the project requires the student to work closely with that person. Frequent oral and written proposals and status reports keep the student engaged in honing their communication skills, culminating in a final project report and presentation.

This paper will describe in detail some of the learning goals of the course, how we address them, and assess the outcomes.

2. BACKGROUND

The course is designed for 3rd or 4th year students in computer science, information systems, or electrical and computer engineering. However, any students with some technical background are welcome and can benefit from the course. The student will not develop new technical skills in the course, but rather use the technical skills they have already developed as a context to develop professional leadership, communication, and more broadly, knowledge about the social context of computing.

SIGCSE'10, March 10–13, 2010, Milwaukee, Wisconsin, USA.

For example, a student with knowledge of Facebook, YouTube, and Twitter, could use those skills (developed outside the classroom) to consult with a mentoring organization interested in using social networking to market to a younger set of volunteers. Or for students in the technical majors, a student who has taken a database class can help an organization design their database to maintain their client information, or to evaluate proposals that have already been made for the development of such a project.

2.1 Course's Role in the Curriculum

For computer science or information systems majors, the course serves as an "in-major" elective. For other students, the course satisfies a general elective.

Prior to taking this course, students have had a course in writing, and some have taken a course in technical communication, but that is currently not a pre-requisite for the course.

2.2 Consulting Partnerships

Each student in the course is individually matched with a leader in a local community organization. This is typically a nonprofit organization, school, or a department of municipal government. The student and the partner are expected to spend at least 3 hours a week together, typically onsite at the organization, and each will be doing work outside of that time as well.

Organizations are solicited via word of mouth and postings to local nonprofit email lists. The leader of an interested organization is engaged in conversation to determine the potential needs of the organization and the organizations' ability to work with a student consultant. The leader is an equal partner in the project, is expected to work hand-in-hand with the student, and gives a large portion of the final presentation.

2.3 History

The course has been taught in fall and spring semesters since spring 1998, with 10-25 students in most semesters. In that time, the course has had over 350 partnerships with 250 different nonprofit organizations, schools, and municipal agencies. Many organizations wish to partner with the course multiple times, which we are happy to do as long as we are not re-solving the same problem.

3. LEARNING GOALS

The course learning goals cover the full process of engaging with a client in order to solve a problem using technology.

Many of these goals overlap the "Social Context of Computing" learning goals contained in [1] and revised in [6]. In the following sections, we will describe the major learning goals of the course, and discuss where they overlap with the Social Context goals.

3.1 Lead a Diverse Working Team

Students seldom get a chance to lead a working team, let alone one that involves anyone other than students. Similarly, "work in interdisciplinary teams" is an oft-stated general education goal, but in practice this most often is reduced to teams of students with different majors. Upon graduation, these students will likely be working in teams that cross many differences, including age, race, gender, language, and technical expertise to name a few.

CS2001 articulates this learning objective as part of the Social Context of computing as:

> *Indicate the role of cultural issues in considering team-work.*

Similarly it addresses the flip side of diverse representation not being included in :

> *Articulate the impact of the input deficit from diverse populations in the computing profession.*

TCinC addresses both of these learning goals by having students lead a diverse team of non-technical (and sometimes technical) professionals of diverse backgrounds and experience. With the student, the team always includes someone in a leadership position in the client organization, and often includes additional management and staff.

To prepare students to assume this role, we begin by discussing the importance of relationship building. We discuss in class the concepts of common ground, shared experience, trust, and social capital, as well as strategies for developing each.

We also have students consider the alternative consulting roles they could play. Most students would default into being an expert-for-hire. This is most closely related to the typical jobs and internships they have held; they have some labor or skill to provide, and so they should get on with providing it. Instead, we teach a capacity-building model of consulting. In this case, the student's goal is help an organization expand its ability to use technology to better meet its mission, in a way that is sustainable after the student consultant leaves. System development is not the goal. Rather the goal is mission focused, for example:

- To improve mental health services by using a database to better track patient assessments of health care providers.
- To feed more hungry families by helping a food bank more effectively use the web to inform donors of the need.

We assess how student consultants have achieved this goal in a number of ways:

- Clients provide survey feedback not only on student performance, but also on how the student increased their ability to manage the technical advances on their own.
- The client and student consultant do a joint presentation, in which the client speaks to the outcomes to them and their organization resulting from the student's leadership.

This feedback is almost always very affirming to the student. Before the semester begins, there are often some students who express concerns that they don't know enough to be useful as a "consultant" to an actual organization. Near the end of the semester they document their perception of the outcomes in a final consulting report, and in person sometimes fret that their results were not technically sophisticated enough. But in many cases, it is not until they hear their client speaking about how their help has impacted the organization that they get a full appreciation of the value of the leadership role they played. The clients typically leave happy because when the student is focused on building capacity, then invariably they provide some residual value, even if their technical solution is sometimes lacking (which is inevitable in a student population).

3.2 Assess a Complex Technical Environment

A second challenge students seldom get the chance to experience is how to implement a technical system in an authentic organization. Technical systems live (or die) within social systems. Users needs change with time; companies release new software updates regularly; new hardware is purchased every few years. It is impossible to create a robust system that takes all potential social changes into account. Rather, computing professionals need to understand and account for the social systems in which the technical systems are embedded.

Furthermore, the value of technology is not intrinsic, but is derived from its ability to solve individual, organizational, or societal problems.

CS2001 includes two related learning objectives:

> *Interpret the social context of a particular implementation.*
>
> *Identify assumptions and values embedded in a particular design including those of a cultural nature.*

We introduce students to the problem of neglecting the social context by using a documentary video that tells the story of two approaches to providing clean drinking water to a village in Togo [7]. In the first approach, a well is drilled and a pump installed without any allowance for maintenance and repair. Of course, the pump eventually breaks and villagers must return to collecting disease-laden surface water. In the second story, government extension workers take into account the social context and work with villagers to build a social system to support the technological water system. We drive the point home by using a short video taken from the final presentations of an earlier TCinC class in which the client discusses how a student team from another project course built them a system that did not take their organizational culture into account, and the system failed. In contrast, TCinC student consultants helped his organization build a solution in Microsoft Access that they could manage and evolve. In the client's words:

> *"What impressed me the most was their ability to listen and to help assess our needs and then to help us to think about them critically. And they didn't really come up with this solution for me, I felt like I was able to come to this myself. Again, just like good counseling or therapy, you come to that and you can use it in life. If someone gives you a magical solution like the other group did it doesn't work."*

But just being aware that there is a social context is not enough; students have to have tools and strategies to investigate and understand it.

Students begin by reviewing local and national benchmarks on how technology is used by nonprofit organizations. This gives some context with which to assess what they observe with their client. We also provide a broad framework for investigating how technology impacts an organization. This framework includes suggested areas to explore along on 10 dimensions, including:

1. Organization – e.g. mission, history, governance structure
2. Programs – e.g. day care, job training
3. Staff – e.g. what applications do they use regularly
4. Facilities – e.g. adequate power and lighting
5. Technology infrastructure – e.g. hardware & software
6. Technology management – e.g. troubleshooting & support
7. Technology planning – e.g. is there a planning committee
8. Information management – e.g. databases or paper forms
9. Communications – e.g. staff email addresses, web site
10. Business systems – e.g. accounting or inventory systems

We teach students to use both interviewing and observation[8].

In terms of evaluating students learning, students articulate their assessment of the organization in a working document that goes through a repeated write-review-revise cycle. This cycle is discussed in more detail in Section 3.4. and is the basis for providing not one but multiple evaluations of the student's ability to meet this goal. In general, students do not have much trouble providing a descriptive account of their client's organizational context. Sample assessments of other organizations are helpful for students to model their work on. Of course, some follow the example too closely. One semester it was curious why several students had included an accounting of the number of bathrooms in an organization until it was found that the first example report provided to them had mentioned a bathroom while describing the facilities.

3.3 Structure a Complex Problem

A third useful challenge for students to learn from is to have to wrestle ambiguity and complexity while structuring an otherwise unstructured problem. All instructors know that problems outside the classroom tend to not be as tidy as those we use for homework assignments.

Students in TCinC do not receive a clear problem statement, because the client often does not have one. Rather, the student consultant has the interesting task of working with their client to investigate problems in the organization, decide which of those problems are important to solve, and what alternatives exist to solve them.

We help students to structure these unstructured problems in a number of ways:

- We practice multiple diagramming techniques, including Cross-Boundary Causality Maps [9], causal flow diagrams, and work process diagrams [10] in order to analyze problems within the context of the organization.
- We differentiate between problems (e.g. losing patient information) and solutions (e.g. a database).
- We emphasize the primacy of mission in any organization, and that the only reason to implement a technical solution is because it will positively impact their mission (e.g. by solving a problem that is hindering them from achieving their mission more fully).
- We assess alternative solutions in terms of maximizing positive impact while still being feasible.

In this way we lead the student through a process by which they define a scope of work. Ideally the scope of work clearly prescribes a solution to a problem that is important to the organization because it impacts their mission; and they can argue why that solution is better in terms of impact, feasibility, and risk than the alternatives.

The student documents this scope of work in a report that is circulated to the client and the instructor, and is the basis for evaluating the students attainment of this learning goal. Therefore it is straightforward to assess how each student has or has not been able to clearly structure and communicate the reasoning that backs the solution path they are taking. Not all students are highly successful at this. All carry on and do something with their client, but the reasoning and planning behind what they are doing is not well defined. Therefore the degree of mastery of this skill is a significant differentiator of students' overall performance in the class. And there is certainly room for finding better ways to help students systematically structure complex problems.

3.4 Communicate Professionally

A fourth useful challenge for students to learn from is to communicate professionally. There are a few aspects to this communication that TCinC helps students develop:

3.4.1 Use Writing Skills to Maintain Working Documents that Describe, Plan, Persuade, and Coordinate Work With Others

TCinC is a very writing intensive course, but it is writing for which we provide clear guidelines and examples. For students who prefer coding over writing, we joke that TCinC is not a writing course, it is a programming course in which the programming language is English. We model in the class that the same writing can be used for multiple purposes:

- To help the writer clearly understand their own reasoning.
- To allow the client to validate or correct the consultant's understanding.
- To share thinking and coordinate the work of the project team.
- To inform stakeholders of the progress of a project.
- To provide an archival record for others to refer to in similar situations.

In TCinC, the student maintains working documents that serve these purposes. By working documents, we mean that the documents are repeatedly updated and shared as the project progresses in a write-review-revise cycle.

For example:

- The student consultant produces a description of the organizational context they are working in and share it with peers, the teaching assistant, and a volunteer mentor.
- The peers, teaching assistant, and volunteer mentor provide written feedback, as well as oral feedback in a small-group meeting.
- The student consultant adds the scope of work to the document and again circulates it, this time also to the client.
- In a small group meeting, a peer orally presents the student consultant's scope of work to the group and it is discussed. In this way the student consultant can observe and listen more closely to the feedback.
- The student consultant revises the description of the context and the scope of work and submits it to the instructor. The instructor provides extensive written feedback and a grade.

Nearer the end of the semester, this write-review-revise process is repeated with the student's documentation of outcomes and recommendations for future work.

Finally, the student consultant takes all the pieces and synthesizes them into a final consulting report. This is distributed to all stakeholders and some are archived on the course web site for future reference.

Students are given clear guidelines for the expected content of the reports, and these guidelines are used to evaluate the students success in meeting the communication goal.

The quality of the students' reports varies, as do the grades they receive; nevertheless, the documents do provide a basis for the student, their client, and the instructor to have a common understanding of the project. Rarely does the client report that the document is significantly flawed, and most of the time find it mostly accurate, complete, and ultimately publishable. In that respect, all students experience the role working documents play in coordinating project work.

3.4.2 Communicate Technical Ideas to a Non-Technical Audience

Another aspect of communicating professionally is to be able to communicate technical ideas to a non-technical audience. Students are immersed in a sea of technical terms, and may have been their whole lives, so that they might fail to realize that those who are not so immersed may have no idea what they are talking about. Most students have not stopped to think that "semaphore" and "daisy chain" are only metaphors taken from the physical world, and that others may not understand the association.

In order to help students be aware of and plan for communicating clearly, the class:

- Discusses the use of metaphors in computing and ways of assessing their value in communicating.
- Recommends that the student models technical skills while subtly giving a verbal think-aloud protocol so that others can learn while watching.

The write-review-revise cycle also helps to flag where communication is unclear to non-technical readers. Throughout the process, the client is asked to review and comment on the clarity of the document.

Finally, the student is expected to make an oral presentation, with the client, in a public forum at the conclusion of the semester. This event is another opportunity for the student to practice communicating to a larger audience in a formal presentation, and provides another assessment opportunity for the instructor.

This is an area of the class that students uniformly do well at. Because it is treated as a priority, and one that is not difficult to carry out, students are good at communicating to their non-technical clients. Clients routinely comment on how much they value the patience with which students help them to understand bewildering technical concepts.

3.4.3 Document Outcomes Objectively

The final communication challenge for students it to learn to document outcomes clearly and objectively.

It is very easy to document outcomes poorly. For example, by:

- Leaving out detail: "the process is faster"

- Using summary statements: "the reporting activity is now more efficient"
- Describing what was done instead of what resulted from that action: "I trained the staff to use of the database."

It is easy to leave the reader with impressions of outcomes without providing any clarity on what exactly the final state was. It leaves this interpretation up to the reader. This is useful when trying to gloss over imperfect results, but it is not useful in providing a clear assessment that in turn can guide future work.

CS2001 articulates a similar learning objective:

> *Evaluate a particular implementation through the use of empirical data.*

We use several practices to help students meet this learning goal:

- When crafting their scope of work, students are taught to define measurable expected outcomes.
- We explicitly review and discuss how language can be used to present clear and concrete evidence about an outcome.
- The write-review-revise cycle is used in order to give feedback to students on where their outcomes are not clear.
- We emphasize the value of negative results alongside positive outcomes, for negative results are useful new information about approaches that have not been successful.
- We try to reassure the student that a well documented negative outcome is far superior (and is graded such) to an ambiguously worded outcome that suggests success.

Students often have difficulty documenting outcomes objectively. And like the ability to structure a complex problem, this skill is a second significant differentiator of students' overall performance in the class.

4. IMPLEMENTATION EXAMPLES

What we have not described in this paper is the implementation of the actual project, for it follows more conventional lines. After completing the scope of work, the student generates and executes a work plan. The type of projects students complete are quite varied for they are custom to the needs of each organization. Nevertheless we will mention a few representative ones:

- Developed a system to better manage the production process of Braille books by improving coordination of information among employees involved in the production process .
- Defined requirements for a library management system, researched alternative solutions, then installed and configured the open source Koha system.
- Designed and implemented a web site using the open source Joomla content management system. Extended Joomla with the open source CiviCRM to keep client, partner, and donor information, and integrated LimeSurvey to accept applications to their program.
- Developed a system to enable patients to make requests for Medical Alert Jewelry on-line. The system was implemented using Microsoft SQL Server and Cold Fusion.
- Developed a system to support coaching feedback to swimmers using video. The project involved choosing appropriate equipment, testing camera locations, integrating hardware and software systems for editing and archiving the video, and training the coach on its operation.
- To support the management of multiple real estate re-development projects, researched shared project-management solutions and helped the organization adopt the hosted Ace Project tool. To help the organization better manage versions of documents related to each project, installed, configured, and trained staff in the use of the open source tools Sub Version and Tortoise SVN.

5. CONCLUSION

This course has been taught continuously each spring and fall since 1998. Clients often will repeat with the course because of the value they get from the student consultants. The median "Overall Course Evaluation" by students is over 4 out of 5.

In conclusion, we have developed a course that successfully teaches our students professional communication and leadership skills that are important for leaders in the discipline. By involving them with actual clients in the community and providing a structured consulting class to support their engagement, students are able to develop many of the Social Context of computing skills that are necessary for leaders of the future.

More information about the course can be found at our web site: http://cmu.edu/tcinc

6. REFERENCES

[1] Computing Curricula 2001: Computer Science, Final Report, December 2001. The Joint Task Force on Computing Curricula, IEEE Computer Society, Association for Computing Machinery (2002).

[2] Adams, J. B. and Runkles, E. 2004. "May we have class outside?": implementing service learning in a CS1 curriculum. J. Comput. Small Coll. 19, 5 (May. 2004), 25-34.

[3] Rosmaita, B. J. 2006. Accessibility first!: a new approach to web design. In Proceedings of the 37th SIGCSE Technical Symposium on Computer Science Education (Houston, Texas, USA, March 03 - 05, 2006). SIGCSE '06. ACM, New York, NY, 270-274. DOI= http://doi.acm.org/10.1145/1121341.1121426

[4] Brooks, C. H. 2008. Community connections: lessons learned developing and maintaining a computer science service-learning program. SIGCSE Bull. 40, 1 (Feb. 2008), 352-356. DOI= http://doi.acm.org/10.1145/1352322.1352256

[5] Christensen, K., Rundus, D., Perera, G., and Zulli, S. 2006. CSE Volunteers: A Service Learning Program to Provide IT Support to the Hillsborough County School District. SIGCSE Bull. 38, 1 (Mar. 2006), 229-233. DOI= http://doi.acm.org/10.1145/1124706.1121412

[6] Computer Science Curriculum 2008: An Interim Revision of CS 2001. Report from the Interim Review Task Force includes update of the CS2001 body of knowledge plus commentary. Association for Computing Machinery, IEEE Computer Society (2008)

[7] The Water of Ayole: Togo, West Africa. [videorecording] Directed by Sandra Nichols, Sandra Nichols Productions, USA. (1988)

[8] Beyer, H. R. and Holtzblatt, K. 1995. Apprenticing with the customer. Commun. ACM 38, 5 (May. 1995), 45-52. DOI= http://doi.acm.org/10.1145/203356.203365

[9] To Think Bigger Thoughts: Why the Human Cognome Project Requires Visual Language Tools, Robert E. Horn, http://www.stanford.edu/~rhorn/a/recent/SpchNBICHrnSpks.html

[10] Contextual Design: Defining Customer-Centered Systems By Hugh Beyer, Karen Holtzblatt, Morgan Kaufmann Publishers, 1997.

Digital Visualization Tools Improve Teaching 3D Character Modeling

Mark van Langeveld
University of Utah
School of Computing
50 S. Central Campus Dr. #3190
Salt Lake City, UT 84112
801-376-9071
longfieldstudio@gmail.com

Robert Kessler
University of Utah
School of Computing
50 S. Central Campus Dr. #3190
Salt Lake City, UT 84112
801-581-4653
kessler@cs.utah.edu

ABSTRACT

Many Universities are building interdisciplinary programs that overlap engineering and fine art departments that focus on games, special effects, animation and other forms of interdisciplinary efforts. With increasing demands for education linking the Engineering Sciences and Fine Arts, fueled by the competitive nature of the industries that recruit graduates, educators need to become more efficient and effective in their task of educating engineering and art majors in cross-disciplinary courses.

CS3650 at the University of Utah is a digital character production course. This course is interdisciplinary and draws from several disciplines including computer science, graphics, anatomy, sculpture, art, and entertainment. It is a prerequisite for our machinima class, which immerses students into 3D game engines. Visualization tools are used in the course to help students learn to create better digital models.

Presented in this paper is an experimental comparison between traditional visualization tools and digital visualization tools, which are less expensive, easier to distribute, arrange/procure and transport than the traditional tools. Traditional visualization tools include lifelike skeleton reproductions, wooden body mass structures, actual live human models, and anatomy drawing books. The digital visualization tools that are contrasted in this paper are: a layered anatomically correct, digital human model (skin, muscles, masses and some bones adapted from several sources) and a VisTrails version of a properly produced human figure (interactive animation). The digital tools are used to replace the traditional visualization tools used in the same educational curriculum, which teaches students to design, model and produce digital characters for games, machinima, and animation. The quantitative experiment demonstrates that digital visualization tools help to improve a student's understanding of the complex software packages used to produce characters, helps to improve specific techniques used to model 3D characters, and it helps to improve understanding of 3D form, more than the traditional tools within the context of this educational curriculum.

Categories and Subject Descriptors: K.3.2 [Computer and Information Science Education]: Computer Science Education, Curriculum.

General Terms: Management

Keywords
Digital entertainment industry, video games, Machinima, 3D character modeling, education, interdisciplinary curriculum, anatomy, form, visualization, instructional technologies.

1. INTRODUCTION

Many universities and colleges are building interdisciplinary programs that overlap engineering and fine art departments allowing a focus on games, special effects, animation and other similar interdisciplinary efforts [1][2][3]. Just recently New York University created the NYU Game Center [4]. In 2007 we began our Entertainment Arts and Engineering (EAE) program [5]. This new academic emphasis was created partially due to the digital entertainment industry's demand (including both game and animation) for new employees that are trained in disciplines from both the engineering and fine arts and partially from the extremely strong draw the program has on a diverse set of interested students [6]. A key to a successful program (according to our industrial colleagues) is that students graduate as either excellent computer scientists or excellent artists with the additional skills of having worked extensively with "the other side." These interdisciplinary classes form the heart of bringing the two sides together.

Typical cross-disciplinary classes include CS1 that focuses on games and graphics [7][8][9] and beginning drawing for non-art-majors. Both curriculums are usually designed to alleviate anxieties associated with "walking to the other side of campus." The classes are also designed to fast track students to a beginning level of competency and to help promote understanding and communication between the two areas. At the University of Utah we have designed a series of two classes that are equally based in knowledge and practices from both the engineering and fine art fields of study. The first is the Digital Character Production Course (CS3650) that feeds into the second, a Machinima [10] class (animation shorts created using a 3D game engine). Both classes are evenly split between art/design principles and engineering/technology principles.

CS3650 provides an extraordinary applied learning experience for students [11] by combining learning concepts that are not commonly taught together. The curriculum is designed to teach students complex problem solving by learning to breakdown the extremely difficult problem of creating a digital character into manageable segments. This promotes understanding diverse concepts that range from computer graphics fundamentals to sculptural ideology and from graphic algorithms to 3D design elementary concepts and most importantly algorithmic thinking. It is a process that provides a direct view of the correlation between many technical concepts and the application of the concepts that solidifies essential knowledge. It also allows for engineers and artists to gain an appreciation and understanding of each other's roles in and contributions to entertainment arts and engineering production, hence, improving teamwork.

The Digital Character Production Course is taught in a guild-style. Guild-style education is project-based and incorporates multiple disciplines and areas of study with the goal and focus of inducing an exceptional learning experience while producing an important and complex product. The learning objectives and outcomes of CS3650 course include teaching students the production pipeline for CG character development, introducing students to the applications for computer graphics used in the game and animation industries, and introducing students to algorithms used in specific modeling techniques including smoothing, polygon decimation, vertex merging, edge loops selections and edge loop inserts. Other learning objectives are to help students: improve their understanding of form, structure, and anatomy of anthropomorphic characters; understand proper contour design for 3D models; learn the critical elements of digital figure modeling that distinguish levels of sophistication in character modeling; learn to translate design concepts into physical representations (paper, words, images and clay); and finally the translation into a digital representation for input to gaming engines and animation tools.

The curriculum is based on techniques for modeling the anatomically correct human figure. All lectures, examples and demonstrations are taught using the human figure as a representation of anthropomorphic characters. This choice was made because the human figure is complex and requires a tremendous understanding of form, structure and visual relationships. Also, most students can tell the difference between accurate human models and non-accurate human models. Even with characters that have extreme proportions (such as characters in "The Incredibles") an understanding of visual human anatomy is essential to make characters that we as viewers want to relate.

A final project assignment is included which accounts for 80% of the student's final grade. The project is to produce a digital character. The students are shown how to break the task into manageable parts that begins with designing a character of the student's choosing with drawings, clay sculpture and words as devices for working out designs and representing design ideas. The next stages include using Adobe's PhotoShop, a 2D software program, and AutoDesk's MAYA, a 3D software program. One of the learning objectives of the course is to teach the students to take the abstract ideas of a chosen character and realize them into drawings and clay sculptures as a learning process, and then to translate the drawings and clay into digital characters. This applied process creates strong intellectual connections between the two disciplines allowing students to solidify important engineering principles.

Courses that are similar to this digital character course are typically taught using traditional visualization tools. Visualization tools provide opportunities for understanding and involve cognitive functions such as recognition, learning, and memory. When objects or characters are visualized, they are easier to understand because they become more tangible in the mind [12]. Typical traditional visualization tools are shown in Figure 1 and serve as 2D and 3D references for aiding the students in producing anthropomorphic characters that have the physical qualities that promote the viewer's ability to relate to the character with sympathy. These tools permit exploration of complex physical relationships of the human figure and also provide concrete examples of comparisons of form, structure and mechanics from 2D to 3D. Digital character classes also require a large amount of one-on-one time with teachers and students, which can limit the number of students in a class.

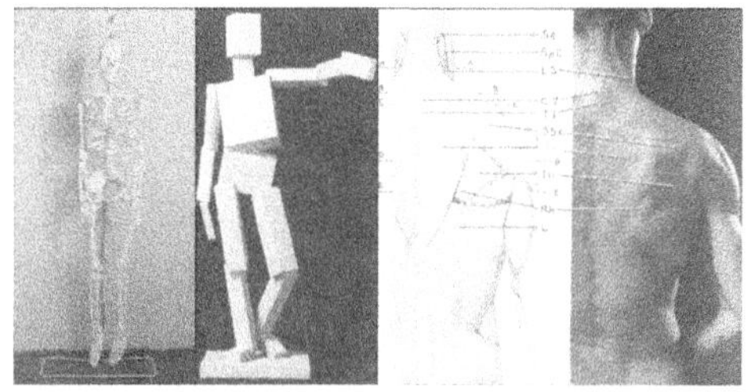

Figure 1: Traditional visualization tools—half-sized skeleton, block figures of anatomical masses, anatomy books[13] and live models.

Recently there has been work completed on digital visualization tools at the University of Utah that seem suited to improve the learning experience in our digital character production course. The Human Reference Model [16][17] (HRM) is a virtual representation of the human figure that allows students to interactively reference it from MAYA. The HRM is a 3D layered anatomically correct, digital human model (bones, skin, muscles, masses and some bones). The model was adapted from the University of Pennsylvania's Digital Figure Modeling Course and anatomical models from a commercial modeling firm. The second tool is a VisTrails [15] MAYA version of a properly produced human figure/character that enables interactive animation (figure 2). This version allows the student to visually review exactly how a model is constructed by following the exact steps taken by an instructor as they work on a sample model. An important advantage is that the student can proceed interactively through the steps of the sample model at any rate they choose.

Our hypotheses is that using digital visualization tools as a replacement for traditional visualization tools will improve the students learning experience without reducing the quality of their final character projects. We also believe that the students who use the digital visualization tools will be able to demonstrate improvement in their understanding of the complex software packages used to produce characters, improvement in specific techniques used to model 3D characters and improvement in understanding of 3D form/visual relationships, more than the traditional tools within the context of this educational curriculum.

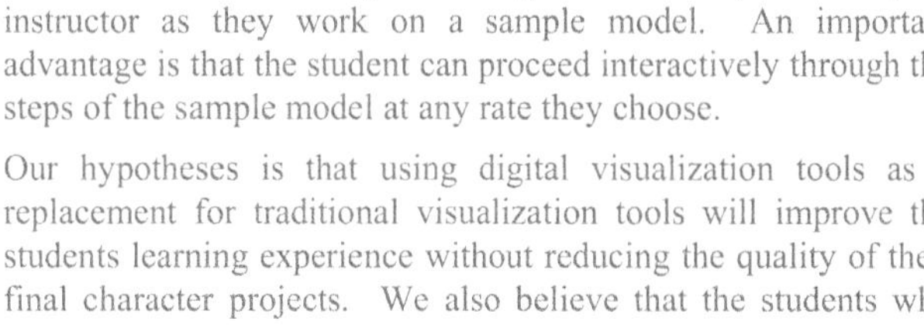

Figure 2: HRM Muscle layer reference screen shot (left) VizTrails—Head Interactive Animation screen shot (right).

2. STATEMENT OF PROBLEM

The Digital Character Production course curriculum at the University of Utah is designed, in part, to help students learn MAYA, a complicated 3D design tool from AutoDesk Corporation that is considered an industry standard for 3D graphics software, for the purpose of producing an anthropomorphic, digital character. The task of creating a successful 3D digital character can be divided into four skill sets: the vision and understanding of the original character, the understanding and ability to control the MAYA software system, the understanding and ability to apply particular techniques to well-organized character models, and the understanding of anatomical form and structure of an anthropomorphic character. The learning objectives for the course are partially derived from the goal for students to acquire the necessary skill sets to produce a successful 3D digital character.

The new digital visualization tools developed at the University of Utah hold great promise as replacements for more traditional tools typically used in digital character production courses.

Within the context of interdisciplinary 3D digital character production courses, the specific questions being addressed in this study are:

- Are the VisTrails—MAYA plug-in and the HRM better than the traditional visualization tools for instructing students to attain the skill set of understanding and ability to control the MAYA software for character production?
- Are the VisTrails—MAYA plug-in and the HRM better than the traditional visualization tools for instructing students to attain the skill set of designing and manipulating contours for well-organized models?
- Are the VisTrails—MAYA plug-in and the HRM better than the traditional visualization tools for instructing students to attain the skill set for understanding the anatomical form and structure of an anthropomorphic characters?
- Are the VisTrails—MAYA plug-in and the HRM better than the traditional visualization tool based curriculum for instructing students to produce 3D digital characters?

3. METHODOLOGY

An experimental methodology was used for this study. The methodology measures include:

- All participants were assigned a term-long modeling project of a character of their own choosing. During the semester the students learned how to use MAYA for polygonal character modeling, how to design and organize contours on character models, and how to model anatomically based forms adapted to their characters. They were also taught to shape the entirety of their character model. They were informed that they would be graded on the overall quality of their models and that would include: their ability to use MAYA to make their model, their ability to organize contours on their model, and their ability to adapt the anatomical forms to their model. The length of the project alleviated the potential stress from short, timed exams (Figure 6).
- All participants were assigned an end-of-term technical exam of a MAYA modeling exercise. The exam was to model a wooden duck. It was different from the humanoid form and structure of their project characters. At the time of the exam, the students were shown an example of a well-done model (Figure 3) and the actual wooden duck that they were to use as a physical reference. Each participant was given a project folder that included photographic and drawn references. They were given exactly ninety minutes. There was no communication between students or proctors during the test. This exam provided a different enough challenge from the final anthropomorphic character project to assess the depth of learning of the students that would be required for extension to a different model. It also mandated an exact time control on the assignment.
- Pre and Post Drawing tests were assigned to all participants to help qualify student's understanding of complex forms, relationships and structure. At the first of the semester the students drew five drawings in one hour: a front-view of a human figure in prone position (from memory), a side view of a human figure in prone position (from memory), a front view of a human head (possible for some reflection in monitor), a side view of a human head (possible for short glimpses of fellow students), and a hand drawn in any position (could use own hand as reference). There were no references allowed except those that naturally occurred with the hand drawings and possibly glimpses of other student faces during the assessment. The instructions were given that they would have an hour to do their very best drawings of a realistic representation of a human. The students were told that they would be graded on effort. At the end of the semester they were given the exact same instructions.

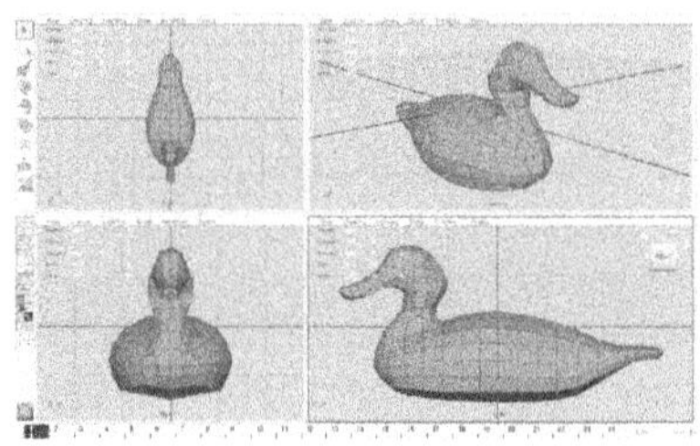

Figure 3: end-of-term technical exam example.

4. PARTICIPANTS AND STRUCTURE

A restricted self-selecting sampling method was used to populate the sample pool. Section 001 was held on Tuesdays at 3:45 to 6:20PM with Lab from 6:30 to 9:00PM and section 002 was held at the same times on Thursdays. By the flipping of a coin, section 001 was assigned the digital visualization tools (Digital Group) and section 002 (Traditional Group) was assigned the traditional tools for the independent variable. The classes and labs were kept completely separate and virtually identical except for the difference in visualization tools. Both classes met 15 times independently and once together for the final presentations of character projects. Each group was randomly assigned 17 engineering majors and 3 non-engineering majors.

The same instructor and two teaching assistants taught the classes. The curriculum included lectures, demonstrations and one-on-one instruction. The only differences at all in the classes were based on the visualization tools. For instance, the Traditional Group was provided with anatomy books, skeleton models and a fieldtrip to the Body Worlds Exhibit and the Digital Group was not. Also the

Digital Group was provided with VizTrails examples and HRMs for references and the Traditional Group was not.

Instruction in the class began with a simple start to the body that lets the students become familiar with many of the MAYA and modeling concepts. Next, the hand is a type of algorithmic instruction. It is step-by-step and all students follow the exact procedures. This teaches techniques by repetition and replication. After that, the face starts off similarly with algorithmic instruction for the nose, but the eyes and lips are one step removed from step-by-step approach. They are more like "here is an example of how to do it, now apply that to the your particular eyes and lips." This allows the students to use their newfound modeling skills and mix them with their own creativity and ingenuity. This gives them the ability to figure out complex modeling problems with less help. Then finishing off the head is a chance to learn new techniques and review several approaches already taught. At this point the students finish the details on the body and complete the character at the level expected for the class.

5. RATERS

Three individuals that have relative academic, and professional industry experience rated the projects, technical exams and pre-post drawings. These raters had no relationship with the participants in the study. Every precaution was taken to insure the raters had consistent viewing experiences and importantly, there was no way for the raters to determine group assignment.

The raters were given additional instruction on the areas of criterion measurements. For the project, each rater was required to give a grade between 0 and 100 on four different criterions: (1) MAYA proficiency, (2) contour design and manipulation, (3) form description, (4) and overall character model. This was the same for the technical exam. For the pre-post drawings, each judge was required to give a grade between 0 and 100 on each of the five different drawings and also a grade on the overall drawings combined for each participant. The raters also compared the first set of drawings to the second set. They graded each drawing for improvement by comparing each participant's pre drawing with the same participant's post drawing. The five drawings completed in the hour exam were: (1) front body, (2) side body, (3) front face, (4) side face, and (5) hand from any angle.

The grades from the raters were subjective. To measure legitimacy of the grades, a Spearman Correlation was completed comparing each grading criterion for all three judges. The nature of the correlation coefficient is to indicate the relationships of the ratings of the raters. The correlation coefficient ranges from -1 to 1. A correlation of 1 signifies that all grades were rated exactly the same, whereas, a correlation of -1 signifies a negative correlation. A 0 correlation signifies no correlation at all. In educational research, an intraclass correlation coefficient of .6 is considered strong enough for reliability. For comparison, highly trained professional Olympic judges for gymnastics usually have an intraclass correlation coefficient of nearly .9. For this study, the expectations of intraclass correlation coefficients are greater than .6 for each criterion. Because of this correlation, we can average each grade from the three raters for the analysis.

6. RESULTS

The first comparison analyzed was the overall final projects. The Digital Group's N = 20 with a mean score of 79.03, a standard deviation of 9.27, and standard error mean of 2.07. The Traditional Group's N = 20 with a mean score of 69.26, a standard deviation of 12.56, and a standard error mean of 2.81. The independent samples t-test was t(38) = 2.79, p = .00805 and a mean difference of 9.76 (Figure 4). The Digital Group's scores were significantly higher than the Traditional Group's scores in the Overall Character Model category. The MAYA proficiency category average scores, the contour design and manipulation category average scores, and the form description category average scores were similar to the final projects. They also had significant t-tests.

Overall Model Averages

	N	Mean	Std Dev	Std Error Mean
Digital Visualization Tools Group	20	79.03	9.27	2.07
Traditional Visualization Tools Group	20	69.26	12.56	2.81

Overall Model Independent Samples Test

t	Sig (two tailed)	Mean Diff
2.79	0.008	9.76

Figure 4: Final Character Model Statistics.

The second comparison analyzed was the end-of-term technical exam. In the MAYA proficiency category, the Digital Group's N = 20 with a mean score of 64.27, a standard deviation of 11.79, and standard error mean of 2.64. The Traditional Group's N = 20 with a mean score of 51.22, a standard deviation of 12.36, and a standard error mean of 2.76. The independent samples t-test was t(38) = 3.41, p = .00150 and a mean difference of 13.05. The Digital Group's scores were significantly higher than the Traditional Group's scores in the MAYA proficiency category. In the contour design category, the Digital Group's N = 20 with a mean score of 65.83, a standard deviation of 10.81, and standard error mean of 2.42. The Traditional Group's N = 20 with a mean score of 49.67, a standard deviation of 11.87, and a standard error mean of 2.65. The independent samples t-test was t(38) = 4.50, p = .00010 and a mean difference of 16.16. The Digital Group's scores were significantly higher than the Traditional Group's scores in the contour design category. In the form description category, the Digital Group's N = 20 with a mean score of 66.55, a standard deviation of 10.79, and standard error mean of 2.41. The Traditional Group's N = 20 with a mean score of 50.85, a standard deviation of 11.39, and a standard error mean of 2.55. The independent samples t-test was t(38) = 4.47, p = .00010 and a mean difference of 15.70. The Digital Group's scores were significantly higher than the Traditional Group's scores in the form description category. In the overall model category, the Digital Group's N = 20 with a mean score of 66.10, a standard deviation of 11.22, and standard error mean of 2.51. The Traditional Group's N = 20 with a mean score of 50.08, a standard deviation of 11.68, and a standard error mean of 2.61. The independent samples t-test was t(38) = 4.2, p = .00010 and a mean difference of 16.01. The Digital Group's scores were significantly higher than the Traditional Group's scores in the overall model category [18].

The third comparison was the pre/post drawing assessment. There was no significant differences found between the two groups in this comparison; however, it was interesting to note that both groups improved at similar rates (Figure 5).

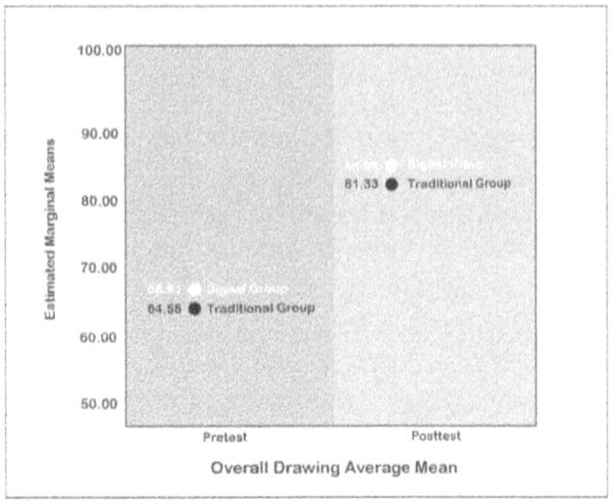

Figure 5: Pre/post Drawings similar rates of improvement.

7. Discussion

Our motivation for this study was influenced by our desire to extend and improve the digital character production course. We wanted to open it to more of the students that were requesting it. We also wanted to extend it further by figuring out how to teach this subject to individuals who wanted the learning experience without attending my classroom. To accomplish this goal of handling more students or helping students to learn the subject using distance learning, there are many obstacles that are hard to overcome and still give the students the same level of learning experience. We focused on one practical obstacle—the physical visualization tools that we use in the classroom to enhance the learning of the students. They work well for classes with limited enrollment of a dozen or less; however, lose their effectiveness as enrollment increases due to their physicality and costs.

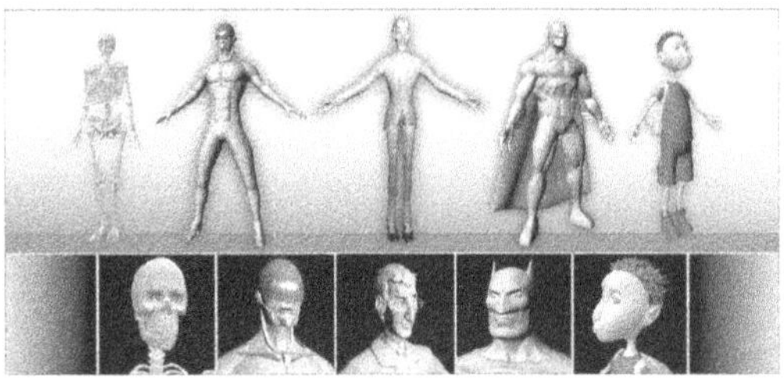

Figure 6: Sample of final projects from engineering students

The VisTrails plug-in is particularly suited to help teachers provide students with interactive animations as examples to help them work through complex modeling concepts. VisTrails gives the students opportunities to review the material at their own pace and as many times as required to learn the material. We think the advantage of the HMR is that it is in the same virtual space as a MAYA project and is accurately recognizable as human. The students have a great capacity to recognize the human figure in great detail. When they see a virtual human form in 3D it is easier for them to mentally translate what they know of the actual human form into the virtual space because of comparison. This seems to improve there understanding of form in general. We had an intuition; born from our experiences using MAYA to produce human forms, that the student's ability to draw the human form would improve. The fact that there was similar improvement from both groups of students, even though they had no drawing instruction or practice between the pretest and posttest, leads me to think that the overall interdisciplinary curriculum of the digital character production course, including the 3D graphic production experience, is responsible for the improvement to the mental model of the human figure for the students; and therefore, they improve their drawing of the human form.

This evidence supports the claim that these digital tools can help to increase the effectiveness and efficiency of digital character production courses that are taught using similar curriculum.

8. FUTURE WORK

In future research, we want to make a comparison between CS students who have taken this course and who go on to take our advanced CS graphics programming class with those who are in the advanced CS graphics that didn't take this course.

9. ACKNOWLEDGMENTS

Thanks to Ryan Vance and Joshua Lee Bross for helping to teach the Digital Character Production Course and also thanks the students that participated in this study. Thanks to Daz3D Productions, Inc. for models and textures for the HRM. Thanks to VisTrails, Inc. for their MAYA plug-in and support.

10. REFERENCES

[1] http://cg.cis.upenn.edu/dmd/

[2] http://cg.cis.upenn.edu/cggt/

[3] http://interactive.usc.edu/research/games/White

[4] http://www.nyu.edu/public.affairs/releases/detail/2394

[5] http://eae.utah.edu/

[6] Kessler, R. van Langeveld, M. and Altizer, R. 2009 Entertainment Arts and Engineering (or How to Fast Track A New Interdisciplinary Program). *Proceedings of the 40th SIGCSE* (Mar. 09). ACM, USA, 539-543.

[7] Gestwicki, P.V. 2007. Computer Games as Motivation for Design Patterns. In *Proceedings of the 38th SIGCSE* (Mar 07). ACM, USA, 233-237.

[8] SIGCSE Bulletin, "Ucigame, A Java Library for Games", University of California, Irvine—Frost, 2008

[9] Leutenegger, S. and Edington, J. 2007, A Games First Approach to Teaching Introductory Programming. In *Proceedings of the 38th SIGCSE* (Mar. 07). ACM, USA, 115-118.

[10] Lowood, H. 2006. High-performance play: The making of machinima. In *Journal of Media Practice*, 7:1, July 2006, pp25-42.

[11] van Langeveld, M. and Kessler, R. 2009 Two in the Middle: Digital Character Production and Machinima Courses. *Proceedings of the 40th SIGCSE* (Mar. 09). ACM, USA, 463-467.

[12] Technology Teacher, Applications and Tools for Design and Visualization, Hall and Obregon, 2002

[13] Human Anatomy for Artists, The Elements of Form, Eliot Goldfinger, Oxford Press, 1991

[14] Anatomy for the Artist, Jeno Barcsay, Barnes and Knoble Books, 1999

[15] www.vistrails.com

[16] www.daz3d.com

[17] www.design.upenn.edu, Digital Figure Modeling, 2003

[18] van Langeveld, M., Educational Impact of Digital Visualization Tools on Digital Character Production Computer Science Courses, Dissertation-Univ. of Utah, 2009

Teaching Web Information Retrieval to Undergraduates

Frank McCown
Harding University
Computer Science Dept
Searcy, Arkansas, USA 72149
fmccown@harding.edu

ABSTRACT

Courses centered around the field of Web Information Retrieval (IR) and web search are slowly being introduced at the undergraduate level. In this paper, we show how the curriculum for a new undergraduate course on web search engines was developed, and we share our experiences in having students develop their own search engine components from scratch or modify and extend a popular open source search engine. We hope our experiences will be helpful to other Computer Science departments that are looking to develop an undergraduate Web IR course.

Categories and Subject Descriptors

K.3.2 [**Computer and Information Science Education**]: Curriculum

General Terms

Algorithms, Experimentation

Keywords

open source, search engines, teaching, Web IR

1. INTRODUCTION

The utility and ubiquity of web search is making Web Information Retrieval (IR) an increasingly popular research topic. The incredible success of Google is a striking example of how important it is for academia and industry to foster innovation in the field of Web IR. Other tech companies like Yahoo and Microsoft continue to make significant investments in web search, and Tim Berners-Lee et al. have begun promoting the study of Web Science [2] in which Web IR is a strong component.

While Web IR is often taught at the graduate level, it is increasingly being introduced at the undergraduate level as an elective (see [10] for a complete discussion of IR curriculum issues in CS). Web IR is often an appealing subject to computer science (CS) students who use search engines like Google and Bing on a daily basis and are curious as to how they function. Using data structures learned in CS 2, an undergraduate student can build a complete web search engine in a semester's time. This can provide extra motivation for students when they are able to apply theoretical concepts to a practical application.

At Harding University, we began preparing in the fall of 2007 to offer an elective undergraduate course called *Search Engine Development*. We wanted to develop a course for undergraduate students in CS with a minimal amount of prerequisites so as to maximize the course's potential audience. We made CS 1/2 and our core Internet Development 1 course the only prerequisites. This allowed sophomores, juniors, and seniors to enroll.

When developing the content for this course, we looked for similar offerings at other universities to determine what subjects should be included and what types of programming assignments should be given. From our survey, we created a curriculum which covered a majority of the topics taught at the undergraduate and graduate levels at many universities, and we experimented with two different approaches to the class programming projects. In 2008, we required students to build a complete search engine from scratch (as suggested in [6] and [8]). In 2009, we required students to modify and extend the open source search engine Nutch [21].

In this paper, we present the curriculum for an undergraduate course focusing on web search which we developed from our survey of thirteen graduate and undergraduate Web IR courses. We discuss text books and reading material for the course, and we share our projects and our experiences having students build a search engine from the ground-up and modifying a complex open source search engine.

2. CURRICULUM

Although the instructor who would be teaching the search engine course had performed extensive research in using search engines for preserving the Web (see, e.g., [19]), he had never taken a Web IR course and had only studied IR independently. Having no base materials from which to develop a Web IR course, it was decided that a curriculum survey should be performed of existing course offerings in Web IR.

The courses listed in Table 1 (sorted by course title) were found using word-of-mouth, Google, and referring links from class web pages. This list is not meant to be an exhaustive list of all Web IR courses, but it is representative of the types of courses that focus mainly on Web IR issues. Sev-

SIGCSE'10, March 10–13, 2010, Milwaukee, Wisconsin, USA.

Table 1: A selection of Web IR courses offered to graduates and undergraduates.

Title	Instructor	University	Audience
Information Retrieval	Susan Gauch	University of Arkansas	Grad
Information Retrieval and Search Engines	C. Lee Giles	Penn State	Undergrad
Information Retrieval and Web Search	Raymond J. Mooney	University of Texas at Austin	Undergrad
Information Retrieval and Web Search	Rada Mihalcea	University of North Texas	Grad
Search Algorithms	Christian Schindelhauer	Univ of Paderborn (Germany)	Unknown
Search Engine Technologies	Nigel Ward	Univ of Texas at El Paso	Both
Search Engine Technology	Dragomir R. Radev	Columbia University	Grad
Search Engines	Bruce Croft	Univ of Massachusetts Amherst	Undergrad
Search Engines: Tech., Society, & Business	Marti Hearst	Univ of California, Berkley	Both
Web Information Retrieval	Xiannong Meng	Bucknell University	Undergrad
Web Search and Mining	C. Manning and P. Raghavan	Stanford University	Grad
Web Search Engines	Ernest Davis	New York University	Grad
WWW Search Engines	Brian D. Davison	Lehigh University	Both

eral courses that came up during the search only focused on IR with little Web application or were non-technical in nature; these were excluded from the list. We noted if the course's audience was primarily graduate, undergraduate, or both. This helped us pick topics more readily accessible to undergraduate students.

Many of the courses listed in Table 1 contained extensive websites with syllabi and project guidelines which greatly helped us in preparing our curriculum. In a few cases, we contacted the instructors of the course to inquire more about the course's content.

We pulled together a core curriculum for our search engine course based on the curriculum surveyed and based on the instructor's research interests. The course had several high-level learning objectives:

1. Students should have a basic understanding of how the Web is organized and its fundamental properties.
2. Students should understand how search engines collect Web content, index it, and present the most relevant results for a given query. They should also understand the technical, legal, financial, and social obstacles that make web search a very difficult problem.
3. Students should understand how to design and construct software that implements several significant Web IR concepts.
4. Students should be aware of new research directions in the field of Web IR and the new features being developed by today's commercial search engines.

To meet these learning objectives, the course covered (in order) the following topics:

- Web IR background
    1. Web IR vs. traditional IR
    2. Web search history
- Web Characterization
    1. Structure of the Web (Bow-tie, scale-free and small world networks, power-law distributions)
    2. Deep web and surface web
    3. Linkrot and web archiving
- Search engine characteristics
    1. Metasearch, vertical, and universal search engines
    2. Organic results, paid inclusion and placement
    3. Types of web search queries
    4. Commercial search engine query characteristics
    5. Evaluating search engine effectiveness (relevancy, precision, and recall)
- Web crawling
    1. Crawler architecture
    2. Politeness policies (robots.txt)
    3. Selection policies (URL characteristics, spider traps, repository freshness)
    4. URL normalization
    5. Sitemap protocol
- Indexing
    1. Boolean retrieval model
    2. Vector space model
    3. Inverted index and implementation issues
    4. Stemming and stop lists
    5. Synonyms, homographs, and misspellings
    6. Term frequency and inverted document frequency
- Ranking
    1. Link analysis algorithms (HITS and PageRank)
    2. Rank fusion algorithms (Borda and Condorcet count)
    3. Eye tracking studies
- Other
    1. Web spam and adversarial IR
    2. Search engine optimization (SEO)
    3. Detecting near-duplicate pages
    4. Personalized search

There were a number of other topics that we would like to introduce into our course, time permitting, in later offerings. These include: text mining (document classification, clustering, etc.), search interfaces, Semantic Web, latent semantic indexing, collaborative filtering, query log analysis, distributed computing issues (Google File System, Hadoop), web agents, and machine learning.

One of our CS department alumni who is now a developer for a major search engine company looked over our curriculum and had few suggestions for improving it. This curriculum is representative of other Web IR courses described in the literature [6, 20].

3. TEXTBOOKS

Many of the courses listed in Table 1 required one or more of the following text books (ranked by popularity):

1. *Introduction to Information Retrieval* by Manning, Raghavan, and Schütze (2008) [17]

2. *Modern Information Retrieval* by Baeza-Yates and Ribeiro-Neto (1999) [1]
3. *Mining the Web: Discovering Knowledge from Hypertext Data* by Chakrabarti (2003) [7]

An early edition of the text by Manning et al. [17] was made freely available on the Web, and that could account for some of its popularity. A number of other texts were also listed as recommended texts but not primary texts (e.g., [14, 12, 24]). Most instructors supplemented class readings or used exclusively the research papers that originated many Web IR topics (e.g., shingling [5], PageRank [22], HITS [15], and the bow-tie structure of the Web [4]). As Mizzaro [20] points out, these papers are usually easy for students to read and understand.

We were surprised that none of these courses used the text *An Introduction to Search Engines and Web Navigation* by Levene (2005) [16]. This text provides a good overview of many topics mentioned in the curriculum list, contains complete references to the many research papers cited in each chapter, and uses language appropriate to an undergraduate audience. Levene's book is currently out of print which could account for its lack of adoption.

We used Levene's book as our primary text (students had no problems finding used copies online). The instructor would occasionally require other readings that were found online about a given topic (Wikipedia provided a good starting point for many topics). We pointed students to many of the classic research papers mentioned previously but did not make them required reading.

A book just released in 2009 by Croft, Metzler, and Strohman entitled *Information Retrieval in Practice* [9] was written specifically to an undergraduate CS audience. It presents pseudocode for implementing a number of Web IR concepts and contains a number of exercises at the end of each chapter that use Galago [11], an open source search engine written by the book authors in Java. We may use this text in a future offering of our Web IR course.

4. HOMEWORK AND EXAMS

A number of homework assignments were given throughout the semester that would reinforce understanding of the day's subject material. Many of these exercises were assigned in the sampled courses or appeared in various forms in the books discussed in the previous section. Two exams and a final comprehensive exam assessed the students' understanding of the material; they used many questions similar in nature to the homework assignments. A brief summary of several homework assignments follows:

1. Experiment with a commercial search engine, use various boolean queries and special operators, and compare the differences in how items are ranked.
2. Calculate the precision and recall for several queries. Calculate the P@10 for queries on Google, Live Search, and Yahoo.
3. Create a term-document incidence matrix and inverted index for the given document corpus, and determine which documents are returned by the given boolean queries.
4. Calculate the TF-IDF scores for the documents returned by Google for the given queries.
5. Calculate the PageRank and hub and authority scores for the given Web graph after one iteration.
6. Calculate the cosine similarity between the two given documents and the Jaccard coefficient using shingles of length n.

5. CLASS PROJECTS

The programming projects used by the sampled courses in Table 1 vary greatly. Some courses require the students to build a fully-functional search engine as suggested in [6, 8], and other courses use independent projects that implement a particular concept. Sometimes the students are to write all their code from the ground-up, sometimes instructors provide some code that must be modified or enhanced, and other instructors encourage students to find freely available code on the Web to implement their projects. Most instructors assigned projects to be completed in small groups using popular programming languages like Perl and Java.

For our search engine course, we devised a number of small individual projects and some larger ones to be completed individually or in teams of two. Although we teach our CS 1/2 courses in C++, we required the projects to be coded in Java, thus giving students exposure to a new language. Some in-class time was allocated to teach Java and servlet basics, but the students were mainly left to learn the nuances of the language on their own.

5.1 Using Search Engine APIs

We initially required our students to create a search engine using the freely available web search APIs by Yahoo. (Google and Microsoft have similar APIs [18].) The Yahoo BOSS API [27] is REST-based and allows simple HTTP requests to be made which return back an XML-formatted set of search results. This relatively small assignment gave students experience in using Java servlets to create a fully functional search engine.

Our students later modified their search engine to create a "universal" search engine, incorporating news and image results along with regular web page results. This assignment made our students more aware of current efforts to enhance the search experience.

5.2 Search Engine from the Ground-up

The first time we offered our search engine course, we required our students to write nearly all of the code to implement a crawler, indexer, and retriever with a web interface. Each of these large project built on the previous project which required the students to re-use code for each new project. The only code given to them by the instructor was a simple web crawler which had to be greatly enhanced. A brief description of each project follows:

1. **Crawler** – Enhance the given crawler to obey robots.txt, limit crawls to a given depth, normalize URLs, and store pages in a local repository. The crawler should replace previously crawled content that resides at the same normalized URL.
2. **Indexer** – Create a program which will create an inverted index on the crawled corpus using TF/IDF and a weighing criteria based on URL, title, and metatags. It uses smart parsing of HTML, stemming, and removal of stop words.
3. **Retriever** – Create a program that can return the first 10 results for a Boolean query executed on the inverted index. Create a web interface for the retriever

which shows a Google-style results page. Extra credit is available for implementing phrase search.

Each project was similar in difficulty and consisted of several hundred lines of code. When the final project was completed, our students had a fully functional search engine which could crawl, index, and search a sizeable web corpus. While all the students were successful in completing at least a somewhat functional search engine, some of the implementation details regarding efficiency became very pronounced as some search engines could retrieve a document significantly faster than other students' implementations.

5.3 Modify an Open Source Search Engine

The second time we offered our search engine course, we decided to approach the search engine projects from the opposite direction. Rather than have the students create a search engine from scratch, we had them take an already existing open source search engine and make some enhancements. We envisioned several goals for our students:

1. Gain experience working on "real" software that is currently being used by many individuals and companies.
2. Observe how many professional software developers write code and how well/poorly they document their code.
3. Gain experience learning to understand what someone else's code is doing.
4. Learn about open source development, including bug tracking, making enhancement requests, version control systems, and code submission.
5. Make a significant contribution to an open source project.

Several of the surveyed courses used open source software, but we were unaware of any course that required their students to make a significant contribution to the software. In a personal correspondence with Bruce Croft, his students have made some contributions to Galago in the past.

We examined a number of open source search engines and finally settled on Nutch, an Apache project built on top of Lucene, a popular IR system. Nutch has a very active developer base and is used by a number of organizations. It is written in Java which, as explained earlier, allowed our students to be exposed to a new language with which they were not yet comfortable. Nutch includes a configurable crawler which can handle multiple content types and an indexer and retriever (which uses Lucene). Nutch uses Java servlets to present a web interface that can return results formatted in an aesthetically pleasing format. Nutch also uses Hadoop [3] and can therefore run efficiently on a distributed system.

Our students were first required to give a presentation on how to become a Nutch developer. This was a team assignment which required a lot of independent research. Some required components of the presentation included detailed steps on how to submit a bug fix or new extension to Nutch (including how JIRA works), how the various main classes of Nutch work together, and how to run JUnit tests for the classes in Eclipse (a popular Java IDE). The students were also to join the user and developer mailing lists and start monitoring the messages distributed daily.

After coming up-to-speed on Nutch, a few small projects and one major project were assigned:

1. **Crawler** – Learn how to run Nutch in Eclipse, and modify Nutch so it will output to a file all the URLs it successfully crawled.
2. **NutchBean** – Learn how NutchBean (the class responsible for querying the crawled corpus) works. Add some command-line parameters so NutchBean can search a user-supplied crawl collection.
3. **Site Query** – Modify Nutch's "site:" query operator to return all results from the given website even if no query term is provided.
4. **Sitemap Support** – Satisfy the outstanding Nutch enhancement request to support the Sitemap Protocol [26], a URL-discovery protocol supported by all the major search engines.

The first three projects required a great amount of code inspection, but only 10-20 lines of code were needed to complete the project requirements. The final project, adding Sitemap support to Nutch, required several hundred lines of code including vigorous JUnit tests to ensure the code was working properly. The final project was released open source as the Java Sitemap Parser [13] on Sourceforge.net, but time did not permit integration with Nutch.

6. DISCUSSION

Both the 2008 and 2009 search engine course offerings covered the same core curriculum given in Section 2, but they both used very different programming projects as outlined in Sections 5.2 and 5.3. The exams given in both offerings covered the same topics and were void of any programming-related problems. The exam averages were nearly the same for both offerings (83% in 2008, 82% in 2009), so choice of projects did not seem to have any impact in learning the overall concepts. The class sizes were too small, however (eight in 2008, three in 2009), to show statistically significant findings.

The instructor asked the students' opinions of the assignments given in both offerings, and several "grass is greener" remarks were made by students in both classes. The students that built the search engine from the ground-up felt they really knew the inner details of how a search engine worked, but all the code they wrote would likely never be used again outside of class. The Nutch students appreciated working on a real-world project, but they were not as aware of the implementation particulars of building a crawler, indexer, or retriever.

The Nutch students often expressed being overwhelmed by the complexity of the Nutch project. The instructor humorously referred to this as the "Nutch burn" since Nutch was relatively new to him as well. There was a large learning curve to getting Nutch properly configured and running, much less understanding its underlying code base which often contained poor documentation. One entire class period (75 minutes) was spent entirely on showing the students how to run Nutch in Eclipse and resulted in the instructor creating a lengthy wiki article on the topic [25]. The students' lack of Java proficiency also was problematic; much of the code used advanced programming concepts which even seasoned programmers might be slow to understand completely.

Overall, the Nutch-based course accomplished all the goals listed in Section 5.3, but it fell short in instilling an interest in Nutch that extended beyond the classroom. In [23], students showed a desire to continue working with the open source projects they had used in class assignments after the course had ended. None of our students expressed any desire to ever use or contribute to Nutch again. Most of our students still felt overwhelmed with Nutch's complexity, even after completing the projects.

Several lessons were learned from teaching this course twice:

1. Too much class time was spent teaching Java instead of Web IR topics. Students would have been able to complete the assigned projects more successfully and with less effort if they had entered the course with more Java programming experience. Therefore, future offerings of this course will require students to complete the department's OOP course that introduces Java.
2. The projects using Yahoo's BOSS API were excellent starting points and provided a gentle introduction into programming Java servlets. Students were able to build useful search engines with little effort and could play with how the search results were presented.
3. From a learning perspective, neither of the project approaches (search engine from scratch or modifying an open source search engine) is clearly better than the other. While the Nutch group learned more about open source software development, the other group had a better understanding of the programming details involved in building a search engine from the ground-up. Students from both groups learned the course subject material equally as well and satisfied the course's learning objectives.
4. From a teaching perspective, the instructor found it significantly more difficult to create class projects based on open source software. Most of this difficulty can be attributed to the very steep learning curve of the open source project which required the instructor to invest a significant amount of time becoming familiar with the code base. Students needed some hand-holding to gain a similar understanding of the code. Now that the instructor is more familiar with Nutch, it would be easier to reuse it in a future offering of the course. However, time must be exerted to keep up with changes in the continuously shifting code base.

We believe that in an ideal course students would create their own search engine and later use and modify an open source engine. From our experience, this is probably more than an undergraduate could accomplish in one semester's time. However, if a less demanding open source project were used (e.g., Galago), maybe a small project could be completed at the end of the semester.

7. CONCLUSIONS

We have described the process by which we developed a curriculum for an undergraduate course on Web IR. The course has used ground-up projects to build a search engine from scratch and projects that involve modifying an open source search engine, and we have shared some of the benefits and problems with both of these approaches.

We are planning to offer the search engine course again in the spring of 2011. We will likely use another open source search engine like Galago in this offering. We anticipate this course will continue to grow in popularity as opportunities in the field of web search continue to expand.

8. REFERENCES

[1] R. Baeza-Yates and B. Ribeiro-Neto. *Modern Information Retrieval*. Addison Wesley, 1st edition, May 1999.

[2] T. Berners-Lee, W. Hall, J. Hendler, N. Shadbolt, and D. J. Weitzner. Creating a science of the web. *Science*, 313(5788):769–771, August 2006.

[3] D. Borthakur. The hadoop distributed file system: Architecture and design. 2007. `http://projects.apache.org/projects/hadoop.html`.

[4] A. Broder, R. Kumar, F. Maghoul, P. Raghavan, S. Rajagopalan, R. Stata, A. Tomkins, and J. Wiener. Graph structure in the web. *Computer Networks*, 33(1-6):309–320, 2000.

[5] A. Z. Broder, S. C. Glassman, M. S. Manasse, and G. Zweig. Syntactic clustering of the Web. *Computer Networks & ISDN Systems*, 29(8-13):1157–1166, 1997.

[6] F. Cacheda, D. Fernández, and R. López. Experiences on a practical course of web information retrieval: Developing a search engine. In *Proceedings of the Second International Workshop on Teaching and Learning of Information Retrieval (TLIR 2008)*, 2008.

[7] S. Chakrabarti. *Mining the Web: Discovering Knowledge from Hypertext Data*. Morgan Kaufmann, 1st edition, October 2002.

[8] M. Chau, Z. Huang, and H. Chen. Teaching key topics in computer science and information systems through a web search engine project. *AMC Journal of Educational Resources in Computing*, 3(3), 2003.

[9] B. Croft, D. Metzler, and T. Strohman. *Search Engines: Information Retrieval in Practice*. Addison Wesley, 1 edition, February 2009.

[10] J. Fernández-Luna, J. Huete, A. MacFarlane, and E. Efthimiadis. Teaching and learning in information retrieval. *Information Retrieval*, 12(2):201–226, April 2009.

[11] Galago. `http://www.galagosearch.org/`.

[12] J. Han, M. Kamber, and J. Pei. *Data Mining: Concepts and Techniques*. Morgan Kaufmann, 2nd edition, 2005.

[13] Java Sitemap Parser. `http://sourceforge.net/projects/sitemap-parser/`.

[14] K. S. Jones and P. Willett, editors. *Readings in Information Retrieval*. Morgan Kaufmann, 1 edition, July 1997.

[15] J. M. Kleinberg. Authoritative sources in a hyperlinked environment. *Journal of the ACM*, 46(5):604–632, 1999.

[16] M. Levene. *An Introduction to Search Engines and Web Navigation*. Addison Wesley Publishing Company, November 2005.

[17] C. D. Manning, P. Raghavan, and H. Schütze. *Introduction to Information Retrieval*. Cambridge University Press, 1 edition, July 2008.

[18] F. McCown and M. L. Nelson. Agreeing to disagree: Search engines and their public interfaces. In *Proceedings of JCDL '07*, pages 309–318, June 2007.

[19] F. McCown, J. A. Smith, M. L. Nelson, and J. Bollen. Lazy preservation: Reconstructing websites by crawling the crawlers. In *Proceedings of WIDM '06*, pages 67–74, 2006.

[20] S. Mizzaro. Teaching of web information retrieval: Web first or IR first? In *Proceedings of the First International Workshop on Teaching and Learning of Information Retrieval (TLIR 2007)*, 2007.

[21] Nutch. `http://lucene.apache.org/nutch/`.

[22] L. Page, S. Brin, R. Motwani, and T. Winograd. The PageRank citation ranking: Bringing order to the Web. Technical report, 1998.

[23] M. Pedroni, T. Bay, M. Oriol, and A. Pedroni. Open source projects in programming courses. *SIGCSE Bulletin*, 39(1):454–458, 2007.

[24] C. J. V. Rijsbergen. *Information Retrieval*. Butterworth-Heineman, 2 edition, March 1979.

[25] Run Nutch in Eclipse. `http://wiki.apache.org/nutch/RunNutchInEclipse1.0`.

[26] Sitemap Protocol. `http://www.sitemaps.org/protocol.php`.

[27] Yahoo! Search BOSS. `http://developer.yahoo.com/search/boss/`.

Electronic Commerce Virtual Laboratory

Joel Coffman
Department of Computer Science
University of Virginia
Charlottesville, VA 22904
jcoffman@cs.virginia.edu

Alfred C. Weaver
Department of Computer Science
University of Virginia
Charlottesville, VA 22904
weaver@virginia.edu

ABSTRACT

Website security is essential for successful e-commerce ventures, but the vital "how-to" components of security are often lacking in academic courses. This paper describes our attempt to instill an awareness of security concerns and techniques by having the students develop an Artist eXchange website, a social networking site that permits the posting and sharing of pictures, music, and text, including an end-user rating system. The six-homework set progresses through HTML, JavaScript, PHP, MySQL, file uploads, and security testing. An innovative feature is that each assignment is evaluated via automated testing, which guides the student toward detecting and correcting mistakes, especially with regard to common attack vectors.

Categories and Subject Descriptors

K.3.2 [**Computers and Education**]: Computer and Information Science Education—*Computer science education, Curriculum*

General Terms

Design, Security

Keywords

Electronic commerce, software laboratory, virtual labs, hands-on programming, guided instruction, evaluation

1. INTRODUCTION

Successful e-commerce depends upon many elements, not the least of which is well-trained computer scientists to design, maintain, repair, and innovate e-commerce technology. Over the past four years, we developed materials to support the education of computer science students who are prepared to work on the components of e-commerce stores. What we learned from that project—to be discussed later—points in the direction of a significant need for expanded education focused on the security of e-commerce systems.

SIGCSE'10, March 10–13, 2010, Milwaukee, Wisconsin, USA.

The need for a focus on security in e-commerce education is consistent with a broader trend in computing. Security has been identified as a grand challenge in the field. At the CRA "Conference on Grand Research Challenges in Computer Science and Engineering" (23–26 June 2002), one of the five grand challenges selected was "Systems You Can Count On." Quoting from the conference presentation on that topic [1]:

> Today, information technology is *the weakest link* in many of our most critical applications and services. Digital computing and communications increasingly pervade our lives, our economy, and our nation's critical infrastructure. In many applications this technology simply can't be trusted; it creates problems that range from chronic aggravation to unacceptable vulnerability.

In his keynote address at ACM SIGCSE in March 2004 entitled "What is Information Security?" [5], Professor Eugene Spafford from Purdue University identified information security as one of society's grand challenge problems for the next decade. Along with security, a pervading theme in these discussions has been the need to educate our students about their ethical responsibilities to themselves, their employers, and society at large. There is simply no doubt that security is a crucial topic that must be taught as part of the computing discipline in general and in the context of e-commerce in particular.

1.1 Existing Course Materials

In keeping with the work of Weaver [9, 8, 10], we adopted a software laboratory to support a computer science course on e-commerce technologies. Core material is first presented in lecture and then immediately reinforced with lab exercises. In an initial course offering, all students found physical labs helpful, but the overwhelming majority (87%) disliked the fixed lab times, preferring instead to do the work on their own schedule. These virtual labs, which may be completed at the student's own pace, center around ten web technologies—including HTML, JavaScript, PHP, ASP, and Flash—that students peruse based on their personal experience. Students who feel comfortable with the material may skip immediately to the intermediate or advanced exercises on each topic. Due to the virtual labs being viewed as a resource rather than a requirement, none of these exercises are graded; instead, a series of homework assignments and a course project are responsible for integrating the disparate concepts into a functional e-commerce website.

Six assignments compose the homework portion of the class, and these assignments are primarily responsible for demonstrating student mastery of material presented in the course lectures and virtual labs. These homeworks typically span multiple weeks, and we allow them to be completed either by individuals or by teams of two. Course feedback strongly confirmed that students prefer a series of integrated assignments that work toward a complete e-commerce site rather than independent exercises completed in isolation. In addition to the homework assignments, the course project allows students to demonstrate their understanding of the underlying concepts. Several of these course projects have transitioned into successful e-businesses.

Nevertheless, we have discovered a consistent shortcoming in the area of security. Even when specifically including security topics in lectures, we find that students fail to incorporate this material in their course projects. Students neither apply coding techniques that prevent common attacks nor use the security tools that are provided as part of our computing infrastructure.

In regards to the first flaw, SQL injection is one of the most common attack vectors across all software systems accounting for 14% of flaws targeted by attackers in 2006 [3]. While class lectures have covered this attack vector even to the depth of a live demonstration of an SQL injection attack against a website mockup, students still frequently omit sanitizing user input. This trend suggests that lectures alone fail to provide sufficient motivation for security. We believe that the homework assignments themselves should provide students with a hands-on learning experience so they fully understand the dangers of lax security.

Beyond this first deficiency, we have found that students do not apply the provided resources for securing their websites. Our classroom setting provides a common (*NIX) web server cluster for students. Because the web servers are a shared resource, the default permissions often provide a means for discovering private information, e.g., database passwords. Students routinely fail to secure their web directories and files so that they are only accessible to themselves and the web server and not all other system users. The suPHP extension,[1] which allows PHP scripts to be read and to be executed only by their owners, is installed on the web server, but students do not take advantage of this ability. It is not uncommon to discover private information simply by reading the PHP source code from an interactive shell.

In part, student failures may only be indicative of the abstract nature of the presentation and a failure to observe these phenomena in the real world. After all, it is well-established that programmers frequently make mistakes in infrequently executed code [11]; perhaps students lack the motivation (expressed via concrete test cases) to invest their time and efforts in website security, which is frequently not considered until after a data breach. Students themselves have picked up on this deficiency (e.g., covering cryptography in the abstract) by critiquing the fact that the e-stores that are created during the existing homework assignments do not implement any security, making them inadequate training for the real world. Thus, our experience suggests security topics should be incorporated into the course not only through lectures but also though the hands-on homework assignments.

[1]http://suphp.org/

1.2 Contributions

Our goal is to integrate security into the course material so security topics are covered in lecture and homeworks in tandem. The correct time to emphasize proper coding practices is while initially learning a language, not included as an afterthought after other topics are exhausted. Common errors and mistakes should be guarded against by explicitly providing working examples (preferably with the students' own code) of possible threats and by giving students the opportunity (or requiring them) to correct any such problems that are revealed. In section 2, we present a case study that builds on the success of virtual labs to create a series of homework assignments designed to introduce web technologies and cover the various security topics associated with each. Section 3 covers our testing methodology for identifying security vulnerabilities and for requiring students to correct any errors revealed by the test suites.

2. ARTIST EXCHANGE CASE STUDY

One of the challenges presented in teaching an e-commerce course is how best to present the myriad of available web technologies. Students taking the course are typically third or fourth year undergraduates with a considerable amount of programming experience, typically in Java. Unfortunately, Java is not one of the languages traditionally associated with web programming or e-commerce software. While there are Java-based technologies for creating dynamic web pages, they do not enjoy the prominence of the Linux, Apache, MySQL, and Perl / PHP / Python (LAMP) software stack. The latter scripting languages are almost universally supported on web servers whereas the former solutions typically require special resources making them ill-suited for a course designed to garner practical experience for students.

The Artist eXchange case study is patterned after wildly successful social networking sites that students are likely to use daily (e.g., Facebook or MySpace). The website provides a location for musicians to create an artist profile, uploading pictures and musical samples of their work. Users have the ability to search for artists and rate the music samples so over time each artist receives an electronic reputation for the quality of his or her music. Our reference implementation is programmed using a variety of the major web technologies (HTML, CSS, JavaScript, and PHP to name a few), but there are no requirements that mandate these technologies. We simply believe that the predominance of the LAMP software stack makes its solutions preferable as part of a general introduction to web programming.

The pedagogical goal of the Artist eXchange website is to familiarize students with languages that may not have been previously encountered, not to introduce programming. Thus, the approach taken in lab write-ups is to introduce a topic, provide a code snippet that illustrates how to use it, and ask students to demonstrate their understanding by incorporating a similar feature in a different location on the website. For example, the HTML DOM is introduced via form validation with JavaScript. Students see a code fragment that verifies that a password and password confirmation input both contain the same value and that displays an alert if the values do not match. Once the student has integrated the code fragment into his or her own website, the lab follows up with a series of additional exercises which increase in complexity. For example,

Figure 1: A screenshot of an Artist eXchange profile. The musician has uploaded a photograph and a music sample, and users may submit feedback regarding their opinion of the music.

1. Clearing the contents of the password and password confirmation input when the values do not match
2. Checking that all of the required fields have received values
3. Verifying that an email address is valid by ensuring that it conforms to a regular expression

Our intent is to provide a ladder of exercises for students to demonstrate their mastery of the material, an approach that has been well-received in the course's existing virtual labs.

The scope of the Artist eXchange website is kept intentionally small for two reasons. First, we recognize that many students may already have significant experience in web development. These students should not be overly burdened by requiring them to conform to a specification instead of learning new material. In addition, the case study itself is not the course project: the case study only serves as a means to learn popular web technologies. Students should focus their time and energy on a project that is of interest to them. Second, a minimal scope allows the Artist eXchange website itself to be modular. If additional activities are desired on any particular technology (e.g., ASP and .NET or Flash), it is trivial to add this technology to the existing site. Hence, the lab activities can adapt to student interests with whatever level of coverage is deemed appropriate by the instructor.

Because one of the major goals of the case study is web application security, the labs work toward correcting common vulnerabilities found in websites, particularly SQL injection vulnerabilities. The Artist eXchange website is constructed from a minimal code base provided to students; the skeleton code provides little beyond the names of files and directories. By constructing the website from the ground up, students have an invested interest in proper security practices. Moreover, integrating security topics in the individual lab assignments allows students to understand the "defense in depth" aspect of security.

Finally, the case study itself reflects an opinion that has been clearly expressed by students: homework assignments should not be independent throwaway exercises but should instead build upon each other. By coalescing the flexibility provided by virtual labs with the in-depth coverage demanded by existing homework assignments, we hope to combine the best aspects of each while reducing the workload on students. Moreover, we hope that modeling the case study around popular social networking sites will enable students to see the practical application and social value of the assignment. Both Teague [6] and Treu and Skinner [7] state that women in particular become more interested once they understand a project's personal or societal relevance. The Artist eXchange website also provides an ideal starting place for discussing computing ethics (simply consider that the website potentially allows users to download an artist's work gratis), which—as stated in the introduction—is itself an important part of teaching security in the classroom.

3. AUTOMATED TESTING

Accompanying the Artist eXchange website is an extensive suite of automated tests that verify that each task is completed correctly. We deem an automated testing framework essential for a number of reasons. First, it enables students to receive real-time feedback on the quality of their work. This feedback comes before any assignment is graded by the instructor, which allows students to correct errors before turning their attention to the next task. The immediate feedback is critical, for each assignment builds upon the previous one. Any errors must be corrected before moving on to the next task. Second, as security topics are introduced, it is essential that the existing services provided by the website not be impacted. A student could easily make a site resilient to SQL injection attacks by removing all database-related code. This "solution" clearly contradicts the goal of the exercise and is expressly guarded against by the myriad of functionality tests. Regression testing also gives students confidence that the modifications required by the lab exercises are completed correctly. Finally, today's websites are extraordinarily difficult to test by hand. Web applications combine client-side and server-side scripting and checking one frequently involves disabling the other, a process impractical when grading between 50 and 100 individual assignments. Fortunately, there are frameworks that allow both to be verified in an automated fashion.

The TestNG framework [2] was chosen for constructing the Artist eXchange test suites for two major reasons. First, TestNG is not a simple unit-testing framework—it is designed to cover all categories of tests, including unit, functional, and integration testing. Because most of the development work that would traditionally be covered by unit testing is included in server-side scripts, the test suites cannot test this functionality directly. Instead, most test cases cover an entire script (e.g., the content of a page or authorization via the websites login forms), which hampers the use of traditional unit-testing frameworks. Second, TestNG supports the notion of test dependencies, which are pervasive in web application tests. Most of the test cases depend on the successful completion of other tests. For example, if the login form prompts for an email address and password instead of a username and password, none of the tests that depend on the presence of the latter elements should be executed. TestNG's dependencies allow these complex relationships to be stated, and a failure in any dependency results in the dependent test cases being skipped instead of failed.

The test cases themselves make extensive use of the Selenium framework [4] for web application testing. Selenium allows static HTML as well as dynamic client-side and server-side scripts to be tested. Developers (students) run a local Selenium RC (remote control) server on their machine, and this server actually executes each test. The Selenium RC server enables tests to be run using a variety of browsers (e.g., Firefox, Internet Explorer, Chrome, Safari, and Opera), which gives the tests additional flexibility. Selenium RC discourages students from coding only to pass the test case in two ways. First, the cost for each test execution is relatively high when compared to traditional unit tests. Creating new browser sessions means that the complete test suite requires between 30 seconds and 5 minutes to complete, instead of the few seconds required in many unit testing scenarios. Second, each new browser session appears on the student's computer; the pop-ups make it difficult to run the tests mindlessly in the background. In addition, by executing each test on the student's machine, the cost of the test in terms of server resources (CPU and memory) is minimized. The cost is born almost completely by the developer.

The combination of TestNG and Selenium again facilitates the modularity goal of the case study. Should an instructor choose to add additional assignments that cover different web technologies, it is simple to incorporate additional test cases for these exercises.

Automated Testing Example

Students start by logging in to the virtual labs website, which contains a list of lab activities. A student selects a specific lab; the website then prompts for the location of the student's code that implements the lab specifications. Once this information is provided, the student may execute the lab's test cases.

The test cases for a lab are typically grouped by specification. For example, the first lab exercise includes test cases for static HTML content and client-side scripts performing form validation. Students select the test cases they wish to execute and click the start button (figure 2). The page displays the status of each test case as soon as it finishes execution. Following completion of the entire test suite (the exact test cases included in the suite are determined by the student's selection), a detailed report is generated.

Figure 3 displays an example report that is automatically created after completing a test suite. The report homepage contains a pie chart of the number of test cases passed, failed, and skipped (top of figure 3). A test case may be skipped if it requires the successful completion of another test case; when the other test case fails, it is not sensible to execute the dependent test. For example, the login test cases are divided into checking the login form's input elements and actually attempting to log into the website using existing login credentials. When the login form does not contain all of the required elements, the attempt

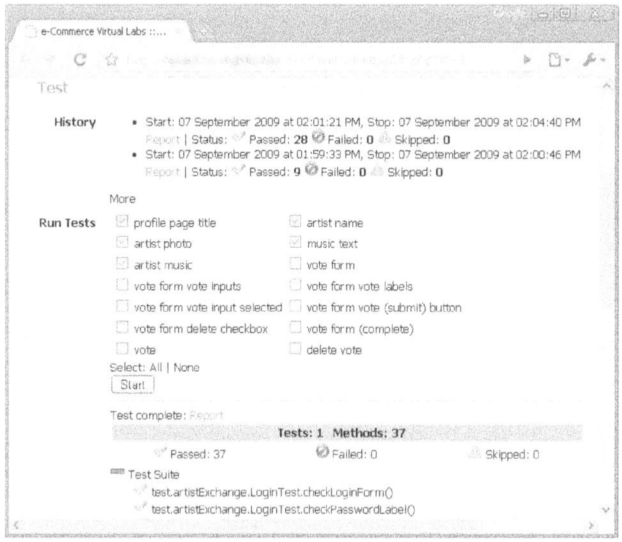

Figure 2: A screenshot of the automated test framework. Students select the test cases they wish to run and see the status of each test case when it finishes execution. A complete history of the student's tests is also provided, and the student may view a more detailed report for any of these tests (see figure 3).

to log in is skipped—if it was executed, it would fail because an element on the login page is not present. The report provides detailed error messages regarding the exact failure (bottom of figure 3). A missing username input generates the error message "Missing username input ('//form[@id='loginForm']//input['@id=usernameInput']')," which not only specifies the missing element but also identifies the XPath expression used to find the element on the page. The XPath expression is particularly helpful for identifying when an element is present but one of the attributes required by the specification (e.g., an id) is missing or incorrect.

After reading the report to identify any implementation mistakes, the student makes the necessary corrections and may execute the test suite again. We do not limit the number of times the test suite may be executed because 1) each test is actually executed on the student's machine (which minimizes server load) and 2) the repeated feedback can help students implement all of the specifications. Once all of the test cases are passed, students are assured that their implementation meets the requirements outlined in the lab assignment.

4. CONCLUSION

We have developed an innovative series of assignments that merge the best aspects of an existing course's virtual labs and homework exercises. The Artist eXchange case study provides an introduction to web technologies, and its automated tests allow students to view their progress toward completing lab objectives in real time. Our Fall 2009 offering of Electronic Commerce Technologies will be the first to incorporate this work. Hence, we will solicit student feedback throughout the process to gather student comments, complaints, and suggestions.

Based on previous feedback, we expect students to appre-

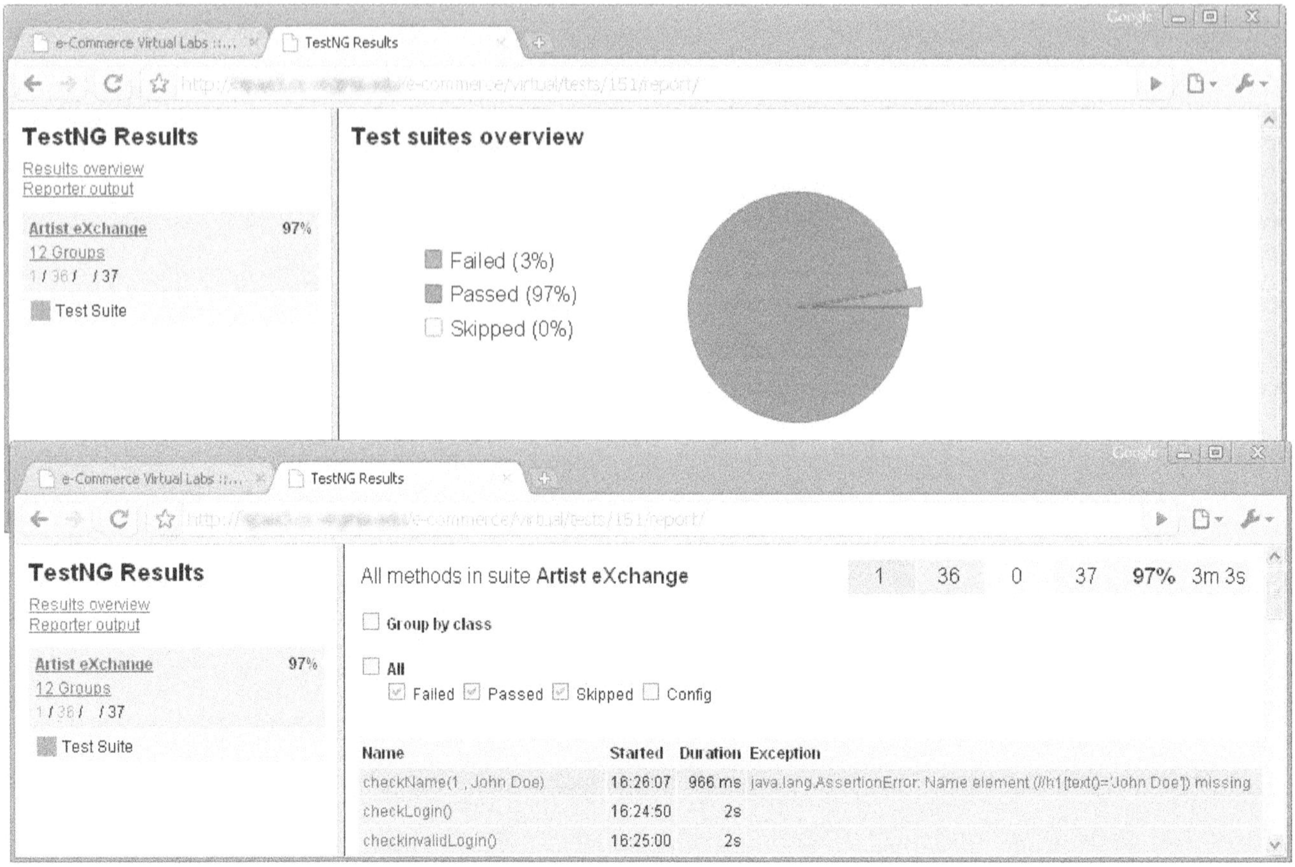

Figure 3: A detailed report generated after executing a series of test cases. The pie chart (top) presents a quick overview on the percentage of test cases passed, failed, and skipped (shown in the colors green, red, and yellow respectively). Clicking on the test provides a more detailed report (bottom) that indicates the cause of failure for each failed test case.

ciate the virtual nature of the assignments since it does not require attendance at fixed lab times. In addition, we think that students will be interested in incorporating other web technologies into the case study—e.g., Flash, ASP, or the .NET framework. The hands-on, practical nature of each assignment should make the experience more exciting to students in general and particularly to women in computing. Finally, by integrating security topics into the assignments, we hope to encourage students to consider this vital aspect of computer science and to incorporate it into their future projects.

5. ACKNOWLEDGMENTS

The authors gratefully acknowledge this project's generous support provided by the National Science Foundation's funding of proposal 0717739, "Secure eCommerce: A Modular Course Supported by Virtual Laboratories."

6. REFERENCES

[1] Systems you can count on, June 2002.
[2] C. Beust and H. Suleiman. *Next Generation Java Testing: TestNG and Advanced Concepts*. Addison-Wesley Professional, 2007.
[3] K. J. Higgins. Cross-Site Scripting: Attackers' New Favorite Flaw. *DarkReading*, September 2006. http://www.darkreading.com/story/showArticle.jhtml?articleID=209904050.
[4] A. Holmes and M. Kellogg. Automating Functional Tests Using Selenium. In *AGILE '06*, pages 270–275, July 2006.
[5] E. H. Spafford. What is Information Security?
[6] J. Teague. Women in Computing: What brings them to it, what keeps them in it? *SIGCSE Bulletin*, 34(2):147–158, June 2002.
[7] K. Treu and A. Skinner. Ten Suggestions for a Gender-Equitable CS Classroom. *SIGCSE Bulletin*, 34(2):165–167, June 2002.
[8] A. C. Weaver. A Programming Laboratory for Electronic Commerce. In *FIE '04*, volume 1, pages 25–30, October 2004.
[9] A. C. Weaver. Electronic Commerce Software Laboratory. In *SIGCSE '04*, pages 453–456, March 2004.
[10] A. C. Weaver. Experience with Teaching Electronic Commerce. In *FIE '05*, number T2H, pages 18–23, October 2005.
[11] W. Weimer and G. C. Necula. Mining Temporal Specifications for Error Detection. In *TACAS '05*, pages 461–476, April 2005.

Developing a Validated Assessment of Fundamental CS1 Concepts

Allison Elliott Tew and Mark Guzdial
School of Interactive Computing
Georgia Institute of Technology
Atlanta, GA 30332-0760
{allison, guzdial}@cc.gatech.edu

ABSTRACT

Previous studies of student programming ability have raised questions about students' ability to problem solve, read and analyze code, and understand introductory computing concepts. However, it is unclear whether these results are the product of failures of student comprehension or our inability to accurately measure their performance. We propose a method for creating a language independent CS1 assessment instrument and present the results of our analysis used to define the common conceptual content that will serve as the framework for the exam. We conclude with a discussion of future work and our progress towards developing the assessment.

Categories and Subject Descriptors

K.3.2 [**Computers and Education**]: Computer and Information Science Education—*computer science education, curriculum*

General Terms

Experimentation, measurement

Keywords

Assessment, CS1, programming, validity

1. INTRODUCTION

Measuring student learning is fundamental to any educational endeavor. Many STEM disciplines have standard validated assessment tools that allow educators and researchers to use the instruments to accurately measure student learning and evaluate curricular innovations (e.g., [10, 4, 14]). However, computer science does not have a similar set of validated assessment tools, and practitioners must devise their own instruments each time they want to investigate student learning.

SIGCSE'10, March 10–13, 2010, Milwaukee, Wisconsin, USA.

Consider the following recent studies of student programming ability with carefully designed, albeit non-validated, assessment plans:

A well-cited study by McCracken, et al asked students to write a program, in a laboratory setting, to build a simple calculator [19]. Students performed much worse than expected earning an average of only 20.8% of the possible points on the assessment. The researchers concluded that students did not possess the basic programming skills expected at the end of the introductory sequence. They reasoned that the students lacked problem solving ability and had difficulty abstracting a potential solution from the problem description.

Lister, et al explored an alternative hypothesis for the students' poor performance in the McCracken study by assessing students' code comprehension and tracing ability, claiming these were prerequisite skills to problem solving [16]. The assessment consisted of twelve multiple choice questions (MCQs) focusing on arrays and iteration. Overall, an average of 60% of the students answered the questions correctly, and the researchers concluded that students struggled with the preliminary, basic skills of reading and analyzing code.

Tew, et al investigated the impact of different CS1 courses on the conceptual knowledge students demonstrate at the end of the course [24]. Their multiple-choice question assessment found statistically significant differences in knowledge understanding after CS1 in several fundamental introductory concepts (e.g., conditional, array, sorting), with only 42.3% of the students answering questions about the introductory material correctly. They repeated their assessment at the end of a common second course and found that the differences in concept understanding were no longer distinguishable.

A common theme among these studies is that students are not performing as well as we would expect and are not demonstrating mastery of fundamental material, often considered to be some of the most basic ideas covered in the introductory curricula. Rather than providing a clear consensus or direction, these studies raise a number of questions. Do students comprehend the computing concepts we cover in our introductory courses? Are students able to demonstrate programming problem solving ability? Is code comprehension a prerequisite skill for other programming activities? Perhaps the study results are more indicative of our lack of precise measures, rather than an accurate measure of students' ability and knowledge.

Valid measures would enable us to know for sure that we are measuring the results of student learning, would enable direct comparison of pedagogical approaches, and would permit investigation of curricular innovations. Computing education and research suffer from the lack of such instruments, and we seek to develop a validated assessment for CS1 that would be widely applicable across curricular approaches.

This paper begins with a argument for the importance of valid assessment instruments in computing and then proposes a method for developing such an instrument in Section 3. Our current progress towards developing the assessment is presented in the following sections. Section 4 contains the results of our document analysis used to identify common introductory concepts, and the test specification and question development is outlined in Section 5. We conclude with a discussion of future work.

2. VALIDITY OF ASSESSMENT

Validity is a measure of "how well the test serves the purpose for which it is used" [15, p. 621]. In other words, validity is the evidence that assures us that questions about a particular concept are indeed measuring that concept. For instance, a question about arrays should require a student to have knowledge about arrays, but should not require knowledge about another concept, such as recursion. In addition, it is important that the question cannot be answered correctly without knowledge of arrays.

In general, there are two classes of evidence used to support validity claims. *Content* related evidence ensures that the assessment's content appropriately operationalizes the constructs it is intended to measure. A test designed to assess CS1 knowledge would therefore identify a number of topics to be measured, and its content validity would be determined by whether the set of topics is a reasonable operationalization of CS1.

Construct related evidence provides the second set of support for validity. A construct is "the concept or the characteristic that a test is designed to measure" [2, p. 173]. Empirical analysis of responses to individual questions provides evidence that the items in the assessment are indeed measuring the desired constructs, rather than something more or less than intended. Together, content and construct validity enable a test developer to provide evidence that the instrument is accurately measuring student knowledge and skills as intended.

Current assessment practices in computing are limited in a number of ways. Most of the measures used by researchers in our field, like the questions used in the McCracken, Lister and Tew studies mentioned previously, are not validated, so we cannot be sure that we are measuring the desired outcomes. On the other hand, the CS Advanced Placement exam has been validated but is tied to a particular programming language and is therefore not widely applicable across different approaches or courses. Similarly, Decker [5] developed an assessment for the introductory sequence of programming courses, also tied specifically to the Java programming language. The instrument was developed and tested at a single institution and therefore its validity claims cannot be generalized beyond that context. Other validated tests in our field are end of program assessments (e.g., GRE Subject Test, Major Field Test) and have psychometric or predictive aims that do not focus on assessing learning.

Building upon the success of concept inventories in physics and other STEM fields, Zilles, et al have begun development on a set of inventories for computing [8]. They assembled a group of experts and are using the Delphi process to identify sets of difficult and important concepts to develop assessments in three areas: discrete math, logic design, and programming. However unlike natural sciences, computer science knowledge has no real world analog, and it remains an open research question as to whether a set of common misconceptions, upon which concept inventories are built, can be identified for computing.

Our work differs from these efforts in that we aim to create a rigorously validated exam that could be widely adopted and used in any introductory CS course. Our goal is to create an exam to measure understanding of fundamental computing concepts, independent of programming language, that would not be overly biased by any particular pedagogical paradigm.

3. METHOD FOR DEVELOPING A VALIDATED CS1 ASSESSMENT

To build our assessment instrument we are adapting the standard educational test development guidelines [2]. In order to achieve language independence, we have augmented these procedures with an additional step. The steps in the resulting process are outlined below:

1. Define Conceptual Content
2. Expert Review of Test Specification
3. Build Test Bank of Questions
4. Verify Language Independence
5. Pilot Questions
6. Establish Validity
7. Establish Reliability

The first step in test development is to establish the purpose and definition of the test—what is to be measured and what the scores mean. The test specification includes the definition of the conceptual content, or constructs, that are to be measured, the format of the questions, and the scoring procedures. The test specification should be reviewed by a panel of experts to provide content validity evidence and ensure that all constructs are adequately represented and extraneous constructs are not included.

After the test specification has been developed and verified, a test bank of questions should be developed to cover all constructs identified in the specification. To achieve language independence for a CS1 exam, we utilize a verbose psuedocode as the exam programming language. Piloting of the questions in both pseudocode and the language of instruction, for example Java or Python, then takes place. This testing is required to ensure students are able to appropriately transfer understanding from their programming language of instruction to pseudocode. Pilot tests also examine the suitability of the questions, allowing necessary revisions to be made prior to the selection of the final candidate questions.

The last stages of test development are empirical studies of individual responses to establish validity and reliability. Validity testing ensures that the test is measuring the intended constructs, and reliability testing verifies that the results are consistent over repeated tests, and thus are dependable.

The following sections of the paper present our results to date. We have completed work defining the conceptual content of the assessment and have built the test bank of questions.

4. DEFINING THE CONTENT

Given our goal of developing a widely applicable CS1 assessment, our strategy for defining content was to identify concepts that a wide variety of introductory courses and approaches had in common. We chose textbooks as the external artifact representing the content of a course because other measures such as course syllabi or assignments are not feasible to analyze on a large scale. We began by conducting a document analysis of the table of contents of the two most widely adopted CS1 textbooks from each of the major publishers of computing textbooks (Addison Wesley, Thomson/Course Technology, Franklin Beedle & Associates, McGraw Hill, Prentice Hall, Wiley & Sons)—12 books in total [3, 6, 11, 12, 13, 17, 18, 20, 22, 23, 25, 26].

Topics listed in the table of contents were aggregated into a list, noting which concepts were covered by which texts. The goal of this bottom-up approach was to identify the set of topics most commonly covered in CS1 courses, as specified by textbooks faculty chose to adopt. However with the increasing breadth in introductory textbooks, the topic list quickly became unwieldy with over 400 concepts, ranging from low level concepts such as byte code and computer architecture to advanced topics traditionally covered later in the curriculum (e.g., relational databases and multi-threaded processes).

We used the framework of the Computer Science volume of Computing Curricula 2001 [1] to revise our initial list of topics. CC2001 provides guidelines for the conceptual content to be covered in the introductory year sequence of computing courses. By providing a variety of models and pedagogical approaches to achieve these goals, the guidelines do not designate any concepts specific to the first or second CS course. Although a list of CS1 topics is not specified, the framework did enable revisions by providing a high level organization for the concepts identified in the first phase of analysis. We chose to eliminate any concepts outside of the scope of the introductory sequence. We further narrowed the intended scope of our assessment by concentrating on the identified concepts that were in the programming fundamentals (PF1, PF3, and PF4) and object-oriented programming (PL6) areas while removing categories such as discrete structures, algorithms and complexity, and software engineering.

Unfortunately, the resulting list of 188 concepts was still too large to be practical for test development. We further refined the list by analyzing the content of canonical texts representing each of the common introductory approaches (objects-first [13, 6], functional-first [7], and imperative-first [26]). A concept was included in this step of revision if it was covered by all of the texts or excluded by only one of the canonical texts. The list of fundamental computing concepts common across languages and pedagogical approaches is listed in Table 1.

The topics in Table 1 have been refined to a scope that fits within the material traditionally covered in CS1. However it is impractical to sufficiently evaluate student knowledge of each of these 29 concepts in a single test setting. We therefore performed additional analysis and synthesis with the aim of generating a small handful of constructs that were

Table 1: Common Fundamental CS1 Concepts

Concept	Lewis & Loftus	Deitel & Deitel	Felleisen et al	Zelle
Variable	x	x	x	x
Simple I/O	x	x		x
Recursion	x	x	x	x
EXPRESSIONS				
Mathematical Operators	x	x	x	x
Relational Operators	x	x	x	x
Logical Operators	x	x	x	x
Assignment	x	x	x	x
CONTROL STRUCTURES				
Selection Statement (if/else)	x	x		x
Definite Loop (for)	x	x	x	x
Indefinite Loop (while)	x	x		x
Nested Loops	x	x		x
FUNCTIONS/METHODS				
Definition	x	x	x	x
Parameters - Pass by Value	x	x	x	x
Return Values	x	x	x	x
DATA TYPES & STRUCTURES				
Primitive Data Types	x	x	x	x
Integer	x	x	x	x
Floating Point	x	x		x
Boolean	x	x	x	x
String	x	x	x	x
Array	x	x	x	x
Tree	x	x	x	
OBJECT-ORIENTED PROGRAMMING				
Object/Class	x	x	x	x
Constructor	x	x	x	x
Instance/Local Variables	x	x	x	x
Accessor Methods	x	x	x	
Mutators Methods	x	x	x	
Encapsulation	x	x	x	x
Inheritance	x	x		x
Polymorphism	x	x		x

amenable to testing. A number of basic concepts were combined into one *fundamentals* construct that includes all of the basic semantic topics (e.g., variables, assignment, mathematical expressions). The primitive data type concepts (e.g., integer, boolean) provide useful information for the kinds of data commonly available for manipulation in test questions, but we chose not to dedicate separate questions to these topics. Procedures for processing simple input and output are often very language specific, so this topic was removed over concern for generalizability across languages and paradigms. Finally, in order to avoid biasing a particular paradigm and to limit the scope of constructs to those most fundamental and widely applicable across any introductory approach, we chose to limit the object construct to the basics of class definitions and method calls. The final list of constructs which serve as the basis of the test specification are as follows:

- Fundamentals (variables, assignment, etc.)
- Logical Operators
- Selection Statement (if/else)
- Definite Loops (for)
- Indefinite Loops (while)
- Arrays
- Function/method parameters
- Function/method return values
- Recursion
- Object-oriented Basics (class definition, method calls)

5. TEST SPECIFICATION AND QUESTION DEVELOPMENT

A test specification is a detailed description of the instrument that specifies the percentage of questions dedicated to each construct, the question format, and the scoring procedures [2]. We have chosen to weight each construct equally with 10% of the questions devoted to each topic and have elected to use a multiple-choice question format. MCQs, when constructed carefully, can provide the same information about conceptual knowledge as short answer or open response questions with significant advantages in test administration and scoring [9]. We have also specified that test scores should be criterion-referenced, interpreted based on individual performance and not rated relative to the performance of peers.

A group of experts in CS education was empaneled to review our test specification. Specifically they provided feedback on the list of constructs to be tested, the standardized multiple-choice question format, and the scoring method to be used. An initial draft of sample questions was provided to help concretize the testing constructs. Based on their feedback, the operational definitions for the constructs were finalized and question development began.

In order to evaluate different kinds of conceptual understanding, three different types of questions about each construct were developed. Definitional questions explore the student's general understanding of a construct. Tracing questions examine a student's ability to predict execution of code using a particular concept (e.g. the value of a variable after loop completes execution). Code completion questions are fill-in-the blank type questions to evaluate a student's ability to write code. For each construct, we built multiple versions of each type of question for the test bank[1].

6. FUTURE WORK AND CONCLUSION

At this stage we have specified the content of our CS1 assessment and the nature of the test's format. We have also developed the bank of questions which cover the common CS1 concepts identified through the analysis of introductory texts. Our next steps in the process are to conduct pilot studies which will allow us to gather evidence for language independence and construct validity. We briefly outline the plans for these studies below.

To achieve the goal of having a language independent CS1 assessment that can be widely adopted, we have an additional burden of investigating the effect of pseudocode as the examination language. We will conduct this inquiry in two stages. The first will compare students' answers to open-ended versions of the questions written in the programming language of their CS1 instruction. Student answer patterns between classes of languages and paradigms will then be compared for similarities and differences in their responses. Common student answers, particularly the incorrect ones, suggest common errors regardless of programming language, and they will be used to generate and verify distractors (i.e., wrong answers) for the multiple-choice questions on the assessment.

The second stage in piloting our assessment will be comparing student performance on analogous versions of the assessment, one written in pseudocode and one written in their CS1 programming language. Ideally, with a brief introduction to the pseudocode, students should be able to transfer their knowledge of computing concepts to the syntax of the pseudocode and perform comparably on the two versions of the assessment.

Empirical analysis of item responses gathered during the pilot phases may suggest revisions. Final candidate questions for the instrument will be selected after any necessary revisions are made. This candidate instrument will then be deployed at multiple institutions for full-scale validity and reliability testing. Construct validity evidence will be gathered by correlating assessment scores with other measures of CS1 learning, such as final exam scores. Additional data will be collected through think aloud protocols to ensure students interpret questions as intended. Reliability of the instrument will be measured using split-half testing. The instrument will be divided into two equivalent tests, administered at 1–2 week intervals, and correlations between the two scores computed.

The method presented above outlines essential steps towards achieving the goal of producing a validated and reliable assessment instrument for introductory computing concepts. The creation of such assessment tools, similar to those available in other STEM disciplines, is an important endeavor for our developing field. As Moss, et al state "assessment practices do far more than provide information, they

[1]Unfortunately, until we have established the validity of the assessment instrument, exam questions must remain private and cannot be published. This prevents potentially biasing participants involved in the validation studies.

also shape people's understanding about what is important to learn, what learning is, and who learners are" [21, p. 111]. No one assessment could, or should, sufficiently define the scope of computing education, so partnerships with practitioners and researchers encouraging the development of new validated assessment instruments are vital for our discipline.

7. ACKNOWLEDGMENTS

This material is based upon work supported by the National Science Foundation under Grant Nos. 0512213 and 0634629. Any opinions, findings, and conclusions or recommendations expressed in this material are those of the author(s) and do not necessarily reflect the views of the National Science Foundation.

8. REFERENCES

[1] Computing curricula 2001. *Journal on Educational Resources in Computing*, 1(3es):1–240, 2001.

[2] American Educational Research Association, American Psychological Association, and National Council on Measurement in Education. *Standards for educational and psychological testing*. American Educational Research Association, Washington, DC, 1999.

[3] J. Cohoon and J. Davidson. *Java 5.0 Program Design*. McGraw Hill, Boston, MA, 2006.

[4] C. H. Crouch and E. Mazur. Peer instruction: Ten years of experience and results. *American Journal of Physics*, 69(9):970–977, September 2001.

[5] A. M. Decker. *How Students Measure Up: An Assessment Instrument for Introductory Computer Science*. PhD thesis, University at Buffalo (SUNY), Buffalo, NY, 2007.

[6] H. Deitel and P. Deitel. *C++: How to Program*. Prentice Hall, Upper Saddle River, NJ, 5th edition, 2005.

[7] M. Felleisen, R. B. Findler, M. Flatt, and S. Krishnamurthi. *How to Design Programs: An Introduction to Programming and Computing*. MIT Press, Cambridge, MA, 2001.

[8] K. Goldman, P. Gross, C. Heeren, G. Herman, L. Kaczmarczyk, M. C. Loui, and C. Zilles. Identifying important and difficult concepts in introductory computing courses using a Delphi process. In *SIGCSE '08: Proceedings of the 39th SIGCSE Technical Symposium on Computer Science Education*, pages 256–260, 2008.

[9] T. M. Haladyna. *Developing and validating multiple-choice test items*. Lawrence Erlbaum Associates, Inc., Mahwah, NJ, 3rd edition, 2004.

[10] D. Hestenes, M. Wells, and G. Swackhamer. Force concept inventory. *The Physics Teacher*, 30:141–158, March 1992.

[11] C. Horstmann. *Java Concepts*. John Wiley and Sons, Hoboken, NJ, 4th edition, 2005.

[12] C. Horstmann. *Big Java*. John Wiley and Sons, Hoboken, NJ, 2nd edition, 2006.

[13] J. Lewis and W. Loftus. *Java Software Solutions (Java 5.0 version): Foundations of Program Design*. Addison Wesley, Boston, MA, 4th edition, 2005.

[14] J. C. Libarkin and S. Anderson. Assessment of learning in entry-level geoscience courses: Results from the geoscience concept inventory. *Journal of Geoscience Education*, 53:394–401, 2005.

[15] E. F. Lindquist, editor. *Educational measurement*. American Council on Education, Washington, D.C., 1951.

[16] R. Lister, E. S. Adams, S. Fitzgerald, W. Fone, J. Hamer, M. Lindholm, R. McCartney, J. E. Moström, K. Sanders, O. Seppälä, B. Simon, and L. Thomas. A multi-national study of reading and tracing skills in novice programmers. In *ITiCSE-WGR '04: Working group reports from ITiCSE on Innovation and technology in computer science education*, pages 119–150, 2004.

[17] D. S. Malik. *C++ Programming: From Problem Analysis to Program Design*. Thompson Course Technology, Boston, MA, 2nd edition, 2004.

[18] D. S. Malik. *Java Programming: From Problem Analysis to Program Design*. Thompson Course Technology, Boston, MA, 2nd edition, 2006.

[19] M. McCracken, V. Almstrum, D. Diaz, M. Guzdial, D. Hagan, Y. B.-D. Kolikant, C. Laxer, L. Thomas, I. Utting, and T. Wilusz. A multi-national, multi-institutional study of assessment of programming skills of first-year CS students. *SIGCSE Bulletin*, 33(4):125–180, 2001.

[20] R. Mercer. *Computing Fundamentals with Java*. Franklin Beedle and Associates, Wilsonville, OR, 2002.

[21] P. A. Moss, B. J. Girard, and L. C. Haniford. Validity in Educational Assessment. *Review of Research in Education*, 30(1):109–162, 2006.

[22] W. Savitch. *Java: An Introduction to Problem Solving and Programming*. Prentice Hall, Upper Saddle River, NJ, 4th edition edition, 2005.

[23] W. Savitch. *Problem Solving with C++: The Object of Programming*. Addison Wesley, Boston, MA, 5th edition edition, 2005.

[24] A. E. Tew, W. M. McCracken, and M. Guzdial. Impact of alternative introductory courses on programming concept understanding. In *ICER '05: Proceedings of the 2005 International Workshop on Computing Education Research*, pages 25–35, 2005.

[25] C. T. Wu. *Intro to Object Oriented Programming using Java*. McGraw Hill, Boston, MA, 4th edition, 2006.

[26] J. M. Zelle. *Python Programming: An Introduction to Computer Science*. Franklin Beedle, Wilsonville, OR, 2004.

Creating the Digital Logic Concept Inventory

Geoffrey L. Herman, Michael C. Loui, and Craig Zilles

glherman,loui,zilles@illinois.edu, University of Illinois at Urbana-Champaign

ABSTRACT

A concept inventory (CI) is a standardized assessment tool that evaluates how well a student's conceptual framework matches the accepted conceptual framework of a discipline. In this paper, we present our process in creating and evaluating the alpha version of a CI to assess student understanding of digital logic. We have checked the validity and reliability of the CI through an alpha administration, follow-up interviews with students, analysis of administration results, and expert feedback. So far the feedback on the digital logic concept inventory is positive and promising.

Categories and Subject Descriptors

K.3.2 [**Computers & Education**]: Computer & Information Science Education—*Computer Science Education*

General Terms

Human Factors

Keywords

Curriculum, Concept Inventory, Assessment, Logic Design

1. INTRODUCTION AND BACKGROUND

A significant difficulty in judging the success of pedagogical interventions is the ability to directly compare performance between cohorts and institutions. Because of this difficulty, computing educators have issued a general call for the adoption of assessment tools to critically evaluate computing education research [2].

Concept inventories are standardized assessment tools that evaluate how well a student's conceptual framework matches the accepted conceptual framework of a discipline. It is critical to accurately assess conceptual understanding, so that instructors can match instruction to their students' needs. Increasing conceptual learning is important, because students who can organize facts and ideas within a consistent conceptual framework are able to learn new information quickly and are able to more easily apply what they know to new applications [3].

The potential for good assessment tools is clear from the impact of the Force Concept Inventory (FCI), a multiple-choice test in which students choose between the Newtonian conception of force and common misconceptions. The FCI demonstrated that even students who had excelled on conventional examinations failed to answer the simple, conceptual questions on the FCI correctly, and it exposed fundamental flaws in instruction [10]. The results of administrations of the FCI to thousands of students led physics instructors to develop and adopt "interactive engagement" pedagogies [6]. Due to the impact of the FCI, "concept inventory" (CI) tests are being actively developed for a number of science and engineering fields [4].

In this paper, we report the development and validation of a digital logic concept inventory (DLCI). We do not provide the whole DLCI, however. For security reasons, the DLCI is available only on paper by request to the authors. Because CIs are not yet commonly used and there are misconceptions about their use, we first define what a CI is and is not.

A CI is a short multiple-choice test that can classify the examinee as someone who thinks in accordance with accepted conceptions in a discipline or in accordance with common misconceptions [11].

A CI is a standardized test. It must meet the demands of statistical analysis and be broadly applicable to many programs. A CI covers each concept multiple times to strengthen the validity and reliability of measurement. This requirement contrasts with a typical classroom exam, which may cover each concept only once during the exam. To be considered a successful instrument, a CI must also be approved by content experts and be widely adopted.

A CI is not a comprehensive test of everything a student should know about a topic after instruction. CIs selectively test only critical concepts of a topic [11]. If students demonstrate understanding of these critical concepts, then it is reasonable to believe they satisfactorily understand all other concepts of the topic. For example, the FCI tests only a student's knowledge of force after a course in mechanics, which also covers topics such as inertia, momentum, and energy [9].

A CI may complement but not replace a final examination, because a CI is not comprehensive.

A CI is not a teacher evaluation. CIs are intended to measure the effectiveness of teaching methods independent of teacher qualifications [1, 9]. As such, a CI can stimulate the adoption of new pedagogies as it provides an objective measure to compare pedagogies.

SIGCSE'10, March 10–13, 2010, Milwaukee, Wisconsin, USA.

A CI reveals students' misconceptions. It does not evaluate their problem solving skills.

2. CONSTRUCTION OF THE DLCI

The DLCI was created by incorporating previously found digital logic misconceptions [7, 8], results from administrations of an alpha version DLCI to 203 students, and a survey of digital logic instructors [5]. The concepts tested by the DLCI were selected using instructor feedback and guidance; the distractors (wrong answers) were created from misconceptions and administration results from the DLCI.

2.1 Concept selection

We used a Delphi consensus rating of what instructors believed to be the important and difficult concepts that students should know after completing a first course in digital logic [5] to choose topics for inclusion. We chose topics that were considered to be highly important by the instructors, but we chose topics independent of the Delphi difficulty ratings in order to check whether the general perceptions of instructors matched reality for the students.

The DLCI has been administered and revised. The current version has 19 items covering topics from four main categories: number representations, combinational logic, functionality of medium-scale integration (MSI), and state and sequential logic. Some topics from the Delphi ratings were not included in the DLCI because they are design based rather than conceptual. The list below shows what concepts are tested and how many items cover each of those concepts (note: the number of items in each sub-category do not add up to the number of items for the larger categories because some items cover multiple sub-categories)

- Number representations (4)
  - Understanding the relationship between representation (pattern) and meaning (value) (3)
  - Conversions between number systems (2)
  - Overflow (1)
- Combinational logic (4)
  - Converting verbal specifications to Boolean expressions (3)
  - Incompletely specified functions (1)
- Functionality of MSI components (2)
- State and sequential logic (9)
  - Converting verbal specifications to state diagrams (2)
  - State transitions (3)
  - Timing diagrams relation state machines (3)
  - Knowing how a sequential circuit corresponds to a state diagram (4)
  - Memory organization (2)

The number of items per concept was motivated by two factors: instrument reliability and student interviews. In order to bolster the reliability of a standardized test, it is necessary for multiple items to test a single concept or ability. So while one concept may be more important than another, the importance of that topic might not correlate with the number of items addressing that concept. A second factor also determined the number of items per concept: the misconceptions found during student interviews. In the DLCI, all distractors should reflect student misconceptions discovered through interviews and early administrations of the DLCI. Items were written only if compelling misconceptions were found to create effective distractors.

The next two questions refer to a sequential circuit *T* that has 0 inputs, 3 flip-flops, and 2 outputs.

18) What is the maximum number of distinct states *T* can potentially be in over time?

a) 6 states b) 8 states c) 10 states
e) 16 states e) 32 states f) ________

19) At an instant of time, how many states is *T* in?

a) 1 state b) 2 states c) 3 states
d) 4 states e) 5 states f) ________

Figure 1: DLCI items with write-in responses

2.2 Item creation

We created the distractors for the DLCI from misconceptions found during problem solving interviews with students [7, 8]. Additional misconceptions were gathered during the alpha administration. On the alpha DLCI, students were given the opportunity to write-in their own answers if they did not like any of the pre-written answers. This option allowed us to uncover misconceptions that did not surface during the interviews. If several students provided the same write-in answer, we deemed the write-in answer to be a new misconception that needed to be investigated with later follow-up interviews. Revised versions of the DLCI include common write-in answers as standard distractors.

2.3 Example item constructions

We explain how we constructed two items of the DLCI.

Students hold multiple misconceptions about the number of possible states in a sequential circuit. Students struggle to understand what allows a circuit to have state, and which circuit components compose state. Some students believe that combinational logic has state, and other students assert that the number of inputs or outputs would affect how many states a sequential circuit might have. Finally, students know that each flip-flop in a system has a state, but they have difficulty with abstracting flip-flop states to system state: the system has only one composite state encoded by the flip-flops [8].

These misconceptions led to the creation of two items on the DLCI (see Figure 1). Item 18 tests whether students correctly understand which components compose state and whether they understand the exponential relationship between flip-flops and circuit state. Item 19 tests whether the students can abstract from individual flip-flop states to the composite circuit state as well as whether inputs and outputs are part of the state. We found that 79% of 108 students answered item 18 correctly and 62% answered item 19 correctly. The write-in response for these items revealed a misconception that had not been found during interviews as 10% of students decided to write-in the answer '0' for both items 18 and 19. Because so many students chose '0' for the answer to 18 and 19, the newest version of the item now includes "0 states" as a standard distractor. Follow-up interviews are needed to know *why* students chose '0'.

For test construction purposes, we decided that each item should have at least four choices to minimize the effect of

7) Alice and Bob have the following requirements for their sandwiches.

Alice must have a sandwich with bacon by itself.

Bob must have a sandwich that does not have both lettuce and bacon.

Which set of Boolean expressions correctly specifies all sandwiches that satisfy their individual requirements?

Use the following variables.

b = bacon; l = lettuce; t = tomato

a) $\boldsymbol{Alice} = b$ $\quad$ $\boldsymbol{Bob} = l \oplus b$

b) $\boldsymbol{Alice} = b$ $\quad$ $\boldsymbol{Bob} = \overline{l\,b}$

c) $\boldsymbol{Alice} = b\,\bar{l}\,\bar{t}$ $\quad$ $\boldsymbol{Bob} = l \oplus b$

d) $\boldsymbol{Alice} = b\,\bar{l}\,\bar{t}$ $\quad$ $\boldsymbol{Bob} = \overline{l\,b}$

Figure 2: Compound concept DLCI item

guessing, which can artificially inflate scores. This requirement was challenging because many concepts had only one misconception and hence only one possible distractor. Using the same process described previously, we created the item in figure 2. Interviews have revealed that when students were asked open-ended questions, they conflated the NAND concept and XOR concept. Students also typically omitted negated variables when translating English specifications into boolean expressions [7]. In both of these cases and many other Boolean problems, we identified only one misconception for each concept. Because we wanted most distractors to be based in real student misconceptions and because we wanted to fully assess students' understanding of Boolean algebra, we decided to combine multiple concepts into one item. While it is ideal to examine only one concept per item, we decided it was better to test multiple concepts per item to fully assess what misconceptions students hold rather than practically eliminate items on Boolean logic.

3. DLCI ADMINISTRATION

In Spring 2009, 203 students from the University of Illinois at Urbana-Champaign were given 25 minutes to complete the alpha DLCI near the end of the semester, before taking their final exams. These students were taking either CS 231 or ECE 290 (introductory digital logic courses for second year students). The CS 231 and ECE 290 students were given slightly different forms of the DLCI. The two versions differed by which experimental items we included, but 15 items were the same on both versions. Summative statistics on student performance on the DLCI can be seen in Table 1.

Because the inventory needs to be a quick assessment of conceptual knowledge, we measured how long students took to complete the DLCI. All students were able to complete the inventory in the 25 minutes allotted, and several students took less than ten minutes.

4. RELIABILITY AND VALIDITY

We checked the validity and reliability of the DLCI through several methods. All measures and data in this section are preliminary, but demonstrate the development process.

4.1 Reliability

We are estimating reliability in two ways: single administration measures and multiple administration measures.

ECE290	Metric	CS 231
111	N	92
8.3	Mean	8.2
2.4	STD DEV	2.7
8	Median	8
1	Minimum score	2
15	Maximum score	14
Normal	Distribution	Normal

Table 1: Distribution of scores on the alpha DLCI administration

To measure single administration reliability we used the Kuder-Richardson Formula 21 (KR-21). The CS 231 student administration had a KR-21 reliability rating of 0.505 and the ECE 290 student administration had a KR-21 reliability rating of 0.639. These preliminary findings indicate that the inventory has acceptable (above 0.4 is acceptable) single administration reliability after the first administration.

To estimate multiple administration reliability, we conducted follow-up interviews with 11 self-selected students two or three weeks after they took the DLCI the first time. Students retook the DLCI in an exam-like situation. After recompleting the inventory, students retook the DLCI one more time in a modified think-aloud format. We compared the students' scores on the retakes with their original scores. Only one student's scores on the first two administrations of the DLCI varied by more than one point. This student had the lowest score of all students interviewed and performed three points worse on the retake. All other students performed the same or one point better on the second administration. Some improvement on the retest is expected, because students had studied for and/or had taken their final exam between administrations. The time gap between administrations and the small number of students that we have been able to recruit to retake the DLCI prohibits any strong conclusions, but the results thus far are promising.

4.2 Validity

Reliability is a necessary (but not sufficient) condition to show that the instrument is valid. Because the preliminary estimates of reliability are positive, we also checked to see whether the instrument is an unbiased estimator of student conceptual knowledge, accurately reflects student misconceptions, and is perceived by experts to measure digital logic conceptual knowledge.

4.2.1 Bias

We checked for bias on two levels: the inventory as a whole and individual items. A 2-tailed t-test revealed that there was no significant difference ($p{=}.8$) between the performance of the CS 231 students and the ECE 290 students, and hence no evidence of bias.

To compare the performance of the different departments on individual items we used the χ^2 test. We found that CS 231 students performed significantly better ($p{=}0.001$) on only one item, which focused on student understanding of conditional logic. We hypothesize that CS 231 students performed better on this item, because they, unlike ECE 290 students, are required to take a discrete mathematics course prior to or concurrently with the digital logic

Question	a	b	c	d	e	f
1	73	45	46	20	19	
2	63	13	31	96		
3	126	46	25	5		
4	11	69	91	32		
5	29	58	92	24		
6	70	26	33	74		
7	14	15	83	91		
8	33	51	13	105		
9	19	155	4	2	18	5
10	3	47	3	45	105	
11	29	141	8	24		
12	29	146	12	16		
13	22	36	101	9	31	
14	31	16	121	5	4	22
15	3	189	8	0	0	

Table 2: Item responses from alpha DLCI (highlighted choices represent the correct answer)

course. Because the computer science students are exposed to conditional logic in multiple courses, we believe their prior knowledge improved their performance on this item. Because students performed poorly on this item, and because our follow-up interviews revealed that students chose their answers based on misconceptions, we believe that this item can be used to assess conceptual knowledge, but it may be better placed on the discrete mathematics concept inventory that is also being developed.

4.2.2 Student content validity

Because we tried to base the distractors in the DLCI on student misconceptions, one measure of validity was to check whether all or most of the distractors were chosen, and whether distractors were chosen because of misconceptions or because of ambiguity in the inventory items. In Table 2 we show that every distractor was chosen by the students except for two distractors on item 15. We also found that items 9 and 15 were answered correctly more than any other items. Both items concerned multiplexers. We suspected that these items revealed that student misconceptions were not widely held for these problems.

After conducting our follow-up interviews, we confirmed that students could accurately and quickly answer item 15 using conceptual arguments, but we learned that many students were answering item 9 correctly using "plug and chug" without understanding the fundamental concept underlying the item. We decided to alter item 9 and drop item 15 from future versions. Using a similar methodology of watching how students solved various items, we determined which other items needed to be altered or dropped.

We also checked to see if better performance on the whole DLCI correlated with better performance on individual items. We evaluated item quality by constructing item response curves (IRCs). Students were grouped into quintiles based on their DLCI total scores. Students in the first quintile had the highest scores, and students in the fifth quintile had the lowest scores. A student's quintile was taken to be the

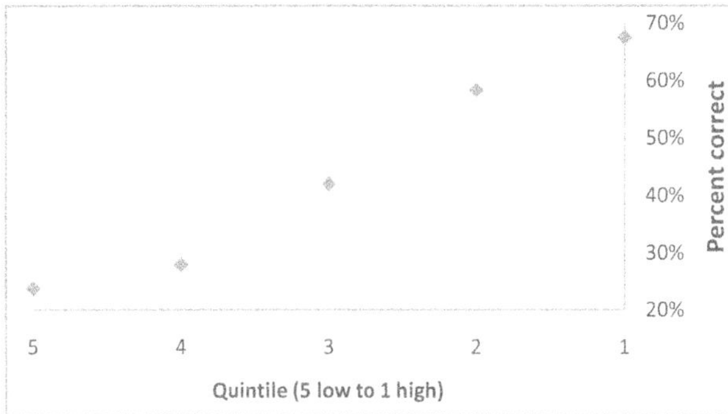

Figure 3: Item response curve of DLCI item 7

Quintile	a	b	c	d	# of students
1	0%	0%	33%	67%	43
2	0%	2%	40%	58%	48
3	13%	6%	39%	42%	31
4	9%	14%	49%	28%	43
5	16%	16%	45%	24%	38

Table 3: Student responses for DLCI item 7 by quintile (correct answer highlighted)

student's level of conceptual knowledge. The IRC for item 7 (Figure 2) is shown in Figure 3 and is typical of all items. This IRC demonstrates the desired correlation between conceptual knowledge and item performance.

In addition to examining the IRCs, we examined which distractors the different quintiles chose. Table 3 shows that students in the first quintile never chose the "bacon-by-itself" misconception distractors (a and b), but students chose these distractors with increasing frequency as the quintile increased. We see similar behavior (although less pronounced) with the "not both" misconception distractors (a and c) as students chose these distractors with increasing frequency as the quintile increased. Students with a stronger conceptual understanding of digital logic don't struggle with omitting visible negated variables, but still struggle with the translation of "not both" into logic, while weaker students struggle with both concepts. The difference in prevalence of the two misconceptions may indicate which concepts need to be stressed more in instruction. In order to accurately assess how common and robust these misconceptions are, however, we need to administer the DLCI to a few thousand students at multiple institutions.

4.2.3 Expert content validity

To check content validity, we collected feedback from 9 experts. We chose experts who had not only taught the material frequently, but who had published textbooks or rigorous pedagogical articles. We strove to find experts with a diversity in race, gender, geography, and type of institution. The experts were asked for feedback on revised items, newly proposed items, and the DLCI as a whole.

On individual items the experts were asked to (1) answer the DLCI item, (2) decide whether the item reflects core concepts that students should know after completing a first course in digital logic design, and (3) rate the quality of the item. At most one expert chose an answer that we did not expect for all but one item.

For 14 of 15 items in the DLCI, at least eight of nine experts concurred that the item reflected core concepts that students should know after a first course in digital logic. For the 15th item, seven of nine experts agreed it represented core knowledge for a first course. Negative expert comments expressed concerns that students would not know the material in the item after a first course. Based on the Delphi ratings and majority opinion of the experts, we believe that each item on the DLCI accurately reflects what students should know after a first course in digital logic.

The experts also provided feedback on the wording and quality of the items by rating each item on a scale of "do not use," "use with major changes," "use with minor changes," or "use as is." A majority of experts rated every item with "use with minor changes" or "use as is." Only three items received votes of "do not use' and none of these items received more than one vote for "do not use." The "do not use" votes were always accompanied by comments that the item would not be covered in a first course. Because of the general support of the items, we believe that each item was generally well written although we will try to further improve clarity and accuracy.

Finally, the experts were asked to provide their opinions about the DLCI as a whole. The experts were asked to (1) decide if the DLCI as a whole reflects core conceptual knowledge after a first course in digital logic, (2) comment on the topic coverage, and (3) indicate how confident they would be that a student who performed well on the DLCI would perform well in a digital logic course.

The majority of experts indicated that the DLCI reflects core conceptual knowledge. The majority also indicated that they were moderately confident or greatly confident that the DLCI would be a good predictor of student performance. Most experts noted that the DLCI is not a comprehensive assessment and that it did not test problem solving skills and design. Experts explained lowered confidence ratings because of these comments.

Our experts' comments about the DLCI all reflect concerns that the DLCI is not a typical exam. This commentary emphasizes the necessity of communicating what a CI is and is not. The DLCI does, however, assess whether students possess core conceptual knowledge. The DLCI is well positioned to be widely adopted at most institutions that teach digital logic.

5. CONCLUSIONS

Based on the expert feedback, student performance, and methods of construction, we believe that the DLCI is on its way to becoming a valid and reliable instrument that can be used at most institutions that teach digital logic. The DLCI is a short (less than 30 minutes to complete), multiple-choice instrument that has passed the initial tests for reliability and validity. Our experts' comments also indicated that the DLCI evaluates core conceptual knowledge that is taught in digital logic at most institutions. The DLCI is meeting not only the structural design qualities we desire for the instrument, but also meets the standards of being broadly applicable and informative. Once fully validated through beta testing at multiple institutions, we believe that the DLCI will be a standardized instrument that can be used to compare how different pedagogies affect conceptual learning.

In order to motivate the adoption of the DLCI, we will need to accurately communicate what a CI is and is not. Once fully validated through administration to over 3,000 students, we expect that the DLCI will show that even students who perform well on traditional digital logic tasks possess robust, commonly held misconceptions.

6. ACKNOWLEDGMENTS

We thank our experts for their multiple rounds of feedback and input. We thank Donna Brown and Maria Garzaran for graciously allowing us to administer the alpha DLCI to their classes. We also thank Joe Handzik and Tabitha Kim for their help in transcribing the interviews.

This work was supported by the National Science Foundation under grant DUE-0618589. The opinions, findings, and conclusions do not necessarily reflect the views of the National Science Foundation or the University of Illinois.

7. REFERENCES

[1] V. L. Almstrum, P. B. Henderson, V. Harvey, C. Heeren, W. Marion, C. Riedesel, L.-K. Soh, and A. E. Tew. Concept Inventories in Computer Science for the Topic Discrete Mathematics. In *ITiCSE '06: Proceedings of the 11th annual SIGCSE Conference on Innovation and Technology in Computer Science Education*, pages 163–167, Bologna, Italy, 2006. ACM press.

[2] M. Ben-Ari. The Concorde doesn't fly anymore. In *the Technical Symposium on Computer Science Education (SIGCSE), keynote address*, Feb 2005.

[3] J. D. Bransford, A. L. Brown, and R. R. Cocking. *How People Learn: Brain, Mind, Experience, and School.* National Academy Press, Washington, DC, 1999.

[4] D. Evans et al. Progress on Concept Inventory Assessment Tools. In *the Thirty-Third ASEE/IEEE Frontiers in Education*, pages T4G–1–T4G–8, Nov 2003.

[5] K. Goldman, P. Gross, C. Heeren, G. Herman, L. Kaczmarczyk, M. C. Loui, and C. Zilles. Identifying Important and Difficult Concepts in Introductory Computing Courses using a Delphi Process. In *Proceedings of the 39th annual ACM technical symposium on Computer Science Education*, pages 256–260. ACM SIGCSE, March 2008.

[6] R. Hake. Interactive-engagement vs traditional methods: A Six-thousand-student Survey of Mechanics Test Data for Introductory Physics Courses. *Am. J. Physics*, 66:64–74, 1998.

[7] G. L. Herman, L. Kaczmarczyk, M. Loui, and C. Zilles. Proof by Incomplete Enumeration and Other Logical Misconceptions. In *Proceedings of the Fourth International Computing Education Research Workshop (ICER 2008)*, Sydney, Australia, September 6-7 2008.

[8] G. L. Herman, C. Zilles, and M. C. Loui. Work in progress: Students' Misconceptions about State in Digital Systems. In *Proceedings of the Frontiers in Education Conferenc*, San Antonio, TX, October 18-21 2009.

[9] D. Hestenes, M. Wells, and G. Swackhamer. Force Concept Inventory. *The Physics Teacher*, 30:141–158, 1992.

[10] J. P. Mestre. Facts and Myths about Pedagogies of Engagement in Science Learning. *Peer Review*, 7(2):24–27, Winter 2005.

[11] G. Rowe and C. Smaill. Development of an Elecromagnetics Course Concept Inventory. In *Proceedings of the 2008 American Society for Engineering Education Annual Conference and Exposition*, pages AC 2008–242–266, 2008.

Identifying Student Misconceptions of Programming

Lisa C. Kaczmarczyk
University of California, San Diego
Sixth College, MC0054
lisak@acm.org

Elizabeth R. Petrick
University of California, San Diego
Department of History, MC0104
erpetric@ucsd.edu

J. Philip East
University of Northern Iowa
Department of Computer Science
east@cs.uni.edu

Geoffrey L. Herman
University of Illinois at Urbana-Champaign
Dept. of Electrical and Computer Engineering
glherman@illinois.edu

ABSTRACT
Computing educators are often baffled by the misconceptions that their CS1 students hold. We need to understand these misconceptions more clearly in order to help students form correct conceptions. This paper describes one stage in the development of a concept inventory for Computing Fundamentals: investigation of student misconceptions in a series of core CS1 topics previously identified as both important and difficult. Formal interviews with students revealed four distinct themes, each containing many interesting misconceptions. Three of those misconceptions are detailed in this paper: two misconceptions about memory models, and data assignment when primitives are declared. Individual misconceptions are related, but vary widely, thus providing excellent material to use in the development of the CI. In addition, CS1 instructors are provided immediate usable material for helping their students understand some difficult introductory concepts.

Categories and Subject Descriptors
K.3.2 [**Computers and Education**]: Computer and Information Science Education – *Computer science education.*

General Terms
Human Factors.

Keywords
Curriculum, Concept Inventory, Programming, Misconceptions, Pedagogy, CS1.

1. INTRODUCTION
Most Computer Science Educators will recall times when they were completely baffled by how their students expressed their understanding of a critical topic. Clearly, understanding a student's inaccurate conceptualization is a necessary prerequisite for helping them move toward an accurate conceptualization. Unfortunately we cannot read minds and we cannot speak in depth with every struggling student. Thus, it would be very useful to have a reliable method of rapidly gauging the most important areas of conceptual difficulty, and to reveal in what form these difficulties manifest themselves.

A promising assessment approach is the use of a concept inventory (CI). The original CI was developed by physics educators (Hestenes, et al.) and addressed concepts of Newtonian Force as taught in introductory physics [10]. The authors had previously discovered that many students did not develop correct conceptions of critical topics. In response, the authors produced a multiple-choice examination that could be used by all physics instructors to determine whether their students appropriately understood the concepts of Newtonian Force. Perhaps their most critical contribution has been that instructors can use the inventory results to gain "on the ground" insight into not only the concepts their students are struggling with, but what specific misconceptions they hold. This information can be immediately leveraged to adjust instruction.

Prior to the project of which this paper is part, there was some discussion and preliminary attempts to develop a CI for discrete mathematics [1]. A digital logic CI is currently being developed and is nearly complete [9]. No other CIs have been fully developed for any area of introductory computing.

The results reported here are part of a multi-institutional project to develop concept inventories for three introductory computing topics: digital logic, programming fundamentals, and discrete structures. The process is as follows: previously, Delphi studies were conducted to identify concepts considered both important and a source of difficulty for students [7]. The next step involves interviewing students who have been instructed on each topic to identify their misconceptions. Results for digital logic have been published [8]; initial findings from interviews on programming fundamentals are reported here. As will be discussed in Section 6, these data and additional data currently being collected, will be used to develop, test, and validate the CI instrument.

2. BACKGROUND
Student misconceptions of programming and closely related topics have been studied for some time. Early studies, such as Mayer's work on mental models of the actions of programming statements [16], were followed by Bayman and Mayer examining misconceptions related to individual program statements in

BASIC [2]. They found that many students had incorrect understandings or outright misconceptions of "much" of even very simple statements. Bonar and Soloway looked more generally at groups of statements to examine student understanding of programming [3]. They recognized that student "step-by-step natural language programming knowledge" interacted negatively with the programming knowledge of formal instruction. These studies touched upon misconceptions, but their primary focus was on larger mental models and theories of cognitive representation, or in some cases discoveries of misconceptions were not fully followed up pedagogically.

Spohrer and Soloway [20] examined the source of programming errors or bugs to see if they result from "misconceptions about the semantics of programming language constructs". They concluded that bugs are more likely to arise from student errors in reading and analyzing specifications and failures to see negative interactions between segments of code. Pea [18] looked beyond language constructs altogether, seeking insight into misconceptions. He found a "superbug"—students' tendency to expect computers to correctly interpret student actions and do the right thing. Confrey [5] examined both theoretical and empirical literature on misconceptions in mathematics, science, and programming and noted that the primary focus of the research was to avoid misconception development though changes in teaching. These studies focus primarily on misconceptions and present important results, however for a wider pedagogical use in CS1, they provide insufficient breadth and depth.

More recent work has often been narrowly focused. Ma, et al. [14] examined the correctness of mental models of assignment (of values and references) that are held by students at the end of a programming course and found a substantial number or erroneous models for even simple assignment. Fluery [6] and Madison and Gifford [15] focused specifically on parameters. Holland, et al. [11] presented misconceptions related to Objects and recommendations for addressing them, however their results were anecdotal and not supported with data.

A variety of other work on misconceptions exists, but from the perspective of providing data needed to develop a CI for CS1, they either replicate the problematic issues above, or else focus on other areas of program related conceptions (correctness and grading) rather than programming conceptions (e.g. Kolikant and Mussai [12] and Sanders and Thomas [19]). Thus there remains a need to investigate student misconceptions across a wide variety of CS1 topics. Conducting in-depth interviews with methodological rigor is one way to provide the broad cognitive understanding needed. In the following sections, we report a first set of results to rectify this situation.

3. INTERVIEW & ANALYSIS PROTOCOL

Eleven students took part in interviews conducted at the University of California, San Diego (UCSD) in spring 2009. Students were recruited from the undergraduate student population who were currently or recently enrolled in Computer Science or Computer Engineering introductory courses CSE8a or CSE11 (two versions of CS1). Participation was voluntary; subjects were recruited through announcements made in courses and via email to CSE lists. Students were compensated for participation in the project.

The primary purpose of the interviews was to reveal misconceptions held by students on an initial group of ten of the thirty-two concepts identified by the Delphi experts [7]. There were eighteen problems, covering the following concepts:

1. Memory Model, References, and Pointers (MMR)
2. Primitive and Reference Type Variables (PVR)
3. Control Flow (CF)
4. Iteration and Loops I (IT1)
5. Types (TYP)
6. Conditionals (COND)
7. Assignment Statements (AS)
8. Arrays I (AR1)
9. Iteration and Loops II (IT2)
10. Operator Precedence (OP)

A secondary purpose of the interviews was to validate the Delphi experts' conclusions that these concepts were indeed difficult.

The interviews were semi-structured and used a modified think-aloud protocol [4]. Choosing a language for code examples was an unavoidable necessity in spite of an overarching goal to develop as language neutral a CI as possible. We selected Java for three reasons. First, Java is currently one of the most widely used introductory programming languages. Second, our Delphi experts explicitly identified a subset of troublesome concepts as Object Oriented (OOP) based. Third, our student population had been taught in Java. It is important to note that not all concepts required that actual code be presented to students in order to reveal misconceptions. A full list of the problems is available from the authors and is expected to be published in a subsequent longer article. In addition, we will address the language dependence issue further in Sections 5 and 6.

There were multiple problems per concept, in order to guarantee that results did not depend on a single question. The majority of problems were covered in at least two distinct variations. Pilot interviews revealed that some concepts were closely related (e.g. Control Flow with other concepts). Thus, misconceptions emerged for some concepts within discussion of problems designed for another concept. Additional interviews and analysis on several of these "overlap" concepts are underway.

Each student was given a subset of the problems. Each interview lasted approximately one hour. With a few exceptions, every student was provided questions for all ten concepts. The exceptions occurred when students worked slowly and time limitations prevented full coverage. To avoid order bias, the problems were given in a semi-random order to each student. The caveat to the randomness of problem ordering is that each student was given one or two simple questions in the beginning to reduce anxiety and acclimate them to the interview process. Students were given the problems on paper, and provided scrap paper to work on if they desired. At no time did the interviewer reveal correct or expected answers to the problems. We collected audio and video recordings of the interviews, along with any written work the students produced. The audio tracks of the interview recordings were transcribed verbatim. Video was used as a back-up and as a visual resource if needed.

We analyzed transcripts and written work from ten of the interviews. Due to equipment failure, one interview was lost. The interviews were analyzed using the following steps of grounded theory and qualitative data analysis as described by Kvale [13], Strauss and Corbin [22], and Miles and Huberman [17]:

1. All of the survey responses were selected for coding in order to avoid bias in selection.
2. All of the survey responses were read and analyzed independently by three researchers: the first and second authors, and a researcher from one of the project's partner institutions (the fourth author).
    a. Each researcher developed codes, operational definitions, and themes grounded in the textual responses.
    b. The three researchers compared their coding and thematic decisions. When there were divergent findings, only those encodings were retained in which all researchers agreed. An inter-rater reliability rating of 96% was achieved.
3. Thirty-two codes with operational definitions were agreed upon. Twenty-five codes addressed the ten targeted concepts.
    a. The codes describe the misconceptions students held and were grouped according to the important and difficult concepts identified by the Delphi experts.
    b. Additional codes addressed other concepts from the full Delphi expert list have been specifically targeted in further interviews during summer and fall 2009.

4. RESULTS

Four themes emerged from the students' misconceptions (see Table 1). Themes 1 and 4 are highly language independent and cover general misunderstandings. Theme 2 involves a number of misconceptions all related to an inability to properly understand the process of while loop functioning. Though not truly language independent, this theme and its misconceptions are applicable across several commonly used contemporary and historic languages. Finally, Theme 3 is a basic lack of understanding of the most fundamental aspects of Object-Oriented Programming.

For the purpose of building a CI, misconceptions are the key data, as they are used to create authentic distracter questions on the instrument. In this paper, we focus on three of the six misconceptions within Theme 1: "Semantics to semantics," (MMR1), "Primitive no default," (PVR1) and "Uninstantiated memory allocation" (MMR4) (see Table 2). Both of the Delphi process concepts these misconceptions fall under (MMR, PVR) were highly ranked overall for importance and difficulty. Of the ten concepts addressed in this set of interviews (see Section 3), these two concepts were ranked highest by the Delphi experts for difficulty.

The first misconception, "Semantics to semantics," (MMR1) occurred when the student inappropriately assumed details about the relationship and operation of code samples, although such information was neither given nor implied. This misconception is language independent although every language will manifest the misconception differently. For example, when examining a list of Java variable definitions and declarations whose inter-relationships are unstated (see Appendix: Problem 1), Student2 explains: "And then have the names of the songs in here, which – but this would be stored in library, I'm assuming, or in the library class. I don't know how they're linked together exactly."

In another example, with a different problem (see Appendix: Problem 2b), Student3 makes incorrect assumptions about connections between variables to the extent that the student makes a mistake concerning the types of the variables. As a result, the student places Objects of different types in an array whose type matches none of them: "And so because there's two arrays, cheese and meats, uh, all those turkey and ham and roast beef are gonna be sorted into the meats array."

In a third example, Student8 completely and repeatedly ignores a variable, because it does not fit with her/his assumptions of how these variables must relate. In a lengthy discussion of the supposed relationships between the variables (see Appendix: Problem 2a), the sole reference (verbally or written) to "sauceType" was the following statement at the very start of the problem discussion: "Usually all the variables go to describing the Object, but I don't think it would describe a sauce."

It should not be surprising that students bring their own assumptions to problems. The Educational Psychology literature has solidly established this basic function of human cognition (e.g. [21]). However, we found it surprising where these assumptions led in terms of confusion between syntax and semantics. Even when an assumption based confusion led to clearly contradictory beliefs and conclusions, the students still could not recognize that their assumptions caused a problem. In one example, a student realized that the syntax did not fit his/her semantic assumptions and, instead of questioning those assumptions, he/she assumed that the syntax must be logically incorrect. Fortunately, this problematic cognitive behavior (for the purposes of learning programming) has also been discussed in the psychological literature and we should be able to draw upon that

Table 1. Themes Emerging From Student Misconceptions

T1: Students misunderstand the relationship between language elements and underlying memory usage.
T2: Students misunderstand the process of while loop operation.
T3: Students lack a basic understanding of the Object concept.
T4: Students cannot trace code linearly.

Table 2. Misconceptions About the Relationship Between Language Elements and Underlying Memory Usage

MMR1	Semantics to semantics	Student applies real-world semantic understanding to variable declarations.
MMR2	All Objects same size	Student thinks all Objects are allocated the same amount of memory regardless of definition and instantiation.
MMR3	Instantiated no memory allocation	Student thinks no memory is allocated for an instantiated Object.
MMR4	Uninstantiated memory allocation	Student thinks memory is allocated for an uninstantiated Object.
MMR5	Off by 1 array construction	Student thinks an array's construction goes from 0 to length, inclusive.
PVR1	Primitive no default	Student thinks primitive types have no default value.
PVR2	Primitives don't have memory	Student thinks primitives without a value have no memory allocated.

field's expertise and resources to customize solutions for computing education.

The second misconception, "Primitive no default," (PVR1) relates to lists of instance variables. This misconception is related to OOP and is a Java specific misconception. Student3 discusses two boolean variables without assigned values (see Appendix: Problem 2b) and states: "I don't think any value is being created for them because there's no assignment there. You know, it's just being declared as a variable." Student5 similarly discusses an integer which is not assigned a value (see Appendix: Problem 2a): "And then int is empty too and it's just creating space to later store an integer."

The third misconception, "Uninstantiated memory allocation," (MMR4) reveals itself when students think that memory is allocated for Objects which have been declared, but not instantiated. This misconception is also related to OOP. For example, Student5 explains how the computer handles memory for the uninstantiated Object "turkey" (see Appendix: Problem 2a): "it's just going to be this blank turkey because we're not setting it to be anything but we're creating like free space to the mater [*sic*] later on declare it."

In another example, involving a similar problem, Student2 discusses the memory allocated for the uninstantiated Object "artist" (see Appendix: Problem 1): "I'm thinking it goes to wherever artist is defined and looks at that class. And I feel like the class would set aside memory.

5. DISCUSSION

We found both unsurprising and surprising results in these interview data. The primary unsurprising, but welcome, result is that the misconceptions we uncovered confirmed the Delphi experts' choice of concepts as difficult for CS1 students.

Two surprising outcomes relate specifically to student misunderstandings. First, the breadth of misconceptions about memory models was unexpected. Memory models are very difficult, but we did not expect such a high number and variety of misconceptions. This finding has an important implication for pedagogy. There are likely to be a diversity of strategies to address memory model misconceptions, without any one quick or universally applicable fix. This challenge is particularly apparent regarding the misconception about students applying semantic assumptions to syntax (MMR1). It will take creative thinking by each instructor, as well as further research, in order to determine the most effective way to leverage these results.

The second surprising outcome relates to Theme 3, not otherwise discussed in this paper: a dearth of even basic conception of an Object. Some students had not formulated misconceptions about Objects, as they had no conceptions at all. During the interviews, they either froze, admitted with some embarrassment to having no idea what an Object was, even when prompted in several ways, or simply changed the subject. This extreme difficulty is being further investigated and results will be reported in a future publication. Meanwhile, one important implication of a lack of knowledge about Objects is that perhaps, within the context of particular student populations, instructors can take a step back and re-think how to introduce the concept of Objects, and focus explicitly on what they consider most critical about Objects in their particular incarnation of CS1.

6. FUTURE WORK

Our findings are representative of our participant population. However, many of the misconceptions we found are generally believed to be universal, but play out differently in different languages, and as such will need to be dealt with in the inventory. As we move forward in developing the inventory, we will further address issues of language dependence. We are currently evaluating options to address this concern. We will also need to address issues of OOP. OOP was an important category of concern to the Delphi experts, and thus must be included. However, we also want to make the inventory as flexible as possible, because at some point in time OOP may no longer be the dominant paradigm. The tension between these competing needs may be our most challenging task.

In following good grounded theory based protocols we have already used the data gathered so far to inform our next steps. First, we have completed a set of interviews conducted in Summer, 2009 that address the remaining Delphi expert concepts as well as the "overlap concepts". We also conducted interviews in the Fall, focusing on concepts which we determined needed additional investigation. Additional interviews are currently taking place at a partner institution to broaden the demographic of student subjects. Next, we will build and test the inventory. Pilot tests will take place at multiple institutions with diverse populations and multiple languages. Many of the original Delphi experts have expressed interest in taking part in initial field tests. Pilot inventory test results will provide feedback about how to improve the inventory questions so that the instrument will be useful to the broadest population and demographic possible.

7. CONCLUSION

We have presented initial results describing three important misconceptions held by CS1 students, along with four broad themes encompassing a larger group of misconceptions. The misconceptions detailed in this paper explore memory model representation and default value assignment of primitive values. These data provide immediately useful information for CS1 instructors to help them understand their students' misconceptions. Finally, these results will be merged with additional data being gathered, and used in the development and validation of a CI for Programming Fundamentals.

8. ACKNOWLEDGMENTS

This work was supported by the National Science Foundation under Grants DUE-0618589, DUE-0618598, DUE-0943318, and CAREER CCR-03047260. The opinions, findings, and conclusions do not necessarily reflect the views of the National Science Foundation or the authors' institutions.

9. APPENDIX

Problem 1. You are setting up a database of information about all the songs you own. Each song has certain information associated with it. Diagram (or use pseudo-code) how this information would be stored in memory:

```
Library library = new Library();
SongList[] songList = new SongList[3];
Genre genre;
Artist artist;
Title title;
Album album;
```

```
int trackNumber = 2;
int year = 1961;
int rating = 5;
```

Problem 2a. You are setting up a database of information about sandwich ingredients. There are a number of information items associated with your database. Diagram (or use pseudo-code) how this information would be stored in memory:

```
Cheese[] cheeses = new Cheese[4];
Meat[] meats = new Meat[2];
Turkey turkey;
Ham ham;
RoastBeef roastBeef;
boolean lettuce = true;
boolean tomato = true;
SauceType sauceType = new SauceType();
int numMeat;
int numCheese;
```

Problem 2b was identical to 2a except for the following two declarations:

```
boolean lettuce;
boolean tomato;
```

10. REFERENCES

[1] Almstrum, V. L., Henderson, P. B., Harvey, V., Heeren, C., Marion, W., Riedesel, C., Soh, L., and Tew, A. E. 2006. Concept inventories in computer science for the topic discrete mathematics. In *ACM SIGCSE Bulletin*, 38, 4 (Dec. 2006), 132-145.

[2] Bayman, P. and Mayer, R. E. 1983. A diagnosis of beginning programmers' misconceptions of BASIC programming statements. *Commun. ACM* 26, 9 (Sep. 1983), 677-679.

[3] Bonar, J. and Soloway, E. 1985. Preprogramming knowledge: a major source of misconceptions in novice programmers. *Hum.-Comput. Interact.* 1, 2 (Jun. 1985), 133-161.

[4] Bowen, C. W. 1994. Think-Aloud Methods in Chemistry Education. In *Journal of Chemical Education*. 71, 3 (Mar. 1994), 184-190.

[5] Confrey, J. 1990. A review of the research on student conceptions in mathematics, science, and programming. *Review of Research in Education*. 16, 3 (1990), 3-56.

[6] Fleury, A. E. 1991. Parameter passing: the rules the students construct. In *Proceedings of the Twenty-Second SIGCSE Technical Symposium on Computer Science Education* (San Antonio, Texas, United States, March 07 - 08, 1991).

[7] Goldman, K., Gross, P., Heeren, C., Herman, G., Kaczmarczyk, L., Loui, M. C. and Zilles, C. 2008. Identifying important and difficult concepts in introductory computing courses using a Delphi process. In *Proceedings of the Thirty-Ninth SIGCSE Technical Symposium on Computer Science Education* (Portland, OR, United States, March 12-15, 2008).

[8] Herman, G. L., Kaczmarczyk, L., Loui, M. C., and Zilles, C. 2008. Proof by incomplete enumeration and other logical misconceptions. In *Proceedings of the Fourth International Workshop on Computing Education Research* (Sydney, Australia, Sep. 06 - 07, 2008).

[9] Herman, G. L., Loui, M. C., and Zilles, C., Creating the Digital Logic Concept Inventory. In *Proceedings of the Forty-First ACM Technical Symposium on Computer Science Education*, Milwaukee, WI, March 10-13, 2010.

[10] Hestenes, D., Wells, M., and Swackhamer, G. 1992. Force concept inventory. *The Physics Teacher*, 30 (Mar. 1992), 141-158.

[11] Holland, S., Griffiths, R., and Woodman, M. 1997. Avoiding Object misconceptions. In *Proceedings of the Twenty-Eighth SIGCSE Technical Symposium on Computer Science Education* (San Jose, California, United States, February 27 - March 01, 1997).

[12] Kolikant, Y. B-D. and Mussai, M. 2008. "So my program doesn't run!" Definition, origins, and practical expressions of students' (mis)conceptions of correctness, *Computer Science Education*, 18, 2 (Jun. 2008), 135-151.

[13] Kvale, S. 1996. *Interviews: An Introduction to Qualitative Research Inquiry*. Sage Publications, Thousand Oaks, CA.

[14] Ma, L., Ferguson, J., Roper, M., and Wood, M. 2007. Investigating the viability of mental models held by novice programmers. In *Proceedings of the Thirty-Eighth SIGCSE Technical Symposium on Computer Science Education* (Covington, Kentucky, United States, March 07 - 11, 2007). SIGCSE '07.

[15] Madison, A. and Gifford, J. 2003. Modular programming: Novice misconceptions. *Journal of Research on Technology in Education*, 34, 3 (Spr. 2003), 217-229.

[16] Mayer, R. E. 1981. The Psychology of How Novices Learn Computer Programming. *ACM Comput. Surv.* 13, 1 (Mar. 1981), 121-141.

[17] Miles, M.B. and Huberman, A.M. 1994. *Qualitative Data Analysis: An Expanded Sourcebook, 2nd Edition*. Sage Publications, Thousand Oaks, CA.

[18] Pea, R. D. 1986. Language-independent conceptual "bugs" in novice programming. *Journal of Educational Computing Research*, 2, 1 (1986), 25-36.

[19] Sanders, K. and Thomas, L. 2007. Checklists for grading Object-oriented CS1 programs: concepts and misconceptions. In *Proceedings of the Twelfth Annual Conference on Innovation and Technology in Computer Science Education* (Dundee, Scotland, June 25 - 27, 2007).

[20] Spohrer, J. C. and Soloway, E. 1986. Alternatives to construct-based programming misconceptions. In *Proceedings of the SIGCHI Conference on Human Factors in Computing Systems* (Boston, MA, United States, April 13 - 17, 1986).

[21] Stanovich, K. E. 2003. The Fundamental Computational Biases of Human Cognition: Heuristics That (Sometimes) Impair Decision Making and Problem Solving. In *The Psychology of Problem Solving*, J. E. Davidson and R. J. Sternberg, Eds. Cambridge University Press, Cambridge, UK, 291-342.

[22] Strauss, A. and Corbin, J. 1998. *Basics of Qualitative Research*. Sage Publications, Thousand Oaks, CA

Social Networking: The New Computer Fluency?

Tarsem S. Purewal Jr.
Department of Computer Science and Engineering
University of Tennessee at Chattanooga
semmy-purewal@utc.edu

ABSTRACT

This paper describes a course in online social networking that is flexible enough to meet the needs of most CS0 courses. Two sections of the course were taught at the College of Charleston during the Spring 2009 semester. We describe our experiences, we outline the topics and we offer suggestions on how the topics can meet the objectives of more traditional CS0 offerings.

Categories and Subject Descriptors

K.3.2 [**COMPUTERS AND EDUCATION**]: Computer and Information Science Education

General Terms

Human Factors

Keywords

Social Networks, Computer Science Education, CS0

1. INTRODUCTION

Hooray! Shout it from the rooftops! Undergraduate enrollments in Computer Science have bottomed out, and in many instances have started to increase [21, 17]!

As we cautiously enjoy increased enrollments and a renewed interest in our field, it's important not to lose sight of two looming problems. First, the increased interest might be short-lived, particularly if we don't find ways of making the discipline more relevant to those who may have discovered it through what some of us might refer to as unconventional means – their Facebook account, for instance. Second, the news is not entirely good; the Taulbee Survey indicates that diversity in our discipline has not increased along with this recent resurgence in interest [21].

The first problem has a relatively straight-forward solution. All one has to do is find the topics that have sparked this rekindled interest and incorporate them into introductory computer science courses. In addition to engaging students, this can give them a context or framework for further studies in the discipline.

The second problem, of course, appears more challenging. It is well-known that females often have developed certain attitudes towards computer science by the time they reach college although the mechanism behind this is not completely clear. This makes it difficult to even get them through the door of any computer science class, much less a course designed around object-oriented programming. It has been argued that – again – by framing the discipline in a more relevant context might assist in drawing more diversity to the discipline [10].

In my view, one of the best current topics to provide this context in order to address both issues is online social networks. This was also advocated quite clearly in a recent paper by several faculty members from Duke University [2], where the authors argue that social networks can provide relevant context and broaden participation in computing. They give a convincing argument that this is indeed the case, and they describe the potential of such a course in very general terms. They also outline three content modules that might be used in such a course.

In this paper, I describe my implementation of a course centered around online social networks. The contribution beyond [2] is twofold. First, I explicitly describe how my course can meet traditional CS0 course objectives. Second, I outline the topics and the flow of the course in detail. Furthermore, the majority of the topics and course content that I present here are not described in [2].

This particular course has evolved over the years at the College of Charleston from a course called "Communications Technologies and the Internet." During the Spring 2009 semester, it was renamed and advertised as "Social Networking." Two sections were taught, servicing approximately 47 undergraduate students from varied majors. No prerequisites were enforced, but recommended skills included keyboarding and experience with e-mail.

2. TRADITIONAL MODELS FOR CS0

There are no explicit models for a CS0 course that are recommended or documented by the ACM/IEEE curricular guidelines [1], but these courses are offered by many Computer Science departments at institutions ranging from small liberal arts colleges to major research universities. The current objectives for such courses generally fall into three categories:

SIGCSE'10, March 10–13, 2010, Milwaukee, Wisconsin, USA.

Objective 1: A service course that teaches some practical computing knowledge and/or meets a general education requirement at the institution [6].

Objective 2: A course that improves retention and success in subsequent CS courses, particularly CS1 [7, 8].

Objective 3: A course that is designed to recruit a more diverse group of students to the major [3, 15].

Topics and course materials vary depending on the instructor and which of these objectives that the course is meeting. For example, at an institution that requires a basic computer course as part of the general education requirement, there may be some expectation that the use of a word processor, a spreadsheet, and presentation software are covered since students may be expected to use these tools in future classes. A CS0 course at this type of institution would thus be designed to meet the first objective.

In terms of the second objective, it appears that several institutions are moving towards a CS0 course that covers algorithmic thinking using tools such as Randy Pausch's Alice language[1], MIT's Scratch[2], and Processing[3]. Recent papers demonstrate some level of success using these tools as a gentler introduction to programming and show that they do meet this objective – they seem to improve student success in subsequent programming courses [8].

Topics meeting the third objective can vary substantially, but one of the major underlying themes has been to make computing fun and more relevant to a new generation of students [11]. I am aware of CS courses taught as part of a freshmen first year experience program, for example, in topics ranging from Computer Graphics in Films, Computers Music and Art, and Robotics.

These three objectives seem to encompass the general thinking when it comes to designing a CS0 course with no pre-requisites, but I'd argue that there is one more objective that should be considered in designing any course that we hope would appeal to a more general population than our usual clientele. That is the broader impact of the technical topics we are covering.

Objective 4: A course that prepares students to analyze and address the current ethical, social and legal implications of the growing ubiquity of and increased reliance on technology.

The case for a course that covers social, ethical and legal issues for computer science majors has been argued numerous times before, and now appears as part of the ACM/IEEE curricular guidelines [1]. In addition to this, however, I believe that it is also essential that courses that cover these topics be offered to a wider audience and that such courses should include faculty who understand the technology itself. In the book *Code and Other Laws of Cyberspace*, Lawrence Lessig argues that computer code can, in fact, be a social regulator for good and for bad, in the same way that government legislation can [12]. If one agrees with his arguments, then this clearly fixes this topic – at least partially – in the domain of computer science.

Furthermore, the need for a public that is well-informed in these areas is beginning to be more important now that organizations and corporations are finding ways of compromising first amendment rights on the web [4] and politicians are working to further extend intellectual property laws in ways that may impede the progress of the public arts [13]. A well-informed populace has always been one of the goals of higher education; these days being well-informed in the basics of technology is essential to the preservation of our freedom and our democracy.

In a previous paper, I've also argued that the third and fourth objective are not mutually exclusive [16].

3. MEETING THESE OBJECTIVES

During the Spring 2009 semester, I offered two sections of a course entitled 'Social Networking.' This offering subsumed a course that had traditionally been called 'Communications Technology and the Internet.' In the past, the catalog description has been:

> *An introduction to digital communications technology. Topics include networking concepts, Internet and intranet tools, protocols and security. Also included are the infrastructure and governance of the Internet, with emphasis on personal, business, social, legal and ethical implications. Recommended skills are keyboarding and experience with e-mail and web browser software.*

This description lends itself well to the study of online social networks, since every topic in the description can be discussed or described in that context. My syllabus description for this particular offering of the course reads as follows:

> *This course will examine the phenomenon of the Internet through the lens of social networking and social media. We'll primarily focus on Social Networks, including social, legal and ethical implications. Along the way we'll experiment with various social networks and social media technologies.*

After the course description was solidified, the topics flowed fairly quickly. Below I describe eight topic sections that were covered roughly in order, and also a brief description of the term project that the students were required to complete.

Overview of Online Social Networks

The core of the course was designed around online social networks, so we began by examining an article by danah boyd and Nicole Ellison that covers, in some detail, the history of online social networks, their defining characteristics, recent research and lingering questions [5]. This article laid the groundwork of the entire course for us, with the exception of some of the more technical and entrepreneurial topics.

The real beauty of this article, however, is that it illustrates that something so familiar and prevalent in a college student's life (their Facebook account) can be examined from an academic perspective. The relevance of this topic, one that students may not often associate with computer science or even technology in general, along with the

[1] `www.alice.org`
[2] `scratch.mit.edu`
[3] `processing.org`

academic tone of the article can easily assist in meeting the third objective.

Practical Uses of Web 2.0 Technologies

For the second topic, we switched from the academic to the more practical. We examined Facebook and Twitter, exploring their uses beyond simply keeping up with friends. We asked whether they could be effectively used for advertising a business or professional networking in a job search, for example. We also discussed the differences between using the technology for broadcasting versus using the technology for communication.

Next we moved on to discussing Google Docs. While not a Web 2.0 technology or website in the strictest definition, the fact that Google Docs allows students to more effectively collaborate on assignments made it a useful addition to the course. This is the same week that the first parts of the term project were assigned, so students immediately began using Google Docs to collaborate on the assignment.

This also led into a discussion of building collaborative knowledge using sites like Wikipedia. Discussions focused on the reliability of collaborative knowledge tools as references in the context of the Stephen Colbert *Wikiality* incident [20] and the widespread belief that Wikipedia should never be used as a primary source[4].

The course content in this section, particularly the use of Google Docs, can be expanded to meet the needs of courses that need to teach word processing, spreadsheet and presentation software meeting the first objective.

Mathematical Models of Social Networks

Approaching this topic from the perspective of the 'six-degrees of separation' or the 'small-world' hypothesis was described in [2]. I had two objectives in introducing this hypothesis. First, I wanted to give the students a concrete example of modeling complex phenomena using graphs, since graphs were later discussed in the context of computational thinking. Second I wanted the students to observe, differentiate and be critical of experimental evidence, mathematical evidence, and anecdotal evidence for hypotheses. In this case, the small-world hypothesis has been tested experimentally in the physical world by Stanley Milgram [14]; these experiments were later repeated in the digital world by Duncan Watts at Columbia University. Both of these experiments have shortcomings and we examined them critically [18].

Mathematically, one can argue that the six-degrees of separation hypothesis holds by making a couple of assumptions that seem rather implausible in the real world. I showed them the argument, which illustrates both trees and exponential growth, and we examined the assumptions critically. In terms of anecdotal evidence, it was fairly easy to pair up the students in the class and have them attempt to find a connection using their Facebook profiles. Several pairs of students were able to demonstrate a connection without too much work, and several others had interesting personal stories to share. We discussed whether or not it was appropriate to draw more general conclusions from anecdotal evidence such as this.

This topic can meet the second objective if the discrete mathematics is emphasized, or it can meet the third objective if the sociological and experimental aspects of the hypothesis are studied in more detail.

[4]the irony is intentional

Networks, Technology and the Cloud

Next we moved on to technology. In particular, we discussed the TCP/IP protocol suite and how the Internet works at a fairly abstract level. Furthermore we discussed cloud computing in general, and how Facebook and Google Docs can be thought of as programs that live on the web in the application layer. We contrasted this with traditional software models, and described how developing non-cloud online social networking software would be challenging.

This topic can meet the first two objectives quite nicely, depending on the depth and approach to the coverage. Several textbooks used for courses focused on computer literacy have chapters that cover these topics very well.

Security and Privacy Online

At the end of our discussion of network technology, we talked very generally about wireless networks and how easy it is to intercept unencrypted transmissions. I briefly touched on the WEP and WPA encryption protocols in very practical terms (e.g. how to turn them on in your home wireless router) and made it known that WEP is a very weak protocol. Further topics for discussion included phishing attacks, and how both MySpace and Facebook leave open the possibility for online trackers to be installed in a user's profile (meaning that a MySpace user can record your IP address when you visit their profile).

Last, but not least, we discussed the importance of picking good passwords not only for your own security and privacy, but for your online 'friends' as well. In particular I illustrated how a dictionary attack can be used to crack passwords. This dovetailed nicely into a discussion of computational thinking.

Computational Thinking

I developed a simple one-way "encryption" scheme to demonstrate a dictionary attack. Each letter of the alphabet is assigned a number, and the encrypted version of a password is the sum of these numbers multiplied by the product of these numbers. Developing an algorithm that computes this is a straightforward exercise even for students not familiar with programming. Using this encryption scheme, one can illustrate an algorithm for a dictionary attack with ease.

After letting the students complete a worksheet where they discovered that they were able to crack passwords using their computational method by hand, I generalized their approach to a true dictionary attack, and showed them an implementation in the Python language. Following that we played with MIT's Scratch software, where the students learned how it could be used to construct a program that computed the encrypted value for each password.

Facebook has a wealth of interesting aspects that illustrate various aspects of computational thinking. In our class, one of the features of Facebook that we spent quite a bit of time discussing is the "People You May Know" tool. This tool generates suggestions for people you may know by analyzing local aspects of your social network graph.

The simplest way that Facebook's tool might work would be to make attempts to 'complete the clique[5].' As Facebook collects its data about its network, it can look for very dense sub-graphs and add people that are not connected in those very dense sub-graphs to their 'people who likely

[5]In a graph, a clique is a complete sub-graph – a set of vertices for which every pair of vertices contains an edge.

know each other' list. This is certainly an oversimplification of the real approach that is used, but discussing this opens up a tremendous number of interesting computational topics. Specifically the problem of counting the number of edges in a clique opens up recurrence relations, and the problem of finding a clique opens up NP-completeness. The former problem was discussed in some depth; the latter topic was discussed briefly.

In general, this topic area is flexible enough to be expanded to meet the second objective.

Modern Web Entrepreneurship

An underlying theme of the course involved questioning how one can create useful technologies in order to start businesses. This was reflected in the term project assignment but we also spent some amount of class time discussing them. Serendipitously, the Economist magazine published an articles [19] on this topic right around the time we reached it in class. One of the articles asked if the Web 2.0 craze could lead to a second dotcom crash, and another described the difficulty in creating online business models based around advertisements. All of these topics were discussed, along with current approaches to making money through Internet businesses (micro-transactions for example).

Most importantly, we discussed how technology shapes businesses and industries, and how fighting technology in order to hold onto outdated business models often fails. The perfect case study for this is the Recording Industry Association of America's strong-armed approach to fighting digital copyright infringement. In doing so they created the perfect opportunity for Apple, a computer company, to succesfully corner the digital music market.

This topic was chosen in an effort to meet the third objective.

Social, Legal and Ethical Issues

The bulk of the last third of the semester was spent discussing social and ethical issues that arise in social networks and through technology in general. This portion of the class was devoted to meeting the fourth objective.

One of the most interesting incidents to happen in online social networking while I was teaching the course was Facebook's change in its terms of service. In March of 2009, Facebook quietly altered their terms of service so that its users no longer retained full control or ownership of any content posted on its site. Interestingly, it took a week before this information reached news outlets. At this point there was an uproar and Facebook changed the terms of service back to the way they were originally [9]. This framed an interesting discussion over website terms of service, and whether or not they can and should be enforced.

Another major topic was the Megan Meier case. Megan Meier was a twelve year old girl who was harassed by an adult posing as a twelve year old boy on MySpace. She committed suicide, and the case made national headlines, particularly when the adult was only found guilty of violating MySpace's terms of service. This, of course, furthered the discussion of the enforceability of terms of service agreements and opened up discussions about cyberbullying. It framed debates about online behavior and whether it is ever appropriate to pretend you're someone else on the Internet.

The last major topic of the course was the debate over intellectual property laws. Readings were taken from Lawrence Lessig's book Free Culture [13], and discussions centered around the debate over whether current intellectual property laws are outdated in the age of the Internet. This is particularly interesting in the context of websites that contain user-generated content – who owns and controls your Facebook status updates?

Term Project

Much of the out-of-class work for the course was based around the open-ended term project. In this project, the students worked in groups to develop an idea for a Web 2.0 application or website. The goal was to brainstorm the idea in the context of business models, web technologies, and user-interface design. Furthermore, they had to give two presentations – a midterm presentation on their idea, their research and their design. The final presentation was a more formal "investor presentation" that described the business model behind the idea and demonstrated a mock-up in front of an "investor" – a local expert in youth entrepreneurship.

The learning objective of this activity was to get the students to think about developing a web-application at a very high level. It was my intention that this would inspire some of the students to take further Computer Science courses so that they could learn how to actually build their applications.

4. REFLECTION

Overall, I was pleased with the outcome of the course. Though I was initially afraid that the topics were too disparate to form a cohesive structure, I ended up very happy with the course flow. The most exciting aspect of the course, for me, was the fact that I was reading relevant articles in the news on a daily basis that I could bring in and share with the class. In fact, many of the required readings weren't even written before the course began! In a field like computer science, where we often make the statement "technology changes so quickly," you would expect this to be the case in many of our classes. Perhaps tellingly, I had never had that experience in computer science before teaching this course.

Comments and ratings on the aggregated student evaluations and voluntary course surveys demonstrate that there was a substantial amount of enthusiasm for the topics, the projects and the course in general. The primary complaint from students seemed to involve the more challenging technical and mathematical content, which is to be expected in an introductory CS course that is designed for non-majors. Surprising to me, however, these complaints were very minimal. Forty-two of the 47 students completed the final course evaluation. All of them agreed with the statement "I would give this course a positive rating," and 32 of them agreed strongly. Likewise, all of them agreed with the statement "This course stimulates critical thinking," and 31 of them agreed strongly.

If I were to teach this course again, I would likely make the term project a much more formal, structured endeavor, perhaps teaching tools such as Photoshop that would allow the students to create a professional mock-up of their idea. I would also be interested in pairing this course with a senior-level software engineering or web programming course. The senior-level computer science students would presumably have the skills to build the technologies that were designed by the social networking students. This type of collaboration experience might benefit both groups.

According to [2] topics relating to social networks could generate more interest in computing-based careers among females. Of the 47 students that signed up for my course last Spring, 16 were females. While this made the course more diverse than most computer science courses in which I've been involved, it certainly leaves a little to be desired. This may, however, be an anomaly – the name of the course was changed after registration began in the Fall 2008 semester, and advertising for the new topics in the course was limited to our college newspaper and word of mouth.

I'm positive that officially changing the course title from "Communications Technologies and the Internet" generated more student interest. Departments that are struggling with enrollments in courses called "Computer Fluency," or something similar might see an immediate turnaround after implementing this type of change.

As an interesting aside, while I was teaching this course I was also making regular trips to local and regional high schools to share with students my view of computer science and computational thinking. During the presentations I often talked a little about Facebook and other online social networks; the high school students would often speak up to interject their thoughts on the topic. When I told them that I was teaching a course about it, they were thrilled to hear that such a course existed.

More generally speaking, I firmly believe the primary message of this article: *framing CS0 in the context of online social networking can re-energize the course while still meeting all of the necessary objectives.* The beauty of the topic lies in its flexibility, its relevance, and its draw. I'm hopeful that exploring how traditional computing topics closely relate might propel otherwise uninterested students further along in the discipline, but I don't currently have any data to support that.

On a longer time-line, however, I will admit that online social networking phenomenon may prove to be a fad and therefore it may not always be suitable for an introductory computer science course. That doesn't change the fact that it is a good topic now, and that now is when we need it the most. So while we're enjoying our time teaching these social networking topics we can also be on the lookout for the next technology that will capture the public's imagination. At that point we'll need to start figuring out how to frame our introductory topics in that context. After all, the fact that things change so rapidly in our discipline is part of the fun of computer science, right?

5. ACKNOWLEDGMENTS

Thanks to the CS Department at the College of Charleston for allowing me to teach this course while I was visiting. Also thanks to Brian Giarrocco, a student at CofC, for several discussions on social networks and entrepreneurship which sparked ideas for the course. Finally, thanks to several anonymous reviewers for very helpful feedback.

6. REFERENCES

[1] Computer Science Curriculum 2008: An Interim Revision of CS 2001; Report from the Interim Review Task Force. `http://www.acm.org/education/curricula/ComputerScience2008.pdf` Retrieved December 6, 2009.

[2] C. Alt, O. Astrachan, J. Forbes, R. Lucic, and S. Rodger. Social Networks Generate Interest in Computer Science. *SIGCSE 2006.* 438-442.

[3] K. Anewalt. Making CS0 fun: an active learning approach using toys, games and Alice. *Journal of Computing Sciences in Colleges.* Volume 23, Issue 3. 98-105. 2008.

[4] Chilling Effects Clearinghouse. `www.chillingeffects.org` Retrieved September 10, 2009.

[5] d. boyd and N. Ellison. Social network sites: Definition, history and scholarship. *Journal of Computer-Mediated Communication* 13(1), article 11. 2007.

[6] D. Cliburn. A CS0 course for the liberal arts. *SIGCSE 2006.* 77-81

[7] C. Cook. A computer science freshmen orientation course. *ACM SIGCSE Bulletin.* Volume 28, Issue 2, June 1996.

[8] C. Dierbach, B. Taylor, H. Zhou, and I. Zimand. Experiences with a CS0 course targeted for CS1 success. *SIGCSE 2005.* 317-320.

[9] Facebook Yields to User Outrage: Reverts to Old TOS. PC World. February 18, 2009. `http://www.pcworld.com/article/159720/facebook_yields_to_user_outrage_reverts_to_old_tos.html` Retrieved September 10, 2009.

[10] A. Fisher, J. Margolis, and F. Miller. Undergraduate women in computer science: Experience, motivation and culture. *SIGCSE 1997.* 106-110.

[11] D. Garcia, R. Cutler, Z. Dodds, E. Roberts, and A. Young. Rediscovering the passion, beauty, joy, and awe: making computing fun again, continued. *SIGCSE 2009.* 65-66

[12] L. Lessig. *Code and Other Laws of Cyberspace, Version 2.0.* Basic Books. 2006.

[13] L. Lessig. *Free Culture: The Nature and Future of Creativity.* Penguin. 2005.

[14] S. Milgram. "An experimental study of the Small World Problem." Sociometry, Vol 32, No 4, pp. 425-443. 1969.

[15] J. Pearce and M. Nakazawa. The funnel that grew our CIS major in the CS desert. *SIGCSE 2008.* 503-507.

[16] T. Purewal Jr, C. Bennett, and F. Maier. Embracing the Social Relevance – Computing, Ethics and the Community. *SIGCSE 2007.*

[17] S. Reges. CS Intro Data. `http://www.cs.washington.edu/homes/reges/sigcse/intro.html` Retrieved September 10, 2009.

[18] S. Schnettler. "A small world on feet of clay? A comparison of empirical small-world studies against best-practice criteria." Social Networks, 31(3), pp. 179-189. 2009.

[19] Six years in the Valley. The Economist Magazine. May 19th, 2009.

[20] Wikipedia in Culture. `http://en.wikipedia.org/wiki/Wikipedia_in_culture\#Wikiality` Retrieved September 10, 2009.

[21] S. Zweben. 2007-2008 Taulbee Survey. Computing Research News, Volume 21, Number 3. May 2009.

Educating the Next Generation of Spammers

Joel Sommers
Colgate University
Hamilton, NY, USA
jsommers@colgate.edu

ABSTRACT

Compelling experiences in introductory courses make a key difference in whether non-majors develop an interest in computer science, possibly even converting them into undergraduate majors or minors. In this paper we advocate integrated hands-on laboratory style activities to provide such pivotal experiences. In the lab activities we describe, students do not engage in programming, yet they learn to think computationally by engaging in computational activities. The course in which these labs are implemented is oriented around three aspects of the the internet's *underside*: its techno-scientific underpinnings, environmental and energy problems and promise brought on by its rapid growth, and security threats associated with its use. We describe the goals and content of the lab activities, as well as various challenges encountered through their implementation. We also discuss student responses and future directions.

Categories and Subject Descriptors

K.3.2 [**Computer and Information Science Education**]: Computer science education; C.2.5 [**Local and Wide-Area Networks**]: Internet (*e.g.*, TCP/IP)

General Terms

Experimentation, Measurement

Keywords

Non-Majors, Computational Thinking, Active Learning, Problem-based Learning

1. INTRODUCTION

Introductory courses play a pivotal role in whether students develop an interest for continuing to take courses within a discipline, especially non-majors with no prior experience. Early student experiences can invigorate an existing interest, open up a new one, or, alas, cause a student to seek intellectual stimulation elsewhere. Departments in institutions with core curriculum requirements (*e.g.*, liberal arts colleges) are often presented with golden opportunities each semester: through curiosity, the fate of scheduling, or acts of serendipity, students enter our classrooms. While they are there ostensibly to fulfill a requirement, the favorable circumstance presented to us is simply that *they are there*. In computer science these opportunities are not insignificant [11, 22].

In this paper, we describe a course for non-majors that was designed to introduce students to scientific practices from the perspective of computer science. The course is oriented around the internet (the author's own research area), and follows a theme of exploring *undersides* of the internet: the technical and scientific underpinnings of the modern internet; environmental problems and social challenges brought on by the internet's rapid growth as well as promising efforts to mitigate these problems; and the many security challenges facing the internet— botnets, denial of service attacks, worms, viruses, spam, etc.—as well as the responses by the scientific and operations community to try to address these threats. In this context, students learn what sorts of questions can be addressed through scientific means, the nature of scientific inquiry and debate, and how scientific practices actually work on the ground. A primary method by which this is accomplished is through in-class laboratory sessions. Through these activities, students learn about computer science by *doing it*. Indeed, the key goal for these sessions is for students to learn to approach problem solving from a computational perspective [14, 23].

One of the main challenges with teaching and learning computer science, especially with non-majors (and the potentially computer-phobic) is that much of our subject matter is rather abstract. The first time the term "packet" is introduced to students, there is visible consternation: the internet is modern magic to most students. It can be hard to picture a packet, or a path that a packet might take through the internet, or what the internet looks like (indeed, characterizing the topology of the internet has been a source of compelling research questions for some time). In-class laboratory exercises provide a way to complement the conceptual knowledge that students gain through readings, discussion, and lecture. Lab exercises also provide a focal point for addressing issues like scientific methodology, designing an experiment, measurement instrument quality and data quality, data gathering, hypothesis testing, and many other issues that come up when performing experiments or when thinking about the process of science.

In his book *Representing and Intervening*, the philosopher of science Ian Hacking introduces the concept of scientific realism. He relates an anecdote of a physicist friend who describes an experiment in which the friend "sprays" electrons on an object. Leading up to this description, Hacking discusses whether an electron is "real" or merely a convenient theoretical construction. He then states: "So far as I'm concerned, if you can spray them then they're real" [16]. His point aptly describes why hands-on exercises are critical for students in introductory computer science courses: until students can *do* something with their knowledge, that knowledge remains lifeless and somehow unreal.

An important design decision for the labs is that there is no direct programming involved. Instead, students work in pseudocode and bring other resources to bear (*e.g.*, a combination of net-accessible and custom software tools provided to the students) when investigating particular phenomena and when attempting to formulate questions and hypotheses. As such, our approach differs from more conventional CS0-style courses that emphasize aspects of computer literacy or that introduce students to a selection of topics in computer science through simple programming, *e.g.*, in javascript.

While our hands-on approach presents interesting learning opportunities, there are some key challenges as well. In particular, there are logistical challenges involved in designing substantive laboratory activities that can be accomplished within the confines of a standard 50 minute class period. Moreover, set up of laboratory hardware and software demands technical resources, system administration expertise, and time. Even for a class of modest size, the setup overhead costs can be significant. Our goal is to release our tools and materials to the community so that others may take advantage of and build upon our approach.

As part of our effort we have developed several laboratory activities, six of which are described in this paper. Qualitative data have been collected thus far on student experiences and whether students feel that the lab exercises contribute to their understanding of course material. We are encouraged by the fact that student feedback has been overwhelmingly positive. Indeed, several students have since enrolled in other computer science courses. We believe, moreover, that our course structure could serve as a model for institutions with similar curricular requirements.

The rest of this paper is organized as follows. In Section 2 we describe the laboratory activities and discuss challenges associated with their implementation. We follow in Section 3 by describing student experiences and feedback. Section 4 presents work related to ours. We conclude and consider future directions in Section 5.

2. AN OVERVIEW OF THE LABS

While each lab is designed to enable students to gain hands-on experience with concepts and ideas from readings, lecture, and class discussion, there are also a number of learning goals that transcend any particular lab. These goals are aligned with the larger context of the course, which is to introduce students to the methods and practices of science through a particular disciplinary lens. In particular, one goal is for students to gain experience in carefully collecting and analyzing data. Moreover, since many kinds of internet data tend to be noisy, a related goal is for students to learn to assess data quality and the validity of a measurement. Such an ability can be challenging to attain, as it can require deep domain knowledge and/or a full understanding of a measurement tool and the assumptions built into it. Our position is that although non-majors are not likely to fully grasp all the issues at stake (indeed, these are difficult for *any* non-expert to understand), they are capable of learning enough to appreciate the importance of evaluating the quality of an experiment's outcome. Through this, it is hoped that they will learn to see science not as a black box that yields answers, but as an imperfect yet powerful process by which to understand the world. A goal that follows from the problem of evaluating measurement data is for students to be able to analyze the design of an experiment and to suggest ways in which an experiment might be improved given limitations of the instruments or data at hand, or a refinement of the question of interest. Finally, we note that although our labs are designed within a particular academic context, we view our approach as well as the specific content of the labs to be more widely applicable.

For each lab, students work in pairs. In some of the labs, there are numbers, symbols, and equations. Having students work in pairs helps to ease the problem of confronting these scary creatures. After performing the hands-on part of each lab, students work through a number of synthesis-type questions which essentially ask students to make sense of what they did in the lab activity and to connect ideas from class with the labwork. Sometimes these questions were completed as part of the lab activity, sometimes they were assigned as homework problems, and in a few instances these questions appeared as exam questions.

2.1 Brief laboratory descriptions

2.1.1 What does the internet look like?

One of the basic definitions of the internet that is introduced early in this course is that *the internet is a network of networks.* This is to say that the internet is composed of many separate, administratively independent networks. The collection of these networks and the connections among them are what forms the internet. In this lab, students use the well-worn internet measurement tool `traceroute` (more specifically, the `paris-traceroute` variant [7]) to learn more about the topology of the internet and how the internet routing algorithms result in specific paths that packets take through the internet.

Students choose two separate remote hosts, one in the US, and one outside of the US, and use the `traceroute` tool to each of these destinations. The non-US destination must be a looking glass `traceroute` server [4] so that students can evaluate two directions of a route. They then analyze the data from `traceroute`, as well as gather some additional data based on the `traceroute` output, such as the estimated geographic location of each router and the autonomous system to which each router belongs. There are two interesting things about `traceroute` that students are made aware of: first, that it is one of the only methods that the research and network operations community has for discovering the path that a packet takes through the internet; and two, that there are many limitations and pitfalls associated with its use. While `traceroute` is designed to give a hop-by-hop listing of the routers through which a packet passes on its way from a sender to a receiver, the data produced can be very noisy, confounding interpretation of the output.

For the purposes of the lab, though, the noisy data is useful. Prior to the lab, we discuss in class some of the reasons behind why `traceroute` data can produce difficult-to-interpret results. For example students learn about packet loss, packet filtering, and challenges presented by the fact that network providers can configure routers in their networks in ways that limit the usefulness of `traceroute`. Thus, one of the key learning goals for this lab is for students to critically analyze the data at hand and to evaluate its validity and meaning.

2.1.2 Spam, spam, spam

First, let us be clear: the lab that inspired title of this paper actually has to do with *stopping spam*, not facilitating its spread. One of the main goals for this lab is for the students to learn how a modern spam filter works, and more generally to learn to think algorithmically about how something like a spam filter can be implemented in a computer. Interestingly, some students think that since they do not receive much spam in their email inbox, it is no longer a serious problem. In reality, over 90% of all email on the internet is unsolicited bulk mail. Clearly, spam continues to be a significant problem.

The main activity in this lab is for students to learn how a widely used spam filtering engine called SpamAssassin [3] works. At the heart of SpamAssassin is a large set of rules that are matched against every incoming email to a mail server. These rules test various parts of an email for known characteristics of spam, or for characteristics that suggest that an email is not spam. These rules contain scores that collectively contribute to an email's overall score. A simple threshold is used to classify an email as spam or not. Another key algorithmic component of SpamAssassin is a machine learning algorithm that enables the system to adapt to evolving trends in features of spam and to be tuned to the kinds of email that a given user receives. Thus, students also learn some of the basic ideas behind statistical classification.

For better or worse, the best way to learn the basics of how SpamAssassin works is by creating and sending spam. As part of this lab, students had to construct spam within certain parameters to sell counterfeit watches and prescription painkillers. Their spam was relayed through an anonymous remailer (with built-in checks on the destination address so that students could only send spam to designated addresses) and passed through SpamAssassin. It is important to note that all the spam generated by the students was processed within a (nearly) closed network in order to minimize the possibility of their spam escaping into the rest of campus and the internet. Their goals were to create some messages that would be tagged as spam by SpamAssassin, and some that would not be tagged, and more importantly to investigate *why* in each case.

2.1.3 Web performance prediction

Use of a web browser has become second nature to students. Indeed, students entering college today have hardly known a time when the web did not hold the position as the central resource for information. Although they may be comfortable using the web, many students are acutely aware of how shallow their knowledge is about how the web functions. When something happens that is unexpected — a web page takes a long time to load or does not load at all — the limits of their knowledge become all too apparent.

The ability to make predictions is fundamental to science. Leading up to this lab, students learn about web protocols, general concepts about underlying transport protocols, and the basics of how web pages are constructed. With that knowledge, their task in this lab is to try to evaluate the factors behind what causes some websites to load quickly and others to load more slowly. The end goal of their evaluation is to try to build a prediction model for web performance.

The main tool the students use for gathering data to evaluate performance and build a model is the firebug extension [5] to the firefox web browser. Firebug provides the ability to measure how long different elements of a web page take to download, and how long the entire page takes to download and display. These measurements can be displayed in real time as a page is loaded, making them quite visually compelling for students learning how the web functions. (Note that students are shown how to disable caching in order to evaluate effects due to the network and remote server.)

To build their prediction model, students can use the data collected from firebug, as well as simple round-trip delay measurements using `ping` and topology measurements using `traceroute`. Students can also make use of measurement tools available from the Measurement Lab [1] in order to test network performance between their computer and a measurement lab host near a target website (if one is available). Tools are provided to create simple 2D scatter plots of different combinations of their data; these scatter plots form the basis for their predictions. For some website selections, a clear set of clusters arises in the scatter plot. For others, the patterns are less obvious. In any case, a learning goal of building this model is for students to recognize that they can develop a hypothesis for why a given site (or cluster) exhibits the performance it does, and using the tools at hand to test their conjecture.

2.1.4 Estimating personal power consumption

Electronic devices of all kinds pervade modern existence. Many students regularly use laptops, smartphones, gaming consoles, and various other devices, each of which consumes some amount of electricity. Although some students are keenly aware of their power consumption footprint (even though they might not be able to quantify it), others are not. This lab consists of two parallel components. In one, students keep a journal of their use of high-tech devices over several days. They log how long they use each device and record some basic information about the device itself. The second component begins partway through the time during which students keep their journal. They are asked to bring a variety of devices into class in order to measure their power consumption. At the end of their journalling, they use the measurements taken in class along with their journal entries to form an estimate of their average daily consumption of power due to high-tech devices.

The power measurements are taken using handheld digital multimeters which have the capability to download the measurements to a computer for graphing. The devices brought into class are measured under different usage scenarios, *e.g.*, while playing an intensive game, watching a video, or allowing the system to remain idle. Server-class systems are also brought into class for measurement in order for students to see the kinds of computers that run commonly used cloud services and to motivate the massive amount of power used by internet services and infrastructure.

Once the journalling period is over and an average daily power consumption is computed, students are asked to quantify the amount of power in terms of the number of pounds of coal that would need to be burned in order to support their power needs. For some, making this calculation results in a rather disturbing image, but helps to achieve a goal of bringing an awareness to students that may or may not have been there previously.

2.1.5 Breaking simple ciphers

One of the key security technologies behind why the internet has been successfully harnessed by the business world is cryptography. While students can clearly grasp *why* cryptography is important and what it generally accomplishes, the details of how different cryptographic ciphers work can be challenging to grasp, especially for the math-phobic. Our position is that focussing on the mathematical details in a course designed for non-majors can be counterproductive. On the other hand, working with relatively simple ciphers can help to provide a concrete context for students to understand the terms and basic process of encryption and decryption. Thus, in this lab students learn how simple cryptographic ciphers work, and attempt to decode two ciphertexts given knowledge of the cipher used to encrypt each of them but without knowledge of the keys.

Two ciphertexts are used. One is encrypted using a monoalphabetic subsititution cipher, the second is encrypted using a Vigenere cipher. Prior to the lab session, cryptanalysis of these basic ciphers is discussed in class and students discover ways in which they can be broken. Breaking the Vigenere cipher is the more difficult one of the two. To solve this challenging problem, students are led to consider the fact that if they can estimate the length of the key, then breaking the ciphertext boils down to the simple task of breaking a series of Caesar ciphers. A standard method for estimating key length is provided as a reference, thus enabling students to break the code.

A web page with some javascript is used to enable students to evaluate letter frequencies and to specify how letters are to be substituted (in the case of the monoalphabetic substitution cipher). The page also enables students to reorganize the ciphertext into a specified number of columns and to perform frequency analysis on each column (these features are useful for breaking the Vigenere cipher).

2.1.6 Scanners and intrusion detection

There are few people who have never experienced having their computer infected with a virus, worm, or other form of malware. For many, such an event motivates questions such as: *Why doesn't operating system vendor X produce a better product? Why is my computer a target of hackers? Why is malware so pervasive?* and *What can I do next time so that my computer doesn't get hosed?* In this lab, students initially play the role of trying to identify vulnerabilities in networked-computers and to understand some of the causes and implications of those potential problems. To do that, they use the Nessus [2] and Nmap [12] tools to scan a set of hosts in a closed, relatively small network, that are known to have vulnerabilities. Using these tools, they are able to discover the set of vulnerabilities that exist in the (mini-)network, and the basic implications of those vulnerabilities.

They then switch roles and try to identify ways in which to mitigate the threats posed by the vulnerabilities that they've identified. A simple and standard defense mechanism that students learn about is a firewall. Through the exercise, students learn how a firewall might be configured to mitigate a vulnerability. Perhaps more importantly, they learn about various shortcomings of firewalls and why they are an ineffective means of defense against a large class of attacks.

One of the goals for this lab is for students to experience first-hand how easy it is for a remote attacker to gain information about a potential target. The motivation for using such powerful and potentially dangerous tools is two-fold: first, to help students recognize the importance of open exchange of information, even if that information could be used for harm, and second to encourage them to configure their own machines in responsible ways.

2.2 Challenges Faced

Of the various challenges posed by instituting in-class labs, probably the most significant is the time constraint. Executing a meaningful laboratory exercise within the confines of a standard 50 minute class period has proved difficult. Indeed, students have also recognized and commented on this problem. While we expect that some of the time constraint problems will be resolved as the labs are refined and revised over time, we also expect that there will continue to be a fundamental tension between providing meaningful and thought-provoking problems to grapple with and overwhelming students with too much to try to accomplish in the time allotted.

For each of these labs, we have spent quite a bit of time setting up or creating tools that are accessible to the students through a standard web browser. While there are many tools that advanced students might be expected to use to accomplish various tasks, our goal was to provide a familiar environment from which to base student activities. Another key logistical challenge has been setting up the laboratory infrastructure, including an isolated network, various servers, student accounts, honeypot machines for vulnerability testing, and the like. Our hope is to generalize and package our configurations where possible so that others can more easily set labs up.

3. EVALUATION

Thus far, qualitative feedback that has been collected from students has been overwhelmingly positive. By these measures, the labs have been very successful and the students have responded very positively to them both in terms of actually enjoying them and feeling like the lab activities contributed to their knowledge base. Below, we provide a representative selection of comments provided by students in response to the following prompt: *Please comment on how the in-class lab exercises contributed to your learning in this course.*

- I really liked the labs. They weren't overly stressful or long, but they did help me to understand the material better because it was a hands on experience with the tools [we] talked about in class.
- I think the labs helped my understanding of the course material because it was a more hands on approach rather than just reading about it.
- The labs definitely helped me understand the material. I learn better when I see things in actions and can see how they work so the labs really helped me.
- Yes...very much so....Although more time should be given in class for lab completion. Maybe make them a 2-day process...
- We actually learn things, instead of watching a teacher flaunt their knowledge.

Finally, although we do not yet have long-term data, our initial experience also suggests that our approach has been instrumental in drawing in students to take further computer science courses, a not insignificant motivation behind our efforts. Approximately 15% of students who have taken this course have subsequently enrolled in a programming-based introductory course. Given the fact that students were enrolled in the course described in this paper ostensibly to fulfill a requirement, we view this as a highly encouraging development.

4. RELATED WORK

There have been many innovative efforts over the years to develop compelling ways to introduce non-majors to computer science. Naturally, our use of in-class laboratory exercises builds on these prior efforts. Moreover, we draw inspiration from problem-based approaches that do not use programming.

More specifically, although the process of design for a non-major's course described in [15] is directed toward a course in which students do programming, their general approach is applicable. In particular, the aspects of topical relevance and choice of a compelling context, and of making the classroom experience a social experience have been underlying goals throughout the development of our laboratory activities. Similarly, our effort is comparable to [19] in which a course for non-majors is designed explicitly around the internet. Indeed, it should not be surprising that many others have noted that the internet, network security, and related areas provide a compelling frame of reference for introductory courses [13, 17, 18].

The problem-based nature of our laboratory activities organized around current events has similarities to the course described by Astrachan [6]. The focus in [6] is for students to ponder larger computational issues rather than focussing on details that they are likely to forget. We believe that an approach that includes meaningful activities in which students can grapple with different problems in a tangible way can help to create a bridge between low-level details on the one hand, and implications on the other.

While it is widely held that students learn best by doing, how and exactly what students should do in an introductory course for non-majors has been the subject of much debate. Many introductory approaches favor a programming-based experience, but others advocate a non-programming-based approach; recent examples may be found in [10,20,21]. While a programming-based approach may certainly be appropriate for certain institutions, it may not be for others that have unique curricular constraints, *e.g.*, in some liberal arts colleges [8, 9, 24].

5. CONCLUSIONS AND FUTURE WORK

In this paper we describe in-class lab activities created for a course for non-majors. The labwork is designed to enable students to grapple with scientific problems in the context of different aspects of the internet, and to provide them with tangible experiences with what are often rather abstract entities. While we contend that hands-on labwork can provide an effective complement to other classroom activities, there are two significant challenges that we have faced with this approach: time and setup costs.

In the future, we hope to develop open courseware materials to assist others wishing to adopt such activities. We also intend to investigate ways in which our approach could be scaled to large classes. Finally, a question we will consider is whether a course like ours for non-majors could be developed entirely around hands-on experiences, and how such a course might be orchestrated.

6. REFERENCES

[1] Measurement lab. `http://www.measurementlab.net/`.

[2] Nessus. `http://www.nessus.com/`.

[3] SpamAssassin. `http://spamassassin.apache.org/`.

[4] traceroute.org. `http://www.traceroute.org/`.

[5] Firebug: web development evolved. `http://getfirebug.com/`, 2009.

[6] O. Astrachan. Pander to ponder. In *SIGCSE '09: Proceedings of the 40th ACM technical symposium on Computer science education*, pages 192–196, March 2009.

[7] B. Augustin, X. Cuvellier, B. Orgogozo, F. Viger, T. Friedman, M. Latapy, C. Magnien, and R. Teixeira. Avoiding traceroute anomalies with Paris traceroute. In *IMC '06: Proceedings of the 6th ACM SIGCOMM conference on Internet measurement*, pages 153–158, October 2006.

[8] A. Brady, P. Cutter, and K. Schultz. Benefits of a CS0 course in liberal arts colleges. *Journal of Computing in Small Colleges*, 20(1):90–97, 2004.

[9] C.D. Cliburn. A CS0 course for the liberal arts. In *SIGCSE '06: Proceedings of the 37th SIGCSE technical symposium on Computer science education*, pages 77–81, 2006.

[10] T. J. Cortina. An Introduction to Computer Science for Non-majors Using Principles of Computation. In *SIGCSE '07: Proceedings of the 38th SIGCSE technical symposium on Computer science education*, pages 218–222, Covington, Kentucky, USA, March 2007.

[11] A. L. Foster. Student interest in computer science plummets. *The Chronicle of Higher Education*, 51(38):A31, May 27, 2005.

[12] Fyodor. Nmap. `http://www.nmap.org/`.

[13] C. Gurwitz. The Internet as a motivating theme in a math/computer core course for nonmajors. In *SIGCSE '98: Proceedings of the twenty-ninth SIGCSE technical symposium on Computer science education*, pages 68–72, 1998.

[14] M. Guzdial. Paving the Way for Computational Thinking. *Communications of the ACM*, 51(8):25–27, August 2008.

[15] M. Guzdial and A. Forte. Design process for a non-majors computing course. In *SIGCSE '05: Proceedings of the 36th SIGCSE technical symposium on Computer science education*, pages 361–365, 2005.

[16] I. Hacking. *Representing and Intervening*. Cambridge University Press, 1983.

[17] A. M. Holland-Minkley. Cyberattacks: A Lab-Based Introduction to Computer Security. In *SIGITE '06: Proceedings of the 7th conference on Information technology education*, pages 39–45, Minneapolis, MN, USA, October 2006.

[18] C.D. Knuckles. A net-centric curricular focus. *Journal of Computing in Small Colleges*, 17(6):75–81, 2002.

[19] S. Kurkovsky. Making computing attractive for non-majors: a course design. *Journal of Computing in Small Colleges*, 22(3):90–97, 2007.

[20] J. Marks, W. Freeman, and H. Leitner. Teaching applied computing without programming: a case-based introductory course for general education. *SIGCSE Bulletin*, 33(1):80–84, 2001.

[21] S. Pollard and J. Forbes. Hands-on labs without computers. In *SIGCSE '03: Proceedings of the 34th SIGCSE technical symposium on Computer science education*, pages 296–300, 2003.

[22] J. Vegso. Low Interest in CS and CE Among Incoming Freshmen. `http://www.cra.org/wp/index.php?p=104`, February 6 2007.

[23] J.M. Wing. Viewpoint—Computational Thinking. *Communications of the ACM*, 49(3):33–35, 2006.

[24] B. Zimmerman. Content and laboratories of a computing science course for non-majors in the 21st century. *Journal of Computing in Small Colleges*, 19(5):68–77, 2004.

Teaching the Principles of the Hacker Curriculum to Undergraduates

Sergey Bratus
ISTS
Dartmouth College
sergey@cs.dartmouth.edu

Anna Shubina
ISTS
Dartmouth College
ashubina@cs.dartmouth.edu

Michael E. Locasto
CSIS
George Mason University
mlocasto@gmu.edu

ABSTRACT

The "Hacker Curriculum" exists as a mostly undocumented set of principles and methods for learning about information security. Hacking, in our view, is defined by the ability to question the trust assumptions in the design and implementation of computer systems rather than any negative use of such skills.

Chief among these principles and methods are two useful pedagogical techniques: (1) developing a cross-layer view of systems (one unconstrained by API definitions or traditional subject matter boundaries) and (2) understanding systems by analyzing their failure modes (this approach works well with learning networking concepts and assessing software vulnerabilities). Both techniques provide a rich contrast to traditional teaching approaches, particularly for information security topics.

We relate our experience applying Hacker Curriculum principles to education and training programs for undergraduates, including the Secure Information Systems Mentoring and Training (SISMAT) program and the Cyber Security Initiative at Dartmouth College, which allows undergraduates to perform supervised red team activities on Dartmouth's production systems.

Categories and Subject Descriptors

K.3.2 [**Computers and Education**]: Computers and Information Science Education

General Terms

Experimentation, Measurement, Security

Keywords

security, information assurance, networking, SISMAT, Hacker Curriculum, teaching failure modes

1. INTRODUCTION

An understanding of information security and assurance holds an increasingly important place in the education of Computer Science students, many of whom will be asked to deal with new security and control challenges arising from a variety of problems, ranging from the privacy challenges of social networks and the use of Electronic Medical Records to a new Smart Energy Grid linked with and controlled by commodity networks and computing systems.

To meet the challenges of modern computer security practice, students must be able to switch from their conditioning by traditional computer science and software engineering curricula to the attacker's way of thinking. Successful work in the field of information security and assurance requires developing a specialized mindset: the essence of real security issues often lies in the complex interplay between **trust**, **models**, and **control**. It is precisely the skill to question trust relationships and the assumptions underlying controls and models that a budding security specialist must nurture.

Over the years, the hacker community has had a great deal of success doing so, and as a result, it has produced an informal but highly coherent and efficient "curriculum" that approaches the same topics as the traditional curricula from a variety of unusual angles. Far from being a haphazard collection of *ad hoc* "hacks", this curriculum exhibits a complex and rich — although often implicit — structure. The hacker community has developed "cross-layer, cross-field" methods of approaching computer systems that we can and should learn from [1, 2].

In order to be meaningful and practical, we believe that the computer security curriculum must include both "defender" and "attacker" perspectives and skills in each of the sub-areas of computing (e.g., systems, networks, human-computer interaction, relevant aspects of social engineering). Yet, teaching skills popularly associated with the hacker community still carries a substantial stigma. Many educational institutions frown on the courses taught within their walls having something to do with "hacking," a topic which they deem to be synonymous with unethical or illegal behavior.

This stigma results from serious misunderstandings that surround the hacker community. In this paper we hope to highlight these misunderstandings and to lay the groundwork for a more productive approach to the discussion about the hacker community's role in computer security research and practice.

1.1 Overview

This paper relates our experiences stemming from collecting and applying Hacker Curriculum principles to the education of our students and interns. These experiences mainly stem from two programs: the Dartmouth Cyber Security Initiative, a home-grown red team of students (guided by research personnel and Dartmouth IT staff) that help to secure the university's production networks, and the SISMAT (Secure Information Systems Mentoring and Training) educational outreach program.[1] We will give a brief overview

SIGCSE'10, March 10–13, 2010, Milwaukee, Wisconsin, USA.

[1] `http://www.ists.dartmouth.edu/projects/sismat.html`

of SISMAT [6], introduce the notion of the "Hacker Curriculum", enumerate some Hacker Curriculum Principles, and describe the "failure modes" teaching principle as we applied it to the SISMAT program during the summer of 2009.

1.2 "Ethical" Hacking

We use the term "hacker" in the most non-pejorative sense possible. From this perspective, ***hacking* is the skill to question trust and control assumptions expressed in software and hardware, as well as in processes that involve human(s)-in-the-loop (a.k.a. "social engineering").** The ethical hacker community promotes the development of such skills in many ways and venues open to the public, such as conferences, e-zines, and websites. Hacking can be seen as a branch of engineering knowledge, and it shows the makings of an engineering discipline in (rapid) development.

Unfortunately, *hacking* has become a loaded term, particularly since the media has found it to be a convenient description of criminal mischief. We, however, see a need to separate the special knowledge, mindset, and skill from ill-advised, nuisance, or criminal behavior that might abuse this knowledge. Hackers possess valuable knowledge, a fact that certain governments understand and appreciate, although initiatives to recruit and hire hackers often meets with sharp criticism [4], with popular and vocal perception that hackers are somehow inherently threatening. This perception dominates in the media and periodically feeds into sensationalist reports of imminent cyber-terror and similar themes, such as occasional calls on the public to "give up certain freedoms" in order to "fix the Internet." [8]

As a community, hackers are defined by their skills and specific knowledge, similar to locksmiths, doctors, or martial artists. A doctor knows ways to harm humans, and might criminally abuse this knowledge. A locksmith is equipped to crack banks' vaults. A policeman is trained to use and is armed with deadly weapons. Yet none of them is defined by the potential misuse of the special skills they possess. Similarly, hacking is a special technological skill that can be misused, but should not be defined by its misuses.

We believe that this *knowledge-centric* or *skill-centric* approach best explains the activities, successes, and aspirations of the hacker community, and it inevitably leads to the imperative to learn from this community rather than shun it.

1.3 Culture Shock

Our experience teaching computer security in the SISMAT program and elsewhere leads us to believe that the most important service we can perform for our students is a *security culture shock*. Teaching students to question their assumptions, however, takes a great deal of effort: they simply cannot be told "question everything" because this spare advice provides them with no roadmap, specific principles, common tools, or peer-reviewed methods for intelligently questioning security assumptions. The Hacker Curriculum contains just such material, albeit largely uncurated.

Since the early days of personal computing, teaching environments in which aspiring young programmers learn their trade have gotten increasingly more efficient at imparting marketable skills without having the students "waste" time on puzzling out various computing failures unrelated to their intended learning tasks. But just as teaching environments that hide the underlying engineering complexities and challenges get better, something is lost: an experience of the many *failure modes* of computing environments.

This approach conditions many students to implicitly trust their programming environment — whether or not it is a real production environment or one constructed explicitly for teaching to mask complexity and to minimize potential confusion. Students also treat API layer interfaces as boundaries of exploration and desirable competence. **Nothing can be more damaging for the development of a security mindset than this type of conditioning.**

For example, software engineers tend to formalize their trust assumption in "layer models:" or patterns that their system designs follow (*e.g.,* the 7-layer OSI (Open Systems Interconnection) networking model). The borders of these layers become natural boundaries of trust (*i.e.,* blocks below boundaries are counted on by developers to not present surprises — changes in behavior, syntax, or semantics), and therefore become limits of expertise. **It is the hacker mindset and skill to question such assumptions of engineering trust in real world systems.**

2. SISMAT 2009

The SISMAT program provides a comprehensive approach to education and outreach for undergraduates and their faculty mentors who are interested in information security and assurance topics, but who lack the necessary local resources and expertise to gain traction in the area. SISMAT provides undergraduates with an intensive, two-week seminar and laboratory course in computer security. In addition, we arrange summer internships on information security topics for each SISMAT participant, and we coordinate with their faculty mentor to design a research project for the next academic year. The SISMAT program also includes a mentor development weekend; participants' mentors are invited for discussions and curriculum development.

While we have reported on our experiences with the pilot year (2008) of SISMAT elsewhere [6], in this paper we focus on how we applied Hacker Curriculum principles to specific lessons in the SISMAT lecture and lab agenda. For further details on SISMAT itself, we refer the interested reader to our previous paper [6]. The lecture and lab exercises for SISMAT 2009 focused largely on specific network security and ethical hacking skills, including traffic manipulation, PKI (Public Key Infrastructure), and code exploitation of C/x86 programs.

The academic world has long struggled with how to best incorporate information security topics and education in the classroom; providing hands-on training is challenging [9, 7, 10] from practical, ethical, and legal standpoints. In SISMAT, the focused nature and full day length of the labs and lecture allowed for more leisurely exploration of corner cases and difficult concepts [5]. We recognize that typical semester-length courses do not necessarily enjoy this advantage in pace.

Finally, the *Cyber Security Initiative* (CSI) is a joint undertaking of our campus IT and the Department of Computer Science. It actively involves students in the ongoing campus-wide security assessment of this large and diverse network infrastructure. Members of the CSI group, guided by senior researchers in computer security, are thereby exposed to the complexities and engineering challenges of a real-world production network, which provides another essential form of culture shock to students never previously exposed to such environments and the practicalities of administrating them [12].

3. A CROSS-LAYER APPROACH

The use of abstraction plays a fundamental role in computer system design. This fundamental principle of software engineering serves as the primary tool for managing complexity in computational systems, and it leads to the construction of systems organized in layers, with clearly defined interfaces between each layer. From the point of view of a programmer working within one layer, other layers are trusted to behave as specified, and he does not have to worry about *their* complexity. Thus interfaces at layer boundaries become not only contracts but also natural boundaries of programmer specializations and core competencies. Examples of layer boundaries include those defined by the OSI (Open System Interconnection) network model, those separating application code from libraries, userland and kernel code separation defined by system calls, and kernel modules from the Windows DDK/WDK.

Naturally, most courses designed to develop a core competence concentrate on programming entirely within one layer of the system or the network. Indeed, from the point of view of managing the complexity of teaching a subject or managing a software project, this approach is probably the most efficient. As a consequence, the students or trainees have enough non-trivial logic in their programs to worry about and cannot also afford excursions into substantially different and differently structured material. Eventually, this approach becomes ingrained and remains an important side-effect of their professional training. The process of building or creating computing and information systems requires the careful use of abstraction to manage an overwhelming amount of complexity.

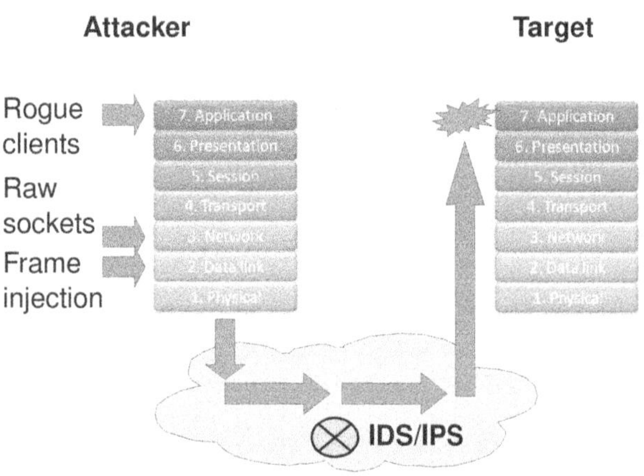

Figure 1: Hackers take the *cross-layer* view of systems and networks. They trace, examine, and craft data flows through layers and interfaces.

Although abstraction proves useful for building things, it can hinder the process of breaking, decomposing, repairing, or otherwise analyzing them. For example, the ability to develop an understanding of a basic software attacks and achieve successful delivery of an exploit to a target requires an almost completely orthogonal approach. We illustrate this approach in Figure 1, using exploitation of a user-level application as an example.

The key observation is that the attack payload (*e.g.*, a shellcode embedded within crafted input to the target) will be acted upon by multiple layers of the sending (attacker) system, the transmitting network (which may include an IDS (Intrusion Detection System) or IPS (Intrusion Protection System) that must remain unaware of the attack) and, finally, the target. None of the transformations of data in transit occurring in these layers should interfere with the exploit payload for the attack to succeed, and additional transformations might need to be applied so as to avoid detection and reaction by the IDS or IPS.

We note that the IDS or IPS has to treat the data streams flowing through it differently than the targets by taking various heuristic shortcuts, because it is typically responsible for examining traffic to many targets, and thus does not operate on the same computational power "budget" as an individual target, and cannot match its data processing precisely. Both Ptacek and Newsham's famous paper [11] and Paxson's paper [3] discuss different IDS evasion techniques that leverage differences in network stack implementations between the targets and the IDS to create different views of the packet stream at the IDS and the target. As a result, the IDS sees the attack stream as innocuous (or at least something that fails to trigger any known attack signatures), and in the worst case can cause the IDS to silently fail open.

We also note that while the payload must take the usual path to the targeted application, the attacking machine is under no such constraints: data it *produces* need not follow normal processing paths and packet composition rules. An attacker's program, therefore, may be instrumented to (1) form the attack packets and send them directly, bypassing the kernel's session and transport layers, or even the network layer (for LAN attacks) to inject straight into the link layer (as shown on the attacker side of Figure 1; and (2) suppression of some of the system's normal functionality (so that the attack tool's responses do not get accidentally invalidated by the kernel's normal reactions to malformed or unsolicited input).

Thus, successful engineering of exploits requires sufficient understanding of all the transformations that take place on the path from the attacker to vulnerable code in a running process on the target. Consequently, successful defenses must incorporate the same **cross-layer** understanding.

Not surprisingly, attack and network security tools in general depend on several libraries that provide ways to bypass the standard flow of data through the network stack. An example of the network security toolchain (described in great detail in Michael Schiffman's book "Building Open Source Network Security Tools: Components and Techniques") can be found in Figure 2.

Nurturing the ability to understand the limitations of algorithms, libraries, APIs, tools, and software systems requires a significant investment of time. Nevertheless, if we do not encourage and permit students to exercise this freedom within the formal curriculum, we run the risk of continuing to produce students that lack an appreciation of software security issues [13].

4. FAILURE MODES ACROSS NETWORK LAYERS

Typical CS network exercises seldom start with a mission of discovery: having to find out such facts about a network as what hosts are present in it, which services are actually available on them, what kinds of packets get filtered on entry ("ingress") or exit ("egress"), and similar reconnaissance activities. Instead, most network introductions center on abstract models of communication, brief glimpses of protocol diagrams and packet header layout charts, particular APIs or client-server libraries. Furthermore, such exercises typically assume that the transaction endpoint(s) are known in advance and available, *i.e.*, communications are not hindered, fully or partially, by adverse network conditions, misconfiguration, router access lists, firewall settings, server configuration, and the like. While such an approach suffices for a gentle introduction to the topic of network communication, it almost wholly concentrates on the way things *should work* rather than the ways that they might be *made to fail*.[2]

[2]Admittedly, failure modes may not necessarily be appropriate for teaching some topics: for example, teaching CS 1 by enumerating all the possible Java compiler warnings and errors does not seem practical, although students probably would appreciate some commentary on and interpretation of these common warnings.

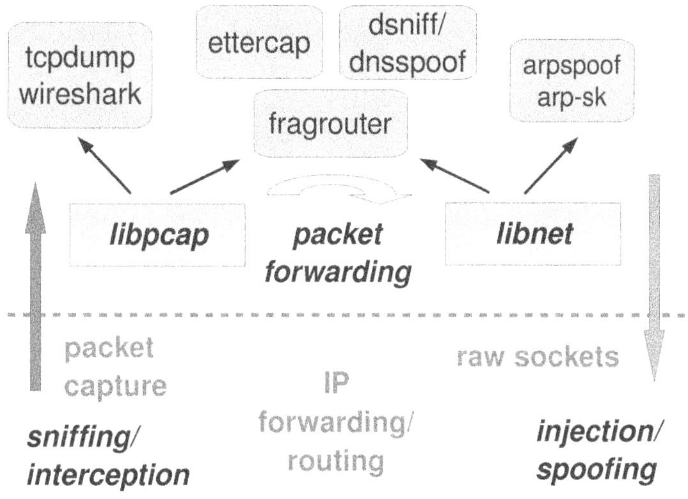

Figure 2: Open source network security toolchain allows bypassing OS network stack layers, enabling extraction and injection of packets from and into the kernel.

In contrast, hackers concentrate on failure modes of network communications, because distinguishing between different kinds of and reasons for transaction failures is critical for network reconnaissance (identifying potential targets and obstacles to exploitation). For example, scanning tools such as *nmap* crucially depend on interpreting signs of connection failure, firewall probing tools such as *firewalk* imitate routing failures, and so on.

In the SISMAT training, we direct the students to explore a variety of network failure modes, and, as a side effect, discover basic port scanning and firewalking techniques. In particular, we direct them to observe the result of attempted connections to non-existent hosts within and outside their LAN, to services not available on a host or filtered via different mechanism, in the presence of invalid and missing routes, *etc.*

As a result, the students gain enough confidence to start looking for failure conditions specifically rather than dismissing them as unintelligible, and to extract valuable reconnaissance information from those conditions.

4.1 Beyond the Socket

Typical CS curricula start with network programming APIs such as sockets and the client-server application model, and then expands "upward" to application protocols and distributed applications, and "downwards" to the details of TCP and mathematical models of congestion control. These topics, however, tend to be taught in separate courses and, as a result, tend to exist separately in the minds of most students.

Hacker analysis takes a different approach, connecting the different networking layers and programming abstractions from the outset. In particular, it is typical for a hacker to acquire an early understanding of which specific kinds of packets and OS network stack data structures result from each of the system calls involved in establishing a socket, and how different stacks differ in this regard.

An intermediate level step (although sometimes taken as a first one in hacker-style networking), is to build the capability for crafting arbitrary packets and injecting them into the network. This step is extremely important from the "culture shock" perspective – it helps the student realize that (1) network packets and frames are malleable and (2) the network by itself is merely a medium that would happily carry along any packet that looks well-formed to the equipment it is comprised of; the network contains hardly any trust guarantees.

The next step is the understanding of how to affect the OS network stack's states and thereby exploit them by sending crafted packets. Ptacek's paper [11] provides a good introduction to the topic and the source for the tool fragrouter gives an excellent and concise set of practical examples. These resources start the students thinking on how traffic patterns they describe could be generated. We then introduce them to *libnet* and *libnet*-based tools from simple ones such as *sendip*, *nemesis*, and *packetdude*, to advanced environments such as *scapy*. As a further example of the type of "problem" that arises with this "failure mode" teaching pattern, the students must consider how to suppress their OS stacks' natural reactions to incoming packets generated as a side-effects of the above manipulations. A simple example is presented by disabling ICMP redirects that would normally accompany ARP poisoning; `http://sockstress.com` provides a more comprehensive example. This pattern allows us to introduce some of the rich capabilities of the iptables/netfilter architecture and discuss its system of hooks within the Linux network stack, as well as the paths taken by a packet through that stack.

5. ROOTKITS: DECEPTION IN DEPTH

Similar to the cyber-defender maxim of "defense in depth", attackers also employ multi-layer deception schemes to throw the administrators off their trail and conceal evidence of malfeasance. In fact, this defense maxim may have been shaped by attacker practices that pre-dated it. We illustrate this "defense in depth" principle – critical for defenders to understand, since a lower level deception can be protecting a higher level one, and vice versa, in Figure 3.

We note that developing efficient rootkits is a task that requires careful understanding of a number of kernel data structures, as well as the ways those are used by different functions of the kernel, such as the difference between how scheduling and reporting code paths

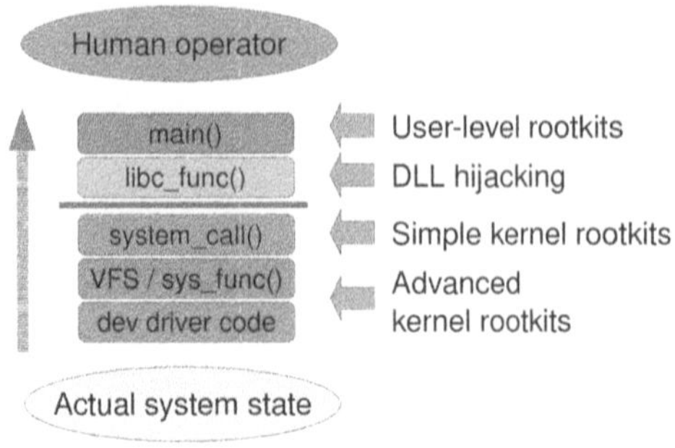

Figure 3: Compromising lower layers of the OS enables deception along the normal data flow path to human operator.

access and affect these data structures. Thus reading of openly available rootkit code not only helps the students to familiarize themselves with these threats, but also may provide valuable insights into OS kernel architecture itself. As with networking, a recommended reading list of helpful hacker materials on rootkits can be found at the Web site `http://hackercurriculum.org/`.

6. CONCLUSION

We posit that the largely undocumented and informal "Hacker Curriculum" contains a number of principles and methods that can prove useful in educating undergraduates in the art of ethical computer security assessment. We applied the "failure mode" principle during a summer cyber-security training camp for undergraduates. By enabling them to view the state of the OS network stack and the network itself as they made both crafted and legitimate requests for resources, they gained an appreciation for the limits and outlines of networks as well as a measure of competence with standard network details and technology.

Hacking involves the ability to develop and nurture a cross-layer view of systems rather than one where abstraction, APIs, or traditional subject domain limits create artificial boundaries. In addition, we find that exploring and understanding the failure modes of CS concepts and computer systems (particularly with regard to networks) provides a useful teaching technique.

Acknowledgments

The authors would like to thank the SIGCSE reviewers for their suggested revisions to the paper and particularly for their suggestions for our presentation during the conference. The authors would also like to thank Greg Conti for his help in organizing the CISSE working group in June of 2009, from which many of the ideas for this paper grew. In addition, we would like to thank the student participants in the SISMAT 2009 course for their willingness to explore these techniques with us. The authors would also like to acknowledge the support of the I3P, Dartmouth College, and DHS for the work described in this paper. This material is based upon work supported by the U.S. Department of Homeland Security under Grant Award Number 2006-CS-001-000001. The views and conclusions contained in this document are those of the authors and should not be interpreted as necessarily representing the official policies, either expressed or implied, of the U.S. Department of Homeland Security.

7. REFERENCES

[1] S. Bratus. Hacker Curriculum: How Hackers Learn Networking. *IEEE Distributed Systems Online*, 8(10), 2007.

[2] S. Bratus. What Hackers Learn That the Rest of Us Don't: Notes on Hacker Curriculum. *IEEE Security and Privacy*, 5(4):72–75, 2007.

[3] M. Handley, V. Paxson, and C. Kreibich. Network Intrusion Detection: Evasion, Traffic Normalization, and End-to-End Protocol Semantics. In *Proceedings of the USENIX Security Conference*, 2001.

[4] M. E. Kabay. Hiring hackers (part 1): British Government Puts a Foot In It. `http://www.networkworld.com/newsletters/sec/2009/081009sec2.html`, August 2009.

[5] D. L. Knox, P. J. DePasquale, and S. M. Pulimood. A Model for Summer Undergraduate Research Experiences in Emerging Technologies. *SIGCSE Bull.*, 38(1):214–218, 2006.

[6] M. E. Locasto and S. Sinclair. An Experience Report on Cyber-Security Education and Outreach. In *Proceedings of the Annual Conference on Education in Information Security*, 2009.

[7] P. Y. Logan and A. Clarkson. Teaching Students to Hack: Curriculum Issues in Information Security. In *SIGCSE '05: Proceedings of the 36th SIGCSE Technical Symposium on Computer Science Education*, pages 157–161, New York, NY, USA, 2005. ACM.

[8] J. Markoff. Do We Need a New Internet? `http://www.nytimes.com/2009/02/15/weekinreview/15markoff.html`, February 2009.

[9] P. Mateti. A Laboratory-based Course on Internet Security. In *SIGCSE '03: Proceedings of the* 34th *SIGCSE Technical Symposium on Computer Science Education*, pages 252–256, New York, NY, USA, 2003. ACM.

[10] B. A. Pashel. Teaching Students to Hack: Ethical Implications in Teaching Students to Hack at the University Level. In *InfoSecCD '06: Proceedings of the 3rd annual conference on Information security curriculum development*, pages 197–200, New York, NY, USA, 2006. ACM.

[11] T. H. Ptacek and T. N. Newsham. Insertion, Evasion, and Denial of Service: Eluding Network Intrusion Detection. In *Snort.org*, January 1998.

[12] R. Speers and E. Tice. Cyber Attacks on the Dartmouth College Network. *Dartmouth Undergraduate Journal of Science (DUJS Online)*, Fall 2009. `http://dujs.dartmouth.edu/fall-2009/cyber-attacks-on-the-dartmouth-college-\network/`.

[13] G. White and G. Nordstrom. Security Across the Curriculum: Using Computer Security to Teach Computer Science Principles. In *Proceedings of the* 19th *National Information Systems Security Conference*, pages 483–488, October 1996.

What Everyone Needs to Know About Computation

John Barr
Ithaca College
barr@ithaca.edu

Steve Cooper
Purdue University
coopers@acm.org

Mike Goldweber
(Moderator)
Xavier University
mikeyg@cs.xu.edu

Henry Walker
Grinnell College
walker@math.grinnell.edu

Categories and Subject Descriptors

K.3.2 [**Computers and Education**]: Computer and Information Science Education—*Computer Science Education*

General Terms

Design, Experimentation

Keywords

Non-major courses, Curriculum, Computational Thinking

1. SUMMARY

For a variety of reasons there has been a renewed interest in non-major level computer science courses. One reason for this is that non-major courses are seen as potentially increasing both interest and enrollment in computer science courses. Another reason is the rising popularity of "computational thinking." Furthermore, as computation becomes the cornerstone of research methodologies, if not professional practice, in the natural, physical and social sciences, including, as well, a growing influence in the humanities, the demand from external departments/programs for non-major level service courses has began to rise, albeit slowly.

This raises some interesting questions to the CSE community. Given that one offers a single non-major level course, what should be the topics covered as distinct from the technologies used to convey those topics? What learning outcomes are most desired? Finally, the competency, or at least serious introduction of which technological skills, if any, should be considered mandatory (e.g. programming).

In short, what should a non-major/minor student who takes one course in computer science come away with knowing and being able to do? Possibly orthogonal to this is the question: What should any liberally (college) educated person know about computation at this point in time?

This panel will outline four different perspectives on this important question in addition to engaging the audience in a discussion regarding the answers to the questions raised.

2. JOHN BARR

Our experience at Ithaca College is that students entering from high school have, over the last 10 years, become less computer literate. Ten years ago we could assume that students knew what a folder or directory was, how to create, rename, and move files, how to install programs, and even how to change basic operating system settings. Today we find that none of these skills are prevalent. Instead, students are experts at finding papers on the Web, installing apps on their cell phones, and are masters at all sorts of communication and social networking technologies from cell phones to texting to Facebook.

The traditional view of computer literacy sees this trend as an unfortunate development that needs to be reversed through computer literacy/non-major level courses. Students should be forced to learn computation, abstraction (such as folders and files), and the basics of maintaining their operating system. But is this true? What do students really need to know?

The discipline of computer science is dedicated to developing computational tools. One aspect of this goal is to make the tools more accessible and flexible. As the discipline matures, the tools it produces have also become more mature. Compare, for example, the iPhone against all previous smart phones. Certainly the iPhone is no less useful or powerful than previous phones. Yet users no longer need to know the arcania of folders, the simultaneous use of multiple buttons, and stupefying navigation techniques.

The lesson to take from this simple look at cell phone technology is not that users are becoming less adept. Rather the lesson is that users have mastered the technology that exists today, not the technology that existed ten years ago. The gritty details of computation and communication have been abstracted out and users no longer need to master these details to use these tools effectively. Just as some people would argue that computer scientists do not need to be masters of assembly language programming to be successful today, the average user of technology no longer needs to master the details of computation to be an effective user of computation-based technology.

3. MICHAEL GOLDWEBER

It is instructive to consider a proposed course, not just against other proposed courses, but against no course at all. After all, both automotive and telephone technology are as ubiquitous as computation, yet the vast majority can successfully utilize both technologies without any grounding, i.e. non-majors college course, in either physics or mechanical engineering. Taking this argument further one might conclude that other disciplines which require knowledge of computation would be satisfied by either requiring an intro-

SIGCSE'10, March 10–13, 2010, Milwaukee, Wisconsin, USA.
ACM 978-1-60558-885-8/10/03.

ductory major-level CS course or covering what aspects of computation are needed in their own courses.

This position argues that a meaningful non-major level CS course should therefore not be concerned with skill acquisition. Instead it should focus on the discipline's deep intellectual contributions; which may be described as algorithmic problem solving, harnessing abstraction to manage complexity, and the automation of an algorithmic solution. Of these, I believe that algorithmic problem solving is not only the most important, but also the one where the greatest success can be achieved.

Algorithmic problem solving has a number of standard paradigms; brute force, greedy, divide and conquer, dynamic programming, etc. In addition to these techniques are the important notions of problem reduction, when a new problem can be recast as an instance of a different, previously solved problem, and the recognition and handling of "hard" problems. Whether or not one ever intends to automate a given problem's solution, being able to approach and eventually solve a given problem using one or more of these techniques is a highly valued skill.

Consider a non-major level course that involves no programming, no discussion of objects, encapsulation or polymorphism, but examines a wide variety of problems drawn from a plethora of problem domains and has students practicing how to develop solutions to these problems. Just as a liberally educated person should be versed in how mathematicians determine truth/solves problems; conjecture and proof, or how natural and social scientists do the same; reproducible experiments informed via the scientific method, they should also be versed in how computer scientists do the same; application of problem reduction and/or the use of standard algorithmic paradigms.

4. HENRY WALKER

Much discussion by panelists here and by others throughout the computing community supports the view that introductory computing courses should involve problem solving. In principle, I too support the idea that problem solving should be central to computer science courses — for non-majors, majors, and anyone else. In courses, I would hope that students would tackle problems and gain experience at finding solutions. However, I wonder how students (or the general citizenry) will state and explain their solutions, and how they will know their proposed solutions are correct.

I think much is lost if people (students, the general public) do not have to be precise in stating their solutions. It is reasonably easy to write high-level outlines for many problems in English, but it does not follow that these approaches can be refined to actually work in practice. Algorithmic problem solving illustrates the maxim, "the devil is in the details."

This difficulty leads to a dilemma. Although courses for both majors and non-majors should emphasize problem solving, omitting some type of programming allows people to be sloppy. This observation leads to the conclusion that programming of some type is needed to sharpen problem-solving skills.

Of course, one can become caught up in details of programming languages (some courses seem overly focused here), but there needs to be some way to make solutions precise. Whatever the language, students should be able to write careful and detailed solutions, and the language should have sufficient expressibility and precision that students and their instructors can analyze the correctness of any proposed solutions. While not essential, machine-executable instructions also can be helpful in determining reviewing correctness.

In this regard, pseudo-code is no better than a formally-defined programming language. If the pseudo-code is defined tightly enough, then it might as well be machine readable. If pseudo-code is not tightly defined, then it is open to the same ambiguities as English or another natural language. Overall, I conclude introductory courses for both non-majors and majors should include a significant component of programming as a mechanism to express ideas carefully and precisely.

5. STEVE COOPER

J. Wing has indicated that she considers computational thinking to be the process of abstraction. Though Wing goes on to focus on the "goodness" of abstractions from an engineering point of view (examining such measures as efficiency, correctness, and software engineering considerations such as simplicity, elegance, usability, modifiability, maintainability, cost, etc.), the bottom line is that any approach towards presenting computational thinking for the masses needs to focus on the process of abstraction. Of course, teaching the process of abstraction is a daunting task, attempting to tackle one of Brooks' essential difficulties (referred to as software invisibility) inherent in software engineering.

If a non-majors course needs to help students understand the process of abstraction, it seems to me to be necessary to provide the students meaningful contexts from which they are comfortable in exploring abstraction. Certainly my own work with Alice (`www.alice.org`, `www.aliceprogramming.net`) provides the context of animation and storytelling from which to explore abstraction. Scratch (`scratch.mit.edu`) is an alternative. Guzdial's work with media computation uses the manipulation of sound, images, and video as an alternative context from which to explore abstraction. Roberts' work with the ACM Java Taskforce provides instructors with a powerful library of graphics and other routines from which to construct their own contexts. Robots are another context, as is the programmable clothing of Lilypad Arduino. And there are many others. It is also not necessary to focus on programming in providing the context. It is certainly possible to explore abstraction through the contexts of networking and/or communication. It is also possible to explore computational thinking and the process of abstraction through domain specific examples/contexts from the geo-sciences, economics, politics, biology, physics, etc. Instructors can demonstrate how computational thinking can be used to provide abstractions for the modeling of behavior.

Guzdial's media computation is used as an example context by which to explain what I mean by the exploration of abstraction. A picture is an abstraction for a collection of pixels. A pixel is an abstraction for a 3-tuple consisting of x and y coordinates and a color. A color is an abstraction for a 3-tuple, say of red, green, and blue. And the abstractions can continue, by considering how a collection of images can be considered as a video, etc. The bottom line is that a concrete example, meaningful to the student, provides a potential context from which to help students explore the process of abstraction.

Understanding NSF Funding Opportunities

Scott Grissom
National Science Foundation
Undergraduate Education
1-703-292-4643
sgrissom@nsf.gov

Joan Peckham
National Science Foundation
CISE
1-703-292-7344
jpeckham@nsf.gov

Harriet Taylor
National Science Foundation
CISE
1-703-292-7973
htaylor@nsf.gov

Guy-Alain Amoussou
National Science Foundation
Undergraduate Education
1-703-292-4645
gamousso@nsf.gov

Victor Piotrowski
National Science Foundation
Undergraduate Education
1-703-292-5141
vpiotrow@nsf.gov

ABSTRACT

This session highlights programs in the National Science Foundation's (NSF) Education and Human Resources (EHR) and Computer and Information Science and Engineering (CISE) directorates. The focus is on providing descriptions of several programs of interest to college faculty, and discussing the requirements and guidelines for programs in these areas. It includes a description of the proposal and review processes as well as strategies for writing competitive proposals. Participants are encouraged to discuss procedural issues with the presenters.

Categories and Subject Descriptors

K.3.2 Computer and Information Science Education

General Terms

Documentation.

Keywords

Grants, awards, proposals, National Science Foundation, education.

1. INTRODUCTION

NSF supports projects to improve education in science, technology, engineering, and mathematics through several programs in its Education and Human Resources (EHR) directorate, as well as in its research directorates, including Computer and Information Science and Engineering (CISE). This forum presents a description of some education-related programs in the EHR and CISE directorates, and enables participants to interact with the presenters concerning specific project ideas that could be appropriate for the various programs.

2. SPECIFIC PROGRAMS DISCUSSED

Complete details about each of the following programs can be found on the NSF websites for the Division of Undergraduate Education (DUE) [1] and the Directorate for Computer & Information Science & Engineering (CISE) [2].

SIGCSE'10, March 10–13, 2010, Milwaukee, Wisconsin, USA.
ACM 978-1-60558-885-8/10/03.

2.1 Advanced Technological Education (ATE)

ATE is a program specifically geared for community colleges, or for four-year schools working closely with community colleges. This program focuses on improvement in the "education of science and engineering technicians at the undergraduate and the secondary school levels. [2]" Specific technological fields include computer and information technology, cybersecurity, forensics, and telecommunications.

2.2 Broadening Participation in Computing (BPC)

BPC aims to significantly increase the number of U. S. citizens and permanent residents receiving post secondary degrees in computing disciplines, with an emphasis on students from communities with longstanding under-representation in computing. BPC has three components: Alliances, Alliance Extensions, and Demonstration Projects.

2.3 Course, Curriculum, and Laboratory Improvement (CCLI)

CCLI supports innovation in student learning in the classroom, and improvements in educational practice. Particular emphasis in CCLI is on creating new learning materials and strategies, developing faculty expertise, implementing education innovations, assessing student achievement, and conducting research on undergraduate STEM education. The NSF showcase presents innovative CCLI projects.

2.4 CISE Pathways to Revitalized Undergraduate Computing Education (CPATH)

CPATH focuses on transforming undergraduate computing education on a national scale to meet the challenges of producing a global economy U. S. workforce. CPATH projects apply core computational thinking concepts, methods, technologies, and tools to a broad range of societal challenges. CPATH supports two levels of projects, Class I and Class II.

2.5 Federal Cyber Service: Scholarships for Service (SFS)

This program seeks to increase the number of qualified students entering information assurance and computer security and to increase the capacity of the US higher education enterprise to continue to produce professionals in these fields. The SFS program is has two tracks: (1) the Scholarship Track that provides funding for scholarships to students in information assurance and computer security, and (2) the Capacity Building Track that provides funding for professional development of information assurance and computer security faculty and for the development of academic programs in these fields.

2.6 Information Technology Experiences for Students and Teachers (ITEST)

While there are four main components to ITEST, the two most likely to be of interest are youth-based projects for students in K-12, and comprehensive projects for K-12 teachers and students. "It is anticipated that projects funded under the ITEST program will not only increase interest in IT through the creation of effective student education programs in both school and non-school contexts, but also maintain interest through supportive activities that include parental involvement, career exploration, externships, research, and multi-year programs."

Two other programs in the Division of Research on Learning in Formal and Informal Settings (DRL) for supporting K-12 students and teachers are Informal Science Education (ISE) and Discovery Research K-12 (DRK-12). These will both be briefly covered.

2.7 Research Experiences for Undergraduates Sites (REU Sites)

Research experience is one of the most effective ways of attracting talented undergraduates to, and retaining them in careers in science and engineering, including careers in teaching and research. The REU Sites program aims to provide appropriate and valuable educational experiences for cohorts of 8-10 undergraduate students in the summer through participation in research and professional development activities. REU projects involve students, most who are from other than the host institution, in meaningful ways in ongoing research programs or in research projects specifically designed for the REU program. REU projects feature high-quality interaction of students with faculty and/or other research mentors and access to appropriate facilities and professional development opportunities.

2.8 Scholarships in Science, Technology, Engineering and Mathematics (S-STEM)

This program makes grants to institutions of higher education to support individual scholarships of up to $10,000/year for academically talented, financially needy students, majoring in science and engineering disciplines. It is expected that scholarship recipients will achieve at least one of the following by the end of the scholarship award period: (1) receive an associate, baccalaureate, or graduate degree in one of the S-STEM disciplines; (2) transfer from an associate degree program to a baccalaureate degree program or from an undergraduate program to a graduate program in one of the S-STEM disciplines; or (3) successfully complete a stage within an associate, baccalaureate, or graduate degree program in one of the S-STEM disciplines.

2.9 STEM Talent Expansion Program (STEP)

STEP grants fall into two categories of activities. Type 1 activities are aimed at implementing recruitment or retention strategies that will lead to a measurable increase in the number of students obtaining STEM degrees in baccalaureate or associate degree programs or completing credits toward transfer to a baccalaureate degree program in STEM fields at community colleges. Type 2 activities focus on educational research on factors affecting associate or baccalaureate degree attainment in STEM.

3. WRITING COMPETITIVE PROPOSALS

NSF programs are quite competitive but there are simple strategies you should be aware of when writing proposals to improve your chances of success. First and foremost, read the Program Solicitation carefully. Your goal is to help reviewers quickly understand *what* you intend to do and that you have given sufficient thought of *how* you intend to do it. Organize the proposal to address the essential components described in the solicitation. Use headings, boldface and bulleted lists to help the reader quickly understand the organization of the proposals. Address each point thoroughly but succinctly. And finally, start well before the submission deadline. Include sufficient lead time to allow colleagues to provide feedback and for your research office to approve the proposal. Specific directions for completing your proposal can be found online [3].

4. REFERENCES

[1] http://nsf.gov/div/index.jsp?div=DUE

[2] http://nsf.gov/dir/index.jsp?org=CISE

[3] http://nsf.gov/funding/preparing/

A Web Service-Oriented Approach to Teaching CS/IS1

Billy Lim
Illinois State University
Normal, IL 61790
bllim@ilstu.edu

Bryan Hosack
Illinois State University
Normal, IL 61790
bhosack@ilstu.edu

Paul Vogt
Illinois State University
Normal, IL 61790
wpvogt@ilstu.edu

SUMMARY

Web services technology is a burgeoning technology that has received much attention in the software industry in recent years under the broader umbrella of service-oriented architecture (SOA). The popularity of the service-oriented paradigm is echoed by Microsoft's Bill Gates, where in a memo to Microsoft's top managers and engineers, he states "The broad and rich foundation of the internet will unleash a 'services wave' of applications and experiences available instantly over the internet to millions of users" [1]. While Web services have been incorporated in many industries in the market place, they are only beginning to appear in the academia, primarily in upper division and graduate CS/IS curricula [2,3]. In this special session, we share our belief that Web services technologies can and should be introduced early in CS/IS curricula. We describe and demo a number of scenarios that illustrate how Web services can be integrated into CS1/IS1 to make these courses more interesting and more importantly, make the students better prepared for upper division classes and for the industry upon graduation. This special session also shares the results of our preliminary findings involving the aforementioned integration and introduces participants to the related courseware. Participants will also receive hands-on experience with some of the scenarios experimented in our study. The intended audience is CS/IS educators who are interested in a novel way of teaching CS1/IS1. *NOTE: Participants are encouraged to bring a laptop with wireless access to the Web and with NetBeans.*

Categories and Subject Descriptors
K.3 [**Computers& Education**]: Computer & Information Science
Education – Computer Science Education

General Terms
Design, Experimentation, Languages

Keywords
Web services, service-oriented architecture, Teaching CS1/IS1

1. OVERALL OBJECTIVE

The overall objectives of this special session are to: (1) disseminate the use of Web service-oriented approach to teaching CS1/IS1, (2) to explore educational innovations for indoctrinating students the state-of-the-art software development practices using SOA, and (3) to build a learning/research community of service-orientation-in-CS1/IS1 enthusiasts.

SIGCSE'10, March 10–13, 2010, Milwaukee, Wisconsin, USA.
ACM 978-1-60558-885-8/10/03.

2. SESSION OUTLINE

The special session includes the project rationale, introduction to courseware using Web services, researcher experience report, brief hands-on demonstration for participants, and concludes with a group discussion/feedback component.

2.1 Project Rationale

Presenters: Drs. Billy Lim, Bryan Hosack, ISU.
Duration: 10 minutes

The rationale for the project, which began with research presented by Lim et al. in 2005 [4] and currently funded by a NSF CCLI grant [5], will be discussed. The importance of how current CS/IS curricula need to incorporate the current software practices (i.e., SOA), without compromising the core materials presently covered in many CS/IS introductory sequences, will be highlighted.

2.2 Courseware Showcase

Presenters: Drs. Billy Lim, Bryan Hosack, ISU.
Duration: 10 minutes

The presenters will briefly present the courseware, which consists of a collection of PowerPoint slides, lab exercises, programming assignments, and tutorials. These are freely available for use and can be downloaded from the project website. Sample student work for various labs and programming assignments will also be showcased. An educational compendium of Web services, WS4Intro, will be presented. WS4Into is hosted on the presenters' server and offers services that are freely available for educational use.

2.3 Experience Report

Presenters: Drs. Billy Lim, Bryan Hosack, ISU.
Duration: 10 minutes

Presenters will summarize the experiences of using the Web service-oriented approach in our CS1 and IS1 courses. Quantitative and qualitative data will be presented on the preliminary use of Web services in CS1/IS1. Analysis of student and faculty evaluation will be presented as well as student perceptions of Web services in the classroom. Presented data will include student demographics, student course performance, and pre-/post questionnaire comparison results.

2.4 Hands-On Experiments with Exercises

Presenter: Dr. Billy Lim, ISU.
Duration: 20 minutes

Participants are encouraged to bring a laptop with wireless access to the Web and with NetBeans (version 6.7.1 as of this writing, Web and Java EE edition; the NetBeans IDE can be freely downloaded from www.netbeans.org.) Participants can experiment with the various Web services incorporated into the courseware so far. Also, participants will experience as a student user, completing a programming assignment to get a feel of what it is like to engage in Web service-oriented approach. A possible sample module would function as follows:

Table 1: Web service scenario for the topic "Control Structures"

Module Name:	**Sequence, Iterative, and Decision Structures**
Typical Delivery:	These topics are typically covered by traditional discussion of scenarios that (1) necessitate a certain ordering be imposed to solve a problem, (2) require a loop be used, and (3) need an if-else structure be employed.
WS Delivery:	Instead of merely processing a collection of numbers or strings that may not resonate with students, one could present a scenario where the goal is to solve a problem by using the three fundamental structures and existing Web services to form a solution.
Example:	A plausible scenario would be to solve the problem of finding the warmest temperature in the entire U.S. by zip code. Further, the warmest area of the country needs to be plotted on a map. Lastly, get a route to go to the warmest area from a given location. This scenario may seem intractable in the traditional introduction environment. But there exist various publicly available Web services that can be composed together to solve this problem rather effortlessly. There exist Web services that retrieve all the US zip codes, finds the temperature for a given zip code, plot a particular area on a map given a zip code, and plot the route given two endpoints (MapPoint Web service, Google Maps API). Thus, one can cover the topic using a more interesting approach. 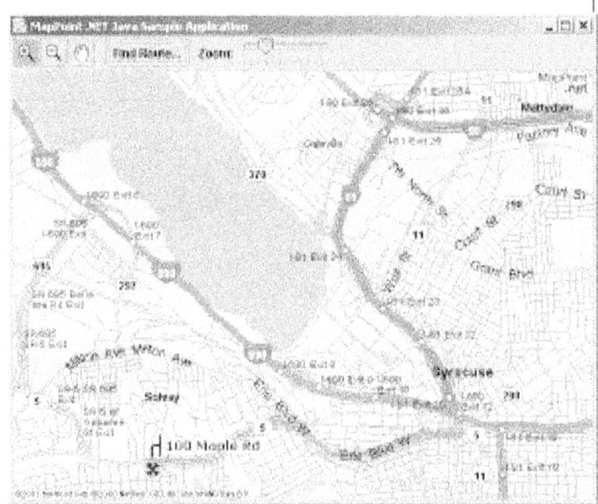

2.5 Group Discussion

Leader: Dr. Bryan Hosack, ISU.
Duration: 20 minutes

We would like to hear suggestions and feedback to the Web service-oriented approach from the attendees and the community at large. This discussion will focus on the presented material and activities, as well as the interest of the community in incorporating this approach at their institutions. The future plans of the project, including a faculty workshop in the summer of 2010, will be discussed.

3. EXPECTATIONS

The intended audience is CS/IS educators who are interested in a novel way of teaching CS1/IS1. It is expected that a fruitful discussion of how the pedagogical approach for CS1/IS1 can be advanced will result. The session provides a complete coverage of the preliminary project findings, from the fall 2009 semester up to the presentation, which would include part of the spring 2010 semester. In addition, companion courseware, user experience report and analysis, future plans, and several related research directions will be provided. The hands-on experience will allow participants to experiment with the Web service-oriented approach used in the classroom by students.

Given how SIGCSE attendees are typically very passionate about topics surrounding CS1, we anticipate about 25-30 participants in this special session.

Feedback from participants will be collected via a brief voluntary single page paper-based survey after the session.

4. MATERIALS PROVIDED

Each participant will receive a CD, containing a package of supporting materials, including (1) detailed notes of all presentations, (2) handouts for the hands-on experiments with the Web service-oriented scenarios, (3) screencast and step-by-step instructions on how to incorporate Web services. Laptops are recommended for the participation in hands-on experiments.

5. SUITABILITY FOR SPECIAL SESSION

The format and the organization of this proposal make it an ideal candidate for experimenting with the SIGCSE special session format. Unlike a regular paper or panel, the session is a mixture of short presentations, group reports, hands-on experiments, and group discussions. The interactivity planned will allow for a much better means to achieve the session objectives.

6. ACKNOWLEDGMENTS

This material is based upon work supported by the National Science Foundation under Grant No. 0837056. Any opinions, findings and conclusions or recommendations expressed in this material are those of the author(s) and do not necessarily reflect the views of the National Science Foundation (NSF).

7. REFERENCES

[1] Gates, W., "Internet Software Services," memo, http://www.scripting.com/disruption/mail.html, Retrieved May 16, 2008.

[2] Humphrey, M., "Web Services as the Foundation for Learning Complex Software System Development," *35th SIGCSE Technical Symposium on Computer Science Education*, Norfolk, Virginia USA March 3 - 7, 2004.

[3] Lopez, N., Casallas, R., Villalobos, J., "Challenges in Creating Environments for SOA Learning," IEEE Proceedings of the International Workshop on Systems Development in SOA Environments, May 2007.

[4] Lim, B., Jong, C., Mahatanankoon, P., "On Integrating Web Services from the Ground Up into CS1/CS2," *ACM SIGCSE 2005*, St. Louis, MO, Feb., 2005.

[5] Lim, B., Hosack, B., NSF-DUE-0837056, "Integrating Service-Oriented Paradigm into Introductory Information Technology Curricula," 2009 – 2011.

Teaching Computer Networks in a Real Network

The Technical Perspectives

Jianping Pan
Dept of Computer Science
University of Victoria
Victoria, BC, Canada
pan@uvic.ca

ABSTRACT

Experimenting in courses such as operating systems, computer networks, and distributed systems is challenging due to the need to access system kernels and network infrastructures, as well as the distributed nature of these experiments. In this paper, we design and develop a laboratory platform that can be rapidly and economically adopted in any educational institutions to teach introductory computer networks courses. By using commercial, off-the-shelf hardware and open-source software, and together with our technical solutions, the platform gives students an opportunity to experiment in a real, flexible and scalable network, and to interact with the network both as a network user and more importantly as a network operator. These features can help students to better understand the algorithms, protocols and practice of computer networks. This easy-to-use lab platform has been received favorably by students. Also, the low-cost platform is easy to maintain, and can be repeatedly used in multiple, back-to-back lab sections.

Categories and Subject Descriptors

K.3 [**Computers and Education**]: Computer and Information Science Education; C.2 [**Computer-Communication Networks**]: Network Architecture and Design

General Terms

Experimentation

Keywords

Computer networks, network experimentation, lab platform

1. INTRODUCTION

"I hear and I forget;
I see and I remember;
I do and I understand." — *Chinese Proverb*

Experimentation is very important for systems-oriented courses in computer science curricula, which can give students a hands-on opportunity to understand the existing systems and their initial design tradeoffs, to answer many *what-if* questions for emerging scenarios, and to potentially improve these systems in both functionality and performance. Experimentation has been credited as a key to an active, engaging learning experience [1–6].

However, experimenting in courses such as operating systems, computer networks and distributed systems is known to be challenging, due to the need to access system kernels and network infrastructures. This requirement is hard to fulfill in most universities, unless there are separate, dedicated network testbed and system sandbox available for teaching purposes (often quite rare). Also in many cases, due to the distributed nature of these experiments, coordination is required (very hard to achieve if not impossible).

Modeling, analysis, simulation, emulation and experimentation are known approaches to computer networks research and education [1,2], where the latter three are more attractive in introductory computer networks courses. However, both simulation and emulation only give students another layer of abstraction to what they encounter in the real world. Also, students have to get familiar with simulation or emulation environments, which can add considerable overhead in introductory courses. On the other hand, experimentation usually is very expensive and needs heavy maintenance, which is normally beyond the reach of universities and colleges both budget and personnel wise.

In this paper, we design and develop a laboratory platform that can be rapidly and economically adopted in any educational institutions to teach introductory computer networks courses. By using commercial, off-the-self products and open-source software, exampled by Linksys WRT54GL broadband home router[1] and OpenWRT firmware[2] in this paper, and together with our technical solutions, the platform gives students an opportunity to experiment in a real, flexible and scalable network, and to interact with the network both as a network user and a network operator, which can help them to better understand the algorithms, protocols and practice of computer networks. The easy-to-use platform has been received favorably by students.

Our contributions in this paper are threefold. To the best of our knowledge, this is the first time that such a low-cost and low-maintenance lab platform is reported in the open literature. Second, due to the use of commodity hardware

[1] `http://linksysbycisco.com/US/en/products/WRT54GL`
[2] `http://openwrt.org/`

SIGCSE'10, March 10–13, 2010, Milwaukee, Wisconsin, USA.

and open-source software, the platform is easy-to-use and easy-to-modify. Last but not least, the platform provides high fidelity and high interactivity that are often only available from certification programs with expensive, proprietary hardware and dedicated maintenance personnel. In fact, this lab platform has been used in multiple, back-to-back lab sections, with virtually no maintenance at all.

The remainder of this paper is organized as follows. In Section 2, we briefly overview the related work on the approaches to computer networks education, with a focus on simulation, emulation and experimentation. We then describe our platform design in Section 3 and present our technical solutions in Section 4. We report our recent experience of using this platform in Section 5, followed by further discussion and concluding remarks in Section 6.

2. RELATED WORK

Modeling, analysis, simulation, emulation and experimentation are known approaches to computer network research and education; however, modeling and analysis usually are less attractive for the first undergraduate networks course [1, 2], so we *only* focus on simulation, emulation and experimentation in this section and overview the most related work.

`ns-2` is an open-source simulator[3] and is widely used in network research communities. `OPNET` is a commercial simulator (free for university teaching and research)[4]. `OMNet++`[5] and `GloMoSim/QualNet`[6] are also often used. However, most simulators have their own user interface and level of abstraction, which creates a steep learning curve at the beginning. Furthermore, simulation normally only focuses on specific issues of the network under investigation, and the observation can be different from what appears in a real network.

Emulation is closer to reality, which is normally better received by students. There are some network emulation platforms available (e.g., `GINI`[7] and `VNS`[8]), among which `Emulab/Netlab`[9], `Planetlab`[10] and `ONL`[11] are the ones with remote, open access. By using commodity computers or network processors with virtualization techniques, network elements such as routers, switches and links are emulated, as well as a variety of end hosts. `Planetlab` is an overlay network over the actual Internet with geographical diversity as well. However, there is a limited provisioning of such emulation platforms, and even research projects have to be scheduled and prioritized. Therefore, it is unlikely for all universities and colleges to use these platforms for teaching introductory courses. In addition, remote emulation platforms lack the "look and feel" experience usually expected by students on hardware devices.

Experimentation gives the closest observation on reality. In fact, nowadays many students already have experience with network devices at home or on campus. However, due to the need to access system kernels (e.g., to use raw `socket` [3]) and the concerns of security and privacy (when observing network traffic [4]), most education institutions do not allow students to have privileged access to lab computers and campus networks. Separate, dedicated network testbed and system sandbox have been built, mostly together with network vendor's certification programs, due to the high cost of network equipment. Supported by NSF and with industry contributions, CAIDA helped build about two dozens of University Internet Teaching Labs (ITL)[12]. Even though, only very few universities have such facilities, with a price tag around $15–17.5K per seat or experiment [5,6], and the majority of universities and colleges is still left out.

Although Linksys WRT54GL and OpenWRT have been very popular in broadband Internet user and hacker communities, not much work has been done for teaching labs yet (other than [7] with a very different purpose and setting from ours). Since many students also use such low-cost DSL/cable routers at home for broadband Internet access, they are not intimidated by strange devices. With a Linux-based OpenWRT firmware, students can use many software tools that they are already familiar with in regular Linux computers, thus easing the learning process. With OpenWRT, Linksys WRT54GL can perform many advanced network operations, which are usually only found in high-end, expensive network switches and routers. Bringing all these features together, we believe the platform we have designed and developed is novel and deserves external dissemination for the benefit of the entire computer science education community.

3. PLATFORM DESIGN

In this section, we first enumerate the design criteria of such a laboratory platform to teach introductory computer networks courses, and then detail the main components of our design. Some technical challenges and our solutions will be presented in the next section.

3.1 Design Criteria

The primary goal of our platform is to support the teaching of the first undergraduate computer networks course in computer science, computer engineering and software engineering majors, where experimentation has been considered as a key to an active, engaging learning experience.

In today's computer science curricula, the first computer networks course normally covers the Internet architecture, services and protocols, particularly TCP/IP protocols and their applications. Technically speaking, the lab platform should support activities in application layers (e.g., HTTP and DNS), transport layer (TCP and UDP), network layer (IP addressing and routing) and link layer (majorly Ethernet and wireless Ethernet). To achieve this goal, we have defined a list of criteria for the lab platform.

High fidelity and high interactivity: First, the platform should be as realistic as possible, preferably close to what are actually used in the real world, so students can easily correlate the algorithms and protocols learned in lectures to what they encounter on a daily basis using the Internet. The observation they have in the lab can be easily found at their home or in work place as well. Second, the platform should provide enough flexibility to allow students to interact with the network directly, e.g., capturing network traffic, analyzing packet headers, changing protocol settings, and so on, just as what a network operator normally can do.

[3]`http://www.isi.edu/nsnam/ns/`
[4]`http://www.opnet.com/`
[5]`http://www.omnetpp.org/`
[6]`http://www.scalable-networks.com/`
[7]`http://www.cs.mcgill.ca/~anrl/gini`
[8]`http://yuba.stanford.edu/vns/`
[9]`http://www.emulab.net/`
[10]`http://www.planet-lab.org/`
[11]`http://onl.wustl.edu/`
[12]`http://www.caida.org/projects/itl/` (The project has ended.)

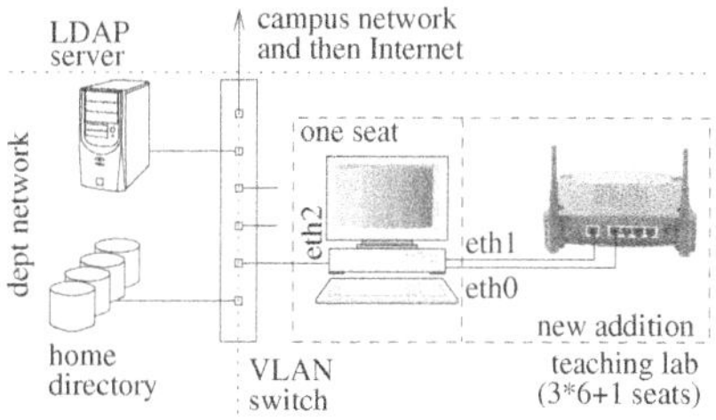

Figure 1: An illustration of the lab platform.

Table 1: Host-Router Connectivity

Host iface	IP address	Router iface	IP address
eth0	192.168.1.100	br0 (LAN)	192.168.1.1
eth1	10.10.1.100	vlan1 (WAN)	10.10.1.1
eth2	public IP	-	-

Easy-to-use and easy-to-modify: Next, the platform should also be easy to use, preferably close to what students have been using in other teaching labs, at home or in workplace. In this sense, there is virtually no initial learning curve for students to start using this platform. Also the platform should be easy to modify without physically recabling to meet the need of introductory networks courses with a focus on TCP/IP protocols and applications.

Low cost and low maintenance: Low cost is important for educational institutions with limited teaching budget and personnel. Normally consumer-grade electronics are more cost effective than those used by enterprise or service providers. Also the platform should have minimum maintenance, especially when one teaching lab usually has to serve multiple and possibly back-to-back lab sections.

3.2 Main Components

To meet these criteria, we use Linksys WRT54GL router with Linux-based OpenWRT as the experimentation platform attached to each student computer (also in Linux) already in the teaching lab, as shown in Figure 1.

3.2.1 Host Computer

The host computer is a regular Linux system[13] but with additional network interfaces (i.e., Ethernet cards). As shown in Figure 1, the host is the main platform for students to access the router and complete their lab assignments, with graphical user interfaces such as KDE and having their home directory automatically mounted no matter which computer they login to. Students only have regular user privilege on these computers. If necessary, the login to these computers can be controlled by the LDAP system, and the VLAN switch can lock down the entire lab.

Each host has at least three network interfaces. One is connected to the campus network, therefore the host is accessible from the Internet through secure shell (SSH) and students can work on their lab assignments off campus. The other two interfaces are both connected to the Linksys router, specifically to its LAN and WAN port, respectively, as listed in Table 1. Another interface can be used to connect between the host and the router, if remote access and file system traffic is desired to be in a separate network.

In our teaching lab, there are three rows of lab benches with chairs, and each row has six student computers, i.e., hosting 18 students at most in one lab section. Each student uses one computer, connected to both the campus network and one Linksys router. In addition, there is an instructor desk with the same setting, as well as a video data projector to display lab tutorial slides and instructor's screen when necessary. Therefore, multiple lab sections, usually back-to-back, have to be offered to accommodate a large class.

3.2.2 Linksys WRT54GL

Linksys WRT54GL is a Linux-compatible home router often used together with a DSL or cable modem for residential or small office and home office (SOHO) broadband Internet access. It has a 200 MHz MIPS CPU with 16 MB RAM and 4 MB flash storage, a 5-port Fast Ethernet switch (by default, one WAN port and four LAN ports) and a built-in IEEE 802.11b/g wireless access point. The switch is VLAN capable, which allows us to flexibly partition these five ports and the wireless interface into different logical networks. The firmware running on the router adds a lot of features to fulfill the role of a residential gateway (e.g., PPPoE, DHCP client and server, NAT and port forwarding, and so on).

Being a consumer device, WRT54GL has many desirable features in addition to low cost (around $50 each unit). For example, its configuration is stored in a separate NVRAM and its bootloader has a separate partition; therefore the device is very robust, which is also advantageous for teaching labs. By pressing the reset button on the back of the router, the router can go back to the default setting specified in NVRAM. By pressing the reset button in a specific sequence during bootup, the bootloader can download and flash a new firmware image from the network, which is very convenient for system recovery in teaching labs.

In our teaching lab, we connect the router to the host through a pair of Ethernet cables with its WAN and LAN port, respectively. From the viewpoint of the router, the host is both inside the home network and on the "Internet". This makes the coordination easier, but creates a technical challenge for the host operating system, which we will solve in the next section. We also disable the wireless interface, since we do not have wireless lab modules in the introductory course and we want to avoid interference between these routers and with the campus wireless network.

3.2.3 OpenWRT Firmware

OpenWRT was initially developed for Linksys WRT54G series, but now has been extended to become a generic operating system for embedded systems, supporting a wide range of home routers from different vendors and with different chipsets. OpenWRT is based on Linux kernel, and almost all Linux applications can be easily ported to OpenWRT with cross-compilers. The default OpenWRT contains many more features missing in the stock firmware, and with OpenWRT, WRT54GL becomes a very powerful (and usually expensive) layer 2 and 3 network device (normally priced in several hundreds to one thousand dollars range).

The stock firmware of Linksys WRT54GL can be replaced through its built-in Web interface or by following a specific bootstrap sequence when powered on. We actually built a customized OpenWRT distribution with only 30 packages, which contains all the features we need in the lab with configuration, patches and add-on packages listed in Table 2. The customized firmware is preinstalled in lab routers, but

[13] we have used both Scientific Linux and Ubuntu, two mainstream Linux platforms based on RedHat and Debian distributions, and the same as those used in our other teaching and research labs.

Table 2: Add-on OpenWRT Packages

Package	Purpose
ip	for routing control
iptables	for NAT and firewall
maradns	a secure DNS server
tc	for network emulation
tcpdump	for network monitoring
ttcp	to test TCP/UDP performance

we also provide the image[14] and installation instructions to students, since they are also interested in replicating such a low-cost experimentation platform at home.

OpenWRT also has a light-weight Web-based interface called `webif`, which allows our students to get familiar with the router at the beginning. After that, students can access the router through SSH, which is essentially the same as their host Linux computer, but they have privileged access to the router other than NVRAM, and it is safe for students to capture traffic in the isolated network. Our experience shows that for students who are already familiar with mainstream Linux environments such as RedHat or Ubuntu, they do not have any difficulty in using the OpenWRT-powered router even in the first lab session.

4. TECHNICAL CHALLENGES

Although the design of the lab platform seems straightforward, we did encounter some technical difficulties when putting these components together, mainly due to the reason that the host computer and the home router are not normally connected in the way that we use in our lab.

4.1 Parallel Links

The first challenge is the parallel links between the host computer and the Linksys router. In our design, we want to send traffic of ordinary applications from the LAN interface of the host (i.e., `eth0`), going through the router from LAN to WAN port, and eventually arriving at the WAN interface of the host (`eth1`). In this case, the host plays a role of a home computer behind the router, as well as the role of a remote computer on the "Internet". From the viewpoint of network protocols, there is no problem with this design.

However, modern Linux kernels have incorporated many extra features, many of them as counter-attack measures. Specifically, when the WAN interface of the host receives a packet coming from the router's WAN port, it will examine the source IP address of this packet (in this case, `192.168.1.100`, the IP address of the LAN interface of the host computer). By default, the kernel will do a reverse shortest path check to see whether the incoming interface is the same as the outgoing one if the kernel is to send a packet to this IP address; if not, the kernel treats it as a source address spoofing attack and will drop the packet silently. Unfortunately, although there is no attack at all, since the source address is `192.168.1.100`, the IP address in the same host, the kernel thinks the packet should come from the local interface (`lo`), rather than an external interface such as `eth1`. Therefore, the dual connection between the host and the router is in fact broken by default.

To deal with this issue, we need to apply a small kernel patch on the host computer (unfortunately, the reverse path check is hard coded in Linux kernel and cannot be configured dynamically). To that end, we used the `send-to-self` patch made available by Julian Anastasov[15], which creates a configurable interface through `sysctl` utility to enable or disable the reverse path check on a per interface basis. In our setting, we disable the check on `eth0` and `eth1`, without compromising the system security, since the actual external interface on the host is only `eth2`, i.e., in `/etc/sysctl.conf`

```
net.ipv4.conf.eth0.loop=1
net.ipv4.conf.eth1.loop=1
```

Depending on whether to specify the source IP address (e.g., `-I` for `ping`, `bind()` in `socket` programming, etc), we can instruct the host to bypass or to go through the router. As shown in below, when going through the router (i.e., with `-I 192.168.1.100`), the round-trip delay is increased from 0.025 to 0.784 ms, which is also confirmed by `tcpdump`.

```
$ ping -c 3 10.10.1.100
PING 10.10.1.100 56(84) bytes of data.
64 bytes from 10.10.1.100: icmp_seq=1 ttl=64 time=0.035 ms
64 bytes from 10.10.1.100: icmp_seq=2 ttl=64 time=0.025 ms
64 bytes from 10.10.1.100: icmp_seq=3 ttl=64 time=0.017 ms
--- 10.10.1.100 ping statistics ---
rtt min/avg/max/mdev = 0.017/0.025/0.035/0.009 ms

$ ping -c 3 -I 192.168.1.100 10.10.1.100
PING 10.10.1.100 from 192.168.1.100 : 56(84) bytes of data.
64 bytes from 10.10.1.100: icmp_seq=1 ttl=63 time=0.821 ms
64 bytes from 10.10.1.100: icmp_seq=2 ttl=63 time=0.766 ms
64 bytes from 10.10.1.100: icmp_seq=3 ttl=63 time=0.766 ms
--- 10.10.1.100 ping statistics ---
rtt min/avg/max/mdev = 0.766/0.784/0.821/0.034 ms
```

4.2 Proxy ARP

Applying the `send-to-self` patch alone still cannot fully solve the parallel links problem, since `eth0` and `eth1` are not in a simple, direct loop assumed in `send-to-self`. In fact, the router is inserted between `eth0` and `eth1` of the host with interface `br0` and `vlan1`, respectively. In this way, the ARP address resolution messages cannot go through the router and reach the host interfaces. In order to deal with that, we have enabled the proxy ARP in the routers, so the ARP request and response messages will be relayed by the router when necessary, i.e., in the router's `/etc/sysctl.conf`:

```
net.ipv4.conf.br0.proxy_arp=1
net.ipv4.conf.vlan1.proxy_arp=1
```

4.3 Network Emulation

With the `send-to-self` patch and proxy ARP, the lab platform is working as expected. However, to provide a "real" Internet environment, we still need to introduce packet impairments such as delay, loss, duplication, reordering and corruption often seen in a real wide-area network.

To achieve this, we adopted the `tc` utility in Linux for traffic control and network emulation. `tc` allows delay, jitter, drop and duplicate probability and correlation to be specified on each network interface, with uniform, normal, Pareto or Pareto normal distribution, as well as using gap to introduce packet reordering. Although `tc` is not as powerful as hardware network emulators, it does serve the purpose in a teaching lab for introductory networks courses.

By introducing network impairments, students can have a realistic network environment (otherwise, the isolated Ethernet is almost error free with negligible delay) and observe how network protocols (e.g., TCP) deal with packet errors and ensure a reliable, in-sequence data transfer.

5. RECENT EXPERIENCE

We started the design and development of the lab platform three years ago, and integrated the new platform gradually

[14] `http://lab.pan.uvic.ca/webb/download.php?id=5434`

[15] `http://www.ssi.bg/~ja/send-to-self.txt`

Table 3: Lab Modules for the Lab Platform

#	Lab activities
1	to get familiar with the platform and `tcpdump`
2	to capture and analyze HTTP traffic with `webif`
3	recursive and iterative DNS query with `maradns`
4	UDP protocol header analysis with DNS traffic
5	TCP connection management with `ttcp`
6	TCP flow and error control with `tc`
7	TCP congestion control with `sysctl`
8	IP addressing and NAT with `iptables`
9	IP routing with asymmetric links and `ip`
10	Ethernet, ARP and interworking

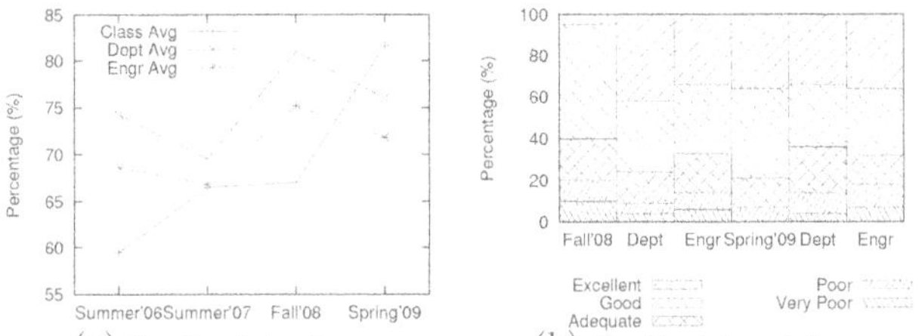

(a) Feedback tendency (b) Feedback breakdown

Figure 2: Student feedback on the (new) platform.

along the way, with the full integration in Fall 2008[16], Spring 2009[17] and thereafter. Here we report our recent experiences to solicit more feedback from the entire community.

5.1 Lab Assignments

Our introductory networks course focuses on TCP/IP protocols and follows a top-down approach [8]. We have developed 10 lab modules, synchronized with the 10-week, in-class lectures that mainly focus on network algorithms and protocols. Such an arrangement has been received favorably by students for them to better understand course materials and then experiment in a real network.

Due to the page limit, we will not detail each lab module listed in Table 3, but use the DNS module as an example[18]. In this lab, students run `maradns` on the router, which is configured as a DNS cache server, and use `nslookup` as a DNS client on the host to do DNS lookup with the DNS server on the router. Using `tcpdump` on `br0` and `vlan1` interfaces on the router respectively, students can observe the recursive DNS queries between `nslookup` and `maradns`, and the iterative DNS queries between `maradns` and the real root, top-level domain and authoritative DNS servers on the Internet, and understand the tradeoff between recursive vs iterative DNS queries, which was hard to convey previously by only slides and blackboard. After each lab, a simple reset can return the router to default settings for the next section.

5.2 Student Feedback

Students have responded to the new lab platform enthusiastically and favorably, and some of them are also interested in replicating such a platform for themselves at home. We started to introduce this lab platform gradually since Summer 2006. As we can see from Figure 2, the student feedback on the lab platform has become increasingly favorable, and surpassed the department (`Dept`) and the engineering (`Engr`) school's average in Spring 2009. Figure 2 also shows the detailed breakdown of student feedback in Fall 2008 and Spring 2009, when the lab platform was fully integrated into the introductory networks course. As we can see, 60% of the students rated the lab platform adequate, good and excellent to contribute to their understanding of the course material in Fall 2008, and in Spring 2009, that percentage went higher than 80%, which was considered significant due to the heavy workload (three hours lectures and two hours labs every week) of this introductory course. We are glad that the new platform does lead to an active, engaging learning experience both in class and in lab: as one of the metrics to indicate student success, the class grade point average has been increased from below 70% (B-) in Summer 2006 and 2007 to above 75% (B+) in Fall 2008 and Spring 2009.

[16]http://www.cs.uvic.ca/~pan/csc361f08

[17]http://www.cs.uvic.ca/~pan/csc361s09

[18]Student/instructor's lab manuals are available on request.

6. CONCLUSIONS

The lab platform we have designed and developed is very powerful and flexible. In addition to the introductory computer networks course, we also plan to introduce it to the operating systems courses due to the open-source Linux kernel on the router, and to the advanced computer networks courses, as well as to the wireless mobile networks course by taking advantage of the wireless interface on the router, which can work in either infrastructure or ad hoc mode.

In summary, we have designed and developed a low-cost (the total cost in addition to the existing computer is less than $100 per seat) and low-maintenance lab platform for introductory computer networks courses. The platform provides a high-fidelity and high-interactivity environment for students to experiment in a real network, which is unprecedented in a regular university teaching lab. Due to commodity hardware and open-source software, the platform is also easy to use, modify and expand for follow-on courses.

Acknowledgment

This work was supported in part by a teaching grant from the University of Victoria's Learning and Teaching Center. We want to thank Drs. L. Cai, S. Ganti, D. Hoffman, E. Manning and K. Wu for their discussion leading to the initial design of this platform, D. Li, M. Lu, M. Daneshi and K. Jahanbakhsh for their contribution to the development or delivery of this platform, and A. Trumpour, R. Taylor, T. Bednar and B. Douglas for their assistance when creating the new computer networks teaching lab.

7. REFERENCES

[1] *ACM SIGCOMM Workshop on Computer Networking: Curriculum Designs and Educational Challenges*, 2002. http://www-net.cs.umass.edu/sigcomm/education

[2] *ACM SIGCOMM Workshop on Networking Education: How to Educate the Educators? (NetEd)*, 2003.

[3] D. Comer, *Hands-on Networking with Internet Applications*, 2nd Ed, Prentice Hall, 2004.

[4] J. Matthews, *Computer Networking: Internet Protocols in Action*, Wiley, 2005.

[5] J. Liebeherr and M. El Zarki, *Mastering Networks: An Internet Lab Manual*, Addison Wesley, 2003.

[6] S. Panwar, S. Mao, J. Ryoo and Y. Li, *TCP/IP Essentials: A Lab-Based Approach*, Cambridge University Press, 2004.

[7] D. Brylow, "An experimental laboratory environment for teaching embedded operating systems," in Proc *38th ACM SIGCSE*, pp.192–196, Portland, OR, USA, March, 2008.

[8] J. Kurose and K. Ross, *Computer Networking: A Top-Down Approach*, 5th Ed, Addison Wesley, 2009.

IPsecLite: A Tool for Teaching Security Concepts

Niakam Kazemi Shiva Azadegan
Department of Computer and Information Sciences
Towson University, Towson MD, U.S.A.
nkazemi@adabtek.com, sazadegan@towson.edu

ABSTRACT

Active learning and using visualization tools provide an effective approach in computer science education. Without meaningful hands-on exercises or access to training tools, it is usually difficult for students to understand or elaborate on complex algorithms, protocols, and concepts underlying different aspects of computing. This paper introduces a tool, IPsecLite, which demonstrates the inner-working of IP Security (IPsec) standard. Built on many networking technologies and cryptographic techniques, IPsec provides services to secure network communication. We introduce IPsecLite through a series of labs that can be used in several security courses. IPsecLite is fully developed and can be easily integrated into curriculum.

Categories and Subject Descriptors

K.3.2 [**Computers and Education**]: Computer and Information Science Education – *Computer science education.* C.2.0 [**Computer-Communication Networks**]: General – *Security.*

General Terms

Performance, Experimentation, Security.

Keywords

IP security, IPsec, network security, visualization, curriculum

1. INTRODUCTION

In recent years, there has been much emphasis on computer security education to meet the demands for skilled personnel in the computer security field. Our institution has been a leader in computer security education and, since year 2002, it has offered specialized security tracks for graduate and undergraduate computer science programs. The courses in tracks were designed to provide strong hands-on experience with security tools that are commonly used in industry [1, 8].

Developing interesting and meaningful laboratory exercises for the security courses has been one of our main challenges during the past 7 years. IPsecLite was one of the tools that we developed to address this problem. This tool is primarily used for teaching IP Security (IPsec). IPsec is a standard for securing network communications at Internet (network) layer of Transmission Control Protocol/Internet Protocol (TCP/IP). IPsecLite can also be used for teaching basic concepts of communication networks, replay and tampering (such as spoofing) attacks, cryptographic algorithms, and IPsec performance evaluation and analysis.

In creating IPsecLite we emphasized on effectiveness, feasibility, and efficiency. *Effectiveness* refers to the tool's contribution in accomplishing lessons' Learning Objectives (LOs) when teaching (or studying) a topic. *Feasibility* refers to whether the user can provide the required resources to use the tool. *Efficiency* refers to the ratio of a) learning objectives that are met (when the tool is used) to b) the resources that are required to use the tool. An effective tool is not necessarily efficient. For example, a general purpose tool may be used to build models that are effective in teaching a topic. However, it may require acquiring skills to work with the tool and efforts to build the models. When these activities are not directly relevant to accomplishing the learning objectives, they may result in inefficiency. Taking the above criteria into account, our design objectives for IPsecLite were: 1) to require (only) minimal knowledge in networking and cryptography; 2) to require no programming and unrelated setup; and 3) to function similar to the real-world IPsec solutions.

In this paper, we introduce IPsecLite and we show how it may be used in teaching network security concepts. We propose three Learning Objective Groups (LOGs): 1) IPsec fundamental concepts; 2) attacks and protection mechanisms; and 3) IPsec performance and overhead analysis. Then, we propose three sample labs that use IPsecLite to accomplish the LOs.

The rest of this paper is organized as follows. In Section 2, we provide an overview of IPsec, briefly introduce IPsecLite, and review the related work. In Section 3, we present the LOGs and the sample labs. In Section 4, we present the future work. And, we present our conclusion in Section 5.

2. BACKGROUND

2.1 IPsec

IPsec is a standard for protecting IP datagrams. It is mainly described in Request For Proposals (RFCs) 4301, 4302, 4303, and 4306. IPsec provides three primary security services: 1) data-origin authentication; 2) data-integrity verification; and 3) data confidentiality. It also supports mechanisms to protect against packet replay and (limited) Denial of Service (DoS) attacks.

IPsec defines two protocols to provide its security services: Authentication Header (AH) and Encapsulating Security Payload (ESP). AH mainly provides data-origin authentication and data-integrity verification services. ESP provides data confidentiality service, in addition to providing AH services.

SIGCSE'10, March 10–13, 2010, Milwaukee, Wisconsin, USA.

IPsec may operate in two modes: transport and tunnel. In transport mode, IPsec protects upper layer protocol packets. In this mode, the endpoints of a connection are also the endpoints of communication. In tunnel mode, IPsec prefixes the datagram with an additional IP header. In tunnel mode, at least one connection endpoint is usually a security gateway (or router) that implements IPsec. In this mode, connection endpoints and communication endpoints are not necessarily the same.

IPsec architecture includes a Security Policy Database (SPD). SPD maintains the rules that govern traffic protection. IPsec architecture also includes a key management part whose main function is to manage Security Associations (SAs). SAs are manifestation of secure connections. An SA contains information that is used to process the corresponding network traffic. There are two types of SAs: 1) IKE-SAs for processing the Internet Key Exchange (IKE) messages; 2) CHILD-SAs for processing data (application) traffic. SAs are unidirectional and therefore an IPsec connection is associated with four SAs (one IKE-SA and one CHILD-SA in each direction). SAs are maintained in the Security Association Database (SAD). SAs may be maintained manually, however, scalable IPsec implementations require automated mechanisms to manage SAs. IKE version 2 (IKEv2) is the default automated mechanism for SA management in IPsec. IKEv2 is a message exchange scheme. Each IKEv2 message includes one or more payloads. A payload is identified by its type. Examples are: Security Association (SA), Key Exchange (KE), and Nonce (N). To establish a shared secret, IPsec endpoints perform a Diffie-Hellman (DH) exchange via IKE messages. The shared secret is used by a Pseudo-Random Function (PRF) to generate several keys for cryptographic algorithms that are used to provide IPsec services. The PRF and the cryptographic algorithms are negotiated using SA payloads.

How IPsec is configured determines its behavior, performance, and the security level it provides. For example, using ESP results in IP datagrams whose payloads are encrypted. Another example is that providing data confidentiality using Data Encryption Standard (DES) requires less computation (cost) than providing the same service using Triple-DES. The former algorithm provides better performance, but the latter algorithm provides better confidentiality.

2.2 IPsecLite

IPsecLite is a tool designed for experimentation with IPsec. It enables the user to efficiently model a network with several host and gateway nodes. Once a network is modeled, IPsecLite enables the user to 1) configure the nodes for IPsec-secure communications; 2) generate traffic among the nodes and observe the inner-working of network operations; 3) simulate attacks and observe mechanisms by which IPsec provides protection; and 4) collect packet processing data (and statistics) for conducting cost (overhead)-benefit analysis. IPsecLite's friendly and intuitive user interface enables the user to complete all of these tasks without any special training or programming.

IPsecLite is not a discrete-events simulator. In IPsecLite network communication takes place in real-time. Also, in IPsecLite key exchange and packet protection operations physically take place. For example, IP datagrams that are protected by ESP, include encrypted payloads, ESP headers, and (optionally) Message Authentication Codes (MACs).

IPsecLite supports modeling of multiple network nodes on the same PC, without Virtualization Software (VS). It also supports simulation of network deficiencies, such as of packet loss, packet corruption, and out-of-sequence packet delivery.

IPsecLite supports ESP and AH in both transport and tunnel modes. Only one secure connection, between each pair of nodes, is supported.

IPsecLite provides visual presentation of IPsec concepts including IKEv2 messages, SAs, and protected packets (AH and ESP). For example, a user may select an incoming (or outgoing) protected packet and observe its parts.

IPsecLite provides processing overhead of IPsec operations per packet or at aggregate level (averages and standard deviations). Before calculating statistics, IPsecLite detects outliers and excludes them from calculations.

IPsecLite implements (minimal) IKEv2 messages that are needed for starting and ending IPsec connections. These messages and their payloads are displayed in detail.

IPsecLite supports several cryptographic algorithms (Figure 3) and it uses Pre-Shared Key (PSK) method for peer authentication.

2.3 Related Work

To provide hands-on experience [3] developed a laboratory environment, referred to as SEED, and a set of laboratories, which included one for IPsec design and implementation. In this lab students develop IPsec software with limited features. The lab only requires support for ESP in tunnel mode and Advanced Encryption Standard (AES) encryption so the implementation is feasible in one semester. More than one machine is needed to test the implementation. VS may be used to alleviate this requirement.

Reference [7] discusses the use of OPNET simulation tool for teaching IP encryption and decryption. After a couple of introductory classes on OPNET, teams of students are asked to create Virtual Private Networks (VPNs) using IPSec. The authors conclude that there is an advantage of using OPNET versus non-interactive teaching methods. They also acknowledge that the tool is insufficient in its focus on certain aspects of IPsec. For example, "the OPNET simulation tool is insufficient to display all the details of the IPsec header/trailer-encapsulated packets." The authors address this deficiency by using additional tools, such as a network sniffer. In OPNET tool, simulation of some IPsec concepts requires changes which require a "significant level of expertise in OPNET and a programming language like C++."

Reference [5] has developed an Integrated Internet Simulation Framework (NIIST) that includes IPsec and IKE protocols. This framework is integrated in the Scalable Simulation Framework (SSF) and SSF Network Model (SSFNet) to provide a modeling framework for large-scale networks. SSF's focus is scalability and high-performance in simulating protocols behavior in such networks. A Data Modeling Language (DML) is used to simulate network operations. Another tool, NIIST Player, enables the user to review the results, IPsec state, and IKE events. In NIIST actual key exchange and actual cryptographic security functionalities are not implemented.

Other general purpose network simulators, such as NeSSi [1], NS-2 [4], and GTNetS [6], provide mechanisms to model a network and simulate its operations. However, they are usually designed to study the behavior of protocols in large networks. Also, they require familiarity with computer simulation concepts. Some also require programming skills.

3. Teaching IPsec by Using IPsecLite

To teach IPsec we first propose three LOGs in Section 3.1. In Section 3.2 we provide three sample labs that use IPsecLite's features to accomplish the LOGs. Each lab may be conducted by students (hands-on activity) or by teachers (IPsec demonstration).

3.1 Learning Objectives

Based on the IPsec overview in Section 2.1 we propose the following LOGs.

3.1.1 Group 1: Fundamental Concepts

The LOs in this LOG are to learn about 1) host and gateway nodes; 2) SPD, IKE, SAD, IKE-SAs, and CHILD-SAs; 3) IPsec protocols and their differences; and 4) transport and tunnel modes (and their applications).

3.1.2 Group 2: Attacks and Protection Mechanisms

The LOs in this LOG are to learn about 1) packet replay attacks and Anti-Replay Window (ARW); and 2) packet tampering attacks and MACs.

3.1.3 Group 3: Overhead Analysis

The LOs in this LOG are to learn about 1) factors that affect cost of IKE operations; and 2) overhead of IPsec security services.

3.2 Using IPsecLite

In this section we propose three sample labs to accomplish the LOGs in Section 3.1. Each lab corresponds to one LOG. In these labs, we use "the user" to refer to the individual who performs the activities (the teacher or the student). Also, we use a sample network that is shown in Figure 1.

3.2.1 Lab 1: Fundamental Concepts

This lab includes four activities to accomplish LOG 1. Estimated time for this lab is 45 minutes.

3.2.1.1 Hosts and Gateway Nodes

In this activity the user simulates the network and generates traffic between two nodes. To do this, they use **IPsecLite Instance Configuration Tool (IPLICT)** (Figure 2) and **Network Traffic Generator Tool** (NTGT) (not shown).

Step 1: The user launches an instance of IPsecLite. They use **IPLICT** to configure a node (for example, G1). Then, the user uses **Start** button to enter the main window (not shown) inside which **IP Traffic Monitor (IPTM)** (not shown) is displayed.

Step 2: The user repeats Step 1 to launch three more instances (in any order) to configure nodes: G2, H1, and H2.

Step 3: On H1, the user uses **NTGT** to send a message from H1 to H2. Then, they observe that **Trace** box reports the arrival of a response from H2.

Step 4: To observe the routing, the user uses **IPTM** on G1, and verifies that the message was routed to G2. Optionally, the user may inspect the traffic on G2, and H2 to follow the message path.

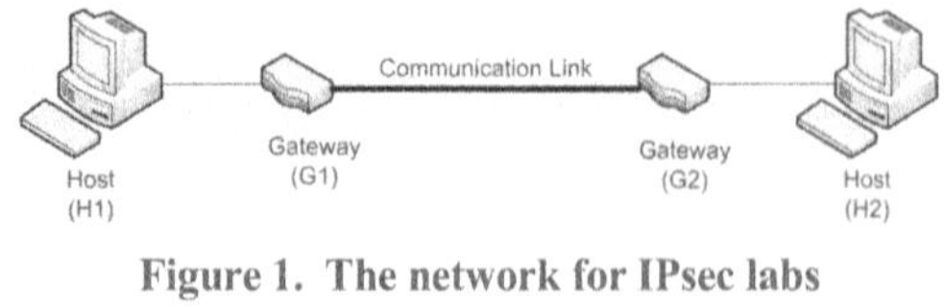

Figure 1. The network for IPsec labs

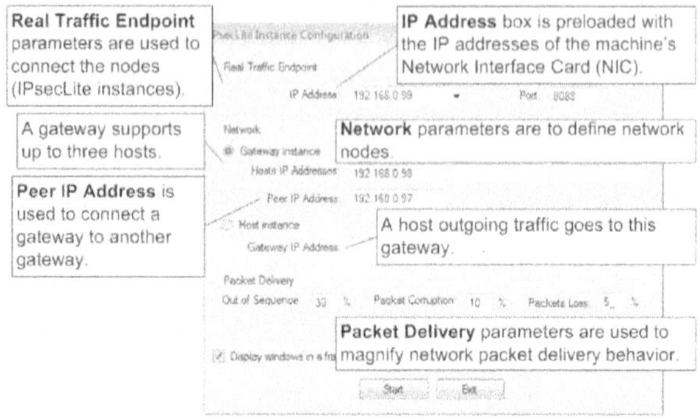

Figure 2. IPsecLite Instance Configuration Tool

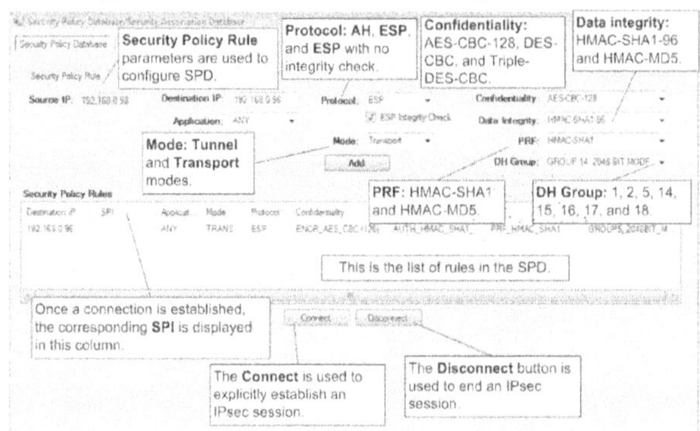

Figure 3. Security Policy Database Manager

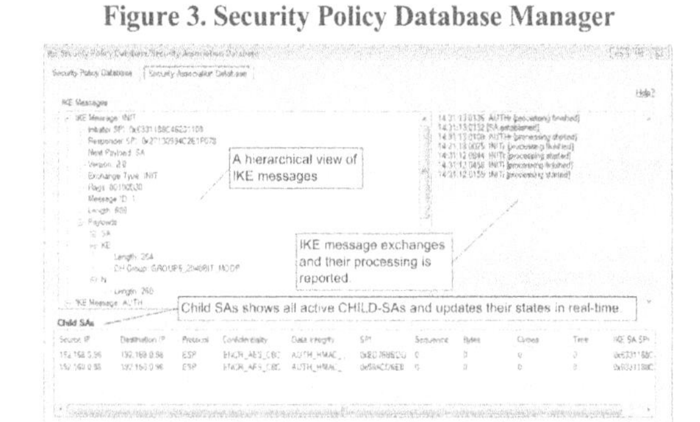

Figure 4. Security Association Database Monitor

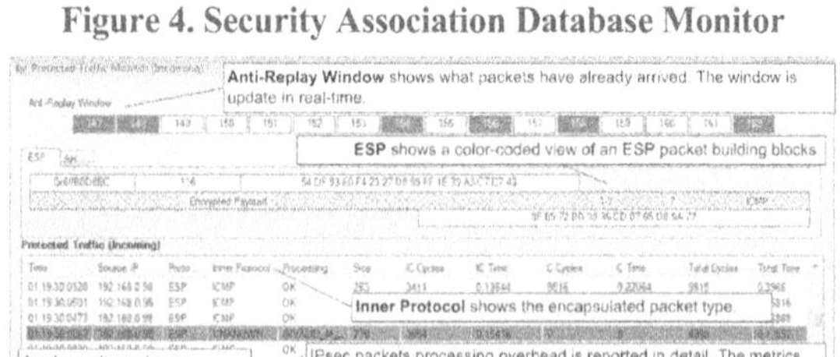

Figure 5. Protected Traffic Monitor (Incoming)

3.2.1.2 SPD, IKE, SAD, IKE-SA and CHILD-SA

In this activity the user uses **Security Policy Database Manager (SPDM)** (Figure 3) and **Security Association Database Monitor (SADM)** (Figure 4) to 1) define traffic protection rules; 2) establish an IPsec connection and observe the corresponding IKE messages; and 3) observe the resulting SAs.

Step 1: The user uses **SPDM** to add a rule for protecting packets between H1 and H2. They enter H2's address in **Destination IP** box, they select ESP from **Protocol** box, and they keep other parameters unchanged. Then, they click on **Add** button and verify that the rule is added to **Security Policy Rules (SPRs)** list.

Step 2: The user selects the rule in **SPR** list and clicks on **Connect** button to start an IKE message exchange for establishing an IPsec connection. IPsecLite switches to **SADM**.

Step 3: The user observes the message exchange events (right pane) and verifies that an **SA Created** event occurred. They also observe the IKE messages (left pane) and inspect the payloads.

Step 4: The user observes that two CHILD-SAs are created.

Step 5: The user selects **Security Policy Database** tab to switch to **SPDM** and verifies that **SPI** column in **SPRs** list contains a value. This value is used to identify the corresponding IKE-SA.

3.2.1.3 IPsec Protocols and Their Differences

In this activity the user generates traffic that is protected by the connection that was established in the previous activity. Then, they establish another connection to protect the packets with AH. In both scenarios, they use **IPTM** and **Protected Traffic Monitor (Incoming) (PTMI)** (Figure 5) to inspect the protected packets and to learn about the differences between AH and ESP.

Step 1: The user uses **NTGT** to send a message from H1 to H2 and they verify that there is a response from H2.

Step 2: The user uses **IPTM** to verify that the message was protected. Using **Network Data** list, the user compares the payload of the corresponding datagram with the payload of the datagram corresponding to the message that was sent to H2 in the first activity. The user observes that the payload of the datagram is not readable and that its protocol is ESP.

Step 3: The user opens a **PTMI** on H2. Then, they send several messages from H1 to H2. They observe values in **Protocol**, **Next Protocol**, and **Processing** columns to learn about 1) the IPsec protocol that was used to protect a packet; 2) what type of packet was encapsulated in the protected packet; and 3) whether the packet was successfully processed, that is, if the packet passed the data-integrity verification and if it was decrypted successfully. They also observe the updates to **Anti-Replay Window (ARW)**.

Step 4: The user selects an item from the **Protected Traffic (Incoming) (PTI)** list and inspects the corresponding ESP packet in **ESP** tab above **PTI** list.

Step 5: The user ends the connection by clicking on **Disconnect** button on **SPDM**. They also inspect the new IKE message.

Step 6: They establish an AH connection between H1 and H2.

Step 7: The user repeats Step 1 to Step 4 and observes the differences. In Step 2, they compare the ESP packets with the new packets (now protected by AH).

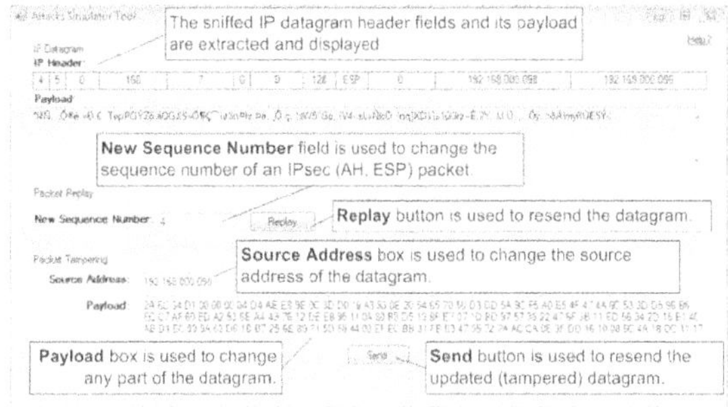

Figure 6. Attack Simulator Tool

3.2.1.4 Transport and Tunnel Modes

In this activity the user establishes a secure tunnel between gateways G1 and G2.

Step 1: The user establishes a secure connection, using ESP, between G1 and G2. Then, they verify the connection by repeating the appropriate steps in previous activities.

Step 2: The user sends one message between H1 and H2 and monitors the datagrams carrying the message between H1-G1, G1-G2, and G2-H2 links. They observe that the communication through G1-G2 link is protected by ESP.

Step 3: The user explains the differences between this scenario and scenarios in activity 3 (Step 2).

3.2.2 Lab 2: Attacks and Protection Mechanisms

This lab includes two activities to accomplish LOG 2. In both activities, the user uses **Attack Simulator Tool (AST)** (Figure 6) to play the role of an adversary. Using **AST,** the user captures a transmitted IP datagram, and retransmits it to its destination. Estimated time for this lab is 20 minutes.

3.2.2.1 Packet Replays

In this activity no changes to the captured datagram is made.

Step 1: The user establishes an IPsec connection between H1 and H2.

Step 2: The user opens **AST** on H1 and **PTMI** on H2. Then, they use **NTGT** to send a message from H1 to H2.

Step 3: **AST** captures the corresponding IP datagram. The user observes that **ARW** includes a packet whose Sequence Number (SN) is included in **New Sequence Number (NSN)** box. Then, they use **Replay** button to retransmit the datagram to H2.

Step 4: The user observes that the datagram is rejected and that its **Processing** status is **REPLAYED**. They also inspect the cost of data-protection services.

Step 5: To get around this problem the user (the adversary) attempts to assign a new SN to the IPsec packet (by using **NSN)** and resend the datagram. However, they observe that the datagram is rejected and processing status is **INVALID-MAC**. Also, the user observes that the cost of data confidentiality service is zero.

3.2.2.2 Packet Tampering

This activity is similar to the previous activity, except that, in one experiment, the user uses **IP address** box to change the source address of the datagram (spoofing), and in another experiment, they use **Payload** box to change the content of the packet. They observe that the IP datagrams are rejected. When the datagram is spoofed, processing status is **NO-SA**.

3.2.3 Lab 3: Overhead Analysis

This lab includes two activities to accomplish LOG 3. Estimated time for this lab is 45 minutes.

3.2.3.1 Key Exchange Overhead

In this activity the user learns how the selection of **DH Group** affects the time that is required to establish an IPsec connection.

Step 1: The user establishes a secure connection between H1 and H2. To define a rule they use **SPDM**, select DH group 1 (768 MODP), and leave the other parameters unchanged.

Step 2: On H1, the user uses **SADM** to capture and log the event times of three events: **INITi [processing started]**, **INITi [processing finished]**, and **SA established**. Then, they end the connection.

Step 3: For each remaining DH group, they repeat Step 1 and Step 2.

Step 4: Using the collected data, they plot a chart with two series such that X-axis represents the length of DH MODP and Y-axis represents duration. The series show the elapsed time between the first two events, which includes the DH exponentiation, and the elapsed time between the first and the last event (in Step 2), which is the time to establish the connection, respectively.

3.2.3.2 IPSec Security Services Overhead

In this activity the user compares the overhead of ESP protocol under different encryption algorithms.

Step 1: The user establishes an ESP connection between H1 and H2 using AES-CBC-128 for data-confidentiality service (and leaving the other parameters unchanged).

Step 2: The user opens the **PTMI** on H2 and **NTGT** on H1.

Step 3: The user sets the **Out of Sequence**, **Packet Loss**, and **Packet Corruption** boxes to 0.

Step 4: With the help of **Repeat** box, the user sends many (for example, 1000) messages of length 512 bytes to H2.

Step 5: The user uses **Recalculate** button on **PTMI** to calculate traffic statistics. Then, they log the results in a spreadsheet.

Step 6: They repeat Step 1 through Step 5, for two other supported encryption algorithms (DES and Triple-DES).

Step 7: They use the collected statistics to plot normal curves.

Figure 7 shows the result when we used a PC (with 2.13 GHz Intel dual core processor and 2MB RAM) for H2. The PC ran 64-bit Windows Vista operating system. We used MS Excel 2007 to plot the normal distributions for CPU cycles for packet decryption. This result shows that in average ESP's overhead is least when AES is used (compare to DES and Triple-DES).

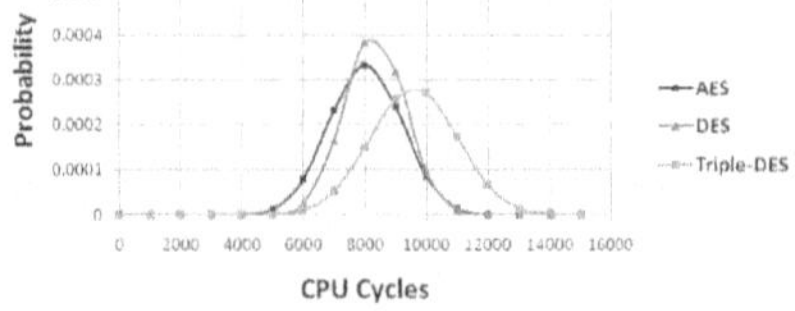

Figure 7. ESP overhead under different encryption algorithms

4. FUTURE WORK

To provide further evidence on effectiveness of using IPsecLite and to explore more ways that this tool can be used, we are currently testing IPSecLite (and the labs) in the Network Security and Applied Cryptography courses at our school.

The users may need to change the sample labs to comply with the resources that are available to them and to support other LOs. Also, other labs may be developed, for example, labs to demonstrate more complex IPsec configurations.

5. CONCLUSION

In this paper we introduced a new tool, IPsecLite, and presented an approach, which uses this tool, to teach (or study) network security concepts (primarily IPsec). We developed IPsecLite to enable effective and efficient teaching of these concepts, especially, when resources are limited. To show how IPsecLite may be used, we defined three learning objective groups and we proposed sample labs to accomplish the objectives.

Further information on IPsecLite and (free) software licenses may be obtained by contacting the authors.

6. REFERENCE

[1] Azadegan, S., Lavine, M., O'Leary, M., Wijesinha, A., and Zimand, M. 2003. An undergraduate track in computer security. In Proceedings of the 8th ACM ITICSE. (Greece, 2003).

[2] Bye, R., Schmidt, S., Luther, K. and Albayrak, S. 2008. Application-level simulation for network security. In Proceedings of the 1st international conference on simulation tools and techniques for communications, networks and systems & workshops. Article 33. (Marseille, France, March 03-07, 2008).

[3] Du, W. and Wang, R. 2008. SEED: A suite of instructional laboratories for computer security education. ACM J. Educ. Resour. Comput. 8, 1, Article 3 (March 2008), 24 pages. DOI=10.1145/1348713.1348716. http://doi.acm.org/10.1145/1348713.1348716.

[4] Lacage, M. and Henderson, T. R. 2006. In Proceedings from the 2006 workshop on ns-2: the IP network simulator. Article 12. (Pisa, Italy).

[5] NIST IPsec and IKE Simulation Tool. http://www.antd.nist.gov/niist.

[6] Riley, G. F. 2003. The Georgia Tech Network Simulator. In Proceedings of the ACM SIGCOMM 2003 Workshops. (Karlsruhe, Germany, August 25 & 27, 2003).

[7] Ryoo, J. and Oh, T. H. 2008. Teaching IP Encryption and Decryption Using the OPNET Modeling and Simulation Tool. In Proceedings of the 12th Colloquium for Information Systems Security Education (University of Texas, Dallas, Dallas, TX, June 2 – 4, 2008).

[8] Taylor, B. and Azadegan, S., 2007. Teaching Security through Active Learning, Frontiers in Education: Computer Science and Engineering. (Las Vegas, NV, 2007).

Teaching Simplified Network Protocols

Dave Feinberg
Carnegie Mellon University
5000 Forbes Avenue
Pittsburgh, PA 15213
(412) 268-4731
fberg@cs.cmu.edu

ABSTRACT

We created a course that, beginning from a hypothetical shared light bulb as our physical layer, introduced students to a hierarchy of simplified versions of network protocols, including Ethernet, IP, and TCP. This paper describes those simplified protocols, along with the Java framework students used to implement and simulate them.

Categories and Subject Descriptors

K.3.2 [**Computers and Education**]: Computer and Information Science Education – *computer science education.* C.2.2 [**Computer-Communication Networks**]: Network Protocols – *protocol architecture (OSI model).*

General Terms

Algorithms, Design

Keywords

Network, Protocol, Simulation, TCP, IP, Ethernet, Programming

1. INTRODUCTION

This paper describes the content of a course entitled "Network Programming," which we taught in the spring semesters of 2006 and 2008 to a total of 48 high school students at The Harker School, an independent school in San Jose, California. In the first half of the course, we introduced students to simplified versions of low-level network protocols (Ethernet, IP, and TCP) which students simulated using a Java framework we provided. At the midpoint of the class, students used their simulated networks to implement their own sockets. In the second half of the course, we switched over to using Java's built-in support for real socket connections. Students worked together in small groups, using sockets to write their own network applications, including networked games, chat programs, etc.

This paper focuses on the first part of the course–particularly the simplified network protocols we developed for teaching Ethernet, IP, and TCP. Lab-based networking courses typically fall into two categories: those in which students configure and experiment with networks, and those in which students implement network protocols [4]. Because we were teaching students who were not likely to continue studying computer networks beyond this course, there was no reason to provide practical training with real network traffic. Rather, we wanted to give our students a hands-on experience with network protocol concepts. We therefore decided to have students implement low-level network protocols on a simulated computer network. Although a number of network simulation frameworks have been developed for use in teaching, none met the precise needs for our course. Some simulation tools required students to implement subsets of the TCP/IP protocols, which could interoperate with industry implementations [1]. However, we felt that this would be unnecessarily detailed and time-consuming work for our students, and that it might obscure the main concepts. Some network simulation frameworks left only one layer for students to implement [3], while others allowed students to implement multiple layers of protocols [5, 7]. But at their lowest level, even the most flexible network simulation tools we looked at were based on the transmitting and receiving of frames. We felt this concealed too much of the physical layer and its relation to the data link layer. To allow students to explore unreliable networks, many tools could be configured to corrupt and drop frames at random. Such a feature, although clearly beneficial, also seemed contrived. We wanted to use a simulation model in which collisions could arise naturally.

In light of all this, we set out to create our own simplified protocol stack, spanning the layers from sockets down to bit detection. To minimize implementation times and remove confusing details, we chose to simplify common protocols so that they became small enough that our students could fully implement them in just half a semester, using our network simulation framework. Students would need to understand the purpose of every bit we used, so we wanted to reduce the protocols to their most essential features, focusing on those bits that really count. We made sure that students understood that we were omitting many details in the real Ethernet and TCP/IP specifications. We believe that our idealized protocols were more effective than the real ones for teaching our students to master fundamental networking concepts.

2. PHYSICAL LAYER: LIGHTS

Our physical layer began from perhaps the simplest possible entity that could support communication: a shared bit. This layer took two forms: a story about flashing lights, and a set of black-box Java classes that simulated those flashing lights. In the story, we imagine a dozen people know they will be imprisoned, one person per cell. Each cell has a single light panel, featuring a light bulb, on/off buttons, and a unique ID number. Pressing the "on" button on one light panel turns on the light bulbs in every cell. Likewise, the "off" button turns off everyone's lights. In other words, all light panels are connected to a single light system, as illustrated in Figure 1.

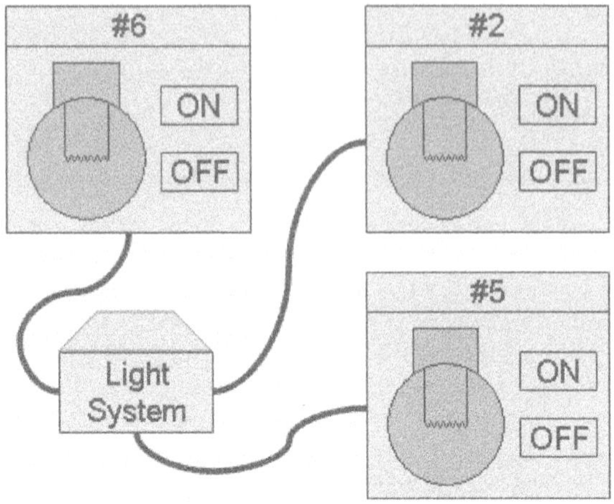

Figure 1. Three hypothetical light panels connected to a light system

Knowing all this, the dozen people conspire to use the light system to communicate with each other. They know they can represent any information as a string of bits. We asked students to consider how the light panels could be used to transmit bits, and what difficulties would arise. The results of that discussion served as the basis for introducing our simplified Ethernet protocol.

3. DATA LINK LAYER: ETHERNET

First we focused on the sending and detecting of bits, using Manchester code (Phase Encoding). To transmit a "0" in t seconds, we turned the light on for $t/2$ seconds and then off for $t/2$ seconds, and vice versa for a "1". To eliminate potential ambiguity, we agreed to begin each transmission with an extra "0". Thus, to send the bits "1100", we turned the light on and off in the pattern shown in Figure 2. In between transmissions, the light bulb was left off, indicating network silence.

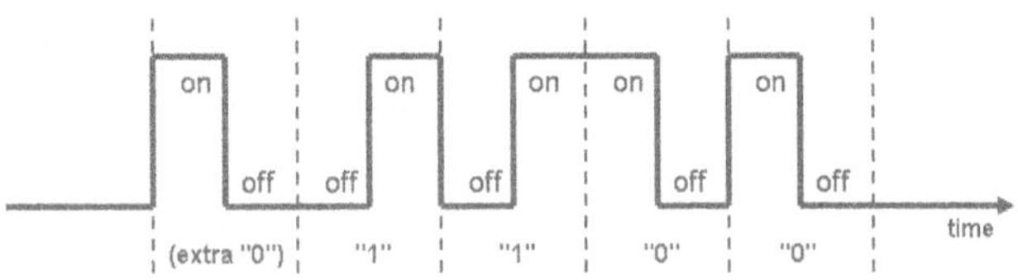

Figure 2. Pattern of on/off transitions to transmit "1100"

We chose Ethernet [6] as our layer 2 protocol, because of its widespread use in homes and schools. Using 48-bit MAC addresses seemed unnecessarily tedious, given that we did not plan to have more than a handful of network interfaces on our simulated network. Therefore, to facilitate learning the fundamentals of the protocol, and to simplify our implementation, we decided to use just 4 bits to represent a MAC address. This allowed us to examine a full Ethernet frame and easily identify the roles played by individual bits. Our 4-bit MAC addresses ranged from #1 to #15, where address #0 was reserved for broadcast frames.

Thus, the Ethernet frames in our simplified protocol consisted only of a 4-bit destination address, 4-bit source address, n-bit payload, and 2-bit checksum, as shown in Figure 3. A frame's payload could consist of any number of bits, but in practice, just 23 bits proved to be sufficient for our simplified protocol suite. For the checksum, we simply counted the number of 1s in the addresses and payload, and then found the remainder when this number was divided by 4. (This checksum function is a substantial simplification over the cyclic redundancy check used by the real Ethernet protocol.)

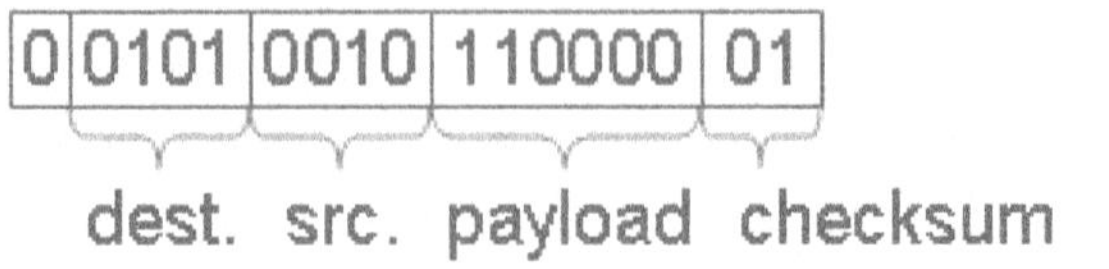

Figure 3. Simplified Ethernet frame for sending "110000" from address #2 to address #5.

To avoid collisions, we waited for silence before transmitting, and watched the state of the light bulb during transmission, to make sure what we set it to matched what we saw. If not, we knew a collision had occurred, in which case we sent a few extra bits to ensure the other transmitting party also detected a collision, before waiting to re-transmit the same frame. On the receiving end, we discarded any frames consisting of fewer than 10 bits, and any frames with invalid checksums.

4. NETWORK LAYER: IP

In our very simplified Internet Protocol, we used two 2-bit values to represent an IP address. For example, the binary value 01.11 represented the IP address 1.3. This was sufficient to let us talk about the value of hierarchical logical addresses. Each of our simplified IP packets consisted only of a destination IP address, a source IP address, and a payload. Each IP packet was transported as the sole payload of an Ethernet frame, as shown in Figure 4.

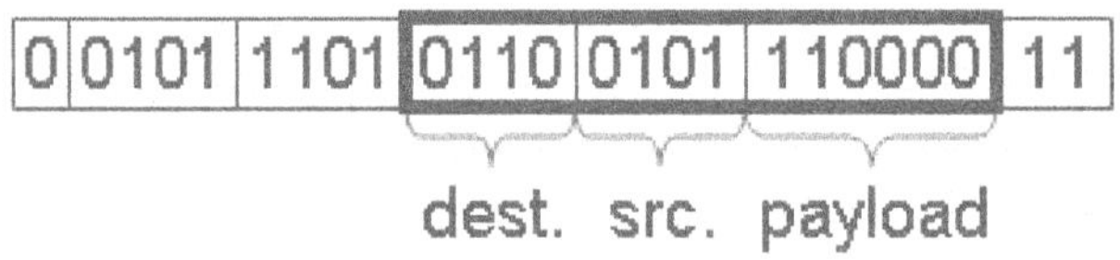

Figure 4. Simplified IP packet carrying "110000" from IP address 1.1 to 1.2. The packet is itself the payload of an Ethernet frame.

For all the technical details we were able to omit in constructing our simplified protocol suite, we found we could not introduce IP packets into our Ethernet simulation without presenting an Address Resolution Protocol (ARP). Using our simplified version of ARP, one could request an unknown MAC address by broadcasting an Ethernet frame to address #0 with a 4-bit payload, corresponding to the requested IP address, as shown in Figure 5. The corresponding ARP reply would contain the same 4-bit payload, with the requested MAC address now appearing as the Ethernet frame's source address, as shown in Figure 6.

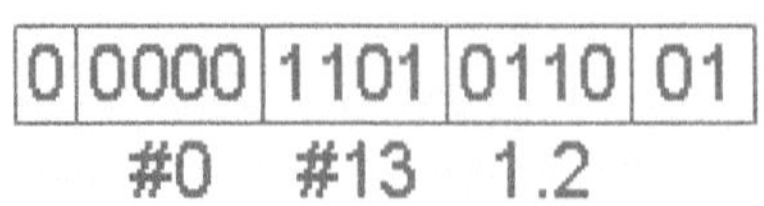

Figure 5. ARP Request for 1.2's MAC Address

Figure 6. ARP Reply from 1.2

5. TRANSPORT LAYER: TCP

We presented TCP [2] as a completely independent layer from IP, where a TCP packet was the payload of an IP packet, as shown in Figure 7. We first focused on the functionality common to both TCP and UDP: inter-process communication. We chose to represent each process's port number as a 2-bit value. Each TCP packet therefore began with a 2-bit destination port number and a 2-bit source port number.

Figure 7. TCP packet embedded inside an IP packet, embedded in an Ethernet frame

We gave each TCP packet a 2-bit sequence number. Thus, in our model, a large message broken down into many TCP packets would begin with sequence #0, then #1, #2, #3, #0, #1, and so on. Next, we used a 1-bit flag to indicate whether this was the final packet in the message. Finally, we chose to have each TCP packet carry the 8-bit ASCII code for a single character as its payload. For example, the message "HELLO" would be broken down into 5 TCP packets, with the first carrying the 8-bit code for the letter "H", and so on. The receiving party would send an ack (acknowledgement packet) for each received letter. Each ack in our simplified TCP model consisted only of the port numbers and sequence number, as shown in Figure 8.

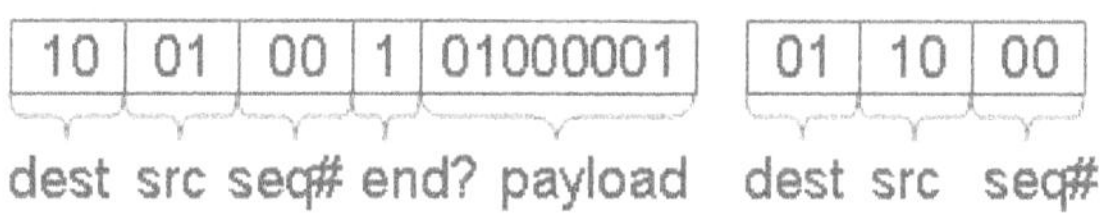

Figure 8. TCP packet #0 (carrying the letter "A") and corresponding ack

In class, we introduced students to the idea of a sliding window, in which a number of TCP packets would be sent before any are acknowledged, and where an ack from the receiving party might acknowledge several packets at once. However, in our implementation, we restricted ourselves to a 1-packet window.

So, in order to transmit "HELLO", we would first send the letter "H", and then wait for an ack. If no ack is received after some timeout, we would re-transmit the "H". Once an ack is received for the "H", we would then go on to transmit the "E". (This is essentially a stop-and-wait protocol.)

6. IMPLEMENTATION

Because the students had already completed an AP Computer Science course, we used Java to implement our network simulation software. Students were provided with two black-box classes: a LightSystem and a LightPanel. Upon running the LightSystem, students could instantiate new LightPanels, which would automatically connect to the LightSystem. Together, these two classes formed the physical layer of our network. (The LightSystem itself was implemented as a server, and could be connected to by LightPanels across the real Internet, using sockets. This allowed us to grade student work by testing that they could interoperate with our correct implementation of the simplified protocols.) The LightPanel API included methods for switching the light on, switching it off, and testing if it is on. The LightPanel could also be asked for its ID, which served as its MAC address.

In implementing our protocol stack, we divided the traditional layers into a number of classes, as shown in Figure 9. Students implemented these classes from the bottom up, starting with the BitHandler class, which could broadcast and detect bit strings.

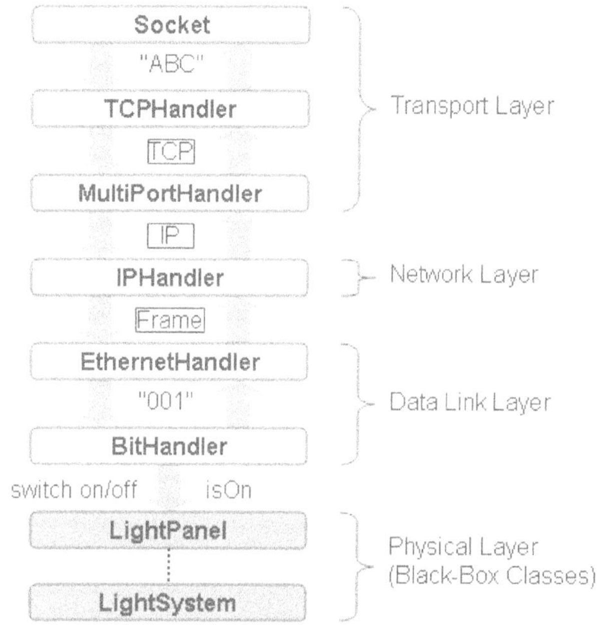

Figure 9. Layers of classes used to implement our network simulation

At the highest level, we created a Socket abstraction (along with a ServerSocket class). The Socket class allowed the user to establish a connection to a given IP address and port, and then send and receive text, one line at a time, until the socket was closed. To send a line of text, the Socket passed that text down to its TCPHandler, whose job it was to wrap each character in its own TCP packet, and to ensure the reliable transmission of each of those packets. To do so, each TCP packet was passed down to a MultiPortHandler, whose job it was to wrap the TCP packet in an IP packet, and pass that down to an IPHandler. The IPHandler would then place the IP packet in an Ethernet frame addressed to the appropriate MAC address (as found in its ARP table or determined from an ARP request), and would pass the frame down to an EthernetHandler. The EthernetHandler would convert the frame into a string of bits, and pass these down to a BitHandler (and handle collisions). The BitHandler's job was to inject those bits into the network by switching the light on and off with the appropriate timing (and to detect collisions).

On the receiving side, the BitHandler used a thread which would regularly poll the LightPanel to determine if the light was on or off. Using a state machine, the BitHandler determined the string of bits received, and passed these up to an EthernetHandler. The EthernetHandler's job was to parse those bits into a frame, verify its checksum, and pass the frame up to an IPHandler (if the frame was addressed to this LightPanel's MAC address, or to the broadcast address #0). The IPHandler would then extract the frame's payload and handle any received ARP request or response appropriately. If the frame contained an IP packet, that packet would be passed up to a MultiPortHandler. This class would then extract a TCP packet from the payload of the IP packet, and examine the destination port number. The MultiPortHandler maintained a table, with each port number registered to a different TCPHandler. Using this table, the TCP packet would get passed up to the appropriate TCPHandler. If the packet was an acknowledgment, the TCPHandler would send the packet containing the next letter in the message (if any). On the other hand, if the packet contained a letter, that letter would get added to a received message string, and an acknowledgment packet would be sent back. When the entire string was received, it would be passed up to the Socket, and eventually returned to the user as the next received line of text.

7. USER INTERFACE

Students were provided with a LightDisplay class–a user interface for controlling and monitoring a light panel, as shown in Figure 10. The LightDisplay served as an invaluable tool for monitoring network activity.

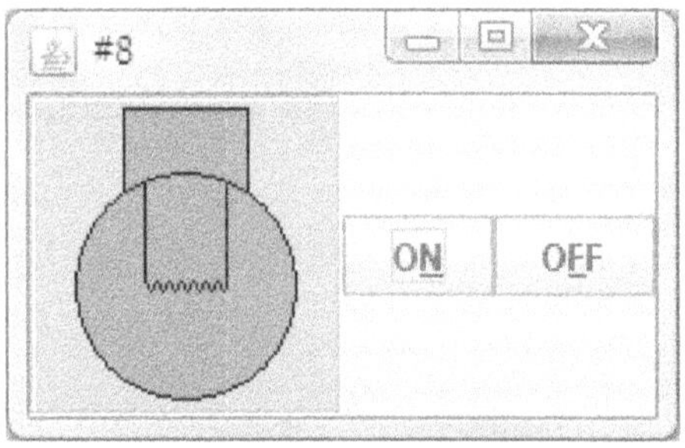

Figure 10. Screenshot of LightDisplay window

Whenever bits were received by a BitHandler, it would pass that bit string up to its registered BitListener. Students were provided with a BitDisplay class (shown in Figure 11), which implemented the BitListener interface. The BitDisplay showed the most recently received bit string, and allowed a user to enter a string of bits to send. The BitDisplay proved to be a valuable debugging tool, allowing us to sniff and spoof Ethernet frames.

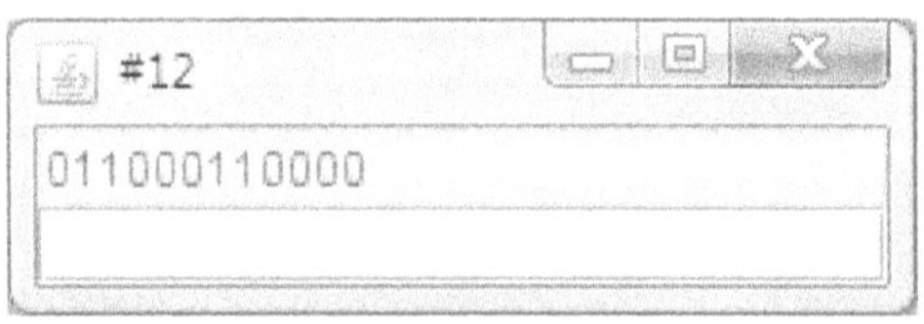

Figure 11. Screenshot of BitDisplay window

Later on, students programmed the EthernetHandler class to implement the BitListener interface, thus allowing an EthernetHandler to register to listen for any string of bits detected by its BitHandler. This architecture repeated itself at each layer, so that an EthernetHandler passed a received frame up to a registered EthernetListener, which might be an EthernetDisplay or an IPHandler, and so on.

8. SWITCHING AND ROUTING

We briefly discussed Ethernet switching in the course. Our more advanced students implemented a simple Ethernet switch, which consisted of several EthernetHandlers–each one on a different LightSystem. The switch snooped on Ethernet traffic to unobtrusively build up a table that kept track of which MAC addresses could be reached from which EthernetHandler. Using this table, the switch would attempt to forward each received frame to the appropriate EthernetHandler(s), if necessary.

We did not go into much detail concerning routing, as our primary goal for the course was to present the workings of the Internet at its endpoints–the students' computers. Thus, we emphasized that each machine knew which range of IP addresses would be found on its local area network (LAN), and that packets destined for all other IP addresses must be sent to the gateway machine (a router on the LAN whose IP address was already known to each machine on the LAN). Advanced students implemented a simple IP router, which consisted of several IPHandlers. The router was configured to know which range of IP addresses could be reached through which IPHandler. Unlike many traditional networking classes, we did not discuss routing algorithms and associated complexities.

9. METAPHORS

In our lessons, we employed a number of metaphors to teach networking concepts. As already emphasized, we used the light system metaphor as a physical layer on which to build our Ethernet protocol. We also compared Ethernet to a room full of people, all trying to talk at once, to motivate solutions to develop strategies for handling collisions. We then extended this metaphor to include multiple rooms of people, where each room played the role of an Ethernet segment, so that a designated person could play the role of an Ethernet switch by running between rooms to relay inter-room messages.

To introduce IP, we compared IP packets to postcards, each carried on its own mail truck (Ethernet frame) destined for some building (host) connected by a network of roads (the physical layer). Here, post offices played the role of routers. This allowed us to emphasize that the IP packet was addressed to the packet's final destination, while the Ethernet frame (truck) carrying that packet (postcard) might be headed to some router (post office) along the way. We extended this postcard metaphor for TCP, by discussing the problem of sending the text of a long book written on a large collection of individual postcards.

Later in the course, we implemented simple applications using client/server architectures. Here, we compared a server to a person waiting to answer calls placed to a published telephone number, and a client to a person calling that number. When a call is established, each person's connected telephone plays the role of a socket. Many students chose to implement network games as their final projects. To teach them how to use sockets to create their own application-specific protocols, we had students act out a 2-player game played over the telephone (simulated with cups and string), where two students acted as clients calling in to play a game, and a third student played the role of a server receiving their calls and passing the necessary information between them. We wrote down the various messages that students spoke into their phones, and used these as the basis for implementing a protocol to play the game over the network.

10. OMITTED TOPICS

In our course, we presented only those areas of computer networking that students needed to know in order to implement socket-based network applications, and to understand how those sockets might be implemented in a simple network model. In choosing to focus on this slice of computer networking, we omitted a number of networking topics that would have been relevant for our students, including HTTP, email, network security, DNS, DHCP, network address translation, home networking, and wireless Ethernet. We also left out a number of topics that are traditionally covered in an introductory computer networking class, including information theory, network topology, routing and inter-router protocols, network flow and congestion, and Internet infrastructure. We only briefly touched on the history of the Internet, and we did not discuss the impact of the Internet on society or related ethical issues.

11. REFLECTIONS

Over all, we felt the course was successful in teaching the key ideas behind network protocols. As we introduced each new topic, the students were engaged in class discussions, anticipating communication difficulties and developing protocols to address them. Ultimately, it wasn't hard to steer the conversation toward the simplified protocols we designed for students to implement. At the midpoint of the course, students performed very well on a comprehensive exam covering the four layers of our simulated network protocol stack.

The implementation of our simulated network required the students to work with several advanced Java programming concepts from the very beginning of the course, including exception handling, multithreaded programming, and the use and implementation of listener objects. Unfortunately, all of these topics were needed for the very first programming assignment.

Although students enjoyed the challenge of running a simplified Ethernet protocol over the light system, their interest declined as we implemented IP and then TCP. Much of the same coding issues repeated themselves at each layer, and therefore later assignments seemed less novel to the students. Not surprisingly, the highlight of the course for our students proved to be the final project, in which students worked in small groups to implement their own network applications.

Our greatest difficulty in the course concerned the first assignment, in which each student's program needed to examine a blinking light panel to determine the received sequence of bits. Unfortunately, later assignments were very sensitive to subtleties in the implementation of the bit detection algorithm. It was not uncommon for a student's algorithm to work well enough for the Ethernet assignment, only to cause problems on the IP assignment. We therefore eventually provided students with an alternative implementation of the physical layer, which transmitted and received bursts of bits, instead of using flashing lights. This implementation solved our reliability issues, but noticeably lost the magic of communicating by flashing light.

We have considered implementing a physical layer that shows flashing lights, but which detects single bits and network silence automatically, and provides a higher level API. Perhaps the light system is too low-level, but it certainly proved to be a helpful metaphor and a great starting point for our discussions. And there was definitely something very satisfying about building so much functionality on top of a flashing light.

12. REFERENCES

[1] Casado, M. and McKeown, N. 2005. The virtual network system. In *Proceedings of the 36th SIGCSE Technical Symposium on Computer Science Education* (St. Louis, Missouri, USA, February 23 - 27, 2005). SIGCSE '05. ACM, New York, NY, 76-80. DOI= http://doi.acm.org/10.1145/1047344.1047383

[2] Cerf, V. and Kahn, R. 1974. A protocol for packet network intercommunication. *IEEE Transactions on Communications* 22, 5 (May 1974), 637-648.

[3] Elsharnouby, T. and Shankar, A. U. 2005. Using SeSFJava in teaching introductory network courses. In *Proceedings of the 36th SIGCSE Technical Symposium on Computer Science Education* (St. Louis, Missouri, USA, February 23 - 27, 2005). SIGCSE '05. ACM, New York, NY, 67-71. DOI= http://doi.acm.org/10.1145/1047344.1047381

[4] Kurose, J., Liebeherr, J., Ostermann, S., and Ott-Boisseau, T. 2002. Workshop report: ACM SIGCOMM workshop on computer networking: curriculum designs and educational challenges (Pittsburgh, Pennsylvania, USA, August 20, 2002).

[5] McDonald, C. 1991. A network specification language and execution environment for undergraduate teaching. In Proceedings of the Twenty-Second SIGCSE Technical Symposium on Computer Science Education (San Antonio, Texas, United States, March 07 - 08, 1991). SIGCSE '91. ACM, New York, NY, 25-34. DOI= http://doi.acm.org/10.1145/107004.107012

[6] Metcalfe, R. M. and Boggs, D. R. 1976. Ethernet: distributed packet switching for local computer networks. *Commun. ACM* 19, 7 (Jul. 1976), 395-404. DOI= http://doi.acm.org/10.1145/360248.360253

[7] Tymann, P. 1991. VNET: a tool for teaching computer networking to undergraduates. In Proceedings of the Twenty-Second SIGCSE Technical Symposium on Computer Science Education (San Antonio, Texas, United States, March 07 - 08, 1991). SIGCSE '91. ACM, New York, NY, 21-24. DOI= http://doi.acm.org/10.1145/107004.107011

Problem-Directed Discrete Structures Course

Norman Neff
Computer Science Department
The College of New Jersey
Hillwood Lakes, N.J.
609 771 2268
neff@tcnj.edu

ABSTRACT
The "2007 SIGCSE Report On the Implementation of a Discrete Mathematics Course" recommends relocating some discrete structures topic areas to other courses, for the sake of coherency. Our implementation of the one semester course also relocates topics, but additionally features a focus on a significant computer science problem: regular language acceptors. This problem-directed course model promises superior coherency, motivation, and integration with computing.

Categories and Subject Descriptors
K.3.2 [**Computers and Education**]: Computer and Information Science Education – *Computer science education, Curriculum*; G.2.0 [**Mathematics of Computing**]: Discrete Mathematics – *general*.

General Terms
Algorithms, Languages, Theory

Keywords
CC2001, computing curriculum, course models, discrete mathematics, discrete structures

1. INTRODUCTION
Shortly after the dissemination of the Joint ACM/IEE Task Force Report on Computing Curricula 2001 [1](CC2001), SIGCSE recognized the need for detailed implementation recommendations for a coherent one semester discrete structures course[2]. This effort culminated in the 2007 SIGCSE Report On the Implementation of a Discrete Mathematics Course[7]. Taking into account the core topic recommendations from CC2001, as well as responses from its survey of undergraduate Computer Science Departments, the 2007 Report found that it was "not possible to develop a coherent package and cover all of the core topics". Adopting a strategy of relocating topics to other courses in order to improve coherency, the 2007 Report recommended three models for a one semester Discrete Structures course. The three models exhibited varying allocations of emphasis among the six topics. Each of the models relocated one or two entire topics from discrete mathematics to other courses in the curriculum. This paper describes a new model for Discrete Structures, in which content allocation is relaxed in order to further improve focus and coherency. The theme of the model is a deep understanding of a single computer science *problem*. In subsequent sections we detail such an approach to Discrete Structures via the problem of regular language acceptance.

2. CURRICULAR FRAMEWORK
In designing the course implementation, we sought a course that

* utilizes one semester

* is accessible to underclassmen in computer science and computer engineering

* in combination with the rest of the curriculum, provides coverage of the required CC2001 discrete mathematics topics

* integrates mathematics with computer science applications

* possesses a coherent computer science theme: mathematics related to regular languages

To accomplish all of the above, we begin with students who have some experience in computing, and build on that experience. The prerequisite for the course is sophomore status, which in our curriculum implies some experience with Java, data structures, and some college level math..

A second curricular issue is the existence of a requirement that Computer Science majors complete one semester of probability and statistics. This frees the Discrete Structures course of responsibility for two of the six CC2001 topic areas. One might argue that the combined probability and Discrete Structures courses effectively constitute a two semester Discrete Structures sequence, but we believe that our organization is much more desirable, for the following reasons:

i) The probability course covers discrete *and* continuous probability, seen as two models of the general axioms for probability measures. Such a grouping makes for a more complete treatment of modern probability theory than would be likely within a two semester Discrete Structures course.

ii) The one semester Discrete Structures course and the probability course may be taken in any order or concurrently.

iii) By relocating the probability related topics, we enable the Discrete Structures course to deeply cover regular languages. This contributes credit hours to the rest of the Computer Science curriculum by permitting rapid coverage of the regular language material in later courses, such as Theory of Computing and Compilers. Therefore, the *net* cost of covering the six CC2001 topic areas is less than two semesters.

3. COURSE ORGANIZATION

The theme of the course is the study of regular language acceptors. We apply the two technologies of finite automata and logic programming to this problem. Section 5 provides evidence that the mathematics underlying the two technologies subsumes the necessary discrete mathematics requirements of the CC2001 report.

Given a finite alphabet A, the set of *regular languages* over A is the closure, with respect to union, language concatenation, and Kleene star, of the set $\{\phi\} \cup \{ \{\text{"s"}\} : s \in A \}$. *Regular expressions* are well-formed formulas representing individual regular languages [6, 10].

The course consists of three sections.

The first section is a motivational unit called "Introduction to egrep" (2 weeks). It engages students in discovery activities using the *egrep* [3] regular expression pattern matching utility. Lab activities include mining html files for particular types of tags or answering questions like "How many entries in the online dictionary file are words containing exactly one 'a' and exactly one 'n'? .

The second section, "Inside egrep" (7 weeks), explores the design of an "egrep" implementation together with the supporting theory. The theory includes constructive proofs that build finite automata to accept regular languages. Figure 1 exhibits the top level of the algorithm for converting any NFA to a DFA with the same acceptance set.

The third section of the course, "Regular Languages through Logic" (4 weeks), covers resolution proof and shows that regular language questions can be reduced to searches for proofs. Figure 2 exhibits a logic program for predicate *mbr/2*,which checks whether a particular string (in list form) is a member of a given regular language. The program is closely based on predicate logic definitions of the regular language operations. The logic program serves as a language acceptor, and can also generate all strings from a given language if executed under a breadth-first implementation of Prolog. Under SLD resolution, the exhibited program is a decision procedure, but [8] gives a similar logic program that is only a semidecision procedure.

4. PEDAGOGICAL TACTICS

Where possible, the course provides hands-on, concrete experience to improve the accessibility of abstract mathematical ideas. In addition to the egrep work mentioned above, the course includes lab experiences with JFLAP[9], with an "automaton node browser", and with a Prolog interpreter.

Sequencing of the discrete structures mathematics topics is primarily determined by their relation to the development of the regular language application. For example, detailed coverage of

```
Set qq, qqt, qq0 // DFA states
Set DFAstateSet = new Set( ) // set of DFA states
        // each element is a set of ints
Queue queue = new Queue( )

qq0 = lambda({NFA.startState})
queue.add(qq0)
DFAstateSet.add(qq0)
repeat

    qq = queue.remove( )
    for each alphabet symbol  s
        qqt  = TD(qq, s) // apply DFA transition fn
        DFAedgeSet.addEdge( qq, s, qqt)
        if qqt ∉ DFAstateSet
            queue.add(qqt)
            DFAstateSet.add(qqt)
until (queue.isEmpty( ))
```

Figure 1. Pseudocode for NFA to DFA conversion

```
mbr([Ch],char(Ch)).  mbr([ ],emptyStrLang).

mbr(Str,union(S1,S2)):-mbr(Str,S1).
mbr(Str,union(S1,S2)):-mbr(Str,S2).

mbr(Str,concat(S1,S2)):-
  mbr(First,S1),mbr(Second,S2),
  append(First,Second,Str).

mbr([ ],star(S)).      (* Case 1 : arg 1 empty *)
mbr([W | Ws],star(S)):-  (* Case 2: arg1 nonempty *)
  mbr([ONCE | ONCEs],S),
  append([ONCE | ONCEs],Rest,[W | Ws]),
  mbr(Rest,star(S)).

append([ ],S,S).
append([S | R],T,[S | U]):-append(R,T,U).
```

Figure 2. Logic program for regular language acceptor

relations is postponed until minimization of automata, which extensively uses equivalence relations.

The prerequisite for the course is sophomore status, which in our curriculum implies some experience with Java, arrays, and linked lists. The programming ability of the students varies widely, but that is not a problem, as Java programming is not among the course activities. What the Java does provide is a basis for an understandable pseudocode notation when discussing computer applications. When appropriate, the student sees new mathematical notations together with related, but more familiar,

Java-based notations. Figure 3 exhibits the mathematical definition of set image together with a corresponding definition in terms of the Java container class.

```
f(S) = { f(s) : s ∈ S }

Set imageOf(Set S){
    Set answer = new Set( );
    Iterator iS = S.iterator( );
    while (iS.hasNext())
        answer.add(f(iS.next( )));
    return answer; }
```

Figure 3. Mathematical and Java-based notations

5. COVERAGE OF DS CORE TOPICS

The CC2001 report identifies six topics in discrete mathematics as the knowledge base for discrete structures: (DS1) functions, relations and sets, (DS2) basic logic, (DS3) proof techniques, (DS4) basics of counting, (DS5) graphs and trees, and (DS6) discrete probability.

Our problem-directed course omits DS6 and most of DS4. The next section discusses our curriculum's handling of these omissions in the context of the 2007 Report recommendations.

In this section, our intent is to show that the regular language problem affords ample opportunity to study *and use* all of foundational discrete mathematics (DS) topics, excepting the topics we have assigned to other courses.

Each regular expression implicitly presents the question: "Exactly what set of strings does the expression match?" Within the first, exploratory, part of the course, students are asked to create a grep pattern that generates a particular set of strings. Discussion of proposed solutions leads to coverage of informal *proof techniques* such as breaking arguments into cases, establishing bidirectional implications, and searching for counterexamples.

For the remaining parts of the course, we can give a sense of the correspondence between the regular language related topics and foundational DS topics. To conserve space, we will give detail only for the second section, "Inside egrep". Figure 4 lists the principal definitions and proofs in the second section of the course. In the following lines, we comment on the connections between items in Figure 4 and DS topics.

i) Definitions of string, language use: *sequence, set, functions*

ii) Regular language definition uses: *set operations, closure, inductive definition.*

iii) Regular expressions are defined by a *uniquely-readable inductive definition.* A good introduction to *proof by induction* arises from proving that each regular expression contains equal numbers of left and right parentheses. A *recursive function* over the set of regular expressions defines the regular language denoted by each regular expression.

iv) A finite automaton is formally a *tuple* consisting of, a set of states, a start state, a set of final states, and a transition function.

Definitions:

- string
- language
- regular language
- regular expression
- nondeterministic finite automaton (NFA)
- deterministic finite automaton (DFA)

Constructive proofs:

- regular expression → NFA
- NFA → DFA
- DFA minimization

Nonconstructive Proofs:

- $\{ a^n b^n : 0 \leq n \}$ is not a regular language

Figure 4. Automata approach to regular languages

It is also representable as a *labeled digraph*, with certain nodes designated "start" and "final".

v) regular expression → NFA. One can prove the correctness of the NFA construction by *inductive proof* over regular expressions.

vi) NFA → DFA. Each DFA state is a set of NFA states. To generate new DFA states from an existing DFA state, we first take the *image* under an appropriate function, and then perform *closure. Transitive reflexive closure* with respect to the NFA's *∈-relation* is computed by *fixed point iteration* or *breadthfirst* search. The algorithm of Figure 1 builds a *breadthfirst spanning tree* of the DFA digraph.

vii) DFA minimization. A sequence of *equivalence relations* and *partitions* is defined on the set of DFA states. *Well- foundedness* implies that the sequence of successive *refinements* reaches a *fixed point*, which is the solution to minimization.

viii) Proof that the language is not regular uses: *indirect proof, pigeonhole principle.*

Figure 5 lists the topics covered in the third section of the course. A similar consideration of the items in Figure 5 shows considerable support for coverage of the formal logic topics, as well as further use of inductive definition, recursion, and inductive proof. Additionally, graphs and trees are involved in the treatment of unification and of logic programming computation trees and termination analysis.

Coverage of the three sections of the problem-directed course implies coverage of all DS foundational topics, other than those topics relocated to other courses.

Propositional logic
syntax and semantics
equivalences
conjunctive normal form
clausal form
resolution proof
Predicate logic
syntax and semantics
equivalences
clausal form wrt satisfiability
unification, SLD resolution
Horn clause specification, regular language
logic program for regular language

Figure 5. Logic programming approach to regular languages

6. COMPARISON WITH 2007 REPORT

The 2007 SIGCSE Report recommendations include two computer science-focused models and one mathematics-focused model. One of the computer science-focused models omits DS6, Discrete Probability, to be covered in a separate probability course. The other computer science-focused model omits DS5, Trees and Graphs, to be covered in an algorithms/data structures course.

Our problem-directed model best matches the first computer science-focused model, with the additional relocation of DS4, basics of counting. The principal relocated subtopics of DS4 are basic combinatorics and recurrence relations. For our majors, the combinatorics are covered within the probability course, and recurrence relations are covered in analysis of algorithms. In both cases, our arrangement provides superior temporal locality between the presentation of the mathematical topic and its application. Relocating the DS4/DS6 material buys us time for adequate coverage of regular languages, which saves time elsewhere in the curriculum.

Our model can be viewed as an extension of the 2007 Report strategy of outsourcing some topics to enhance coherency in the remaining material. However, none of the 2007 Report models replicates the focus on a single computer science problem area.

7. CONCLUSION

The problem-directed course design is meant to be flexible. One can adjust the relative concentrations on the automata and logic programming technologies. One can investigate chosen DS topics more deeply than is required by the application. One can focus on other difficult problems, such as data mining or market basket analysis [12]. The invariant is organization around a significant computing application.

In our previous experience with math-centric versions of Discrete Structures, some computer science students invariably questioned the necessity of studying the mathematics. It's hard to satisfactorily answer this concern for underclassmen. In fact, the appropriate nature and extent of mathematics content remains an important subject of discussion in the discipline [4, 5, 11].

We believe that our focus on a useful, concrete computer problem results in greater interest and achievement for computer science majors. For many of our students, the problem-directed course design answers the question "Why do we study math?" in the most convincing way— by *experience*.

8. REFERENCES

[1] ACM/IEEE Task Force Report on Computing Curricula 2001-Computer Science, Volume, December 2001.

[2] Baldwin, D., Marion, B., and Walker, H. 2004. Status report on the SIGCSE committee on the implementation of a discrete mathematics course. In *Proceedings of the 35th SIGCSE Technical Symposium on Computer Science Education* (Norfolk, Virginia, USA, March 03 - 07, 2004). SIGCSE '04. ACM, New York, NY, 98-99.

[3] Bambenek, J. and Klus, A. 2009 *Grep Pocket Reference*. O'Reilly Media, Inc.

[4] Bruce, K. B., Drysdale, R. L., Kelemen, C., and Tucker, A. 2003. Why math?. *Commun. ACM* 46, 9 (Sep. 2003), 40-44.

[5] D'Antonio, L., Baldwin, D., Ford, F., Henderson, P., and Wyatt, R. 2002. Panel: is there too much math in the computer science curriculum?. *J. Comput. Small Coll.* 17, 3 (Feb. 2002), 97-102.

[6] Hein, J. L. 1994 *Discrete Structures, Logic and Computability*. Jones and Bartlett Publishers, Inc.

[7] Marion, B. and Baldwin, D. April 2007. SIGCSE Committee Report On the Implementation of a Discrete Mathematics Course. http://www.sigcse.org/resources/discrete-mathematics/DiscreteMathReport.pdf

[8] Neff, N. 1993. A logic programming environment for teaching mathematical concepts of computer science. In *Proceedings of the Twenty-Fourth SIGCSE Technical Symposium on Computer Science Education* (Indianapolis, Indiana, United States, February 18 - 19, 1993). SIGCSE '93. ACM, New York, NY, 20-24

[9] Rodger, S. H., Wiebe, E., Lee, K. M., Morgan, C., Omar, K., and Su, J. 2009. Increasing engagement in automata theory with JFLAP. In *Proceedings of the 40th ACM Technical Symposium on Computer Science Education* (Chattanooga, TN, USA, March 04 - 07, 2009). SIGCSE '09. ACM, New York, NY, 403-407.

[10] Sipser, M. 1996 *Introduction to the Theory of Computation*. 1st. International Thomson Publishing.

[11] Tucker, A. B., Kelemen, C. F., and Bruce, K. B. 2001. Our curriculum has become math-phobic!. In *Proceedings of the Thirty-Second SIGCSE Technical Symposium on Computer Science Education* (Charlotte, North Carolina, United States). SIGCSE '01. ACM, New York, NY, 243-247

[12] Wick, M. R. and Wagner, P. J. 2006. Using market basket analysis to integrate and motivate topics in discrete structures. In Proceedings of the 37th SIGCSE Technical Symposium on Computer Science Education (Houston, Texas, USA, March 03 - 05, 2006). SIGCSE '06. ACM, New York, NY, 323-327.

Reinventing CS50

David J. Malan
Harvard University
School of Engineering and Applied Sciences
Cambridge, Massachusetts, USA
malan@post.harvard.edu

ABSTRACT

Computer Science 50 is Harvard College's introductory course for majors and non-majors alike, enrollment in which both rose and fell along with the dotcoms. Although enrollment peaked in 1996 at 386 students, it had settled by 2002 in the neighborhood of 100.

We set out in 2007 to combat that trend by tackling two problems. We hypothesized that CS50 suffered from two, one of perception and one of design. Although, per end-of-term surveys, the course had never lacked for good teachers or good content, the consensus on campus for years had been to beware this particular course. And the course's own syllabus may very well have been dated in the eyes of students who had begun to carry regularly modern hardware and software in their backpacks and pockets.

Not only did we proceed to revamp every one of CS50's problem sets, we brought its syllabus more in line with technological trends already familiar to students. And we altered the tone of the course to appeal to those "less comfortable" with computing on campus. But we took care to preserve the course's rigor and underlying fundamentals, lest we do our own students a disservice.

Our new approach appears to be working. Between 2006 and 2007, enrollment in CS50 more than doubled from 132 to 282 (+114%). Between 2007 and 2008, enrollment increased another 17% to 330, though even more striking was that year's 48% increase in female enrollment. By 2009, enrollment remained strong at 338.

We present in this work what we have done and why we have done it.

Categories and Subject Descriptors

K.3.2 [**COMPUTERS AND EDUCATION**]: Computer and Information Science Education—*Computer science education*; K.3.2 [**COMPUTERS AND EDUCATION**]: Computer and Information Science Education—*Curriculum*

SIGCSE'10, March 10–13, 2010, Milwaukee, Wisconsin, USA.

General Terms

Design, Experimentation, Human Factors

Keywords

CS0, CS1, CS2, curriculum, pedagogy

1. INTRODUCTION

Computer Science 50 is Harvard College's "introduction to the intellectual enterprises of computer science and the art of programming" for majors and non-majors alike, a one-semester amalgam of courses generally known as CS1 and CS2. Although enrollment in CS50 spiked to 386 in 1996 (on a campus of 6500), our numbers, like most universities', not only rose but also fell with the dotcoms.[1] In 2002, enrollment dipped below 100 and, by 2006, had settled at 132. Of course, ten years prior, our numbers were in precisely that neighborhood too. What might, at first glance, have been a worrisome decline may, in fact, have been mere restoration of equilibrium.

But clearly there was an audience for computer science out there, even though external forces may have coaxed some members our way. And so we asked ourselves in 2007 whether we could recreate the excitement that the dotcoms instilled in so many students and whether we could attract similar numbers with forces more internal than external. To be sure, some of that era's students might have enrolled for academically wrong reasons (*e.g.*, dreams of getting rich quick). So we did not necessarily want all of them back. But among those 386 were some good computer scientists, some of whose potential might not have ever been realized had they not been coaxed from other departments. We wanted to find precisely those students in 2007.

We hypothesized that CS50 suffered from two problems, one of perception and one of design. Although the course was highly regarded, most everyone on campus seemed to think that it should only be taken with caution, not unlike similar courses elsewhere. Opinions were mixed on whether the cause for concern was the course's workload or difficulty, but the result was the same. The consensus was to beware. And it probably did not help that we began each semester from the ground up, introducing students first to assembly language and later to C. Not only does "hello, world" tend to underwhelm students who now carry iPhones and iPods, the syntax of these (and most languages, for that matter, Java

[1] We were fortunate in 1996 to have Brian Kernighan at the helm of CS50.

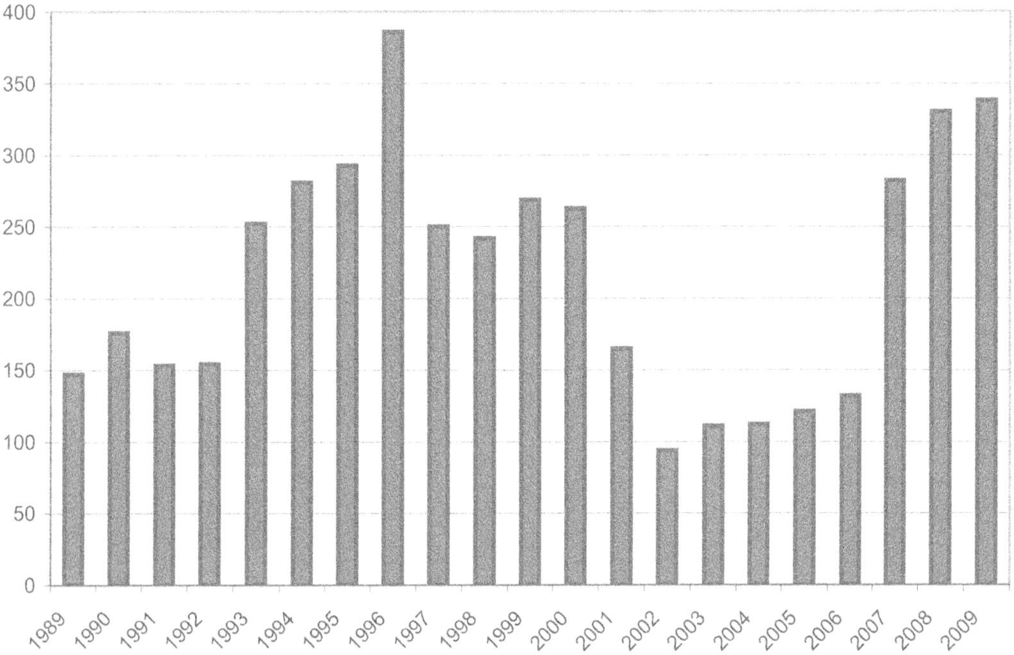

Figure 1: Enrollments in CS50 both rose and fell along with the dotcoms. But they have since risen again in lockstep with changes we began to implement in 2007. Between 2006 and 2007, enrollment increased 114% from 132 to 282. Between 2007 and 2008, enrollment increased another 17% to 330, though more striking was that year's 48% increase in female enrollment. By 2009, enrollment remained strong at 338.

included) tends to distract students from more interesting fundamentals in an introductory course's first weeks.

And so we set out to tackle both problems at once. Not only did we reorganize our syllabus, we modernized our problem sets, tying each one to a real-world domain more familiar to today's students. And we altered the tone of the course, embracing in Week 0 those "less comfortable" and "more comfortable" (with computing) alike. In a word, we set out to make the course more "accessible," while still preserving its content and rigor. We daresay it is easy to create a popular gut, but we had no such intention. Although CS50 is a terminal course for many non-majors, it is a gateway to higher-level courses for majors and minors and must still, therefore, provide no less strong a foundation. More "accessible" has not meant "easier" or "less work" but, rather, more friendly to those who might otherwise worry that they do not belong.

Thus far, our approach appears to be working, per Figure 1. Between 2006 and 2007, enrollment in CS50 increased 114% from 132 to 282. Between 2007 and 2008, enrollment increased another 17% to 330, though even more striking was that year's 48% increase in female enrollment. By 2009, enrollment remained strong at 338. In total, CS50's enrollment has increased by 156% since 2007. To be sure, enrollments in computer science programs have been on the rise nationally since 2007, but not by nearly as much (6.2%) [7].

We present in this paper the new CS50. In the section that follows, we offer background on the students who have begun to take this particular course. In Section 3, we discuss CS50's current philosophy and motivation for the same. In Section 4, we detail the course's curriculum. In Section 5, we survey the problem sets we have modernized. In Section 6, we present our results and, in Section 7, we conclude. Although we happen to spend most of CS50 in C, we suspect the lessons we've learned are no less applicable to courses in Java and other high-level languages.

2. STUDENT BODY

Although some students who take CS50 have one or more prior courses under their belt (*e.g.*, AP Computer Science), most of them (72%) do not. When asked to describe their level of comfort with computing (or the mere idea of being in CS50), 34% of Fall 2008's students described themselves as among those "less comfortable," 14% described themselves as among those "more comfortable," and 52% described themselves as somewhere in between.

Although more than half of the course tends to be male, female enrollment appears to be on the rise. Whereas female students composed 29% of Fall 2007's student body, they composed 36% of Fall 2008's thanks to an increase of 48% in raw numbers. In fact, almost all growth in enrollment between 2007 and 2008, from 282 to 330, was the result of more female students in 2008.

Although students gather twice weekly for large lectures, CS50 implements apprenticeship learning [1,2], whereby each student is apprenticed at term's start to a teaching fellow (TF) who grades that student's work and leads a weekly "section" (*i.e.*, recitation) for that student and a dozen or so others. Almost all of the course's 30 TFs are still undergraduates themselves who took CS50 one or more years prior.

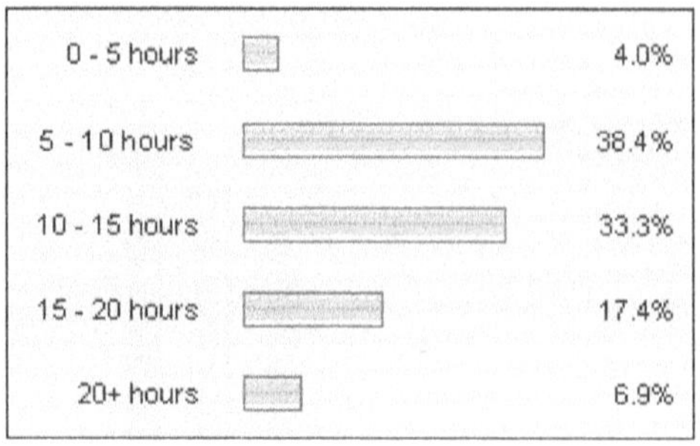

Figure 2: CS50 is known for its workload. Most students spent at least 10 hours outside of class on each week's problem set, with some spending as many as 20.

3. PHILOSOPHY

It is not our intention in CS50 to weed students out but, rather, to open as many eyes as possible to a field we ourselves love. In exchange for their time, the course promises to get every student from Week 0 to Week 12. And the course's own syllabus assures them that "what ultimately matters in this course is not so much where you end up relative to your classmates but where you, in Week 12, end up relative to yourself in Week 0." We provide students with every resource they need to succeed, including lectures and sections (and videos thereof), in-person office hours, virtual office hours [4], code walkthroughs for problem sets (*i.e.*, programming assignments), an anonymized bulletin board, scribe notes, and more. Not only do these resources provide a support structure that empowers students to tackle each week a problem set that demands upwards of 15 hours of work outside of class, per Figure 2, they allow students to engage with the course from any number of angles. Students for whom lectures move quickly can review videos at home. Students who learn best in one-on-one contexts can find precisely that structure at office hours. And students who fear asking the proverbial dumb question can turn to the bulletin board and ask it anonymously. Sections, moreover, are offered in three different flavors: some for those "less comfortable," some for those "more comfortable," and some for those somewhere in between.

But the course plays as hard as it works students. We introduce students in lectures and problem sets not only to computer science but also to geek culture. Lolcats [6] exist alongside linked lists. Internet memes break the ice at classes' start. And YouTube clips allow students to breathe during what might otherwise be 90 intense minutes of lecture.

The course takes its curriculum seriously but not itself too much so. Of course, years from now, we may very well grimace at our conflation of science and geekery. But we think the rewards worth those particular risks. To date, this course is renowned as having one of the heaviest workloads at Harvard. But this same course is nonetheless now Harvard's fifth largest. There's much to be said for that spoonful of sugar. We expect much of our students (cf. Figure 2) in return for the fun that we have. And we get it.

4. CURRICULUM

We discuss in this section the overall arc of the course, including the topics (italicized) covered in lectures each week. Omitted below are weeks with vacations or quizzes. The course covers an unusual number of topics, some in more detail than others. The course's breadth is accompanied by depth in a subset of topics. But it's worth noting that we rely on problem sets to reinforce, hands-on, the topics we feel most important to students' foundation, per Section 5. Lectures are not the course's sole delivery mechanism for content.

4.1 Week 0

Introduction. Bits. Binary. ASCII. Programming. Algorithms. Scratch. Statements. Boolean expressions. Conditions. Loops. Variables. Threads. Events.

Though everyone's favorite canonical program, it's perhaps fair to say that "hello, world" fails to excite most students today. And converting Fahrenheit to Celsius is not terribly interesting. But it's hard to compete in Week 0 with the hardware and software that students carry in backpacks and pockets. There is only so much one can do with C's (or Java's) most basic syntax before it is time to introduce more sophisticated constructs (*e.g.*, arrays). Implementation (and comprehension) of GUIs is generally weeks, if not semesters, away. And so we do not use C in CS50's first week. We use instead Scratch [5], a drag-and-drop programming language developed by MIT's Media Lab, similar in spirit to Alice [3] *et al.*, but whose learning curve is much lower. Although designed for youth in after-school programs, we use Scratch to excite our students in Week 0. With it can they implement their own animations, games, and interactive art without the frustration of semicolons and other syntactical distractions that just aren't interesting in the first days of a course. And yet among Scratch's "puzzle pieces" are precisely the constructs we want to introduce in this first week of class: statements, Boolean expressions, conditions, loops, and variables. Scratch even allows us to discuss threads and events, topics generally reserved for non-introductory courses.

But we spend just one lecture and one problem set on Scratch, after which we immediately transition to C in Week 1.

4.2 Week 1

C. Source code. Compilers. Object code. SSH. SFTP. GCC. Functions. Comments. Standard output. Arithmetic operators. Precedence. Associativity. Local variables. Types. Casting. Standard input. Libraries. Boolean expressions, continued. Conditions, continued. Loops, continued.

In Week 1 do we dive head-first into C, but we feel comfortable waving our hand at certain syntactic details that might otherwise bog down the course's momentum. Yes, `for` loops are cryptic at first glance, but, thanks to Scratch, students already have a mental model into which they can fit that new "piece." We daresay the parentheses and semicolons intimidate them less because the underlying idea is already familiar. And so we spend this week discussing more interesting topics like standard input and output, functions and libraries, and Linux itself. We take care during lecture, though, to provide students with dozens of bite-sized examples with which to pick up C's particular syntax.

4.3 Week 2

Functions, continued. Global variables. Parameters. Return values. Stack. Frames. Scope. Arrays. Strings. Command-line arguments. Cryptography.

In Week 2, we continue to look at more sophisticated topics, including parameters and return values, stack frames and scope, and even arrays. But we also introduce the first of several real-world domains, namely cryptography. That particular topic allows us to challenge students this week to implement a number of ciphers as well as crack passwords using heuristics of their choice. Both activities reduce to some standard input and output, some loops, and some typecasting between `char`s and `int`s, all quite accessible to students at this point in the course. But the problem domain is intellectually "sexy," and that is what motivates.

4.4 Week 3

Linear search. Binary search. Asymptotic notation. Recursion. Pseudorandomness. Bubble sort. Selection sort. Insertion sort. Merge sort. Debugging.

In Week 3 do we transition away from syntax and details specific to C, instead elevating the discussion to algorithms and data structures. We discuss searching and sorting. We discuss efficiency and measurement thereof, including O, Θ, and Ω. Though, perhaps most importantly, we have students act out each of the algorithms. Students remember that bubble sort is slow after they've seen it acted out (not only inefficiently but awkwardly too) by volunteers on stage. We then reinforce those visuals with animations that contrast the algorithms' run times side by side.

4.5 Week 4

Structures. Dynamic memory allocation. Stack and heap. Pointers. Debugging, continued.

In Week 4 do we then discuss how to implement those algorithms in memory. And we discuss memory management in C as well as pointers, the latter of which absolutely takes time to sink in. And so we revisit that particular topic throughout the following weeks.

4.6 Week 5

File I/O. Forensics. Linked lists. Stacks. Queues.

We next introduce students to some file I/O so that their problem sets can finally read from and write to actual disks. We introduce yet another problem domain, this time digital forensics. And we introduce a handful of new structures, including linked lists.

4.7 Week 7

Valgrind. Bitwise operators. Hash tables. Trees. Binary search trees. Tries. Huffman coding.

In Week 7, we introduce students to more sophisticated data structures still, among them hash tables and tries. And, per Section 5, we don't have them implement those structures for the sake of the structures themselves but, rather, to solve more interesting problems.

4.8 Week 8

HTTP. XHTML. PHP. SQL.

In Week 8, we transition away from C altogether and begin a brief look at Web programming. We present the basics of XHTML and then move on to PHP, whose syntax is similar enough to C that we spend most of our time on the features it boasts over C. Moreover, `php.net` offers what may very well be the best documentation of any language today. It certainly facilitates students' picking up a language as of yet unfamiliar to them. We also familiarize students in this week with SQL, including `SELECT`, `INSERT`, `UPDATE`, and `DELETE`, as well as the basics of schema design, but only enough so that they have an ability to store and retrieve data for the week's problem set.[2]

Our motivation for PHP in this week is twofold. Not only do we want to empower students to implement, at term's end, final projects that just so happen to be Web-based, we want them to realize that they are not taking a course about C but, rather, about programming and computer science itself. We want them to experience, with training wheels still on, how one goes about learning new languages, lest they assume, to their detriment, that they must wait for some subsequent course to teach them an additional language.

Other languages might fulfill these same goals. But we happen to like PHP, if only because `php.net` is such a good teacher.

4.9 Week 9

CSS. JavaScript. Events, continued. Ajax.

In Week 9, we both continue and conclude our look at Web programming, introducing students to DOM (yet another application of data structures already covered earlier in term) as well as to JavaScript, whose syntax is quite similar to PHP's own. Thanks to both are yet more possibilities for final projects accessible to students.

4.10 Week 10

Preprocessing. Compiling. Assembling. Linking. CPUs.

In Week 10 do we tease students with what's been underneath the hood all term long. We discuss what it really means to compile, assemble, and link code. And we discuss what "Intel inside" has meant all along.

5. PROBLEM SETS

But it is by way of the course's problem sets that the course's lessons truly sink in. We present in this section the challenges students now take on in each week.

Problem Set 0 invites students to implement most any Scratch project of interest to them, subject only to a few constraints. The aim of this first problem set is to get students excited, to do with Scratch what "hello, world" simply cannot. But the mere act of designing their own animation, game, or interactive art exposes them to statements, Boolean expressions, conditions, loops, and more, all of which prove fairly intuitive when so easily dragged and dropped.

Problem Set 1 next introduces students to Linux. It challenges students to implement a handful of bite-sized C programs, among them validation of ISBNs or credit cards, greedy change-making, and Super Mario's pyramid.

Problem Set 2 then presents that first real-world domain: cryptography. Students must either implement a pair of old ciphers (Caesar and Vigenère) or crack a copy of `/etc/passwd`.

Problem Set 3 is the first that provides students with skeletal code (for the Game of Fifteen) that they must first understand and whose blanks they must proceed to fill in.

[2]We provide each student with a MySQL database that they manage with phpMyAdmin, whose user-friendly GUI lowers the bar considerably to managing tables.

Problem Set 4 hands students even more skeletal code (over 600 lines) for Sudoku, whose implementation they must finish. This problem set also introduces students to APIs, in this case's ncurses's.

Problem Set 5 then has student dabble in the domain of forensics. We first stroll about campus with a digital camera, taking photos of indentifiable but non-obvious locations on campus. We then "accidentally" format the camera's CompactFlash card, at which point we make a "forensic image" of the same (using `dd`) and beg students to recover as many of its JPEGs as they can by writing C code. The problem set then evolves into a course-wide scavenger hunt, as students are also enticed (as via pizza) to find the photos' locations on campus (and photograph themselves there).

Problem Set 6 fosters a friendly competition among students, who are handed a dictionary with 143,091 words and challenged to implement the fastest spell-checker possible (that uses minimal memory). Students (who opt in) are then ranked on the course's homepage according to their code's runtime. Students report spending more time on this problem set than any other, but only because so many are determined to out-do their friends.

Problem Set 7 has students implement, in PHP and SQL, an E*Trade-like site for "buying" and "selling" stocks. Thanks to freely available stock quotes from Yahoo Finance, students integrate actual prices (via CSV feeds) into their own sites.

Problem Set 8, finally, challenges students to implement a "mashup" using tiles from Google Maps and RSS feeds from Google News. Not only does this last project serve as a stepping stone to similarly Web-based final projects, it exposes them to yet another wonderfully documented API, this one from Google.

6. RESULTS

Not only has CS50's enrollment grown by 156% in three years, so have courses downstream grown in size too. Between 2006 and 2007 did CS51 (a LISP-based follow-up to CS50) almost double in size. Similarly did subsequent courses in theory increase their ranks, one by 33% and another by 122%. So has CS1, an optional lead-in to CS50, nearly tripled in size, from 31 to 90 this past year. To be fair, some of these same courses' enrollments have since dipped, though the department has begun offering many more next steps for students emerging from CS50, so we actually now "compete" with ourselves for students some terms.

Whether or not higher enrollments in CS50 and these other courses translates to more majors remains to be seen. Majors tend to take CS50 in their freshman or sophomore year, so a year or two hence will we have a better sense of any such trend.

7. CONCLUSION

In Fall 2007, we set out to reinvent CS50. Not only had the course suffered for years from a fear factor on campus, its problem sets were no longer consistent with topics genuinely of interest to students. And so we aspired to right both, while still preserving the course's historical rigor and underlying fundamentals. Two years' of end-of-term surveys indicate that we have indeed preserved the former, and careful attention to the course's curriculum has ensured that we have preserved the latter as well.

As the course's sheer size now attests, we appear to have transformed what was once, for many students, a course not to be taken into one that must be. Undoubtedly that mindset will not persist forever, as enrollments do seem to ebb and flow. But, for now, many more students do seem excited by computer science on campus.

APPENDIX

The address of CS50's website is:
`http://www.cs50.net/`

8. REFERENCES

[1] O. Astrachan and D. Reed. AAA and CS 1: The Applied Apprenticeship Approach to CS 1. In *SIGCSE '95: Proceedings of the Twenty-Sixth SIGCSE Technical Symposium on Computer Science Education*, pages 1–5, New York, NY, USA, 1995. ACM.

[2] O. Astrachan, R. Smith, and J. Wilkes. Application-Based Modules Using Apprentice Learning for CS 2. *SIGCSE Bull.*, 29(1):233–237, 1997.

[3] S. Cooper, W. Dann, and R. Pausch. Teaching objects-first in introductory computer science. In *SIGCSE '03: Proceedings of the 34th SIGCSE technical symposium on Computer science education*, pages 191–195, New York, NY, USA, 2003. ACM.

[4] David J. Malan. Virtualizing Office Hours in CS 50. *SIGCSE Bull.*, 41(3):303–307, 2009.

[5] J. H. Maloney, K. Peppler, Y. Kafai, M. Resnick, and N. Rusk. Programming by Choice: Urban Youth Learning Programming with Scratch. In *SIGCSE '08: Proceedings of the 39th SIGCSE technical symposium on Computer science education*, pages 367–371, New York, NY, USA, 2008. ACM.

[6] Pet Holdings, Inc. I Can Has Cheezburger? http://icanhascheezburger.com/.

[7] Stuart Zweben. 2007–2008 Taulbee Survey. Technical Report 3, Computing Research News, 2009.

Broadening Student Enthusiasm for Computer Science with a Great Insights Course

Marie desJardins
University of Maryland Baltimore County
Department of Computer Science & EE
Baltimore MD 21250
mariedj@cs.umbc.edu

Michael Littman
Rutgers University
Department of Computer Science
Piscataway NJ 08854
mlittman@cs.rutgers.edu

ABSTRACT

We describe the "Great Insights in Computer Science" courses that are taught at Rutgers and UMBC. These courses were designed independently, but have in common a broad, engaging introduction to computing for non-majors. Both courses include a programming component to help the students gain an intuition for computational concepts, but neither is primarily programming focused. We present data to show that these courses attract a diverse group of students; are rated positively; and increase students' understanding of, and attitudes towards, computing and computational issues.

Categories and Subject Descriptors

K.3.2 [**Computers and Education**]: Computer and Information Science Education—*computer science education, curriculum*

General Terms

Design, Human Factors, Measurement

Keywords

introductory courses, attitudes towards computing

1. INTRODUCTION

Most computer science degree programs include an introductory course sequence that focuses on teaching students how to program. Many colleges also have introductory courses designed for students majoring in other disciplines, and students who have not yet decided on a major. However, these courses are typically still programming centered.

Several studies over the past few years have identified the emphasis (some would say overemphasis) on programming in introductory courses as one of the problems with CS degree programs [17]. A heavy emphasis on programming often does little to attract non-majors into the major, and may "turn off" some students who had intended to major in CS. Women and underrepresented minorities are more likely to be affected by this situation [16]; one hypothesis is that these students are more motivated by a desire to help other people in their careers (rather than by a prior interest in programming and computers *per se*), and are therefore less likely to feel that the programming-heavy introductory sequence is relevant to their long-term goals.

The emphasis on programming in courses designed for non-CS majors may also unintentionally turn students off to CS. In the long run, because CS is inherently interdisciplinary, and because computing is becoming increasingly important across disciplines, it is essential—both for the field of CS and for society as a whole—that *all* college graduates have an appreciation for the capabilities and limitations of computing. Therefore, not only is it problematic if an exclusive focus on programming reduces students' interest in CS, but these programming-centered courses may not lead to the learning outcomes that are most important for a broad student population: namely, an understanding and appreciation of the basic and applied *science* of computer science. Recently, some institutions have begun offering courses that are "contextualized" to different interest areas, such as engineering or multimedia computation [12], or that offer a "breadth-first" approach to computer science rather than a purely programming-centric pedagogy [1, 2, 10]. However, while intended to be more appealing to non-CS students, these courses are still centered around programming.

At Rutgers University and UMBC, the authors have designed and taught courses for non-majors that focus on what we call the "Great Insights" of computer science. These courses have been very popular at both schools, have attracted a number of students to take additional programming-focused CS courses, and have had a positive effect on students' attitudes towards computing as a discipline. The courses have attracted a higher percentage of female and minority students than the traditional programming-centered introductory courses for majors and non-majors. While the courses we describe do include a programming component, we introduce "student-friendly" visual programming paradigms (Scratch and Alice) only to illustrate the idea of programming to the students, not with an intention to give them proficiency in programming *per se*.

One of the key aspects of the courses we describe is that they are not "lightweight" or "high-level": while they are meant to be engaging and accessible for students with a wide range of backgrounds, they do not shy away from topics that are conceptually challenging and mathematically rigorous. At the same time, the courses make no attempt to "weed out" students, but focus on exposing *all* students to the deep and interesting ideas underlying the discipline.

The idea that programming and technologies are not philosophically at the core of computing and computational thinking is not new. Denning [7] argues that we should move away from the "classic" division of computing into technology categories (networking, compilers, etc.) and towards developing a model that is focused on core scientific and engineering principles. Denning identified five such "core principles" of computing: computation, communication, coordination, automation, and recollection; in later work, two additional principles—those of evaluation and design—were added [8]. Wing [18] argues persuasively that understanding principles of computation and "computational thinking" is important for everyone, not just computer science. We were also partly inspired by "Great Ideas" and breadth-first programming-centered courses [2, 6, 10].

In this paper, we describe the shared structure of our courses, discuss some of the specific topics and teaching techniques that each of our courses has incorporated, and present data supporting the success of the classes in both schools. We conclude by discussing some of the ongoing improvements that are planned for both courses and our recommendations for other faculty who may be considering introducing similar courses at their institutions.

2. GREAT INSIGHTS COURSES

The two "Great Insights" courses that we describe here are Rutgers's CS105, "Great Insights in Computer Science," and UMBC's CMSC 100, "Introduction to Computers and Programming."[1] The intention of both courses is to give students from a variety of backgrounds a broad exposure to the scientific principles and mathematical aspects of the discipline of computer science.

The essence of the courses is a key principle of computer science: the notion of *abstraction* (or, viewed the other way, problem reduction). The message is "it's all just bits"; the key to computer science is that those bits can be composed in highly complex ways through abstraction layers, resulting in today's sophisticated hardware and software.

Both classes use Google and universal product codes (UPCs) as case studies that touch upon many of the "Great Insights" that drive computer science. Specific topics that both courses cover include logic circuits, Boolean algebra, binary numbers, algorithms (including top-down design and searching/sorting), computer organization, theory of computation (finite state machines, the halting problem, complexity classes, and NP-completeness), data compression (including Huffman codes), AI and heuristic search, and computer graphics. The differences between the two classes, and specific pedagogical techniques that each of the authors has used in their classes, are discussed in the next sections.

2.1 Great Insights at Rutgers

The Rutgers course was created in the Spring of 2006 to respond to a perceived need to reach out to non-majors and

[1] UMBC's original CMSC 100 taught students how to use Microsoft Excel and other application tools, and covered the basics of programming in various languages. The author completely redesigned the course in 2008, but the course title has not yet changed to reflect the revised course contents.

Week	Topics
1	Course Overview; Barcodes
2–3	Bits; Boolean Algebra; Logic Blocks
4	Binary Arithmetic; State Machines
5	Programming in Scratch
6	Machine Language; Subroutines; Recursion
7–8	Randomness; Self-contradiction; Halting
9–10	Midterm; Decision Problems on Lists
11	Growth Rates: Songs, Algorithms; NP
12	Algorithms: Reachability, Sorts, Binary Search
13	Heuristics; Huffman Codes
14	Parallelism; Images; Learning
15	Robots; Reinforcement Learning; Genetic Algorithms

Table 1: Topics by Week for Rutgers's CS105

present the "science" side of computer science. Existing introductory classes at Rutgers were concerned with societal issues, programming, and software applications, but not academic computer science. (Table 1 summarizes the topics covered.)

Everyday Examples. We used a short book by Danny Hillis [13] that provides an engaging account of the inner workings of computers, from logic gates up to parallel and learning systems. The book uses personal anecdotes to make the material more accessible. For example, the section on algorithms begins with a story in which Hillis's college roommate announces, "I have decided to use a better algorithm for matching my socks." The book then describes how two different solutions to the same problem can have different properties.[2]

The class elaborates on this example, carrying out a live demonstration, soliciting ideas for other approaches to the same problem, presenting the algorithms themselves as programs, considering different objectives for optimality, and going through the analysis of the different options.

Other examples in the class's algorithm-analysis section include analyzing song growth [5], decision problems on lists ("Who can be the first to tell me if the median of this list of 19 numbers is 47?"), and graph search in web spidering. The emphasis is on engaging the students to look at familiar problems from a (novice) computational perspective.

Programming in Scratch. Although the class does not emphasize programming, it is difficult to convey computational ideas without some concrete means for expressing algorithms. In the first year, we used Python for all in-class examples because, to our eye, it looked like executable pseudocode. When it became clear that beginning students still struggled with the syntax, we tried dropping the examples, but that made the class too vague. When we found Scratch (scratch.mit.edu), however, our search was over. Scratch was designed around three core principles: "Make it more tinkerable, more meaningful, and more social than other programming environments" [11].

Although Scratch is pitched at a younger audience, it can be used successfully in a college-level course [15]. We found that the simplicity of the *appearance* of the language made it possible for students to absorb the basic ideas very quickly

[2] The book's strength is its broad and engaging exploration of computer science concepts. Its primary weakness is that it is not actually a textbook; it lacks exercises and reviews that students could use to cement their understanding.

Week	Topics
1	Course Overview; Deconstructing Google
2	Deconstructing a Computer; "It's All Just Bits"
3	Huffman Codes; Introduction to Alice
4	Algorithms
5	Computer Organization; Computational Efficiency
6	Operating Systems and Networks
7–8	Algorithms; Presentations; Midterm
9	Data Abstractions and "Movie Day"
10–11	Databases, AI, and Game Playing
12	Graphics and Theory of Computation
13	Secure Computing
14–15	Computing Tomorrow and Student Presentations

Table 2: Topics by Week for UMBC's CMSC 100

and to be able to start thinking about simple programs right away. In the first year that we adopted Scratch, students began insisting that we use Scratch not just for the actual programming examples, but as the pseudocode as well.

Because of the ease with which Scratch control structures can drive simple media (sounds and animation), we were able to illustrate concepts such as loops and recursion in a way that was more perceptual and less abstract. As a concrete example, students were asked to determine whether a simple loop would halt. When this material was presented using Python, most students answered these questions correctly no more often than random guessing, even at the end of the semester. When we switched to a live demonstration using Scratch, and placed an annoying sound effect inside the loop (on each iteration, it would make a loud pop), students began taking a greater interest in distinguishing halting and non-halting loops ("No, don't start *that* one!"), resulting in increased student performance on these tasks.

Another benefit of Scratch is the community website (see http://scratch.mit.edu/users/cs105). Scratch programs can be posted on a YouTube-like website and shared with friends, even those who have not installed the Scratch development environment. The class included an assignment in which students used this facility to create an animated holiday card. We demonstrated the best cards in class for a "Scratch Off"—students voted to decide which program would receive a prize and be posted on the class Scratch site.

Videos. Another mechanism that we used in the class to engage students with ideas from computer science was the creation of music videos on several pertinent topics, roughly one per chapter of the book. The current videos (youtube.com/mlittman) include Octopus's Counting (binary numbers), The Sorter (sorting), Paintcan (recursion), The Answer Man (computability), and an end-of-class review. Some of these videos have been picked up for use in other classes, including at UMBC—the Octopus video has been viewed over 32,000 times.

The class has been offered a total of eight times, five of these by the second author (who was the original course designer). Each semester brings new experience and examples.

2.2 Great Insights at UMBC

UMBC's CMSC 100 uses as a textbook Brookshear's *Computer Science: An Overview* [3]. The textbook covers many of the topics in the course, but we omit much of the "technology-centered" material and add more of illustrations of the core scientific principles of computation (e.g., Huffman codes, finite state automata, minimax game trees, and Google as a case history). We also supplement the course material heavily with additional lecture notes, handouts, and relevant articles from the scientific and popular press. A high-level outline of the course topics by week is given in Table 2.

By way of comparison, UMBC's course is slightly more applied than the course at Rutgers, and has an added focus on CS and society, as well as applications of computing in a variety of domains.

CMSC 100 is currently in its second offering, with the author (and original designer) still teaching the class. In 2010, we expect the course to be taught by other instructors, so one of the main course-development activities this year is to create a "course package" that can easily be reused by other instructors.

Applications. The UMBC course spends time throughout the semester discussing how computing affects society. Specific topics include privacy, environmental impacts, security and computer viruses, validation of autonomous systems, and the ethical and philosophical issues surrounding AI and the possibility of true intelligent computers.

Students are required to write a research paper on the applications of computing in a field of interest to them. This assignment includes a short proposal, a preliminary bibliography, an in-class one-minute topic presentation, a draft paper that is read and critiqued by two other students, a final paper, and a short (3-minute) in-class presentation of their findings. Topics in 2008 ranged from autonomous vehicles to theatrical lighting and pyrotechnics to motion-capture technology for testing bowling balls and bowling technique. This assignment not only gives the students important writing practice (with significant feedback to improve their writing and paper organization), but it also gives them a much broader and deeper exposure to the possibilities and importance of computing (particularly since they learn about what all of the other students have researched as well).

Programming in Alice. The courses uses Alice [4] to teach basic programming concepts. The first two assignments simply ask the students to download Alice 2.2 and run the three included tutorials, answering a few short questions about the tutorials to make sure they are paying attention. After that, there are two very open-ended programming assignments: the students create their own movie/story that includes a certain number of objects, classes, and methods. There are a few other requirements to make sure that students use the whole "toolkit" of programming constructs (e.g., they must at some point iterate using a "for" loop).

The resulting programs are shown in class, and the students have the opportunity to vote on their favorites. This "movie day" is very popular with the students, since it gives them the chance to "show off" their own work and to see what the other students were able to create with the Alice environment.

Given our experiences in the two classes, both Alice and Scratch seem to be good environments for beginning programmers to experiment and apply what they have learned about algorithmic techniques in practice. Scratch's interface is perhaps a bit easier to use (the drop-down menus in Alice for setting parameters, and mechanisms like the camera angle, are not always intuitive for the students to understand). Scratch's syntax is also intuitive enough to be used as the pseudocode standard in Rutgers's CS105; since training students to read and understand pseudocode (or even the concept of a sequential or iterative algorithm) is quite challenging, we are considering trying out Scratch as an alternative to Alice in the 2010 offering.

Nifty Lectures and Assignments. Several of the lectures and assignments have been particularly effective and popular. Students were especially engaged by the "Deconstructing Google" and "Deconstructing a Computer" lectures. In the former lecture, we start from "how Google works" and peel away the layers of abstraction, bringing the discussion down to the level of server farms and the amount of storage required to crawl and index the web. In the latter lecture, we literally take apart a computer and talk about the components, how modular the design is, and how the pieces are configured to make a computer work.

As part of the final homework assignment, students are required to submit three proposed exam questions on the course Blackboard website. As an incentive to design good (but fair) questions, students are told that 30% of the final exam will consist of questions from the website. Students can see each other's questions, which helps them to prepare—and the instructor gains valuable insights into what students thought the course was actually about.

Honors Section. UMBC has an Honors College program for academically talented students who wish to pursue a more intensive and engaging option throughout their college career. All Honors College students are required to take a certain number of "Honors"-designated courses. CMSC 100H, the Honors section of CMSC 100, is offered as a weekly discussion session/lab in addition to the regular CMSC 100 lectures. The honors section alternates seminar-style discussion sessions with "programming boot camp"—a fast-paced introduction to Linux and Python (the programming language used in our CS 1 class) that is designed to prepare students for the introductory programming course for CS majors. (In 2008, all of the eight honors students continued into that course; one withdrew from the course for personal reasons, but the others all passed the course with a B or higher.) Over the course of the semester, as the students' algorithmic problem solving skills improve, they incrementally design and implement a player agent for the game of Mastermind. In the second year, we used pairs programming in some of the labs, which proved very effective in this accelerated learning environment.

"Social impact" discussion topics have included privacy and security, the environmental impact of Google's large-scale search operations, and Asimov's "Three Laws of Robotics" and whether it is ethically acceptable to treat intelligent robots as servants.

3. OUTCOMES

In the Fall of 2008, we engaged in some simple evaluations to assess how well our introductory courses were meeting our goals. We had introductory students at UMBC and Rutgers fill out entrance and exit surveys. These surveys collected some basic data about the students, their educational background, their familiarity with computers, and their attitudes towards the class, computer science, and computers more generally.[3] Surveys were offered in paper form for some classes and via an online site (surveymonkey) for others. Students were not required to complete surveys, and exit surveys in particular had a low rate of return. (As a result, we were unable to form strong conclusions about how the courses *changed* student perceptions—other than anecdotally—but have more substantial data about the populations that the courses attract.)

	Programming	Insights	Programming	Insights
UMBC	17% (36)	30% (46)	24% (34)	33% (46)
Rutgers	14% (21)	50% (66)	10% (19)	84% (44)
Combined	16%	42%	19%	65%

Table 3: Percentage (and total survey responses, in parentheses) students who are female (left) and who feel they would not enjoy being a computer scientist (right) in two kinds of introductory courses (traditional programming-based and Great Insights) at the two schools.

In the results below, we distinguish between the new introductory Insights courses described in this paper—Rutgers-I (CS105) and UMBC-I (CMSC 100)—and two more traditional introductory programming courses offered at the same time—Rutgers-P (CS111/112) and UMBC-P (CMSC 104).

The composition of the classes themselves varied (Table 3). At both schools, the Great Insights courses attracted a substantially greater percentage of female students than the traditional programming-based courses (left part of table, 16% vs. 42%). (In the Rutgers case, the difference is significant, $p < .01$ by a two-tailed Fischer's exact test).

Although the survey did not ask for the respondents' race, we have statistics for the UMBC courses. There was a noticeably higher percentage of minority students in the UMBC-I course than in UMBC-P. The latter course usually has very few Hispanic and African-American students, typically less than 10%. (UMBC's undergraduate student population is 16.5% African American and 4% Hispanic.) By contrast, in 2008, 13% of the students in 100/100H fell into these categories; this year, 22% of the students are Hispanic or African-American. The course also attracts an extremely diverse group of students in terms of their majors: over the two years the course has been taught, we have had students from economics and financial economics, psychology, engineering, computer science, biology, visual arts, history, public policy, media communications, mathematics, and political science. UMBC-I also has a relatively large percentage of undeclared students (nearly 20%).

One of the questions on the survey asked students whether they agreed with the statement, "I think I would enjoy being a computer scientist." The percentage who *disagreed* with the statement (answering either "Disagree" or "Strongly Disagree") are shown in the right of the table. There are a number of interesting trends here. First, the traditional programming-style courses attracted students who were more convinced they would enjoy being computer scientists (with only 19% of the students disagreeing, compared with 65% of the Insights students disagreeing). The Great Insights students may have been interested in computer science, but not necessarily as a career. Second, the Rutgers class in particular seems to have reached a wider community, the vast majority of whom were not expecting to enjoy a career in

[3]The "attitudes" questions all used a five-value Likert scale: Strongly Agree, Agree, Neutral, Disagree, and Strongly Disagree.

computer science. It is worth noting that the percentage of such students dropped in the post-survey from 84% to 67%, indicating that the idea of being a computer scientist seemed at least somewhat less unappealing.

Less quantitatively, our effort to include accessible and engaging material appears to be working. The number of students has grown with each offering of both classes. We have also received a number of very supportive and unsolicited statements from students via email, including:

- *"i'm a History and English buff, total opposite side of the spectrum...lol but i must say i truly LOVED this class."*
- *"Thanks to you I'm minoring in CS now. You made it even more enjoyable and made it a lot easier so that even an art major like me could understand."*
- *"I am currently a majorless sophomore who really enjoyed your class, however I'm not a huge math fan. Your class made me think of majoring in something computer related ... Thanks for a great class!"*
- *"Thanks to your wonderful teaching in CMSC 100H, not only am I in CMSC 100H, but my first day of MATH 301 [Analysis I, a notoriously difficult class required for mathematics majors] was a breeze."* (CMSC 100H student)
- *"I would absolutely be taking more CS classes had I not graduated. Already, the small amount that I do know has given me tangible results both personally and professionally. I am considering following up my education with a CS program because so few classes bore such great results."*

4. CONCLUSIONS / RECOMMENDATIONS

We have described two courses, at Rutgers and UMBC, that use the idea of Great Insights in computing to teach non-majors about computational thinking and the science of computation. These courses have been very successful at increasing student interest in and engagement with computing. However, the popularity and success of the courses also depend heavily on the degree of engagement and enthusiasm that the instructors bring to the courses. This is particularly true in a course of this type, because non-CS majors are not necessarily intrinsically motivated or predisposed to understand the importance or relevance of CS concepts to their own interests. Capturing the key pedagogical techniques and methods that make these courses successful is a focus at both UMBC and Rutgers as the courses begin to be taught by new instructors. We have also considered the possibility of writing a textbook to carry the ideas of these courses to other institutions.

At UMBC, we are discussing the possibility of offering a variation of CMSC 100 that is specifically designed for majors. On the practical side, this course would likely include somewhat more programming (probably in Python) and an exposure to Linux. On the conceptual side, the topics would likely stay the same, but in some cases with more depth and/or mathematical rigor. The CS majors that have taken the Insights classes have been extremely positive about them, since many of the concepts discussed in the class are otherwise not mentioned until late in the degree program, if at all.

We are enthusiastic about "spreading the word" to other institutions about the success of the Great Insights approach to introductory courses for non-majors at Rutgers and UMBC. We encourage other faculty to consider introducing similar classes into their curriculum as an alternative to traditional programming-centered computing classes for non-majors. Further information and many course materials are available on both course websites [14, 9].

Acknowledgements

The course development at UMBC was completed during Prof. desJardins's sabbatical leave, supported by UMBC and the CS&EE department. Prof. desJardins's time was also supported by NSF CAREER #0545726. Prof. Littman's time was supported in part by NSF ITR-0325281.

Thanks to Chaitra Satharayanara, who organized and helped to analyze the student response data.

5. REFERENCES

[1] A. W. Biermann. *Great Ideas in Computer Science.* MIT Press, 1997.

[2] A. W. Biermann and D. Ramm. *Great Ideas in Computer Science with Java.* MIT Press, 2001.

[3] J. G. Brookshear. *Computer Science: An Overview (10/e).* Addison Wesley, 2008.

[4] Carnegie Mellon University. Alice website, 2009. Alice.org.

[5] D. Chavey. Songs and the analysis of algorithms. *ACM SIGCSE Bulletin*, 28(1):4–8, 1996.

[6] T. J. Cortina. An introduction to computer science for non-majors using principles of computation. In *SIGCSE'07*, pages 218–222, 2007.

[7] P. Denning. Great principles of computing. *CACM*, 46(11):15–20, November 2003.

[8] P. Denning and C. Martell. Great principles of computing website, 2009. http://cs.gmu.edu/cne/pjd/GP/.

[9] M. desJardins. CMSC 100 Syllabus, Fall, 2009. http://www.cs.umbc.edu/courses/undergraduate/100/Fall09/.

[10] Z. Dodds, C. Alvarado, G. Kuenning, and R. Libeskind-Hadas. Breadth-first CS 1 for scientists. *SIGCSE Bulletin*, 39(3):23–27, September 2007.

[11] M. R. *et. al.* Scratch: Programming for all. *Communications of the ACM*, 52(11), November 2009.

[12] M. Guzdial. Teaching computing to everyone. *Communications of the ACM*, 52(5):31–33, 2009.

[13] D. Hillis. *The Pattern on the Stone: The Simple Ideas that Make Computers Work.* Basic Books, 1998.

[14] M. Littman. CS105: Great Insights in Computer Science, 2009. http://www.cs.rutgers.edu/m̃littman/courses/cs105-08/.

[15] D. J. Malan and H. H. Leitner. Scratch for budding computer scientists. In *SIGCSE'07*, 2007.

[16] J. Margolis and A. Fisher. *Unlocking the Clubhouse: Women in Computing.* MIT Press, 2001.

[17] E. H. Turner, E. Albert, R. M. Turner, and L. Latour. Retaining majors through the introductory sequence. In *SIGCSE'07*, pages 24–28, 2007.

[18] J. Wing. Computational thinking. *CACM*, 49(3):33–35, March 2006.

Coaching Via Cognitive Apprenticeship

Ray Bareiss
Carnegie Mellon Silicon Valley
Building 23, NASA Ames Research Park
Moffett Field, CA 94035
011-650-335-2801
ray.bareiss@sv.cmu.edu

Martin Radley
Carnegie Mellon Silicon Valley
Building 23, NASA Ames Research Park
Moffett Field, CA 94035
011-303-818-3283
martin.radley@sv.cmu.edu

ABSTRACT

At Carnegie Mellon's Silicon Valley campus we employ a learn-by-doing educational approach in which nearly all student learning, and thus instruction, is in the context of realistic, team-based projects. Consequently, we have adopted coaching as our predominant teaching model.

In this paper we reflect on our experience with the nature of teaching by coaching using a framework derived from Cognitive Apprenticeship, and explain how we employ the techniques it suggests in our teaching. We also discuss a range of instructional tensions that arise in teaching by coaching and present a survey of student attitudes regarding the effectiveness of our approach.

Categories and Subject Descriptors

K.3.2 [**Computer and Information Science Education**]: Active Learning. Pedagogy. Software Engineering.

General Terms

Human Factors.

Keywords

Software Engineering, Active Learning, Learning by Doing, Story-Centered Curricula, Cognitive Apprenticeship, Information Systems, Graduate Studies, Instructional Technologies, CS Ed Research, Professional Practice, Experience Report

1. INTRODUCTION

Carnegie Mellon's Silicon Valley campus offers an MS in Software Engineering with Technical and Development Management tracks targeted at working software professionals [2]. We also offer an MS in Software Management intended to be a "technical alternative to an MBA" for mid-career software professionals.

The Carnegie Mellon Silicon Valley Software Engineering curriculum comprises six semesters worth of project-based courses. Working both in teams and individually, students act as employees of a fictional company hired to architect, design, and implement or manage multiple releases of a complex application on an aggressive schedule. Within this structure, and with support from faculty members, students confront realistic technical and business problems, including conflicting requirements, limited time and resources, team leadership challenges and ineffective communication.

Given the nature of the knowledge and skills being taught and Cognitive Science research suggesting that the most effective teaching is delivered during active problem solving (see, e.g., [3]), we have adopted coaching as our predominant teaching model (Our teaching model is actually somewhat more complex than we present in this paper, employing subject-matter experts and role playing faculty in addition to coaches. Please see [2] for a more complete discussion.)

Our early approach to teaching through coaching emphasized open-ended questioning (cf. [6], [10]), encouraging students to figure out how to complete assignments on their own with coaches providing guidance almost exclusively by asking questions. While this appeared to produce good learning outcomes, we observed that students became frustrated with this approach and wanted more direct guidance on how to complete their work successfully, balancing the pain of discovery and the amount of effort required to master the subject matter. We began a search for a more varied and balanced model of teaching through coaching and found one in Cognitive Apprenticeship.

2. COACHING VIA COGNITIVE APPRENTICESHIP

Cognitive Apprenticeship transfers the instructional techniques of apprenticeship from their traditional realm of physical activities, such as carpentry or metal work, to mental activities which have historically been taught via traditional classroom techniques:

> "While there are many differences between schooling and apprenticeship methods, we will focus on one. In apprenticeship, learners can see the processes of work: They watch a parent sow, plant, and harvest crops and help as they are able; they assist a tradesman as he crafts a cabinet; they piece together garments under the supervision of a more experienced tailor. Apprenticeship involves learning a physical, tangible activity. But in schooling, the "practice" of problem solving, reading comprehension and writing is not at all obvious -- it is not necessarily observable to the student. In apprenticeship, the processes of the activity are visible. *In schooling, the processes of thinking are often invisible to both the students and the teacher. Cognitive apprenticeship is a model of instruction that works to make thinking visible.*"[4] (Italics are ours.)

Cognitive Apprenticeship suggests that problem solving skills can be taught in the context of scaffolded problem solving by observation of modeling by expert practitioners, appropriate

SIGCSE'10, March 10–13, 2010, Milwaukee, Wisconsin, USA.

removal of the scaffolding (fading), and by reflection on student experiences. Collins, et al, [4, see "Method" beginning on page 13] provide a coherent and seemingly comprehensive catalog of teaching techniques. We have diverged from their model in one key regard which we found to be problematic: Collins, et al, identify "coaching" as an instructional technique, but its description subsumes the other techniques enumerated in the model, implying that coaching is indeed a superordinate category. We have, therefore, dropped coaching as a distinct category.

The following sections discuss how we have interpreted and implemented each technique in our teaching context:

2.1 Modeling

When modeling problem solving, a coach "thinks aloud", verbalizing the thought process as he or she solves an authentic problem. For example, when teaching a Requirements Analysis course, one of the authors modeled analyzing the "whole product" required to solve a customer's entire business problem by walking through Moore's model [8, p. 113] using the example of the products produced by the author's previous eLearning company to show how eLearning software alone does not solve companies' training problems and to articulate what a complete solution would entail. Note that the students were being asked to develop requirements for quite a different application, a social software application for ridesharing. We have found that it is important to model by analogy so students cannot directly copy the answer, but rather they must process what they observe and transfer it to a new problem-solving context.

We have also found storytelling to be a compelling approach to modeling, one that makes coaching vivid and memorable for students [9]. For example, during our Requirements course, students complained about the difficulty of getting interview subjects to describe their work processes specifically during requirements elicitation. The coach responded with the story of an experience interviewing design engineers during which he encountered the same problem. He explained to the students that he solved the problem by having each engineer literally hold, during the interview, an artifact that the engineer had designed and focusing the interview on the specific process by which that artifact had been designed. True stories conveying the coach's real-world experience are especially powerful as a source of guidance, and when we find good stories we tend to reuse them.

2.2 Scaffolding & Fading

Collins, et al [4], describe scaffolding as "the supports the teacher provides to help the student carry out the task." We have implemented three forms of scaffolding: task design, direct guidance, and feedback:

2.2.1 Task Design

In the bulk of our courses, we define the scope the tasks and provide input material our students need to do meaningful work while focusing on targeted knowledge and skills. In doing so, we eliminate peripheral, time-consuming, and (sometimes) overly difficult aspects of the work to be done. For example, in our Introduction to Human-Computer Interaction (HCI) course, students are given a product vision and requirements documents (including well-organized interview data) to enable them to focus on interaction design rather than having to conduct the entire requirements process as a prelude. The coach may also decide to adjust the students' assigned tasks on the fly, relieving the burden on students who are struggling while further challenging students who are excelling. For example (again from the HCI course), an advanced group of students might be asked to storyboard a mobile version of the desktop application they were originally assigned.

2.2.2 Direct Guidance

The coach must constantly monitor a team's progress to ensure that they are not "spinning their wheels" and, thus, becoming frustrated and losing motivation. In such situations, the coach will provide "just-in-time hints" to a team, or if a student team is really struggling, the coach may provide even more specific direction. In doing this, the coach must prioritize the key learning objectives to be mastered based on the team's skills, capabilities, and available time.

2.2.3 Feedback

While coaching, we constantly provide verbal and written feedback to a team of students. In particular, we have found written feedback to be quite effective, and we employ a "limited mastery approach" in which teams submit a deliverable, receive detailed feedback, and are permitted to revise and resubmit it before it is graded. Feedback ranges from directly correcting minor errors to pointing out common errors, which are left to the team to correct, to asking open-ended questions to encourage them to think more deeply (e.g., "You specified that the system *must* respond to all queries within 2 seconds. What if it took the system 3 or even 4 seconds to respond to 25% of queries? Would the system be a failure?"). In one author's courses, the density of comments is approximately seven per page on first drafts of a typical written deliverable. We have found verbal feedback to be especially impactful if provided by role playing faculty members [2] in the context of a meeting, such as a presentation to management, in which students' work is evaluated as it would be in an industrial context.

As students gain mastery, scaffolding is gradually *faded*, i.e., removed (generally later in the curriculum rather than within a single course), and the students are expected to take more direct responsibility for planning and monitoring their own work. Scaffolding is almost completely faded when students undertake a real-world Practicum (i.e., capstone) Project at the end of their studies. During the Practicum, students are not provided with supportive curricular materials (although they can and should refer back to the material provided in previous courses), and the coach no longer gives directive guidance, instead reminding the team that they now own the entire process and its outcomes. That said, however, the coach does continue to observe the team closely and is ready to intervene when major problems arise (especially problems with real-world clients which may be particularly difficult for the team to address themselves).

2.3 Articulation

Articulation involves getting students to verbalize their knowledge and reasoning. We continue to rely heavily on questioning for this aspect of instruction. For example, when students in the HCI class are beginning to think about conducting usability tests, the coach will encourage them to articulate their thought process by asking such things as: "Do you agree with Krug's assertion in *Don't Make Me Think* [7] that "the importance of recruiting representative users is overrated"? "When do you think this does and doesn't matter?" "What types of user attributes are most likely to matter in your project?" After completing their project, they are asked to articulate what they have learned in the form of a presentation to faculty roleplaying senior management in which each team proposes best practices in interaction design drawn from and justified in terms of their experience. (Note that this activity also promotes reflection.)

Many of our courses also require student teams to present their recommendations to faculty role playing as company executives. For example, in our Project and Process Management course, student teams are asked to recommend an appropriate software development methodology for a specific project and to articulate their knowledge by justifying their recommendations in a presentation that will be accepted or rejected by their executive based on the quality of their justifications.

2.4 Reflection

Reflection helps students to critique their own performance with the goal of extracting general lessons from a recent specific experience. Collins, et al [4], suggest this most often occurs in the context of comparing their work and thinking to that of others. For example, when a task in any of our courses culminates in a presentation, students may observe the presentations of other teams including the faculty's feedback, which highlights strengths and weaknesses of the work. As previously noted, students receive comprehensive written feedback on all deliverables which provides another basis for reflection. Finally, at the end of most courses, the coach facilitates a "reflection session" during which the team discusses its work processes and their outcomes, as well as their performance as a team, and the team is encouraged to articulate general lessons learned which will be applicable to similar work in the future. We should note that we do not always promote reflection adequately, and we consider this to be one of the major areas for improvement in our teaching.

2.5 Exploration

Exploration involves pushing students to become independent problem solvers, requiring them to frame their own problems and to define and execute the processes for solving those problems. In our curricula, such exploration is largely restricted to the final Practicum Project in which student teams must interact with real-world clients to understand requirements and negotiate the scope of work and then to define and manage their own work processes, and as noted earlier, to own the results of their decisions. We are considering options for such things as independent study projects and using real-world projects earlier in the curriculum to enable students who are ready to engage in exploration earlier in the curriculum.

3. INSTRUCTIONAL TENSIONS

Over the past six years, we have encountered a range of tensions while teaching by coaching:

3.1 Does the Coach Need to be a Subject-Matter Expert?

In our experience, the coach does not need to be a subject-matter expert (SME); however the coach must be adequately versed in the subject matter to facilitate student learning.

The coach must exceed a threshold of expertise to get and maintain buy-in and respect from the students and to know if a team is "fooling" him or her. This threshold can change depending upon the expertise of the students. For example, one of the authors has coached teams through a Foundations of Software Engineering course in which the students develop a software product using an agile methodology and tools. The author is not a hands-on software developer at the same level as many of the students; however the author has managed agile software development projects and is very familiar with agile methodologies. This has enabled the author (as a coach) to resolve the majority of student questions. Technical questions that the author cannot answer are forwarded to another faculty SME for resolution. We see this as being analogous to professional sports where many successful coaches cannot play the sport at the level they coach.

If the coach is not an SME, the coach and any SME faculty involved in the course must be on the same page in terms of the course learning objectives and the current thinking on industry best practices to avoid conflict between what the SME espouses and what the coach implements.

We support faculty coaches who are not SMEs by creating coach's notes. Coach's notes provide a description, by week, of the key topics, points and logistics that the coach must cover with their student teams. However, providing coach's notes brings the overhead of maintaining the notes and may lead to "prescriptive coaching" (in which the coach leads the team to answers based on the coach's notes) rather than "adaptive coaching" (in which the coach helps guide the team to an outcome which is the appropriate culmination of its own work).

3.2 Should Coaches Grade?

After a coach guides a student team in creating quality deliverables and pre-reviews those deliverables, it is difficult to objectively critique the final version of those deliverables. Of course, the coach is in the best position to know how and where the team has been guided and whether the team paid adequate attention to that guidance. At the same time, the coach wants the team to do well, and so may interpret what they read or hear in more positive terms. Correspondingly, students may lose trust and confidence in their coach if they perceive that their coach is not setting them up for success in the course.

3.3 Student Buy-in

Students, especially those new to this teaching approach, are used to faculty providing them with prescriptive answers through lectures and are expecting to be tested on remembering the answers. We have found that students quickly become experts at getting coaches to provide "the answers" instead of learning on their own (for example, telling their coach: "I don't get it…I don't know what to do…You have to help me.").

In addition, the goal for some students becomes completing the work as quickly as possible while still getting a good grade rather than maximizing learning.

Coaches need to proactively acquire student buy-in to the instructional approach and to shift the discourse from grades to the value of learning outcomes. One effective technique has been to invite alumni to talk about their learning experiences during new student orientation to the program. Another is to acknowledge that a fictional learning context can never match reality, and to ask the students to "suspend their disbelief" about the fictional project scenarios and act fully in their fictional roles.

3.4 Individual Mentoring

Coaches uncover a remarkable breadth of student needs, ranging from addressing lack of confidence to career mentoring to resolving personal problems. Such issues are outside the scope of the curriculum, and time for coaches to address these issues is not an "official" part of the coach's workload, so it is up to each coach to determine how much time they spend on these issues each semester. For many faculty the prospect of working personally with the students is what makes teaching rewarding, even if he or she has to use personal time to do so.

3.5 Team Issues

Coaches also uncover a remarkable breadth of student teaming issues, from lack of interpersonal skills to students who do not pull their weight to (in rare occasions) students who are verbally or psychologically abusive. Unlike individual issues, resolving these issues is part of the curriculum; however it is still up to each coach to determine how much time he or she spends on these issues each semester.

One author calls team members individually once in the middle of each semester just to see if the student has something they might share privately but will not share in a group session. In most cases, no new information emerges, but occasionally a student will open up and provide information that enables the coach to provide the student with specific guidance, address team issues, or take other actions as warranted.

3.6 Coaching Remote Students

Thirty to forty percent of our students are remote (i.e., they live far enough away that they cannot regularly come to campus). Having remote students on teams is an instructional virtue for our programs since virtual work is increasingly the professional norm, and our students can develop their virtual teaming skills as part of their studies.

Coaches must be careful to not favor local students, who participate more visibly, to the detriment of remote students. Coaches can level the playing field between local and remote students by:

- Holding coaching meetings by phone (and collaboration software), whether students are local or not.
- Proactively querying the students in all team conversations. Do not let students sit silent.
- Learning about virtual teams and virtual body language [5]
- Watching for bias in the evaluation and grading of local students over remote students.

3.7 Is a Coaching-Based Approach Scalable?

In our experience, a single faculty member can both coach and provide subject-matter expertise to a small course (25 or fewer students); however some of our courses have 60 students with even larger classes predicted in the future. Instead of attempting to hire multiple subject-matter experts to teach different sections of these large courses, we have used one faculty member to act in the roles of the supervising faculty, fictional role player (e.g., the VP of Engineering), and subject-matter expert, and we have used other, sometimes less expert, faculty as coaches to work with as many sections of students as needed.

To validate the viability of this model we collected faculty effort data during the offering of a 58-student course that used 5 faculty working with 12 student teams over 7-weeks. One faculty member coached 4 teams, while the other faculty members coached 2 teams each.

Two faculty averaged less than 1 hour per week per student (.72 and .94), while the other three faculty averaged much higher (1.67, 1.81 and 1.92). If we assume that 75% of the coach's preparation work goes away the second time they coach a course (this was the first time that this course had been taught), then all coaches would be under 1.5 hours per student per week. We have thus set a goal of spending a maximum of one faculty hour per student per week (since we know such efficiency is possible).

Of course, gathering teaching time metrics puts pressure on the coaches to limit their "face time" with students and, in fact, may cause coaches to be more directive in order to reduce student time demands. To avoid this unintended consequence we regularly reflect with the coaches in our larger classes about their interactions with students and other faculty, framing the discussion of time spent in terms of "high quality" (focused on facilitating key learning outcomes) versus "low quality" hours. Our goals are to achieve a crisper definition of good coaching practices and to build camaraderie and rapport among the faculty.

4. DOES OUR COACHING APPROACH WORK?

During June 2009, we surveyed our current students and *all* alumni (since 2003) to ascertain their attitudes towards our teaching methods, and 116 of 375 responded. Overall, 75% believe our teaching methods are more effective than what they have experienced in other university education; 13% believe they are neither better nor worse; and 12% believe they are worse. With respect to teaching specific types of skills:

- Technical skills: 65% believe they are effective, while 19% are neutral, and 16% believe they are ineffective
- Business skills: 82% believe they are effective, while 11% are neutral, and 7% believe they are ineffective
- Professional skills (e.g., teamwork, communication, negotiation): 88% believe they are effective, while 9% are neutral, and 3% believe they are ineffective.

The most frequent reasons respondents cited (via free text comments) for believing our methods are worse than traditional methods include:

- Too much emphasis on what the students think and too little on what the faculty think during discussions
- Faculty do not (typically) present an overview to provide a conceptual framework for learning new material
- Limited individual feedback (in contrast to team feedback which is copious)
- Faculty do not track teams carefully to ensure balanced contributions by all members.

(And three of 116 thought that the use of conventional lectures would improve teaching.) The first two reasons are most notable because they imply that some faculty do not adequately balance the use of various teaching options; in particular, some faculty may continue to overuse the technique of open-ended questioning and underuse techniques such as modeling and providing direct guidance when appropriate to scaffold a struggling team. The second two reasons primarily reflect a limitation, we recognize, of available faculty time.

In contrast, students who believe the methods are effective cite the initial frustration but ultimate benefit of faculty not simply providing answers. Our goal as teachers is perhaps best illustrated by this quote from an alumnus:

> *The student seems to absorb the material. It becomes very much a part of you without you realizing it until you find yourself in a situation that requires application of some aspect of what you learned.*

5. CURRENT THINKING ON THE IDEAL COACH

We have established a mature curricular framework; however we still leave many teaching decisions to the intuition of individual coaches, resulting in a variety of styles and range of effort, with corresponding variations in effectiveness. That said, our current thinking about the definition of an "ideal coach" is that ideal coaches:

- Adjust to use different teaching methods based on their assessment of a student team's specific situation and needs
- Allow students to diverge from course planned content if/as warranted
- Balance the use of Cognitive Apprenticeship techniques (e.g., open-ended questioning) appropriately given a team's situation, abilities, and mental state
- Have an adequate level of subject-matter knowledge
- Ensure that the students develop and use appropriate work processes and apply what they are learning to their work
- Are flexible with their student scheduling and availability
- Are willing to engage with the students to address and resolve individual as well as team issues
- Are experienced in facilitation
- Are able to establish an empathetic relationship with individual students and teams
- Are comfortable with virtual teams and distance learning.

Are coaches born or produced? We argue that smart, empathetic people can be taught to be good coaches assuming we can codify which teaching techniques are likely to be most effective in which situations and we can train coaches in areas such as:

- Teaching smart people how to learn [1]
- Providing a Cognitive Apprenticeship
- Modeling and coaching effective leadership, teamwork, communication, etc. as well as technical knowledge and skills
- Handling problem students and teams
- Gaining student buy-in to our educational model and teaching approach.

Our program initially employed part-time industrial practitioners as coaches; however because of the wide variability in quality and high administrative overhead, we have evolved to a small group of full-time faculty. This might be the end of the story if the plan was to not grow the student enrollment. Given planned enrollment growth, our ability to codify and impart our teaching methods to new coaches is critical to our successful growth as well as to the replication of these methods to other institutions.

6. ACKNOWLEDGMENTS

Our thanks to the Carnegie Mellon Silicon Valley faculty, past and present, for their dedication, energy and innovation that have made this program a success.

7. REFERENCES

[1] Argyris, C. Teaching Smart People How to Learn, Harvard Business Review. May-June, 1991

[2] Bareiss, R. and Griss, M. 2008. A Story-Centered, Learn-by-Doing Approach to Software Engineering Education. Proceedings of SIGCSE 2008 (Portland, Oregon, March 12-15, 2008).

[3] Bransford, J. D., Brown, A. L., and Cocking, R. R. (Eds.). 2000. How People Learn: Brain, Mind, Experience, and School. National Academy Press, Washington, DC.

[4] Collins, A., Brown, J.S., and Holum, A. 1991. Cognitive Apprenticeship: Making Thinking Visible. American Educator (Winter 1991), pp. 1-18.

[5] Croasdell, D., Fox, A. and Sarker, S. 2003. Systems Development by Virtual Project Teams: A Comparative Study of Four Cases. *Annals on Information Technology, Volume 5*, pages 447 – 463.

[6] Hmelo-Silver, C. and Barrows, H. Goals and Strategies of a Problem-based Learning Facilitator. Interdisciplinary Journal of Problem-Based Learning 1, 1 (Spring, 2006), 21-39

[7] Krug, S. 2006. Don't Make Me Think, Second Edition. New Riders Publishing, Berkeley, CA.

[8] Moore, G.A. 2002. Crossing the Chasm, Revised Edition. Harper Business, New York, NY.

[9] Schank, R.C. 1995. Tell Me a Story: Narrative and Intelligence, Northwestern University Press, Evanston, IL

[10] Staff, Harvard Business School. 1998. Case Method Teaching, Report 9-581-058 (November 6, 1998).

Increasing Technical Excellence, Leadership and Commitment of Computing Students through Identity-Based Mentoring

Kristy Elizabeth Boyer
Department of Computer Science
North Carolina State University
Raleigh, NC, USA

E. Nathan Thomas
Diversity Office
University of South Florida Polytechnic
Lakeland, FL, USA

Audrey S. Rorrer
Department of Computer Science
University of North Carolina at Charlotte
Charlotte, NC, USA

Deonte Cooper
Division of Applied Arts and Sciences
University of South Florida Polytechnic
Lakeland, FL, USA

Mladen A. Vouk
Department of Computer Science
North Carolina State University
Raleigh, NC, USA

{keboyer@ncsu.edu, nathomas@lakeland.usf.edu, arorrer@uncc.edu, dcooper@lakeland.usf.edu, vouk@ncsu.edu}

ABSTRACT
Recent years have seen a growing awareness in the computing education community that initiatives outside the classroom are vital for retaining students and preparing them for a collaborative and dynamic professional environment. Particularly important are programs that develop rich technical skills while increasing students' interest in computing disciplines. We present Computing Identity Mentoring, an intervention designed to increase commitment to computing while enhancing students' technical and leadership skills. This program was implemented at seven universities during 2008-2009. Preliminary results suggest that Computing Identity Mentoring contributes to students' self-efficacy regarding computing and leadership, and solidifies students' commitment to a career in computing. This paper presents early findings on the effectiveness of the approach and illustrates Computing Identity Mentoring in the context of three of the seven institutions where it has been implemented.

Categories and Subject Descriptors
K.3.2 [**Computer and Information Science Education**]: *Computer Science Education*

General Terms
Human Factors

Keywords
Mentoring, project-based initiatives, computing pipeline, diversity, broadening participation

1. INTRODUCTION
Computing students face myriad challenges while moving through their higher education. These students, like those in other disciplines, must adjust to life at a college or university while balancing academic, social, and personal concerns. While computing educators and computing education researchers are actively investigating pedagogical questions that relate directly to students' academic success, there is growing recognition that initiatives beyond the classroom or laboratory may be key to retaining the talented, diverse individuals who will become the technology innovators of tomorrow (*e.g.*, [2, 3, 7]).

In addition to the challenge of retaining students who go on to graduate with the computing degree they set out to obtain, computing educators have the privilege of preparing students for future employment as computing professionals. Today's computer scientist is regularly placed in interdisciplinary settings where leadership skills such as teamwork and collaborative accountability are of paramount importance. These rich technical skills are recognized as critical components of the computing curriculum by some accreditation organizations (*e.g.*, ABET). In this paper, we present a mentoring program designed to increase retention of students in computing majors while reinforcing and expanding technical and leadership skills.

This paper describes Computing Identity Mentoring, an intervention through which students engage in mentoring relationships designed to increase the students' sense of *computing identity* as defined by a set of cultures, values and practices. Computing Identity Mentoring is an instance of Identity-Based Mentoring [8] with implementation guided by the Thomas Principles for mentoring success (Identity Development, Psychological, Social, and Academic Support, Sense of Belonging, and Leadership Development) [6, 17]. The goals of this program include increasing retention in the major and enhancing technical and leadership skills in computing. The initial implementation of Computing Identity Mentoring has been carried out in the context of the STARS Alliance (Students and Technology in Academics, Research, and Service), a partnership of more than twenty colleges and universities primarily in the southeastern United States. Supported by the National Science Foundation, the STARS Alliance aims to increase the number and diversity of students enrolled in computing disciplines [6].

Based on related educational psychology research, we hypothesize that Computing Identity Mentoring holds benefits for students including:

- Increasing computing knowledge and technical proficiency [7, 12, 16].
- Enhancing skills such as leadership and collaboration.
- Increasing students' commitment to computing majors [4, 5, 9, 15].

Preliminary findings on student perceptions regarding Computing Identity Mentoring at seven U.S. universities support the above hypotheses.

2. RELATED WORK

A variety of mentoring programs exist for computing students, from widespread distributed mentoring models that span across continents, to local peer mentoring programs that meet the needs of an individual department. Computing Identity Mentoring adds an identity-based component to these approaches by basing mentoring activities on a set of Computing Identity Core Values, which we will describe in Section 3.

2.1 Existing Mentoring Programs

Mentoring occurs when a *mentor* serves as a trusted role model, counselor, or teacher for a *mentee*. While mentoring relationships can develop spontaneously in personal or professional settings, Computing Identity Mentoring is an example of an organized program that involves training mentors, formally assigning mentors to mentees, and holding participants accountable for the mentoring activities. This section gives examples of other formal mentoring programs.

The Computing Research Association (CRA) sponsors a number of research-oriented mentoring programs. Among these is the Distributed Mentor Project[1] (DMP) in which female undergraduates spend the summer following their sophomore or junior year working with a faculty research mentor in an area of the student's technical interest. This long-running project has been highly successful in helping participants better understand and feel prepared for graduate school, and to more clearly define their career goals [11]. The CRA DMP is a program for outstanding undergraduates who are able to commit a summer to immersion in a research project, usually in a location other than the student's home city.

MentorNet[2] is an electronic mentoring program that pairs undergraduate and graduate students with professional mentors. These mentor/mentee pairs exchange correspondence electronically in eight-month mentoring relationships. MentorNet provides training, coaching, and support for the interaction. MentorNet mentees regularly report increased confidence in science or engineering and an increased desire to pursue a career in the mentee's field of study [14].

Mentoring programs implemented within academic departments have also shown success with improving student learning and retention. These programs are designed to help students with coursework while smoothing the transition into college or university [10, 13, 16]. Such programs have shown success in measures of diversity, retention, and technical skill enhancement.

2.2 Identity-Based Mentoring and the Thomas Principles

In identity-based mentoring, mentoring relationships form around a group's values, practices, and culture [8]. These cultural considerations can include a student's ethnicity, gender, age, disability status, and field of academic study. In the case of Computing Identity Mentoring, the field of study is the focus of the mentoring relationships, with attention paid to all cultural aspects of the mentees. Thomas' research [17] has identified a set of principles that are significantly related to student's college adjustment and academic success. These principles include 1) Identity Development, 2) Psychological Support, 3) Social Support, 4) Academic Support, 5) Sense of Belonging, and 6) Leadership Development. Computing Identity Mentoring as implemented in the STARS Alliance explicitly addresses these principles in its curriculum. Some of these principles have been considered in previous computer science education research; for example, fostering a sense of belonging has been shown important for students' choice to remain in the major [1]. Computing Identity Mentoring also facilitates open communication about important issues that arise in a mentee's college adjustment [3].

3. COMPUTING IDENTITY MENTORING

This section features an introduction to the Computing Identity Core Values and presents case studies from three of the seven universities that deployed the program during the 2008-2009 academic term. These case studies illustrate how the program was implemented within different institutions' infrastructures.

3.1 Core Values

We define *computing identity* as a sense of pride and belonging to the community of researchers and practitioners in computer science and information technology. In order to build a mentoring program that fosters a sense of computing identity, we utilize a set of core values based on the core values of the STARS Alliance for broadening participation in computing [6]. Table 1 presents these core values and the corresponding four components of computing identity: technical excellence, leadership, civic engagement and service, and community outreach.

3.2 Mentor and Mentee Training

The core computing values described above are implemented within the Computing Identity Mentoring program. Students' year long involvement with the program begins with a training workshop, designed by an ecological-community psychologist, that is intended to engage students in their own identity development. Another important aspect of the training program involves teaching students to learn from each other during a series of targeted exercises. In post-workshop interviews, students who attended the workshop reported substantial benefit from the activities. One important aspect of the training workshop is highlighted by the words of one attendee, "I really liked sharing experiences so that even though we only just met, we already know a lot about each other."

---

[1] http://www.cra.org/Activities/craw/dmp/index.php

[2] http://mentornet.net/documents/about/programs/one_on_one.aspx

Table 1: Components of Computing Identity

Computing Identity Component	Associated Values
Technical Excellence	Increasing skill and competence in computing [required by all CS curricula]
Leadership	Professional development and teamwork to develop rich professional skills for success in the workforce [ABET/CAC required]
Civic Engagement and Service	Activities that help change the image of computing from a machine-centered to a people-centered discipline
Community Outreach	Efforts to develop students into computing professionals regardless of gender, ethnicity, or disability status

The training workshop includes two developmental phases. In the first phase, Student Adjustment, students discuss what it means to be a computing student. This phase includes modules about college adjustment, personality styles and interaction, and views on diversity in computing. The second phase, Mentoring Skills using the Thomas Principles, includes modules on identity development, psycho-social and academic support, developing a sense of belonging, and leadership skills for mentoring relationships. The training workshop is an important aspect of Computing Identity Mentoring in part because the event serves as a powerful shared experience on which to establish the mentoring relationship.

3.3 Implementation at NC State University

The Department of Computer Science at North Carolina State University implemented Computing Identity Mentoring with graduate students who mentored between one and three undergraduate students each. All mentors and mentees were participants in the broader STARS Alliance. During the 2008-2009 academic year, NC State had four graduate student mentors and ten undergraduate mentees.

Each mentee chose a project that would be the focus of the mentoring relationship throughout the year. The projects were designed to reflect the core values of computing identity and to complement the leadership skills already included in the undergraduate curriculum. As part of Computing Identity Mentoring, each mentee chose from the following types of projects:

- **Research projects** involve conducting undergraduate research, usually in the subject area of the graduate student mentor. Research areas to date have included Artificial Intelligence, Graphics, and Networking. *(Technical Excellence)*
- **Community service** projects involve completing work or performing service for a community organization. For example, one team of mentors and mentees went regularly to a residential retirement facility and rehabilitation center where they conducted technology education sessions with residents. *(Civic Engagement and Service)*
- **Outreach** projects are designed to foster interest in computing discipline among younger students. One such project involved mentoring teams visiting a nearby middle school and conducting educational hands-on activities with computing and robotics. *(Community Outreach, Leadership)*

This project-centered mentoring approach yields a valuable shared experience because the mentor and mentee collaborate on a worthwhile project designed to foster a sense of computing identity. At the end of each semester, all the students gave presentations of their work so that the components of computing identity were visible, in compelling and socially relevant ways, to the other mentoring teams.

3.4 Implementation at USF Polytechnic

The University of South Florida Polytechnic implemented its mentoring through a tiered structure. At the top level was the advisor who oversaw the program. The next level included student facilitators, comprised of past STARS mentors, who supported and led the mentor teams and collected and analyzed logs of the mentoring activities. The mentor and mentee teams were made up of university, community college and collegiate high school students. Together, the mentoring teams and facilitators conducted outreach activities. One outreach activity was a week-long middle school math and technology summer camp designed to build and sustain academic and social excellence. Another outreach activity involved volunteering with the local annual Science Olympics. These projects, conducted by teams of facilitators, mentors, and mentees, create shared experiences that help build students' sense of the computing identity core values.

3.5 Implementation at UNC Charlotte

The Department of Computer Science at the University of North Carolina at Charlotte implemented undergraduate student mentoring through a credit-bearing service-learning course. The course was structured as a repeatable elective seminar for STARS Alliance participants, who selected from a menu of service projects in which to participate. Mentoring was a service project that was combined with K-12 outreach, and had objectives targeted to mentors and mentees. Community building and computing identity were the primary objectives for mentors, who were STARS Alliance participants enrolled in the seminar course. Community building and recruitment into computing disciplines were the primary objectives for mentee participants, who are younger undergraduate students not enrolled in the seminar. During the 2008-2009 year, a total of eight students mentored six undergraduate students. Low performing students who were enrolled in an entry level computer science course were invited to participate as mentees.

Student mentors enrolled in the course chose from one of four outreach service-learning projects to coordinate throughout the semester. Outreach projects consisted of *GameCATS*, using gaming to attract K12 and college students computer science, *High School Outreach* bringing a number of sophisticated computing presentations and hands-on workshops, *COOKIES*, promoting safe computing practices to the community, and *Team Hope*, showing robotics demonstrations to middle school students. The mentors worked with their mentees throughout the term to engage in campus seminars, conduct outreach, and hold monthly in-person meetings. Contact by phone and email were made on a weekly basis to develop the mentoring relationship and discuss the activities. The mentors also participated in additional mentor training seminars throughout the semesters to enhance leadership within the relationship.

The tiered mentoring approach provides benefits to both mentors and mentees. Mentors receive training and are placed in leadership roles within the relationship and the service projects while obtaining academic credit. Mentees receive academic and social support provided within the framework of computing outreach. Both mentors and mentees develop deeper understanding of the computing discipline through their outreach and mentoring activities, in an effort to enhance their commitment to computing majors.

4. DATA COLLECTION AND RESULTS

The 2008-2009 academic year saw the first widespread implementation of Computing Identity Mentoring. In total, seven institutions across the STARS Alliance participated: Auburn University, University of South Florida Polytechnic, University of North Carolina at Charlotte, Georgia Southern University, North Carolina State University, North Carolina A&T State University, and Florida A&M University. The previous section has described Computing Identity Mentoring as implemented in three institutions. A total of 56 students from all seven institutions participated in Computing Identity Mentoring.

4.1 Methods

Student outcomes are measured with a repeated measures pre- and post-survey, quasi-experimental study design with survey responses measured by a six point Likert scale. Students at all STARS Alliance institutions were invited to complete the surveys, but participation was voluntary. The number of respondents who completed the entire post-survey was 111, which constitutes a total response rate of 43% of all STARS Alliance students for 2008-2009. Of these respondents, 30 participated in the Computing Identity Mentoring program, while 54 reported participating in a different mentoring program during the year. The remaining 27 students reported no involvement in any mentoring program. In order to gain insight as to the effectiveness of Computing Identity Mentoring in particular, the results in this section are based on comparing the responses of the 30 Computing Identity Mentoring students ("participants," from this point forward) with the 54 students who had been involved in other mentoring programs ("non-participants," from this point forward).

4.2 Results

Figure 1 displays the differences between participants and non-participants. Students who participated in Computing Identity Mentoring felt, to a significantly stronger degree than non-participants, that they developed their computing skills and knowledge in the past year. The same trend emerged for students' beliefs about their leadership skills. While student knowledge and leadership skills are accumulated as they move through the curriculum, a stronger agreement with these statements on the part of the participants indicates a differential effect of Computing Identity Mentoring.

Participants felt more committed than non-participants to a career in computing and believed more strongly that computing would allow them to get a job they like. The activities involved in Computing Identity Mentoring require a nontrivial time commitment, so it is not surprising that Computing Identity Mentoring participants felt more strongly than their non-participant counterparts that the program had been demanding of their time. On the other hand, participants also felt more strongly (though with weaker statistical significance) that the program had improved their performance in their major, which suggests that the extra time required was not harmful to the students' overall success.

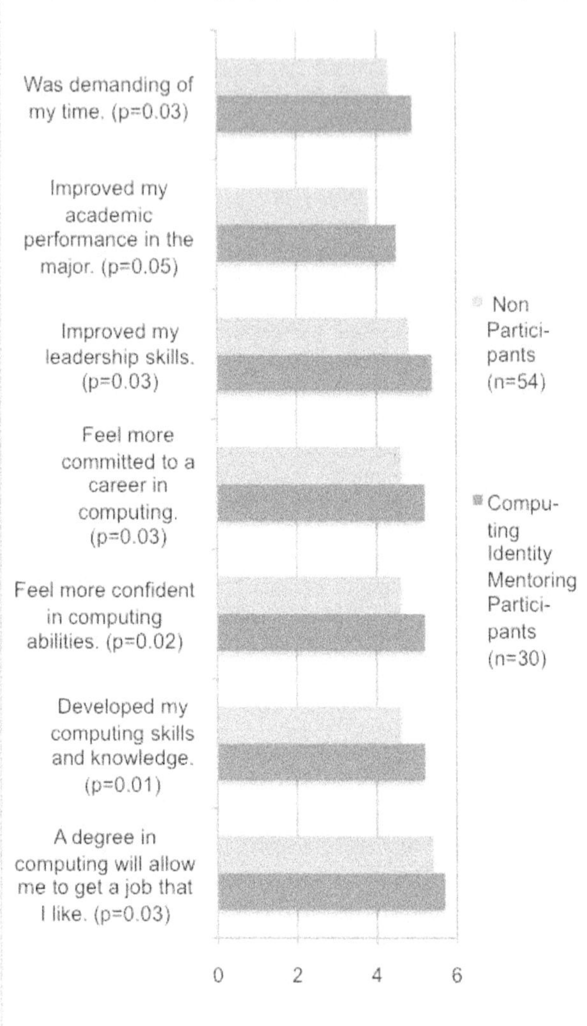

Figure 1. Significant Differences in Post-Program Survey Between Computing Identity Mentoring Participants and Non-Participants. All Respondents were STARS Alliance Participants. (0=lowest agreement; 6=highest agreement; p-values from two-tailed *t*-test)

4.3 Limitations

The findings from the first year of full Computing Identity Mentoring implementation indicate statistical trends that support the hypotheses regarding the effectiveness of the program. Some limitations require caution in generalizing the results. First, the overall response rate to the surveys was low, which means that the students who responded may not be representative of the larger population of students who participated in the STARS program. This issue of representativeness is of additional concern because STARS students, who were selected based on applications to the NSF-funded program, were likely not representative of the overall student populations although the program was open to all students regardless of gender or ethnicity. However, the sampling problem applies to both participant and non-participant groups, so the results clearly indicate a differential effect from participating in the mentoring program.

It is also important to note that the analysis was conducted with item-by-item averages rather than by scale averages; however, future study is expected to provide confirmation of a computing identity scale because of the significance of these initial findings. Additionally, student maturation is a confound for mentor training participants, as most of the participants engaged in mentoring for more than one year. This effect would suggest that computing identity is developmental, which is supportive of the overall hypothesis that computing identity can be facilitated through mentoring.

5. CONCLUSIONS & FUTURE WORK

Computing Identity Mentoring is designed to increase students' sense of *computing identity*. Within the program, this identity is defined by core values pertaining to technical excellence, leadership, civic engagement and service, and community outreach. We have described the implementation of Computing Identity Mentoring in three different academic departments to illustrate the adaptability of this program to a wide variety of institutional structures. When compared to students who participated in other mentoring programs through the STARS Alliance for broadening participation in computing, Computing Identity Mentoring students showed significantly stronger agreement to survey items addressing computing self-efficacy, leadership skills, and commitment to a career in computing. Though these results can only speak to student perception, they indicate that participating in Computing Identity Mentoring positively impacts students in a variety of ways.

Survey data from the first year of widespread implementation indicate that participants of the program feel more strongly than their non-participant counterparts that their technical skills and computing knowledge have increased. The survey results also suggest that Computing Identity Mentoring increases students' confidence in their leadership skills. Finally, mentored students felt, to a significantly stronger degree than non-participants, committed to a career in computing and that a computing field will give them a job they like.

Directions for future work include moving beyond survey responses to collecting data about student performance. Such quantitative data will allow us to more precisely gauge the benefits of Computing Identity Mentoring on student learning, technical skill development, and academic achievement. Retention data for mentoring participants is being collected longitudinally, and will shed light on the retention impacts of the program over time.

6. ACKNOWLEDGMENTS

This work is supported in part by the STARS Alliance (NSF CNS-0540523). Additional support is provided by the NCSU Department of Computer Science and an NSF Graduate Research Fellowship. Any opinions, findings, conclusions, or recommendations expressed in this report are those of the participants, and do not necessarily represent the official views, opinions, or policy of the National Science Foundation.

7. REFERENCES

[1] Bean, J. and Eaton, S. B. The Psychology Underlying Successful Retention Practices. *Journal of College Student Retention: Research, Theory and Practice*, 3, 1 (2001), 73-89.

[2] Bell-Watkins, K., Barnes, T. and Thomas, N. Developing Computing Identity as a Model for Prioritizing Dynamic K-12 Computing Curricular Standards. *Journal of Computing Sciences in Colleges*, 24, 3 (2009), 125-131.

[3] Biggers, M., Brauer, A. and Yilmaz, T. Student Perceptions of Computer Science: A Retention Study Comparing Graduating Seniors with CS Leavers. In *Proceedings of the 39th SIGCSE Technical Symposium on Computer Science Education*, 2008, 402-406.

[4] Chavous, T. M. The Relationship Among Racial Identity, Perceived Ethnic Fit, and Organizational Involvement of African American Students at a Predominantly White University. *Journal of Black Psychology*, 26, 1 (2000), 79-100.

[5] Cohoon, J. M. Just Get Over It or Just Get On with It. In *Women and Information Technology: Research on Under-Representation*. MIT Press, 2005.

[6] Dahlberg, T., Barnes, T. and Rorrer, A. The STARS Leadership Model for Broadening Participation in Computing. In *Proceedings of the IEEE Frontiers in Education Conference*, 2007, 17-22.

[7] Dahlberg, T., Barnes, T., Rorrer, A., Powell, E. and Cairco, L. Improving Retention and Graduate Recruitment through Immersive Research Experiences for Undergraduates. In *Proceedings of the 39th SIGCSE Technical Symposium on Computer Science Education*, 2008, 466-470.

[8] Dollarhide, C. Mentoring Using Identity Development Theory: Retaining Students of Diversity. In *Proceedings of the Michael Tilford Conference on Diversity and Multiculturalism*, 1997.

[9] Dozier, G., Biggers, M. and McCrickard, D. S. Building Diversity in the Undergraduate Computer Science Research Pipeline. In *Proceedings of the 46th Annual ACM Southeast Regional Conference*, 2008, 532-533.

[10] Frieze, C. and Blum, L. Building an Effective Computer Science Student Organization: The Carnegie Mellon women@SCS Action Plan. *ACM SIGCSE Bulletin*, 34, 2 (2002), 74-78.

[11] Harrold, M. J. Distributed Mentor Project: Evaluation of Impact and Experiences of Participants. *Computing Research News*, (September 2000), 2-9.

[12] Hrabowski, F. A. and Maton, K. I. Enhancing the Success of African-American Students in the Sciences. *School Science and Mathematics*, 95, 1 (1996), 19-27.

[13] Miller, A. and Kay, J. A Mentor Program in CS1. In *Proceedings of the 7th Annual Conference on Innovation and Technology in Computer Science Education*, 2002.

[14] Single, P. B., Muller, C. B., Cunningham, C. M., Single, R. M. and Carlsen, W. S. MentorNet: E-Mentoring for Women Students in Engineering and Science. *Journal of Women and Minorities in Science and Engineering*, 11, 3 (2005), 295–309.

[15] Stephenson, P., Miguel, L., Peckham, J., Herve, J. and Hutt, R. Using Undergraduate Interdisciplinary Research to Promote Computer Science. *Journal of Computing Sciences in Colleges*, 22, 3 (2007), 98-104.

[16] Tashakkori, R., Wilkes, J. T. and Pekarek, E. G. A Systemic Mentoring Model in Computer Sciene. In *Proceedings of the 43rd Annual ACM Southeast Regional Conference*, 2005, 371-375.

[17] Thomas, N. The Effects of an Ethnic-based Mentoring Model on College Adjustment, Grade Point Average, and Retention Among First Year African American College Students Attending a Predominantly White Institution. Ph.D. Dissertation, Department of Psychology, Michigan State University, (2005).

Teaching with Robots: a Service-Learning Approach to Mentor Training

R. Brook Osborne, Antony J. Thomas, and Jeffrey Forbes
Dept. of Computer Science
Duke University
Durham, NC 27708-0129
rbo@duke.edu, antontyt@cs.duke.edu, forbes@cs.duke.edu

ABSTRACT
This paper describes a program in which undergraduates mentor teams of local middle and high school students on robotics projects. These teams learn and apply the scientific, mathematical, and computing fundamentals behind the construction of robots and the design of control algorithms. The mentors play a crucial role in the effectiveness of the program. Mentor training has evolved over the five-year life of the program from ad-hoc preparation to a service-learning course where students learn both the technical skills required to design, construct, and test, mobile robots and the pedagogical techniques necessary to mentor middle and high school students. We provide an overview of the program and some evaluation results.

Categories and Subject Descriptors
K.3.2 [**Computers and Education**]: Computers and Information Science Education

General Terms
Human Factors.

Keywords
Service-learning, robotics, outreach.

1. INTRODUCTION
In describing the elements of a successful outreach program, Dodds and Karp note that, "Undergraduate involvement is not merely helpful, but crucial to maintain a dynamic, long-term outreach program [3]." Since September 2004, undergraduate students from Duke University have mentored middle and high school students from Durham Public Schools as part of Duke RoboCupJunior, a project-oriented and team-based academic enrichment program. Mentors work closely with a team of 3-4 students and help develop new lesson plans. Experienced mentors can work as teaching fellows and produce new project materials and evaluate program activities. Each year, a particularly capable teaching fellow takes the lead of the program and serves as program coordinator, managing all program activities, connecting with teachers and parents, and developing a vision for the program.

SIGCSE'10, March 10–13, 2010, Milwaukee, Wisconsin, USA.

Our goal in outreach is to foster interest and improve competence in STEM disciplines, specifically computing. Robotics is a popular domain for attracting students to computing and engineering [7]. Developing mobile robots is an intellectual endeavor that can excite students of all ages and backgrounds [6]. Seeing a program realized in robot behavior can be a fascinating experience in which ideas and computer code meet the physical world. Robots can be used in education to motivate further study in mathematics and computing [7], demonstrate the interplay between technology and society [4], and broaden participation among underrepresented groups [14].

The intersection of a traditional learning environment with the real world application of newly acquired knowledge makes this program a unique experience for the undergraduate students who serve as mentors. The program provides exceptional opportunities for young students who would likely not otherwise be exposed to the endless possibilities found within robotics. This reciprocal payoff differentiates Duke RoboCupJunior from other similar robotics and engineering curricula.

2. ROBOCUPJUNIOR
RoboCupJunior is an international endeavor aimed at pre-college students that seeks to cultivate interest in science and technology through a multifaceted and unconventional approach to competition [11]. RoboCup promotes cooperation and the exchange of ideas among researchers from various universities and organizations while encouraging clever and practical solutions to challenging situations [1]. RoboCupJunior seeks to engage primary and secondary school students through one of three competitions: soccer, rescue and dance. Soccer calls for mobile robots to compete in a two-on-two tournament that mirrors the RoboCup competitions. In rescue, robots race to rescue "victims" from mock disaster scenarios. The third competition, dance, requires students to design and construct robots that move in conjunction with their own choreographed dance. RoboCupJunior is a formative learning experience for students from a variety of backgrounds, helping to develop skills and interests while fostering academic creativity [10].

Figure 1: RoboCupJunior Dance, Rescue, & Soccer

The Duke RoboCupJunior program is a collaboration between the Duke Department of Computer Science and Durham Public

Schools (DPS) that has four major components: afterschool sessions, Science Days, competitions, and teacher workshops.

2.1 Afterschool Sessions

Over the academic year, once a week after school, a team of Duke student mentors meets at Durham School of the Arts to work with Durham Public Schools students on robotics exercises. Each mentor is assigned a group of four students whom they supervise. In early sessions, the students are introduced to the robotics kit (Lego MINDSTORMS NXT) and the basics of robotics programming (through Robolab, NXT-G, or RobotC). Students are also exposed to simple concepts from engineering, math, and computer science, such as modular design, gear ratios, and input vs. output. Over time, they learn more advanced programming techniques, such as control flow and multithreaded programming. Midway through the term, teams select a project to work on for the rest of the semester—dance, soccer, or rescue. Teams create and follow their own schedule in order to produce solutions to the particular challenges of each project. Moreover, students control the structure and functional workings of their teams. Mentors are still on hand to supervise, answer questions, and provide motivation, but do not take over projects or provide solutions.

2.2 Science Days

The mentors conduct weekend workshops at Duke where students learn about the applications of science and technology from practicing scientists. These workshops feature presentations by professors as well as graduate students from the university. Workshop topics are determined by student interest and speaker availability. For example: students have joined their mentors in discussing study skills and the life of a college student; a professor from the medical school spoke about opportunities in the health sciences and how the human body works in ways similar and dissimilar to robots; and undergraduate students taking part in a design competition sanctioned by the Society of Automotive Engineers explained how building a miniature race car is similar to the construction process of RCJ

2.3 Competitions

Periodically, students demonstrate their progress by exhibiting the proposed solution to their project during a regional exhibition. Soccer teams face off in a robot soccer tournament. Dance teams perform their routine for a panel of judges who evaluate performance on creativity and complexity. Rescue teams run their robots through a simulated disaster scenario, receiving points for both speed and accuracy. Teams from RoboCupJunior programs from around the region are invited to compete in the three events. Winners are eligible to attend the RoboCupJunior World Finals.

2.4 Teacher Workshops

Teachers serve a crucial role in the robotics program: recruiting students and serving as an advisor for teams. We host annual one-day workshops for teachers from local schools interested in using mobile robots in their classrooms. The training session introduces teachers who are unfamiliar with the program to both the hardware and software platforms, and provides an outline of the goals for the coming year. This workshop includes breakout sessions where teachers build and program a robot to complete a given task. This orientation to the program also serves as a sounding board for returning teachers to discuss their experiences with incoming school representatives and to open lines of communication between teachers and Duke mentors.

3. WHY RCJ?

RoboCupJunior can be differentiated from similar youth-oriented competitions such as FLL and Botball [6] in three major ways. First, RCJ consists of three standard competitions that remain static or change only slightly from year to year. This consistency results in familiarity with each task, which in turn encourages students to refine project outcomes over time—an important skill for future researchers.

This standardization of competition topics leads to the second important difference: cooperation between teams. An integral part of RoboCup—on both the Junior and Senior levels—is the implicit expectation that ideas will flow between teams. This coordination is visible both in the scoring system (inter-team pairings are common in both rescue and dance) and the structure of the conferences (World Finals stress collaboration through both a series of meetings and the physical set-up of the staging and competition areas).

Finally, the World Finals of RCJ take place in conjunction with RoboCup, which is attended by hundreds of scientists and engineers from around the world, giving young students the opportunity to interface with researchers working on real-world problems. For example, participants in RoboCup soccer are working to create a robotic soccer team that can defeat the World Cup Champions by 2050, while rescue bots navigate disaster scenes and recover life-size victims. This exposure to scientists performing real research and exhibiting real solutions provides students with the invaluable experience of witnessing possible career paths and areas of interest for the future.

4. MENTOR TRAINING

Undergraduates can become mentors for the Duke RoboCupJunior program by taking a service-learning course offered jointly through the Department of Computer Science and the Program in Education. At the program's inception, mentors were recruited through the Duke chapter of the National Society of Black Engineers and worked on a volunteer basis. Some students would turn their mentoring work into an independent study course. Other students mentored as part of an introduction to programming course, but formalized lessons on mentoring were not given. The ad-hoc mentor training resulted in uneven mentor preparation, participation, and quality.

As the program grew and demand increased, we created a course, CompSci 89S "Computer Science Education Research Seminar - Teaching with Robotics," to properly train an adequate number of mentors. After taking this course, students should be able to:

- design and implement the software and hardware architecture of a LEGO robot to perform tasks such as line following and simple map building
- formulate a lesson plan for an after school robotics enrichment program for middle or high school students
- formulate and support a hypothesis on how access to and proficiency with computing technology affects education
- effectively mentor students from diverse cultural and educational backgrounds.

This class developed into a service-learning opportunity—a class that links traditional teaching with at least 20 hours of community service. Service learning also emphasizes reading, personal reflection and analysis [5]. Mentors maintain and share an online journal wherein they contemplate the impact of their actions both on individual students and on the program as a whole. Mentors are responsible for reading and commenting on their peers' journals, which leads to further discussion and deliberation. Reflection is a crucial component of the service-learning experience, as it creates and perpetuates both internal thoughtfulness and open dialogue. The course fulfils the four requirements established by the Duke Service Learning Program:

1. **Each student will participate in at least 20 hours of service** through afterschool mentoring sessions and weekend workshops.
2. **The service experience is integrally related to the academic subject matter of the course.** Mentors must learn how to build and program robots in order to effectively mentor their student teams. Furthermore, mentors will learn about teaching techniques and discuss the social ramifications of technology in education.
3. **Coursework involves critical reflection on the relationship between academic course content and the service experience.** Mentors complete journals on Blackboard after each RCJ session and discuss the relationship between course material and their teaching experiences.
4. **Coursework involves critical reflection on the ethical and civic dimensions of the service experience.** Mentors develop a new lesson plan for the program that specifically addresses the purported need for afterschool science and technology enrichment programs and how they may or may not contribute to educational and social goals.

The service-learning approach to teaching to training mentors is innovative because it is not typically used in conjunction with technical coursework [2,9]. More commonly social science courses – education or psychology, for example— integrate volunteerism into their curricula. Service-learning doesn't explicitly define "service" as school-oriented, and many social science and humanities courses are well equipped to complete the community service requirement in settings other than the classroom. For example, common volunteer activities include working at nursing homes and basic tutoring. In these situations, students often directly apply the knowledge and skills discussed in class to their tutoring or volunteerism. However, this program requires that mentors invest more into the service component. While mentoring is integral to the learning experience, it is not a simple extension of what is discussed in class. Rather, students must synthesize material mastered in class with firsthand experiences to create an effective lesson plan. The payoffs for mentors, however, are large; this method of learning leads to greater appreciation and comprehension of relevant course material, while serving a public need [10].

4.1 Mentor Effectiveness

In 2007 and 2008, students were invited to participate in a focus group conducted by an external evaluation agency, Compass Consulting, who compiles the results and returns a summary of responses. These group discussions serve as an opportunity for students to voice their concerns along with their praises of the program. One of the questions that the focus groups addressed was how the students perceived their undergraduate mentors. The spring 2007 results were very positive:

- "Duke students give us confidence to prepare us for competitions."
- "They're very nice...inspired us."
- "[Name] would always say, 'look back at what you did wrong,' would try to make you figure it out versus doing the work for you...teaching us versus doing it for us."

This last comment is especially interesting, as the 2007 focus group was conducted before the program adopted the service-learning model, yet it seemed that the volunteer mentors nevertheless used effective teaching techniques.

The 2008 focus group, which was conducted after the service-learning model was adopted, netted some similar responses:

- "[Mentors] really push us to figure things out on our own, but they are there to help if you really get stuck."
- "[My mentor] was all about getting you to learn instead of doing the work for you."
- "[Mentor] will tell you what's wrong and then help you figure out how to figure it out, but [he/she] wouldn't fix it for you...challenge."

Three comments stood out from the 2008 focus group:

- "Last year, mine didn't help, but this year mine helped a lot."
- "I really hope that [name] gets to teach me robotics another year because we are like best friends."
- "I wish [mentors] were teachers at our school."

The increased enthusiasm for the mentors between 2007 and 2008 suggests an improvement in the quality of the program's mentor training. The fact that several students pointed out that the mentors taught the student without giving away solutions corroborates this change. The results of the focus group remained very positive between the two years, affirming the viability and effectiveness of the service-learning model.

5. PROGRAM EFFECTIVENESS

The program is evaluated annually in two ways. First, students complete individual, anonymous surveys designed by the Burroughs Wellcome Student Science Enrichment Program to measure the three stated goals of Burroughs Wellcome. Specifically, surveys measure the extent to which program activities were successful in: (1) improving students' competence in science and math, (2) nurturing enthusiasm for math and science, (3) as well as measure any change in students' interest in pursing science-related careers. Second, data is collected during the previously mentioned focus groups. Through these two modes of data collection, mentors and coordinators are given a preliminary view of the strengths and weaknesses of the program

5.1 Participation

Students who participate in the program are recruited through the teachers who attend the teacher workshops and through other contacts with Durham Public Schools. In the past three academic years, participation in the robotics program has been as follows.

Year	Gender		Race/Ethnicity				
	Male	Female	White	African-American	Latino	Asian-American	Other
'06-'07	13	11	5	18	1	0	0
'07-'08	34	22	26	18	2	2	8
'08-'09	29	11	14	20	3	2	1

In addition to having a diverse student population, we have uncharacteristically high minority enrollment in the mentor training course. From the 2006-2007 school year through the spring of 2009, mentors were made up of 20%, 62.5% and 40% women. Over those same three years 33%, 25% and 20% of our mentors were African-American.

5.2 Self-Efficacy

In the survey, the majority of the students in the program report agreeing or strongly agreeing with the following statements:

- This program has helped me learn science better.
- Because of this program, I feel better about being able to learn science.
- I learned some things in this program I can use in science class at school.

In 2007, focus groups found that "All students believed that participating in RoboCup had improved their building, programming, and debugging skills." Interviews conducted in 2008 found that students perceived a measurable increase in science skills as a result of participating in the program. One student commented on the multifaceted skill set acquired as a result of working with robots, saying that the program helped to "be more logical and to go through things one step at a time, which has helped make me better in math." In addition to facilitating logic-driven thinking, students attributed involvement with the program as a major factor in becoming more "focused" and "creative" in other subjects and to "think about how things work." In addition to these obviously positive ramifications, it is notable that these changes in self-efficacy are the result of internal reflection in conjunction with the synthesis of the effects of multifarious factors. That is, students who experience a positive change in what they believe they are capable of accomplishing are actually benefitting from increased self-efficacy. The fact that students are able to attribute this change to their participation in the program speaks to their powers of self-regulation and reflection—both skills important for life-long learning.

5.3 Interest & Motivation

There exists evidence that the RoboCupJunior program facilitates increased interest in STEM fields of study and careers [7,11]. *Mindstorms: Children, Computers, and Powerful Ideas,* a canonical text in favor of the integration of technology into the classroom by Seymour Papert, describes the connection between hands-on experimentation and increased learning potential [8]. Papert argues that widespread use of computers in the classroom "could contribute to mental processes not only instrumentally but in more essential, conceptual ways, influencing how people think even when they are far removed from physical contact with a computer (just as the gears shaped my understanding of algebra although they were not physically present in the math class)." [8]

Data collected in program evaluations provide a favorable argument for Papert's assessment of the positive effects of hands-on learning experiences on student interest. The results suggest that as a function of the program, students are more enthusiastic about science as a whole. The majority of students surveyed agreed or strongly agreed with the following questions on the BWF Student Feedback Survey:

- Because of this program, I think I am more aware of the importance of science in everyday living.
- I tell my family or friends about the things we do in this program.
- Because of this program, I am more excited about science.
- Because of this program, I think I have a better understanding of what scientists do.

Similarly, most students indicated that they are "thinking more about getting a job in a science-related career."

The results of the 2008 focus group mirror those found in the student surveys. All of the students said that they were interested in science and math prior to starting RoboCupJunior. It is to be expected that a program rooted in computers and technology would draw an audience with an interest in such closely related subjects. However, all but one student noted that the project led them to either develop or strengthen their interest in robotics, technology, engineering, or science as a career. One student commented on the usefulness of speakers, noting, "they had people come meet with us about college majors and stuff that we could do." Another student pointed out that RoboCupJunior helped to foster a nascent interest in programming.

5.4 Competence

The impact of RoboCupJunior on competence is measured in two main ways: competition results and mentor comments. The former paints an incomplete but promising picture of the effectiveness of the program. Participation in the 2007 RoboCupJunior championships in Atlanta provided us with some insightful data. Unfortunately, no data are compiled from other teams competition on the international level, which precludes us from making direct comparisons to other teams. However, direct analysis of competition results provides a partial explanation of the effectiveness of the program. In 2007, 8 students participated in the primary divisions of the dance and rescue events. The dance event does not provide individual rankings, but only the top 9 teams out of a field of 26 make the final. The DPS dance team made the final cut, outperforming the other US team competing in the primary division. The rescue event utilizes group scoring, where each team's score is an aggregate of the various teams it is partnered with. The Duke-mentored rescue team placed 13th in a field of 23, finishing higher than the other two teams representing the United States. A team of four DPS students competed in rescue at the 2008 RoboCupJunior international competition, held in Suzhou, China. The students again performed well, better than the other US team and in the middle of the field overall.

Each participant was given a rating at the beginning and end of the year ranging from 1-5 (1=poor, no experience, 5=expert) in six areas: programming, building, systematic thinking, teamwork, communication, and flexibility within the group. In 2007, the program coordinator found that the average student improved in teamwork by .875, communication by .625, and systematic thinking ability by .375 points. Retrogression is not observed in any of the six measurements. Observed gains were significantly more pronounced for males than females across the board, and this difference in performance between genders presents an important area for further study.

In the future, we hope to better assess skills relevant to programming. Through the use of the Test of Logical Thinking conducted at multiple points in students', we will be able to measure changes in students' capacity with controlling variables, proportional reasoning, combinatorial reasoning, probabilistic reasoning, and correlational reasoning. [13]. These measures are crucial, as these five skills demonstrate and predict the ability to perform critical thinking processes required for many STEM courses.

6. FUTURE WORK & CONCLUSIONS

The current program is limited to local students because each team of 4 students meets with a mentor each week. In order to broaden the reach of the program, the project staff is currently in the process of producing a RoboCupJunior Primer for educators interested in starting a similar program at their institution. This Primer will unify available resources and bodies of information concerning both RoboCupJunior and educational robotics in general. This Primer will take the form of a website designed for students, teachers, and mentors that will link with the existing TeachEngineering digital library [12]. This Primer will provide the following information:

- a training manual with the requisite materials, and software needed for running a RCJ program
- a guide on to how produce fun, effective, and challenging curriculum for the students
- a gallery of student-contributed robot designs, programs, and videos of robots in action
- a section on how to foster a spirit of teamwork and cooperation through careful use of project deadlines, assigned roles, and scheduled exhibitions.

The proposed RoboCupJunior Primer will be useful to students, teachers, and parents interested in RoboCupJunior or other educational robotics activities [7]. While there exist many robotics books, tutorials, online guides and the like, our aim is to create a unified resource that will cover all facets of building and maintaining a RoboCupJunior program. The Primer goes beyond a tutorial explaining programming syntax and building plans. Rather, the Primer teaches participants on all levels to consider multifaceted solutions to larger, more involved problems. In addition to instructional sections, the Primer has a section dedicated to discussing individual, robot related feats. Teams will be able to post pictures of their robots in a gallery, share useful bits of code in the repository, and ask and answer questions in the forum. The dynamic and interactive nature of the site, along with implicit openness with ideas and solutions and strong community component sets the RoboCupJunior Primer apart from similar robotics education websites [7].

In the five years since its inception, the program began as a small-scale, volunteer run program serving only one middle school classroom, and has since grown into an interdepartmental course that reaches an average of 40 students from five middle and high schools across the DPS district. The local program will be used as a model for other school districts and individual schools interested in starting a similar program of their own. Through widespread dissemination of the RCJ Primer, potential coordinators will have access to detailed instructions ranging from program creation and maintenance to proper methods of dealing with group dynamics as well as a direct line of communication to seasoned mentors and other coordinators.

7. ACKNOWLEDGMENTS

This work is generously supported by an award from the Burroughs Wellcome Fund Student Science Enrichment Program.

8. REFERENCES

[1] M. Asada, H. Kitano, I. Noda, and M. Veloso. RoboCup: Today and tomorrow: What we have have learned. Artificial Intelligence, 110:193~214, 1999.

[2] E.J. Coyle, L.H. Jamieson, L.S. Sommers. EPICS: A Model for Integrating Service-Learning into the Engineering Curriculum. *Michigan Journal of Community Service Learning*, 4:81-89, Fall 1997.

[3] Z. Dodds, and L. Karp. The Evolution of a Computational Outreach Program to Secondary School Students. In *Proceedings of the 37th SIGCSE Technical Symposium on Computer Science Education,* Houston, TX, 2006.

[4] E. Hamner, T. Lauwers, D. Bernstein, I. Nourbakhsh, and C.F. DiSalvo, Robot Diaries: Broadening Participation in the Computer Science Pipeline through Social Technical Exploration, *AAAI Spring Symposium on Using AI to Motivate Greater Participation in Computer Science*, ,2008

[5] B. Jacoby and Associates. *Service-Learning in Higher Education: Concepts and Practices.* Jossey-Bass, San Francisco, CA, 1996.

[6] B. Lester. Robots' Allure: Can It Remedy What Ails Computer Science? *Science* 16 November 2007: Vol. 318. No. 5853, pp. 1086 – 1087.

[7] M.J. Mataric, Nathan Koenig, and David Feil-Seifer. Materials for enabling hands-on robotics and STEM education. In *Proceedings of the AAAI Spring Symposium on Robots and Robot Venues: Resources for AI Education*, Stanford, CA, 2007.

[8] S. Papert. *Mindstorms: Children, computers, and powerful ideas.* Basic Books, Inc., New York, NY, USA, 1980.

[9] R. Renner and B. Juliano. Integrating Service Learning with Undergraduate Robotics Research. In *Proceedings of the AAAI Spring Symposium on Robots and Robot Venues: Resources for AI Education*, Stanford, CA, 2007.

[10] E. Sklar, A. Eguchi, and J. Johnson. RoboCupJunior 2002: Learning with educational robotics. In *RoboCup-2002: Robot Soccer World Cup VI*, 2002.

[11] E. Sklar and S. Parsons. RoboCupJunior: a vehicle for enhancing technical literacy. In *AAAI-02 Mobile Robot Workshop*, 2002.

[12] Sullivan, J.F., M.N. Cyr, M.A. Mooney, R.F. Reitsma, N.C. Shaw, M.S. Zarske, and P.A. Klenk. 2005. The TeachEngineering Digital Library: Engineering Comes Alive for K–12 Youth. In *Proceedings of the ASEE Annual Conference*, Portland, OR, 2005.

[13] Tobin, K., Capie, W.. 1981. The Development and Validation of a Group Test of Logical Thinking. *Educational and Psychological Measurement*, 41(2,): 413-423 , 1981

[14] Williams, A.B., Touretzky, D.S., Manning, L., Walker, J.J., Boonthum, C., Forbes, J., and Doswell, J.T. The ARTSI Alliance: Recruiting Underrepresented Students to Computer Science and Robotics to Improve Society. In *Proceedings of the AAAI Spring Symposium on Using AI to Motivate Greater Participation in Computer Science*, 2008.

The Weiner Lecture Archives: An Ontology-Driven Interface for Viewing Synchronized Lectures and Notes

Daniel D. Garcia, Gene Zhang, Sean Carr, Sameer Iyengar, Hava Edelstein, Albert Liu
University of California, Berkeley
777 Soda Hall
Berkeley, CA 94720-1776
+1 510-642-9595
{ddgarcia,albert_j_liu}@berkeley.edu, {genezhang,seancarr,sameeriyengar,hbe123}@gmail.com

ABSTRACT
For several years, the lectures in our introductory Electrical Engineering and Computer Science (EECS) courses have been videotaped and webcast, mainly as an aid to students with time conflicts that prevent them from attending class. We present the Weiner Lecture Archives -- a project to identify, archive, filter, and make available the best of these lectures with their notes on the web. We provide a hierarchical, ontology-driven interface to entire courses, which allows users to choose any topic and/or subtopic to view, from a small snippet of one lecture to one that spans many lectures. Once the topic is chosen, our system launches RealPlayer to play the lecture video in one window while showing synchronized lecture notes or slides in another window. By the spring of 2007, we had finished encoding our department's entire four-course introductory sequence into this system. Student and worldwide use was greater than 100,000 views last year alone, direct feedback has been encouraging, and we hope to expand to other EECS courses in the future.

Categories and Subject Descriptors
K.3.1 [**Computer Uses in Education**]: Distance Learning

General Terms
Documentation, Design, Human Factors

Keywords
Distance learning, webcast, Synchronized Multimedia Integration Language, SMIL, slide synchronization, topic hierarchy, ontology

1. BACKGROUND
In the mid-1990s, colleague Larry Rowe and his students in the Berkeley Multimedia Research Center were designing two systems that would serve as the architectural foundations for this project. First, they were building the hardware and software infrastructure of the Berkeley Internet Broadcasting System (BIBS) [10], which provided live remote viewing and on-demand replay of course lectures through streaming audio and video over the web. We were one of the earliest to offer free university lecture webcasts, and it pushed the limits of bandwidth and processor capabilities of the day.

Figure 1. Larry Weiner

In parallel, Rowe and his students were working on the Berkeley Continuous Media Toolkit (CMT), which provided synchronized continuous media playback [7]. The media could be anything: video, audio, text, and even commands to control the Tcl-based client (say, to load a particular lecture slide in a window at a certain moment). BIBS became so successful that the University's Educational Technology Service (ETS) [3] took it over and grew its capabilities and capacity[1]. The computer science four-course introductory sequence was webcast and archived every semester. This was a great resource to students who missed class or wanted to review a confusing lecture, and even to autodidacts from around the globe who wanted to learn computing on their own. However, the webcast system had several shortcomings.

First, only the *raw* lecture webcasts were available, replete with deprecated semester-specific information (e.g., announcements

[1] ETS currently offers free webcasting and archived playback, in RealMedia streaming format [9], and more recently, .mp3 (audio) and .mp4 (video) format, for 47 of the biggest lecture courses on campus, as well as hundreds of special events by guest speakers and luminaries.

SIGCSE'10, March 10–13, 2010, Milwaukee, Wisconsin, USA.

for talks or midterms that occurred years ago) and wasted lecture time (e.g., fumbling with a USB drive, mid-lecture breaks, etc.). Second, slides / notes for these lectures were not linked to the webcast, so viewers always had to go hunting through outdated class websites to find them. Once the notes were downloaded, there was no way of synchronizing them with the video in RealPlayer [9], so viewers had to manually scroll them in a separate window while watching the lecture. There was also no connection to our anonymous course surveys [1,5], so semesters that were highly rated were indistinguishable from those that were duds. Finally, the webcasts were presented by date recorded instead of by curriculum topic, so content that spanned lectures required extra downloading, and there was no easy way to quickly jump to a short snippet within a lecture.

In June of 2002, UC Berkeley alumnus Larry Weiner (Figure 1) passed away, but left a trust fund to our department for educational resources. We decided to honor his name by building a system, the Weiner Lecture Archives (WLA) [11], to augment the existing free webcast infrastructure but address all the problems we'd noted.

We began by consulting the course surveys to find the most recent, highest-rated semester for each of the intro courses. We then gathered and posted all the notes for that semester, and hired a former A+ student for each course to go through all the lectures to encode the appropriate time-code slide transitions, allowing for synchronized playback of slides and video. During this process, the student filters out all but the purest curriculum content (by not recording the time-codes for the offending segments or by recording them under a special category such as "administrative" or "obfuscated"), essentially *cleansing* our webcast. This process can be done in real time, so this step requires approximately 45 hours for a 15-week semester-long course. Finally, we wrap our content with the gentle, navigable interface of an ontology tree based on all of the course topics, labeling each node by topic as well as playback length.

In the following sections, we describe our interface and provide a detailed description of the implementation of all the varied components that make up the project. We'll have a discussion of the usage we've noted, feedback we've received, reflection on a critical architectural decision, and conclude with a discussion of where the project will go in the future.

2. INTERFACE

From the WLA home page, a student selects one of the four lower-division computer science classes we currently offer from the big tabs at the top and is taken to a dedicated class page. From there, they see all of the main topics covered in that course for that semester. We present a hierarchical navigation familiar to our users, mimicking the cascading directory structure from the Apple Finder and Windows Explorer interfaces. Our contribution is the re-use of this time-tested interface for curriculum navigation.

Exploration of the tree reveals that each main topic branches off into several sub-topics. Figure 2 shows this for the CS3 course ontology. Once the user chooses the topic (or sub-topic, or sub-sub-topic, etc.) they wish, they click the link.

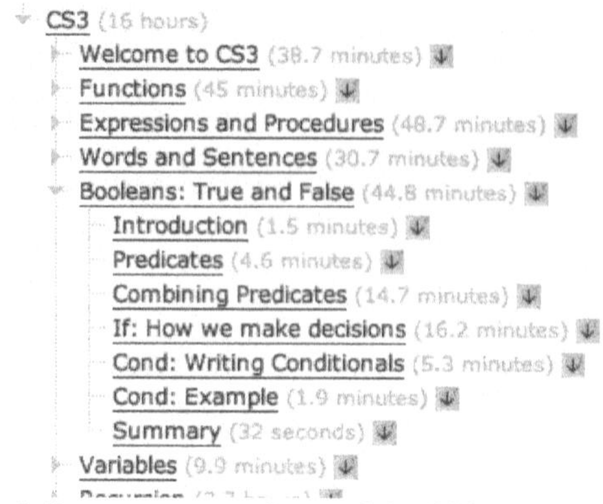

Figure 2. Screen capture of part of the CS3 course ontology, after the user has chosen to expand the "Booleans: True and False" subtopic. The clip length for each topic is shown in parenthesis. The down-arrow at the right of each topic displays only that sub-tree.

This brings up RealPlayer with the video cued exactly to the requested clip in one window and the synchronized notes in the right. As the video proceeds, the notes auto-advance. Figure 3 shows what results if the user clicks the "Introduction" subtopic under the "Booleans: True and False" topic for CS3 and watches for 19 seconds. Note that the overall displayed video length is exactly the length of the clip requested, with 0:00 labeling the start and 1:31 (1.5 minutes, as advertised) the end. We abstract away all information about the originating source video files (e.g., the actual time within the webcast(s) that the clip was extracted, from which webcast(s) they were culled, etc). If the clip happens to contain lectures from multiple webcasts recorded on different days, the user notices nothing when the video seamlessly crosses a day boundary, aside from the fact that the instructor instantaneously changes clothes (hopefully)! The user need only consider course content, and leave the heavy lifting (of determining the sources required to *deliver* that content) to us.

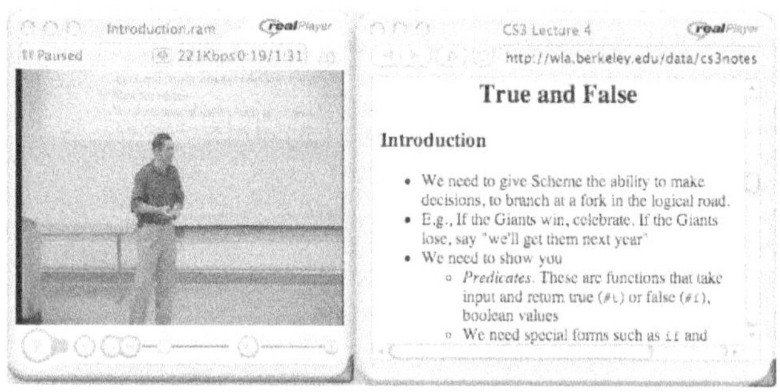

Figure 3. The lecture webcast video synchronized with HTML notes. As the lecture progresses, the notes auto-scroll to the current topic via web anchors. The video can be scrubbed, and the video and notes will re-sync.

2.1 Integration into UC-WISE

UC-WISE is an interactive collaborative learning environment [2] currently used in some of our intro CS courses. In a UC-WISE course, students have a very lab-centric experience: they spend one hour in lecture per week instead of the traditional three, and *six* hours per week in lab instead of just two. Lab activities range from taking online quizzes, reading web pages, engaging in collaborative "brainstorms", responding to directed questions in a communal newsgroup setting, and interacting with an interpreter.

Now, thanks to WLA, that can include watching a short lecture video clip! This can also address the loss of two hours per week with the esteemed "sage on the stage" (who may be a gifted, inspirational speaker). The curriculum developer can easily locate the relevant clips by navigating through our ontology just as a normal user would. However, instead of *clicking* on the link, they copy the link *location* and paste it into the UC-WISE authoring environment. They can choose to make the video compulsory or optional, depending on the context. There are some subtleties still to be worked out (e.g., we now need to make headphones required to watch the clips in lab, how do we let them know when content has been updated, etc.), but this integration with UC-WISE holds great promise.

3. IMPLEMENTATION

3.1 Slide Synchronization

WLA uses the Synchronized Multimedia Integration Language (SMIL) [12] for most of its synchronization between lecture slides/notes and streaming videos. SMIL lets us declare sequences of multiple video files (useful for viewing lecture topics that span multiple days of lecture), and start & end times for playback for each video file. It also lets us specify various actions for RealPlayer at arbitrary points during playback. For example, we use this to synchronize all of our lecture slides, by instructing RealPlayer (via a SMIL extension developed by RealNetworks, Inc) to display a different URL for a different lecture slide at specific times during video playback.

All notes are first located from the course web page or individual instructor and copied to our web server. WLA currently supports HTML and raw text notes without any pre-processing. In our system by way of SMIL, time codes are linked to different URLs, so scrolling is made possible through URLs that link to page anchors peppered throughout the document. PDF files require a pre-processing script step that splits each one into individual pages (which themselves are assigned a unique URL). PowerPoint slides require must be first converted to a 1-up PDF file, and processed accordingly. Most slide transitions can be preserved if the PDF creator chooses the "save *with* animations". The most common technique for putting PowerPoint slides on the web involves rasterizing each slide into images, a far inferior solution to PDFs that preserve the object properties of the presentation.

3.2 Ontology System Design

In this section we will describe the internals of our system and what factors and decisions led us to the current design. Starting with the low-level data structures, we will build up to the algorithms that power the core of the user interface.

3.2.1 Data Structures

The main data structure in our system is a tree of topics. We chose MySQL because we were familiar with it, it was already set up on our servers, and it would likely be on any servers we might migrate to in the future. The three main database entities we have are *videos*, which reference external video files and contain meta-data about them; *video clips*, which define clips within a video using a specific start and end time and link the clips with their places in the lecture notes; and *tree nodes*, which define the relationships between nodes that create the ontology structure, store a topic name for each node, and reference any video clips associated with the node.

3.2.2 Database Abstraction Layer

Given the complexity of the relational tree structure we built and the redundancy and synchronization requirements it has, we decided to build an abstraction layer so the application code does not have to deal with managing it. The idea is similar to the *Model-View-Controller* paradigm, although we did not decouple our controller code from our view. Having a clear data abstraction layer with a defined interface saved us countless development hours as we re-factored the system several times. Initially, the abstraction layer consisted of low level *getters* and *setters* for all of our entities. As the application became more complex, however, we added higher and higher-level methods so that complicated data manipulation tasks still seemed simple to the application code. For example, moving an entire sub-tree from one place in the tree to another is as simple as making a call to: `moveSubtree(src_node_id, new_parent_node_id)`. Other than being easier to use, providing methods for complex tasks like this allows the abstraction layer to be responsible for managing transactions rather than relying on the application code to do it, which eliminates the problems of nested transactions.

3.2.3 AJAX On-Demand Loading

The first iteration of our ontology-driven interface loaded an entire topic tree (or sub-tree) before displaying it and therefore was extremely slow for a tree of any reasonable size. Once the tree was loaded, expanding and collapsing sub-trees was relatively quick, although it required looping over all descendants (of the clicked node) and hiding or showing them. The current design eliminates the need to always load the entire tree. Using AJAX, we delay the loading of sub-trees until they are needed, only load one level of the sub-tree at a time, and only load more when it is requested. In addition, expanding/collapsing a sub-tree is faster because we now only hide/show the immediate children of the sub-tree. Using AJAX on-demand loading was a big performance win and changed the feel of the site from sluggish to responsive.

3.2.4 Lineage Field Optimization

To efficiently select all the clips for a given sub-tree we created a "lineage" field that lists all the node's descendents. Having this field allows us to select, with a single database query, all nodes with the same ancestry. Therefore, when the user clicks on a topic to watch the video we can select all nodes that are descendants of that topic node in a single query. We also have another field that defines the absolute ordering of these nodes. We use this to efficiently sort the results so the aggregated video clips are shown in the correct order. The key benefit here is we only need one query, whereas if we had only kept track of a node's parent and/or children, we would need to traverse the tree using several queries.

3.3 Architecture

Due to certain constraints, our PHP web server, MySQL database server, and video-streaming server are all on separate machines and networks. The speed of a single MySQL query doesn't suffer much from this setup, but there remains a fair amount of overhead involved, which is one of the reasons we made all possible efforts in our application to reduce every task to a single query. We use a laptop on the same network as the web server as a backup database server. Nightly backups are made from our master server to the backup server, and also to our test server to ensure that the test data closely mimics our production data. The basic components of our architecture are fairly generic and are readily available in most web application environments without having to navigate around our server constraints. Thus, it would be fairly easy to replicate WLA in another setting, provided that a high-bandwidth RealVideo streaming server were available to power the actual video delivery, as ETS does for our project.

3.4 Data Entry and Ontology Layout

3.4.1 Topic Tree Delineation

To facilitate the data entry process, we created a standard text file format which allowed the editors to specify all necessary video, clip, and node information, as described in 3.2.1. After uploading the timing files, the topic tree is fine-tuned if needed using a web-based topic tree editor.

3.4.2 Ontology Development

The process of developing a final configuration of nodes in the topic tree from the raw videos and lecture notes involved several steps and decisions, each with its own considerations. We chose start and end times of each clip so that each corresponded to a single topic, ideally lasting around three to four minutes. Keywords were used in the naming of nodes to aid searches; for instance, all nodes corresponding to examples in lecture began with "Example". By the nature of the topic tree, nodes representing broader topics occupied shallower positions in the tree. Where possible, each of the siblings in a group represented roughly equally important/broad topics, and each non-leaf node branched off into five to seven children in order to limit the depth of the tree without confusing users with too many choices at each node [8]. Siblings were arranged so that topics that were more basic, broad, important, and/or earlier in the course appeared first.

3.4.3 Data Entry Personnel, Resources, & Strategies

One student was assigned to each course to be presented on the website. These students had each achieved a grade of A+ in the course that they were assigned. To facilitate the viewing of the webcasts, instead of streaming the webcasts from the server, each student was given a local copy of all the webcasts for their assigned course on DVD. Some strategies were used to speed up the production of timing files. For example, we discovered Enounce 2xAV [4], a plug-in for RealPlayer that allowed videos to be played back at speeds greater than real time. The accuracy of lecture start and end times were later spot-checked by jumping to those precise times in the raw video to confirm that the times were exactly the ones desired.

4. DISCUSSION

We went live with WLA in the spring of 2005. It featured an early, non-ontology-based interface design, and listed only CS3, our computer science service course. We advertised it heavily to the students in that semester's UC-WISE lab-centric CS3, and waited eagerly to see the adoption. The usage statistics showed three distinct 100+ view spikes: one right after our announcement, one before the first midterm, and one before the final exam.

By the spring of 2007, we had finished encoding all four of our computer science lower division courses. The webcasts for the semesters featured on WLA continue to receive thousands of hits per semester [Table 1], despite many (1, 8, 5, and 5 respectively) more recent semesters available on the main webcast site. CS3's Fall 2001 raw webcasts are no longer directly available, so these numbers are *directly* the result of WLA access. Although the logs do not show what ratio comes from WLA access for the other three courses, we are confident the vast majority do, since there would be no good reason to visit the raw webcasts from a course that was 3-4 years outdated. We have also gained an active global community of distance learners. Here are a few of the many thanks we've received:

"Just a quick note to thank you and Berkeley University [sic] for putting Machine Structures CS61C on the web. ... Great stuff, thanks. I'm a 55 year old computer tech/engineer"
– Tony Atkinson, Norwich Norfolk UK

"I am a 35 year old electronics engineer. I have always loved programming and as a hobby. I just wanted to say...great stuff!"
– Naim Lesmer, DENMARK

"Thank you for making the web casts and much of the course material available online for free. I am learning a great deal from your lectures alone. Having the lecture slides available separately is a plus. I am an autodidact that greatly appreciates having learning resources, such as your lectures, freely available via the internet" – Gary Buczkowski, Tennessee, USA

"I am currently a student at the University of Houston and watch the Webcast to supplement my computer architecture class material. Once again thank you and the University of California Berkeley for making this service available."
– Carlos J. Restrepo, Texas, USA

Table 1. Webcast Viewership Statistics

	Hits During Semester	
Class	**Fall 2008**	**Spring 2009**
CS3 (Fall 2001) intro to programming (for non-majors) in scheme	9115	6561
CS61A (Spring 2005) "big ideas" in scheme	8686	20115
CS61B (Fall 2006) data structures in java	41417	30755
CS61C (Fall 2006) machine structures in C	32691	21966

5. FUTURE WORK

One issue is keeping up with new developments in video formats and hosting. In the years after WLA first went live, campus ETS has moved away from the Real format toward the .mp4 format and YouTube. We are exploring ways to support these new file formats and hosting services so that users can enjoy the same functionality with these videos that we now provide with Real.

For example, by using the YouTube APIs [6], it should also be possible to sequence and play segments of lectures and synchronize them with the appropriate lecture notes.

One issue we have yet to deal with is what to do with deprecated content, e.g., a Java 1.1 demo. Our current practice is to mark it as obsolete (making it unavailable to a user), and replace it with updates if available. Ideally, we would provide a natural way to navigate through our deprecated material as well ... heck, some of our viewers may still be running Java 1.1! We have yet to decide how to present this content in a way that is clean and consistent with our current design.

Another limitation of our system is that we do not support arbitrary meta-data tags for ontology nodes. This has great benefits for search, especially if combined with tags that users could supply. While we're letting users contribute content (Web 2.0 meet WLA. WLA, Web 2.0), why not release the keys to the castle and let them submit their own webcast annotations? Certainly the clips and accompanying ontology would have to go through an approval process, but opening up the indexing process could make it much easier to add other courses to our archive. A huge step in this direction would be to find or develop PowerPoint-embedded software that automatically records slide transition time-codes during lecture. One would still need to filter an instructor's "back, back, back, (oops too far!), forward, (long pause for explanation), forward, forward" clicks into "jump-back-2-slides, (long pause), jump-forward-2-slides", but it might be possible to write scripts to help automate that process to search for common instructor patterns.

We do intend to add more courses to our archive, probably starting with our Electrical Engineering introductory courses and then moving on to the EECS upper-division and maybe even graduate courses. We also hope to add one-time lectures, culled from our weekly colloquium series, research group talks and thesis presentations. In the long term, following in the footsteps of BIBS, we hope to eventually become adopted by the campus and become fully integrated in their webcast infrastructure.

6. CONCLUSION

We have presented the Weiner Lecture Archives, a system built by U. C. Berkeley undergraduates over the course of several years, that provides an ontology-driven interface to synchronized webcast video and slides of the "greatest hits" of our computer science introductory courses. Our hierarchical topic tree allows the viewer to easily navigate to the content they want, and with the click of a single link, watch anything from a 1-minute clip for a simple demo to the 1.5-day video of an entire course. This feature has been critical to the integration of our repository with the UC-WISE lab-centric instruction project, which will be infusing our synchronized video snippets into its curriculum. The usage exceeds 100,000 views per year, feedback we have received from all over the globe has been unanimously positive, and is quite encouraging. In the near term, we hope to add more courses and one-time lectures to our archive, to provide an even richer experience for our worldwide community of distance learners.

7. ACKNOWLEDGMENTS

We wish to acknowledge the generous support of the Larry Weiner Trust for funding this project. Thanks to Lecturers Mike Clancy and Brian Harvey for useful feedback throughout, to the helpful folks at ETS for hosting our video streams, and to project alumni Cassandra Guy, Babak Pahlavan, Matthew Ng, Jun Kitagawa, Aaron Steele and Steven Chan for their work developing early versions of WLA. Finally, thanks to Larry Rowe for his leadership and foresight with the BIBS and CMT projects that got the webcasting and slide-synchronization balls rolling on campus.

8. REFERENCES

[1] Chen, Carl, GoodProfOrNot: About, http://goodprofornot.sourceforge.net/about.html

[2] Clancy, M., Titterton, N., Ryan, C., Slotta, J., and Linn, M. 2003. New roles for students, instructors, and computers in a lab-based introductory programming course. In *Proceedings of the 34th SIGCSE Technical Symposium on Computer Science Education* (Reno, Nevada, USA, February 19 - 23, 2003). SIGCSE '03. ACM Press, New York, NY, 132-136. DOI= http://doi.acm.org/10.1145/611892.611951

[3] Educational Technology Services, Webcasting, http://ets.berkeley.edu/webcastberkeley

[4] Enounce, Enounce 2xAV, http://www.enounce.com/myspeed

[5] Eta Kappa Nu, Course Surveys, http://hkn.berkeley.edu/student/CourseSurvey/

[6] Google, YouTube APIs and Tools, http://code.google.com/apis/youtube/overview.html

[7] Mayer-Patel, K., Simpson, D., Wu, D., and Rowe, L. A. 1996. Synchronized continuous media playback through the World Wide Web. In *Proceedings of the Fourth ACM international Conference on Multimedia* (Boston, Massachusetts, United States, November 18 - 22, 1996). MULTIMEDIA '96. ACM Press, New York, NY, 435-436. DOI= http://doi.acm.org/10.1145/244130.244458

[8] Miller, G. A. (1956). "The magical number seven, plus or minus two: Some limits on our capacity for processing information". *Psychological Review*, 63, 81-97

[9] RealNetworks, http://www.real.com/realplayer

[10] Rowe, L. A.; Harley, D; Pletcher, P; and Lawrence, S. "BIBS: A Lecture Webcasting System". *Berkeley Multimedia Research Center, TR 2001-160*, June 2001. http://bmrc.berkeley.edu/research/publications/2001/160/

[11] University of California, Berkeley, The Weiner Lecture Archives, http://wla.berkeley.edu/

[12] World Wide Web Consortium, Synchronized Multimedia, http://www.w3.org/AudioVideo

The Design of an Online Environment to Support Pedagogical Code Reviews

Christopher Hundhausen, Anukrati Agrawal, and Kyle Ryan
Visualization and End User Programming Laboratory
School of Electrical Engineering and Computer Science
Washington State University
Pullman, WA 99164
+1 509-335-4590

hundhaus@wsu.edu, aagrawal@eecs.wsu.edu, kdryan@wsu.edu

ABSTRACT

Inspired by the *formal code inspection* process commonly used in the software industry, we have been exploring the use of *pedagogical code* reviews (PCRs), in which a team of three to four students, led by a trained moderator, (a) walk through segments of each other's programming assignments, (b) check the code against a list of best coding practices, and (c) discuss and log issues that arise. We have found that PCRs not only improve the quality of students' code, but also positively impact students' communication and sense of community. However, implementing PCRs also presents a key logistical challenge: how to make code solutions and review results accessible to team members before, during, and after the team reviews? To address this challenge, we are developing an online environment specifically tailored to support PCRs. Our environment enables students to submit their code solutions; to review team members' code solutions on-line prior to PCRs; to carry out PCRs; and to resubmit their solutions based upon the results of the PCRs. In an empirical evaluation of the environment in a CS1 course, we found that it not only eased the logistics of implementing PCRs, but also improved the organization and efficiency of the PCR process.

Categories and Subject Descriptors

K.3.1 [**Computer Uses in Education**]: *Collaborative Learning, Computer-Assisted Instruction*; K.3.2 [**Computer and Information Science Education**]: *Computer science education, Curriculum.*

General Terms

Design, Experimentation, Human Factors.

Keywords

Studio-based learning and instruction, pedagogical code review, code inspection, CS1, online peer review environment

1. INTRODUCTION

New jobs in the computing field are increasingly requiring design, critical thinking, communication, and teamwork skills in addition to programming skills. We believe that traditional approaches to teaching computing, which aim to develop programming skills through a series of individual programming assignments, inadequately prepare students for such jobs. In order to better prepare students for jobs in the computing profession, we believe computing courses need to emphasize design, communication, and collaboration skills as well as programming skills.

To that end, we have been exploring *studio-based* instruction as a means of engaging students more actively in the learning process and helping them to develop design, communication, and collaboration skills [6]. Adapted from architectural and fine arts education, our studio-based instructional approach emphasizes learning activities in which students construct solutions to assigned computing problems, and then present their solutions to their instructors and peers for review and discussion.

One possible adaptation of studio-based instruction for lower-division computing courses is the *pedagogical code review* (PCR) [5]. Based on the *formal code inspection* process (see, e.g., [4]) commonly used in the software industry, PCRs have small teams of students first review each other's code individually, and then come together as a team both to log issues (defects and improvements) that they encountered, and to identify additional issues as a team. Students can then be given an opportunity to resubmit their assignments based upon the results of the review.

In previous work, we implemented PCRs in a CS 1 course at Washington State University in the Spring Semester of 2008 [5]. Our empirical evaluation produced evidence that PCRs (a) positively impacted the quality of students' code; (b) stimulated discussions about increasingly sophisticated programming issues, including issues of design; and (c) inspired students to seek help from other students and work together outside of the PCRs.

In addition to documenting these educational benefits of PCRs, our empirical evaluation identified two key logistical problems with implementing PCRs purely with paper-based materials:

1. *Distribution of student code solutions was difficult.* Running a PCR requires that all members of a review team have a copy of each team member's code. We found it both logistically challenging and wasteful to print out all of this code. Moreover, we were unable to distribute code printouts to students such that they had sufficient lead time to review each other's code prior to the face-to-face reviews—one of the keys to the success of code reviews [10].
2. *Distribution of code review results was difficult.* A PCR yields an issue log, which documents in detail the issues that were found. We required the code author to fill in and retain a paper-based issue log of the issues that arose within the review of his or her code. However, we did not copy and distribute these issue logs to other students, as it would have required more effort and paper than we were willing to sacrifice. Thus,

SIGCSE '10, March 10–13, 2010, Milwaukee, Wisconsin, USA.

students missed out on a potentially valuable educational activity: that of reviewing each other's issue logs in order to verify their accuracy and identify commonalities between their and others' issues.

To address these problems, we present here a preliminary design and evaluation of OSBLE (Online Studio-Based Learning Environment), an online environment specifically tailored to support PCRs. The Instructor interface allows instructors to set up a course, add students and review teams, and to specify programming assignments. The Student interface allows students to upload assignment solutions, and to review and log issues on team members' solutions online. The Moderator interface allows a moderator to assign team roles, and to run a PCR. In an empirical evaluation, we found that OSBLE not only succeeded in overcoming the logistical obstacles identified above, but also improved the organization and efficiency of the PCR process.

2. RELATED WORK

The on-line environment presented here (OSBLE) supports both asynchronous reviews performed by individual students, and face-to-face PCRs performed by teams. Educators in many fields have become increasingly interested in incorporating online components into their courses. In addition to supporting both asynchronous and synchronous discussions, widely-used course management systems such as Blackboard [1] allow the instructor to post course announcements, materials, and assignments; students can hand in assignments and even take quizzes online through these systems. While not designed to support general course management, OSBLE is similar to these systems in that it does support some basic course management features. For example, it allows instructors to post course announcements, provide links to course materials, and configure course assignments for online submission.

Several computing educators have developed web-based systems specifically to facilitate asynchronous online peer review. For example, RRAS [9] enables instructors to develop online assessment rubrics for programming assignments, and to assign student reviewers to assignments. After submitting their assignments online through RRAS, students can anonymously review the assignments to which they were assigned by filling in and submitting the assessment rubric.

In a similar vein, Peer Grader [2] allows students to submit an assignment for review by their peers. Reviewers can anonymously provide both written feedback and a grade to authors. Peer Grader allows authors to revise and resubmit assignments, in order gradually to converge upon a more polished product. In addition, to encourage reviewers to perform high-quality reviews, Peer Grader requires a set of students to assess and grade each review. Review grades are then factored in to students' final assignment grades. Peer Grader is used as a foundation for Expertiza [3], which uses peer review as a basis for building up repositories of reusable learning objects from which students in subsequent courses can benefit.

More recently, Reily *et al.* [7] describe an environment designed specifically to support online peer review of student programming assignments in introductory computing courses. Like RRAS, the Reily *et al.* environment requires reviewers to submit reviews based on a rubric that is specified by the instructor. Like Peer Grader, the Reily *et al.* environment also allows peer reviews to be rated; however, the review ratings may be provided only by the author who receives the reviews—not by others, as is the case for Peer Grader. Unlike both RRAS and Peer Grader, the Reily *et al.* environment requires reviewers to specify, as part of their reviews, specific test cases and the results of executing those test cases. The test case results, along with the rubric-based assessment, are combined into a peer review score. In an empirical evaluation of their environment, Reily *et al.* found that (a) the peer review scores of students well matched those of teaching assistants; (b) students generally preferred the reviews of students who had less programming experience than they had; and (c) students who wrote peer reviews performed significantly higher in the course than students who did not.

OSBLE has much in common with the environments just reviewed—most notably, its support for the on-line submission and review of programming assignments. However, because OSBLE is specifically tailored to support the PCR process, it has two key differences: (a) it allows reviewers to anchor structured review log entries to specific lines or line ranges (thus supporting a form of "artifact-centered discourse"; see [8]); and (b) it supports both asynchronous code reviews performed by individuals, and face-to-face code reviews performed by teams.

3. USING OSBLE TO SUPPORT PCRs

Through an iterative, *user-centered* design process, we developed OSBLE in C# using ASP .NET 3.5. OSBLE is designed specifically to support the following usage scenario, which involves five key steps:

1. Instructor creates an assignment. The instructor logs in and creates a course assignment. This entails specifying several assignment details, including the due date and the precise files that students must submit as part of their solutions (see Figure 1).

2. Students submit solutions. Prior to the assignment due date, students log in and submit the specific deliverables required for the assignment, "locking" them once they have reached their final form. Once a student's solution has been locked, the student can no longer modify it, and the code solutions of the student's team members become available to the student for review.

3. Students perform online reviews. Once the due date passes, those students who have submitted assignment solutions are charged with individually reviewing the solutions of their team members. To review the code solution of a team member, a student locates the team member in a list, and then selects a specific component of the solution to view. To log an issue that pertains to a specific line of code, the student can either click on the line or on the "Log an issue" button (Figure 2), both of which bring up a dialog box that can be filled in with the details of the issue (Figure 3). Once an issue is logged, the line(s) to which it pertains are highlighted in yellow; highlighted lines can be clicked on to view the issue(s) associated with them.

4. Students perform face-to-face PCRs with moderator. PCRs are typically held in a regularly-scheduled lab period that takes place after the assignment is due. At the beginning of each PCR, the team moderator assigns the team members to specific PCR roles (*author*, *reader*, *inspector*, *recorder*), and then clicks the "Start Inspection" button to commence an in-lab review (see Figure 2). OSBLE makes it easy, within this review, for teams to review the issues logged by individual members of the teams, and to transfer those issues upon which they agree to the team review log. To do this, the team can choose the "View Issue Log" button, which brings up a list of the issues logged by team members ahead of time (see Figure 4). Next to each issue is a link entitled "To Lab"; if clicked, this link adds the corresponding issue to the team review log, and changes the highlighting of the issue from yellow to orange to indicate that it was logged by the team (see Figure 5).

5. Students resubmit solution based on PCR. After a PCR is completed, students are given an opportunity to review the issue logs for their assignment solutions, and to resubmit a solution based upon those logs.

4. EMPIRICAL EVALUATION

The original motivation for our development of OSBLE was to make the PCR process easier to implement and more effective for students. In particular, we were interested in exploring the following three research questions:

RQ1. As compared to implementing PCRs with paper, will implementing PCRs with OSBLE improve access to student code and issue logs?

RQ2. As compared to implementing PCRs with paper, will implementing PCRs with OSBLE improve the organization and efficiency of the PCR process?

RQ3. Will students' ability to use OSBLE to review team members' code solutions prior to face-to-face PCRs enable teams to log more issues than they can with paper, which does not easily support "ahead-of-time" reviews?

To address these research questions, we ran an empirical study in the spring, 2009 offering of CptS 121 ("Program Design and Development"), the CS 1 course at Washington State University. Our study (henceforth referred to as the "OSBLE Study") nearly replicated the one we ran in the Spring, 2008 offering of CptS 121 [5] (henceforth referred to as the "Paper Study"). The key difference was that, instead of using paper to implement the PCRs that took place in the course, we used the version of OSBLE presented in the previous section. Running this follow-up study allowed us to make direct comparisons between a paper-based and OSBLE-based implementation of PCRs.

The CptS 121 courses in which both studies took place were nearly identical: they had the same instructor (who was not involved in this research), textbook, assignments, schedule, and grading scheme. In addition, both CptS 121 courses required students to participate in three PCRs that took place in course labs in the eighth, eleventh, and thirteenth weeks of the fifteen week semester. The dates of the code review labs immediately followed (by two to five days) the due dates of three (of the eight total) course assignments. Below, we summarize key details of the studies, and report our main findings.

4.1 Participants

The Paper Study focused on three review teams consisting of 10 students enrolled in one section of the spring 2008 offering of CptS 121. That section enrolled a total of 22 students. In contrast, the OSBLE Study focused on six code review teams consisting of 26 students enrolled in two sections of the spring 2009 offering of CptS 121. These two sections had a total of 40 students.[1]

[1] The numbers of participants in each study reflect the fact that only a subset of students signed an informed consent form to release their data for analysis in our study.

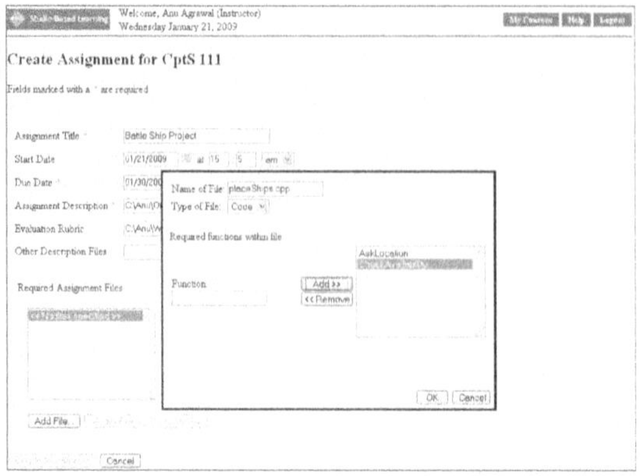

Figure 1. Instructor interface for creating assignments

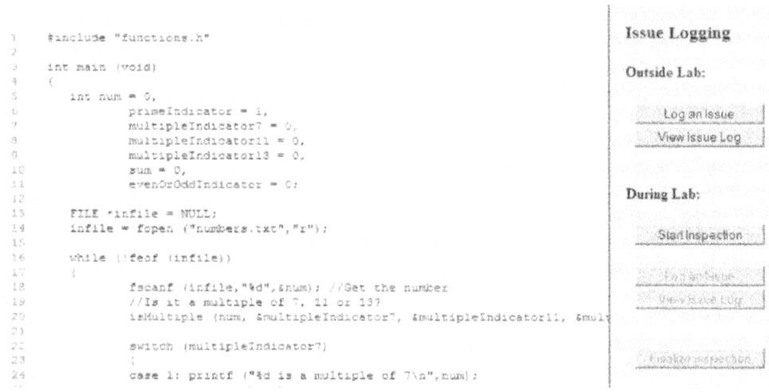

Figure 2. Student Interface for reviewing code

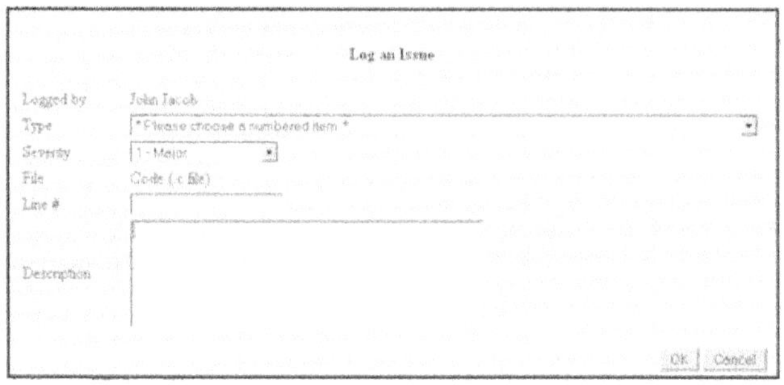

Figure 3. Issue logging form

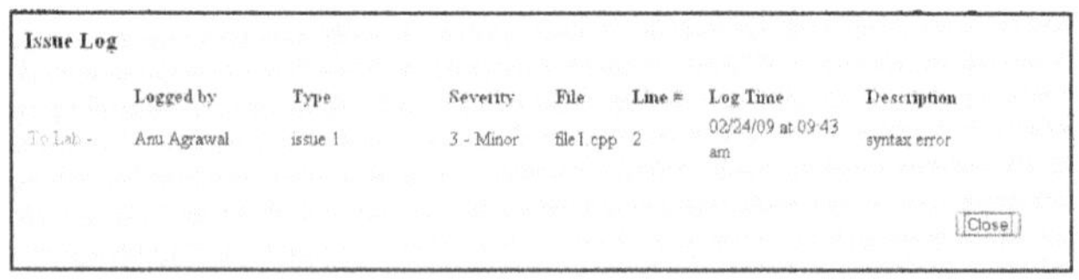

Figure 4. Transferring an issue to in-lab log

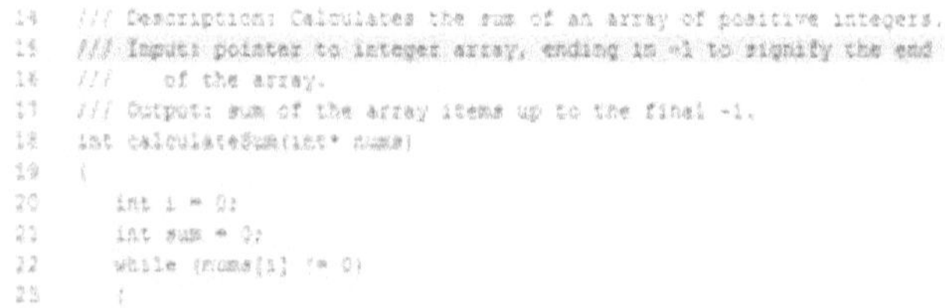

Figure 5. OSBLE highlighting scheme: Yellow Issues were found outside of lab; orange issues were found in lab (PCR)

In addition, we hired five computer science graduate students to serve as moderators in the Paper Study, and six computer science graduate and upper-division undergraduate students to serve as moderators in the OSBLE Study. Three of these moderators were common across both studies. We required the moderators to attend a one hour training session prior to the first PCR. We paid moderators $40 to $50 for each code review lab they worked.

4.2 Formation of Code Review Teams

Students were divided into code review teams of three to four. To form code review teams, we created an ordered list of students based on their course grades as they stood the day before the first scheduled PCR. We then assigned students to teams in a round-robin fashion, so that the teams were roughly equivalent in terms of the abilities of their members.

4.3 PCR Materials and Procedure

Students in both studies completed all course assignments in the C programming language, the instructional language for the course. The three course assignments that were the focus of the PCRs in both studies varied in complexity and length. The first assignment had students process numbers in a file and solve equations in different forms; it required roughly 150 lines of code. The second assignment, the longest and most complex (roughly 500 lines of code), had students implement the game of battleship. The final assignment required students to implement a nine-function string library; it required roughly 250 lines of code.

In the Paper Study, students did not have access to each other's solutions prior to the PCRs. In contrast, in the OSBLE Study, students were asked to review their team members' assignment solutions ahead of time in OSBLE.

In the OSBLE study, both moderators and students were provided with training on OSBLE. Prior to the first PCR, moderators and students were given a brief (fifteen-minute) demonstration of how to use OSBLE to perform PCRs. In addition, a nine-page tutorial on how to use OSBLE was available online by clicking on the "Help" button in OSBLE.

4.4 Data Collection Methods

In both studies, we employed three primary data collection methods. First, we attended all of the PCR sessions, and noted key observations. Second, we videotaped one code review performed by each team in each of the three PCR sessions. Third, we collected and analyzed all code review logs generated by the teams. In addition, in the OSBLE study, we instrumented OSBLE to collect user activity and usage data.

4.5 Results

We organize the presentation of our results around the three research questions posed for this study. For each research question, we present and compare relevant data and observations collected in the Paper and OSBLE Studies.

RQ1: As compared to implementing PCRs with paper, will implementing PCRs with OSBLE improve access to student code and issue logs?

In the Paper Study, the code solutions of other students were not available prior to the PCRs, thus preventing students from reviewing each other's code ahead of time. Moreover, after a team reviewed a given student's code solution, only that student (the *code author*) retained a copy of the team issue log; other team members could not review the issue log at a later time.

In contrast, in the OSBLE Study, students were able both to review the code solutions of others online, and to log issues online, immediately after the assignment due date passed. All team members were able to view issues so logged. Further, since teams used OSBLE to log issues during the PCRs, all team members could access the issue logs generated in the PCRs at any time after the PCR took place.

RQ2: As compared to implementing PCRs with paper, will implementing PCRs with OSBLE improve the organization and efficiency of the PCR process?

In the Paper Study, we required students to bring four printouts of their code solution to each PCR lab. However, students frequently forgot to bring the printouts. As a result, we observed that the team moderators, in collaboration with students, generally spent the first 15 to 30 minutes of each PCR lab making the printouts necessary to perform the code reviews. In addition, in the Paper Study, the course instructor had to print out and distribute two copies of the issue log to each student: one that was filled out and retained by *code author*, and a second that was filled out by the team *recorder* and retained by us for research purposes.

In contrast, in the OSBLE Study, students accessed each other's code solutions during the PCR labs using their own laptop computers, or one of those available in the lab. While logging in to OSBLE and accessing the code solutions of authors incurred a minimal amount of delay, we observed that the process went much more smoothly than in the Paper Study. Moreover, since issue logs were filled out maintained online through OSBLE, the instructor did not have to print out paper issue logs, nor did students have to retain (and potentially lose) paper copies.

To determine whether OSBLE might enable teams to log issues more quickly, we wanted to use our video data to compare the amount of time teams needed to log issues in both studies. Unfortunately, the video recordings from the Paper Study were of such a poor quality that we were unable to obtain timing data from them. However, we did obtain high quality recordings of all the review sessions of two teams that were enrolled in the Spring, 2009 offering of CptS 121, but that were in a different section from the teams that participated in the OSBLE study. These teams used OSBLE to view each other's code, but logged all issues (both ahead of time and within the PCR) on paper. Under the circumstances, the video data of these teams provided us with a reasonable basis for comparing the efficiency with which teams can log issues with paper versus OSBLE.

Based on 27 issues logged, the two teams that used paper took an average of 66.4 seconds (sd = 23.6 seconds) to log an issue. In contrast, based on 52 issues logged, four OSBLE teams took an average of 42.0 seconds (sd = 24.4 seconds) to log an issue. (We failed to gather complete video data on two of the OSBLE teams, so their data were not included in this analysis.) According to an independent samples t-test, this difference is statistically significant ($df = 77$, $T = 4.31$, $p < 0.0001$). In practical terms, OSBLE enabled teams to log issues 37 percent faster than paper, resulting in a more efficient PCR process.

RQ3: Will students' ability to use OSBLE to review team members' code solutions prior to face-to-face PCRs enable teams to log more issues than they can with paper, which does not easily support "ahead-of-time" reviews?

To address this question, we first wanted to determine the extent to which OSBLE Study participants actually logged issues prior to the PCRs. To our astonishment, our OSBLE log data indicated that *no* students reviewed team members' code prior to any of the PCRs. We speculate that this was the case because students had no incentive to do so. Indeed, while students were told that logging issues ahead of time could make the PCRs more valuable, they received no course credit for performing such reviews.

Thus, our data suggest that teams in both the Paper and OSBLE studies were on equal footing: students in neither study prepared for the PCRs by reviewing code ahead-of-time. Given that OSBLE appeared to improve the efficiency and organization of the PCRs, we nonetheless wondered whether OSBLE might enable teams to log more issues than paper. To explore this possibility, Table 1 presents the average number of issues recorded per team in the three code reviews, along with the overall total, in the Paper and OSBLE Studies. Because of the small sample sizes, we used non-parametric Kruskal-Wallis tests to determine whether statistically significant differences existed; however, we found no such differences in either PCR 1 ($df = 1$, $H = 1.07$, $p = 0.30$), PCR 2 ($df = 1$, $H = 0.60$, $p = 0.44$), PCR 3 ($df = 1$, $H = 2.40$, $p = 0.12$), or overall ($df = 1$, $H = 0.82$, $p = 0.36$).

5. SUMMARY AND FUTURE WORK

We have presented OSBLE, a new online tool that supports PCRs. In an empirical evaluation of OSBLE, we found that the tool not only addressed the logistical obstacles of implementing PCRs with paper, but also improved the organization and efficiency of the PCR process. However, while the tool successfully allowed students to submit their assignments online, we also found that students did not take advantage of the ability to review each other's code asynchronously prior to the PCRs.

Accordingly, in future work, we would like to explore new community-based incentive mechanisms for engaging students in asynchronous peer reviews. To that end, we are presently developing a new version of OSBLE that (a) enables students to upload a profile picture of their choosing, (b) allows students to comment on each others' log issues, and (c) requires peers to rate each other's reviews with respect to their helpfulness. We translate students' helpfulness ratings to a four-star scale, and the quantity of their reviews (number of issues logged and comments posted) to a seven-color scale that is calibrated based upon the total activity of all students in the course. Whenever a student posts a comment or issue, the student's name, picture, and rating are displayed.

The new OSBLE is being designed to be highly configurable. For example, the instructor can set the level of student anonymity, with levels ranging from completely anonymous (no identifying information available on any students, as in [7]), to partially anonymous (user-selected pseudonyms and non-identifying profile pictures), to relatively non-anonymous (students can see the names, profile pictures, and ratings only of their team members). This configurability will enable us to explore the impact of several variables, including anonymity, on the quality and quantity of peer reviews in introductory computing courses.

We invite interested educators to join us in this research. OSBLE is under active development, and is freely available at osble.sourceforge.net under the GPL open source license. Educators who are interested in tailoring OSBLE to their own courses are encouraged to contact the authors for assistance.

Table 1. Mean (Std. Dev.) Issues Logged by Teams in Each PCR Session and in Total, by Condition

Condition	*n*	PCR 1	PCR 2	PCR 3	Total
Paper	3	13.7 (10.5)	16.0 (7.2)	9.3 (1.5)	39.0 (2.6)
OSBLE	6	20.5 (3.5)	12.3 (7.2)	15.0 (6.0)	47.8 (18.3)

6. ACKNOWLEDGMENTS

We are grateful to the anonymous instructor who allowed us to implement and study PCRs in his CptS 121 course. This project is funded by a National Science Foundation CPATH Award (CNS-0721927). Contributions to this work by other members of the research team—Mike Trevisan, Dana Fairbrother, N. Hari Narayanan, Martha Crosby, Margaret Ross, Rita Vick—are gratefully acknowledged.

7. REFERENCES

[1] Blackboard, Inc. 2008. http://www.blackboard.com.

[2] Gehringer, E. Electronic peer review and peer grading in computer science courses. In *Proc. 32nd SIGCSE Technical Symposium*. ACM Press, New York, 2001, 139-143.

[3] Gehringer, E., Ehresman, L., and Skrien, D. Expertiza: students helping to write an ood text. In *OOPSLA '06: Companion to the 21st ACM SIGPLAN symposium*. ACM Press, New York, 2006, 901-906.

[4] Gilb, T. and Graham, D. *Software Inspection*. Addison-Wesley, Menlo Park, CA, 1993.

[5] Hundhausen, C., Agrawal, A., Fairbrother, D., and Trevisan, M. Integrating pedagogical code reviews into a CS 1 course: an empirical study. In *Proc. 40th SIGCSE Technical Symposium*. ACM, New York, 2009, 291-295.

[6] Hundhausen, C., Narayanan, N., and Crosby, M. Exploring studio-based instructional models for computing education. In *Proc. 39th SIGCSE Technical Symposium*. ACM Press, New York, 2008, 392-396.

[7] Reily, K., Finnerty, P.L., and Terveen, L. Two peers are better than one: aggregating peer reviews for computing assignments is surprisingly accurate. *Proc. ACM 2009 International Conference on Supporting Group Work*, ACM (2009), 115-124.

[8] Suthers, D. and Xu, J. Kukakuka: an online environment for artifact-centered discourse. In *Proc. Eleventh World Wide Web Conference*. WWW2002, Honolulu, 2002, 472-480.

[9] Trivedi, A., Kar, D., and Patterson-McNeill, H. Automatic assignment management and peer evaluation. *Journal of Computing Sciences in Colleges 18*, 4 (2003), 30-37.

[10] Wiegers, K. Improving quality with software inspections. *Software Development 3*, 4 (1995), 55-64.

A Visualization Tool for Tutoring the Interactive Learning of Data Structures and Algorithmic Schemes

Rafael del Vado Vírseda
Dpto. de Sistemas Informáticos y Computación
Universidad Complutense de Madrid
rdelvado@sip.ucm.es

ABSTRACT

We present a visualization tool for the interactive learning of data structures and algorithmic schemes which can be used as a useful educational environment in Computer Science. The different parts of this tool intend to transmit to the students the importance of separating the specification and the implementation of data structures, facilitating the intuitive comprehension of the most typical implementations by using algorithmic schemes, and providing examples where such structures are used. The tool has been designed to allow teachers to monitor the whole educational process of the students, providing a personal training assistant and a range of tutoring techniques according to the student's response. Along the academic course 2008/09 we have evaluated the part of the tool concerning data structures. The tool evaluation is carried by means of tests, some of them managed from a Virtual Campus, with open access to all the students, and another one managed in a computer laboratory with a controlled group. In this paper, we show the results of this educational experience about the benefits that the students get from the tool in the current teaching of Computer Science.

Categories and Subject Descriptors

I.3.3 [**Picture/Image Generation**]: Display algorithms; I.3.6 [**Methodology and Techniques**]: Graphics data structures and data types; K.3.2 [**Computer and Information Science Education**]: Computer science education

General Terms

Algorithms, Human Factors, Performance

Keywords

Computer science education, data structures, algorithmic schemes

1. INTRODUCTION

The study of data structures and algorithmic schemes is both essential and complex for Computer Science students. In this paper we present a tool which intends to facilitate the understanding of all these topics by means of the visualization and the interaction with the user, allowing teachers to monitor the educational process. Additionally, it tries to promote a continuous and personal work of the student along the academic course in a context where the convergence with the *Bologna process* and the new guidelines of the *European Higher Education Area*[1] imply innovative education methods centered in the student.

The tool has been made available through a Virtual Campus for the students of a *Data Structures* course, taught in the second year of the Computer Science studies at the Faculty of Computer Science of the Complutense University of Madrid (UCM). In particular, it may be used by the students of three groups of the Computer Science degree and by another group of the Computer Science technical degree in Management. Consequently, along this academic year we only evaluate that part of the tool concerning Data Structures.

These students have been provided with a guide for learning with the tool some of the data types included in the course programme. Additionally they have received some flash animations illustrating particular applications of the data types. Afterwards the students may check their level of knowledge by answering some tests. The development of the abstraction ability and the capacity of solving new problems requires practising individually the reasoning and also solving a big amount of exercises. These tests promote the individual work fundamental for assimilating the concepts. Their accomplishment is completely volunteer and its main aim is to help the students to learn. Additionally they may answer some questions about the usefulness of the tool, also available through the Virtual Campus.

In this paper we present the tool's development and its educational capacities in Computer Science Education, and also present some results obtained from the experience along the academic course 2008/09. The tool, the animations, and the tests are given in Spanish so that the students do not consider the language as an added obstacle in the learning process. In Section 2 we show both the usage and the implementation of the tool. In Section 3 the flash animations are described. Section 4 describes a tutoring system for the tool to address the whole self-learning process. Section 5 describes in detail the experiences with the students. Finally, in Section 6, we conclude and present plans for future work.

2. THE VISUALIZATION TOOL

2.1 Tool Usage

The students may download the tool from the UCM Virtual Campus[2]. Currently it may be executed in Windows environments with Java Virtual Machine JDK1.5 (o higher) but we have also generated a multi-platform version.

[1] `http://www.ond.vlaanderen.be/hogeronderwijs/bologna/`
[2] `http://www.fdi.ucm.es/profesor/rdelvado/SIGCSE2010/`

SIGCSE'10, March 10–13, 2010, Milwaukee, Wisconsin, USA.

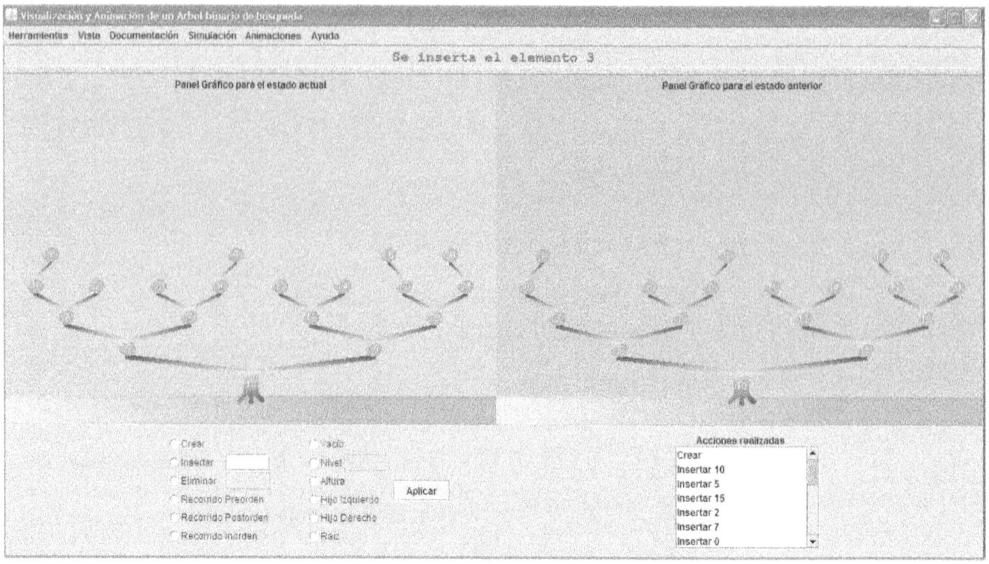

Figure 1: User view of the tool for binary search trees.

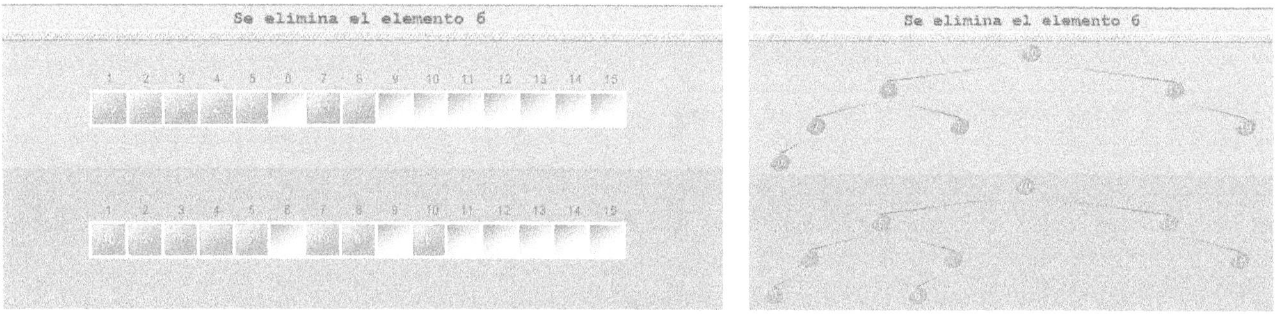

Figure 2: Static and dynamic implementations of binary search trees in the tool.

When the application is started the user selects one area: data structures or algorithmic schemes. We concentrate in this section on data structures. The student must choose the particular data structure, being now available: stacks, queues, binary search trees, AVL trees, priority queues, ordered tables and hash tables. When a data type has been selected, for example the binary search tree data type, we may view in a drawing panel the behavior of the structure, see **Figure 1**. It is divided in four parts:

- The Graphical Panel for the **current state**, after the execution of the last action.
- The Graphical Panel for the **previous state**, before executing the last action.
- A text box where the **executed actions** are shown, and a checkbox where the **methods** of the data structure may be chosen.
- On the upper part, a label showing the **result** of the actions execution.

The user may choose the *Simulation* option, and then a sequence of operations provided in a text file are executed without interruption. Such file may be modified by the user. On the contrary, if the user wants to execute the operations one by one, she/he must start by creating an empty structure. The student may choose one of several simple types for the elements of the structure (e.g. integers, strings) and then he/she can execute the different methods over the structure and introduce the elements interactively.

At the same time the structure is being created, the user can select the *View* of the data type: either an abstract view of the data type at the level of its algebraic specification (*User View*) or the structure's state used in its implementation (*Implementation View*). In the user view the behavior of the structure is shown independently from the implementation. For example, **Figure 1** shows the user view for binary search trees. In the implementation view the tool shows how the data are kept in a particular implementation. For example, two implementations for the binary search trees are given: a static implementation by means of an array, and a dynamic implementation by means of pointers. They are shown in **Figure 2**.

The main difference with respect to other related tools [2] is that we intend that the students assimilate a key concept of the course: the difference between the behavior description of a data structure given by the algebraic specification, and its implementation in a particular programming language. Additionally, the flash animations, which we will describe in detail later, provide among other things, examples of the use of data structures to solve problems. In this way, the three fundamental aspects of the course are covered:

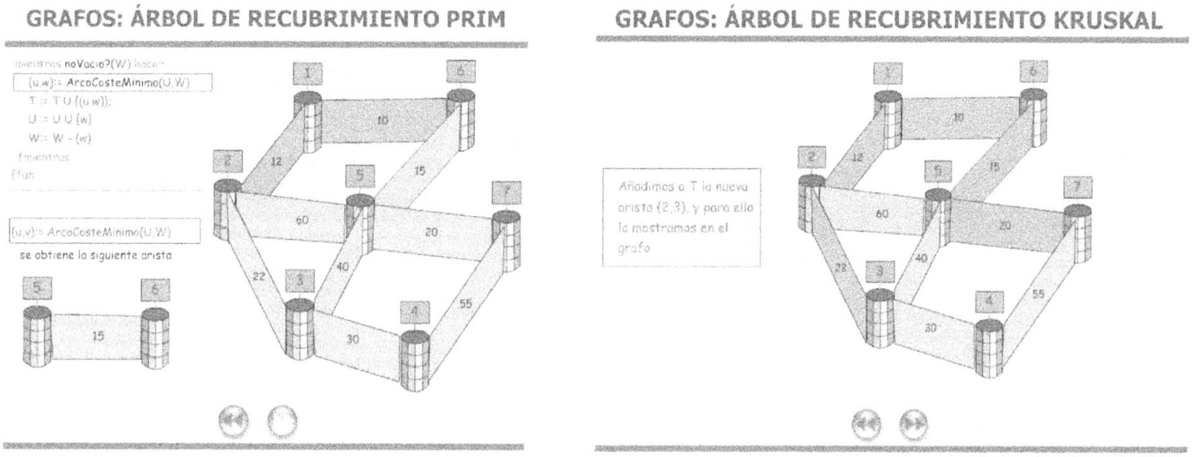

Figure 3: Prim's and Kruskal's algorithm animations integrated into the tool.

behavior, implementation, and usage of data types. The tool has documentation about the data structures including algebraic specifications, implementations using Java and cost of the algorithmic methods in a given implementation.

We have shown in this section binary search trees as a representative example, but the tool also shows: stacks, queues, AVL trees (including visualization of the rotations), priority queues and its implementation using binary heaps on an array (including visualizations of the up and down movements), ordered and hash (open and closed) tables.

2.2 Tool Implementation

The tool was originally implemented in the context of the course *Software Engineering* in the last year of the Computer Science degree. It has been implemented in Java and designed in a modular way, so that adding new data structures (and algorithms) is as easier as possible for the programmer. Its main components are: the **interface package**, the **graphical package**, and the **implementation package**.

The user communicates with the tool through the interface package, which consists of an interactive module and a **panel** where the animations are shown. The interactive part (depending on the operations applied by the user) calls the corresponding function of the implementation module and also the panel functions responsible for painting the action. The panel communicates with the graphical package, where the graphics for each different data structure have been implemented as well as the animations controlled by Java threads. This modular design allows to easily incorporate new knowledge to the tool.

3. ALGORITHM ANIMATIONS

The algorithm animations have been developed in flash to allow us to show graphically the use of data structures in solving problems [1, 2, 4, 5]. They can be classified in three groups:

(1) Animations of algorithms that use data structures; e.g., the algorithm that transforms an infix expression to a postfix expression.

(2) Animations about the operations of a data structure; e.g., Kruskal and Prim algorithms for computing the minimum cost spanning tree of a graph.

(3) Tutorials about the behavior of a data structure and animations of some of its operations: stacks, queues, binary search trees, red-black trees, and priority queues.

Animations complement the tool and are offered to the students with it. Whenever possible, due to the screen size limitations, the algorithm code is written in the left-hand side of the screen while the animation occurs in the right-hand side to facilitate the students following the algorithm. Most of the algorithms have been written in a high level pseudocode description, independent of any particular programming language. The input data for the animation have been chosen such that the algorithm executes as many cases as possible. Besides, the animations execute the algorithm in detail, instruction by instruction, showing the result of the boolean expressions that control the execution flow.

In **Figure 3** we show pictures of the Prim's and Kruskal's Algorithms. These animations were given to a group of students to obtain the minimum spanning tree. The results of this experience are shown in Section 5.2. Other algorithms and data types animations can be accessed independently form from the tool in `http://www.fdi.ucm.es/profesor/rdelvado/SIGCSE2010/`.

4. TUTORING SYSTEM

The integration of an intelligent tutoring system turns our visualization tool into an innovative instrument of high pedagogical interest in Computer Science Education in comparison to other related approaches [2, 4, 5]. This tutoring system attempts to address the whole self-learning process of the main data structures and algorithmic schemes, from the algebraic specification until the real implementation.

The students have their first contact with the data structures and algorithms that they are going to study by means of the usage of this tutoring system for the tool. In order to control the student's self-learning process correctly, an **online database** has been built on the tool. For this purpose, an additional module (which can be obtained from `http://gpd.sip.ucm.es/rafav/`), has been designed to allow teachers to monitoring the progress of their students (see **Figure 4**), according to the information stored in the database (time spent on each animation, or most consulted documents on the help on the tool). Moreover, the tutoring system also allows seeing detailed information of each specific student, by selecting their identification number.

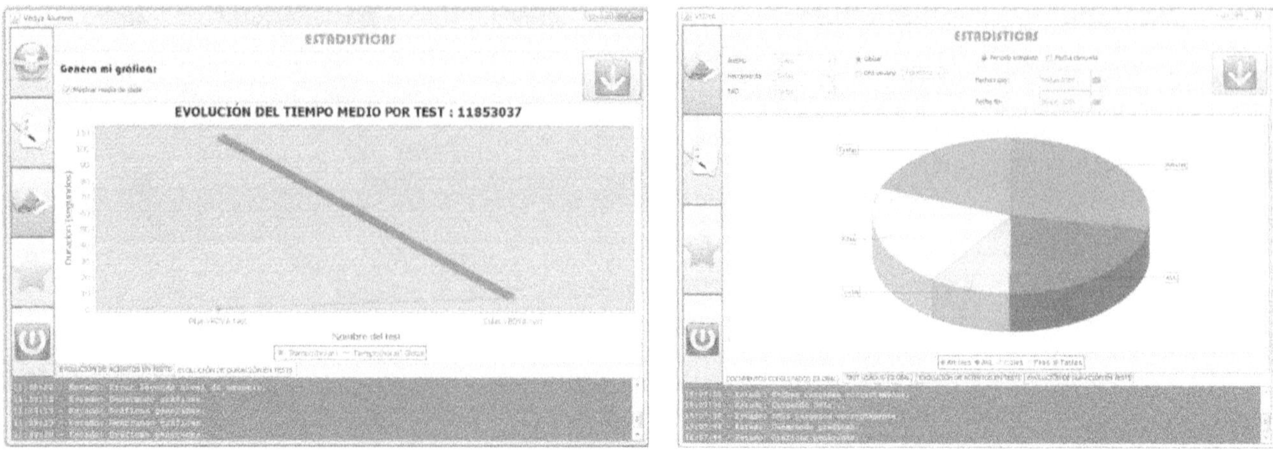

Figure 4: Tutoring system for the visualization tool.

5. EXPERIENCES AND RESULTS

As we have mentioned before, the tool is available for the students of the topic *Data Structures* in the Computer Science Faculty of the Complutense University of Madrid through the Virtual Campus (`http://campusvirtual.ucm.es/prof/EDI0809.html`). In total they are 486 students.

5.1 Design of the Experiences

We have done two different experiences:

- One **non-controlled** experience: all the students may access the Virtual Campus and participate freely in the experience: download and use the tool, and answer different kinds of tests.
- One **controlled** experience: two groups of students must answer a test in a controlled ambient from the point of view of the time and the access to the material.

With respect to the **non-controlled** experience, the students may freely access the Virtual Campus without any restriction of time (but the last delivery time at the end of the course) or material (slides, tool, bibliography) and answer the questions of several tests.

For each of the following data structures we have provided a test (which can be obtained from `http://www.fdi.ucm.es/profesor/rdelvado/SIGCSE2010/`) that evaluates the knowledge of students about the structure: stacks, queues, binary search trees, balanced trees (AVL and red-black), and priority queues. Tables have been not included in the experience as they have been added to the tool very recently. The students may use these tests to verify their advances in the understanding of the different concepts. The questions are structured in three blocks: *behavior* of the structure, *implementation* of the structure, and *use* of the data type by an algorithm.

The resolution of the tests by the students is controlled by the Virtual Campus and our tutoring system. The students are recommended to use the tool and the animations to complement the study of the data structures and then to answer the test to check their knowledge. However, if needed, they can consult the educational material: course slides, bibliography [3, 6], the tool. Each test consists approximately of 24 questions distributed between the three blocks, except the test about AVL and red-black trees which only pays attention to implementation, as they are taught as efficient implementations of binary search trees. Some of the questions have two possible answers: *true* or *false*, while other has several alternatives. After each question, the student tells us whether she/he has needed to consult some material to answer the question and in that case which one. When the delivery time is over the students may know their marks and the correct answers also through the Virtual Campus and the tutoring system.

Additionally, we have elaborated tests about the usefulness of the tool for each of the data structures, where the students manifest the time dedicated to study the structure, the time dedicated to answer the test, and also which material is more interesting for them. The aim of these other tests is to obtain the subjective opinion of the students about the help given by the tool to learn about the data structures and to know their study preferences.

In the **controlled** experience we try to evaluate more objectively the usefulness of the animations. In particular we have chosen the animations of the Kruskal and Prim algorithms for obtaining a minimum spanning tree of a graph. We choose two groups of students: approximately half of the students are only given the slides of the course and the data structure books at class; and the other half are given only the animations at a computer laboratory. Then, all the students answered the same questions in one hour about these algorithms.

5.2 Obtained Results

5.2.1 Non-Controlled Experience

We outline here the main conclusions from the results of the non-controlled experience. With respect to the material the students used to study, as long as the structure is more complicated the use of the tool (simulation, case execution, and tool help) increases considerably. The better results are obtained in the AVLs and the red-black trees. The tool helps to visualize the rotations in these balanced trees. In the rest of the structures they used class material or bibliography [3, 6].

When answering the tests questions, the students were also asked whether they needed additional help to answer them. In the case of binary search trees and AVLs they use the tool as much as the class material, which means that visualization of the operations, such as eliminations and rotations, are useful for them. In the case of red-black trees, they used "other" material a bit more than the tutorial animation, which presumably consists of a colleague advice.

	All the questions						Excluding cost questions					
	Correct answers		errors		don't knows		Correct answers		errors		don't knows	
	media	σ	media	σ	media	σ	media	σ	media	σ	media	σ
Animations	9.63	2.37	6.18	2.2	3.3	2.9	9.18	2.1	4.26	1.7	0.55	1.57
Slides	11.9	3	4.9	2.2	1.1	1.9	9.25	2.6	4.1	2	0.65	1.53

Figure 5: Medias and standard deviations (σ).

We can say that although only a small percentage of students have followed the experience, those who have done it, both consider the tool as an interesting material and have used it to complement the rest of the available material, including the class explanations. The tool is specially useful for visualizing the most "complex" operations.

5.2.2 *Controlled Experience*

This experience was carried out with 59 students. We gave 32 of them the slides of the course and the data structure books [3, 6]. The rest were taken to a laboratory, where they could execute the animations. We gave the same test to both groups, consisting of 18 questions, 12 of them about execution aspects of the algorithms, and the rest about their cost.

In **Figure 5** (left) we provide the media and the standard deviation of the number of correct answers, the errors, and the number of *don't knows*. First, we observe that students using the animations, answer in media less questions than the other ones. Besides, they make more errors than the others. This is due to the fact that most of the *animations students* do not answer the questions about the cost of the algorithms, while in the other group they give correct answers to these questions. The reason is that students of the *slides/books* group obtained the costs of the algorithms directly from the material, while the *animations students* had to deduce it from the code. **Figure 5** (right) gives the results excluding questions about costs. Now both groups present a similar behavior. The standard deviation of the students belonging to the *animations group* is slightly lower than that of the other group. The explanation for this results may be that students who use animations assimilated the concepts in a more homogeneous way, while the use of more conventional learning material, such as books or slides, leads to greater differences among the students. Finally, we observe that most of students of the *animations group* have failed the same questions about the algorithm. This may be attributed to the fact that the example displayed in the Kruskal animation does not exhibit some cases of the algorithm. We can conclude that although there are not big differences between both groups, animations constitute an optimum complement to facilitate the comprehension of the different algorithms. Besides, it has helped us to detect in the students difficulties to derive the algorithms costs.

The most positive aspect of this experience is that all the students who used the animations indicated the benefits of using them to understand the implementation of the algorithms. They also mentioned that consulting written material would also be helpful to answer the questions about the algorithms costs. Some of them also complained about the example of the Kruskal algorithm, as it was not as representative of all cases of the algorithm as it was desirable. The examples must exhibit the complete behavior of the algorithm, avoiding possible misunderstandings of it. Otherwise, students may be guided by the animation to make wrong assumptions about the algorithms.

6. CONCLUSIONS AND FUTURE WORK

In this paper, we have presented an interactive tool for the visualization of data structures and algorithmic schemes which can be used for tutoring students in the first years of Computer Science Education. The main benefit of this kind of software is to facilitate the student's grasp of the target procedures in Computer Science, and to facilitate teamwork and communication between teachers and students.

We have made two different kind of educational experiences. In a non-controlled experience we have priorized that all the students may access the tool and so get benefit of it and of the tests. This is the reason why they do not have restrictions of time or material. However they are also given questions in order to evaluate the usefulness of the tool. In a controlled experience however the time and the material are restricted in order to evaluate directly the usefulness of the tool and/or the animations.

In our opinion the experiences have been very positive for those students who decided to participate, although we would have liked the number of volunteer participants was higher. We confirm that the tool is complementary to both the class explanations and material, making easier the visualization of some operations over data structures and algorithmic schemes.

In the next academic year we will continue using the tool, not only in the *Data Structures* course but also in the *Algorithms* course, in which the part of the tool dedicated to algorithmic schemes (dynamic programming, divide and conquer, greedy methods, branch and bound) will be as well evaluated. We will also intend to generate a multi-platform version of the tutoring system and improve those aspects signaled by the students in the test.

7. REFERENCES

[1] M. H. Brown and J. Hershberger. *Color and Sound in Algorithm Animation*. j-COMPUTER 25(12), pp. 52-63, 1992.

[2] T. Chen and T. Sobh. *A tool for data structure visualization and user-defined algorithm animation*. Frontiers in Education Conference, 2001.

[3] T. H. Cormen, C.E. Leiserson, and R. L. Rivest. *Introduction to Algorithms*. The MIT Press/McGraw-Hill, 2001.

[4] R. Fleischer and L. Kucera. *Algorithm Animation for Teaching*. Software Visualization, International Seminar Dagstuhl Castle 2001, Revised Lectures, Springer LNCS 2269, pp. 113-128, 2002.

[5] C. Kehoe, J. Stasko, and A. Taylor. *Rethinking the evaluation of algorithm animations as learning aids: an observational study*. In International Journal of Human-Computer Studies, 54(2), pp. 265-284, 2001.

[6] M. A. Weiss. *Data Structures and Problem Solving Using Java*. Addison-Wesley, 3rd Edition, 2005.

Comparing Alice, Greenfoot & Scratch

Sally Fincher (moderator)
School of Computing
University of Kent
Canterbury, Kent, UK
+44 (0)1227 824061
S.A.Fincher@kent.ac.uk

Stephen Cooper
Computer Graphics Technology
Purdue University
West Lafayette, IN, USA
coopers@acm.org

Michael Kölling
School of Computing
University of Kent
Canterbury, Kent, UK
+44 (0)1227 827570
M.Kolling@kent.ac.uk

John Maloney
Media Laboratory
Massachusetts Institute of Technology
Cambridge, MA, USA
jmaloney@media.mit.edu

SUMMARY
This panel will showcase and compare three leading Initial Learning Environments (ILE): Alice, Greenfoot and Scratch.

Categories and Subject Descriptors
D.1.7 [**Programming Techniques**]: Visual Programming, D.2.6 [**Programming Environments**]: Interactive Environments. K.3.2 [**Computer and Information Science Education**]

General Terms: Design, Languages

Keywords
ILE, Alice, Greenfoot, Scratch.

1. INTRODUCTION
Although designed at different times and in different contexts, these three environments—Alice, Greenfoot and Scratch— can be classified together as sharing similar characteristics. All are visual, all aim to foster immediate engagement in an attractive activity, and all aim to introduce pre-University students to programming. We describe these as "Initial Learning Environments".

As well as being used by individuals and in face-to-face group situations, these environments can also support remote community in the form of "galleries", webpages where students can post and share their materials. Characterized as the *fridge door* approach ("at the end of a day at kindergarten, youngsters like to have a painting to take home to show the family and to have it displayed on the door of the refrigerator" [1]), the Scratch team describe this as "deep shareability" [2].

In this session, we will give a short demonstration of each ILE. We will then pose a series of the same questions to each ILE, to expose the particular strengths of each.

The purposes of this panel are threefold:

- Firstly, we seek to showcase ILE software, demonstrating the maturity of this type of environment.
- Secondly, by including the three major ILEs, we show the breadth of approach in the area.
- Thirdly, by interrogating each ILE in turn, we allow comparison of their features and encourage educators to select the resource most suited to their needs and their situation.

Each ILE is represented by a panelist who is central to the design team for their environment and so may authoritatively speak to features, goals, desires and wish-lists. They can not only demonstrate features of the environment, but also can speak about why they were put there. Equally, they are knowledgeable as to the directions that each environment might develop in the future.

2. ALICE
http://www.alice.org

Alice is a 3-dimensional interactive animation program visualization environment. Novice programmers build animated 3-D movies and author games as they learn introductory object-oriented programming concepts.

Alice provides a drag-and-drop development environment, to prevent students from making syntax errors. The software (and the source code, for the more adventurous) is freely available from the Alice website, and instructional/curricular materials are freely available to teachers at www.aliceprogramming.net.

Alice was originally designed as a tool to improve at-risk computing undergraduate students' ability to succeed in CS1 and beyond (see [3] for greater detail). It is currently being used in hundreds of colleges and secondary schools, in pre-CS1, CS1, pre-AP, and non-majors courses.

The Alice development team is currently building the next version of Alice, Alice 3. Alice 3 will enable the typing of Java code to build Alice worlds (as well as an ability to move between Alice's IDE and a more traditional one, such as NetBeans), as well as including characters from Electronic Arts' popular game, The Sims.

3. GREENFOOT
http://www.greenfoot.org

Greenfoot is an educational development environment highly specialized for the development of interactive, graphical applications. It is based on the Java programming language. Using Greenfoot, students from high school age can develop engaging and interesting programs, such as games and simulations, quickly and easily while learning fundamental programming concepts.

The use of text based programming based on Java makes very sophisticated applications possible, matching students' high

SIGCSE'10, March 10–13, 2010, Milwaukee, Wisconsin, USA.
ACM 978-1-60558-885-8/10/03.

expectations, and prepares them for progression to more general programming environments.

4. SCRATCH

http://scratch.mit.edu/

Scratch is a media-rich, networked environment originally designed for use in "computer clubhouses", a network of afterschool learning centers for youth from economically-disadvantaged communities. Scratch's focus on media springs from this initial situation, as clubhouse participants were observed to be "creating and manipulating graphics, animations, videos, and music (and often integrating multiple media)"[2] Thus "Scratch emphasizes media manipulation and supports programming activities that resonate with the interests of youth, such as creating animated stories, games, and interactive presentations". [4]

A Scratch project is built from a background and a number of movable sprites. Programming is based on a metaphor of building blocks, and, influenced by previous systems such as LegoBlocks, is accomplished by dragging blocks from a palette and assembling them, like puzzle pieces, to create "stacks" of blocks. These "stacks" then determine various behaviors of the objects.

5. REFERENCES

1. Fincher, S. What are we doing when we teach programming? In Frontiers in Education '99, pages 12a41-5. IEEE, November 1999
2. Resnick, M., Kafai, Y., Maeda, J. A Networked, Media-Rich Programming Environment to Enhance Technological Fluency at After-School Centers in Economically-Disadvantaged Communities. Proposal to National Science Foundation, 2003
3. Moskal, B., Lurie, D., Cooper, S. Evaluating the effectiveness of a new instructional approach. In SIGCSE '04: Proceedings of the 35th SIGCSE technical symposium on Computer science education, pages 75-79, 2004
4. Maloney, J. H., Peppler, K., Kafai, Y., Resnick, M., Rusk, N. Programming by choice: urban youth learning programming with Scratch In SIGCSE '08: Proceedings of the 39th SIGCSE technical symposium on Computer science education, pages 367-371, 2008

Panel

Multicore Education: Pieces of the Parallel Puzzle

Organizer and Chair:

Joel C. Adams
Calvin College
Grand Rapids, MI 49546
+001-616-526-8666
adams@calvin.edu

Daniel J. Ernst
U. of Wisconsin–Eau Claire, WI, USA
ernstdj@uwec.edu

Thomas Murphy
Contra Costa College, CA, USA
tmurphy@contracosta.edu

Ariel Ortiz
Tecnológico de Monterrey, Mexico
ariel.ortiz@itesm.mx

PANEL SUMMARY

Although *Moore's Law* continues to hold at present, *Moore's Dividend* – where software developers could rely on increasingly faster CPUs to make their software faster – has expired [5]. Instead of manufacturing uni-core CPUs with faster clocks, hardware manufacturers are producing *multi-core* CPUs, and *many-core* CPUs (with 32 or more cores) have begun appearing. Traditional sequential applications will not take advantage of these new hardware capabilities, and thus will not run any faster. To gain performance on these new and future hardware platforms, applications must be designed and written in pieces that run simultaneously on different cores. Ideally, the performance of such *parallel applications* should *scale* as the number of available cores increases.

As computer science educators, it behooves us to prepare our students for this brave new parallel world. In this session, the panelists will discuss different aspects of doing so, including:

- How do we integrate parallelism into the CS curriculum? What aspects of parallelism do we cover, and where?
- What available technologies (e.g., programming languages, libraries, etc.) facilitate parallel application development?
- What resources are available for CS faculty members to learn how to design and build parallel applications?

Each panelist will focus on one of these aspects of the problem.

Categories and Subject Descriptors

K.3.2 [**Computer and Information Science Education**]: Computer Science Education, Curriculum

General Terms

Algorithms, Design, Languages, Performance

Keywords

Concurrency, Curriculum, Faculty, Many-core, Multi-core, Parallel, Programming, Languages, Training, Workshops

SIGCSE'10, March 10-13, 2010, Milwaukee, Wisconsin, USA.
ACM 978-1-60558-885-8/10/03.

Chair Joel Adams, *Calvin College*

Joel Adams is Professor and Chair of the Department of Computer Science at Calvin College. He has been teaching students about concurrency and parallelism for 20 years. To provide platforms for his students to experience the benefits of distributed parallelism, he has designed and built a variety of Beowulf clusters over the past decade, ranging from small clusters like Microwulf [1] to a terascale cluster at *dahl.calvin.edu*.

As chair, he will introduce the session and each of the other panelists. If (and only if) time permits, he will provide a brief overview of how OpenMP (see *openmp.org*) can be used to parallelize hotspots in legacy (i.e., sequential) C or C++ code.

Panelist Daniel Ernst, *U. of Wisconsin – Eau Claire*

The recent shift in computing towards ubiquitous parallelism raises several questions for computer science educators. Most of these questions relate to how we can best prepare students for a world where parallel resources are always available, and where, as the number of cores increases, sequential applications and single-threaded performance will become less and less acceptable in practice.

Traditionally, parallel programming concepts have been kept in the realm of upper-level electives and/or reserved for students who plan to work in the realm of high-performance scientific computing. This curricular placement within computer science has naturally led to these concepts being taught in an advanced way, appropriate to the level of the students.

As has been observed by others [6], in order to bring parallelism and concurrency to the mainstream, educators need to re-frame parallelism using simpler concepts, preferably ones that students can think about and understand in a natural way.

A few years ago, Daniel initiated and helped begin the implementation of changes to the curriculum at the University of Wisconsin – Eau Claire to attempt to address this deficiency in their curriculum [4]. The approach they adopted was to provide a consistent and integrated exposure to parallelism, spread across the curriculum, in a platform-agnostic manner.

In his presentation, Daniel will share guidelines and lessons he and his colleagues at Wisconsin – Eau Claire have learned. In particular, he will share their initial experiences with their recent curricular changes, and insights stemming from the many discussions they have had with other educators on this topic.

Panelist Thomas Murphy, *Contra Costa College*

Thomas Murphy is a professor and chair of Computer Science at Contra Costa College (CCC). He is director of the CCC High Performance Computing Center, which has supported both the Linux cluster administration program and the computational science education program. Since 2003, Thomas has been an instructor with the National Computational Science Institute Parallel and Distributed Working Group, which presents several three to seven day faculty workshops each year. He also helps coordinate the SC07-11 Education Program. He helps maintain the Bootable Cluster CD software platform, the LittleFe hardware platform, and the CSERD (Computational Science Education Reference Desk) curricular platform.

As a panelist, Thomas will describe multicore and parallel computing resources and opportunities for computer science educators. These include:

- *The SC Education Program*, which provides summer workshops and other opportunities for educators to learn about parallel computing and develop curricular materials;
- *BCCD*, a mechanism for turning a lab of personal computers into a network of workstations (NOW) multiprocessor;
- *LittleFe*, a portable and inexpensive Beowulf cluster;
- *CSERD*, a collection of resources for computational science, including parallel / cluster computing.

If time permits, Thomas will provide a brief overview of success integrating parallelism into a community college CS program.

Panelist Ariel Ortiz, *Tecnológico de Monterrey*

Ariel Ortiz is a fulltime faculty member at the Tecnológico de Monterrey, Campus Estado de México. He has been teaching different programming styles and languages for more than two decades. In 2007, he started to use the *Erlang* language (see *erlang.org*) in his Programming Language course in order to teach functional, concurrent and distributed programming. He has also recently begun covering Google's *MapReduce* model (see *labs.google.com/papers/mapreduce.html*) in the concurrent portion of this course. In this presentation, he will compare and contrast these technologies.

Erlang simplifies parallel programming by modeling a problem as a collection of parallel processes that can only communicate with each other by sending and receiving messages. Erlang has parallel processes, but no locks, and no possibility of shared memory corruption (since there is no shared memory). Concurrency is supported by the Erlang virtual machine and not by the operating system. This means that applications behave the same way regardless of the deployment platform.

What follows is a list with some guidelines for efficient multi-core programming in Erlang. By following them, a program might run *n* times faster on an *n*-core processor – without any changes to the program itself [2]:

- Avoid side effects.
- Use lots of processes.
- Avoid sequential bottlenecks.
- Favor CPU bound processes and small messages.

MapReduce is a programming model that can be used in order to adhere to these guidelines. It involves specifying a map function that processes a key/value pair to generate a set of intermediate key/value pairs, and a reduce function that merges all intermediate values associated with the same intermediate key [3]. Mappings and reductions are executed in parallel.

REFERENCES

[1] J. Adams, T. Brom. Microwulf: A Beowulf Cluster For Every Desk. *39th SIGCSE Technical Symposium on Computer Science Education*, March 2008. 121-125.

[2] J. Armstrong. *Programming Erlang: Software for a Concurrent World.* Pragmatic Bookshelf, Raleigh, NC. 2007.

[3] J. Dean and S. Ghemawat. *MapReduce: Simplified Data Processing on Large Clusters.* http://labs.google.com/papers/mapreduce.html Accessed September 2, 2009.

[4] Daniel J. Ernst and Daniel E. Stevenson. Concurrent CS: Preparing Students for a Multicore World. *13th Annual Conference on Innovation and Technology in Computer Science.* June 2008. 230-234.

[5] J. Laurus. Spending Moorre's Dividend. Communications of the ACM (52) 5. May 2009. 62-69.

[6] Michael L. Scott, "Don't Start with Dekker's Algorithm: Top-Down Introduction of Concurrency," *Workshop on Multicore Programming Education* (held in conjunction with ASPLOS 2009), March 2009.

Recognizing the Most Influential CS Education Papers

David G. Kay
Department of Informatics
Donald Bren School of Information and Computer Sciences
University of California, Irvine
Irvine, California 92697-3440
kay@uci.edu

Invited Participants:
Kim Bruce
Pomona College
Michael Clancy
University of California, Berkeley
Nell Dale
University of Texas, Austin
Mark Guzdial
Georgia Institute of Technology
Eric Roberts
Stanford University

SUMMARY

This special session is devoted to identifying the CS education papers of the 20th century that have had the greatest influence on our practice of CS education today. The point is not primarily to produce the list of papers; rather it is to derive criteria, principles, and practices for identifying valuable contributions to CS education. This will provide a basis for establishing of awards or other recognition for influential contributions to CS education; it may also clarify the criteria for reviewing all papers. Invited participants will identify influential papers and their criteria for selecting them; the audience will also be encouraged to nominate papers and propose selection criteria. The results of this session will be communicated to the SIGCSE leadership, who will decide whether, and how, to implement any actual awards.

Categories and Subject Descriptors

K.3.2 Computer and Information Science Education

General Terms

Documentation

Keywords

Influential papers, publication process, recognition of excellence, awards

SIGCSE'10, March 10–13, 2010, Milwaukee, Wisconsin, USA.
ACM 978-1-60558-885-8/10/03.

1. OVERALL OBJECTIVE OF THE SESSION

Two separate threads led to this session.

The first is a view that seems widespread in the SIGCSE community, at least among those who have been SIGCSE participants for many years. They feel that SIGCSE papers too often don't adequately take prior work into account; they often show no awareness of results or experiences that were established and published more than a few years back. In fact, the new review process with assistant program chairs is one approach to addressing this issue.

The second event that prompted this session was a colleague of the organizer who won an award at the International Conference on Software Engineering (ICSE 2008): Most Influential Paper from Ten Years Ago. The ICSE conference organizers each year look at the ICSE conference of ten years ago and decide which paper at that conference had the greatest influence on the field in the intervening period.

We think that SIGCSE should establish a similar award; besides recognizing the best work, the award would raise awareness of past work and prompt educators to look further back for solutions and insights, thereby reinventing fewer wheels. Having a SIGCSE award for most influential paper of ten years ago would also build a sense of CS education as a discipline with a history and an established body of published results. While college teachers in most subfields of computer science have spent many years of graduate study in their subfields, few computer science educators have done graduate study in computer science *education.* Thus, this additional opportunity for exposure to significant past work in CS education would be particularly valuable.

By asking invited participants and the audience to identify influential papers, this session will begin the discussion of how to determine which contributions should win such an award.

It is important to note that the purpose of this session is not primarily to determine what the most influential papers are. Rather, it is to undertake a rather loose prototype process for selecting influential papers. We expect this activity to bring forth the range of criteria that any actual, eventual selection process would have to establish. These might include the following:

- What counts as a publication for this recognition? Do we include SIGCSE workshops or panels or special sessions? Do we include software?
- From which journals or conferences should publications be considered? Might we recognize an innovation published in a venue not oriented towards education?
- Should the recognition be categorized ("CS education research" vs. experiential reports vs. tools, for example)?
- If a tool is influential, is the paper describing it necessarily influential?
- Must the influence be broad, or is significant influence on one particular area (e.g., programming languages or nontraditional students) sufficient for recognition?
- Is ten years the right length of time for a proper perspective in CS education?

These questions are only representative; the reason to have this session is to bring out questions that we cannot anticipate in advance.

For purposes of the session, the invited participants and the audience at large will be asked to identify the three CS education papers published before 2000 that they believe have had the greatest positive influence on our practice of CS education today. They would also be asked to reflect on their selection process and the criteria they had to resolve.

Each invited participant is a computer science educator of long experience; among them they have won major SIGCSE awards, taught graduate courses on computer science education, and made influential contributions themselves. They will launch the discussion with their paper nominations.

In advance of the conference we will also poll the SIGCSE community via the mailing list, describing the session and its motivation, collecting paper nominations, and inviting participation in the special session to discuss their criteria. As the timetable below indicates, the largest block of time at the session would be an "open mike" session at which anyone will be invited to describe their selection process.

The results of this session will be communicated to the SIGCSE leadership; they will decide whether, and how, to implement an actual award.

2. OUTLINE OF THE SESSION

0:00 to 0:10: Organizer describes the motivation and goals of the session and the schedule.

Throughout the session, the organizer or an assistant will record the issues, processes, and criteria that are raised.

0:10 to 0:35: Invited participants present the influential papers they identified and describe the criteria they used.

0:35 to 0:65: Audience members present their influential papers and describe their selection process.

0:65 to 0:75: The organizer will summarize the selection criteria that emerged during the session, possibly taking straw votes on issues where alternative approaches have been suggested.

3. EXPECTATIONS

The audience might include anyone at SIGCSE, especially anyone who has submitted papers to SIGCSE or other CS education conferences. Everyone likes talking about awards and recognition, so the consideration of particular papers will likely be a draw.

4. SUITABILITY FOR A SPECIAL SESSION

We propose this as a special session because of its high degree of audience participation and the potential open-endedness of the discussion. It would not be impossible as a panel, but under the typical panel format there are fewer invited panelists, the panelists are eager to take up most of the time, and audience participation is typically relegated to a few minutes at the end.

Keynote Talk

Science Education for the 21st Century: Using the Insights of Science to Teach/Learn Science

Carl E. Wieman
Director of the Carl Wieman Science Education Initiative and Professor of Physics, University of British Columbia
Director of the Science Education Initiative and Distinguished Professor of Physics, University of Colorado at Boulder

Abstract

Guided by experimental tests of theory and practice, science has advanced rapidly in the past 500 years. Guided primarily by tradition and dogma, science education meanwhile has remained largely medieval. Research on how people learn is now revealing how many teachers badly misinterpret what students are thinking and learning from traditional science classes and exams. However, research is also providing insights on how to do much better. The combination of this research with modern information technology is setting the stage for a new approach that can provide the relevant and effective science education for all students that is needed for the 21st century. I will discuss the failures of traditional educational practices, even as used by "very good" teachers, and the successes of some new practices and technology that characterize this more effective approach, and how these results are highly consistent with findings from cognitive science.

Categories & Subject Descriptors: K.3.2 [Computers and Education]: Computer and Information Science Education – computer science education

General Terms: Human Factors

Bio

Carl Wieman is currently the director of the Carl Wieman Science Education Initiative at the University of British Columbia and a similar program at the University of Colorado at Boulder. These collaborative initiatives are aimed at achieving departmental-wide sustainable improvement in undergraduate science education. He has carried out research in a variety of areas of atomic physics and laser spectroscopy. His research has been recognized with numerous awards and honorary degrees including the Nobel Prize in Physics in 2001 for the creation of Bose-Einstein condensation.

His work in science education has been recognized by being named the US University Professor of the Year in 2004 by the Carnegie Foundation for the Advancement of Higher Education and receiving the National Science Foundation's Distinguished Teaching Scholar Award in 2001 and the American Association of Physics Teacher's Oersted Medal in 2007. He is an elected member of the National Academy of Sciences and serves on the Academy Board on Science Education. He is also a member of the U.S. National Academy of Education.

SIGCSE'10, March 10–13, 2010, Milwaukee, Wisconsin, USA.
ACM 978-1-60558-885-8/10/03.

What Do "CS1" and "CS2" Mean? Investigating Differences In the Early Courses

Matthew Hertz
Computer Science Department
Canisius College
Buffalo, NY 14208
hertzm@canisius.edu

ABSTRACT

Thirty-one years ago, the ACM Computing Curricula used the terms "CS1" and "CS2" to designate the first two two courses in the introductory sequence of a computer science major. While computer science education has greatly changed since that time, we still refer to introduction to programming courses as CS1 and basic data structures courses as CS2. This common shorthand is then used to enable students to transfer between institutions and as a base of many research studies.

In this paper we show that while there is wide agreement on the connotation of CS1 and CS2, there is little agreement as to the denotation of these terms. Surveying CS1 and CS2 instructors, we find little agreement on how important various topics are to each of these course and less agreement on how well students master the material. Even after limiting the analysis to whether a topic has ANY important or students complete a course with ANY mastery of the material, we continue to find significant disagreements between instructors.

Categories and Subject Descriptors

K.3.2 [**Computers and Education**]: Computers and Information Science Education—*Computer science education; Curriculum*

General Terms

Standardization

Keywords

CS1, CS2, Survey, Curriculum Design

1. INTRODUCTION

The introductory sequence of Computer Science courses includes a first course introducing students to programming fundamentals and an additional one or two courses teaching data abstractions/data structures. Using the terminology originally developed by the ACM's 1978 Computing Curricula [2], the introductory course is commonly referred to as *CS1* and the latter course(s) are called *CS2*. While earlier Computing Curriculum had been developed [6, 1] and changes continue to be made to the (now joint ACM-IEEE) curriculum [13, 12, 11], these concepts endure. The accepted nature of CS1 and CS2 can further be seen in how these ideas have been incorporated into other model curricula that have been developed [3, 14, 5].

The names and general principles of CS1 and CS2 have continued, but the past 30 years have changed the concepts covered in these courses. Between the Liberal Arts Curricula and the most recent ACM-IEEE curricula there are 3 proposed ways to organize CS1 and CS2 courses. Each of these curricula includes courses organized in an object-first manner. The ACM-IEEE curricula also defines an imperative-first approach to these courses while the liberal arts curricula defines a functional-first model. Many departments deviate from these models focusing more than required on specific topics, introducing new topics, or ignoring topics.

Given all of these potential differences, we must ask whether the terms "CS1" and "CS2" actually convey any real meaning anymore. The answer to this question is very important. Each year at SIGCSE and other computer science education conferences there are many papers examining student performance in CS1 and CS2 (for example, [7, 8, 10]). This research assumes a common understanding of these courses. The validity of cross-institutional studies also rely upon a single definition of CS1 and CS2. Whenever students consider transferring and faculty evaluate the transcripts of transfer students, they rely upon the common agreement of these topics. For all these situations, it is important to verify that these assumptions are valid. If there is no common understanding, it is important that this fact be understood and we always make explicit the information needed to evaluate a course.

To investigate whether there is any underlying agreement on what occurs in CS1 and CS2 courses, we examined a range of topics from the ACM Small College and ACM-IEEE Computing Curricula. Respondents to our survey were asked to rate both the importance and student achievement on each topic in their CS1 and CS2 courses. Using Fleiss' kappa [9], we then determine the level of overall agreement between instructors. We further examine the level of agreement of whether instructors felt topics had any importance and students left their course with any ability on each topic.

As we show, there is little of the agreement suggested by

SIGCSE'10, March 10–13, 2010, Milwaukee, Wisconsin, USA.

Control constructs	Testing
Methods, functions, subroutines	Debugging
Variables, types, expressions	Recursion
Error handing (e.g., exceptions)	Arrays, strings
I/O (e.g., files, printing to screen)	Sorting
Style (e.g., indentation, variable names)	Trees
Stacks, queues, lists	Graphs
Abstraction mechanisms (e.g., interfaces, abstract classes)	Other data structures
Object-oriented programming (e.g., inheritance, class anatomy)	

Table 1: List of Topics Used in the Survey

use of the terms CS1 and CS2. While some general agreement exists on the most basic of topics, beyond this we found little to suggest any common definitions of CS1 and CS2. Even at the coarsest of granularities, there is little agreement on which topics are taught in each of these courses. So while we often discuss CS1 and CS2, these courses are taught so differently as to make them nearly meaningless.

Section 2 explains the design of the survey and the steps taken to minimize survey error. Section 3 presents our results and Section 4 discusses what the results mean. Finally, Section 5 presents our conclusions and discusses future work.

2. SURVEY DESIGN

In order to determine what, if any, agreement exists on the content of CS1 and CS2 courses, we developed a survey. Our first step in developing this survey was to create a list of topics by which we could evaluate the courses. We examined existing curricula and chose to base our list on the division of topics presented in the LACS Model Curriculum for a Liberal Arts Degree. This outline is itself based upon the ACM-IEEE Model Curriculum, but is more detailed in specifying each topic. This topic listing is still general enough for to be mapped to courses taught using either object-oriented or functional languages. We therefore thought this made it ideal to analyze the range of introductory courses taught under aegis of CS1 and CS2. Starting from this list, we then made several small changes to insure the accuracy of our results. The list of topics we used in our survey can be found in Table 1 and the changes made can be found in Table 2. Our changes largely fit into 4 categories. The first set of changes was splitting possibly unrelated topics. These changes help insure we collect results at the finest grain possible. We also tried to generalize topics to best match all the programming languages that could be used. These resulted in our second set of changes. Our third set of changes combine closely related topics. These changes keep our survey to a reasonable reasonable size. Finally, we added a topic that we felt was frequently taught, but not included in any curricula.

Given the final list of topics, we next needed to determine how to best collect data that would enable us to see if there was agreement on these topics. We were interested in whether a universal definition of CS1 and CS2 exists. This focuses more on peoples' perception of these courses than on objective standards. We therefore used a subjective scale for instructors to rate their own courses. Instructors marked how important each topic is for success in their course from 1 ("unrelated") to 5 ("critical"). Instructors also rated how capable students were on each topic at the completion of their course from 1 ("none") to 5 ("mastered"). While these results are subjective (instructors may differ on what it means for a topic to be "important" rather than "critical" or for students to be "knowledgeable" on a topic rather than "demonstrate mastery"), we believe this to be an important consideration.

To gather respondents, we used a targeted snowball sample [4]. Initial invitations were repeatedly posted to the SIGCSE e-mail discussion list. Within this invitation was a request that the invitation be forwarded to other related mailing lists or forwarded directly to CS1 or CS2 instructors. This led to 143 respondents to the survey. (This and all future numbers treat a single respondent who answered questions about both the CS1 and CS2 as if they were two separate responses. As we are analyzing these two data sets separately, we feel this is less likely to cause confusion). Incomplete surveys were then pruned. After pruning we had 58 completed surveys about CS1 and 41 completed surveys on CS2.

3. RESULTS

It was clear, even before the survey response period was complete, it would be difficult to find any common definition of CS1 or CS2. Several respondents either added comments at the end of the survey or e-mailed us directly to discuss their difficulty responding to their survey. Most of these comments questioned our combining arrays and strings in a single topic. While agreeing that strings are important, the respondents either teach in languages that do not include arrays, such as Python, or utilize a heavily object-oriented style which prefers lists. Respondents suggested that this grouping showed a historical bias that was no longer reasonable. While these comments were too late for us to change our survey to capture these differences, they clearly point to an important deficiency in how even the most recent curricula describe what is learned in CS1 and CS2.

The responses we received about mixing arrays and strings provided a clear showing of how wide a range of material is subsumed under the CS1 and CS2 monikers. The comments left by respondents to the questions about CS2 more clearly showed the diversity of meanings of "CS2". Using the common [12, 5] and historical [1] definitions, we referred to the course as *CS2/Data Structures* throughout our survey. Yet, 5 out of 64 individuals (7.8%) added comments stating that CS2 was not their primary data structure course. At their institutions, CS2 now means "the course after CS1" and is stripped of any other connotation.

Given these two early findings, we also wanted to see if there was any agreement on either what topics were important in CS1 and CS2 courses or the capability of students at the end of these courses. To quantify this level of agreement, we evaluated our data using Fleiss' kappa [9]. Fleiss' kappa

Topic in LACS Curriculum	Topic in Survey
Split Topics	
Tracing, testing, debugging	Testing Debugging
Arrays, lists, strings	Arrays, strings
Searching, sorting	Sorting
Generalized Topics	
Streams, files	I/O (e.g., files, printing to screen)
Interfaces	Abstraction mechnisms (e.g., interfaces, abstract classes)
Exceptions	Error handling (e.g., exceptions)
Advanced structures	Other data structures
Combined Topics	
Anatomy of a class Inheritance	Object-oriented programming (e.g., inheritance, class anatomy)
Stacks, queues	Stacks, queues, lists
Added Topics	
	Style (e.g., indentation, variable names)

Table 2: Starting from the topics for CS1 and CS2 in the LACS Model Curriculum, we then made these changes to create our final list. The changes here are grouped by the reason for making the change.

evaluates the consistency of judges using categorical ratings and returns a score from 0 to 1. A score of 0 on Fleiss' kappa denotes complete disagreement amongst the judges; a score of 1 arises when the judges are in complete agreement. While there is no agreed upon standard for how to interpret these results, one guideline uses a linear binning of the results [15]. Each topic is evaluated independently using this metric, but we are interested in examining all of the results for each course. We therefore plotted these results using a radar plot. The results from CS1 can be seen in Figure 1(a) and the plot of CS2 results are found in Figure 2(a).

Fleiss' kappa is defined only for nominal data and treats all disagreements equally. In reality, the difference between whether a topic is "important" or "critical" is much less significant than the difference between a topic being "beneficial" and "unrelated". This could result in Figures 1(a) and 2(a) providing an overly dismal view of the level of agreement that actually exists. We therefore generated a second set of results to examine if there was at least agreement on the topics covered in each course. To perform this measurement, we recoded responses as 0 if a topic was unrelated to their course or students were incapable with the material and recoded the response as a 1 for all other responses. Thus encoded, Fleiss' kappa measures the agreement that the topic belongs in the course at all or that students end the course with any ability to perform this work. The results of this second analysis can be seen in Figure 1(b) for CS1 and Figure 2(b) for CS2.

4. ANALYSIS

The results seen in Figures 1 and 2 are very telling, especially when combined with the qualitative responses from the previous section. As we now discuss, there would appear to be little agreement as to what it means to be a CS1 or CS2 course. While there is more agreement as to which topics are important for CS2 students, this agreement comes with the significant caveat that few of the agreed upon topics include any data structure. We will now discuss the results from each course in turn.

Figure 1(a) shows that there is very little agreement as to either importance of topics in CS1 or students' ability after CS1. While there was some agreement on how important some of the most basic underpinning of programming (control constructs; methods, functions, subroutines; variables, type, expressions) were to respondents CS1 courses, that was about all that could be agreed upon. The next 4 topics with the highest levels of agreement are ones for which 57% to 78% of respondents stated that the topics had nothing to do with their courses. When examining students' abilities after CS1, there was only agreement on those topics which a majority of respondents never cover. The next highest kappa was only a 0.38 for control constructs. This low-level of agreement suggests that there is little common skill levels among students across different institutions.

We continue to see very little agreement when we limited our analysis to look at if topics were at all related to their course or students passing this course had any ability with the material. As Figure 1(b) shows, most agree that basic programming concepts are part of their CS1 course and that student passing CS1 have some ability in them. But there are still very significant disagreements on about half of the possible topics. These results show that while we can expect all students coming out of CS1 to have some knowledge of basic programming concepts, exactly which topics and the level of this expertise is going to vary greatly.

Figure 2(a) shows that CS2 has even less agreement than we found in CS1. While there continued to be some agreement on the four most basic topics, the next highest kappa we measured was a 0.46 for object-oriented programming concepts. These results show that there is less agreement on both the importance of these topics and on students ability after passing the course. Most of this decrease is explained by the increasing rate respondents reporting that a topic is at least partially related and that students complete their course with at least some ability. This effect can better be witnessed by the greatly increased agreement in Figure 2(b). Even when limiting our analysis to this binary analysis, we still find strong disagreements on several important data structures such as trees, graphs, and other data structures. These kappas all stay below 0.82 and several remain below 0.5.

These results are not due to the range of languages used

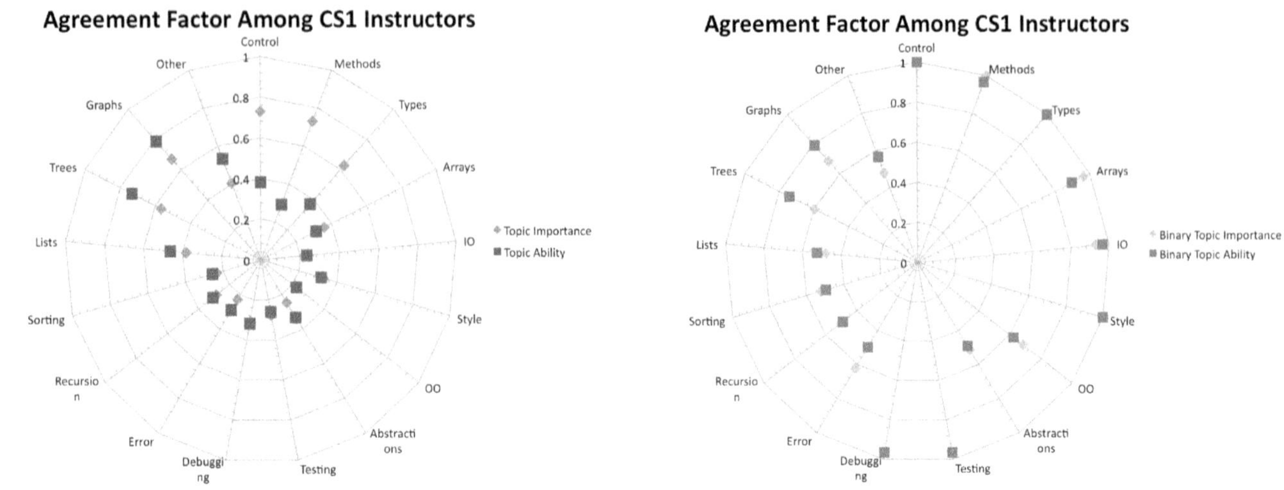

(a) Graph showing the level of agreement among CS1 instructors.

(b) Graph showing how much CS1 instructors agree that a topic has any importance or students had any ability in a topic.

Figure 1: Graph showing the level of agreement among CS1 instructors as to the importance of each topic in their CS1 course and how capable students were at the completion of that course. The level of agreement was measured using Fleiss' kappa. A result of 1 denotes perfect agreement and a result of 0 denotes no agreement.

in these courses. When we examined the results for object-oriented, procedural, and functional languages separately, our results were identical. This finding was true for every analysis: both CS1 and CS2 and both the importance and student abilities. Rather than being a result of the language used, these differences arise from the wide variety of styles and methodologies used by the respondents.

There are a number of important conclusions that one can draw from these results. While it appears that CS1 continues to be synonymous with an "Introduction to Programming" course, CS2 is no longer used strictly as another name for a course on data structures. Further, both CS1 and CS2 have been stretched to include a much wider range of activities than when originally proposed. As a result of these changes, there is little agreement on what topics are important to these courses and whether students passing these courses will have any knowledge of this material.

Continuing to use the CS1/CS2 terminology could cause more harm than good in the long run. These terms gives students a false sense that the skills learned in CS1 at one institution will automatically prepare them for CS2 at another school. Similarly, faculty need to know more than whether a class at another institution was called CS2 to determine if it could be used to replace a data structures course they offer. These results also suggest that we, as education researchers, must do more to place our results in context. To understand how others' research would apply at our own institutions, or to explain how our own research would apply to others, we must understand what the content of the course really is – just saying it is a CS1 or CS2 course provides very little explanation. By providing this extra information, we can make explicit the pedagogical assumptions that underlie the research and enable everyone to better understand the results.

5. CONCLUSION

While the community continues to use the terms CS1 and CS2, the reality has moved away from these terms having any meaning. In our survey of educators, we found that there is little agreement about how important a range of topics are to these courses. Moreover, we show that there exists only very weak agreement as to whether these topics even apply to each course. Sadly, there is even less agreement as how capable students are with these concepts after passing each courses. We think that these disagreements are part of, and vital to, the continued evolution of how we teach computer science. Rather than try and pigeonhole courses into terms we, as a community, have outgrown we instead propose that in research, course descriptions, and other important works, we provide more complete descriptions of the course and provide the context needed for others to understand what it includes.

Acknowledgements

The authors would like to thank Sarah Ford, R. Mark Meyer, Paul Gestwicki, the survey respondents, and the anonymous reviewers for their help in improving this paper.

6. REFERENCES

[1] W. F. Atchison, S. D. Conte, J. W. Hamblen, T. E. Hull, T. A. Keenan, W. B. Kehl, E. J. McCluskey, S. O. Navarro, W. C. Rheinboldt, E. J. Schweppe, W. Viavant, and D. M. Young, Jr. Curriculum 68: Recommendations for academic programs in computer science: a report of the acm curriculum committee on computer science. *Commun. ACM*, 11(3):151–197, 1968.

[2] R. H. Austing, B. H. Barnes, D. T. Bonnette, G. L. Engel, and G. Stokes. Curriculum '78: recommendations for the undergraduate program in

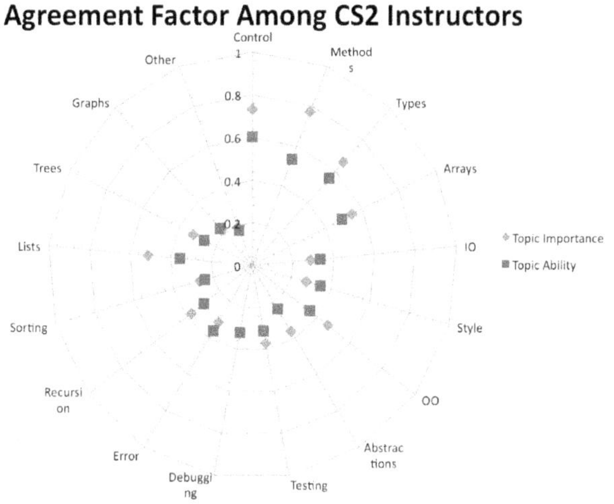

(a) Graph showing the level of agreement among CS2 instructors.

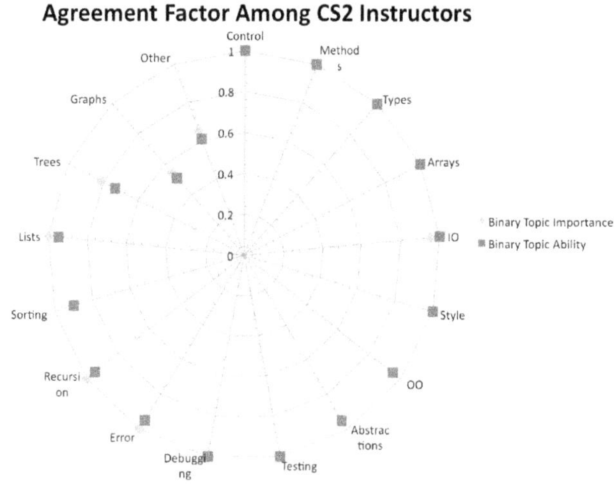

(b) Graph showing how much CS2 instructors agree that a topic has any importance or students had any ability in a topic.

Figure 2: Graph showing the level of agreement among CS2 instructors as to the importance of each topic in their CS2 course and how capable students were at the completion of that course. The level of agreement was measured using Fleiss' kappa. A result of 1 denotes perfect agreement and a result of 0 denotes no agreement.

computer science— a report of the acm curriculum committee on computer science. *Commun. ACM*, 22(3):147–166, 1979.

[3] J. Beidler, R. H. Austing, and L. N. Cassel. Computing programs in small colleges. *Commun. ACM*, 28(6):605–611, 1985.

[4] *Implementation and Analysis of Respondent Driven Sampling*, New York, NY, Nov. 2006. Springer New York.

[5] L. A. C. S. Consortium. A 2007 model curriculum for a liberal arts degree in computer science. *J. Educ. Resour. Comput.*, 7(2):2, 2007.

[6] S. D. Conte, J. W. Hamblen, W. B. Kehl, S. O. Navarro, W. C. Rheinboldt, D. M. Young, Jr., and W. F. Atchinson. An undergraduate program in computer science—preliminary recommendations. *Commun. ACM*, 8(9):543–552, 1965.

[7] J. Gal-Ezer, T. Vilner, and E. Zur. Has the paradigm shift in cs1 a harmful effect on data structures courses: a case study. In *SIGCSE '09: Proceedings of the 40th ACM technical symposium on Computer science education*, pages 126–130, New York, NY, USA, 2009. ACM.

[8] E. Howe, M. Thornton, and B. W. Weide. Components-first approaches to cs1/cs2: principles and practice. In *SIGCSE '04: Proceedings of the 35th SIGCSE technical symposium on Computer science education*, pages 291–295, New York, NY, USA, 2004. ACM.

[9] J. J. Randolph. Free-marginal multirater kappa: An alternative to fleiss' fixed-marginal multirater kappa. In *Joensuu University Learning and Instruction Symposium*, Joensuu, Finland, 2005. Available at: `http://www.eric.ed.gov/contentdelivery/servlet/ERICServlet?accno=ED490661`.

[10] H. Roumani. Practice what you preach: full separation of concerns in cs1/cs2. In *SIGCSE '06: Proceedings of the 37th SIGCSE technical symposium on Computer science education*, pages 491–494, New York, NY, USA, 2006. ACM.

[11] SIGPLAN programming language curriculum workshop. *SIGPLAN Notices*, 43(11), 2008.

[12] C. The Joint Task Force on Computing Curricula. Computing curricula 2001. *J. Educ. Resour. Comput.*, page 1, 2001.

[13] A. B. Tucker. Computing curricula 1991. *Commun. ACM*, 34(6):68–84, 1991.

[14] H. M. Walker and G. M. Schneider. A revised model curriculum for a liberal arts degree in computer science. *Commun. ACM*, 39(12):85–95, 1996.

[15] Fleiss' kappa. In *Wikipedia*, Retrieved 4 Sept. 2009. Available at: `http://en.wikipedia.org/wiki/Fleiss'_kappa`.

Braided Teaching in Secondary CS Education: Contexts, Continuity, and the Role of Programming

Arno Pasternak
Fritz-Steinhoff Gesamtschule Hagen and
Technische Universität Dortmund
44227 Dortmund, Germany
arno.pasternak@cs.tu-dortmund.de

Jan Vahrenhold
Technische Universität Dortmund
Faculty of Computer Science
44227 Dortmund, Germany
jan.vahrenhold@cs.tu-dortmund.de

ABSTRACT

In this paper, we propose a new approach to thinking about and implementing Computer Science curricula in secondary education. The characteristic feature is to organize the items to be taught into what we call "strands" which then can be interlaced during the course. This naturally leads to a spiral curriculum in secondary Computer Science education. In the view of our proposed approach, we also comment on the role of programming in secondary education.

Categories and Subject Descriptors

K.3.2 [**Computers and Education**]: Computer and Information Science Education

General Terms

Theory

Keywords

Curriculum, Contexts, Continuity, Programming

1. INTRODUCTION

In response to the diminishing or simply non-existent curriculum credit for Computer Science in secondary education, educators and researchers have developed transdisciplinary or multidisciplinary approaches to introduce and teach Computer Science concepts in Science or Arts classes [14, 15, 18]. The subject matter of such a course, e.g. Bioinformatics, then provides a natural context in which Computer Science concepts can be embedded.

Recently, a multi-year effort of a large group of German educators and researchers resulted in "Educational Standards for Computer Science in Lower Secondary Education" (see [4] for an overview). These standards were modeled after the National Council of Teachers of Mathematics' standards for Mathematics [19] and describe the competence standards that should have been reached at the end of tenth grade (assuming that Computer Science is taught at least one session per week starting in fifth grade). An open research and implementation issue, however, is to define concrete teaching units that can be used to achieve these goals.

Contexts.

The contributors to the above-mentioned German standards have suggested that teaching units should be context-based: students should be able to see how the subject matter taught in class relates to everyday life. The contributors suggest to follow the "Context-based Chemistry" approach proposed for secondary Chemistry education [21]; a closer look at these two fields shows, that Chemistry indeed is facing almost the same problems as Computer Science—see the synopsis by Gilbert [12] who discusses four different concepts of "context".

It has been reported that contextualized courses on college level lead to an increasing motivation of the students and effectiveness of the course—see, e.g., [1, 15, 25]. Unfortunately, Computer Science in secondary education can also be implemented as an Information and Communication Technology class (see [17] for a discussion of the implications thereof), and thus a purely application-based context such as word processing is not suited to foster the understanding of Computer Science in the spirit of *Computational Thinking* [29]. What is needed is a concept that subsumes the notion of "contexts" but prevents them (and thus Computer Science) from being misinterpreted as a collection of isolated applications of Information and Communication Technology.

Continuity.

One of the distinguishing features of Computer Science is the breadth of the field which encompasses subject matters close to Engineering as well as subject matters from (Discrete) Mathematics. This breadth provides a rich source of topics for secondary education and gives educators the potential of reaching out to students with widely varying interests and aptitudes. The lack of (sufficient) curriculum credits, however, has actually turned this breadth into a major impediment to implementing a curriculum that follows the "spiral" approach advocated by Bruner [5]. In his seminal work, Bruner elaborates on the hypothesis that "any subject can be taught effectively in some intellectually honest form to any child at any stage of development" [5, p. 33]. Consequently, this approach requires multiple iterations over the subject to reach an understanding at adult level. The philosophy behind Bruner's approach is widely accepted and has led to the identification of, e.g., *fundamental ideas* [24]

SIGCSE'10, March 10–13, 2010, Milwaukee, Wisconsin, USA.

and - with some grain of salt - *great principles* [8] in Computer Science—see [30] for a empirical determination of such concepts present in Computer Science courses on university level. If Computer Science is taught with little curriculum credit or as an elective, there is little room for an educator to visit subject matters more than once while at the same time covering the variety of subject matters deemed "necessary" by administrators, parents, and students.

The Role of Programming.

Programming has always been an integral part of Computer Science up to the point that well-designed visual programming languages and environments such as Alice, Logo, Scratch, or Greenfoot are used as entry points to Computer Science in primary and (lower) secondary education. Also, open source software projects have been used to increase interest and improve retention at college level [16].

In the general public's view, however, Computer Science often is misidentified with programming exclusively: In a recent issue of the *Communications of the ACM*, Felleisen and Krishnamurthi observed that a "large part of the [enrollment and acceptance] problem is due to how computing is portrayed to schools, parents, the people who allocate the education budgets, and the students" [9]. Freeman's immediate rebuke [10] of their viewpoint that "programming [...] is our field's single most valuable skill" [9] (instead bringing up the ability to abstract) clearly shows the differentiation of programming and algorithmics and, in this respect, is exemplary of several non-programming based approaches to outreach and curriculum (re-)design—see, e.g., [3, 29]. In passing, we note that a study undertaken in 1999 reported on a significant decrease in the percentage of introductory Computer Science courses for *non-majors* on college level that actually taught programming [27]. Unfortunately, no data more recently acquired is available.

In recent years, the main question related to programming was not whether or not to teach programming but *when* to teach programming and when to introduce object-orientation; as an illustrative example, see [2]. Independent of which answer to the above question a particular educator prefers, he or she must judge any new suggestion for how to implement a given Computer Science curriculum also by how programming can be embedded in the resulting course.

2. STRANDS AND BRAIDED TEACHING

Definition.

The central concept of our approach is to organize the subject matters to be taught in secondary education not by topic but along what we call *strands*. This organizational concept is general enough to subsume the concept of a *context* and, as we will demonstrate, allows for a smoother linkage of different subject matters in class.

DEFINITION 1. *A* strand *is a sequence of items addressed in class that satisfies the following criteria:*

1. *The items can be assigned to a well-defined subject matter (by their structure or their content).*

2. *The subject matter is identifiable and recognizable to the students throughout the sequence.*

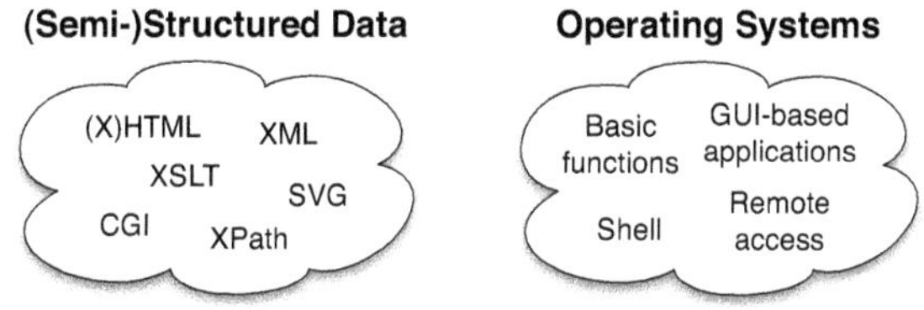

Figure 1: Strands: Sequences of items assigned to a subject matter by structure (left) or content (right).

3. *The subject matter is being presented from more than one point of view or embedded in more than one context.*

4. *The sequence of items is addressed in more than one teaching unit.*

While the first criterion is of an objective nature, the remaining three criteria depend on structural and pedagogical decisions made by the educator responsible for the course. Most notably, the above definition does not impose any particular order on the items in the sequence. As the examples given below will illustrate, the particular order of teaching the items in a strand will be subject to external factors such as curriculum design or personal preferences of the educator.

Another important aspect is that a strand is defined to appear in more than one teaching unit. While, as we will sketch below, one can construct a strand for a clearly delineated subject matter such as *operating systems*, our approach forbids this subject matter to be taught *en bloc* and thus isolated from other topics and concepts in Computer Science. At first, this may seem overly restrictive; in practice, however, it provides the educator with more leeway to present concepts from different viewpoints (or, in the terminology of Denning's *Great Principles* [8], through different windows of computing mechanics) and thus to better reach out to students with varying interests and aptitudes.

Braided teaching then aims at covering the contents in a given curriculum by a collection of strands that are interlaced wherever appropriate. Interlacing the strands and presenting the items embedded in more than one context has to be planned carefully, since using too many context switches will present a ragged, incoherent, and confusing image of Computer Science. On the other hand, findings from the "Chemistry in Context" project indicate that teaching units that stay too long within a single context lead to a rapid decline in the students' interest [23]. Furthermore, staying too long within a context may result in misidentifying the concept taught with the context and thus counteract the spiral curriculum's intended effect of enabling transfers of principles across contexts.

Examples.

As a first illustrative example, we present a strand that contains items related to *(semi-)structured data* (Figure 1, left). The structural concept behind all of these items, the hierarchical or semi-structural organization of data is easily identifiable and recognizable; in fact, it represents the fundamental idea of *structured dissection* [24]. Also, the subject matter can be visited more than once and be taught in increasing complexity from static and dynamic HTML to queries on data represented in XML. Since the strand contains *scalable vector graphics* and may be extended to also address automata for validating XML documents according to a given schema, it is not restricted to web data.

The occurrence of SVG in the strand on (semi-)structured data illustrates another consequence of our approach: due to the requirement that strands must not be taught *en bloc*, the subject matters will be presented interlaced. Also, items may be assigned to more than one strand. In the above example, SVG may be a point where the strand on (semi-) structured data can be linked with a strand on multimedia.

Another (content-based) strand which has been used by one of the authors in class is organizing topics related to *operating systems* (Figure 1, right). The details of this course will be presented in Section 3.

Related Concepts.

It remains to discuss how the concept of strands relates to other organizational concepts in Computer Science education. Besides the canonical topic-by-topic sequence which can be trivially distinguished from a strand, the two most relevant concepts are *contexts* and *fundamental ideas.*

In the terminology of the Gilbert's discussion [12], *contexts* as they are used (not only) in Computer Science on college level and (higher) secondary education are mainly a "reciprocity between concepts and applications" [12, p. 967] whereas contexts in (lower) secondary education mainly relate to "topics and people's activities that are considered of importance to the lives of communities within the society" [12, p. 969].

In the terminology of our approach, a context (or a much larger project) can be defined as a sequence of items groups by content. Since, in general, the presentation of these items from multiple viewpoints and their distribution over more than one teaching unit will introduce unpleasant continuity breaks, we prefer to think of a context (in the traditional sense) as a temporally coherent frame in which items from one or more strands can be interleaved and related to applications or social circumstances.

A *fundamental idea* [5, 24] is a concept that is general enough that its mastery allows for transfers of principles (as opposed to transfers of instructions to activities). Fundamental ideas (such as *modularity* or *verification*) thus represent concepts of the underlying science and are exemplified by well-chosen items; these items, just as the items in a strand, can be arranged according to a spiral curriculum, and in this respect, the strand on (semi-)structured data has a close resemblance to exemplifications of a fundamental idea. On the other hand, a strand (for instance the strand on operating systems) may also be comprised of items that belong to the same content, and thus not every strand resembles a fundamental idea. The major difference, however, between a strand and a fundamental idea is that by design a fundamental idea organizes items exclusively from the perspective of an educator. To qualify as a strand in the sense of Definition 1, the sequence of items must be arranged and taught in a way that is identifiable and recognizable by the students as well.

The concept of strands appears to be closely related to the concept of *threads* that has been implemented, e.g., at Georgia Tech [11]. In this system, students are given a choice from a collection of sequences of courses to fulfill the curriculum requirement and to prepare for their chosen career path. The concepts are related in the sense that each strand and thread has to fulfill the requirement that the items taught have to be coherent and not restricted to a single subject matter. Furthermore, the union of threads as well as the union of strands is required to cover the respective curriculum. In contrast to the concept presented in [11], our approach does not provides means for assembling a career-specific set of courses but is a concept for educators that wish to (re-)organize items to be taught in class according to a spiral curriculum, embedded into different contexts and possibly interlaced. Due to the fact that secondary education and education on university level are organized quite differently, the final distinguishing feature is that in a thread-based setting the choice which thread to follow is made by the students, whereas the strands to be used in teaching are selected by the educators.

3. PROGRAMMING AS A STRAND?

It may seem trivial to present any current *programming* course as a strand encompassing, e.g., "Sequence", "Control Structures", "Variables", and "Object/Class". A closer look, however, at Definition 1 reveals several shortcomings of this straightforward approach: the requirement that the common subject matter be identifiable and recognizable by the students can only be fulfilled if both students and educators are willing to accept programming as a higher-ranking concept on its own. It will be hard if not impossible, to present, say, control structures from more than one point of view. Finally, most current courses known to the authors that include programming do so in a blocked fashion, either as an entry point (see Section 1), as a programming-only course, or as a hands-on teaching unit in which the (algorithmic) concepts previously taught in class are being realized in a programming language.

In these shortcomings, the following assessment of programming (in contrast to algorithmics) made by the K–12 Computer Science curriculum task force is manifested:

> "While programming is a central activity in computer science, it is only a tool that provides a window into a much richer academic and professional field." [26, p. 6]

Interlacing Programming and Strands.

Especially in (lower) secondary education, students are able experience the power of computers and software without having to program themselves. Furthermore, the extent to which the average student can realize programs is unlikely to result in assignments that can compete (regarding their attractiveness) with easy-to-access free software available on the internet. In this respect, Astrachan's Law ("Do not give an assignment that computes something that is more easily figured out without a computer." [22]) may have to be phrased even more restrictive when applied to lower secondary education.

We propose to break with the traditional habit of teaching programming *en bloc* and to treat programming as if it were just another strand where the items are embedded in more than one context. Admittedly, this still does not provide us with multiple perspectives on `if`-statements; it tremendously helps, however, with presenting programming as a tool in the sense of the above assessment.

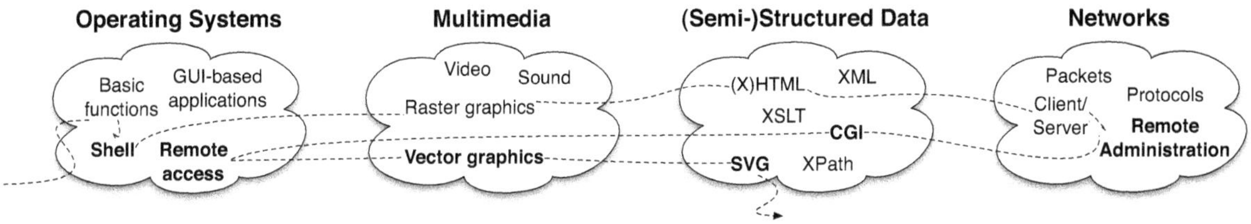

Figure 2: Braided teaching: In the (abbreviated) example depicted here, the educator has decided to visit various strands along the dashed line. Algorithmic concepts and items from "programming as a tool" are interlaced with the items in bold face.

Example.

One of the authors has designed classes for grades 9 and 10 organized according to four major strands: *operating systems*, *multimedia*, *(semi-)structured data*, and *networks* (see Figure 2; note, however, that the collection of items depicted is reduced for ease of presentation and thus not comprehensive. Most notable, the interlaced strand on *algorithmics* is left out to unclutter the picture). In an introductory phase, students learn how to use shell commands for working with files and directories as well as for an exemplary installation of a small software package. Elementary programming concepts are introduced as means of automating certain tasks in shell scripts. After a short switch to the *multimedia* strand, a first visit is paid to *(semi-)structured data* strand where students experience (X)HTML not only as means for encoding web pages but also for representing structured data. The following teaching units obviously are located in the *networks* strand.

In the next phase of the course, the students revisit the *(semi-)structured* strand and learn how to use CGI for structured documents automatically and with dynamically varying content. These scripts then must be uploaded to servers. Coming full circle to one of the initial parts of the course, vector graphics and their structured representation using the SVG format are discussed and used for again interlacing with "programming as a tool".

4. IMPLICATIONS

An intended side-effect of interlacing programming with strands is that programming is put on the same level of importance as all other strands and thus is no more (but also no less) important than any specific strand. Consequently, the question of which programming language to use (or whether and when to introduce objects) is no more important than which other strands to teach. If an educator wishes to do so, he or she can actually choose a programming language such that it supports the contexts in which items are embedded and not vice versa.

Braided Teaching Using Tcl/Tk.

To illustrate the flexibility stated above, we point out that an approach to braided teaching could be based, e.g., on the Tcl/Tk programming language [20]. This particular choice is not due to features of this language *per se* (but see Warren [28] advocating the use of scripting languages) but motivated by the fact that Tcl/Tk seamlessly integrates with a shell. In the context of braided teaching, this is a major advantage over other languages or microworld-based environments, since the student do not regard programming as switching to a different environment. Furthermore, the Tcl/Tk shell allows for an interpreter-based approach to Logo-like graphics, thus providing the agreed-upon advantages [6] of having direct interaction and visual feedback—see also [13] for comments on how to reach out to students with Tcl/Tk. We note in passing that even the answer to whether and when to introduce object-orientation is not preempted by our selection of the programming language.

As mentioned above, the collection of strands reflects a pedagogical and sometimes personalized decision of the educator (for example, to start from an operating systems strand), and this is especially true for the choice of the programming language. One could just as well imagine a collection of strands that naturally leads to a completely different selection of a programming language. To some extent, the development of Alice [7] can also be seen as the selection of a programming language based upon the requirements of a *virtual worlds* context.

5. CONCLUSIONS

In this paper, we have advocated what we call *braided teaching*: a new way of thinking about the organization of items when implementing a Computer Science curriculum in secondary education. This approach relies on grouping the items along strands, and its main conceptual advantage is that it allows for an easier implementation of a spiral curriculum while at the same time giving the educator more leeway with didactical decisions. We have exemplified our approach and observed that it allows for a more seamless integration of programming giving it the role delineated in the ACM K–12 Computer Science curriculum.

Our approach as formulated in this paper pertains to (lower) secondary education, and thus two directions for future research present themselves: The obvious task is to demonstrate both in theory and in practice that braided teaching can be instantiated with a reasonable collection of strands and that the effects expected by following the spiral curriculum can be observed as well. The first author's experience with teaching along single strands leads us to believe so. Also, it remains to investigate how this concept can be extended to propaedeutic pre-college or freshman courses and how it might be combined with existing organization concepts on college level.

6. REFERENCES

[1] C. Alt, O. Astrachan, J. Forbes, R. Lucic, and S. Rodger. Social networks generate interest in computer science. In D. Baldwin, P. Tymann, S. Haller, and I. Russel, editors, *Proceedings of the 37th SIGCSE Technical Symposium on Computer Science Education*, pages 438–442, 2006.

[2] O. Astrachan, K. Bruce, E. Koffman, M. Kölling, and S. Reges. Resolved: Objects Early has failed. In W. Dann, T. Naps, P. Tymann, D. Baldwin, and J. D. Dougherty, editors, *Proceedings of the 36th SIGCSE Technical Symposium on Computer Science Education*, pages 451–452, 2005.

[3] T. Bell, I. H. Witten, and M. Fellows. Computer Science Unplugged: An enrichment and extension programme for primary-aged children. `http://www.google.com/educators/activities/unpluggedTeachersDec2006.pdf`, 2002.

[4] T. Brinda, H. Puhlmann, and C. Schulte. Bridging ICT and CS: Educational standards for computer science in lower secondary education. In *ITiCSE '09: Proceedings of the 14th Annual ACM SIGCSE Conference on Innovation and Technology in Computer Science Education*, pages 288–292, 2009.

[5] J. S. Bruner. *The Process of Education.* Harvard University Press, Cambridge, MA, 1960.

[6] D. H. Clements and J. S. Meredith. Research on Logo: Effects and efficacy. *Journal of Computing in Childhood Education*, 4:263–290, 1993.

[7] W. P. Dann, S. Cooper, and R. Pausch. *Learning to Program with Alice.* Pearson Education, London, UK, second edition, 2009.

[8] P. J. Denning. Great principles of computing. *Communications of the ACM*, 46(11):15–20, Nov. 2003.

[9] M. Felleisen and S. Krishnamurthi. Viewpoint: Why computer science doesn't matter. *Communications of the ACM*, 52(7):37–40, July 2009.

[10] P. A. Freeman. Letter to the editor: Computer science *Does* matter. *Communications of the ACM*, 52(9):8, Sept. 2009.

[11] M. Furst, C. Isbell, and M. Guzdial. Threads^{TM}: How to restructure a computer science curriculum for a flat world. In I. Russell, S. Haller, J. D. Dougherty, S. Rodger, and G. Lewandowski, editors, *Proceedings of the 38th SIGCSE Technical Symposium on Computer Science Education*, pages 420–424, 2007.

[12] J. K. Gilbert. On the nature of "context" in chemical education. *International Journal of Science Education*, 28(9):957–976, July 2006.

[13] S. Graham and C. Latulipe. CS girls rock: Sparking interest in computer science and debunking the stereotypes. In S. Grissom, D. Knox, and D. Joyce, editors, *Proceedings of the 34th SIGCSE Technical Symposium on Computer Science Education*, pages 322–326, 2003.

[14] S. Hambrusch, C. Hoffmann, J. T. Korb, M. Haugan, and A. L. Hosking. A multidisciplinary approach towards computational thinking for science majors. In S. Fitzgerald, M. Guzdial, G. Lewandowski, S. Wolfman, and T. J. Cortina, editors, *Proceedings of the 40th SIGCSE Technical Symposium on Computer Science Education*, pages 183–187, 2009.

[15] M. Hart, J. P. Early, and D. Brylow. A novel approach to K-12 CS education: Linking mathematics and computer science. In S. Rodger, J. Dougherty, M. Guzdial, S. Fitzgerald, and E. Walker, editors, *Proceedings of the 39th SIGCSE Technical Symposium on Computer Science Education*, pages 286–290, 2008.

[16] G. W. Hislop, H. J. C. Ellis, A. B. Tucker, and S. Dexter. Panel: Using open source software to engage students in computer science education. In S. Fitzgerald, M. Guzdial, G. Lewandowski, S. Wolfman, and T. J. Cortina, editors, *Proceedings of the 40th SIGCSE Technical Symposium on Computer Science Education*, pages 134–135, 2009.

[17] J. Hromkovič. Contributing to general education by teaching informatics. In R. Mittermeir, editor, *Proceedings of the Second International Conference in Informatics in Secondary Schools - Evolution and Perspectives*, volume 4226 of *Lecture Notes in Computer Science*, pages 25–37. Springer, 2006.

[18] C.-C. Lin, M. Zhang, B. Beck, and G. Olsen. Embedding computer science concepts in K-12 curricula. In S. Fitzgerald, M. Guzdial, G. Lewandowski, S. Wolfman, and T. J. Cortina, editors, *Proceedings of the 40th SIGCSE Technical Symposium on Computer Science Education*, pages 539–543, 2009.

[19] National Council of Teachers of Mathematics. *Principles and Standards for School Mathematics.* National Council of Teachers of Mathematics, 2000.

[20] J. K. Ousterhout. *Tcl and the Tk Toolkit.* Addison-Wesley, Reading, MA, 1994.

[21] I. Parchmann, C. Gräsel, A. Baer, P. Nentwig, R. Demuth, B. Ralle, and the ChiK Project Group. "Chemie im Kontext": A symbiotic implementation of a context-based teaching and learning approach. *International Journal of Science Education*, 28(9):1041–1062, July 2006.

[22] N. Parlante. Astrachan's law. *Inroads – the SIGCSE Bulletin*, 35(4):26–27, Dec. 2003.

[23] B. Ralle, D.-S. Di Fuccia, and W. Schwarz. Lehrer planen gemeinsam - Ein Einblick in die Arbeit des Projektes Chemie im Kontext. *Der mathematische und naturwissenschaftliche Unterricht*, 58(7):388–393, 2005. In German.

[24] A. Schwill. Fundamental ideas – rethinking computer science education. *Learning and Leading with Technology*, 25(1):28–31, Sept. 1997.

[25] A. E. Tew, B. Dorn, W. D. Leahy, Jr., and M. Guzdial. Context as support for learning computer organization. *ACM Journal on Educational Resources in Computing*, 8(3), Oct. 2008. Article 8, 18 Pages.

[26] A. Tucker, F. Deek, J. Jones, D. McCowan, C. Stephenson, and A. Verno. A model curriculum for K-12 computer science: Final report of the ACM K-12 task force curriculum committee, 2004.

[27] M. Urban-Lurain and D. J. Weinshank. Is there a role for programming in non-major computer science courses? In *Proceedings of the 30th Annual ASEE/IEEE Conference on Frontiers in Education*, pages T2B-7–T2B-11, 2000.

[28] P. Warren. Teaching programming using scripting languages. *Journal of Computing Sciences in Colleges*, 17(2):205–216, 2001.

[29] J. M. Wing. Computational thinking. *Communications of the ACM*, 49(3):33–35, Mar. 2006.

[30] A. Zendler and C. Spannagel. Empirical foundations of central concepts for computer science education. *ACM Journal on Educational Resources in Computing*, 8(2), June 2008. Article 6, 15 Pages.

Writing in an Upper-Level CS Course

Alan Garvey
Truman State University
100 E. Normal St.
Kirksville, MO 63501
660-665-9195
agarvey@truman.edu

ABSTRACT

This paper discusses the use of writing as a teaching approach for an upper level computer science course. In describing my experiences, I hope to encourage those schools/teachers who are considering incorporating writing into such a course. Many different kinds of writing are compared and contrasted. Attention is paid to practicalities of the writing process and of the demands made of faculty in these writing-based courses.

Categories and Subject Descriptors

K.3.2 [**Computer and Education**]: Computer and Information Science Education – *computer science education*

General Terms

Documentation, Management, Theory

Keywords

Writing to Learn, Writing Across the Curriculum, Writing in Computer Science Classes, communication skills

1. INTRODUCTION

I have been teaching Programming Languages as a writing-enhanced course at my public liberal arts and sciences university for 8 years. Over the years I have incorporated writing into the course in many different ways. This paper looks at some of those kinds of writing, plus a number of other ideas about how to incorporate writing into this or other courses.

To summarize, at my university a "writing-enhanced" course has desired *outcomes* relating to: *cognition* (using writing as a mode of learning, exhibiting critical thinking, showing audience awareness), *process* (engaging in deep revision, assessing their own writing, copy-editing as a regular habit) and *product* (being able to write clear, coherent, well-organized prose; demonstrating a command of syntax, style and tone; and exhibiting mastery of punctuation, usage and formatting conventions). One major goal in these courses is to facilitate critical thinking on the part of the student.

These desired outcomes leave quite a bit of freedom for the instructor to incorporate writing into the course in many ways.

SIGCSE'10, March 10–13, 2010, Milwaukee, Wisconsin, USA.

Perhaps the most obvious is the traditional 20 page research paper and that is still a possibility, but there are many other ways to teach using writing.

The topic of writing in computer science classes comes up fairly often in the computer science education literature [2, 3, 5, 6, 7, 9] (and many other papers not cited here). Often there is an assumption that writing for computer science students should be taught in a writing class [2, 6, 7], perhaps one that is team taught with a writing teacher [2, 5, 7]. These papers are full of helpful ideas about how to teach writing, how to evaluate student writing and why writing is important for our students. The history of the *writing across the curriculum* (WAC) [1] movement as it relates to computer science is very interestingly discussed in a recent SIGCSE paper [5] and clearly my university's writing enhanced requirement is a direct response to the WAC initiative.

In this paper, I attempt to illustrate how writing can be used for teaching in a standard, upper level computer science major course: Programming Languages. One motivation for writing this paper is as a response to that recent SIGCSE paper [5] which suggests that there is a distinction between the kind of writing suggested by WAC initiatives [1], which primarily are about using "writing to learn" (WTL), and the kind of "writing in the discipline" (WID) that is expected of computer professionals. These are seen as being so distinct as to require "bridge" assignments to get from one to the other. I don't question the usefulness of the assignments described, but I question the discrete distinction made between the categories and would suggest that there is really more of a continuum. Perhaps my discomfort is just with the somewhat limited idea of what counts as "writing in the discipline". Different kinds of writing are appropriate and useful in different contexts, but I think that practicing computer scientists in industry and academe are best served by being familiar with a broader selection of writing approaches and styles. And we need to recognize that even the most formal, technical writing often starts with an informal process of just getting the words written down.

2. KINDS OF STUDENT WRITING

Many kinds of writing assignments are available to instructors using writing as a way to teach a computer science course. This section attempts to define several categories of assignment and lists particular examples of each category in several subsections.

2.1 Summarizing Assignments

a. abstracts
b. reaction statements and questions
c. textbook summaries
d. lecture summaries

The idea with this category is to briefly summarize some kind of longer material. Being able to read a complex work, pick out the most important concepts and explain those in understandable language is difficult for many students. It often requires not just being able to understand and digest complex readings, but being able to fit them into a larger context of ideas.

Abstracts are formal, impersonal brief summaries usually of formal papers or texts. Learning to write in this formal, impersonal, unopinionated, factual style is useful in many other contexts in life. Being able to fairly summarize the position of another when describing your own position, for example, can be helpful.

Reaction statements are almost the opposite of abstracts. Here the focus is on the personal, perhaps informal reaction of the student to the material. If badly done this can just lead to rants, but carefully thought out reactions can facilitate deep thinking about a topic. I find that having the students come up with questions that they have after reading a paper can be a good way to get them to think critically and not take everything they read at face value. Questions can range from "what does this concept mean" to "why didn't they consider this alternate approach to this issue" to "how does this idea fit with that other idea we've discussed previously".

Textbook and lecture summaries are a way to force students to spend some time thinking about class-related materials. Among other things, these can be great aids in preparing for exams.

For all but the lecture summaries, these kinds of writing can be required of the students BEFORE the material is discussed in class, as a way to get the students to come to class prepared to engage in meaningful discussions of the concepts.

2.2 Programs as Writing

a. documentation requirements in assignments

b. organization as a grading criteria

c. code walkthroughs

d. peer reviews of code

Presumably all CS professors should always evaluate all student programs as writing at some level. It is never acceptable for a student to submit undocumented, badly organized, incomprehensible code. But, in practice, we often focus on functionality over form.

The idea with focusing on programs as writing is to emphasize the importance of the human side of code readability. It is important that code compile and execute correctly (the computer side of readability) but it is equally important that code be understandable for other humans.

One way to approach this is through code walkthroughs. These are quite common in industry these days, but perhaps not as typical in the classroom. We often present students with what we consider to be high quality code and use that to explain and illustrate concepts. But with a code walkthrough the idea is to get the students to evaluate code critically and decide as a group whether a particular implementation is clear, well organized (and, of course, whether it is functionally correct).

A somewhat more unusual (in my experience at least) way to think about programs as writing is to adapt a standard Writing Across the Curriculum idea of *peer review* to programs. Have students produce "first drafts" of a solution to a programming assignment, then give each other feedback on those solutions. This approach has some interesting ramifications:

- It broadens students awareness by showing different ways of solving a problem.
- It helps those students who were seriously struggling with an assignment (and whose own peer evaluations will probably be quite negative) to see a way of solving the problem. This also brings to the fore an opportunity to discuss plagiarism and how it is okay to adapt the idea of another person, but not okay to "steal their code".
- It grounds more abstract discussions of desirable programming practice in particular examples: "here's why this particular organizational strategy doesn't work in this case", "this variable name is ambiguous in a way you might not have considered", "this particular code layout is irritating to read".

2.3 Reviews/critiques of the writing of others

a. review of CS books and articles

b. review/discussion of popular writing about technical subjects

c. reviews that compare/contrast multiple articles and introduce students' own opinions (can be creative, but also requires some argument to defend the opinion)

Section 2.1 describes the summarizing of technical texts. This category is focused on more critical/review kinds of writing. In some ways this kind of writing is much harder. The writers have to both understand the other writing well enough to explain it, and then, in addition, add their own critical commentary on the writing.

One way to do this is to have the students read a technical article or book, say a CACM article or an article from a technical collection or a conference paper. Finding articles from these kind of publications that are at a level where an undergraduate can make sense out of them can sometimes be difficult, but such articles exist. Of course, finding articles that students can understand well enough to criticize effectively can be daunting.

Perhaps a somewhat easier way to approach this issue is to have students critique popular writing about technical issues. Articles from *Time Magazine* or *Newsweek*, or from the *New York Times* can be examined for their accuracy and clarity. Sometimes these articles are quite good, but often they are at least garbled if not just plain technically inaccurate. Getting students to realize that media coverage of something they are familiar with isn't always accurate can have the useful side effect of making them more critical of articles they encounter from outside of their expertise.

My favorite kind of writing assignment in this category has students compare and contrast multiple articles that address the same topic. For example, I give them two articles that address the issue of what programming languages will look like far in the future. Figure 1 shows an example of an assignment in this category. This particular assignment has worked well to focus discussion about the future of programming languages. Sometimes it is necessary to push students to do more than list issues from each paper and just say "I agree" or "I disagree". A well written paper of this sort will demonstrate critical and creative thinking about a complex topic.

Programming Language of the Future Assignment

```
This writing assignment asks you to briefly
(5-7 pages, 1500 to 2000 words) write about
what you think the programming language of
the future will look like, while also
commenting on the thoughts of Paul Graham
and Gregory Wilson on this topic.
```

One form of writing that is encountered quite regularly in magazines such as the *New Yorker*, the *Atlantic*, the *New York Review of Books* and others is the book review essay. In this form of writing the reviewer discusses a recent book (or, often, more than one book on a related topic) while also injecting their own, often strongly felt, opinions about the topic the books address. When this is done well the reader comes away with the feeling that they understand, at least vaguely, what the reviewed books are about, as well as seeing them from the unified perspective provided by the reviewer.

For this assignment, I want you to write in this format about the programming language of the future. The two works that I want you to discuss as part of your essay are The Hundred-Year Language by Paul Graham (also available in his book *Hackers and Painters* which is available through Safari) and Extensible Programming for the 21st Century by Gregory V. Wilson from ACM Queue Magazine. (Be sure to notice that the Wilson article has six sections, each with their own webpage.) I should come away from your paper with some idea of what Graham and Wilson think about this topic, as well as a clear idea of what you think.

You should write this paper for an audience of informed computer scientists (rather than a typical *New Yorker* reader, for example) who have not read the articles in question. You are expected to follow the conventions of academic prose. You are not required to cite other sources besides the two papers you are given, but, if you do refer to other sources, you should cite them using a standard academic citation style.

Figure 1. Sample Assignment

2.4 More creative kinds of writing

a. speculative writing about the future

b. taking a side and arguing for a particular perspective on a controversial issue

c. any writing that involves opinions rather than just "facts"

The previous writing categories described here involve either paraphrasing or commenting on or otherwise responding to the words of other writers. Later categories often involve writing in a style that is carefully prescribed and not particularly open to creative expression. (Some may see this as a criticism of these writing styles, but that is not my intention here.) Both of these kinds of writing are useful, but in this category I'm gathering together the kinds of writing that require true creativity on the part of the student. In my experience, many students find this a particularly scary prospect.

The assignment shown in Figure 1 involves students reviewing papers that comment on what future programming languages might look like, as well as speculating themselves on the topic. That speculative aspect of the assignment probably best fits into the category I'm describing here. Well done responses to this prompt will not just comment on and slightly extend the ideas in the reviewed papers. Instead they will define whole new categories or perhaps find ways to organize the possibilities that open up new ways of thinking about them.

Another kind of paper in this category doesn't directly bring in the works of others, but simply asks the student to take a side and argue for a position on a controversial issue. The best prompts in this area don't have "right answers" and are open to disagreement. That might be because they involve ethical issues that society as a whole doesn't agree on, or because they involve more aesthetic or subjective concerns. Still the best papers in this category won't just be rants about the writer's particular opinions on an issue. They will be organized, well argued stands that try to persuade others to agree with them on the issue at hand. An example of this is a paper that advocates the use of a particular programming language for CS 1, making persuasive arguments, but perhaps invoking the students' own experiences as well.

I will limit myself to non-fiction prose writing for this paper, but obviously there is a whole category of creative technical writing that falls under the heading of sci-fi/fantasy. On rare occasion I've had students respond to a writing prompt by producing a dialogue or other short work of fiction. While this is often not an appropriate response to the given assignment, there are certainly real-world situations where such writing can be very effective. The trick is recognizing when more fictional approaches might succeed. One of the best replies to Searle's Chinese Room argument that I have ever encountered is in an extra short story by Terry Bisson in which two sentient computers discuss these beings they encounter that appear to be "sentient meat". (quoted in [8], pg 96)

2.5 Scientific method research papers

Probably one of the most common kinds of writing assignment given in computer science classes is the classic scientific method paper, meant to be in the style of journal articles that introduce, say, a new algorithm or architecture, argue for why it is superior to previous state of the art, then conduct some kind of statistical experiments to quantify the scientific results. Since most journal and conference articles are (at least ideally) of this form, we see a need to include this kind of writing in our classes.

Having undergraduate students truly write a paper of this sort (including coming up with the innovation that the paper is about) is probably beyond what these students are able to do, especially in a classroom setting. One strategy to address that includes using this kind of writing for a simple lab exercise, where there is no need for true innovation, just investigation on the students' part.

Another strategy I sometimes use is to have the students do a write up of this sort for an already well-known algorithm or data structure, for example, Quicksort or SkipLists. Even with this simplification, the experimental results section is usually still not achievable, due both to the time constraints and students' statistical abilities. But we can talk at length about what such a section SHOULD look like and getting them thinking about these issues, preparing at least a few of them for the time in graduate school when they might be ready to make such a contribution.

2.6 Interdisciplinary writing

Along with the commitment to writing in my university's curriculum there is a strong commitment to exposing students to interdisciplinary thinking and requiring them to engage in this kind of thinking themselves. Every student is required to take a junior-level interdisciplinary seminar that looks at a particular topic from the integrated perspectives of multiple disciplines. These classes have few prerequisites (other than junior standing) and are not discipline-specific, so they have to be understandable by a general student audience. For many years I have been teaching a kind of introductory cognitive science class that looks at human and (perhaps) machine intelligence from the perspectives of artificial intelligence, psychology, neuroscience, philosophy and other disciplines. This class is regularly taken by students who are CS, math, business, psychology and several other majors.

All of the kinds of writing described above are potentially useful in this kind of context. Since these classes often tend to involve readings of primary sources (rather than the use of traditional textbooks), the various summarizing kinds of writing, particularly abstracts, are especially useful. I regularly have students do 500 word abstracts of a reading, and let them hold on to these abstracts to help them organize their thoughts during class discussions of the paper.

Another kind of writing that tends to be particularly useful in these classes is explanatory writing that gathers information from multiple sources and synthesizes it into a coherent discussion of a topic, preferably from the perspectives of multiple disciplines. Doing this requires students to attain a certain level of expertise in disciplines with which they are only passingly familiar. (This is not the place to describe the demands on faculty in teaching such courses.) But, as I regularly tell my students in classes, "life is interdisciplinary". Even in their future careers that will presumably be at least somewhat based on what they studied in school, they will be required to analyze and synthesize material from outside of their immediate areas of expertise. And in regular living they will constantly be required to make decisions that weigh inputs from various perspectives and ways of thinking.

2.7 Team-based writing

As with interdisciplinary writing, the issues here are somewhat orthogonal to those of previous categories. Since most software development these days is done by teams, CS students can expect to often be part of a team that is asked to perform tasks that frequently involve writing.

In particular, software specification and design involves extensive documentation. Code itself continues to require documentation and organization. Code requires programmer-level documents written for those trying to extend or maintain the code. And, of course, applications require user-level documentation, perhaps written by a professional writer, but still requiring significant inputs from the software developer.

One issue that regularly comes up in team-based writing is trying to produce a document that fairly distributes the writing workload, while still not sounding like it was produced by 10 different people. One way to approach this issue is to have strict and detailed style guidelines that prescribe as much as possible how the writing should be done. This is often most easily accomplished for software documentation, but it is also useful for more general audience documents.

I think it is a useful exercise for every student to be required, at least once in their undergraduate experience, to write to a very detailed and prescribed standard. And then have their writing mercilessly reviewed with respect to that standard. This is not pleasant or enjoyable for anyone involved, but is a very real-world kind of assignment.

3. THE WRITING PROCESS

This paper is primarily focused on kinds of writing assignments that can be particularly useful in an upper level computer science major course. But the writing *process* students go through is at least as important as the writing *products* that they eventually produce.

Unfortunately, in my experience, for many students the perceived optimal writing *process* is to sit down the night before a paper is due and crank it out in one extended writing session. In fact, the ability to churn out 5 pages of reasonably decent prose in an evening probably correlates strongly with being a successful college student. And in one sense there is nothing wrong with this. Being able to produce grammatically correct, reasonably well organized prose quickly is a useful life skill.

The main problem with this process is that it isn't conducive to the kind of deep, critical thinking we would like our students to engage in. Texts written quickly tend to reinforce the student's ingrained beliefs and ideas, rather than getting them to think things through in a fresh way.

But there is at least a partial solution to this problem: in a word, *revision*. The idea is to have students produce multiple drafts of a text, revising earlier drafts to produce later drafts, based on feedback received from the professor or from peers in the class or from an institutional Writing Center or from wherever such feedback can usefully be provided. (Some of my students have been successful with having a parent provide feedback on drafts of papers. While I would never require this of all students, for some it can be quite helpful.)

In my experience, there are two major difficulties getting students to engage in deep revision. One issue is the student who produces a "rough draft" that is nowhere near complete, perhaps just a short outline of what the final product will be. If there is nothing to be reviewed, it is unlikely that these students will get useful feedback. The second issue is the student who produces a strong first draft and gets feedback that basically says "this is great". To help avoid the first case, I usually tell students that their "first draft" (I studiously avoid the term "rough draft") will not be graded, but that their completed paper will receive a lower grade (regardless of quality) if they do not hand in a serious effort for the first draft. The second issue is harder (for me at least) to address. If a student gives me a first draft that is essentially an "A" paper, what can I realistically ask them to do? Fortunately (or perhaps unfortunately?) this problems doesn't arise as often. Sometimes I will use this as an opportunity to suggest that the student might want to engage with the same topic in a later, longer paper assignment or perhaps consider the topic for their senior capstone project.

One way that the writing process can go drastically wrong is when students plagiarize. On occasion I have had students argue that, if someone else already said it better, why should they be required to rewrite an idea in their own words? But usually when students plagiarize it is for much more mundane reasons such as lack of time management skills, laziness or fear of a lower grade. The only things I will say about plagiarism is that it has to be dealt with severely (meaning, for example, that the penalty needs to be worse than just a zero grade on the plagiarized assignment) and that the earlier it is caught the better. Catching plagiarism early is greatly facilitated by the revision process. If I see something in an early draft that looks suspicious, I immediately point it out to the student. More often than not, this makes the issue go away before any more significant response on my part is necessary.

4. FACULTY EVALUATION OF STUDENT WRITING

One question/concern that sometimes gets raised about having students do the kind of writing described in this paper is the expectations it makes of faculty. The two concerns I hear the most are faculty who feel unprepared to evaluate writing and faculty who see evaluating writing as requiring huge amounts of time and energy.

One response to the first issue is that some schools, at least sometimes, seem to encourage team teaching of these courses with both a computer science instructor and a writing instructor [2, 5, 7]. I think team teaching is great and I am all for it, but, at least at my school, the resources are rarely available to support it. And, again in my experience, it isn't necessary. I'm teaching Programming Languages, not a writing class. I'm using writing as a way to get students to learn computer science.

One aspect of this concern is that most computer science professors are not trained copy editors. We don't know the correct terminology for the kind of writing errors we encounter. But my response to this is that copy editing is NOT what using writing to teach is about in any significant way. On those (relatively rare) occasions when I encounter a grammatically incomprehensible paper, I will usually do simple copy editing of a page or two, to make sure the student understands what the issues are, then either have them copy edit their own work or send them to the Writing Center for detailed assistance.

This relates to the second concern mentioned, that of faculty time and energy. I find that interesting, creative papers that explore innovative solutions through writing are much more enjoyable to evaluate than twenty-five Java programs that are all attempting to do exactly the same thing. A good paper induces more energy in me, the evaluator, than the evaluation process consumes.

But, realistically, it does take time to carefully evaluate student writing. Where does that time come from? One answer is that I don't carefully evaluate ALL the writing a student does for the class. For example, some abstracts might get careful evaluation and detailed feedback, while some get cursory checks. For example, some first drafts might be evaluated by peers (or the Writing Center) rather than by the professor. Also, writing assignments sometimes replace other assignments or exams in the class. Finally, my university has made a commitment to make Writing Enhanced classes have an (at least somewhat) reduced enrollment, so there may be fewer students to evaluate.

5. CONCLUSION

Writing is a life skill that all educated people should have, including computer scientists. By incorporating many kinds of writing into an upper level CS class, it is possible to both teach the students the important content of the course and to improve their writing and critical thinking abilities.

6. ACKNOWLEDGMENTS

Thanks to those who helped me overcome my fears about using writing to teach computer science.

7. REFERENCES

[1] Bean, J.C. 2001 Engaging Ideas. Jossey-Bass, San Francisco

[2] Dugan, R. F. Jr. and Polanski, V. G. 2006. Writing for Computer Science: A Taxonomy of Writing Tasks and General Advice. JCSC (21,6) pp 191-203.

[3] Gersting, J. L. and Young, F. H. 2001. Shall We Write? SIGCSE Bulletin (33, 2) pp 18-19.

[4] Graham, P. 2003. The Hundred-Year Language. http://paulgraham.com/hundred.html Also appears in Hackers and Painters, O'Reilly, 2004.

[5] Hoffman, M. E., Dansdill T. and Herscovici, D. S. 2006. Bridging Writing to Learn and Writing in the Discipline in Computer Science Education. Proceedings of the Thirty-Seventh SIGCSE Technical Symposium on Computer Science Education, pp 117-121.

[6] Kay, D.G. 1998. Computer Scientists Can Teach Writing: An Upper Division Course for Computer Science Majors. Proceedings of the Twenty-Ninth SIGCSE Technical Symposium on Computer Science Education, pp 117-120.

[7] Pesante, L.H. 1991. Integrating Writing Into Computer Science Courses. Proceedings of the Twenty-Second SIGCSE Technical Symposium on Computer Science Education, pp 205-209.

[8] Pinker, S. 1997. How the Mind Works. W.W. Norton.

[9] Walker, H. M. 1998. Writing Within the Computer Science Curriculum. SIGCSE Bulletin (30,2) pp 24-25.

[10] Wilson, Gregory V.2004. Extensible Programming for the 21st Century. ACM Queue Magazine vol. 2, no. 9

A Breadth-First Course in Multicore and Manycore Programming

Suzanne Rivoire
Sonoma State University
Department of Computer Science
Rohnert Park, CA, USA
suzanne.rivoire@sonoma.edu

ABSTRACT

The technique of scaling hardware performance through increasing the number of cores on a chip requires programmers to learn to write parallel code that can exploit this hardware. In order to expose students to a variety of multicore programming models, our university offered a breadth-first introduction to multicore and manycore programming for upper-level undergraduates. Our students gained programming experience with three different parallel programming models, two of which are less than five years old and targeted specifically to multicore and manycore computing. Assessments throughout the semester showed that the course gave students a broad base of experience from which they will be able to understand ongoing developments in the field.

Categories and Subject Descriptors

K.3.2 [**Computers and Education**]: Computer and Information Science Education; D.1.3 [**Programming Techniques**]: Concurrent Programming—*parallel programming*

General Terms

Human Factors, Languages

Keywords

parallel programming education, multicore programming education, OpenMP, TBB, CUDA

1. INTRODUCTION

Over the past five years, processor manufacturers have abruptly shifted their method of scaling performance from increasing clock speeds to increasing the number of cores on a chip. Two- and four-core processors are common now, and the number of cores is expected to scale into the manycore range of tens and even hundreds in the coming years [2]. If these hardware improvements are to translate into software performance gains, programmers must learn how to write parallel code.

SIGCSE'10, March 10–13, 2010, Milwaukee, Wisconsin, USA.

Researchers have proposed many programming models for harnessing multicore and manycore processors. However, despite increasing consensus that undergraduates should learn parallel programming, these newer models are generally presented only at the graduate level. Furthermore, it is unclear which of these models will prevail in the long term.

At Sonoma State University, a mostly undergraduate U.S. public university with approximately 125 computer science majors, we created an elective course to give our undergraduates a broad-based background in multicore programming. We wanted the students to gain plenty of programming experience but to avoid committing to a single model of parallel programming. Instead, our course aimed to give students the broad perspective necessary to understand future developments in this rapidly changing field and to effectively use whichever programming models win out. In order to meet this goal, we offered a unique breadth-first introduction to multicore and manycore programming, giving students hands-on experience with three programming models: OpenMP, TBB, and CUDA. The unusual organization and content of this course allowed our students to achieve these learning objectives, and the students' feedback has provided us with clear indications of what worked and what decisions should be revisited in future offerings of the course.

This paper first reviews related work in parallel programming education in Section 2. Section 3 then discusses the content and structure of the course. Section 4 examines student feedback on the course organization and content, and Section 5 discusses lessons learned.

2. RELATED WORK

While the multicore era has introduced new urgency and complexity to parallel programming education, undergraduate parallel programming courses are not new [3, 8]. One approach to teaching undergraduates parallel programming is to inject it in snippets throughout the CS curriculum, as the University of Wisconsin at Eau Claire has done [7]. Another way to introduce new parallel programming models is in the operating systems class, where undergraduates traditionally encounter concurrency for the first time, as UT-Austin has done with transactional memory [19]. This paper presents an alternative approach: a single undergraduate elective course devoted to studying a range of parallel programming models. The advantages of this approach are a sustained focus on parallel programming, exposure to a variety of programming models, and ease of implementing the course without requiring systemic changes to the curriculum.

Beyond the undergraduate level, several studies [13, 14]

have considered best practices for parallel programming instruction. At the graduate level, a course at the University of Central Florida examined several graphics processors and programming models [9]. The course described in this paper examines a broader variety of programming models with less emphasis on the hardware implementation. Because our course targets a less experienced undergraduate audience, the pedagogical techniques and assessments also differ.

A related body of research tracks the productivity of novice programmers with different parallel programming models [10, 11]. These studies target the high-performance computing domain, a relatively specialized area. However, as multicore processors become mainstream, the usability of parallel programming models will become even more important.

3. COURSE DESIGN

CS 385, Multicore and Manycore Programming [18], was offered as a special-topics upper-division elective for computer science majors at Sonoma State University. The course prerequisites were CS2 and introductory computer organization. Eighteen students, all junior- and senior-level undergraduates, enrolled. The class met for a total of two hours of lecture and two hours of supervised lab each week.

3.1 Subjects covered

The course content comprised five modules of two to three weeks each. The first module was a lecture-based crash course in parallelism, the memory hierarchy, and performance analysis. Because junior-level computer architecture was not a prerequisite for this course, an introduction to these topics was needed to ensure that all of the students had sufficient background.

The next three modules covered three different parallel programming models, which were chosen on the basis of their accessibility to our students (who are most proficient with C++), the robustness and user-friendliness of their implementations, and their potential scalability to tens if not hundreds of cores. Students completed labs and programming projects using each of these three models.

The first model covered was OpenMP [4]; the idea was to get the students up to speed using a simple and widely supported shared-memory programming model. OpenMP allowed the students to quickly express task- and data-level parallelism as well as some ability to tune the performance of their code through scheduling directives.

The next model was Intel's Threading Building Blocks (TBB) [12], which supports parallelism using STL-like C++ generic programming abstractions. TBB supports a greater variety of parallel patterns than OpenMP, and it largely takes low-level scheduling out of the programmer's hands.

The final programming model was nVidia's CUDA [16], a model for general-purpose programming of graphics processors (GPUs) that has been widely used to harness their ample data parallelism for scientific computing. Unlike current CPUs, GPUs are already able to handle thousands of hardware threads, which makes the mapping of tasks to threads substantially different than on CPUs. GPUs also require more explicit memory management on the part of the programmer, and all but the simplest tasks require some low-level hardware knowledge.

The remaining portion of the course was a qualitative overview of other parallel and multicore programming models. Students read and discussed technical papers on GPU computing in general [17], MapReduce [6], and transactional memory [1]. The students thus gained a wider perspective than would be possible with programming alone, and they also were exposed to reading technical papers and graduate-style discussion for the first time.

3.2 Assignments

3.2.1 Labs

In each weekly lab session for the first four modules, students wrote parallel code to perform a specific task, and they were asked to measure the performance of their sequential and parallel code at different data set sizes in order to understand speedup and overheads.

The lab assignments given during the initial background module required the students to mimic some of the thought processes of parallel programming before they were introduced to a specific programming model. The students wrote straightforward sequential versions of two very simple algorithms: incrementing all of the elements in an array, and finding the maximum element of an array. Both algorithms are "embarrassingly parallel," although the second requires a reduction at the end. The students then modified their code to operate on a chunk of the array at a time based on a "thread ID" parameter passed into their function, which introduced them to the problem of mapping elements of the array to "threads" correctly and efficiently.

In the next module, when they learned OpenMP, they actually parallelized this code and experimented with the effect of different data set sizes and scheduling directives on speedup and performance. They also implemented a simple task-parallel program. The final OpenMP lab presented a task with significant interaction between threads. The problem was to parallelize a program that scans through a character array and does the following:

- If the ith character is 'q' or 'Q', it encrypts character i and the next 15 characters using an algorithm similar to AES, then copies the result into the output array and resumes with character $(i+16)$.
- Otherwise, it copies character i to the output array unmodified.

This seemingly simple problem requires significant interaction between threads to ensure that the parallel version yields the same result as the sequential version, due to the difficulty of determining whether a given 'q' will begin a 16-character block, or whether it will be passed over because it is contained in the block triggered by a previous 'q'.

The TBB lab assignments used the array increment, array max, and "encryption" problems as well as specific smaller problems to exercise the timing features and concurrent containers unique to TBB.

The CUDA labs focused on the problem of finding the Euclidean distance between two N-dimensional points. This problem has an embarrassingly parallel phase followed by a reduction, which the students optimized extensively, gaining intimate knowledge of the hardware.

The final "labs" were writeups of the technical papers the students read in the final module of the course. Following the "just-in-time" teaching method successfully employed by Davis in upper-division CS courses [5], I prepared a list of questions for the students to answer by electronic submission, due a few hours before class. I then designed the in-class discussion around their responses. The assignments also included guidelines on how to read these papers and what the students should be looking for, since they had not read detailed technical papers before.

3.2.2 Projects

In addition to the supervised labs, the students were also assigned four longer-term projects. Three were programming projects: one for each of the three programming models studied. In these projects, the students were asked to parallelize matrix multiplication using the chosen model and then further tune the performance with at least four optimizations. Students were also asked to measure the of each version of the program and analyze the results. Finally, open-ended qualitative comments about the project or programming model counted for 5% of the assignment grade.

The fourth project was not initially planned as part of the course. Rather, it occurred to me midway through the course as a way to diversify the projects and to give students practice in technical communication. Since students had found that the existing documentation and resources for some of the programming models failed to address novice parallel programmers, I assigned them to write tutorials about one of the three programming models studied. The students worked in groups of 2-3 students (8 groups total). Each group was assigned a programming model based on their stated preference and on a random drawing to be sure that each model was equally represented. This project was a valuable addition to the course and a useful assessment of the students' high-level understanding. However, because it was not initially written into the course schedule, the students ended up with an unnecessarily heavy workload when it was assigned toward the end of the semester.

3.2.3 Other assessments

The only other assessments in the course were 4 narrowly focused quizzes (one for each module except the introduction) and a comprehensive final exam requiring students to synthesize their knowledge of all of the different programming models studied.

4. STUDENT FEEDBACK

4.1 Course organization and content

I solicited qualitative and quantitative student feedback on the course organization and content in an informal survey at the end of the semester. I also examined the qualitative responses from our standardized institutional course evaluations; unfortunately, the quantitative portion of our institutional evaluations is focused solely on the instructor rather than the course. The data show an overall positive response to the course, although they indicate possible areas for improvement the next time this course is offered.

Figure 1 shows the results of the quantitative portion of this student survey, which was answered by 15 of the 18 students. Students were asked to rate the three major instructional components of the course—lectures, labs, and projects—on their helpfulness in four major categories: understanding parallel algorithms, analyzing the performance of code, understanding the latest developments in the technology industry, and increasing programming skills.

Option	# students
Would have preferred depth-first (studying one model in great detail)	0
Would have preferred depth-first with a little bit of breadth	7
Liked the course as is	7
Would have preferred a little more breadth (more topics, shallower coverage)	0
Would have preferred a lot more breadth	0
Don't care/don't know	1

Table 1: Student opinions of course breadth

The figure shows that the project portion of the course was most polarizing, with high variation in student ratings across all four of the questions. Projects also received the lowest average ratings of any course component in three of the four categories. Furthermore, in the category of "helped me understand and analyze the performance of my code," at which the projects were specifically targeted, they were rated as no more helpful than the lab assignments. A look at the students' qualitative remarks provides no easy answers; students commented both in favor of and against using the same problem for all of the different programming models, and only one student complained about the choice of matrix multiplication. One possible explanation is the students' understandable frustration with competing with other students for the limited hardware resources available to extensively test the performance of their code, which one student summed up as "a lesson in agonizing frustration."

The labs, on the other hand, were rated as the most helpful component of the course in three of the four categories shown, and they seem to have succeeded where the projects failed. Since the lab exercises presented the students with a variety of types of parallelism, it is not surprising that students rated them highly in the category of parallel algorithms. Similarly, the increase in programming skills may be attributable to the cooperative setting of the lab portion of the course, which allowed students to quickly get feedback from peers and the instructor.

Finally, the evaluations showed that students were highly enthusiastic about learning a topic that they perceived as relevant and cutting-edge. The lack of a textbook and the relative paucity of beginner-level tutorials about TBB and CUDA did not seem to bother the students; in fact, the only qualitative comment on this subject urged me to continue encouraging the students to find and read online documentation in lieu of a textbook in the future.

Perhaps most importantly, I solicited student feedback on the choice to make this course breadth-first instead of pursuing a single parallel programming model (see Table 1). Students' responses to this question divided evenly between "keep as is" and "would prefer depth-first with a little bit of breadth." In the qualitative comments, students mentioned that they appreciated being able to compare parallel programming models, but some students did suggest studying two models in detail instead of three.

4.2 Programming models studied

I also obtained student feedback on the three program-

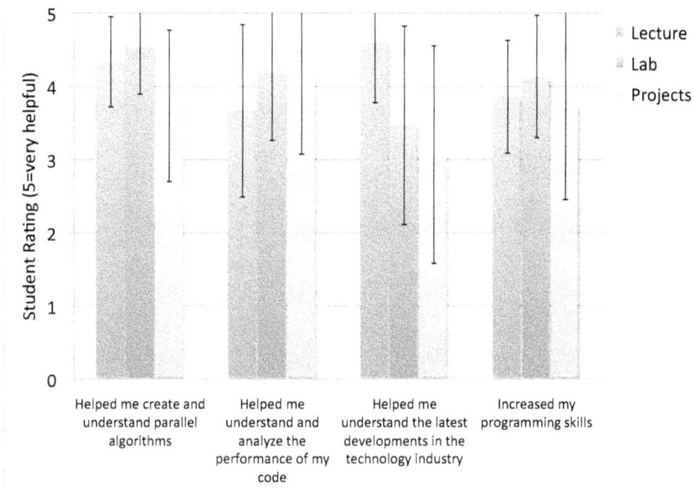

Figure 1: Results of end-of-semester student survey

	OpenMP	TBB	CUDA
1st choice	0	1	7
2nd choice	6	1	0
3rd choice	1	6	0

Table 2: Number of groups choosing each programming model for the final project

ming models we studied from their three programming project writeups and from their preference ordering of the three models for the tutorial project.

Table 2 shows the students' order of preference for tutorial topics. CUDA was the first choice of seven of the eight groups; the group that chose TBB did not specify a second or third choice because they were well aware that they had no competition for their first choice. OpenMP was the clear second choice, and TBB the third. The qualitative end-of-semester feedback, as well as student comments on project writeups, further underscored this order of preferences. These preferences also correlate with the degree of low-level detail the programmer is concerned with: CUDA requires the programmer to understand the hardware on which it runs at a fairly low level, while TBB nudges the programmer toward a higher level of abstraction and less concern with the low-level details of thread mapping and scheduling. Their preference for lower-level models, surprising given their prior experience with the STL and their lack of similar background in computer architecture, was summed up by one student in his CUDA writeup:

"My opinions on CUDA have changed since we first began working with it. At first, I didn't like it because it was for GPUs, and I'm not really interested in graphics... Then we started learning a bit more about GPUs, and I've realized that they are for so much more than graphics now... I began to like CUDA more and more, as I began to really understand how I am working with the hardware at such a low level. TBB was thinking in terms of high-level programming, object-oriented, but with CUDA, I really have full control of what's going on. I think that this class in general has prepared me for Architecture and Operating Systems so much, and working with CUDA is a perfect example of this. I've really come to understand CPU and GPU hardware, and I'm starting to like it."

5. LESSONS LEARNED

5.1 Breadth-first?

While I continue to believe that undergraduate students are better served by exposure to a variety of multicore programming models than a semester-long commitment to a single model, experience with this course shows that 3-week modules may be too short for students to get an adequate feel for a programming model. One possibility is to focus the programming projects on two models but introduce breadth through the readings, since the final phase of the course, in which we discussed papers on other programming models, went better than expected, . Another alternative, also suggested by some students, would be to require more programming and architecture background of the students, requiring less time for introductory material and allowing more time to study each model. Unfortunately, the latter alternative is probably impractical at our institution given its relatively small size; we are unlikely to have a sufficient number of students who meet a significantly more stringent prerequisite.

The choice of programming models remains an open question for future offerings of the course. I would definitely include a GPU-based programming model, whether CUDA, OpenCL [15], or something else; the high degree of parallelism gave students the satisfaction of seeing dramatic speedups, and the low-level control required pushed the students to understand hardware at a deeper level. The other model(s) are less obvious; using OpenMP as a gentle introduction to parallel programming turned out to probably be unnecessary, but TBB was roundly disliked and students found it difficult to understand the performance of their TBB programs. Since this area is evolving so quickly, perhaps the right platform has not yet been developed.

The paper discussions were another means of achieving breadth, and the specific papers chosen gave students a wider perspective on parallel programming at a level that they were able to understand. In the future, we would make up for decreasing breadth in the programming projects by budgeting time for a wider range of readings on parallel programming. This method would give the students the desired exposure to several programming models without the overhead of repeatedly mastering new syntax.

5.2 Improving the course components

Student feedback shows a clear opportunity to improve the projects. Most significantly, as important as it is for students to learn how to optimize code with the assistance of thorough performance measurements, contention for hardware resources can render the experience both meaningless and frustrating. Matrix multiplication is also a rather staid problem for the students to optimize. The right solution may therefore be to give students a more complicated but more interesting problem and emphasize getting a working implementation at the expense of optimizing and tuning.

The lab activities were mostly intended to get students comfortable with the syntax of the different programming models, but the data in Section 4 show that they were integral to achieving the conceptual learning objectives of the course. This indicates an opportunity to revisit the content of the labs to increase their effectiveness in that role.

Finally, the students' engagement with the readings far exceeded my expectations, largely due to the reading guides and the just-in-time teaching methods used for that component of the course. Due to the success with the reading guides in this class, I have begun to prepare reading guides for other, textbook-based, courses as well; after all, college textbooks may be as unfamiliar for beginning students as technical papers are for advanced students.

6. CONCLUSION

In conclusion, a breadth-first introduction to multicore programming models satisfied my objectives of giving students a broad-based perspective on parallel programming, and students indicated general satisfaction with the course. The organization of the course and the specific combination of models studied were novel and proved effective for our students, with some caveats.

The choice of a GPU programming model was pedagogically effective and popular with students; in fact, students enjoyed and learned more using low-level models than high-level ones. This counterintuitive observation will help me select the other programming models more effectively in the next course offering. The success of the reading portion of the course also suggests that we could cover two models in depth instead of three and compensate by reading about a wider range of models. While there is plenty of room for adjustment, this initial version of the course successfully prepared our undergraduate computer science students for productivity with emerging parallel programming models.

7. ACKNOWLEDGMENTS

I am grateful to the faculty of the Sonoma State University CS department for the opportunity to offer this course, to Christos Kozyrakis for his advice on the course content, and to Roger Mamer and Gina Voight for their technical and administrative support throughout the semester. In addition, this paper benefited from the comments of John Davis, Joy Tang, Kathy Charmaz, Sheila Katz, Richard Senghas, Tom Rosin, and the anonymous reviewers. Finally, I am especially grateful to the students who took CS 385 in Spring 2009 for their enthusiastic participation in, and their patience with, this experimental course.

8. REFERENCES

[1] A.-R. Adl-Tabatabai, C. Kozyrakis, and B. Saha. Unlocking concurrency. *Queue*, 4(10):24–33, 2007.

[2] K. Asanovic, R. Bodik, et al. The landscape of parallel computing research: A view from Berkeley. Technical Report UCB/EECS-2006-183, EECS Department, University of California, Berkeley, Dec 2006.

[3] R. M. Butler, R. E. Eggen, and S. R. Wallace. Introducing parallel processing at the undergraduate level. *SIGCSE Bull.*, 20(1):63–67, 1988.

[4] L. Dagum and R. Menon. OpenMP: an industry-standard API for shared-memory programming. *IEEE Computational Science & Engineering*, 5(1), 1998.

[5] J. Davis. Experiences with Just-in-Time Teaching in systems and design courses. In *SIGCSE*, 2009.

[6] J. Dean and S. Ghemawat. MapReduce: simplified data processing on large clusters. In *OSDI*, 2004.

[7] D. J. Ernst and D. E. Stevenson. Concurrent CS: preparing students for a multicore world. In *ITiCSE*, 2008.

[8] A. L. Fisher and T. Gross. Teaching the programming of parallel computers. *SIGCSE Bull.*, 23(1):102–107, 1991.

[9] H. Gao, M. Dimitrov, et al. Experiencing various massively parallel architectures and programming models for data-intensive applications. In *Workshop on Computer Architecture Education*, 2008.

[10] L. Hochstein, V. R. Basili, et al. A pilot study to compare programming effort for two parallel programming models. *Journal of Systems and Software*, 81(11):1920–1930, 2008.

[11] L. Hochstein, J. Carver, et al. Parallel programmer productivity: A case study of novice parallel programmers. In *Supercomputing (SC)*, 2005.

[12] Intel. Intel Threading Building Blocks (TBB). `http://software.intel.com/en-us/intel-tbb/`.

[13] M. C. Jadud, J. Simpson, and C. L. Jacobsen. Patterns for programming in parallel, pedagogically. In *SIGCSE*, 2008.

[14] D. A. Joiner, P. Gray, et al. Teaching parallel computing to science faculty: best practices and common pitfalls. In *PPoPP*, 2006.

[15] Khronos Group. OpenCL - the open standard for parallel programming of heterogeneous systems. `http://www.khronos.org/opencl/`.

[16] nVidia. CUDA zone. `http://www.nvidia.com/object/cuda_home.html`.

[17] J. D. Owens, M. Houston, et al. GPU computing. *Proceedings of the IEEE*, 96(5):879–899, May 2008.

[18] S. Rivoire. CS 385: Multicore and manycore programming, Spring 2009. `http://rivoire.cs.sonoma.edu/cs385/`.

[19] C. Rossbach, O. Hofmann, and E. Witchel. Is transactional programming really easier? In *PPoPP*, 2010.

Test-First Java Concurrency for the Classroom

Mathias Ricken
Dept. of Computer Science
Rice University
Houston, TX 77005, USA
+1-713-348-3836
mgricken@rice.edu

Robert Cartwright
Dept. of Computer Science
Rice University
Houston, TX 77005, USA
+1-713-348-6042
cork@rice.edu

ABSTRACT
Concurrent programming is becoming more important due to the growing dominance of multi-core processors and the prevalence of graphical user interfaces (GUIs). To prepare students for the concurrent future, instructors have begun to address concurrency earlier in their curricula. Unfortunately, test-driven development, which enables students and practitioners to quickly develop reliable single-threaded programs, is not as effective in the domain of concurrent programming. This paper describes how ConcJUnit can simplify the task of writing unit tests for multi-threaded programs, and provides examples that can be used to introduce students to concurrent programming.

Categories and Subject Descriptors
D.1.3 [**Programming Techniques**]: Concurrent programming.
D.2.5 [**Software Engineering**]: Testing and debugging – *Testing tools.*
K.3.2 [**Computers and Education**]: Computer and information science education – *computer science education.*

General Terms
Reliability, Languages.

Keywords
CS education, Java, JUnit, unit testing, concurrent programming, tools, software engineering.

1. INTRODUCTION
In test-driven development, tests are written for a unit of code before the code itself is written, and all tests must succeed before a new revision can be committed to the code base, facilitating the early detection and repair of program bugs [7]. This approach to software development is steadily gaining popularity both in computer science education [6] and industrial practice [1][13].

Unfortunately, unit testing is much less effective for programs with multiple threads of control than for sequential (single-threaded) programs. The importance of concurrent programming, however, is rapidly growing as multi-core processors replace older single core designs. To exploit the power of these new processors, programs must run several computations in parallel. Unless there is a breakthrough in processor design or language implementation technology, writing and testing concurrent code will become a skill that all software developers must master. Several schools have already responded to this trend and introduced concurrent programming concepts early in their curricula [2][3].

Furthermore, multi-threading not only occurs in applications designed to exploit multi-core CPUs. GUI frameworks like AWT/Swing and SWT access components and react to user input in a separate *event thread*. As a result, most applications with GUIs already involve multi-threading.

Developers of large Java applications like DrJava [11] have identified two obstacles to applying test-driven development to concurrent programs: (*i*) the standard unit testing frameworks make it easy to write bad tests and (*ii*) thread scheduling is non-deterministic and machine-specific, implying that the outcome of a test can change from one run to the next [12].

Test-driven design increases programmer confidence [14], which is especially important in introductory programming courses. The fact that tests with failed assertions may succeed is particularly troubling, because it could give students a false sense of security. It is therefore crucial to identify how concurrent unit tests may report false successes and what can be done to address this issue.

Contributions In this paper, we present a course module introducing concurrent Java programming, which is suitable for inclusion at the beginning of a software engineering course that only presumes the CS 1/2 sequence as prerequisite. In this module:

1. We identify the shortcomings of the standard JUnit [8] framework (and its competitors [15]) in the context of concurrency and describe how an extension of JUnit called ConcJUnit [9] remedies these problems (Section 2).
2. We present a series of small examples that elucidate common problems in concurrent programming. First, we study a trivial program that increments a counter from multiple threads to stress the importance of atomicity when performing operations on shared data (Section 3). Next, we write and analyze a program that requires access to two pieces of shared data, introducing the possibility of deadlock (Section 4). To assess the students' understanding of the covered topics, we assign the implementation of a bounded buffer and a readers-writer lock as homework (Section 5).
3. We discuss why concurrent programs remain difficult to test because of nondeterministic thread scheduling (Section 6).

2. IMPROVING TESTING FRAMEWORKS

All popular unit testing frameworks for Java including JUnit behave pathologically with regard to concurrency: failed assertions and uncaught exceptions in threads other than the main thread are ignored and do not cause a test to fail. The unit test in Figure 1, for instance, succeeds even though the child thread unconditionally calls JUnit's `fail()` method.

Inexperienced programmers unfamiliar with this pathology typically write unit tests for multi-threaded units of code that report success when assertions in auxiliary threads fail. Even experienced programmers may fall prey to this problem when they move code out of the main thread. The AWT/Swing and SWT GUI frameworks, for example, mandate that GUI components and the associated documents be accessed from the event thread. A unit testing harness is supposed to provide a rigid foundation for refactoring, but fails to do so if thread boundaries are crossed.

The unit test in Figure 1 reveals another design flaw in JUnit: even when a test creates an exception handler for a child thread, there is no guarantee when the child thread fails that the test has not already ended and falsely reported as a success. JUnit does not warn if some child threads spawned in a test do not terminate on time.

A well-written test ensures that all child threads have ended before the test outcome is determined. The most common ways to achieve this property are (a) using `Thread.join()`, (b) using `Object.wait()` and `Object.notify()`; or (c) by monitoring a shared `volatile` variable in a busy-loop. While option (c) is usually avoided for performance reasons, both (a) and (b) can be efficiently used to control thread lifetimes. These two options, shown[1] in Figure 2 and Figure 3, are equivalent as long as the child thread terminates immediately after the call to `notify()`.

However, only the first option, using `join()`, ensures that the other thread has truly terminated. To support robustness under refactoring, a well-formed unit test should require that all child threads are joined with the test's main thread. This action can be done directly, with the main thread invoking `join()` for all child threads, or indirectly, through the transitive property of `join()`, as long as all join operations together ensure that each child thread terminates before the test ends [12].

2.1 Unit Testing with ConcJUnit

ConcJUnit is an open-source project designed as a replacement for JUnit. Since it is backward-compatible with JUnit, replacing the `junit.jar` file with the appropriate version of ConcJUnit enables support for concurrent unit testing while preserving existing testing behavior.

ConcJUnit installs a default exception handler for all child threads spawned in a test, as well as for the AWT/Swing event thread. The framework can therefore properly detect uncaught exceptions and failed assertions in any thread. When run with ConcJUnit, the test in Figure 1 fails as expected.

ConcJUnit also tracks all child threads and causes the test to fail if any of them are still alive when the main thread terminates. To

```
1.  public void testException() {
2.    Thread t = new Thread() {
3.      public void run() {
4.        // should cause failure but does not
5.        fail();
6.      }
7.    };
8.    t.start();
9.  }
```

Figure 1: Test Should Fail But Does Not

```
public void testWithJoin() {
  Thread t = new Thread() {
    public void run() {
      // ...
    }
  };
  t.start();
  t.join();
}
```

Figure 2: Lifetime Control Using Join

```
public void testWithJoin() {
  final Object sign = new Object();
  Thread t = new Thread() {
    public void run() {
      // ...
      synchronized(sign) { sign.notify(); }
      // no more code here
    }
  };
  t.start();
  synchronized(sign) { sign.wait(); }
}
```

Figure 3: Lifetime Control Using Wait/Nofity

```
1.  public void testException() {
2.    Thread t = new Thread() {
3.      public void run() { /* no op */ }
4.    };
5.    t.start();
6.    Thread.sleep(5000); // long wait
7.  }
```

Figure 4: Child Thread Gets Lucky

help the developer determine which threads these are, ConcJUnit records the source location where each child thread is started and reports this information for any thread that does not properly terminate. For example, in Figure 1, ConcJUnit reports that the thread started in line 8 did not terminate.

Furthermore, ConcJUnit analyzes the join operations that are performed and issues a warning when a child thread terminates but is not absorbed by a join. For instance, for the test in Figure 4, ConcJUnit reports that the thread started in line 5 terminated, but only because of the vagaries of thread scheduling.

The analysis of join operations is conservative and enforces the policy that all child threads must be joined with the main thread. As a result, ConcJUnit will emit a warning for some correctly synchronized tests, such as the one in Figure 3 employing `wait()`

[1] `join()` and `wait()` may resume *spuriously* (§17.8.1 JLS [4]). For brevity, the loop necessary to handle this has been omitted.

and `notify()`. At the programmer's option, these warnings can be suppressed. In our experience, the conservative analysis is helpful, because it catches improperly synchronized tests. Moreover, it is easy to ensure that child threads terminate using join operations.

Thread creation coordinates are helpful in analyzing uncaught exceptions and failed assertions in child threads as well. If a unit test fails in a child thread, ConcJUnit provides a stack trace of the failed child thread, as well as the stack trace of all ancestor threads up to the point where the child thread was started. In Figure 5, for example, the failure occurs in a named helper class, and it is not immediately obvious which thread failed, `t1` or `t2`. The extended stack trace with the thread creation context, however, shows that the child thread was started in line 11; therefore, the failure occurred in thread `t2`.

ConcJUnit has recently been integrated into the DrJava IDE, making it easy for beginners to use. Given a testing framework that is well equipped for multi-threaded programs, we subsequently discuss some small examples with our students.

3. MULTI-THREADED COUNTER

We explain that concurrency, while helpful for many tasks, improves performance when it is used to break down a computation into smaller pieces, which are processed in parallel by different CPU cores and then combined into a final value. Communication between threads is required to coordinate the assembly of the final value from the results produced by the individual threads.

This communication is usually performed using shared data. To illustrate this technique, we present a very simple example: a computation that increments an integer counter 10 million times. We initially write a single-threaded test program for this task. At the end of the program, we assert that the counter has indeed reached the expected value. The source code for this unit test is given in Figure 6. After this test has been written, the students develop the code for the actual counter, shown in Figure 7.

When multiple cores are available, it should be possible to distribute the work of incrementing the counter. Figure 8 shows a test program that spawns 10 helper threads, each incrementing the counter a million times. The test waits for all helper threads to finish (using the `join()` operation), and then asserts that the integer variable contains the expected number. To the students' surprise, this test fails because the actual value of the counter is typically less than the expected value. More interestingly, the actual value changes from one execution to the next.

To discover the cause of the failure, we ask the students to describe in detail what operations the expression `count++;` actually performs. They discover that, if one assumes addition can only be performed in a CPU register, the previous line can be re-written in pseudo-code as

```
long register = count;
register = register + 1;
count = register;
```

Shown this way, it becomes evident that the increment expression is not atomic and may be interleaved with operations in other threads. If thread A first reads the counter, but then gets preempted by another thread B also incrementing the counter before A can write the changed value back to memory, then the

```
1.  class Helper extends Thread {
2.    boolean toFail;
3.    public Helper(boolean b) { toFail = b; }
4.    public void run() { if (toFail) fail(); }
5.  }
6.
7.  public void testTCC() {
8.    Thread t1 = new Helper(false);
9.    Thread t2 = new Helper(true);
10.   t1.start();
11.   t2.start();
12.   t1.join(); t2.join();
13. }

junit.framework.AssertionFailedError:
    at TCCTest.Helper.run(TCCTest.java:4)
    at ...parent called Thread.start()...
    at TCCTest.testTCC(TCCTest.java:11)
```

Figure 5: Thread Creation Context for Uncaught Exceptions

```
public class SingleIncTest extends TestCase {
  static final long N = 10000000;
  public void testSingle() {
    Counter c = new Counter();
    c.incNTimes(N);
    assertEquals(N, c.count);
  }
}
```

Figure 6: Single-threaded Counter Test

```
public class Counter {
  public long count = 0;
  public void incNTimes(long n) {
    for(int i=0; i<n; ++i) { count++; }
  }
}
```

Figure 7: Counter Implementation

```
public class MultiIncTest extends TestCase {
  static final long N = 1000000;
  static final int T = 10;
  public void testMulti() throws Exception {
    final Counter c = new Counter();
    Thread[] ts = new Thread[T];
    for(int i=0; i<T; ++i) {
      ts[i]=new Thread() {
        public void run() {
          c.incNTimes(N);
        }
      });
      ts[i].start();
    }
    for(Thread t: ts) t.join();
    assertEquals(T*N, c.count);
  }
}
```

Figure 8: Multi-threaded Counter

```
A1      long register₁ = count;       // register₁==0
   B1   long register₂ = count;       // register₂==0
A2      register₁ = register₁ + 1;    // register₁==1
A3      count = register₁;            // count==1
   B2   register₂ = register₂ + 1;    // register₂==1
   B3   count = register₂;            // count==1
        final result                  // count==1
```

Figure 9: Problematic Interleaving

work done by thread A is lost. Figure 9 shows one such problematic interleaving.

This is an example of a *data race*. A data race occurs when (1) two threads access the same shared data, (2) at least one of the accesses is a write access, and (3) the accesses are unsynchronized (nothing prevents the order of the accesses from changing). The accesses in our example are the read access of B1 and the write access of A3: If A3 happens before B1, the program performs as expected; however, if B1 occurs before A3, as shown in Figure 9, then the increment performed by thread A is lost. The actual interleaving is nondeterministic and changes from one run to the next, which also explains why the final value of the counter varies.

To eliminate this concurrency bug, we need to ensure that the instructions A1; A2; A3 cannot be interleaved with the same instructions in another thread. We do this by introducing a synchronized block requiring a lock object to be acquired before the increment operation may be performed. Threads compete for ownership of the lock object, and only the thread owning it is allowed into the synchronized block protected by the lock. The instructions A1; A2; A3 in the synchronized block are not atomic—thread A may be preempted by other threads—but once thread A has ownership of the lock object, no other thread may execute code protected by the same lock object.

Once the students allocate a lock object as a field of the `Counter` class and enclose the increment operation in a synchronized block, the unit test will pass.

```
private Object lock = new Object();
// ...
synchronized(lock) { count++; }
```

It is important to emphasize that the code needs to be protected by the same *runtime* object for the synchronized block to be effective; therefore, the lock object cannot be the value of a local variable in the `incNTimes()` method, because a local variable will be bound to a different object in each call.

4. MULTI-THREADED BANK

After the students have correctly synchronized the multi-threaded counter, we present them with another problem: in a concurrent simulation of a bank's checking accounts, we would like to make arbitrary transfers from one account to another. This implies subtracting a value x from the balance of account A and adding it to the balance of account B. We use the notation ($A \rightarrow B$, x) for this transfer.

One drastic approach would be to have one lock object protecting the access to all accounts; however, this would eliminate concurrent transfers and essentially serialize the program. We would like to allow several transfers at the same time, as long as they don't involve the same accounts. For instance, it should be

```
1.  final int NUM_ACCOUNTS = 5;
2.  final int NUM_TRANSFERS = 1000000;
3.  long[]    accounts = new long[NUM_ACCOUNTS];
4.  Object[]  locks = new Object[NUM_ACCOUNTS];
5.  Random    r = new Random();
6.  class TransferThread extends Thread {
7.    public int from, to;
8.    public void run() {
9.      for(int i=0; i<NUM_TRANSFERS; ++i) {
10.       from = r.nextInt(NUM_ACCOUNTS);
11.       to   = r.nextInt(NUM_ACCOUNTS);
12.       synchronized(locks[to]) {
13.         synchronized(locks[from]) {
14.           int x = r.nextInt(100);
15.           accounts[from] -= x;
16.           accounts[to]   += x;
17.         }
18.       }
19.     }
20.   }
21. }
```

Figure 10: Nested Synchronized Blocks

```
class CheckThread extends Thread {
  public void run() {
    while(true) {
      Thread.sleep(5000);
      for(TransferThread t: ts) {
        System.out.println(t.from+"->"+t.to);
      }
    }
  }
}

Output:   0->1
          1->0
```

Figure 11: Diagnostic Background Thread and Output

allowed to execute the transfers ($0 \rightarrow 1$, 10) and ($2 \rightarrow 3$, 20) concurrently, but the transfer ($1 \rightarrow 2$, 15) should block until accounts 1 and 2 are not in use anymore.

Most students will suggest one lock object per account acquired in two nested synchronized blocks, as shown in Figure 10. It is worthwhile to point out that Java locks are *re-entrant*, i.e. if a thread has already acquired ownership of a lock, attempting to do so again is a no-op; therefore, it is not problematic if `from == to`. When a student runs a unit test that issues random transfers and checks that the total amount of money remains constant, it is almost certain that the program will "hang" after a few seconds without finishing all transfers.

Unfortunately, it is difficult to determine what exactly happened without using additional tools such as a debugger. Adding a print statement after line 8 to show the values of `from` and `to` is not helpful because performing console output inadvertently synchronizes competing threads, eliminating the "hanging" problem in typical schedules. However, it is possible to run an additional diagnostic thread, shown in Figure 11, in the background and periodically print the current `to` and `from` values of all the transfer threads. When the students analyze the diagnostic output, they realize there is a cycle: For instance, one thread has claimed lock object 0 and needs lock object 1, while the other thread owns lock object 1 and requires lock object 0; neither thread can proceed. This situation is called *deadlock*.

It is interesting to note that there would be no deadlock if the second thread had also attempted to procure lock object 0 first. In that case, the second thread would just have to wait until the lock object is released again. The order in which the lock objects are sought is critical. This observation leads students to the realization that lock objects must be acquired according to the same global order.

In our account transfer example, one way to ensure this is to always acquire the lock with the lower account number first:

```
synchronized(locks[Math.min(to,from)]) {
  synchronized(locks[Math.max(to,from)]) {
```

Any total order on lock objects will work.

5. HOMEWORK ASSIGNMENT

To assess the students' understanding of the topics covered, we assign the implementation of a bounded buffer and a readers-writer lock as homework. We provide unit test suites for both, allowing students to test their programs before they turn in their assignments.

While we primarily grade for correctness, which among other things involves checking that the implemented methods are correctly synchronized, we also consider efficiency and fairness. For example, a bounded buffer implementation should maximize concurrency, yet avoid awakening more waiting producers or consumers than can be accommodated. For the readers-writer lock, readers and writers should be put in a queue to ensure that readers cannot starve writers.

The assignment, along with the solutions, is available at [10]. Note that we also discuss synchronized methods, `volatile` and `final` variables, and the `Object.wait()`, `Object.notify()` and `Thread.interrupt()` methods before we assign this homework. Brief notes are contained in the assignment.

6. NONDETERMINISTIC SCHEDULING

We also inform our students that ConcJUnit can only detect problems in the schedule (the interleaving of operations on shared data) [12] chosen by the JVM for each test. ConcJUnit does not detect all defects that *could* occur; only those in the executed schedule are found. Even when a ConcJUnit test passes without failures or warnings, the same test could fail on the next run.

Conventional unit testing assumes the program behavior is deterministic, a property that is lost for concurrent programs. The ordering of competing accesses to shared data is non-deterministic – even when those accesses are synchronized. The Java Memory Model [5] does not even ensure that program execution corresponds to a serial interleaving of its threads unless the program is free of data races. The simplest strategy for avoiding data races in Java is to mark all shared variables as `final` or `volatile`. Both dynamic and static data race detectors have been developed for Java [5], but this is still an active area of research. We are not aware of any lightweight, practical race detection tools suitable for use in the classroom or in routine software development.

Since concurrent program execution is non-deterministic, a unit testing framework should ideally run each test under all possible schedules. Unfortunately, the number of possible schedules increases exponentially with the size of the program. A practical alternative to exhaustively running each test under all schedules might be to run each test under a set of schedules generated using heuristic methods. The design and construction of such a heuristic tool is one of our primary research interests.

7. CONCLUSION

As mainstream processor designs become more explicitly parallel and include more cores, concurrent programming will become more prominent in both computer science education and industrial practice. It is therefore essential to educate students about the challenges involved in writing efficient and reliable concurrent programs. Using ConcJUnit and the examples presented in this paper, instructors can temper the conflict between test-driven development and concurrent programming.

8. REFERENCES

[1] Bowers, A. N., Sangwan, R. S., and Neill, C. J. 2007. *Adoption of XP practices in the industry—A survey: Research Sections*. Softw. Process 12, 3 (May. 2007), 283-294.

[2] Ernst, D. J. and Stevenson, D. E. 2008. *Concurrent CS: preparing students for a multicore world*. In Proceedings of the 13th Annual Conference on innovation and Technology in Computer Science Education (Madrid, Spain, June 30 - July 02, 2008). ITiCSE '08. ACM, New York, NY, 230-234.

[3] Fekete, A. D. 2009. *Teaching about threading: where and what?*. SIGACT News 40, 1 (Feb. 2009), 51-57.

[4] Gosling, J., Joy, B., Steele, G. L. and Bracha, G. *The Java Language Specification*. 3rd Ed. Addison-Wesley, Reading, MA, USA, 2005.

[5] IBM. *ConTest*. http://www.alphaworks.ibm.com/tech/contest

[6] Jeffries, R. and Melnik, G. 2007. *Guest Editors' Introduction: TDD—The Art of Fearless Programming*. IEEE Softw. 24, 3 (May. 2007), 24-30.

[7] Jeffries, R. http://www.xprogramming.com/

[8] JUnit Project. *JUnit*. http://junit.org/

[9] Rice JavaPLT. *ConcJUnit*. http://concutest.org/concjunit/

[10] Rice JavaPLT. *Concurrent programming assignment and solution*. http://concutest.org/download/sigcse2010-java-concurrency.zip

[11] Rice JavaPLT. *DrJava Web Site*, http://drjava.org/

[12] Ricken, M. and Cartwright, R. 2009. *ConcJUnit: unit testing for concurrent programs*. In Proceedings of the 7th international Conference on Principles and Practice of Programming in Java (Calgary, Alberta, Canada, August 27 - 28, 2009). PPPJ '09. ACM, New York, NY, 129-132.

[13] Rumpe, B. and Schroeder, A. *Quantitative Survey on Extreme Programming Projects*. In Proceedings of International Conference on Extreme Programming and Flexible Processes in Software Engineering (XP2002). (Alghero, Italy, May 2002) 95-100.

[14] Spacco, J. and Pugh, W. 2006. *Helping students appreciate test-driven development (TDD)*. In Companion To the 21st ACM SIGPLAN Symposium on Object-Oriented Programming Systems, Languages, and Applications (Portland, Oregon, USA, October 22 - 26, 2006). OOPSLA '06. ACM, New York, NY, 907-913

[15] TestNG Project. *TestNG*. http://testng.org/

Introducing Concurrency in CS 1*

Kim B. Bruce
Department of Computer Science
Pomona College
Claremont, CA 91711
kim@cs.pomona.edu

Andrea Danyluk
Department of Computer Science
Williams College
Williamstown, MA 01267
andrea@cs.williams.edu

Thomas Murtagh
Department of Computer Science
Williams College
Williamstown, MA 01267
tom@cs.williams.edu

ABSTRACT

Because of the growing importance of concurrent programming, many people are trying to figure out where in the curriculum to introduce students to concurrency. In this paper we discuss the use of concurrency in an introductory computer science course. This course, which has been taught for ten years, introduces concurrency in the context of event-driven programming. It also makes use of graphics and animations with the support of a library that reduces the syntactic overhead of using these constructs. Students learn to use separate threads in a way that enables them to write programs that match their intuitions of the world. While the separate threads do interact, programs are selected so that race conditions are generally not an issue.

Categories and Subject Descriptors

K.3.2 [**Computer and Information Science Education**]: Computer Science Education; D.1.3 [**Concurrent Programming**]: Parallel programming

General Terms

Design, Algorithms

Keywords

CS 1, concurrency, Java, objectdraw

1. INTRODUCTION

The issue of how to effectively write concurrent and parallel programs has become increasingly important. Over the last several years, the Computing Research Association has sponsored a number of conferences on Grand Research Challenges in Computer Science and Engineering. The most recent of these, "Revitalizing Computer Architecture Research", held in December of 2005, identified four grand challenges. One of those was making parallel programming more mainstream. The report states:

> "The grand challenge is to make parallelism pervasive and parallel programming mainstream in order to enable software to make effective use of the widely available parallel hardware and continue the performance improvement trend of the past several decades. ... The goal is to make parallel programming accessible to the average programmer. *The development of parallel software should be a core component of the undergraduate computer science and engineering curriculum.*"[1]

Given the the rapid proliferation of multi- to many-core architectures and the fact that increases in processor speed are slowing, it is clear that all students need to learn parallel programming as an essential skill. In the past, programmers could count on new generations of processors to speed up their programs' execution time with little or no intervention by the programmer. However, increases in the number of processors on a chip will not necessarily speed up existing sequential programs. Programmers will have to rewrite sequential programs to take advantage of multiple processors. While hard problems will likely continue to be solved by specialized "gurus" in parallel programming, all of our students must be familiar enough with the ideas of parallel programming to solve the sort of problems they will encounter in their professional careers.

Good overviews of the importance of concurrent programming are available in recent articles by Sutter and Larus [8, 9]. The following text is excerpted from the latter article:

> "For several reasons, the concurrency revolution is likely to be more disruptive than the OO revolution. First, concurrency will be integral to higher performance. ...
>
> The second reason that concurrency will be more disruptive than OO is that, although sequential programming is hard, concurrent programming is demonstrably more difficult."

Comments such as these have helped convince many computer scientists that we are heading into (yet another) crisis of software development. However, most students do

*Research partially supported by NSF CCLI grant DUE-0088895.

SIGCSE'10, March 10–13, 2010, Milwaukee, Wisconsin, USA.

[1] Emphasis added.

not yet obtain much exposure to high-level concurrent programming. While Computing Curricula 2001 [1] and the recent 2008 [5] revision specify a four-hour knowledge unit PF/EventDriven-Programming, few schools appear to be teaching this material in their introductory course sequences.[2] Most students likely see a brief mention of concurrency in operating systems or architecture courses,[3] while many programs provide advanced electives in parallel programming and concurrency.

We believe that an introduction to the ideas and difficulties of parallel programming can and should take place in the traditional CS 1 – CS 2 course sequence. In this paper we report on our experiences on introducing concurrency as an integral part of a CS 1 course. As explained below it is our experience that students find (simple) concurrency a very natural concept that matches well with their world view. It is more productive to take advantage of their intuition rather than trying to force program designs into a single-threaded sequential mode.

2. CONCURRENCY IN CS 1

There has been a great deal of interest in introducing concurrency in a more central way in the undergraduate CS curriculum.[4] But how early can these ideas be introduced? Does it even make sense to attempt this in the first two CS courses?

In the fall of 1999, the authors implemented a major update of the Williams College CS 1 course. With the support of the specially designed `objectdraw` library for Java, this course takes an objects-first approach, uses truly object-oriented graphics, incorporates event-driven programming techniques from the beginning, and includes concurrency quite early in the course. The authors now have ten years of experience teaching this course first at Williams and later at Pomona Colleges, and have authored a text book [3] using this approach.

Our course introduces event-driven programming on the very first day of class. Students define simple methods that respond to a variety of input events including the mouse button being clicked and the mouse being moved. Event-handling systems typically handle events sequentially. If the code executed to respond to a mouse click takes a long time, the system will not be able to react to other events until it is complete. As a result, code executed in response to such events must execute quickly or it will destroy the responsiveness of the system.

We also make extensive use of graphics and animations. The display of an animation is often triggered by an event like a mouse click. Displaying an animation, however, inherently takes a long time. Therefore, it is not reasonable to execute all of the code to produce the animation in the method that responds to the event. In particular, because screen updates are done by the event-handling thread, performing an animation in the event-handling thread will generally result in only the last frame being displayed.

The standard solution to this problem is to include code in the event handler to create a separate thread to display the animation. It is possible to design libraries that disguise this use of concurrency in performing animations by defining a type of event that occurs each time the next frame of an animation should be displayed. We wished, however, to provide an introduction that taught students the correct programming techniques so that they would not later have to learn an entirely different way of programming in standard Java.

As a result, in the third week of the semester we teach students how to create and execute separate processes. Students create classes that extend an `objectdraw` library class `ActiveObject`. `ActiveObject` is a trivial extension of the standard Java `Thread` class. The new class is necessary only because the standard `sleep` method of `Thread` throws an `InterruptedException` and we don't introduce exception handling until late in the term. The only new feature in `ActiveObject` is a `pause` method that does not throw exceptions. Students write their first simple program using separate processes in the fourth week of the term. This program implements a simple game that involves dropping a ball into a box. The `Ball` class from this program is illustrated in Figure 1.

When the ball is created, a filled oval is drawn on the screen, and the other instance variables are initialized using the parameters (omitted in the code displayed). At the end of the constructor, the `start` message is sent, which results in the creation of a new thread that begins executing the `run` method. The `run` method results in the ball falling to the bottom of the screen, where it is determined whether or not it is completely contained in a box that was passed in with the constructor.

While this assignment introduces students to the creation of threads, it is not a very compelling example of a concurrent program. While a separate thread is necessary for the animation to be displayed, there are really never two programmer-controlled threads active at the same time while this program is running. The event-handling thread awakens to launch the `Ball` thread when the user clicks and then it waits until another input event occurs.[5] Other than the creation of the thread, there is no interaction between the thread created in the `Ball` object and the main event thread. However, the `BoxBall` example provides an introduction to the mechanics of creating threads that prepares the students to complete a program that depends heavily on concurrency the following week.

In the fifth week of the term, students implement a simple version of the `Frogger`™ game (see Figure 2). For those who have not played it, this game involves guiding a frog across a four-lane highway without getting hit by a car. The program involves the creation of a separate thread for each car as well as one thread for each lane whose purpose is to periodically generate new cars.

The interactions between the cars and frog are very simple. Every time a thread associated with a car moves the car, it checks to see if the car has run over the frog. If so,

[2]Somewhat puzzlingly, the description of the knowledge unit does not mention concurrency even though concurrency is needed for non-trivial event-driven programs.

[3]There is a 6 hour knowledge unit OS/Concurrency in Curricula 2001, but it is more concerned with the support of concurrency in operating systems rather than writing concurrent programs. The Curriculum 2008 interim report expresses much concern about the growing importance of concurrency, but makes no changes in the core curriculum to reflect this importance.

[4]See for example the Workshop on Curricula for Concurrency and Parallelism at OOPSLA 2009.

[5]The event thread is busy updating the window, but this is outside of the programmer's control.

```
import objectdraw.*;

public class Ball extends ActiveObject {
   private static final int PAUSE_TIME = 50;
   private static final int DROP_DIST = 10;

   private int size;
   private FilledOval theBall;
   private Box theBox;
   private int bottom;

   // Create ball and start it falling
   public Ball(int size, Location pt, DrawingCanvas c,
               Box theBox, int bottom, Text score)  {
      theBall = new FilledOval(pt,size,size,c);
      ...
      start();
   }

   // Drop the ball to the bottom of the playing area.
   // At bottom, check if it landed in the box.
   public void run() {
      while (theBall.getY() < bottom - DROP_DIST) {
         theBall.move(0,DROP_DIST);
         pause(PAUSE_TIME);
      }
      if (insideBox()) {
         score.setText("You got it in!");
         theBox.moveBox();
      } else {
         score.setText("Try again!");
      }
      theBall.removeFromCanvas();
   }

   // Return true iff this ball is inside theBox.
   public boolean insideBox()  {
      double leftPoint = theBox.getLeft();
      double rightPoint = theBox.getRight();
      boolean leftIn = theBall.getX() > leftPoint;
      boolean rightIn = (theBall.getX() + size
                                       < rightPoint);
      return (leftIn && rightIn);
   }
}
```

Figure 1: Simplified version of Ball class from BoxBall game.

it sends a `kill` message to the frog, which results in setting its instance variable `isAlive` to false. When the user clicks to move the frog, the program tests to see if the frog is still alive. If so, then it is moved appropriately. If not, the click is ignored unless the user has clicked in a special part of the screen to reincarnate the frog.

To introduce concurrency at this early point in a student's education we must carefully select examples that limit how much students need to know about concurrency. All of our example programs are designed so that race conditions will generally not be an issue. Variables are typically only set by a single thread or are set consistently by threads with access to the variable, so the relative timing of threads does not make a difference in the results of program runs. For example, in Frogger, the fact that all a car does when it thinks it has killed the frog is set a boolean variable to be false means that interference is not an issue even if two cars detected that they overlapped with the frog's position at almost the same time.

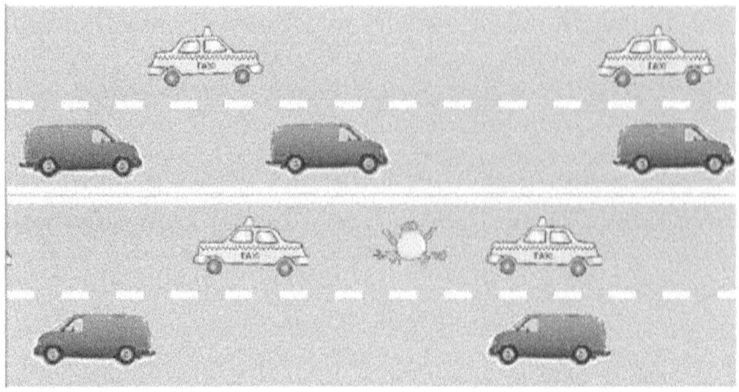

Figure 2: The Frogger game uses separate threads.

Our experience has convinced us that students find that concurrent programming matches well with their intuitions. When students look at a game like Frogger, they see the cars as independent entities. Forcing them to implement the combined motion of all of the cars in one sequential thread would seem less natural.

This is exactly what would happen if we tried to avoid introducing threads by instead using a library that provided a form of "animate" event that occurred each time a new frame of an animation needed to be drawn. All the cars would need to be moved one step each time this event occurred. To do this, the students would have to maintain an array of car positions and write a loop to update the array and the screen at each step. The resulting solution would not only seem less natural, it would in fact be more complex. In the concurrent solution, on the other hand, the class used to implement the motion of the cars is no more complicated than the `Ball` class shown in Figure 1. In particular, because each car moves independently (all cars in the same lane move at the same speed so that they don't run into each other), we are able to introduce this lab before we introduce arrays or other techniques to handle collections of objects.

If we avoid introducing concurrency early, we force students to learn to sequentialize naturally concurrent processes. If we instead introduce concurrency early using examples designed to avoid complex synchronization problems, we enable our students to appreciate the power of this approach while it still seems natural to them.

Threads are used pervasively in the course after the `BoxBall` and `Frogger` examples. In some programs presented or assigned in the course, concurrency is necessary in order to support the timely response to controls in event-driven programming, while in others it is used in support of many interacting objects and threads. Examples include labs to play the Simon game (where a separate thread is used to play a sequence of notes stored in an array) and the Nibbles™ game (where a separate thread is used to move the snake around the screen – under the control of a user who employs arrow keys to determine the direction to move). Concurrency also plays an important role in most of the final projects for the course – typically variations on games like PacMan™, Space Invaders™, Tetris™, Brickout™, Centipede™, etc.

Finally as part of our discussion of streams, students learn about web and mail servers, as well as about sockets and general client-server programming. In one of their lab assignments they write a simulator for the "Pictionary"™ game in which the program is started on two different computers. One is designated by a user as a server and the other is run as a client that connects via a socket. The user interacting with the server draws a picture which is transmitted one line segment at a time to the client, where it is drawn on a canvas. The client then sends guesses to the server until the client guesses the correct answer. While quite primitive, it gives the students a feel for how distributed computing works.

Thus by the end of our first course students have a general feel for the use of concurrent threads and simple client-server programming.

3. AN INFORMAL EVALUATION

While we worried a great deal about the introduction of concurrency during the first offering of the course in the fall of 1999, we discovered that most students found the notion of concurrency very natural, with traditionally difficult issues, such as parameter passing, overwhelming concurrency issues.

While we did not perform a formal evaluation of the material, we do have several indicators that suggest that the introduction of concurrency material was successful. At the end of the spring 2009 term we asked our students to rank our labs on educational value, difficulty, and fun. We used a scale of 1 to 5 where 1 is low and 5 is high.

Lab	Ed Value	Difficulty	Fun
Intro/eclipse	3.3	1.5	2.8
Laundry/conditionals	3.8	2.3	3.1
Magnets/class	3.4	2.7	2.8
Boxball/parameters	3.7	2.8	3.3
Frogger/concurrency	4.4	3.7	3.8
GUI	3.8	1.9	3.0
Recursive Picts	3.8	3.1	3.2
Recursive Lists	4.3	3.3	3.5
Simon/arrays	3.7	3.3	3.6
Nibbles/2-dim arrays	4.3	3.7	4.1
Datamining/strings	3.8	3.9	2.0
Pictionary/streams	3.6	2.3	3.5
TestProg 2 (**Tetris**)	3.9	4.4	3.6
Overall Average	3.8	3.0	3.3
Average/Concurrency	3.9	3.4	3.7
Average/Nonconcur.	3.7	2.7	2.9

Figure 3: Student evaluation of CS 1 labs. Labs with significant use of concurrency are in boldface.

The laboratories that involved concurrency were heavily weighted toward the end of the course, including the final test program and both array programs, no doubt impacting student ratings of difficulty. Nevertheless, we found the comparisons interesting. Because they involved some of the most complex programs, it was not a surprise that the average difficulty of the concurrent programs was distinctly above those of the others (3.4 versus 2.7). However the educational value of the concurrent programs were slightly higher than the others, while the "fun" rating was considerably higher. Interestingly, the highest scores in "fun" were also associated with higher levels of difficulty and educational value, as seen with the Frogger and Nibbles labs.

As another data point, for the final project in the 2009 spring term offering of the CS 1 course at Pomona College, students had a choice of writing a version of the Tetris game where the tetris pieces are animated by separate threads (the main event thread handles user interactions – key presses – with the game) or of writing a simplified facebook-style application that involved no concurrency. 26 of the 28 students enrolled in the course chose to do the Tetris game. The average grade on the assignment was 91.9 out of a maximum of 100. Other semesters have resulted in similar scores. The final project at Pomona in the fall of 2007 was a simplified version of the centipede game. In that game, one thread animated all of the pieces of the centipede, separate threads animated the movement of each of the bullets shot to destroy the centipede, and the main event thread responded to user interactions via the keyboard. That semester the average score for the final project was 98.4 (extra credit resulted in a top score of 103 for that assignment).

These grades, while not a perfect measure of student learning, do indicate that students were able to succeed in writing relatively sophisticated programs that use simple forms of concurrency. In particular the concurrency was used in the programs to animate motion of game components in the games and to respond to user input during this animation. Moreover, threads were able to communicate by calling methods that resulted in changes to instance variables whose values were accessed by other threads. While race conditions were avoided in the programming assignments, they were discussed in class and are tested on most final exams.

4. WHAT ABOUT RACE CONDITIONS?

As noted above, we are able to hold off on the discussion of race conditions and the need to use synchronized methods by carefully assigning programs that minimize opportunities for interference. However, as a matter of principle, we do introduce the problem of race conditions and the use of `synchronized` later in the semester as we want students to be aware of the complexities of concurrent programming.

We introduce a simple example to illustrate race conditions. We demonstrate a program to simulate two ATMs that are simultaneously accessing the same account. One ATM withdraws \$100 from the account a total of 200 times, while the second deposits \$100 to the account the same number of times. When the program is run, the students are surprised when the final balance of the account is different from the initial balance. They are even more surprised when running the program multiple times results in different final balances.

The difficulty lies in the (unsynchronized) method that changes the balance in response to a deposit or withdrawal.

```
public void changeBalance(int amount) {
  int newBalance = balance + amount;
  display.setText("" + newBalance);
  balance = newBalance;
}
```

The problem with this code (which is written a bit oddly in order to increase the odds that a race condition will result)[6] is that between the first line and last line of the method, another thread can come in and reset the balance.

We then illustrate how, with only one transaction on each ATM, we can obtain a balance of the expected $1000 or the unexpected values of $900 or $1100. The unexpected values result when one process starts executing the `changeBalance` method while the other is in the midst of executing the same method – having updated `newBalance`, but not yet resetting `balance`.

The students find this a compelling example (they all interact with ATM machines regularly and tend not to think of them as behaving randomly!). A question on the final exam consistently illustrates that the vast majority of students understand the issue and how to fix it (in this case by simply making the `changeBalance` method `synchronized`).

While this doesn't address all the possible problems with concurrent programming, it sets students up to understand that there are issues, which can be explored in later courses.

5. RELATED WORK

There are many possible approaches to introducing concurrency in a CS 1 course. We discuss a few here.

Lynn Andrea Stein's approach [7] is the most similar to ours. She proposed focusing the introductory course on interactions, using concurrency. More recently that course seems to have shifted from Java to Python, while still emphasizing interaction. We have not shifted our course as dramatically as hers to focus on interaction, but instead emphasize concurrency as a natural way of modelling problems and of programming solutions to them.

Ernst and Stevenson [4] describe their efforts to integrate concurrency into their undergraduate curriculum, including CS 1. Their focus is on traditional data parallel processing where processing a collection of data is divided into several threads, each of which handles a subset of the data. Generally there is little to no interaction between threads aside from the main thread waiting for all of the subthreads to finish their computations before resuming. This is the traditional style of concurrency that shows up frequently in scientific computation, but leads to limited kinds of programs compared with those where different objects interact more significantly. Our approach is different in that we provide a more task-parallel approach where different threads are performing different kinds of actions and have some (limited) interactions while executing, rather than waiting for subtasks to terminate.

Yet another approach is exemplified by Sanders & van Dam [6], who choose to hide concurrency by using a timer class to trigger regularly-spaced events that can be handled. Students write simple methods that are designed to react to a single event. However, as these events can be generated frequently, they can trigger animations generated as the responses to these events.

Ben-Ari and Kolikant [2] describe a course on concurrent and distributed systems designed for high school students. This was a much more specialized course that introduced students to more of the difficulties of concurrency with more emphasis on topics such as mutual exclusion, deadlock, and livelock. We expect that their work will be helpful in designing follow-up courses to the one described here.

There are indeed many ways that concurrency can be integrated into an introductory course. Our own approach has the advantage of matching students' intuitions of agents interacting while executing concurrently. While we limit the interactions between threads to avoid race conditions, students learn how to use concurrent processes to solve problems in ways more natural than attempting to sequentialize the processes.

6. CONCLUSIONS

In this paper, we have described the treatment of concurrency in the CS 1 course that the authors have taught over the last ten years. Students have reacted very positively to this course and informal evidence presented indicates that students both enjoy this material and find it educationally valuable. We hope to see many more groups experimenting with how to introduce concurrency early in students' undergraduate careers so that they will learn to think of concurrency as a natural approach to problems.

With the increasing importance of many core computers, it is becoming critical that our students become more comfortable and knowledgeable about concurrency. While what we have described here is only a first step for students, and many important complications are not addressed, we believe that it ise an important first step that can be built on in more advanced courses, starting with CS 2.

7. REFERENCES

[1] Computing curricula 2001. *J. Educ. Resour. Comput.*, page 1.

[2] M. Ben-Ari and Y. B.-D. Kolikant. Thinking parallel: the process of learning concurrency. In *ITiCSE '99: Proceedings of the 4th annual SIGCSE/SIGCUE ITiCSE conference on Innovation and technology in computer science education*, pages 13–16, New York, NY, USA, 1999. ACM.

[3] K. B. Bruce, A. Danyluk, and T. Murtagh. *Java: An eventful approach.* Prentice Hall, 2006.

[4] D. J. Ernst and D. E. Stevenson. Concurrent CS: preparing students for a multicore world. In *ITiCSE '08: Proceedings of the 13th annual conference on Innovation and technology in computer science education*, pages 230–234, New York, NY, USA, 2008. ACM.

[5] Interim Review Task Force. Computer science curriculum 2008: An interim revision of CS 2001. Technical report, ACM / IEEE CS, 2008.

[6] K. E. Sanders and A. van Dam. *Object-Oriented Programming in Java: A Graphical Approach.* Addison-Wesley, 2006.

[7] L. A. Stein. What we've swept under the rug: Radically rethinking CS 1. *Computer Science Education*, 8(2):118–129, 1998.

[8] H. Sutter. The free lunch is over: a fundamental turn toward concurrency in software. *Dr. Dobb's Journal*, 30(3), 2005.

[9] H. Sutter and J. Larus. Software and the concurrency revolution. *Queue*, 3(7):54–62, 2005.

[6]The `setText` method executed in the second line refreshes a value displayed on the screen, providing a likely opportunity for another thread to grab the processor and resume executing.

A Technology Infused Science Summer Camp to Prepare Student Leaders in 8th Grade Classrooms

Youwen Ouyang
Computer Science and Information Systems
California State University
San Marcos, CA
ouyang@csusm.edu

Katherine Hayden
College of Education
California State University
San Marcos, CA
khayden@csusm.edu

ABSTRACT

Technology-enhanced science curriculum has potential for introducing fundamental computing concepts to adolescents. iQUEST (investigations for Quality Understanding and Engagement for Students and Teachers) is designed to transform middle school science teachers into advocates for technology being a critical part of student learning. It targets 7th and 8th grade science classrooms that serve high percentages of Hispanic students. To prepare student leaders in iQUEST teachers' classrooms, a group of 24 Hispanic students from project schools were invited to participate in a weeklong technology infused science summer camp. These students would continue on in project classrooms where teachers receive intensive technology training and support over the next year. This paper describes the camp activities and reports how the camp impacted students' aptitude and attitude toward technology and science.

Categories and Subject Descriptors

K.3.2 [**Computing Milieux**]: Computers and Education – Computer and Information Science Education

General Terms

Design, Economics, Experimentation, Human Factors.

Keywords

Computing foundations, middle school, science curriculum, summer camp.

1. INTRODUCTION

To broaden participation in computing by diverse populations, the computing community has long recognized the need for outreach activities for students at the middle school level [2]. The "Gr8 Designs for Gr8 Girls" project at University of Toronto offers one-day programs where girls rotate through four different activities that focus on design and creativity [5]. The "Increasing Student Participation in Research Development" program at Lamar University held one-day computing academies where female and minority middle school students work in teams of two or three in completing hands-on activities [6]. A 5-day summer workshop called I*Wear was offered by the Hong Kong Polytechnic University to use wearable computing and e-textiles to teach middle school students about technology and computing in a context that is futuristic, innovative, and creative [10]. The "Build It, Trust It, Use It" project at the Northern Kentucky University offers a series of three eight-week workshops on Sunday afternoons for selected recent immigrant families of middle schoolers to build computers together [7]. The "Digispired" project at Virginia State University offers a 3-year program for 89 middle school students where they meet two weeks during summer and 10 – 15 Saturdays during the year to learn about programming, computer graphics, and animation [8].

However, afterschool programs or summer camps have the inherent disadvantage of the number and types of students they can reach as well as the contact hours each student can receive. Excitements and knowledge gained from summer and afterschool activities can be diminished over the next few months if they are isolated from regular classroom experience. Inside middle schools, technology related electives often focus more on keyboarding, Microsoft Office, and Internet searching. Movement for integration of technology in regular curriculum has been largely promoted by Education Technology faculty who focus on pedagogy instead of fundamental computing concepts underlying hardware, software, and applications. The ACM K-12 Task Force Curriculum Committee recognized that the lack of integration of computer science into the K-12 curriculum played an important role in the serious shortage of information technologists at all levels [4].

The *investigations for Quality Understanding and Engagement for Students and Teachers* (iQUEST) project at California State University San Marcos (CSUSM) targets 7th and 8th grade science classrooms that serve high percentages of Hispanic students and low socioeconomic populations. It is designed to deliver learning modules that are rich in both computing and science content for these students through science classrooms. The computing curriculum for iQUEST modules includes Level I (Foundations of Computer Science) and Level II (Computer Science in the Modern World) of the ACM K-12 Model Curriculum.

The main iQUEST components are shown in Figure 1. Professional development activities are designed for science teachers to embed Information and Communication Technology (ICT) in their curriculum. With support from computing, education, and science experts, teachers collaboratively design classroom activities that engage their students in the use of ICT to support their learning of science. Fundamental computing concepts are explained to teachers and students in the context of the adopted ICT-enhanced resources. Support for teachers and students are provided by CSUSM students for classroom implementation of iQUEST modules. Online collaboration and videoconferencing allow students and teachers to interact with each other as well as ICT-savvy science experts. Outreach activities will focus on career education for counselors, students and their parents. High school media arts classes will visit local technology businesses and produce career education videos to be used in outreach activities. These videos will be accessible on the project Web site.

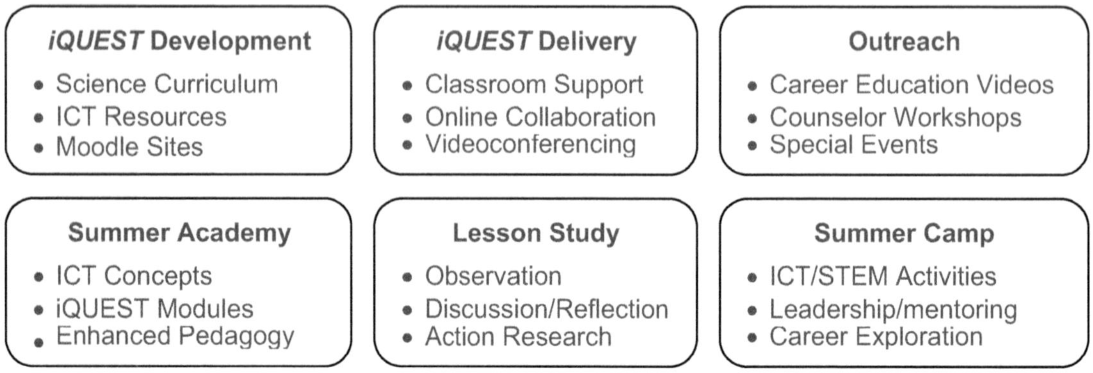

Figure 1Main Components of iQUEST

In May 2009, iQUEST welcomed seventeen 8th grade teachers to a one-day orientation where teachers were introduced to each other, project leadership, and the main components of the project. These teachers committed to the project for two years. Professional development for teachers includes a 3-day Academy during summers of 2009 and 2010 as well as two annual collaborative lesson study rotations and monthly afterschool workshops throughout the school year. In addition, the project provides continuous support for teachers as they design and implement iQUEST modules in their classrooms. This paper focuses on a weeklong student summer camp held in July 2009 to prepare student leaders in project classrooms. Section 2 describes the student demographics in the summer camp, the overview of camp activities, and highlights of activities that integrate computing and science curriculum. Section 3 reports on the analyses of two surveys administered to students at the beginning and end of the camp. The concluding remarks are presented in Section 4.

2. WEEKLONG SUMMER CAMP

2.1 Demographics

All students who were invited to the iQUEST Student Summer Camp were Hispanic with 50% girls and 50% boys. There were 12 students from each of the two school districts closest to campus and the two largest partner school districts involved in the project. Each of these districts has an average of about 50% Hispanic students in their schools. Teachers invited applications from students who were considered would most likely to benefit from the experience as well as likely to be committed for the entire week experience. Students were required to submit a short essay for why they wanted to attend as part of the application. Site administrators made the final selection and a waiting list was created in case of attrition. A family orientation was scheduled and offered in both English and Spanish.

2.2 Camp Overview

The iQUEST Summer Camp is designed to produce student leaders in project classrooms who are excited and knowledgeable about using technology to support their learning of science. A guiding principle for iQUEST is that technology must be introduced in the context of science content to make its way to classrooms. Although the 2009 iQUEST Summer Camp served only incoming 8th graders because the iQUEST focus for the 2009/2010 school year is 8th grade, iQUEST is scheduled to also work with 7th graders in the 2010/2011 school year. Therefore, we were looking for a theme that could be applied to both grade levels. The Science Content Standards for California K-12 Public Schools [3] includes an "Investigation and Experimentation" strand throughout all grade levels. The National Science Education Standards [12] also identify "Unifying Concepts and Processes" as a strand that transcends disciplinary and grade boundaries. Therefore, we identified "Scientific Observations and Process" as the theme for our summer camps. Students learn what constitutes being good observers in a variety of venues through activities that require them to record scientific data accurately. One key objective for the camp is for students to develop an appreciation for how technology enhances science discovery. Students are constantly engaged in activities that use technology to assist data recording, visual record keeping, organization, and scientific measurements.

The 2009 iQUEST Summer Camp was held on the campus of CSUSM from Monday, July 13 through Friday, July 17. The university campus was chosen to be the location for the camp to provide students with state-of-the-art technology experiences in university science labs and classrooms. Many students had never been to a university campus before, so hosting the camp at the university helped these students see college as within reach. Buses were arranged to pick up and drop off students from three schools because transportation to campus can be difficult and time consuming for some families. Camp activities started at 9:00 am and ended at 3:00 pm.

Throughout the camp, students experienced the fun and excitement of science in a shared community of peer learners. Students worked in pairs to observe and classify live crabs that were captured by camp teachers the day before. (Teachers returned the crabs to the ocean at the end of the day.) Group activities were designed for students to use probes to measure the electromagnetic spectrum. A videoconference with an imaging scientist from Rochester Institute of Technology guided students through the process of taking apart a consumable camera. Within the eye dissection lab, students participated in both virtual and physical dissection of a cow/sheep eye to investigate and observe the geometric shapes and angles associated with its anatomy and physiology. Geocaching took students through an interesting adventure on campus with the help of Global Positioning System (GPS) receivers. A career panel was also presented to students where professional men and women shared the use of technology in their daily work. Each day ended with students writing their reflection as blog entries.

It is important to note that instructors for the summer camp were science teachers, not computer scientists or technologists, to reflect the reality of middle school science classrooms. The team included two high school, and one middle school teacher, each with a different expertise in science including physics, life science and physical science. Project leadership worked closely with instructors to identify technology resources and to help teachers integrate appropriate components of the ACM K-12 Model Curriculum into science activities. The following section highlights some of such components.

2.3 Computing Concepts in Science Activities

Marc Prensky, a frequent speaker at K-12 education conferences, recommends that teachers rethink their strategies and pedagogy to meet the needs of the "digital native" students [13]. Technology has been introduced to teachers through the use of project based, real world activities where experiences are often shared in online environments such as wikis, blogs and online communities [1]. A transformed classroom environment is to be rich in technology experiences and provide immediate classroom access to information [14]. Unfortunately, computer science education has not been able to ride on the wave of technology integration in classrooms to promote understanding of fundamental computing concepts. The following summer camp activities demonstrate how technology integration in science can present engaging opportunities for computer science education as described in the ACM K-12 Model Curriculum. The key is to provide necessary content knowledge in computing concepts to teachers so that they can apply such knowledge during teachable moments throughout the school year.

Moodle [11] is an open source course management system that has been widely adopted by many universities and school districts to support online collaboration among teachers and students. Currently, most iQUEST partner districts do not have any course management system in place for their teachers, and the ones that do, have had little acceptance due to lack of training. iQUEST hosts Moodle for project teachers and creates a Moodle shell for each participating teacher to implement for student learning activities. A Moodle shell was created for the 2009 summer camp for camp instructors to post camp schedules, online resources, and reflection prompts. Each student received an account to access the camp Moodle shell, not only during the camp day in the computer lab, but also from home. This presented the opportunity for teachers to share with students the basic components of computer networks and organization of Internet elements. At the end of each day, students were asked to use the Moodle Blog feature to write reflectively about their experiences and share them with others as Web content. The exercises of including images, sound, text, and links in students' blog entries provided the opportunity to discuss Web page design, hypermedia and common formats for data transmission.

For the crab activity, each student pair was assigned a live crab to create detailed observations of the crab that would allow others to identify the crab by studying the observation notes. The observations then were collected and distributed among student pairs. Prior to the distribution, teachers and students discussed the identification system for the records and crabs as well as different distribution algorithms to ensure no student pair would be assigned their own observation record and crab. Once students received their assigned observation records, they rotated through all the stations and attempted to match the observation record with the right crab. This prompted students to apply the concepts of logic and set to problem solving. When a match between crab and observation was reached, both the pair that found the match and the pair that recorded the observation were rewarded. This reward system motivated students to carefully describe key characteristics that would distinguish their crab from the rest.

Geocaching was the most popular camp activity for the students. GPS receivers drew students' attention to computing technology beyond standard desktop and laptop computers. Students learned about how technology advancements and the system of satellites provided positioning data related to longitude and latitude. As students traveled around campus with their GPS receivers to find cache containers hidden by camp instructors, they recognized the delay of GPS reading caused by communication between the receivers and the satellites. The fact that two people standing next to each other would get different readings on their receivers if they had come from different directions, prompted discussions of computers as models of intelligent behavior and what distinguishes humans from computers. A campus map was given to students so that they could strategize the shortest path to get to the proximity of each cache container. Students were also asked to place containers and provide clear step-by-step directions to help others locate their "treasure". This process allowed students to gain insights into algorithms writing.

3. IMPACT ANALYSES

To assess the impact of the Summer Camp activities on students' attitude toward science and technology, two surveys were administered both at the beginning and end of the iQUEST Summer Camp week. The Test of Science Related Attitudes (TOSRA) survey [9] contained 28 items related to student attitudes toward science. The Information and Communication Technology Attitude (ICTA) survey focused on attitudes toward technology integrated instruction and technology in general. It contained 49 questions. For each question, a five point Likert scale was utilized with 1 being strongly disagree and 5 being strongly agree. Some questions were worded positively while others were worded negatively. When calculating the score to represent a student's overall attitude, reverse coded items were rescored to ensure that a participant's higher score corresponded to positive attitude. Since ICTA has many more questions than TOSRA, we decided to divide the overall score for each student by the number of questions to allow same scales for comparison. A score close to 3 indicates the student felt neutral about science or technology but a score close to 5 indicates strong interest toward science or technology.

There were 12 boys and 12 girls in the camp program. A randomly generated ID was assigned to each student so that the scores on TOSRA and ICTA could be compared. Figure 2 compares the pre and post TOSRA scores for every girl in the camp. Each dot on the line reflects an average TOSRA score for one student. Similarly, Figure 3 compares the pre and post TOSRA scores for every boy in the camp. The pre and post ICTA scores for girls and boys are compared in Figures 4 and 5 respectively. Scores in all four charts were arranged according to the ascending order of student IDs. As a result, the first pair of dots on Figure 2 and the first pair of dots on Figure 4 belong to the same girl. Two boys' responses for TOSRA were not completed properly. We decided not to include their scores for ICTA in Figure 5 for it to be comparable to Figure 3. One boy's pre and post TOSRA scores were both below 3 and, therefore, were not shown in Figure 3.

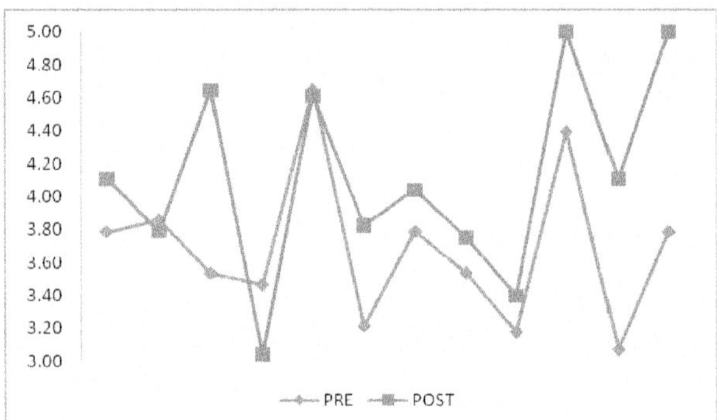

Figure 2 Pre & Post TOSRA Scores for Girls

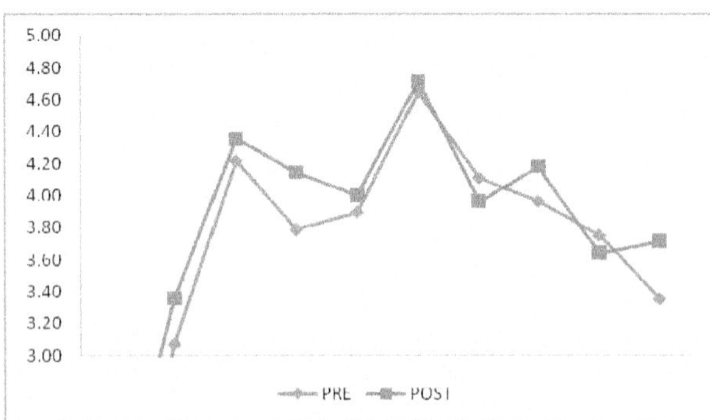

Figure 3 Pre & Post TOSRA Scores for Boys

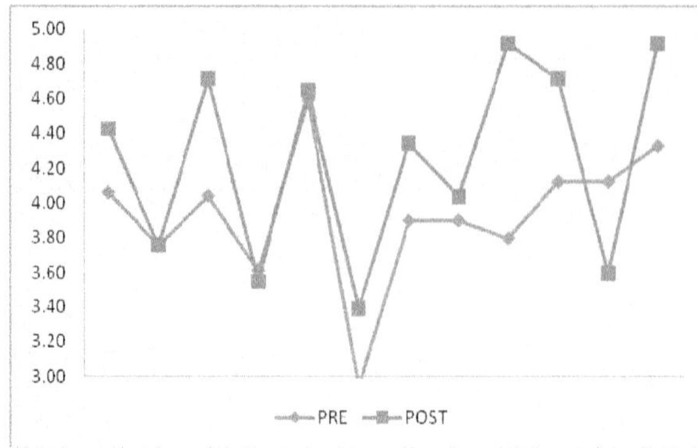

Figure 4 Pre & Post ICTA Scores for Girls

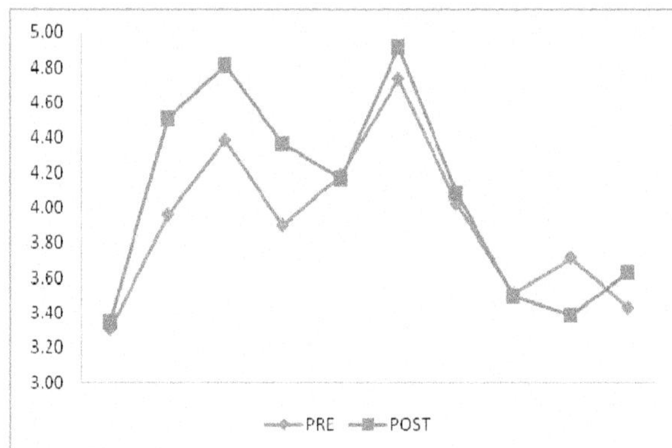

Figure 5 Pre & Post ICTA Scores for Boys

Due to the small size of our sample, we have been advised by our external evaluator to present the data descriptively rather than inferentially. Most student scores indicate a positive impact on their attitude toward science as well as interest and competency in technology as a result of attending the summer camp. There was one noticeable negative change of scores on TOSRA and two noticeable negative changes of scores on ICTA. Student TOSRA scores and gains seemed to follow a similar pattern as their ICTA scores and gains. Students scoring high on TOSRA also scored high on ICTA. Students whose scores dropped on TOSRA also dropped on ICTA. The only exception is the second to last girl in the charts.

Factor analysis of the ICTA indicates that the survey contains several subgroups of questions. The largest proportion of ICTA questions were based on a "computer competency" factor. Results for competency questions mirrored the overall scale, with about half a standard deviation increase overall from pre to post surveys. However, questions related to career interest showed no significant differences. These results were consistent with focus group conversations held near the end of the camp by the external evaluator. Students expressed appreciation for the exposure to technology tools, but in discussing their career objectives, they often cited long-standing interests that had existed prior to the camp experience. Often these interests were influenced by prior relationships with parents or siblings. It is likely that a brief camp experience is not sufficient to have a dramatic influence on most students' career goals. Ongoing evaluation of the project will track camp participants and other students to identify factors in the iQUEST project that may be salient to influencing career interests among middle school students.

4. CONCLUSIONS

The 2009 iQUEST Summer Camp confirmed the premise for the iQUEST project that middle school science curriculum presents excellent opportunities to integrate various components of the ACM K-12 Model Curriculum. The integration of computer science education and science activities as illustrated in Section 2.3 provided evidence that, with proper support, science teachers can become advocates for both computing concepts and technology related careers. The iQUEST project will continue to follow the students from the summer camp throughout the school year. As these students participate in project activities in their science classrooms, we will be able to further study the impact of the summer camp activities on their leadership in adapting technology to support learning. Classroom observations will provide the opportunity to closely look at the classroom environment created by the project teachers. The TOSRA and ICTA surveys will also be administered to all students in project classrooms at the beginning and end of the school year. Such data will allow comparison of the impact of a yearlong intervention with that of the summer camp experience.

5. ACKNOWLEDGMENTS

The iQUEST project is funded by the National Science Foundation (DRL 0833753). The opinions expressed in this paper are those of the authors and do not represent the views of NSF.

Talbot Bielefeldt and Greg Sampson-Gruener, Senior Research Associates at the International Society for Technology in Education (ISTE), are the external evaluators for the iQUEST project. The authors wish to thank them for their valuable input in data analyses and interpretation. Special thanks go to camp instructors Jorge Hirmas, Traves Oneill, and Kimberly White as well as the wonderful camp assistants, Elizabeth Montes and Antonio Sanchez. Both Elizabeth and Antonio are Hispanic students from the Computer Science and Information Systems Department at CSUSM. They not only provided valuable technical support but also were excellent role models for the kids.

6. REFERENCES

[1] Boss, S. and Krauss, J. 2007 *Reinventing Project-based Learning*, International Society for Technology in Education, Eugene, OR

[2] Broadening Participation in Computing Research and Education: Report of Computing Research Association Workshop on Broadening Participation (October 2004), DOI=http://www.cra.org/Activities/workshops/broadening.participation/report.html

[3] Bruton, S. and Ong, F. editors *Science Content Standards for California Public Schools, Kindergarten Through Grade Twelve*, California Department of Education (CDE) Press DOI=http://www.cde.ca.gov/BE/ST/SS/documents/sciencestnd.pdf

[4] Computer Science Teacher Association (CSTA), *A Model Curriculum for K-12 Computer Science: Final Report by the ACM K-12 Task Force Curriculum Committee,* 2nd ed. October 2003, DOI=http://www.csta.acm.org/Curriculum/sub/ACMK12CSModel.html.

[5] Craig, M. and Horton, D. "Gr8 Designs for Gr8 Girls: A Middle-School Program and Its Evaluation", in *Proceedings of 2009 SIGCSE*, March 3 – 7, Chattanooga, Tennesse pp 221 – 225

[6] Doerschuk, P., Liu, J., Mann, J. 2009 "INSPIRED Computing Academies for Middle School Students: Lessons Learned", in *Proceedings of 2009 Tapia*, April 1 – 4, Portland, Oregon, pp 52 – 57

[7] Doyle, M., Kirby, K. G., Newell, G. 2008 "Engaging Constructions: Family-Based Computing Experiences for Immigrant Middle school Students", in *Proceedings of 2008 SIGCSE,* March 12 – 15, Portland, Oregon, pp 58 – 62

[8] Javidi, G., Sheybani, E. 2009 "DIGISPIRED: Digital Inspiration for Interactive Game Design and Programming" *Journal of Computing Science in Colleges*, Vol. 24, No. 3, pp 144 – 150

[9] Joyce, B. A. and Farenga, S. J. 1999 "Informal Science Experience, Attitudes, Future Interest in Science, and Gender of High-ability Student: An Exploratory Study", *School Science and Mathematics* Vol. 99, No. 8, pp 431 – 437

[10] Lau, W., Ngai, G., Chan, S., and Cheung J. "Learning Programming through Fashion and Design: A Pilot Summer Course in Wearable Computing for Middle School Students", in *Proceedings of 2009 SIGCSE*, March 3 – 7, Chattanooga, Tennessee, pp 504 – 508

[11] Moodle, DOI=http://moodle.org/

[12] National Committee on Science Education Standards and Assessment, *National Science Education Standards*, National Research Council, 1996

[13] Prensky, M. 2001 "Digital Natives Digital Immigrants", *On the Horizon*, Vol. 9, No. 5 MCB University Press, October 2001

[14] Warlick, D. F. 2004, *Redefining Literacy for the 21st Century*, Linworth Publishing Inc., Worthington, Ohio

Design and Evaluation of a Computer Science and Engineering Course for Middle School Girls

Gabriela Marcu[1], Samuel J. Kaufman[2], Jaihee Kate Lee[3], Rebecca W. Black[2], Paul Dourish[2], Gillian R. Hayes[2], Debra J. Richardson[2]

[1]HCI Institute
Carnegie Mellon University
gmarcu@cs.cmu.edu

[2]University of California, Irvine
{kaufmans, rwblack, jpd, hayesg, djr}@uci.edu

[3]Global IT Academy
Brea Olinda High School
jaihee.kate_lee@yahoo.com

ABSTRACT

A significant focus in the United States recently has been to increase engagement and interest in STEM curricula, particularly among girls and underrepresented minorities [3]. In this work, we take an approach to teaching and learning that supports flexibility, experimentation, and play with technology. With this approach, we aim to make STEM curricula more comfortable and engaging for all types of children and teens, with a particular emphasis on lower socio-economic status female students. We designed and tested a computing course for middle school girls, and this work resulted in three best practices: hands-on work incorporating creativity through crafts into engineering and computing, the frequent presence of an audience to motivate engagement, and engineering-focused individual roles structuring group work. Pre- and post-surveys and exit interviews revealed significant changes in attitudes and an enthusiasm for engineering projects and careers as a result of participation in the course.

Categories and Subject Descriptors

K.3.2 [**Computers and Education**]: Computer and Information Science Education – *computer science education, information systems education, curriculum.*

General Terms

Measurement, Experimentation, Design

Keywords

Computer science and engineering education, gender issues, diversity in computing, hands-on curriculum.

1. INTRODUCTION

A major challenge to middle and high school computer science curricula stems from the differences in the way girls and boys engage with the material. Margolis and Fisher have described a "'magnetic attraction' that motivates many boys to engage in intense self-guided exploration of computing" while "girls … then are often sitting shoulder to shoulder in classes with boys who have spent endless hours learning everything they can about computers and who have friends to turn to when they want to learn even more" [7]. With a focus on hands-on activities that result in meaningful products related to real-world applications, girls can become more engaged. In addition, increased confidence with STEM and interest in its applications can help girls experiment and learn. In this work, we take an approach to teaching and learning that supports flexibility, experimentation, and play with technology. With this approach, we aim to make STEM curricula more comfortable and engaging for all types of children and teens, with a particular emphasis on lower socio-economic status female students. This approach includes an emphasis on sharing and presentation of projects, based on the idea that performance for an audience can motivate at-risk children and teens to engage with technology [5].

We developed and tested a four-week course on computing and engineering for middle school girls—primarily Latinas and other minorities from low-income families. We used several innovative pedagogical tools in the curriculum designed to improve the attitudes of participants towards engineering and computer science, improve confidence with these activities, and increase interest in these careers. In particular, we found three features of our course to be particularly successful: hands-on work incorporating creativity through crafts into engineering and computing, the frequent presence of an audience to motivate engagement, and engineering-focused individual roles structuring group work.

2. CURRICULUM

This engineering instruction was offered as part of Eureka!, a four-week summer camp held each year for middle school-aged girls affiliated with Girls Incorporated of Orange County, a non-profit organization inspiring girls to be strong, smart and bold. 53 girls participated in the Monday to Friday camp and all of them took our required course, along with a variety of courses with themes ranging from body image, to film, to college preparation. Instruction lasted an hour a day twice a week and one half-day, totaling approximately 12 hours of instructional time. The 53 girls were divided up into three consecutive class periods.

A female recent college graduate served as the primary instructor for the course, facilitating activities and enforcing timelines and rules. One male undergraduate student and eight female high school students provided additional instructional support. The high school girls, who had taken classes in computer science, served as mentors and role models to the girls in the course. At the same time, the high school volunteers were mentored by the undergraduate student and recent graduate who were in turn mentored by the three female and one male professors involved in this work. At least four high school volunteers were present at each class session, providing hands-on help for each of the four groups of students in a class. This one-on-one attention for the groups created a supportive environment for learning through exploration, including minimal troubleshooting support.

SIGCSE'10, March 10–13, 2010, Milwaukee, Wisconsin, USA.

2.1 Pedagogical Design

The curriculum was based on the principle that students learn best when they are actively involved in the process [1][10]. We designed the curriculum to be entirely hands-on, embracing both Piagetian and Vygotskian perspectives on learning. Specifically, we drew on Piaget's formulation of learning and cognitive development as constructed through hands-on experience of the world [9]. Further, we drew on Vygotsky's emphasis on how children imagine and play [11]. In his view, they begin their play with pivots (*e.g.,* sticks, dolls) and can then move on to imaginative play without any props. In our curriculum, we wanted a focus on tangible devices to provide pivots to allow students to begin through playful interaction, and move eventually into the deeper understanding and imagination required for abstract programming and engineering abilities.

Thus, we found Papert's development of Piaget's work to be particularly influential. Building from constructivism, Papert described the educational theory of constructionism in which learning is a *reconstruction* as opposed to a *transmission* of knowledge [8]. He further extended these ideas to include manipulation of materials and technologies with the idea that students learn best when the learning is associated with the creation of a real-life product. We thus wanted the curriculum to involve design projects and the creation of final, presentable products.

To accomplish these educational goals, we used PicoCricket Kits[1], which combine basic programming concepts, electrical devices, and creative designing, as the focus of our course. These kits include electrical devices such as a light, speaker, motor, light sensor, and sound sensor, which are connected to a computer through USB cables (see Figure 1, left) and controlled using composable drag-and-drop programming elements (see Figure 1, right). Legos ® and craft supplies are also included to involve artistic design and to foster creativity. All devices in the PicoCricket Kit have a Lego ® base, allowing them to be integrated into Lego ® construction.

We divided the girls into small groups and created a role for each group member that was conceptually linked to a component of the kit and a related field within engineering. The roles were: software engineer, electrical engineer, civil engineer, and design engineer. The girls rotated through the roles, taking on a different one each class until each group member had performed each role at least once. One of our goals was to help the girls gain an understanding of what it means to be an engineer through experiencing both the hands-on and conceptual work of several different kinds of engineers, thereby showing them a path to a career in computer science and engineering. Working on small group projects with designated roles also had the benefit of allowing each girl to master a particular task and conceptual domain of knowledge before moving on to the next role [2]. Moreover, students working in small groups tend learn more of what is taught and retain it longer than they do when the same information is presented in a more traditional one to many lecture format [6].

The roles were defined solely by designated tools from the PicoCricket Kits. In this way, we hoped to facilitate learning about the roles and tasks through objects, and thereby ground understanding of these abstract professional identities. No further explanation or description of the roles was given other than of the purpose of the tools. The software engineer used a laptop to write programs using the PicoCricket software, PicoBlocks. The electrical engineer was responsible for the devices (light, speaker, motor, light sensor, sound sensor) and cables. The civil engineer was tasked with building a structure for the devices using materials such as Legos ® and Play Doh ©. The design engineer was encouraged to bring an artistic perspective to the design of the project with a variety of craft materials including pipe cleaners, fuzzy balls, feathers, popsicle sticks, and glue. Each girl wore a small, color-coded pin to help her formally embody her role.

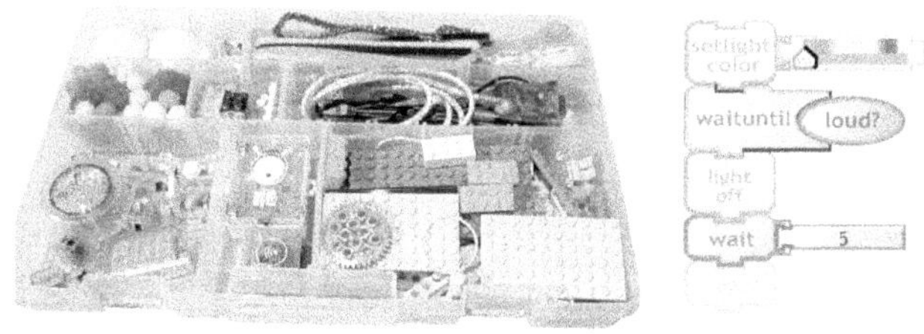

Figure 1. The contents of a PicoCricket Kit. Left, all physical parts: devices, cables, Legos, and craft supplies. Right, a sample program written using PicoBlocks software.

2.2 Schedule

The course met eight times and was divided into four parts: introduction to PicoCrickets, one-day assigned activities, a larger creative project, and preparation for final project presentations. The first one-hour day was intended as a non-structured introduction to PicoCrickets. Girls were divided into groups of four and each group was provided with a PicoCricket Kit. The girls were instructed to open the kits, see what was inside, and try experimenting with the parts to see how they worked. No roles were assigned at this first session, because the focus was on the girls learning about the PicoCrickets.

Over the next two class periods, the girls completed "out of the box" PicoCricket projects and began rotating through the roles. Assignments included making a musical instrument by conducting electricity through a pickle and creating a kinetic sculpture that moves based on sensor inputs (*e.g.,* noise or light). Groups were tasked with following the instructions included in the kit while being as creative as possible. One project was assigned per session resulting in varying degrees of "completeness" from groups that were completely polished to those that were only partly finished. Many groups added a lot of their own creative ideas to design a more complex product. A future audience was emphasized by holding project demonstrations at the end of each class session. These were lively, positive events, and the instructor took photographs and videos as each group presented.

The second half of the course was devoted to a longer-term group project of the girls' design. The girls brainstormed collectively about different things in the world they could build using PicoCrickets, which they then turned into a project idea in their small groups. Over the next three class periods they completed their projects and continued rotating roles each day. The projects included such diverse ideas as an amusement park, the internal organs of the human body, and a fairy tale house in the woods.

At the end of the third week, the girls spent a day at our university. A panel of professionals representing the four engineering roles spoke about career paths and daily activities. The girls watched demos of research projects. They then divided into groups based on their favorite roles to prepare posters about each career.

[1] http://www.picocricket.com/

During the final class day, we video recorded the girls demonstrating their projects. On the last day of camp, at an all day celebration, this video was shown for family and friends.

3. ASSESSMENT METHODS

We used a mixed-method approach to evaluating the course: pre and post-surveys, observation of in-class activities, and interviews with both the girls in the course and the high school student mentors. This approach enabled us to collect a large amount of empirical data even within the constraints of only a four-week course during which we could not interfere with class instruction time substantially. Girls in the course were between the ages of 11 and 14. More than half (30 of 53) self-identified as Hispanic. Girls enrolled in camp pay tuition for the entire four week course on a sliding scale, with most girls served by the organization coming from low income families. The high school girls came from relatively higher income families and were aged 15 to 17. One had limited knowledge of Spanish.

A pre-survey was administered at the beginning of the first class and a post-survey at the beginning of the final class. Both surveys took approximately 10 minutes to complete and included questions on a five-point Likert scale about attitudes towards engineering and computer science, confidence with engineering and computing, and interest in these careers. The post-survey also included assessment questions about the workshop itself. To test changes in participant perceptions, we used Mann Whitney's U Test for significance to analyze the pre and post-surveys. This choice is appropriate for independent, ordinal data, and also allowed us to compare our significance levels with those reported in previous work [4].

Extensive field notes were used to document a total of 30 hours of observation. All students and instructors were observed for the duration of the course, at each class session.

Optional interviews were conducted with fifteen girls during the final class session either individually (n=6) or in groups of 3 or 4. The interviews were semi-structured in nature to allow the girls to lead the discussion to those issues they found most important. Topics included what they liked about the course, what they learned, and how they envision an improved course in the future. A group interview was also conducted with the high school student instructors, focused on what they enjoyed about their experiences, their challenges, and what they learned.

4. RESULTS

Interview and survey results indicate the course was both fun and educational. All 15 girls interviewed reported that they had fun, learned new things, and would participate in the course again. Their favorite reported aspects of the course were using the PicoCrickets, using their creativity, and being able to choose their final projects.

Post-survey questions evaluating the course yielded positive responses. In response to "this workshop was fun", 41 of the 53 girls (78%) either agreed or strongly agreed. When asked if they learned something from the workshop, 45 (85%) either agreed or strongly agreed. The girls also reported an increased interest in STEM because of the workshop. When asked about an increased interest in computers, 31 (59%) either agreed or strongly agreed, and in response to engineering, 34 (65%) either agreed or strongly agreed. In addition, 34 (65%) of the girls agreed or strongly agreed that they would recommend the workshop to their friends. Furthermore, the girls reported more positive attitudes towards, perceptions of, and confidence and interest in engineering and computer science after the course (see Table 1). The most significant survey items focused on understanding what programmers and engineers do, suggesting that one of the greatest strengths of this course was making participants feel that they have a better understanding of these careers. The second highest significance was in the survey items regarding the difficulty of programming and engineering, and the girls' answers lowered by almost one full point on the five point Likert scale. These changes indicate that the course raised girls' confidence. The rest of the survey items that are significant focus on the girls' interest in, and confidence with, engineering and computing. These survey results suggest that we improved perceptions and attitudes, and this was further demonstrated in interviews with the girls.

Table 1. Survey Items with Mann-Whitney U Significance Levels, Ordered by Significance. The darkly shaded values are significant at the p < .01 level, and the lightly shaded values are significant at the p < .05 level.

Survey Item	Pre Mean (St. Dev)	Post Mean (St. Dev)	*p*
I understand what programmers do.	2.94 (.99)	3.85 (.92)	.0000
I understand what engineers do.	3.16 (.99)	4.12 (.73)	.0000
Engineering is hard.	3.21 (.83)	2.47 (.98)	.0001
Programming is hard.*	3.12 (.75)	2.56 (.71)	.0003
I know more than my friends about computers.*	3.10 (.92)	3.63 (.91)	.0032
I like engineering.	3.39 (1.0)	3.96 (.89)	.0037
Engineering jobs are boring.	2.53 (.83)	2.06 (.88)	.0076
Engineering is fun.	3.52 (.99)	4.00 (.96)	.0095
Computer jobs are boring.*	2.54 (.90)	2.06 (.81)	.0105
I am good with computers.**	3.82 (.91)	4.22 (.80)	.0300
I like the challenge of engineering.	3.39(.98)	3.78(1.0)	.0545

** Questions replicated from previous work [4] with similar levels of significance. ** Question replicated from previous work [4] in which we found significant results, but others did not.*

Towards the end of the camp, most girls expressed having a more positive understanding of engineering. For example, one girl was so excited about the prospects of programming that she wanted to use her new knowledge on an older piece of hardware:

> *P08: "My dad has this old calculator... and I kind of want to program it!"*

Even those girls who continued not to perceive computing or engineering as potential career paths still expressed more positive views than when they began camp four weeks earlier:

> *P06: "I like it. I mean, I don't think it would be the career for me, but I think it's definitely better than what I used to think it was. Just building stuff."*

4.1 Hands-On Work

Results suggest that the hands-on work with PicoCrickets changed the girls' understanding and perceptions of engineering and computer science. Interviews revealed that the girls were able to express important concepts about the nature of engineering work, particularly in relation to their roles.

P08: "[With programming], you want a certain thing, and you have a certain thing in your head. But... you have to make it, and you have to figure out how do you make it."

P02: "[Civil engineers] make sure it all works together and...the foundation is strong and it doesn't fall over."

These concepts and challenges inherent to engineering fields were learned through the manipulation of objects and hands on problem solving – never through lectures or explicit teaching. The girls exchanged the real world actions of developing software or building a new road for the playful actions of creating an Ice Cream Shop from PicoCrickets and crafts. These pivots allowed them to learn about engineering in a safe, fun environment in the short term that lays the scaffolding for later more complex concepts upon returning to school or even in subsequent workshops [11].

In addition, when the panel of engineers discussed their jobs and their enjoyment of daily activities, the girls were able to connect their own tasks to the real-world ones being described. They discussed the significance and impact of engineering, as well as the relevance of the engineering activities they themselves took part in.

P02: "[This course is] not like the big engineering that adults do, but it's a step towards it"

P10: "There's so much things (sic) you can do with [engineering]."

In interviews, the girls explicitly cited the hands-on work as the source of their learning about general engineering concepts. They expressed surprise and amazement at uncovering all the different things they could do with engineering through working with the PicoCrickets. These comments suggest that their hands-on work served as significant exposure to new concepts and was a perception altering learning experience.

P02: "Programming? I thought it was all just html and stuff. I didn't really think there was programming for making things move and light up and stuff... I think it's cool how you can do almost anything.... Make it do what you want."

P04: "I didn't know that we could do that. I could never imagine us doing that."

Some interview participants framed the changes in their perceptions and attitudes within the context school, pointing out the potential failure of school-based STEM curricula to provide positive exposure to computing and engineering.

Figure 2. A sample PicoCricket project. PicoCricket devices are connected with cables. Legos ®, Play Doh ©, and craft supplies complete the project.

P05: "I thought [engineering] was just computer stuff. And I don't like computers at my school. But after we went through this, it was really fun."

P04: "At school they should have this. I would love that class."

These views indicate that a shift in school-based STEM curricula towards hands-on exploration could impact girls' interest in computing and engineering more broadly. As Papert noted, "Learning in our schools today is not significantly participatory—and doing sums is not an imitation of an exciting, recognizable activity of adult life." [8, p.179]. In this course, however, we created a participatory learning environment in which young girls who were novices worked alongside young women and adults who were more expert to develop projects jointly. Multiple times during the course, the authors—all who have advanced degrees—learned something unexpected from working alongside the girls. Whether it be that a pulley controlled by a simple PicoCricket motor could be made to hold the weight of a large platform or that music could be looped to create multi-layered songs, the young girls contributed to the discovery and co-creation acts and taught the mentors as well.

4.2 Roles and Group Work

Interviews also revealed that having specified roles for each group member improved the group work experience, particularly by structuring collaboration, facilitating expertise sharing, and allowing the girls to mimic each other and their mentors when they were not sure about the right course of action [11]. The girls expressed an appreciation for the benefits of working on a project in a group rather than individually.

P01: "You just can't do it all on your own. You really have to rely on the people you're working with. And it could turn out better than just you working by yourself."

P11: "When you work in a group, other people have different ideas. So it adds more to what you already had."

Having gained a better understanding of engineering through the course, the girls were also able to apply their appreciation for group work to real-world engineering.

P06: "You have a bunch of different engineers, and you can't just have one building the whole entire building. You have to have different ones do it."

Results demonstrate that the knowledge and understanding the girls gained about engineering made the field much more appealing to them. Girls reported coming into the course with very little knowledge about engineering, being ignorant about what it even is, often thinking that engineering is equivalent to math. They also were unaware before the course that there are different types of engineering. The results of our surveys and discussions with the girls indicate that these initial perceptions led them to view engineering as uninteresting.

P01: "I thought [engineering] was like a lot of building and math. I didn't used to like it. Cause it was math....[now] it's fun.... Engineering is a lot of things.... Its not just math."

Many of the girls reflected on what they learned about working with others on a collaborative project, demonstrating the valuable life skills that were emphasized for them during the course.

P07: "I learned that some people might be a little bit harder to work with than others, but you just have to – everybody has to have respect for each other and it'll work out."

The girls also gained engineering skills through their group work. If one girl either already had a particular skill, or learned it through taking that role during the course, as roles were rotated she would share her expertise with the others.

P10: "Basically we just helped each other out with all of the jobs." P11: "She was really good at the computer, so if it was our turn or something, she would be the expert in it." P10: "I learned a lot."

P10: "I did not know how to make the things rotate or change color until... I think it was her... I think she was the one who taught me. I'm like, Oh! Okay! I get this!"

By working together and miming what they saw each other do, the girls were able to accomplish much more than any one individual's skills and development might make her independently capable of [11]. Furthermore, the girls learned about engineering even through group conflict. For example, through a persistent struggle with conflict in her group, one of the girls learned an important lesson about documenting design decisions and requirements: *"Put it on paper!"*

4.3 Audience

Throughout the course, we used performance for various audiences to motivate the girls to work hard on their projects and be as creative as possible. This emphasis on presenting to an audience helped the girls develop pride in their work. This pride was important in reinforcing what the girls learned and establishing confidence in the knowledge and skills they gained. One of the girls exuded this pride and confidence in her interview:

P02: "It feels good. I actually built something...it looks nice and it actually works. I'm proud of myself and my whole group."

The girls yelled and cheered during the presentation of posters describing their favorite roles and potential career paths (Figure 3). For example, the poster about software engineering reads that they "enjoy programming because… it is easy … it's like magic! … [you are] responsible for making it work! … it's fun!!!"

With occasional reminders of the requirement of presenting their project at the end of each class session, girls were motivated to be more creative, and finish on time. Reminders were met with exclamations and a sudden sense of urgency and hurriedness to their work. The girls would say their projects weren't ready yet and they wanted more time, demonstrating care and pride in their work.

Figure 3. Two girls enthusiastically presenting their poster about why software engineering was their favorite role.

5. CONCLUSION

In this work, we took an approach to teaching and learning that supports flexibility, experimentation, and play with technology. We developed a course featuring hands-on building of projects combining crafts with technology, engineering-focused roles structuring group work, and the frequent presence of an audience to motivate engagement. Results indicate that this approach helped students gain an understanding of what it means to be an engineer through experiencing both the hands-on and conceptual work of several different kinds of engineers. This knowledge and understanding led to significant improvements in the perceptions of girls enrolled in this course towards computer science and engineering, and significant increases in their confidence and interest in these fields. Despite entering the course with largely negative views towards computing as "boring" and "all about math," the girls finished the course with enthusiasm and appreciation for these subject areas and the careers they might obtain through them. Our results indicate that a shift in school-based STEM curricula towards hands-on exploration, group work, explicit consideration of future careers or roles, and a focus on an audience to consume their end products could impact girls' interest in computing and engineering more broadly.

6. ACKNOWLEDGEMENTS

We thank Microsoft, the NCWIT Seed Fund, and Google for their generous support of this project. Thanks to Khai Truong and David Kay for their thoughtful critique of earlier drafts.

7. REFERENCES

[1] Beckman, M. (1990) Collaborative Learning: Preparation for the Workplace and Democracy, College Teaching, 38(4), 128-133.

[2] Cohen, E. (1994) Designing groupwork: Strategies for the heterogeneous classroom. Teachers College Press, Columbia University, NYC, NY.

[3] Ericson, B., Guzdial, M., and Biggers, M. (2007) Improving secondary CS education: progress and problems. SIGCSE Bull. 39, 1, 298-301.

[4] Ericson, B., McKlin, T. Girl Scouts Compute! (http://gacomputes.cc.gatech.edu/Members/jpdimond/girlScouts2009-sigcse-barb.pdf) Retrieved Sept 11, 2009.

[5] Hayes, G.R., Piper, A.M., Amar, B., Bevis, K.J., Newstetter, W., and Bruckman, A.S. (2004) Audience in Computer Learning: A Constructionist Interpretation. Proceedings of the International Conference of the Learning Sciences. (June 22-26, 2004, Santa Monica, CA, USA).

[6] Kohn, A. (1986) No Contest: The Case Against Competition. Boston: Houghton Mifflin.

[7] Margolis, J. and Fisher, A. (2002) Unlocking the Clubhouse: Women in Computing Cambridge, Massachusetts: MIT Press.

[8] Papert, S. (1980) Mindstorms: Children, Computers, and Powerful Ideas. Basic Books, Inc.

[9] Piaget, J. P. (1962). *Play, dreams, and imitation in childhood.* New York: Norton.

[10] Slavin, R. E. (1990) Cooperative learning: Theory, research and practice. Englewood Cliffs, NJ, Prentice-Hall.

[11] Vygotzky, L.S. (1978) Mind in Society. New York: Cambridge University Press.

Computational Thinking via Interactive Journalism in Middle School

Ursula Wolz
Dept. of Computer Science
The College of New Jersey
Ewing, NJ 08528
+1 609 771 2766
wolz@tcnj.edu

Meredith Stone
Independent Evaluator
41 Nassau Drive
Lawrencevillle, NJ 08648
+1 609 895 1239
MeredithKStone@aol.com

Sarah M. Pulimood
Dept. of Computer Science
The College of New Jersey
Ewing, NJ 08528
+1 609 771 2788
pulimood@tcnj.edu

Kim Pearson
Dept. of English
The College of New Jersey
Ewing, NJ 08528
+1 609 771 2692
kpearson@tcnj.edu

ABSTRACT

To address the critical shortage of students entering computing fields, as well as broaden participation in computing, we present a summer and afterschool program in Interactive Journalism through which middle school students and their teachers develop an appreciation for and competence in computational thinking. We report on the outcomes of our first year in which three middle school language arts teachers, a technology teacher and a guidance counselor collaborate with college faculty to publish a school magazine of the future. Students and their teachers research and conduct interviews to develop news stories that are then presented as story packages with text, video, and procedural animations in Scratch. Results of formal data collection show changes in students' perceptions of what it means to program, as well as their emerging confidence in their ability to design computational solutions and to program.

Categories and Subject Descriptors

K.3.2 [**Computing Milieux**] Computer and Information Science Education

K. 4.0 Computers and Society

General Terms

Human Factors

Keywords

K-12 CS Education, Computational Thinking, Scratch, Writing and Computing, Broadening Participation in Computing

1. INTRODUCTION

Research on the computing pipeline and mathematics education inform the position that women and minorities self-select out of computing related fields because they (1) do not see themselves as "computer types," (2) do not successfully navigate the culture of a traditional computing classroom, and (3) are ill-prepared academically for entry into existing undergraduate programs [2,7]. The profound shift in journalism due to the Internet provides a venue through which to engage these students in computing via writing, information gathering and analysis, as well as a range of digital media from graphics to still images to procedural animation (e.g., Flash [6], Scratch [16], Alice [1]), interactive graphics and enhanced video. Our emphasis on socially responsible activities (e.g., news reporting), rather than consumerist focused activities (e.g., video games and entertainment) provides a foothold into activities deemed appropriate for school. There is also growing evidence that socially relevant activities attract girls.

Jane Margolis et al. [10] present a troubling picture that members of underrepresented groups (e.g., women as well as all people of color) are enthusiastic about pursuing careers in computing but are barred because they cannot obtain the necessary preparation in high school to succeed in the requisite college majors, or to enter college at all. Efforts are underway (e.g. via the CSTA) to change national and state policy.

The program presented here demonstrates how to infuse computer science into the existing culture and curriculum of mainstream public education, rather than attempt to dramatically change it through public policy. It also provides a solution to the most critical challenge facing an over-burdened K-12 curriculum: to add computer science will either require removing something else (probably the arts), or watering down the experience so as to render it meaningless to long term pedagogical goals.

We asked the question: how can we *infuse* computer science and computational thinking through an existing rather than novel venue? We have found that the school newspaper, with its socially responsible agenda, its need for 21st century technology overhaul, and its isomorphism to the process of software design, has proven to be remarkably effective in communicating the message to young people, their teachers and parents, that computational thinking skills are accessible to anyone, and that computer science offers critical skills for the 21st century workforce that should be actively pursued by students.

2. RATIONALE

We posit that the existing school culture, in its belief systems, processes and support structures, is inadequately prepared to implement the extensive change in curriculum assumed by proponents of broad-based computational thinking. As Margolis et al. describe so eloquently [10], the technology, teacher expertise and technical support required to implement a broad-based computing curriculum in K-12 is in crisis. They focused on the Los Angeles School District and describe three schools ranging from inner city to affluent suburban. Their stories resonate with teachers we have talked to throughout the country: teachers are not empowered or trusted to use technology in a way that models computational thinking or promotes concepts of computer science. Yet there is significant evidence from the last 20 years that genuine buy-in from teachers, school administrators,

SIGCSE'10, March 10–13, 2010, Milwaukee, Wisconsin, USA.

technology support staff, parents, and students is necessary for educational innovation, especially technology-based innovation to take place [4, 17].

2.1 K-12 Computing

To attract a broad constituency to even the best high school computing experiences requires consistent exposure to computational ideas beginning in kindergarten. Broadening participation requires exposing young people to computing in sustainable ways. Extracurricular experiences such as summer camps and after school programs (affiliated with school or national organizations) can inspire young people, but there is significant evidence that ultimately career path choice is influenced and motivated by parents and school [7,15].

This presents a particular problem for computer science education because it is currently all but absent from state curricula. We address the problem of classroom instruction in a forthcoming paper. Afterschool programs strongly tied to mainstream curriculum provide a vehicle through which students, teachers, parents, and school policy makers (e.g., administrators and board members) can develop an appreciation for the need to include solid, deep, sustained instruction in computing in the mainstream curriculum, not as a "special" such as art, music, technology or physical education.

Unless computing becomes mainstream, computer science will remain marginalized as the domain of an elite, for example those predisposed to and academically successful in traditional STEM disciplines. While we wholeheartedly support the robotics movement as supplementary to standard curriculum, it is still not sufficiently in the mainstream to dispel the prejudices of a generation of policymakers. Video game design is even less likely to find its way into the mainstream curriculum. Broadening participation in computing requires casting a wide net and abandoning stereotypes about who is and is not cognitively capable of computational thinking. This requires thinking beyond traditional STEM disciplines and considering applications in media, journalism and the arts. It also requires thinking about the community and culture of the classroom [14, 18].

2.2 21st Century Journalism

Evidence is mounting that a 21st century journalist will require a strong computing background [8, 11], and 21st century computing professionals will increasingly apply their skills to information dissemination through an as yet to be imagined collection of venues, processes and media. Underlying both disciplines are foundational principles of information access and dissemination, fact analysis, process description and decision-making for results presentation. These neutral terms are equally embraced by journalists and computer scientists to describe how to construct a news item and a software artifact respectively. Consequently, we ascribe to a broad view of computing: one that embraces both the creator of software to support journalism as well as the journalist programmer[1] who can competently embrace emerging digital media. This viewpoint reflects the growing recognition of the importance of computing within the news industry [13]. Journalists are increasingly expected to create and extract information from databases. They construct social network maps to unearth relationships and patterns of behavior. News presentation is also increasingly computer-driven, in the form of content management systems, procedural (e.g., Flash) animations, and user-customization tools. Fundamentally, as programmer-journalist Adrian Holovaty has observed, journalism and computing are both concerned with gathering, organizing and presenting structured data [8].

To attract young people into such careers we need to start early, because they will need well-established skills in writing, computational thinking and quantitative reasoning. By the time they reach college, many students have segregated themselves into "good writers" or "good mathematicians." Women traditionally will gravitate toward the former. Keeping them, as well as minority boys in math and science is a national problem [2, 7]. We address the computing pipeline problem by focusing on the critical point of middle school (particularly 8th grade), when students make career dependent decisions on high school course selection based on preconceptions and misconceptions about computing careers and requisite preparedness for those careers.

3. THE IJIMS PROGRAM

The Interactive Journalism Institute for Middle School (IJIMS) is a yearlong demonstration project funded by the National Science Foundation Broadening Participation in Computing program (CNS 0739173) [9]. We recruited middle school teachers through their principal, Ms. Barbara Brower, who emphasized the technology and writing components of our project. Our student recruiting procedures explicitly identified the students who are not the school "math stars," but rather those who have a creative bent in visual media and writing or whose talents do not necessarily predict success in the traditional math and science classroom. In other words, we recruited ordinary kids rather than those self-selecting into computing disciplines. In the second year we invited a cohort of students nominated by their teachers to an information meeting at the middle school that was led by members of our teacher cohort and current IJIMS middle school participants. At the behest of the teachers we included 7th graders to develop a stronger sense of community through a two, rather than one-year experience.

3.1 Pilot Program in the First Year

In its first year, we offered a one-week institute for five teachers (all white women, three language arts: Laura Fay, Suzanne Gallagher, Jean Gardner; one technology: Mary DiSimone; one guidance counselor: Jill Schwarz), followed immediately by an identical institute for 16 rising 8th graders at which the teachers participated as mentors to the students. The demographics of the middle school students was 2/1 female/male, with almost half identified as Latina/o or black. Through NSF and College of New Jersey support we also recruited five undergraduate research assistants (3/2 male/female, 2/1 white/non white) for an 8-week undergraduate research program that culminated in the two weeks with the middle school teachers and students.

During the subsequent academic year the teachers and students, with our active support, developed an afterschool program to run a 21st century, online school newspaper. Approximately two thirds of the students continued to attend throughout the year (maintaining both gender and ethnic/racial proportions of the summer program.).

---

[1] This new professional description was first used by Adrian Holovaty [8].

The afterschool program began as twice monthly, 45-minute meetings. By mid-year we increased contact to once per week. At the insistence of the teachers and students, we invited students who had not participated in the summer program to attend as well. One language arts teacher dropped out of the program in late February due to an emerging leadership role in another program. The remaining teachers supported and gradually took ownership of the afterschool program. Our guidance counselor did not participate during the school year because of a scheduling conflict.

3.2 The Second Year Revised Program

To date we have completed the summer program of the second year with 29 middle school students (18 girls, 11 boys, 12 7th graders, 17 8th graders) with approximately the same ethnic/racial composition as the first year. This past summer (July 2009), the remaining three teachers recruited two new teachers, a female language arts teacher (Marcy Tucker) and a male math teacher (Rober Kohut), both white. We held a weeklong informal preparation session where we worked one-on-one with all the teachers to prepare for the second summer session with the students. This year through NSF funding we again supported six undergraduate research students (5/1 male/female, 5/1 white/Hispanic.)

3.3 Immersive, Active Learning

The weeklong summer institute is a model for immersive, active skills learning. In teams, referred to in the news industry as "beats," students and teachers are assigned a topic, research that topic on the Internet, then prepare for, execute and video tape an interview with someone related to the topic. Summary notes are then compiled into a formal news report that includes selecting graphics, still images and editing video clips. The connection to computing, especially programming, occurs when team members develop procedural animations that support the story line as side bars. Students learn about database use, privacy and security via "CAFÉ" (Collaboration And Facilitation Environment) [3] through which they develop, edit, and ultimately file their stories.

We chose Scratch [16] as the most appropriate vehicle for procedural animation. This syntax-free programming environment supports novice users as they quickly build expertise in telling stories through traditional programming constructs such as statements, control structures, events and expressions. With almost no formal instruction (less than two hours in our summer program) novices can build animations and simple interactive games to support the narrative line of their journalism work. We considered both Alice and Flash, but the steeper learning curve of these more complex environments could not provide the immediate immersion of the Scratch environment or the strong culture of "remixing" in the online Scratch community.

In our pilot summer (2008) the five teachers each partnered with an undergraduate already experienced in interactive journalism to develop a story that included video and Scratch animation. Each partnership then led a team of three or four middle school students in the subsequent week. Their work is published on an online magazine "F.I.S.H." (Fisher's Interesting Stories Here) [5].

In our second summer (2009) the six teachers prepared for the week with middle school students by each working through a story with informal support from the six undergraduates. During the subsequent middle school institute each teacher partnered with an undergraduate and worked with four to five middle school students. Their work is published as "N.E.W.S." (New Ewing Web Stories) [12].

4. PROGRAM GOALS AND OUTCOMES

The primary goal of our project is to demonstrate how expository writing, and journalism in particular, can be used to cast a wide net to broaden participation in computing.

4.1 Goals

By directly engaging students who do not necessarily view themselves as "computing types" our program is designed to change their perspective on career options in the expanding computing disciplines. More specifically we set out to:

1. Change their perceptions about what programming is.
2. Show them that software design (e.g. creating projects in Scratch) is like news reporting.
3. Empower them to feel competent in software design and using their new computing skills.
4. Convince them that programming can be fun.
5. Give them a sense of accomplishment in doing worthwhile, socially responsible work.

A secondary goal was to ignite enthusiasm for computational thinking in their teachers. Outcomes for this goal are summarized in a forthcoming paper. We focus here on the student outcomes and compare our pilot summer project with the more recent summer experience. We will analyze the results of the year-long program after we complete our second academic year.

4.2 Methodology

Throughout the first year and second summer, our independent evaluator, Meredith Stone, developed and administered (a) pretests of computer efficacy, (b) attitudinal surveys, (c) a non-computer-based media construction assignment. Rubrics are also under development to assess the sophistication of their Scratch programs both quantitatively and qualitatively. We are in the process of validating these instruments. Finally, extensive formal observation and interviews were conducted throughout. Each summer we asked both the teachers and students to comment on the day's activities and what they did, aligning these questions to our targeted outcomes. We also asked them to rank their sense of accomplishment from 1 (nothing much) to 5 (an amazing amount).

4.3 Results

4.3.1 Change Perceptions about Programming

Our data suggests that we changed the students' perceptions about programming. Specifically, after the summer institutes in 2008 and 2009 our students did not espouse the generally held beliefs that programmers work by themselves or that working on a computer means you cannot be creative. When students were asked to circle ALL that applied, their responses to the following items were as seen in Table 1. We noted that many who circled "work all by myself" in 2009 also circled "work with others."

Table 1. Attitudes about working with computers

Working with computers means I:	July 08 N=13	July 09 N=27
Work all by myself	1	7
Work with other people	6	16
Can be creative	10	19

4.3.2 *Software Design and News Reporting*

We believe that the process involved in good writing is the same as the process involved in creating good procedural animations. Our students are beginning to think so too. Table 2 shows the response to a survey question asking them to rank their agreement with the statement "During the past week, I learned that Computer Science and Journalism are a lot alike" on a scale of 5 = Strongly Agree to 1 = Strongly Disagree. Since their rating is going up, we assume our teachers are getting better at showing them the relationship.

Table 2. Relationship between Computer Science and Journalism

Average score 5 = Strongly Agree to 1 = Strongly Disagree	July 08 N=16	July 09 N=27
During the past week, I learned that Computer Science and Journalism are a lot alike	3.6	4.0

4.3.3 *Empower Them to Feel Competent*

In 2009, we directly assessed student perceptions' of their ability to program through a survey given the first morning of the institute and the last afternoon. Our data indicate that we increased the students' confidence in their ability to create computer programs. The results are given in Table 3 below. Note that not only did the number of students who either Agreed or Strongly Agreed with the statement "I believe I can create a computer program" rise from 66% to 88%, but the number who Disagreed or Strongly Disagreed went from 14% to 0%. We believe that the initial 66% is higher than typically would be expected as five of the rising 8th graders (17%) had worked with Scratch prior to the summer program.

Table 3. Beliefs about ability to program

I believe I can create a computer program			
	Agree/ Strongly Agree	No Opinion	Disagree/ Strongly Disagree
First Day	19	5	4
(N=29)	66%	17%	14%
Last Day	23	3	0
(N=26)	88%	12%	0%

With respect to their new computer skills (Scratch animation, video editing, CAFÉ management system), students were asked to rank their agreement with the two statements "During the past week, I learned enough about the Interactive Journalism process that I could teach it to others" and "I believe I will use the computer skills I learned during the past week in whatever career I choose" on a scale of 1 to 5, with 5 = Strongly Agree and 1 = Strongly Disagree. The students recognized that they had learned new computer skills which they could teach others and which they would be able to use in the future in whatever career they chose. Their ratings appear in Table 4.

Table 4. Beliefs about competence as programmers

Average score 5 = Strongly Agree to 1 = Strongly Disagree	July 08 N=16	July 09 N=27
During the past week I learned enough about the Interactive Journalism process that I could teach it to others	3.9	4.1
I believe I will use the computer skills I learned during the past week in whatever career I choose	4.2	4.0

4.3.4 *That Programming Can Be Fun*

As seen in Table 5, for both the 2008 and 2009 summer institutes, the majority of the students reported that they had had the MOST FUN during the week working on their Scratch projects. In addition, when asked on another survey "what would you like to continue doing next year in school," Scratch was one of the most frequent answers both years, tied with "writing news stories and interviewing people." Note that another option was video production.

Table 5. Most fun activity was Scratch

Scratch	July 08 N=16	July 09 N=27
MOST Fun	9 (56%)	19 (70%)

Further, when asked to rank their agreement with the statement "During the past week, I learned that Interactive Journalism can be a lot of fun," on a scale of 5 = Strongly Agree to 1 = Strongly Disagree, the students' average was greater than 4 both years as seen in Table 6 below.

Table 6. Interactive journalism is fun too

Average score 5 = Strongly Agree to 1 = Strongly Disagree	July 08 N=16	July 09 N=27
During the past week, I learned that Interactive Journalism can be a lot of fun.	4.1	4.4

4.3.5 *A Sense of Accomplishment for Work*

During both the 2008 and 2009 summer institutes, the students' sense of accomplishment increased each day with only one temporary downturn due to a server crash on day 4, 2009. Students were asked to rate their accomplishment on a scale of 1 to 5, where 5 was labeled "an amazing amount," 3 was labeled "Enough," and 1 was labeled "Nothing much." The results are in Table 7 below.

Table 7. Sense of Accomplishment

	Day 1	Day 2	Day 3	Day 4	Day 5
July 2008 (N=16)	3.75	3.87	3.88	4.00	4.63
July 2009 (N=27)	3.96	4.35	4.43	4.18	4.93

5. FUTURE WORK AND SUMMARY

The formal results reported here only begin to tell the story of our experience over the past eighteen months. Systematic observation by Meredith Stone, as well as formal interviews (via scripted protocols) indicate that the teachers as well as the students fully appreciate the relationship between computer program design via Scratch and the process of constructing a magazine news or feature story. Two of the language arts teachers, Laura Fay and Suzanne Gallagher, have incorporated Scratch programming into the New Jersey standards-based language arts curriculum, for 8th grade research report writing and 7th grade poetry writing respectively. The results of their brief introductions to programming will be reported in a subsequent paper.

Of concern is the degree to which this middle school is typical of what Margolis et al. describe as "the shallow end" where students and teachers have almost no access to real computing power. It is a significant hurdle for the teachers to get time in antiquated computer labs with severely restricted Internet access due both to site filtering and narrow bandwidth. For example, it takes months to get new software such as Scratch updates because the installs are done manually on each machine only by the IT staff. We gently offer solutions, sometimes suggesting ways to better negotiate with IT staff, sometimes helping to circumvent roadblocks. For example, we provide sufficient USB drives containing Scratch and support materials for a class so that lab time is used efficiently rather than waiting for software to download. Respecting the culture of the school is as essential to infusion as understanding what can realistically be accomplished and how to promote change.

We have raised the question of whether the Scratch projects developed by the middle school students do indeed demonstrate computational thinking. Are they "really" programming? We are developing both a quantitative (counting programming constructs) and qualitative (using human analysis with inter-rater reliability) protocol comparing the work of our various cohorts (July 08, July 09, AY 09-10, 8th grade report writing, 7th grade poetry) with programs written by TCNJ undergraduates in introductory computer science classes and with selected random samples from the Scratch website. Informal analysis by computer science faculty who teach lower level introductory classes suggests that the Fisher students are producing Scratch projects on par with CS 0 level undergraduates. Results of our formal analysis will be reported in a subsequent paper.

All five teachers at Fisher Middle School have developed action plans for incorporating programming into their curriculum in the coming year. Each one filed a research proposal with us as part of our continuing project. Teachers throughout the building are being casually introduced to Scratch by our collaborating teachers and their students. Our 8th grade cohort dispersed into five different high schools (that we have been able to track). At least one young person going to each school is committed to continuing to study programming and computer science. We have indeed begun to infuse computational thinking into a middle school in way that enriches rather than subsumes existing curriculum.

6. ACKNOWLEDGMENTS

A heartfelt Thank You to Dr. Janice Cuny, Director of the Broadening Participation in Computing Program at NSF. This work would not be possible without our program manager, Mary Switzer, the 11 undergraduates who devoted their summers to our work and the awesome teachers and staff at Fisher Middle School. This work is supported by NFS CNS 0739173.

7. REFERENCES

[1] Alice: http://www.alice.org/

[2] Barker, L. J., E. Snow, K. Garvin-Doxas, T. Weston, Recruiting Middle School Girls into IT: Data on Girls' Perceptions and Experiences from a Mixed-Demographic Group, in Women and Information Technology: Research on Underrepresentation, Cohoon & Aspray, The MIT Press, Cambridge MA, 2006. pp. 113-136.

[3] CAFÉ: http://highered.commandprompt.com/cafe/

[4] Corcoran, T. (1995, June). Helping teachers teach well: Transforming professional development. CPRE Policy Briefs. Rutgers, NJ: Consortium for Policy Research in Education, 69-79.

[5] FISH: http://highered.commandprompt.com/fish/

[6] Flash: http://www.adobe.com/products/flash/

[7] Goode, J., R. Estrella, and J. Margolis, Lost in Translation: Gender and High School Computer Science, in Women and Information Technology: Research on Underrepresentation, The MIT Press, Cambridge MA, 2006. pp. 89-113.

[8] Holovaty, A., "A fundamental way newspaper sites need to change." Holovaty.com. September 6, 2006. http://holovaty.com/blog/archive/2006/09/06/0307/?highlight=structured%2520data.

[9] The Interactive Journalism Institute for Middle School: http://www.tcnj.edu/~ijims

[10] Margolis, J., Estrella, R., Goode, J., Holme, J.H., and Nao, K. (2008). Stuck in the Shallow End: Education, Race, and Computing. MIT Press.

[11] Murray, J. H. Hamlet on the Holodeck, The Future of Narrative in Cyberspace, MIT Press, Cambridge MA, 1997.

[12] NEWS: http://highered.commandprompt.com/news/

[13] Niles, R. The Journalist as Programmer: Q & A with Adrian Holovaty. Online Journalism Review June 5, 2006, http://www.ojr.org/ojr/stories/060605niles/index.cfm

[14] Pulimood, S. M. and Wolz, U. Problem Solving in Community: A Necessary Shift in CS Pedagogy. In Proceedings of the 39th Technical Symposium on Computer Science Education (ACM SIGCSE), Portland, Oregon, March 12 – 15, 2008.

[15] Simpson, J.C., Segregated by Subject: Racial Differences in the Factors Influencing Academic Major between European Americans, Asian Americans, and African, Hispanic, and Native Americans. The Journal of Higher Education, Vol. 72, No. 1. (Jan. - Feb., 2001), pp. 63-100.

[16] Scratch: http://scratch.mit.edu

[17] Tenenberg, J. and S. Fincher, "Opening the Door of the Computer Science Classroom: The Disciplinary Commons," SIGCSE Symposium, Covington, Kentucky, USA P 7-10 March 2007

[18] Wolz, U. and Pulimood, S. M. An Integrated Approach to Project Management through Classic CS III and Video Game Development, in Proceedings of the 38th Technical Symposium on Computer Science Education (ACM SIGCSE), Covington, Kentucky, March 7 – 10, 2007

Compatibility of Partnered Students in Computer Science Education

Joshua Sennett
University of Virginia
Department of Computer Science
Charlottesville, VA 22904
+1-434-982-2688
jas7wh@virginia.edu

Mark Sherriff
University of Virginia
Department of Computer Science
Charlottesville, VA 22904
+1-434-982-2688
sherriff@virginia.edu

ABSTRACT
This paper details the results of an investigation into the compatibility of partnered computer science students. The study involved approximately 290 students at the University of Virginia (UVA). This study builds on the work of researchers at North Carolina State University (NCSU). NCSU researchers have conducted a number of studies on the compatibility of pair programmers. We examined many of the factors that the NCSU researchers explored in their studies (including personality type, learning style, skill level, programming self esteem, work ethic, and time management choices) in order to determine whether the conclusions of the research at NCSU also hold true at UVA. Consistent with the NCSU studies, we found that skill level continues to be the most important factor in student compatibility.

Categories and Subject Descriptors
K.3.1 [**Computers and Education**]: *Collaborative learning,*
K.3.2 [**Computer and Information Science Education**]: Computer science education

General Terms
Measurement, Experimentation, Human Factors

Keywords
Pair Programming, Computer Science Education, Pair Evaluation

1. INTRODUCTION
Pairing students together for group work has long been used in schools and classrooms as a pedagogical tool to increase students' comprehension of subject material. This strategy has been applied to computer science education in the form of "pair programming," wherein two students work together at one computer on programming assignments [3]. Research has shown that involving students in pair programming activities can lead to increased comprehension of the material and higher success rates in the associated class [7]. Unfortunately, incompatibility between students can limit the method's effectiveness [7].

This problem has prompted researchers at North Carolina State University (NCSU) to explore the possible factors contributing to partner compatibility in computer science education [3, 4, 5, 7, 10]. These factors include personality type, learning style, skill level, programming self esteem, work ethic, and time management choices [10]. The goal of this study is to contribute to the body of knowledge on student compatibility. By analyzing many of the same factors examined in the NCSU studies we hope to determine whether the conclusions of the NCSU researchers also hold true in University of Virginia (UVA) computer science classes.

In conjunction with this study, we set out to design and implement a web-based tool to facilitate the use of groups and the collection of compatibility data. The tool used in UVA classes to gather data for this study is the "PairEval" tool made available by the NC State researchers. The tool we designed was based on PairEval and expands the original system's functionality. This new system allows professors to more easily add questions to the surveys posed to the students. It also simplifies the group forming process. These new features should make the use of group work and pair programming easier for computer science professors, as well as facilitate the collection of student compatibility data for use in future work.

In Section 2 we provide a discussion of the relevant background material and related work. Section 3 describes the details of our study and its methodology. The results of the study are presented in Section 4. In Section 5 we describe the additions we have made to the PairEval web tool. Section 6 presents our conclusions and possibilities for future work.

2. RELATED WORK
This section discusses the related work and background information for the Myers-Briggs personality types, the Felder-Silverman learning styles, pair programming, and student compatibility research.

2.1 Myers Briggs
The Myers-Briggs Type Indicator (MBTI) was developed by Isabel Briggs Myers and Katharine Briggs in the 1940s and first published in the MBTI Manual in 1962[6]. It aims to place Carl Jung's theory of psychological types into a usable and understandable format. The Myers-Briggs personality test classifies a respondent into categories representing their personality traits in four different dimensions, or dichotomies, consisting of opposite personality qualities. For each of the four dimensions an individual receives a classification and a number

(from 0 to 100) that indicates how strongly they respond to that classification. The four dimensions of the Myers-Briggs Type Indicator are Introvert-Extrovert, Sensing-Intuition, Thinking-Feeling, and Judging-Perceiving.

2.2 Felder-Silverman

In 1988 Felder and Silverman proposed a model to describe student learning styles that would be particularly relevant to engineering students [2]. Recent publications of the original paper include a 2002 preface by Felder, explaining a few changes made. The Felder-Silverman learning style model borrows from a number of other systems, including the Myers-Briggs personality type indicator and a learning style model developed by Kolb. Like Myers-Briggs, the Felder-Silverman learning styles model consists of four dimensions (although, it was originally five). Individuals are placed into a given classification for each dimension based on their responses to a number of questions. The scale for each dimension ranges from -11 to 11, with values given at the odd integers (-11, -9, -7, etc.). The four dimensions of the Felder-Silverman learning styles model are Sensing-Intuitive, Visual-Verbal, Active-Reflective, and Sequential-Global.

2.3 Pair Programming

Pair programming is a practice wherein two programmers sit at the same computer to work on a program, algorithm, or piece of code [8]. One programmer, the "driver", controls the keyboard and types code while the other, the "navigator", observes, watching for errors. The two programmers switch roles frequently (every 20-30 minutes). A large amount of research into pair programming has shown it to be an effective tool in computer science education [1, 3, 7, 9].

Nagappan et al. [7] provide the results of a pair programming study conducted over three semesters at NCSU. In this study some lab sections were taught using pair programming, while other sections retained solo programming, functioning as a control. The study found that in all cases the pair programming lab sections had an equal or higher percentage of students finish the course with a grade of C or better. This indicates that pair programming can promote increased comprehension and retention of course material. Nagappan et al. also conclude that the pair programming students had a positive view of their group learning experience, that participation in pair programming does not harm students' future performance on individual assignments, and that pair programming reduces work load for instructors and teaching assistants.

Ferzli et al. [3] present the trends they observed during several focus group discussions regarding pair programming. The focus groups were conducted with students and teaching assistants after working with pair programming in their lab sections over the course of the semester. The overall impressions were positive, with students commenting on the method's effectiveness in helping them learn. Some, however, commented on the negative experiences that resulted from incompatible partners. Teaching assistants also found the method effective for facilitating student learning. They also commented that the method resulted in less work for them, as students were able to figure out more on their own and did not have to continuously seek help from their teaching assistants.

2.4 Student Compatibility

There is already a significant body of research into student compatibility in pair programming. These studies examine the factors that may lead to student compatibility. The goal of this body of research is to maximize the group learning experience by minimizing incompatibilities between students. Here we summarize several of the studies into pair compatibility.

In 2004, Katira et al. [5] released the results of a study conducted at NCSU over the Fall 2002 and Spring 2003 semesters. The study involved 564 students, both graduate and undergraduate. The courses involved were a freshman introductory computer science course (CS1), an upperclassman software engineering course (SE), and a graduate level object-oriented programming course (OO). The study looked at the significance of several factors in the compatibility of students in the different classes: Myers-Briggs personality type, skill level, students' perceived skill level, and self esteem. The study concludes that the significance of personality type differed depending on the course, with personality type being found to be significant in the introductory course, but not in software engineering course (this hypothesis was not tested on the graduate course). The researchers found that skill level (based on midterm scores) was only significant in the graduate course. Students' perception of their partner's skill level was found to be significant in all courses. The significance of students' programming self esteem was only tested in the introductory course and was found not to be significant.

A study released in 2006 by Williams et al. [10] continues to build upon this body of work. Their study incorporated the data from the Fall 2002-Fall 2003 CS1, SE, and OO courses (Phase 1 of the study) as well as data from Fall 2004-Fall 2005 SE courses (Phase 2). In Phase 1, the study looked at the significance of actual and perceived skill level in all three classes and personality type and programming self esteem in the two undergraduate courses. In Phase 2 the study examined Felder-Silverman learning style, work ethic, and time management skills in the SE course. The researchers found personality type to be insignificant, except in Phase 2, where individual dimensions were analyzed. The researchers found the pairing of a Sensor and Intuitor to be more likely to result in a Very Compatible rating. Similarly, in the Felder-Silverman learning styles, the sensing-intuition dimension was the only one to be found significant. Actual skill level was insignificant except for in Phase 1 SE courses. Perceived skill was significant in all cases. Programming and problem solving self esteem was found to be significant in Phase 1 and 2 SE. Work ethic was found to be significant in SE Phase 2. Time management skills were not found to be significant in the Phase 2 portion of the study.

3. STUDY DETAILS

In this section we detail the courses that contributed to the data pool used in this study, our hypotheses, and the methodology.

3.1 Course Description

The data used in this study is taken from two courses at the University of Virginia: CS150 and CS201.

CS150 is an introductory computer science course titled "Computing: From Ada to the Web". It is intended for students with no previous computer science background and generally aimed at non-engineering students. The data from CS150 used in this study was gathered during the Spring 2008 semester, when the course had an enrollment of 68 students. Students were assigned group homework assignments. The students filled out partner evaluations after submitting each assignment.

CS201, "Software Development Methods", is also a lower-level computer science course. It is generally the second programming computer science course students will take. CS201 is aimed at engineering students. The data incorporated in this study from CS201 was gathered from two sections of the course taught during the Fall 2008 semester and one section during the Spring 2008 semester. Each lecture session has several lab sections associated with it. The total enrollment across the three sections was 226 students. The partner evaluation data received from the CS201 came from several group homework assignments and a final group project.

3.2 Hypotheses

The goal of this study was to reproduce the results of the previous work in this field at NCSU (discussed in the Related Work section). Our data did not contain race or gender information. Therefore, these factors have been omitted from our hypotheses. Our data also did not include the test scores or GPA information used by the NCSU studies as metrics for "actual skill". As such, this hypothesis has been excluded as well.

The following table lists our research hypotheses:

Table 1: Research Hypotheses

Hypothesis: Pairs are more compatible if students with … are grouped together.	
H-1	… different personality types …
H-2	… different learning styles …
H-3	… similar perceived skill levels …
H-4	… similar programming self-esteem …
H-5	… similar work ethic …
H-6	… similar time management skills …

3.3 Methodology

We used a similar methodology to test the viability of each hypothesis. As part of their partner evaluation, students gave their teammate an overall compatibility and effort score. For each hypothesis we ran a Spearman rank-order correlation with the overall score and number of different scenarios.

For personality type we examined the partners' values for each dimension of the Myers-Briggs type indicator. First, we ran a Spearman correlation with the overall score and a value representing whether the partners fell in the same category for that dimension (i.e. both Extrovert, both Sensing, etc.). Then, we ran a Spearman correlation with the absolute value of the difference between the two partners' numeric Myers-Briggs score for the given dimension. Finally, we created a number of binary variables representing how close two users were in this dimension. If the difference between the two users numerical scores was less than or equal to a given number, the variable would be 1, otherwise 0. These variables were created in the range from 0 to 200 (the maximum possible difference in two Myers-Briggs numerical scores) in intervals of 10. We ran a Spearman correlation for each of these variables.

The method used for the learning styles is almost identical to that used for personality type; each dimension was examined individually. The only difference in methodology between personality type and learning style is that the range of binary variable spans from 0 to 22 in intervals of 2.

The methodology used to examine perceived skill levels is much simpler. On the partner evaluation form students were asked to rate their partner's technical competency in relation to their own as better, about the same, or worse. In examining the relationship between perceived skill and compatibility we ran a Spearman correlation with the overall score and skill rating.

For hypotheses four through six, students provided answers at the beginning of the course to a self evaluation survey which included questions regarding their programming self esteem, work ethic, and time management skills (the questions relating to programming self esteem were split into separate questions). For these questions students placed themselves on a scale that ranged from 1 to 9. These hypotheses were analyzed in the same fashion as the personality type and learning style hypotheses, with the difference being that the range binary variables tested ranged from 0 to 8 (the maximum possible difference) .

4. RESULTS

In this section we summarize the results found in performing the Spearman rank-order correlations discussed in the previous section.

4.1 Personality Type

Overall, we found personality type to be insignificant in student compatibility. There were no significant correlations in any of the four dimensions based on the category match or the numerical difference between partners.

While there are some scattered statistically significant results ($p < .050$) among the binary variables, the correlation coefficients in these cases indicate a very weak correlation. For example, the variable indicating that a pair is within 130 on the Sensing-Intuition dimension is statistically significant, but has a correlation coefficient of -0.049, not a very strong correlation. This is typical of the correlation numbers we observed, generally somewhere in the range of 0.050 to -0.050. Also, if this were truly an indicator of compatibility, we would expect to see other significant results near this one.

There is, however, a group of significant values present in the judging-perceiving dimension when using a one-tailed significance test. The variables representing partners within 60, 70, 80, and 90 of each other on the judging-perceiving scale are all significant. Still, the correlation is not extremely strong, with the highest coefficient being 0.074 at variable 80. The results of our study do not indicate any strong correlation between personality type and partner compatibility.

4.2 Learning Styles

The results of our learning styles correlations were even less significant than for personality type. There were no significant correlations in any of the four dimensions based the category match or the numerical difference. The active-reflective and sensing-intuitive dimensions had no significant results in their binary variables. The visual-verbal dimension had no significant results using a two-tailed significance test and only a few scattered significant results with weak correlations ($\rho < 0.050$) using a one-tailed significance test. The sequential-global dimension had one significant correlation when the difference between partners is within ten. This produced a correlation coefficient of 0.082. This still a very slight correlation and there are no other significant results surrounding this one. The results seem to indicate that there is no correlation between learning style and compatibility.

4.3 Skill Level

Perceived skill level was by far the most accurate predictor of partner compatibility. The Spearman correlation of the overall rating and skill rating resulted in a statistically significant correlation ($p = 0.000$) with a $\rho = -0.464$. This is a fairly strong correlation, indicating that students do not enjoy working with partners who they feel to be less technically competent than them.

4.4 Programming Self Esteem

The survey questions regarding programming self esteem are split into four questions which required students to place themselves somewhere on a scale from 1 to 9 (the names with which we refer to them by are in brackets):

- [Speed] When working on a programming assignment, do you think that: 1) It takes me longer to complete programming tasks than my colleagues. 9) I am much quicker at solving programming tasks than others.
- [Problem Solving] When working on a programming problem: 1) I have difficulty knowing where to begin on new programming problems. 9) I have no difficulty in starting the problem.
- [Helping] When helping others with their computer science work, do you: 1) Feel that you do not know enough to help others. 9) I know enough to help others.
- [Roadblock] When I run into a roadblock in my thinking: 1) My mind goes around and around in circles. 9) I know that I will find the answer somewhere.

For each of these four questions we ran Spearman correlations as described in the methodology section. The speed and problem solving questions did not return overall significant results. There were a few significant results, but as with the personality types and learning styles they were scattered and had weak correlation coefficients. The roadblock question had significant results for partners within 3, 4, and 5 of each other. The correlation was fairly weak (between -0.050 and -0.060), but this may improve in further investigations.

The helping question returned significant results ($p = 0.023$) for the Spearman correlation with overall score and the difference between the partners' helping responses using a two-tailed significance test. The correlation is slight ($\rho = 0.056$), however this result is still worth noting. Future investigations may find stronger correlations between students' responses to this question and partner compatibility. This question may prove an accurate indicator of how students perceive skill level, as the question requires them to relate their computer science experience to that of their peers.

4.5 Work Ethic

Work ethic does not seem to be a significant factor in compatibility. We received one significant result ($p = 0.048$), when the difference between the two numbers is 0 (a perfect match). This correlation resulted in a ρ of .049. This is not a very strong correlation, but this factor may prove more telling in future work.

As an interesting aside, a Spearman correlation with the overall score and only the work ethic response of the person being evaluated returns a significant result ($p = 0.000$) with a correlation coefficient of $\rho = 0.128$, indicating that students with stronger work ethics tend to receive more positive reviews from their partners.

4.6 Time Management Skills

Our results did not show time management to be a significant factor in compatibility. No results where statistically significant. Williams et al. [10] also found time management to be insignificant. They theorized that students' busy schedules dictated that they meet whenever both partners where available. Since these windows of time are most likely rare, students have to disregard their personal time management habits and meet whenever those times may be.

5. PAIREVAL

In conjunction with this study we began developing a web-based tool in PHP and MySQL that would facilitate the use of group work in computer science courses. This app is based off of the open source tool from NCSU called PairEval. NCSU's PairEval provided functionality that allowed students to respond to pre-course surveys (including taking a Myers-Briggs personality test and a Felder-Silverman learning styles test), enroll in courses and evaluate their partners for a given assignment. Our version of PairEval aims to extend the functionality of NCSU's app to make it more usable by professors. The two key functionalities added to the system are survey customization and group formation.

5.1. Survey Customization

In NCSU's PairEval tool the student pre-course survey questions are hard-coded in. If a professor wanted to add or remove questions from a survey he/she would have to modify the application code containing the questions and update the database accordingly. We have simplified the process of adding and removing questions and surveys by providing an interface to do so within the application. With our expanded functionality, professors can create and delete surveys and add and remove questions from their surveys without having to edit the application code or database. Our hope is that this will make the system easier for professors to use and foster the gathering of student compatibility data for future research.

5.2 Group Formation

The PairEval tool provided by NCSU does not provide an easy way for professors to form student groups for assignments. The professor must enter the number of groups he/she wishes to create and then manually place each student into a group. In our app, the formation of groups has been automated. In this system the professor selects the course and assignment, enters a desired number of students per group (obviously, it will not always be possible to have exactly the requested number per group), and clicks a button to have groups automatically generated for that assignment. This should make the use of groups in computer science courses easier for professors, hopefully encouraging the use of pair programming. As the research into the field of partner compatibility progresses we also hope to include an algorithm that will incorporate this new knowledge in order to maximize the compatibility of the created groups.

6. CONCLUSIONS AND FUTURE WORK

The main finding of this study is that students' perceived skill level continues to be the most accurate predictor of partner compatibility. The other categories were found to be insignificant on the whole. The results of our study are summarized in the following table:

Table 2: Summary of Results

Hypothesis: Pairs are more compatible if students with … are grouped together.		Result
H-1	… different personality types …	No
H-2	… different learning styles …	No
H-3	… similar perceived skill levels …	Yes
H-4	… similar programming self-esteem …	No
H-5	… similar work ethic …	No
H-6	… similar time management skills …	No

We plan to continue to gather data in University of Virginia computer science courses. This data will be used in future studies to analyze any changes in trends. In addition to continuing to gather data in the courses discussed in this study we would like to expand our efforts into other courses. We would like to gather data from higher level programming courses to see if the conclusions found for the introductory level courses examined in this study also hold in upper level classes. We would also like to gather data from non-programming courses, such as UVA's Digital Logic and Design (DLD) course. DLD is an introduction to the design and implementation of logic circuits. The lab sections for this class more closely resemble a traditional science lab. We would like to examine whether the factors that affect compatibility between partners in a more traditional lab setting are similar to those affecting pair programmers.

We would also like to continue to refine the questions presented to students in the beginning of course surveys. The new PairEval tool should make this process easier with its ability to easily modify the surveys. We would like to introduce new questions that could possibly serve as indicators of compatibility or of students' perceived skill level and examine their correlation with pair compatibility.

We also plan to continue to expand the functionality of the PairEval system. As more information becomes available on the factors that lead to compatibility between students we plan to update the system with an algorithm that will pair students together for maximum compatibility.

7. REFERENCES

[1] Cockburn, Alistair and Williams, Laurie. *The Costs and Benefits of Pair Programming* in *Extreme Programming Examined.* Addison Wesley, 2001.

[2] Felder, R. M. and Silverman, L. K., "Learning and Teaching Styles in Engineering Education," *Engineering Education*, vol. 78, 1988, pp. 674-681.

[3] Ferzli, M., Wiebe, E., and Williams, L., "Paired Programming Project: Focus Groups with Teaching Assistants and Students", NCSU Technical Report, TR-2002-16, November 25, 2002.

[4] Katira, N., Williams, L., and Osborne, J., "Towards Increasing the Compatibility of Student Pair Programmers", International Conference on Software Engineering (ICSE) 2005, pp. 625-626.

[5] Katira, N., Williams, L., Wiebe, E., Miller, C., Balik, S., and Gehringer, E., "On Understanding Compatibility of Student Pair Programmers", ACM Technical Symposium on Computer Science Education, SIGCSE 2004, pp. 7-11.

[6] Myers, I.B., McCaulley, M., Quenk, N., and Hammer, A. *MBTI Manual: A Guide to the Development and Use of the Myers Briggs Type Indicator.* 3rd ed. Consulting Psychologists Press. 1998.

[7] Nagappan, N., Williams, L., Wiebe, E., Miller, C., Balik, S., Ferzli, M., and Petlick, M., "Pair Learning: With an Eye Toward Future Success", *Extreme Programming/Agile Universe* 2003, pp. 185-198.

[8] Williams, L. and Kessler, R. *Pair Programming Illuminated*, Addison Wesley, 2003.

[9] Williams, L., Kessler, R., Cunningham, W., and Jeffries, R. "Strengthening the Case for Pair-Programming", *IEEE Software*, 2000. 17: p. 19-25.

[10] Williams, L., Layman, L., Osborne, J., and Katira, N., "Examining the Compatibility of Student Pair Programmers," Proceedings of Agile 2006, Minneapolis, MN, July 23-28, 2006, pp. 411-420.

The Benefits of Pairing by Ability

Grant Braught, John MacCormick, and Tim Wahls
Dickinson College, Carlisle, PA 17013
{braught, jmac, wahlst}@dickinson.edu

ABSTRACT

An analysis of data from 259 CS1 students is performed to compare the performance of students who were paired by demonstrated ability to that of students who were paired randomly or worked alone. The results suggest that when given individual programming tasks to complete, lowest-quartile students who were paired by ability perform better than those who were paired randomly and those who worked alone.

Categories and Subject Descriptors

K.3.2 [**Computer and Information Science Education**]: Computer science education; D.2.3 [**Software Engineering**]: Coding Tools and Techniques

General Terms

Experimentation, Human Factors

Keywords

Pair programming, pairing methodology, collaborative learning

1. INTRODUCTION

Controlled experiments on the effects of pair programming have been reported from a variety of institutions and for a wide range of different courses. These studies present convincing evidence that students who pair program are more likely to successfully complete the course [, ,], have increased confidence in their solutions [,], are more likely to continue with computer science [ ], and develop better individual programming skills [ ]. Additionally, some studies have shown that pair programming is particularly beneficial for female and minority students [, ,], and also for students with lower SAT scores [ ].

Numerous studies have also investigated the factors that affect pair compatibility when pair programming is used. The majority of these studies paired students randomly and then used quantitative and/or qualitative methods to identify correlations between the students' ratings of their pairings and factors such as ability, perceived ability, confidence, personality type, work ethic, gender and ethnicity. By far the most common conclusion is that pairs are most likely to be compatible when students are paired with a partner who they perceive as being of equal or higher ability [, , , ,]. The results are considerably less clear for pairs with similar actual ability (as measured by some combination of GPA, SAT/GRE and midterm exam scores) — some studies report a positive correlation with pair compatibility [ ], while others could not establish a consistent correlation [,]. Several of the studies included personality tests such as the Myers-Brigs Type Indicator, Felder-Silverman Learning Style or Keirsey Temperament Sorter and concluded that pairs comprising students with different personality traits were more likely to be compatible than homogeneous pairs [, ,]. A number of the studies also examined the effects of self-esteem or confidence on pairing, producing mixed results. One study found that pairing students with similar self-esteem did not influence the likelihood of pair compatibility [ ], another found that the most confident students reported enjoying pairing more than less confident students [ ], while another found the opposite [ ]. One study that considered gender and ethnicity found that for female and minority students, being paired with another female or minority student was positively correlated with pair compatibility [ ].

The factors affecting pair compatibility have been investigated quite extensively, but surprisingly few studies have attempted to directly measure the effects of the pairing methodology on student achievement. Thomas, Ratcliffe and Robertson [ ] studied the effects of pairing students by their confidence in their own coding skills. Pairs in which both students had similar confidence (e.g. high/high or low/low) received the highest scores on assignments, and further significant differences were not found between the scores of low/low pairs and high/high pairs. They also report that high/low pairs received the lowest scores. Sfetsos *et al.* [ ] created pairs with similar and dissimilar temperaments, as measured by the Keirsey Temperament Sorter. They found that heterogeneous pairs communicated more often, produced better designs and wrote code that passed more acceptance tests than homogeneous pairs.

Both of the studies just described measure the impact of the pairing methodology on the quality of the work produced by the *pairs*. One might also ask how different pairing methodologies impact the *individuals* within the pairs. In the remainder of this paper we present evidence suggesting that when students are paired with a partner of similar ability, the individuals within the pair each learn at least as much as if they had either worked with a random partner or worked alone. The evidence also suggests that for the bottom quartile of students, pairing by similar ability may result in increased learning for the individuals in the pair. Some limitations of the dataset prevent us from drawing firm conclusions, but we do believe our analysis provides useful insights into the benefits of by-ability pairings and will motivate more carefully controlled studies in the future.

2. DESCRIPTION OF THE DATASET

Our dataset consists of 13 sections of a one-semester, entry-level Java programming class, taught by four different instructors between 2005 and 2008. The content and format of the class, including homework and programming assignments, was virtually identical in each section. Only students who completed the course are included in the dataset (that is, we eliminate students who withdrew, but not those who failed). Enrollment in each section was capped at 24 students. An average of 20 students completed each section, resulting in a dataset of 259 students.

Students are graded on four different types of work: (i) weekly written homework exercises; (ii) weekly programming assignments; (iii) three written exams; (iv) two programming exams. Because the programming exams are of special importance in our analysis, we describe them in some detail here. The required task in a programming exam is to complete the fields and method bodies of the skeletons of one or more Java classes, and also to write unit tests for each method. The provided skeletons contain the method signatures and detailed JavaDoc comments. During a programming exam, students work individually in a proctored room, receive essentially no assistance, and have a fixed amount of time (two hours) to complete the exam. Grading of the exam is mostly automatic (via Web-CAT [ ]), although instructors can deduct a small number of points for poor programming style. The automatic grading assesses formatting and documentation, runs reference tests to verify correctness, and checks for code coverage of unit tests. Although the actual content of the programming exams changed each semester, considerable efforts were made to keep the structure, length, difficulty, and grading of these exams as uniform as possible over the study period.

In contrast to the programming *exams*, which were administered uniformly over all sections, the weekly programming *assignments* were administered quite differently in different sections. In particular, three different approaches were used: (i) *ability pairs* – students work on programming assignments in pairs assigned by ability, with students of similar ability (as measured by overall performance in the course to date) working together; (ii) *random pairs* – students work on programming assignments in pairs assigned randomly; and (iii) *no pairs* – students work on programming assignments individually. In the two pairing approaches, students are required to rotate the "driver" (i.e. typist) role every 15 minutes during the 2-hour laboratory session. Students were not aware of the criteria for assigning pairs. Of the 13 sections in the dataset, 7 paired students by ability (142 students), 2 paired students randomly (41 students), and 4 used no pairs (76 students).

We will refer to students as being "trained with" one of the three approaches, and for additional brevity will use phrases like "ability-pair students" to refer to students trained with ability pairs. The main purpose of this paper is to assess the effect of these three training strategies on student outcomes.

3. ANALYSIS

We are interested in the hypothesis that students trained with ability pairs achieve better individual outcomes than students trained with random pairs or no pairs — especially for less able students. The "outcomes" will be the scores achieved by students on the final programming exam of the semester, given in the 14th week. It is important to note that this outcome measures a student's skill when programming *alone*, regardless of which of the three training approaches was used by the student in previous assignments. Previous work [ ] has shown that ability pairing benefits the lowest quartile of students, compared with using no pairs. We would like to investigate whether the same is true for random pairings. Therefore, our hypothesis tests will focus on the lowest quartile of students, as measured by their programming exam scores. For concreteness, the hypothesis test comparing random and ability pairs is described in detail; the test comparing no pairs with ability pairs is perfectly analogous. Specifically, the null hypothesis for random pairs will be, "the 25th percentile of programming exam scores for students trained with random pairs is the same as for students trained with ability pairs."

The test statistic used in this experiment, denoted n_{25}, is very simple: it is the number of students trained with random pairs who scored less than the 25th percentile of the scores for students trained with ability pairs. Figure 1 shows the numerical results for our dataset. The 25th percentile of scores for the 142 students trained with ability pairs is 82/100 (i.e. 25% of the 142 students scored less than 82 on the programming exam — this is the intersection of the ability-pair line and the dashed horizontal line in the figure). Of the 41 students trained with random pairs, 14 scored less than 82 (i.e. are left of the vertical line) on the programming exam. Therefore, the test statistic is $n_{25} = 14$. The conventional approach is to compute the p-value of the test statistic, and reject the null hypothesis if the p-value is lower than a given level of significance, such as 0.05 or 0.01.

How can we convert this test statistic into a p-value? Intuitively, if the null hypothesis were true and the 25th percentile for random-pair students was the same as for ability-pair students, then approximately 10 (i.e. one quarter of 41) of the random-pair students should have scored less than 82. The fact that considerably more than 10 students (actually 14) scored below 82 immediately raises suspicions that the null hypothesis may not hold. To quantify this suspicion and obtain a p-value, we compute the probability that a value of $n_{25} \geq 14$ would have occurred if the null hypothesis were true. This probability can be calculated as the tail of a binomial distribution: $p = \sum_{k=n_{25}}^{N} \binom{N}{k} \pi^k (1-\pi)^{N-k}$. Here, $N = 41$ is the number of random-pair students and $\pi = 0.25$ is the value of the percentile used in the null hypothesis. Each term in the sum is the chance that k of N students would score less than 82 if, as stated by the null hypothesis, the chance of doing so is 25%.

For this experiment $p = 0.12$, which means that there is a 12% probability that a discrepancy of at least this amount (between the expected number of students scoring below 82,

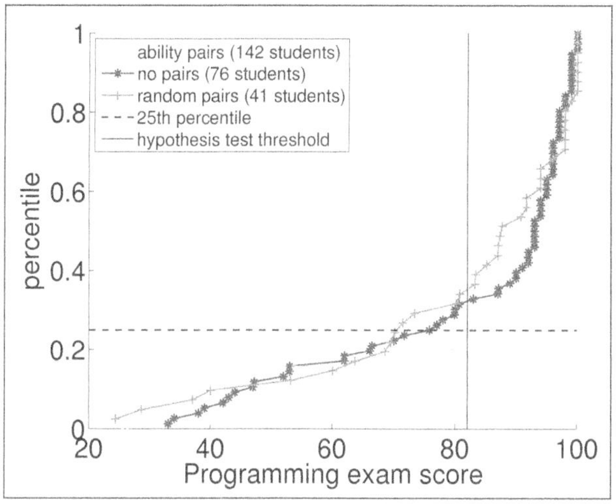

Figure 1: The method of pairing students for assignments has potentially significant effects on the performance of the bottom quartile of students. Below the 25th percentile (dotted line), the difference between ability pairs and the other two methods has mild statistical significance (p-values ranging between 0.02 and 0.12).

and the actual number doing so), would have arisen if the null hypothesis were true. It is conventional in statistical analyses to reject the null hypothesis only if the p-value is considerably lower than this (say, 0.01 or 0.05). However, given the small amount of data available for this study, we regard the p-value of 0.12 as providing some evidence that the null hypothesis may be false, and that more extensive studies of such hypotheses would be worthwhile. On the other hand, it should also be noted that p-values in post-hoc studies such as this one are frequently more extreme than they would have been in a controlled study, so some care must be taken in assessing the significance of this result.

Some additional remarks on our choice of statistical tests are in order. First, a more conventional way to test the difference between two distributions (such as the distributions of scores for ability-pair students and for random-pair students) would be to apply the Kolmogorov-Smirnov (KS) test. But because we have a priori reasons to believe the differences will be concentrated in the lower quartile [ ], KS is less than ideal for this application. Indeed, KS has lower power than the hypothesis test described above, and yields a p-value of 0.39 for the hypothesis that the two distributions coincide. A p-value this high provides no evidence for rejecting the null hypothesis. Second, the above test based on binomial probabilities assumes that the 25th percentile of ability-pair scores (82/100 in this case) is the true 25th percentile for the population of students trained by ability. In fact, 82/100 is merely an estimate for this quantity based on the 142 ability-pair students in our dataset. A more sophisticated test taking this uncertainty into account could be applied. However, given the relatively high number of ability-pair students we believe the simpler approach taken here still yields useful results.

3.1 Tests related to the main hypothesis

The previous subsection described the concrete details of one particular hypothesis test, comparing the lowest quartile of students trained with ability pairs and students trained with random pairs. Naturally, we can perform the same test comparing ability-pair students with no-pair students, and both tests can be done for any desired percentile instead of the 25th percentile discussed so far. The following table gives the p-values for some representative points in this space of hypothesis tests, using the same data from Figure 1.

percentile	random pairs	no pairs
10%	0.11	0.02
15%	0.04	0.03
25%	0.12	0.12
50%	0.17	0.36

It should be clear that below the 25th percentile, there are potentially significant differences between training with ability pairs and training with the other two approaches (random pairs and no pairs). Any differences at the 50th percentile are much less clear. Hopefully it is also clear from these results that we have not simply cherry-picked one particular percentile (in this case, the 25th percentile) for our discussion because it happens to yield statistical significance. In fact, we see much stronger significance at the 10th and 15th percentiles — but the very small number of students in the tails of these distributions makes us reluctant to draw conclusions about this.

3.2 Other hypotheses

The main thrust of our analysis has been to test the hypothesis that pairing by ability improves the performance of weaker students on solo programming tasks, but our dataset is suitable for testing numerous other interesting hypotheses. For example, given the extensive evidence in the literature on the educational benefits of pair programming, one might expect to see a significant difference between students trained with random pairs and students trained with no pairs. However, a quick glance at Figure 1 should be sufficient to demonstrate that our dataset cannot validate this hypothesis. It may well be true that random pairings generally produce better outcomes than no pairings at all, but in our data the bottom quartile of random-pair students and no-pair students have very similar performance on the programming exam.

We are also interested in whether the choice of pairing method affects student performance on all individual activities in the course. To investigate this, we re-ran the analysis of Section 3, substituting the students' score on all solo assignments (homework, programming exams, and written exams) for the final programming exam score. The results using this "solo activity score" are shown in Figure 2. Based on an informal visual assessment of the graph, there does appear to be a noticeable difference between ability pairs and the other two approaches in the lowest quartile — though perhaps not as striking as the difference for the programming exam shown in Figure 1. In fact, if we compute the p-value of the 25th percentile statistic n_{25} defined above, we find the difference is somewhat significant for no-pair students (p-value 0.12), but insignificant for random-pair students (p-value 0.45).

Finally, one might consider the effect of pairing method on student performance in pair programming assignments themselves. Again, a very similar analysis can be performed, this time measuring student outcomes by their total score on all pair programming assignments, termed a student's

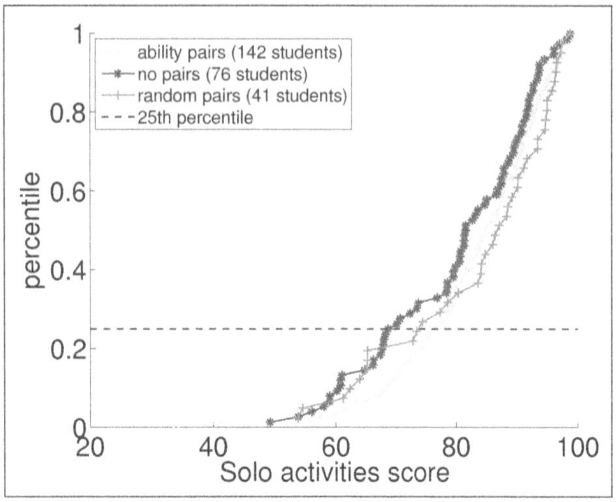

Figure 2: Pairing method may have a mild effect on the lowest quartile of students. In contrast to Figure 1, which measured student performance on a programming exam only, this figure shows their performance on all individual activities including homework, programming exams, and written exams. In the lowest quartile, there do appear to be noticeable differences in performance.

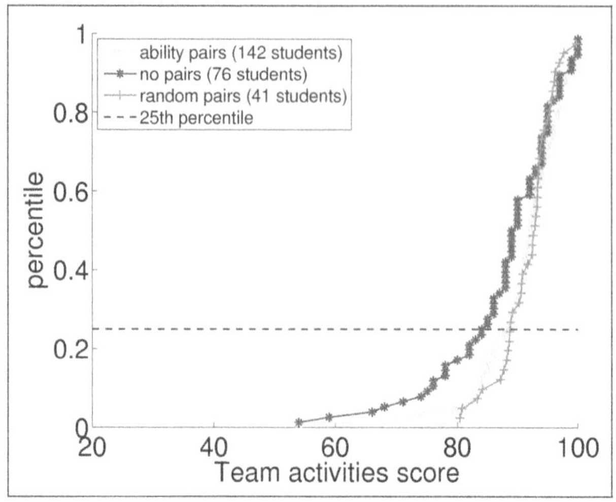

Figure 3: In the lowest quartile, there is overwhelming statistical evidence that students working alone achieve lower scores on a given set of assignments than students working in pairs (whether random or by ability) on the same set of assignments. In other words, below the dotted line representing the lowest quartile, the red and green lines are statistically indistinguishable but the blue line exhibits a highly significant difference.

"team" score. (Obviously, for students trained with no pairs, there are no pair programming assignments. But we can still collect the scores of the no-pair students on the assignments that were done in pairs by students in other sections. This results in a comparable number that is still referred to as the "team" score for no-pairs students.) Figure 3 shows the results. Here we see that outcomes for ability pairs and random pairs are virtually indistinguishable (p-value 0.96), whereas a highly significant difference does exist in the lowest quartile between no-pair students and the other two approaches (p-value $< 10^{-3}$ for no-pair vs random, and for no-pair vs ability). In fact, there is high significance for differences at the 50th percentile too (p-value ≈ 0.014 in both cases).

The stark difference in team scores for no-pair and paired approaches is not at all surprising. The instructors in our study have observed strong anecdotal evidence that students are much less likely to give up on a challenging assignment when working with someone else, and this tends to dramatically improve the performance of the bottom quartile.

3.3 Confounding factors

We believe our dataset provides useful and novel insights, but it possesses some limitations that should be acknowledged clearly. First, this is a partially post-hoc study, in the sense that the random pairing technique was not part of the original design. The majority of the data was collected from a carefully-controlled study that compared pair programming using by-ability pairs with individual programming [ ]. The same course was subsequently taught twice using random pairings, resulting in a dataset with potentially useful information about different pairing strategies. Second, the pairing strategies themselves were not applied with perfect consistency: instructors used different combinations of automatic grade-based scripts and their own subjective impressions in assigning pairs. In any case, ability pairs are not used early in the semester when the instructors have no grades or impressions on which to base them. Therefore, the first four or five weekly programming assignments are always completed using random pairings.

A further potential weakness in the dataset is the fact that the two sections that employed random pairings were also exceptional in another respect: in both cases, these sections were taught by instructors who had not taught the course before. Therefore, inferior performance by students in random-pair sections might be due to the relative unfamiliarity of the instructors with the course material. To investigate whether this is indeed a serious problem, we analyzed the outcomes of the *first* programming exam. This exam is given in week 7 of the semester, so students in the ability-pair sections have worked on only one or two assignments in by-ability pairs. If the effect of first-time instructors dominated the effect of random pairings, we would expect a difference between the random-pair sections and ability-pair sections on *both* programming exams. However, the 25th-percentile difference on the first exam is not significant (p-value 0.41), which suggests the instructor effect is not dominant and adds credibility to the previous analysis.

4. DISCUSSION

The evidence presented suggests that pairing students of similar ability may improve the performance of less able students on individual programming tasks as compared to random pairings. Why might this be the case? We can envision several reasons.

First, because our ability metric of performance in the course to date includes some direct measures of the tasks to be completed in pairs (actual programming), it seems likely that students who are paired together will perceive each other to be of similar ability, and thus are likely to be compatible. Each of the studies cited earlier that did not observe a correlation between actual ability and pair compatibility used less specific measures of actual ability such as GPA, SAT/GRE scores and midterm exam scores. In fact, one of these studies alludes to exactly this, saying that while pair compatibility did not correlate with metrics such as GPA, SAT/GRE and midterm scores, more specific metrics such as computer science GPA and total GPA are predictors of perceived ability [ ]. Thus, we suspect that our mechanism for pairing by ability is in fact forming more compatible pairs than pairing randomly.

Second, and of particular relevance to the performance of the weaker students in the class, are the implications of working with a partner of similar ability. One might be tempted to pair a weaker student with a stronger student so that the weaker student can learn from the stronger. But in our experience, and in that of others [,], the stronger student instead takes over, and either does the work or simply gives direction. Thus, in random pairings that contain a stronger and weaker student, the weaker student will not actually experience the process of resolving whatever difficulties arise — instead simply observing how the stronger student handles the problem. Even worse, when the stronger student is the driver in the pair, the weaker student may not even be exposed to problems that he/she would face if working individually. When two students of similar ability work on such a problem together, they are more likely to resolve it in a collaborative way that seems likely to result in deeper understanding and a better learning outcome for both students.

5. CONCLUSIONS

If pairing by ability can improve outcomes for the students who have demonstrated the least aptitude for the course material, further investigation certainly seems warranted, particularly since this approach requires no extra class time and little administrative overhead, and appears to have no harmful effects on higher-ability students [ ]. A more tightly controlled study comparing the performance of students in sections that are paired randomly to those that are paired by ability would not be difficult to perform. If such an investigation were to be conducted it should also include self-pairing, as at least one study found that when students are allowed to self-pair they tend to choose partners that have a similar ability level [ ]. Thus, perhaps any benefits of ability pairing could be obtained without the even minimal administrative overhead of assigning pairs.

6. ACKNOWLEDGMENTS

Partial funding for this research was provided by the National Science Foundation under a CCLI-A&I grant (DUE-0511264). We would also like to thank Dr. Stephen Edwards of Virginia Tech for supporting our use of WebCAT, which provided quantitative data on student program quality and testing.

7. REFERENCES

[1] G. Braught, L. M. Eby, and T. Wahls. The effects of pair-programming on individual programming skill. In *SIGCSE*, pages 200–204, 2008.

[2] G. Braught, T. Wahls, and M. Eby. The case for pair programming in the computer science classroom. *Submitted to Trans. Computing Education*, 2009.

[3] Carver, Henderson, He, Hodges, and Reese. Increased retention of early computer science and software engineering students using pair programming. *CSEET*, pages 115–122, 2007.

[4] E. A. Chaparro, A. Yuksel, P. Romero, and S. Bryant. Factors affecting the perceived effectiveness of pair programming in higher education. In P. Romero, J. Good, S. Bryant, and E. A. Chaparro, editors, *Psychology of Programming Interest Group 17th Workshop*, pages 5–18, 2005.

[5] B. Hanks. Student attitudes toward pair programming. In *ITiCSE*, pages 113–117, 2006.

[6] N. Katira, L. Williams, and J. Osborne. Towards increasing the compatibility of student pair programmers. In *ICSE*, pages 625–626, 2005.

[7] N. Katira, L. Williams, E. Wiebe, C. Miller, S. Balik, and E. Gehringer. On understanding compatibility of student pair programmers. In *SIGCSE*, pages 7–11, 2004.

[8] C. McDowell, L. Werner, H. E. Bullock, and J. Fernald. The impact of pair programming on student performance, perception and persistence. In *ICSE*, pages 602–607, 2003.

[9] C. McDowell, L. Werner, H. E. Bullock, and J. Fernald. Pair programming improves student retention, confidence, and program quality. *Commun. ACM*, 49(8):90–95, 2006.

[10] G. Melnik and F. Maurer. Perceptions of agile practices: A student survey. In *Proc. Extreme Programming and Agile Methods*, pages 241-250, 2002.

[11] E. Mendes, L. Al-Fakhri, and A. Luxton-Reilly. A replicated experiment of pair-programming in a 2nd-year software development and design computer science course. *SIGCSE Bull.*, 38(3):108–112, 2006.

[12] R. Nicolescu and R. Plummer. A pair programming experiment in a large computer course. *Romanian J. Inf. Sci. and Tech*, 6(1-2):199–216, 2003.

[13] P. Sfetsos, I. Stamelos, L. Angelis, and I. Deligiannis. An experimental investigation of personality types impact on pair effectiveness in pair programming. *Empirical Softw. Eng.*, 14(2):187–226, 2009.

[14] L. Thomas, M. Ratcliffe, and A. Robertson. Code warriors and code-a-phobes: a study in attitude and pair programming. In *SIGCSE*, pages 363–367, 2003.

[15] Web-cat research server front page. `http://web-cat.cs.vt.edu/`, 2009.

[16] L. L. Werner, B. Hanks, and C. McDowell. Pair-programming helps female computer science students. *J. Educ. Resour. Comput.*, 4(1):4, 2004.

[17] L. Williams, L. Layman, J. Osborne, and N. Katira. Examining the compatibility of student pair programmers. In *Proc. AGILE*, pages 411–420, 2006.

[18] L. Williams, L. Layman, K. M. Slaten, S. B. Berenson, and C. Seaman. On the impact of a collaborative pedagogy on african american millennial students in software engineering. In *ICSE*, pages 677–687, 2007.

Making Contact with the Forgotten K-12 Influence: *Are You Smarter Than YOUR 5th Grader?*

Mindy L. Hart
Purdue University Department of Computer Science
K-12 Outreach Program
305 N. University Street
West Lafayette, IN 47907 USA
mindy@purdue.edu

ABSTRACT

This paper is an experience report that describes a computer science based workshop titled *Are You Smarter than YOUR 5th Grader?* and targeted at fourth through sixth grade female students and parents. The novel approach of including parents as a pair programmer with the student is highlighted. Additionally, the paper probes the impact of this workshop and plans for revision and replication of future workshops.

Categories and Subject Descriptors

K.3.1 [**Computer Uses in Education**]: collaborative learning.

K.3.2 [**Computer and Information Science Education**]: computer science education.

General Terms

Design, Human Factors, Theory.

Keywords

K-12 instruction, computer science education, pair programming, workshops, parent involvement.

1. SUMMARY

After years of soaring enrollments in Computer Science at Purdue University, the last seven years have shown a 52% decrease in the number of high school students interested in pursuing CS as a major and career. The number of women choosing CS in our department has dropped from 13% to 7% [10]. A similar picture is reflected across the nation and is problematic for companies trying to recruit students with CS degrees. The Department of Computer Science at Purdue University has a number of interrelated initiatives that are designed to increase the awareness of computer science among girls in the K-12 environment. Most of the current programs focus on supporting teachers and inspiring students through summer camps, professional development workshops for K-12 educators, and in-class presentations throughout the state of Indiana.

Anecdotally, many of our current CS undergraduates have shared that it was a parent who first encouraged individual interest in computing beyond general computer use. Likewise, Margolis and Fisher have documented similar stories in *Unlocking the Clubhouse*. To quote the authors, "Parents impart their computer enthusiasm and skills to their children, and through early mastery acquired at home children gain a competence and confidence they carry with them into school" [6]. Toward this effort, the Purdue University Department of Computer Science K-12 Outreach Program has developed a workshop designed to engage this influential layer. Through funding received from NCWIT's Academic Alliance Seed Fund Grant Program, we developed the program we are calling *Are You Smarter Than YOUR 5th Grader?* The program seeks to engage parents alongside their children, thus creating a support system beyond the walls of school. We recognize in today's society, many students are often more skilled at general computer tasks than their parents due to the emergence of technology use in schools. This program uses activities that level the playing field for all involved, and allows the child and parent to develop understanding and experience success alongside each other, no matter the skill level of either party. In turn, we hope mutual respect and encouragement will continue throughout the years as the parent and child become more enthusiastic about computing opportunities.

The *Are You Smarter Than YOUR 5th Grader?* Program is targeted at girls in grades 4-6 and their parent or guardians. The pilot workshop consisted of six sessions during the Fall 2008 semester. The children experience pair programming with their adult counterpart while participating in activities such as the Alice [1] storytelling challenge and PicoCricket [9] design studio. Additionally, children partake in CS Unplugged [4] activities while parents are offered special sessions on topics such as college admissions or encouraging technology use in their children.

This paper will discuss the details of the workshop as well as the outcomes discovered from the program and attitudinal surveys. We will share information discovered about the value of including the parents in the child's education experience and any obstacles we encountered in trying to make this a true pair programming experience.

1.1 Related Work

There are countless studies detailing the benefits of using pair programming in the post-secondary environment, especially CS0,

SIGCSE'10, March 10–13, 2010, Milwaukee, Wisconsin, USA.

CS1, and CS2 level courses in collegiate settings. Most concur with the findings of McKinney and Denton that using pair programming is beneficial in that it provides for deeper learning, desirable career skill development, fun learning environments, higher retention, higher interest in CS, higher success rates in courses, higher achievement, and a sense of belonging [8]. Additionally, Braught et.al. conclude that pair programming has a positive effect on students with lower SAT scores and that these students are more likely to have significantly improved individual programming skills after participating in a collaborative setting [2].

Just as there are many studies highlighting the effects of using pair programming, there are also many reports on the effect parents have on children's interest and eventual career choices in STEM (Science, Technology, Engineering, and Mathematics) based disciplines [3,7,11]. Messersmith et.al. further suggests some of these interests and career choices are developed through experiences in homes, schools, and other contexts such as early interactions with parental social networks and the provision of key experiences involving computing.

A unique paper highlights an attempt to bring parents and students together in Taiwan much in the way we have attempted in the *Are You Smarter Than YOUR 5th Grader?* workshop. Parents and children attended a computer camp and used MSWLogo programming. This research randomly chose three participating pairs to observe and recorded behaviors and attitudes during the camp. Findings from this research include that parents and children naturally take on the assumed roles in pair programming, parental involvement helped children spend more time on analysis and design rather than just trial and error, program output was more well-structured, reflection on actions and problem-solving was emphasized, and children tended to proceed with caution because of parental supervision and interaction [5].

2. WORKSHOP LOGISTICS

2.1 Recruitment and Design

Participants were recruited via brochures and poster placement at local schools as well as through local press releases. Due to lab constraints, we were only able to accommodate 26 pairs. Of these 26 students, 22 were female. Our university allows us to target a specific group, however we cannot limit enrollment to that group. Therefore, we had 4 male students also enroll in the program. While the workshop was offered free of charge, families were asked to submit a $25 refundable deposit to hold their spot. Originally participants were asked to commit to coming to six sessions- two each month for each of three months. Realizing this may not be realistic, we loosened that requirement to attending 4 of the 6 sessions. If that milestone was reached, the parents would have their deposit returned and the family would be able to keep the PicoCricket kit.

To keep with the game show theme of the title, each of the six sessions started with an interactive trivia contest. Participants were given an eInstruction clicker upon arrival and would use it to submit their answers to the trivia questions. Trivia questions revolved around general computer trivia, computer history, Purdue University trivia, and logic games. Prizes, obtained from corporate sponsors, were awarded to the top scorers each week.

Pairs were then dismissed to the labs and given some general instruction for the day. Lab sessions were led by local teachers, current Purdue computer science students, and other departmental employees. Two sessions focused on PicoCrickets, two sessions focused on Alice, and in the final two sessions, pairs were given an open challenge where they could choose to use either option (or both) to design a project around a given theme.

Each session ended with a lunch and learn session. Lunches were provided for the families. Some of the activities during these lunches included: student presentations of created works, university admissions presentations, CS Unplugged activities, viewing of a short version of Randy Pausch's last lecture for the parents, and tours of the departmental visualization lab.

2.2 Workshop Staff

We were fortunate to have a variety skills and interests among our staff. Knowing that we would have approximately 50 participants each week, we needed to have sessions in two separate labs with parallel instruction. To do the parallel instruction, we hired a local teacher who was familiar with the programs and has used them in her classroom and partnered her with the K-12 outreach coordinator to design and plan the sessions. Two concurrent and identical sessions were then conducted in two labs. Additionally, students from the CS 290- Service Learning in Outreach course volunteered time as a service learning activity and acted as lab assistants. A few additional college students were hired to help as lab assistants when the CS 290 students were not available. Having 5-6 staff members available each week helped develop rapport with the families and ensured that pairs were able to get the support they needed when questions arose.

2.3 Cost of Delivery

The original NCWIT Seed Fund Grant was for $15,000. We came in just a few dollars under that budget. A large portion of the funding was spent on PicoCricket kits for the families. The other large portions of the budget came in the form of staff wages and lunches each week. It is possible to do the workshop for less if using another project other than the PicoCrickets and limiting the amount spent on food. We felt strongly about giving the students something that they could take home with them and continue to use after the workshop was completed, hence the purchase of the PicoCricket kits.

2.4 Workshop Activities

Each week, participants were asked to be available from 9am-1pm. There was considerable variance in the actual arrival time since many families were traveling considerable distances to attend. The interactive quiz at the beginning allowed for the families to arrive within a reasonable time frame and lab instruction to be given all at one time. Some weeks included a theme and participants were encouraged to dress in the theme and create their projects around that theme. Table 1 shows the schedule of each week's activities. Alice and PicoCrickets were chosen because of the ease of use with this age group and potential interest to girls, but could easily be replaced with other programs or activities more readily available.

Week 1 and 2 focused on programming using Alice. The promotional materials indicated that participants would engage in an Alice Storytelling Challenge. The Alice Storytelling Challenge was designed to give students an avenue to express their imaginative side. This activity combined the use of creativity and programming with the Alice 3D graphic design program. In this challenge students created their own digital world to tell a story. The exercise taught programming with a drag-and- drop interface which allowed students to see the relationships between the animation they created and the programming statements. In week 1, participants were given a general introduction to the program and then were guided through the built-in tutorials. At the end of each tutorial, participants were given time to explore the concepts learned and practice using them. The session ended with participants being encouraged to work within the parent/child pair to create a commercial. Week 2 encouraged the pairs to retell a common story with a twist using Alice. Time was given for presenting each project at the end of the session.

Week 3 and 4 introduced the PicoCricket kits to the participants. Participants were told they would take part in a PicoCricket design studio. PicoCrickets bring art to life. With a PicoCricket set a student can elicit an action or reaction from their art based on stimuli. This robotic set uses lights, motors, sensors, and other devices to plug into the PicoCricket to create a performance. It involves an art and craft element to actually build and design the devices too. Week 3 was conducted similar to week 1, where participants were guided through some general activities under the concepts of sound, light, and motion and were given time to play with each concept before moving to the next instruction. Week 3 ended with a challenge to create a burglar alarm using two of the three main concepts. Week 4 was an opened-ended challenge using the PicoCricket kit and participants were asked to create an assistive device that would help them in school. Examples of projects include a time test countdown timer and an automatic textbook retrieval and shelving device.

Week 5 and 6 took more of an open lab approach. Participants were given a challenge to create a holiday themed project using Alice or PicoCrickets. Examples included a PicoCricket representation of the New Year's Eve ball drop countdown and an Alice Christmas tree sale commercial.

Table 1: Weekly Activities

Week 1
• Staff Introductions • Program Description • Pre-test • Interactive Computer Trivia Challenge • U. of Washington "Power to Change the World" • Computer Science Unplugged Activities • Introduction to Alice Programming
Week 2
• Alice Tea Party/ Mad Hatter Theme- Crazy Hat Day • Interactive Computer Trivia Challenge • Alice Project Assignment: Retell a Common Story • Tea Party Luncheon • Children Participate in more CS Unplugged activities • Parents watch abridged version of The Last Lecture
Week 3
• Interactive Purdue Trivia Challenge • Introduction to PicoCrickets Lab • Visualization Lab Tour
Week 4
• BOILER UP! Purdue Theme Week • Interactive Purdue Trivia Quiz • Pico Cricket Challenge- "School" Themed Assistive Device Development • University Admissions Presentation
Week 5
• Interactive Logic Puzzle Trivia Challenge • Open Challenge- choose either Alice or Crickets to design a 'Holiday' themed project.
Week 6
• Holiday Themed Week- Wear something that represents your favorite holiday • Best of the Best Interactive Trivia Challenge • Project Show and Tell • Completion Banquet
Spring Follow-Up Workshop
• Ultimate Spring Break Adventure- Hawaiian Themed • Create a representation of your Ultimate Spring Break Adventure using either Alice or Crickets

3. PARTICIPANT WORK AND ACTIVITY

The students and parents involved in the workshop seemed to be quick learners and pleasantly surprised each other with their abilities after one small session. Below is a sample of student work after exposure to specific programs. The ease of use and cognitive understanding at the 4th-6th grade level were important factors in considering the media chosen for these projects for each pair.

Figure 1: Final Alice Project in Week 6

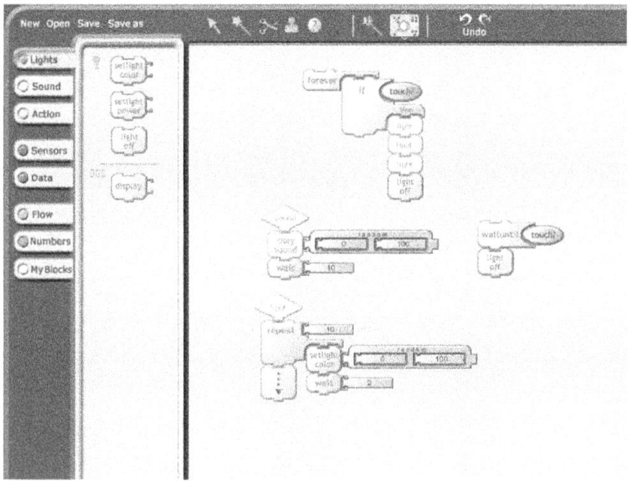

Figure 2: Student work on day 1 of PicoCricket exposure

4. WORKSHOP OUTCOMES

Parents and students were given an attitudinal survey during the first and last session of the workshop. Questions centered on general computer use, the potential for a career as a computer scientist, and perceived ability differences based on gender. For the pre-survey N=48, for the post survey N=39. The statements that showed the most change from pre- to post- survey are as follows in Table 1. The survey was based on a 5 point scale were 1= strongly agree, 2= agree, 3= neutral, 4= disagree, and 5= strongly disagree.

Table 2: Results of Sampling of Survey Questions

Statement	Pre-Test	Post-Test	Delta
I like to use computers	3.96	1.33	2.63
I use a computer everyday	3.98	1.96	2.06
Computers help me learn	3.98	1.49	2.49
Computers can help solve problems	4.08	1.38	2.70
Girls can be computer programmers	4.46	1.31	3.15
Boys like computers more than girls do	3.98	4.31	-.33
Computer programming is fun	3.65	1.72	1.93

Additionally, parents were asked to comment on what they liked best about the workshops. Here is what a few had to say:

> *"The opportunity for my daughter to learn skills she isn't getting in school. I think it broadened her idea of computer science and got her excited about this field. The challenges were open-ended enough to provide brainstorming and creativity."*

> *"Learning something new with our daughter...one-on-one. Getting to talk about, and learn how to employ real technology in real-life scenarios. The contests were always fun and challenging.. We loved bringing our daughter to Purdue - which she loves. She loved getting to be a part of a university campus & wanted to spend a little time after class sightseeing each week."*

> *"It was enthralling to have a computer activity that stimulated my child's interest beyond watching videos on the computer or playing games. I especially enjoyed participating directly with them and attending the sessions as there are few activities, in this town, designed for parents and children to participate together."*

5. LESSONS LEARNED

Some of the realizations made by the program staff are as follows:

1) Need to have more formal evaluation process to determine effectiveness of program.
2) We should have coded each participant with a number so we could trace individual change in attitudes on the survey.
3) 6-session format was nice in that it brought about continued contact with families and support for projects.
4) 6-session format was a deterrent for many families to sign up because of too long of a time commitment spread out over three months.
5) Follow-up session the following semester was a good idea and ensured continued use of tools.
6) Additional opportunities for these participants should be crafted to continue to expand the skills and interest of parents and students.
7) Entire families wanted to come to the program; we were only expecting one adult and one child per group. It made for some interesting planning and space issues.
8) Additionally, families with more than one child in this age group had trouble 'pairing' with just one child during the activities.
9) Guest speakers need to be coached on how to talk to and interest 4th-6th grade students.

6. FUTURE WORK

The program has been funded by a Motorola Innovation Generation Grant to continue development through the 2009-2010 school year. Plans are being made to repeat the workshop in January and February 2010 with minimal changes to the original format. Additionally, plans are in the works to create a teacher/student version of the workshop for fall 2010.

7. CONCLUSIONS

The intent of this paper is to share this novel program with others such as K-12 educators and university faculty, staff, or students who may be looking for additional ways to engage the K-12 environment in computer science education. All in all, this seems to be a worthwhile idea. Much of the feedback we received from parents was positive in that we were hitting an age group where it was still fun for students to do activities with their parents. Additionally, by making the parent the 'expert' on a subject, there was less hassle for a student to want to download a program such as Alice at home and continue to use it. Also, if the child got stuck on something, the parent was able to help troubleshoot more so than if it were just something the child had studied in a traditional classroom.

There was a lack of awareness of the goldmine of data we could be collecting with a program such as this. For future workshops, we are looking into actual research quality data that could be collected and used beyond anecdotal items. The reproduction of this sort of workshop series in other locations could easily be done on a smaller budget and varied timeframe. However, the contact with the families over time vs. a onetime event was desirable and lauded by the parents.

We would be delighted to work with others that may have similar interests and goals.

8. ACKNOWLEDGMENTS

We wish to thank NCWIT's Academic Alliance and Microsoft Research for the generous funding of this pilot program and Motorola Foundation for continued funding.

9. REFERENCES

[1] Alice Programming Language. Available at: www.alice.org

[2] Braught, G., Eby, L., and T. Wahls. 2008. The Effects of Pair-Programming on Individual Programming Skills. *In SIGCSE '08: Proceedings of the 39th SIGCSE Technical Symposium on Computer Science Education*, Portland, Oregon, March 2008, ACM Press, 200-204.

[3] Cavanagh, S. 2007. When It Comes to Math and Science, Mom and Dad Count. *Education Week 27*(9), 8-8.

[4] Fellows, M., Bell, T., and I. Witten. 2002. *Computer Science Unplugged.* Computer Science Unplugged, http://www.csunplugged.org

[5] Lin, J., Liu, S., and W. Tzeng. 2009. Parent-Child Collaboration in MSWLogo Programming. *Proceedings NECC '09: National Educational Computing Conference*, Washington, DC, June 2009. Available at: http://center.uoregon.edu/ISTE/uploads/NECC2009/KEY_43193604/Lin_NECC2009_UploadFile_20090414_RP.pdf

[6] Margolis, J. and Fisher, A. 2002. *Unlocking the Clubhouse: Women in Computing.* MIT Press.

[7] Messersmith, E., Garrett, J., Davis-Kean, P., Malanchuk, O., and J. Eccles. 2008. Career Development from Adolescence through Emerging Adulthood: Insights from Information Technology Occupations. *Journal of Adolescent Research, 23*(2), 206-227.

[8] McKinney, D. and L. Denton. 2006. Developing Collaborative Skills Early in the CS Curriculum in a Laboratory Environment. *In SIGCSE '06: Proceedings of the 37th Technical Symposium on Computer Science Education*, Houston, TX, March 2006, ACM Press, 138-142.

[9] PicoCricket design kit. Available at: www.picocricket.com

[10] Purdue Data Digest. https://www.science.purdue.edu/component/content/article/28-undergraduate-task-force/446-data-about-science-students-at-purdue

[11] Sonnert, G. 2009. Parents Who Influence Their Children to Become Scientists: Effects of Gender and Parental Education. *Social Studies of Science, 39*(6), 1-15.

Report on the Future of Computing Education Summit

Mark Guzdial (Moderator)
School of Interactive Computing, Georgia Tech
85 5th Street NW
Atlanta, GA 30332-0280
+1-404-894-5618
guzdial@cc.gatech.edu

Jane Prey
Senior Research Program Manager
Microsoft Research
Seattle, WA
+1- 425.703.5485
jprey@microsoft.com

Lucy Sanders
CEO NCWIT
UCB 322
University of Colorado at Boulder
Boulder, Colorado 80309
Lucinda.Sanders@Colorado.EDU

Heikki Topi
Bentley University
175 Forest Street
Waltham, MA 02452
+1-781-891-2799
htopi@bentley.edu

Joseph Urban
Texas Tech University
Department of Computer Science
Lubbock, TX 79409
+1-806-742-1193
joseph.urban@ttu.edu

Categories and Subject Descriptors
K.3.2 [**Computing Milieux**]: Computers and Education – *Computer and Information Science Education*

General Terms
Design, Experimentation

Keywords
Curriculum, Education, Professional Societies

SUMMARY

Computing education is facing fierce challenges today. Our undergraduate enrollments are below what is needed to supply the needs of the marketplace in trained computing professionals. The enrollment we have (at least in the United States, and in most of the Western world) is mostly male and lacks ethnic diversity. How do we face these challenges?

In many other domain-specific education fields, the professional organizations of those domains lead the charge to address challenges. Organizations like the National Council of Teachers of Mathematics (NCTM) and American Society for Engineering Education (ASEE) serve to gather attention on challenges in their fields. These organizations work at improving K-12 education, at improving teacher professional development, and at supporting (and sometimes reforming) post-secondary education.

SIGCSE'10, March 10–13, 2010, Milwaukee, Wisconsin, USA.
ACM 978-1-60558-885-8/10/03..

With that model in mind, the Association for Computing Machinery (ACM) Education Board was funded by the National Science Foundation program in CISE Pathways to Revitalized Undergraduate Computing Education (CPATH) to organize a summit of professional organizations in computing. The summit was held June 25-26, 2009, in Washington, DC. The goals of the summit were:

- To develop a consensus view of the challenges facing Computing Education.
- To agree on a shared set of strategies for addressing these challenges.
- To establish plans for a coordinated effort for implementing these strategies.

1. PROFESSIONAL ORGANIZATIONS
Fourteen professional computing organizations submitted position papers that described their view of the challenges, how they were addressing these challenges, and an initial set of strategies and plans for coordinated effort.

- ACM Education Board
- ACM SIGCSE
- ACM SIGITE
- American Society for Engineering Education (ASEE)
- Association for Information Systems (AIS)
- Coalition to Diversify Computing (CDC)
- CompTIA
- Computing Research Association (CRA)

- Computer Science Teachers' Association (CSTA)
- EDUCAUSE
- iCaucus
- IEEE Computing Society Educational Activities Board
- National Center for Women & Information Technology (NCWIT)
- Society for Information Management (SIM)

2. PROCESS AND OUTCOMES

The representatives from these organizations met in a series of three breakout sessions on the first day of the meeting. In the first round, we identified the *Challenges* based on the position papers. In the second round, we identified potential *Strategies* for addressing those challenges. In the third round, we identified *Actions* that the organizations alone or collectively could take to implement these strategies.

On the second day, the proposed Action Items were listed, and representative of organizations signed up as "owners" of that item (i.e., committed to making it happen) or as "participants" on that item (i.e., expressed an interest in being part of making it happen).

The final action items that gained owners included:

- To establish a new entity to speak for computing education, e.g., to work with Congress on "The Computing Education Act of 2012."
- To develop a white paper identifying the top five research questions whose answers would most advance computing education.
- To develop a better way to archive and identify findings on computing education resources and research.
- To identify audiences and messages for public relations work to improve the impact and perception of computing education.
- To develop mini-grants for teachers that will trigger local press coverage of computing education in their community.
- To develop a study by a representative group of industries of what they need and want in computing student preparation.

3. PANEL

At this panel, Mark Guzdial will be the moderator. He was the PI on the grant from the NSF funding this effort.

- While at NSF, Joseph Urban, with Harriet Taylor, approached the ACM Education Board with the idea for the summit. He will present the reason for the summit.
- Heikki Topi, a co-PI on the NSF grant, will present the planning process and how the summit was organized.
- Lucy Sanders, CEO of NCWIT and a participant at the summit, will describe her experience at the summit and the action items that her organization agreed to "own."
- Jane Prey, a co-PI on the NSF grant, will present the follow-on plans and activity.

4. ACKNOWLEDGMENTS

Our thanks to Harriet Taylor and the NSF CPATH program for funding this effort (CNS-0849355).

Surfacing Computer Science in STEM Education

Robert Schnabel
(moderator)
Indiana University
Bloomington, IN
schnabel@indiana.edu

Susan Rodger
Duke University
Durham, NC
rodger@cs.duke.edu

Mark Stehlik
Carnegie Mellon University
Pittsburgh, PA
mjs@cs.cmu.edu

Chris Stephenson
CSTA Executive Director
Eugene, OR
cstephenson@csta.acm.org

John White
ACM Chief Executive Officer
New York, NY
white@hq.acm.org

Categories and Subject Descriptors

K.3.2 [**Computer and Information Science Education**]: Computer Science Education

General Terms

Standardization, Legal Aspects

Keywords

Computer Science Education, Education Policy, K-12 curriculum

1. Summary

Discussion regarding proposals and polices to improve Science, Technology, Engineering, and Mathematics (STEM) education in K-12 now span from local school boards up to the President of the United States [1]. It is no longer a question of whether STEM education will be a focus within K-12 education; it is how the United States and other nations are going to accomplish reform. Despite this attention, the computing education community still has important questions about whether STEM really includes all disciplines and whether the push toward "core" subjects [2] will leave sufficient room for rigorous and engaging computer science courses. This special session will present new research reflecting how computer science education is treated in each of the 50 states coupled with perspectives on the national education policy landscape and strategies for reform. It will connect the broad SIGCSE community to the policy issues by giving them new data and a call to action to help surface computer science within STEM in the discussions that are now happening around the country.

SIGCSE'10, March 10–13, 2010, Milwaukee, Wisconsin, USA.
ACM 978-1-60558-885-8/10/03.

2. Overall Objectives of the Session

This special session reports on the recent activities of ACM's Education Policy Committee (EPC) [3]. The EPC's purpose is to develop policy positions and educate policy makers on behalf of the ACM, CSTA, and the broader computing community with the goal of improving the opportunities for quality education in computing and computer science. It will focus initially on steps to ensure that computer science education is identified as a critical component of K-12 education policy in the U.S. at both federal and state levels. Specifically the EPC will:

- Review issues that impact science, math, and computer science education in K-12 and higher education systems
- Determine if current policies are adequately serving the computing field and recommend improvements
- Comment on proposals before governmental bodies that impact computing issues
- Educate policymakers on the role and importance of computing education
- Provide expertise on key computing and education issues to policymakers

This session seeks to continue and extend a dialog started with the community at the 2008 SIGCSE conference [4]. Its primary goals are to educate SIGCSE attendees on the national landscape for education policy [5]; provide current information on where computer science fits; and present new, compelling research – collected on behalf of ACM's EPC – on the substantial gaps in the ways in which states treat computer science education in grades K-12. This session is also designed to engage the audience in a broader discussion of the how ACM, and the community at large, can move forward with outreach and reform strategies to address these gaps.

3. Outline of the Session

This special session will present three topics, each followed by a discussion. After each presentation, additional members of the EPC will discuss related issues facing the field as reform moves forward.

The first topic – presented by John White, ACM's Chief

Executive Officer – will cover the different components of ACM's education activities and how they fit together.

The second topic will explore education policy landscape and the Education Policy Committee's plans for reform.

The third topic will cover two new pieces of research: 1) how the ACM K-12 Computer Science Model Curriculum Standards [6] have been (or have not been) integrated into grade 9-12 math, science, and technology standards across the United States; and 2) the extent to which computer science courses are or are not mapped into state graduation requirements The session will also cover issues such as teacher certification and perspectives on how to reform education from the local level.

After the report from the committee there will be an extended dialog with the audience.

4. Expectations

This session is intended to engage the broad constituency of SIGCSE, that is, computer science educators from K-12 to higher education. As a result of the presentations and the broader discussion, the participants will have a deeper understanding of the current gaps in how computer science fits into the STEM education discussion and potential reforms that the ACM Education Policy Committee is moving forward. The discussion will also give members of the broader computer science education community an opportunity to provide critical feedback regarding these policy initiatives and to consider them in the broader context of providing consistent messages to policy makers with regard to the nature and importance of the discipline.

5. Suitability for Special Session

There is broad interest within the community about the state of computer science education in K-12 and the need to address the well-known issues [7,8]. A special session is sought because of the nature of the discussion, its reach across the community, and the need to engage the entire community in the important discussion about how public policy decisions affect computer science learning in the classroom.

6. REFERENCES

[1] President Barack Obama, April 27, 2009, Accessed 9/11/09 at http://www.whitehouse.gov/the_press_office/Remarks-by-the-President-at-the-National-Academy-of-Sciences-Annual-Meeting/

[2] National Governors Assocation and Council of Chief State Schools effort – *Common Core State Standards Initiative*. Accessed 9/11/09 at:

http://www.corestandards.org/

[3] The Education Policy Committee's resources can be accessed at: http://www.acm.org/public-policy/education-policy-committee

[4] "An Open Dialogue Concerning the State of Education Policy in Computer Science", Schnabel, R., Buell, D., Goode, J., Moore, J., and Stephenson, C., Thirty-ninth SIGCSE Technical Symposium on Computer Science Education (2008), 114-115.

[5] Wilson, C. and Harsha, P., The Long Road to Computer Science Education Reform, *Communications of the ACM. ACM* 52,9 (Sept. 2009), 33–35.

[6] ACM K-12 CS Model Curriculum, 2nd Edition http://www.csta.acm.org/Curriculum/sub/ACMK12CSModel.html

[7] Stephenson C., Gal-Ezer, J., Haberman B., and Verno A., *The New Education Imperative: Improving High School Computer Science Education*, ACM/CSTA, 24-32.

[8] Goode, J., Reprogramming college preparatory computer science. *Communications of the ACM* 51,11 (Nov. 2008), 31–33.

If ______________, You Might Be a Computational Thinker!

Daniel D. Garcia (moderator)
Colleen M. Lewis
University of California, Berkeley
{777,387} Soda Hall
Berkeley, CA 94720-1776
+1 510-642-{9595,1042}
{ddgarcia,colleenl}@cs.berkeley.edu

John P. Dougherty
Haverford College
370 Lancaster Avenue
Haverford, PA 19041
+1 610-896-4993
jd@cs.haverford.edu

Matthew C. Jadud
Allegheny College
520 N. Main St.
Meadville, PA 16335
+1 814-332-2565
matthew.c@jadud.com

SUMMARY

Computational Thinking (CT) has been articulated as a "fundamental skill for everyone, not just for computer scientists" [10]. Almost all agree with the lofty goals of the initiative, to teach humanity the ability to see the world through the sharpened eyes of a computer scientist. Others have shared their vision of what CT is, how to pave the way [7], weave it into a curriculum [1, 2, 9], and what the effects might be [8]. However, what does it *really* mean to be a computational thinker? While it is helpful to see examples that show we're already engaged in CT (e.g., using a backpack is pre-fetching and caching), it is perhaps more valuable to see everyday situations that are *transformed* when viewed through a computational thinker's trained eyes (e.g., writing dates as *YYYY-MM-DD* so they'll sort correctly). We hope to present enough examples to satisfy a growing chorus of those who need more grounding, using a unique delivery format.

Jeff Foxworthy is a popular and successful stand-up comedian, especially in rural areas of the southern United States [5]. His signature bit is to find subtle aspects of life that are common to "rednecks", a term used to describe "uneducated white farm laborers" (whose neck is red from sunburn) [3]. These observations are never meant to be mean-spirited, are told with acute comic timing, and audiences love them. Here are some of his best [4], using his template:

"If ______________________________, you might be a redneck!"

...you think the last words to the Star Spangled Banner are *'Gentlemen, start your engines'*...

...you get stopped by a state trooper, and when he asks you if you have an I.D. and you say, *'Bout what?'*...

...you carried a fishing pole into Sea World...

We will use a similar template and each of the four "stand up computational thinkers" will riff on observations of life as seen through CT eyes. We hope to provide enough examples that the (mostly CT) audience will feel compelled to join us in an "open mike" format and share their experiences. Whenever possible, we will channel Mr. Foxworthy and aim for the funny bone.

Categories and Subject Descriptors

K.3.2 [**Computer and Information Science Education**]: Computer Science Education

SIGCSE'10, March 10–13, 2010, Milwaukee, Wisconsin, USA.
ACM 978-1-60558-885-8/10/03

General Terms

Algorithms, Design, Documentation, Economics, Experimentation, Human Factors, Languages, Legal Aspects, Management, Measurement, Performance, Reliability, Security, Standardization, Theory, Verification.

Keywords

Computational Thinking, stand-up comedy, Jeff Foxworthy

1. OBJECTIVE

This special session has a singular objective: to provide contextualization through examples to support the growing CT movement. All the situations presented by the speakers as well as the audience contributions will be compiled and made publicly available through a wiki. This allows for a wealth of material to share with others (including/especially the general public) to explain the benefits of CT, perhaps even uncover a few budding computer scientists. The session will be organized as a topic-driven, open mike, stand-up comedy experience.

2. OUTLINE

In the spirit of CT, here is the outline, in pseudo-code:

(Before the conference...) Collect the union of all the CT topics for all the examples from all the presenters into a topic pool (e.g., "Boolean Logic", "Testing and Debugging", "Concurrency", etc.)

Begin the session with the moderator explaining the session and format, emphasizing the importance of audience participation throughout (5 min).

All four stand-up computational thinkers ascend the stage; open mikes are made available to the audience.

Repeat until 75 minutes are up:

- Remove an un-chosen topic from the topic pool and display it on the screen for all to see
- All presenters who have ideas for this topic take turns, share their example, with opportunities for the other three to riff on what was just said.
- Audience members are free to contribute / comment at any time

Here are three samples from each presenter with the CT topic in parentheses. Each should be placed into the modified template:

"If ________________, you might be a computational thinker!"

2.1 Daniel D. Garcia

...in order to guarantee you'll be woken up for the next day's SIGCSE keynote by your hotel alarm clock, you set it to one minute more than the current time, *test* to see if the volume is ok, and then *change one thing* – the alarm time... (testing, debugging)

...in response to a gleeful *"Trick or Treat!"* from neighborhood ghouls and goblins, you hand out some candy then hope that they meant *exclusive* or and not *inclusive* or... (Boolean logic)

...you're working with three outstanding educators to submit a proposal for a special session entitled "If _____, you might be a computational thinker" and you use a Google Docs [6] live shared document instead of sending copies of a Word file around and worrying about who has write lock... (recursion, concurrency, single source of truth)

2.2 John P. Dougherty

...you do not *stack* your clean dishes or clothes, you *queue* them; (on a related note, you understand why inspired supermarket milk fridges have open backs so they can load milk from the *back* of the fridge not the front ... and also why you should reach to the *farthest back* of a column of milks to get the freshest carton)... (stacks vs. queues)

...you applauded during *Jurassic Park* when the girl uttered the line *"It's a UNIX system! I know this!"*, then you groaned because you realized it was actually *IRIX*... (pop culture, UNIX)

...you realize that Three Dog Night had it wrong; *One* is not the loneliest number, *Zero* is... (integer representation)

2.3 Matthew C. Jadud

...you rooted for the computer in *War Games*... (pop culture, AI)

...you've ever caused everyone's dinner to get cold while you explain the glories of the *Dining Philosophers* problem using a friend's chop stick, and then discovered that most philosophers like their take-out warm, thank-you-very-much... (concurrency)

...you look at an onion and weep ... because it has no base case... (recursion)

2.4 Colleen M. Lewis

...you call someone and you get their roommate because they're not home, and instead of saying you'll call *them* back in an hour, you ask them to call *you* back... (polling vs. interrupts)

...you think that the joke *"There are 10 kinds of people in the world, those who understand binary numbers and those who don't."* is funny... (binary numbers)

...you think you have a way to beat the house in Blackjack, so you write a simulator to stress-test it... (simulation, probability)

3. EXPECTATIONS

The intended audience for the special session is the broad community of computing educators, including those who have and have not joined the CT campaign. They will hear (and hopefully, contribute) many varied situations of what computational thinkers do in real life, and should take away concrete, grounded examples of how CT could positively affect the lives, behavior and perceptions of everyday people.

4. SUITABILITY

Our format involves all four presenters on stage at once, one-upping each other with their prepared and ad libbed examples, with audience contributions through an open mike. A special session affords and encourages this unique format with the most audience involvement.

5. REFERENCES

[1] Astrachan, O., Hambrusch, S., Peckham, J., and Settle, A. 2009. The present and future of computational thinking. In *Proceedings of the 40th ACM Technical Symposium on Computer Science Education* (Chattanooga, TN, USA, March 04 - 07, 2009). SIGCSE '09. ACM, New York, NY, 549-550. DOI= http://doi.acm.org/10.1145/1508865.1509053

[2] Curzon, P., Peckham, J., Taylor, H., Settle, A., and Roberts, E. 2009. Computational thinking (CT): on weaving it in. In *Proceedings of the 14th Annual ACM SIGCSE Conference on innovation and Technology in Computer Science Education* (Paris, France, July 06 - 09, 2009). ITiCSE '09. ACM, New York, NY, 201-202. DOI= http://doi.acm.org/10.1145/1562877.1562941

[3] Dictionary.com. *Redneck Definition*. 2009-09-10. http://dictionary.reference.com/browse/redneck

[4] FortOgden. *You might be a redneck if...* 2009-09-10. http://www.fortogden.com/foredneck.html

[5] Jeff Foxworthy. *Official Website*. 2009-09-10. http://www.jefffoxworthy.com/

[6] Google. *Google Docs*. 2009-09-10. http://docs.google.com/

[7] Guzdial, M. 2008. Education. Paving the way for computational thinking. *Commun. ACM* 51, 8 (Aug. 2008), 25-27. DOI= http://doi.acm.org/10.1145/1378704.1378713

[8] Henderson, P. B., Cortina, T. J., and Wing, J. M. 2007. Computational thinking. In *Proceedings of the 38th SIGCSE Technical Symposium on Computer Science Education* (Covington, Kentucky, USA, March 07 - 11, 2007). SIGCSE '07. ACM, New York, NY, 195-196. DOI= http://doi.acm.org/10.1145/1227310.1227378

[9] Lu, J. J. and Fletcher, G. H. 2009. Thinking about computational thinking. In *Proceedings of the 40th ACM Technical Symposium on Computer Science Education* (Chattanooga, TN, USA, March 04 - 07, 2009). SIGCSE '09. ACM, New York, NY, 260-264. DOI= http://doi.acm.org/10.1145/1508865.1508959

[10] Wing, J. M. 2006. Computational thinking. *Commun. ACM* 49, 3 (Mar. 2006), 33-35. DOI= http://doi.acm.org/10.1145/1118178.1118215

Scalable Game Design and the Development of a Checklist for Getting Computational Thinking into Public Schools

Alexander Repenning
University of Colorado
Computer Science Department
Boulder 80309-430
+1 (303) 492-1349
ralex@cs.colorado.edu

David Webb
University of Colorado
School of Education
Boulder 80309
+1 (303) 492-0306
dcwebb@colorado.edu

Andri Ioannidou
AgentSheets Inc.
6560 Gunpark Drive
Boulder, CO, 80301, USA
+1 (303) 530-1773
andri@agentsheets.com

ABSTRACT

Game design appears to be a promising approach to interest K-12 students in Computer Science. Unfortunately, balancing motivational and educational concerns is truly challenging. Over a number of years, we have explored how to achieve a functional balance by creating a curriculum that combines increasingly complex game designs, computational thinking patterns and authoring tools. Scalable Game Design is a research project exploring new strategies of how to scale up from after school and summer programs into required curriculum of public schools through game design approaches. The project includes inner city schools, remote rural areas and Native American communities. A requirement checklist of computational thinking tools regarding curriculum, teacher training, standards and authoring tools has been developed and is being tested with thousands of students.

Categories and Subject Descriptors

K.3.2 Computer and Information Science Education

General Terms

Design, Human Factors, Languages

Keywords

Game design, computational thinking, computational science.

1. INTRODUCTION: THE SCALABLE GAME DESIGN INITIATIVE

Scalable Game Design is an initiative with the goal to expand opportunities to motivate, engage, and educate students about Computer Science through game design, starting at the middle school level. For over 15 years, funded mainly by the National Science Foundation (NSF), we have carried out investigations on new approaches to programming resulting in game and simulation authoring systems such as AgentSheets [1, 2] and AgentCubes [3]. While the goal has largely remained the same, the degree of ambition has steadily increased, in that we have gradually moved away from communities of self-selected users towards what is perhaps the most challenging educational context: implementing new IT curricular as part of the regular public school program.

The main goal of our latest NSF-funded ITEST project called "Reforming IT Education through Game Design: Integrating Technology-Hub, Inner City, Rural and Remote Regions" (iDREAMS[1] for short) is to bring Computer Science to middle schools with the ultimate aim of developing a larger IT workforce. Numerous problems with existing high school advanced placement courses have been discussed [4], but Computer Science education at the middle school level has received comparably little attention. As a result, programming has almost completely disappeared from the middle school curriculum. Existing IT opportunities at the middle school level often include little more than keyboarding, web browsing, and use of application training.

The rapidly increasing number of summer camps, after-schools programs, female and minority focused special programs, and computer clubs at the middle school level strongly suggests that there is a demand from students for such opportunities. Many, including numerous ITEST projects [5] and our own projects [1], have invested a great deal of time and effort in broadening participation through motivational extracurricular activities. We believe this is an important first step. However, we also believe that now is the right time to bring Computer Science into middle school curricula to develop a stronger and bigger IT workforce. One reason to do this is that motivational concerns need to be addressed at the middle school level, using early IT experiences to support future career choices. The middle school years are critical for students in reaching conclusions regarding their own skills and aptitudes [6, 7]. This is the age at which children prematurely and often falsely conclude that math and science is not for them, or that Computer Science is all about programming or is a field that is hard as well as boring. Another reason to do this is to expose all students, including minorities and women, to Computer Science at a level of participation that no combination of extracurricular programs could achieve. After all, one should not forget that participation in extracurricular programs is based on self-selection and typically involves additional fees. Students showing up at these events usually are already excited about information technology. What about the large majority of students who are skeptical towards IT or may not have the resources to participate? While many extracurricular programs have been successful, they only reach out to a small subset of children compared to the number of students enrolled in middle schools.

Skepticism towards programming in schools [8] is entirely justified. A student running towards us when we entered a school with an early prototype of the LEGOsheets [9] perhaps best summarized the programming in school situation in 1996. Excited to see the LEGO blocks, he asked us what we would be doing. We explained we would do programming. "Programming, oh no!" he replied, "I know what is going to happen. The teacher writes a program onto the blackboard, we type it into the computer and it

SIGCSE'10, March 10–13, 2010, Milwaukee, Wisconsin, USA.

[1] http://scalablegamedesign.cs.colorado.edu

never works." This points out that programming, as an educational activity, must be heavily scaffolded, but also grounded in students' interests, insights, and creativity. Ultimately, programming in schools is not just about picking the right software, but about a process reconceptualizing what the right skills to teach are and what kinds of pedagogical and motivational models need to be employed to make Computer Science a feasible and integral part of K-12 education.

Given the less than ideal track-record of programming in schools in general and specifically in middle schools [10], the question arises: why should we bring programming to middle schools in a systematic way? And by systematic, we mean initiatives involving entire school districts, as opposed to grass root efforts of individual teachers. We believe that the field of Computer Science education may approach a critical tipping point [11]. Results of the 2009 CSTA National secondary CS survey indicate that in only two years high schools offering courses featuring game design have increased from 0.6% in 2007 to 10% in 2009. Many interesting strategies, tools and curricula have been explored in isolation. It is time to investigate how to integrate some of these results in a way that would make them sustainable for public schools at a large scale. In particular, the notion of Computational Thinking [12-14] has refueled research in IT education by re-examining the core values of Computer Science education.

Our iDREAMS project is specifically exploring a number of pragmatic dimensions related to computational thinking of how to bring Computer Science education to public schools. The project started in early 2009 with the goal to provide game design and programming experiences to over 2000 students over three years. Specifically, the project engages a vertical segment of diverse inner city, remote rural and Native American communities from South Dakota to southern Colorado including some of Colorado's poorest rural school districts. A major research question for this project is whether it is possible to introduce computational thinking at the middle school level through game design to diverse communities of non self-selected teachers and students.

While, conceptually speaking, computational thinking is at the core of this project we are less interested in creating a new definition of what computational thinking is (or is not), and are mostly concerned with the pragmatics of computational thinking. How can we use tools, train teachers, scaffold game design education, support teachers in the classroom, and motivate the general student, teacher, parent, and school administrator populations? If we want to advance the notion of computational thinking beyond self-selected groups of teachers and students, what kind of conceptual computational thinking tools do we need?

This paper describes what we call the computational thinking tool checklist. This is an early and evolving version of suggested requirements that conceptual tools should satisfy to facilitate computational thinking in public schools. A discussion section briefly talks about experiences with the iDREAMS project so far.

2. COMPUTATIONAL THINKING TOOLS CHECKLIST

The version of the computational thinking tools checklist presented here is the result of building and using computational tools, e.g., AgentSheets, for many years for game design and computational science [15] applications. Our latest initiative, Scalable Game Design, enhances K-12 education by creating game design based curricula and teacher training aligned with computational literacy frameworks and standards [16, 17]. *Scalable* refers to the scope of applications starting with simple game design in middle schools and advancing along a gentle learning slope [18, 19] all the way to graduate school. At the middle school level, Scalable Game Design consists of two modules. In 6th grade a one-week module is integrated into an existing required course. In 7th grade a four-week module in elective courses allows students to move on to more complex games or computational science simulations.

We have started to use and evolve the notion of *computational thinking tools* as a combination of curriculum based on a computational thinking pattern inventory, authoring tools, and teacher training. We claim that for systemic impact, a computational thinking tool used in K-12 must fulfill *all* these conditions:

1) ***has low threshold***: a student can produce a working game quickly.
2) ***has high ceiling***: a student can make a real game that is playable and exhibits sophisticated behavior, e.g., complex AI.
3) ***scaffolds Flow***: the curriculum provides stepping stones with managed skills and challenges to accompany the tool.
4) ***enables transfer***: tool + curriculum must work for both game design *and* subsequent computational science applications as well as support transfer between them.
5) ***supports equity***: game design activities should be accessible and motivational across gender and ethnicity boundaries.
6) ***systemic and sustainable***: the combination of the tool and curriculum can be used by *all* teachers to teach *all* students (e.g. support teacher training, standards alignment etc).

The following sections describe these requirements in detail.

2.1 Low Threshold

An ideal strategy to include Computer Science in a way that will be inclusive to women and minorities may be to make it part of existing required courses (e.g., computer power or exploratory wheel courses[2]). In this context it is typically feasible to squeeze in a one-week (5x45 minutes) module. In that time it must be possible for students to make one complete game such as Frogger. If even a simple game is hard to build and game design activities lead to frustration, then little progress towards computational thinking will be achieved. With AgentSheets, many students finish a simple Frogger-like game (cursor controlled frog, moving cars, some kind of collision handling between frogs and trucks) in the first three sessions, and additional game creation activity follows.

To make this possible, one may have to differentiate between a programming tool and a computational thinking tool. As pointed out by Wing [12], computational thinking should not be considered a synonym for programming. Given the experience of many teachers (who have never made a game, never programmed, and in many cases, not even played a game), it is essential that computational thinking offers a simple mapping between problem and solution. For example, if the task is to simply program the frog in Frogger, a user-controlled object trying to cross a busy highway, then we would expect a relatively simple solution.

[2] Exploratory Wheels are courses that cover a variety of topics so that students can get a taste of different technical domains and decide if they are interested in pursuing the topic in more detail. Typically the topics covered in the exploratory wheel are offered as subsequent elective courses.

The true challenge for a low threshold is not a question of whether there is some kind of drag and drop programming, but whether the resulting program includes excessive need to *code*, rather than to *represent* the problem description. In comparing implementations of a cursor-controlled character in AgentSheets and Scratch (in Figure 1 and Figure 2 respectively), both systems feature a drag and drop programming style, but in the Scratch solution, the use of doubly nested loops and "magic" constants (e.g., where is the value of -162 coming from?) cannot be conceptually traced back to the original problem description. In other words, in one case we have a program that is closer to a computational thinking level whereas in the other case it is at a much lower code level.

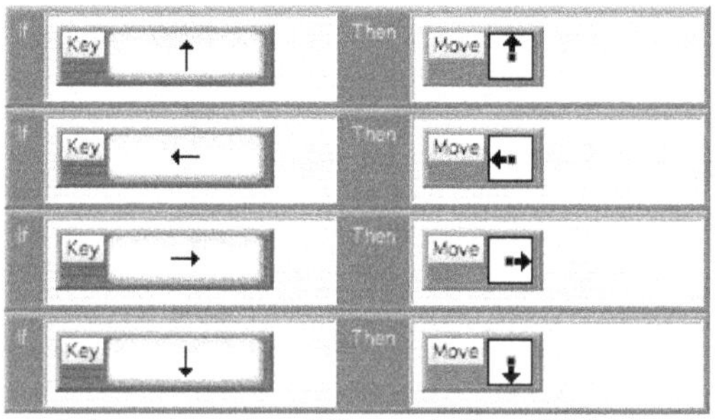

Figure 1. Programming at Computational Thinking level: Program to make a cursor-controlled frog

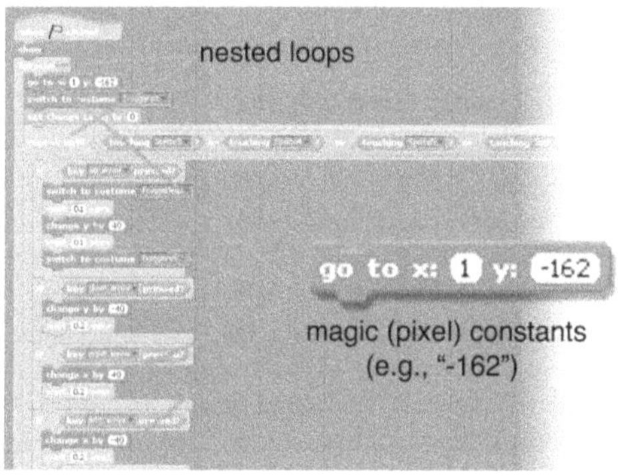

Figure 2. Programming at Code level: program contains many elements that cannot be traced back to problem.

The main point of low threshold is not to compare programming languages, but to illustrate that the notion of thresholds may mean vastly different things to different people. A computational thinking tool must include a design scaffold for teachers and students to transparently map a problem description into solution. Pragmatically speaking, the most important aspect of a low threshold tool is not if – in theory – a programming language may allow a simple solution but whether or not teachers with little or no programming background can be systematically trained to teach their students to find solutions to computational thinking challenges.

2.2 High Ceiling

If the students cannot make interesting, playable games, then their initial excitement quickly gives way to disappointment. Students need ways to create games with complex behavior using sophisticated math and Artificial Intelligence. How can my characters find the shortest path in a maze? How can I make them collaborate and compete? This type of sophistication may seem out of the reach of middle school students, but we have found ways to scaffold game design, including 3D visualizations (Figure 3), with computational thinking patterns to the point where middle school students can build games that not too long ago would have been challenging for Computer Science university students.

Collaborative Diffusion [20] is a collaborative agent programming approach based on diffusion equations initially used in graduate and undergraduate Computer Science courses on educational game design [21]. This approach can be used to make highly sophisticated games with Sims-like behaviors. The need to deal with advanced math concepts, i.e., the need to program, tweak and debug diffusion equations, did not dissuade middle school students [22]. On the contrary, students in many cases found math, for the first time, to be useful because math became a tool that allowed them to build their video game. Of course, not all students progress to this point at the middle school level. However, we believe it is essential not to trap students into toy-like programming languages that may provide a short burst of enthusiasm, but ultimately fail to help them progress from motivational game design to educational STEM applications.

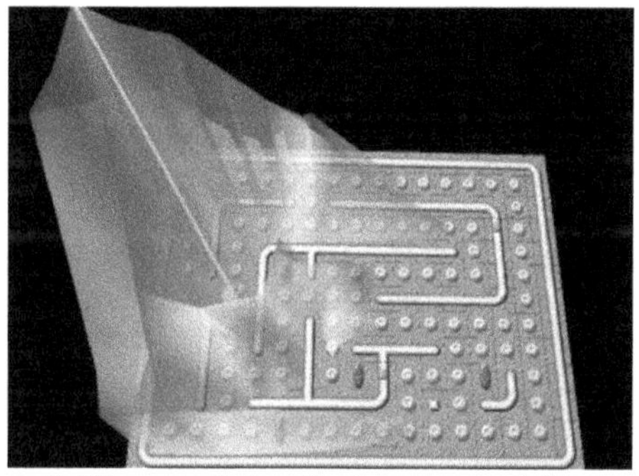

Figure 3: The use of visualization can explain complex concepts such as diffusion and how they can be used for Artificial Intelligence applications.

2.3 Scaffolds Flow

Low threshold and high ceiling are important but what is the process to effectively progress from basic to sophisticated game design? Working with teachers and students worldwide, we have analyzed the kinds of games they have built in terms of challenges and skills. Optimal flow [24] in game design requires balancing design challenges and developing skills by scaffolding the process with well-defined stepping stones based on increasingly complex computational thinking patterns, e.g.:

- **Collision**; in Frogger: frog meets truck
- **Push**; in Sokoban: person pushes boxes
- **Transport**: in Frogger: logs and turtles transport frogs
- **Generate**: in Space Invaders: defenders shoot rockets
- **Absorb**: in Frogger: tunnel absorbs cars
- **Choreography**: in Space Invaders: mothership coordinates alien ships movement and descent
- **Polling / Counting**: in Pac-Man: game ends when all the dots are eaten
- **Diffusion**: electricity, heat, rumors, toys: spread of information
- **Path Finding**: in The Sims: people finding food
- **Collaborative Diffusion**: in a soccer game: players collaborate and compete
- **Hierarchy of Needs**: Maslow's model of human motivation.

These computational thinking patterns are language as well as application independent. For instance, once a student understands how to conceptually represent a collision in one programming language, e.g. Java, then the student is more likely to be able to create a corresponding solution in a different language.

The Scalable Game Design curriculum is based on a number of increasingly demanding game designs, for instance, moving from a game like Frogger, to Pac-Man, SimCity, and all the way to The Sims. Each design, in addition to tutorials and sample solutions, offers links to computational thinking patterns[3]. The curriculum covers an extended duration of the Computer Science education pipeline ranging from middle school to graduate school, but does not prevent advanced students from moving ahead. Indeed, many of the advanced middle school students build sophisticated games compared in complexity to ones found typically at the undergraduate level.

2.4 Enables Transfer

"Now that you can make Space Invaders can you build a science simulation?" teachers ask their students. Perhaps, this question really gets to the core of computational thinking. While the jury is still out on defining what computational thinking really is, this kind of pragmatic interpretation provided by teachers essentially provides a litmus test for what computational thinking should be able to achieve. Educators believe it should be able to achieve transfer. How can game design skills transfer to model building, which is part of computational science and STEM education? Many educators are willing to explore the idea of game design for its motivational benefits. If, however, students can only make a game using a particular software tool, then ultimately game design will not be accepted at a large scale in K-12. One could argue that if there is no transfer to STEM there is no computational thinking.

Of course, we know that transfer does not just happen [25]. What does random movement in a game have to do with Brownian motion in a computational science model? These connections need to be established explicitly by teachers and integrated into a set of interconnected computational thinking courses including, for instance, game design, computational science, and robotics. We have been using AgentSheets extensively to teach students game design and computational science but have not yet systematically explored mechanisms of transfer. We have started to develop a higher-level computational thinking pattern inventory that is explicitly connects these patterns to different applications such as game design and computational science (Figure 4).

Figure 4. Computational Thinking Inventory: an inside out gradual and iterative exploration of transferable computational thinking patterns.

At a technical level computational thinking tools would also have to include certain affordances to be truly useful. According to the President's Information Technology Advisory Committee, computational science has tremendous potential for STEM education [15]. However, even the most basic computational science applications require tools for numerical analysis including the ability to define sophisticated mathematical expressions, the ability to collect and export data, and support for visualizing data.

2.5 Supports Equity

Tools have to be effective in both motivating and educating students across ethnicity and gender in a variety of educational settings, including elective classes or programs, and required courses within the curriculum. Formal studies (e.g. an independent research study by the Stanford School of Education [26]), concluded that both boys and girls express the same high levels of desire to continue with game design using AgentSheets. In our local school district (which is the first district in Colorado to bring programming to its middle schools by using an early version of our Scalable Game Design curriculum and AgentSheets in all its middle schools), teachers already report that, after students complete AgentSheets units in their Exploratory Wheel courses, both boys and girls are motivated by their experiences and so energized that they go to the counseling office to put computers as their first elective choice. They also report that participation of girls in elective courses significantly increases. As one teacher reported, "I used to only have 2 or 3 girls in my elective classes, now half of the class is girls." In iDREAMS schools, the participation of women is close to 50% because in many of these schools these courses are required.

2.6 Systemic and Sustainable

For computational thinking tools to be successfully integrated into K-12 education, they need to be systemically adopted by schools and districts. We have developed teacher training and curricula aligned with ISTE NETS standards [17] and have integrated Scalable Game Design into the middle school computer education curriculum of entire school districts. The Scalable Game Design wiki pages include specific links from each game design activity to ISTE standards covered. The game design activities with their intrinsic need to engage students in problem solving including accessing, compiling and integrating information, are also consistent with learning outcomes suggested by the K-12 Computer Science model curriculum[4] recommend by the ACM.

Integration with standards is essential, especially when trying to reach a tipping point for a Computer Science education strategy that is more systemic and sustainable. When shifting towards implementation models that move away from self-selected teachers and students, participation can reach critical levels. The iDREAMS project takes place in 16 schools. Some schools have multiple IT teachers with some schools teaching Computer Science to an estimated 600 students per semester.

3. DISCUSSION

Currently there are 19 middle school teachers participating in the iDREAMS project. Over the course of the 2009-10 school year, based on responses received from teachers, there will be approximately 75 cycles of the Frogger unit taught to over 2,000 students. Twelve community college students are also serving as classroom support liaisons in select classrooms.

Prior to the 2009-10 school year, community college students completed one week of training that included an opportunity to design five games from Frogger to The Sims, design a science

[3] http://scalablegamedesign.cs.colorado.edu/wiki/Frogger_Design

[4] http://csta.acm.org/Curriculum/sub/CurrFiles/K-12ModelCurr2ndEd.pdf

simulation of an ecosystem, and observe a summer session game design class. During the second week of the institute, the community college students were joined by participating teachers to design similar games and further explore the methods and activities proposed for middle school students to construct games.

Teachers who have already started to implement the Frogger unit in their classes have been completing daily lesson logs to document their observations of students, monitor the pacing and activities completed, and indicate how they have adapted the proposed unit to address perceived student needs. Even though we are at the early stages of implementation and data collection, four teachers have already reported that the lessons went exceptionally well, with unusually high engagement: students who are usually not engaged, are showing strong interest. Students also seemed to comprehend ideas that had previously been troublesome.

The computational thinking tool checklist presented here is an early framework of evolving recommendations for introducing computer science into the regular school program through game design. We invite interested parties to participate, challenge and refine this framework through the Scalable Game Design wiki.

4. ACKNOWLEDGEMENTS

This material is based in part upon work supported by the National Science Foundation under grant numbers 0833612 and DMI-0712571. Any opinions, findings, and conclusions or recommendations expressed in this material are those of the authors and do not necessarily reflect the views of the National Science Foundation.

5. REFERENCES

[1] A. Repenning and A. Ioannidou, "Broadening Participation through Scalable Game Design," in Proceedings of the ACM Special Interest Group on Computer Science Education Conference, (SIGCSE 2008), Portland, Oregon USA, 2008, pp. 305-309.

[2] A. Repenning and A. Ioannidou, "Agent-Based End-User Development," Communications of the ACM, 47(9), pp. 43-46, 2004.

[3] A. Repenning and A. Ioannidou, "AgentCubes: Raising the Ceiling of End-User Development in Education through Incremental 3D," in IEEE Symposium on Visual Languages and Human-Centric Computing (VL/HCC'06), Brighton, United Kingdom, 2006, pp. 27- 34.

[4] Board of Directors, Computer Science Teachers Association, "Achieving Change: The CSTA Strategic Plan," 2005.

[5] ITEST Learning Resource Center, "ITEST Project Abstracts: Cohorts 1, 2, 3, 4 & 5," 2008.

[6] E. Gootman, "The Critical Years: For Teachers, Middle School Is Test of Wills," New York Times, March 17, 2007.

[7] S. J. Sears, "Career and Educational Planning in the Middle Level School," NASSP Bulletin, April 1995, 1995.

[8] T. Oppenheimer, The Flickering Mind: The False Promise of Technology in the Classroom and How Learning Can Be Saved. Toronto, Canada: Random House, 2003.

[9] J. Gindling, A. Ioannidou, J. Loh, O. Lokkebo, and A. Repenning, "LEGOsheets: A Rule-Based Programming, Simulation and Manipulation Environment for the LEGO Programmable Brick," in Proceeding of Visual Languages, Darmstadt, Germany, 1995, pp. 172-179.

[10] R. S. Cohen, "Logo in the Primary Classroom: Should Simplified Versions Be Used?," The Computer Teacher, pp. 41-43, 1990.

[11] M. Gladwell, The Tipping Point: How Little Things Can Make a Big Difference: Back Bay Books, 2002.

[12] J. M. Wing, "Computational Thinking," Communications of the ACM, 49(3), pp. 33-35, March 2006.

[13] S. Papert, "An Exploration in the Space of Mathematics Education," International Journal of Computers for Mathematical Learning, 1(1), 1996.

[14] G. H. Fletcher, and J. J. Lu, "Education, Human computing skills: rethinking the K-12 experience," Communications of the. ACM, 52(2), pp. 23-25, 2009.

[15] President's Information Technology Advisory Committee (PITAC), "Report to the President: Computational Science: Ensuring America's Competitiveness," June 2005.

[16] Committee on Information Technology Literacy, National Research Council, Being Fluent with Information Technology. Washington, D.C.: National Academy Press, 1999.

[17] International Society for Technology in Education (ISTE), National Educational Technology Standards for Students (NETS), 2nd ed., 2007.

[18] M. Dertouzos, "Creating the People's Computer," MIT Technology Review, Cambridge, MA, 100(3), pp. 20-28, 1997.

[19] A. I. Mørch, "Three Levels of End-User Tailoring: Customization, Integration, and Extension," in Computers and Design in Context, M. Kyng and L. Mathiassen, Eds. Cambridge, MA: The MIT Press, 1997, pp. 51-76.

[20] A. Repenning, "Collaborative Diffusion: Programming Antiobjects," in OOPSLA 2006, ACM SIGPLAN International Conference on Object-Oriented Programming Systems, Languages, and Applications, Portland, Oregon, 2006, pp. 574-585.

[21] C. Lewis and A. Repenning, "Creating Educational Gamelets," in Educating Learning Technology Designers: Guiding and Inspiring Creators of Innovative Educational Tools, C. DiGiano, S. Goldman, and M. Chorost, Eds. New York: Routledge, 2008, pp. 203-229.

[22] A. Repenning, "Excuse me, I need better AI!: employing collaborative diffusion to make game AI child's play," in ACM SIGGRAPH symposium on Videogames, Boston, Massachusetts, 2006, pp. 169-178.

[23] K. Schneider and A. Repenning, "Deceived by Ease of Use: Using Paradigmatic Applications to Build Visual Design," in Proceedings of the 1995 Symposium on Designing Interactive Systems, Ann Arbor, MI, 1995, pp. 177-188.

[24] M. Csikszentmihalyi, Flow: The Psychology of Optimal Experience. New York: Harper Collins Publishers, 1990.

[25] S. M. Barnett and S. J. Ceci, "When and where do we apply what we learn? A taxonomy for far transfer," Psychological bulletin, 128(4), pp. 612-37, 2002.

[26] S. Walter, B. Barron, K. Forssell, and C. Martin, "Continuing Motivation for Game Design," in CHI 2007, San Jose, California, USA, 2007, pp. 2735-2740.

Game-Themed Programming Assignments For Faculty: A Case Study*

Cinnamon Hillyard
U. of Washington, Bothell
chillyard@uwb.edu

Robin Angotti
U. of Washington, Bothell
rrider@uwb.edu

Michael Panitz
Cascadia Comm. College
mpanitz@cascadia.edu

Kelvin Sung
U. of Washington, Bothell
ksung@uwb.edu

John Nordlinger
Microsoft Research
johnnord@microsoft.com

David Goldstein
U. of Washington, Bothell
dgoldstein@uwb.edu

ABSTRACT

Despite the proven success of using computer video games as a context for teaching introductory programming (CS1/2) courses, barriers including the lack of adoptable materials, required background expertise (in graphics/games), and institutional acceptance still prevent interested faculty members from experimenting with this approach. The *G*ame-*T*hemed programming *A*ssignment (GTA) modules are designed specifically for these faculty members such that they can selectively pick and choose a subset to experiment with and gradually adopt the materials in their own classes. The design and academic merits of the GTA modules have been verified and presented previously [24]. This paper begins by describing results from GTA workshops for CS1/2 faculty and goes on to detail the results of our year-long project in adopting the GTA modules in classes. In this case, we have demonstrated that introductory programming concepts can be examined, practiced, and learned based on GTA modules when neither the faculty nor the students involved have backgrounds in graphics or games. More importantly, our results showed that it is straightforward to *blend* the GTA modules into existing classes with minimum alterations. The GTA modules are excellent catalysts enabling faculty to begin exploring teaching with game-themed materials.

Categories and Subject Descriptors

K.3.2 [**Computers and Education**]: Computer and Information Science Education – *computer science education*

General Terms

Design, Experimentation

Keywords

CS1/2, Assessment, Games, Assignments, Adaptation

*This work is supported in part by Microsoft External Research under the Computer Gaming Curriculum in Computer Science RFP, Award Numbers 15871 and 16531.

SIGCSE'10, March 10–13, 2010, Milwaukee, Wisconsin, USA.

1. INTRODUCTION

Proper integration of interactive graphical games into introductory programming (CS1/2) courses can motivate and engage students and build excitement and enthusiasm for the Computer Science (CS) discipline as well as accomplish desired student learning outcomes (e.g., [19, 3]). Most of the existing research in this area is based on pioneering exploratory projects by faculty members with expertise in computer graphics and games [20]. With few exceptions, these projects are "*student-centric*" where the main goals of study are student engagement and various learning outcomes. Adaptability and generality of the resulting materials are not primary concerns. For general faculty members teaching CS1/2 courses, few of which have computer graphics or games backgrounds, it can be challenging to take advantage of these results.

One way to support faculty members to explore teaching CS1/2 courses in the context of interactive graphical games is by building and freely disseminating game-themed educational modules that are *limited in curriculum scope* and *self-contained*. Such modules would allow faculty members to experiment and gain experience with game-themed materials in a well-defined sub-topic area as part of their normal classes and to demonstrate results to assist the decision-making process of institutional oversight committees [24]. The CS1/2 *G*ame-*T*hemed *A*ssignment (GTA) modules are *limited in curriculum scope* because each module is a programming assignment designed around a core computer science (CS) concept (e.g., binary search tree). In addition, each GTA module is completely independent and is a *self-contained* unit with extensive supporting materials including a detailed implementation tutorial.[1] In this way, faculty members can choose to experiment with any subset of the GTA modules to combine with their own assignments in their classes.

In the first of our two-phase project we have successfully designed, developed, and verified the academic merits of the GTA modules [24, 23].[2] This paper describes the en-

[1]Other materials include: a description of the assignment, prerequisite knowledge, and expected student learning outcomes; sample pre- and post-tests; a technically equivalent traditional console-based assignment; sample solutions for both the console-based and game-themed versions; sample grading rubrics; frequently asked questions; and sample student starter projects.
[2]All GTA modules are freely available at:
http://depts.washington.edu/cmmr/Research/XNA_Games/.

couraging outcomes from our on-going GTA workshops for CS1/2 faculty and then presents the results from our year-long adoption of the GTA modules. It is important to note that there is nothing magical about teaching with games. As highlighted by Bayliss [4], faculty buy-in and experience are some of the most important factors in realizing the student engagement potentials of game-themed teaching approach. GTA modules are designed as catalysts for development of faculty expertise in the area. For this reason, in our study we do not anticipate evidence of overwhelming student engagement. Instead, the goals of our study are to verify that GTA modules can be adopted with minimal effort by a faculty member with no background in computer graphics or games, and with minimal disturbance to an existing course. We want to verify that the GTA modules ***"do no harm"*** while faculty members experiment with and develop experience in game-themed contexts.

The GTA modules are simple "real-time interactive graphics programs." Strictly speaking, these programs do not qualify as "games" because they have unknown entertainment value. However, in our current implementation, since the programs run on both PCs and the XBox 360 gaming platform, we use the term, "game-themed."

2. BACKGROUND

Existing work on presenting CS1/2 concepts in the context of computer games can be broadly categorized into three approaches [23]. First, little or no games programming (e.g, [11]) where students learn by *playing* custom games. Second, per-assignment games development (e.g., [3, 24, 17]) where individual programming assignments are computer games designed around technical topics being studied. Third, extensive games development where faculty and students work with custom games engines (e.g., [5, 16]), specialized programming language (e.g., [8]), environments (e.g., [13]), or specific curricula (e.g., [14]), etc.

As discussed by Levy and Ben-Ari [15] and Ni [18], issues that faculty consider when examining new and innovative teaching materials for adoption include: preparation time, material contents, departmental oversight committee, and compatibility of programming languages. Adopting/adapting results from an extensive games development approach requires a significant investment of time which includes faculty understanding a game engine or significantly reworking existing curriculum. This work intensive adoption/adaptation is not suitable for limited scope investigation, especially for faculty members with no backgrounds in computer graphics and games. Projects and results from the per-assignment games development approach are typically from faculty members with expertise in graphics/games and are *"student-centric"* where the main goals of study are student engagement and various learning outcomes. Most instructors of CS1/2 courses do not have the time or expertise to adapt and/or implement these projects in their courses.

The GTA modules are limited curriculum scope, self-contained CS1/2 assignments, that require no existing knowledge of games or graphics from the faculty and require minimum changes to existing classes in order to be adopted. These modules are *"student-centric"* because they allow students to practice CS concepts in context. More importantly, these modules are *"faculty-centric"* because they are the stepping stones for faculty to begin experimenting with a promising new approach to teaching CS1/2 courses.

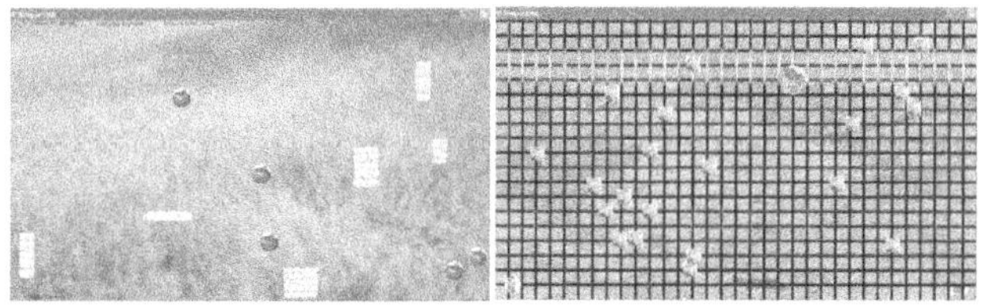

Figure 1: Games by Faculty with no prior backgrounds.

3. GTA WORKSHOPS FOR FACULTY

Outside of classrooms, GTA-related workshops had been offered for interested faculty members at regional and national (e.g., [21]) conferences, and at institutions internationally (e.g., [22]).[3] These workshops guided faculty to develop game-themed applications based on tutorials from the GTA modules. Images in Figure 1 are screen shots of a *"Worm-like"* and a *"Pizza Delivery"* games resulting from the second day of multi-day version of the workshops (e.g., [22]). Although relatively simple, these games were designed and developed in a matter of hours by CS1/2 faculty members with no prior background in graphics/games.

The workshops have received overwhelmingly positive feedback from the participants. For example, written feedback on *"the appropriateness of material difficulty,"* included: *"I found the materials challenging but able to comprehend,"* and *"good balance of complexity and new materials."* While the written feedback on *"the presented materials will help me develop game-themed applications,"* included: *"For sure!"* and *"In this environment [GTA], YES!."* The results and feedback from these workshops showed that, though they found the GTA materials to be non-trivial, faculty participants with no prior expertise in graphics/games were able to comprehend and begin developing game-like applications within a matter of hours.

4. ASSESSMENT TOOLS AND PROCEDURES

Based on the positive feedback and promising outcomes from the GTA workshops, we began in-classroom adoption of GTA modules. Because the modules are designed as catalysts for faculty development, faculty members needed to have the reassurance of consistent student learning outcomes when experimenting this potentially powerful approach to teaching. This project utilized exam scores, qualitative evaluation of projects, student attitude survey, and success rates [7, 9] to assess student learning outcomes and perceptions when the GTA modules were adopted in existing classes.

For long-term effects, new teaching materials are tracked over multiple semesters of the same course via course enrollments (e.g., [19]) or continual student successes (e.g., [3]). In the case of GTA modules, one goal was to demonstrate the feasibility of simple replacement of selective assignments in existing classes. The same classes were followed over different semesters where different GTA modules were adopted. The assessment procedure was designed around existing *console-based*[4] CS1/2 classes.[5] These were well established courses producing many successful alumni in advanced CS courses and in the industry [1].

[3]Refer to *http://faculty.washington.edu/ksung* for workshop lecture notes.

[4]*Console-based"* or *"console assignments"* refer to programming assignments based on keyboard and character driven console monitors. A *"console course"* is a course based on console assignments.

[5]The involved instructor has no background in graphics/games.

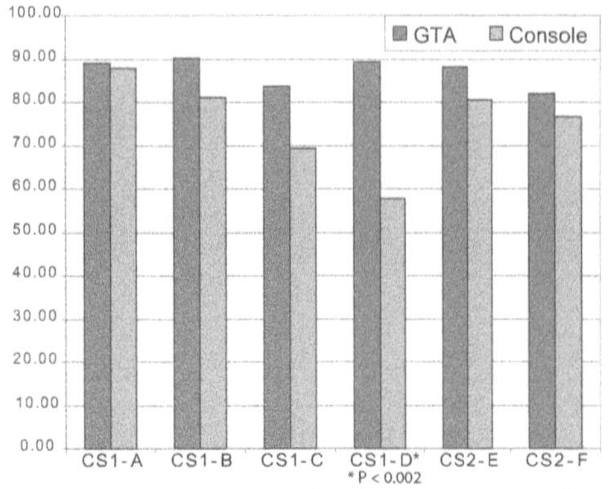

Figure 2: Average Assignment Results.

Each GTA module included a non-game console assignment and a game-themed assignment. To facilitate the assessment procedure, in phase one of the GTA project the console versions of the assignment was designed to be technically equivalent to the ones in existing CS1/2 courses[6]. In this way, the GTA replaced corresponding assignments without incurring any changes to the courses.

Of the six GTA modules developed thus far, four were targeted for CS1, and the other two were designed for CS2. The game-themed versions of these assignments were integrated into existing CS1/2 courses over three academic quarters. Two existing CS1/2 courses were offered without modification and served as control groups. In the experimental classes, two of the four existing console assignments were replaced with GTAs. Each GTA course consisted of a mixture of two existing console and two GTA modules in combinations which varied from class to class. This verified that a faculty member could select and replace some or all existing assignments with GTAs. To minimize variation between students in the classes, the modifications to the courses were not advertised, thus students did not know they were registering for a class using the GTAs.

5. RESULTS AND ANALYSIS

Throughout the experiment the instructor *avoided* any extra effort when adopting the GTA modules. For example, no lecture time was spent covering graphics or games aspects of the GTAs. In all cases, the *exact* same assessment instruments were administered under similar conditions for both GTA and console courses.

Success Rates

The success rates of these CS1/2 classes have fluctuated between 65% to 85% historically. In addition, because we do not offer CS2 in the Winter quarter, the Spring-CS2 class always has a higher enrollment than the Fall offering. With this historic perspective in mind, we began our analysis by examining the overall success rates of all the classes:

	Pass	Fail	Drop
CS1-F(G)	13 (72%)	5 (28%)	3
CS1-S(G)	13 (76%)	4 (24%)	2
CS1-W(C)	13 (65%)	7 (35%)	4
CS2-S(G)	18 (86%)	3 (14%)	2
CS2-F(C)	11 (79%)	3 (21%)	2

In the above table, the left column indicated the class (*CS1* or *2*), academic quarter (e.g., F for Fall) and types of class ("*G*" and "*C*" for GTA and console). The next columns show number and percentage that passed, failed, or dropped. The first three rows were results from the CS1 classes and the bottom two were from the CS2 classes. If examined closely, the *Pass* averages of GTA classes (72% and 76% for CS1 and 86% for CS2) were higher than the console classes (65% for CS1 and 79% for CS2). Caution should be used when examining these figures since they are well within the historic ranges. Because of the small number of female students, to ensure strictest anonymity, we did not analyze the results from the these students separately. The above analysis includes all of the students in our classes.

Assignment Scores

Figure 2 plots the average scores on assignments for all of the six assignments.[7] The left bar above each assignment displays the results from GTA while the right is from the console assignment. The scores from GTA were consistently better than the corresponding console version. From the written feedback (to be detailed later), it was clear that students spent more time *playing* with the GTA assignments and thus resulted in smaller number of errors in their final submissions. In addition, we observed an interesting *trend* in the score differences. At the very beginning of CS1 when the assignment was trivial (CS1-A, simple arithmetic), the difference between GTA and console were small. By the end of CS1, the assignments became more challenging (CS1-D, 2D array), and the difference in scores also became more prominent (89% vs. 58%). As widely recognized (e.g., [6]), interactive graphical feedback encourages experimentation and this trend in assignment score differences reflected students' further engagement with the assignment. However, this increase in score differences became less prominent by CS2 assignments (88% vs. 81% for CS2E, and 82% vs. 77% for CS2F). As observed by Guzdial [10], CS2 students are more experienced and often prefer assignments without elaborate setups. Our results verified this observation that as students became more proficient, the advantage of interactive graphical feedback diminished.

Self-Reported Time Spent on Assignments

Figure 3 shows students self-reported time spent on the assignments. When we looked at the time spent on the four CS1 assignments, it was interesting to note that students reported more than twice the amount of time spent on CS1-B, C and D console assignments. From the average scores and success rates, we know students were learning comparable materials. These large discrepancies seemed to suggest *game-themed* assignments were much more efficient learning tools. While it may be true that visual feedback is an important learning tool, we do not believe that alone it could

[6]The *technical equivalency* of the game-themed and console versions of the assignments has been verified by an independent faculty evaluator [24]. In the rest of this paper, *GTA* refers to the actual game-themed assignment, while *GTA module* refers to the entire collection of materials. Each GTA module contains a game-themed assignment (GTA) and a technically equivalent console version of the assignment.

[7]Note that each assignment has a GTA and console versions. For example, the GTA version of *CS1-A* was offered during Spring while the corresponding console version was offered in the control course, Winter.

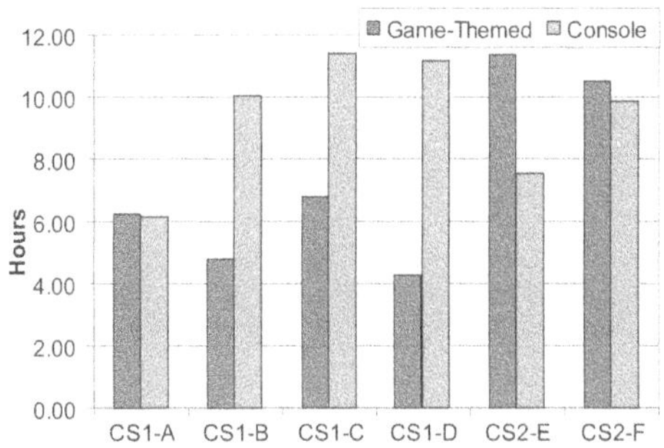

Figure 3: Self Reported Time Spent.

accomplish such impressive results. From the written feedback (e.g., "*counting only the time I actually "worked" on and not "played" with it*"), it appeared that some students discounted the time they spent *playing* with the sample solution and starter project. We believe the correct numbers for GTA should be closer to those from console assignments. In the case of CS2, the large time difference between the first GTA (CS2-E) reflected the fact that the assignment was more complicated and demanded time for familiarization. The similar amount of time spent for the second CS2 assignment (CS2-F) showed that students were able to take advantage of their initial time investment.

Per-Assignment Survey

After students handed in their assignments and before they received their grades, the exact same questions were asked to all students: *clarity* and *difficulty* of the assignment, amount they have *learned* from the assignment, if completing the assignment made them feel *satisfied*, and if the assignment was *interesting*.

Figures 4 and 5 represent the average of all results from GTA and console courses for all the CS1 and CS2 courses, respectively. Results in Figure 5 showed CS2 students found the console assignments easier to understand, slightly more challenging, and contrary to intuition, they found working on console assignments more satisfying and that the console assignments were more interesting.

Fortunately, written feedback from students helped explain the above observations. In both CS1 and CS2 GTA courses, students complained that they had to spend extra time understanding the given GTA starter project. However, in all cases, once they understood the given system, students reflected that completing the assignment was not "*as complicated as it first appears.*" In CS2 assignments, many students expressed frustration at not able to *improve* on the assignments (e.g.,"*it was interesting to have an end result you can play with, I wish I was able to improve the boring game,*" or "*I did learn a lot about BST [Binary Search Tree] doing this assignment. However the 'game' parts were useless as we don't actually get to do gaming.*").

The GTA modules were designed to be *expertise neutral* to prevent superfluous graphics user interaction programming and inappropriate gaming contents (e.g., violence) [25, 12]. We have made a conscious decision to restrict students' access to such functionality [24]. This feedback showed that we were successful, however, the feedbacks also told us that we had literally taken "the fun" out of games programming. We are currently investigating the delicate balance between allowing creativity and discouraging excessive graphics programming.

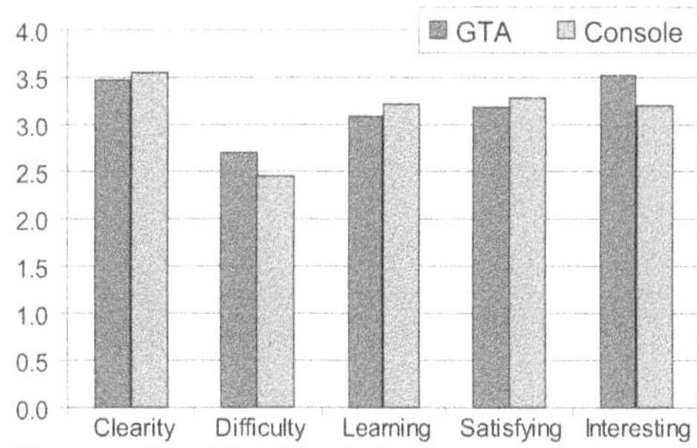

Figure 4: CS1 Post Assignment Survey.

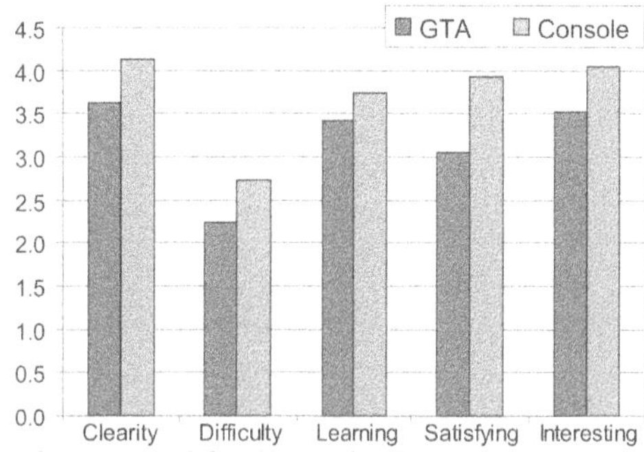

Figure 5: CS2 Post Assignment Survey.

Pre- and Post-Course Survey

We designed course survey forms to understand students' background, self-perception, interests, and general attitudes towards the CS discipline. Students completed these forms during first day of class (*pre*-course) and before the final exams (*post*-course). Tables 1 and 2 show the averages of all students from the *GTA* and *Console* classes separately.[8]

It is interesting that replacement of *some* assignments in our CS1/2 classes was almost *transparent*. The only exception was the "*Well prepared*" question for CS1 students. In this case, after the class when asked about "*in hindsight, how well do you think you are prepared for the class,*" there was an obvious spike in self-confidence for GTA students. These data, in combination with the better performance results from GTA (e.g., CS1-C and D in Figure 2) and the indifference attitude from Figure 4, implied an interesting and potentially important observation. CS1 students performed better because the interactive graphical application supported experimentation and visualization. Since the applications were not really fun or flashy they did not find the assignments especially interesting. However, after the class, they did become more confident about their abilities. Together these data suggested that targeted "*uninteresting*" interactive graphical assignments can be a good tool for teaching CS1 students.

Feedback From Faculty

After grading each assignment the instructor filled out a feedback form detailing his efforts specific to the assignments (e.g., lecture time, answer questions, grading time), and impressions on student learning. As mentioned, the instructor did not have prior background in computer graphics/games and purposely avoided specific lecture time and extra help for GTAs. As a direct result, his feedback showed no significant difference in efforts between the GTA and console assignments. However, he reported students' verbal com-

[8]Students had the option to not participate in these surveys.

		Like CS	Career	Coding	Prepared	Difficulty	Scope
GTA (N=22)	Pre	4.50	4.64	3.91	2.90	2.61	3.41
	Post	4.50	4.68	3.68	3.86	3.41	3.77
	Change	**0.00**	**0.05**	**-0.23**	**0.96***	**0.80**	**0.36**
Console (N=10)	Pre	4.17	4.73	3.65	3.04	3.09	3.41
	Post	4.40	4.70	3.20	3.10	3.80	3.50
	Change	**0.23**	**-0.03**	**-0.45**	**0.06**	**0.71**	**0.09**

*P < 0.02

Table 1: CS1 Pre- Post- Course Survey.

		Like CS	Career	Coding	Prepared	Difficulty	Scope
GTA (N=18)	Pre	4.64	4.82	3.86	4.27	2.64	3.59
	Post	4.61	4.94	3.89	4.56	3.06	4.11
	Change	**-0.03**	**0.13**	**0.03**	**0.28**	**0.42**	**0.52**
Console (N=9)	Pre	4.54	4.38	3.46	3.54	3.08	3.69
	Post	4.44	4.78	3.67	4.11	3.44	3.78
	Change	**-0.09**	**0.39**	**0.21**	**0.57**	**0.37**	**0.09**

Table 2: CS2 Pre- Post- Course Survey.

ments on GTAs to be more work and more difficult[9]. In the end, because the GTAs were "*dropped*" into the classes without any dedicated lecture time, the assignments had minimal effect on the class as a whole. It is encouraging that as the instructor became more comfortable with GTAs, he did begin experimenting with graphics/game programming and developed a simple card matching game based on the provided tutorials. Currently, the instructor is experimenting with incorporating game-themed instructional modules in his CS1 classes [2].

6. CONCLUSION

The resulting games and survey feedback from GTA workshop participants indicated that it is straightforward for faculty without graphics/games background to understand and begin working with GTA modules. Our classroom case study demonstrated that it is possible for a CS faculty member with no background in graphics/games to integrate GTA modules in an existing course without adverse effects on student learning. These results are exciting because interested faculty can confidently begin limited curriculum scope experimentation with selected GTA modules in their own courses. To further support these faculty members, we have developed limited curriculum scope, self-contained "Game-Themed Instructional" (GTI) modules for teaching individual programming concepts (e.g., linked-lists, or arrays) [2]. We envision interested faculty members experimenting with selected GTA and GTI modules in their existing classes, becoming comfortable with game-themed teaching approach, consulting the tutorials provided with GTA and GTI modules, and beginning to develop their own game-themed materials. We believe the true potential of engaging and exciting students can only be realized when the instructor becomes proficient in and feels ownership of the instructional materials [4].

Currently, we are designing a multilingual and API-independent platform to support GTA/GTI modules in multiple programming languages and APIs. In addition, we are working on sharing our results with colleagues from community colleges and high schools and continuing to offer workshops for interested faculty members.

7. REFERENCES

[1] BIT142/143: Intermediate programming and data structure, 2007. Cascadia Community College.

[2] R. Angotti, C. Hillyard, K. Marino, M. Panitz, K. Sung, and J. Nordlinger. Game-themed instructional modules: A video case study. November 2009. Work in progress.

[3] J. D. Bayliss. The effects of games in cs1-3. *Journal of Game Development*, 2(2), 2007.

[4] J. D. Bayliss. Using games in introductory courses: tips from the trenches. In *SIGCSE '09*, PP. 337–341, 2009.

[5] K. Bierre, P. Ventura, A. Phelps, and C. Egert. Motivating oop by blowing things up: an exercise in cooperation and competition in an introductory java programming course. In *SIGCSE '06*, PP. 354–358, 2006.

[6] S. Cooper, W. Dann, and R. Pausch. Teaching objects-first in introductory computer science. In *SIGCSE '03*, 2003.

[7] J. Cromack and W. Savenye. Learning about learning in STEM education, 2007. *http://research.microsoft.com/ur/us/AssessmentToolkit/*.

[8] W. Dann, S. Cooper, and R. Pausch. *Learning to Program with Alice*. Prentice Hall, Upper Saddle River, NJ, 2006.

[9] M. Eagle and T. Barnes. Experimental evaluation of an educational game for improved learning in introductory computing. In *SIGCSE '09*, PP. 321–325, 2009.

[10] M. Guzdial. Contextulized computing education. In *Invited Presentation, Microsoft Research Faculty Summit, http://home.cc.gatech.edu/guzdial/169*, July 2008.

[11] P. Haden. The incredible rainbow spitting chicken: teaching traditional programming skills through games programming. In *ACE '06*, PP. 81–89, 2006.

[12] S. Haller, B. Ladd, S. Leutenegger, J. Nordlinger, J. Paul, H. Walker, and C. Zander. Games: good/evil. In *SIGCSE '08*, PP. 219–220, 2008.

[13] M. Külling and P. Henriksen. Game programming in introductory courses with direct state manipulation. In *ITiCSE '05*, PP. 59–63, 2005.

[14] S. Leutenegger and J. Edgington. A games first approach to teaching introductory programming. In *SIGCSE '07*, PP. 115–118, 2007.

[15] R. B.-B. Levy and M. Ben-Ari. We work so hard and they don't use it: acceptance of software tools by teachers. *SIGCSE Bull.*, 39(3):246–250, 2007.

[16] M. C. Lewis and B. Massingill. Graphical game development in cs2: a flexible infrastructure for a semester long project. In *SIGCSE '06*, PP. 505–509, 2006.

[17] A. Luxton-Reilly and P. Denny. A simple framework for interactive games in cs1. In *SIGCSE '09*, PP. 216–220, 2009.

[18] L. Ni. What makes cs teachers change?: factors influencing cs teachers' adoption of curriculum innovations. In *SIGCSE '09*, PP. 544–548, 2009.

[19] I. Parberry, T. Roden, and M. B. Kazemzadeh. Experience with an industry-driven capstone course on game programming. In *SIGCSE '05*, PP. 91–95, 2005.

[20] K. Sung. Computer games and traditional computer science courses. *Communications of the ACM*, 52(12):74–78, December 2009.

[21] K. Sung. Xna game-themed applications for teaching introductory programming courses. *Invited Pre-Conference Workshop, FDG*, April 2009.

[22] K. Sung. Xna game-themed applications for teaching introductory programming courses. *Invited 3-Day Workshop, Digital Arts University, Mexico*, February 2009.

[23] K. Sung, M. Panitz, R. Reed-Rosenberg, and R. Anderson. Cs1/2 game-themed programming assignments for faculty. *Journal of Game Development*, 3:27–47, March 2008.

[24] K. Sung, M. Panitz, S. Wallace, R. Anderson, and J. Nordlinger. Game-themed programming assignments: the faculty perspective. In *SIGCSE '08*, PP. 300–304, 2008.

[25] H. M. Walker. Do computer games have a role in the computing classroom? *SIGCSE Bull.*, 35(4):18–20, 2003.

[9]The instructor did not have access to any survey information during the classes.

What Game Developers Look for in a New Graduate: Interviews and Surveys at One Game Company

Michael Hewner
Georgia Institute of Technology
School of Interactive Computing
85 5th St. NW
Atlanta, Georgia
hewner@gatech.edu

Mark Guzdial
Georgia Institute of Technology
School of Interactive Computing
85 5th St. NW
Atlanta, Georgia
guzdial@cc.gatech.edu

ABSTRACT

Video game development is an attractive career objective for many computer science students. Colleges are starting degree programs and specializations to serve this interest, but faculty may not have an informed idea of what game programming is like or how to advise students interested in the field. This paper describes the results of interviews with developers, managers, and artists at one company to determine what qualifications were most significant when evaluating college hires for jobs in game development. The qualifications we elicited formed the basis of a company-wide survey.

Categories and Subject Descriptors

K.3.2 [**Computers and Education**]: Computer and Information Science Education—*Curriculum*; K.8.0 [**Personal Computing**]: General—*Games*

General Terms

Human Factors

Keywords

Game curriculum, Game concentration

1. INTRODUCTION

If you want to know how to 'break into' video game programming, you can take your pick of popular press books on the topic. These books advise aspiring game programmers to "explore schools with strong computer science departments" and check out game programming books and web tutorials [3]. For educators in computer science departments looking to advise their students, the question is more difficult—there is very little research into what qualifications the video game industry considers important. As many schools establish video game specializations and degree programs to attract new students [9], this lack of research is becoming more of a problem. Though the fundamentals of computer science is a good starting point, we can better inform curricula for these video game programs if we know what game companies are really looking for.

This paper describes the results of a series of interviews and a survey at one game company. The game company (which asked not to be identified) employs over 100 people and produces primarily 1st-person shooter games for mainstream consoles. The goal of the research was to understand what qualifications game developers look for when evaluating college hires.

2. RELATED WORK

The most commonly referenced resource in designing video game curricula is the International Game Developers Association (IGDA) Curriculum Framework [5] (see [2] for an example of a program that used this). This document was produced by a team of educators and game developers in workshops and other venues. The framework lays out 16 broad topics in their "Game Programming" section. Included in this list are mainstream CS topics like Artificial Intelligence and Networks as well as more game specific areas like Game Engine Design and Design/Technology synthesis. While the curriculum framework is a good start, it is difficult to guess the relative importance of its items.

Monica McGill has published several papers [7][8] on game developer qualifications. Her work is based on content analysis of game developer job postings. This research provides detailed breakdowns about the use of languages and tools in game industry. She also reports that game development companies frequently list communication and interpersonal as important in their job postings.

In the broader area of IT careers, a variety of different studies have attempted to understand the needs of industry (e.g. [6], [10]). These studies employ a similar method: a set of focus groups with industry professionals to identify categories that are used to build a larger scale survey instrument. These studies have found a significant difference between the expectations of academics and industry, with a particular lack of education in project management and coordination activities. Begel and Simon [1] provide a more detailed analysis of this mismatch in their observations of newly hired engineers at Microsoft. They found new developers had the technical skills to succeed, but had difficulty using the resources of their team and integrating into the company culture.

3. METHOD

Our method consisted of two rounds of interviews followed by a larger scale survey. We interviewed a cross-section of the company: developers of varying seniority and department, developer managers and artists. Altogether nine employees participated in the interview process.

The first round of interviews began with the prompt "Say you were going to interview some new college hires and you decided to put together a document about what was important to look for in a new hire. What would be in that document?" The interview would proceed with the interviewer occasionally asking the participant to clarify something that was unclear or asking the participant to elaborate on a general category they had identified. In general participants had a lot of opinions and little prompting was necessary. Near the end of the interview, the participant was invited to look over the interviewer's notes and identify approximately five items they thought were most important in the various characteristics they had identified.

After the first round of interviews we extracted a list of qualifications identified by our participants. We combined commonly mentioned items into single items, but generally included even qualifications just mentioned in passing in our final list. Where possible we used the wording of our participants rather than our own descriptive categories. The result of this was a list of short phrases we felt corresponded to the qualifications that were mentioned in the first round.

The second round of interviews began with each participant from the first round going through our qualifications list and ranking their importance. We instructed the participants to think aloud as they did this exercise, especially with regard to items that were confusing. Oftentimes as part of this process individuals would expand on areas that others had mentioned but had been absent from our first interview. Then we showed participants our notes from their previous interview and asked them to make sure the points they raised were adequately represented in the list. We used the feedback to revise and add to the list before presenting to the next interviewee.

A similar method has been used previously to elicit qualifications for generalized IT jobs (see [6], [10]). These studies generally elicited qualifications using focus groups rather than the two interview process we used. Similar to the focus group, participants had the opportunity to reflect on the written results of others (from the 1st round interviews) and revise their qualifications. Conducting the interviews privately allowed participants to express dissenting opinions more freely: the responses of their co-workers was anonymous, and therefore there was no social pressure to defer to more experienced peers or managers. This allowed us to focus on what might have been a touchy subject in a focus group: whether there was disagreement within the company about what qualifications were most important.

Using interviews instead of focus groups also allowed us to revise the qualification list more frequently during the second round. When one participant found a particular phrasing confusing and suggested a revision, we could revise the item. Then we would check in a later participants think-alouds that they were interpreting the new phrasing as intended.

Once the interviews finished, we used the qualification list we developed to create a survey. To keep the survey to a reasonable length, we could not include every item from our interviews. Qualifications that were ranked as highly important and provoked disagreement or interesting discussion in interviews were included. We removed qualifications that most of our interviewees ranked as less important. Survey respondents were recruited by a company-wide email message. The survey was conducted online. In the survey participants ranked each of elicited qualifications on a Likert-type scale ranging from "Not important" to "Essential, would not hire without good skills in this area". The qualifications were presented in a random order.

4. RESULTS

Table 1 provides a detailed breakdown of the survey results, including the complete list of qualifications we elicited. Thirty-two participants completed the online survey. Twenty-seven identified themselves in a software development role, four said they manage software developers, and one listed himself/herself as a technical artist. Respondents ranged between 2 and 18 years experience in the game industry, with the average being 8.3 years. Sixty-three percent said that they had participated in the interviewing/hiring of a software developer in the last two years. The following section provides more details on the qualifications as they were elicited in our developer interviews.

4.1 Programming

Skill with C++ programming was frequently the first skill participants would mention in their interviews. They emphasized that knowledge of every language feature was not necessary—simple code was considered more efficient and easier to maintain. Knowledge about the STL (C++ Standard Template Library) was not generally ranked as very important. Other languages such as perl, C#, and Lua were in use at the company but not mentioned by the participants in our interviews.

Ranked even higher than C++ in the survey results was data structures. This was something that a few interviewees mentioned in passing during the interviews but did not elaborate on. Unfortunately, it's not clear exactly what aspects of data structures were considered most useful for game programming.

An ambiguous qualification that frequently came up in interviews was sometimes called "problem solving" by participants. The company's interview process involved the interviewee working through tricky algorithm-oriented questions. Several participants said that getting the right solution was not as important as how an interviewee approached the problem:

> The important part is not if you know the answer to the question. It's how you attack a question, if you get frustrated with it. If you just stammer on and go off in some complete random direction. Or if you can just make...'hey this is kind of relevant, this is relevant, and that's what I know.' That's all anybody is really looking for.

Part of the evaluation of these questions focused on how well the interviewee interacted with the interviewer and took guidance. We revised the description of this qualification several times during the second round of interviews. The final version "being able to solve algorithmically challenging problems" was ranked highly in the online survey but does

Table 1: Rankings of each qualification's importance from online survey. [n = 32]

		Not useful	Sometimes useful but not required or evaluated in interviews	Important, has an impact on the hiring decision	Very Important, has a large impact on a hiring decision	Essential, would not hire without good skills in this area
Programming	Proficiency with the C++ language including basic knowledge of features like templating	0.0%	0.0%	19.4%	**51.6%**	29.0%
	Knowledge about data structures	0.0%	3.1%	15.6%	**43.8%**	37.5%
	Being able to solve algorithmically challenging problems	0.0%	0.0%	31.3%	**53.1%**	15.6%
	Debugging and familiarity with debugging tools	0.0%	15.6%	25.0%	**43.8%**	15.6%
	Professional programming experience of any sort (e.g. an internship)	0.0%	12.5%	34.4%	**46.9%**	6.3%
Optimize	Understanding the performance implications of particular language constructs and hardware platforms; familiarity with how to optimize code	0.0%	6.3%	31.3%	**53.1%**	9.4%
	Algorithm analysis using big O (e.g. determining an algorithm is O(n log n))	3.1%	25.0%	**40.6%**	25.0%	6.3%
Design	Ability to build a good object design for a large system and understand the implications	0.0%	6.3%	37.5%	**46.9%**	9.4%
	Willingness to write a "good enough" solution, rather than spending a long time engineering an elegant solution	0.0%	12.5%	**59.4%**	25.0%	3.1%
	Writing clean code	0.0%	0.0%	15.6%	**65.6%**	18.8%
Specializations	Basic familiarity with the implementation of renderers and the graphics pipeline	0.0%	34.4%	**46.9%**	9.4%	9.4
	Linear Algebra	0.0%	12.5%	**40.6%**	25.0%	21.9%
	Understanding how a compiler works and its limitations	0.0%	**43.8%**	**43.8%**	9.4%	3.1%
	Multithreaded Programming	0.0%	**34.4%**	**34.4%**	31.3%	0.0%
	Newtonian physics and how to simulate it	9.4%	**50.0%**	40.6%	0.0%	0.0%
	Assembly language programming	15.6%	**62.5%**	18.8%	3.1%	0.0%
	Network programming	3.1%	**56.3%**	37.5%	3.1%	0.0%
	Deep knowledge in a particular specialization (e.g. AI, Audio)	0.0%	31.3%	**53.1%**	15.6%	0.0%
	Flexibility to work on any part of a game project	0.0%	21.9%	**50.0%**	28.1%	0.0%
People Skills	Ability to work with others and check your ego at the door	0.0%	0.0%	15.6%	9.4%	**75.0%**
	Ability to work with someone in a different part of the organization and understand their requirements	0.0%	6.3%	31.3%	**40.6%**	21.9%
	Being able to communicate clearly to both technical and nontechnical audiences	0.0%	15.6%	31.3%	**37.4%**	15.6%
Game Industry	Enthusiasm for building video games	0.0%	6.3%	28.1%	**37.5%**	28.1%
	Modding games as a hobbyist or other extracurricular game projects	21.9%	**53.1%**	15.6%	9.4%	0.0%
	Willingness to put in extra hours to complete a feature on time	0.0%	0.0%	37.5%	**43.8%**	18.8%
	Knowledge about the game industry	6.3%	**56.3%**	34.4%	3.1%	0.0%
	Having contacts within the gaming industry	34.4%	**56.3%**	3.1%	6.3%	0.0%
	A bachelor's degree in computer science	3.1%	25.0%	**43.8%**	18.8%	9.4%

not express the complex way these questions were evaluated by interviewers.

4.2 Optimization

"Performance doesn't just apply to making a computer program fast...You wouldn't even need to specifically teach performance if you taught people to understand the implications of what they are doing. If people really understood that putting one little include brings in a whole bunch of code..."

Optimization techniques were mentioned nearly as often in our interviews as C++, though they were ranked less highly. A frequent complaint was that students did not understand how the compiler might produce poorly optimized code. The performance optimization the participants talked about generally focused on improving the speed of frequently called functions; this often required a understanding of the hardware, operating system or the compiler. Distributing work correctly across multiple processors also was mentioned as a technique that was becoming more important. Memory optimization was also discussed: optimizations focused on reducing the size of frequently allocated objects and finding ways to limit the number of objects. Being able to optimize C++ code was considered a very important skill although participants varied in how much they expected students out of college to be able to do this.

One optimization technique that received varying response was big-O. This optimization technique did not often come up in interviews. When prompted participants frequently said that while big-O might be useful under certain circumstances they didn't think about it frequently. In the online survey, big-O was one of two qualifications that was rated as both "not useful" and "essential". This may reflect a divide in the game industry as to the usefulness of academic computer science—the other qualifications that similarly spanned all rankings was "a bachelor's degree in Computer Science".

4.3 Design

Being able to develop an object design to solve a particular problem was another commonly mentioned skill. Many interview participants emphasized that a good designer was willing to compromise and build a "good enough" solution rather than wasting time overengineering things the "right" way. A few mentioned that they were particularly wary of overengineering in applicants with advanced CS degrees.

Some interview participants stressed that they considered object oriented design questions to be more appropriate for more senior interviews. What they expected from college students was enough understanding of design to make sense of the codebase and the ability to write clean easy to understand code. The ability to write clean code was ranked more highly by our survey participants than object oriented design—85% ranked writing clean code as "very important" or "essential", compared to 56% for design.

4.4 Specializations

Computer graphics is often considered to be the computer science field closest to game programming, and interview participants did mention that some familiarity with the way the rendering pipeline works could be useful. However, participants generally also agreed that rendering in general was handled by a specialized team and not every programmer needed to be an expert. Experience with linear algebra was also frequently mentioned. Linear algebra was ranked much higher on the survey, with 47% ranking it as essential or very important, compared to 19% for rendering.

Other subfields of computer science were mentioned by interview participants. Compliers, multithreaded programming, physics, and assembly language were all brought up as skills that were useful. However, generally these skills were ranked much lower by survey respondents than programming, design, and optimization. Interview participants also did not agree on whether a deep knowledge of a particular field was useful, or if candidates who could move between all areas of game development were valuable. Participants agreed that when interviewing for a particular specialized team deep specialty knowledge was important—beyond that there seems to be disagreement.

4.5 People Skills

> "Many of us don't have the ability to walk into the room with a complete stranger and start up a conversation. We don't necessarily need that level of skillset. Just somebody who's not intimidated to really get in and figure out the problem rather than just implement what's on the sheet."

Several kinds of people skills where ranked extremely high by the participants—usually higher than C++ and other technical skills. Several participants mentioned that assessing culture fit was what they considered the primary goal of interviews, with technical qualifications being secondary. Technical skills could even be learned on the job.

Of the people skills mentioned in interviews, the skill that was consistently ranked highest was the ability to work on a team without excessive ego. This was the highest ranked skill in the online survey, with 75% of respondents ranking it as "essential" (by contrast, only 29% ranked C++ proficiency as essential). Participants individually emphasized that too much ego and unwillingness to take advice was against the company culture. Since the interviews were only at one company, it is difficult to know whether this concern with ego is shared across the game industry.

Another area frequently ranked as essential was the ability to communicate clearly with coworkers in other departments. Developers were frequently in the position of explaining game behavior or building tools for testers, artists, and game designers. These groups were often quite technically sophisticated themselves and would script or use complex in-house game development software. Participants frequently talked about how a good developer would design a solution that was technically feasible and satisfied the other stakeholders rather than simply coding from a bug report or specification document.

A question we asked most of the participants was "Do you think that most people at the company agree about the kind of game developer candidate that should be hired?" Participants who saw competing viewpoints often identified two camps—those who focused on technical skill and those who focused on culture fit. Those in the culture fit group often commented that the technical aspects of the job was learnable while social aspects of the job were not. They felt that their peers often attached excessive weight to success on algorithm-oriented questions and college degrees.

4.6 The Game Industry

Another highly ranked qualification was enthusiasm for building video games. Video game modding and other extracurricular projects were considered evidence of this enthusiasm—but not everyone agreed how important a consideration this was for an applicant. A few participants also mentioned a willingness to work extra hours when necessary and this was ranked highly in the survey. Long hours are part of the mythos of the gaming industry; at this company people worked longer days and weekend hours during crunch times. The IGDA conducted an industry-wide survey that focused on the topic of long hours [4]; their results showed that long hours during crunch times are widespread.

Two items that were not highly ranked were knowledge about the game industry and having game industry contacts. A few participants mentioned that they felt having contacts was given inappropriate weight in the hiring process, but this does not appear to be a widespread concern given the survey results. Some others commented that although contacts are not important for a college hire, because the game industry is small interviewers often call friends at other game companies to check on experienced candidates.

5. DISCUSSION

Although our goal was to discover results that were as generalizable as possible, our method has some limitations. One obvious limitation is that the interviews and survey occurred only at one game company. Although some of the results we found are similar to other, broader game developer studies [8], it is still difficult to extract what may be part of this particular company's culture from the game industry as a whole. Similar to this, our effort to get the viewpoints of those across the company may not reflect the real hiring process. Some viewpoints may carry more weight than others: this was outside the scope of this study.

Our participants seemed to favor candidates with good C++ programming skills and some experience with object oriented design. Understanding how to write efficient code was also important, which requires abstract topics like data structures, compilers, and multithreaded programming. But in general our participants stressed that students interested in the game industry were better off building strong general coding skills rather than learning deep knowledge of specialized areas like rendering.

Another area almost all our participants agreed on was that students interested in the game industry need to be able to work on a team. Interpersonal skills were ranked as highly as technical skills by almost all our participants. The idea that developers need strong team skills is echoed in McGill's [8] game developer work and other studies on developer qualifications in general [6][10][1].

Of the game-specific qualifications that came up in our interviews, a basic familiarity with rendering and linear algebra was most consistently ranked high. Our participants also looked for candidates who could show they were excited about building games. But overall one of the most interesting results of this study is how similar the qualifications we elicited from our participants were to any industry-oriented computer science curriculum. Participants did not mention things like level design knowledge, experience with particular console platforms, or advanced knowledge of rendering and computer graphics. One reason for this may be because video game companies usually have to recruit from traditional CS programs and are used to having to teach game specific skills on the job. But this is good news for schools looking to recruit students pursing game programming careers: if professors focus on coding skills, efficiency, and team interactions their graduates should be attractive to the game industry.

6. CONCLUSION

There is a lot of mythology about game programmers. Some of it seems to be borne out by our interviews—game companies are looking for C++ programmers who can write efficient code. Some of the mythology seems to discredited—you don't need to have mastered every assembly language instruction on your video card's GPU, nor can you be a egotistical recluse who only communicates in code. Some seems to be half-true–game developers do favor pragmatic programming over theory, but many still value a college degree.

Although other studies have provided broad surveys of industry qualifications (e.g. [5] [8]) interviews provide more nuanced view of what game development companies are looking for and why. The qualifications elicited here also provide a starting point for research on a larger scale. One of the key results is that even at one company building one kind of game, there is disagreement about what qualifications are most important. To understand what skills are important across different kinds of games and different companies industry-wide research is necessary. Video game curricula is already being developed [9] and students who are attracted to game development specializations and degree programs expect their professors to prepare them. With larger scale research into understanding game developer qualifications, hopefully soon we can live up to our students' expectations.

7. ACKNOWLEDGMENTS

The authors sincerely thank our interview and survey participants for taking time to share their experiences with us.

8. REFERENCES

[1] A. Begel and B. Simon. Novice software developers, all over again. In *Proceeding of the fourth international workshop on Computing education research*, pages 3–14, 2008.

[2] L. Ficocelli and D. Gregg. B. sc. computer game development...why not? In *Changing Views*, pages 16–20. DiGRA (Digital Games Research Association), 2005.

[3] A. Gershenfeld, M. Loparco, and C. Barajas. *Game Plan*. St. Martin's Griffin, 1st edition, May 2003.

[4] International Game Developers Association. Quality of life in the game industry. `http://www.igda.org/qol/whitepaper.php\#source`, 2004.

[5] International Game Developers Association. Curriculum framework v. 3.2 beta. `http://www.igda.org/academia/curriculum\_framework.php`, 2008.

[6] D. Lee, E. M. Trauth, and D. Farwell. Critical skills and knowledge requirements of IS professionals. *MIS Quarterly*, 19(3):313–340, 1995.

[7] M. McGill. Critical skills for game developers. In *Proceedings of the 2008 Conference on Future Play*, pages 89–96, 2008.

[8] M. McGill. Weighted game developer qualifications for consideration in curriculum development. In *Proceedings of SIGCSE 2009*, pages 347–351, Chattanooga, TN, USA, 2009. ACM.

[9] B. B. Morrison and J. A. Preston. Engagement: gaming throughout the curriculum. In *Proceedings of SIGCSE 2009*, pages 342-346, Chattanooga, TN, USA, 2009. ACM.

[10] E. M. Trauth, D. W. Farwell, and D. Lee. The IS expectation gap: Industry expectations versus academic preparation. *MIS Quarterly*, pages 293–307, 1993.

Parallel Computing: At the Interface of High School and Industry

Robert Chesebrough
Intel Corporation
1390 15th street SE
Rio Rancho, NM 87124
(505) 891-8158
robert.a.chesebrough@intel.com

Ivan Turner
Brooklyn Technical High School
29 Fort Green Place
Brooklyn, NY 11217
(718) 804-6400
iturner@schools.nyc.gov

ABSTRACT

This paper is an experience report describing the interaction between parallel programmers from industry and a select group of 16 high school students and six faculty from a Technical High School during a three-day "Clubhouse Parallel Universe Boot Camp" held summer 2009. Based on observations of what worked, this whitepaper offers next steps for getting parallelism topics taught at the high school level around the country.

The paper also explores elements in the area of experimentation and human factors and touches on algorithms taught and languages used at this camp. The paper evaluates role playing exercises and hands-on labs presented by industry parallelism experts. We also explore how this specific group of high school kids responded, and draw some conclusions about next steps based on the teaching experience of the co-authors.

Categories and Subject Descriptors

K.3.2 Computer and Information Science Education: Computer science education

K.3.2 Computer and Information Science Education: Curriculum

General Terms

Algorithms, Experimentation, Human Factors, Languages

Keywords

Intel Parallel Studio, OpenMP, Threading Building Blocks, concurrency, critical sections, deadlocks, domain decomposition, high school, parallelism, race conditions, reductions, role playing, synchronization, task decomposition

1. INTRODUCTION

This paper is an experience report which will focus on the material covered each day with some observations about how the boot camp was received and how it might be improved in a future incarnation. The paper is a collaborative effort between the lead Intel instructor and a teacher from Brooklyn Technical High School who attended and evaluated the training.

SIGCSE'10, March 10–13, 2010, Milwaukee, Wisconsin, USA.

2. BACKGROUND ON BROOKLYN TECHNICAL HIGH SCHOOL

BTHS is a school of 5000 students and 225 faculty with over 200 junior and senior Computer Science students. Our students were primarily CS-focused students entering their senior year or, in some cases, about to enter college, having graduated from BTHS. One boot camp student was from Hunter High School was about to enter his sophomore year. All students had some experience with programming.

BTHS CS majors typically have taken Java programming and database classes by the end of their junior year.

Since the number of slots for the boot camp was limited, BTHS staff and principal chose 16 of the brightest to attend.

For this pilot event, seven different instructors taught over the three day span. There were typically 22 individuals in the audience on a given day. This unusually favorable instructor to student ratio is a bit misleading. Due to scheduling conflicts of many of our parallelism experts, several instructors were only able to teach a portion of a day. For future boot camps the targeted number of instructors is one instructor for every eight students participating in lab activities.

3. BOOT CAMP CURRICULUM

The language choice for the boot camp was C/C++. This choice was driven by the decision to focus more on data level parallelism [4] in the form of OpenMP. The choice of C/C++ was further supported by the availability of threading diagnostic tools for C/C++ that were not yet available for languages such as C# or Java. Use of the DirectX based 3D game demo determined that much of the camp would be run on Windows platforms.

In hindsight, given the backgrounds of many of the students, developing at least one implementation module in Java may have been advantageous.

The entire curriculum has been posted under K-12 Courseware to http://software.intel.com/en-us/courseware/mod/resource/view.php?id=79

The material may be downloaded and used by members of Intel Academic Program. Participation in this program only requires an online registration at the following URL:

https://ssl.software.intel.com/en-us/register/academic/.

3.1 Day One

The synopsis of the first day would be: "How do I begin to think in parallel"? Day one was primarily conceptual in nature but students were also introduced to one implementation of parallelism through OpenMP. The agenda for day one is shown in Table 1.

Table 1. Agenda for day one

Sequence	Duration	Topic
1	1 hour	Introducing Parallel Programming
2	3 hours	Thinking Parallel
3	0.25 hour	Puzzle Du Jour
4	3 hours	OpenMP

"Introducing Parallel Programming" amounted to a demonstration of a multi-core gaming system and showcased how taking advantage of multiple cores can lead to visibly impressive performance gains for games. This module echoes Herb Sutter's explanation for why the "free lunch" is over and why we now face such a fundamental turn towards concurrency in software [8]. His case is made based on performance reasons and also on the ubiquity of parallel hardware. In class, we pointed out that eventually all programmers would have to grapple with concurrency, either as a result of their own direct coding, or more likely from the need to maintain and troubleshoot parallel codes written by others. From this standpoint, all programmers and software architects need to be trained in concurrency issues such as race conditions so that they are aware of their causes and prescribed treatments.

The "Thinking Parallel" module defined terminology and explained parallelism concepts such as processes, shared memory, tasks, threads, domain and task decomposition, race conditions, synchronization, critical sections, and deadlocks [6].

According to Hartman and Sanders[4], data parallel programming is recommended to ease the transition from serial to parallel computing. That is one reason we focused heavily, though not exclusively, on domain decomposition during this camp.

During the "Thinking Parallel" module, the students did role playing worked with hands-on props (e.g., envelopes and folded newspapers) to illustrate parallelism concepts. The impetus for using games and role playing to illustrate parallelism concepts can ultimately be traced back to a paper by Kitchen, Schaller, Tyman entitled *Game playing as a technique for teaching parallel computing concepts [5]*. The authors argue convincingly that static drawings on a blackboard do not effectively convey the more dynamic and complex inter-workings of parallel computations, whereas role playing, where students play the role of a processing core, illustrates parallelism concepts more easily and naturally.

In the camp, students were assigned into teams of four and were shown how to decompose the task of stuffing and addressing envelopes using both task and domain decomposition. The inspiration for this example came from the second chapter of Reinder's book [7]. In domain decomposition, each student "core" performed the jobs of folding, stuffing, sealing, addressing, stamping and mailing envelopes using his individual stack of letters.

To demonstrate task decomposition, each student was asked to take on one or two particular tasks, such as stuffing or folding, or stamping envelopes. As a team of "cores" all the tasks were accomplished in pipeline fashion. As one core completed a task he fed his result to the next stage of execution.

A similar exercise using index cards as manipulatives had the class add all the elements of a virtual vector to compute a vector sum written on a globally shared index card. When illustrated with few rules, race conditions abounded. Gradually, rules or policies were implemented to avoid race conditions. The first policy instituted was to declare a special pen as a "critical section". The policy mandated that no student "core" could write to the global index card without first acquiring the special "critical section" pen. Once a global result was written the student "core" could relinquish control of the critical section so other cores could have a turn.

Students observed a substantial performance impact from using a critical section.

Next, students were shown how to use reduction to compute the vector sum. In this case, a partial sum was computed by each student "core" using his own local memory (each student had his own scratch pad for calculations). Each core would then update a global index card specifically designated for that core (a partial sum variable). At the end of the exercise, a "master thread" student would collect all partial sums and update the global index sum by himself. Effectively this was a reduction calculation and students observed a significant increase in performance (over the critical section) while still ensuring no race conditions.

Five role playing activities were demonstrated by students during this Thinking in Parallel module as are described more fully by Chesebrough [2].

For the last three hours, we introduced OpenMP as a pragma-based approach to parallelism, whereby a program can be parallelized incrementally – parallel region by parallel region. The key topics and labs were: OpenMP *parallel sections*; work sharing constructs such as *omp for* and *omp task*; and a variety of clauses such as *private*, *shared*, *reduction*, and *schedule*. We also introduced the students to the topics of *critical sections*, *atomics*, *single* constructs, and *nowait* clauses [6]. Student labs included 1) a parallel version of helloworld that demonstrates that printf is not thread safe 2) an unbounded loop traversing a linked list parallelized with omp tasks, 3) a mandelbrot calculation that was easily parallelized with and omp for, 4) a matrix multiply example that was easily parallelized with omp for, and 5) an evaluation of pi using an integral of 4/(x^2+1) that was solved using omp for with appropriate reduction and private clauses.

3.2 Day Two

The second day of the boot camp explored a different way to implement parallelism and also explored diagnostic tools for parallel correctness and performance. The agenda for day two is presented in Table 2.

Table 2. Agenda for day two

Sequence	Duration	Topic
1	0.25 hour	Puzzle Du Jour
2	4 hours	Threading Building Blocks
3	1.5 hour	Threading Correctness
4	1.5 hour	Threading Performance

The Intel® Threading Building Blocks module for C++ programs was covered for the first half of the day. Students were introduced to Amdahl's and Gustafson's laws[6]; Generic Parallel Algorithms; the TBB *parallel_for*, *parallel_reduce*, *parallel_sort* parallel algorithms; and the TBB task scheduler, generic highly concurrent containers, scalable memory allocators, and low-level synchronization primitives [7].

Students performed hands-on labs using TBB templates in exercises such as matrix multiplication, numerical integration, recursive tasks, concurrent hash maps, and scalable memory allocation. These exercises were probably a little too advanced for the students, for whom Java had been their only programming language. A handful of the students, however, thrived on these challenges.

The second half of day two was an exploration of software threading tools used to detect race conditions and threading performance issues such as deadlocks and threading load imbalance. The class explored how to use Intel® Parallel Studio, a suite of threading and optimization tools. We demonstrated how to use Intel® Parallel Inspector to locate sources for race conditions in their C/C++ OpenMP code.

The class used Intel® Parallel Amplifier to identify hotspots where parallelism might be useful. Further, the class used the software to identify locks and wait conditions that impacted code performance due to over-synchronization and threading load imbalance.

3.3 Day Three

Day Three brought all the elements from the first two days together to give students the chance to thread a demo game application called "Destroy the Castle." The agenda for day three is listed in Table 3.

Table 3. Agenda for day three

Sequence	Duration	Topic
1	0.25 hour	Puzzle Du Jour
2	4 hours	Game Threading
3	1.5 hour	Lock Free Queues
4	0.5 hour	Threading Challenge and Wrap up

We presented a high level overview of a "typical" 3-D game. We then showed how the Destroy the Castle game was comprised of physics, AI, particle, and rendering components that could all be parallelized using a task decomposition approach. We next showed how to use domain decomposition to further parallelize the AI portions of code. By applying these approaches for parallelizing the application students were able to thread the Destroy the Castle game, utilize all the cores to work during the game execution, and dramatically improve the game's performance as measured by frame rate. The lab examples were heavily annotated with "//Activity X, insert code here" instructions, and the instructor demonstrated the code change in front of the class prior to sending the students back to work on the lab machines.

Following this session, we reviewed one approach to lock free queues. This was essentially an instructor demo and code walk through of code developed by a software architect from the financial services industry to implement a "Lock Free Queue" using atomic compare and swap operations.

3.4 Puzzles du Jour

We challenged the students with two Puzzles du Jour. Each challenge was offered one day and the students asked to ponder a solution over night. Students would then participate in discussion about how to solve the problem the next day.

The first Puzzle du Jour was called the "Friendly Numbers" challenge [1], and had been used in an online Intel threading challenge contest a few months prior to the boot camp.

In this challenge, the program accepts a range of integers. For each integer in the given range, the code finds all the factors of the integer, computes the sum of all the factors, and then computes the ratio of the sum to the given integer, which is also called the *abundancy [1]*. Finally, the code needs to find all pairs of integers within the range that have the same abundancy ratio. Once they understood the serial algorithm, students were asked to devise a parallel solution to the problem. The following day, the class discussed possible parallel approaches, then, examined one possible parallel solution in a lab exercise. Students found two areas of the serial code that could be executed in parallel. In the first portion, the students correctly identified the factoring step as computation that could be done concurrently using domain decomposition. The second code portion identified was the search through the list for matching pairs as another portion of the code that could be parallelized.

For the second Puzzle du Jour, students had to find a parallel solution to the quicksort algorithm [1]. A brief explanation of quicksort was given along with a role playing exercise, in which students play the part of a processor core. They walked through the serial quicksort recursive algorithm and left for the day to ponder a parallel solution.

The next day's class discussion revealed one parallel solution to the quicksort algorithm and had the students do a role playing exercise to demonstrate the approach. One student was asked to pick a pivot, and sort all index cards into piles to the left and to the right of the pivot depending on the relative size of the value on the index card. The student then handed the stack of cards on the left to a student "core" to sort the stack concurrently with yet another student "core" assigned to sort the right hand stack. This process was done recursively with more and more students getting involved.

4. OBSERVATIONS

Overall observations about the effectiveness of this pilot were made by the co-author and by written feedback from other BTHS faculty as well as from written feedback from the students. There were no formal exams given to determine proficiency. Rather, verbal quizzes, inspection of code samples, and student and teacher discussions as well as formal classroom feedback forms were used to evaluate success.

A co-author reported that this boot camp was a great experience for the teachers and students at Brooklyn Technical High School. The presenters were knowledgeable and articulate and the students actually learned about parallel programming.

One key observation about the boot camp was that parallelism concepts were readily understood by these students. This was evidenced throughout the camp by frequent verbal quizzes and also by observing that terms and concepts had been adopted into the student's vocabulary throughout the camp. They could readily identify race conditions and suggested domain or task decomposition parallelization strategies during the puzzle de jour discussions.

The concepts presented during the first day were repeated throughout the boot camp, and students were regularly quizzed verbally to test understanding. By the end of the boot camp most students had a firm grasp of race conditions, deadlocks, task and domain decomposition, tasks, and synchronization. They could explain these terms and identify instances of these terms in algorithms or in code, or both.

By the end of the boot camp, the terminology and underlying concepts were second nature to the students.

4.1 Role Playing is a Double-edged Sword

Several students wrote in their course evaluations that the best part of the camp was the use of role playing, and the conceptual analogies used to illustrate new ideas. The role playing exercise helped drive concepts home. However, a couple of the more advanced students confided to a co-author that the role playing seemed too childish.

The key takeaway from this feedback is that teachers need to gauge their audience and select activities that are appropriate. Role playing may work better with less experienced students but the exercises may "put off" more experienced programming students. Advanced and experienced students, like those chosen to participate, may often be bored by demonstrations that would be necessary in a more standard classroom environment. They really just want to get their hands dirty by programming.

A second issue that was noted regarding role playing was that not enough detailed instruction given on how to execute each role. This caused confusion. For example, during one role playing exercise (vector summation), students were each asked to play the part of an individual processor core with the goal of demonstrating what a race condition is. All cores overwrote a common "shared" index card containing the global sum.

While several groups of students did observe a race condition and actually saw how incorrect values can be accumulated in a shared variable, one group of students failed to observe a race condition. This group, by instinct, took turns adding their values to the global sum, and avoided any race condition at all. For this group, it was not as obvious why it is so easy to fall into situations where race conditions exist. For them, it just seemed that the cores should just "know" how to avoid them. It was suggested that if role playing is used in the future, a short script needs to be written for each actor to explicitly follow.

4.2 Ease of Use: OpenMP

The students gave the OpenMP module high marks for simplicity of implementation. This seemed to be one of the favorite modules from the first two days as judged from the feedback sheets. Students and faculty commented on how easy it was for students to make the transition from Java to using C/C++ and OpenMP. BTHS faculty experience has shown that transitioning from C++ to Java is easier than transitioning from Java to C++. Fortunately, OpenMP blended into the language without making use of too many of C++'s unique features and the students were able to see it and make it work very easily.

4.3 Challenge of Teaching Intel® Threading Building Blocks

The Intel® Threading Building Blocks turned out to be one of the more challenging sets of labs during the three-day camp. The more advanced students seemed to relish the challenge of learning how to implement parallelism using Threading Building Blocks and learned how to use it quickly. However, for many in the class, having never taken a C++ class, Threading Building Blocks proved to be quite a challenge.

It was observed that the concepts associated with C++ class templates were a little foreign, and without a firm grasp on C++ classes, the students got lost more frequently in these labs than they did in OpenMP. One other high school teacher in attendance suggested that these labs would be much more palatable with a prior, week-long C++ primer.

4.4 Value of Teaching Thread Correctness and Thread Performance Tools

Software tools training was provided so that students could use tools to help them find race conditions, deadlocks, and performance limiting synchronizations. Each tool was covered for about an hour with hands-on labs given for an additional half an hour.

Instructors and BTHS faculty noted that the tools coverage was overwhelming. Students saw the value in having a software tool that identifies race condition for them – but most had never been in a situation where they had to analyze someone else's code, let alone seeing new code for the first time ever and being asked to find the specific race conditions in the code. Most students were able to complete the lab exercises but without continued use of the software tools the risk is that they will forget how to use it before long.

While debugging is an essential part of learning to program, the use of Intel® Parallel Inspector was very difficult to grasp because the students didn't have enough experience with parallel programming itself. Students could see that there were a number of uses for the software and they could understand the results. However, it would take more experience with the errors before students could really start using a tool to fish them out.

4.5 Capturing Student Attention with Game Threading Examples

The game threading portion of class was well received by the students and one of the key motivational reason for students to take the class. Some students were disappointed that the class wasn't more about how to create a game from scratch.

The threading concepts used were developed over the previous two days of training and most of the students were able to follow to concepts being used. They used task decomposition to do physics, AI, particle calculation concurrently. They also used domain decomposition to get more parallelism from the AI computations. The heavy use of C++ was certainly a challenge for most of the students. All threading exercises used code that had been marked with comment lines indicating where to make code changes, which eased some of the stress of needing to understand C++ code.

Typically there would be 20-30 minutes of lecture then hands on labs to make these code changes. Student feedback indicated that this segment could have been lengthened from 4 hours to all day to give more time for understanding and applying the concepts and to make the coding changes.

4.6 Stretching Students' Abilities with Lock Free Queues

The lock free queue was the most challenging portion of the three-day class. Some students seemed to be able to follow the instructor's code review, but without continued exposure to the code, the details of the lesson were lost. The bigger takeaway was the instructor's challenge that there may be new ways to parallelize an algorithm that are much more efficient than current approaches, if students are willing to "do the experiments."

General feedback was to remove this module in future revisions or revise it to be more conceptually focused. A line by line code review made it difficult for students to stay engaged particularly because it did not provide any hands on lab time.

5. RECOMMENDATIONS

The recommendations below are based on the co-author's experience and observation of student responsiveness during the boot camp.

5.1 Teach Parallelism Concepts

In all cases, we recommend that conceptual parallelism be added to programming curricula. We found that bright high school students picked up the concepts of parallel tasks, domain and task decomposition, race conditions, critical sections, reductions, and many other concepts from a purely conceptual standpoint, apart from code.

5.2 Teach at Least One Implementation method

In order to provide necessary lab time, we note that at least one parallel implementation needs to be taught. In out case, OpenMP was the most desirable implementation, but in other circumstances it could be the java.util.concurrent package, or Threading Building Blocks. Students need to be armed at least one way to express parallelism in code.

In high schools still teaching C/C++, the OpenMP implementation can be easily adopted by students. For such schools we would recommend at least adding OpenMP to their C/C++ materials covering loops.

5.3 Add Parallelism to College Board AP Tests

The College Board is the company that distributes the Advanced Placement exams. They are a major influencer in what is taught in high school curriculums. To date, parallelism topics such as threads or synchronization are not taught in the AP curriculum. According to the AP course description threads are explicitly excluded from AP Computer Science Java Subset [3].

With such a large influence on high schools and universities, the College Board's Advanced Placement exam needs to be revamped to include parallelism concepts and some implementation on parallelism. The authors urge College Board to consider adding parallelism as a key part of the Advanced Placement Exam.

5.4 Role Playing should be used judiciously

As noted earlier, some high school students, particularly more advanced students, may view the role playing as childish. Some younger and less experienced students enjoyed the role playing demonstrations and found them to be instructive.

6. ACKNOWLEDGMENTS

Our thanks to Randy Asher, principal at Brooklyn Technical High School for working with Intel to make this pilot boot camp take place. Also, our thanks to the other faculty and students at BTHS who attended the boot camp and who provided feedback on how to make future camp a bigger success.

7. REFERENCES

[1] Breshears, C. *The Art of Concurrency* O'Reilly Press, 2009 138-142, 169-182,

[2] Chesebrough, R. *Five role playing exercises to introduce parallelism concepts,* Retrieved Nov 5, 2009 from Intel Software Network Software Blogs http://software.intel.com/en-us/blogs/2009/11/05/five-role-playing-exercises-to-introduce-parallelism-concepts/

[3] College Board AP Computer Science A Course Description, May 2010, May 2011 Retrieved Nov 5, 2009 from apcentral.collegeboard.com http://apcentral.collegeboard.com/apc/public/repository/ap-computer-science-course-description.pdf

[4] Hartman, J. and Sanders D. *Data parallel programming: a transition from serial to parallel computing,* Technical Symposium on Computer Science Education archive, Proceedings of the twenty-fourth SIGCSE technical symposium on Computer science education (1993)

[5] Kitchen, A., Schaller, N., Tymann, P. *Game playing as a technique for teaching parallel computing concepts,* ACM SIGCSE Bulletin Volume 24, Issue 3 (1992)

[6] Quinn, Michael J.,*Parallel Programming in C with MPI and OpenMP* McGraw Hill Higher Education press, 2003 ISBN- 978-0071232654

[7] Reinders, J. *Intel Threading Building Blocks* O'Reilly Press, 2007 ISBN-978-0-596-51480-8

[8] Sutter, H. *The Free Lunch Is Over: A Fundamental Turn Toward Concurrency in Software* Dr. Dobb's Journal, 30(3), March 2005

Using Microlabs to Teach Modern Distributed Computing

Barry L. Kurtz, Rahman Tashakkori, John Helfert, Michael Sage
Appalachian State University
Boone, NC 28608
828-262-2370
{BLK,RT}@cs.appstate.edu

ABSTRACT
Closed labs have become a common feature in computer science education because they provide hands-on experience in a supervised setting. Microlabs extend this approach into the lecture format with very short hands-on activities in the "middle of" the lecture. This approach was developed for a modern distributed computing course that integrated all levels of parallelism (multicore, cluster, and grid) into a single course and required a substantial course project that used all these levels. After presenting the current status of our activities, we will discuss future directions that include stand-alone distributed computing modules and a distributed computing repository. This work is supported, in part, by a National Science Foundation grant.

Categories and Subject Descriptors
K.3.2 [Computer and Information Science Education] Computer Science Education, Curriculum

General Terms
Algorithms, Performance, Human Factors

Keywords
Distributed Computing, Computer Science Labs, Multicore Computing, Cluster Computing, Grid Computing

1. INTRODUCTION
We first review some historical trends in teaching distributed computing followed by a discussion on the use of labs in computer science education.

1.1 Historical Trends in Teaching Distributed Computing
In the 1980s and the early 1990s instruction in high performance computing emphasized computer architectures for parallelism. Topics included Flynn's taxonomy (SIMD, MIMD, etc.) and very expensive, special purpose computers that supported high performance computing.

By the mid-1990s it became evident that special purpose machines could not be justified on a cost basis and a workstation "farm" was a much more cost effective approach to distributed computing within the reach of ordinary universities. Courses in cluster computing, at first using PVM [11] and then MPI [8], emphasized a message passing paradigm in a distributed memory system.

Threads are lightweight processes that can distribute work over multiple processors or cores. Modern object-oriented languages, such as Java and C#, support threads directly. In other environments, libraries, such as PThreads [10] and OpenMP [9], supported shared memory, threaded programming. As multicore chips become the norm rather than the exception, there is renewed interest in shared memory approaches to distributed computing.

Grid computing emerged in the early 21st century largely in response to the needs of businesses to tie together their diverse computing resources. Globus [6] became a de facto standard in the academic community because it was a freeware application; however, due to its steep learning curve and lack of support, it has not been a commercial success. Courses on grid computing have emerged in the undergraduate curriculum [14]. The Common Object Request Broker Architecture (CORBA) was an early attempt at using heterogeneous computers hooked to a network transparently, but it has been replaced by the widespread acceptance of web services based on the Simple Object Access Protocol (SOAP) model. The Internet is too slow to support high performance computing directly, so grid computing applications often stress data parallelism. For some "embarrassingly parallel" applications that don't require constant message passing, a worldwide network of computers "at home" has proved to be very effective; perhaps the two best known examples are seti@home [12] and folding@home [5]. Software frameworks, such as BOINC [2], have been developed that allow this approach to be extended into computer science education.

In this paper we use the term "distributed computing" in an umbrella sense to include all forms of parallelism ranging from shared memory approaches (threads, OpenMP) and distributed memory approaches (clusters, web services). Many of the example labs are classical; our use of the word "modern" refers to the integration of all these levels in a single course and a single course project.

1.2 Use of Labs to Teach Computer Science
The traditional approach to computer science education is to have students complete programming assignments outside of class. Open lab environments, perhaps with a lab monitor to provide general assistance, are provided so students can access computing resources. The closed lab environment is modeled after Chemistry or Physics

labs where students meet once or twice a week at a scheduled time to complete programming activities under supervised conditions. These closed labs are common in the introductory CS1 and CS2 courses. Students are often required to complete a lengthy sequence of activities with a lot of hand holding to guarantee early success in computer science. These labs are usually supplemented with traditional programming assignments to be completed outside of scheduled class time.

A variation of the closed lab is a testing environment where students have to complete small program components under strictly monitored and possibly timed conditions. Ken Bowles [3] at the University of California San Diego (UCSD) introduced the use of drills and programming quizzes to support instruction in UCSD Pascal in the CS1 course. Kurtz has used this approach at three universities: the University of California Irvine, New Mexico State University [1,7], and Appalachian State University [4].

An increasingly popular approach to computer science instruction is to hold the entire class, both lecture and lab, in a classroom/laboratory environment. In this environment there is usually a projection system to support lecture, the seats are arranged in a forward-facing position to make viewing the lecture convenient, and every student has immediate access to a computer. Typical classroom environments may be limited to 20-30 students and does not support large lecture formats. The instructor's computer is often running software that allows monitoring, displaying and/or taking control of student screens. The microlabs described in this paper were used in this environment.

2. THE STRUCTURE OF MICROLABS

2.1 Characteristics of a Microlab

Our microlab approach is a form of active learning and in this sense is nothing new. However the consistent application of this approach throughout a course integrating distributed and parallel computing is unique. Microlabs are designed to be completed in the middle of a normal lecture, thus they are short duration and require a limited amount of coding. A 5 minute microlab may require only a few lines of new code to be put into a skeleton program while a 15 minute microlab might involve writing one or more methods. Students are given the opportunity to work in pairs but our experience indicates that most students prefer to work individually. Not everyone will finish a microlab during the allotted time period, but these students are allowed to work on the microlabs after class and check them off the next class period. Initially students were hesitant to give up trying and go back to lecture mode, but once they realized the ground rules after the first few microlabs, they were willing to switch back to lecture mode even when their microlab wasn't completed.

Development of microlabs does require extensive work by the instructor and lab assistants (if available). An entire framework must be provided to incorporate the student modifications into a complete program and testing environment. The student must correct all compile errors on his/her own. This is relatively easy for a programming environment a student is familiar with, but when using a new language (e.g., C) and a new set of library routines (e.g., MPI), this can be a challenge. Developing carefully chosen test cases assists students in finding any logical errors once the program compiles and executes. In our development environment the instructor and lab assistant were available to help with problems in a small class, but this approach may not scale well to a lecture hall environment with a large number of students. We will discuss these issues in more detail in section 2.3.

2.2 How Microlabs Differ from Closed Labs

Microlabs differ from typical closed labs in several ways. First, they occur during a lecture and are intended to give students some immediate hands-on experience with the lecture topic. They are much shorter and more focused than a closed lab activity. After the brief interlude, the class must continue on in lecture mode. As explained above, students who have not finished the activity must be willing to suspend their efforts until after the class period. The microlabs also require a more substantial support environment than normal closed lab activities in order to be completed in a short period of time.

2.3 The Feasibility of Using Microlabs in a Large Lecture Environment

The mixture of lecture and lab activities is most easily carried out in a lab environment that is also set up as a classroom (projector, forward-facing seats, etc.). What about a pure lecture environment with no installed equipment and a large class of students? Won't the microlabs just be demonstrations by the instructor or work by a single student asked to come work in front of the class? Five years ago these might have been the only choices, but that is not true today. A majority of students, particularly computer science majors, own laptop computers that can connect wirelessly to a local area network. Students can be asked to work with a classmate if they don't have a laptop with them. This approach can establish a virtual network of machines even in a large lecture hall.

The next problem to be solved is to insure the students use their computers in the manner intended by the instructor. Fortunately commercial companies have developed software, such as DyKnow Monitor or SmartSync, to solve these management problems. Not only can instructors observe what students are doing, they can also block access to undesired activities.

A final problem is to provide feedback to students who are working on a microlab. As discussed in section 1.2, there is a long history of automated testing environment to administer, grade, and provide feedback to students working on programming quizzes. We are adapting this approach to provide similar support for microlabs in a distributed computing environment. This is discussed in section 5.2.

3.0 THE DISTRIBUTED COMPUTING COURSE

3.1 Multicore Computing

The first topic covered in Multicore Computing was the use of threads in Java. There were ten lecture presentations where topics ranged from mutual exclusion and semaphores to message passing using array blocking queues.

There were ten microlabs for threads in Java, as listed in Table 1. As a detailed example, in ML05 students had to complete a class called Semaphore that used the lock and condition variables available in Java 1.5 to simulate the behavior of a counting semaphore. The constructor and the methods for P and V in the class are initially empty. The skeleton program contains a simple application that runs two threads each incrementing a shared global variable fifty times. With a non-functioning semaphore class the results varied from 50 to 100. Once the students get the Semaphore simulation running correctly, the result is always 100. The steps students had to complete were:

- complete the constructor that stores the number of allowed permits, creates a re-entrant lock and a local condition variable called nonzero
- complete the P method that obtains the lock, waits until the semaphore count is greater than zero, decrements the semaphore count, and releases the lock
- complete the V method that obtains the lock, signals the condition variable nonzero if the semaphore count is zero, increments the semaphore count, and releases the lock

Most students completed this microlab in 20 minutes.

Table 1: Microlabs for Java Threads

Lab	Task
ML01	Taking Turns
ML02	Dekker's Algorithm
ML03	Dinning Philosopher
ML04	Sleeping Barbers
ML05	Semaphore Simulation with a Monitor
ML06	Bounded Buffer
ML07	Prime Number Sieve Using Message Passing
ML08	Bounded Buffer Using Message Passing
ML09	Laplace Grid Using Message Passing
ML10	Laplace Grid Using Shared Memory

There were five programming assignments for this portion of the course. These assignments ranged from P01 (The Bakery Algorithm) through P05 (The Game of Life).

The next approach for shared memory threads was using OpenMP [9] in C. Our students are Java literate and, at this stage, only have limited experience in C. This section of the course provided a good introduction to C before more intensive experiences with MPI using C. There were six lecture topics: an introduction to OpenMP, clauses, directives, synchronization, handling global data, and runtime commands.

There were five microlabs for OpenMP, as listed in Table 2. In ML15 students were given a skeleton program that contained the following code fragment:

```
#pragma omp for reduction(+:sum)
for (i=0; i < N; i++)
{
    sum = sum + (a[i]*b[i]);
}
```

The directions to the student state "if you run the program multiple times you will find that the sum printed out may differ between each execution. You need to introduce one more pragma to control the updating of sum so that the correct result is returned each time." (Note: students were not told which pragma to use.) The easiest solution was to put `#pragma omp atomic` before the assignment to sum; an alternative was to use the pragma named critical. This is an example of a very short microlab that most students completed in 5 minutes. There were three programming assignments using OpenMP: Matrix Multiplication, Calculating PI using Monte Carlo Techniques and Gray Scale Conversion.

Table 2: Microlabs for OpenMP

Lab	Task
ML11	Hello World
ML12	A Row Vector times a Matrix
ML13	Using FirstPrivate and LastPrivate
ML14	Fixing an Orphan Process
ML15	Protecting a Critical Region

Cluster Computing

The MPI lectures covered Basic Operations, Global Operations, an MPI Application, Derived Datatypes and Communicators. There were seven microlabs in MPI, as listed in Table 3.

Table 3: Microlabs for MPI

Lab	Task
ML16	Hello World
ML17	Taylor Series using Scatter and Gather
ML18	Factorial using Reduction
ML19	Implementing a Prime Number Count
ML20	Dot Product
ML21	Using Groups
ML22	Using MPI_Split

In ML17 students were told: "You are to calculate sine for the values 0.1, 0.3, 0.5, 0.7, 0.9, 1.1, 1.3, 1.5. Put these values in a vector and scatter them to eight processes. Have each process calculate the sine using the Taylor expansion." An algorithm in high level psuedocode was provided. "Gather the results back into the main program and print out the values:
sin(0.1) = 0.0998334
sin(0.3) = 0.29552
: : : : "

Students had 15-20 minutes to complete this microlab; they were given a skeleton program that contained:

```
MPI_Init(&argc, &argv);
MPI_Comm_size(MPI_COMM_WORLD, &size);
MPI_Comm_rank(MPI_COMM_WORLD, &id);
   //your code goes here
if(id == 0)
// the for loop to print results was given
```

Most students were able to complete this lab in the allotted time.

There were four programming assignments in MPI: Total Count of Images (later integrated into the course project), Numerical Integration using the Trapazoid Method, Sparse Matrices, and Fox's Algorithm for Matrix Multiplication.

Grid Computing and Web Services

These lectures covered Condor, Directed Acyclic Graph Manager, an Overview of Globus [6], and Web Services. There were only two microlabs, as listed in Table 4, that involve Condor, a workload scheduler that can be used under Globus.

Table 4: Microlabs for Grid Computing

Lab	Task
ML23	Grid - Using Condor
ML24	Grid - Directed Acyclic Graph Manager

At this time, students had been introduced to the course project involving image processing; programming assignments now became project assignments. There were two intermediate checkpoints on the course project: "Searching for a SubImage Using MPI" and "Searching for a SubImage at Multiple Websites Using Web Services."

The Course Project

The project used several of the tools developed during the course. Students had to access two URLs that each contained a distinct collection of grayscale mammograms. Each website had four quadcore computers connected by a 1 Ghz LAN. These images were approximately 3000 x 4000 pixels. Students were given a variety of target images, ranging from 9 x 9 pixels to 17 x 17 pixels, and they had to search for the best match in the mammograms. Each web service was implemented in Java; it had to call a C program that used MPI over the local area network. The images had to be striped horizontally with overlapping rows (the number of overlapping rows was (t-1)/2 where t was the target image size). Recent versions of MPI detect whether MPI is running on a multicore machine and automatically distribute tasks over these cores. In the latest version of this project we have introduce some OpenMP pragmas to increase parallelism at the single machine level. Java threads were used by the client program that called the web services; there was a separate thread for each web service call. An initial web service call started the search process. A repeated web service call checked for results. If null was returned, it tried again after a short delay (useful processing at the client could have been done at this time, but for simplicity students put in sleep statements). Results for the best match for each image were passed back from the C program to the Java program, which in turn returned this non-null result from the web service (if the results were not known yet, null was returned). The printing process had to be put into a separate thread using a lock to insure that printing results was atomic and not intermixed.

3.5 Other Activities

There was one week remaining in class by the time all topics necessary to complete the project were finished. Students expressed interest in learning about tools available in the .NET development environment. There were two lectures: use of the Semaphore Class in C# and use of the Task Parallel Library [13] (similar to OpenMP in C). Two microlabs allowed students to experience hands-on activities, as shown in Table 5.

Table 5: Microlabs for the .NET Environment

Lab	Task
ML25	.NET - Dining Room Semaphore in C#
ML26	.NET - Calculating Correlation Using the Task Parallel Library

There were no programming assignments associated with C# and the .NET environment.

EVALUATION OF THE MICROLAB APPROACH

A few microlabs had two separate activities that were graded independently. There were 31 microlab grades spread throughout the course; each component was graded on a satisfactory/not satisfactory basis. If a student did not finish a microlab during the allotted time, the student could complete it after class and check it off the next lecture period. Eighty four percent of students earned 90% or higher on the microlabs; sixteen percent of students earned between 80 to 90%. The most frequent cause of not completing a microlab was absenteeism during the lecture that introduced the lab activities.

Our first year grant activities were evaluated by an independent external evaluator [see Acknowledgements]. In the introduction of the report, the evaluator said:

The course developers followed the Chinese proverb, "I hear and I forget, I see and I remember, I do and I understand", by allowing the students to be active learners during the class period through the use of the microlabs.

There was a sequence of questions associated with each of the major topics covered in the course. Table 6 shows the results for the question dealing with microlabs.

Table 6: Evaluation Results

The microlabs helped me understand the lecture materials.					
Topic	**SD**	**D**	**N**	**A**	**SA**
Threads	0.0	0.0	0.0	33.3	66.7
OpenMP	0.0	0.0	0.0	66.7	33.3
MPI	0.0	0.0	0.0	50.0	50.0
Web Services	0.0	0.0	33.3	33.3	33.3
SD(strongly disagree),D(disagree),N(neutral),A(agree),SA(strongly agree)					

It can be seen that students reacted very favorably to the use of microlabs. Only the web services microlabs, which did not relate to the course project, received any neutral evaluations. When asked in a free-form input text box the question "What was the best part of the course?" 50% of the students explicitly said the microlabs. The evaluator concluded:

Overall, the short-lecture/mcirolab approach designed by the grant participants is a strong pedagogical tool for teaching students distributed computing.

FUTURE DEVELOPMENTS

The Distributed Computing Modules

Our NSF grant is organized into two phases:

- During year one materials were developed as part of a complete course that was taught in the summer 2008 and the spring 2009
- During year two materials will be modularized and introduced into existing courses as separate learning modules

We strongly believe that distributed computing education has to permeate the entire computer science curriculum and not just be an upper division elective course. These modules will allow instructors to introduce distributed computing concepts into many courses in the curriculum. Here are some characteristics of these modules:

- They last 2 to 3 weeks
- They include presentations, microlabs, and program assignments
- There will be a wide variety of materials available that will allow instructors to pick and choose particular items to suit the course needs

- Materials can be easily modified and expanded to allow the instructor to have a feeling of ownership

During the Fall 2009 semester we have tested the following modules:

- Java threads in our CS2 course; these results were mixed as the instructor did not want to use the more complex examples (he said students "were not ready yet")
- MPI in our Programming Languages course plus one lecture on Java threads; these results appears to be more positive with students completing the assigned microlabs
- An expanded version of our .NET materials in our software engineering course; all levels of parallelism (threads, the task parallel library, MPI.NET, and web services) were integrated into a single programming environment using C# and used in the course project; trouble with setting up Windows Server and HPC Server limited the use of MPI.NET

Our external reviewer had the following comment about module development:

It will be interesting to see how the course materials will be used as independent modules or lectures in lower-level computer science courses during the second year of this grant.

The Use of Microlabs

To make the microlabs practical in for a large lecture section we need both a virtual wireless network with associated management software and an automated grading system. We have developed programming quiz grading systems in the past [4] but adaption of such systems to a distributed computing environment is challenging. We have started this work and here are some of the problems that need to be overcome:

- Extend the automatic compilation to handle multiple languages such as Java, C, and C#
- Check intermediate results returned by individual program components as well as the final result
- Allow for some non-determinism regarding the order results are reported
- Check for correct deployment of a web service even if the client program is not functioning properly
- Take into account any randomness used to generate test data

We have made a start on tackling these issues by introducing an automated grading program for MPI programs written in C during a summer workshop. Work is currently in progress during the second year of our grant.

5.3 The Distributed Computing Repository

Another component of our grant activities is the establishment of a distributed computing repository. It will not only contain materials directly developed as part of this grant but will also contain materials developed by researchers at other universities. Our initial focus has been on lecture presentations that can be searched using a keyword system. In addition to the lectures referenced in this paper, the repository also includes lectures from the following researchers:

- Dr. Barry Wilkinson, UNC Charlotte, Parallel Computing (ITCS 4145)
- Dr. Yaohang Li, North Carolina A&T, Distributed Systems (COMP750)
- Dr. Barry Wilkinson, UNC Charlotte, Grid Computing (ITCS 4146)

We will expand these materials to include programming assignments and projects associated with these courses. The repository can be accessed at:

http://www.cs.appstate.edu/distributedComputing.

Our external reviewer reacted positively to our initial version of the distributed computing repository as indicated by the following comment:

In conclusion, the course materials developed for the integrated course and their initial inclusion in the distributed computing repository, started by the grant participants, is a wonderful beginning of an invaluable resource for instructors of distributed computing.

ACKNOWLEDGMENTS

The activities presented in this paper were partially supported by a NSF grant (0737355) entitled *Modern Distributed Computing Education* funded as a Phase 1 (Exploratory) proposal under the Course, Curriculum, and Laboratory Improvement (CCLI) program. The funding level was $150,000 for two years commencing July 2008. The graduate assistant position associated with this grant was funded 50% by the NSF and 50% by the Office of Research and Sponsored Programs at Appalachian State University.

The annual evaluation of our first year activities was performed by Joel Hollingsworth at Elon University.

REFERENCES

[1] J.M. Adams, B. Kurtz, A State-of-the-Art CS Undergraduate Lab, *Software Engineering Education – Lecture Notes in Computer Science #423*, Springer-Verlag, 1990, 85-94

[2] BOINC - BOINC.berkeley.edu

[3] K. Bowles, A CS1 course based on Stand-Alone Microcomputers, *SIGCSE Bulletin*, Vol. 9, No. 1, February 1978, 125-127

[4] C. Ellsworth, J. Fenwick, B. Kurtz: The Quiver system. *SIGCSE Bulletin*, Vol. 35, No. 1, March 2004: 205-209

[5] Folding@home - http://folding.stanford.edu/

[6] Globus - http://www.globus.org

[7] B. Kurtz, H. Pfeiffer, "Developing Programming Quizzes to Support Instruction in Abstract Data Types", *SIGCSE Bulletin*, Vol. 21, No. 1, February 1989, pp. 66-70

[8] MPI - http://www.mcs.anl.gov/research/projects/mpich2/

[9] OpenMP - http://openmp.org

[10] PTreads - http://sourceware.org/pthreads-win32/

[11] PVM - http://www.csm.ornl.gov/pvm/

[12] Seti@home - http://setiathome.ssl.berkeley.edu/

[13] Task Parallel Library - http://msdn.microsoft.com/en-us/concurrency/default.aspx

[14] B. Wilkinson, C. Ferner, Towards a top-down approach to teaching an undergraduate grid computing course, *SIGCSE Bulletin*, Vol. 38, No. 1, February 2008: 126-130

Is Teaching Parallel Algorithmic Thinking to High School Students Possible? One Teacher's Experience

Shane Torbert
Thomas Jefferson High School for Science and Technology
Fairfax County Public Schools
Fairfax County, VA
smtorbert@fcps.edu

Uzi Vishkin
The University of Maryland
Institute for Advanced Computer Studies (UMIACS)
College Park, MD 20742
vishkin@umd.edu

Ron Tzur
University of Colorado Denver
ron.tzur@ucdenver.edu

David J. Ellison
Indiana University
Bloomington
djelliso@indiana.edu

ABSTRACT

All students at our high school are required to take at least one course in Computer Science prior to their junior year. They are also required to complete a year-long senior project associated with a specific in-house laboratory, one of which is the Computer Systems Lab. To prepare students for this experience the lab offers elective courses at the post-AP Computer Science level. Since the early 1990s one of these electives has focused on parallel computing. The course enrolls approximately 40 students each year for two semesters of instruction. The lead programming language is C and topics include a wide array of industry-standard and experimental tools. Since the 2007-2008 school year we have included a unit on parallel algorithmic thinking (PAT) using the Explicit Multi-Threading (XMT) system [11, 12]. We describe our experiences using this system after self-studying the approach from a publicly available tutorial. Overall, this article provides significant evidence regarding the unique teachability of the XMT PAT approach, and advocates using it broadly in Computer Science education.

Categories and Subject Descriptors

K.3.2 [**Computers and Education**]: Computer and Information Science Education—*computer science education*

General Terms

Design, Human Factors, Algorithms

Keywords

Parallel Algorithmic Thinking, High School, XMT, PRAM Algorithms

1. INTRODUCTION

Thomas Jefferson High School for Science and Technology is a member of the National Consortium for Specialized Secondary Schools of Mathematics, Science, and Technology. Admission is competitive and students are drawn from a region whose total population is over one million people. Through a national contest in the early 1990s the Computer Systems Lab won an ETA supercomputer and subsequently created a one-semester elective course in Supercomputing Applications.

The original ETA was damaged by a leaky roof and later replaced with a cluster of Linux workstations running PVM and MPI. In 2003 the ETA was exchanged for a Cray SV1 which is still housed in the lab, but the main environment for computing continues to be approximately 50 mixed-use Linux workstations, a few dedicated high-performance Linux and Solaris servers, and a recently acquired eight-node cluster. System administration and maintentance are handled by a small group of the high school students themselves.

The recognition that parallel programming is becoming mainstream Computer Science knowledge is supported by texts such as [4] that wrote: "for the first time in history, no one is building a much faster sequential processor. If you want your program to run significantly faster..., you're going to have to parallelize your program". In 2007 this evolution of the field led us to expand the offering from one semester to two semesters and change the name of the course to Parallel Computing.

2. STUDENT POPULATION

The students in our course have either already completed or are currently enrolled in AP Computer Science and many have also taken two-semesters of another elective in Artificial Intelligence. Thus they typically come into the Parallel Computing course with two years experience in Java and one year in Python, as well as exposure to Big-Oh analysis and data structures including queues, heaps, trees, and graphs. Mathematically they are at least through Algebra II and many are in Calculus, so they are familiar with matrices, exponentials, and logarithms. They are highly motivated in this area and many will eventually become undergraduate Computer Science majors.

3. GOALS OF THE COURSE

Essentially all aspects of the course have changed from the original conception and continue to change as needed.

3.1 Language and Tools

At various times the course has been taught in C, C++, and Fortran. We currently teach the course in C and one major goal is to expose students to aspects of C (e.g., pointers) that they would not have seen in either Java or Python. This choice also facilitates discussions of system-level architecture which play a minor but important role in the course.

We have long abandoned PVM but still spend a semester covering MPI at the level of send/receives, focusing first on the Manager-Worker paradigm for the embarrassingly parallel problems and then later on more complicated communication schemes. In the second semester we cover XMT, pthreads, OpenMP, sockets, and Nvidia's CUDA [2].

3.2 Principles

We begin with embarrassingly parallel problems such as parameter search, fractal generation, and cellular automata, using 2-D OpenGL graphics (students have previously used Java's Swing) to visualize speedup when possible. Then we move to coupled problems such as heat transfer and orbital mechanics, before returning again to such problems as iterative matrix solvers, image compression, and ray tracing.

We want students to appreciate the breadth of parallel computing's current landscape while at the same time see some depth in the context of classic problems, their solutions in parallel, and a generalizable approach to writing parallel code. Formal analysis, which has long been an integral part of our serial algorithmic thinking courses, has only been included in the parallel course since our introduction of XMT.

4. EXPLICIT MULTI-THREADING

The parallel random-access machine/model (PRAM) theory of algorithms [6, 7], developed mostly in the 1980s, provides a well-established, easy approach to parallel algorithmic thinking (PAT). The Explicit Multi-Threading (XMT) system from the University of Maryland was designed to implement PRAM-like programming. As such, XMT provides students a simple-to-use alternative to MPI. As has been noted by others [3, 5, 8, 9, 10] the complexity of coding in MPI or even OpenMP can be quite overwhelming for a beginning student. With XMT the coding overhead is instead very light.

The programming language for XMT, called XMT-C, adds only two constructs to ANSI C: `spawn` and prefix-sum. So far we have only used the spawn construct, within which the dollar-sign ($) variable acts like an MPI rank or a thread ID, and shared access to previously declared arrays makes send/receives of data unnecessary. Installation of the emulator [1] is easy and provides cycle and time estimates for comparison calculations. Most importantly from an instructional perspective, XMT has allowed us to cover a range of algorithms that we had never considered covering using MPI.

5. ALGORITHM ANALYSIS

We make extensive use of timing data to show speedups for embarrassingly parallel problems but had not ventured

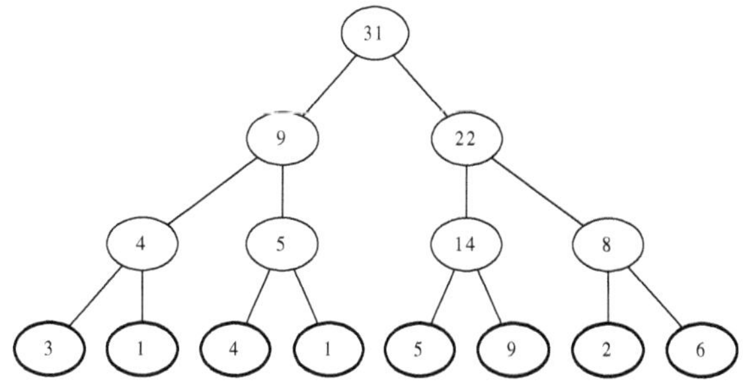

Figure 1: Tree representation of a simple sum.

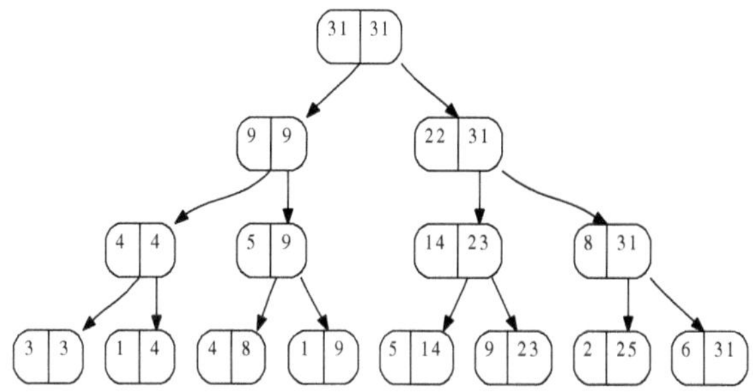

Figure 2: The widely used prefix-sum calculation.

into formal analysis of algorithms until we began using XMT. The main reason for parallel algorithms is performance and it was important to be able to match their performance analysis with that of serial algorithms.

5.1 Summation Example

We began our XMT unit with a simple example: calculating the sum of an array of integers. A serial version can be constructed easily and runs in $O(N)$ time. In parallel we take advantage of a tree structure as shown in Figure 1. The operations at each level of the tree are independent and can be done in parallel using a spawn block in $O(1)$ time. If we then run a loop over the levels we will arrive at the top node of the tree in $O(\log N)$ time. Note that the amount of work (i.e., total number of operations) is still $O(N)$ but the amount of time has been reduced drastically. A code listing is provided in the Appendix.

5.2 Prefix-Sum

We do not have the students code the simple summation example. Instead we use it as a basis for discussing the prefix-sum problem whose main idea will be used for many other algorithms. For a given position in the array the prefix-sum is the sum of all the values up to that point. Having completed a bottom-to-top pass of the tree to calculate the overall sum we then complete a top-to-bottom pass to calculate all the prefix-sums, as shown in Figure 2. Again the operations at each level can be done independently in parallel. We walked through the parallel algorithm with the students, modified the summation pseudocode to calculate these prefix-sums, and the students then wrote their own XMT-C code. This served as a first check for us as to whether or not the system was working properly and also that the students understood the basic style of approach we planned to follow.

5.3 Matrix Multiplication

At this point we were able to have a very powerful discussion about matrix multiplication. How can we multiply two $N \times N$ matrices in parallel? We began from the perspective of the N^2 elements in the resulting matrix. Each of these elements is calculated by taking the dot product of a given row and column from the input matrices. Since each of these dot products is independent they can all be done in parallel. In turn, each dot product consists of N multiplications and a summation. The multiplications are independent and each summation, as we have seen, can be done in $O(\log N)$ time and independently of the other summations. Thus the entire matrix multiplication takes the normal $O\left(N^3\right)$ work but an astonishingly low $O(\log N)$ time. The "wow" factor resulting from this discussion cannot be overstated.

5.4 Other Examples

The students next solved a series of problems related to prefix-sum. We did not reveal any solutions until the students had a chance to attempt the problems themselves, which included prefix-min, compaction, nearest-one, and segmented prefix-sum. Even without fully knowing where all of this was leading the students became very engaged in these problems. One student even coined the term "micro-parallelism" to describe the radically different approach we were taking with XMT as compared to MPI. Not only were they successful at solving the problems but the students also realized immediately that this bottom-up approach to building algorithms in parallel was of a fundamentally different nature from what they had previously seen.

5.5 Communication Schemes

No one wanted to try coding these algorithms in MPI with send/receives and the careful up-and-down tree-based communication that would be needed to pass data, manage tasks, and avoid deadlock. Since communication is a major difficulty in writing MPI code we wait as long as possible to attempt even simple schemes like nearest-neighbor and round-robin. The ease of implementing tree communication is a major difference between XMT and MPI.

5.6 Student Work

Not only was the language overhead far less with XMT than it had been with MPI but it was small enough that upon returning from a week-long winter break students required essentially no review before resuming productive work. In addition, the algorithmic problems considered sparked real creativity. It was no longer the case that everyone in the lab was chasing the same canonical solution but instead students were actually inventing different methods for solving these problems.

6. RANKING AND MERGING

6.1 Big-Oh Analysis

Once the students had gained some experience coding in XMT we attempted a much more ambitious problem but one whose big-picture usefulness they could immediately grasp. When the students were introduced to Big-Oh analysis in the AP Computer Science course, the first application they saw was sorting. That course considers the selection, insertion, merge, quick, and heap sorts. This made writing a mergesort for XMT a natural fit and a powerful example of how to evaluate the quality of a parallel algorithm. Our goal was to find an algorithm that balances a small amount of work with a small amount of time.

Table 1: Big-Oh comparison for rank-merge.

	Serial	Binary Search	Partitioning
Work	$O(N)$	$O(N \log N)$	$O(N)$
Time	$O(N)$	$O(\log N)$	$O(\log N)$

6.2 Statement of the Problem

The problem was presented as follows: given two sorted arrays merge them into one sorted array. Due to their prior experience learning the mergesort the students knew that a parallel solution to this problem would lead to a technique for sorting in parallel. We discussed the idea of determining for each element from one list where it would fall in the other list, and that once we knew where it fell in both lists (we already knew where it fell in its own list) we could calculate its ultimate location in the sorted list. We could also move everything into place with a single spawn block in $O(N)$ work and only $O(1)$ time. This concept, known as ranking, tells us how many elements are smaller than we are, which in turn tells us our index in the merged array.

6.3 A First Attempt

We can calculate the rank of each element using a binary search on the other list. This takes $O(\log N)$ work for each of N elements for a total of $O(N \log N)$ work. The binary searches are all independent so they require only $O(\log N)$ time. Already students were impressed by this result because if a mergesort requires $O(\log N)$ levels of recursion then we have just described a parallel sort that runs in a mere $O\left(\log^2 N\right)$ time! But we can still improve the amount of work being done; a serial merge takes only $O(N)$ work which our first parallel attempt has increased by a factor of $\log N$.

6.4 Big Idea: Partitioning

We consider breaking the rank-merge problem into pieces in order to reduce the asymptotic behavior of the work without changing the time. We partition each of the sorted input arrays into $O(N/\log N)$ pieces of size $O(\log N)$ and perform the binary search ranking process on only the endpoints of these partitions. This still takes $O(\log N)$ time but now only $O\left(\log N \cdot (N/\log N)\right) = O(N)$ work. To rank the remaining elements we perform $O(N/\log N)$ serial-style merges, all of which are independent and can be done in parallel.

Each serial-merge is linear in both work and time. That is, the serial-merge is linear in terms of the amount of data being merged by this particular instance of the serial-merge code. We are not merging all the data at once but rather in small pieces, the partitions. Since the partitions have been carefully constructed so that their sizes are $O(\log N)$ this amounts to only $O(\log N)$ work and time for each merge instance.

This critical point must be explained with great care or only the best students will catch it. Then, multiplying by the $O(N/\log N)$ number of partitions gives us a total of $O(N)$ work. Since we're still only using $O(\log N)$ time this means the parallel mergesort will be as good as serial in terms of work, $O(N \log N)$, for only $O\left(\log^2 N\right)$ time.

6.5 Comparison of Algorithms

A summary of these three approaches is shown in Table 1. This kind of development of a non-trivial algorithm, drawing from previous experience and refining with subtle ideas, was in no way a part of our program prior to using XMT. Students continue to be impressed by the timing data speedups of a big MPI run but now we can also appeal to their more sophisticated abilities of anaylsis, to extend those skills in a parallel environment, and to build general purpose techniques in a highly-coupled context.

7. TEACHER PREPARATION

Prior to the emulator being available for download a pilot was conducted during the spring semester of 2008 as a proof-of-concept. After XMT proved to be a viable tool the instructor self-taught himself the material only by reviewing a series of online video lectures in preparation for the 2008-2009 year. He was in regular contact with the XMT team before, during, and after the five-week instructional unit.

8. CONCLUSIONS

The students in this course would be classified as very good in Computer Science even if they weren't studying parallel computing. Our challenge is to present them a broad array of meaningful, inspiring, real-world, eye-opening experiences. Our use of XMT as described here has provided them with a level of insight that MPI just couldn't do given their backgrounds and the instructional timeframe we have to work with. It has earned itself a permanent place in our curriculum and we look forward to improving our presentation of this material each year. Specifically, we plan on extending our instructional unit to include the selection problem (that will require use of the prefix-sum construct) and the general technique of accelerating cascades. For the 2009-2010 school year this will begin the first week of February at the start of the second semester and continue until the first week of March, covering five weeks of instruction.

Compared to OpenMP, which requires a laundry list of preprocessor directives that are also hardware specific, we found the XMT interface was easier for students to pick up and use. Compared to CUDA, we found the additional syntax features to be far more intuitive in XMT with the added benefit that no specialized graphics cards had to be purchased, installed, and configured in order to run student programs.

As a high school we have the luxury of assuming that an undergraduate education will follow anything we do with our students. Thus, our end-product goal is not a ready professional heading into the job market but rather a motivated, activated, and stimulated teenager entering a university setting prepared for many more years of learning. While our presentations do not always contain the same level of abstraction that might be found in a college-level lecture, wherever possible we want to challenge our students with the most rigorous problems they can reasonably be expected to solve. The XMT system has allowed us to expand these offerings with both a new style of question and a user-friendly environment for writing parallel code.

Overall, this article provides significant evidence regarding the unique teachability of the XMT PAT approach, and advocates using it broadly in Computer Science education.

9. POSTSCRIPT

In response to SIGCSE reviews, we describe also experiences and strategies teaching more typical groups of K-12 and a freshman course to college students.

9.1 K-12 Settings

D. Ellison, a K-12 mathematics teacher, taught more typical students with minimal or no programming experience at:

1. Baltimore Polytechnic Institute, a majority African-American high school. The class met bi-weekly over two months and was offered to 11th grade students who happened to take AP Chemistry as an alternative to their Lego Mindstorms robot programming class.
2. Montgomery Co. Public Schools, middle-school summer camp for underrepresented students. The class met nine mornings from 8:30 AM until 12:30 PM.

9.2 Pedagogy

Consistent with a constructivist theory of learning and reform education methods at this elementary level we posed problem solving tasks designed to prompt student construction of algorithms, generally in small groups of 3-4. During class discussions we considered students' proposed algorithms especially in light of the following three questions designed to promote an understanding of parallelism:

- How can I introduce parallelism into my algorithm?
- How can I measure the benefits of parallelism?
- How can I justify when parallelization is exhausted?

Quantifying operations in algorithms proved useful as we guided students to an understanding of a PRAM computer model and more general notions of work and depth. Again we posed questions:

- What is this serial algorithm doing for us? What is enabling it in the computer?
- What is this parallel algorithm doing for us? What is enabling it in the computer?

9.3 Findings

Under these methods we find typical students, even at the middle school level, are capable of viewing the computer as PRAM and are able to gain deeper understandings of their algorithms including time complexities. We found students' initial struggling with C coding can be rather tedious. After some problem solving activities described in detail below we supplied them with nearly completed XMT-C code to speed things along. With help from the XMT team at the University of Maryland we produced elegant and understandable code representing both serial and parallel algorithms.

The next phase of the curricula included compiling and executing the XMT-C code during class. We encouraged students to compare serial and parallel time cycles and number of operations by running progressively larger data sets. Students analyzed their results via spreadsheets. The purpose of examining the data in this way was to help students quantify the benefit of the parallelism over serial, to form and test their conjectures regarding the PRAM model, to test the limit of parallelism's benefit, and to help them develop a sense of the time complexity of their algorithms. These activities strengthened the impact of previous discussions.

9.4 Activities

From our presentation at the 2009 CS4HS workshop [11]:

1. Introduction to algorithms (via problem solving activities from the CSTA Curriculum Statement, 2007)
2. MS LOGO activities, especially at the middle school level as a warm-up to coding algorithms in XMT-C
3. The Exchange Problem (introduces the use of variables and exchanging array values in serial and parallel)
4. The Bill Gates Problem (Mr. Gates completes morning activities illustrating that independent tasks can be conducted simultaneously under parallelism)
5. Vector + Vector addition (naive parallelism compared to serial for constant time operations)
6. Parallel addition (the binary tree technique supported students understanding of algorithms and strengthened their mathematical notions of the binary exponential and its logarithm)
7. Matrix Multiplication (and exploring the potential of log time using nested spawn commands)
8. Merge Ranking (middle school students actually formed themselves into two lines and performed the ranking)

9.5 College Freshman Setting

U. Vishkin taught an elective freshman course at the University of Maryland in Spring 2009. Most of the 19 students were not Computer Science or Computer Engineering majors. Programming assignments included parallel algorithms for radix sort, finding the median, sample sort (an extension of Quicksort), and merge sort. Similar assignments would be acceptable in a serial programming course for freshmen. Pedagogy: Revisiting the performance (complexity) analysis of an assignment after completion was helpful towards the next assignment. Findings: We found that nearly all students were able to produce correct working code that achieved satisfactory speed-ups for each of the assignments.

10. ACKNOWLEDGMENTS

Help by the XMT team, and support by National Science Foundation grants 0325393, 0811504, and 0834373, are gratefully acknowledged.

11. REFERENCES

[1] Emulator for xmt-c. sourceforge.net/projects/xmtc.
[2] Toolkit for cuda. nvidia.com/cuda.
[3] D. Ernst, B. Wittman, B. Harvey, T. Murphy, and M. Wrinn. Preparing students for ubiquitous parallelism. *SIGCSE '09: Proceedings of the Fortieth SIGCSE Technical Symposium on Computer Science Education*, pages 136–137, 2009.
[4] J. L. Hennessy and D. A. Patterson. *Computer Architecture: A quantitative approach, 4th edition.* Morgan Kauffman, 2007.
[5] C. Jacobsen and M. Jadud. Towards concrete concurrency: occam-pi on the lego mindstorms. *SIGCSE '05: Proceedings of the Thirty-Sixth SIGCSE Technical Symposium on Computer Science Education*, pages 431–435, 2005.
[6] J. JaJa. *Introduction to Parallel Algorithms.* Addison-Wesley Professional, 1992.
[7] J. Keller, C. Keller, and J. Traff. *Practical PRAM Programming.* Wiley-Interscience, 2000.
[8] A. Kimball, S. Michels-Slettvet, and C. Bisciglia. Cluster computing for web-scale data processing. *SIGCSE '08: Proceedings of the Thirty-Ninth SIGCSE Technical Symposium on Computer Science Education*, pages 116–120, 2008.
[9] J. Paul, M. Kouril, and K. Berman. A template library to facilitate teaching message passing parallel computing. *SIGCSE '06: Proceedings of the Thirty-Seventh SIGCSE Technical Symposium on Computer Science Education*, pages 464–468, 2006.
[10] C. Pheatt. An easy to use distributed computing framework. *SIGCSE '07: Proceedings of the Thirty-Eighth SIGCSE Technical Symposium on Computer Science Education*, pages 571–575, 2007.
[11] U. Vishkin. umiacs.umd.edu/users/vishkin/xmt.html.
[12] U. Vishkin. Using simple abstraction to guide the reinvention of computing for parallelism. *Comm. ACM*, to appear.

APPENDIX

A. CODE LISTING FOR SIMPLE SUM

```
#include <xmtc.h>
#include <xmtio.h>
#define n 8
#define log_n 3
int main()
{
   int h,p,B[log_n+1][n+1];
   int A[n+1]={0,3,1,4,1,5,9,2,6};

   // copying elements of an array to be summed A
   // into the leaves of a balanced binary tree B
   spawn(1,n)            // for i, 1<=i<=n pardo
   {
      int i;             // index for left-to-right
      i=$;               // XMT-C uses dollar sign
      B[0][i]=A[i];
   }

   // at each point in time p=2^h and n/p gives the
   // number of nodes at level h of the binary tree
   h=1;
   for(p=2;p<=n;p*=2)    // move up the tree
   {
      spawn(1,n/p)
      {
         B[h][$]=B[h-1][2*$-1]+B[h-1][2*$];
      }
      h+=1;             // h goes from 1 to log_n
   }

} // output uses printf and is not shown here
```

Introductory Computing Students' Conceptions of Illegal Student-Student Collaboration

Michael Stepp, Beth Simon
Computer Science and Engineering Dept.
University of California, San Diego
La Jolla, CA
{mstepp, bsimon}@cs.ucsd.edu

ABSTRACT
Academic integrity and cheating are issues of specific importance in computing courses due to the restricted nature of much of our assigned work. Additionally, use of valued pedagogical and professional practices such as pair programming can muddy the waters when it comes to students' understandings and experiences with collaboration. In this study we report on 112 students at the beginning of a second programming course being asked to describe a scenario of student-to-student collaboration that "crosses the line" in terms of what should be allowed in the course. We find that students describe inappropriate acts involving sharing of code and sharing of information, with the former being more prevalent. Additionally, about half of the scenarios include mitigating circumstances that should not affect the propriety of those acts. Finally, when presented with other students' (often vague) scenarios, students have little consensus on whether those reflect appropriate or inappropriate collaborations.

Categories and Subject Descriptors
K.3.2 [**Computer Science Education**]: Introductory programming – *academic integrity.*

General Terms
Human Factors.

Keywords
CS1, Cheating, Plagiarism, Academic Integrity.

1. INTRODUCTION
The academic integrity or collaboration policy for a computer science course is perhaps more interesting than in other disciplines, because programming assignments are often structured in restricted ways. Educators give introductory programmers straightforward tasks, and encourage them to write code in one particular style. Furthermore, the compiler catches a wide range of mistakes, giving greater similarity through enforced correctness. This greatly reduces the solution space, meaning that there are far fewer acceptable answers to a programming assignment than, say, an English essay.

Additionally, a clear and explicit policy is especially important for beginning students, since they may have little or no experience in "programming for a grade". Their previous experiences in other disciplines collaborating on homework may have a different "look and feel" than those with a programming assignment.

Though at first it may seem trivial to create a collaboration policy, there are many elements to consider. For instance, if Student A asks Student B for help, should B be allowed to look at A's code? Can A look at B's code? In either case, should the student be allowed to look at the whole program, or a limited portion? Can the helper describe the solution, or is she limited to explaining the high-level concepts involved? How would students know the difference between those two situations? Is debugging collaboration considered differently than code-creation collaboration? Most importantly, how can these various situations be described in a way that novice students can understand and, hopefully, apply in their actual programming experiences?

In this paper, we take a different tack from much of the related literature which asks students to evaluate pre-defined (and expert-defined) situations. We asked 112 students at the beginning of a second computing course to invent scenarios regarding "appropriate" collaboration practices between students. We find that students discuss a range of practices that generally fall into two categories regarding sharing of *code* or *information*, and that students are more likely to describe the former. We also find little consensus in students' ability to determine the propriety of other students' scenarios. Through this exercise, we identify students' lack of attention to key details when creating scenarios, and suggest value in both training of students in this area and class discussion of such scenarios. Our hope is that improved student ability at creating and evaluating scenarios may make their collaboration with each other more thoughtful, and perhaps more in line with local norms. Alternately, such scenarios, as coming from the student perspective, may be more effective in defining a collaboration policy that is meaningful and useful for students and we provide a handout for students to support such discussion.

2. RELATED WORK
[1] studied first year students' ability to detect plagiarism from predefined scenarios, in contrast to student-generated ones. In addition, the students rated 15 scenarios relating to copyright violation and plagiarism, based on the seriousness of the infraction. They found students tend to consider some forms of

plagiarism as more serious than others, and that they would be more likely to admit to the ones they considered less serious. Students also had difficulty identifying which scenarios involved plagiarism and which didn't.

[2] conducted a study of 1206 students and 190 academic staff asking about four issues (seriousness, penalty, prevalence, personal history) about 20 different scenarios relating to academic integrity. For every scenario, the students rated the seriousness as lower, the penalty as lower, and the prevalence as higher than the staff did. Staff underestimated the actual prevalence of these acts (as reported by personal history).

[3] had 103 students at Monash University rate 18 different scenarios relating to academic integrity violations. Students were very homogeneous in their views of what counted as academic integrity violations, but those views did not correspond well with university policy -- many students rated a variety of policy violations as acceptable. In this study, novices are not found to have homogenous views when shown student-described scenarios.

Our work seeks to bring greater authenticity and student reflection to the "scenario technique" by engaging students in developing their own collaboration or academic integrity scenarios. We also seek to develop instructional support in effective discussion and student application of academic integrity guidelines.

3. METHODOLOGY

3.1 Subjects

Data reported here is from two terms (Winter 2009 (Class A) and Spring 2009 (Class B)) of a CS1.5 course (2nd 10 weeks) at the University of California, San Diego. The previous CS1 course (for students with no prior programming experience) required the use of pair programming for assignments. Thus, this was students' nominal first experience programming independently. The same instructor (Simon) taught both CS1 and CS1.5 (both terms). A total of 164 students submitted answers but we report on 112 scenarios. We removed 16 student responses because they didn't answer the question, and 36 responses from Class A because we asked them a slightly different question (described below).

3.2 Assignment

Our experiment took the form of a survey presented to the students in both Class A and B. The exact text of the survey for Class A is given in Figure 1. Class A had the option of describing either an appropriate or an inappropriate collaboration scenario between two students in the class. We chose to focus on collaboration between students in the class based both on students' previous experience in pair programming and our common "lab culture" -- most students do their programming in a common room on campus.

For Class B, the assignment changed to exclude the "appropriate" response option, based on excessive vagueness in those responses from Class A. Specifically, it stated "[T]he goal of this description should be to outline the 'cross over line' where the kind of help you might seek from another student in the class is not allowable or fair." In addition, we presented 5 situations generated in Class A (4 "appropriate", 1 "inappropriate") to Class B students to be rated as one or the other. These situations, chosen for the "less than clear" situations they presented, were:

1. You've been trying to finish your assignment but are stuck on one of the methods and cant [sic] figure out how to do it. You call over another student and ask for help and they let you see what they did for there [sic] method to help you get started. [W35]
2. When it is a bug you have narrowed down where it can be to a small portion of the code. Just a couple of lines perhaps, or maybe its [sic] just in one method. This way hopefully you don't to show your whole code to the other person. [AltW31]
3. When my code does not work, I would ask my friend to give me a hint. So, when my friend comes by to help me on the code, he and I would generate a code as we discuss through the process. [AltW07]
4. Student A is working on his program but he has no idea what to do, then he asks student B about it. After listening to the explanation of the assignment and student B's idea of how to do it, student A is inspired and starts to do his own work without copying exactly what B tells him. [AltW34]
5. Student A and Student B are both assigned a program. Student A completes it and it works perfectly. Student B is struggling with the assignment and asks Student A for help. Student A comes over and skims the code, gives advice, but not directly telling Student B what to do. (i.e. "Take another look at your loops") or, Student A can also draw a diagram or something to help Student B understand the assignment more clearly. [AltW22]

The purpose of this activity is for everyone in the class to consider the reasons and value of having rules for what constitutes legal or "OK" ways of collaborating with other CSE8B students on programs. This does NOT address interactions with tutors for CSE8B. On one side, we know that it can be very valuable to get a "second set of eyes" when going after a difficult bug. It can be wasteful to spin your wheels forever when you might make progress much faster with someone else's quick comment. On the other side, we know that you, as a professional, have an expected level of personal effort and debugging that you are expected to be able to perform. This DOES involve struggling and trying to debug on your own. Additionally, program grades are part of your assessment in this course, and your personal hard work should be rewarded fairly. Below, **tell us about a debugging scenario you can imagine encountering in this class and tell us whether YOU think it should be legal to collaborate with another 8B student in that scenario (or not).**

Figure 1. Assignment posed to Class A (emphasis added)

3.3 Analysis Methodology

The authors developed an initial set of categories by reviewing the entire data set. Refining the categories led to complete agreement in coding responses. Based on students' descriptions of "inappropriate acts", we found 9 common categories of inappropriate acts, with a 10th included as "Other" to capture the remaining. The categories are given by example on the final page. Every student response fit into at least one inappropriate act category, but we coded them with as many categories as were applicable (max: 3).

Of their own accord, some students noted "mitigating circumstances." Only 55 students included mitigating circumstances. These are also given by example on the final page.

4. RESULTS

4.1 Generated Scenarios

Inappropriate Acts. Figure 2 shows the breakdown of inappropriate acts as identified from student-generated scenarios in the two classes. There were two main categories of inappropriate collaboration, involving either sharing *code* or *information*. Examples of categories are shown on the last page.

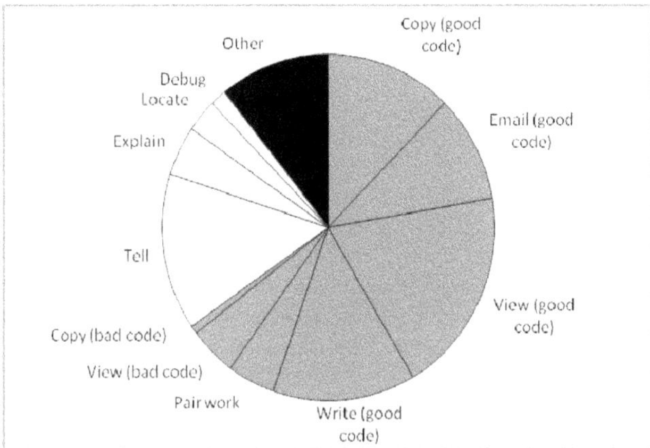

Figure 2. Freq. of Inappropriate Acts in Student Scenarios

65% of the inappropriate acts identified in student scenarios involved sharing of *code* (dark grey). The grand majority of code sharing acts (85%) occur "directionally" from a knowledgeable student to a less knowledgeable student (Copy, Send, View, or Write "good code"). Relatively few acts described students working together (often as a holdover from the previous class' pair programming technique) or having a more knowledgeable student working in some way with the less knowledgeable students' code (View or Copy "bad code").

24% of acts involved sharing of *information* (light gray) from a knowledgeable student to one less knowledgeable (Tell, Explain, Locate or Debug a bug). We classified the remaining 11% of acts as Other, either because they were too vague to classify or because they did not reflect two students collaborating (e.g. "google for some codes" [S01]).

Mitigating Circumstances. Just under half of all students (47%) also went on to give, as part of their scenario, a notable mitigating circumstance that might more clearly explicate when an inappropriate act may occur. The variety of these mitigating circumstances is interesting in helping to understand the expected situations in which students may be pressured to cheat.

Table 1. Mitigating Circumstances Frequencies

Mitigating Circumstance	Frequency
Stuck	31
Being at Different Places	16
Procrastination	15
Amount of Code	6
Asking Fails	2
Not Exhausting your own Resources	2

We categorized mitigating circumstances into six groups, shown in Table 1. Examples of the categories are shown on the last page. *Stuck* was one of the most common mitigating circumstances. Additionally, variations on being stuck sometimes mentioned frustration as a result of being stuck or, specifically, a student having exhausted their resources (having asked a TA, or having no TA available) in addition to being stuck. A surprising and common circumstance involved when two students have worked "different amounts" or were in "different places" with respect to completing their code – often cited as an aspect that makes collaboration inappropriate. We did not code as "different places" the most common case of one student being "completely done" with their program, as this was ubiquitous in most responses (either explicitly or implicitly).

4.2 Student Evaluation of Scenarios

As shown in Figure 3, when asked to evaluate other student-generated collaboration scenarios, only once was there solid consensus from students. Again, in this question, we ask students to say whether acts were "appropriate" rather than "legal" because we encouraged the students to think for themselves about the value and consequences of collaborating with others. The instructor and TA for the course (the authors) both agreed on the kind of collaborations they could expect to allow in this course. They agreed with the majority of students on all scenarios except Scenario 3, where they thought the phrase "he and I would generate a code" was beyond what was acceptable.

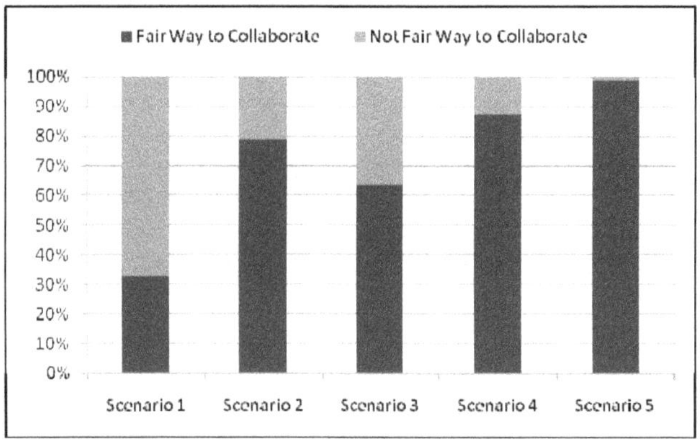

Figure 3. Spring Student Assessment of Provided Scenarios

5. DISCUSSION

Generating Collaboration Policies. Most previous work has looked at student ability to identify and rate violation of academic integrity policies and has shown students struggle to appropriately apply such rules. Might we reach a better outcome if we involved students in the process more generatively? Here we engage students in "defining" policy by "consider[ing] the reasons and value of having rules for what constitutes legal or 'OK' ways of collaborating" as part of consideration of their professional development and academic value of course assessment.

This process for generating local or course-specific policy has potential benefit for *instructors*. Students had, in a previous course, signed a computing-specific academic integrity statement which included standard wording on plagiarism and prohibited specifically "providing, procuring or accepting assignments in part or in whole" to/from other students, required that code be "student's original work", and outlined that "collaboration with other students to develop, complete, or correct course work is limited to activities explicitly authorized by the Instructor". Recognizing that she lacked a list of "explicitly allowable" collaboration activities to provide to students, the instructor asked students to help generate such a list that she would then endorse for the course.

This process for generating local or course-specific policy has potential benefit for *students*. Another consideration is to engage students in considering the implications of collaboration activities on their overall learning process, given recognized positive aspects of collaborations for novice programmers. Part of the motivation for pair programming in CS1 is to help students struggle less with getting stuck (especially debugging), and to develop skills in discussing and evaluating multiple solutions to a problem specifically as that process positively influences learning [4]. From this viewpoint, the instructor approved collaboration decisions (based on the 5 scenarios in Spring and their discussion in class) help students draw the line in interpreting the phrase "student's original work" (e.g., discussion up to a point is valued, generating code together crosses the line). Viewing others' code to help debug is "reasonable collaboration" as long as the amount of code viewed is small. While these scenarios leave significant room for improvement, their discussion does allow for reflection on positive valuation of collaboration targeted at improved understanding, versus "simple sharing" of code or information.

Code versus information. By instructor standards for this class, all code sharing activities (except possibly those that have the more knowledgeable student viewing the less knowledgeable student's code, for say restricted debugging) were clearly inappropriate acts. As **clearly** inappropriate acts, it is concerning that so many student responses are of this type, rather than exploring the more interesting "borderline" cases. Certainly, discussion of the difference in "tell" and "explain" scenarios would be quite valuable in class. Students described "Telling" as a form of "speaking in code", compared to "explain" which implied more algorithmic or higher level discussion, and also often implied more 2-way discussion rather than "dumping" of information from a knowledgeable source to a less knowledgeable one. In this class, many cases of "explain" (and also "locate" and "debug") were in fact considered allowable by the instructor – or at least could be with small modifications to the described scenario (see [S38] on last page).

Often two scenario characteristics applied that made View (bad code), explain, locate, and debug reasonable: limited scope of assistance and lack of "use" of knowledgeable student's "good" code. Specifically, having a more knowledgeable student view, explain or work with (in a limited way) a less knowledgeable student's code was more likely to be seen as appropriate, valuable collaboration – compared to engaging the less knowledgeable student with the "good code".

Evaluation of Scenarios. Though students achieved little consensus evaluating each other's scenarios (replicating reports when evaluating pre-defined scenarios), we chose those scenarios for their vagueness and, hence, discussion potential. In future work, this sort of "peer review" might be a valuable process in helping students develop better scenarios. Future work would then be required to see if resultant student-generated scenarios are, in fact, more likely to be understandable and consistently evaluated by other students, perhaps even at different institutions.

6. IMPLICATIONS FOR INSTRUCTORS

Developing Skill in Describing and Assessing Collaboration. From reviewing the scenarios we find that students commonly lack skill in specifying details of collaboration scenarios to make them clearly assessable. Often, the degree of interaction and other important characteristics are missing or muddied. This can leave open issues for discussion (see below), but makes it difficult to define explicit, easily-followed rules. If we want students to accurately follow a set of behaviors, we should consider explicitly developing their skills in both describing and evaluating such scenarios. Perhaps introductory computing courses should engage students in writing detailed scenarios as both a goal in itself and to provide them greater opportunity to reflect on their behavior. One might provide students with a set of "sample" scenarios that are worded too vaguely, then ask each student to "elaborate" both an appropriate and an inappropriate version of them. Making this a class assignment could help develop more contextualized, institutional, or course-specific sets of guidelines.

Class Discussion. Even without adding explicit educational goals as outlined above, having students generate their own scenarios regarding collaboration may have value. For an instructor, review of such responses may highlight common behaviors at your institution or specific cases where students are clearly mistaken in understanding local accepted practices. For students, a valuable class activity could be a discussion of their own results, or even those provided by students in this study (which may make the conversation less loaded, especially in small classrooms). The last page of this paper provides student-generated scenarios as a starting point for classroom discussion, which we invite instructors to use verbatim or modify for their own purposes.

7. CONCLUSIONS

In this work we report on the experience of asking students in an introductory computing class to define their own inappropriate collaboration scenarios. Results feature the sharing of *code* and *information* as distinct situations. We consider the possibility of this first experience for future, more comprehensive instructional processes for improving both collaboration policies and students' abilities to recognize and evaluate them.

8. REFERENCES

[1] Marshall, S., Garry, M. (2005). How well do students really understand plagiarism?. In H. Goss (Ed.), Proceedings of the 22nd annual conference of the Australasian Society for Computers in Learning in Tertiary Education (ASCILITE) (pp. 457-467). Brisbane, Australia, 4-7 December.

[2] Brimble, M., Stevenson-Clarke, P. (2005), Perceptions of the prevalence and seriousness of academic dishonesty in Australian universities, *Australian Educational Researcher*, Vol. 32 No.3, pp.19-44.

[3] Dick, M., Sheard, J., and Markham, S. 2001. Is it okay to cheat? - the views of postgraduate students. *SIGCSE Bull.* 33, 3 (Sep. 2001), 61-64.

[4] Simon, B., Hanks, B. First Year Students' Impressions of Pair Programming in CS1. JERIC 7, 4. 2008.

Student guide to unfair collaboration scenarios

These scenarios are students' own words describing possible situations where they might work together in ways that would not be fair based on university standards and their goals for professional development.
Do you agree with them -- are these inappropriate ways to collaborate? Do they provide enough detail for you to decide?

Illegal Acts: sharing information

- ***Tell*:** One student encounters a failure with his code and seeks help from surrounding peers. He finds another student who has had the same failure and that student has identified the defect. The student asks this student to **tell him exactly what it is that he changed** to make it work. [W23]
- ***Explain*:** I am working on an assignment that is due in 2 hours and panicking and just need to do one last part before I finish. I see my friend in the lab as well and I go over to him and ask him for some quick help. I notice he is stuck on a part that I finished and he did the part I need. I tell him we should just **explain in words how we did our own sections in words away from the code** and he agrees. This is crossing the line because it is not friendly debugging help (which might be ok) but it is actually an unfair help in a crucial step in completing the code. [S38]
- ***Locate*:** Let's say you get an out of bounds error. You don't know why that is. You can ask your friend for possible reasons, but if you get your friend to actually **go up to your computer and point out, "your problem is here"**, that crosses the line. [S32]
- ***Debug*:** **Asking someone else for help debugging** when you have not exhausted your own resources of finding the bug. [W29]

Illegal Acts: sharing good code

- ***View*:** You've been trying to finish your code but are stuck on one of the methods and can't figure out how to do it. You call over another student and ask for help and **they let you see what they did for their method** to help you get started. [W35]
- ***Copy*:** One individual is having trouble figuring out an assignment. He has started on it and has been working on it for awhile, but cannot seem to finish the last part. He asks another student in the class for help. **He copies/pastes the last section to his program directly from the other student's program.** [S07]
- ***Send*:** Student A asks student B to debug a code. **Student A gives student B the whole code through e-mail** because it's late at the lab. Student B does debug some of the code, but there is a risk of student B keeping most of the code for himself. [W44]
- ***Write*:** You are having a problem with your code because it is having an out of bounds error and you are not sure why. You ask a friend and **he fixes the line that is messing up your code**. [S17]

Illegal Acts: coding together

- ***Pair*:** Student A needs help debugging and Student B realizes he has made a similar mistake. Both students have completed their program. **They work together to solve the bug** but student

Illegal Acts: sharing bad code

- ***View*:** Classmate A has a runtime error on his code and doesn't know what's wrong. He is about 90% done, and needs someone to **skim over his code to see what he did wrong**. He contacts his friend, classmate B, to check over his code. He sends it to Classmate B via e-mail, and just asks him to find out what's wrong and email him back. [W06]
- ***Copy*:** A scenario that would not be okay would be if the debugging involves errors in most parts of the program so that none of the program is executing. This is because then a peer reviewer would have to go through and understand all parts of the students program and would see exactly how they did their work. I think that would make it too easy and tempting **for the reviewer to copy if they hadn't started working on their project yet**. [W33]

Mitigating Circumstances

- ***Stuck*:** Student A is finished with the body of the code but when he/she runs the code the expected result does not occur. Student A has **spent a considerable amount of time trying to figure out where the bug is** and what he/she has done wrong; however, he/she is unsuccessful in fixing the program. Student A asks Student B for assistance in locating where the code is going wrong. [S63]
- ***Different Places*:** Sally, a good friend of mine, had been working on her program for a couple of days. When she compiles her code, everything is alright except for a logic error. **She wants me to check over her code when I haven't even written mine yet.** I should tell her she should look for a tutor for her problems because I'd be tempted to use some of her code. [S21]
- ***Procrastination*:** **It's late at night and the assignment is due tomorrow**, I email a classmate and ask if they can help out by sending part of the program they made to help me figure out my error and finish my code. [S60]
- ***Amount of Code*:** If someone has a code that is riddled with errors which they cannot spot and they ask for help it's ok, but as soon as they start letting the other person **rewrite parts of it beyond a line or two** it starts becoming questionable. [S09]
- ***Asking Fails*:** Let's say a person gets stuck on their code for quite some time. They **have been asking for help from fellow students, and finally the person helping gets frustrated** and lets them see their own code. The person then understood his/her mistake and used what he/she saw to fix his bug. [S18]
- ***Not exhausted resources*:** When you have **spent minimal time examining the problem yourself** and ask for help after like 5 minutes of looking at it. When you know the other person is already done and maybe willing to help push you in the right direction. [W34]

Harnessing Surprise: Tales from Students' Transformational Biographies

Lynda Thomas
Department of Computer Science
Aberystwyth University
Aberystwyth, Wales, UK
ltt@aber.ac.uk

Carol Zander
Computing and Software Systems
University of Washington Bothell
Bothell, WA, USA
zander@u.washington.edu

Anna Eckerdal
Department of Information Technology
Uppsala University
Uppsala, Sweden
Anna.Eckerdal@it.uu.se

ABSTRACT
Transformational biographies are used to shed light on situations when students have experienced 'surprise.' These biographies are examined in light of a philosophical position that surprise is useful in engendering learning, and, that as educators, we should try and set up situations in which our students experience it more often. The paper reports on a grounded-theory inspired examination of 108 students' transformational biographies for evidence of surprise. Students clearly perceived an 'anomaly or contradiction to a previous belief or understanding' in just under half of them. The paper then goes on to further identify different kinds of surprise and the triggers that caused them and concludes with suggestions for enhancing learning by capitalizing on students' surprise.

Categories and Subject Descriptors
K.3.2 [**Computers and Education**]: Computers and Information Science Education - *Computer Science Education*

General Terms
Human Factors.

Keywords
Surprise, Student Biographies, Attitudinal factors, Threshold Concepts, Transformation, Work Experience.

1. INTRODUCTION
Do students learn better if they experience 'surprise' during their learning process? And if so, how can we as educators use surprise in our teaching?

In this empirically based work, we examined written biographies collected from students in the second half of their degree programs in Sweden, Wales, and the United States. The students were asked about "transformational learning experiences", and we were interested to note that many of the experiences that they described involve a clear element of surprise. This caused us to specifically analyze the biographies for further evidence of surprise, and to dig deeper in order to determine how student surprise can be harnessed for the purpose of enhancing the learning experience. A theoretical basis for this work is discussed in Section 2. The methodology is described in Section 3 and our findings are reported in Section 4. If we accept that surprise is a useful learning tool, then what caused it in our students? This is examined further in Section 5. Section 6 comprises a discussion of how instructors can use these results to help students learn computing concepts inside and outside the classroom.

SIGCSE'10, March 10–13, 2010, Milwaukee, Wisconsin, USA.

2. BACKGROUND
This research was initially motivated by a search for *threshold concepts* in computing. In this section, we begin by discussing how surprise might be incorporated into theories of learning, and then go on to relate this to threshold concepts.

Lucas [6] discusses surprise in the context of critical reflection in accounting education, and points to moments of surprise as involving:

> ... perceptions of anomalies or contradictions ... This involves discrepancies between one's expectations and one's perceptions of an experience and a trigger event is needed. Secondly, there is a stage of appraisal. This may involve, on the one hand, a minimisation or denial or, on the other, an opening up to unknown possibilities. The third stage involves exploration. This might involve the development of new identities and role models, a public declaration of a change of state, and the testing of new ways of thinking and acting. The fourth stage requires the development of alternative perspectives.

Adler, in a philosophical paper about the use of surprise in education, defines surprise as occurring when one "recognizes an occurrence or event that is contrary to one's expectations." [1] The response to surprise that encourages learning is that one's reasoning was faulty but 'correctable.' This then provides intrinsic motivation to learning, and also helps the learner to focus their attention on important concepts.

How *can* such important concepts be identified? Meyer and Land [8] have proposed using threshold concepts as a way of characterizing particular concepts that might be used to organize the learning process. Threshold concepts are a subset of the core concepts within a discipline, and are characterized as being:

- *Transformative*: they change the way a student looks at things in the discipline
- *Integrative*: they tie together concepts in ways that were previously unknown to the student
- *Irreversible*: they are difficult for the student to unlearn
- *Potentially troublesome* (as in Perkins [10]) for students: they are conceptually difficult, alien, and/or counter-intuitive

- Often *boundary markers*: they indicate the limits of a conceptual area or the discipline itself

In previous work, it has been determined that although the idea of threshold concepts may be quite appealing, these concepts are less easy to pinpoint in computing than one might assume. A number of potential threshold concepts have been discussed, however, particularly: object-orientation and pointers/memory management in [2] and abstraction in [9]. In addition, students' experience of learning these concepts has been characterized as the 'Liminal Space', which corresponds to some of the aspects Lucas refers to above, particularly those relating to identity and change of state [3].

There seems to be synergy here with the idea of surprise. When Adler says that surprise helps the learner focus on 'important concepts' perhaps where we see surprise, we are also seeing potential threshold concepts.

Recent advances in neurology, and the use of MRI scans, have provided researchers with more evidence that at least memory and the learning of concepts is enhanced by surprise and that this has implications for teaching and learning [4]. In terms of harnessing the power of surprise in teaching and learning we may also make reference to the ideas of variation theory, as developed by Marton and others [6]. In variation theory, learning is understood as developing richer ways to see phenomena in the world. This involves seeing new features of phenomena, not discerned before. Variation theory emphasizes *variation* and *discernment* as key words in this process. A necessary, but not always sufficient condition for discerning new features is that the student has the opportunity to experience variation in the learning situation in a way that highlights these specific features.

Variation theory emphasizes that it is possible to create learning conditions that enable students to discern new features of phenomena by varying some things and keeping others invariant. Marton et al. [7 p.16–17] discuss so called *patterns of variation*. These patterns describe different combinations of systematic variation and invariance. One of the patterns, the *contrast* pattern, is explained by Thuné and Eckerdal [11] as contrasting "a phenomenon P to other related phenomena, to make it possible to discern P as a phenomenon distinct from other phenomena." Surprise can appear when students experience a distinct contrast.

3. METHODOLOGY

Data were collected as written biographies from computing students. Students were asked to identify and describe a computing concept that transformed the way they see and experience computing. Included in the instructions were two sample transformation biographies: the first talked about writing long, repetitive code, and learning about functional decomposition; the second described learning about complexity analysis. A copy of these instructions may be found in [12].

These data were collected from 108 students from 5 institutions in Sweden, the United Kingdom, and the United States. For analysis, the student biographies, where necessary, were translated into English by the researcher. Biographies were collected in a Technical Communication class at Institution A in the U.S.A. (62), in an Agile Methodologies class in the U.K. (35), in an Ethics class at Institution B in the U.S.A. (8), and from students in Sweden (3) who were not associated with a particular class.

Nearly all of the biographies were collected as a regular assignment associated with a course taken by computing majors in the second half of their computing degree programs. The students at Institution A, although in the second half of their program had only completed two programming courses; they were generally older, however, and often had industry experience. These biographies, since they were collected from a Technical Communication course, had been reviewed by the instructor for style only and were then revised by the student.

The data led the authors to consider the relationship between learning and surprise. Many students either used the words 'surprise' or 'amaze', or variations on these terms, or else their biography indicated surprise in some other way.

The emergence of theories from the data is part of a grounded theory approach that originates in the work of Glaser and Strauss [6], who outline grounded theory as a way to "[discover] theory from data systematically obtained from social research" (p. 2). Theories may emerge organically from the data through a process of collection, coding and analysis of data. In this sense, this paper then uses a grounded theory approach to discover a preliminary theory that links surprise and learning in computing.

Biographies that used obvious words were easily pulled from the others for further analysis. In addition, all the biographies were examined by at least two researchers looking for other examples of manifestations of surprise. For the latter biographies, when the rare conflict arose, two researchers worked together to consensus

The resulting 52 biographies (30 using a keyword and 22 with other indicators) were then examined more closely to determine in what *way* surprise was a factor identified by the writer. While this work has some quantitative aspects, it primarily uses qualitative research methods, specifically, a thematic approach.

4. SURPRISE IN CONTEXT

In Table 1, we present the simple quantitative analysis of which biographies used words or phrases such as 'surprise' 'opened my eyes', 'amaze', etc. and their variations. In addition we have counted the number of biographies that give an 'impression' of surprise without using specific identifiable words.

Table 1: Number of biographies exhibiting surprise

Word Used	**Number of Bios**
Surprise	6
Opened my eyes	11
Amaze	11
Epiphany	6
Others (awe, unexpected)	2
Total number of biographies with words (some had more than one word)	**30**
Number of biographies identified by 'impression' (without a specific word)	**22**

From this simple count we can see that transformation was often accompanied by surprise. Words that could have been used in a surprise sense were not counted if the context did not indicate surprise. For example, 'wonder' in the sense of 'I wondered' was not counted. The biographies that were identified by 'impression' all indicated a radical change of view. For example:

> *S2 - It was so self-evident. I don't understand how I could have missed it. Everything became so simple.*

This was important because the larger dataset had already been analyzed from the point of view of transformation [12] and the analysis presented here is different in that we looked very specifically for situations where students perceived an anomaly or something that contradicted their expectation.

After identifying which biographies to focus on, we identified the manifestations of surprise as breaking down into three main categories: surprise at an idea or concept; surprise associated with behavior or a technique; and surprise at the student's own ability to perform in a given situation.

4.1 Surprise associated with a concept

The students were asked to identify computing concepts that transformed the way they see and experience computing. In investigating what concepts were related to students' experience of surprise, a number of concepts were found. Several concepts appeared more than once, but the majority of concepts were only discussed in one biography, for example, security, binary search trees, the halting problem, and TCP/IP.

Object-orientation and concepts related to it, such as inheritance, polymorphism, encapsulation and object were by far the most common concepts mentioned. About 20 biographies discuss one or more of them.

One example where surprise is related to object-orientation is when subject 21 experienced a positive surprise when finally understanding the idea of modeling in object-orientation. This left a lasting impression:

> *S21 - My code became very long and hard to understand as just a long list of commands. After realising that this was not the right way to go about making the program I thought back to one of the first lectures I was given on Object Orientation. It then dawned on me that the classes were representing real world objects, the dog class could be thought of as an actual dog, with a name and colour represented as attributes in the class. This was a major breakthrough in the development of that worksheet.*

Similarly, subject 50 discusses inheritance:

> *S50 - While working on the assignment I was amazed by how much less code I had to write to complete the same programming project.*

With this new insight the student shows appreciation:

> *S50 - If only I had this knowledge at the beginning of the course, who knows what kind of headaches inheritance might have saved me.*

4.2 Surprise associated with behavior

Sometimes the surprise that students evinced was associated not with a concept *per se*, but with something else such as a technique, or a modification of behavior.

Biographies that mentioned a technique usually referred to it in terms of surprise at its efficacy. Students had been introduced to the technique before but that they had never seen the value of it. Designing before coding and elegance in coding were very common here:

> *S13 - This really opened my eyes to the major difference that uni was going to make on the way I coded, ... I began to see the importance of fore-thought when writing a program rather than just diving in _head-first_ and coding something that in the end could be completely replaced by something much easier and more efficient.*

It is heartening to see students eventually grasping this kind of technique. Other techniques that caused students surprise included running queries through a query analyzer, including good source code comments, and using Open Source Software:

> *S79 - It was almost 300 times faster than my previous query. The performance increased exponentially and I was enchanted by the improvement I made.*
> *S93 - The uncommented four page code took me twelve straight hours to figure out what the program was trying to do, and how to make it compile correctly. In contrast, the commented six page source code took me two hours.*
> *S85 - For years, I happily ran their inefficient, proprietary, closed-source software, oblivious to alternatives...my eyes were opened to alternatives, and I began to experiment.*

4.3 Surprise with student's own performance

Some students were surprised that programming was easier than they had expected, for example:

> *S8 - I really did surprise myself though, and I learned enough in just a few hours to create the framework of a working interactive website with secure login.*

Others discovered that they were not as good as they had thought:

> *S69 - Within the first couple days I realized I was in way over my head. I had spent my time on a Windows machine playing video games, and thought I knew everything because I could update a video card driver. ... I knew so little I was pretty sure I was going to be fired. This was surprising and scary for me, because I came into the job thinking I was settling for a position I would quickly get bored with.*

The students quoted above continued on in Computer Science with success. The negative experience reported by S69 caused him to reevaluate his preparation for the job: *"It has been almost two years since I started and I have absorbed as much knowledge as possible in that time."*

A few students mentioned Internet or gaming communities and the power of social involvement in drawing them into computing:

> *S57 - I decided to go try out this new concept called ``chat rooms" and when I entered there were hundreds of people chatting away about anything and everything...*
> *This form of socialization was very new and exciting and it was the beginning of my passion for computers and internet.*

One student, however, reported a different result from his surprise experience, one that made him think about his career:

S107 - Before this experience, I thought I was never `bad" at anything. In my experience in academics…I was never truly ``stuck" at any assignments. or projects. ... because of that, I was never forced to find something that I was good at doing. However, this experience of failing to implement a complete program, ...made me think about what I actually wanted to do for my career.

5. TRIGGERS FOR SURPRISE

We investigated where students were and what they were doing at the time of their surprise. The list of these triggers is not unexpected:

- Instructors
- Comparing to previously-learned material
- Working on a project or other work
- Peer pressure
- At a job
- Something external (not job or school)

But digging deeper gives us insight into the triggers for their surprise. **Instructors** make an impression on students. Some were quoted, e.g., *"There's no point in reinventing the wheel all over again"* in the context of inheritance. After pointing out that an instructor showed the comparison of a O(n) vs. O(log n) algorithm, a student relays surprised delight: *"I had no idea that such a process could be optimized to such a great extent."* Other instructors made an impression as though they were personally responsible: *"Then, to my relief, my professor introduced me to the concept of model-view-controller […]."* Moreover, professors can be a catalyst for students' imagination:

S92 - Earlier this year, I sat in […], trying hard to listen to the professor's dissertation on the fundamentals of C++ pointers. As I listened, I began to visualize the world of computing differently. ... In my mind, I could see a massive, interconnected web of arrows pointing around a great room with many boxes. The boxes were of all different sizes and shapes -- each with its own functionality.

While most of the triggers that directly came from instructors are seen positively, there is often a fine line. One student clearly relays this: *"Following the instructor made it easy to do the assignment, but I really didn't know what I was doing at first."*

Students displayed surprise with relation to **previous things they had learned.** Many students who had learned procedural programming first, commented positively on object-oriented programming: *"This new concept was completely unlike the disorganization my previous efforts epitomized."* and *"Sure, object-oriented design had been used for several years before I discovered it, but for me, it was as if I had just invented the wheel or something. Eureka!"*

One student had a major revelation when learning about the architecture of processors and how logical gates can be arranged to create complex circuitry:

S43 - I had always been confused by how the programs I wrote could ultimately be reduced to nothing but electrical signals, but I suddenly saw how you could create a simple adder.

Another student, upon seeing the proof of the Halting problem's undecidability, said it *"changed my view of computers and their capabilities."*

Projects were often catalysts. An assignment to simulate a traffic intersection and another to simulate a lunar lander helped students understand the interaction of objects in object-oriented programming. Similarly, a student found the modularity of a Sudoku problem-solving program *"amazing"* and a group project solving a Trivial Pursuit team quiz application highlighted the importance of object-oriented concepts.

Working on recursion, one student describes how writing out a visual representation helped: *"Writing the function calls and blocks of memory allocated out on paper finally allowed me to understand."*

Peer pressure was a trigger. A student describes how a classmate *"was horrified"* upon seeing the student's finished code and says *"after seeing my classmate's expression and his code, I was truly embarrassed […]."* Another student came to fully appreciate software design practices after **tutoring a peer**. Previously, he *"lazily"* completed the required design documents after the coding, but came to understand the purpose of designing and when *"the design process was taken seriously,"* less time was spent on the assignments.

Triggers also occurred through a **job**. One student used inheritance to enhance the security of their web-based application. Another realized *"I had no experience with important website applications like IIS, Apache, or MySQL."* And another discovered artists who were incorporating computer programs into their artwork and realized that *"artistic creativity also exists in computer programming."*

Lastly, triggers could be **external** to anything that happened at school or work. For one student a network crash forced a learning experience that eventually led to being *"reborn"* with the knowledge of how networks communicated. Another student was *"excited"* to do *"surfing on the Internet Highway."* Still another had an *"epiphany"* while working on a hobby project to convert an old program over to C++, realizing inheritance and polymorphism could be used to easily manipulate data.

6. DISCUSSION

To some extent surprise is serendipitous. One student noted this himself *"Was it my randomness that one class had become my stepping stone in my life?"* But, as educators, how can we harness it in our teaching and curriculum design?

A surprising suggestion from the new literature on brain activity is to **begin lectures with something novel** "…novelty seems to promote memory. This finding gives teachers a potential tool for structuring their lessons more effectively. Although most teachers start a lesson by going over material from the previous class before moving on to new subject matter, they should probably do just the opposite: start with surprising new information and then review the older material."[4] There is some evidence of this in the biographies. Students noted when something that an instructor did "opened their eyes"; it would be interesting to know at what point in a lecture this occurred.

Some things instructors already know and try to do – incorporate **meaningful challenging assignments** in our courses. Can we do more? Students react differently to different projects. While some students react to games, others prefer practical applications, so the best compromise is to vary the assignments at an attempt to appeal to all students.

As faculty, we also know how much is learned by teaching, by the action of **explaining out loud to someone else**. In the biographies students relay gaining much from peers in different ways. Can this be productively channeled? Group projects facilitate peers learning from each other. Having to discuss problems forces students to discuss issues out loud that they might otherwise only mull over in their heads. Also, having undergraduate assistants for lower-division courses allows students to tutor.

What peers think about students and their work appears to have an impact and therefore peer interaction can provide a strong motivation to change. However, this is a delicate situation. On the one hand, peer interaction is potentially very effective, but if students may feel embarrassed in these situations. As teachers, we must provide students a comfortable atmosphere where they can trust each other with their work. For example, code could be reviewed anonymously.

The evidence showing surprise for students **starting with procedural programming and changing to object-oriented** is powerful. This could be interpreted as a reason to teach a fundamentals approach first. Without comparison, students may not understand or appreciate the need for what they perceive as complexities of the object-oriented paradigm. One student describes this sentiment as *"Love at first sight"* with object-oriented programming. He describes how satisfaction with basic data types did not last and eventually it was difficult to keep track of all the variables. Fortunately, *"the most exciting programming class"* on object-oriented programming gave him the tools.

The **contrast pattern**, discussed in Section 2, is a useful tool for introducing surprise [11]. Teachers can use this pattern in a different context to help students discern important aspects of the learning goals that otherwise might be less obvious. In varying some aspects of the experience, students can be led to learn through experiencing surprise. For example, one subject, in discussing inheritance, described an assignment: "*The final class assignment was to take a prior programming project and rewrite the program by only using pre-existing classes provided by Sun Microsystems. [...] While working on the assignment I was amazed by how much less code I had to write to complete the same programming project"* This contrast helped the student to discern one important idea behind inheritance.

Similar experiences were reported by the students quoted in Section 4.2. One instructor assigned students the problem of debugging two programs, one commented and one without – the uncommented code took six times longer to debug.

There is certainly evidence in this research that what we do as instructors, in introducing new concepts, setting assignments, and supervising work experience and peer tutoring, makes a difference; particularly if we can encourage our students to experience surprise, leading to a desire to correct their faults and hence providing intrinsic motivation to learning.

7. ACKNOWLEDGMENTS

Thanks to our students for allowing us to use their work, to Chris Loftus for collecting biographies, and to Jonas Boustedt, Robert McCartney, Jan Erik Moström, and Kate Sanders for their work on the initial analysis. Thanks also to Uppsala University and to Umeå University for physical and electronic meeting places.

8. REFERENCES

[1] Adler, J.E. 2008. Surprise. Educational Theory, 58(2) (May 2008). 49-173.

[2] Boustedt, J., Eckerdal, A., McCartney, R., Moström, J. E., Ratcliffe, M., Sanders, K., and Zander, C. 2007. Threshold concepts in computer science: do they exist and are they useful?. In Proceedings of the 38th SIGCSE Technical Symposium on Computer Science, SIGCSE '07. ACM, New York, NY, 504-508.
DOI = http://doi.acm.org/10.1145/1227310.1227482

[3] Eckerdal, A., McCartney, R., Moström, J. E., Sanders, K., Thomas, L., and Zander, C. 2007. From Limen to Lumen: computing students in liminal spaces. In Proceedings of the Third international Workshop on Computing Education Research, ICER '07. ACM, New York, NY, 123-132.
DOI = http://doi.acm.org/10.1145/1288580.1288597

[4] Fenker, D. and Schütze, H. 2008. Learning by Surprise. Scientific American. (Dec 17, 2008).

[5] Glaser, B.G. and Strauss, A.L. The discovery of Grounded Theory: Strategies for qualitative research. Aldine: Chicago, 1967.

[6] Lucas, U. 2008. Being "pulled up short": Creating moments ofsurprise and possibility in accounting education. Critical Perspectives on Accounting 19 (2008) 383–403.

[7] Marton, F. and Tsui, A. 2004. Classroom Discourse and the Space of Learning. Lawrence Erlbaum Ass., Mahwah, NJ.

[8] Meyer, J. H. and Land, R. 2005. Threshold concepts and troublesome knowledge (2): Epistemological considerations and a conceptual framework for teaching and learning. Higher Education, 49 (2005), 373–388.

[9] Moström, J. E., Boustedt, J., Eckerdal, A., McCartney, R., Sanders, K., Thomas, L., and Zander, C. 2008. Concrete examples of abstraction as manifested in students' transformative experiences. In Proceeding of the Fourth international Workshop on Computing Education Research, ICER '08. ACM, New York, NY, 125-136.
DOI=http://doi.acm.org/10.1145/1404520.1404533

[10] Perkins, D. 1999. The many faces of constructivism. Educational Leadership, 57(3) (1999), 6–11.

[11] Thuné, M. and Eckerdal, A. 2009. Variation Theory Applied to Students' Conceptions of Computer Programming. European Journal of Engineering Education. [to appear].

[12] Zander, C., Boustedt, J., McCartney, R., Moström, J. E., Sanders, K., and Thomas, L. 2009. Student transformations: are they computer scientists yet?. In Proceedings of the Fifth international Workshop on Computing Education Research Workshop, ICER '09. ACM, New York, NY, 129-140.
DOI = http://doi.acm.org/10.1145/1584322.1584337

Collaborative Research in Computer Science Education: A Case Study

Sue Fitzgerald
Metropolitan State University
Information and Computer Sciences
St. Paul, MN 55106 USA
sue.fitzgerald@metrostate.edu

Brian Hanks
Fort Lewis College
Computer Science Info. Sys.
Durango, CO, 81301 USA
hanks_b@fortlewis.edu

Renée McCauley
College of Charleston
Computer Science
Charleston, SC 29424 USA
mccauleyr@cofc.edu

ABSTRACT
This paper describes a process for establishing and maintaining a computer science education research group. Its purpose is to tell the story of one long-standing group, describe the benefits afforded by collaborative research groups and provide advice about how to form such a group. The intended audience is faculty members at teaching-intensive institutions who wish to establish or revive a research program in computer science education. We discuss establishing and maintaining a computer science education research agenda in a teaching-intensive environment.

Categories and Subject Descriptors
K.3.2 [**Computer and Information Science Education**]: Computer Science Education

General Terms
Human Factors.

Keywords
Collaborative research, computer science education research, case study, qualitative research

1. INTRODUCTION
For those of us who genuinely care about teaching and learning, teaching institutions are rewarding environments in which to work. Computer science education research is often valued at such institutions because of the teaching focus. However, due to high concomitant teaching loads and service expectations, it can be a challenge to maintain a scholarship program. We conquered this obstacle by forming a multi-institutional collaborative research group (the Debug Group). We have met weekly, via VoIP, since 2005. As a group, we've 1) studied debugging, mindsets, pair programming and qualitative research methods, 2) organized an ITiCSE working group and two NSF-sponsored workshops and 3) published nine papers. Our goal is to offer this as a possible model for other educators who, like us, might be unable to persist in their research without the support of such a group. We have found group collaboration to be both professionally and personally rewarding.

SIGCSE'10, March 10–13, 2010, Milwaukee, Wisconsin, USA.

We use a case study research approach to relate our experiences. Using source documents including emails, meeting minutes and semi-structured interview questions, we reconstructed the history of our research group and tell its story here. We include our reflections on both the challenges and benefits of our collaboration. Section 2 describes our methodology and Section 3 outlines our history. Sections 4 and 5 describe the benefits and drawbacks of belonging to such a group and Section 6 provides practical advice for organizing a collaborative group and pursuing research in computer science education.

2. METHODOLOGY
The case study is one of the primary qualitative research approaches. When using this approach, researchers observe and interview participants and examine documents and reports in order to "understand an issue or problem using the case as a specific illustration" [2, p. 73]. A few key themes which shed light on the case are identified. The researcher describes the case in detail and discusses the themes. At the end, he or she reflects on the lessons learned. Context is important [5].

Qualitative research projects commonly collect large amounts of data from a few participants. The participants are actively involved in the research and may be asked to verify the accuracy of the report before it is published [2]. The goals of qualitative research methods are to explore, to generate insight and to create theory rather than to prove hypotheses. Because we want to illustrate the value of collaborative research groups, describe how one such group succeeded and encourage others to collaborate, we chose to tell the story of our ongoing research collaboration as a case study.

In order to recreate the process of forming and maintaining our collaborative research group, we examined minutes from weekly meetings (October, 2005 through August, 2009) and semi-annual face-to-face meetings, traced email conversations and solicited responses to these questions from eleven group members.

- How did you come to join the Debug Research Group?
- Why did you seek out research partners and form or join this group?
- What benefits have you seen from being part of the group?
- Besides the "Debugging" series of papers, what papers or other scholarly achievements have resulted from your participation in this group?
- Have your research practices improved/disintegrated/stayed the same as a result of participating? How and why?
- If you are no longer 'officially' part of the group, why did you leave? What impact has being a member of the group had on you, since you left?

- What interesting thoughts do you have to share with others with regard to this group?
- What practical advice would you give to someone who is interested in forming a similar sort of research group?
- Is there anything else you would like to say?

One group member attended meetings only briefly and declined to answer the questions. Another member who attended for only a few months responded but did not directly answer the questions. In all, nine members responded in detail. Responses to the questions were analyzed by the three authors using thematic analysis. The authors identified themes and argued their analyses to consensus.

3. HISTORY

The Debug Group has been a very successful collaboration for its members. But this didn't occur overnight. How did this group form, evolve and work together to achieve this success?

3.1 Group Formation

The Debug Group first met in October, 2005, but our story began earlier. All of the original members of the group previously participated in the Bootstrapping [1] or Scaffolding [6] projects. In 2002, Sally Fincher, Marian Petre and Josh Tenenberg set out to create a "community of practice of researchers in computer science education" by organizing the Bootstrapping Research in Computer Science Education project [4]. Fincher, Petre and Tenenberg led two intensive workshops on the design, conduct and management of computer science education research. In the year between the workshops, participants collected data for a joint multi-institutional study. The Bootstrapping project was designed to "foster a community of discourse, in which ideas can be generated, tested, examined and extended" [1]. They repeated the experiment in 2003 and 2004, calling it Scaffolding Research in Computer Science Education [6]. Both the Bootstrapping and Scaffolding projects were highly successful; they spawned a community of scholars eager to engage in computer science education research.

During the SIGCSE 2005 conference, members of the Bootstrapping and Scaffolding groups met to share research ideas. Attendees were encouraged to find others with like interests. One participant expressed interest in novice debugging but noted that extensive research literature existed. She recommended a study of the literature before engaging in debugging research. Later, at an informal working day before ICER 2005, a research agenda was developed and the Debug Research Group subsequently began to meet via teleconference. Originally 10-15 people expressed interest in the group. Of those, eight formed a core group who met regularly.

Our initial goals were to:

- review literature on debugging, focused primarily on novice debugging; secondarily comparing novices with experts; not including debugging environments per se but including any qualitative or quantitative assessments of debugging environments;
- publish our findings as a literature review;
- look for a feasible study to replicate.

We were initially motivated to join the group for a variety of reasons, including both an intrinsic interest in the topic as well as an interest in working with this particular group of people:

> I was interested in the topic of debugging and this seemed like an enjoyable way to work in this area.

> My research interest is novice programmers, and debugging is a very important skill that many novices do poorly. So the interest area of the research group was of interest to me.

> I knew about the group because I knew one of the members very well, and when I was invited to join [in late 2007] I jumped at the chance.

Some participants felt isolated at their home institutions:

> I wanted to work with [another participant] since our [earlier] collaboration ... was fun. To be honest I wasn't as interested in Debugging as I am in many things. I am isolated in my job and working with other people gives me the chance to talk about issues, do research etc.

> I did this for two reasons: 1) to keep me making progress, 2) to have some people to work with, which I enjoy. There was no one at my institution who I wanted to work with.

Other motives for participating were mentioned as well:

> The larger group gave us a wider range of students, larger numbers for finding subjects, and more people with whom the work could be shared.

> I recall that we did decide to start with reading and literature review and I thought that was a great excuse to force myself to read background papers BEFORE doing a project, rather than after.

3.2 Group Process

Our group used web-based teleconferencing software for one-hour weekly meetings. The teleconferencing facility permitted voice and video transmissions and included a shared white board for note taking and diagramming. We disabled video transmissions for performance reasons.

We designated one participant as meeting organizer and discussion leader. During the meetings, reading homework was assigned to each participant. Each week participants presented summaries of their assigned papers. These summaries evolved into an annotated bibliography which later served as the basis of our published literature review on novice debugging. The summaries and weekly minutes were initially posted to a website. In 2008, an interactive wiki which could be edited by any group member replaced the website.

3.3 Evolution of the Group

Our initial group of eight members met weekly as a reading group for over a year. Two additional participants attended meetings briefly. One did not find the group to be a good fit; the other was unable to attend at the inconvenient local time. Another group member stopped attending after one year, "because of other commitments. It wasn't that the group was low on my priorities, but that I felt that I wasn't consistently pulling my weight."

Three other group members left in 2008, for a variety of reasons:

> I did not have time to be as functional a member of the group as I felt necessary to stay in the group. Also, the topic of the group was starting to drift from debugging and, while also interesting, it gave me an excuse to pull back.

As the only European member I sometimes felt a bit out of the loop, and my other research group had several Europeans, so it was easier for me to meet with in person and I thought it would be more likely to lead to things European, grants, colleagues, kudos at work etc. ... We were at a place where it seemed like I could bow out easily, so I did.

I left due to overload of research projects and reduced enjoyment in weekly meetings. ... Also, at the time, the group was in a "re-start" phase, where exactly what we wanted to do next was unclear.

A new group member joined in 2008. At present there are five active group members.

3.4 Publications and Other Activities

Collectively, we've been quite productive.

As mentioned, we began by studying the novice debugging literature to learn about previous research and to pinpoint what we wanted to investigate further. We identified papers of interest and kept a list of them. When we presented paper summaries in the weekly meetings, we rated some as "must read" for everyone. Many papers led to the identification of other readings, which were added to our list. After many months of reading, we organized our summaries into a literature review, which was published in the journal *Computer Science Education*.

As we read, we identified studies we thought were suitable for replication while simultaneously generating and recording our own ideas. Concurrent with the writing of our literature review, we began to design and implement a research study of novice debugging[1]. We planned for one semester, collected data the next semester and then met, face-to-face, for four days to analyze our data and organize a report on our findings. We spent the next two semesters working remotely, followed by another multi-day face-to-face meeting to further analyze the data and write-up our findings. The results of this study were published in two journals (*Computer Science Education* and *IEEE Transactions on Education*) and in two conferences (SIGCSE and ITiCSE). We also organized an ITiCSE working group in 2007 that was related to debugging.

Our study of novice debugging led to many discussions about how novices learn to program and about retention in computing. One of our members encountered Carol Dweck's work on mindsets [3] and the effect that student mindset has on persistence in a course or major. Additionally, as we discussed attitudes toward programming and how they affect persistence and success, our reading broadened. The discovery of the mindset research led a subset of the group to teach students about mindsets and to conduct a simple survey to see if student mindsets had changed as a result. We learned that the simple intervention did not produce the change we had hoped for, but it did lead to useful information which was published as an ICER conference paper. This study led several of us to change the way we speak to students about how they should expect to learn challenging, new material.

Thinking more about novices and specifically about those who survived their introductory programming course, we asked the survivors to provide advice to future novice programmers. This advice was presented at the SIGCSE conference.

We also published research on student attitudes toward programming in which we were able to compare attitudes of students learning to program in different languages or under different teaching models (traditional, media computation, etc.).

As we dug deeper into our investigations of novices, we found it necessary to learn more about how to conduct good educational research. Our backgrounds as computer scientists, we discovered, did not always prepare us for the research we wanted to conduct. With external support we organized two workshops: a statistics bootcamp and a workshop on qualitative research methods, both held in conjunction with ICER conferences. These workshops brought in many like-minded researchers in addition to our group.

4. BENEFITS

Group members identified many benefits of participation. Perhaps the most commonly cited benefit was that participation in the group made it easier to get things done and to make progress on research projects:

Being in the group helps me keep my research moving forward, because the weekly meetings provide 'mini-deadlines' that help motivate me to accomplish something.

The regular meetings force me to do something research-related every week. Without this group, or something similar, I would focus almost exclusively on teaching.

Related to this was the notion of sharing the workload, especially when outside commitments interfered with research time:

Having different people be able to take 'the lead' in time critical things (editing a paper, etc.) when personal teaching deadlines keep me from doing something.

It also turns out to be easier to hit deadlines because there are others around to pick up the ball when you cannot.

Group members also discussed how being in the group has improved their research:

You develop better research studies because more people critique them.

My research practices have improved. I have learned what makes for good/bad data and good/bad questions. What makes a study low or high cost is clearer to me.

I've learned a lot about educational theories that I would not know otherwise, and I've used research techniques, particularly qualitative ones, that I would probably not otherwise [have] used.

Some members noted that participation in the group made them more productive.

Another common benefit cited by the participants was the sense of community that developed, and how being in the group helped members avoid isolation:

The group provides a set of people to talk to about CS Ed research. As I am in a small department in a college that is geographically isolated, this is extremely important to me.

[1] This study was supported, in part, by an NSF grant that covered data transcription costs and travel costs for two face-to-face meetings.

> I have no research colleagues in education at my own institution, so the weekly meetings were great in terms of giving me a community to belong to and that 'spoke the same language'.

Several members felt that participation in the group allowed them to work on larger projects:

> The larger group gave us a wider range of students, larger numbers for finding subjects, and more people with whom the work could be shared.

> ...gathering much larger data sets than I would be able to alone, and multi-institutional ones.

> I teach at a small institution, so one of the great benefits is being able to collaborate on larger multi-institutional studies.

The research led to changes in teaching:

> I think this has helped broaden my perspective and also led to improvements in my teaching.

> I would take suggestions and ideas from our discussions and immediately incorporate them into my everyday teaching.

Finally, participating in a group is fun!

> Our weekly meeting is often the highlight of my week.

> I enjoy the meetings - it has added to my social life!

> Paper writing by committee can be fun and easy.

5. CHALLENGES

There have been a few challenges along the way. As time passed, we've struggled a bit to stay focused. Progress slowed at times as we discussed what to investigate next.

> As the group evolved, so did our interests. Some of the group members were very busy with other commitments and several were engaged in research projects with other partners. I think the group was just tired of reading about debugging so we started exploring several different ideas. We became more fragmented and less focused on debugging specifically. At that point, several group members left. Those remaining were a bit fatigued and it's taken us a while to refocus.

Technological support is key to meeting productively across long distances. Our experiences with teleconferencing software have been stressful at times as we attempt to communicate from a variety of platforms, operating systems, browsers and locations. It is not uncommon for one or more participants to have problems hearing or speaking during meetings. Despite the technical challenges, we regret that our current software product has been discontinued. We expect to invest both time and effort in finding and learning its replacement.

Finding a commonly acceptable meeting time is our largest ongoing challenge. As discussed earlier, having a weekly meeting is important to maintain progress and to provide a sense of community. However, finding a common time is problematic. We reschedule the weekly meeting at the beginning of every academic term in order to find a time that works for everyone. Often, someone has to leave a few minutes early to prepare for class, or has the meeting occur during their lunch hour.

Originally, the group included members from outside of North America. However, the wide range of time zones led to very inconvenient meeting times for some members:

> Right now I don't remember if that meant that the meetings would be at 23:00 - 24:00 or 24:00 - 01:00 my time but the end result was that before I was able to go to sleep the clock would be 01:00 or 02:00 (wind-down time) ... which meant that I would get 4 or 5 hours sleep those days.

6. ADVICE

Having persevered as a group since 2005, we offer the following guidance to colleagues who may be interested in traveling a similar path. This guidance is as much about being successful in education-based research as it is in being successful as a group.

6.1 Distributed collaboration

Our productivity is due, in great part, to our effectiveness as a group. We believe that the following advice will allow others to form similarly effective research groups.

Be active in searching out others with interests similar to your own. Research partners provide motivation and keep us on task. When we have spoken at meetings such as the CRA-W Mentoring workshop about our experiences, several participants expressed an interest in forming similar groups, so the question is, how do you find collaborators? Potential collaborators attend SIGCSE symposia and often participate in BOFs, ITiCSE conferences and working groups, CCSC conferences and NSF-sponsored workshops. They also read the SIGCSE list. Intensive workshops are good places to make lasting connections.

Establish a regular meeting time. How can a group keep going, despite the daily pressures of teaching that swamp us all? Our group meets for one hour each week. Our weekly meeting motivates us to set personal deadlines and make progress. Meeting times may change from semester to semester, as teaching schedules change. We recommend weekly or bi-weekly meetings.

Determine a meeting interaction-strategy. Our meetings are democratic, but we do depend on a leader to establish the meeting agenda, keep and post minutes and assign action items. Because teleconferencing requires a higher than normal degree of respectful listening, we find it useful for our leader to moderate our discussion, bringing us back on-topic when needed. Other groups manage successfully without a specified leader. Be flexible, the appropriate interaction-strategy may have to be determined over time.

Set goals. At the start of each term, we agree on goals and set deadlines for various activities.

Be flexible. As busy, engaged teachers and researchers, we juggle multiple demands. The demands vary over time and from person to person. As a group, we've come to realize that each individual's contribution will vary from project to project. Members engage most fully with those projects which match their interests and availability. We keep multiple projects going in parallel so projects are often at different stages of evolution. The leadership role changes from project to project.

Use collaboration tools. The Internet and collaborative technology have made it possible for us to work together effectively. As noted above, we use a VoIP teleconferencing program for our weekly meetings. Other technologies that we find useful include Google docs for maintaining shared documents and spreadsheets, CiteULike (www.citeulike.org) for managing citations and web sites and wikis for organizing our experimental resources. These tools facilitate sharing and help ensure that we are all using the same version of documents or data.

Meet face-to-face at least once a year. We meet annually during the SIGCSE symposium and other conferences if several of us attend. These face-to-face meetings revitalize the group and add an enjoyable social element. We were fortunate enough to receive external funding for two intensive four-day face-to-face meetings in 2007 and 2008, where we were analyzed data, wrote-up results and made plans for the future. These intensive meetings were highly productive.

Enjoy your research collaboration. Our group members continue to enjoy each other although some group members have moved on to other topics or groups.

6.2 Education-based research

When we discuss education research, we mean empirical research related to learning, teaching methods, tools and learning environments, rather than experiential reports on pedagogy or classroom practice. In particular, computer science education research investigates educational practice within the context of teaching computer science. Our experiences suggest useful advice on doing computer science education research well, in addition to the practicalities for forming and running a group.

Learn about qualitative research methods. Over the past thirty years or so, educational research has evolved to include qualitative as well as quantitative explorations. Quantitative research, such as experiments with control and treatment groups, is useful for determining whether a pedagogical technique or tool works. However, it does not offer insight into why or how things works; this is where qualitative research comes into play. Qualitative methods are more focused on the participant's view of a situation, rather than placing them into artificial or contrived experimental situations [2].

Trained as computer scientists, we were familiar with quantitative methods but had little exposure to qualitative ones. To fill this gap, we read about and discussed these techniques as a group. One group member took an education research course at her university. We also organized a workshop so that we and others could learn from an expert.

Find a local statistician. For quantitative research projects, having a contact or a group member who is comfortable with statistical techniques is very helpful. We found it especially helpful to have access to such a person when critically analyzing published literature as well as our own findings.

Pick a topic of interest and start reading. Problem identification happens naturally in an educational setting. We found our research questions when we observed problems among our students, struggled with techniques for teaching a concept, or realized we were dissatisfied with results at the end of a course. We picked topics we truly cared about and did not limit ourselves to reading only computer science journals. The other sciences have well-established education research journals and conferences from which we learned.

Keep an annotated bibliography. The natural place to start, in attempting to solve a problem, is to review the literature and look for previously identified solutions to it. Our practice is to write a brief summary of everything we read – it helps us keep the information organized (and not forgotten) and in more than one instance has formed the basis of the background research for a paper or grant proposal. Through review of the literature, we have found studies that we wanted to replicate or refute.

Do not assume that everything published is good. We critically assess the research that we read. Not all published research is of high quality or worthy of replication. Building on existing work is necessary, but it is important that the research that we build upon be valid. We constantly question procedures and conclusions that are not convincing.

7. CONCLUSION

Participation in the Debug Group has been incredibly rewarding. We have learned a lot about students' struggles, motivations, and attitudes, we've become better researchers and we have published extensively. By focusing our research on issues in computer science education, we believe that we have also become better teachers.

We hope that our experiences might serve as a model for other computer scientists who would like to conduct education-based research, but find it difficult to do in teaching-oriented institutions.

8. ACKNOWLEDGMENTS

Our thanks go to the present and former members of the Debug Research Group for generously sharing their time and opinions and to Jan Erik Moström and Umeå University, Sweden, for graciously allowing us to use their web-based Marratech teleconferencing facility. Our collaboration, research and other activities were supported in part by two NSF grants, DUE #0122560 and DUE #0923592, for which we are grateful.

9. REFERENCES

[1] Bootstrapping Research in Computer Science Education, http://depts.washington.edu/bootstrp/ (last accessed Aug. 30, 2009).

[2] John W. Creswell, J. 2007. Qualitative Inquiry & Research Design: Choosing Among Five Approaches, Sage Publications.

[3] Dweck, C. S. 1999. Self-Theories: Their role in motivation, personality and development. Taylor & Francis.

[4] Fincher, S. and Tenenberg, J. 2006. Using Theory to Inform Capacity-Building: Bootstrapping Communities of Practice in Computer Science Education Research, Journal of Engineering Education 95, 4 (Oct. 2006), 265-278.

[5] Patton, M. Q. 1990. Qualitative evaluation and research methods. Newbury Park, CA: Sage.

[6] Scaffolding Research in Computer Science Education, http://depts.washington.edu/srcse/ (last accessed Aug. 30, 2009).

Development and Application of a Web-based Programming Learning System with LED Display Kits

Seok-Ju Chun
Seoul National University of Education
1650, Socho-dong, Seocho-gu, Seoul, Korea
chunsj@snue.ac.kr

Jungwoo Ryoo
The Pennsylvania State University-Altoona
147 LRC 3000 Ivyside Park, Altoona, PA 16601
jryoo@psu.edu

ABSTRACT
This paper describes a new programming learning system. It consists of a Web-based flowchart application and Light Emitting Diode (LED) display kits. The LED kits produce various animations or static images according to a flow chart. The flowchart tool allows students to manipulate program elements through a Graphical User Interface (GUI). Survey results show that the proposed system makes learning how to program less challenging and more interesting for beginners. Encouraged by these initial findings, the authors are developing a system with add-on features including sensor accessory options and compatibility with well known LEGO® products.

Categories and Subject Descriptors
K.3.2 [**Computer and Information Science Education**]: Computer Science Education

General Terms
Algorithms, Experimentation

Keywords
Programming, Flowchart, Web-based Learning, LED Display Kit

1. INTRODUCTION
Early programming education helps nurture prolific and creative software developers who can make significant contributions to our increasingly information-centric global economy. Teaching beginners how to program presents a great challenge since a student must have an experience that goes well beyond simply learning the syntax of a programming language. However, students tend to spend most of their time struggling with syntax errors rather than solving a problem [6].

Students of non-English speaking countries have even more difficulty in becoming skillful in programming languages such as Visual Basic, C or Java, because they are forced to write their programs using English statements and reserved words. Therefore, a visual programming language based on flowcharting may greatly improve their learning effectiveness by allowing them to bypass some of the language-related obstacles as a non-English speaking person.

Several tools provide flowchart-based programming environments [2, 3, 5, 7, 10]. All these tools claim that they are effective in reducing the cognitive burden of programming learning by shrinking the conceptual distance between actions in the real world and programming. Among them, RAPTOR [3] allows students to create programs by combining basic flowchart symbols and an environment that visually displays the location of the currently executing symbol and the contents of all variables. RAPTOR has many new features compared to its predecessors. Nevertheless, the existing tools including RAPTOR are designed mainly for college students and inappropriate for K-12 students.

This paper introduces a new programming learning system geared toward K-12 students and the students of non-English speaking countries. The learning system consists of a Web-based flowchart application and an LED display kit. Students can display static outputs (e.g., LED lights turned on diagonally from left to right) or animations after creating a flowchart by dragging and dropping icons representing different program elements. The LED display kit acts as an output device that displays images according to a set of instructions automatically generated by the online flowchart program. Our system adopts the problem-based learning (PBL) approach [8] that encourages students to solve a well defined problem and to learn on their own during their attempt to find a solution to the problem.

The remainder of this paper is organized as follows. The LED display kit is described briefly in section 2. Section 3 discusses our fully developed Web-based flowchart application. Section 4 presents the results of our survey administered among diverse student groups to measure the effectiveness of our new programming learning system. Section 5 concludes this paper with a discussion of our future research plan.

2. LED DISPLAY KIT
A light emitting diode (LED) is a semiconductor diode that emits light when electrically biased in the forward direction of the *p-n* junction [9]. Nowadays LEDs are popular in many applications such as traffic signals and electronic display boards due to their

low price and relatively lower maintenance cost. The LED display kit consists of an 8×8 LED matrix panel, a microprocessor (CPU), and a serial communication module. Figure 1 shows the system architecture of our LED display kit. The LED display kit, an 8×8 dot matrix produces a visual output as instructed by the code generated by the Web flowchart application.

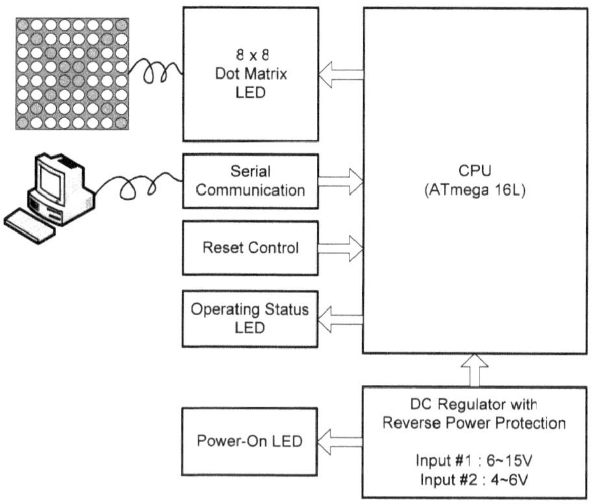

Figure 1. System Architecture of the LED Display Kit

Each row of the 8×8 LEDs represents 8 bits in a binary number system, and thus it can display values between 0 and 255. For instance, assuming that an input number of the LED display kit is 10001111_2, the corresponding row of the LED panel is lighted as follows: on, off, off, off, on, on, on, and on). Note that the LED panel has 64 LEDs, and therefore the LED display kit can produce 2^{64} different patterns. Figure 2 shows an example (letter X) of the many possible outcomes and a photo taken during a programming class in an elementary school.

Although the program output can also be displayed to a standard monitor, using the LED display kit has many advantages over the use of a regular computer screen due to the following reasons:

- Students appear to be much more engaged in their activities when they instantly see, on our LED display kit, the results of algorithms they create via the Web flowchart tool. Particularly, the LED display kit seems to invoke the curiosity of the students due to its novel appearance.

- Students can also arrange multiple LED display kits into a bigger display to produce a mosaic effect, more complex shapes, or animations. This feature of the LED display kit encourages collaborative learning and is not possible when using a computer monitor

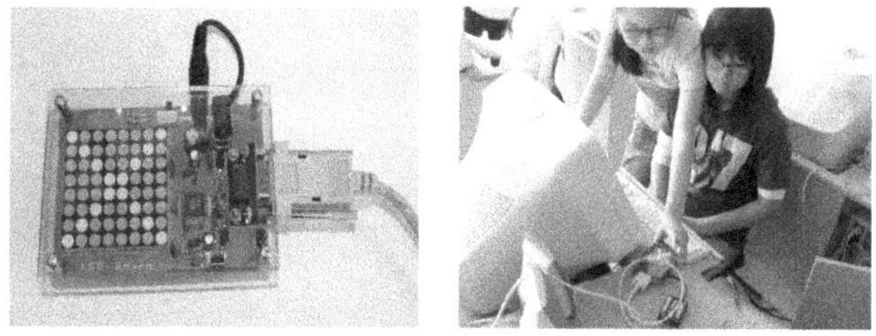

Figure 2. LED Display Kit and Programming Class

3. WEB-BASED FLOWCHART SYSTEM

The Web-based flowchart system (also referred to as Web-flowchart) has been implemented in Microsoft Visual Basic 6.0 and HTML 4.0. The core ActiveX module of the flowchart system is automatically downloaded into client computers when users visit our programming education Web site (http://www.ilogic.kr) for the first time. The Web-flowchart supports basic programming constructs such as variables, if/else, loops, one-dimensional arrays, and functions. We developed two courses using the proposed system: one for beginners and the other for advanced users. In the beginner's course, a learner is allowed to use only the first row (8 dots equivalent to 1 byte of information) of the display apparatus and a wait-timer command. Each physical LED light can be turned on by either selecting the check boxes in a Web-flowchart LED icon or using a variable initialized with a value. With this basic setup, students can already create a simple animation. For example, they can make a dot move from right to left by continuously multiplying a value (e.g., 1) in a variable by 2. The speed of the dot movement can be controlled by a wait-timer in milliseconds. To code this animation, students do not need to know any special print command syntax (e.g., one used in Java or C programming language). Therefore, students can just focus on the logic of the algorithm behind the animation, receive instant feedback, and become familiar with core programming concepts more easily. In the advanced course, a learner can use all eight rows (64 dots) of the LED display kit, which leaves much more room for creativity.

The use of variables in computer programming is one of the common weaknesses of novice programmers [7]. In the Web-flowchart environment, students use symbols that represent variables (□, ○, △, ☆, ♤, ♡, and ♧) for simple calculations and can produce still images or animations after creating a flowchart in a drag-and-drop fashion. Figure 3 shows our Web-based flowchart system and an algorithm that displays a triangle.

In conjunction with our programming education system, we also adopt the problem-based learning (PBL) approach [8]. As part of this effort, we developed a comprehensive set of programming challenges (6 for beginners and 15 for advanced users) that encourage students to use their imagination and creativity.

These problems include asking students to:

(1) Create a flowchart for the LED lights to be turned on diagonally from left to right,

(2) Create a flowchart for the LED lights to be turned on diagonally from right to left,

(3) Create a flowchart for the LED lights to be turned on in an X shape, that is, the combination of (1) and (2), and

(4) Create a flowchart for a triangle rotating clockwise.

Figure 4 shows students collaborating to do a group assignment.

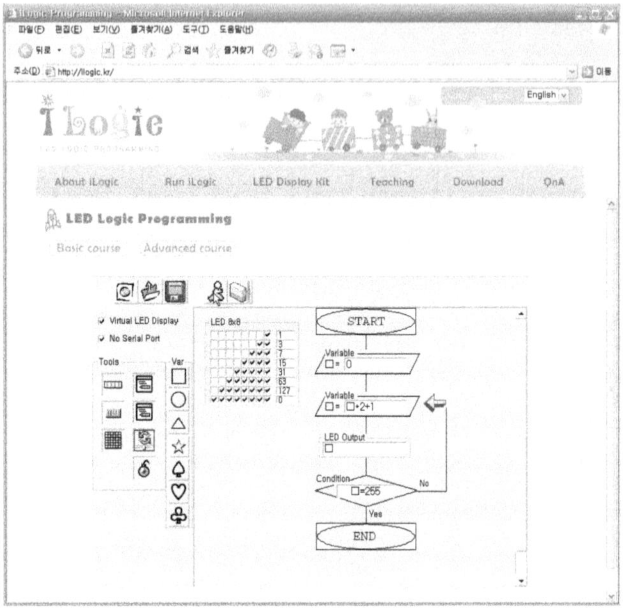

Figure 3: Web-Flowchart

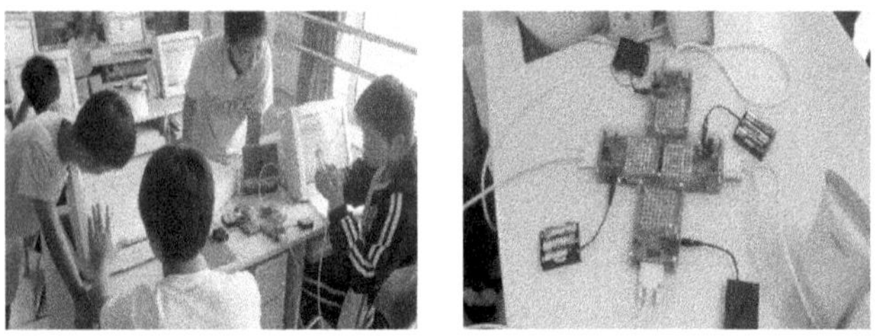

Figure 4: Students Collaborating to Do a Group Assignment Using Four LED Display Kits

4. SURVEY

This section describes the results of surveys administered in various programming classes from Fall 2005 through Spring 2009. The programming courses were offered for diverse groups of students including elementary school students, gifted students, college students, and teachers. As part of this pilot project, we designed a prototype LED display kit and made 20 copies of it. The first year (beginner's) programming course was tried at the Sin-sang-do elementary school and Woo-i elementary school during the Fall 2005 and Spring 2006 semesters respectively. Approximately, 35 students attended the 30-hour programming course during 15 weeks (2 hours per week), and one LED display kit was shared by two students.

For the second year (advanced) programming course, we modified the LED display kit and made 85 of them. The course was offered at the Sin-sang-do elementary school and Joong-ang elementary school during the Spring 2007 semester simultaneously. The course outline was the same as the first year course. We developed our own textbook that introduces programming concepts and describes how to use the Web-flowchart tool and LED display kits. The textbook consists of 3 parts: basic concepts for programming, Web-flowchart, and PBL-based algorithm exercises.

4.1 Elementary-School Students

We have 2 year experience of teaching at three elementary schools from Fall 2005 through Spring 2007. A total of 126 elementary school students participated in our programming courses. At the end of each course, student feedback was collected in the form of written answers to the following questions:

(Question 1) Do you think that our programming course using the Web-flowchart tool and the display apparatus is interesting?

(Question 2) What is your opinion about our problem-based learning (PBL) approach in which an instructor assigns challenging problems (e.g., animation problems) to students, and then students try to solve the problems using the display apparatus and Web-based flowchart tool?

(Question 3) Do you think that these programming education tools helped you understand programming concepts or algorithms?

(Question 4) Are you going to take a more advanced programming course again next semester?

(Question 5) Are you going to recommend this programming course to your friends?

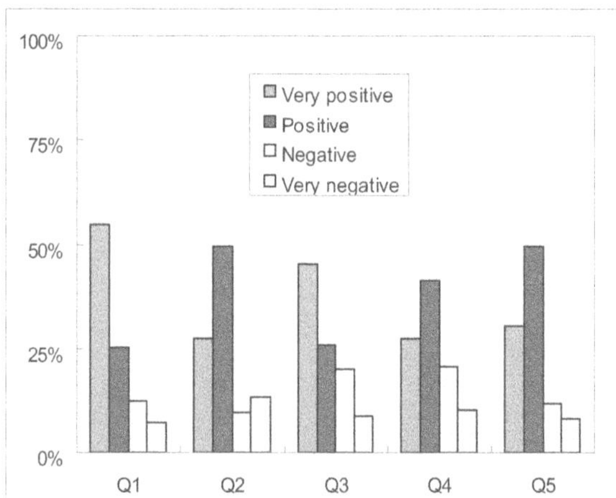

Figure 5: Survey Results of Three Elementary Schools

The survey results of the 126 students are shown in Figure 5. The figure shows that the programming learning method using the LED display kits and the Web-flowchart tool is engaging students and helping them understand programming concepts or algorithms.

4.2 Undergraduate Students

We also offered our programming course to undergraduate students during the Fall 2007 semester. A total of 35 students attended the 8-hour programming course during 4 weeks (2 hours per week). The students who took the course were all seniors from the department of computer education at Seoul National University of Education (SNUE). The course was offered as part of another course on topics in elementary school computer education. Seventy percent of graduates from SNUE become teachers at 500 public schools in Seoul city. The course was intended to prepare the seniors for being able to teach elementary school students how to program. Most of the students stated that the course was interesting, and that they would be able to reuse the course materials in teaching their students in the future.

4.3 Teachers

Ten elementary school teachers also took our programming course. These teachers were all enrolled to a Master degree program in Computer Education at SNUE. There were 2 male and 8 female teachers. They attended our 6 hour programming course during the Fall 2007 semester. Before taking the class, the teachers already had some basic understanding of programming concepts and could solve programming problems with moderate difficulty level. However, they were having difficulties in teaching programming to their students. Five (1 male and 4 females) out of 10 teachers who took the course responded to our survey.

The respondents had to use a number between 1 (the lowest score) and 4 (the highest score) to answer each of the 5 questions on our programming learning method using the LED display kits. The five questions used for our survey are shown below:

(Questions 1) Do you think our programming education approach using the LED display kits was interesting?

(Question 2) Do you think the Web-flowchart system was easy to use?

(Question 3) Do you think teaching how to program is necessary for elementary school students?

(Question 4) Do you think the PBL-based programming teaching method will help students develop creative thinking skills?

(Question 5) Will you offer a programming course using our LED display kits at your school next semester?

Table 1: Results of the Survey Administered to Teachers

	Very positive	Positive	Negative	Very Negative
Q1	5	0	0	0
Q2	5	0	0	0
Q3	3	1	1	0
Q4	0	4	1	0
Q5	2	2	1	0

4.4 Gifted Students

The same programming course was made available for gifted students at the SNUE Gifted Institute during the Spring 2008 semester. A total of 33 gifted elementary school students participated in the programming class. 12 students from an advanced science program and 11 students from the institute's advanced math program attended 3 hours of the programming class. They were either 5th or 6th graders. Most of those who took the class had prior experience in programming in Visual Basic or C. Students were engaged in learning basic Web flowchart uses and concepts and given five problems sequentially. The difficulty of each question increased as they solve their problems. Students who solved all five problems received 5 points while those who solved 1 problem received 1 point.

The grader also assigned a score ranging from 1 to 5 based on his/her subjective evaluation of a student and the student's participation level (e.g., their attitude, the questions they asked, and how responsive they were) in class. Table 2 shows the evaluation results of the students. The advanced math group had higher overall GPA than the advanced science group. However, the science group students participated in the class more actively, and they therefore demonstrated superior ability to solve the given problems.

Table 2: Evaluation Results of the Gifted Students

	Problem-Solving capability	Class Participation
Science-intensive class	3.5	4.58
Mathematics-intensive class	3.25	4.38

5. CONCLUSION AND FUTURE WORK

This paper proposed a new programming learning approach using an LED display kit and a Web flowchart tool. We tested the system with various audience groups in a number of courses. The responses from our in-class surveys were generally positive.

We are planning to add the following new features to the learning system we discussed in this paper. The first set of new features will include infrared, touch, and other sensors as well as sound and mobility. We are also investigating the feasibility of introducing a new interface so that combining our system with LEGO® blocks and an NXT robotics kit is possible. Figure 6 shows different possible combinations of the LED display kit and the existing LEGO® products.

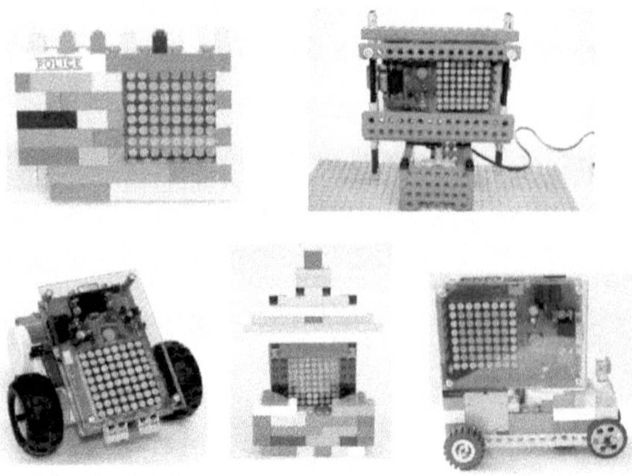

Figure 6: Diverse Combinations of the LED Display Kit and LEGO® Products

6. ACKNOWLEDGMENTS

We would like to thanks three teachers, Soo-Poong Chae at the Woo-i elementary school, Jin-Sook Ryu at the Sin-sang-do elementary school, and Ju-Hwa Lee at the Sin-bong elementary school for teaching the programming courses and administering student surveys in their classes.

7. REFERENCES

[1] Al-Barakati, N. M., and Al-Aama, A. Y. 2009. The effect of visualizing roles of variables on student performance in an introductory programming course. *ACM SIGCSE Bulletin 41(3)*, 228-232.

[2] Calloni, B. Iconic programming proves effective for teaching the first year programming sequence, In *Proceedings of the 28th ACM Technical Symposium on Computer Science Education (SIGCSE'97)*, San Jose, CA, USA, February 1997, 262-266.

[3] Carlisle, M. C., Wilson, T. A., Humphries, J. W., and Hadfield, S. M., RAPTOR: a visual programming environment for teaching algorithmic problem solving, In *Proceedings of the 36th ACM Technical Symposium on Computer Science Education (SIGCSE'05)*, St. Louis, MO, USA, February 2005, 176-180.

[4] Chun, S. A Web-based programming learning system for elementary school students using LED display kits, In *Proceedings of the 39th ACM Technical Symposium on Computer Science Education (SIGCSE'08)*, Portland, OR, USA, February 2008, Poster.

[5] Crews, T., and Murphy, C. *Programming Right from the Start with Visual Basic .NET.* Pearson Prentice Hall, 2004.

[6] Jones, S., and Burnett, G. 2007. Spatial skills and navigation of source code. *ACM SIGCSE Bulletin 39(3)*, 231-235.

[7] Levitin, A. Analyze that: puzzles and analysis of algorithms, In *Proceedings of the 36th ACM Technical Symposium on Computer Science Education (SIGCSE'05)*, St. Louis, MO, USA, February 2005, 171-175.

[8] Schmidt, H. G. 1993. Foundations of problem-based learning: some explanatory notes. *Medical Education 27*, 422-432.

[9] Schubert F. E. Light-Emitting Diodes. Cambridge University Press, 2003.

[10] Ziegler, U., and Crews, T. An integrated program development tool for teaching and learning how to program, In *Proceedings of the 30th ACM Technical Symposium on Computer Science Education (SIGCSE'99)*, New Orleans, LA, USA, February 1999, 276-280.

A Strategy for Collaborative Outreach: Lessons from the CSbots Project

Tom Lauwers
Carnegie Mellon University
5000 Forbes Ave.
Pittsburgh, PA 15213
001-412-268-6723
tlauwers@andrew.cmu.edu

Emily Hamner
Carnegie Mellon University
5000 Forbes Ave.
Pittsburgh, PA 15213
001-412-268-6723
ehamner@cmu.edu

Illah Nourbakhsh
Carnegie Mellon University
5000 Forbes Ave.
Pittsburgh, PA 15213
001-412-268-2007
illah@cs.cmu.edu

ABSTRACT

Many efforts are being made to improve computer science education in order to address the retention and motivation of students. These efforts rely on the development of educational tools and environments, tools that, when successful, require many years to integrate into the computer science education community. We introduce a strategy that both speeds uptake in the community and improves the chances of the project creating an educationally successful tool. The strategy hinges on creating an initial community of educators before an educational tool is fully mature but at the point at which it becomes usable by teachers. While this is somewhat analogous to the beta-testing communities in software development, our aim is for the community to drive the underlying design in significant ways. Our context is CSbots, a project to develop a robot, software environment, and associated curricula for introductory computer science education. We detail our collaborative outreach effort, which resulted in the concurrent creation of a community of 30 invested educators and a well aligned educational tool ready for broad dissemination.

Categories and Subject Descriptors

K.3.2 [**Computer and Information Science Education**]: Computer Science Education and Curriculum.

General Terms

Documentation, Design, Experimentation, Human Factors

Keywords

Outreach, High School, Teacher Training, Robotics, Workshop, CSbots, Computer Programming, Participatory Design

1. INTRODUCTION

One of the most important problems confronting secondary education nationally is a declining interest in computer science among high school students, especially girls. Not surprisingly, this decline translates directly into a 50% decline in the number of Americans deciding to major in computer science since 2000 [2]. The solution to this problem lies in identifying methods for making computer science interesting to a broader and more diverse group of high school students, and in training high school teachers in these methods.

Several mature efforts are underway to tackle this problem; Alice [3] and Scratch [9] are visual programming languages that provide an environment for programming that allows students to create rich visualizations and animations within minutes. The Lego Mindstorms robotics kit coupled with powerful open source software environments for visual and textual programming allow students to program robots in addition to computers [8]. Finally, CS Unplugged introduces CS concepts through physical and paper based games, preparing students for the conceptual challenges of computer science [1]. All of these programs rely on mature, release versions of software, hardware, and/or curriculum and are supported by a network of trainers and training workshops. Though these efforts have had positive measurable impacts on students [5,7,8,10], the problem of low interest and motivation is by no means solved. We believe that many different approaches are necessary and that new efforts should be brought to the attention of educators as soon as possible.

This paper is about a strategy to create an initial community of secondary school educators before a project is fully mature but at the point at which it becomes usable by teachers. While this is somewhat analogous to the beta-testing communities in software development, our aim is for the community to drive the underlying design in significant ways. Although it may seem somewhat counterintuitive to try to build a community around something as it is still evolving, doing so makes it possible for the community itself to begin directing the evolution. As the community is a representative sample of the group of end users, this process can lead to a better alignment of the final release version of the software, hardware, and curricula. Furthermore, by creating an initial community of educators around the project, adoption of the final version of the project may be accelerated.

We introduce this strategy in the context of CSbots, a project to develop a robot, software environment, and associated curricula that are aligned with the learning goals of computer science education, specifically at the AP and introductory college level. Over the course of two years we engaged in a collaborative outreach experiment, working with a small community of teachers in the first year, holding a workshop at the end of this year, and then scaling the community to roughly 30 involved teachers. This outreach effort occurred while our system of educational tools was developing, and in many ways drove the evolution of that development. This paper is devoted to describing how we started the community in the initial project year, how we recruited and trained a larger community through a workshop, how we scaled the community during the second project year, and how the community affected our project's development.

2. INITIAL PROJECT YEAR

At the start of our outreach effort, we had 1) an initial robot, dubbed 'alpha', 2) a set of potential assignments co-developed with a partner at a local community college, and 3) a Java API and environment. Though we were still making revisions to all three of these elements, we felt that the project had reached a sufficient level of maturity to introduce it to classrooms and teachers.

Over the 2007-2008 school year, we worked with five high school teachers in a participatory curriculum-development process. We were fortunate to be able to work with teachers from locations across the United States. Through this process the high school teachers gave us feedback on our curriculum and robot system; wrote additional assignments which utilized the robot; and tested the robot with students in the classroom, both as an extracurricular activity, and as a recruitment tool for their computer science programs.

2.1 Instructor Recruitment

Our goal was to recruit five teachers to actively participate during the initial year. We recruited teachers to work with us by offering a short, one and a half hour session at Carnegie Mellon's CS4HS summer workshop for high school teachers [4]. During this workshop, we trained teachers on how to use the robot platform and associated software and tasked groups of teachers to write programs that responded to different colors of flash cards. We announced during this session that we were looking to partner with several teachers to develop curricula and inform hardware and software changes to the platform. Of the 35 teachers at the CS4HS session, 22 signed up for additional information about the partner program. We emailed these 22 several weeks later and asked them to complete a survey to help us determine their initial ability to work on the project; eight of the teachers responded to the survey and seven were able to partner with us. We sent robots to all seven, but two of the seven teachers dropped out of the program several months in due to lack of time, leaving us with exactly the number of partners we initially sought.

2.2 The Robot Platform

The alpha robot sent to our partner teachers was an intermediate design in the CSbots project. It was designed to be maximally instrumented, so as to allow us to discover which features appealed to teachers and students. The platform that we used in the alpha cycle was an iRobot Create[1] and a Qwerk controller[2] (Fig. 1). Together, these two off-the-shelf components provided a rich set of features:

- A wireless connection between computer and robot
- Programmability in standard Java through a Java API
- Bumpers for simple obstacle detection
- Position and velocity control
- Vision via a USB webcam
- Audio, including text to speech
- Response through RSS feeds to real-time internet data

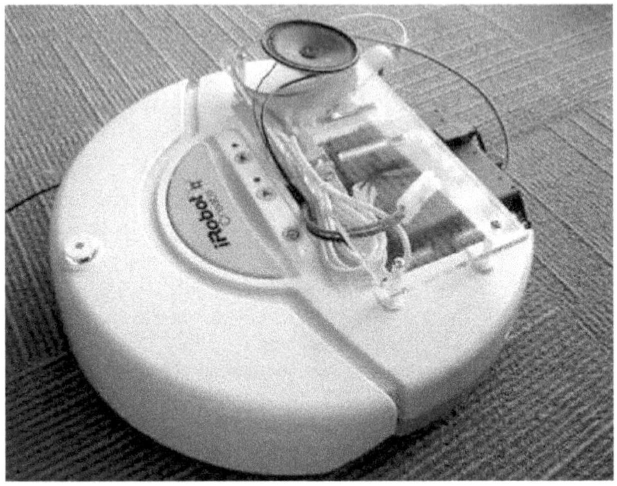

Figure 1: The Alpha Robot Platform

2.3 Communication and Instructor Support

At the beginning of the project we realized that frequent communication between the partner teachers and project team would be necessary. As our partners were distributed over the continental US face to face meetings could not occur. We began the year by mailing each teacher a robot and instructions on how to set up the robot at their school. Four teachers had no problems with setup, while the fifth had technical difficulties due to restrictive school policies on installing new software. These problems were resolved by calling the school's technical support..

Once teachers had received their robots, we kept to a schedule of monthly individual phone calls to get an idea of how each teacher was using the robot and to deal with any problems that might have arisen. These phone calls were crucial in maintaining the relationships between us and the teachers, as they created a series of monthly goals that drove both our group and the teachers to work on the curricula and software API.

In addition to phone calls, we also kept in touch using a wiki. Teachers used the wiki to provide information about their schools, upload pictures of themselves and their students, and later to share activities and assignments they had developed for the robot.

2.4 Structure of the First Year

Teachers were sent robots at the end of September and most began using the robots as soon as they arrived. In addition to the robots, we also sent twelve assignments targeting common high

[1]http://www.irobot.com/sp.cfm?pageid=305

[2]http://www.charmedlabs.com/

level concepts in the AP curriculum: control structures, arrays, variables, and classes. Our goals for the fall semester were to have the teachers set up the robot and attempt the assignments in order to become familiar programming with the robot. Most teachers went beyond this, inviting their students to try out some of the assignments and providing feedback regarding the activities, software API, and robot hardware.

December marked the end of the training phase of the program, as by this time all had tried out a majority of the assignments and were becoming familiar with robot programming. The relationship between the teachers and us became less prescriptive and more cooperative. Teachers began creating additional activities and assignments for the robot. As their comfort with the robot grew, all the teachers involved their students to a great extent. Despite having only a single robot, they were able to integrate robot activities into their spring curricula, and were able to use the robot extensively in out-of-class settings. As part of the purpose of our study was to discover which hardware features were most useful to teachers and students, we sent supplementary kits of sensors and actuators and asked the teachers to try using them; these kits included light sensors, a distance sensor, and servos with which teachers could build robot arms. The teachers used these supplementary kits, and they, or in some cases their students, upgraded the robot hardware with them.

3. WORKSHOP AFTER YEAR ONE

The successes that our pilot teachers had with a single robot per classroom supported a belief that the program could be scaled, and we decided that a workshop after the initial project year was the best way to do so. We had support to host a summer 2008 workshop with up to twenty five teachers; as well as to subsidize the cost of alpha robots for all attendees. The workshop was centered on training teachers on the alpha robot used in the first year and on the curricular materials that were generated by the partner teachers and project team during that year.

3.1 Recruiting Participants

We recruited participants by emailing the SIGCSE and the Collegeboard's AP Computer Science teacher mailing lists. We also worked with the CS4HS organizers to email their list of attending teachers. We co-located with CS4HS and held the workshop directly before CS4HS. This was essential to recruiting an adequate number of participants to a new and unknown workshop; as nearly all of our participants also attended CS4HS.

Twenty-four new teachers attended the workshop, and four of our existing partner teachers attended to share their experiences. Collectively, these teachers teach at least 1500 students per year. We were pleasantly surprised at the wide reach of the workshop which attracted teachers from 12 states and one foreign country (a teacher attended from the American Embassy School in India).

3.2 Workshop Composition

The workshop took place over one full and one half day near the end of July and was composed of a number of lectures, panel discussions, and directed and open ended robot activities.

3.2.1 Lectures

Two one-hour lectures were given during the first day. The first lecture was given at the start of the workshop and described the robot's hardware, explained the wireless network configuration, and detailed the software API necessary to write programs. The second lecture concerned the curricular activities and assignments already created, and explained how certain high level CS1 concepts mapped well onto certain features of the robot's hardware (for example, looping works well with reading in sensors).

3.2.2 Panel Discussions

Two 45 minute panel discussions were held on the first day. The panels consisted of the four teachers who took part in the pilot, allowing peer to peer discussion of common concerns related to teaching CS1 in high schools. The panel topics included:

- How the robot is used effectively at different schools.
- Challenges to setting up the robot in different contexts.
- Involving students out of class.
- How to maximize the limited resource of a single robot
- How the robot was used for community outreach.

3.2.3 Directed Robot Activities

Teachers worked on two directed robot activities during the workshop. These activities were relatively brief at 30 minutes each and allowed teachers to become familiar working with the hardware during the morning and early afternoon of the first day. The activities were based on some of the assignments created by our partner teachers during the pilot year.

3.2.4 Open-Ended Activities

The last hour and a half of the first day and the entire second day were devoted to allowing teachers to work in small groups to develop robot assignments and activities (and to write solutions to these with the robots present). This time was structured only in so much that a goal was presented to the participants: Create one or more potential assignments that involve the robot. These activities produced a long term beneficial result for the community, as all the participants shared their assignments with the group at the end of the workshop. The open-ended structure also allowed groups to focus on areas of personal interest (for example sensing or text-to-speech), to work at their own pace, and to receive individual assistance from us and the experienced teachers on an as-needed basis.

3.3 Evaluation

We evaluated the workshop through a post-workshop survey of participants. The goal of the post-workshop survey was to anonymously allow teachers to provide feedback about the workshop. The survey was conducted online, and 16 out of 24 teachers responded to our request to complete it. Our conclusion from the survey feedback was that the workshop effectively trained the teachers in use of the robot and accompanying materials. Twenty one out of 24 attendees purchased a robot at the end of the workshop, further confirming the workshop's effectiveness.

3.3.1 Workshop Ratings

We asked teachers to rate a number of aspects of the workshop on a scale from 1 (Poor) to 5 (Excellent). Table 1 summarizes the mean ratings for each aspect.

Overall, teachers were very positive about the workshop in their ratings, and were fairly consistent as well – almost all teachers rated every aspect of the workshop as either 'good' (a rating of 4) or 'excellent' (a rating of 5).

Table 1: Summary of Teacher Ratings of Workshop

Workshop Aspect	Mean Rating
Technical lectures on robot, software, and curricula	4.6
Discussion panels	4.1
Guided hands-on activities	4.8
Open-ended activities/brainstorming	4.4
Overall workshop experience	4.8

We also asked teachers about our effectiveness at teaching them how to use the robot and curriculum developed for the workshop. Specifically we asked them to agree or disagree with the following statement: "*The CSbots workshop gave me the appropriate information to effectively use the Create robot and associated curriculum at my school.*" On a scale from strongly disagree to strongly agree, all teachers marked 'agree' or 'strongly agree'.

4. SECOND PROJECT YEAR

Although in many outreach programs a training workshop is the culminating event, our project continued throughout the 2008-2009 school year. Our aims during the year were to build and support the community sparked by the summer workshop, gather feedback from the community about the design of a second generation robot, and evaluate the robot's success in schools.

4.1 Building Community

Our group continued to support the community that developed during the summer workshop during the entire second year. Our motivation in maintaining communication with teachers after the workshop was two-fold. Firstly, we hoped to strengthen the young community by remaining available to participants for ongoing support. Secondly, continuing contact allowed us to monitor the effectiveness of the training received during the workshop, teachers' use of the robot, and the robot platform's robustness and performance during the year.

4.1.1 Community website

During the workshop we introduced teachers to a website where they could download software and sample assignments. We also encouraged them to use the site to share any assignments they developed which used the robot. The initial website, which was part of a larger robotics community site, was not well utilized by participants and received low ratings on participant surveys. This prompted us to develop a new community site targeted exclusively at the CSbots community. The new site, csbots.org, utilized wetpaint, an off the shelf community website building platform. Although we hoped this new site would elicit more assignment contributions from the community, teacher contributions remain relatively low though the new site is visited frequently to access documentation and posted assignments.

4.1.2 Documentation and Support

Over the course of the year, we continued to clarify documentation as questions arose and promulgated the new documentation through the website. We also added significant features to the software, notably standalone ("no robot required") software packages for audio and Internet RSS feeds. We emailed teachers to alert them when significant new features became available via the website.

Though we expected to receive requests for technical support, most teachers were able to begin using the robots without additional help, and in the few cases where problems did arise, typically teachers resolved them independently.

4.2 Gathering Feedback

The teachers' experiences during the initial project year with the robot and software, as well as on-going studies at a community college [6], provided us with insights into the next robot design. We began developing the hardware for this design after the summer workshop, and produced 100 robots in the spring of 2009. The community of teachers influenced the design of this second generation robot, known as the Finch (Fig. 2), in a number of ways:

- Teachers' experiences adapting a single robot to a classroom of 30 students suggested that the Finch should be sufficiently low cost to enable schools to purchase one for every student.
- The Finch robot's sensors and actuators were determined partially from the teacher's experiences with the first generation robot and hardware kit during the first year.
- We sent teachers designs for the shell of the second generation robot and solicited feedback from teachers and their students to determine the aesthetics of the robot.
- In spring of 2009, ten teachers volunteered to receive Finch robots and tested these robots with their students in much the same spirit as the first year's teachers. These experiences are informing the software API, documentation (especially with regards to instructionally supporting multiple operating systems and IDEs), and hardware modifications to the Finch.

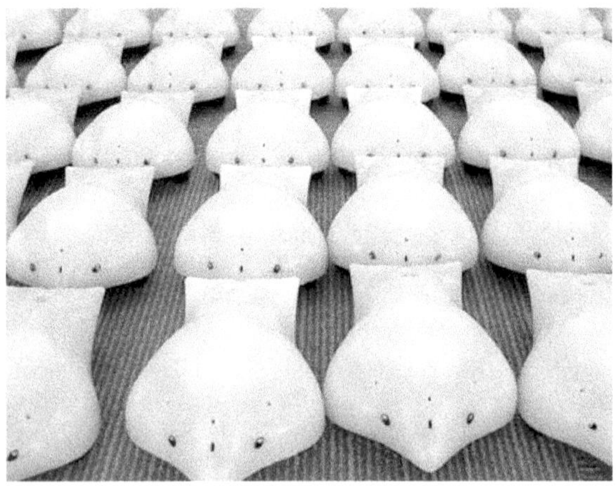

Figure 2: A Flock of Finches

4.3 Evaluating the Program

We asked teachers to complete two surveys during the course of the second year; one at the end of 2008 and one at the end of the academic year. These surveys were designed to gauge how the robots were being used and by whom.

4.3.1 Mid-year survey

Seventeen teachers responded to the mid-year survey. The two most common uses for the robot were as motivation for students and as a recruitment tool. Teachers reported that students used the robot in class assignments and for extra credit. Students also used the robot as an extra-curricular activity. Gifted and advanced students who were no longer challenged by the traditional curriculum particularly enjoyed working with the robot.

We asked teachers how many students had used the robot in the past semester. The mean result was about 3.5 students per teacher, with a total of 55 students spread across 16 responding teachers. This is not too surprising, as there is only one robot at every school, and the way the robots were used appears to be to motivate small groups of students.

We asked teachers if they faced technical or logistical difficulties setting up their robots. Overwhelmingly teachers reported no problems, but two teachers did have trouble as their schools did not allow the creation of an independent wireless network, which is required to run the robot. The teachers eventually worked around this problem. No teachers reported broken robots.

4.3.2 *End-of-year survey*

Teachers participated in an end-of-year survey conducted in June 2009 to determine changes in the way they used the robot since our last survey at the end of 2008. Fifteen teachers participated in the survey. We also asked teachers who had been provided with a Finch to fill out a separate survey; 8 teachers responded.

As before, most teachers used the robot as a recruitment tool – 11 of the 15 teachers mentioned this as a use. Nine of the 15 teachers had students actively using the robots; in a few cases, these students were given full control of the robot for a few weeks or a month to do an extended project. Once again, it seems that gifted and advanced students were the main users of the robot. Teachers with a Finch also reported use primarily for recruitment and with small groups of students.

The total number of students using the alpha robot was 37, with most teachers who used the robot with students reporting groups of 4-6 using the robot. Among teachers who had also received a Finch, a total of 56 students used the Finch, with an average of roughly 10 students per teacher using the Finch in spring 2009. It appears that the Finch, perhaps because it is more portable, was used by a larger number of students for smaller, shorter projects.

Technical problems were somewhat rare and were typically resolved by the teacher. Problems were fairly idiosyncratic, with no teacher reporting the same problem as someone else. The problems reported were: Poor battery life, failed charger (a replacement was sent), setting up the software environment, compatibility problems with Mac OS, struggling to set up the hardware properly, bumpers that didn't respond when hit, and getting wireless networking working. These problems, in all but one case were temporary and resolved by the teacher. Teachers who had a Finch generally reported fewer problems, and no hardware-related problems at all. Three of the eight responding teachers indicated some level of technical difficulty – one had trouble setting up the USB driver on their Mac, and two had trouble using software IDEs with the Finch. All three teachers resolved these problems on their own without contacting us

4.3.3 *Analysis*

Of teachers completing the surveys, it seems that the training workshop was successful in achieving its goals; teachers were able to set up the robots at their school, integrate them into the school environment in a worthwhile and contextually appropriate manner, and when technical difficulties did appear, teachers mostly managed to solve these problems independently.

5. CONCLUSIONS

Though considerable effort was required to develop an alpha design that was usable in educational settings, involve teachers in a pilot program, and organize a workshop, the payoff was significant. The work done with our community of teachers has laid the foundation for a thriving program that has the potential to impact many students. This foundation includes all of the necessities for applicability to educational settings: Curriculum, software, a robust robot platform tailored to the needs of an introductory CS class, a community of educators, and a successful strategy for training teachers that could be scaled up in the future. Since this work was performed concurrently with the design of the robot and software API, the end result is a well-aligned educational tool developed in a relatively short period of time. After only three years the robot and accompanying software and curriculum are ready for mass production and distribution. We are pursuing plans to expand teacher training opportunities and look forward to a growing community of educators using this technology to teach and inspire their students.

6. ACKNOWLEDGMENTS

We thank our partner teachers for many insightful suggestions, activities, and assignments. We also thank Chris Bartley for providing software support to the project. We thank the Arthur Davis Foundations for fully funding this work.

7. REFERENCES

[1] Bell, T. and Fellows, M., http://csunplugged.org, 2009

[2] Bizot, B., US CS New Majors, Enrollment Both Rise in 2007-2008, Computing Research News, Vol. 21/2. 2009.

[3] Cooper, S., Dann, W., & Pausch, R.Teaching objects first in introductory computer science. Proceedings of the 34th SIGCSE Technical Symposium on Computer Science Education (SIGCSE 2003), Reno, NV

[4] Blum, L., Cortina, T., Lazowska, E., and Wise, J., "Special Session: The Expansion of CS4HS: An Outreach Program for High School Teachers", SIGCSE 2008, Portland, OR.

[5] Kelleher, C. and Pausch, R.. "Lowering the barriers to programming: A taxonomy of programming environments and languages for novice programmers." ACM Comput. Surv., 37(2), pg 83-137, 2005..

[6] Lauwers, T., Nourbakhsh, I., and Hamner, E., "CSbots: Design and Deployment of a Robot Designed for the CS1 Classroom", SIGCSE 2009, pg 428-432, Chattanooga, TN

[7] Maloney, J. H., Peppler, K., Kafai, Y., Resnick, M., and Rusk, N. Programming by choice: urban youth learning programming with scratch, pg 367-371, SIGCSE 2008,

[8] M. McNally. "Walking the grid: Robotics in CS2" In Proceedings of the 8th Australian conference on Computing education, pages 151-155, 2006.

[9] Monroy-Hernández, A. and Resnick, M. "Empowering kids to create and share programmable media" Interactions 15, 2 Mar. 2008,

[10] Taub, R., Ben-Ari, M., and Armoni, M. 2009. The effect of CS unplugged on middle-school students' views of CS. SIGCSE Bull. 41, 3 (Aug. 2009 pg 99-103)

A K-12 College Partnership[1]

Stephen Cooper
Purdue University
Computer Graphics Technology
West Lafayette, IN 47906 USA
1.765.494.6130
coopers@acm.org

Wanda Dann
Carnegie Mellon University
Computer Science Department
Pittsburgh, PA, 15213 USA
1.412.268.9959
wpdann@andrew.cmu.edu

John Harrison
Princess Anne High School
Virginia Beach, VA, 17837 USA
1.757.648.5600
John.Harrison@vbschools.com

ABSTRACT
To combat the decline of teaching computing courses in high schools, a plan was created to offer professional development (in both content and pedagogy) to high school computing teachers, and to have college faculty partner with those high school teachers to implement innovative curricula. This paper describes a pilot program that was run in support of an NSF Innovative Technology Experiences for Students and Teachers (ITEST) project that funded this plan of action. Professional development activities were offered during summer 2006 and the resulting curriculum was taught in high school the following academic year (2006-2007).

Categories and Subject Descriptors
K.3 [**Computers & Education**]: Computer & Information Science Education – Computer Science Education.

General Terms: Languages

Keywords: Object-oriented, Programming, Alice, K-12, Program Visualization.

1. INTRODUCTION
There has been a significant decrease in the number of Computer Science (CS) students since the peak in 2000-2001. According to the Higher Education Research Institute at the University of California at Los Angeles, "the percentage of incoming undergraduates indicating that they would major in CS declined by more than 60 percent between the fall of 2000 and 2004, and is now lower than … in the early 1980s" [15]. Over the past 3 years, the overall number of baccalaureate students in CS seems to have bottomed out, but at a level nearly 70% lower than the number of students in 2000. The Computer Research Association's Taulbee study reports similar declines [20]. (The Taulbee survey does report a slight uptick in the number of students enrolled in Bachelor's programs this past year, and a decline of only 10% of students receiving BS degrees in computing between 2007 and 2008. However, the Taulbee survey has changed its data collection to include a broader number of degree programs.) Recent data provided by College Board further indicates a significant drop in the number of high-school students that complete advanced placement (AP) tests in CS relative to overall test takers. While the number of AP tests taken increased by 82% between 2000-2006, the number of students taking AP CS A increased by 7% during this time [22]. The situation in CS in high school has deteriorated so much that the College Board recently cancelled offering the CS AB exam, starting this academic year.

As this data suggests, CS is decreasingly viewed as a "hot" career. Attracting students to computing has become an issue for undergraduate CS departments across the US and the situation shows little signs of improvement. Compounding this problem is that many states, at the high school level, are moving computing from the college track to the career and technical track, with a corresponding movement of existing computer teachers back into mathematics and science departments, and the assignment of the teaching of CS increasingly is given to business teachers or any certified teacher, many of whom have no academic preparation in CS [21].

This precipitous drop in interest in CS stands in sharp contrast with job demand data from the US Bureau of Labor Statistics, which predicts that, in the decade 2006-2016, and after accounting for job losses due to outsourcing, there will be more than 700,000 new jobs created just in computer systems and information [9]. This number is much greater than the anticipated number of computing-related degrees granted in the US. Thus, there is a crisis looming on the horizon. Under the current conditions, the US will be unable to satisfy the IT industry's labor demands.

Many colleges have attempted to combat this decline through two main mechanisms. The first has been to improve the quality of the introductory course offerings, in content as well as pedagogic approach. And, there have been many reported successes, both in terms of keeping a higher percentage of declared majors, as well as in convincing students with other majors to take at least a concentration of courses in computing. While it is beyond the scope of this paper to list all of the innovative approaches being tried, a few of the more influential ones are mentioned here. Guzdial [10] has used the approach of students using multimedia to excite them about computing. Both Karel the Robot [2] and some of its offshoots, such as Jeroo [14] use movement of a robot in 2D space as a program visualization to help students to see their programs. Scratch [12], developed at MIT, is a similar tool targeting younger students (and encourages them through animation and storytelling). The Eventdraw library [3] uses the "hook" of GUI building to encourage students in computer

---

[1] This work was partially supported by NSF grant NSF-0624654. Any views and opinions expressed are those of the authors and do not necessarily represent those of the National Science Foundation.

SIGCSE'10, March 10–13, 2010, Milwaukee, Wisconsin, USA.

programming. The How To Design Programs [8] approach uses functional programming to engage students. The use of programmable clothing [4] may well provide a very strong motivation to encourage women to consider computing. There are numerous approaches to attract students to computing using robots. And while the emphasis of many of these approaches has been in college, it is likely that many of them could be effectively refocused towards high and middle school.

The second approach has been to offer K-12 outreach, most commonly through summer camps or workshops. Here the primary audience is high school and middle school students, though a few efforts have targeted middle and high school teachers. The Computer Science Teachers Association has been very supportive of this approach, both through their Java Engagement for Teacher Training and through Teacher Enrichment in Computer Science workshops [19].

The approach presented here fits into the latter category (focusing on teacher professional development), though with an eye toward building longer term mentoring and support. Rather than limiting the high school teacher professional development to a summer workshop, the approach described in this paper is to build a partnership between a college and nearby school districts, with continued support and interaction throughout the academic year. The remainder of this paper describes a pilot program, funded as part of an ITEST grant, involving a partnership between Saint Joseph's University (Cooper's home institution at the time) and ten of the eleven high schools that make up the Virginia Beach School District.

2. ITEST

NSF's Innovative Technology Experiences for Students and Teachers (ITEST) program "responds to current concerns and projections about the growing demand for professionals and information technology workers in the U.S. and seeks solutions to help ensure the breadth and depth of the STEM [Science, Technology, Engineering and Mathematics] workforce." [18] A focus is on designing programs for K-12 students and/or providing professional development for their teachers.

The project description and project summary from our ITEST proposal are each available from [23]. The plan was to develop partnerships between a college/university and its nearby school districts, and thereby to provide professional development and assistance to middle and high school computer teachers. During the summer, two one-week workshops were to be run, styled on the TECS standard established by the Computer Science Teachers Association [16]. Although details about these workshops are beyond the scope of this paper, we can briefly summarize that the first week focused on Alice [24] content and the second week focused on curriculum development. A third-week workshop would be held in which the K-12 teachers could work with a small group of summer students, to practice using the curricular materials they had just developed. During the following academic year, the college faculty would regularly meet with the middle/high school teachers.

Our ITEST grant proposed six sets of such workshop and mentoring relationships. One of these six was a pilot in Virginia Beach (high schools in partnership with Saint Joseph's University). In following summers, five other workshop and mentoring partnerships were run in Oxford, MS (high and middle schools in partnership with the University of Mississippi), Durham, NC (middle schools in partnership with Duke University), Charleston, SC (high schools in partnership with the College of Charleston and Columbia College), Golden, CO (high schools in partnership with Colorado School of Mines), and San Jose, CA (high schools in partnership with Santa Clara University). Virginia Beach was an ideal location for the pilot program. The nearby naval base helped to ensure significant ethnic and economic diversity among the students. The first two one-week workshops were run during summer 2006. Due to the late awarding of the ITEST grant, the third week workshop was not possible to schedule at the pilot site.

3. VIRGINIA BEACH

The Virginia Beach City Public Schools (VBCPS) serve approximately 70,535 students in grades K-12. The school system includes 57 elementary schools, 14 middle schools, 11 high schools, and a number of secondary/post-secondary specialty centers, including the Advanced Technology Center, Technical and Career Education Center, Center for Effective Learning, Virginia Beach Central Academy, Adult Learning Center, and Open Campus. In addition, the school division presently operates several academy and magnet school programs. In high school, there is a Health Sciences Academy, a Global Studies and World Languages Academy, a Legal Studies Academy, a Technology Academy, a Visual and Performing Arts Academy, a Mathematics and Science Academy, and an International Baccalaureate Middle Years and Diploma Program (Princess Anne High School, PAHS). Harrison, co-author of this paper, is a computing teacher at PAHS.

Demographics: The VBCPS demographics show a culturally and racially diverse population with approximately 56% of the students Caucasian, 28% African-American, 6% Hispanic, 6% Asian, and the remaining 4% divided among Pacific Islanders, and Native American students. Approximately 49% of the students are female. Approximately 27% of the students are considered economically disadvantaged. The 11 high schools reflect the local neighborhoods and vary significantly in cultural makeup, ranging from 80% Caucasian and 11 % African American to 44% Caucasian and 37% African American.

CS Course Offerings – Background: VBCPS offers Computer Programming, Advanced Placement CS, International Baccalaureate Standard Level (IBSL) CS, and International Baccalaureate Higher Level (IBHL) CS. All courses satisfy graduation requirements in Mathematics with the AP and IB CS Courses satisfying graduation requirements for the Virginia Advanced Diploma.

CS courses have been offered by VBCPS at the various high schools since the early 1990s. IBSL and IBHL CS were introduced in 1999 and 2003, respectively, with AP CS following the transition from Pascal to C++ in 1998 and from C++ to Java in 2003.

The computer programming course has varied greatly in content and purpose. In the late 1990s the course consisted of one semester of Qbasic followed by one semester of C++. For the 2000 - 2001 school year, the course transitioned to a full year of C++, emphasizing procedural programming and numerical solutions.

Computer Programming Course – a Ten Year History at Princess Anne High School, PAHS: When computer programming was first taught in the 1999 – 2000 school year, approximately 25 students in two sections were enrolled in the course. Of these 25 students, only about one-half chose to continue the study of C++ during the second semester. Discussions with other computer programming teachers in VBCPS indicated a similar trend.

With the transition of the AP CS Course from Pascal to Java in 1998, VBCPS decided to change the computer programming curriculum to a full year course in C++. The course was taught at a much slower pace than the AP Course, covered one-dimensional arrays as the data structure, and emphasized numerical computation using real world problems. During the first three years, the number of students enrolled in computer programming rose dramatically, peaking at nearly 100 students at PAHS in the 2002-2003 school year. During this time, AP CS numbers remained fairly constant also, with about 20 students studying some combination of AP and IBSL CS.

Following the 2002-2003 school year, computer programming and AP CS enrollment dropped significantly, not only at PAHS, but across the VBCPS division. The decrease in enrollment was attributed to three main factors: transition to Java in the AP Curriculum, the number of students attempting to earn the Virginia Advanced Diploma by taking Algebra II (computer programming does not satisfy the Advanced Diploma requirement until the student has completed Algebra II), and the perceptions of students and parents that (1) CS is hard and (2) there are no jobs in CS. The 2004-2005 school year saw barely 30 students enrolled in computer programming, 10 in AP CS, and 5 in IBHL CS at PAHS. Numbers were similar at other high schools across the division. VBCPS CS teachers recognized the need to make significant changes in the curriculum to save CS in Virginia Beach.

Fortunately, 2006 marked the beginning of the textbook adoption cycle for Computer Programming. The textbook adoption committee, supported by the Mathematics Instructional Specialists, recognized that there was a unique opportunity to change the structure of the Computer Programming course so as to address the needs of students who desire to pursue the entire CS curriculum as well as those who have completed Geometry and need an additional mathematics credit to satisfy their graduation requirements. The committee decided that C++ was not the answer to the problem.

First, the committee looked at using Java in the computer programming course, perhaps with the BlueJ development environment, [1] focusing on more interesting but less mathematically challenging problems. Karel J Robot [2], among other approaches, was examined and rejected for the course. GreenFoot [11], at that time, was considered too immature, and there was little textbook support. Finally, the committee came across Alice, described at [5, 6, 7] with the results of a college-level study available from [13]. Alice seemed to be a potential answer to this dilemma. With Alice's drag-and-drop interface, the syntax errors that plague and frustrate beginning programmers were eliminated. Interesting problems could be explored from the beginning of the course. Complex animation was possible with the built in Alice commands. Interactive programming using the mouse and keyboard was easy, allowing students to create interactive programs without learning about listeners, events and other complex constructs.

The four members of the VBCPS textbook adoption committee attended an Alice workshop, which confirmed opinions concerning using Alice at the high school level as the first programming course. Upon consultation with Cooper and Dann, the VBCPS teachers were invited to be the pilot testing ground for the proposed ITEST grant. The goal was to provide faculty professional development in the form of Alice workshops and curriculum development workshops for high schools in Virginia Beach, and to use this as a model for the remaining five sites.

4. THE COURSE

The course and curricular materials developed at the Virginia Beach pilot session are based on the entire Learning to Program with Alice [7] textbook and approach. Chapter 8, Recursion, was specified as an optional unit in the curriculum. Approximately 27 weeks are allotted to cover the 11 chapters of [7]. This was planned to allow for 9 weeks to explore Java using BlueJ. The Java exploration focuses on the BlueJ Shapes and Picture project, introducing students to the Java programming constructs of selection and repetition using a familiar but significantly different interface. (It was decided to make the students' Java experiences as visual as possible, after having worked with the visual Alice for the major portion of the school year.) Most students quickly grasped the similarities, though they became frustrated with the same issues (syntax, lack of realism) that affect many beginning programming students.

The course is broken into five major sections consisting of 14 Units of instruction. Each unit covers a specific set of programming concepts or constructs, with spiraling built-in to refresh student understanding of previous topics. Programming concepts are presented using PowerPoint slides and illustrated with Alice program segments. Students then try these concepts using the examples developed in class before moving on to additional programming exercises. Each unit concludes with a programming project of greater scope and complexity than the programming exercises. Students construct either visual or textual storyboards depicting their program before actually writing the program and present their project to the class. This reinforces problem solving and algorithmic thinking, which are two major concepts of the course. VBCPS high school courses are taught on the alternating day block schedule. Each class meets alternate days for 95 minutes for the entire school year. Students are provided ample time to work on their programs in class. A brief course description follows:

Section 1 is an Introduction to Alice. *Unit 0 – Introduction to Computer Programming, History of Computing*: In this unit, students are introduced to the discipline of CS. They explore the history of the subject by constructing timelines of hardware and software development, discuss computer ethics, and research famous computer scientists. *Unit 1 – Getting Started with Alice*: Students explore the Alice programming environment by completing the four tutorials and appendix exercises. They are exposed to a number of computer programming terms, storyboarding and modify existing Alice Programs. *Unit 2 – Program Design and Implementation:* Students create storyboards to solve a variety of problems. They are introduced to simple Alice statements and the concept of a method. Working in teams of two, they develop a storyboard for a more complex scenario and present their solution to the class. Students then use their storyboards to create their first Alice program. *Unit 3 – Putting the*

Pieces Together: Students are introduced to control structures such as If/Else and Loop statements and functions. They use these structures and built-in functions to create storyboards and Alice programs. Student teams then complete and present a storyboard design and program as the culminating exercise for this unit.

Section 2 introduces object-oriented concepts. *Unit 4 – Classes, Objects, Methods and Parameters*: Building on the concepts developed in units 2 and 3, students more fully explore the differences between a class and an object. The concept of passing information to a method using parameters is developed using the built-in methods for each object. Students create their own methods and functions as part of the problem solution. They create a Halloween themed project and present their storyboard and project to the class. *Unit 5 – Interaction: Events and Event-Handling*: Students are introduced to the concepts of interactive programming using mouse and keyboard events. They create interactive programs and develop unit projects that require user interaction.

Section 3 focuses on functions and control statements. *Unit 6 – Functions and If/Else*: Students use functions to control decision making in If/Else statements. Incorporating previous concepts, the programs and projects become increasingly complex. Storyboards start to become more textual and algorithmic in nature due to the non-linear program flow as interactivity and decision making are added. *Unit 7 – Repetition: Definite and Indefinite Loops*: Students use both for and while loops to create more interesting programs. The concept of using functions to control the repetition either as a counter in the for loop or condition in the while loop is explored. Student projects continue to increase in complexity.

Section 4 covers advanced topics. *Unit 8 – Recursion (Optional Unit)*: Students are introduced to recursion using classic problems such as the Towers of Hanoi or game play where the number of moves is not known at the beginning. Students explore the concepts of base case and recursive case and discuss the pros and cons of recursive solutions. *Unit 9 – List Processing*: Students are introduced the concept of list data structures by creating lists of objects. Using the built-in Alice programming statements for-all-in-order and for-all-together, students process lists of objects. The advantages of using a list instead of multiple individual objects are discussed and illustrated. *Unit 10 – Variables and Revisiting Inheritance*: Students are introduced to mutable variables and use these variables as scorekeepers or timers. The concept of inheritance is revisited from earlier chapters where student created methods are added to an object to create a more capable object. This new object may be saved and used in later projects.

Section 5 transitions to Java. *Unit 11 – Transition to Java*: Students use the Java Style of the Alice programs to begin to explore Java syntax. They are introduced to the BlueJ Java programming environment and explore simple graphical Java programs. Students add constructors and create new programs using existing classes. *Unit 12 – Understanding Class Definitions*: Students explore existing Java classes and related Java concepts to Alice concepts. Object state, methods and functions are explored as are the programming constructs of decision-making and repetition. Real world examples are used to illustrate these concepts. *Unit 13 – Object Interaction*: Students explore more complex situations that require multiple objects in the solution. They explore how these objects interact by passing information to solve the problem.

The interested reader is invited to visit [17] to see the entire course curriculum. The zip files contain a course plan (including a schedule), unit plans, lesson plans, power points, laboratory exercises, project assignments, exams, and grading rubrics. Individual teachers at different high schools taught slight variations of the course, available from [17], but all covered nearly identical content.

5. RESULTS

The new Computer Programming Course is now in its fourth year, confirming the enduring effects of this project at Virginia Beach. PAHS is maintaining a solid 40 to 45 student enrollment in two sections. Many of these students are seniors who may have only completed Geometry. Classes are typically 35 – 50 percent female, 10 – 15 percent African American with a few high achieving ninth and tenth grade students. In addition, a small number of students with various learning challenges, such as those with Asperger's syndrome or other high-performing types of Autism, have participated in the course. All ten high schools are showing similar gains. All but one school has multiple sections of Alice, with marked increases in female and minority student enrollment. Two high schools, Kellam and Kempsville, offer four or five Alice sections, attracting those students who have struggled in mathematics courses by offering them the opportunity to fulfill their mathematics requirements in an interesting but challenging manner.

The new computer programming course is also showing some positive impact on the AP and IB CS courses. At PAHS, enrollment in AP CS is up for the second year, increasing from nine students in 2006 – 2007 to 18 in 2007 – 2008 and now 33 in 2008 – 2009. Four Computer Programming students were among the 18 AP Students in 2007 – 2008 and five are among the 33 in 2008 – 2009. While not large numbers, the success of the Alice project seems to be carrying over to attract students to AP CS.

6. CONCLUSION

The ITEST pilot project has been remarkably successful. In the third year after introducing Alice across the school district, all ten high schools are continuing to use Alice, offering significantly larger numbers of sections to significantly larger numbers of students. While the number of students taking the AP CS exam A is flat nationwide [22], there is a significant increase in the Virginia Beach schools.

Several lessons have been learned. (1) The first is that it would be extremely helpful if the secondary schools were close (geographically) to the university partner. While there were several advantages to having one of the original Alice researchers running the workshops, the 300 mile distance between Virginia Beach and Philadelphia meant that follow-up mentoring contacts were limited to once every 3 to 4 weeks, and it was not possible for students from Saint Joseph's University to work closely with the Virginia Beach teachers, to help them to build virtual worlds for use in the high school classes. (2) To disseminate the results of the workshops and of the course and of the teacher experiences to other Virginia high school teachers, it would have been helpful to have Virginia State Department of Education officials involved in the workshops or in the implementation of the project. (3) One of the side highlights of this project has been the community building within the Virginia Beach computing teachers. Often, there is only one computer teacher for an entire high school. That teacher is typically responsible for a different subject (in Virginia Beach, most of the computer teachers were also mathematics teachers), and would teach four preparations (introductory computing, AP computing, and two mathematics preparations) among the five classes. This higher number of preparations and being the only computer teacher often leads to an increased sense of isolation. Getting together with other teachers to discuss Alice every few weeks was beneficial to the teachers' sense of community.

Despite the successes of the Virginia Beach pilot program, several challenges for the future are anticipated. (1) All of the Virginia Beach teachers were also either mathematics or science teachers, and most had previous programming experience. Workshops that are held after this project concludes must be cognizant that many of the high school teachers will likely be business teachers, with no previous programming experience and, indeed, with very little prior STEM exposure. The movement of computing (as taught within high school) from the college-track to the career and technical track practically guarantees that this will be the case. Thus it is likely that the pace of the presentation of the Alice content within the workshops will need to be slower. (3) Future workshops will include teachers from multiple school districts (where all of the teachers at the Virginia Beach workshops taught at schools within the Virginia Beach School District). Thus, it will likely be more difficult for the teachers to develop the same sense of community that has been developed as part of the pilot. (4) There will likely be challenges moving to school districts that are more urban and rural. For example, computer access (both inside and outside of school) will likely be a challenge in many rural schools. (5) It will be essential to involve state Department of Education officials involved in the projects, as they have an important role to play in the dissemination of results throughout their states. (6) There is also a need to build a community of presenters, teachers who will be able to present Alice workshops throughout their state, and assist other teachers with the teaching of Alice. There are over 30,000 high schools in the United States, and offering workshops that "teach the teachers" will be essential to successfully disseminate project results.

7. REFERENCES

[1] Barnes, D. and Kolling, M (2009). *Objects first with Java: A Practical Introduction Using BlueJ*. Prentice Hall.

[2] Bergin, J., Stehlik, M., Roberts, J., and Pattis, R. (2005). *A Gentle Introduction to the Art of Object-Oriented Programming in Java*. cafepress.com.

[3] Bruce, K., Danyluk, A., and Murtagh, T. (2005). *Java: An Eventful Approach*. Prentice Hall.

[4] Buechley, L., Eisenberg, M., Catchen, J., and Crockett, A. (2008). The LilyPad Arduino: using computational textiles to investigate engagement, aesthetics, and diversity in computer science education. In *Proceeding of the Twenty-Sixth Annual SIGCHI Conference on Human Factors in Computing Systems* (Florence, Italy, April 05 - 10, 2008). CHI '08. ACM, New York, NY, 423-432.

[5] Cooper, S., Dann, W., and Pausch, R. (2003). Teaching objects-first in introductory computer science. In *Proceedings of the Thirty-fourth SIGCSE Technical Symposium on Computer Science Education*, Reno, NV, February.

[6] Cooper, S., Dann, W., and Pausch, R. (2003). Using animated 3D graphics to prepare novices for CS1. *Computer Science Education*, 13(1).

[7] Dann, W., Cooper, S., and Pausch, R. (2005) *Learning to Program with Alice*. Prentice Hall.

[8] Felleisen, M., Findler, R., Flatt, M., and Krishnamurthi, S. (2001). *How to Design Programs: An Introduction to Computing and Programming*. MIT Press.

[9] Figueroa, E. and Woods, R. (2007). Employment Outlook: 2006-2016. Industry output and employment projections to 2016. *Monthly Labor Review*, 130(11):53–85.

[10] Guzdial, M. (2005). *Introduction to Computing and Programming in Python: A Multimedia Approach*. Prentice Hall.

[11] Kölling, M. (2008). Greenfoot: a highly graphical ide for learning object-oriented programming. In *Proceedings of the 13th Annual Conference on innovation and Technology in Computer Science Education* (Madrid, Spain, June 30 - July 02, 2008). ITiCSE '08. ACM, New York, NY, 327-327.

[12] Malan, D. J. and Leitner, H. H. 2007. Scratch for budding computer scientists. *SIGCSE Bull.* 39, 1 (Mar. 2007), 223-227.

[13] Moskal, B., Lurie, D., and Cooper, S. (2004). Evaluating the Effectiveness of a New Instructional Approach. In *Proceedings of the Thirty-fifth SIGCSE Technical Symposium on Computer Science Education,* pages 75-79. ACM, Mar.

[14] Sanders, D. and Dorn, B. 2003. Jeroo: a tool for introducing object-oriented programming. In *Proceedings of the 34th SIGCSE Technical Symposium on Computer Science Education* (Reno, Navada, USA, February 19 - 23, 2003). SIGCSE '03. ACM, New York, NY, 201-204.

[15] Vegso, J. (2005). Interest in CS as a major drops among incoming freshmen. *Computing Research News*, 17, 3, 6-1.

[16] http://tecs.acm.org/ Accessed 8/27/2009

[17] https://www.aliceprogramming.net/ITEST/vb/index.html Accessed 8/27/2009.

[18] http://www.nsf.gov/pubs/2009/nsf09506/nsf09506.htm Accessed 8/28/2009.

[19]http://csta.acm.org/ProfessionalDevelopment/sub/TeacherWorkshops.html Accessed 8/26/2009.

[20] http://www.cra.org/CRN/issues/0905.pdf Accessed 8/29/2009.

[21]http://www.csta.acm.org/ComputerScienceTeacherCertification/sub/State_Certification_Files/requirementsbystate.html?CFID=42722&CFTOKEN=78079580 Accessed 8/26/2009.

[22]http://professionals.collegeboard.com/data-reports-research/ap Accessed 8/28/2009

[23] http://visualization.sju.edu/grants.html Accessed 8/27/2009

[24] http://www.alice.org

Novel Approaches to CS 0 with App Inventor for Android

Ellen Spertus
Mills College
5000 MacArthur Blvd.
Oakland, CA 94613
+1 510-430-2255
spertus@mills.edu

Mark L. Chang
Olin College
Olin Way
Needham, MA 02492
+1 781-292-2559
mark.chang@olin.edu

Paul Gestwicki (Moderator)
Ball State University
Dept of Computer Science
Muncie, IN 47306-0450
+1 765-285-8668
pvg@cs.bsu.edu

David Wolber
University of San Francisco
2130 Fulton St.
San Francisco, CA 94117
+1 415-422-6451
wolber@usfca.edu

Categories and Subject Descriptors
K.3.2 [**Computers and Education**]: Computer and Information Science Education.

General Terms
Human Factors, Languages

Keywords
CS 0, education, introductory computer science, mobile application development, visual programming environments, social aspects

1. SUMMARY
Google's App Inventor for Android (AIA) is a visual programming environment for creating mobile phone applications that is designed to be accessible and appealing to college non-majors taking introductory courses in computer science. Specifically, AIA provides a development environment similar to StarLogo TNG [7], Scratch [5], and Alice [2] but enabling users to create mobile applications incorporating social networking, location awareness, and Web-based services for Google's Android platform [1].

Faculty at twelve different colleges and universities used AIA in a wide range of introductory computer science courses for non-majors in the fall of 2009. After a short visual introduction to AIA, panelists from four of these schools will present:

- their different curricular approaches
- ways in which AIA was successful or unsuccessful in helping them meet their educational goals
- projects created by their students
- what they learned from their experiences that can be applied to other introductory computer science courses
- whether AIA was effective in interesting students who would otherwise not take computer science courses
- results of pre- and post-surveys of the students

SIGCSE'10, March 10–13, 2010, Milwaukee, Wisconsin, USA.
ACM 978-1-60558-885-8/10/03.

2. POSITIONS
2.1 Mark L. Chang, Olin College
Mark L. Chang, Lynn Andrea Stein, and Mark Sheldon delivered a collaborative, student-led first experience course designed to engage non-programming-oriented students in developing applications for mobile devices. The goal for the course was to observe how the different contexts of the participating students affected their design of mobile applications, as well as how having a tool that eases the learning curve empowers students and engages them in the creative process of building applications. From this, we hoped to be able to design a new set of tools and interfaces that not only eased the mechanics of development, but adequately captured the creative input of individuals who do not necessarily think in terms of code.

Students with existing experience developing for the Android platform were selected to lead a four-week mini-course. The students in the mini-course took part in a lightweight design exercise that involved paper prototyping and scenario sketching to fuel the brainstorming process. After candidate applications were proposed, the student mentors led technical sessions that introduced the students to the AIA programming environment with the goal of developing at least some part of their initial applications.

2.2 Paul Gestwicki, Ball State University
Paul Gestwicki modified his existing Visual Programming course to use AIA. The course introduces the basics of computing to non-majors through the development of graphical user-interfaces, conventionally using Microsoft VisualStudio to write Windows applications. Using AIA allowed students to work in the even more compelling domain of mobile smart phone applications.

The experimental section used AIA in the context of studio-based learning (SBL), a pedagogic approach that is characterized by representation construction, presentation, and discussion [3]. Specifically, the students created their own Android applications and presented these for discussion to both peers and instructors.

Gestwicki hypothesized that the combination of AIA and SBL would result in high student motivation and positive attitudes towards computing, which he formally evaluated using qualitative research methods and the Motivated Strategies for Learning Questionnaire [6].

2.3 Ellen Spertus, Mills College

Ellen Spertus taught a course at Mills, a women's liberal arts college, entitled "Technology for a Better World", in which she invited students to look beyond the applications of information and communication technology (ICT) to education and commerce that students were most familiar with and to consider ways in which ICT has changed and will continue to change life for relatively disempowered people, such as the use of Twitter in the aftermath of the Iranian elections, the One Laptop Per Child initiative, and how ICT is driving economic development at the bottom of the ladder, such as through enabling micro-finance and increasing the availability of pricing information [3]. Spertus chose this approach because of her own interest in the subject and because of her belief it would appeal to Mills students, known for their political activism and concern for social justice.

In addition to incremental reading, writing, debating, and lab assignments, students were assigned a final project in which to design, prototype, and present an Android application to empower, and not just to entertain, its target audience.

Spertus was also a developer of AIA while employed by Google full-time while on leave from Mills College and part-time while teaching the course.

2.4 David Wolber, University of San Francisco

David Wolber of the University of San Francisco taught a special section of a CS0 course entitled "Robots, Computing, and the Web" using Android phones as the "robots" and AIA as the programming environment. He hypothesized that students would be especially motivated to learn programming if they were able to build applications that they and others might actually use on their most used computing devices.

In lab, students learned programming concepts and problem solving through the development of simple games and convenience applications. They were also assigned readings and blog responses focusing on how mobile and cloud computing is changing society. Their final project was to design and build a mobile application that helped someone.

3. REFERENCES

[1] Abelson, H. 2009. App Inventor for Android. Google Research Blog, July 31, 2009. URL= http://googleresearch.blogspot.com/2009/07/app-inventor-for-android.html.

[2] Dann, W., Cooper, S., and Pausch, R. 2008. *Learning to Program with Alice*. 2. Prentice Hall Press.

[3] Torero, M. and von Braun, J., eds. 2006. *Information and Communication Technologies for Development and Poverty Reduction*. Johns Hopkins University Press, Baltimore.

[4] Hundhausen, C. D., Narayanan, N. H., and Crosby, M. E. 2008. Exploring studio-based instructional models for computing education. In Proceedings of the 39th SIGCSE Technical Symposium on Computer Science Education (Portland, OR, USA, March 12 - 15, 2008). SIGCSE '08. ACM, New York, NY, 32-396. DOI= http://doi.acm.org/10.1145/1352135.1352271

[5] Monroy-Hernández, A. and Resnick, M. 2008. FEATURE Empowering kids to create and share programmable media. *interactions* 15, 2 (Mar. 2008), 50-53. DOI= http://doi.acm.org/10.1145/1340961.1340974

[6] Pintrich, P., Smith, D.A..F., Garcia, T., and Mckeachie, W.J. 1993. Reliability and Predictive Validity of the Motivated States for Learning Questionnaire. *Educational and Psychological Measurement*, 53 (August 1993), 801-813. DOI=10.1177/0013164493053003024

[7] Wang, K., McCaffrey, C., Wendel, D., and Klopfer, E. 2006. 3D game design with programming blocks in StarLogo TNG. In Proceedings of the 7th international Conference on Learning Sciences (Bloomington, Indiana, June 27 - July 01, 2006). International Conference on Learning Sciences. International Society of the Learning Sciences, 1008-1009.

Effective Delivery of Computing Curriculum in Middle School – Challenges and Solutions

Youwen Ouyang (moderator)
Comp. Sci. & Information Systems
California State University
San Marcos, CA
ouyang@csusm.edu

Ursula Wolz
Comp. Sci. & Interactive Multimedia
The College of New Jersey
Ewing, NJ
wolz@tcnj.edu

Susan H. Rodger
Computer Science Department
Duke University
Durham, NC
rodger@cs.duke.edu

Categories and Subject Descriptors
K.3.2 [**Computing Milieux**]: Computers and Education – Computer and Information Science Education

General Terms
Design, Economics, Human Factors, Languages.

Keywords
Alice, computing foundations, middle school, Scratch.

1. SUMMARY
The ACM K-12 Task Force Curriculum Committee recognized that the lack of integration of computer science into the K-12 curriculum played an important role in the serious shortage of information technologist at all levels [2]. Much effort from the computing community has been devoted to improve the content and delivery of AP Computer Science. However, AP Computer Science is an elective at the high school level, isolating computer science from the standard curriculum. Jane Margolis argued that this has led to minority students "stuck in the shallow end", missing the opportunities to engage in a computer science experience prior to college [3]. After-school and summer camp activities designed for underrepresented groups are wonderful venues for students to participate in fun and exciting computer science activities. However, only a limited number of students may be reached by extracurricular programs. This panel brings together principle investigators of three National Science Foundation projects to share their experience of working with middle school language arts, mathematics, science, and social studies teachers. The panelists' presentations will be followed by open discussion on the challenges and solutions for effective delivery of computing curriculum in middle schools.

2. URSULA WOLZ
Ursula Wolz is the lead PI (with Monisha Pulimood and Kim Pearson) on the NSF funded project "Broadening Participation in Computing via Community Journalism."[8] (CNS 0739173) The goal is to entice middle school teachers to integrate computational thinking into their classroom instruction via an afterschool program. Pearson is a journalism professor. Pulimood is a computer scientist, who, with Wolz studies problem solving in community [4]. Wolz has written extensively on the teaching of introductory computer science.

SIGCSE'10, March 10–13, 2010, Milwaukee, Wisconsin, USA.
ACM 978-1-60558-885-8/10/03.

Wolz will report on a demonstration program with Fisher Middle School, Ewing, NJ. In the summer of 2008, four teachers (three language arts, one technology) and a guidance counselor spent a week learning interactive journalism, including procedural animation in Scratch [7]). In the following week these teachers led 16 Fisher rising 8th graders in researching, interviewing for and creating news stories for an online magazine. The stories were told via text, graphics, video and procedural animation. During academic year 08-09 the teachers took control of the afterschool magazine. Two of the teachers also integrated procedural animation into their language arts curriculum supplementing expository writing and poetry with Scratch projects.

In summer 2009, three of the language arts teachers returned as did the guidance counselor. They recruited an additional language arts teacher and a math teacher. Twentyeight rising 7th and 8th graders participated in the second run of our program in July and will continue in the second year of the afterschool program. All of the teachers are supporting further research on procedural animation in their curriculum via continued NSF funding.

Our project goal is to *infuse* computer science into existing curriculum by empowering teachers to adapt our principles and techniques in highly personal ways. Results of our formal study show that both the students and teachers understand the value of computational thinking skills, that they are confident they can master those skills, and that they develop rudimentary computational thinking skills. The primary impediment is access to technology. Our program suffers from the same roadblocks as those described by Margolis. Despite a solid technology framework in the school, teacher expertise is woefully inadequate. The IT staff mistrusts the teachers, who in turn are deeply frustrated at their inability to get both the computing and human resources necessary to adequately support computing in their classrooms.

3. SUSAN RODGER
Susan Rodger is leading the Adventures in Alice Programming project in Durham, NC. Eight universities in six regions of the country are integrating Alice into K-12, funded by an NSF ITEST grant ESI-0624642 and IBM. . The NC site specifically focuses on integrating Alice [1] into a diverse set of subjects in Middle School and High school. In summer 2008 Rodger trained thirty-five teachers in Alice in an extensive three week session and ran two one-week summer camps on Alice for middle school kids [6]. In summer 2009 she trained 100 teachers in one-week workshops and met with many of the teachers from the previous year for a 3-day follow-up workshop. Teachers attending these workshops

have included many disciplines: language arts, foreign language, science, math, social studies, business, music, art and media.

Rodger's approach is to teach both computer science concepts such as objects, functions and parameters along with basic Alice animation constructs such has how to glue two objects together, or how to move the camera to follow a moving object. We developed over 40 short tutorials. Some of them are starter tutorials that in 1-4 parts give students enough starting information to create a simple Alice world. The rest of the tutorials are specific about a computer science concept such as Lists, topic specific such as creating a 3D Helium Molecule which includes using lists, or Alice specific such as changing scenes by fading to black and fading back in. Younger students are likely to stick with the starter tutorials, whereas older students could be challenged more with the advanced tutorials. All of our tutorials are available for free on our website [5].

We see the majority use of Alice for K-12 in a course as a project (in place of a poster, model, or report). In language arts a student might create an Alice world for a book report or about a story they wrote. In science, a student might create an ecosystem. In a foreign language such as Spanish, the student might create a story that shows words of objects in the story in Spanish. Teachers from our workshop planned to use Alice in many ways. Some teachers built Alice worlds to show for a lecture (how a hot spot volcano is formed, school safety). Other teachers created an interactive Alice world for students to view and interact with such as a math world on area and perimeters of different shapes. Still other teachers have students build an Alice world either from scratch or using a template world to help them get started.

4. YOUWEN OUYANG

The CyberTEAM and iQUEST projects partner computer science and education experts to deliver learning modules that are rich in both computing and science curriculum to local middle schools. The computing curriculum focused by the projects includes Level I (Foundations of Computer Science) and Level II (Computer Science in the Modern World) of the ACM K-12 Model Curriculum [2]. The design of both projects is based on these guiding principles:

1. Technology intensive science investigations provide great opportunities for deeper understanding of computing and science concepts.
2. Students' best chance to experience technology-enhanced learning comes from technology-savvy teachers.
3. Technology must be introduced in the context of science curriculum in order to attract teachers and administrators.

Teachers participate in professional development activities that engage them in hands-on experiences that connect Information and Communication Technology (ICT) with their curriculum. Scientists are also invited to demonstrate effective use of ICT in their own research. Teachers then design classroom activities that engage their students in the use of ICT to support their learning of science. As teachers adopt ICT-enhanced learning resources into their curriculum, the projects help teachers understand the appropriate fundamental concepts underlying hardware, software, algorithms, and their adopted ICT-enhanced resources. Such knowledge is then transferred to middle school students as teachers guide their students in related classroom activities. Computer science students are deployed into classrooms as middle school students engage in ICT-enhanced learning activities. Such support is critical for teachers who hesitate to face ICT challenges on their own and who are concerned about technology glitches in the middle of their class activities.

Partner districts for the CyberTEAM and iQUEST projects have high percentages of Hispanic students and students from families of low socioeconomic status. These students have limited access to structured ICT activities beyond classrooms. At the beginning of the project, it is common to see teachers and students who treat technology as magic and simply sigh that "technology just does not like me" when they encounter a problem. Project activities have helped them understand that the magic of technology is created by humans according to certain underlying principles. As a result, they are more willing to trouble shoot technical problems and look for solutions that overcome the limitation of their access to technology. In addition, as students experience how ICT-enhanced resources advance their own learning, they become more motivated to explore ICT related career options.

5. ACKNOWLEDGMENTS

The panelists' works are partly supported by the National Science Foundation through CNS-0739173 (Wolz), ESI-0624642 (Rodger), OCI-0753422 (Ouyang) and DRL-0833753 (Ouyang). The opinions expressed are those of the panelists and do not represent the views of NSF.

6. REFERENCES

[1] Alice 2009, http://www.alice.org

[2] Computer Science Teacher Association (CSTA) 2003, *A Model Curriculum for K-12 Computer Science: Final Report by the ACM K-12 Task Force Curriculum Committee,* 2nd ed.

[3] Margolis, J., Estrella, R., Goode, J., Holme, J. J., Nao, K. *Stuck in the Shallow End: Education, Race, and Computing*, The MIT Press, Cambridge, MA 2008.

[4] Pulimood, S. M. and Wolz, U. 2008. *Problem solving in community: a necessary shift in cs pedagogy.* 39th SIGCSE March 12 - 15, 2008)

[5] Rodger, S. *Duke Adventures in Alice Programming*, http://www.cs.duke.edu/csed/alice/

[6] Rodger, S. et. al., *Engaging Middle School Teachers and Students with Alice in a Diverse Set of Subjects*, Fourtieth SIGCSE Technical Symposium on Computer Science Education, p.271-275, 2009.

[7] Scratch, http://scratch.mit.edu

[8] Wolz, U., Stone, M., Pulimood, M., Pearson, K. *Computational Thinking via Interactive Journalism in Middle School,* 41st SIGCSE, March 10-13, 2001

Re-imagining the First Year of Computing

Owen Astrachan
Duke University
ola@cs.duke.edu

Kathleen Haynie
External Evaluator
kchaynie@stanfordalumni.org

Chris Stephenson
Executive Director, CSTA
cstephenson@csta.acm.org

Lien Diaz
College Board
ldiaz@collegeboard.org

Amy Briggs
Middlebury College
briggs@middlebury.edu

Categories and Subject Descriptors
K.3.2 [**Computer and Information Science Education**]: Computer Science Education

General Terms
Design, Standardization, Management.

Keywords
Computer Science Education

1. Summary
The Advanced Placement (AP) Computer Science program is intended to reflect enough of a common core of a first semester or year of university-level computer science so that placement or credit can be awarded for work done before college. The SIGCSE symposia have a long history of providing forums for discussing the evolution of the AP program from its inception [1] to the transition in languages from Pascal to C++ to Java [2,3,5,7,8,9]. In [15] a report on the beginning of the project we report on here was presented. This proposed special session is a report on a new direction, with the potential for widespread adoption, for a new course in computer science for high schools and colleges; a course with the potential to be a new AP course attracting a larger and more diverse audience than typical introductory programming courses. In this session we will report on the process that has led to this new direction, the potential for piloting the new course, and the need for complete disclosure and dialog that will be part of this session.

2. Background
In April of 2008 the College Board announced the elimination of the AP AB exam (roughly corresponding to CS2). On the cusp of that announcement a *redesign commission* of high school and college educators was convened to examine the AP Computer Science program. The original charge to the commission was to develop learning claims with associated evidence to help assess what students know and to help ensure that the AP program is aligned with university programs. The elimination of one AP exam led to changes in the expectations of and charge to the commission. In August of 2008 the College Board received supportfrom the National Science Foundation (NSF) to examine new pedagogies and curricula that might impact the AP program.

SIGCSE'10, March 10–13, 2010, Milwaukee, Wisconsin, USA.
ACM 978-1-60558-885-8/10/03.

For example, philosophies and approaches in [12,13] could have an impact on both college and high school programs.

The NRC report [14] has led to potential changes in AP Science Courses that might engender changes at the University level, a potentially new and exciting direction. Large-scale changes at the high school level funded by NSF and based on work from [10,11] may have an impact on AP and pre-AP programs. As part of the 2008 NSF support to the College Board's AP Computer Science program an advisory group of college and high school educators met with the commission in September of 2008 subsequent to and in anticipation of a faculty colloquium that was held in October of 2008. The audience for that faculty colloquium was department chairs, curriculum developers, and in general those responsible for the design and implementation of the first year of university computer science programs. In this symposium we will report on the outcomes of a survey from that symposium.

The results of that survey led to a large project overseen by the College Board, funded by NSF, and with PIs from college and university settings. The commission overseeing the project includes college and high school teachers, an external evaluator, and College Board personnel. This new project, which is the subject of this proposed special session, also has an expanded board including representatives from SIGCSE, CRA, CSTA and related communities. The project that we report on in this session is the beginning of this new course and potential AP exam, a course that re-imagines the first year of instruction in computer science in the sense that the course does not correspond directly to any existing course, but pulls elements from several courses currently taught. The project will develop a curricular framework and support that could facilitate the widespread adoption of the approach, ultimately including professional development if the approach is to succeed both in the piloting and wide-spread adoption phases.

3. Session Details
Members of the commission, the advisory board, the College Board, and NSF may report on the logistics and process by which possible changes to the AP program are being developed. Part of this development includes communication with the constituencies involved with and impacted by AP --- precisely the SIGCSE community. This session will include reports from the different groups represented in this process: educators from both high schools and colleges in addition to the sponsoring groups for this process. Much of the session will be dedicated to hearing questions and concerns from the audience as well as from those not in attendance whose comments we will solicit before the SIGCSE symposium.

4. Audience and Expectations

Questions relating to the AP Computer Science program will have wide-ranging interest among SIGCSE attendees at both the post-secondary and K-12 level. College and university educators are specifically concerned with the extent to which any new AP CS curriculum and exam will lead to credit or placement when there is no current course on which the proposed course is based. The pilot program on which we report will try to demonstrate that the approach is feasible at the post-secondary level and that credit and/or placement is appropriate. The proposed course is neither a standard CS1 course nor a CS0 course in the traditional models of these courses. Instead, the new course re-imagines what a first course could be. This course is not meant to replace a programming-based CS1 course, but to augment offerings for students interested in computing. High school educators are also deeply invested in proposed changes to the curriculum and how such changes will impact their students and drive the need for increased professional development. At present there is considerable interest in the future directions of the program especially in light of recent changes announced by the College Board. This session will provide an opportunity for the computer science community to better understand the scope and possible directions currently being considered for a new course in computer science, to continue a dialog about the process and proposed content for the course, and to begin to solicit interest in the piloting process that will be necessary to ensure the success of the project.

As part of the project we will also provide extensive information relating to the evaluation of the proposed project, including the process used in evaluating the project and the methods by which success will be measured and determined.

5. REFERENCES

[1] David Rine, J.R. Jefferson Wadkins, and Steven Garland. Advanced Placement Program in Computer Science. Proceedings of the Fourteenth SIGCSE Technical Symposium on Computer Science Education (Orlando, FL, 1983), 204.

[2] Mark Stehlik, Susan Rodger, Kathy Larson, Alyce Brady, and Chris Nevison. Current and Future Directions of the Advanced Placement Exam. Proceedings of the Thirtieth SIGCSE Technical Symposium on Computer Science Education (New Orleans, LA, 1999), 358.

[3] Christopher Nevison, Joe Kmoch, Robert Noonan, Tim Corica, Sarah Fix, and David Kay. Changes in the Advanced Placement Computer Science Course: Case Studies and C++. Proceedings of the Twenty-Sixth SIGCSE Technical Symposium on Computer Science Education (Nashville, TN, 1995), 374-375.

[4] Jacabo Carrasquel, Joyce Currie Little, Allen Tucker, and James Collofello. Advanced Placement Computer Science Exam: How Universities are Handling Placement. Proceedings of the Sixteenth SIGCSE Technical Symposium on Computer Science Education (New Orleans, LA, 1985), 238.

[5] Owen Astrachan, Robert Cartwright, Rich Kick, Cay Horstmann, Fran Trees, Gail Chapman, David Gries, Henry Walker, Ursula Wolz. Recommendations for Changes in Advanced Placement Computer Science. Proceedings of the Thirty-First SIGCSE Technical Symposium on Computer Science Education (Austin, TX, 2000), 416.

[6] Barbara Boucher Owens, Fran Hunt, Stuart Reges, and Cary Laxer. The University Perspective: Awarding Credit for Advanced Placement (AP) in Computer Science. Proceedings of the Thirty-Second SIGCSE Technical Symposium on Computer Science Education (Charlotte, NC, 2001). 396-397.

[7] David Gries, Kathleen Larson, Susan Rodger, Mark Weiss, and Ursula Wolz. AP CS goes OO. Proceedings of the Thirty-Second SIGCSE Technical Symposium on Computer Science Education (Charlotte, NC, 2001). 423-424.

[8] Scot Drysdale, Judith Hromcik, David Reed, and Reg Hahne. The Year in Review: Changes and Lessons Learned in the Design and Implementation of the AP Exam in Java. . Proceedings of the Thirty-Sixth SIGCSE Technical Symposium on Computer Science Education (St. Louis, MO, 2005). 323-324.

[9] Reg Hahne, Cay Horstmann, David Reed, and Don Allen. Growl...roar...are we ready for tiger?: review of the current climate and changes to be implemented for the 2007 AP CS exam. Proceedings of the Thirty-Seventh SIGCSE Technical Symposium on Computer Science Education (Houston, TX, 2006). 378.

[10] Jane Margolis, Rachel Estrella, Joanna Goode, Jennifer Jellison Holme, Kimberly Nao. Stuck in the Shallow End. MIT Press, 2008.

[11] Jane Margolis and Allan Fisher. Unlocking the Clubhouse: Women in Computing. MIT Press, 2003.

[12] Wilson, G. Alvarado C., Campbell J., Landau, R., and Sedgewick, R. CS-1 for scientists. Proceedings of the SIGCSE Technical Symposium on Computer Science Education, SIGCSE Bulletin 40, 1 (March 2008), 36-37.

[13] Wing, J. 2006. Computational Thinking. CACM. 15, 5 (March 2006), 33-35.

[14] Learning and Understanding: Improving Advanced Study of Mathematics and Science in U.S. High Schools, Committee on Programs for Advanced Study of Mathematics and Science in American High Schools, National Research Council, 2002.

[15] Owen Astrachan, Henry Walker, Chris Stephenson, Lien Diaz, Jan Cuny. Advanced Placement Computer Science, the Future of Tracking the First Year of Instruction. SIGCSE Proceedings 2009, 397-398.

Peer Review in CS2: Conceptual Learning

Scott Turner
Department of CIS
ECPI College of Technology
Hampton, VA
scturner@vt.edu

Manuel A. Pérez-Quiñones, Stephen Edwards
Department of Computer Science
Virginia Tech
Blacksburg, VA
{perez, edwards}@cs.vt.edu

Joseph Chase
Information Technology
Radford University
Radford, VA
jchase@radford.edu

ABSTRACT

In computer science, students could benefit from exposure to critical programming concepts from multiple perspectives. Peer review is one method to allow students to experience authentic uses of the concepts in a non-programming manner. In this work, we examine the use of the peer review process in early, object-oriented, computer science courses as a way to develop the reviewers' knowledge of object-oriented programming concepts, specifically Abstraction, Decomposition, and Encapsulation.

To study these ideas, we used peer review exercises in two CS2 classes at local universities over the course of a semester. Using three groups (one reviewing their peers, one reviewing the instructor, and one completing small design or coding exercises), we measured the students' conceptual understanding throughout the semester with concept maps and the reviews they completed. We found that reviewing helped students learn Decomposition, especially those reviewing the instructor's programs. Overall, peer reviews are a valuable method for teaching Decomposition to CS2 students and can be used as an alternative way to learn object-oriented programming concepts.

Categories and Subject Descriptors

K.3.2 [**Computers and Education**]: Computer and Information Science Education – *Computer science education.*

General Terms

Measurement, Design, Experimentation, Human Factors

Keywords

Peer Review, CS Education, Learning, Object-oriented Concepts

1. INTRODUCTION

Teaching computer science, much like in other disciplines, we continually expose students to concepts in the discipline, to prepare them for professional activities and to teach them how to learn. One common way to do this is to have students create programs.

Students early in the computer science curriculum often define a successful program as one that one that compiles and runs. So, while they will be concerned about style guidelines and the requirements laid out in the specifications, if the program produces the correct output (i.e. the instructor's output), they consider it correct. These working programs, however, may be poorly designed and poorly implemented.

This creates a need for ways to expose students to critical programming concepts from another perspective, one that rewards students for understanding appropriate uses of the concepts and reasons for applying them. In other words, we want to use a non-programming activity to explore the fundamental aspects of programming. Peer review is one solution to the problem. It has many known benefits [14], and is used in many other fields [4] but there is no consensus on how beneficial the review process is in helping students learn object-oriented programming concepts in early computer science courses.

Specifically, we are interested in how reviewing can improve novice students' learning of the abstract, high-level concepts of Abstraction, Decomposition, and Encapsulation. These three were chosen because they are central to object-oriented programming [1] and good design. They are also meta-concepts that are likely to be new to students and misunderstood by them [11]. Increasing the students' understanding of these concepts early in the curriculum gives them a better foundation for the rest of their classes and for their future careers.

Based on earlier work [9], we are exploring the implementation in terms of the *type* of review. In this context, the review's *type* is either a peer review where students interact with each other or a training review where students practice on teacher provided materials. The decision to use a training review or a true peer review affects the social interaction between the students and may have effects on the learning of the students [9]. A better understanding of these issues is needed so that peer review may be effectively used in the computer science classroom.

2. RELATED RESEARCH

2.1 Peer Review

In the computer science education literature, there are a number of studies detailing the benefits of using peer review activities. There have also been a number of studies involving the creation of software applications to assist the peer review. Studies found in the literature have commonly evaluated how closely student reviews matched other students or instructor reviews [4, 12], basic student motivation and attitudes towards peer review [12, 13] and systems for performing reviews [14].

What is missing, in general, is a focus on the reviewer and learning. Many studies approach peer review from the view of the

SIGCSE'10, March 10–13, 2010, Milwaukee, Wisconsin, USA.

administrator and provide programs to address those concerns. Others look at the feedback and what those being reviewed have to gain. How the reviewer learns and otherwise benefits from the act of reviewing is not typically central to the literature. Studies into motivation and improvements in class work do relate to the reviewer but do not necessarily show that it improved learning. Exploring this unaddressed issue helps round out the literature and understanding of peer review.

To complicate matters, research and experiences in other fields may not translate into the computer science classroom. Theories of peer review [8] and some of the research in attitudes towards peer review [13] indicate that how the review is done and with what materials, can influence the outcomes. A better understanding of how the reviewer benefits from the review *in the computer science classroom* is needed.

2.1.1 Motivation
One reason for using peer review in the classroom is that it is an active learning exercise that offers a different type of learning activity. This has the benefit of breaking the monotony of a class in a typical lecture format. Our use of the reviews as another way to explore programming concepts provides a different perspective to the students and can help challenge their preconceived notions of computer science.

2.1.2 Peer Review Theories and Frameworks
One way to look at the process is from a cognitive viewpoint. Bloom's taxonomy [2] can be used for this. Peer review supports higher-level learning skills such as synthesis, analysis, and evaluation. Piaget's [7] and Vygotsky's [3] work provide a (social) constructivist approach to peer review. Peer review is an active process that engages the students in learning and can provide new perspectives to challenge current beliefs. Interaction between reviewer and reviewee allows for the creation of knowledge as the differences in knowledge and experiences provide an opportunity for dialogue. There are also numerous ways in which peer reviews can be carried out. Topping [8] provides a solid foundation in which to explore the peer review activity with a 17 dimension topology of the process.

In our work, we focused our attention on Topping's *Product/Output*, *Objectives* and *Directionality* dimensions. The *Product/Output* dimension is important in computer science classes. Reviewing design diagrams or code is not necessarily the same as reviewing a term paper, a film, or anything else. The concepts being reviewed and the methods being used (such as reading or running code) can be very different. This restricts what we can infer from peer review experiences in other disciplines. If we want to understand how reviewing programs helps students, we have to have them review programs.

We are actively exploring the dimensions of *Objectives* and *Directionality* which are related to the *type* of review: peer or training. For peer reviews, students work with other students and comment on their work and provide feedback through mutual social interaction. Training reviews are designed to help students learn to assess others before interacting with their peers but they limit the sociality. For both *types*, we want students to learn, but there are different emphases in the ways they are done.

2.2 Object-oriented Programming Concepts
One of the reasons for using peer review is to improve student understanding of the discipline's concepts. While there are many aspects of computer science we could enumerate and explore, we narrowed down the possibilities by examining those that are used early in an objects-first curriculum. We decided to focus on three broad concepts that are core to object-oriented programming: Abstraction, Decomposition, and Encapsulation.

Because we are specifically looking at these three concepts, it is important to clearly define them as we are going to use them. Our definitions are loosely based on work by Armstrong [1].

Definition: Abstraction—Using classes to represent logical, cohesive, and coherent ideas or items. Methods have a logical fit with the class's abstraction and provide common actions for that class. Implementation may not be known but can still be used.

Definition: Decomposition—Dividing the functionality, data, and responsibilities of a program into manageable portions. This includes creating classes to perform a specific task and grouping them with association and aggregation to form more complex structures. This also involves the use of inheritance to separate out and take advantage of commonalities between classes.

Definition: Encapsulation—Hiding information and restricting access to portions of a class. While this involves setting the correct scope for methods and variables, it also concerns what can be accessed or changed, and when those actions can occur.

These are interesting concepts both because they are central to the discipline, because they require high-level thinking and advanced mental development [7], and because they can be directly expressed in designs and code.

It is also worth noting that students use these concepts in their projects whether they understand them or not. Part of the importance of the concepts is that they are essential in building robust, elegant, and extensible program. On the other hand, understanding them is *not* required to build *working* programs. Research in this area has found that students can perform well in a class (as measured by grades, program completion, etc.) while carrying significant misunderstandings about the topics [11]. It is important these concepts are learned early and well.

Abstraction, Decomposition, and Encapsulation are critical concepts for the students to understand. Understanding them will help students understand the entire object-oriented programming process better. So, it would be greatly beneficial to the students to learn these ideas early. With peer review, there is the opportunity to give students more exposure to the concepts in authentic use. To use the process well, more information is needed to understand how the learning of the concepts is related and how the review process can be used to aid that learning.

3. METHOD

3.1 Participants
Participants were computer science students enrolled in selected sections of a CS2 course at two local universities. There were 64 students at one university and 70 from the other that participated in the study. The students' class level varied from freshman to senior (with just a few seniors). Most were Computer Science majors (75%) but there were also several students considering majoring in CS. There were a total of 13 females in the study.

3.2 Design

For each class, the reviews were designed to fit into and support the educational goals of the class. In this case, reviews were a mixture of code and design reviews. We had each reviewer evaluate two programs or designs for each activity using a rubric to guide them. The same rubric was used for all of the exercise. We also had students create and update a concept map to help us gauge student learning over the length of the study.

3.2.1 Concept maps

Before starting the study, the students were given a brief (10-15 minute) introduction to concept mapping. As an assignment, the students were then asked to draw a single concept map about their knowledge of Abstraction, Decomposition, and Encapsulation. They were also asked to update this map between the second and third study assignments and at the end of the semester.

Concept maps, as discussed in the literature, are a way to display an understanding of a body of knowledge graphically [5]. The creators of the maps select concepts that they think are part of a topic and connect those concepts according to their understanding of the relationships between them. This explicitly requires students to enumerate their knowledge and show how they think those ideas work together. This provides opportunities to find misconceptions.

There have been a number of studies that have looked at the changes in concept maps over time as an indication of changes in understanding over time [5]. Differences in what concepts were used and how they were linked show that the creator reevaluated the material in some way.

3.2.2 Groups

We used the same three groups in our experiment at both universities: a Peer review group, a Training review group, and a Control group. The peer review group reviewed the work of their classmates for each assignment. The training review group evaluated materials provided by the instructor. All of these resources were deliberately designed to have some strong and some weak points without being obviously a "good" or "bad" project. Both review groups were explicitly told who they were reviewing. The control group completed homework assignments, design or coding work, that were typical for the course. These exercises were designed to take about as long as the review tasks. Groups ranged in size from 15 to 26. For the complete experimental design details, see [10].

3.2.3 Study Activities

The sequence of activities in the study included a brief introduction to concept mapping and the creation of an initial concept map. This was followed by two review assignments. The original concept map was then updated and another two reviews were completed. Finally, the concept map was updated again near the end of the semester. Our work used a methodology similar to that found in Hay, Wells et al. [5]. The intervention was given as homework, spread over roughly ten weeks of classes. The timing of the assignments was worked into the routine of the class.

3.3 Data Analysis

Since concept maps can be used to display knowledge, this also makes them a good way to measure the students' understanding of object-oriented concepts. As discussed earlier, we can measure change in that understanding by looking at the differences in what concepts were used and how they were linked.

To analyze the concept maps, we had to assign values to several aspects of the maps. These values were calculated for the portion of the maps addressing Abstraction, Decomposition, and Encapsulation. As one value, we used the Novak and Gowin score [6], which rewards connections between concepts. As our second value, we counted the concepts in each group. This rewards the use of concepts in the maps rather than the connections. Our third value, the standard concepts count, recorded the presence of those concepts that should be in all maps. These are terms or ideas that come from our definitions of Abstraction, Decomposition, and Encapsulation, from basic object-oriented theory (e.g. class), and from the literature [1]. Students who did not complete one of the concept maps were excluded from the analysis.

4. RESULTS

Once we had coded and measured the Novak score, the count of concepts, and the count of standard concepts for each concept, the values were analyzed using a MANOVA with repeated measures over time. The school and group the students belonged to were used as factors in the analysis. To look at effects at each university, we also applied a MANOVA with repeated measures over time to each school's data. We used the scores from those students that completed all three maps. After the initial analysis, a post hoc analysis was completed on the significant factors. For most of our measures of the concept maps, there were significant changes over time and between schools.

4.1 Abstraction

Looking at the combined data for the concept of Abstraction, the mid- and post-map values for the Novak score and the number of concepts were significantly different from the pre-test ($p<0.01$, $p<0.05$ respectively). There were no differences found between the mid- and post-maps. We did not find any differences between the groups. There were significant differences between schools for the number of valid concepts ($p<0.05$) and the Novak score ($p<0.05$). The maps at Univ-2 were generally larger and with more connections but did not contain significantly more standard concepts. With the data separated by school, we saw the same basic patterns at both universities but, at Univ-1, they were not as large and not significant.

4.2 Decomposition

Decomposition provided us with a much different picture. In the combined data, school was a significant factor for all of the measures ($p<0.05$). As we have seen before, Univ-2 had higher scores than Univ-1. Viewing the schools separately, we found evidence of improvement over time at both universities.

More interesting than the differences between the schools are the differences between the groups over time. We looked at the individual groups over time and compared the groups at each point in time. The control group did not significantly change over time but the other groups did. For the Peer group, the mid-map Novak value was higher than the pre-map's ($p<0.05$). The post-map's Novak value is slightly lower than the mid-map's and is not significantly greater than the pre-map's. The changes in the Training group were more dramatic. Each score is greater than the last ($p<0.001$). As can be seen from Figure 1, the Training group is definitely diverging from the others. This is a good indication that the Training group understood the concepts faster than the other two. It should be noted that the Peer group also appears to be understanding the concepts better than the Control group, but it is fairly slight.

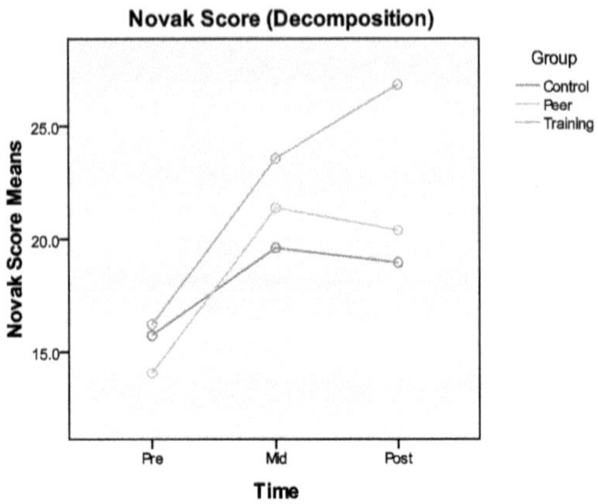

Figure 1: Decomposition Novak Score by Group (All)

We did not see this difference in groups when analyzing the data from each university. We only saw effects over time. However, looking at the data, we see a very similar effect. For Univ-2, both the Peer and Training groups have similar growth. It seems likely that both groups are experiencing benefits from the reviews but it also appears that the Training group is benefiting somewhat more.

We also compared the values for each map across groups. There were no significant differences at any of the three times. This seemed somewhat at odds with the changes found within the groups. After examining the data, it became apparent that there was a high level of variance within each group. So, while there are definitely changes in two of the groups, it is not visible when looking at the data only in terms of groups. We found similar interactions and results with the standard concepts value.

4.3 Encapsulation

When we looked at Encapsulation, we saw results over time similar to those with Abstraction but slightly more pronounced. Time was a significant factor for all the measures. Aside from the valid concepts, the mid- and post-map values were both significantly greater than the pre-map values ($p<0.005$) but were not different from each other. With the valid concepts score, there was also a significant difference between the mid- and post-maps ($p<0.01$). We did not find significant differences between schools except with the standard concepts ($p<0.05$). Univ-2's scores are still higher than Univ-1's overall, but with a smaller gap than seen earlier.

4.4 Comparison between Concepts

In the previous section, we looked at how the concepts changed over time. In this section, we compared the three concepts. This was done to contrast the students' relative understanding of Abstraction, Decomposition, and Encapsulation. Previous work [9] has found differences in how students reviewed these concepts. That was an indication that the students may understand them at different levels or be learning them at different rates. Here, we are exploring that idea further to better define what those differences are. This will help us determine if peer review is equally useful for all the concepts or if it is better for some than others. It also gives us additional insight into the students' understanding of the object-oriented concepts.

To do this, we compared the Abstraction, Decomposition, and Encapsulation Novak scores across each test. We used a MANOVA with repeated measures by concept for the pre-, mid-, and post-maps. As before, the school and group the students belonged to were used as factors in the analysis. The analyses were run on the entire data set and on the data from the individual schools. After the initial analysis, a post hoc analysis was completed on the significant factors.

First, we examined the Novak values. For the pre-map, we found interactions between the concept and the school ($p<0.01$). At Univ-1, there were differences between Encapsulation and Decomposition ($p<0.001$). From the results for each school, it appears that Univ-1 came into the class with a weaker understanding of Decomposition and Univ-2 entered with a more balanced knowledge of the concepts.

Examining the mid- and post-maps, we just saw the differences by school and by concept. All the scores from the universities were significantly different ($p<0.05$) with Univ-2 having the higher values. The more interesting finding was with the concepts. The Novak score for Encapsulation was significantly higher than either the Abstraction or Decomposition scores ($p<0.05$). Viewing the data by school, these differences are reflected at Univ-1. They were not significant at Univ-2, however. The data shows the same general trend as found at Univ-1, but it is much more modest. It appears that students find Encapsulation easier to understand and explain than the other two concepts. The change in the concepts' Novak scores over time supports this claim.

5. CONCLUSIONS

From its uses in other situations and in other disciplines [14], we had expected to see bigger gains from those reviewing (peer or training reviews) as they were exposed to more and more varied examples of the concepts in actual use. When looking at the concept maps, we, again, found no sign of an effect from the different groups except with Decomposition.

With Decomposition, however, we found effects between the groups. Both of the reviewing groups showed signs of improvement over those that did not review and the students who were reviewing the instructor-provided material proved to have the most growth. Although the nature of the growth was somewhat different at each school, the effects are plain. Reviewing program designs and code can help students learn and understand the concept of Decomposition at this level. For the other concepts we were measuring, Abstraction and Encapsulation, we did not find any noticeable differences (significant or otherwise) that would lead us to believe that the reviews affected them in the same, perhaps smaller, way. With those two concepts, the students that reviewed fared about as well as those who were doing additional design or coding exercises.

Exploring the differences between the students' understanding and learning of these concepts helped us shed some light on our findings. Looking at the concept maps and the rubric data, we started to see specific distinctions between the concepts. Based on its changes over time and on its comparison to the other concepts, students seemed to have the best understanding of Encapsulation and seemed to be learning it well. Their understanding grew over time and appeared to be stronger than that of the other two concepts. On the other hand, the students' knowledge of Abstraction seemed to be progressing the least. The data suggests that the students do not have a strong grasp on what it means to create classes that form a clear representation of a concept or real world object. When it comes to Decomposition, there were signs that students were actively trying to learn it.

Among other things, this suggests a partial ordering to the concepts. Teaching Encapsulation early and then devoting more time to Decomposition might be beneficial to the students as they seemed to have picked up Encapsulation quickly. The ideas behind Abstraction may need to be introduced early, but may not be understood until later classes. From the data, it is not clear how Abstraction relates to the other concepts. This ordering provides us with more information about to how focus our efforts.

To understand why this review process is effective for only one of the three concepts, we considered the nature of the ideas they portray. Abstraction and Encapsulation can both be applied very locally, for instance, to a single class [1]. Either the class represents a coherent real world object or ideas or it does not. The same is true of Encapsulation. Visibility is specific to a class as are the ways in which the class's data is accessed and modified. Both of these concepts are also relatively easily mapped to language constructs. Abstraction can be thought of as the collection of variables and methods in a class. Basic Encapsulation can be achieved through a small number of key words. Students can (and should) understand each of these two concepts on a broader scale so that they can see how simple, well defined classes simplify the program and improve reuse as they work together and how the correct protection of a class's inner workings reduces errors and unneeded dependences with other classes. But, as they are learning these concepts, they do not have to look at those wider perspectives.

Decomposition is different. By its very nature, it involves a bigger picture. Student must understand how classes can work together to build something more than the individual parts and they must see how problems can be divided into smaller and smaller pieces until they are solvable. It cannot be done at the class level and it does not map as nicely to language constructs. Yes, there are plenty of features that make Decomposition easier to achieve but there is nothing that helps a novice designer decide how to divide the functionality. The same computations could be done as part of a method, as its own method, as part of another class, in a completely separate class, and so forth. There are multiple possible approaches that are supported by the language that may or may not be appropriate for any given situation. Decomposition requires the student to identify the pieces of a problem and to consider how they are connected.

So, why are reviews helpful for this concept? Reviews provide students with someone else's interpretation of the big picture for a problem. They can get experience working at this higher level by analyzing and comparing the design choices with their own [3]. As they try to understand why a solution is the way it is, they can start to develop their knowledge of good and bad design choices.

This proposed explanation also helps us understand why Training reviews (instructor-provided material) appear to be more effective than Peer reviews. The instructor's designs and code can provide a richer experience and a wider selection of design decisions than are likely to be found in a student's work at this level in the curriculum. It can give students practice with ideas and techniques they have not been taught nor have thought of yet. The difference between the student's level of understanding and the instructor's (even in work with poor decisions deliberately inserted, as we did in the study) offers an opportunity for learning.

In closing, we found that the use of reviews can be a valuable tool for helping students learn OO Decomposition.

6. REFERENCES

[1] Armstrong, D. J. The Quarks of Object-Oriented Development. *Communications of the ACM*, 49, 2 2006), 123-128.

[2] Bloom, B. S. *Taxonomy of educational objectives*. Allyn and Bacon, Boston, MA, 1984.

[3] Doolittle, P. E. Vygotsky's Zone of Proximal Development as a Theoretical Foundation for Cooperative Learning. *Journal on Excellence in College Teaching*, 8, 1 1997), 83-103.

[4] Falchikov, N. and Goldfinch, J. Student Peer Assessment in Higher Education: A Meta-Analysis Comparing Peer and Teacher Marks. *Review of Educational Research*, 70, 3 (Autumn, 2000 2000), 287-322.

[5] Hay, D., Wells, H. and Kinchin, I. Quantitative and qualitative measures of student learning at university level. *Higher Education*, 56, 2 2008), 221-239.

[6] Novak, J. D. and Gowin, D. B. *Learning how to Learn*. Cambridge University Press, 1984.

[7] Piaget, J. *The Psychology of Intelligence*. Harcourt and Brace, New York, 1950.

[8] Topping, K. Peer Assessment Between Students in Colleges and Universities. *Review of Educational Research*, 68, 3 (Fall 1998 1998), 249-276.

[9] Turner, S. and Pérez-Quiñones, M. A. *Exploring Peer Review in the Computer Science Classroom*. Computing Research Repository, 2009 http://arxiv.org/abs/0907.3456v1.

[10] Turner, S. A. *Peer Review in CS2: the Effects on Attitudes, Engagement, and Conceptual Learning*. Virginia Tech, Blacksburg, 2009 http://scholar.lib.vt.edu/theses/available/ etd-08272009-003738/.

[11] Turner, S. A., Quintana-Castillo, R., Pérez-Quiñones, M. A. and Edwards, S. Misunderstandings about Object-Oriented Design: Experiences Using Code Reviews. In *Proceedings of the 39th SIGCSE Technical Symposium on Computer Science Education* (Portland, Oregon, 2008). ACM Press.

[12] van Hattum-Janssen, N. and Lourenco, J. M. Peer and Self-Assessment for First-Year Students as a Tool to Improve Learning. *Journal of Professional Issues in Engineering Education & Practice*, 134, 4 2008), 346-352.

[13] Xiao, Y. and Lucking, R. The impact of two types of peer assessment on students' performance and satisfaction within a Wiki environment. *Internet & Higher Education*, 11, 3/4 2008), 186-193.

[14] Zeller, A. Making students read and review code. In *Proceedings of the 5th annual SIGCSE/SIGCUE ITiCSE Conference on Innovation and Technology in Computer Science Education* (Helsinki, Finland, 2000). ACM Press.

Turning Exams Into A Learning Experience

Benjamin Yu, George Tsiknis, Meghan Allen
University of British Columbia
Department of Computer Science
2366 Main Mall
Vancouver, BC
Canada V6T 1Z4
benyu, tsiknis, meghana @cs.ubc.ca

ABSTRACT
Most students see exams as a stressful experience, having crammed as much as they possibly can and hoping that the material they have studied would indeed be on the exams, and the material that they did not have the time to study for, nor understand, would be overlooked by their professors. At the same time, instructors see exams as formal assessments of student learning. Exams are seldom thought of as a learning experience. In this paper, we report our experiences in the use of two-stage exams as a learning experience for the students in two different courses. In a two-stage exam, students write an exam individually, then they rewrite the same exam in collaboration with three or four other students. One of the main objectives is to encourage peer instruction and promote learning even during the exams. Students obtain immediate feedback during the exam, and initial results have shown that this type of exam format produces some positive effects in later assessment.

Categories and Subject Descriptors
K.3.2 [**Computers and Education**]: Computer and Information Science Education – *Computer Science Education, Self-Assessment.*

General Terms
Design, Experimentation, Measurement, Human Factors.

Keywords
Two-stage exams, learning, peer-instruction, assessment, midterms.

1. INTRODUCTION
Traditionally, learning is thought of taking place only in the classroom, labs, or when students are engaged in their homework assignments, or readings, whereas midterms and final exams are thought of only as student assessments so students can demonstrate what they have learned. Learning is not emphasized during exams, but perhaps takes place as a by-product after the exams. However, learning can take place during exams if the exams are conducted in such a way to foster learning rather than solely focusing on recall of material or concepts learned in preparation for the exams. A shift of focus on learning rather than on testing can also reduce the anxiety most students associate with exams. This paper discusses the use of two-stage exams, which turn the exams into a learning experience, in the midterms of two different computer science courses. We will report the students' comments on the midterms and how their performances on the midterms correlate with the final exam that consists of isomorphic questions as those in the midterms. We will also discuss how the administration of two-stage exams can be improved.

This paper is organized into the following sections. Section 2 provides the background information of the two-stage exam. Section 3 describes the courses which we administered the two-stage exam. Section 4 provides the details of what transpired during the exams. Section 5 includes both anecdotal comments from the students on the two-stage exams as well as analysis of their performance in the two-stage exam and the correlation with isomorphic questions on the final exam. Finally, section 6 is a discussion of the experiments, with concluding comments and future work in section 7.

2. TWO-STAGE EXAM
The idea of a two-stage cooperative exam is that students take the same exam twice during an extended period of time but in different settings. These settings can be individual in the beginning, followed by working in pairs, or collaboratively in a larger group. The goal is to turn these testing sessions into a learning experience. Cooperative group problem solving has been shown to be an effective technique for helping students learn a complex skill [5, 6, 7]. However, the authors are not aware of two-stage exams having been extensively conducted and studied in too many contexts.

An example of how two-stage exam is implemented in a large class for midterm or final exams as reported in [8] is as follows: during the first 30 minutes of the class period, the students take a multiple-choice exam with about 20 - 25 questions in it individually. They hand in the answer sheets at the end of the exam. Then right away, they are given the same multiple-choice exam but with added questions in it, and are asked to work on it collaboratively with someone close by for 45 minutes. They can use books, notes, and other resources. The grade of the exam is calculated based on a weighted average of the first submission (75%) and second submission (25%) of the exam. However, if this grade is less than the grade in the first submission (i.e. from the solo effort alone), then the final score of this exam is based solely on the first submission.

With this simple change in exam format throughout the term, it was reported that there was a large improvement in the final exam scores from a mean of 74% to 80%, based only on the solo part of

SIGCSE'10, March 10–13, 2010, Milwaukee, Wisconsin, USA.

the exam. Although it seems that the collaborative component of the exam may have boosted the final score, a statistical comparison with grades from previous years with no collaborative component in the exams shows that there is no dramatic change in grade distribution. The number of students at the bottom rungs of the ladder is fewer with the two-stage cooperative exam strategy, but there is no increase in the upper rungs.

There is another significant benefit of the two-stage exam, which is the immediate feedback the students receive during the group discussions. It has been reported that the single most powerful influence for student achievement is feedback [1, 4]. But it is not just any feedback. Informative, timely, concise feedback, which the students can actually follow up on, is what really counts. In particular, timely feedback received by students while it still matters to them and in time for them to pay attention to further learning or receive further assistance is especially important for student growth and learning [3]. While the group discussions do not guarantee that the students will come up with the correct answers to all the questions in the exam, the group discussions provide ample opportunities for the students to collaborate in solving the problems from different angles and perspectives, thus fostering an enriched environment for learning.

Given the encouraging results from the research literature and similar experiences of two-stage exams in other courses from other disciplines at our university, we decided to try this exam format in the midterms of two computer science courses offered during the summer sessions of 2009 at the University of British Columbia.

3. COURSES / STUDENT BACKGROUND

This section provides the background information of the two courses where two-stage exams were administered.

3.1 Course 1: Models of Computation

The first course is one of our first year courses on formal models of computation. It covers similar topics as the Discrete Structures knowledge area of the ACM Computer Science Curriculum [2]. The course explores formal modeling systems to understand and explore the capabilities of computers, and, more generally, of any process for solving a problem. Topics include reasoning about formal systems and proving relevant properties, propositional and predicate logic, creating regular expressions, creating and using Deterministic Finite Automatons, justifying behaviors and correctness of some algorithms, etc.

A total of 37 students registered in this course with 11 females and 26 males. The course included three 2.5 hour lectures, four hours of lab, and one hour of tutorial each week for 6 weeks.

3.2 Course 2: Introduction to Software Development

The second course is one of the beginning programming courses for Computer Science majors at the University of British Columbia. It is usually taken after the introductory programming course in the first year. Because of the applied nature of the course material most of its learning goals are at the *application* level of the *cognitive domain* aspect of the learning taxonomy. The course introduces students to the software development process. It covers similar topics as the introductory part of the Software Engineering knowledge area of the ACM Computer Science Curriculum [2]. Topics include design practices, data abstractions, inheritance, testing, concurrency, and distributed computing.

A total of 59 students registered in this course with 24 females and 25 males. The course included three 2.5 hour lectures and two two-hour labs per week for 6 weeks.

4. MIDTERM EXAM

Both midterm exams took place in the lecture theatre. In Models of Computation the students were given 80 minutes to do the test individually, and in Introduction to Software Development the students were given 50 minutes to write the test individually. In both courses after the individual portion of the exam, the students then rewrote the same test in groups of three or four after they handed in their individual work. In both cases, there were significant discussions among the students during the collaborative part of the exam. The following sections provide additional details of what took place in each of the courses.

Models of Computation

The students were given approximately 50 minutes to complete the exam in groups of three or four. The students had been working on problems in small groups during lecture all semester and were therefore already comfortable working with their classmates. They quickly organized themselves into 11 groups. We observed that most of the groups worked through each problem together and discussed the best approach to take for each particular problem. In most groups the students were having interesting discussions and did seem to be learning from one another.

Three of the groups stood out as problematic. The first group was entirely comprised of extremely high-achieving students. Instead of discussing each question, this group split the exam up into four sections and each student completed one section of the exam. They then reviewed each question and handed in their exam early. This was a reasonable strategy for this particular group since each student was strong and able to do quite well without input from the other group members. However, in this particular instance the two-stage exam was not a learning experience for the students, instead it was just a simple re-write of questions they had previously answered.

The second group was comprised of three low-achieving students and one high-achieving student. None of the three low-achieving students were able to provide much useful input so the high-achieving student essentially wrote the entire group exam. This was unfair for the high-achieving student because he greatly assisted the other members of his group and did not receive any reciprocal assistance in understanding the material on the exam.

The third group was comprised of one extremely high-achieving student (female) and three average-achieving students (males). This group had good debates about the questions. However, the extremely high-achieving student was unable to convince the other three group members that her answers were correct. This is consistent with Heller and Hollabaugh's observation that three-member groups with one female and two males do not perform as well homogeneous gender groups or mixed gender groups with two females and one male [6]. This was frustrating for her, and demonstrated that some students would not learn as much as they could from their group members.

Introduction to Software Development

To increase participation and active learning opportunities, a number of group activities are normally included in this course. In each lecture, true-false or multiple choice questions were used during the presentation-discussion of a concept and at least one long group exercise was included at the end of the presentation. During these group exercises, students were asked to work in groups of two or three and use the ideas and techniques they have learned to solve a related problem. After the students have submitted their work, the instructor would ask for input from the groups and present the solution on the board. Typical exercises take up 10 to 15 minutes of the class time.

Since the students already had experience with group work, it was anticipated that they would be pleased with the notion of the two-stage midterm exam when it was announced. However, nearly one third of the students had some concerns with the group exam portion when they were told that their exam mark would be a weighted average of the individual and group exam. A number of good students were afraid that the group work would not provide any significant help for them and it might even slow them down. Some of the low-achieving students felt that they may be embarrassed if they could not contribute enough at the group exam. The concerns diminished considerably when the students were informed that the score of the group exam would not be taken into account if it was lower than the score of the individual exam, and the students could choose their group partners.

As stated before, after the students took the individual exam, they formed groups of three or four and were given a new exam paper with the same exam questions which they had to complete in 30 minutes. It is important to note that none of the questions were multiple choice questions. All the questions required a considerable amount of work to derive the answers which were of the form of short (10 to 15 lines) Java programs, short answers, or mathematical computations.

The first significant notable difference between the group exam and the regular group exercise is that every student actively participated in their group. During the group exercises in the lectures before the midterm exam, five of the students in the class never joined any group; they always worked on their own. Even after a number of attempts to convince them of the benefits of group work, they continued to work on their own. However, during the group exam, it was a pleasant surprise to see these five students not only participated in their groups, but also being very active in the group discussions. A couple of them even took the lead to write out the group's final answers on the exam paper. When they were asked how they liked the new experience, four out of the five replied that they enjoyed it very much. Moreover, these four students started participating in groups during the lecture group exercises after the midterm exam.

The rest of the class was similarly involved in active discussions during the group exam. Because the students had formed the groups by themselves, each student was familiar with their team members, and they were comfortable to openly discuss the exam questions. However, we did notice that there were a few students who took some time to find a group for various reasons. Even in those cases, there were significant discussions among the students during the group component of the exam.

There is another notable difference between the group exams and the individual exams in that the amount of working scribbles is more on the group exams than the individual exams, and occasionally, multiple attempts of the solution of the same question are seen on the group exam papers. This is an indication that even though the time for the group test was less than the time for the individual test, there were significant collaboration and effort from the group to solve the questions.

An analysis of the individual and group responses to each exam question reveals some more interesting facts. The test question on which the group performance had the largest average gain was a programming question on how to use certain data structure for a specific problem. It seems that this type of problems benefit greatly from the group collaboration and the fact that an isomorphic question (more details in the next section) in the final exam shows a 50% improvement above the individual score is a strong indicator that the group activity may have helped in the student learning.

There was also a question in the exam where isomorphic questions have been included in every midterm given for this course. In this question we provide a specification of a method of some class and ask the students to list a minimum set of test cases that comprise a sufficient black-box testing of the method. One of them is on the selection of test cases for a piece of software and the other is on class design. Students have always had difficulties with such questions in the past. The average score on similar questions in the midterm and the final exam were low and the same errors would appear each time. This summer, even though the average group score on the software testing question of the midterm exam was only 11% higher than the individual average, the average score of the isomorphic question in the final exam was 31% higher than the individual average of the corresponding midterm question. Moreover, 72.5% of the students in the class improved their individual score on this question in the final exam, and only 15.5 % of them did worst in the final exam question. It seems that this type of question benefits well from group discussion.

After the midterm exam, the students were asked if they learned anything new from the group exam. More than half of the class indicated that the exam was indeed a learning experience for them. Only three of the 59 students indicated that they were forced to accept an answer without being convinced that it was better than theirs. Finally, all except five students wanted to have a two-stage final exam.

5. DATA ANALYSIS

We have also conducted online attitudinal survey towards the end of the term. Here are some of the results. For the course on Model of Computation, 75.9% of 29 students surveyed responded positively to the midterm, 13.8% responded negatively, and the rest (10.3%) were neutral.

Three isomorphic questions from the midterm were included in the final to see how the students perform on these questions. The final exam was conducted as individual exams and no group discussion was allowed. Surprisingly, there is quite a significant drop in the overall student performance on these questions in the final exam. Overall, there is an average drop of 6% among the three isomorphic questions. One question skews the result quite significantly with a drop of 23%, another question has no change, and the third isomorphic question in the final has a 10% gain.

For the course on Introduction to Software Development, the end of term online attitudinal survey shows that 75.5% of 49 students surveyed responded positively to the midterm, 18.4% responded negatively, and the rest (6.1%) were neutral.

Three isomorphic questions from the midterm exam were also included in the final exam to see how students perform on these questions. Just like the other course, the final exam was conducted as individual exams and no group discussion was allowed. In this case, the result is more encouraging: 72.5% of the students did better in the first question, 51.7% did better in the second question, and 50% did better in the third question. At the same time, 15.5% of the students did worse in the first question, 48.3% did worse in the second question, and 20% did worse in the third question.

5.1 Student Comments

As indicated above, most students are positive about the two-stage exams. Here are some of their comments:

"..we got immediate feedback and thus we immediately were able to learn our mistakes. whereas getting back midterm at a later date makes us care less about the midterm material.."

"..When we did the midterm the second time with our partners, they made me realize certain issues i didn't see before. Also, I learned from them certain techniques they use in handling such questions that is very useful to me now. ..."

"... I learned alot (sic) from others. I was also able to help others who didn't understand something that I did ..."

"...I trhink (sic) that was fun, amazing and very helpful many benefits can come out of that: team work is important, you get to see different point of view and of approaching a problem. It also turns the stress of the exam into something positive. .."

However, there are also negative comments:

"I felt that I couldn`t put 100% of my input because some of my group members were really persistent on their solutions (even though, the answer key indicated, I was closer to the solution than they were). Our score was somewhat similar to my individual grade and so my mark wasn`t boosted as high as some of my group members (because their individual grade was a lot lower) - this is kind of unfair."

"...partnership wastes a lot of time. It helps in boosting the marks, though, which I like. But in terms of learning, less likely to, especially if we have already done it once individually. Better if we have one exam for individual and one or two questions for the partners."

6. DISCUSSIONS

While there are strengths in the two-stage exams, we did encounter challenges in both of our courses.

- As reported in the surveys, high-achieving students claim that they don't seem to get much out of the two-stage exam, while low-achieving students do. Although this may be the case where there is not much of grade improvement for the high-achieving students, their understanding of the material would have been improved due to their discussions and explanations of their solutions in the group portion of the midterm. The imbalance of group member abilities where stronger students have more to contribute than to receive from other members may be one of the factors that need addressing. One possible way to avoid this is to provide other opportunities for students to work with different groups before the exam so they can find a group they are comfortable in working with. Another possibility is to have the instructor assign students of similar GPA to the same group.
- Students who have difficulty in articulating and explaining their answers in the group discussions also do not feel the group exam was beneficial. This may not due to the exam format but more on the opportunities and practices the students need to have in order to communicate effectively their ideas to others. The two-stage exam would have highlighted this to these students so they can take appropriate steps to improve their teamwork and communication skills.
- Time was wasted during the exam period (in the case of Introduction to Software Development) for some of the students to organize themselves into groups. Students should be given ample notice to plan ahead who they would like to work with before the exam rather than trying to find a group in the last minute. Again, instructor assignment of groups may be a solution.
- One of the student comments relate to the difficulty level of the exam. If the exam is too easy and the questions are too straight forward, it defeats the purpose of the two-stage exam. In order to turn the exam into a learning experience, the questions in the exam should be challenging and the solutions non-trivial. Of course this is true for good exams in general.
- In both courses, the same exam was used in the individual section as well as for the group section of the two-stage exam. To foster even more discussions and knowledge transfer, it would be beneficial to add other additional isomorphic question for the group section, as is recommended in the literature..
- In both courses, a number of students commented that the time allocated to the group section was insufficient, especially for discussions. As opposed to [8], the exams conducted in the two courses were not just multiple choice questions. Hence, additional time was required to write out the solutions.

7. CONCLUSION AND FUTURE WORK

The initial feedback from the students as well as their performance in both the midterm exams and the final exam suggest that two-stage exam can be a valuable learning experience. As noted in one of the comments from the students, the two-stage exam "turns the stress of the exam into something positive". There are also some indications that the students do better in the isomorphic questions in the final exam given their experience in the midterm exam. Whether this is due to the learning gain from the two-stage exam or not will require further investigation. At the same time, such performance gain is not evident in all the isomorphic questions. We intend to analyze these questions at greater depth, as well as the student solutions from the solo portion of the two-stage exam, the solutions from the group portion of the two-stage exam, and the solutions from the final exam. We are also conducting two-stage exams at higher level courses of our computer science program. If students see exams as part of the learning process, we hope that their retention of the material will also be greater in later terms, and we plan to conduct longitudinal study that will follow up on this study.

The authors would like to acknowledge funding provided by the Carl Wieman Science Education Initiative for this study.

8. REFERENCES

[1] Black, P. & William, D. (1998). Assessment and classroom learning, Assessment in Education, vol. 5, no. 1, pp 7-74.

[2] Computer Science Curriculum 2008: An Interim Revision of CS 2001. (December 2008). Association for Computing Machinery. Retrieved on September 7, 2009 from http://www.acm.org//education/curricula/ComputerScience2008.pdf.

[3] Gibbs, G. & Simpson, C. (2005). Conditions Under Which Assessment Supports Students' Learning, Learning and Teaching in Higher Education, Issue 1, pp. 3 - 31.

[4] Hatte, J.A. (1987). Identifying the salient facets of a model of student learning: a synthesis of meta-analyses, International Journal of Educational Research, vol. 11, pp. 187-212.

[5] Heller, P., Keith, R., Anderson, S. (July 1992). Teaching Problem Solving Through Cooperative Grouping. Part 1: Group versus Individual Problem Solving. *American Association of Physics Teachers*. 60(7). pp 627 - 636.

[6] Heller, P., Hollabaugh, M. (July 1992). Teaching Problem Solving Through Cooperative Group. Part 2. Designing Problems and Structuring Groups. *American Association of Physics Teachers*. 60(7). pp 637 - 644.

[7] Schwartz, D. L. (1999). The productive agency that drives collaborative learning. *Collaborative Learning: Cognitive and Computational Approaches*, pp. 197-218.

[8] Yuretich, R., Khan, S., Leckie, R., Clement. (March 2001). Active-Learning Methods to Improve Student Performance and Scientific Interest in a Large Introductory Oceanography Course. Journal of Geoscience Education. 49(2), p 111- 119.

Experience Report: Peer Instruction in Introductory Computing

Beth Simon, Michael Kohanfars, Jeff Lee, Karen Tamayo
Computer Science and Engineering Department
University of California, San Diego
La Jolla, CA USA
bsimon@cs.ucsd.edu, {mkohanfa, jwl001, ktamayo}@ucsd.edu

Quintin Cutts
Department of Computing Science
University of Glasgow
Glasgow, Scotland.
quintin@dcs.gla.ac.uk

ABSTRACT
Peer Instruction (PI) is a pedagogical technique to increase engagement in lectures. Students answer a multiple choice question (MCQ) typically using *clickers* (hand-held remote devices with a minimum of 5 option buttons), discuss the question with their peers, and then answer the question again. In physics, PI has years of evidence of increased conceptual learning, as measured by the Force Concept Inventory (FCI)[7]. In this experience report, we describe how PI was applied in CS1 and CS1.5 courses teaching Java. We identify specifics of the standard PI model which were adopted, adapted, or discarded for use in introductory computing, describe the process involved for the instructor, give examples of the types of questions asked of students, report on students' performance in answering these questions, reflect on the value for the instructor, and report the attitudes and opinions of the students. We conclude with observations, advice and suggested improvements.

Categories and Subject Descriptors
K.3.2 [**Computer Science Education**]: Introductory Programming – *abstract programming concepts*

General Terms
Human Factors

Keywords
CS1, peer instruction, clickers, PRS, classroom response, active learning.

1. INTRODUCTION
Peer Instruction (PI) is a well-documented method of instruction which has been shown to improve student performance on conceptual questions in physics for almost 20 years [4]. Specifically, PI challenges students to work with their deep understanding of the core concepts of the subject rather than the simpler rote application of formulae. The specific PI format is to pose students a ConcepTest (a MCQ requiring deep conceptual understanding) to answer individually using clickers, then have them discuss the question in groups, challenging each other on their answers, and after reaching a group consensus, to answer again. Often this process is accompanied by reading quizzes which students complete before class (requiring them to read material that won't be lectured on, to make time for ConcepTests and discussion), mini-lectures before a ConcepTest covering difficult issues from the reading, and post-ConcepTest discussion led by the instructor. Student performance is shown to increase on both standardized measures (such as the FCI) – and on control comparisons of final exam questions [4].

Here we report on the process and results of applying the PI model in introductory computing courses. Our goal was to leverage the benefits the PI model has shown for engaging students in deep understanding of core concepts – but in the context of introductory computing challenges. We describe the process by which ConcepTests were developed, the kinds of questions developed, the way in which they were presented and used in class, how students fared answering these questions, and student valuation of PI assessed through survey questions. We conclude with recommended advice and suggested improvements.

2. RELATED WORK
The seminal work on PI in physics was reported in [4]. However, additional summative reports in other disciplines can be found [2]. Best practices guides are also available [12].

In the computing education context, use of a specialized web application called MessageGrid was reported in an algorithms and data structures course. [10] Pre-lecture reading assignments were given and mini-lectures (10-15 min) were followed by audience questions and discussion using MessageGrid following the PI model. Students reported the process was valuable for learning. However, that work did not evaluate the student performance on MessageGrid questions, discuss how questions were developed, or note how many questions students answered throughout the term.

Clickers are used in [9] in a short course CS1 in Java, asking questions approximately every 15 minutes. However, they did not use the PI instructional model and do not report on student responses to questions. Detailed results are provided in [3] from a one-week experiment using clickers. However, [3] differed substantially from the PI model, using clickers for a 10-15 minute comprehension test at the beginning of class, followed by group work, reported back at the end of class via use of clickers.

Cutts et al. developed a special feedback session of PI questions derived directly from issues arising classwide in a written mid-term exam, in order to engage the students fully with aspects of the course demonstrated to be problematic [5].

3. SETTING

In this section we describe the courses where PI was used and the adaptations we made to the general PI model.

3.1 The Courses

We report on two introductory computing courses taught at a large US research intensive public university on the quarter system (10-week terms). The courses are a Java-based CS1 and CS1.5 (first two terms) of introductory computing intended for students with no prior programming experience. PI was used for the first time in Fall 2008. The courses reported here are from CS1 in Winter 2009 and CS1.5 in Spring 2009, i.e. the second time they were taught. We present these "second trys" as reflecting slightly polished "first attempts" at using PI in introductory computing. The same instructor (Simon) taught both courses, and 60% of the students from CS1 enrolled in CS1.5.

Table 1. Course Size and Pass Rate

Course	Pass	D or F	Withdraw
CS1 (N=94)	86%	7%	7%
CS1.5 (N=69)	88%	3%	9%

3.2 Model Adaptation

The PI model does not simply involve having students answer questions with clickers in class. Within the PI literature (primarily in physics) there are specific implementation features of PI that, when applied, have been shown to have strong positive impacts on learning. The instructor adopted some aspects of the PI model faithfully, but also deviated from the standard model in some aspects. The standard components are itemized below with bold indicating whether they were adopted here.

- Textbook reading **was** assigned before each class
- Reading Quizzes (before or at the beginning of class, to encourage students to complete the reading and self-test their understanding of it) **were not** used due to preparation cost.
- Mini-lectures **were not** used. A common PI tradition is to have 10-15 minute mini-lectures prior to a set of ConcepTests. Here, the instructor felt that textbook reading was sufficient to enable students to immediately engage with PI questions.
- Clicker questions, like the physics ConcepTests, **did** aim to challenge deep understanding.
- The typical PI vote-discuss-vote format on clicker questions **was** used. Students initially had 30-90 seconds to answer; they then discussed the question with their peers, and were expected to come to a consensus before answering again.
- Discussion groups **were not** pre-assigned, but were ad-hoc (e.g. discuss with those people around you) due to implementation costs (lack of numbered seats).
- The result of the first vote **was not** always hidden from students before they entered into discussion. This seemed to promote interest, but may encourage voting for the most popular answer.
- The correct answer **was** indicated on the slide after discussion.
- Students **were** asked to provide reasonable explanations for why wrong answers were wrong, in their own words (in addition to explanations of the correct answer).
- The instructor **repeatedly presented** students with rationale and research results from physics showing the benefits of the PI model for learning.

4. QUESTION DEVELOPMENT

A significant question is whether the clicker questions asked were similar to physics ConcepTests, in testing deep understanding of core concepts. The differences in introductory courses in these two disciplines make this a difficult question to answer.

It is rare in the PI research literature to see analysis of questions posed in class, and therefore difficult to determine precisely the nature of an effective PI question. Physics has the widely-accepted FCI, and so it is clear to physics teachers which concepts should be addressed. There is no such inventory in computing around which to base PI questions. Faced with that lack, therefore, we describe here the process and thought by which the instructor generated questions for these courses and give some examples of the variation in types of questions asked.

PI questions were developed with the expectation that students had completed the textbook reading before class, though perhaps not thoroughly comprehended all of it. To develop a question, the instructor scanned a few pages of the text, identified a concept or programming structure that from prior experience she expected students might not thoroughly grasp, or for which common usage errors often occur – then designed a question to expose that issue, and created 3-4 distracters that would be correct given a specific misconception. In line with the PI literature, questions were written emphasizing application of concepts over, for example, simple language rule knowledge questions. Such simple questions can cause student boredom and resentment [13, 2].

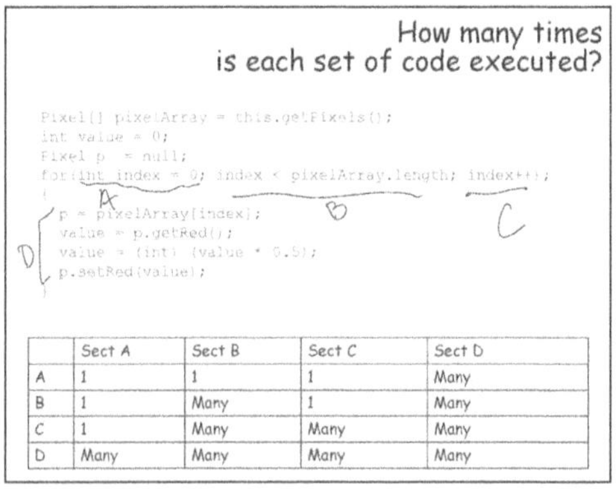

Figure 1. A Language Feature Conceptual Question

Obvious questions are code tracing or "select the right line(s) of code" questions (similar to those reported in [8]). A simple example might be the incorrect use of <= instead of < in a loop condition. More conceptual questions might test programming structure behavior (see Figure 1) or ask students to pick the correct diagram of the order in which a 2-D array was accessed (Figure 2).

Some questions asked students to express higher-level analysis such as explaining in English words what a code fragment does [8] or describing conditions when a particular code structure or feature should be used. In more complex scenarios, a series of

Figure 2. A Conceptual Nested Loop Question

questions can be used to have students "write" code (e.g. after discussion of a recursive algorithm to perform binary search, select the line of code to use as a method header, select the line of code that correctly implements the base case, select the line of code for the recursive case where you are looking for something "earlier", etc.).

Table 2 shows the number of questions given in each class along with an average number per 1 hour 20 minute lecture period.

Table 2. Peer Instruction Questions In Each Class

Course	Total Clicker Questions	Questions per 80 minute lecture
CS1 Wi	71	4.4
CS1.5 Sp	66	4.1

5. THE IN-CLASS EXPERIENCE

Using most commercial clicker systems, the instructor can see student responses as they submit them (often as counts per answer). Whether or not to display these results on the projected screen is usually an option. In class, the instructor always checked to see how students answered on their individual (first) vote on a question. In the rare case that almost all students got it right, the instructor often just reported this to the students and briefly discussed the right answer. This may not have been effectively implemented, as it can be quite challenging, in the middle of class, to make a good judgment on whether a topic has already been mastered by students. In the second running of each course, the instructor was much more likely to simply always have students discuss and revote, being more confident in the quality of the questions or the general value of students discussing answers and putting their explanations into their own words.

Students required a bit of prompting the first class or two – they are not used to talking being a necessary part of the class. Several requests by the instructor of "It should be louder -- talk! Explain why you think the right answer is right and why the wrong answers are wrong" for the most part got an anecdotal 90% or more participation. This last sentence was repeated often. Students were frequently reminded that being able to put into words exactly why wrong answers were wrong would help them cement critical issues in their minds, hopefully helping them identify mistakes while doing programming assignments or answering exam questions.

The amount of time spent on each question, for individual or group voting or discussion, varied. In general, 30-60 seconds were given for the individual vote, though often the instructor had read the question to the students first. Discussion time varied (but was around 3-5 minutes), with the instructor roaming around the room listening in and offering to answer questions. This allowed the instructor to get a feel for when useful discussion was wrapping up. The final vote was usually very quick – less than 20 seconds. Students always want to see the result of the final vote. Discussion always followed. Usually the instructor would confirm that the most popular answer was, in fact, correct (and indicate it with Tablet PC ink on the slide). Often she then (using the vote results either of the final vote or the first vote) asked students about a specific, popular wrong answer (or 2 or 3) – asking a student in the audience to provide an explanation of why that answer would be tempting. Since students worked in groups discussing these issues, they seem prepared and more confident in speaking these explanations in front of the rest of the class. Additionally, perhaps because it was an instructor-selected "mistake" or because they know other students voted for that answer, there seems to be less stigma with explaining the reasoning that made that answer seem plausible (especially when they can go on to say how they figured out it was wrong).

6. PERFORMANCE ON PI QUESTIONS

How did students do on the questions, and did they improve in the "after discussion" vote? The instructor didn't have any firm goals with regards to a target correctness level either for the before or after discussion vote, other than to make questions challenging enough to keep students engaged and to give them impetus to discuss with their peers. However, Mazur reports "the number of students who give the correct answer to a ConcepTest increases substantially, as long as the initial percentage of correct answers to a ConcepTest is between 35% and 70%. (We find that the improvement is largest when the initial percentage of correct answers is around 50%)"[4].

Table 3. PI Question Counts by Initial Vote Correctness

Course	<35%	[35,70]	>70%	Highest
CS1	21%	68%	11%	86%
CS1.5	26%	70%	4%	76%

For these classes 68%-70% of the questions fell within the initial vote correctness recommended by Mazur. Of the rest of the questions, the majority were quite hard for students and no question was answered correctly by more than 86% of the class.

Both CS1 and CS1.5 classes performed consistently with the average correctness in the initial vote to be 47% and 44% and the after discussion vote to be 68% and 63% respectively. Figure 3 shows the correctness on a per question basis for CS1 only (the graph for CS1.5 shows similar characteristics). Each bar along the X-axis reports one question, and questions are sorted from lowest to highest correctness by initial vote (before discussion). The light color bars show correctness level before discussion, the dark "tops" indicate correctness level in the group vote (except when the bar goes negative, that highlights when more people got the question wrong after discussion).

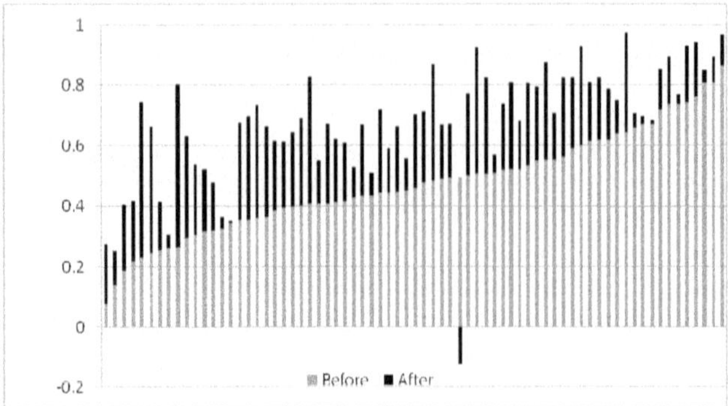

Figure 3. CS1 Correctness Before and After Discussion.

Although one interpretation of this behavior is that only ~20% of students improve via peer discussion, that ignores the students who answered the question correctly before and after discussion. *Normalized gain* gives the fraction of students not answering correctly first time who answer correctly in the after-discussion vote. We calculated normalized gain, NG, using the correctness, C, for each vote, as (A: after discussion, B: before):

$$\text{If } C_A > C_B : NG = (C_A - C_B) / (1 - C_B)$$

$$\text{If } C_A < C_B : NG = (C_A - C_B) / (C_B)$$

The normalized gain for CS1 and CS1.5 was 41% and 35% respectively. Mazur [4] reports normalized gain in one class of 43% and reports a genetics class show 33%[11]. However, these numbers were calculated from class averages, not per question (as ours were). Interestingly, our numbers do not concur with Mazur's report that the gain is largest when the initial percentage of correct answers is around 50%. We find slight increases in normalized gain as the proportion of initially-correct answers for a question increases. Why this is the case, and greater detail on student performance analysis, is a subject for future work.

7. STUDENT SURVEYS

Students answered questions on the use of PI as part of an end of term survey, which was required for a point in the class. Since many of the students in CS1 are also represented in CS1.5 (60% went on to take it) similar results on their perceptions would be expected. In this section, we also report survey results from an earlier CS1.5 course (in Winter 2009) which has a different set of students in it for a better sense of student perception. These numbers are reported in parentheses in Tables 4 and 5.

Overall, students responded positively to PI in CS1 and CS1.5. Table 4 shows that over 60% of students would recommend another instructor to use it; Table 5 shows that 78-87% of them agree that PI was valuable for their learning. We also asked some questions to get students' self-reporting on the fidelity with which they engaged in the PI process. Although the classroom seemed amazingly animated and engaged to the instructor, we find out from students that 9-17% of them rarely discussed and 30-33% only sometimes discussed, whilst the remainder always did so.

Table 4. Would you recommend that other instructors in computing courses use clickers with discussion?

Course	Yes	Maybe, depends on course	No	Don't Care
CS1, N=87	62%	28%	6%	4%
CS1.5, N=60 (N=79)	60% (65%)	35% (25%)	3% (4%)	2% (6%)

Table 5. Clickers with discussion is valuable for my learning.

Course	Agree	Neutral	Disagree
CS1	78%	8%	14%
CS1.5	87% (81%)	7% (11%)	7% (8%)

Based on instructor suspicion, we asked whether students actually read the textbook before class and confirmed that only a minority of the class (20-38%) read most or all of the time. Additionally, of the people who didn't always read before class, about half of them felt this had had a negative impact on their ability to learn in class. These results feed into our suggested improvements.

8. RECOMMENDATIONS AND DISCUSSION

From the reported data we can get a picture of how the PI pedagogy was adapted and adopted in two introductory computing courses. The instructor developed questions which were, by the numbers, challenging for students, but also engendered discussion and learning (based on increased correctness after group discussion). Students, on a survey, reported to finding PI valuable for their learning.

However, the students weren't the only ones who felt they learned more by using PI. Here we summarize some of the value the instructor felt in using PI:

- Preparing Questions: It can be very valuable to review the textbook, looking at it with a critical eye as to how a student would read and likely not quite understand certain concepts. Coming up with possible distracters can be both frustrating and illuminating.
- In Class: It was easy to figure out how much time to spend in discussion of a question, by looking at the correctness of votes both in the solo and group vote. Sometimes the instructor was surprised at both how well or how poorly students did on specific questions.
- Engaging Students in Post-Voting Class Discussion: Since students did vote individually, and often wrongly, it is very easy to say "many of us thought that C was correct originally, why is that reasonable? Why might you think it is C?" This seemed to lead students to be comfortable sharing their own explanations of misconceptions.
- After Class: It was very easy to create challenging exam questions: look for questions with low group vote correctness rates, and make students aware of this method of preparing exam questions. We are in the process of analyzing the data to determine if this is effective.

Based on this experience report, we offer up a few recommendations and mention a few concerns that will be addressing in future uses of PI.

- Getting Started: Look for an advisory document like [1, 12] to make sure that you invest time wisely in creating the right kinds of questions (hard, but meaningful ones) and put in the right motivational structures (points for students) to ensure the students are properly prepared.

- Promoting Student Discussion: At the beginning of discussion say "discuss with those around you. Don't just figure out the right answer. Explain why the right answer is right, put into words why the wrong answers are wrong". Focus students on evaluating all the answers, not just finding the right one.
- Engaging Students in the Process: It is important to inform students about your choice of pedagogy, and explain to them the benefits of using it. Showing graphs from research papers (even in other fields) can be helpful, to provide evidence to students that this non-traditional form of instruction is designed to *help them succeed*.

Issues which we discovered in the use of PI which we plan on addressing in future use include the following:

- Getting Students to Read: We'll implement the suggested PI practice of simple reading quizzes for credit (given online, before class) so that students have an incentive to read the textbook before class.
- Showing Voting: We'll switch to a default of not showing solo vote results – to keep students focused on evaluating all the answers rather than simply switching to the most popular.
- Improve Questions: We'll review and possibly modify questions with low initial vote correctness, especially if they have a low normalized gain.
- Better Student Discussion: We'll assign discussion groups, rather than letting students self-form into groups. We have particular concerns about under-represented groups feeling uncomfortable. We'll choose groups of size 4 to allow for missed classes and attrition.

The PI model is not commonly used in CS. Anecdotally, we know that students struggle to successfully apply introductory programming concepts, exactly the area in physics where PI has been so successful. Yet in CS, traditional lecture models appear to be common with instructors explaining and perhaps working examples for students in an attempt to promote learning and understanding. We hope that this report will give instructors some understanding of how PI may be adapted to computing.

Inevitably, instructors will also value additional evidence of the positive impact of PI on student learning in CS. We have shown here that learning "by peer discussion" (as measured by normalized gain from individual vote to group vote) does achieve similar results to those reported in physics and genetics. Crucially, it should be noted that the 44% "in-class" normalized gain reported in [4] was only *preliminary* evidence of learning – the final normalized gain in that class, based on the FCI, was 74%. Draper [6] and Smith et al [11] both argue that this difference between immediate and final learning gain is to be expected when using PI. An analysis of our students' voting behaviour against their final result is underway; in future work we hope to further elucidate the impact of PI on CS learning. The lack of a validated instrument such as the FCI will add challenges.

9. CONCLUSIONS

This experience report describes the process and results of using Peer Instruction in two introductory computing courses. The instructor developed a set of varied, challenging multiple choice questions based on difficulties and misconceptions students might be expected to have from reading the textbook. Lecture was replaced with a process of asking a series of questions (4-5 in 80 minutes) in the PI vote, discuss, revote model. Finally, the instructor led discussion of the question, engaging students. Students' initial correctness in answering ranged from 15%-86% with an average of 44-47%. Average correctness after discussion was 63-68% with a normalized gain of 35-41%. Students were generally very positive towards PI with 78-87% reporting it was valuable for their learning. The instructor reported value in being able to easily gauge explanation depth after asking questions and in finding key issues students had not yet mastered for developing quizzes and exams. We provide a set of recommendations and issues to address for future use of PI in introductory computing.

10. REFERENCES

[1] Beatty, I, Gerace, W., Leonard, W., Dufresne, R. Designing effective questions for classroom response system teaching. Am. J. Physics 74 (1), January 2006.

[2] Caldwell, J. Clickers in the Large Classroom: Current Research and Best-Practice Tips. CBE-Life Sciences Education, 6 (1): 9-20, 2007.

[3] Carter, P. An experiment with online instruction and active learning in an introductory computing course for engineers: JiTT meets CS. 14th Western Canadian Conference on Computing Education, 2009.

[4] Crouch C. and Mazur, E. Peer Instruction: Ten years of experience. *Am. J. Phys. 69 (9) 2001.*

[5] Cutts, Q., Carbone, A., and van Haaster, K. Using and Electronic Voting System to Promote Active Reflection on Coursework Feedback. In Proceedings of Intl. Conf. on Computers in Education, Melbourne, Australia, 2004.

[6] Draper,S.W. Catalytic assessment: understanding how MCQs and EVS can foster deep learning. *British Journal of Educational Technology 40(2)*: 285-293, 2009.

[7] Hestenes, D., Wells, M. and Swackhamer, G. Force Concept Inventory. *The Physics Teacher 30: 141-158*, 1992.

[8] Lister, R., Fidge, C., Teague, D. Further evidence of a relationship between explaining, tracing and writing skills in introductory programming, *SIGCSE Bulletin 41(3)*: 161-165 2009.

[9] Lopez-Herrejon, R. and Schulman, M. Using Interactive Technology in a Short Java Course: An Experience Report. *SIGCSE Bulletin 36(3): 203-207*, 2004.

[10] Pargas, R. and Shah, D. Things are clicking in computer science courses. *SIGCSE Bulletin 38(3): 474-478.* 2006.

[11] Smith, M., Wood, W., Adams, W., Wieman, C., Knight, J., Guild, N., Su, T. Why Peer Discussion Improves Student Performance on In-Class Concept Questions. Science 323, 122, (2009).

[12] Wieman, C. and the staff of the CU and UBC Science Education Initiatives. Clicker Resource Guide: An Instructor's Guide to the Effective Use of Personal Responses Systems (Clickers) in Teaching. http://cwsei.ubc.ca.

[13] Wieman, C. http://cwsei.ubc.ca/resources/clickers.htm

How Programming Environment Shapes Perception, Learning and Goals: Logo vs. Scratch

Colleen M. Lewis
Graduate School of Education
University of California, Berkeley
Berkeley, CA 94720
1- 510-388-7215
colleenl@berkeley.edu

ABSTRACT

This study compares the attitudinal and learning outcomes of sixth grade students programming in either Logo or Scratch. Given proposed affordances of the visual programming language, Scratch, I hypothesized that those students learning Scratch would demonstrate greater competence in interpreting loops and conditional statements and would have more positive attitudes towards programming. However, differences in performance between the two groups appeared only in the greater ability of the students that learned Scratch to interpret conditional statements. Contrary to our hypothesis, we found that students that learned Logo had on average higher confidence in their ability to program and students were no more likely to plan to continue to program after the course or view the learning of topics as difficult if they learned Logo or Scratch.

Categories and Subject Descriptors

K.3 [Computers and Education]: General

General Terms

Human factors

Keywords

Scratch, Logo, K-12, Programming

1. INTRODUCTION

Programming has been seen as an opportunity for students to develop the intellectual resources to tackle challenging problems [4]. However, many of the studies failed to show expected benefits and the Logo community did not flourish as hoped [1][3]. Many of the challenges faced by students learning to program in Logo can be understood through the limitations of the programming environment. For example, before testing a program in Logo, each line of code must adhere to syntactic constraints. This fragile environment may cause students to focus their attention on the syntax of the code and miss the opportunity to focus on the semantic meaning.

SIGCSE'10, March 10–13, 2010, Milwaukee, Wisconsin, USA.

Building upon the early work on Logo, a new programming environment Scratch [2] offers much of the same functionality as Logo. However in Scratch the code blocks only lock into place in syntactically valid ways, therefore "bugs" are always semantic errors and never the result of a typing error or a misremembered detail of language syntax. Scratch is one of the recently developed visual programming languages that are thought to make complex elements of flow of control, such as loops and conditionals, more natural [5]. This study evaluates the pedagogical value of Scratch in comparison to a well researched tool, the Logo programming environment. We hypothesized that in comparison with students using Logo, students using Scratch would:

- Be more likely to report that programming in general and the learning of individual constructs was easy.
- Feel more confident about their competence writing computer programs and be more likely to report that they plan to continue to pursue computer programming.
- Be better able to trace the flow of control of loops and conditionals.

2. PREVIOUS RESEARCH

New languages, such as Scratch, typically build from previous languages to offer new functionality and claimed pedagogical advantages. This study builds upon a line of research that has begun to explicitly test the pedagogical claims of new programming tools. In a study designed to see if students learning Java will spontaneously develop competency with flow of control constructs in a visual programming language, Alice, the researchers, Parsons and Haden, found that "students struggled to make the connection between work in Alice and 'real programming'."[5]. In an effort to provide fewer syntactic constraints, visual programming languages may be perceived as "simple" and not related to real programming. However, research comparing learning in a more and a less syntactically strict language, Java and Python respectively, attribute the greater success of students in Python to be a result of reduced syntactic complexity [3].

3. METHODOLOGY

3.1 Setting

Participants were students enrolled in the course "Making Music, Movies, and Games with Computers", a summer enrichment program offered through the Academic Talent Development

Program (ATDP) at the University of California, Berkeley. The course met for a total of 36 hours over 12 days. All course participants had completed fifth grade and were between 10 and 12 years old. Students applied to participate in this enrichment program that is designed for academically advanced students.

There were 2 offerings of the course, with the exact same course description. Students indicated in their application a preference for the morning or the afternoon offering and were placed in their preferred offering on a first-come, first-served basis. Each offering of the course was taught by the same instructors, the author with the assistance of two teacher aids.

3.2 Treatment Groups

Each offering of the course became a treatment group in this study and the two treatments differed based upon which language they learned first. Treatment 1 (*Scratch-First*) learned to program in Scratch[1] for 6 days before beginning instruction in Logo. Treatment 2 (*Logo-First*) learned to program in Logo[2] for 6 days before beginning instruction in Scratch. This study focuses on these first 6 days and addresses the students' perceptions, learning and goals before beginning their second programming language.

3.3 Curriculum

Students in each class worked in pairs to complete worksheets designed by the researcher to introduce programming constructs. The first 6 days of instruction focused on the core programming constructs such as conditionals, variables and loops that are shared by both Logo and Scratch. On each of the first 6 days, students worked on worksheets designed to have students in each class accomplish equivalent goals. For example, on the third day of instruction students in each treatment were asked to draw a brick wall. Figure 1 shows the images that were provided on the respective worksheets to demonstrate the goal. Although the images and content of the worksheets differ, the goals on each worksheet were the same.

Figure 1: Demonstration of the goal of drawing a brick wall for Logo (left) and Scratch (right)

A recent multi-national, multi-institution study [6] suggests that it is possible to translate exams between languages while preserving the level of difficulty. A similar methodology is used in this study to create assessments and in-class programming tasks of comparable difficulty.

3.4 Participants

In Treatment 1 (*Scratch-First*) there were 16 males and 10 females for a total of 26 students. In Treatment 2 (*Logo-First*) there were 17 males and 7 females for a total of 24 students.

[1] Students used version 1.4 of Scratch (http://scratch.mit.edu).

[2] The version of Logo used was developed by Guy Haas (http://www.bfoit.org/itp/install.html).

3.5 Data Sources

Written assessments were given on the second and fifth days of class to assess student understanding of concepts and techniques covered the previous class day. Written surveys were given at the end of the sixth day of instruction and beginning of the seventh to gather information regarding the students' evaluation of their experience during class as well as their interests and goals.

4. DATA ANALYSIS

4.1 Similarity of Treatment Groups

When the students applied to the course, they were not aware of any difference between the two versions of the course. Based upon this sampling method, we did not suspect that the two groups would vary greatly. As a precaution, on the first day we administered a survey of prior computer experience. The differences responses of the participants in Treatment 1 and Treatment 2 were not statistically significant at the 5% level ($z=-1.007$; $p=0.3140$) using the Mann-Whitney-Wilcoxon test. Although this does not demonstrate that the two populations are equivalent, we postulate similarity based upon the sampling method and the similarity in distribution of responses regarding prior computer experience. To capture the similarity of the two groups, histograms of their responses to four representative questions are provided below in Figure 2. Participants in Treatment 1 (*Scratch-First*) and Treatment 2 (*Logo-First*) had similar distributions of responses to the following 4-level Likert questions.

- I am good at using the computer
- I find computers frustrating to use
- I am comfortable using a mouse
- I am comfortable typing on a computer

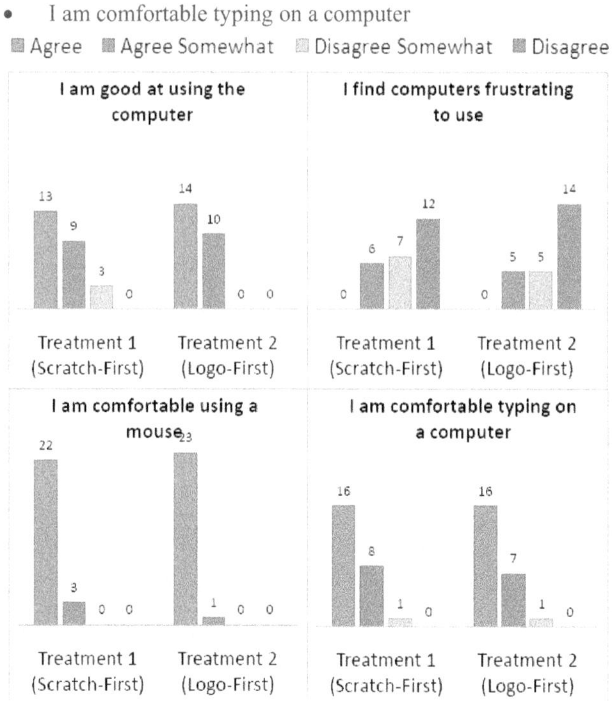

Figure 2: Student responses to 4-level Likert questions regarding prior computer experience

4.2 Student Report of Difficulty

To investigate the hypothesis that students in Treatment 1 (*Scratch-First*) would be more likely to judge programming and the learning of individual constructs to be easy, all students responded to questions regarding their experience of the difficulty of learning various programming commands and constructs. The questions were given on the 7th day of instruction, before introducing students to a second language. There were 8 questions covering the following constructs: `repeat`, variable creation, `if`, and, `forward/move`, set x and y coordinate, set pen color, and set heading. The students responded to a 4-level Likert question in the form of "It was hard to learn how to use [Programming Construct]". A response of "Agree" was coded as a 4 to indicate that the programming command was hard to learn while "Agree somewhat", "Disagree somewhat" and "Disagree" were coded 3, 2 and 1 respectively. The total of the coded scores for the 8 questions were added together to create a rating of perceived difficulty for each student.

Figure 3 below shows the students' rating of difficulty by treatment group. Students from Treatment 1 (*Scratch-First*) had a range of scores between 32 and 46 with a mean rating of 37.62 out of 64 and a standard deviation of 3.43. Students from Treatment 2 (*Logo-First*) had a similar range from 32 to 45 but a slightly higher mean of 38.35 and a standard deviation of 3.70. The difference between the means of the two groups was less than 1 out of 64 and was not significant at the 5% level (z=0.716, p=0.4743).

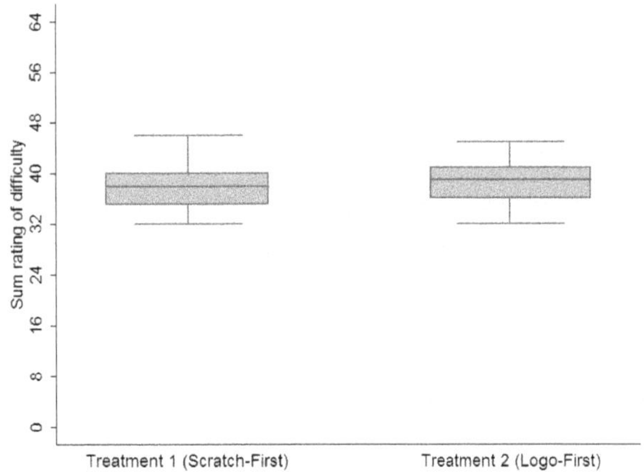

Figure 3: Student cumulative rating of difficulty of programming commands

The unexpected result of no difference between perceived difficulties motivated further investigation. Through an analysis of individual questions, we found that while most students in each treatment group disagreed with the statements "It was hard to learn how to use variables" and "It was hard to learn how to use `repeat`" the groups diverged when asked about learning conditionals. Two questions requested information about the process of learning conditionals: "It was hard to learn how to use `IF`" and "It was hard to learn how to use `AND`". There was a statistically significant response, using a Mann-Whitney-Wilcoxon test, between the two groups when responding to "It was hard to learn how to use `AND`" (z=2.423; p=0.0154). These results match the instructors' perception that students using Logo had a much more difficult time learning `AND`. Figure 4 shows the distribution of responses to four of the Likert questions regarding difficulty of learning. The histograms show the similar responses regarding variables and `repeat` to contrast the difference in distribution regarding the difficulty of conditionals.

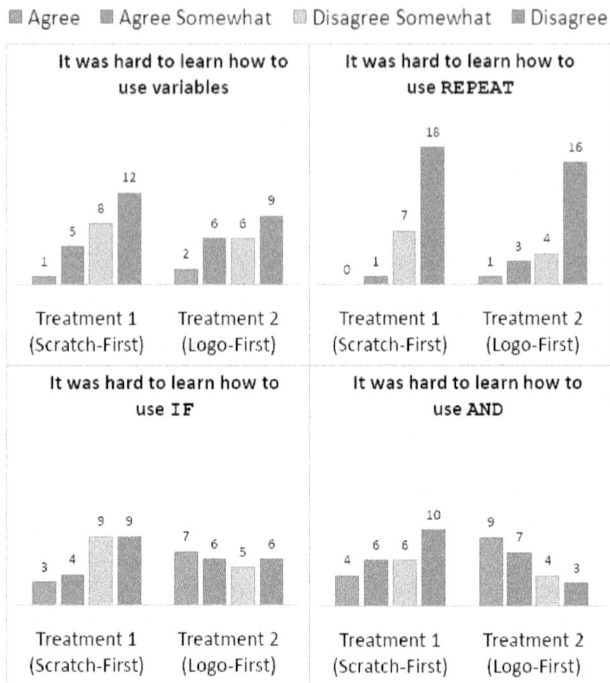

Figure 4: Student responses to 4-level Likert questions regarding the difficulty of learning

4.3 Confidence of Treatment Groups

To investigate the hypothesis that students in Treatment 1 (*Scratch-First*) will feel more confident about their competence writing computer programs and be more likely to report that they plan to continue to pursue computer programming the students were asked to respond to the following questions using a 4-level Likert response:

- Writing computer programs is easy.
- I am good at writing computer programs
- I plan to continue programming after the class is over.
- I want to take another computer programming course.

The results, shown in Figure 5, were analyzed using a Mann-Whitney-Wilcoxon test. Despite the expectation that Scratch makes programming easier, there was no statistical significance between the treatment groups on their response to the question: "Writing computer programs is easy" (z=-1.560; p=0.1189). However in response to the question "I am good at writing computer programs" it was Treatment 2 (*Logo-First*) that answered more positively and the differences between the treatment groups was statistically significant at the 5% level (z=-2.016, p=0.0438). This provides evidence that could prove the counter-hypothesis, that students in Logo will judge their competence at programming higher. It is possible that like the results from [5], the students learning Scratch did not recognize Scratch as "writing computer programs". However, other references to "writing computer programs" in the course presumably serve to cue the student that they are engaged in "writing computer programs". For example, in the same survey, the students responded to the questions (emphasis added) "Writing *computer programs* is easy", "It is possible to know what a *computer program* will do before you run it", "When I run a *computer program* twice in a row it will do the same thing", and "What is the most frustrating thing about *writing computer programs*?"

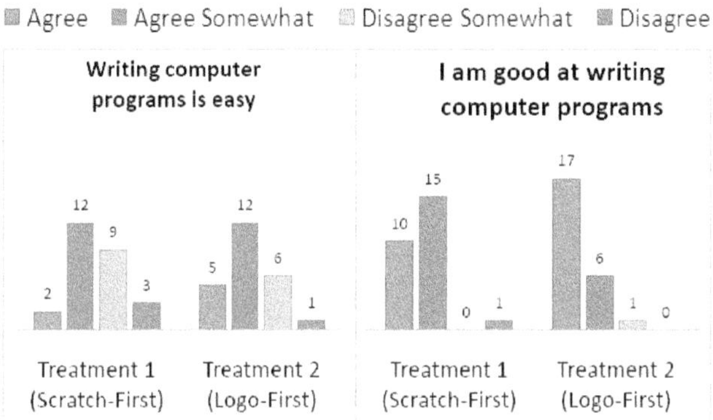

Figure 5: Student responses to 4-level Likert questions regarding competence programming

An alternate explanation is that even after 18 hours of instruction students in Treatment 1 (*Scratch-First)* had not used every command appearing in the Scratch menus, which might have eroded their confidence in their abilities. In contrast students using Logo may have been under the impression that they had learned everything that Logo had to offer. Future research will seek to isolate the effects of these different factors.

As shown in Figure 6, regardless of initial programming language, the majority of students agreed or agreed somewhat with the statements:

- I plan to continue to program after the class is over.
- I want to take another computer programming course.

This suggests that although we hypothesized that students exposed to Scratch would be more likely to plan to continue to program after the course, students indicate a similar level of intention to continue programming or take additional computer programming courses regardless of what languages they have seen.

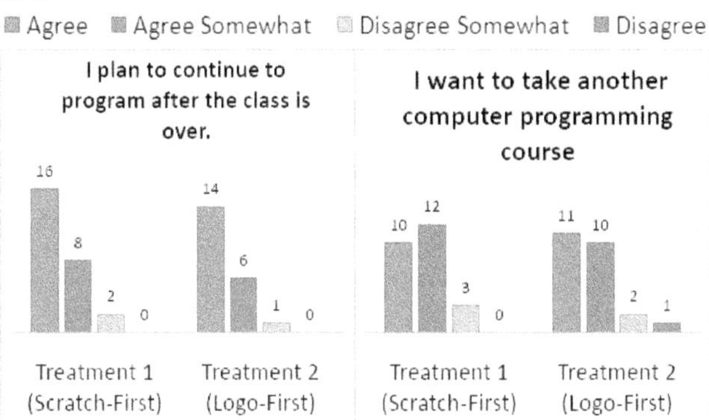

Figure 6: Student responses to 4-level Likert questions regarding their future plans for computer programming

4.4 Student Assessments

4.4.1.1 Student Interpretation of Loops

At the beginning of the 2nd day, after 3 hours of instruction, students were given an assessment where they were asked to describe the results of `repeat` statements. A representative question is shown in Figure 7. This example shows a nested `repeat` statement translated into both Logo and Scratch. Students in each treatment group saw the corresponding `repeat` statement and were asked to write answers to the following questions:

- How many beats/seconds will this example take to run?
- How many times will the example play the note 60?

```
repeat 5 [playnote 67 1 repeat 10 [playnote 60 1]]
```

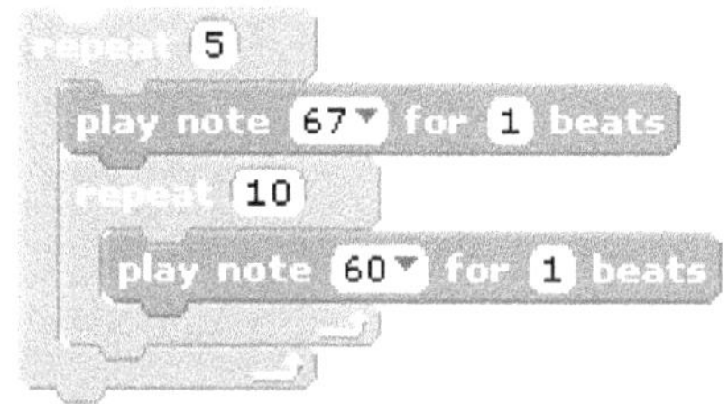

Figure 7: Example question from assessment of ability to interpret loops

We expected that the Scratch question would be easier for the students to answer because of the additional context regarding the meaning of the commands. For example, Figure 8 shows a comparison of the Logo and Scratch syntax to play a note. Whereas the Scratch command can be read like a sentence "play note 67 for 1 beats", in the Logo example there are no cues that differentiate the note to be played from the duration. Despite this apparent complexity, no students answered with a number over 55 on any questions, which might have indicated a student confusing the note number as the duration for the note. As opposed to confusion regarding the `play note` command, it appears that student difficulty was associated with the behavior of the `repeat`.

```
playnote 67 1
```

Figure 8: The `play note` command in Scratch and Logo

The performance difference between the two groups was not statistically significant (z=-0.945; p=0.3448). Students from Treatment 1 (*Scratch-First*) had a mean of 3.0 and a standard deviation of 2.6. Students from Treatment 2 (*Logo-First*) had a mean score of 2.4 and a standard deviation of 2.7.This assessment does not confirm our hypothesis that students using Scratch would outperform students using Logo on their ability to interpret repeat statements.

4.4.1.2 Student Interpretation of Conditionals

At the beginning of the 5th day, after 12 hours of instruction, students were given an assessment of their ability to interpret the result of conditional statements. On the previous day, both groups of students had made a simplified paint program that involved setting the pen color depending upon the location of the mouse. The assessment asked them to consider similar examples of code and predict the final pen color or in some cases say what notes would be played. The most complicated example included interpreting the result of the code shown in Figure 9 for a series of x and y locations for the mouse.

```
setpencolor 1

if greater? mousey    0
     [setpencolor 2]

if less?    mousey    0
     [setpencolor 3]

if greater? mousex  200
     [setpencolor 4]

if greater? mousex  100
     [setpencolor 5]

if less?    mousex -100
     [setpencolor 6]
```

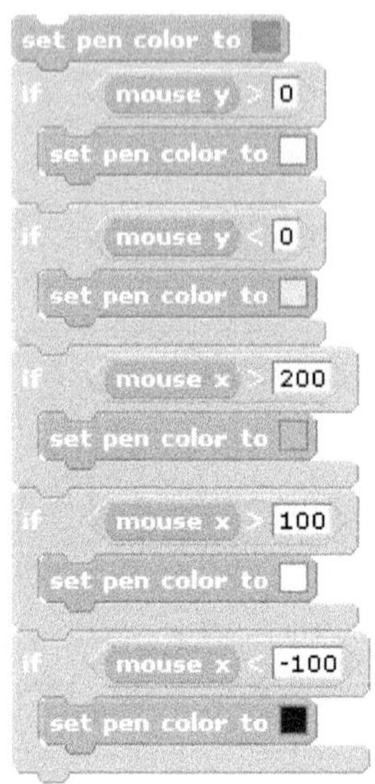

Figure 9: Question from assessment of ability to interpret conditionals expressions

Figure 10 below shows a box plot of the cumulative scores on the assessment of student ability to interpret conditional expressions. The mean score for students in Treatment 1 (*Scratch-First*) was 8.16 out of 13, while the mean score for Treatment 2 (*Logo-First*) was only 5.68. A Mann-Whitney-Wilcoxon test was used to compare the performance of each group and the higher performance of students in Treatment 1 (*Scratch-First*) was statistically significant at the 1% level (z=-2.528, p=0.0115).

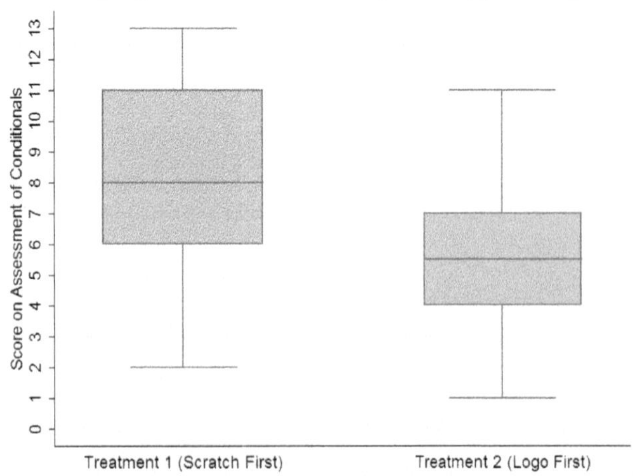

Figure 10: Box plot of student performance on assessment of conditionals

5. CONCLUSION AND FUTURE WORK

While the Logo environment appeared capable of supporting student development of confidence, interest in computer programming, and understanding of the loop construct, the Scratch environment provided a relative improvement in learning outcomes for students learning the construct of conditionals.

Scratch offers a number of affordances that would suggest that it should be easier to learn and interpret. Given these affordances, it is surprising that the students learning Logo and Scratch performed similarly when interpreting loops. For example, in Logo students have only a textual representation and during the learning process would presumably be distracted by low-level details such as syntax. However, perhaps this low-level focus allows students to focus on some important low-level details, such as the role of every command in a larger program. It may be that this low-level focus allowed students learning Logo to compensate for the lack of a visual representation.

There has been a significant amount of research done on student experiences in Logo however, only through a comparison with a different programming environment, such as Scratch, can we begin to isolate the features of student experience impacted by the content of programming and those impacted by the programming environment.

6. ACKNOWLEDGMENTS

I want to thank the study participants, Andrea diSessa, Michael Clancy, Randi Engle, Steven Kisely, George Wang and other members of the Patterns, UC-WISE and Video research groups at the University of California, Berkeley. I want to thank the Scratch team at MIT and Guy Haas for his development and support of JLogo. This work was partially supported by a grant from the Spencer Foundation (grant number 200500036) to Andrea A. diSessa, PI.

7. REFERENCES

[1] diSessa, A. (2000). Changing Minds: Computers, Learning, and Literacy. MIT Press:Cambridge, MA.

[2] Maloney, J., Peppler, K., Kafai, Y. B., Resnick, M., & Rusk, N. (2008). Programming by Choice: Urban Youth Learning Programming with Scratch. *ACM Special Interest Group on Computer Science Education.*, Portland: ACM.

[3] Mannila, L., Peltomaki, M., & Salakoski, T. (2006). What About a Simple Language? Analyzing the Difficulties in Learning to Program. Computer Science Education, 16(3), 211-227.

[4] Papert, S. (1980). Mindstorms: Children, Computers, and Powerful Ideas. New York: Basic Books, Inc.

[5] Parsons, D., & Haden, P. (2007). Programming Osmosis: Knowledge Transfer from Imperative to Visual Programming Environments. In S. Mann & N. Bridgeman (Eds.), Procedings of The Twentieth Annual NACCQ Conference (pp. 209-215). Hamilton, New Zealand.

[6] Whalley, J. (2006). CSEd Research Instrument Design: The Localisation Problem. In S. Mann & N. Bridgeman (Eds.), Proceedings of The Nineteenth Annual NACCQ Conference (pp. 307-312). Wellington, New Zealand.

Teaching Computational Thinking through Musical Live Coding in Scratch

Alex Ruthmann
Dept. of Music
Univ. of Massachusetts Lowell
Lowell, MA 01854
1-978-934-3879
Alex_Ruthmann@uml.edu

Jesse M. Heines
Dept. of Computer Science
Univ. of Massachusetts Lowell
Lowell, MA 01854
1-978-934-3634
heines@cs.uml.edu

Gena R. Greher
Dept. of Music
Univ. of Massachusetts Lowell
Lowell, MA 01854
1-978-934-3893
Gena_Greher@uml.edu

Paul Laidler
Student, Dept. of Computer Science
Univ. of Massachusetts Lowell
Lowell, MA 01854
1-978-934-3634
plaidler@gmail.com

Charles Saulters II
Student, Dept. of Music
Univ. of Massachusetts Lowell
Lowell, MA 01854
1-978-934-3634
kingd615@hotmail.com

ABSTRACT
This paper discusses our ongoing experiences in developing an interdisciplinary general education course called *Sound Thinking* that is offered jointly by our Dept. of Computer Science and Dept. of Music. It focuses on the student outcomes we are trying to achieve and the projects we are using to help students realize those outcomes. It explains why we are moving from a web-based environment using HTML and JavaScript to Scratch and discusses the potential for Scratch's "musical live coding" capability to reinforce those concepts even more strongly.

Categories and Subject Descriptors
K.3.2 [**Computers and Education**]: Computer and Information Science Education — *computer science education, curriculum.*

General Terms
Design, Languages

Keywords
Performamatics, Scratch, computer science education, interdisciplinary courses, musical live coding, generative music, curriculum design.

1. PERFORMAMATICS BACKGROUND
Performamatics is a series of courses intended to attract students to computer science (CS) by tapping their inherent interest in performance and the arts. Toward that end, two CS professors have teamed with five Music, Theater, and Art professors to offer both introductory and advanced courses where assignments designed to reinforce CS concepts center around applications in the Arts. These courses are in the spirit of pioneering work done by Cooper, Dann, & Pausch [3], Guzdial [6], and Yanco et al. [15], and have been described in many other papers and presentations [5, 7, 8, 9, 12]. Readers are also referred to www.performamatics.com for links to online materials.

The most successful Performamatics courses to date (based on enrollment and student feedback) have clearly been the introductory ones. These are general education (GenEd) courses co-listed in two departments, allowing CS majors to earn Arts & Humanities GenEd credit while Arts majors earn Science & Technology GenEd credit. *Tangible Interaction Design* is a collaboration between CS and Art, while *Sound Thinking*, the course on which this paper focuses, is a collaboration between CS and Music.

2. SOUND THINKING
One of the hurdles in getting our first offering of *Sound Thinking* approved for dual GenEd credit was to convince the GenEd committee that Music majors would learn something about technology and CS majors would learn something about music. The committee feared that if project teams had both CS and Music majors, each group would naturally navigate to its own discipline and there might be relatively little true cross-over. We therefore established the following behavioral objectives for all students.

Upon completion of this course, students should be able to:
1. Identify properties of sound and describe the organization of sound into music.
2. Design a simple notation system and describe the differences between formal and informal notation.
3. Distinguish between analog and digital audio.
4. Discuss the basic differences between various audio file formats and sound compression techniques.
5. Create a web-based computer program that plays a music file.
6. Create a web-based computer program that plays a user-definable sequence of music files.

In the first half of the semester, students created compositions for "found" instruments, invented notations for those instruments, recorded the instruments' sounds, manipulated those sounds with audio editors, and remixed and recomposed the sounds into original compositions. In the second half, they created webpages that incorporated music, used a JavaScript Application Programmer Interface (API), and developed interactive web applications in which music played an integral part. Looking back, we see that objectives 1, 2, 5, and 6 held the most interest for students, and that's where we spent most of our class time.

Before the course was taught, there was much discussion among the Performamatics faculty about the development platform to be used for programming assignments. A CS professor said, "The Music majors will cringe if you make them code. You've got to use a visual programming environment." But a Music professor strongly disagreed, saying "One of our goals is to have them overcome any fear they have of code. We *want* them to see real code." Given that we thought students would enjoy creating webpages that they could share with their friends, we therefore chose Dreamweaver as our development platform, because it allowed viewing the page layout and its underlying code simultaneously. This helped students easily see the cause-and-effect relationship between the code and its result. We taught the basics of underlying HTML and JavaScript (with a custom API to play sounds and sound files), and only one of the 13 students had any real trouble doing the webpage development assignments.

On the contrary, most of the Music majors were very technically savvy and the post course student evaluations revealed that they wanted to know *more* about what was "under the hood." They enjoyed referring to the CS professor on the faculty team as a "magician" (because he could almost always make their pages do what they wanted when their CS partners were stumped), and they suggested that when the next the course is taught, the programming should be spread throughout the semester rather than confined to the second half.

We are now revising *Sound Thinking* for its next offering. With the help of students funded through a Research Experience for Undergraduates supplement to our NSF CPATH grant, we investigated a number of other platforms for use in the course. We have settled on Scratch [10, 11]. The remainder of this paper discusses why we feel that Scratch is an appropriate platform for teaching computational thinking through music.

3. MAKING MUSIC WITH SCRATCH

Scratch has the ability to generate and play sounds using various components in its Sound category. But if one wants to begin making *music* with more than one sound line in Scratch, one needs to address the issue of synchronization.

This issue is best addressed once students are familiar with looping, an essential concept in the implementation of many musical models. As students begin working with models where multiple voices are layered, it becomes necessary to maintain the tempo using the Scratch timer. Figure 1 shows a loop that will play a hand clap (MIDI drum instrument #39) every quarter of a beat. However, this example will not have a steady tempo, and if it was used to layer multiple voices, each would eventually fall out of synchronization.

The Scratch timer offers a way to address this problem. We first determine how many seconds our hand claps should be apart and then use the Scratch timer to control when each clap should occur. Figure 2 shows a more complex loop that will remain synchronized with the tempo regardless of the number of iterations performed. Each iteration waits until the Scratch timer reaches the value stored in variable now. This variable holds the time when a hand clap should sound. A message is then broadcast to play the hand clap. This ensures that the loop will complete and return to the "wait until" statement before the next hand clap needs to be played by delegating the actual playing to a "when I receive" event handler. The value of variable now is then changed to contain the time at which the next hand clap should be played. The Scratch timer ensures that the hand claps remain in tempo.

Note that in addition to synchronization, many other computational thinking concepts are touched upon by this example.

- looping
- initialization
- use of variables
- changing variables algorithmically
- modularization
- event processing

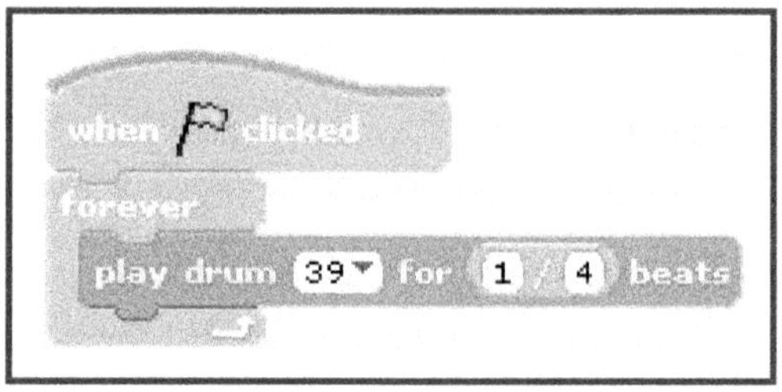

Figure 1. A hand clap loop.

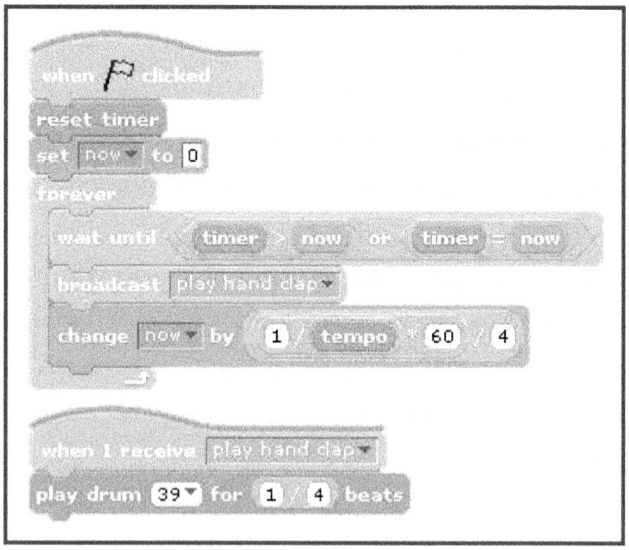

Figure 2. Hand clap loop synchronized via the Scratch timer.

4. FROM CODE TO MUSIC

Once students understand basic note and sound generation in Scratch and can implement synchronization, more musical, generative algorithms for creating and manipulating sequences of notes can be explored.

One possible starting point is to use the "forever" loop to generate random melodies constrained by lower and upper boundaries as shown in Figure 3. In this example, random musical pitches from middle C (MIDI note #60) and the C above that (MIDI note #72) are chosen and played for half a beat. Because the "play note" function is surrounded by a "forever" loop, Scratch continues to generate notes until the Scratch stop button (●) is pressed.

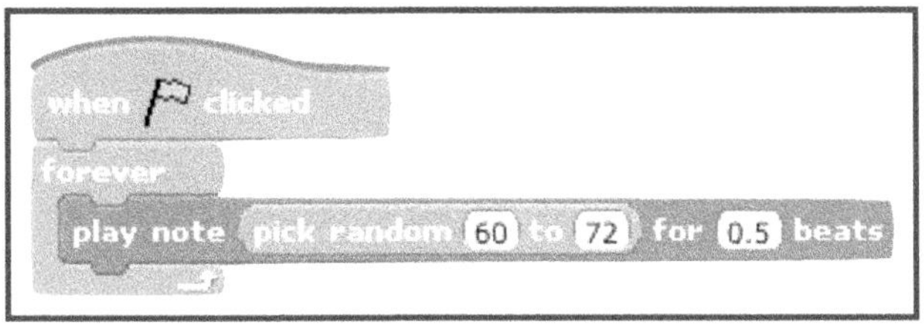

Figure 3. Code for a random melody by boundary constraints.

The fact that Scratch also functions as a live interpreter/compiler makes things more interesting. This feature allows the boundaries of the random pitches as well as the duration of the sound played to be manipulated in real time through "musical live coding" [2, 13, 14] without disrupting the sounds being generated. That is, the resultant melody can be changed in real time by adjusting the upper and lower bounds of the random function and changing the duration value for the beat without stopping program execution.

The code in Figure 3 can be expanded to generate a random melody from notes provided in a pitch set as shown in Figure 4. This code implements a Scratch "list" that contains a Pentatonic (five note) pitch set. It then selects a random note from that pitch set and adds a pitch offset (MIDI note 38). In a real-time performance, the pitch could be changed by manipulating the offset to move the randomly chosen notes higher and lower through the pitch register. Additionally, through the use of the "pick random" function, the bounds of the notes chosen from the Pentatonic pitch set could be further constrained. For example, if we wanted to choose only the 2nd, 3rd, or 4th note of the set, we could change the function to "pick random 2 to 4." This technique enables live coders to create more variety in the resultant musical output.

In most music, melodies do not move by random intervals. If one has a large pitch set, random intervals could result in very large leaps from one pitch to the next. A more natural sounding melody can be generated by implementing a "random walk" algorithm to change subsequent pitches as shown in Figures 5a and 5b. This results in a more musical melody by constraining the interval movement between -4 and +4 of the prior pitch. This approach also enables the melody to move freely across the MIDI pitch spectrum rather than to be constrained by the length of the pitch set as was the case in the prior examples.

Eventually, these techniques can be expanded to model the musical styles of various composers. Our initial explorations have centered on generating music in the style of Arvo Pärt and Philip

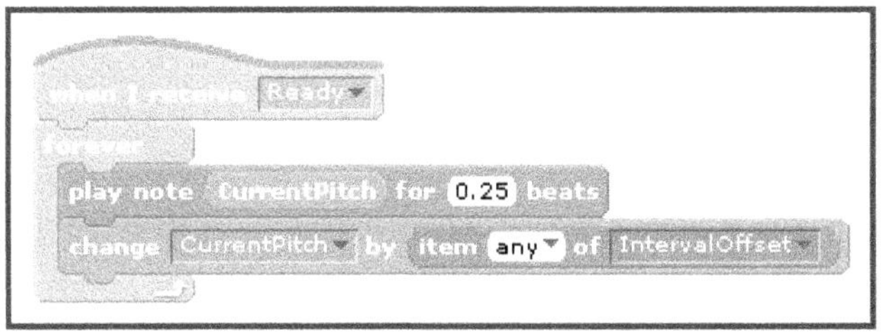

Figure 5a. Code for a melody via a "random walk" algorithm.

Glass. Figure 6 shows a small part of a larger algorithm inspired by Arvo Pärt's *Stabat Mater* [1]. This example iterates through the AeolianPitchSet list (organized as a descending minor scale) to select pitches and then chooses random rhythm values from the RhythmSet list. The values of the RhythmSet list were derived from an aural analysis of the *Stabat Mater* and weight the probability of selecting a whole note twice that of selecting a half note. In the full algorithm, this code is duplicated twice to create three multithreaded musical parts that are triggered via keystrokes. The addition of human control to starting and stopping threads enables the performer to create dynamic variations in musical form and texture by starting and stopping sections of the overall code.

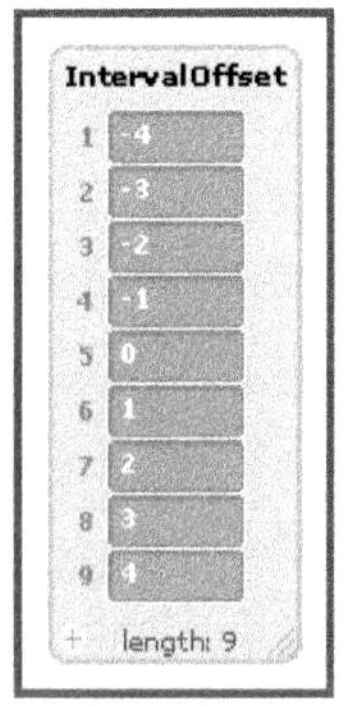

Figure 5b. Interval list for use with the "random walk" algorithm.

In addition to the live manipulation of lists, variables, and offsets shown in prior examples, Figure 6 also enables the selection of multiple pitch set lists, modification of the direction in which the list is iterated, and the ability to choose randomly or to isolate and repeat pitch values. Additional functions from the Scratch Sound and Numbers menus can be added, removed, and manipulated in real time to generate more musical control and expression. For example, a "change volume by x" function could be added to create changes in musical dynamics or to realize dynamic fading in or fading out of sections of the code. Additionally, a "change tempo by x" function could be inserted at various points to slow down or speed up the tempo. This could be set to a discrete value or by a mathematical function as shown in Figure 7.

Performing effective real-time manipulation of code (musical live coding) to create and shape generated music requires both musical and computational understanding. From a musical perspective, one needs to understand how the ongoing, generative music should sound. From a computational perspective, one needs to understand how the code can be adjusted and manipulated in real time to achieve the aural and musical changes and outcomes one

Figure 4. Code for a melody from pitch and rhythm set lists.

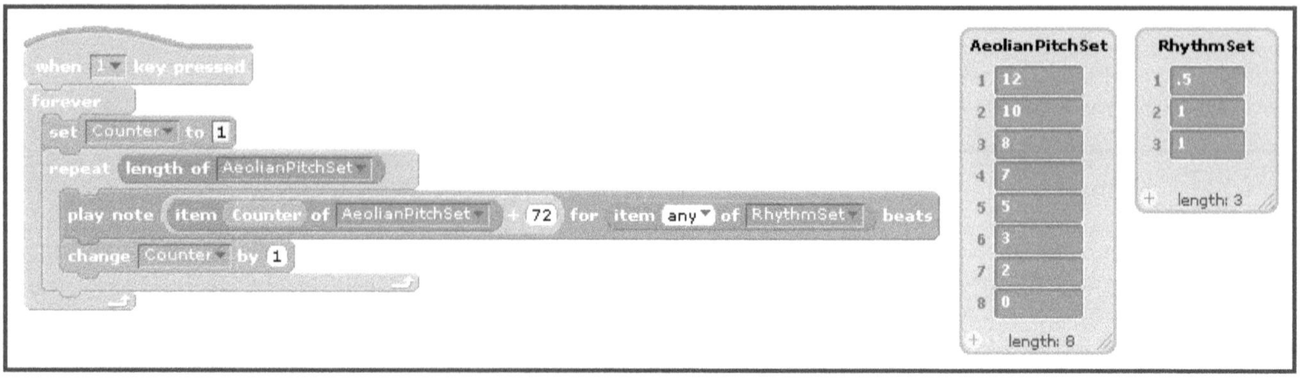

Figure 6. Melodic code inspired by Arvo Pärt's *Stabat Mater*.

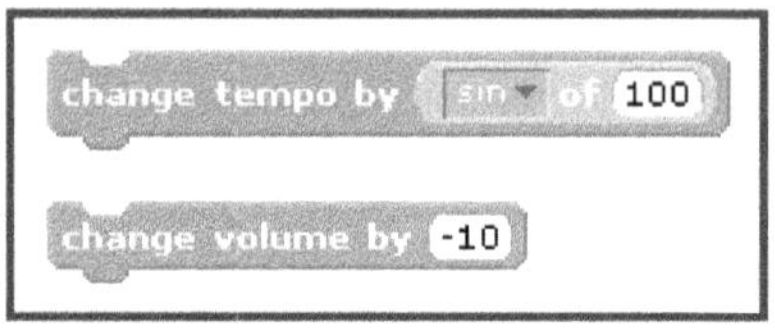

Figure 7. Examples of built-in Scratch functions well suited to musical live coding.

desires. These are advanced skills, but they can be learned through experimentation and exploration that is both educational and fun. Scratch provides a unique, easy-to-learn platform that enables musical live coding by allowing nearly all aspects of the code to be adjusted in real time. Students can then share and showcase their work in live or pre-coded performances, which is the essence of Performamatics.

5. ADDING A TANGIBLE INTERFACE

As the course develops, we plan to integrate tangible computing using IchiBoards [4] (Figure 8). Using these devices' live sensing capabilities, we can implement gestural musical input and design new instruments to perform musical algorithms implemented in Scratch.

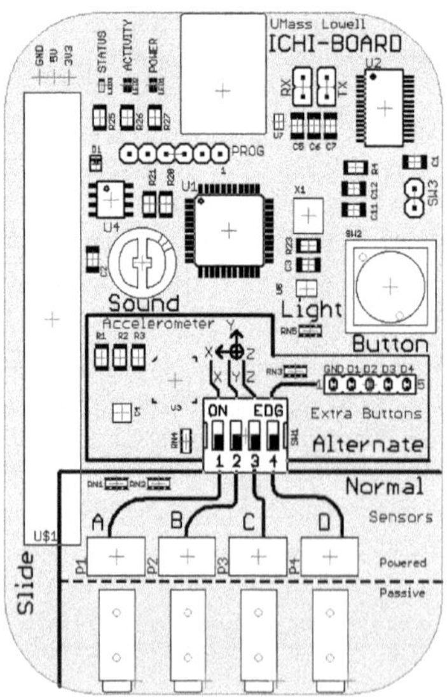

Figure 8. IchiBoard [4].

Figure 9 shows a simple program that converts an IchiBoard into a musical instrument. A "forever" loop is used to enable continuous live sensing of the board's button and slider sensors. When the button is pressed, the slider value is read and a note is played whose pitch corresponds to that value. Computational thinking comes into play because the IchiBoard's slider returns values between 0 and 100. To convert those values to a 7-note whole tone musical scale in which each interval is two equal half-steps apart, the value returned by the slider is combined with a copy of itself on which a modulus 2 operation has been applied. This ensures that when the slider is moved, the pitch of the note being played always jumps by a whole step rather than a half step. With the beat value set to 0.01, a continuous stream of pitches sounds when the button is pressed. The result is a surprisingly expressive instrument with which the user can establish a rhythm through interaction with the button and play gestural pitch sweeps through manipulation of the slider.

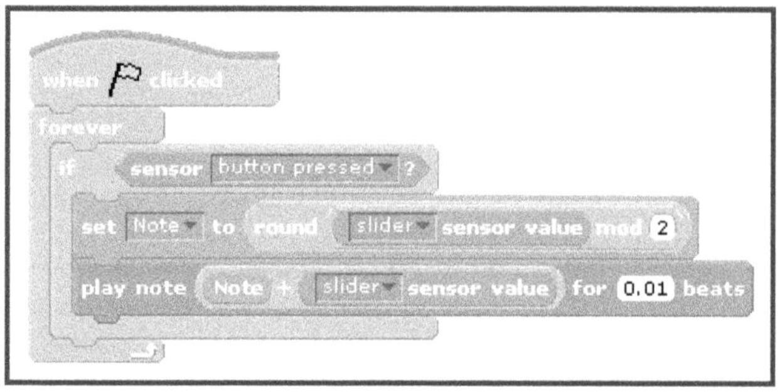

Figure 9. Code for a simple IchiBoard musical instrument.

The previous example only takes advantage of two of the eight possible sensor inputs on the IchiBoard. More complex interface configurations and Scratch code are currently in development that will enable more interesting musical performances and live coding demonstrations of computational thinking.

The integration of IchiBoards as an interface for tangible computing enables discussion of CS hardware concepts such as:

- What is a device?
- What is a sensor?
- What is a signal, and how is it detected in software?
- What is an event, and how is it detected in software?
- What different types of events are triggered by various devices (real and virtual)?

Integrating physical computing with Scratch's graphical coding environment provides a unique platform for expressive computing in real time. Programs can not only be written to create music, but they can be written to model musical environments that are performed through musical live coding or the design and interfacing of tangible computing devices such as the IchiBoard.

6. INTERDISCIPLINARY BENEFITS

After taking *Sound Thinking* in the Spring 2009 semester, Music major Charles Saulters developed a strong interest in using computational thinking as a means of developing more expressive gestural music controllers. He pursued a Research Experience for Undergraduates with us over the summer, exploring ways to apply these Performamatics concepts in even more exciting ways. He describes his work as follows.

> I am interested in enabling others to achieve more than they ever thought possible through the use of computational thinking in real world situations that are relevant and interesting to students. One "hook" that I found particularly interesting is the manipulation of virtual instruments, composing for and performing using nontraditional devices such as the iPod Touch. Now more than ever, we musicians find ourselves in an age where technologically almost anything is possible. It is therefore crucial that we understand what makes computers function and acquire a strong working knowledge of programs and the coding behind them.
>
> Interdisciplinary collaboration helps cultivate new and exciting innovations that can bring about the revitalization of CS education for which Performamatics was conceived. Using music as a hook, we can create innovative live performances and interesting visuals in conjunction with "musical live coding" to tap the imagination of people who might never have considered CS as a possible major. People (like myself) tend to be intimidated by the mystifying technical jargon. However, with more exposure to interesting multi-disciplinary projects, students can start thinking computationally and actively using that new way of thinking in a hands-on way without even realizing they are doing so. At that point, the fear is gone.
>
> Devices such as the iPod Touch and iPhone are ideal tools for exploring computational thinking. They are easy to use, have simple, intuitive user interfaces, and have a wide range of functionality: file transfer, web browsing, MIDI control through accelerometers, light sensors, microphones, and touch sensors.

While no Scratch interface to iPhones or iPods yet exists, these sensor-rich input devices have tremendous potential as expressive interfaces to musical live coding and performance. We see our work in integrating IchiBoards into *Sound Thinking* Version 2 as an initial step in providing these benefits.

7. ACKNOWLEDGMENTS

The work described in this paper is based upon work supported by the National Science Foundation under Grant No. 0722161, "CPATH CB: Performamatics: Connecting Computer Science to the Performing, Fine, and Design Arts" and a complementary Research Experience for Undergraduates (REU) supplement. *Principal Investigator:* Jesse M. Heines. *Co-Principal Investigators:* Fred G. Martin, Gena Greher, Jim Jeffers, and Karen Roehr. *Senior Personnel:* Sarah Kuhn and Nancy Selleck. *Student Researchers:* Paul Laidler and Charles Saulters II. Additional information on the Performamatics project can be found at www.performamatics.org.

Alex Ruthmann's adaptation of musical live coding in Scratch is based on his collaboration with Andrew R. Brown and Andrew C. Sorensen at the Queensland Univ. of Tech., Brisbane, Australia.

Any opinions, findings, and conclusions or recommendations expressed in this material are those of the author(s) and do not necessarily reflect the views of the National Science Foundation.

8. REFERENCES

[1] Brown, A.R. (2005). *Making Music with Java*. Brisbane, Australia: Lulu.com.

[2] Brown, A.R., & Sorensen, A.C. (2009). Interacting with generative music through live coding. *Contemporary Music Review* **28**(1):17-29.

[3] Cooper, S., Dann, W., & Pausch, R. (2000). Alice: a 3-D tool for introductory programming concepts. *Jrnl. of Computing Sciences in Colleges* **15**(5):107-116.

[4] Engaging Computing Group (2009). *IchiBoard*. www.cs.uml.edu/ecg/index.php/IchiBoard/IchiBoard *accessed* Nov. 16, 2009.

[5] Greher, G.R., & Heines, J.M. (2008). Connecting Computer Science and Music Students to the Benefit of Both. *Assoc. for Technology in Music Instruction (ATMI) 2008 Conf.* Atlanta, GA.

[6] Guzdial, M. (2003). A media computation course for non-majors. *SIGCSE Bulletin* **35**(3):104-108.

[7] Heines, J.M., Goldman, K.J., Jeffers, J., Fox, E.A., & Beck, R. (2008). Interdisciplinary approaches to revitalizing undergraduate computing education. *Jrnl. of Computing in Small Colleges* **23**(5):68-72.

[8] Heines, J.M., Jeffers, J., & Kuhn, S. (2008). Performamatics: Experiences With Connecting a Computer Science Course to a Design Arts Course. *The Int'l. Jrnl. of Learning* **15**(2):9-16.

[9] Heines, J.M., Greher, G.R., & Kuhn, S. (2009). Music Performamatics: Interdisciplinary Interaction. *Proc. of the 40th ACM SIGCSE Technical Symposium on Computer Science Education*, pp. 478-482. Chattanooga, TN: ACM.

[10] Malan, D.J., & Leitner, H.H. (2007). Scratch for budding computer scientists. *Proc. of the 38th ACM SIGCSE Technical Symposium on Computer Science Education*. Covington, Kentucky, USA: ACM.

[11] Maloney, J., *et al.* (2004). Scratch: A Sneak Preview. *Second Int'l. Conf. on Creating, Connecting and Collaborating through Computing (C5'04)*, pp. 104-109. Kyoto, Japan.

[12] Martin, F., *et al.* (2009). Joining Computing and the Arts at a Mid-Size University. *Jrnl. of Computing Sciences in Colleges* **24**(6):87-94.

[13] Sorensen, A.C., & Brown, A.R. (2007). aa-cell in practice: An approach to musical live coding. *Proc. of the Int'l. Computer Music Conf.* Copenhagen, Denmark.

[14] Wang, G., & Cook, P.R. (2004). On-the-fly programming: using code as an expressive musical instrument. *Proc. of the 2004 Conf. on New Interfaces for Musical Expression*, pp. 138-143. Hamamatsu, Shizuoka, Japan: National Univ. of Singapore.

[15] Yanco, H.A., Kim, H.J., Martin, F., & Silka, L. (2007). Artbotics: Combining Art and Robotics to Broaden Participation in Computing. *Proc. of the AAAI Spring Symposium on Robots & Robot Venues*. Stanford Univ., CA.

Scratching Middle Schoolers' Creative Itch

Joel C. Adams
Department of Computer Science
Calvin College
Grand Rapids, MI 49546
+001-616-562-8666
adams@calvin.edu

ABSTRACT

Each July since 2003, the author has directed summer camps that introduce middle school boys and girls to the basic ideas of computer programming. Prior to 2009, the author used Alice 2.0 to introduce object-based computing. In 2009, the author decided to offer these camps using Scratch, primarily to engage repeat campers but also for variety. This paper provides a detailed overview of this outreach, and documents its success at providing middle school girls with a positive, engaging computing experience. It also discusses the merits of Alice and Scratch for such outreach efforts; and the use of these visually oriented programs by students with disabilities, including blind students.

Categories and Subject Descriptors

K.3.0 [**Computers and Education**]: General

General Terms

Measurement, Experimentation, Human Factors, Languages.

Keywords

Alice, 2-D animation, computer science, games, gender, middle school, music, programming, Scratch, summer camps, videos.

1. INTRODUCTION

Summer computing camps provide an enjoyable way to introduce young people to computing as a creative endeavor. Such camps provide a relaxed, informal setting where young students – especially young women – can use the computer to express themselves, learn problem-solving skills, have fun, and interact with peers who have similar interests.

Thanks to the broad applicability of computing, summer camp programs have been structured around Alice [1], cryptography [9], robotics [2], web-page authoring [8], and other engaging topics [5]. By providing an early, enjoyable, technology-enriched experience, such camps can provide long-term effects [3], combating the stereotypes that "computing is boring" and "computing is for geeks". Conventional wisdom holds that these stereotypes are entrenched by high school, so many of these programs target middle school students [1][3][5].

SIGCSE'10, March 10–13, 2010, Milwaukee, Wisconsin, USA.

The Imaginary Worlds Camps

Each summer since 2003, the author has directed the *Imaginary Worlds Camps* (IWC): two self-supporting single-sex summer day camps – one for boys and one for girls – in grades 6 and up. A detailed description of these camps is given in [1].

From 2003-2008, IWC campers used Alice 2.0 (see *alice.org*) to create computer-generated movies, and in the process, learned about object-based programming. This approach was very successful, thanks to Alice's integrated development environment (IDE) that lets users create sophisticated 3D animations using drag-and-drop programming. The maximum capacity for each camp is 30 campers; the boys' camp has filled and had a waiting list each summer, while the girls' camp has attracted an average of 15 girls each summer. The feedback has been uniformly positive, and over the years, many campers (boys and girls) have returned and attended the camp multiple years.

1.1 The Repeat Campers Problem

There are positive and negative aspects to these repeat campers:

- On the positive side, campers returning indicate success: their experience has been so positive, they want more.
- On the negative side, campers who return a second time have prior experience, and may be bored with instruction that targets novices. Serving both groups of campers within the limited resources of a summer program is a challenge, and the problem gets worse when campers return a *third time*.

One might simply not accept returning campers. However, this is undesirable as doing so merely turns away young people that IWC has successfully attracted to computing. It is also undesirable when a camp is not full, as is the case with the IWC girls' camp.

A better solution might be to vary the focus of the camp from year to year. For example, instead of repeating the Alice camp each year, the camp's focus might be shifted to a different computing-related activity that is equally fun and engaging. By doing so, all campers – first-timers and repeaters – will be novices with respect to the new activity. The challenge is to find a computer-related activity that campers will find as engaging as Alice.

One contender is **Scratch** (see *scratch.mit.edu*), which has been used in middle schools [10], after-school programs [7] and college introductory CS programs [6]. Scratch supports 2D graphics and events, has strong sound support (integrated music synthesizer / drum machine, predefined audio loops, plays WAV and MP3 files), and an innovative IDE that lets users build programs by dragging and dropping interlocking puzzle pieces. It also has a *social website* where users can easily share projects.

2. A SCRATCH-BASED IWC

Scratch's feature set provides strong support for creating and sharing music videos, slide shows, 2D computer games, and other animations. After a few weeks of experimenting with Scratch, the author decided to try to build the 2009 IWC around it.

2.1 Administrative details

Scratch proved to be a popular choice for IWC 2009. The IWC Boys Camp was the first of the college's many summer camps to fill, and parents asked to be added to a waiting list. One boy was attending IWC for the third time; two others were attending a second time. The Girls Camp registrations trickled in much more slowly, but by July 1, fifteen young women had registered. The college's summer camps program took care of publicity and registration details, including ordering special t-shirts for campers. A 1GB flash drive was ordered for each camper, so that campers could take home a copy of Scratch and their project.

Each camper was sent a letter asking them to come to the camp with an idea for a computer game or music video they would create. By spending time coming up with an idea before the camp, they could spend their time at camp more productively.

To keep the camper-to-staff ratio at 6-to-1, the author hired two college students and two high school students (the latter being past IWC campers) to serve as helpers. The practice of hiring the strongest IWC campers as helpers in subsequent years has proven to be an effective way of recruiting helpers for IWC.

2.2 Syllabus and Pedagogy

Prior to 2009, IWC used an eight-day format (two Monday-Thursday weeks per camp), in which students spent day 1 learning the basics of Alice and story-boarding their movies, spent six days learning object-based programming and creating their movies, and then showcased their movies on day 8. Scratch seemed to be simpler than Alice, so the author decided to try a five-day (Monday-Friday) format in 2009. The shorter format let us reduce the price of attending IWC from $280 in 2008 to $185 in 2009.

The camp began each day at 9:30 and concluded at 2:30. Each day (except the last) was organized as shown in Table 1:

Table 1. IWC 2009 Daily Structure

Time	Activity
9:30	Classroom demo illustrating morning topics
10:00	Move to lab, work on projects
12:00	Activity / Lunch break
12:30	Classroom demo illustrating afternoon topics
1:00	Move to lab, work on projects
2:30	Campers leave; camp staff meet to debrief

Each morning began with a live-demo in a lecture classroom, away from the distractions of the computer lab. Over the course of these classroom demos, the author designed and built a simple "Frogger-style" computer game from start to finish, and used it to illustrate various aspects of software development. For example, the first afternoon's session was on game design and storyboarding (see below), to get the students thinking about the look and structure of their games.

Following each morning demonstration, campers moved to the lab to begin applying what they had seen to their own projects. After a lunch break (outside, weather permitting), campers returned to the classroom for a second demo introducing new topics. Afterwards, they worked on their own projects the rest of the day.

At the end of the first afternoon, the students received their flash drives, and were guided through the steps of copying Scratch and their project to it, so that they could take them home.

Each day, the students were given a reading assignment from a Scratch book [4] that Cengage / Course Technology generously provided at greatly reduced cost. This book provided the campers with a useful reference and the readings covered Scratch topics that were not covered in the live demonstrations.

The author organized the camp's topics as shown in Table 2:

Table 2. IWC 2009 Weekly Structure

Day	Morning Topic	Afternoon Topic
1	*Scratch Overview*	*Design & Storyboarding*
2	*Broadcasts & Messages*	*Variables & Expressions*
3	*Conditional Logic*	*Sound*
4	*Using Randomness*	*User Testing*
5	*Sharing Your Project*	*Project Showcase*

The sequencing of these topics follows the order in which they become useful in developing a game. For example:

- In the *Scratch Overview* demo (#1), the author built a simple "Aquarium" animation to present the basic concepts needed to construct a simple 1-level game, including sprites, backgrounds, event loops, sound, and so on. Campers then spent the rest of the morning exploring Scratch, especially its libraries of predefined sprites and backgrounds.
- In the *Design & Storyboarding* demo (#2), the author sketched storyboards – the sequence of imagined screen shots (title, instructions, level 1, ...) – for a multi-level game called "Cat Splat" in which the user uses arrow keys to guide a cat (with nine lives) across a series of increasingly busy highways. Afterwards, campers spent the afternoon drawing storyboards for *their* games or music videos. When they were done, they had to "pitch" their projects to a helper, who (if necessary) worked with the campers to improve their designs.
- In the *Broadcasts & Messages* demo (#3), the author showed how to use messages to organize and synchronize the actions in a multi-level game. By defining message-handlers for the stage and sprite specifying their behaviors for each level in the "Cat Splat" game, a message-broadcast could be used to initiate a given level. To illustrate, to display the title and instructions, a "level0" message-handler was defined for the stage and each sprite. The stage's behavior was to change its background to the title screen, and each sprite's behavior was to hide itself. Similarly, on receiving a "level1" message, the stage changed its background to a country road; the cat and a car sprites positioned and showed themselves, with the car sprite entering an event-loop that moved it back and forth along the road. Campers quickly saw the benefit of jumping directly to a given level to bypass the preceding levels.

- In the *Variables and Expressions* session (#4), the author added variables to the "Cat Splat" game to store the player's level in the game, and the cat's remaining number of lives. Asked to come up with additional uses for variables, students came up with a game timer, a player's score, and other uses.
- In the *Conditional Logic* session, (#5) the author implemented "level2" as a two-way road for the cat to cross, with two cars traveling in opposite directions. Producing the desired behavior required the introduction of conditions, relational operators (< and >) and the OR operator (*if the cat is touching car1 OR it is touching car2, it gets splatted*). This allowed the difference between OR and AND to be demonstrated in an amusing way – when the OR was replaced by AND, the cat was invulnerable unless it was touched by *both* cars.
- And so on ...

By letting the game development drive the progression of topics, students were introduced to the topics in an "as needed" fashion. This "just in time" pedagogy seemed to work quite well: the need to solve a game-related problem motivated the students to pay close attention as a means of solving that problem was presented.

2.3 The Scratch Website

A strong feature of Scratch is its website – a *social website* – where registered users can post projects, comment on other people's projects, "friend" one another, group projects into galleries, and so on. The last morning, campers did a final review of their projects, created accounts at *scratch.mit.edu*, uploaded their projects, and added them to an IWC 2009 project gallery (*http://scratch.mit.edu/galleries/view/53807/*). Campers were very excited by this ability to have their creations posted publicly for anyone in the world to see, and the ability to e-mail their friends and family a URL to their project.

With the projects uploaded to the Scratch website, IWC moved to the campus theater for a "World Premier Showcase Celebration" to which the campers' families and friends were invited. With the author standing nearby for moral support, each camper gave a brief introduction to his or her project, demonstrated it for the audience, and then talked about the biggest obstacle they had encountered during the camp. This public speaking was itself a great challenge for some of our campers; most chose to talk about technical difficulties they had encountered.

3. ASSESSMENT

The desired outcomes were that campers leave IWC having:

A. had a positive computing experience;
B. learned some basic ideas of computer programming; and
C. a positive view of a career in computing.

To assess the achievement of these outcomes, the author used a direct measure – the campers' projects – and indirect measures including camper pre- and post-surveys. Despite the small sample sizes, IWC 2009 produced some statistically significant results, one of which we share here. The boys' and the girls' responses were similar; in the rest of this section, this paper focuses on the girls' responses unless noted otherwise.

3.1 A Positive Computing Experience

The post-surveys indicate that campers had a very positive experience. Figure 1 presents the girls' responses to the question:

How would you describe your experience at IWC?

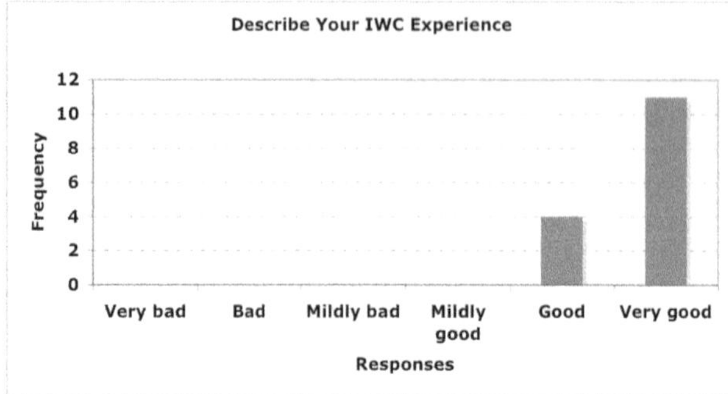

Figure 1. Camper Experience

As can be seen, 73% of the girls chose the best possible response, and 27% chose the next-best response. As a validating measure, Figure 2 presents the girls' responses to a follow-up question:

Would you want to attend a follow-up IWC next year?

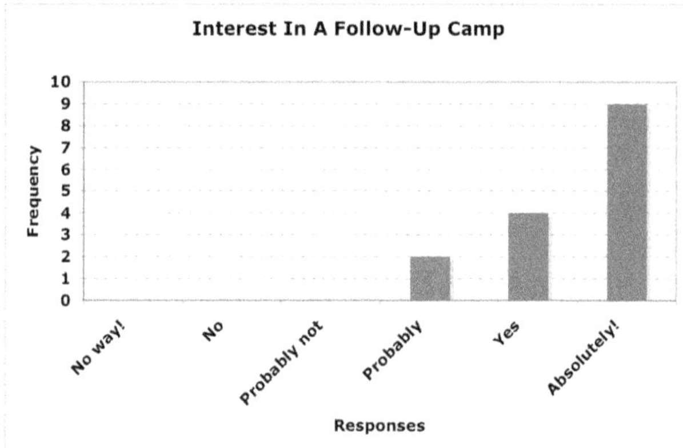

Figure 2. Interested In Follow-Up Camp?

The responses remain uniformly positive, with 60%, 27%, and 13% of the girls choosing the top three responses, respectively.

3.2 Programming Basics

To assess outcome B, campers were asked:

Rate how much you know about programming?

on both the entry- and exit-surveys. Response-choices ranged from *0 (Nothing)* to *5 (Expert)*. Figure 3 presents the *shift* in the girls' answers between the two surveys:

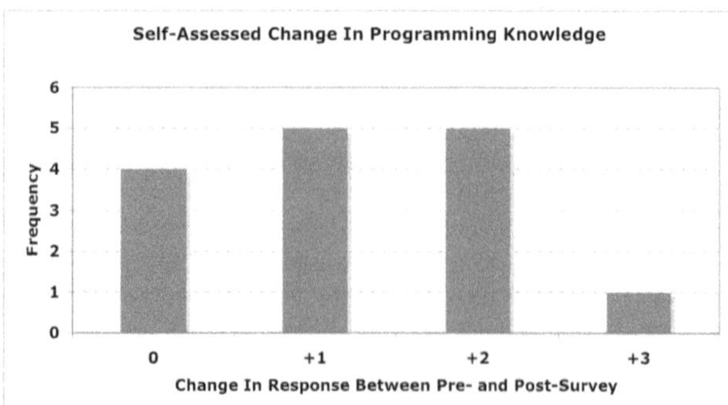

Figure 3. Change In Programming Knowledge

73% of the girls reported an increase in programming knowledge, while 27% reported no change: 33% of the responses had an increase of +1, 33% had an increase of +2, and 7% had an increase of +3. The overall average shift was +1.2, and it *was* statistically significant (p = 0.000218), so most IWC campers understood they had learned something about programming.

The number of scripts and sprites in a project can also provide a rough measure of how much programming a camper has done. *The girls' projects used an average of 16 sprites and 100 scripts.* While the games tended to have more sprites and scripts than the videos, the difference was not statistically significant (p=0.4026).

3.3 Computing Careers

To help IWC campers see the possibilities in computing careers, they were shown the U. of Washington's *A Day In The Life* videos [11]. To assess outcome C, campers were asked:

How do you think it would be to have a job using computers?

on both the entry- and exit-surveys. Choices ranged from *0 (Very bad)* to *5 (Very good).* Figure 4 presents the girls' response-shifts:

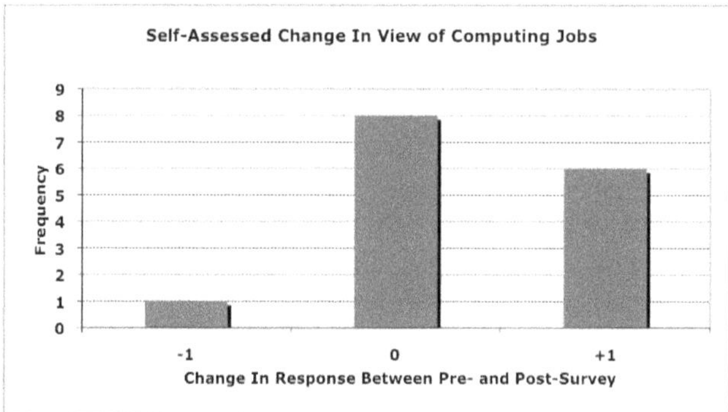

Figure 4. Change In View Of Computing Careers

53% of the girls indicated no change, 40% indicated a change of +1, and 7% indicated a change of -1. However, all 8 of the '0-change' girls gave positive responses on both surveys: one chose *3 (Mildly good),* four chose *4 (Good),* and two chose *5 (Very good)* on their surveys. In all, 14 of the 15 girls responded positively to this question on the post-survey. The average shift was +0.3, but it was *not quite* statistically significant (p = 0.0552).

4. DISCUSSION

This section presents some IWC-related observations.

4.1 Comparing Alice And Scratch

Both Alice and Scratch have drag-and-drop IDEs. They differ in:

- Animation: Alice is 3D; Scratch is 2D. Pragmatically, Scratch projects save and load much more quickly: our Scratch Showcase Session took about ¾ the time as in previous years.
- 3D animations look more polished than 2D animations. However, one of the first questions in every IWC has been, *"Can we create our own characters?"* Thanks to Scratch's 2D sprite-graphics editor, we were able to answer, *"Yes"* for the first time in 2009. Pretty much every camper did so.
- Alice users drag code tiles; Scratch users drag interlocking puzzle pieces. Pragmatically, Scratch seems to have an easier learning curve: once novices see how to drag-drop-lock puzzle pieces and launch a script, they are off and running.
- Alice's 3D entities are objects. Scratch's sprites are object-like, but where Alice provides parameterized methods, Scratch provides only message broadcasts and message-handlers.
- On the post-survey, campers were asked to rate the difficulty of computer programming on a scale of *0 (Very hard)* to *5 (Very easy).* The average response of roughly 220 male and female Alice campers between 2004 and 2008 was 2.7. The average for this year's 45 Scratch campers was 3.1. However, this difference was not statistically significant (p = 0.1566).
- Alice and Scratch can both be used to build games, movies, or videos. However, the prevailing metaphor for Alice projects seems to be visual story telling; Scratch seems to lend itself more to games. Given the choice of creating a music video or a game, *13 of 15 girls and 29 of 30 boys chose to create games.*
- Movies and music videos have a linear structure that requires little in the way of branching behavior. By contrast, games require a great deal of conditional logic and branching behavior. Put differently, when IWC campers create *movies and videos*, almost none of their projects use if statements. However, when IWC campers create *games*, every project employs if statements and conditional logic extensively.

4.2 Students with Disabilities

Each IWC since 2004 has had at least one camper with a serious disability. All have been male campers. The 2009 camp attracted three disabled boys: "Allan" with muscular dystrophy, "Bob" with high-functioning autism, and "Chris" with blindness. (Names have been changed to protect anonymity.) In this section, we discuss how their disabilities affected their experiences at IWC.

4.2.1 "Allan"

Allan was a 14-year-old attending IWC for a second time. His muscular dystrophy affected his legs, and he wore leg braces beneath his jeans. During our daily activity/lunch break, he would play a game like chess or cards with fellow campers, while other boys threw a Frisbee or ran around. Most of Allan's fellow campers were unaware that he had any disability.

Allan's disability had no effect on his ability to use Alice in 2008 or Scratch in 2009. His 2009 project was a game that was very similar to those of his fellow campers, defining custom animations and handling user-events with a techno audio track. As part of our assessment, we asked the campers what they liked best about IWC, and what they liked least. Allan reported that what he liked best about IWC-2009 was "*Scratch*"; and what he liked least was "*It was too short.*"

4.2.2 "Bob"

Bob was a 14-year-old attending IWC for the first time. His autism occasionally produced verbal outbursts when he became excited or frustrated (not uncommon when learning to program), but he generally had very good communication skills. He rarely took part in activities during lunch break, but he would discuss Scratch, computer games, movies, and other topics with his fellow campers. In short, his fellow campers knew he was a little different, but it was not a barrier for him.

Bob's project was an ambitious interactive movie-game, in which, for some parts of the story, the player guided the hero past challenging obstacles; in other parts of the story, predefined animations moved the characters to advance the story.

Bob loved using Scratch's sprite editor to create new costumes for his hero and villain sprites. But he was *very* frustrated by not completing his project prior to the Showcase session. (He was consoled to learn that he could finish his project at home and then *update* his project on the Scratch website.) Bob reported that what he liked best about IWC was "*making my game*"; what he liked least was "*not getting my game done in time*."

4.2.3 "Chris"

Chris was a 13-year-old attending IWC for the first time. His father contacted the author months before the IWC began, explained that his son was blind, but was very interested in music, and would like to create a music video. Was this possible?

The author invited Chris and his father to campus for a Scratch demo. Chris owns a computer with a Braille interface, but Scratch had no accessibility features or support for a Braille interface.

Chris's father decided to take a week of vacation and join Chris at the 2009 IWC, to help Chris create a project by serving as his eyes and hands. Chris and his father attended each classroom session where his father watched and Chris listened to the demo. In the lab, they sat at one of the aisle workstations, where Chris would communicate his ideas for what should happen next, and his father would work at making those ideas happen on-screen. Together, they created an interesting story involving a flying saucer, a vampire bat, and mutant humans. Its sound track was a fascinating mixture of bagpipes, the X-Files theme, sci-fi sound effects, and other interesting sounds. Chris reported that what he liked best about IWC was the "*sounds library in Scratch*"; he left blank the question regarding what he liked least. The author takes that to mean he liked everything!

5. CONCLUSIONS

Having used Alice in previous camps, the use of Scratch in 2009 was fun. Alice's 3D graphics tend to look more polished, but Scratch's 2D graphics offer some advantages, including a less-steep learning curve, faster load/save times, and the ability to create your own characters. As a lead-in to Java, Alice's provision of objects, methods, and parameters seems preferable. But Scratch's lower complexity and strong support for game-creation (requiring branching behavior) seem to make it preferable for teaching conditional logic and branching. In short, both Alice and Scratch can be used to provide young people with a positive introduction to computing, but since Scratch seems simpler than Alice, perhaps middle schools should use it first, to introduce students to the very basics of programming. After students have mastered conditional logic and branching in Scratch, teachers could switch to Alice to introduce object-based concepts.

Students with disabilities who are able to use a mouse can use either Alice or Scratch, thanks to their drag-and-drop IDEs. Likewise, many students with learning or behavioral disabilities will find the creative and graphical aspects of both programs to be deeply absorbing. There have been almost no behavioral problems at IWC over the years, as students find both of these programs to be very engaging.

Both Alice 2.0 and Scratch are highly visual; neither provides accessibility features for students with visual impairments. Either program may be difficult to use for students with visual impairments, and impractical for blind students, unless sighted persons work with such students as their eyes and hands.

From the author's perspective, using Scratch in the 2009 IWC was a great success. All involved had a very positive experience learning about programming, and nearly all left with a positive view of computing careers. The author hopes this record will encourage others to plan their own outreach efforts, and looks forward to reading about them.

6. ACKNOWLEDGMENTS

The author thanks Stacy Hiquet of Course PTR (a division of Cengage Learning), who provided reduced-price copies of [4].

7. REFERENCES

[1] J. Adams. Alice, Middle-Schoolers, & The Imaginary Worlds Camps. *Proceedings of the 38th SIGCSE Technical Symposium on Computer Science Education* (March 2007). pp. 307-311.

[2] K. Cannon, K. Panciera, and N. Papanikolopoulos. Second annual robotics summer camp for underrepresented students. *Proceedings of the 12th SIGCSE Conference on Innovation and Technology in Computer Science Education* (June 2007). pp. 14-18.

[3] M. Craig and D. Horton. Gr8 designs for Gr8 girls: a middle-school program and its evaluation. *Proceedings of the 40th SIGCSE Technical Symposium on Computer Science Education* (March 2009). pp. 221-225.

[4] J. Ford. Scratch Programming For Teens, Course Technology / Cengage Learning, 2008.

[5] W. Lau, G. Ngai, S. Chan, and J. Cheung. Learning programming through fashion and design: a pilot summer course in wearable computing for middle school students. *Proceedings of the 40th SIGCSE Technical Symposium on Computer Science Education* (March 2009). pp. 504-508.

[6] D. Malan and H. Leitner, Scratch for budding computer scientists. *Proceedings of the 39th SIGCSE Technical Symposium on Computer Science Education* (March 2007). pp. 223-227.

[7] J. Maloney, K. Peppler, Y. Kafai, M. Resnick, and N. Rusk. Programming by choice: urban youth learning programming with scratch, *Proceedings of the 39th SIGCSE Technical Symposium on Computer Science Education* (March 2008). pp. 367-371.

[8] L. Pollock, K. McCoy, S. Carberry, N. Handigopal, and X. You. Increasing High School Girls' Self Confidence and Awareness of CS through a Positive Summer Experience. *Proceedings of the 35th SIGCSE Technical Symposium on Computer Science Education* (March 2004). pp. 185-189.

[9] L. Saliga, L. Nelson, and K. Liszka. What's the secret?: an encrypted treasure hunt. Journal of Computing Sciences in Colleges (24) 1, October 2008. pp. 55-61.

[10] P. Sivilotti and S. Laugel. Scratching the surface of advanced topics in software engineering: a workshop module for middle school students. *Proceedings of the 39th SIGCSE Technical Symposium on Computer Science Education* (March 2008). pp. 291-295.

[11] University of Washington CSE Department, "Why Choose CSE?" Online: *http://www.cs.washington.edu/WhyCSE/*. Accessed August 2009.

A Simple Machine Simulator for Teaching Stack Frames

Dino Schweitzer Jeff Boleng
United States Air Force Academy
USAFA, CO 80840
+1-719-333-3945
dino.schweitzer@usafa.edu

ABSTRACT

Stack frames are a fundamental concept in computer science often taught in an operating systems or an assembly language programming course. Computer security courses also rely on an understanding of stack frame concepts when teaching buffer overflow attacks. To assist students in learning the fundamentals of stack frames and related concepts, we have developed an interactive Simple Machine Simulator tool that allows students to step through a C-like language program and watch how memory changes. We have used this tool successfully in various courses to teach different aspects of stack frames and their use. This paper will describe the tool, how it is used to teach stack frame concepts, our experience, and future plans.

Categories and Subject Descriptors

K.3.2 [**Computer and Information Science Education**]: Computer Science education.

General Terms: Experimentation, Languages.

Keywords

Active Learning, Stack Frames, Buffer Overflow, Visualization.

1. INTRODUCTION

Stack frames, or activation records, are a fundamental concept in computer science education. Students need to understand the purpose and operation of stack frames when subroutines are called to understand how parameters are passed, how re-entrant code is enabled, and how recursion is possible. When teaching computer security concepts, buffer overflows most commonly attack a system by "smashing the stack" and inserting malicious executable code directly onto the stack. To understand the threat and details of the attack, students need to understand how stack frames work, and how they can be manipulated to achieve the desired results. In the ACM Computer Science Curriculum 2008, the notion of stack frames, activation records, and subroutine calls appears in multiple places within the curriculum including Programming Fundamentals, Operating Systems, Programming Languages, and Architecture [1].

SIGCSE'10, March 10–13, 2010, Milwaukee, Wisconsin, USA.

At the United States Air Force Academy (USAFA), the basic concepts of stack frames are introduced in various courses and at different levels. Our Computer Organization and Architecture course introduces stack frames at the assembly language programming level to explain the process of passing parameters and a return addresses to subroutines. In the Operating Systems course, stack frames are used to demonstrate process control, concurrency, and reinforce the memory hierarchy introduced in the Computer Architecture course. Finally, in the introductory Computer Security course, stack frames are used in the discussion of buffer overflows.

Unfortunately, in the security course, some of the students are not computer science majors, have never seen stack frames or assembly language, and struggle with the concepts. As a result, in previous offerings, an inordinate amount of time was spent reviewing stack frames rather than focusing on the buffer overflow issue. In addition, we had students performing a hands-on lab in which they intentionally generated a buffer overflow in C, and viewed the results using disassemblers and debuggers. Needless to say, our non-CS majors were confused. To assist in student comprehension and minimize the need to understand additional background material, we developed a Simple Machine Simulator (SMS) interactive tool to demonstrate stack frames and buffer overflows in a hands-on "web lab" environment. Based on the success of the tool, other courses in the major are now using it to introduce stack frame concepts to students in an easy-to-understand context.

The remainder of this paper will describe other approaches found in the literature (Section 2), describe the tool itself (Section 3), demonstrate how the tool was used to teach buffer overflows (Section 4), and conclude with our experience and future plans for the tool (Section 5).

2. OTHER APPROACHES

Visualizing machine registers and internal CPU state is not new. A wide variety of assembly language simulators are available. For instance, SPIM [2] and MIPSTER [3] are both well known and widely used. We use both in our Computer Architecture course. Another related tool is CPU SIM [4].

A specific approach to generating buffer overflow via return address redirection is described in Phillips and Tan [5]. We use a simplified version of this technique in our Computer Security course with the web lab described below. Barnett [6] introduces a scaled down assembly language and assembler used to reduce the required initial knowledge that has influenced our approach. Cribb [7] also describes a similar simulator with a greatly simplified instruction set. Finally, Sundarararaman and Back [9] present a more general purpose memory and data structure visualization technique.

Our approach is different from previously presented tools in the following ways:

1. A common goal of the above simulators is to use them to teach assembly language syntax and programming skills. One of our specific goals was to avoid the overhead and complexity of teaching syntax. Our tool is used to illustrate the concept of stack frames and buffer overflows in only two lessons. By greatly simplifying the instruction set and using a very common language syntax (i.e. C like) our simulator is accessible to students that may never have seen assembly language before. In fact, we have successfully used the simulator in a web lab with non computer science majors and received positive feedback.
2. Another common goal of assembly language or machine simulators is to aid in the teaching of hardware concepts such as memory access modes, cache hierarchies, pipelining, etc. This is not our goal. So again, greatly simplifying the simulator and syntax was possible. We represent memory as a linear array of storage. This is sufficient for our purposes to represent how data can be stored in memory, and how function calls and returns result in program counter changes.
3. Many existing simulators are also developed and used to illustrate the relationship and translation of language statements to assembly instructions, then to binary, and lastly to how the binary flows through the internals of the CPU's logic gates. This detailed flow is important to support a computer organization and architecture course, but is a lower level of abstraction than we require.

Our focus is at a higher level of abstraction than existing simulators. We do not require students to understand the intricacies of special purpose registers or memory layouts common in modern processors. Our simulator implements the minimum amount of detail required to teach the specific concepts of stack frames, function calls, and buffer overflows.

A similar effort to create visualizations for use in teaching security concepts was accomplished by Susan Gerhart at Embry Riddle who created a series of playback animations and applets for specifically demonstrating buffer overflow attacks [8]. These demonstrations along with other security-related visualizations are available at http://nsfsecurity.pr.erau.edu/bom. Some of these tools are similar to our approach. The user is able to interactively stepwise execute a program and see the effects in a visual memory representation. The user can affect the execution by means of inputting different values at prompts. The tools are designed as applets that can be embedded in web pages. The main differences between these tools and our simulator are:

- Memory is limited to 256 locations that uses primarily color coding to represent types of data as opposed to the specific binary contents.
- Individual instructions are not represented in memory.
- Our simulator provides explicit information on the contents of stack memory to teach students stack frames.
- Our simulator represents a von Neumann architecture with instructions and data explicitly sharing memory. This model can be used for a variety of educational applications beyond stack frames and buffer overflows.

3. SIMPLE MACHINE SIMULATOR

3.1 Design Goals

The overall purpose of the SMS is to demonstrate the stepwise execution of a pseudo-high level program and see how memory changes to illustrate various concepts. The original focus of the tool was on stack frame concepts, so lower level assembly language details such as addressing modes, registers, and variable length instructions were avoided. To provide this focus, the language needs to be limited, simple, and similar to languages with which students are already familiar. This avoids the need to learn a totally new language in order to use the tool. There is also a requirement for a highly interactive environment in which students can single step through a program, but at any point in time, stop and back up to fully understand what just happened. This allows for "what if" scenarios and student experimentation. The running of the tool needs to be relatively self-evident with minimal instruction on how to make things happen. Our experience with similar tools is that students want to "get going" and not spend time reading instructions or understanding complex interfaces. Finally, it is desirable to embed the tool in customized web pages so that different scenarios and experiments can be presented to the student using the same tool. Sufficient explanatory material can be placed on the web page for the student to complete the exercises without additional references.

3.2 Implementation

Similar to the work at Embry Riddle, SMS is written as a Java applet that can be embedded in web pages along with text for proposed experiments or descriptions. Figure 1 shows the basic layout of the tool. The code pane on the left side of the window displays the current program loaded in memory and highlights the current instruction to execute. The buttons below the code pane control stepwise execution of the program. Below the buttons are the input console and the output pane for performing input and output operations. The right pane displays the contents of memory, and can be viewed in decimal, hex, binary, or character format. Memory consists of 4,096 16-bit locations. The user can scroll through and view all of memory at any point. The Note field in the memory display provides additional explanatory text about what is contained at that particular memory location. A dropdown Help Menu is also present allowing students to display information on instruction formats and how to execute programs.

One of the goals of the tool is to keep the language simple and at a high-level for understandability. To understand the relationship of code to memory, it is necessary for each high-level instruction to have a binary representation in memory. To maintain simplicity, SMS has only two basic data types (integers and strings) and seven basic high-level instruction types:

Assignment
Input
Output
Call subroutine
Return from subroutine
End of Program
NOP

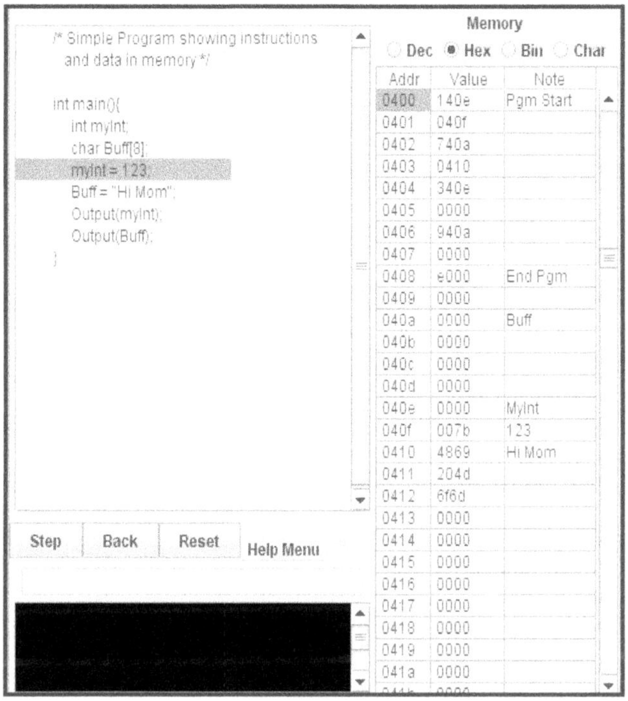

Figure 1. Simple Machine Simulator screen.

The Assignment, Input, and Output instructions can be for either integers or strings. Integers take one memory location (16 bits) and strings are variable length, two characters per word and null terminated. Each instruction takes two words of memory consisting of an op code, and up to two parameters. The source code is designed to look like C with variable declarations and similar syntax. As an example of how the source code translates to memory, Figure 1 shows the instruction "myInt = 123" highlighted in the code pane. The corresponding memory location, at address x0400, is highlighted in the memory pane. The first memory word has four bits representing the op code, which is 1 for integer assignment. The remaining 12 bits are operand 1, which in this example is x40e which is the memory location for myInt. The lower 12 bits of the second word is the second operand, which in this example is x40f. Since our simple language does not have literals, it is necessary to store literal values, 123 in this case, at separate memory locations. The second operand refers to the memory location containing 123.

When the sample program in Figure 1 is executed, the values 123 and "Hi Mom" are printed to the output pane and an "*** END OF PROGRAM ***" message is output when the End of Program instruction at location x408 is executed. As the user steps through the program, the next instruction to execute and corresponding memory location are highlighted to follow what is happening.

In order to use SMS to demonstrate stack frames, it was necessary to add a relative addressing mode. The high order bit of the second instruction word is used to indicate an address relative to the Stack Pointer (SP). When this bit is set, the final address of the operand is calculated by adding the value in the lower 12 bits to the current value for the SP. While more complicated than desirable, this mode is necessary. To help students in understanding it when a program is executing, the current memory location of the SP is identified in the Note portion of the memory display.

3.3 Executing Programs

The programs in SMS are normally predefined by the instructor. When the tool comes up on a web page, the appropriate program is loaded based on the concepts being presented. The student can execute programs using the Step, Back, and Reset buttons at the bottom of the code pane. Students cannot directly change the high level program during the lab, but they can affect the contents of memory based on input values entered. It is very possible, and, in fact, encouraged in certain labs for students to change the contents of instructions in memory. If the students change an instruction to an illegal instruction and attempt to execute it, they will receive a "run time" error message on the console. This occurs frequently when students first attempt to change the return address from a subroutine call and send the program counter to some arbitrary location in memory.

3.4 Calling Subroutines

To maintain the design goal of simplicity, subroutines are called with either zero or one parameters. The second operand of the call instruction is the parameter. When a subroutine is called, the appropriate information is pushed onto the stack. Specifically, the items pushed are:

- return address
- parameter is present
- local variables

This information composes the stack frame, or activation record, associated with the call. In order for the simulator to know how much stack memory to set aside for local variables, the first word of the subroutine is the count of how many positions on the stack to reserve. Figure 2 shows the SMS state after a subroutine call has been executed. The memory locations between the SP, shown in the Notes field, and the address for the start of the routine comprise the stack frame for this call. In this example, the return address, x404, was the first item on the stack, followed by the parameter, a single word integer value, followed by three words set aside for local variables. The SP grows toward low memory. As the user steps through the statements in the subroutine, any changes to local variables are reflected in the stack memory locations. The high order bit of operands associated with local variables is set indicating addressing relative to the SP. Thus, the second operand for the highlighted input instruction at x03f6 is x8000 indicating it will go at the location pointed to by SP plus a zero offset. When the student executes the statement, they will see the appropriate memory location change.

Figure 3 shows the SMS state after the second subroutine is called from the first. There are now two stack frames on the stack reflecting the return addresses, parameters, and local variables for both calls. As the user steps through the execution, they see the SP dynamically change and can verify the meaning of each value on the stack with the assistance of the notes. Different scenarios can be presented to students with subroutines calling other subroutines or calling themselves (recursion). As the student steps through the execution, they can observe the stack growing and shrinking with each call and return.

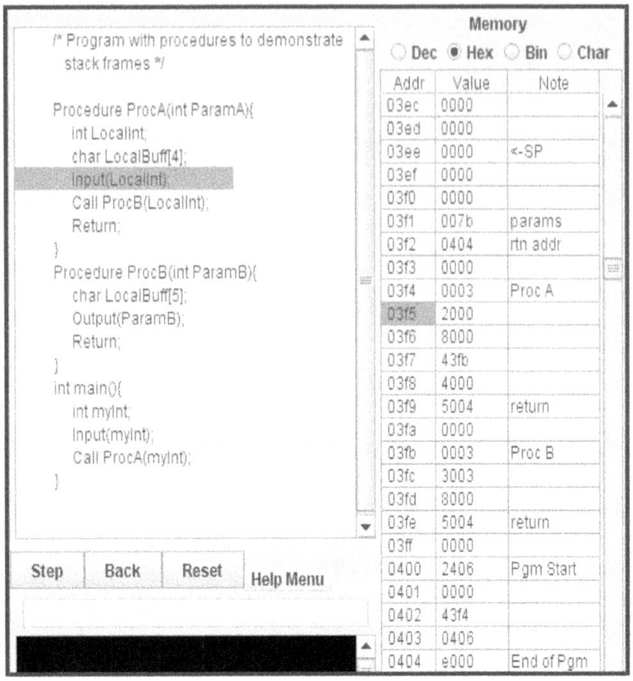

Figure 2. SMS state after subroutine call.

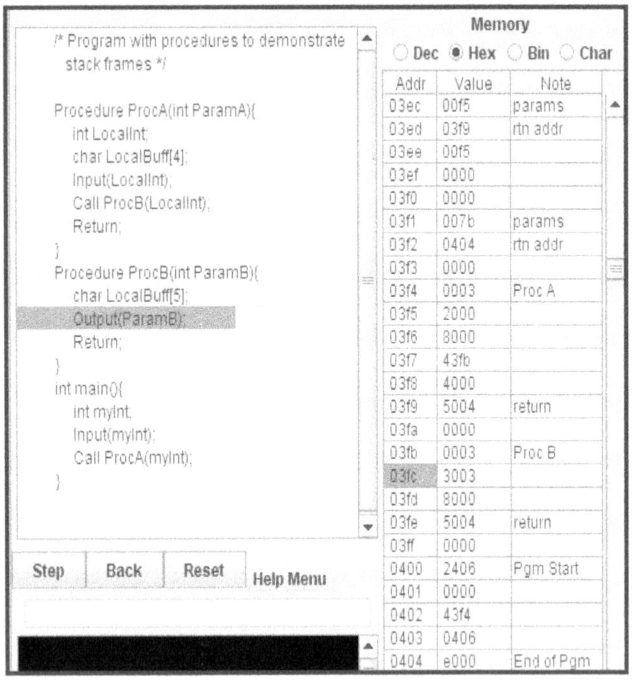

Figure 3. SMS state after second subroutine call.

4. TEACHING BUFFER OVERFLOWS

In the introductory computer security course at USAFA, students receive hands-on training in current tools and techniques for both offensive and defensive aspects of security. Buffer overflows are a primary vulnerability exploited by current attacks and it is important for students to understand what they are, how they are exploited, and how to prevent them. In previous offerings of the course, students conducted a hands-on experiment in which they generated a buffer overflow in a C program. To observe the overflow, students used code debuggers to step through the program, setting breakpoints, and attempting to manipulate stack content based on carefully crafted input strings. To place code on the stack, students wrote Intel assembly code to accomplish some simple task, assembled the code to determine the machine code equivalent of the program, and finally crafted a string input that would place the appropriate bytes on the stack. The process was involved and required three lessons of class time to explain and step students through the process.

In spring 2009, the course was changed to use SMS to teach buffer overflow. Initially, students were provided the simple example shown in Figure 1 to familiarize themselves with the tool and its operation. Next they were presented with a simple buffer overflow situation shown in Figure 4. Four words of memory are set aside for both Buff1 and Buff2 since they were declared as containing up to eight characters. In the instructions for this example, students are encouraged to enter string values greater than eight characters to see how the input is corrupting subsequent memory locations and affecting program execution. This demonstrates the basic concept of buffer overflow and how it can adversely affect program execution.

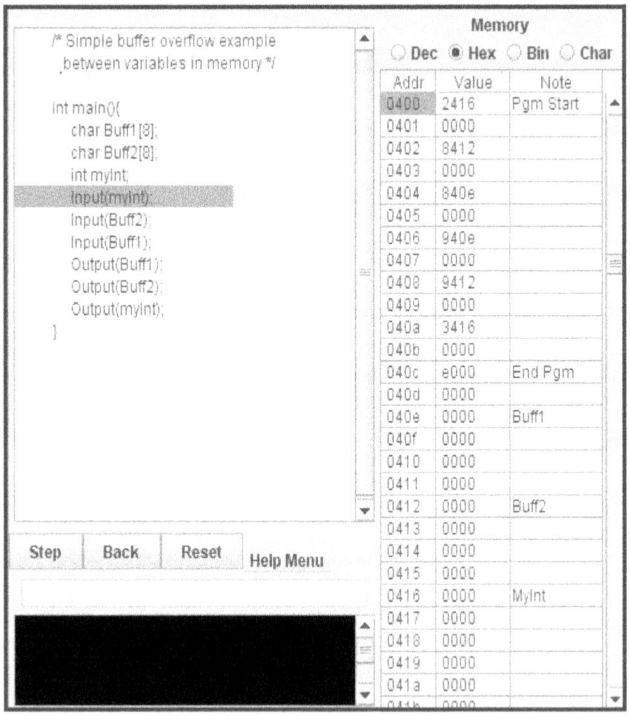

Figure 4. Simple buffer overflow example.

After this example, students were provided the example shown in Figures 2 and 3 along with an explanation of stack frames. This allowed them to re-familiarize themselves (or in some cases see for the first time) how stack frames work and the specific stack contents in this simulator. Next, students were introduced to the concept of "smashing the stack" by stepping through an example in which they input values for a local subroutine variable in an attempt to change the return address on the stack. The goal was to skip the instruction in the main program immediately following the call. This example resulted in many students experiencing the "Illegal Instruction" error code when they jumped to some random location in memory. The final code sample and exericse was more complicated and led the students through the process of inserting code on the stack through a buffer overflow in order to execute arbitrary code. Rather than have students write their own code to insert, they were provided with an instruction that represented a system call to get root privilege. If they successfully inserted the instruction on the stack and were able to get it to execute, they were rewarded with a "root>>" prompt in the output pane.

The entire buffer overflow lab is accomplished using five web pages with the examples described along with explanatory text on each page. Students in the security class, including non-CS majors, were able to comprehend the tool and successfully complete the lab in a single class session.

5. OUR EXPERIENCE AND PLANS

The initial use of SMS in our computer security course proved highly successful. The basic concepts of buffer overflow, why it is a security threat, and approaches to detect or eliminate them were presented in lecture format, followed by a one-class lab using the SMS tool. Students were able to complete the entire lab in a single class session (50 minutes). Thus, two lessons were devoted to the topic as opposed to three lessons in previous semesters. In addition, non-CS majors who struggled to complete the complexity of the previous hands-on demonstration, were able to successfully complete and understand the web lab version with SMS. Although quantitative analysis of student knowledge gained based on exam questions is difficult due to small sample sizes, the buffer overflow web lab was highly rated on student critiques as an enjoyable and useful experience.

Based on this success, we began investigating the use of the tool in some of our other computer science classes. While the tool was initially developed for the buffer overflow problem, by designing it with a general language/memory architecture, we created an environment that can be easily re-purposed for other applications. For example, in our operating systems class, we have successfully introduced the tool as a refresher on the purpose and operation of stack frames when calling routines. In our computer architecture course, which teaches assembly language programming, we are planning on using the tool to introduce the concepts of stack frames and subroutine calling without the details of the specific language.

Some modifications to the tool are planned to accommodate the different ways of using it. For example, an editor is being incorporated to allow students to create their own high-level programs on the fly based on the simple instruction set and then assemble them to memory. This will reinforce the idea of a Von Neumann architecture in which instructions and data coexist in memory. It will also allow students to write simple programs that they can "watch" execute. Other courses are also reviewing the tool to determine applicability in their material. Since computer science majors will have seen and used the tool initially in their sophomore year, it will be a familiar environment for other demonstrations.

The tool is public domain and freely available for use. Please contact the authors for further information.

6. REFERENCES

[1] ACM Curricula Recommendations, http://www.acm.org/education/curricula-recommendations, last accessed Sep 11, 2009.

[2] SPIM, A MIPS32 Simulator, http://pages.cs.wisc.edu/~larus/spim.html, last accessed Sep 11, 2009.

[3] MIPSTER 2.0, http://www.downcastsystems.com/mipster/default.asp, last accessed Sep 11, 2009.

[4] Dale Skrein. CPU Sim 3.1: A tool for simulating computer architectures for computer organization classes. ACM Journal on Educational Resources in Computing (JERIC), Vol. 1, Issue 4, 2001, 46-59.

[5] Andrew E. Phillips and Jack S. E. Tan. Exploring Security Vulnerabilities by Exploiting Buffer Overflow using the MIPS ISA. ACM SIGCSE 2003 Bulletin, Vol. 35, Issue 1, Jan 2003, 172-176.

[6] Barnett, B. L. A visual simulator for a simple machine and assembly language. Technical Symposium on Computer Science Education (SIGCSE, Nashville Tennessee, USA), 1995, 233-237.

[7] A Simple Assembly Language Computer Simulator. http://www.cse.yorku.ca/~peterc/simulator/simulator.html, last accessed Sep 11, 2009.

[8] Gerhart, Susan. Animation of Buffer Overflows and Cryptography. Technical Symposium on Computer Science Education (SIGCSE, Norfolk Virginia, USA), 2004.

[9] Jaishankar Sundarararaman and Godmar Back. HDPV: interactive , faithful, in-vivo runtime state visualization for C/C++ and Java. Proceedings of the 4th Symposium on Software visualization (SOFTVIS, Ammersee, Germany) 2008, 47-56.

In the Zone: Virtual Computing on a Budget

Stan J. Thomas
Wake Forest University
Winston-Salem, NC 27106
sjt@wfu.edu

Paul M. Whitener
Wake Forest University
Winston-Salem, NC 27106
whitenpm@wfu.edu

ABSTRACT

In this paper, we report on our efforts, extending over several years, to provide computer science students experience with a variety of operating system and computing environments. We describe our explorations into the use of virtual machine environments for instructional purposes, explorations that have led to the current multifaceted approach to virtualization. We also demonstrate that implementing a diverse, sophisticated virtual computing environment does not require a large investment in computer hardware, in fact it can lead to a cost saving by extending the useful life of systems and reducing the complexity of system administration.

Categories and Subject Descriptors

K.3.2 [**Computers and Education**]: Computer and Information Science Education; D.4.0 [**Software**]: Operating Systems-General

General Terms

Management, Economics, Experimentation

Keywords

Virtualization, operating systems, computing environments

1. INTRODUCTION

Currently, many colleges and universities struggle to provide students with the latest technologies for learning while working within their budgetary constraints. Computer Science departments, in particular, seek to provide experience with the latest in computing hardware and software for students, whether it be personal computers, mobile devices, high performance computing, or computing in the cloud. However, reality may be a little different. With limited budgets and limited system administration support, programs may believe there is no option but to standardize on one hardware platform and one operating system. This paper reports on our efforts over a five year period to provide a variety of computing experiences for computer science students, culminating in our current multifaceted approach which takes advantage of virtualization tools running on commodity hardware to provide a variety of computing environments at a very reasonable cost. Within this environment we provide students a variety of computing experiences that prepare them for initial employment as well as life-long learning.

SIGCSE'10, March 10-13, 2010, Milwaukee, Wisconsin, USA.

2. UBIQUITOUS COMPUTING

For more than a decade Wake Forest University has been a leader in the campus wide laptop computing initiative in higher education [2,3,5]. The university was the second in the nation to offer a common notebook platform to incoming students and to then replace it with a newer model after two years. This comprehensive plan, initially referred to as the Plan for the Class of 2000 [1], led to the elimination of traditional computer labs, including those labs where computer science students previously had access to SGI and Sun Microsystems workstations, IBM personal computers, and other hardware and software platforms. With the elimination of computing labs, the Computer Science department was forced to identify new approaches to provide multiple computing environments to our students.

Subsequently, the department became an early adopter of dual booting student laptops with both Linux and Microsoft Windows. The dual boot approach allowed students to have access to the application rich Windows software load provided by the university—necessary for general class work across campus—in addition to Red Hat Linux—needed for certain computer science coursework. Using the Linux load, students had *root* access on their own notebooks and could make modifications at the system level. In conjunction with the formal study of operating systems, students gained the ability to "look under the hood" of their own computers. Other classes, beginning with the CS2 course, utilized the Linux load and open source tools for software development in C++. Faculty and support staff from the campus Information Systems group worked to identify a rich set of Linux applications that computer science students could use both for coursework and their own entertainment needs. Students were provided both Linux and Windows updates through university satellite servers and had full access to the software repositories maintained by the campus Information Systems staff.

As time passed there were recurring, hard to diagnose disk instability issues with the dual boot configuration. Knowledgeable students started replacing the university provided Red Hat Linux with other dialects of Linux. Issues arose. Configurations became unsupportable by the campus Help Desk. Faculty and department staff members were frequently asked by students to troubleshoot laptop issues unrelated to the assignment or learning objectives at hand. The dual boot configuration was deemed by the department to be unsustainable. After four years of offering a dual boot laptop load to computer science majors, the decision was made to discontinue providing this option beginning with the Fall 2008 semester. We elected to return to the earlier days when students received their laptops with only the university standard Microsoft Windows load. A new option had to be identified to provide students with experience working in a variety of computing environments in a more engaging way than simply logging into a remote server.

3. VIRTUALIZATION

During the 2007-08 academic year some of our classes were taught using the Linux-like Cygwin environment under Windows. Although Cygwin met some of our needs, it did not provide the full Linux experience desired and it was not an ideal environment for teaching operating system internals. In addition, much like with the dual boot approach, use of Cygwin on student laptops required substantial student cooperation in the installation and maintenance of the software.

During the same time period, three converging developments led the department to explore the use of virtual computing (VC) to provide a variety of computing environments for our students. First, as previously described, the Windows-Linux dual boot option, as well as Cygwin, had proven unsatisfactory. Second, faculty members had very specific computing needs for courses they were introducing, some of which required students to have full system administration or *root* privileges. Third, the department was fortunate to have hired a system administrator with extensive experience managing virtual computing environments and who was eager to use the latest software tools to support our instructional needs.

We investigated successful virtual computing initiatives in higher education, particularly the Virtual Computing Lab (VCL) project at North Carolina State University [4,6] in partnership with IBM, but we were not equipped nor budgeted to build our instructional activities on a centralized high performance computing foundation. As a small department in a small university we did have the flexibility of experimenting with leading edge technologies in a manner appropriate to our local needs and budget; hence we started our virtualization initiatives by targeting two courses with very specific computing needs.

3.1 Initial Experiments

For the Spring semester of 2008 one faculty member was planning a server administration course utilizing AMP (Apache, MySQL, PHP) tools. For this course each student needed a dedicated computer with *root* privileges. In years prior to 2008 we used a collection of older desktop computers for these student learning platforms. This approach had proven to be very time-consuming for the instructors, as systems had to be initially imaged and frequently reimaged during the semester. In addition, these weakly secured systems tended to be attractive to hackers.

For Spring 2008, a second faculty member had very specific software requirements for a senior/graduate level computer graphics course he was teaching. He wanted students to develop applications using OpenGL libraries in a Linux environment. This requirement could have been met by utilizing a single Linux/Solaris server but it was feared that the computational requirements for the class would tax a single server.

3.1.1 Platform

At the time, the department had several Sun Blade 1000 workstations in storage. These circa 2000 workstations had originally served as office systems for faculty. In order to support our virtualization experiments, six Sun Blade 1000 systems were salvaged and put back into service. Each unit was configured with 1GB of ram, a single 32GB hard drive and a single 750MHz Sparc III processor. OpenSolaris (Solaris Express Community Edition) was installed as the operating system (OS). This OS release was chosen primarily because of its support of Solaris Zones and secondarily because of the wide variety of open source tools bundled with it.

Solaris Zones have some unique features that make them extremely easy for administrators to maintain. A Solaris Zone is a kernel level virtualization technique comparable to a BSD Jail. It is a lightweight method that provides complete, isolated, and secure runtime environments for users and applications with negligible resource overhead. Any number of individual *non-global zones* (virtual machines) can be allocated, secured and managed by an instance of Solaris called the *global zone*. Physical hardware resources and kernel operations are managed by the global zone and allocated dynamically to its hosted non-global zones. In the configuration we employed, non-global zones shared common file system directories as read only mount points. This reduced the needed disk footprint per zone to around 150Mb. Each non-global zone can have its own personality, including separate password/shadow files, hostname, and IP addresses, and may be given access to shared or dedicated resources at varying priority levels. Application software packages may be added to individual non-global zones as needed. By design, the non-global zone memory space and disk "user land" are isolated via the kernel from the global zone as well as from other hosted non-global zones. This makes them very secure and allows independent rebooting and "crashing" of the non-global zone without affecting other zones on the box. Each non-global zone is an ideal environment for student work requiring "virtual" root access. At the same time, the environment helps to consolidate common Solaris administration tasks to a small number of Solaris global zone instances.

A non-global zone was designed for the AMP class. Once the configuration was approved by the instructor, the zone was easily replicated with a distinct password/shadow file, hostname, and IP address for each. One zone was created for each student in the class for a total of twelve AMP zones across six Sun Blade 1000s. Each student thus had root access to the equivalent of a full Solaris server but in a virtualized environment.

Similarly, a non-global zone was configured for the graphics class containing the desired development environment and graphics libraries. Once the "load" was approved by the professor, one zone was created for each student in the graphics class for a total of twelve graphics instruction zones across the six Sun Blade 1000s.

Students in these classes used a variety of methods to connect to their virtual machine zones. Students needing only a command line interface simply used *putty* under Windows or *ssh* in a terminal session from other operating systems. Students needing a graphical interface from Mac OS X or Linux used a terminal window to run *ssh* and X-Windows provided the graphical interface. Students running Windows on their client computers had access to both HummingBird Exceed and the open source combination of *xming* with *putty*. A small number of Sun Ray thin clients were also provided for students to access their zones when their personal computer was not available.

While students in the AMP class were not required to utilize their personal zone, their other option was to provide their own hardware, which some students elected to do. Similarly, while students in the graphics course were not required to use their zone for class, if they did choose to use their zone, they could be assured that the professor had tested all assignments and verified operation on the zones. This made debugging and troubleshooting much easier for both student and professor. In addition, students from both classes had full access to the zones, including *root* access. The zones were accessible from both on campus as well as off. Students could reboot their zone at their own will, make changes and administer their own server, all while not affecting other zones on the host or the host itself.

3.1.2 Lessons Learned

Once they were configured and created, the only problem with the zones supporting AMP administration had to do with permissions that had to be modified across all the zones. The problem arose from an oversight in the configuration of the load and not the system itself. The hardware, software platform was stable, performed well, and no substantive issues were reported.

For the graphics course, a few students were hampered by an incompatibility between the version of the OpenGL Utility Toolkit (GLUT) running on their zone and the version running on their own Linux devices. On these systems, some GLUT routines did not interact correctly between the zone and the graphics hardware on the client machines. The issue was not observed on client systems running OpenSolaris or Mac OS X. Again, the computing performance and reliability of the Sun Blade 1000s was adequate, although the network traffic between client and server was, at times, a noticeable bottleneck.

From a system administrator's point of view, managing Solaris Zones is straightforward. From the global zone, the administrator can shut down a non-global zone, reboot it, and change any password without affecting other zones. Software patching is also simplified. Patches are applied from the global zone and automatically pushed to all non-global zones on the box. Likewise, if a new package is added to the global zone it will be available, by default, on all non-global zones on the box. At the end of the semester it was a simple administrative process to sterilize and/or "rezone" the hardware for the upcoming semester.

Table 1. Virtual Computing Platforms – Spring 2008

Course	Computing Need	VC Solution	Quantity
AMP Administration	AMP with root access	OpenSolaris Zones	12
Graphics	C++, GLUT, and libraries	OpenSolaris Zones	12

During the Spring 2008 semester, the use of Solaris Zones allowed 24 virtual servers to be created across six otherwise shelved Sun Blade 1000 workstations, as reflected in Table 1. This resulted in a monetary savings for the department as well as an easily configured, easily managed, and stable work environment for students and the faculty. Students were also able to have their own servers with *root* privileges, an added benefit.

3.2 Year Two

Based on our successful foray into virtualization during the Spring 2008 semester, the department elected to move additional courses to a virtual computing environment for Fall 2008. To prepare for increased dependence on virtualization the department purchased two multiprocessor, multicore servers. These SunFire x4600 servers contained eight dual core AMD64 2.8GHz CPUs with 32GB of ram and dual 146GB hard drives.

In planning for the Fall 2008 semester the faculty identified a need for four different operating system environments in addition to Windows XP: OpenSolaris, Debian Linux, Ubuntu Linux, and a Windows server (to support SQL Server). Although a single Linux/Solaris environment would have been sufficient, we elected to support the specific requests of individual faculty members. For example, Solaris was desired for a course needing the ultimate hardware performance, whereas Ubuntu Linux was desired for an OS course in which students need to study and modify kernel source code. These varying requirements led to a multi-faceted solution.

3.2.1 Multiple Platforms

Once again, the Sun Blade 1000s were a part of the solution. They were reconfigured to provide zones for students in three courses. Three different zone configurations were deployed to support software development in our data structures course; a SAMP (Solaris, Apache, MySQL, PHP) environment for a database management course; and a basic configuration for a class learning Perl and Postgres. The SAMP environment was supported on a single shared zone to facilitate discussion of multiuser database concepts. In all other cases, students had their own dedicated zones.

A second component of the solution utilized our new SunFire x64/x86 servers. These servers were configured with OpenSolaris which offers an additional virtualization tool named xVM specifically for x64/x86 processors. xVM is Sun's release of Xen, the open source virtualization platform. xVM/Xen can be viewed as an open source equivalent to VMware Server and is classified as a Type 1 hypervisor. A Type 1 hypervisor runs on the "bare metal" of the server. The guest VM is made to think it is the only OS running. Sun's implementation of xVM/Xen offered the benefit of being part of the OpenSolaris release, not an add on package. One of the SunFire servers was configured to double as both an xVM virtualization host and to provide native OpenSolaris for a second level course on data structures and algorithms. Using OpenSolaris with xVM, fully virtualized instances of Debian Linux were created on the new servers. These instances were used for an upper division/graduate level operating system class, as well as a graduate level networking class. Students had root access to their own virtual machines and were responsible for administering them. xVM also hosted an instance of Windows running Microsoft SQLServer for a database management class.

The final piece of our virtualization solution for Fall 2008 arose from a need to provide a Linux-on-the-laptop solution without dual booting but while retaining the extensive Windows software load provided by the university. The answer was VirtualBox, another virtualization tool that is free for personal and academic use. Originally developed by the German company Innotek, it is now distributed by Sun in conjunction with the xVM initiative. VirtualBox is a Type 2 hypervisor product much like VMware Server and Workstation. That is, it runs on top of an OS as opposed to being part of the OS. VirtualBox is available for almost all x64/x86 based systems, including Windows, multiple Linux versions, OpenSolaris, and Mac OS X. Once Virtual Box is running, users can then install virtualized installations of Windows, most versions of Linux, or the x64/x86 Solaris strains. The installation and setup of a VM under VirtualBox is simple. In fact, the installation of VirtualBox, as well as the downloading, installation and setup of Ubuntu under VirtualBox served as Lab1 for the students in our CS2 course. We have even used VirtualBox successfully in a Digital Media course with a mixture of CS majors and non-majors. Once installed, Ubuntu runs as a guest OS inside a "window" on the students' Windows standard load, providing a standard GUI interface to Ubuntu within the window. This configuration also allows students to move files between Windows and Ubuntu via a common VFAT folder.

3.2.2 Lessons Learned

As we experienced in Spring 2008, there were very few problems or issues with our use of Solaris Zones in the fall semester, even though they were running on legacy hardware.

Our first experience with the xVM architecture on the SunFire platform was very positive in terms of the capability of the hardware to support a large number of simultaneous virtual machines. We did have an issue with a few of the VMs supporting Debian Linux as the guest OS. These VMs would occasionally go into a sleep state that required them to be "rebooted" from the host server. This condition was random and difficult to reproduce. In fact the exact cause of the problem was never identified. Instances of Ubuntu Linux running on the same system at the same time never exhibited this problem behavior.

The VirtualBox software proved to be remarkably stable and was quickly endorsed by students. We found it to be a very effective replacement for the traditional dual boot configuration. The most significant problem that arose during the semester was caused by students accepting automatic updates to the Ubuntu kernel in the guest OS. In a few cases these kernel updates required reinstallation of the VirtualBox guest addition tools, even though they never caused problems with Windows itself or to the VirtualBox software itself.

During the Fall 2008 semester, the combined use of these three approaches to virtualization created almost 90 virtual machines running on various platforms, including student laptops and legacy workstations. Once again, this clearly resulted in a monetary savings for the department as well as an easily configured, easily managed, and stable work environment for students and faculty.

Table 2. Virtual Computing Platforms – Fall 2008

Course	Computing Need	VC Solution	Quantity
Introduction to Linux	Debian Linux	xVM	8
Linux Administration	Debian Linux w/*root*	xVM	6
Perl&Postgres	Root privileges	OpenSolaris Zones	3
CS2 (C++)	Ubuntu	VirtualBox	12
Data Structures	C++ compiler, libraries	OpenSolaris Zones	8
Algorithms	C++ compiler, libraries	OpenSolaris Zones	8
DBMS	SAMP/ LAMP	OpenSolaris Zones	12
DBMS	SQL Server	xVM	1
Operating Systems	Debian Linux	xVM	8
Network Security	Debian Linux	xVM	12

3.3 Third Semester

By Spring 2009 we had started to rely very heavily on virtualization for our instructional computing needs. The system administrator developed a streamlined process for configuring and deploying virtual machines. Otherwise, the Spring 2009 semester proved to be a repeat of the Fall 2008 semester. The distribution of virtual machines utilized for the semester is shown in Table 3.

Table 3. Virtual Computing Platforms – Spring 2009

Course	Computing Need	VC Solution	Quantity
Web Server Administration and PHP	Root privileges	OpenSolaris Zones	6
CS2 (C++)	Ubuntu	VirtualBox	12
Programming Languages	Multiple Compilers	OpenSolaris Zones	12
Operating Systems	Debian Linux	xVM	22
Data Mining	Standard Login	OpenSolaris Zones	8

4. CURRENT DIRECTIONS

At the current time (Fall 2009) almost all of the instructional computing in the department is supported partially or completely on virtual machines. We are now conducting a pilot using Sun's Virtual Desktop Infrastructure (VDI) server. The product is similar to the North Carolina State Virtual Computing Lab (VCL) platform without the scheduler function [4, 6]. Using either Sun's implementation of VirtualBox or VMware, VDI allows virtual machines to be built and "served up" on a demand basis. So far, VDI has proven to be very flexible. The VDI software allows virtual machines to be made available for one time use and then destroyed or for them to be assigned for an arbitrary length of time. Virtual machines can be built on a Windows system running the special version of VirtualBox that ships with VDI, or they can be built natively on a Solaris server with VDI installed. Any x86 operating system can be loaded on the virtual machines, including Windows, Linux, and Solaris. (Mac OS X is only licensed to run on Apple hardware.) Sun's VDI server has a wide choice of retention and provisioning options that make the system well suited for class use. The initial VDI software install took about an hour and the system was up and running with a working

Ubuntu virtual machine in another 2 hours. The VDI server software only runs on Solaris, but can serve out almost any x86 platform, except for OS X, as mentioned. Students can connect while on campus or from home using the VPN connection provided. As an extension of VDI, Sun's Secure Global Desktop (SGD) software allows students to connect to the VDI server through a web interface from anywhere in the world. We are studying the purchase of licenses for the SGD software but have not yet made the decision to invest in this technology.

Our experience with the use of virtualization for instructional purposes has been very positive. Virtualization has allowed us to provide many different operating systems and environments for faculty and staff with modest investments in new hardware, while putting back into use older, unused hardware. It has allowed us to do more with fewer servers, and hence to reduce overall energy costs. And it has helped to familiarize our students with the types of computing environments they are likely to work in as they enter today's work force.

5. ACKNOWLEDGMENTS
The authors would like to thank the faculty members who have contributed to this learning process by employing virtual computing environments in their courses: Dr. Jennifer Burg, Dr. Daniel Cañas, Dr. David John, Dr. Tim Miller, Dr. Paul Paùca, Dr. William Turkett.

6. REFERENCES
[1] Brown, David G. A plan for the class of 2000. Nultiversity (Spring 1997), 12-16.

[2] Brown, David G., Burg, Jennifer J., Dominick, Jay L. A strategic plan for ubiquitous laptop computing. 41:1 (January 1998), 26-35.

[3] Burg, Jennifer J., Thomas, Stan J. Computers across campus. Communications of the ACM. 41:1 (January 1998), 22-25.

[4] Schaffer, Henry E., Averitt, Samuel F., Hoit, Marc I., Peeler, A., Sills, Eric D., Vouk, Mladen A. NCSU's Virtual Computing Lab: A Cloud Computing Solution. IEEE Computer. 42:7 (July 2009), 94-97.

[5] Thomas, Stan J., Laxer , C., Nishida, T., Sherlock, H. The impact of campus-wide portable computing on computer science education. ACM SIGCUE Outlook. 26:4 (October 1998), 35-40.

[6] http://vcl.ncsu.edu

The Pep/8 Memory Tracer: Visualizing Activation Records on the Run-Time Stack

J. Stanley Warford
Pepperdine University
24255 Pacific Coast Highway
Malibu, CA 90263
Stan.Warford@pepperdine.edu

Chris Dimpfl
Pepperdine University
24255 Pacific Coast Highway
Malibu, CA 90263
Christian.Dimpfl@pepperdine.edu

ABSTRACT
This paper presents a virtual machine simulator with a memory trace facility having two unique features. First, the machine is designed to illustrate the translation from C/C++ to assembly language and from thence to machine language. Instead of the more common memory dump labeled by address, the tracer displays a graphic representation of the cell labeled by its symbol. Second, the simulator displays in real time the growth of the run-time stack on function activation, detects and displays the boundaries of the activation record, and displays all the cells on the run-time stack labeled by symbol. The paper includes download information for the open-source application.

Categories and Subject Descriptors
B.3.3 [**Memory Structures**]: Performance Analysis and Design Aids – *Simulation*. C.0 [**Computer Systems Organization**]: General – *Modeling of computer architecture*. K.3.2 [**Computers and Education**]: Computer and Information Science Education – *Computer science education*.

General Terms
Design, Languages

Keywords
Pep/8, Simulation, Virtual machine, Memory model, Assembly language, Activation record, Visualization, Run-time stack, Heap

1. INTRODUCTION
Virtual machines in computer science are used both for teaching concepts and for implementing algorithms in industry. Yurcik gives a survey of machine simulators in [14], as does Rosenblum in [10]. The most famous virtual machine for teaching is probably Knuth's MIX [3], and the most widespread machine for implementing algorithms in industry is probably the Java virtual machine. [4] Pep/8 is a virtual machine for teaching computer systems concepts [13] based on the seven levels of abstraction popularized by Tanenbaum [12]: application, high-order language, assembly, operating system, instruction set architecture (ISA), microcode, and logic gate.

A common topic in programming language texts such as that by Ghezzi [2] is the implementation of function activation with an activation record, also known as a stack frame, on the run-time stack. Machines are invariably designed to support function activation through architecture features that provide for maintaining the run-time stack. Simulators for teaching computer architecture principles typically include such features. Examples are the SIMPLESIM simulator for the book by Ghezzi [2], the MARIE simulator for the book by Null [6], and the LC-3 simulator for the book by Patt [7]. The classic text by Patterson [8] has spawned many simulators for the MIPS machine, two of which are SPIM [11] and MARS [5].

The memory trace facility of the Pep/8 simulator has two unique features compared to the above simulators. First, the machine is designed to illustrate the translation from C/C++ to assembly language and from thence to machine language. Variable names at the C/C++ level correspond to symbols at the assembly level and to memory addresses at the machine level. Instead of the more common memory dump labeled by address, the tracer displays a graphic representation of the cell labeled by its symbol.

Second, the simulator displays in real time the growth of the run-time stack on function activation, detects and displays the boundaries of the activation record, and displays all the cells on the run-time stack labeled by symbol. The resulting display is similar to figures in textbooks that describe the function activation process. These features are in addition to the availability of the standard memory dump.

Section 2 describes the Pep/8 computer at the assembly and ISA level. Section 3 describes the simulator and shows the symbolic memory trace capabilities. The concluding section includes details about the simulator's availability.

2. THE Pep/8 VIRTUAL MACHINE

2.1 The assembly and ISA levels
Pep/8 is a small 16-bit von Neumann computer with an accumulator (A), an index register (X), a program counter (PC), a stack pointer (SP), and an instruction register (IR). It has eight addressing modes: immediate, direct, indirect, stack-relative, stack-relative deferred, indexed, stack-indexed, and stack-indexed deferred. The instruction set is based on an expanding opcode yielding a total of 39 instructions, which come in two flavors – unary and nonunary. The unary instructions consist of a single 8-bit instruc-

tion specifier, while the nonunary instructions have the instruction specifier followed by a 16-bit operand specifier (OpSp).

For the nonunary instructions, the addressing modes determine the operand from the operand specifier as follows:

Addressing mode	**Operand**
Immediate (`i`)	OpSp
Direct (`d`)	Mem [OpSp]
Indirect (`n`)	Mem [Mem [OpSp]]
Stack-relative (`s`)	Mem [SP + OpSp]
Stack-relative deferred (`sf`)	Mem [Mem [SP + OpSp]]
Indexed (`x`)	Mem [OpSp + X]
Stack-indexed (`sx`)	Mem [SP + OpSp + X]
Stack-indexed deferred (`sxf`)	Mem [Mem [SP + OpSp] + X]

At the assembly level, students learn the compilation process by translating complete C++ programs to Pep/8 assembly language. The Pep/8 addressing modes facilitate teaching the C/C++ memory model:

- Global variables are allocated at a fixed location in memory.
- Parameters and local variables are allocated on the run-time stack.
- Dynamic variables are allocated at run time from the heap.

Global variables are accessed with direct addressing, local variables with stack-relative addressing, local arrays with stack-indexed addressing, and dynamic variables via pointers with indirect addressing.

For example, the following complete program in C++

```
#include <iostream>
using namespace std;

int a, b;

void swap (int& r, int& s) {
   int temp;
   temp = r;
   r = s;
   s = temp;
}

void order (int& x, int& y) {
   if (x > y) {
      swap (x, y);
   }
}

int main () {
   cout << "Enter an integer: ";
   cin >> a;
   cout << "Enter an integer: ";
   cin >> b;
   order (a, b);
   cout << "Ordered they are: " << a << ", "
        << b << endl;
   return 0;
}
```

is translated to the following Pep/8 assembly language program.

```
         BR      main
a:       .BLOCK  2          ;global variable #2d
b:       .BLOCK  2          ;global variable #2d
;
;******* void swap (int& r, int& s)
r:       .EQUATE 6          ;formal parameter #2h
s:       .EQUATE 4          ;formal parameter #2h
temp:    .EQUATE 0          ;local variable #2d
swap:    SUBSP   2,i        ;allocate #temp
         LDA     r,sf       ;temp = r
         STA     temp,s
         LDA     s,sf       ;r = s
         STA     r,sf
         LDA     temp,s     ;s = temp
         STA     s,sf
         RET2               ;deallocate #temp
;
;******* void order (int& x, int& y)
x:       .EQUATE 4          ;formal parameter #2h
y:       .EQUATE 2          ;formal parameter #2h
order:   LDA     x,sf       ;if (x > y)
         CPA     y,sf
         BRLE    endIf
         LDA     x,s        ;   push x
         STA     -2,s
         LDA     y,s        ;   push y
         STA     -4,s
         SUBSP   4,i        ;   push #r #s
         CALL    swap       ;   swap (x, y)
         ADDSP   4,i        ;   pop #s #r
endIf:   RET0               ;pop retAddr
;
;******* main ()
main:    STRO    msg1,d     ;cout << "Enter ..."
         DECI    a,d        ;cin >> a
         STRO    msg1,d     ;cout << "Enter ..."
         DECI    b,d        ;cin >> b
         LDA     a,i        ;push the address of a
         STA     -2,s
         LDA     b,i        ;push the address of b
         STA     -4,s
         SUBSP   4,i        ;push #x #y
         CALL    order      ;order (a, b)
         ADDSP   4,i        ;pop #y #x
         STRO    msg2,d     ;cout << "Ordered ..."
         DECO    a,d        ;      << a
         STRO    msg3,d     ;      << ", "
         DECO    b,d        ;      << b
         CHARO   '\n',i     ;      << endl
         STOP
msg1:    .ASCII  "Enter an integer: \x00"
msg2:    .ASCII  "Ordered they are: \x00"
msg3:    .ASCII  ", \x00"
         .END
```

Variables `a` and `b` are global. Global variables are allocated at assembly time with the `.BLOCK` dot command. The statement `a: .BLOCK 2` allocates two bytes for `a`. The decimal input instruction `DECI a,d` inputs the value `a` using direct addressing indicated by the letter `d`. On the other hand, `x` and `y` are parameters in the `order` function. Stack variables are allocated with the subtract SP instruction. The instruction `SUPSP 4,i` in `main` allocates two bytes for `x` and two for `y` where the `i` indicates immediate addressing. The load accumulator instruction `LDA x,s` in the `order` function uses stack-relative addressing indicated by the letter `s`.

2.2 Trace tags

To trace a variable, the programmer embeds trace tags in the comments associated with the variables and single steps through the program. There are two kinds of trace tags:

- Format trace tags
- Symbol trace tags

Trace tags are contained in assembly language comments and have no effect on generated object code. Each trace tag begins with the # character and supplies information to the symbol tracer on how to format and label the memory cell in the trace window. Trace tag errors show up as warnings when the code is assembled, allowing program execution without tracing turned on. However, they do prevent symbolic tracing until they are corrected.

The global tracer allows the user to specify which global symbol to trace by placing a format trace tag in the comment of the `.BLOCK` line where the global variable is declared. For example, the line from the above program

```
a:  .BLOCK 2    ;global variable #2d
```

has format trace tag `#2d`, which is read as "two byte, decimal." This trace tag tells the symbol tracer to display the content of the two-byte memory cell at the address specified by the value of the symbol `a` formatted as a decimal value.

The legal format trace tags are:

`#1c` One-byte character

`#1d` One-byte decimal

`#2d` Two-byte decimal

`#1h` One-byte hexadecimal

`#2h` Two-byte hexadecimal

Local variables are allocated on the run-time stack with the `SUBSP` instruction. They are defined by their offset from the top of the stack with the `.EQUATE` dot command. In the above program, the lines

```
x:  .EQUATE 4    ;formal parameter #2h
y:  .EQUATE 2    ;formal parameter #2h
```

define `x` at four bytes below the top of the stack and `y` at two bytes below the top. Each of them is given a two-byte hexadecimal format because that is appropriate for addresses. (Note that they are called by reference.) At run time, `x` and `y` are allocated on execution of the instruction

```
    SUBSP  4,i    ;push #x #y
```

and deallocated on execution of the instruction

```
    ADDSP  4,i    ;pop #y #x
```

These instructions show the use of symbol trace tags `#x` and `#y`. The programmer specifies which local variables or parameters are being allocated on the run-time stack with the `SUBSP` instruction and which are being deallocated with the `ADDSP` instruction. The stack tracer uses the symbol trace tags to label the memory cells in the memory trace pane of the application. Furthermore, the assembler verifies that the number of bytes being pushed by the `SUBSP` instruction corresponds to the total number of bytes taken from the format trace tags in the `.EQUATE` statements. If they do not match, a trace tag warning is issued and the symbolic tracer is disabled.

Arrays are handled by an extension to the format trace tags. The letter `a` indicates that a variable is an array, and is prefixed by the number of elements in the array. For example, the global array declared in C++ as

```
int vector[4];
```

is translated to Pep/8 assembly language as

```
vector: .BLOCK 8  ;global variable #2d4a
```

where the format trace tag `#2d4a` is read as "two-byte decimal, four-cell array." The assembler verifies that the number of bytes allocated by the `.BLOCK` (eight) is equal to the product of the cell size and the number of cells (two times four).

If the C++ `vector` array is declared as a local inside the `main` function as

```
int main () {
   int vector[4];
   int j;
```

the corresponding Pep/8 assembly language code fragment is

```
vector:   .EQUATE 2  ;local variable #2d4a
j:        .EQUATE 0  ;local variable #2d
main:     SUBSP 10,i ;allocate #vector #j
```

In this example, symbol `vector` equates to two, which is the offset of the first cell of the array, `vector[0]`, from the top of the stack. Similarly, local variable `j` has offset 0 from the top. As before, the assembler verifies that the total number of bytes allocated by `SUBSP` corresponds to the number of bytes specified in the format trace tags.

We encountered a pleasant serendipity with the implementation of trace tags in the Pep/8 assembler. Previously, we tried to enforce consistent documentation of assembly language code when students translated programs from C++. A nice side effect of trace tags is that the assembler forces students to document their code with meaningful comments. To avoid trace tag warnings, they must specify in their comments the number of bytes allocated for each variable as well as which variables are being allocated for each `SUBSP`. We now require all assembly language programs to contain trace tags with no warning messages from the assembler.

3. THE Pep/8 SIMULATOR

Previous versions of Pep/8 suffered from years of accumulated code added in an ad hoc manner. To add the symbolic memory trace feature the authors, the second of whom is an undergraduate student, rewrote the application from scratch based on the mediator object-oriented design pattern. [1] It is implemented with the C++ class libraries of Nokia's Qt development system. [9]

3.1 Memory tracing with scalar variables

Figure 1 is a screen shot of the application during a trace of the assembly language program in Section 2.1.

The Listing Trace pane, top left, is generated from the source code upon successful assembly. The source code is not visible in this screen shot, but is accessible by clicking the Code tab.

The CPU pane, top right, shows the current content of the registers in hexadecimal and decimal notation. The programmer is single-

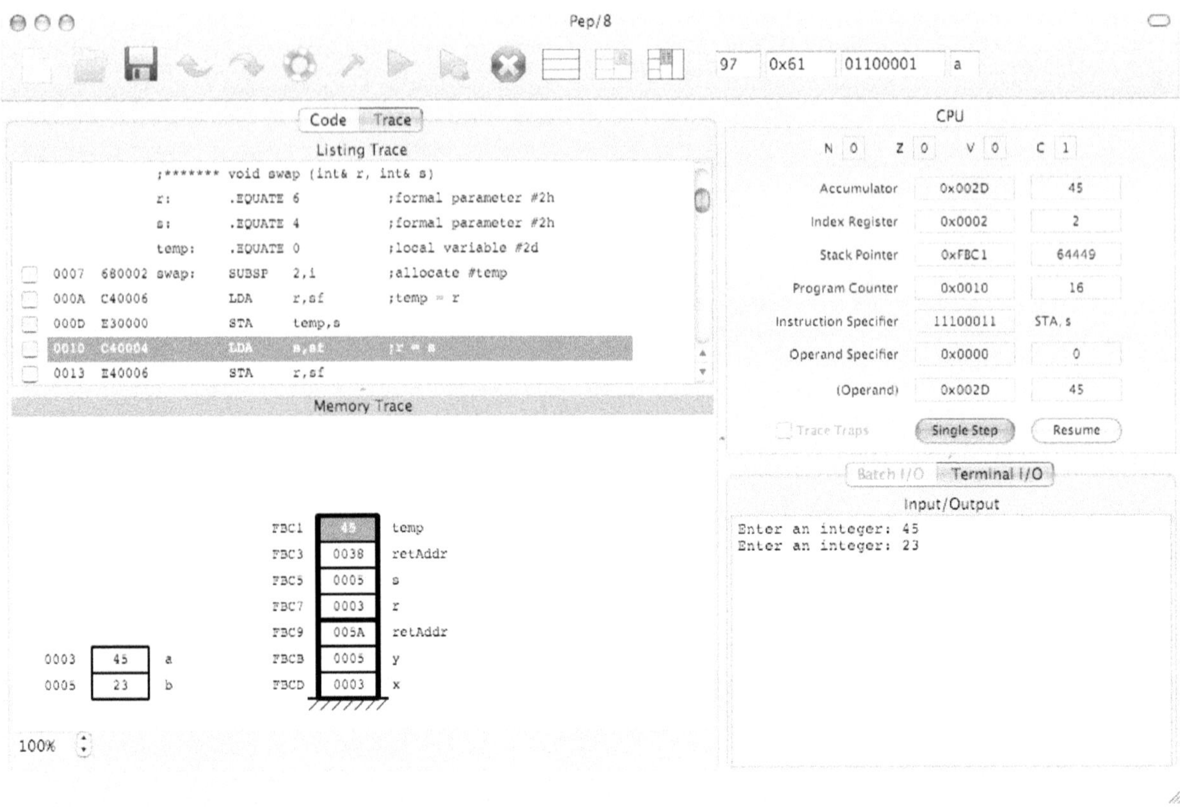

Figure 1. The Pep/8 main window.

stepping through the code and the current value of the program counter is 0x0010. Consequently, the instruction at address 0x0010 in the Listing Trace pane is highlighted, indicating that the `LDA` instruction will execute in the next cycle.

The Instruction Register is divided into two parts—a one-byte Instruction Specifier and, for non-unary instructions, a two-byte Operand Specifier. The CPU pane displays the Instruction Specifier in binary, to help the programmer visually decode the expanding op-code if desired. It also decodes the opcode and the addressing mode and displays the corresponding instruction mnemonic and letter indicating the addressing mode. Figure 1 shows that the `STA` instruction has just executed with stack-relative addressing.

The Pep/8 simulator supports both batch and interactive I/O as can be seen in the I/O pane, bottom right. When prompted, the user entered the two integers 45 and 23 in interactive mode.

The Memory Trace pane, lower left, displays the values of both global and local variables. The global variables, `a` and `b`, are allocated at a fixed location in memory and appear on the left. To the left of each cell is the memory address and to the right is the symbol taken from the trace tag. The format of the value within the cell in this case is decimal, also taken from the trace tag.

The run-time stack is to the right of the globals. As with the globals, each cell on the run-time stack has its address to the left of the cell and its symbol to the right. The `CALL` instruction pushes the incremented value of the PC onto the run-time stack. By default, it generates a label of `retAddr`, which stands for return address. Corresponding to the fact that the `STA` instruction has just stored

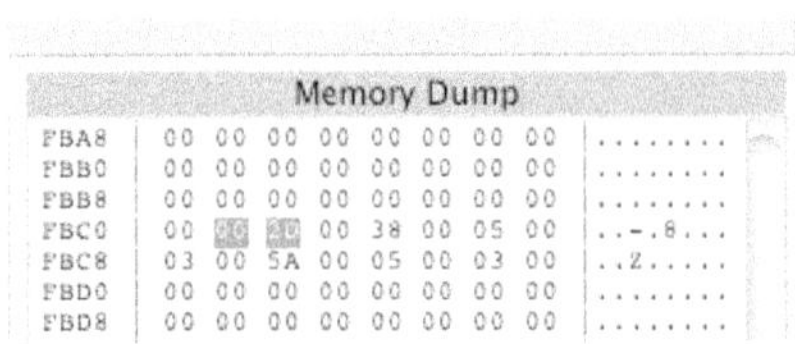

Figure 2. A traditional memory dump.

the value of 45 to local variable `temp`, that cell is highlighted in red on top of the stack.

Figure 1 shows two activation records. First is the activation record for function `order` consisting of the cells for parameters `x` and `y`, and for `retAddr`. Second is the activation record for function `swap` consisting of the cells for parameters `r` and `s`, for `retAddr`, and for local variable `temp`. Figure 2 illustrates how dramatic this visualization is by showing how the programmer confronts the same information in the traditional memory dump, also available in the Pep/8 application.

The functions traced in Figure 1 are both void. The symbolic memory trace handles non-void functions as well, the only difference being an extra cell at the bottom of the activation record to hold the returned value, also specified by the programmer with trace tags. Our naming convention is to label that value `retVal`.

3.2 Memory tracing with array variables

Figure 3 shows two separate screen shots of the Memory Trace pane that correspond to the code fragments for `vector` in Section 2.2. Part (a) shows the case where `vector` is declared to be global

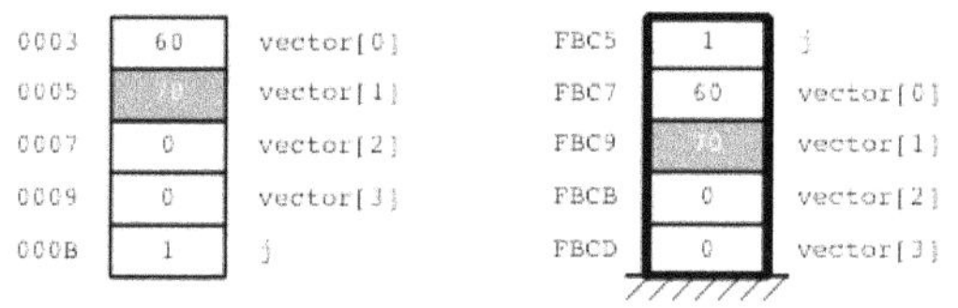

(a) Global (b) Local

Figure 3. Tracing an array

and is allocated with the `.BLOCK` dot command at load time. Part (b) shows the case where `vector` is declared to be local and is allocated with the `SUBSP` instruction at run time.

3.3 Tracing the heap

Pep/8 also features a rudimentary heap that can be traced with the same trace tag system. Figure 4 shows a trace of an assembly language program that is a translation of a C++ program implementing a linked list. A node is a struct with two fields — `data`, which is an integer, and `next`, which is a pointer. The same frame that outlines an activation record on the runtime stack outlines a node on the heap.

A feature not illustrated in this paper but available with Pep/8, is the ability to trace a global `struct`. Each cell of the `struct` is rendered symbolically with a period separating the variable name and the field name.

4. CONCLUSION

While most machine simulators have a standard memory dump facility for tracing the content of memory during program execution, the Pep/8 simulator is unique in its ability to visually show the structure of the activation record on the run-time stack.

This feature has several pedagogic advantages. First, the system of trace tags that are necessary to enable the stack trace forces students to document their assembly language code more precisely than would otherwise be the case. Format trace tags require them to specify the number of bytes for each variable, and symbol trace tags require them to specify which variables are being allocated on the run-time stack. To do these specifications correctly, they must understand the structure of the activation record. This activity is a prime example of the educational principle that students learn better by doing than by simply studying.

A second advantage of the visual representation of activation records is its illustration of the mechanism of recursion. Space limitations in this article preclude showing a lengthy sequence of snapshots to illustrate how the run-time stack grows and shrinks during the execution of a recursive algorithm. Such demonstrations are both enlightening and entertaining in the classroom. A favorite exercise is to have students write the Towers of Hanoi problem in C++ and then translate it to assembly language and run it on the simulator. This is an example of learning the mechanism of recursion by programming the detailed structure of the activation record.

A third advantage is the reinforcement in students' minds of the memory model of C/C++. This paper shows how the Pep/8 simulator displays the memory structure for global variables at a fixed location, local variables and parameters on the run-time stack, and dynamic variables on the heap.

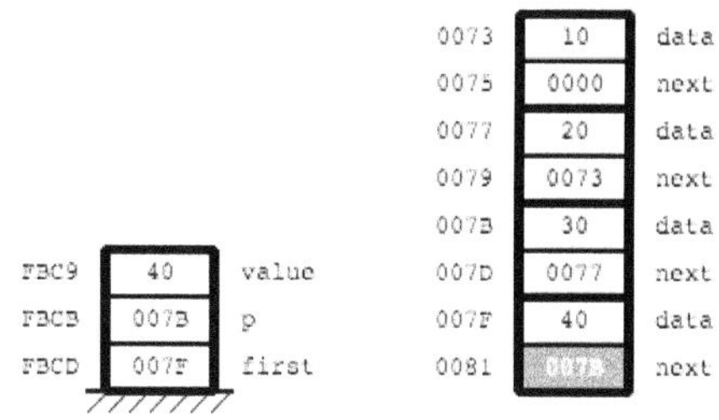

Figure 4. Tracing the heap.

Pep/8 software is available free of charge under the GNU General Public License at

http://code.google.com/p/pep8-1/

The site contains the source code in an SVN repository as well as executable builds for Windows, Mac OS X, and Linux. The Windows build runs under Windows XP, Vista, and System 7. The OSX build is a universal binary that runs on PowerPC and Intel Macs. The Linux build is for Ubuntu, but the source is easily compiled for other flavors of Linux with the Qt Creator IDE from Nokia [9], which we enthusiastically recommend for open-source, free, cross-platform development and deployment.

5. REFERENCES

[1] Gamma, E., Helm, R., Johnson, R., and Vlissides, J. *Design Patterns: Elements of Reusable Object-Oriented Software*, Addison-Wesley Publishing Company, Reading, MA, 1995.

[2] Ghezzi, C. and Jazayeri, M. *Programming Language Concepts*, third ed. John Wily & Sons, Inc., New York, NY, 1998.

[3] Knuth, D. E. *The Art of Computer Programming*. Addison-Wesley, Reading, MA, 1997.

[4] Lindholm, T. and Yellin, F. *The Java(TM) Virtual Machine Specifi cation*. Sun Microsystems, Inc., Palo Alto, CA, 1999.

[5] MARS, http://courses.missouristate.edu/KenVollmar/MARS/

[6] Null, L, and Lobur, J. Computer Organization and Architecture, second ed. Jones and Bartlett, Publishers, Inc. Sudbury, MA 2006.

[7] Patt, Y. N., and Patel, S. J. Introduction to Computing Systems, second ed. McGraw-Hill, New York, 2004.

[8] Patterson, D. A. and Hennessy, J. L. *Computer Organization and Design*. Morgan Kaufmann Publishers, San Francisco, CA, 2005.

[9] Qt, http://qt.nokia.com/

[10] Rosenblum, M. The Reincarnation of Virtual Machines, *ACM Queue*, vol. 2, no. 5, July/August, 2004.

[11] SPIM, http://pages.cs.wisc.edu/~larus/spim.html

[12] Tanenbaum, A. S. *Structured Computer Organization*. Pearson Prentice Hall, Upper Saddle River, NJ, 2006.

[13] Warford, J. S. *Computer Systems*. Jones and Bartlett Publishers, Inc. Sudbury, MA, 2010.

[14] Yurcik, W., ed. Special Issue on Specialized Computer Architecture Simulators, *Journal on Educational Resources in Computing*, vol. 2, no. 1, March 2002.

Monetary Values: Double Trouble or Dollars and Sense?

Aaron Tenenbaum
Dept of CIS, Brooklyn College
2900 Bedford Avenue
Brooklyn, NY 11210
1-718-951-5657
tbaum@sci.brooklyn.cuny.edu

Gerald Weiss
Dept of CIS, Brooklyn College
2900 Bedford Avenue
Brooklyn, NY 11210
1-718-951-5657
weiss@sci.brooklyn.cuny.edu

David Arnow
Dept of CIS, Brooklyn College
2900 Bedford Avenue
Brooklyn, NY 11210
1-718-951-5657
arnow@acm.org

ABSTRACT
It is curious but there is widespread misuse of floating-point types to represent monetary amounts in introductory programming classes. This is evident from a survey of popular CS1 textbooks. It is instructive to examine how dollars and cents and other currency values are represented in actual practice and how we can utilize those techniques in computer science education, for both the sake of correctness and to illustrate important general principles. Furthermore, it is particularly interesting to review the history of CS education and determine how this situation came to pass. The interplay between technology, academic cultures and institutional development turns out to be quite significant.

Categories and Subject Descriptors
D.3.3 [**Programming Languages**]: Language Constructs and Features – *data types and structures, input/output* E.2 [**Data**]: Data Storage Representations – *primitive data items* K.3.2 [**Computers and Education**]: Computer and Information Science Education – *Computer science education, Curriculum*

General Terms
Design, Languages

Keywords
Monetary values, currency representation, numerical types

1. BACKGROUND
A survey of introductory programming texts reveals that in the treatment of accounting problems (for example, bank accounts, hours and wages, and sales, to mention a few), the variables holding the monetary data are usually declared as being of type **real**, **float** or **double**. If any rationale is provided at all, it is usually that, since the monetary numbers are not whole numbers of dollars but often have cents or pence connected with them, they require a fractional part. Numbers with fractional parts are not integers. Since the only other kind of primitive numerical type available is floating-point, it is **real**, **float** or **double** that is selected to do the job, at least in the classroom.

SIGCSE'10, March 10–13, 2010, Milwaukee, Wisconsin, USA.

However, reals are almost never used in actual practice to represent monetary values, because of rounding errors and binary representation. [1,22] For example, if .01 is added 10000 times using real numbers, the result is almost never exactly 100. Sometimes, explicit rounding is used but sometimes even that is inaccurate. Other times, the instructor relies on output statements to produce the correct value in printouts and output files.

In general, floating-point type values are meant to represent either a) *measurements* and quantities that derive from measurements that have an inherent limited precision, or b) approximations of irrational numbers. On the other hand, integer type values represent quantities that are *counted* and can be put into a 1-to-1 correspondence with the integers. Money, of course, is counted, not measured. There is a count of dollars and there is a count of cents. Using a measuring stick to determine an amount of money is quite a rare occurrence indeed (although we often hear about the national budget or debt reaching from here to the moon if piled into a linear line of dollar bills). The English language itself reflects this: the discipline of tracking money is called "ac<u>count</u>ing".

Programming languages and systems that support accounting applications take care to provide non-floating-point numerical types that are suitable for handling money. For example, both MySQL and SQL Server provide a DECIMAL type that can represent as many as 38 decimal digits with a fixed decimal point. This permits to-the-penny representations of the worst projections of the U.S. national debt in Paraguayan Guarani (currently 5000 per USD) for years to come [23,24]. Multiple digits to the right of the decimal point are often needed to facilitate currency conversion or to avoid or minimize roundoff error.

Professional programmers working with languages such as C++ and Java, whose primitive types don't provide this kind of representative power, make use of suitable integer-based classes that they develop themselves or acquire from third parties [29]. These classes are implemented using two or more integers, as needed for their precision. A good discussion of this issue and one solution for actual representation of currency in Java is described in [**1**]. Systems such as Microsoft's Excel and Access also have a currency data type that operates on currency correctly. The operations are no doubt implemented by a scheme such as in [1].

Using non-floating-point numerical types does not remove all concerns for numerical error in accounting. But it reduces them to a controllable set. In some cases, notably interest calculations, it is beneficial to do some intermediate computations using floating point arithmetic. But the fact remains that using non-floating-point types for currency values is industry practice and rightly so.

To get a sense of the pitfalls of using floating-point representation in the context of values that require exact representation (such as currency), consider printing the monetary quantity $93.585 (such a quantity could arise for example from a $110.10 value discounted 15%). Following the customary rules of rounding, this value displayed with two digits should be $93.59. As it turns out, the `%fm.n printf` format specifier does follow the customary rules of rounding to *n* digits. For example,

```
printf("%8.2f", 93.58501)
```

yields 93.59*. Unfortunately,

```
printf("%8.2f", 93.585)
```

yields 93.58. We can readily see why, since

```
printf("%19.15f", 93.585)
```

yields 93.584999999999994. The issue is "representation error" (though using the term "error" here is a bit unfair to the float type which never held out the promise of exact representation of decimals: float promises to represent numerical values up to a certain precision and that is what it has done here). It is tempting to correct for this representational deviation by writing

```
printf("%8.2f", 93.585+0.005)
```

which yields 93.59 but an attempt to do this programatically only leads to more problems:

```
double x=93.585;
double y=0.33;
printf("%8.2f ", x+0.005);
printf("%8.2f\n", y+0.005);
```

yields

```
93.59     0.34
```

instead of

```
93.59     0.33
```

Furthermore, this can arise quite naturally from simple, innocently posed "first week" CS1 problems. For example:

A store is having a sale for the holidays: buy any item and get the second at a 15% discount. Prompt the user for the full price of the item and produce an invoice containing:

- *The full price of the first item*
- *the discounted price of the second item*
- *the total price of the purchase*

Standard rules for rounding are to be used.

Apart from using floating point type, here is a reasonable solution:

```
int main() {
  double firstItem, secondItem, total;
  printf("Price of 1st item? ");
  scanf("%le",&firstItem);
  secondItem = 0.85 * firstItem;
  total = firstItem + secondItem;
  printf("1st item: %8.2f\n", firstItem);
  printf("2nd item: %8.2f\n", secondItem);
  printf("          --------\n");
  printf("Total   : %8.2f\n", total);
}
```

* C examples were compiled with GCC 4.3.0 20080428 (Red Hat 4.3.0-8) targeting x86_64-redhat-linux. Java examples were compiled and run using Sun's Java 2 SE (build 1.5.0_17-b04, mxed mode, sharing)/Java Hotspot Client. Both C and Java examples were run on Linux 2.6.18.8-xen3-U-64 #3 SMP x86_64.

Here are the results of two sample executions:

```
Price of 1st item? 110.20
1st item:   110.20
2nd item:    93.67
          --------
Total   :   203.87
```

```
Price of 1st item? 110.10
1st item:   110.10
2nd item:    93.58   <--
          --------
Total   :   203.69
```

We have already seen that the error in the second execution is caused by the internal representation of the value of `secondItem`. This is not a unique example, and to make matters worse, there is no straightforward way to anticipate problematic values like 93.585. Indeed, to concoct the above example, we generated multiple cases of varying discount percentages and prices until we encountered a situation where the roundoff error produced a discrepancy to two places.

Thus, it is not merely the discrepancy that is problematic, but the fact that the discrepancy seems to arise in an arbitrary fashion (at least at the level of understanding of an intro student). Furthermore, the student's *by-hand* calculations produce a different result, undermining their understanding of the situation.

Here is the same program and results, this time using integer type:

```
int main() {
    int firstItem, secondItem, total;
    printf("Price of 1st item? ");
    scanf("%d",&firstItem);
    secondItem = (85 * firstItem + 50) / 100;
    total = firstItem + secondItem;
    printf("1st item: %8d\n", firstItem);
    printf("2nd item: %8d\n", secondItem);
    printf("          --------\n");
    printf("Total   : %8d\n", total);
}
```

```
Price of 1st item? 11020
1st item:    11020
2nd item:     9366
          --------
Total   :    20386
```

```
Price of 1st item? 11010
1st item:    11010
2nd item:     9358
          --------
Total   :    20368
```

Although the input and output format of this program suffers from cosmetic deficiencies, it has the advantage of being correct. (The deficiencies can be corrected to the degree to which the CS1 instructor or author chooses to address simple parsing and formatting techniques.)

The problem is not confined to C and C++. The following "first week" Java program and resulting output make this clear:

```
public class Sale  {
  public static void main(String[] a) {
    double  chrg = 5.10;
    double  taxrate = .05;
    double  tax = taxrate*chrg;
    double  total = chrg+tax;
    System.out.printf(" chrg=  $%6.2f\n",chrg);
    System.out.printf(" tax=  $%6.2f",
                                   tax,taxrate);
    System.out.printf("total=  $%6.2f\n",total);
  }
}
```

```
charge=  $  5.10
   tax=  $  0.26  <--
 total=  $  5.35
```

Using output integer types and arithmetic thus seems to be the only way to go. True, there are issues of rounding as well (how much do we pay a $100/hour worker for 20 minutes?) but at least the results are uniform and can be predicted at the CS 1 level.

2. THE CS1 CHALLENGE

The languages most commonly used in introductory programming courses, Java, C, C++, C# and Python do not provide the decimal types needed for convenient correct handling of currency values. The CS1 author or instructor then must first decide whether or not to simply avoid examples that involve currency. If such examples are included in the text or course, then another decision must be made: to what extent should currency values be properly handled?

Few, as an abstract matter, would advocate intentionally taking an incorrect approach. Remarkably, however, the erroneous use of double (or other floating point types) to represent monetary quantities is quite widespread. Although we cannot cite what faculty do in the classroom, the common occurrence of this error in a great many textbooks that are otherwise of the finest quality and authored by the most esteemed colleagues in the community strongly supports this contention [8, 9, 12, 17, 18, 19, 26, 28, 32].

3. HISTORY

3.1 Before The Fall

In the United States in the 1960s and through the early 1970s, the primary high-level languages of introductory computing instruction were COBOL and FORTRAN. FORTRAN was viewed as a scientific/engineering programming language, and had no specific provisions that made it easy to represent currency values.

Commercial programming depended on COBOL. Those introductory programming courses that were commercially oriented, in information systems or business programs, were taught using COBOL as well. COBOL did have a tool for representing currency values well. It had a native decimal (as well as binary) number type, with a specification for the number of digits before and after the decimal point. Many computers had decimal numbers implemented in hardware or firmware, and the COBOL data types were designed to take advantage of those facilities. So, COBOL was built to represent monetary values, and its data types do that well. No one used a floating-point data type to represent money in COBOL. Decimal numbers with a fixed number of decimal digits were used invariably.

COBOL, however, was "inelegant." It was wordy, non-mathematical and not very useful for scientific or systems work. Since most of those who developed the computer science discipline came from mathematics or the sciences, COBOL became viewed as a "vocational" or "data processing" language, not suitable for use in scientific higher education.

The dichotomy in programming courses was naturally reflected in introductory textbooks. While we have not undertaken an exhaustive search of the introductory programming literature before 1976, a clear division appears: FORTRAN texts, which illustrated programming using numerical, scientific, engineering, and discrete math problems [2, 7, 10, 11, 20, 21, 30], and COBOL texts, which illustrated programming using administrative, business and financial problems. In the COBOL texts, the availability and use of fixed decimal attributes made the proper handling of monetary values easy and accessible to the beginner. Since problems involving monetary amounts were never or barely discussed in the FORTRAN texts (and presumably the courses that used them), these quantities were almost never misrepresented.

An author of an early leading and influential FORTRAN text, Professor Dan McCracken of City College, wrote us:

> *I did not use any monetary examples in my text because the book, in 1960/61, was aimed at engineers and scientists. I was also aware of the problem with non-exact floating binary for most fractional amounts. The vast majority of authors, in my sampling, still don't understand the issue and cheerfully use doubles, with no warnings. But no bank on the planet uses doubles for monetary amounts. Banks can't be sending out checking account statements that are off by a penny.*

Another language, ALGOL, was used primarily in Europe and in newly created computer science departments that often focused on neither scientific or business applications, but on systems and systems programming. ALGOL, like FORTRAN, did not have decimal representation support built into it, and reals were used in the very few cases where monetary examples were provided in a text.

Many texts in FORTRAN and ALGOL did not even mention an example with monetary values [20, 21, 11] or used them only in connection with modeling [2]. An exception may be found in the very popular FORTRAN text [7] on page 109.

Computer science as an educational discipline arose from users of ALGOL or FORTRAN, not from COBOL users. Examples were primarily oriented towards mathematical, engineering or systems programming. Thus the tradition arose that the few times that money was represented, it was represented by the native data types in those languages—the reals. It was "good enough" for science-bound, introductory programming students. One did not want to confuse them by going into the complexities of how money should be represented, since the "purpose" of programming for this community was not commercial applications in any case and because it added an extra layer of complexity, taking away from the main thrust of the course. Ideas of abstraction and representation did not yet have the prominence in computer science that they gained later.

And thus there were, by the early 1970s, two distinct educational worlds, business computing using COBOL and nascent computer science using FORTRAN and ALGOL— each restricting itself to problem domains that were treated correctly— for the most part.

This world was disrupted by a succession of technological advances in the 1970s. The first of these was the increased availability of PL/1, arguably the first language that, whatever its faults, was equally suitable for scientific, systems and commercial work. PL/1, like COBOL provided a native attribute, **fixed decimal**, with which monetary values could be represented in a satisfactory way– as a number with a specified number of decimal digits. PL/I saw rapid adoption as an initial instructional language. It also made it possible to have a single introductory course for students of business computing and computer science students.

At the same time, the decade-long explosion of undergraduate computer science programs and departments began. With the availability of PL/1, these programs could justifiably claim to offer introductory programming sequences that were appropriate for students of all interests. Introductory programming courses and the textbooks that served them reflected this unification, and most texts used PL/1's **picture** and **fixed decimal** attributes to provide correctly implemented credible examples from accounting that were co-mingled with those from science and engineering [3, 27, 31, 33, 25]. This period of "currency Eden" was not to last very long.

3.2 After The Fall

Then, starting in the late 1970s and early 1980s, introductory programming textbooks appeared, authored by some of the giants in the world of CS education, that returned to the misrepresentation of monetary amounts as floating point values [5, 6, 14, 13]. As it turned out, the misrepresentation error in these seminal texts, which appeared during the birth-phase of most undergraduate computer science programs, has replicated itself, as we have seen, to the present day.

3.3 How Could This Have Happened?

It seems that this occurred as a result of a combination of significant historical events and simple, human oversight. The advent of the microprocessor and the PC replaced the decimal arithmetic supporting mainframes that had been the mainstay of many CS departments. This shift was the death-knell to PL/1 as a teaching language, but the replacement of PL/1 had already begun earlier as the pendulum swung back to "small languages" like Pascal and C, neither of which supported fixed decimal arithmetic.

There is little question that C and Pascal offered improvements over both PL/I and FORTRAN as teaching languages. But in terms of numerical primitive types, they both returned to the world of FORTRAN. However, the university world had moved on: introductory programming no longer lived in EE, Physics or Math departments. It existed in the context of undergraduate CS departments that had mission obligations that transcended the world of math, science and engineering. It was more difficult to take the approach of the accounting-avoiding FORTRAN textbooks and courses of the 1960s and early 1970s.

At least one author [15] did write a Pascal text that avoided all accounting problems, and there was at least one C textbook [16] that managed the same. Ken Bowles, in his text [4] gave an explicit warning about the problem of using **real** values to represent money:

> *Accuracy problems with REAL numbers are also very important in administrative computations. One of the strategies used in most implementations of COBOL, the "Common Business Oriented Language," results in most computation being done with integers, even though the programmer thinks the numbers are really decimal fractions. COBOL provides ways for the programmer to specify how many decimal digits of precisions must be carried. Unknown to the programmer, a <variable> indented to represent Dollars and Cents (2 decimal points of precision) would in fact be carried as an integer representation of cents.*

But his was a lone voice. Most other authors since then have incorporated accounting examples using floating-point types for monetary values. A few authors such as Dale [8] and Deitel [9] make it clear that this is wrong in principle and dangerous in practice. Deitel's admonishes the reader:

> *Notice that lines 17-19 declare the* ***double*** *variables ... We did this for simplicity because we're dealing with fractional parts of dollars, and we need a type that allows decimal points in its values. Unfortunately, this can cause trouble. ...*

and he goes on to provide an excellent, compelling numerical example of how the very code he presented as an example can give incorrect results. In his warning, he also conveys his reason for using doubles: expediency in dealing with fractions. This is probably the reason that most authors have for making this choice.

4. REMEDIES

There is no reason that the CS education community has to continue to make this choice. Rather than shy away from accounting problems or use inappropriate representations to solve them, CS1 instructors and authors can instead use monetary values as an excellent vehicle for teaching many points about programming.

The difference between floating-point and integer representations and between binary and decimal representations can easily be brought home using monetary values, something that every student is familiar with. The fact that every integer within a certain range can be represented, but not every real even when the decimal precision is fixed, is important for students to know. The ideas of precision, rounding and truncation can be introduced as well. Some of the relation of mathematics and computation can be brought home here.

Apart from numerical and mathematical issues is the issue of the meaning behind a primitive type. Reals are the numbers of measurement, integers the numbers of counting. Nothing brings this home to students better than a discussion of currency representation.

Addressing the representation of monetary values provides an excellent segue into use of existing classes (such as Java's BigDecimal) or can motivate the development of simple class definitions that reinforce basic concepts in typing and object-oriented programming. This in turn can be related to currency data types as they exist in real software that many students are already acquainted with (such as spreadsheets), or that they will learn about. It is also a good basis for a lecture about the entire concept of reality, abstraction and representation.

5. THE LESSON

CS1 education has been remarkably successful in keeping up with the fast pace of ever-advancing computer science. The community of authors of the introductory texts have kept up with new languages, and introduced at various periods structured, modular, and O-O programming, graphical user interfaces, web technology, semi-formal methods, and other innovations. However, it is also important not to lose what was once gained. We no longer have the convenience of fixed decimal primitive types in the languages we use in introductory courses, but we need not give in to a false expediency at the expense of giving our students— who may well go on to work in accounting and financial applications— an incorrect view of monetary data. To do so does a disservice to both our students and our community.

6. ACKNOWLEDGMENTS

Our thanks to Dan McCracken for his valuable thoughts on the subject.

7. DEDICATION

In memory of our late colleague, Pat Sterbenz, who could have explained all of this so easily and more clearly.

8. REFERENCES

[1] Armstrong, John N. 2004. Java & Monetary Data. Dr. Dobb's Journal (May, 2004). See: http://www.ddj.com/java/184405653?pgno=1

[2] Basso, D., Schwartz, R. 1981 **Programming with FORTRAN/WATFOR/WATFIV**, Winthrop Publishers.

[3] Bates, F. and Douglas, M. 1975 **Programming Language/One**, Prentice-Hall.

[4] Bowles, K. 1977 **Problem Solving Using PASCAL**, Springer-Verlag.

[5] Conway, R., Gries, D., Zimmerman, E. 1981 **A Primer On Pascal**, Winthrop.

[6] Cooper, D., Clancy, M. 1982 **Oh! Pascal!**, Norton.

[7] Cress, P., Dirksen, P., Graham, W. 1968 **FORTRAN IV with WATFOR and WATFIV**, Prentice-Hall. See page 109.

[8] Dale, N., Weems, C., Headington, M. 2000 **Programming and Problem Solving with C++**, Jones-Bartlett.

[9] Deitel, P., Deitel, H. 2008 C++ **How To Program**, Prentice-Hall.

[10] Didday, R., Page, R. 1974 **FORTRAN for Humans**, West.

[11] Hirsch, S. 1973 **Essentials of FORTRAN IV**, Reston Publishing.

[12] Horstman, C. 2006 **Big Java**, Wiley.

[13] Jensen, K., Wirth, N. 1974 **Pascal User Manual and Report**, Springer-Verlag.

[14] Kay, D. 1985 Programming for People/Pascal, Mayfield.

[15] Keller, A 1982 **A First Course in Computer Programming using Pascal**, McGraw-Hill.

[16] Kelley, A., Pohl, I 1984 **A Book on C**, Benjamin Cummings.

[17] Kelley, A., Pohl, I 2001 **C by Dissection**, Addison Wesley.

[18] Lewis, J., Loftus, W. 2007 **Java Software Solutions**, Addison-Wesley.

[19] Malik, D. 2004 **C++ Programming: Program Design Including Data Structures**, Thomson.

[20] Marateck, S. 1977 **Fortran**, Academic Press.

[21] McCracken, D. 1973 **Guide to FORTRAN IV Programming**, Wiley.

[22] Microsoft Development Network (Office Developer Center) 2009 Currency and Decimal Data Types, http://msdn.microsoft.com/en-us/library/aa164763(office.10).aspx

[23] Microsoft Development Network (SQL Developer Center) 2009 Data Types, http://msdn.microsoft.com/en-us/library/aa258271(SQL.80).aspx

[24] MySQL 5.0 Reference Manual, 11.13 Precision Math, http://dev.mysql.com/doc/refman/5.0/en/precision-math-decimal-changes.html

[25] Richardson, G., Birkin, S. 1975 **Problem Solving Using PL/C: An Introduction for Business and the Social Sciences**, Wiley.

[26] Savitch, W. 2005 **Java: An Introduction to Problem Solving & Programming**, Prentice-Hall.

[27] Shortt, J., Wilson,T. 1982 **Problem Solving and the Computer: A Structured Concept with PL/I (PL/C)**, Addison-Wesley.

[28] Staugaard, A. 2004 **Information Systems Programming with Java**, Prentice-Hall.

[29] Stein, G. 2009 private conversation with lead software project manager in a major Wall Street Brokerage.

[30] Sturgal, J., Merchant, M. 1973 **Applied FORTRAN IV Programming**, Wadsworth.

[31] Weinberg, G 1966 PL/I Programming Primer, McGraw-Hill.

[32] Wu, C. 2004 **An Introduction to Object-Oriented Programming with Java**, McGraw-Hill.

[33] Hume, J., Holt, R. 1982 **Structured Programming Using PL/1**, Reston.

Double Sorting: Testing Their Sorting Skills

Darrah P. Chavey
Beloit College; Dept. of Mathematics & Computer Science
700 College St.; Beloit, WI 53511
chavey@beloit.edu

ABSTRACT

You're teaching elementary sorting techniques, and you would like your students to do a programming assignment that tests their understanding of the ideas. But all of the code for elementary sorting techniques are in the textbook, easily found on the Web, etc. We suggest the use of two "Double Sorting" techniques whose solution is not standardly available, are fairly straight-forward to code, and offer speed improvements over the "straight" sorts. Double Sorting, the idea of processing two chosen elements simultaneously, applies to both Insertion Sort and Selection Sort, with speedups of 33% and 25%, hence are good enough to justify coding, but not good enough to be in Web collections. Code for this can be written in as little as a dozen lines of C++/Java code, and is easily within the reach of introductory students who understand the basic algorithms. In addition, the ideas used for double sorting are natural first steps in understanding how the N^2 sorts can be improved towards the $N \log N$ sorts that they will study later. For more advanced students, these double sorts also generate good exercises in the analysis of algorithms.

Categories and Subject Descriptors

A.1 [**Introductory and Survey**]: CS1/CS2, Arrays, Sorting.

General Terms

Algorithms, Performance.

Keywords

Sorting, Insertion, Selection, Quicksort, CS1.

1. INTRODUCTION

When first teaching students about working with arrays, an excellent programming exercise would be to explain the Insertion Sort, or Selection Sort, algorithm to the students in class, and then require that they convert the algorithm into code on their own. It might even be possible to use such an assignment in a closed lab, where the lab instructor was careful to watch for students who grabbed the code off the web, or from the text, instead of writing it themselves. In most cases, though, we need to resign ourselves to the fact that this is not an effective programming assignment. At least as good, though, is to demonstrate the sorting algorithm *and* how to convert the algorithm into code, then demonstrate a modification of that algorithm, and finally to assign the coding of that modification as a programming exercise. This paper suggests two such simple modifications of these sorting algorithms: Double Insertion Sort, and Double Selection Sort.

SIGCSE'10, March 10–13, 2010, Milwaukee, Wisconsin, USA.

A good programming exercise should, ideally, give the students both programming practice, and help them understand significant concepts. We will argue that each of the double sorts introduces students to concepts that are important in other contexts. Because the double sorting code is substantially different in the cases where the array size is odd or even, these two sorting algorithms provide examples of four programming assignments that are roughly equivalent in difficulty, but almost completely independent of each other, e.g. assign "Double Insertion Sort, odd size arrays" one semester, etc. Consequently, they could provide four semesters of "the same, but different" assignments before recycling a previous assignment, reducing potential plagiarism issues.

Double Insertion Sort does not currently (as of Dec., 2009) have solutions on the Web, and the two available solutions for Double Selection Sort are either less than helpful, or are probably identifiable as copied. Since these sorts do not offer enough substantial improvements over other sorting algorithms, we would not expect that solution code would appear on the Web – assuming that readers of this article do not post their own program solutions on publicly accessible pages (and we ask that they avoid doing this). Since the double sorts do offer substantial speed improvements (33% and 25%) over the standard "single" sorts, we can motivate such an assignment as an improvement on the code that they probably have in their textbooks. In addition, since both QuickSort and MergeSort, done properly, will use recursion on large array sizes, but will have a threshold at which they will switch to one of the N^2 sorts, one can argue that the use of a double sort for these small array partitions will provide a (modest) improvement to these two critical sorting algorithms.

Finally, while these sorting algorithms are aimed primarily at CS 1–CS 2 courses, the analysis of these algorithms can provide useful exercises for a more advanced class doing analysis of algorithms, and we will discuss this later.

2. RELATED WORK

Papers such as [4, 5] have worked to address related problems that we have when trying to construct reasonable assignments involving the $N \log N$ sorts. These assignments suffer from the same difficulty of students Googling their results instead of writing their own, and these authors have interesting suggestions on ways to have students focus on the ideas and concepts of these algorithms, while still having to develop their own code.

In [3], Juhlstrom suggest an interesting approach to getting students to understand these N^2 sorts. In the only paper in the ACM Digital Library with the word "Whimsical" in the title, he suggests looking at N^3 sorts! In particular, he limits candidate algorithms to those which "compare and move values [and where] each operation must plausibly advance the sorting process." By constructing algorithms that create N^3 versions of Bubble Sort, Selection Sort, and Insertion Sort, one can give students assignments whose solutions they surely will not find with Google, but which require an understanding of the algorithm. It seems likely that class discussion of the differences between the "textbook code" and their assigned algorithm would do much to illuminate both the algorithms and the need to plan, and think, before coding.

The Double Insertion Sort problem, as an "Assignment to Use Next Week," was included as part of the tutorial [1], although individual assignments were not published in that journal, and the assignment distributed did not include most of the additional material of this paper. The Double Selection Sort problem is a somewhat well-known problem, as will be discussed in section 6.

3. DOUBLE INSERTION SORT

One problem with Insertion Sort is that we always insert a new element from the top of the array, even if will end up much closer to the bottom. Wouldn't it be faster to insert large elements from the top and small elements from the bottom? An implementation of this idea can be built by sorting an array from the center out. Assume, for simplicity, that the array we're sorting has an even number of elements. Sort the center two elements. Take the two elements on the "fringe" of the sorted portion of the array (the ones immediately before and after the sorted portion); insert the larger element of this pair from the top of the array, moving larger elements up one by one as we would do in regular Insertion Sort, until we find the right location for this new element. Finally, insert the smaller one of this pair from the bottom of the array, moving smaller elements down one by one.

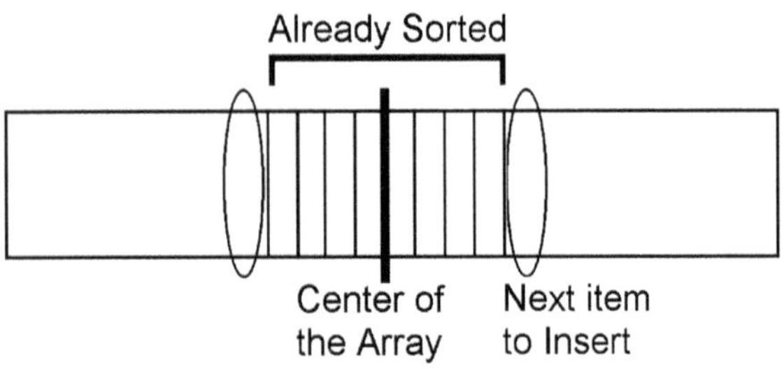

Figure 1. Double inserting the fifth pair of elements.

Pictorially, imagine that we are at the point where 4 pairs of items have been double insertion sorted. Then the middle 8 items of the array are fully sorted, with the next pair drawn as ovals in figure 1. We first interchange the two elements of this pair if necessary. We insert the top item of this pair, exactly as if inserting the 9-th element in Insertion Sort (but with a different "bottom element" then in Insertion Sort). When that is done, we insertion sort the bottom element, moving it up, essentially reversing the code for Insertion Sort. We should note that because of the initial sort of the two "outside" elements, we are guaranteed to have sentinels at both ends of our region of activity, so we are guaranteed never to fall off the array, or to leave the sorted portion of the array. This is both a good teaching example of sentinels, and one way in which the code is somewhat nicer than for straight insertion sort.

The coding requirements for this assignment are not particularly difficult, although it can be simplified by assuming that the size of the array is even (or that it is odd). The insertion sort from one end of the array should follow directly from, say, code in your text or your class. The student needs to infer the insertion sort in the other direction, then spend some time thinking about where the center is and how to move out from there. (With many options for "off by 1" errors.) A useful extra credit option is to ask students to run Double Insertion Sort against Insertion Sort to empirically compare their performance. While we normally recommend assigning only the "odd size" or "even size" array problem for students to program, an interesting paired project (which we have not tried) is to have two students work together, one primarily responsible for the odd case and the other primarily for the even case.

This algorithm generally succeeds in the goal that the larger element tends to be inserted from the large side of the array (e.g., the right side), and the smaller element from the small side (the left). Thus the initial swap of elements, if necessary, tends to move *both* items a large step towards their final destination. This tends to noticeably increase the speed of the algorithm as compared to Insertion Sort. This algorithm can thus be viewed as a conceptual step towards some of the faster exchange sorting algorithms, such as Shellsort and Quicksort. These faster algorithms also begin with the premise that we should often exchange elements that are far apart in the array, so that both are moved a large step closer to their final positions. The principal that speeds up Double Insertion Sort leads naturally to this more general sorting principal.

It is easy, even at this level, for students to understand the improvement in the worst-case time. If we were to insert items k and $k+1$ using straight Insertion Sort, the worst case number of comparisons will be $2k-1$. However, in Double Insertion Sort the smaller element can never move past the final location of the larger one. For example, if the larger item of a pair must be moved 90% of the way down the currently sorted array, then we are guaranteed that the smaller item will be moved no more than 10% of the way up. With the original comparison, inserting two items thus requires at most $k+1$ comparisons, for a 50% worst-case speed-up. Overall, Insertion Sort has a worst-case complexity of $N^2/2 + O(N)$, while Double Insertion Sort has a worst-case complexity of $N^2/4 + O(N)$. We might note also that the worst-case performance for Insertion Sort occurs with the fairly "natural" example of a reverse sorted list, while worst-case performance for Double Insertion Sort does not seem to occur for any such "natural" example. In particular, it runs in linear time on a reverse sorted list.

Although it is more complicated (see section 5), analysis shows that Insertion Sort has an average-case complexity, for both assignments and comparisons, of $N^2/4 + O(N)$. On the other hand, Double Insertion Sort can be shown to have an average case complexity (either measure) of $N^2/6 + O(N)$. Thus the average-case is 33% faster, and the worst-case is 50% faster, than Insertion Sort.

Sample Java code for this problem is shown below. This code works for odd size arrays; code for even size arrays is very similar, and can fairly easily be combined with this into a single method. There are a variety of ways to re-write the six lines of the "if" statement. For example, one could replace this by two conditional assignments, giving an 11 line solution to the problem. This "if" statement involves a certain optimization that a student solution would not likely include: Double insertion requires sorting a pair of elements; Insertion sort pulls out the element before moving others in the array; the code here combines those into a single step. This optimization affects the $O(N)$ constant in a full analysis, but does not change the constant of the N^2 term.

```
public void doubleInsertionOddSize( long toSort[] ) {
    long smallerItem, largerItem;
    int arraySize = toSort.length;
    int toMove, middle = arraySize / 2;

    for (int fringe = 0; fringe < arraySize/2; fringe++ ) {

        // Put the pair being inserted into "smallerItem" and "largerItem"
        if (toSort[ middle - fringe - 1 ] > toSort[ middle + fringe + 1 ]) {
            smallerItem = toSort[ middle + fringe + 1 ];
            largerItem  = toSort[ middle - fringe - 1 ];
        } else {
            largerItem  = toSort[ middle + fringe + 1 ];
            smallerItem = toSort[ middle - fringe - 1 ];
        }

        // Now insert the larger item from the top
        for (toMove = middle+fringe; toSort[toMove] > largerItem; toMove--)
            toSort[ toMove+1 ] = toSort[ toMove ];
        toSort[ toMove+1 ] = largerItem;

        // And insert the smaller item from the bottom
        for (toMove = middle-fringe; (toSort[toMove] < smallerItem); toMove++)
            toSort[ toMove-1 ] = toSort[ toMove ];
        toSort[ toMove-1 ] = smallerItem;
}
```

Figure 2. Java Code for Double Insertion Sort on Odd-Length Arrays

4. DOUBLE INSERTION SORT & THE N log N SORTS

The author prefers to give students programming assignments that have at least some sense of "realistic value," as opposed to being too apparently "make work" assignments. Of course one advantage of double sorting as an assignment is that it *isn't* important enough to appear in places the students will easily find. Better students will realize, however, that by itself double insertion sort is not particularly important: The advantage of any N^2 sort is in the simplicity of the code; if we were willing to put up with more complicated code, we would probably go with an $N \log N$ sort. Even at the CS 1/CS 2 level, we have some students who know this. What most of them don't know, though, is that sorts such as Quicksort and Mergesort have break-even thresholds, below which the N^2 sorts are superior, and that better implementations of $N \log N$ sorts will use the recursive techniques on large array sizes, but switch to an N^2 sort for small array partitions. For example, Quicksort is often used down to a threshold of size 15 (or some number close to that), then Insertion Sort is used for partitions of that size or less. Based on the previous discussion, one would expect that if we replaced Insertion Sort with Double Insertion Sort, we would get some modest amount of speed-up. That does, in fact, happen. We ran 100 trials on lists of size 10,000; 100,000; and 1,000,000, using a threshold of 15, and running Insertion Sort in one case and Double Insertion Sort in another case. (We used identical arrays for these two cases to ensure comparability.) If we scale the number of assignments and comparisons executed by Quicksort + Insertion sort to 100%, the results for Quicksort + Double Insertion Sort are shown in table 1:

Table 1. Quicksort Speedup Using Double Insertion Sort

N	10,000	100,000	1,000,000
Compares	97.5%	98.1%	98.4%
Assigns	89.1%	91.0%	92.3%

Of course as N gets larger, we expect these numbers to increase, because the $N \log N$ component must (asymptotically) overwhelm the N^2 component for these small partitions. While these improvements are quite modest, given the importance of Quicksort and the difficulty in improving it, it is still somewhat impressive that it is possible to get an 8-9% speed-up in it using a introductory student level program.

5. AVERAGE-CASE ANALYSIS OF DOUBLE INSERTION SORT

The average case analysis of Double Insertion Sort is beyond what we would normally expect to present to a CS1/CS2 class. We have, however, used it in an upper-level algorithms class, and it might be appropriate for a Discrete Math course in the CS curriculum as well, so we outline the analysis here, focusing on the number of comparisons only.

Inserting the larger number from the top is symmetrical with inserting the smaller number from the bottom, so we need only consider the cost of the former operation, and then double it. We cannot calculate the insertion cost as we would with Insertion Sort, because the distribution of the final location of this element is not evenly distributed — it is much more likely to be on the right side of the array than on the left. Instead, we begin with the state where we have just completed the sorting of elements $k-1$ and k, so that we now have a sub-array of k sorted items, which we number from 1 to k. We now ask how many comparisons did it take us to get the larger of the last two items into place? In particular, what is the probability that the top item moved $i-1$ steps down this part of the array, and landed in position $k-i$? This probability is given by the number of ways of choosing two elements from this array (i.e. the last pair inserted) with the larger item being in position $k-i$, divided by the number of ways of choosing any two elements from this array. Since the larger one must have been in position $k-i$, and we have $k-i-1$ options for where the smaller element was (see figure 3), this probability is $(k-i-1)/\binom{k}{2}$.

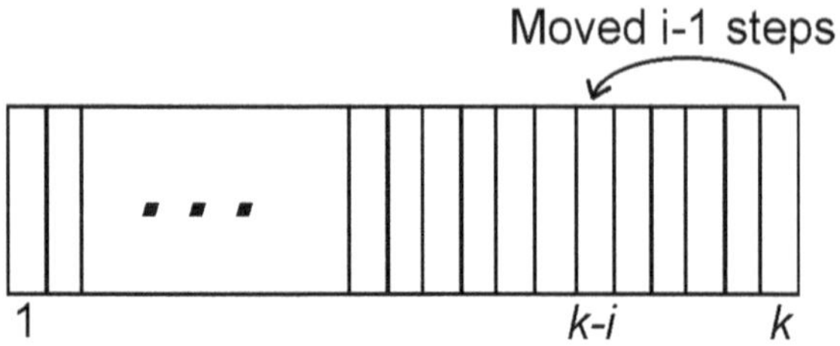

Figure 3. The cost of inserting an item from the top.

It will have taken us i comparisons for this insertion, so summing up the expected value of all such comparisons tells us that the average number of comparisons will be $\sum_{i=1}^{k-1} i\cdot(k-i-1)/\binom{k}{2}$. Standard summation techniques reduce this to $k/3$. Doubling this (for inserting the lower item) and summing for every other value of k (since we add two items at a time) can be written as: $\sum_{k=1}^{N-1}(k/3+O(1))$ which gives $N(N-1)/6 + O(N)$.

6. DOUBLE SELECTION SORT

Unlike Double Insertion Sort, Double Selection Sort has been described before, and can be found in two sources on the Web (and, as best as I can find, only those two sources). One of these sources, [6], has it available, but somewhat difficult to locate, written in Visual Basic, and probably offers more translation problems than writing it in Java or C++ in the first place. The second source, [2], has it in C++, but probably in a style from which plagiarism would be easily detectable. Thus while this as a program assignment is slightly more problematic than Double Insertion Sort, it is still probably usable, and introduces another important algorithm that we often show our students at this level.

Selection Sort finds the minimum, or maximum, of N elements in $N-1$ comparisons. The MaxMin algorithm lets you find the minimum *and* maximum of N elements in $3N/2$ comparisons (keep the current min and max; take 2 more elements, compare them against each other; then compare the two largest and the two smallest). To convert this to a sorting algorithm, we reverse the "build direction" of the Double Insertion Sort algorithm by sorting our array from the outside in. Find the Max & Min in array elements [0 … $N-1$], place them in the two outside positions, then iterate this algorithm with the remaining array elements [1 … $N-2$]. While Selection Sort requires $N^2/2 + O(N)$ comparisons, Double Selection Sort will require $3N^2/8 + O(N)$ comparisons, for a 25% speedup on this measure. Unfortunately, Selection Sort is used primarily when comparisons are much cheaper than assignments, since it uses only $N + O(1)$ assignments. Consequently, this improvement does not have as much of the "real-life value" that Double Insertion Sort has. Nevertheless, it could still be a useful assignment, or for a class that's seen Double Insertion Sort, it would make a useful comparison and an opportunity to demonstrate the MaxMin algorithm.

7. REFERENCES

[1] Cutter, P. and Schultz, K. 2004. Assignments to Use Next Week: Tutorial Presentation. J. of Computing Sciences in Colleges 20(1), Oct. 2004, p. 114.

[2] Gordon, S. 2007. Benchmark of Sorting Algorithms on Arrays. http://pr.stewartsplace.org.uk/d/sortbench.d

[3] Julstrom, J., 1992. Slow Sorting: A Whimsical Inquiry. ACM SIGCSE Bulletin 24(3), Sept. 1992, pp. 11-13.

[4] Merritt, S., and Nauch, C., 1990. Inventing A New Sorting Algorithm: A Case Study. ACM SIGCSE Bulletin 22(1), Feb. 1990, pp. 181-185.

[5] Rolfe, T., 2005. List processing: sort again, naturally. ACM SIGCSE Bulletin 37(2), June 2005, pp. 46-48.

[6] VBExplorer, 2004. Sorting Viewer – Sorting Methods Discussed. http://www.vbexplorer.com/VBExplorer/vb_feature/august2000/sv4.asp

The Baffling CS Notions of "As-if" and "Don't-care"

David Ginat
CS Group, Science Education Department
Tel-Aviv University
ginat@post.tau.ac.il

ABSTRACT

The notions of "as if" and "don't care" are essential notions in computational thinking. The former appears in the reformulation of tasks, reduction between tasks, auxiliary variables, and more. The latter is the core of non-determinism, asynchronous execution, and arbitrary choices in deterministic algorithms. The two notions are not intuitive, and require abstraction. We expect computer science (CS) graduates, who developed computational thinking during their studies, to demonstrate comprehension of these notions. Unfortunately, this may not be the case. In this paper we present a study of CS graduates, which reveals difficulties of limited comprehension and acceptance of these notions. We characterize the difficulties, relate them to cognitive aspects of abstraction, and offer some didactic suggestions.

Categories & Subject Descriptors

K.3: [Computers & Education] Computer and Information Science Education – Computer Science Education.

General Terms

Algorithms, Design, Theory.

Keywords

Abstraction, task reformulation, non-determinism.

1. INTRODUCTION

Consider the following **Ants** task. N ants are located on a rod, in different locations. Each ant moves in a constant speed towards one of the ends of the rod; the leftmost ant moves right, the rightmost ant moves left, and each of the rest moves either left or right. In time ants meet; whenever two ants meet, each switches its moving direction. An ant that reaches one of the rod ends leaves the rod. Given the ants speed v and the N ants' initial locations and moving directions; compute the time in which all the ants will leave the rod (although not obvious, this will eventually happen).

The Ants task describes some algorithmic scenario. The initial, and natural solution approach that comes to mind is the simulation of the described scenario. This indeed is (in our experience) the initial approach demonstrated by CS students. Unfortunately, this may also be the sole approach of many. The more suitable and effective approach requires a change of the task perspective. Yet a new, non canonical perspective may sometimes be confusing or unclear.

The essential point in the above task is to observe that since ants are identical, we actually do not have to explicitly follow the back-and-forth ant meetings. When ants A and B meet, they both switch their moving directions. Yet, we may actually look at ant A as "becoming" ant B and ant B as "becoming" ant A. This implies that we can overlook all the meeting events, and actually view each ant as moving constantly in its initial direction. Thus, the time in which the last ant will leave the rod derives from the maximum among: the time that the ("incarnation" of the) leftmost ant will reach the right end and the time that the ("incarnation" of the) rightmost ant will reach the left end.

The above perspective embeds two notions – the notion of "as if" and the notion of "don't care". The "as if" notion is enclosed in the viewpoint of regarding one ant as "becoming" another. The "don't care" notion is encapsulated in the viewpoint of overlooking the original occurrences, and not caring about N-2 of the ants (as the output is derived only from the data about the two end-ants).

The latter two notions are essential notions in computer science. The notion of "as if" appears in reductions, which are means for showing equivalence between problems (e.g., [6,7]); it also appears with auxiliary variables, which assist in illuminating the picture of distributed and concurrent executions (e.g., [8]); and it appears in algorithmic solutions and theorem proofs in which the original point of view is transformed into an alternative one.

The notion of "don't care" is the core of non-determinism [1,6]; it also is an essential theme in asynchronous executions, in which one may not assume a-priori the order of events [3]; and it is relevant in the design of deterministic algorithms (e.g., an arbitrary starting point in bipartite matching, and other algorithms [2]).

The objective of this paper is to examine CS graduates' use and comprehension of the notions of "as if" and "don't care". These notions involve the essential computational thinking elements of task reformulation and abstraction [10]. Yet, although essential and apparent in a variety of CS courses, these notions are not straightforward, and may be baffling. In what follows we reveal difficulties in comprehending these notions and in accepting their utilization. These difficulties unfold, in a sense, some canonical-perspective impasse in engaging abstraction.

We conducted a study with 19 CS graduates, who were studying for their high-school teaching diploma. We examined the participants' behaviors in two stages: 1. their approaches to given algorithmic tasks, which required a change in the natural solution perspective; and 2. their reactions to the tasks' displayed solutions, which enclosed "as if" and "don't care" notions. We display our results in the next section, and reveal particular difficulties with the two notions. We then relate our results to cognitive aspects of abstraction [4,5,9], and offer some didactic suggestions.

2. "AS IF" AND "DON'T CARE" DIFFICULTIES

We posed to the study's participants a questionnaire with three algorithmic tasks, to be solved in 180 minutes. The tasks did not require any particular algorithmic scheme, but did require some insightful observations, and non-immediate solution perspectives. The participants were first requested to solve each of the tasks. Then, in a following class meeting, they were shown the suitable solutions of the given tasks, and were asked to comment on their understanding of the displayed solutions. We describe our results in each of the three sub-sections below. Each sub-section displays: one task, student attempts of solving the task, student comments in a class discussion on the suitable solution, and our interpretation of the student difficulties. The student comments presented below are only some of those we have experienced. Our interpretation is based on these and additional ones not presented here, due to lack of space.

2.1 TASK-1

The first task is the **Ants** task presented in the Introduction. The task description asserts that eventually all the ants will leave the rod. This assertion is not obvious, and should be realized upon gaining sufficient insight into the task. Unfortunately, only 5 of the study's participants demonstrated the required insight, and offered an explanation similar to the one displayed in the Introduction.

The other 14 participants were wondering about the ant-movement and offered algorithmic solutions which were simulation variants of the movement process. Some of the 14 participants examined the movement process with very few (e.g., 2, 3, or 4) ants and noticed that all the ants eventually reach the rod ends, but they were unable to offer a satisfying explanation and a corresponding algorithmic computation.

We displayed to the participants the solution described in the Introduction, of viewing each ant as "becoming" the ant whom it meets. This viewpoint reduces the original movement process into a process with no meeting events, and simplifies the original task perspective. Those who comprehend and accept this reduction see rather quickly the simple and elegant solution (which actually is just a max computation of two values).

Some of the participants felt comfortable and comprehended our solution, but more than one third continued to wonder; and expressed their vague picture:

R.: "I do not understand how you can suddenly decide that you do not look at the actual objects (ants), but rather on their incarnations ... why are you allowed to do so? ... you should keep following the movement of each of the ants."

A.: "Your explanation sounds strange to me. I may understand that you kind of look at one ant as becoming another ... but when you compute the output, you derive it only from the two end-ants, when actually maybe they won't be the actual ants that will remain in the end, as ants become other ants ..."

T.: "I can believe the new perspective of ants becoming other ants, but the output then depends only on two out of the N ants ... this means that you are not using most of the input data; yet if it is there, it should somehow be used ... perhaps the change in the point of view yielded invalid convictions ..."

The above participants' reactions reflect various difficulties with abstracting the task at hand and accepting the notions of "as if" and "don't care". Analyzing these reactions, we may recognize:

- **Difficulty to divert from concrete objects and occurrences.** R.'s comment reflects a difficulty to divert from the original ants and ant movements, and overlook actual events. A.'s comment encloses a similar difficulty.
- **Difficulty to divert from the intuitive solution scheme.** R.'s comment reflects his difficulty to change the natural solution scheme that comes to mind; in this case – a simulation of the described process.
- **Difficulty with ignoring some of the input data.** Both A. and T. are concerned with performing the computation only with some of the input data; while disregarding the rest (the data of the N-2 ants that are not the end-ants).
- **Difficulty to transform the point of view.** All three participants expressed a difficulty to transform the original task's perspective into a different one, based on some "as if" notion. In particular, T. expresses her thought that the change of perspective may have yielded invalid convictions.

In order to provide some further illumination into the task, we offered the following invariant assertion:

> *At time t after the ants started moving on the rod: there is an ant at distance $t \times v$ from the original location of the leftmost ant, moving right; there also is an ant at distance $t \times v$ from the original location of the second ant from the left, moving in the original direction of that ant; and so on for each ant. (Note: if a new location is beyond one of the rod ends, then its corresponding ant is not on the rod anymore.)*

The above assertion was justified by examining an ant-meeting event, and showing that if the assertion holds before the event, then it also holds after the event. Quite a few of the unconvinced participants felt more comfortable following the above assertion, but not all. It seemed that the main difficulty stemmed from the participants' difficulty to depart from their concrete view of the task objects + events. (We elaborate on it further in the discussion section, after displaying further results in the next two sections.)

2.2 TASK-2

The second task posed to the participants involved the division of a set into two disjoint subsets with specified properties.

> **Diplomats.** Given a group of N diplomats, each having 0, 1, 2, or 3 foes (among the other diplomats), develop an algorithm which splits them into two groups, A and B, such that each diplomat does not have more than one foe in her own group. We consider a rivalry to be symmetric; thus if p is a foe of q, then q is also a foe of p.

At first glance one may wonder if the goal may always be attained. Indeed, attainability is not that obvious. One way of getting convinced of attainability is the design of an algorithm that will always yield the desired goal.

All the participants sought an algorithm that will start from a meaningful starting point, and steadily progress toward the desired goal. The more common algorithm they designed was based on: first handling the diplomats with three foes, then handling the diplomats with two foes, and so on. They put a selected diplomat in group A, and all her foes in group B; then another diplomat in group A and all her foes in group B; and so on. Some conjectured that this scheme is sufficient for correctness. Others noticed that it may yield an erroneous result, as group B may include diplomats who have more than one foe in their group (B).

Those who noticed the difficulty sought another way of starting the assignment of diplomats into groups. They particularly sought a scheme which will not involve transfers of diplomats from one group to another. Unfortunately, they were unable to devise such an algorithm. Seven participants conjectured that since they were unable to devise such an algorithm, perhaps the goal specified in the task specification may not always be attained.

We displayed the suitable solution. This solution allows repeated transfers of diplomats between the two groups. Moreover, it starts from an arbitrary division of the diplomats into the groups A and B, and involves repeated steps that refine this initially arbitrary division. In each step, a diplomat with more than one foe in her group is sought after; and if found, then this diplomat (and not her foes!) is transferred to the other group. When such a diplomat may not be found, the goal is attained. Surprisingly, this process always yields attainability.

Many participants were puzzled. The starting point is arbitrary, and diplomats are repeatedly transferred between groups; but "magically" this process always yields successful termination. How can this be? This seemed intriguing to many.

The key point is that one can define a simple metric, for arguing progression and termination of the algorithm. The metric is:

The num of rivalries in group A + the num of rivalries in group B.

Each step of the above algorithm reduces the value of this metric (since the transfer of a diplomat reduces the num of rivalries in her original group by 2 or 3, and increases the num of rivalries in her new group by at most 1). At the beginning, the value of the metric does not exceed 3N, and this value repeatedly decreases. Since it may not be negative, successful termination is guaranteed.

Some participants were convinced by the above argumentation and felt comfortable with the displayed solution. Yet more than a third still remained puzzled. They expressed their difficulties:

A.: "No matter how you initially divide the diplomats into groups you always succeed … this total randomness (of the starting point) is a bit strange … and vague …"

Y.: "Why is the selection of transferred diplomats handled this way? … a diplomat may go back and forth between the groups … how can we track diplomats in this process … a diplomat should be put as soon as possible in his final group and not be transferred … this is how we can clearly see progression …"

D.: "The displayed metric for convincing us is strange … you do not look at actual diplomats and say … 'we are done with those ones, and now proceed to the next' … that is, there is no currently finalized subset of diplomats, with which you are done during the process, and then proceed …"

S.: "What will the value of the metric be when you are done? … You do not care? How can you not care? It is clear if you say that the metric will eventually reach 0, for example, but you do not specify the value that it will reach … how can this ensure proper termination?"

In this task's solution, the concrete objects (diplomats) remained concrete. Nevertheless, difficulties with diverting from the seemingly natural point of view remained, and further difficulties with "don't care" were displayed:

- **Difficulty with an arbitrary starting point.** A. expresses a difficulty of accepting that any initial division of the diplomats may yield success. The initially random division of diplomats into groups yields some vagueness.
- **Difficulty with accepting a non-concrete eventual value.** S. cannot understand how he is expected to be convinced that the (refinement) process of diplomat transfers will eventually end. He needs to see a concrete value of the metric that will be reached upon termination. The absence of such a value is blurring the picture for him.
- **Difficulty to divert from the intuitive solution scheme.** Both Y. and D. expect the familiar scheme displayed in many algorithms, of inductive progression with a concrete, increasing set of elements.
- **Difficulty to transform the point of view.** The metric displayed for arguing termination is elegant and clear. Yet, it requires one to depart from the concrete view of the actual diplomats in the two groups, and focus only on the amounts of the diplomats in the groups. It seems that all the above participants demonstrated a difficulty with this transition of the point of view.

We exemplified the algorithm, displayed the metric progression with particular illustrations, and yielded further illumination.

2.3 TASK-3

The third task posed to the participants is an optimization task, of computing an optimal starting point in a cyclic path.

> **Car cycle.** N gas stations are located along a cyclic road. In each station, there is a limited amount of fuel. The total amount of fuel in the N stations is sufficient for completing exactly one round of the cyclic road. In some stations the fuel amount may be more than needed for reaching the next station, and in others – less than needed for reaching the next station. A driver should start driving her car, clockwise, from one station and complete one round (while filling fuel in every visited station), without "getting stuck" without fuel. The goal is to find (compute) a suitable starting point, in as efficient computation as possible.

Obviously, if the fuel is evenly distributed among the stations, then any station may be a valid starting point. On the other hand, a station in which the fuel is insufficient for reaching the next station is not a candidate for a starting point.

The participants offered various solutions to this task. Nine participants offered the straightforward solution of trying every station as a starting point, until finding a valid one. This natural solution is correct, but inefficient, as it requires N repeated passes over the input.

Three participants suggested the solution of starting from the station with the maximal amount of fuel. This solution requires only a single pass over the input, but may yield incorrect output. These participants tried to divert from the straightforward solution. They examined some input examples, from which they extracted the above erroneous over-generalized scheme.

Four participants proposed an inductive scheme, in which adjacent stations are grouped, in different locations of the cycle, and form sequences of stations such that in each sequence one may start at the leftmost (clockwise) station and reach the rightmost one. This indeed is a relevant and insightful idea. Yet, those who offered it could not implement it efficiently, as unions of sequences may occur in different locations of the cycle.

Three participants yielded the elegant and efficient solution. They noticed that one may actually perform only one round, while starting from any station and examining the remaining fuel amount upon reaching each station. The special characteristic of a valid starting station is that at such a station the remaining fuel amount (prior to filling, in the station) is the lowest in the round.

That is, if we start the car path from any station (be it valid or not), and follow the remaining fuel amount upon reaching each station on the path (before filling the tank in the station), while allowing negative fuel values; then the amount of fuel remaining upon reaching the valid starting station will be minimal among all the stations on the cycle.

We exemplify the latter observation with the following example. Let the cycle be composed of 8 stations, let the fuel amount required to ride between any two stations be 10, and let the fuel amounts in the 8 stations be: 6 5 15 9 8 17 2 18. We may start our single-round tour in station 1. The (remaining) fuel value before filling fuel in this station is 0. Upon reaching station 2, the remaining fuel value will be -4, since we filled 6 (in station 1) and then consumed 10 (in driving to station 2). Similarly, the remaining fuel amount upon reaching station 3 will be -9 (due to 6-10+5-10). The sequence of the remaining fuel values in all the eight stations will be: 0 -4 -9 -4 -5 -7 0 -8 (and 0 again, upon returning to the first station).

The minimum value (-9) of the remaining fuel is obtained upon reaching the third station. If we start from this station, with the initial (remaining) value 0, we will get exactly the same relative values as in the sequence above, all shifted by +9. The reason for obtaining the same relative sequence is that we perform the same cyclic summation, and only start it from a different point.

Since the lowest relative value of the remaining fuel is in station 3, and we start there with 0, none of the other values will be negative. Thus, station 3 is a valid starting point (and actually the only valid starting point in this example).

The above solution was displayed to the class, with additional elaboration (which we do not display here, due to space limitations). Many seemed puzzled, and were not sure that they were convinced. Some of their reactions were the following:

D.: "I do not get this … how can you allow negative values to the fuel amounts? … with negative fuel values the car cannot advance …"

Y.: "I understand that if you start at different points then you get the same relative sequence, only with shifted values … but why do you not look at absolute values … after all, we are talking about fuel amounts …"

A.: "I do not see why does the minimum imply the valid starting point … it is just the minimal fuel value in the particular round you perform … and this value is anyway artificial … since you allow negative values …"

B.: "I do not understand the point that you may start at any station and perform only one round … how can it be that you allow yourself to pick a station randomly and somehow … like magic … you get the desired result …"

R.: "I understand that you find the minimum point of the remaining fuel … but this applies to the particular round that you just performed … don't you have to check now that indeed, when starting from the point of that minimum you actually succeed in completing a round?"

The above participants' reactions reflect some abstraction difficulties indicated earlier, and additional ones:

- **Difficulty to divert from concrete objects and occurrences.** D., Y., and A. express a difficulty to divert from the original story in the task, which involved real-world fuel values.
- **Difficulty to transform the point of view.** All five participants express a difficulty to transform the original task's perspective into a different one, based on some "as if" notion; this time with artificially negative fuel values.
- **Difficulty with an arbitrary starting point.** Both B. and R. do not fully accept the notion of starting anywhere, and "somehow … like magic …" (B.'s comment) obtaining the desired result.
- **Need to return to the original perspective.** R. can accept, to some extent, the change in the task perspective; but the result in the new perspective is insufficient – it should be verified in the original perspective.
- **Difficulty to relate the original element-to-compute to the one computed in the new perspective.** The original element to compute is a valid starting point, from which a round may be completed; yet the new element computed in the new perspective is some minimum fuel value. B. and R. could accept a change in the point of view, but had a difficulty in relating these two elements to one another.

We elaborated on the elegant one-round computation, with a few more examples. We showed that if we start the cycle in another station, then we get the same relative sequence of values, shifted by some amount (e.g., if we start in the second, rather than the first station in the latter example, then we get the remaining fuel sequence of: 4 0 -5 0 -1 -3 4 -4 (start at station 2, with fuel amount 0; then fill 5 in this station and spend 10; and so on)).

In trying to address the difficulty of negative fuel values, we offered the modification that the car will artificially start the round with a fuel amount that is sufficient for one round. This yields no negative fuel values in the tour, and offers "more concreteness".

3. DISCUSSION

The previous section revealed CS graduates' difficulties with the notions of "as if" and "don't care". The difficulties were revealed upon attempting to solve unfamiliar tasks and upon commenting on these tasks' displayed solutions. The tasks' suitable solutions did not require any competent knowledge of algorithmic schemes, but rather a change in the original task perspective. Unfortunately, the participants' expressed difficulties with the required change, even after it was shown to them.

CS graduates should do better, as throughout their studies they are introduced to a variety of computational thinking elements, which include the notions of task reformulation and abstraction, with "as if" and "don't care" occurrences.

The utilization of "as if" involves departure from (at least some) concrete objects and occurrences in the original task. It also requires possible departure from the natural, or canonical task perspective; and it entails the comprehension of the relationship between the elements in the original task and those of the reformulated task representation.

The engagement of "don't care" requires comprehension and acceptance of the potential irrelevance of: certain task data, a concrete starting point, a concrete eventual value; or the unimportance of additional features, like the ordering of events.

Unfortunately, participants in our study did not demonstrate awareness and understanding of the above, and rather showed:

- Difficulty to divert from concrete objects and occurrences.
- Difficulty to divert from the intuitive solution scheme.
- Difficulty to transform the point of view.
- Need to return to the original perspective.
- Difficulty to relate the original element-to-compute to the one computed in the new task perspective.
- Difficulty with ignoring some of the input data.
- Difficulty with an arbitrary starting point.
- Difficulty with accepting a non-concrete eventual value.

We are not familiar with similar studies of the above difficulties in algorithmics. Some CS education studies on abstraction and non-determinism are related to ours, and we will refer to them below. Mathematics educators examine difficulties similar to those above (involving abstraction) through different angles. One angle involves the "distance" between the thinking person and the object of thought [9]. Another angle involves the complexity of the concept of thought [4,5]. We may examine our results in light of these two angles.

It seems that in all the three tasks, there was a gap between the participants and the objects of thought, which some participants had a difficulty to bridge. In the first and the third tasks (Ants, Car), participants did not accept the gap between the original task objects and the modified objects of the task reformulation. In addition, participants demonstrated difficulties in embedding a non-deterministic point of view, of "don't care" characteristics, in the solutions of the three tasks, that were basically deterministic.

The complexity of the concept of thought appeared in various forms in the three tasks. The first two tasks (Ants, Diplomats) required the acceptance and comprehension of the notion of black-box. One had to focus on the important information (ant movements in Ants, and metric progression in Diplomats), understand why some information may be overlooked (ant meetings in Ants, and back-and-forth diplomat transfers in Diplomats), and overlook this information. The difficulty seemed to stem from the need to make a distinction between the relevant and the irrelevant information. In the third task (Car), one had to realize that the cyclic summation process yields the same sequence of relative values (of remaining fuel) regardless of the summation starting point. This allowed an arbitrary starting point.

The collection of the described difficulties yields the theme of a dominant *canonical perspective*. The participants seemed to repeatedly incline towards the familiar, seemingly "called for" viewpoint, and expressed inconvenience with the less natural one. These findings add-to and widen previous findings of student difficulties with the notion of abstraction in general and the notion of non-determinism in particular (e.g., [1,5]).

One may argue that the participants' difficulties and questions unfolded here are natural and represent critical thinking. While this is true to some extent, we would like our graduates to do better. They should demonstrate fewer difficulties with both reaching and understanding the desired solution. We offer below some didactic suggestions for enhancing students' competence with the "as if" and "don't care" notions:

- Embed the notions of "as if" and "don't care" gradually, throughout the CS curriculum, from the very beginning, starting already in CS1 and CS2; possibly with tasks like those presented here.
- Refer to these notions on relevant occasions, while indicating the non-canonical point of view they may encapsulate.
- Explicitly tie occurrences of these notions to occurrences of the well advocated CS notions of abstraction and non-determinism.
- Be aware of potential student difficulties with these notions (such as those displayed here); and therefore underline their essential characteristics, provide illuminating illustrations and convincing arguments, and aim at making the vague and unfamiliar much more familiar.

4. REFERENCES

[1] Armoni, M. & Galezer, J. 2007. Non-determinism – an abstract concept in computer science studies, *Computer Science Education*, *17*(4) 243-262.

[2] Cormen, T.H., Leiserson, C.E., Rivest, R.L., & Stein, C. 2001. *Introduction to Algorithms*, MIT Press. 2nd Ed.

[3] Dijkstra, E.W. 1975. Guarded commands, nondeterminancy and formal derivation of programs, *Communications of the ACM*, *18*(8) 453-457.

[4] Dubinsky, E. 1991. Reflective abstraction in advanced mathematical thinking, in Tall, D. (Ed.) *Advanced Mathematical Thinking*. Kluger 95-123.

[5] Hazzan, O. 2003. How students attempt to reduce abstraction in the learning of mathematics and in the learning of computer science, *Computer Science Education*, *13*(2) 95-122.

[6] Hopcroft, J.E., Motwani, R., & Ullman, J.D. 2001. *Introduction to Automata Theory, Languages, and Computation*, Addison-Wesley. 2nd Ed.

[7] Lewis, H.R. & Papadimitriou, C.H. 1981. *Elements of the Theory of Computation*, Prentice-Hall.

[8] Lynch, A.N. 1996. *Distributed Algorithms*, Morgan Kaufman.

[9] Wilensky, U. 1991. Abstract meditations on the concrete and concrete implications for mathematical education, in Harel, I., & Papert, S. (Eds.) *Constructionism*, Ablex Pub, 193-203.

[10] Wing, J.M. 2006. Computational Thinking, *Communications of the ACM*, 49(3) 33-35.

Computational Thinking in High School Courses

Vicki Allan
Computer Science
Utah State University
Logan, Utah 84322
vicki.allan@usu.edu

Valerie Barr
Computer Science
Union College
Schenectady, NY 12308
barrv@union.edu

Dennis Brylow
Math, Stat & CS
Marquette University
Milwaukee, WI 53201
brylow@mscs.mu.edu

Susanne Hambrusch
(Moderator)
Computer Science
Purdue University
W. Lafayette, IN 47906
seh@purdue.edu

1. PANEL SUMMARY

The number of undergraduates entering computer science has declined in recent years. This is paralleled by a drop in the number of high school students taking the CS AP exam and the number of high schools offering computer science courses. The declines come at a time when career opportunities in CS continue to grow and computer science graduates are seen as crucial in building a globally competitive workforce for the 21st century. Efforts aimed at reversing the declining interest in computer science include curriculum revisions at the undergraduate level at many institutions, a re-design of computer science AP courses [1], and the inclusion of computational thinking into disciplines outside computer science [3].

This panel discusses four projects of computer science researchers collaborating with high school teachers on integrating computing and computational thinking into their courses. The majority of the high school teachers involved is teaching science and math courses. They are teaching a diverse group of talented and college-bound students. The goal of all projects is to integrate computing into disciplines represented in the high school curriculum and to raise the awareness of computer science as an exciting and intellectually rewarding field.

This panel will outline recent and on-going activities and interaction with high school teachers. Each panelist will describe how he/she got involved and the nature of the interaction. The panelists will talk about their individual projects, outline their visions for future interactions, and how their effort can be replicated by others. The session will briefly describe NSF's RET program which provided teacher support for three of the four projects. The session will then be opened for discussion; the audience will be encouraged to ask questions and contribute additional ideas for the inclusion of computational thinking in high school courses.

Categories and Subject Descriptors

K3.2 [**Computing Milieux**]: Computers and Education – *Computer and Information Science Education*

General Terms

Experimentation

Keywords

Computational Thinking, Education.

2. SUSANNE HAMBRUSCH

The "Science Education in Computational Thinking (SECANT)" project at Purdue University collaborated with two high school physics teachers to incorporate selected material of the Matter&Interaction (M&I) Curriculum with computational thinking principles into high school physics courses [3]. The high school course includes three weeks of Python programming focusing on computational methods and visualizations crucial to the M&I Curriculum. Lab material developed within this project gives a first introduction to programming. Throughout the school year, students use computation to illustrate and simulate physical principles and models, and they apply computational thinking concepts. The computational concepts include designing repeated processes through iterations, determining how data generated is stored and represented, abstracting and generalizing physical processes, and visualizing the collected data to observe patterns and other phenomena.

This approach is currently implemented in the AP Physics course. The high school devotes a full year to AP Physics and has some flexibility on what material to cover. Introducing computation into AP Physics provides a unique opportunity to upgrade the non-prescribed part of the AP course and to interest and expose high-ability students to computation. A future plan is to include selected computational material into Physics 1 and 2.

The panel presentation will describe challenges and successes of this on-going effort. This will include highlights on how decisions were made on what computational material to include, how software installation issues were resolved, how students with widely different problem-solving interests and abstraction abilities were engaged, and how the use of visualization and encouraging creativity played a key role in keeping students interested.

3. VALERIE BARR

The Union College CS department is engaged in a project to "Create a Campus-Wide Computation Initiative". The goal of this project is to interest non-CS students in the role of computation in their field and encourage them to seek a strong computational foundation. Each summer, the project works with a number of faculty-student pairs who design a curricular element (labs, module, or complete course) that will infuse computation into their discipline. The ten academic departments that have pursued this opportunity include Astronomy, Biology, Classics, Economics, Film Studies, and Political Science.

In Summer 2009, the project collaborated with two teachers from Bard High School Early College (a joint project of Bard College and the NYC Dept. of Education). One teaches chemistry, physics, and math while the other teaches math and statistics. Each teacher chose one course into which to initially infuse computation, a 10th grade advance math course and a statistics course. In both cases the infusion will take place across the entire semester, rather than being limited to one discrete part of the course (as an early college program, Bard runs on a college model with two semesters per year). One teacher will be weaving computation into a statistics course, using Sage (built on Python), while the other will be using Python to introduce computation into a 10th grade advanced math course. As with the college courses, computation will be used to support the disciplinary work, but at the same time students will be introduced to programming, problem solving, and computational thinking.

The panel presentation will include discussion of the interactions and on-going collaboration between the high school and college faculty, and the roll out of the revised high school courses. Jane Budimir, of Bard High School, will discuss her experience with her 10th grade math class, share examples of how she integrated computation into her course, and talk about the student response.

4. DENNIS BRYLOW

For five years, the "Linking Mathematics and Computer Science" summer workshop series at Purdue has sought to inform and inspire high school mathematics teachers, arming them with the tools to motivate state-mandated curriculum topics with powerful examples in computer science. This past year, Marquette University has instituted a "Computational Thinking for the Sciences" spin-off workshop aimed at high school science teachers. For both workshop series, our goal is to exploit the natural linkages between existing topics in secondary school math/science and post-secondary computer science and engineering. Rather than concentrate on adding new, additional content into high school courses already bursting with mandates, we seek instead to show the many ways in which current topics are deeply important to students who choose to pursue college degrees in computer science, information technology, engineering, or the hard sciences. We offer enrichment activities that encourage algorithmic thinking and logical exploration. In the laboratory component of the workshops, we also generally teach tools designed to help high school and middle school students explore computation and computer-based problem solving; past tools have included Alice, SketchUp, and VPython.

The panel presentation will describe the challenges inherent in recruiting high school math/science teachers, designing coherent computational content within the strictures of a multitude of state curriculum standards, and making a workshop relevant for teachers ranging from pre-Algebra and Trigonometry to AP Physics and Biology.

5. VICKI ALLAN

Some who are trying to make changes in computer science curriculum have been believers in the "Field of Dreams" motto, "If you build it, they will come" or perhaps "If you build it and design a good book around it, they will come." This fails to account for the fact that we may not understand what "it" we should build, nor the fact that "they" are so busy they may not be able to come.

The Computer Science department of Utah State University has been funded to create and evaluate a collection of Interactive Learning Modules (ILMs) which can be used to transform computer science education (csilm.usu.edu). In addition to using the ILMs to engage Computer Science students in learning, we also seek to use such modules to attract new students to the discipline. Much research has suggested that the effort to entice more students to computer science needs to begin much earlier than the first day of college.

To help us design and evaluate material for use in K-12, four teachers were brought to the USU campus. Benefits of this interaction are many. While college professors know which skills are required to pursue a degree in computer science, they may not know how to get young students to that level of competency. Engaging activities need to be built around competencies specified in the state standards. The RET teachers helped us to understand how those competencies are being interpreted and what support the teachers need to succeed in achieving them. Many of the administrators who decide the curriculum in technology and computers substitute computer literacy for computational thinking. It takes a merger of both viewpoints to find activities that satisfy both state standards and the goals of computational thinking. The panel presentation will discuss ways others can use the customizable ILMs to support computational thinking in local schools.

6. ACKNOWLEDGEMENTS

Susanne Hambrusch would like to thank NSF for support under the CPATH program Grant No. CCF-0722210 and the associated RET supplement. Valerie Barr would like to thank NSF for support under the CPATH program Grant No. IIS-0722203 and the associated RET supplement. Vicki Allan would like to thank NSF for support under the CPATH program Grant No. 0829563 and the associated RET supplement. Dennis Brylow would like to thank Motorola for supporting the Linking workshop at Purdue and the Klingler-Way College of Arts and Science for supporting the workshop at Marquette.

7. REFERENCES

[1] J. Cuny, Transforming High School Computing: A Compelling Need, A National Effort. http://opas.ous.edu/Committees/Resources/Publications/NSF_AP_CS_10000ExecSumm_Ed.pdf

[2] B. Sherwood and R. Chabay, *Matter & Interactions I & II: Modern Mechanics.* Wiley; 2nd edition, 2007.

[3] Wing, J. 2006. Computational Thinking. CACM. 15, 5 (March 2006), 33-3.

Some Developments in Mathematical Thinking for Computer Science Education Since Computing Curricula 2001

Doug Baldwin (Moderator)
SUNY Geneseo
Dept. of Computer Science
Geneseo, NY 14454
+1 585-245-5659
baldwin@geneseo.edu

Bill Marion
Valparaiso University
Dept. of Math & Computer Science
Valparaiso, IN 46383
+1 219-464-5422
Bill.Marion@valpo.edu

Murali Sitaraman
Clemson University
School of Computing
Clemson, SC 29634-0974
+1 864-656-6738
MSITARA@clemson.edu

Cinda Heeren
U. Illinois Urbana-Champaign
Department of Computer Science
Urbana, IL 61801
+1 217-244-2529
c-heeren@illinois.edu

Categories and Subject Descriptors
K.3.2. [**Computers and Education**]: Computer and Information Science Education – *computer science education, curriculum.* G.2.m [**Discrete Mathematics**]: Miscellaneous.

General Terms
Design.

Keywords
Mathematics, Computer Science Education, Computing Curricula 2001.

1. SUMMARY

The Computing Curricula 2001 (CC 2001) computer science volume [1] is the first professional society curriculum model for computer science to include elements of discrete mathematics as part of the core of computer science. In the roughly eight years between the release of that curriculum and SIGCSE 2010, computer science education in general has evolved in many ways, and the CC 2001 recommendations have played an influential role in that evolution. This panel reviews developments in integrating discrete mathematics into the computer science curriculum since CC 2001, how those developments have been influenced by the centrality of discrete math in the CC 2001 core, and how the role of math in computer science curricula may continue to develop in the future. The panel will address both the influence CC 2001's discrete math recommendation has had on curricular changes to computer science courses, and what changes have taken place in the discrete math courses themselves.

The panel format will consist of...

- A 5 minute introduction by the moderator
- 10 minute presentations by each panelist, each describing a specific development with which that panelist has been involved, discussing its relationship to CC 2001, and outlining what it bodes for the future
- 30 minutes for discussion between the audience and panel. Suggested topics for discussion include (in addition, of course, to anything that the audience wishes to introduce) the role of mathematics in computer science, whether math's actual place in computer science curricula has changed since the publication of CC 2001, and if so how. A questionnaire handed out to audience members as they enter the panel session will help them start thinking about these issues.

SIGCSE'10, March 10–13, 2010, Milwaukee, Wisconsin, USA.
ACM 978-1-60558-885-8/10/03.

2. Bill Marion

As an outgrowth of the CC2001 report, in the summers of 2003 and 2004, I organized at Valparaiso University two one-week faculty professional enhancement workshops under the auspices of the Mathematical Association of America's (MAA) PREP project (funded by NSF) for undergraduate mathematics faculty who teach a discrete mathematics course to meet the needs of computer science majors. The purposes were (1) to provide these mathematicians with an understanding of what the implications of the report were for the teaching of discrete mathematics and (2) to illustrate by examples and applications ways to connect the mathematics topics with computer science material their students were learning in CSI and CSII-type courses. Doug Baldwin, Susanna Epp, Peter Henderson, Henry Walker and I were the workshop leaders. One of the outcomes was that, over the course of the next four to five years, some combination of the five of us presented workshops at SIGCSE symposia and CCSC conferences and organized panels at MAA national meetings.

More significantly, some of the PREP workshop participants developed a variety of resources for teaching discrete mathematics, including a textbook, proof builder software and an MAA Notes Volume on discrete mathematics.

In my remarks I will summarize these activities and discuss their effect on the teaching of discrete mathematics. In addition, I will talk about how the CC2001 recommendations have affected the theory and algorithms courses at Valparaiso University.

3. Doug Baldwin

The CC 2001 report's most prominent models for including discrete math in the computer science curriculum are a single course and a two-course sequence. The report's authors prefer the two-course model as the more workable one pedagogically, but acknowledge that some institutions will not be able to devote two full courses to discrete math. The one-course model is an option for such institutions, although it is not as carefully crafted as the two-course model.

In June of 2003, SIGCSE chartered a committee to find or develop practical one-semester model discrete math courses compliant with CC 2001. The committee, co-chaired by Bill Marion and Doug Baldwin, surveyed then-current practice in teaching discrete math. This survey revealed that a large fraction of the respondents did indeed teach discrete math for computer science in a single course. The designs of those courses lay along a spectrum, ranging from courses that were taught with the math itself as the main motivator to courses that were taught with computing applications of the math as the main motivator. As a result of this second observation, the Committee recommended three model courses: two representative of the computer science end of the spectrum, and one representative of the math end.

In June 2007 the committee released a final report, detailing the model courses. The committee also released a collection of exercises and syllabi for teaching discrete math. Both the report and collected materials are available on the SIGCSE Web site (see http://www.sigcse.org/resources/discrete-mathematics); the report also appeared in the June 2007 *inroads*. This presentation will summarize the committee's history and results, and will seek audience opinions of the impact of the committee's work on the teaching of discrete math.

4. Murali Sitaraman

To teach key mathematical concepts effectively and at the same time engage and excite students in the process, analytical reasoning tools are useful. A variety of CS courses including ones on programming, data structures and algorithms, and object-oriented introduction and software engineering courses offer excellent opportunities to introduce mathematical thinking. A reasoning tool can help introductory students understand why their programs fail and how they can be fixed using mathematical analysis, as opposed to a trial and error alternative. In a course where interface specifications are introduced, students can provide specification-based test points to show their understanding of interface contracts and a tool can check if their test points satisfy given specifications. Alternatively, in a programming or software engineering course, students can study and attempt to prove tool-generated verification conditions for correctness to understand the connection between their code correctness and mathematical thinking.

Reasoning tools can be used to introduce one or more mathematical concepts within a week or two in a number of courses, making it possible for educators to experiment with and adapt the ideas without major course restructuring and without significant time investment.

Sitaraman and others have employed mathematical reasoning tools in their classrooms routinely for the past few years at Clemson and elsewhere. Some results from these efforts are reported in recent SIGCSE and ITiCSE proceedings [2]. The feedback from students has been overwhelmingly positive. Students no longer view mathematical thinking as an aside, but as an integral and essential part of computing.

5. Cinda Heeren

In 2007, the National Science Foundation supported the creation of a multiple choice learning assessment tool called a Discrete Math Concept Inventory. The development of this tool is occurring over four phases, the first two of which are complete. Our first objective, to winnow the set of inventory topics to a reasonable few, was completed as the result of a Delphi process, in which experts in Discrete Math instruction were asked to name the most important and difficult topics in the course. The consensus response was a tight subset of the CC2001 syllabus, weighted toward proofs and logical reasoning, especially those types most often employed in proofs of algorithm correctness and complexity. The second phase, in which students were interviewed while solving problems from the important-difficult domain, has exposed many specific areas for instructional intervention, particularly in the areas of mathematical rigor and problem solving strategies. While the original purpose of the interviews was to elicit student misconceptions for use in designing multiple choice questions, we have learned much more about how and what students absorb in a CC2001 Discrete Math course. The panel presentation will be a status update on the Concept Inventory development process, together with a guided ride through the analysis techniques used to evaluate student interview responses.

6. ACKNOWLEDGMENTS

Thanks to Peter Henderson for help planning this panel.

7. REFERENCES

[1] IEEE CS/ACM Joint Task Force on Computing Curricula 2001. Computing Curricula 2001: Computer Science. http://www.computer.org/portal/cms_docs_ieeecs/ieeecs/education/cc2001/cc2001.pdf.

[2] Sitaraman, M., Hallstrom, J.O., White, J., Drachova-Strang, S., Harton, H., Leaonard, D., Krone, J., and Pak, R. Engaging students in specification and reasoning: "hands-on" experimentation and evaluation. In Proc. 14th ACM SIGCSE Conf. on Innovation and Technology in CS Education (ITiCSE), ACM Press, 2009, 50-54.

Rediscovering the Passion, Beauty, Joy, and Awe: Making Computing Fun Again, part 3

Daniel D. Garcia (moderator)
University of California, Berkeley
777 Soda Hall
Berkeley, CA 94720
+1 510-642-9595
ddgarcia@cs.berkeley.edu

Gail Chapman
Computer Science Teachers Association
2 Penn Plaza, Suite 701
New York, NY 10121
+1 212-626-0507
gail.chapman@csta.acm.org

Orit Hazzan
Dept of Education in Technology & Science
Technion - Israel Institute of Technology
Haifa 32000, ISRAEL
+9724 8293-107
oritha@techunix.technion.ac.il

Maggie Johnson
Google
1600 Amphitheatre Parkway
Mountain View, CA 94043
+1 650-253-7707
maggiej@google.com

Leigh Ann Sudol
Carnegie Mellon University
5000 Forbes Avenue
Pittsburgh, PA 15213
+1 914-806-4211
leighannsudol@gmail.com

Categories and Subject Descriptors
K.3.2 [**Computer and Information Science Education**]: Computer science education

General Terms
Experimentation

Keywords
Computer science education

1. SUMMARY

In 2006, computing education was suffering from a crisis – enrollments were dropping sharply at universities and colleges across the United States, and interest in computing from high school and middle school students was waning significantly. At the SIGCSE Symposium in 2007, the ACM Education Board organized a special session to explore the underlying causes [3]; one of the culprits that emerged was the tarnished image of computing and computing professionals. At the same conference, keynote speaker Grady Booch shared that one of the "metaskills" lessons that should be taught is the "passion, beauty, joy and awe" (PBJA) of computing [2]. This led to room-packed special sessions at the following two SIGCSE symposia to explore that idea from different perspectives [4, 6]. The sessions have provided a forum for sharing:

What we've done: Highlighting successful PBJA initiatives the presenters have undertaken or have seen and wish to celebrate.

What we should do (curriculum): Pointing out, as Grady Booch did, where our curriculum is lacking in PBJA, and how to fix it.

How we should do it (pedagogy): Sharing how a change in attitude/focus/behavior/etc. can make strides to improving PBJA.

SIGCSE'10, March 10–13, 2010, Milwaukee, Wisconsin, USA.
ACM 978-1-60558-885-8/10/03

Fortunately, enrollments are rising again, and there are universities where the numbers are so strong (returning to historic highs), that some claim the crisis is over [5, 7]. Many dispute this, however, citing statistics that indicate under-represented students (women and ethnic minorities) have not returned, and there still exist strong negative connotations about the field [1]. This PBJA "movement" was born out of the enrollment crisis, but need not be tied to it. There is always value in sharing novel best practices and advocating techniques to your colleagues to make computing fun for the next generation. We have gathered educators who bring a wide variety of perspectives; this year, we hear from international, domestic, high school, university and industrial representatives.

2. GAIL CHAPMAN

Computer science teachers at the K-12 level rarely have the opportunity to experience the collaborative nature of computer science and all too often forget that what may have inspired passion, beauty, joy and awe for us has little relevance in the lives of today's diverse student population. The isolation that teachers feel can lead to teaching that models their own experiences rather than unleashing the bodies of knowledge related to computer science that students bring from their lives, culture, and communities.

In Los Angeles Unified School District, the K-12 Computer Science Equity Alliance, a University-District partnership funded by NSF to attract and retain more females and students of color in rigorous computing courses, has developed and supported an integrated approach to reframing computer science education; this includes curriculum, professional development for teachers, and ongoing support.

The curriculum builds off of learning theories that draw from students' funds of knowledge, emphasize collaborative inquiry, and develop algorithmic thinking. However, providing curricular resources alone is not enough to support teachers. Teachers need to experience models of engaging computing learning communities, which provide examples of projects that are conceptually grounded, but open-ended enough to allow students to make relevant connections with their own lives. Ongoing professional development is essential to support the teachers. In this session, I will share examples of how this integrated approach to teaching and learning has changed the nature of computer science classrooms in LAUSD and inspired passion, beauty, joy and awe for both students and teachers.

3. ORIT HAZZAN

My perspective is based on my belief that most computer science graduates eventually work as software engineers. If we just admit to this fact, and without changing the definition of what CS is, we might feel more comfortable to expand the scope of the educational offerings of CS programs and eventually let CS students rediscover at least some of the passion, beauty, joy, and awe of computing. According to this perspective, such CS programs should include also some engineering aspects that are manifested in the daily work of software engineers, such as teamwork experience, management skills, and a customer-oriented perspective. These elements, which point to the discipline's social facet, have the potential, in my opinion, to make computing fun, especially in light of the fact that this image clearly contrasts the image of CS that deters many potential students from entering the discipline. Accordingly, it is my belief that in order to generate greater excitement among potential CS students, we should highlight the fact that human aspects, in general, and teamwork, in particular, are at the heart of the actual work of the discipline's graduates. The importance of these skills has already been widely acknowledged by the software industry, which employs most of the CS graduates. In my presentation, I will introduce this perspective by highlighting connections between human aspects of software development & CS curricula.

4. MAGGIE JOHNSON

Google has a commitment to contributing to computer science education initiatives, as well as increasing diversity in the field. At the undergraduate and graduate level, we have created programs such as the Fuse retreat for freshmen, CSSI for rising sophomores, BOLD for rising juniors, and Google Summer of Code. Google sponsors efforts with NSF, NCWIT, CS4HS and CS Unplugged as well as programs that support the educational use of our products and technologies such as Google for Educators, the Google Teacher Academy, App Inventor for Android, and Google Code University. These are all important efforts, but none directly address bridging the achievement and diversity gap in computer science at the K12 level.

One of our current initiatives focuses on bridging this gap. We are developing middle school Algebra and Science curriculum that incorporates simple programming exercises to help students recognize, generalize and represent patterns, and then construct corresponding algorithms. These exercises support and enhance the learning of Algebra and Science through interactive exploration, and by building solutions to problems which students find not only fun, but also very rewarding.

5. LEIGH ANN SUDOL

Although it may seem counter-intuitive, the fact that computers have become ubiquitous could actually have a detrimental effect on student's interest in computer science. The Apple slogan *"There is an App for that"* implies that the majority of useful things people use everyday is already done. The programs that we ask students to write in our introductory classes can be found on Google, already complete, faster than students can open up the editor they are going to write their programs in.

Introductory computer science used to be about getting the computer to do something you wanted it to do that did not exist before. We have moved away from this mentality of creating new programs, to instead become an introductory discipline in recreating existing works. Part of the joy of early computer science is still found in that moment of creation and completion.

With this in mind early introductions to computer science should focus not only on core concepts of the discipline, but what new and exciting things are being created right now with those concepts. Using iGoogle as a way to develop mash up software aimed at a particular audience, motivating early machine learning with Weka and the Netflix prize can help students come to understand and appreciate data. Asking introductory programming students to write programs that will help them with other classes, or support a small piece of current research can help them feel a part of and come to understand the beauty in the larger field of computer science.

6. REFERENCES

[1] ACM, WGBH. Interim report. *New Image for Computing.* April, 2009. `www.acm.org/membership/NIC.pdf`

[2] Booch, G. 2007. Readn', writ'n, 'rithmetic..and code'n. *SIGCSE Bull.* 39, 1 (Mar. 2007), 197-197. `http://doi.acm.org/10.1145/1227504.1227380`

[3] Cassel, L., McGettrick, A., Guzdial, M., and Roberts, E. 2007. The current crisis in computing: what are the real issues?. In *Proceedings of the 38th SIGCSE Technical Symposium on Computer Science Education* (Covington, Kentucky, USA, March 07 - 11, 2007). SIGCSE '07. ACM, New York, NY, 329-330. `http://doi.acm.org/10.1145/1227310.1227426`.

[4] Garcia, D. D., Cutler, R., Dodds, Z., Roberts, E., and Young, A. 2009. Rediscovering the passion, beauty, joy, and awe: making computing fun again, continued. In *Proceedings of the 40th ACM Technical Symposium on Computer Science Education* (Chattanooga, TN, USA, March 04 - 07, 2009). SIGCSE '09. ACM, New York, NY, 65-66. `http://doi.acm.org/10.1145/1508865.1508889`

[5] NY Times. *CS Programs Make a Comeback in Enrollment.* `www.nytimes.com/2009/03/17/science/17comp.html`

[6] McGettrick, A., Roberts, E., Garcia, D. D., and Stevenson, C. 2008. Rediscovering the passion, beauty, joy and awe: making computing fun again. In *Proceedings of the 39th SIGCSE Technical Symposium on Computer Science Education* (Portland, OR, USA, March 12 - 15, 2008). SIGCSE '08. ACM, New York, NY, 217-218. `http://doi.acm.org/10.1145/1352135.1352213`

[7] Reges, S. Email to SIGCSE-members mailing list. *enrollment crisis over?* 2009-05-21.

Undergraduate Computer Science Education in China

Ming Zhang
School of Electronics Engineering
and Computer Science
Peking University
mzhang@net.pku.edu.cn

Virginia M. Lo*
Department of Computer
and Information Science
University of Oregon
lo@cs.uoregon.edu

ABSTRACT

This paper examines the current status of *professional computing education* for undergraduate majors and *fundamental computer education* for non-majors in China. We describe the evolution of computing education over the past decade and its role in meeting society's requirements for IT talent, and we discuss developing trends for computing education at China's universities. We conclude with a description of the Computer Science major at Peking University, one of the nation's leading research-based computer science departments.

Categories and Subject Descriptors

K.3.2 [**Computers and Education**]: Computer science education, curriculum.

General Terms

Design, Management, Standardization

Keywords

Computer science education, China, Peking University, School of Electronics Engineering and Computer Science

1. INTRODUCTION

In the 21st century, information technology has permeated every sector of life in China. The capabilities of collecting, presenting, storing, transferring, processing, controlling, and applying information are fundamental to daily life and have become an important aspect of basic literacy. The field of *computer science and technology* plays a pivotal role in the rapid growth of China's economy through the training of a talented pool of scientists, engineers, and IT professionals.

In this paper, we present developments in *professional computing education* for undergraduate majors and *fundamental computer education* for non-majors in China, as the nation moved from an elite computer education model to a "mass education" model.

While some aspects of the evolution of computer science education are unique to China, many issues are those faced by computer science educators worldwide regarding innovation, internationalization, and relevance to society's needs. As an example of the changes in computer science education in China, we describe the Computer Science major in the School of Electronics Engineering and Computer Science at Peking University, one of the nation's leading comprehensive research-based universities.

2. BACKGROUND IN COMPUTING EDUCATION IN CHINA

The flagship computing discipline in China is *Computer Science and Technology*. Established in 1956, this field has gone through over 50 years' development to become the largest undergraduate major in China [2].

The current curriculum for Computer Science and Technology was proposed in 1996, modeled after ACM Computing Curricula 1991. This curriculum emphasized computer software and computer applications, built on the foundations of computer science and engineering. However, the ACM curriculum model for computing education did not completely meet the economic needs nor the scale of the Chinese educational system.

In 1998, the policies of the Ministry of Education (MOE) in China promoted the transition from "elite education" to "mass education" by dramatically increasing university enrollments. Before 1998, only a very small elite group of students were admitted to China's universities through an intensely competitive national examination system. The change to "mass education" was driven by the huge growth in the high tech economic sector in China as well as the desire to expand educational opportunities to a greater portion of China's talented youth. Correspondingly, more and more universities built up their computer education programs. At the end of 1994, there were only 318 universities offering the computer specialty programs in China; and by 2002, there were 484 programs; by 2003, 505 programs, an increase of 4%; by 2004, 652 programs, an increase of 29% [6].

By the end of 2007, there were 598 universities that had departments of computer science running 847 computing related specialty programs, with total enrollment of over 430,000 undergraduates. In addition to these Computer Science and Technology programs, there were more than 10 computing related

SIGCSE'10, March 10–13, 2010, Milwaukee, Wisconsin, USA.

* Supported in part by NSF Grant #0722341, *CPATHi18n*: Internationalization of Computer Science: the Pacific Rim Community Model.

disciplines and nearly 2,000 related specialty programs with nearly 1,000,000 undergraduates. Table 1 gives the size of some of the key disciplines.

Table 1: Key Computer-related Disciplines (2005)

Discipline	Number of Departments
Computer Science and Technology	771
Information Management and Systems	501
Information and Computing Science	441
E-commerce	280
Educational Technology	202
Software Engineering	149
Geographic Information Systems	137
Network Engineering	115
Information Engineering	51
Information Security	49

Realizing the fact that increasing enrollments had adverse effects on the quality of education, the Ministry of Education in China started the "Quality Engineering Plan" (http://www.zlgc.org/) in 2003. The following six initiatives were carried out to improve and ensure the quality of higher education graduates: approval of novel specialty disciplines; recognition of national best courses, best textbooks and qualified course repositories; innovative practical education and training of China's talent pool; certification of distinguished teachers and qualified educational teams; evaluation of education quality; and higher education backup for China's western region. In addition, efforts were made to reform and improve creativity and to develop excellent quality curricula. In the same year, the Advisory Committee for the Computing Discipline of the Ministry of Education kicked off a program of reform for China's Computing Curricula. The main tasks of the Advisory Committee were as follows: advise the MOE regarding strategic directions for undergraduate disciplines; provide curriculum guidance to educational institutions; and supervise the evaluation of computing education.

Based on a set of field trips to 10 universities and 12 IT companies and based on information obtained through thousands of questionnaires, the following observations were made [7]: First, it takes too much time to train graduates to be ready to work in industry given the nation's intense workforce needs. In 2004, the MOE predicted that the incremental demand for computing talent is 1 million people per year. Second, students are losing confidence in the overall competence achieved through the Computer Science and Technology major, compared with other majors. "What is my core competence? The other majors seem to be able to do all I can do!" Seniors and graduates complain about the education/training received. Third, Computer Science and Technology has fallen from its rank as the 1st or 2nd choice by high school students when they chose majors in university to its current rank of 5th or 6th. Finally, despite government statistics that show a big shortage of IT professionals, the future for graduates is unbalanced. Top-level graduates in China are in very high demand and there is a severe shortage of these highly qualified individuals. Conversely, the unemployment problem for the graduates from lower-level institutions grew significantly after 2000 due to enrollment surges.

The Advisory Committee for the Computing Discipline identified four new challenges for computing professional education: (1) broadening of the discipline's intention; (2) development of greater independence of sub-disciplines within the discipline of computing; (3) addressing the diversity of society's needs for information technology; (4) coping with the popularization and huge scale of computing education. These factors impelled the Ministry of Education to analyze the precise role of computing education within the university educational system and the maximum utility of resources. Merely applying the name "Computer Science and Technology" to hundreds of new departments and programs was clearly not enough.

3. PROFESSIONAL COMPUTING EDUCATION FOR MAJORS

3.1 Pyramid Model of Computing Education

Based on research conducted by the Ministry of Education regarding the role of computing education and society's needs for computing professionals, a new pyramid model of computing education was developed that identified three basic directions for training the nation's high tech workforce: *Science-oriented, Engineering-oriented* and *Technology-oriented*, with the smallest talent pool at the top, and the largest talent pool at the bottom.

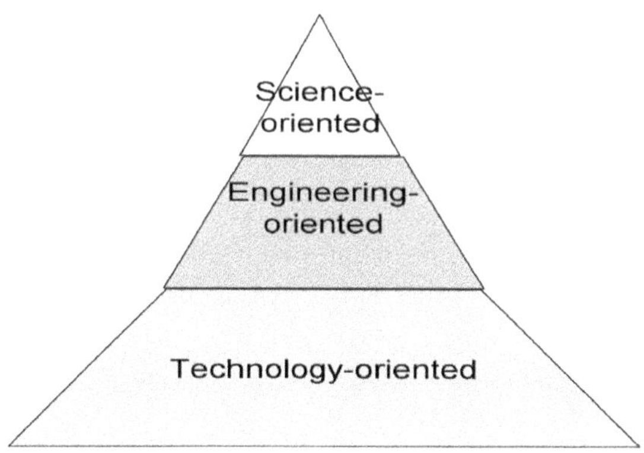

Figure 1: Pyramid Model of Computing Education

According to Denning et. al, the fundamental question underlying the discipline of computing is "what can be automated and how to compute effectively," approached through the three paradigms of theory, abstraction and design [5]. The goal of the pyramid model of computing education is to develop different talent pools working within various sub-disciplines and to utilize appropriate problem-solving methodologies within the three tiers of the pyramid.

Science-oriented talent focuses on "what can be automatically computed effectively." Education in this tier focuses primarily on theory and abstraction paradigms. This group comprises the nation's distinguished scientific talent pool. Their role in scientific discovery is innovation and creativity through research-oriented careers. *Engineering-oriented talent* is concerned with "how to implement automatic computing effectively and at low cost." Their focus is on theory and design paradigms through engineering solutions. Talented students in this pool are trained to master fundamental theories in order to guide engineering design and implementation. *Technology-oriented talent* is concerned with the goal of "making it convenient to use computer systems for automatic computing." The focus here is on the design paradigm. This talent pool learns theories of system construction and receives training in fundamental methods for problem description. With engineering at the forefront, this group is prepared to construct application-based computing systems that meet customers' needs.

3.2 Strategies for Professional Computing Education

Integrating the analysis and ideas of ACM-IEEE CC2005, the Ministry of Education suggested the following development strategies for professional computing education:

(1) Encourage universities to develop a variety of directions under the name "Computer Science and Technology" based on the trade-offs between societal needs and local or regional conditions, allowing local decision-making for curriculum development. Each university could name its departments as it saw fit and were no longer constrained to use the names of the major specialties currently approved by the Discipline Program Approval Committee of the Ministry of Education, shown in Table 1.

(2) Provide further educational opportunities for young teachers, enhancing their academic capabilities. Young teachers can study abroad with support from the China Scholarship Council, MOE and universities; visit other domestic universities; take free courses provided by the High Education Institutions Teacher online training center, paid by MOE, (http://www.enetedu.com/). Many places also provide summer seminar and training courses with very low registration fee. In 2001, the Ministry of Education sponsored the first University Course Forum of Computer Science to encourage teachers to exchange experiences and course materials.

(3) Enhance the practical and hands-on ability of students. With the increasing emphasis on engineering and technological education, experimental courses and internship opportunities are seen as important ways to help students improve their practical skills.

In a 2007 survey of 53 Chinese universities, 49 said the strategy was good for their departments, and 46 departments volunteered to serve as pilot programs. With the endorsement of MOE, the new strategies are being piloted in 14 universities and large scale practice is anticipated in the near future, followed by evaluation of these initiatives. In Section 5, we describe specific strategies employed by the School of Electronics Engineering and Computer Science at Peking University in Beijing.

4. FUNDAMENTAL COMPUTER SCIENCE EDUCATION FOR NON-MAJORS

China is also grappling with the challenge of providing *fundamental computing education* for non-computer science majors [4][5]. In 1999, courses in the fundamentals of computer science became required in most Chinese universities, challenging teachers with the role of educating huge number of students from many disciplines and with diverse computing backgrounds. During the next few years fundamental computing education made significant strides: the knowledge structure became more mature, integrated and systematic; the quality of teachers, textbooks, and the hardware environments greatly improved. However, university-level fundamental computing education has the following essential problems and challenges at present:

(1) The growth of computing-related disciplines. The universities need guidelines to keep abreast of the recent evolution in professional computing curricula into the five major computing areas identified by IEEE-ACM CC2005: CS (Computer Science), CE (Computer Engineering), SE (Software Engineering), IT (Information Technology) and IS (Information Systems) [1].

(2) Relationship to professional education in other disciplines. The requirements for IT skills in support of other disciplines are complex, diverse, and rapidly changing. The problem of designing fundamental computing education to fit the computing needs of a wide range of disciplines is truly daunting.

(3) The quality of fundamental computing education. The training of *huge* numbers of *high quality* IT professionals to meet China's needs has become the problem hotspot of fundamental computing education.

The current trends in fundamental computer education are characterized by "diversification, modularization, networking and integration" [8], meaning *diversification* in educational objectives, knowledge body, and teaching methods; *modularization* of the body of knowledge that is maximally adaptive to developments in IT and "student-oriented" educational ideology; embracing of *network-based* educational technologies available through the Internet; and *integration* of fundamental computer education with the professional education of other disciplines and of fundamental computer education with application-driven computer science. In addition, computer education for non-majors will "orient[ing] to applications, emphasizing on practice, focusing on information literacy and fitness" [8] [9] With the rapid growth of information technology, students should achieve basic information literacy as a foundation for lifelong learning and innovation, which is the final goal of higher education.

5. COMPUTER SCIENCE AT PEKING UNIVERSITY

Peking University, often referred to as the Harvard of China, is one of China's premier research universities.[1] At present, Peking

[1] Peking University and Tsinghua University, China's two most prestigious universities, as well as the Chinese Academy of Sciences, are located in the Haidian District, a western suburb of Beijing. Their campuses are adjacent to Zhonguancun (China's Silicon Valley) providing rich opportunities for interaction with the leading Chinese and international high tech companies.

University has 99 key national disciplines (among them 9 disciplines are nationally ranked number one), 271 research institutions and research centres, including 2 national engineering research centres, and 13 national key laboratories. Peking University is a comprehensive university with research and educational programs in the basic and applied sciences, social sciences, the humanities, engineering, medicine, law, journalism, management, and education. As an example of the many dimensions of computer science education in China, we briefly describe the Computer Science major at Peking University, housed in the School of Electronics Engineering and Computer Science (EECS).

5.1 Computer Science Major Requirements

Each year approximately 3600 new undergraduates matriculate at Peking University of which 340 are admitted to the School of Electronics Engineering and Computer Science.[2] EECS administers four majors: Computer Science and Technology, Electronics, Microelectronics, and Machine Perception. About 140 to 160 choose to major in Computer Science, and 40 to 60 choose to major in Machine Perception which is very close to Computer Science. The School of EECS sits at the top level of the computer education pyramid and provides science-based education for its highly talented group of students.

Those declaring CS as the major must fulfill the course requirements shown in Tables 2-4, and must further specialize in one of 9 subareas: theoretical computer science, software engineering, database and data management, computer networking, computer architecture, digital media and HCI, artificial intelligence and intelligent perceptiveness, knowledge discovery, or natural language processing. About 80% of the undergraduates apply to work in a faculty research lab. All students must complete a one-year experimental thesis and pass an oral defense. These requirements were instituted in 2007 as part of EECS's new strategies for curriculum reform and innovation.

Table 2. School of EECS Foundation Classes

Intro to Information Science and Technology *	
Mathematics Analysis I/II/III Advanced Math I/II Advanced Algebra I/II Linear Algebra	**Physics** Mechanics (A,B) Electromagnetism (A,B) Physics C
Programming Intro to Computing * Programming Lab Data Structures and Algorithms * Data Structures and Alg Lab	**Microelectronics** Microelectronics and Circuit Design Circuit Design Lab

Table 3. Computer Science Major Foundation Classes (in addition to EECS Foundations; * denotes core course)

Software Compiler and Compiler Lab * Operating Systems and Lab * Programming Languages Intro to Networking *	**Hardware** Digital Logic and Lab Microcomputer Architecture and Lab Computer Architecture and Lab
Theory Set Theory and Graph Theory Algebraic Structures and Combinational Theory Mathematical Logic Probability and Statistics Analysis of Algorithms	**Intelligence** Human Brain and Cognition Information Theory Artificial Intelligence Numerical Computing Signals and Systems

Table 4. Computer Science Electives

Programming Problem Solving and Programming Linux Programming MS Windows Programming Java Programming	**Software Engineering** Software Engineering Intro to Object-Oriented Design Intro to Middleware Software Testing Service Oriented Architecture
Theoretical Computing Intro to Theoretical Computer Science Intro to Random Processes Application of Primary Theory of numbers	**Data Management** Intro to Databases(Required) Database Theory and Practice Data Warehouse and Data Mining Web Data Management Spatial and Multimedia Database Systems
Computer Networking Networking (Required) Intro to Web Technology Network and Web Programming Network Protocol Analysis and Design Information Security Network storage	**Digital Media and HCI** Intro to Digital Media Digital Video Processing Computer Graphics Visual Computing and Processing Digital Art Human Computer Interfaces
Computer Architecture Assembly Language Embedded Systems Digital Signals and Multimedia Processing	**Natural Language Processing** Intro to Natural Language Processing Statistical Linguistic Analysis Intro to Modern Information Retrieval
Computer Intelligence and Knowledge Discovery Intelligent Information Processing Intro to Machine Learning Intelligent Information System Lab	**Intelligent Perspectives** Pattern Recognition Biological Signal Processing Digital Signal Processing Voice Signal Processing Digital Graphics Processing
Scientific Writing	**Adv. Information Technologies** Various courses
Senior Thesis (required)	

5.2 Innovation in Computer Science Education

The desire to foster creativity and innovative thinking has motivated redesign of the requirements within EECS to allow more free electives, research mentoring of students, close interactions with industry, and greater exposure to international opportunities. In 2007, the Computer Science Department set up an experimental program, the *Accelerated Course Plan*, to foster the development of a new generation of talented individuals

[2] Peking University is also home to the School of Software and Microelectronics which houses the engineering and application-based departments: Digital Arts and Design, Network and Communication Technology, Embedded Systems Engineering, Software Technology, E-Services, Management and Technology, IC Design and Engineering, Financial Information Engineering. This school was ranked number one of 36 schools of software established by the MOE's national initiative in engineering and technology-oriented education.

whose education emphasizes creativity, leadership, and international competence. The ACP was modeled after Peking University's *Yuanpei Project*, a university-wide initiative designed to train the best and brightest as the nation's future leaders. Under the *Computer Science Accelerated Course Plan*, eight accelerated core courses are offered in lieu of the normal courses: Advanced Introduction to Computer Science, Advanced Programming Practice, Advanced Data Structures and Algorithms, Advanced Operating System, Advanced Database System, Advanced Software Engineering, Advanced Compiler Theory and Advanced Computer Architecture. The nation's stellar high school students are recruited to this intensive program which allows them to quickly move into upper level courses and creative research.

Another area of innovation promotes cutting-edge academic-industry interaction. The department's Advanced Technologies course group sponsors courses to introduce new trends and developments in industry to our students, such as "Advanced IT Technology" taught by researchers from IBM's Computer Research Lab; "Parallel Computing in Multicore Architectures" taught by engineers from Intel; "Fundamental Storage Technology" taught by engineers from EMC.

In the arena of internationalization, our department hosts many international lecturers, and during the summer sends students to international exchange programs at UCLA, UC Berkeley, Stanford, Yale, the University of Illinois at Urbana-Champaign, and the University of Oregon, among others. We also offer a wide variety of international collaborative courses. From 2001 to 2006, we taught the introduction to web technology course in collaboration with the University of New England with total enrollment of over more than 500 students. Supported by University of Zurich, Switzerland, we successfully offered the Artificial Intelligence course broadcast by videoconference in 2004, which will be continued in fall 2009. See http://shanghailectures.org/.

In 2010, we will offer a collaboratively taught course in Global Distributed Software Engineering with the University of Oregon. Project teams made up of students from Peking University and the University of Oregon will work together across geographic, time zone, and cultural differences. This project is affiliated with the NSF CPATHi18n project.

6. CONCLUSION

Reform and innovation in computing education in China faces many challenges. In order to meet China's rapidly changing social and economic needs, higher computing education should update its educational objectives and ideology, rethink and re-invent the knowledge body of computing curricula, address the individualized needs and talents of its students, and be responsive to regional conditions. Furthermore, it is necessary to evolve pedagogical methods, re-educate faculty members and evaluate the efficiency and quality of education.

In addition, China should pursue forums for dialog with colleagues from other countries on the advances in computing education. In 2008, the First ACM Summit on Computing Education in China took place in Beijing, hosted by Tsinghua University. In October 2009, the Ministry of Education convened the 5th University Course Forum of Computer Science featuring leading U.S. computer science educators as the keynote speakers.

During the past decade much of the groundwork was laid for a renaissance in China's approach to computer science education. The next decade will be a time for continuing innovation, increasing internationalization, and broader expansion as we evaluate the outcomes of recent educational initiatives and explore the exciting future of computer science education in China and its role throughout the world.

7. ACKNOWLEDGMENTS

This paper was developed as part of the NSF funded project *CPATHi18n*: Internationalization of Computer Science Education, the Pacific Rim Community Model (www.cpathi18n.org) for the purpose of educating the computer science education community about developments in Pacific Rim computer science departments. Professor Zhang is a CPATHi18n partner, representing Peking University, and Professor Lo is co-PI for the CPATHi18n project. Thanks to Xiaoming Li and Zongli Jiang from the Advisory Committee of Computing Education China; Xiangkui Yao and Kiki Davis, University of Oregon, and the anonymous reviewers for help in the preparation of this paper.

8. REFERENCES

[1] ACM-IEEE CC2005. The overview report of computing curricula 2005

[2] Advisory Committee of Computing Education. 2005. The report of strategic study of computing curriculum in China. China University Teaching 5 (2005), 7-10.

[3] Advisory Committee of Computing Education. The fundamental computing curriculum for higher education in China. To be published by Press of High Education.

[4] Cortina, T. J., An introduction to computer science for non-majors using principles of computation. In Proceedings of the SIGCSE Conference (Covington, Kentucky, March 2007), 218-222.

[5] Denning, P. J. , Comer, D. E., Gries, D. et. al., 1989. Computing as a discipline. Communications of the ACM, 32, 1, 9-23.

[6] Li, X. and Lunt, B., 2006. Undergraduate computing education in China - a brief status and perspective. In Proceedings of SIGITE Conference (Minneapolis, Minnesota, USA, October 19-21, 2006), 35-38.

[7] Li, X., Chen, P., Zhang, M. and Zhu, M., 2004. Report of the social requirement of talents in computer science and technology. Journal of Computer Education 9 (2004), 11-18.

[8] Myers, J. P. Jr , 1989. The new generation of computer literacy. ACM SIGCSE Bulletin Archive, 21,1 (Feb. 1989), 177 – 181.

[9] National Research Council Computer Science and Telecommunications Board, 1999. Being fluent with information technology. Washington, DC National Academy Press, 1999

[10] Urban-Lurain, M. and Weinshank, D. J., 2000. Is there a role for programming in non-major computer science courses? Proceedings Frontiers in Education (Kansas City, Missouri, October 2000).

A Survey of Computer Science Teacher Preparation Programs in Israel Tells Us: Computer Science Deserves a Designated High School Teacher Preparation!

Noa Ragonis
School of Education - Computer Science Department
Beit Berl College, Israel
and Department of Education in Technology and Science
Technion – IIT
noarag@beitberl.ac.il

Orit Hazzan
Department of Education in Technology and Science
Technion – Israel Institute of Technology
oritha@tx.technion.ac.il

Judith Gal-Ezer
Computer Science Department
The Open University of Israel
galezer@cs.openu.ac.il

ABSTRACT

This paper focuses on the development and implementation of computer science (CS) teacher preparation programs, which are among the educational and pedagogical challenges faced by those involved in the current development of CS. It presents a survey that reflects the accumulative knowledge gained in Israel over the past twenty years with respect to CS teacher preparation. We explored nine institutes (six universities and three teacher education colleges) that offer CS teacher preparation programs. The survey indicates that while the programs vary in their implementation details, they are all motivated by the unique characteristics of CS, which play a central role in their design. We suggest that this observation further emphasizes the obvious: CS deserves designated CS teacher preparation programs. We therefore hope that this survey will contribute to the community of CS educators in general and to practitioners involved in developing CS teacher preparation programs in particular.

Categories and Subject Descriptors

K.3.2 [**Computers and Education**]: Computer and Information Science Education – *Computer science education, Curriculum.*

General Terms

Management, Performance, Human Factors.

Keywords

Computer science education, computer science teacher preparation, Methods of Teaching Computer Science course, practicum in computer science.

1. INTRODUCTION

The dynamic development of computer science (CS) poses a variety of pedagogical and educational challenges, including those that address high school CS teacher preparation, which are the focus of this paper. The importance of this topic emerges from the observation that though the international community of CS educators addresses it extensively, specific CS teacher preparation frameworks do not exist in most countries [1,4,8].

The Israeli high school CS curriculum [9] is considered one of the most advanced in the world [21,23,27]. Thus, there is an interest in the factors that foster its success, and particularly in CS teacher preparation programs, which play a critical role in the implementation of the curriculum. This interest motivated us to explore the current situation in Israel with respect to the structure and content of teacher preparation programs.

The survey presented in this paper is based on data collected from heads of CS teacher preparation programs and from instructors of the Methods of Teaching Computer Science (MTCS) course, which is one of the main components of many of these programs. The study addresses the rationale and implementation of the programs and highlights similarities as well as at differences between them. One of the main observations that emerged from the survey is that *the characteristics of the field of CS have a significant impact on the design of the surveyed CS teacher preparation programs*. We also found that most of the programs have a similar structure with relatively small variations in their implementation. In this paper, however, we focus mainly on the common aspects of the programs.

Most of the material presented here does not address a specific high school CS curriculum and, therefore, we suggest that it can be applied to a variety of CS curricula implemented in different countries. Specifically, based on the accumulative knowledge and experience we present, we suggest that each institution can tailor its CS teacher preparation program to fit its specific prospective CS teacher population.

2. SURVEY BACKGROUND

2.1 CS Teacher Preparation in the World

The rapid changes and development in the field of CS pose a huge challenge for designers of high school CS curricula and, consequently, for teacher preparation programs as well [6,15,17,23,26]. This fact is amplified due to the fact that in most countries no CS teacher preparation programs are offered [1,4,8], and further, no requirements for CS teaching certificates are defined. For example, according to a survey published in the USA in 2007 by the CSTA, only 53% of the 45 states that completed the survey declared that they have at least some defined requirements for a CS teaching license [3]. Two partial explanations of this are the fact that different states offer different CS high school curricula [21,27,28] and that no international or national standards exist for CS teacher preparation programs. Accordingly, in places where CS teacher preparation programs do exist, they usually address general principles of teaching science rather than focusing specifically on teaching CS. This lack of designated CS teacher preparation programs can, subsequently, explain why CS is taught in many high schools by mathematics teachers or teachers of other scientific disciplines [5,29].

Thus, the CS education community has expressed its awareness of the need for special teacher CS preparation programs by establishing the Computer Science Teachers Association (CSTA) [27,29], and supporting its various activities. A special CSTA task force report states, for example, that "Teachers must acquire both a mastery of the subject matter and the pedagogical skills that will allow them to present the material to students at appropriate levels." [27, p. 18]. This report also recommends defining standards for a CS teaching license, a fact that will eventually determine the contents to be included in CS teacher preparation programs.

Another CSTA report deals with ways to improve the teaching of CS in the high school, declaring that "It is also clear that teachers are the corner stone of successful curriculum implementation." [24, p. 40]. The report addresses the need to deal with the development of both pre-service and in-service CS teachers, and mentions the role of a professional CS teacher organization in the ongoing support and professional development of CS teachers. One attempt to support in-service CS teachers was reported by Carnegie Mellon University, which conducts a summer workshop for high school CS teachers with the objective of enriching their teaching materials [2].

Our literature review revealed that descriptions of CS teacher preparation programs in the international literature are rare, and if such descriptions exist, they are, in most cases, obsolete [7,14,19,20]. Recently, awareness of the topic has increased and several publications have been published on the topic. For example, Kolczyk (2008) deals with the teaching of basic concepts in algorithms in Poland [16] and Grugurina (2008) addresses CS teacher preparation in Groningen University in Holland [11]. And yet, no detailed descriptions of teacher preparation programs that could serve as a model for other places are to be found.

2.2 CS Teacher Preparation in Israel

Israel has a national-wide high school CS curriculum; thus, all CS high school students study according to the same curriculum. A general model for CS high school education in Israel is presented in [13] (see Figure 1). The model consists of interrelationships between four key components:

- A well-defined **CS curriculum**, including written text books and teaching guides;
- A requirement of a mandatory formal **CS teaching license**;
- **Teacher preparation programs**, including at least a bachelors degree in CS and a CS teaching certificate;
- **Research** in CS education.

We propose that each of these components, as well as the relationships among them, contribute to the infrastructure of the Israeli high school CS curriculum, and together make it one of the leading high school CS curricula in the world.

Figure 1: A model for a high school CS education program

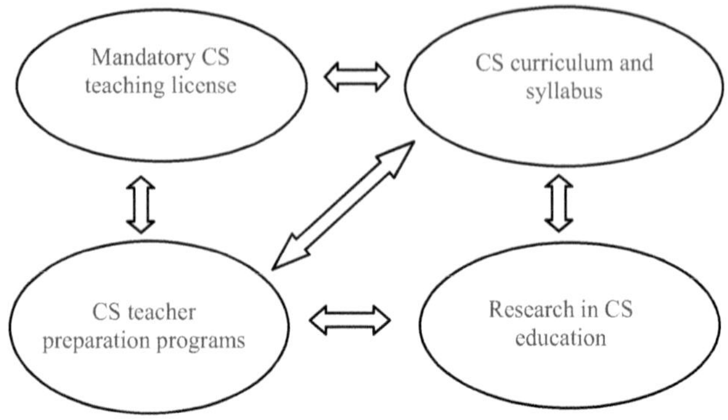

The survey presented in this paper focuses on the third component of the model – CS teacher preparation programs. Teacher preparation programs in Israel have two main frameworks:

a) *Teaching certificate* studies offered to graduate students who already have a bachelor's degree in CS.
b) *Bachelor of Education* (B.Ed.) studies that include disciplinary studies along with broad educational studies, which also provide a teaching certificate.

In both cases, the teacher preparation studies are based on four tires: (1) disciplinary studies; (2) general pedagogical studies (such as psychology and general teaching skills); (3) studies related to the didactics of the teaching of the discipline; and (4) practice teaching the discipline in school classes. The present survey focuses on the third and fourth tires – *the didactics and practice teaching of the discipline*, in our case, the teaching of CS.

According to our literature review, much of the literature on CS teacher preparation is based on the Israeli experience. For example, a series of papers published in *Inroads – The SIGCSE magazine* [12,18] describe the MTCS course at the Technion – Israel Institute of Technology and the CS practicum performed in high schools. Several other papers describe the integration of a tutoring model into the Technion's MTCS course [22] and another series of papers present a teacher preparation program offered by the Israeli Open University [10, 30]. The above-mentioned papers describe mainly teacher preparation programs offered by the Technion and the Israeli Open University; the survey presented in this paper widens the perspective and examines several additional Israeli universities and colleges that offer CS teacher preparation programs.

3. SURVEY DESCRIPTION

3.1 Survey Objectives

The survey objectives are to identify the rationale, core studies, and implementation model of Israeli CS teacher preparation programs.

3.2 Survey Participants

The survey was conducted in nine Israeli academic institutions that offer CS teacher preparation programs: five universities (the Technion – Israel Institute of Technology, The Open University of Israel, the Weizmann Institute, Tel-Aviv University, and Ben-Gurion University); one general college (the Jerusalem College of

Technology[1], with its subdivisions into Machon Lev and Machon Tal[2]), and three academic colleges of education (Beit Berl, Oranim, and Al-Qasemi College of Education[3]).

The participants from each institution included the heads of the CS teacher preparation programs and the instructors of the MTCS course. In total, data was collected from 14 participants (in some institutions the same person serves in both roles).

Among the heads of the CS teacher preparation programs, seven have been serving in this position between 8 to 17 years and seven are also the instructors in the MTCS Course.

Among the ten MTCS instructors, four have been teaching the course for over 10 years, three - between 5 and 9 years, and the other three - less than 5 years. All of them have also been coordinating the high school practicum for between 3 to 17 years.

Further, eight of the participants were and are involved also in the development of the national high school CS curriculum; ten are involved in the professional development of in-service teachers; eight are strongly involved in research in CS education, and seven were or are involved in teaching high school CS.

3.3 Data Resources

Data was collected using the following tools:

1. Open questionnaire distributed to the heads of the CS teacher preparation programs and to the instructors of the MTCS courses. The questionnaire addressed the personal credo of the research participants, the pedagogical objectives of the CS teacher preparation programs and of each of its elements, the professional skills that CS teachers should acquire, and details of how these topics are actually expressed in the program.
2. Documents that describe the rationale and structure of the CS teacher preparation programs.
3. Syllabi of the MTCS courses and descriptions of the practicum.

4. SURVEY FINDINGS

In this section, we present the survey findings with respect to the structure of the programs (Section 4.1), the survey participants' rationale and vision of the characteristics of CS and how they should be expressed and reflected in the teacher preparation programs (Section 4.2), and the programs' main components (Section 4.3).

4.1 The Structure of the Programs

As in any other discipline, CS teacher preparation programs are offered in two frameworks described in Section 2.2: (a) Teaching certificate and (b) Bachelor of Education (B.Ed.).

The surveyed programs are based on the following components (1 unit is ~ 28 academic hours):

(1) CS studies - either as a major or a minor;
(2) General pedagogical studies - 20-27 units;
(3) Didactics of CS - 2-6 units;
(4) Practicum in high school classes - 2-6 units.

It is noteworthy that all of the programs include, in their general pedagogical studies, courses that relate to research methods, and in most of the programs, students practice research skills within the CS discipline. This fact further illustrates the interconnections between the four elements of the Israeli high school CS education model (Figure 1).

4.2 The Essence of CS – The Participants' Perspective

One of the main findings of the survey reveals the common conception of all survey participants regarding the *essence of CS* and how *it inspires the actual implementation of the CS teacher preparation programs*.

In what follows, we present, and illustrate using the survey participants' words, the main characteristics of CS which in their opinion must be understood by prospective CS teachers (PCST).

- **CS is a dynamic field that keeps changing**
  - *PCST should feel comfortable with the frequent developments in the field, which enables them updating their teaching materials.*
  - *PCST should be able to read professional papers (in CS and in CS education research).*
- **CS knowledge and its interconnections with other disciplines**
  - *PCST should have sufficient professional knowledge in order to have the self-esteem required to teach the pupils.*
  - *PCST should have broad perception of the various aspects of CS and of its interconnections with other fields.*
- **The centrality of problem-solving processes in CS**
  - *Problem-solving processes are at the heart of CS and therefore should be at the heart of its teaching.*
  - *Pupils must become familiar with different programming paradigms to provide different perspectives of problem-solving processes.*
  - *CS teachers must be aware of learners' difficulties during problem-solving processes.*

4.3 Main Components of CS Teacher Preparation Programs

The survey participants addressed the importance that the PCST should acquire both *CS knowledge* (Section 4.3.1) and *CS pedagogical knowledge* (Section 4.3.2), and further, with respect to *CS pedagogy* - the importance of *integrating theory and practice*. Table 1 indicates the frameworks within which the PCST learn each component. In what follows, we elaborate on these components as expressed by the survey participants and demonstrate them using illustrative quotes.

Components of CS teacher preparation programs	Frameworks in which the PCST acquire this knowledge	
CS	- CS courses - MTCS - Designated courses offered by science education departments	
CS Pedagogy	Theory	- MTCS - Other designated courses
	Practice	- Practicum - MTCS

Table 1: Components of CS teacher preparation programs – the perspective of the survey participants

[1] The JCT institution combines professional studies with Jewish studies.
[2] Machon Lev is for men and Machon Tal is for women – Students learn in different courses up to the gender.
[3] Al-Qasemi College of Education teaches Arab students.

4.3.1 CS Topics

We start with several illustrative quotes that show the emphasis of CS knowledge in CS teacher preparation programs:

- o *PCST must grasp the connections between different topics in the field of CS.*
- o *PCST must acquire a broad perspective of the discipline at a high level of abstraction.*
- o *PCST must acquire extensive knowledge on topics that are not usually taught in regular CS degrees, such as the history of CS, CS scientists, and a discussion of what CS is.*

This CS knowledge is acquired in addition to courses studied as part of the CS studies, in designated courses offered by the science education departments that offer the CS teacher preparation programs. These courses focus on CS contents with special attention to aspects relevant to high school CS teaching.

4.3.2 CS Pedagogy Topics

This component focuses on pedagogical content knowledge (PCK) [25], i.e., pedagogical knowledge that is specifically relevant for teaching CS. Such knowledge is acquired mainly in the MTCS course and the practicum. The following participants' abbreviated quotes emphasize the need to combine theoretical subjects with their implementation in the teaching of CS in general, and the need to show the PCST ways to apply outcomes of CS educational research in their own teaching in particular.

We present the survey participants' perspective on the two aspects of teaching CS, theory and practice, when asked to describe their perceptions of two main components of the CS teacher preparation program – the MTCS course and the practicum in high school CS classes.

The MTCS Course

The survey participants addressed the following topics with respect to the MTCS course. As can be seen, most of the topics relate the theory with the practice of CS teaching. We note that only illustrative quotes are presented.

CS pedagogic theory

- o *PCST should acquire knowledge and tools for planning, creating and preparing lessons.*
- o *The studies must be based on recent CS education literature. It is important to facilitate guided discussions based on the learned material.*
- o *PCST should explore the main information resources like the ACM Digital Library and the Journal of Computer Science Education.*
- o *PCST must become aware of the need for ongoing learning, ongoing reflection and ongoing professional development.*

Familiarity with the high school CS curriculum

- o *PCST should become familiar with the national high school CS curriculum they intend to teach.*
- o *PCST should become familiar with CS curricula used abroad.*
- o *The curriculum should be broken down into main topics and each topic should be addressed from different perspectives.*

The teacher's perspective

- o *A teaching toolbox should be anchored in the CS learning content: active learning, inquiry learning, peer teaching, teaching in the lab, learning by projects, animation and visualization tools, internet, games, different kinds of questions, patterns.*
- o *[Students'] problems that emerge should be discussed and coping approaches should be offered.*
- o *How to plan a teaching sequence and a lesson for a specific topic defined in the curriculum.*
- o *PCST should acquire strategies to evaluate pupils' products: class assignments, homework, exams, projects.*
- o *PCST should employ ongoing reflective thinking to improve their performance.*
- o *PCST should become familiar with the main online information resources that the CS teachers can use.*

The pupil's perspective

- o *PCST should increase their awareness to pupils' learning processes and difficulties.*
- o *PCST should analyze students' difficulties and typical mistakes in different topics of the curriculum.*
- o *PCST should adapt learning materials to meet the needs of pupils with different cognitive skills.*

The survey participants also referred to the teaching strategies applied in the MTCS course. These strategies should serve as an example for good teaching and should combine all of the above perspectives.

The practicum

The survey participants use the MTCS course as an opportunity to prepare the prospective CS teachers for their practicum in high school CS classes, as is described in what follows:

- o *The practicum provides an opportunity to apply, for the first time, the theoretical knowledge the PCST are exposed to in the* [MTCS] *course. The students prepare and teach mini-lessons to their peers in the course and get their feedback.*
- o *A tutoring project is integrated in which each PCST tutors another university student who is taking an introductory CS course.*

The objectives of the actual practicum that takes place in high school classes, as perceived by the survey participants, address benefits beyond the acquisition of actual teaching experience. As is illustrated in what follows, the participants also address the benefits gained from observing the mentor-teacher teaching and from the actual opportunity of becoming familiar with the school system, from a teacher's perspective.

First teaching experience

- o *PCST gain some basic experience in the preparation of CS lessons.*
- o *PCST gain some basic and initial experience in teaching CS.*

Observing the mentor-teacher

- o *PCST observe the teaching of lessons in the computer lab and in the traditional class.*
- o *PCST observe different aspects of school teaching, such as pupils' behavior, teacher-pupil discourse, class atmosphere*
- o *PCST benefit from the guidance and supervision of an expert.*

Becoming familiar with the school system

- o *PCST are first introduced to high school pupils.*
- o *PCST participate in the different activities that their mentor-teachers are involved.*

5. Discussion

The accumulative experience gained in Israel during the past two decades with respect to CS teacher preparation delivers a very clear message: *Since CS has unique characteristics,* ***designated*** *CS teacher preparation programs should be offered.* This message has two main implications: (1) only teachers with formal CS background should teach CS in the high school; and (2) a general science-teaching certificate is not sufficient for teaching CS. We intend to follow up this survey by interviewing the survey participants and examining additional details of the actual application these programs (e.g., hours allocated to each aspect of the above findings).

ACKNOWLEDGMENTS

We would like to thank all of the survey participants who dedicated time and responded to our questionnaires. Their contribution is highly appreciated.

6. REFERENCES

[1] Armoni, M. (in preparation): Looking at Secondary Teacher Preparation through the Lenses of Computer Science – a Literature Survey.

[2] Blum, L. and Cortina, T. J. (2007). CS4HS: an outreach program for high school CS teachers. *ACM SIGCSE Bulletin*, 39(1), 19-23.

[3] CSTA (2007). Computer Science State Certification Requirements - CSTA Certification Committee Report, http://www.csta.acm.org/ComputerScienceTeacherCertification/sub/TeachCertRept07New.pdf [2009, July]

[4] CSTA (2008). Ensuring Exemplary Teaching in an Essential Discipline: Addressing the Crisis in Computer Science Teacher Certification, *Final Report of the CSTA Teacher Certification Task Force*. http://www.csta.acm.org/Communications/sub/DocsPresentationFiles/CertificationFinal.pdf [2009, July]

[5] Deek, F. P. and Kimmel, H. (1999). Status of computer science education in secondary schools: one state's perspective. *Computer Science Education*, 9(2), 89-113.

[6] Eurydice (2004). Key Data on Information and Communication Technology in Schools in Europe. *Eurydice, The information network on education in Europe*, Belgium. http://www.eurydice.org/ressources/eurydice/pdf/0_integral/048EN.pdf [2009, July]

[7] Frederick, T. J. (1975). Computer science education for students training to be secondary teachers. *ACM SIGCUE Outlook*, 9(SI), 10-14.

[8] Gal-Ezer, J. (1995). Computer science teachers' certification program. *Computers and Education*, 25(3), 163-168.

[9] Gal-Ezer, J. and Harel, D. (1999). Curriculum and course syllabi for a high-school CS program. *Computer Science Education*, 9(2), 114-147.

[10] Gal-Ezer, J. and Zur, E. (2007). Certification via distance learning. *Mathematics and Computer Education* 41(3), 250-265.

[11] Grugurina, N. (2008). Computer Science Teacher Training at the University of Groningen. *Lecture Notes in Computer Science 5090, ISSEP 2008* (272-281).

[12] Hazzan, O. and Lapidot, T. (2004). The practicum in computer science education: Bridging gaps between theoretical knowledge and actual performance, *inroads – the SIGCSE Bulletin*, 36(4), 47-51.

[13] Hazzan, O., Gal-Ezer, J. and Blum, L. (2008). A model for high school computer science education: the four key elements that make it!, *ACM SIGCSE Bulletin*, 40(1), 281-285.

[14] Heeler, P.J. (1983). A master's degree in school computer studies. *ACM SIGCSE Bulletin*, 15(1), 99-103.

[15] Kavander, T. and Salakoski, T. (2004). Where have all the flowers gone? — Computer Science education in general upper secondary schools. Proceedings of the Fourth Finnish/Baltic Sea Conference on Computer Science Education 2004, Koli, Helsinki University,Finland,112-115.

[16] Kolczyk, E. (2008). Algorithm – Fundamental Concept in Preparing Informatics Teachers. *Lecture Notes in Computer Science 5090, ISSEP 2008* (265-271).

[17] Kushan, B. (1994). Preparing programming teachers.. *ACM SIGCSE Bulletin*, 26(1), 248-252.

[18] Lapidot, T. and Hazzan, O. (2003). Methods of teaching a computer science course for prospective teachers. *Inroads – the SIGCSE Bulletin* 37(4), 79-83.

[19] Moursund, D. (1978). Computer science education for preservice elementary school teachers. *ACM SIGCUE Outlook*, 12(4), 3-10.

[20] Poirot, J., Luerhmann, A., Norris, C., Taylor, H. and Taylor, R. (1985). Proposed curriculum for programs leading to teacher certification in computer science. *Communications of the ACM* 28(3), 275-279.

[21] Ragonis, N. (2009). Computing Pre-University: Secondary Level Computing Curricula. In Ed. Benjamin W. Wah. (Eds.): *Wiley Encyclopedia of Computer Science and Engineering* 5(1), 632-648. John Wiley & Sons, Inc., Hoboken, NJ, USA.

[22] Ragonis, N. and Hazzan, O. (2008). Disciplinary-pedagogical teacher preparation for pre-service computer science teachers: Rationale and implementation. *Lecture Notes in Computer Science 5090, ISSEP 2008* (253-264).

[23] Ragonis, N. and Hazzan, O. (2009). Integrating a tutoring model into the training of prospective Computer Science teachers. *Journal of Computers in Mathematics and Science Teaching* 28(3), 309-339.

[24] Stephenson, C., Gal-Ezer, J., Haberman, B. and Verno, A. (2005). The new educational imperative: Improving high school computer science education. Final report of the CSTA Curriculum Improvement Task Force http://csta.acm.org/Communications/sub/DocsPresentationFiles/TCEAPres07.pdf [2009, September].

[25] Shulman, L. S. (1986). Those who understand: Knowledge growth in teaching. *Educational Teacher,* 15(2), 4-14.

[26] Taylor, H. G. (1997). The evolution of standards for accrediting computer science teacher preparation programs. *ACM SIGCSE Bulletin* 29(1), 67-71.

[27] Tucker, A., Deek, F., Jones, J., McCowan, D., Stephenson, C. and Verno, A. (2004). A Model Curriculum for K-12 Computer Science. The ACM K-12 Education Task Force http://www.csta.acm.org/Curriculum/sub/ACMK12CSModel.html [2009, September]

[28] Weinstein, P. and Resnick, M. (1999). Computer programming revisited. *Technology and Learning*, 19(8), 38-42.

[29] White, J. (2004). Computer science teachers association report for ACM's sigs, http://www.acm.org/sigs/sgb/minutes/agenda100304_3_2.ppt [2009, September]

[30] Zur, E. and Vilner, T. (2004). Teaching certificate in computer science – didactics workshop. *ACM SIGCSE Bulletin* 36(3), 24.

The Interaction Between High School Curriculum and First Year College Courses: The Case of Computing

Adnan H. Yahya
Department of Computer Systems Engineering
Birzeit University, Birzeit, Palestine
yahya@birzeit.edu

ABSTRACT

Many countries, including those in the developing world, have introduced mandatory Information Technology (IT) courses for high school (HS) students. This was motivated by the importance of IT skills for the general population in view of the widespread use of computers. The HS curriculum is frequently decided upon by university faculty, with university needs very much in mind. A steady shift of introductory college level material to HS curriculum is observed. With all the positive effects of IT HS education, the issue of how to modify the first year computing courses to account for the material transferred to HS had to be addressed. The problem is complicated by the nonuniform adoption of IT education in high schools even within a single country, the varying emphasis on theory vs. practice in HS courses and the differences in the availability of resources at high schools, inadequacy of testing procedures and, in the case of many developing countries, the language of instruction difference between HS and college. Ignoring the HS curriculum when designing college level courses is a waste of resources and may render the college classes boring for many students. Accounting for the HS computing education at the college level may require a suite of placement tests. Even then, it may not be straightforward to figure out how to modify each of the introductory college courses to account for the HS material. On the example of the completely revamped IT education in Palestinian schools, which introduced mandatory technology education for grades 5-12 for all HS students, we discuss the dilemma of how to account for the HS IT knowledge and skills at the college level, especially the way this should affect the first computing courses at the college level, which has been a topic of debate in the last years.

Categories and Subject Descriptors

K.3.2 [**Computer and Information Science Education**]: *Computer science education, Curriculum*

General Terms

Design, Standardization.

Keywords

High School Curriculum, K12 Computer Education, Computer Science Curriculum, Model Computer Curriculum.

1. INTRODUCTION

In many countries there is strong realization that computing skills are essential for citizens being able to lead their everyday life in an efficient manner and to benefit from the multiplicity of information technology based services that are being offered. The average citizen's need for these skills has been continuously shifting to earlier ages. Even school students find it essential to use the Internet for their research assignments and to use computers to write reports, give presentations and to gain access to the ever expanding IT-enabled educational resources. Web based sources such as dictionaries and the Wikipedia are proving popular with a growing number of students. Internet based social networking is gaining acceptance for many, including kids. Modern communications and gaming are having more of the characteristics of computing. Additionally, computing has established itself as a discipline and potential career path to which students may need to be exposed in sufficient depth and breadth to be able to make informed career decisions in the future.

To meet the demands for computer literacy, many countries have resorted to including Information Technology as a study subject early in their education system. For example, in Palestine, IT studies start as early as the fifth grade and continue, in increasing doses, till high school matriculation. While early on, concentration may be on skills and general concepts, later study shifts to the basics of computing. These are topics that have been traditionally covered at the college level. This applies to both the skills needed by non-IT college students that are very much covered in HS and also some of the material in introductory college computer science courses. This implies a shift of material that has been part of the college IT education to the high school level which may necessitate adjustments in the college curriculum. The adjustment task is not a straightforward matter. It is complicated by factors like the high school material having the breadth, but not necessarily the depth, of college courses, the nonuniform nature of the preparation of incoming students, the differences in the language of instruction, the testing approaches and the rigor in which the material is covered at various levels and the rapidly changing nature of information technology which may render skills/knowledge obsolete fast.

In the remainder of this paper we will discuss the issue of the interaction between high school curriculum and college curriculum on the example of the Palestinian school system which introduced compulsory IT education for grades 5-12. We first describe the Palestinian educational environment then we report on our experience in adapting the college IT material to take into account the skills/knowledge of incoming students and the problems associated with that and the way things may develop in the future.

2. THE ENVIRONMENT

In this section we outline the state of high school and college technology curriculum in Palestine to highlight the issues raised by the recent developments in this area.

2.1 High School Curriculum

The Palestinian educational system has undergone dramatic changes with the introduction of the unified Palestinian curriculum starting 1995. Unified because it was adopted in all Palestinian schools in all parts of the Palestinian territories: the West Bank including East Jerusalem and Gaza. Earlier the former had a curriculum heavily influenced by the Jordanian system and the latter had a curriculum heavily influenced by the Egyptian system. One of the new features of the new curriculum is the adoption of English instruction from first grade and the introduction of technology education from grade 5 on, for all students of all streams (science, arts and vocational) and in all schools (public, semipublic and private). On the average students learn technology for 2 hours a week in every one of grades 5-12. The topics covered include engineering drawing, material sciences, electronics and digital circuits, electricity and protection and information technology. IT features prominently at all levels and in the last 2 grades of high school (grades 11 and 12) only information and communications technology (ICT) education is offered. As is the case for all other subjects, the language of instruction for technology and IT school education is Arabic. The first class of students who completely followed the Palestinian curriculum graduated from HS in 2006 and are currently in their sophomore year at college. Currently, the total number of students in Palestinian schools is 1,104,208 students evenly split between males and females. The number of those getting some sort of instruction in information technology is 571314 of which 285,126 are females (Grades 5-10). 142,481 students, of which 75,312 females, are being instructed in IT alone (grades 11 and 12)[4]. The original plan envisioned that 5.6% of educational hours be allocated to Technology and Applied Sciences[5] with 2 weekly hours devoted to these subjects for the 8 academic years of grades 5-12. The current school curriculum adheres closely to this vision[5].

On average, information technology occupies about one third of technology instruction in grades 5-10. Topics covered include basic Internet search, communications basics, basic computer algorithms and programming (Visual Basic), computer ethics and social implications (though not as a distinct topic) and basic computer construction. Packages covered include word processing, spreadsheets, computer based technical drawing, and more. For grades 11 and 12 the topics covered and the hours devoted to each are given in the following table[5]:

#	Topic	(Grade) Hrs First Semester	(Grade) Hrs Second Semester	**Total Hrs**
1	Basic Computing Concepts	(11) 10	(11) 5	**15**
2	Problem Solving, Algorithms and Programming	(11) 13	(11) 20	**33**
3	Communication Networks and Internet	(12) 11	(12) 10	**21**
4	Multimedia and Web Design	(12) 15		**15**
5	Databases		(12) 15	**15**
6	Computer Maintenance	(11) 15		**15**
Total hours 11th grade		38	25	63
Total hours 12th grade		26	25	51
Total Hours		**64**	**50**	**114**

Table 1: IT Education for 11th and 12th Grades, all Streams[5]

One of the main problems facing technology instruction in Palestinian HS is the insufficient resource availability, both instructors and laboratory equipment. The diverse material covered in the technology curriculum makes it difficult for teachers in traditional disciplines to teach the multiplicity of topics at a reasonable level. The pay levels make teaching unattractive to computer science and engineering graduates. While certain universities are beginning to offer degrees in *teaching technology* at HS, the outcome is still in need of evaluation. Many schools do not have adequate laboratory resources in terms of numbers, availability and quality in the rapidly changing field of IT. Additionally, the need for regular revision of school curriculum to account for technology development and lessons learned was evident from the start. However, for various reasons the revision was substantially delayed and only started recently.

2.2 College Curriculum:

Most Palestinian universities require all their students to take courses in computing, with minor variations between schools[8]. For example, computer instruction is compulsory for all students at Birzeit University (8000 students, 56% of which are females)[3]. Students have to take one of the following two courses:

2.2.1 Basic Computer Programming; for the scientific colleges, in this case colleges of Engineering, Information Technology and Science. This mandatory course teaches basic computer programming with an introduction to computing and algorithms. Calculus is a prerequisite for this course but no computer skills are assumed. The language of choice varies and the course has a major lab components where students practice hands on programming under the supervision of their instructor.

2.2.2 Introduction to Computing: for the social sciences, commerce, law and public administration students the required course is non-technical introduction to computing that surveys basic computer architecture but focuses on the basic skills including operating systems, word processing, spreadsheets, presentation software with emphasis of Microsoft Office suite, and web search and ethics. While this is a freshman level course, many students tend to delay taking it until later in their university education. There are no prerequisites for this course and it assumes no previous computer knowledge or mathematical skills. The language of instruction for the computing courses at the college level is English. However, subject matter instruction at the colleges taking the introductory non-technical computer course is mainly in Arabic. The students taking the non technical computing course are of varied backgrounds in terms of their mathematical knowledge and computer skills, as many college majors accept HS graduates from both scientific and social sciences streams. However, the policy is to have all students, independent of their backgrounds, take the same course in mixed sections. The university has no policy of requiring a placement exam or a waiver for people with computing skills, though the university has an elaborate system with placement tests and varying university requirements for English language proficiency.

Now that the incoming class has been heavily instructed in computing, both at the technical and skills levels, the previous introductory offering is no longer sustainable. Retaining the same course content is a waste of resources since most incoming students have the skill level sought by the course. The situation is more complicated during the current transition stage when students have widely diverse computing backgrounds due to the varied HS experiences.

3. THE PROBLEM

In this section we address the problems facing the interaction between HS and College curriculum at two levels; that of the general, nontechnical computing course mandatory for students outside science and engineering and technical computer courses required for science/engineering students.

3.1 General Computer Skills Course:

The content of the traditional skills based nontechnical college computer course for non science/engineering students is almost fully covered in the HS curriculum, certainly in breadth and to a large extend in depth. One main difference is that the HS curriculum is delivered in Arabic while the college level course is basically in English. Also much of the instruction at the college level is delivered in the lab using a hands-on approach. To account for the overlap between HS and college material three options have been under consideration:

1. Mostly stick with the old college content on the assumption that it never hurts to refresh the required skills, more so that many of the skills have been taught a long time ago, used older versions of the applications and also to account for the language switch and the change in instruction mode. The drawback is the wasted resources, the weak motivation for students to do well at the school level and the false impression this approach creates about the nature of university instruction.
2. Assume that students already have the skills required and scrap the college level computer literacy course in as far as it touches on issues covered in school curriculum. The main drawback here is that the skill level may not be sufficient or uniform for all students because of the different levels of exposure to lab work and the skill levels of the teachers and availability of resources during HS years. This approach will perpetuate the weakness of certain students in IT skills and will make it difficult for the university departments to make assumptions about the IT skill levels of its students and to incorporate that into curriculum design.
3. Build on the HS curriculum and direct the college course to areas not covered in HS be it breadth-wise by selecting topics of interest to students but not covered in HS. Such topics may include discipline specific packages: e.g. SPSS for social sciences, E-commerce for Commerce students, law reasoning programs for law students. Or depth-wise by having students go deeper into topics already covered in high school. Examples are more elaborate use of word processing packages, more advanced features of presentation software, and so on. Once more, the nonuniform nature of student preparation and the difficulty of building on their previous knowledge is an obstacle to such an approach. The need for in depth coverage may not be evident for the regular packages for non-IT experts.

3.2 Technical Computing Courses:

As for the technical IT courses, the intersection between high school material and several college level courses is substantial. However, none of the technical IT college courses is completely covered in high school curriculum. The following points are evident:

1. While students study algorithms and data structures, the depth is not college level. Students touch on basic *sort* and *search* algorithms but without theoretical analysis. The reason is that the high school material doesn't assume the mathematical skill assumed for the college courses since it is delivered to students with widely varying backgrounds. This may apply also to Databases.
2. The programming material may be substantial. However, the language of choice (Visual Basic) is not the same as that for college (C, Java,...). The problems and projects in HS are simpler in nature than those one would expect at the college level.
3. The computer basics covering the foundation of computer construction, CPU components and operating systems are shallower than the material covered in an introductory computer organization course at college. Similar reasoning will apply to database and communications material.
4. The switch in the language of instruction from Arabic in High School to English in college is present in all components.

Nevertheless, two points are clear. The HS material covers the introductory material in several courses and makes some of the concepts offered there familiar to the degree that they can be skipped. Certain students may have done much better than others in HS to the degree that they can skip one of the basic computing courses or they can realistically take an alternative, more advanced, course in place of the basic one.

This content overlap problem is not unique to computing. There is substantial degree of duplication between the HS material and the introductory college courses in the sciences as well. The overlap there is much more evident to the degree that the first mathematics, physics and chemistry college courses are more than 80% covered in high school at similar depth though in Arabic. These courses are prerequisites to more advanced courses in the respective discipline. This is troubling many people designing curricula, say in engineering, where they don't appreciate the need to restudy the HS material before proceeding to new stuff and the associated loss of highly sought after credit hours. One of the factors hindering changes are the comparisons with other countries whose students may not have overlapping material and the fear of loss of teacher load by the respective departments. We believe that any solutions applicable to computing will be more so to introductory science courses.

4. POSSIBLE SOLUTIONS

Here too, we offer the solutions to the problem at hand in two phases: general, nontechnical and technical computing. Our solutions were justified mostly by the local experiences. It seems to us that the widespread computer curricula recommendations for high schools[1] and undergraduate college levels[2] do not explicitly address the issue considered in this article despite the specification of various models for K12 curriculum, including the Advanced Placement (AP) targeting students who plan a career in computer science, business or related fields[1].

4.1 General Literacy Computing Course:

A uniform solution that calls for having all students attend the same course seems to be problematic no matter what the nature of the course offered is. Students mathematical backgrounds are different since several colleges accept both science and arts streams HS graduates. Requiring stronger mathematical content will render the course inaccessible to arts students. A descriptive non-math based course will be too easy, and even dull for the science stream students. Offering two different college courses to account for varying student math skills is another option. However, this may be difficult to justify since both groups are majoring in the same field and their IT needs should be the same. However, if handled properly, having students with varying IT skills beyond the minimum required in a class may be desirable by having students learn by example from their colleagues with more advanced IT skills.

The other option is to have a skill based course, with a clear designation of the skills that a student must develop by the end of the course. The level of the course must reflect the stage at which these skills are required. For example, with the current emphasis on writing, presentation and Internet research skills, the course is better offered at the freshman level. Students will be required to take a placement exam to determine the degree to which they meet the skills proficiency. Those who do well are exempted from the course and those who don't are required to take the course as a remedial, and still skills based course. They need to retake the test once again after they take the course. However, contrary to the current practice, students will be able to repeat the course only once after which they have to pass the test on their own. The testing process may be independent of the college and one may refer to standardized tests such as ICDL to guarantee consistency and test neutrality.

4.2 Technical Computer Science:

Since no single university course is rendered completely redundant by the material covered in HS, the courses with substantial coverage must be modified to account for the overlap, both in depth and breadth. While the instructor can still survey the HS material, that must be done minimally and in a volume that will help students reload the context. Using this approach we estimate that certain courses may be reduced by about 30%, an amount that can be used to go deeper into new material and extend the course coverage. It may be the case that the coverage of the college level material can be accomplished in less courses, or les credit hours, than is currently possible. The savings can be used to add totally new courses to the college curriculum to account for newer trends and more advanced topics. Historically, departments were interested in exceeding the number of hours allocated for the programs they are offering so such an approach will alleviate this restriction. If at any later stage it transpires that certain college courses are (almost) completely covered in HS these courses should be treated as the fully covered non technical course.

One problem with this approach is that the level of incoming students may not be uniform. Instructors may find it difficult to go deeper into the course when not all their students are adequately skilled in high school material. We believe that the way to go around this is to assume that each student has good knowledge of the HS material and for the college curriculum to be based on this assumption. The skill/knowledge level of students must be tested through an entrance/placement exam. Students found to have inadequate skills may be required to have one or more remedial course to bring them up to the required standard.

4.3 Remedial Nature of Introductory Courses:

We would like to emphasize that we are advocating the use of remedial courses to bring all students to the required skill level. The usual practice has been to use the "when in doubt redo the high school material at the college level" approach. We believe that the current approach is counterproductive in more than one way. There seems to be no clear evidence to indicate that the repetition helps improve the skill level substantially. On the negative side, many students find the repetition boring and are getting a false impression about the novelty of university education. On the positive side, under the new approach students will tend to take HS curriculum more seriously and invest more in getting the required skills to avoid the college level repetition and the associated costs. One additional advantage is that if designed well, the entrance exams will reflect positively on the type of material emphasized at the school level where traditionally much memorizing is the common approach as opposed to critical analysis and thinking. High school teachers are bound to take notice of the skills needed and to start stressing them in their instruction. One may even predict a situation where the general HS matriculation exams merge with the entrance exams offered by universities to the advantage of not only the educational system but also to the market through students who do not enroll in college.

We anticipate some difficulties in adopting any of the mentioned solutions. Academic considerations may not be the only factors affecting the decision on the possible solution to the problem. Issues like student and faculty members readiness /resistance to adopt these solutions and the associated changes, the need for monitoring procedures to evaluate the new course content and delivery methods are real obstacles that need to be overcome. Logistics and cost considerations, especially those associated with administering proper, skill-based placement exams for a large student population may also prove a real problem that may require a nationally coordinated effort to minimize overhead and to eliminate duplication and spare students the need to take a multiplicity of exams for several schools they are considering applying to.

5. CONCLUSION

In this paper we have addressed the issue of how the increasing doses of high school information technology education can influence and be influenced by the content of introductory computing courses at the college level. We argued that taking account of the interaction between the two is not a trivial matter and may have profound implications for the types of skills high school students achieve, the mode of course delivery and testing used at HS. We advocated the use of placement tests, initially administered by colleges, to determine the computing knowledge/skill level of incoming students and to require students not passing a given threshold to take remedial courses, thus giving a clear advantage to students with better HS skills as opposed to the current practice of requiring all students to (re)take material generally based on least common HS skills of the incoming students. This approach may be as relevant to two year community colleges[7]. It need not be unique to computing but can be easily extended to other disciplines as well. We believe that this approach has the added advantage of being adaptive to future changes to HS and College curricula, a frequent occurrence in a field characterized by rapid changes in technology and systems. This dynamism is lacking in the traditional educational system characterized by its high inertia, and which has been struggling with how to incorporate into the HS matriculation exams disciplines with a major practical/skills component such as IT courses.

6. REFERENCES

[1] ACM Model Curriculum Committee, *"ACM K-12 CS Model Curriculum", 2nd Edition.* 2003. http://csta.acm.org/Curriculum/sub/ACMK12CSModel.html

[2] ACM Model Curriculum Committee. "Computing Curricula 2005: The Overview Report". 2005. http://www.acm.org/education/curricula-recommendations

[3] Birzeit University. "Facts and Figures". 2009 http://www.birzeit.edu/about_bzu/

[4] Palestinian Ministry of Education. "Preliminary Statistics for the academic year 2007/2008". 2008. http://www.moehe.gov.ps/stats/generalstat2008.xls

[5] Palestine Curriculum Development Center. Palestinian School Textbooks, 2009. http://www.pcdc.edu.ps/ http://www.pcdc.edu.ps/textbooks/index.htm

[6] Palestine Curriculum Development Center and Unesco. First Palestinian Curriculum Plan 1998. http://www.pcdc.edu.ps/first_curriculum_plan.pdf

[7] The Computing Competitiveness Council "21st Century Computing Education for South Carolina: Recommendations for Change". Summer 2007 www.csta.acm.org/Research/sub/New_Folder/ResearchFiles/CCCProposal.pdf

[8] Palestinian Ministry of Education and Higher Education. Information Technology Programs at Palestinian Universities General Evaluation Report. April 2007. http://www.aqac.mohe.gov.ps/EngV/Aqac_Index/AQACfiles/FinalGeneralITReport.pdf

Internationalization of Computer Science Education

Sarah Douglas, Art Farley, Ginnie Lo, Andrzej Proskurowski, Michal Young
Department of Computer and Information Science
University of Oregon, Eugene, OR, USA
[douglas, art, lo, andrzej, michal]@cs.uoregon.edu

ABSTRACT

Internationalization of computer science education involves incorporating awareness, knowledge and skills of professional life in a global environment. Through an NSF CPATH grant[1] we have established a Pacific Rim community of computer science departments, high tech industry and international programs exploring a new model of computer science education that focuses on the knowledge, skills and competencies necessary for professional success and leadership in a global context. This paper describes our progress in building an international community of computer science educators, as well as our efforts in curricular innovation and establishment of international summer schools. Internationalization of computer science education will help attract the best and brightest students and broaden the appeal of computer science to a much more diverse population. Computer science will be seen as a pathway to a career not in an isolated cubicle but in the wide-open world.

Categories and Subject Descriptors

K.3.2 [**Computers and Education: Computer science education, curriculum**]:

Keywords

Computer science education, internationalization, computers in society

1. INTRODUCTION

Today, both scientific inquiry and economic enterprise are global, but computer science education has remained largely parochial in both course content and student experiences. This raises the following important question: *What must we do to transform American undergraduate computer science education to prepare our students to work and to lead in a global community of computing professionals?* We will call this transformation internationalization, or *i18n*, borrowing the abbreviation for "internationalization" from the software development community.

Through a series of workshops and other activities we have established a Pacific Rim community of computer science departments, high tech industry and international programs exploring a new model of computer science education that focuses on the knowledge, skills and competencies necessary for professional success and leadership in a global context. Our community and experience can serve as a resource and model for creating similar communities nationwide. In this paper, we report on the activities of our community and discuss the results of our international collaboration toward building a common understanding of the importance of internationalization for computer science education.

2. COMMUNITY BUILDING

An integral part of our effort to develop an international element to computer science education has been to create a community dedicated to exploring the issues involved. Given our location in the Pacific Northwest, we focused on the Pacific Rim as a domain for creating such a community. Here we review the activities undertaken to create our community and develop ideas regarding internationalization.

2.1 Planning Workshop

In November, 2007 we conducted a planning workshop involving over twenty Pacific Northwest[2] academic and industry partners to refine our plans for community building. We developed a website, http://www.cpathi18n.org, to serve as a clearinghouse for information about our project. We also designed and printed a promotional brochure. During the planning meeting in November 2007 we identified areas of high priority to our Pacific Northwest academic and industrial partners, including a need for 'soft skills' in the areas of cross-cultural communication, team work across international and time-zone boundaries, the importance of face-to-face meetings for global team members,and the lack of international experience for American CS undergraduates.

2.2 Friendship Tour

To reach out to possible Asian partners and form initial connections, in March 2008, we visited several potential academic and industrial partners in China and Japan, to begin

[1]NSF grant CNS-0722341: CPATH CB: *i18n*, Internationalization of Computer Science Education: The Pacific Rim Community Model

[2]*North American PNW*; this US-centric error was pointed out by our Asian partner!

initial discussions of issues of mutual interest and to extend a personal invitation to the upcoming May workshop. The visits included presentations from the *i18n* team and hosts, as well as discussions of the perceived problems and possible resolutions. The institutions visited were Peking University, Tsinghua University, Beihang University, IBM China, Microsoft Research Asia, Kyoto University and Tohoku University. During our Asian visit we discovered that the issues facing us and our students are very similar to those facing our Asian partners. This indicated a strong possibility of developing mutually beneficial activities and projects.

2.3 International Workshops

We conducted three workshops over a one year period to build our Pacific Rim Community and address issues of internationalization of computer science education.

Workshop 1: Assessing the Needs and Challenges of i18n of Computer Science Education

The May 2008 workshop took place in Portland, Oregon. It represented the official launching of the project. Fifty participants from North American Pacific Northwest and Asia, including representatives of the computing industry, were introduced and the i18n management team members presented the project overview. Keynote addresses by Lionel Ni, chair of computer science department at HKUST and Gurdeep Singh Pall, corporate VP of Microsoft, introduced us to cross-cultural issues in academia and industry. The first session had as its theme 'Internationalization: Skills and Challenges'. Small working groups discussed and recorded their candidates for skills needed to perform effectively in a global context and impediments to acquisition of these skills.

The second session was focused on 'International Experiences'. The topics and generated ideas included industrial internships, student and faculty exchanges, a summer school, international volunteer service, sister departments and possible dual degree programs. The third session was dedicated to curricular innovations. Working groups topics included: an i18n model curriculum, international software engineering projects, international software engineering competition, a cross-cultural communication course, a cultural HCI curriculum module and an international ethics curriculum module. We found a strong desire for interaction across the Pacific Ocean and an eagerness for educational collaboration.

Workshop 2: Enhancing Computer Science Education through Pacific Rim Partnerships and International Experiences

Working groups that formed during the May 2008 workshop reported their findings at the next workshop, which was held in Beijing during October 2008 on the campus of Peking University, the workshop co-sponsor. The workshop was attended by over sixty participants that included deans, department heads, professors, and students from our Pacific Rim partner institutions in the U.S., Canada, China, Japan, Korea, the Philippines, and Vietnam. Our keynote speaker was Professor Fuqing Yang, Dean of the Faculty of Information and Engineering Sciences, Peking University, Director of the National Engineering Research Center for Software Engineering, and pioneering founder of the field of computer science in China.

The workshop was again organized around small working groups aimed at developing i18n curricular modules and laying the groundwork for international pilot projects and programs. One significant challenge is communicating internationally about scientific results in any field. One result of the efforts through this workshop was creation of a course on Scientific Writing in English for Computer Science Researchers. This experimental course was taught in Beijing Fall 2008 at Tsinghua University.

Workshop 3: Moving i18n Forward: from Ideas to Implementation

The third workshop was held in Portland, Oregon during May 2009. A keynote address on technical training and skill development programs for Google software and hardware engineers was presented by Maggie Johnson, Learning and Development Director, Google. Working group sessions included Cross-cultural HCI, Global Distributed Software Engineering, International Summer School, and Surveying Computer Science Education in the Pacific Rim. There were also short sessions on International Computer Ethics and a Model i18n Curriculum and Recommendations to IEEE/ACM.

As a result of these three workshops, a strong community of computer science educators was formed with several projects continuing into the future. There are two types of efforts underway: curricular innovations and international summer schools.

3. CURRICULAR INNOVATION

An initial action intended to incorporate the impact of internationalization into the computer science curriculum has been made in the interim ACM/IEEE review completed in July 2008 [3]. The review authors state: *With the increased globalization of computing and the international nature of the workforce it is increasingly important to pay attention in the curriculum to certain related matters.*

The international considerations mentioned in the review include international competitiveness, legal, social, etc issues, and cultural issues. Our experience points to a need for curricular innovation beyond this narrow set of issues, as discussed below.

3.1 Multicultural Communication

The issues in cross-cultural communication are not unique to computer professionals, but are certainly important in the context of the global economy, multinational development teams, and localization of computer applications. Awareness of other cultures and of one's own cultural viewpoint as a viewpoint rather than a universal reality belongs to the general set of skills students must develop. Other skills include language (with attention paid to cultural differences in use of "shared" English), and the process of cross-cultural accommodation. Difficulties of electronically-mediated communication are compounded by cultural differences.

As a common problem in cross-cultural communication we have identified the use of English as effectively the lingua franca of global IT. Native English speakers need to accommodate the difficulties of novice speakers and writers. Since translation can change the meaning of a statement, often frequent cross-checking is needed to ensure shared meaning. (For example, asking the other party to restate what they think was just agreed.) But there are also non-linguistic issues, such as Asian deference to the boss resulting in communication problems with superiors, or misunderstandings where "yes" should not be taken for an absolute answer.

There is a controversy about which culture determines the interaction: the professional IT culture or the national culture [1]? Some studies have shown remarkable consistency of values (motivation for work, views of authority, etc.) for IT professionals regardless of national culture. Other studies [2] have shown distinct national differences within the same professional culture (IBM).

We propose as a learning objective that students, after graduation, possess a set of skills that enable them to work effectively on multi-language, multi-cultural, distributed teams. These skills should include: Know how to work within good management practice and become a good manager oneself. (This mitigates cultural impacts.) Possess strong oral and written communication skills. Know how to assign responsibilities and meet one's responsibilities. While these objectives are not directly related to cross-cultural experience, they are a prerequisite to successfully tackling it. An important means towards acquisition of such skills is to participate in distributed, cross-cultural projects (see the following subsection). As a good starter project we propose work on distributed same-cultural projects (for instance, Free/Open-Source Software, FOSS). International experience, provided either in a more controlled environment by inter-university agreements, or by international internships are another avenue of skill acquisition. For those students with interest and time, departments should provide a track for spending time abroad.

It would be desirable to break down the learning objectives into, say, 6-hour modules, akin to structure of the IEEE/ACM Curricula 2001. These may be often achieved in the context of other computer science courses.

3.2 Global Distributed Software Development

Software today is often produced by global teams, but the conventional software engineering project course or capstone project provides little opportunity for students to learn the necessary skills for software development in a global setting. Students typically work in co-located teams where many of the problems of distributed development do not arise and peer-to-peer communication fills the gaps left by ambiguous specification, misunderstandings, and poor planning. Two overlapping working groups of the CPATH i18n project addressed issues of preparing students for leadership roles in projects that span continents, time zones, and cultures.

One of the working groups concerned itself with modules that could be incorporated into conventional courses in software engineering. The material to be covered in such course modules includes some straightforward practical skills, such as use of distributed version and configuration control systems and multiple forms of synchronous and asynchronous communication. More fundamentally, though, the challenges of globally distributed software engineering require a deeper grasp of core "computational thinking" [4] skills of appropriate separation of concerns, abstraction, and precise interface description. The structure of software artifacts and of the processes that produce software are deeply intertwined with organizational structure. As early as 1968, Conway observed that system structures inevitably reflect the communication structures of the organizations that produce them [5]; his observation was called "Conway's Law" by Brooks in his seminal book on software project management [6]. Parnas's pioneering work on information hiding in modular software structure [7, 8] is motivated by similar observations about the way human organizations conceive, construct, and evolve software systems.

A second working group, sharing several members with the first, considered development of courses in which students would actually collaborate internationally on software projects. A software project course typically tries to simulate, in a short project with a small team of students, the demands and constraints of a more critical project evolving over a longer period of time and with a larger and more diverse set of actors. The simulation is imperfect: The consequences of an inappropriate abstraction, with poorly placed module boundaries or poorly described interfaces, is far less when a homogenous group of students are co-located and have ample opportunity for discussion. A corollary of Conway's law is that modularity and abstraction matter much less for a small, homogenous, co-located development team. As a consequence, the success of a student project is often determined primarily by proficiency in coding alone, undermining the goals of a project-oriented software engineering course. The challenges of a real distributed project make it more difficult to substitute informal communication for abstraction and decomposition and clearly illustrate the interplay between separation of concerns in the software architectural design and organization of work, and between precise interfaces, appropriate formalism, and effective communication.

A handful of institutions around the world have already introduced global software engineering project courses, but there are many challenges to wide adoption, both technical and non-technical. For example, in addition to fundamental issues of working across institutional as well as national boundaries, something as simple as differences in academic calendars can complicate collaboration between student teams in different countries. The initial CPATH working groups recognized that nurturing development of internationally distributed project courses would require the joint efforts of a longer-lived international community, beyond the time frame of the initial CPATH project, but building upon the community established in that project. With support of a second CPATH project grant, a second series of community-building workshops has been planned to grow and maintain this community, along with two pilot offerings of internationally distributed project courses, one teaming students in Vietnam with students in the U.S., and another teaming students in China with students in the U.S.

3.3 Cross-Cultural HCI

We have developed a proposal for a 6 hour curriculum module to introduce undergraduate majors to the concepts of designing for cross-cultural human-computer interaction (HCI). The curriculum emphasizes the following major issues: i) Definition of cultural aspects of universal usability and developing software for international use; ii) Examples of the dominant interface culture and how it affects usability; Examples of culturally sensitive software artifacts; and iii) Cross-cultural software development with guidelines, human-centered development process and usability evaluation. The module will integrate into an HCI, software engineering, or general computer science course.

We see two areas of future activity. First is dissemination of our ideas and curriculum module. The proposed syllabus[3] needs be enhanced with a course description that includes

[3]Douglas, S. et al, Introducing Cross-Cultural Human-Computer Interaction (HCI) into the Curriculum, in preparation

readings, lectures, discussion material, and exercises. The goal of our dissemination plan is to make the CS community aware of the importance in incorporating cross-cultural HCI into the CS curriculum. This includes engendering broader discussion of the relevance of these results at conferences, and organizing workshops on teaching cross-cultural HCI to CS teachers. We have already started an online repository of resources and will continue to make the repository available for researchers and educators. Possible target partners include NSF Broadening Participation in Computing award recipients.

The second activity is the actual teaching and evaluation of the module itself or components of the module. Our repository of resources will allow new partners to both contribute new ideas and to evaluate our curriculum. We propose to make our model curriculum available to faculty members to try out at various institutions in order to solicit their feedback. We plan to seek out culturally diverse partners to help us to continue to understand the impact of culture on computers (and also the influence of computers on their cultures). We plan to utilize social networking tools to connect with our partners and to gather ideas.

Finally, we plan to make a recommendation to ACM/IEEE to include a curriculum module such as this one in the Computer Science curriculum under HCI in the next revisions of the Computing Curriculum, and to advocate for the inclusion of topics on internationalization in the curriculum and professional preparation.

3.4 International Computer Ethics and Social Impacts

The information age in which we live, with the use of networked computers located around the world, has created a global society. The subsequent mixing of cultures and economies has resulted in tensions regarding issues of personal privacy, intellectual property, freedom of speech, access to information, and computer security, among others. There are associated social impacts due to the changing nature of work, the development of online communities, and disruptions of established patterns of communication and control. The newly networked world does not automatically recognize national and cultural boundaries, leading to conflicts as to what is ethical and what are acceptable social impacts.

The internationalization of ethical issues and social impacts due to universal use of computers is the focus for the course module proposed here. Understanding the differing ethical and social expectations of people around the world represents an important element in realizing effective cooperation in cyberspace and will play a significant role in developing information systems that are acceptable and effective across cultures.

Many of these ethical issues have deep cultural and historical roots that go far beyond what can be covered in two weeks of study, as is anticipated for this course module. Therefore, the goal for this course module is to raise student awareness of the existence of cultural differences and the role they can play in the field of computer science, given its international context. To create such a course module, one must select issues to be addressed, review recent cases of controversy, determine the current state of affairs regarding selected issues, and collect materials that explain and discuss a variety viewpoints.

The outline we have devised for the course module is as follows: i) motivate discussion with recent issues in the news; ii) provide an international perspective by reviewing United Nations statements and ACM/IEEE codes; iii) discuss issue areas, by noting international agreements, national laws, cultural norms, business practices, and student attitudes and behavior. For the latter, we are developing questionnaires in various issue areas that students can complete at departments around to world to assess and illustrate differences in student attitudes and behaviors globally. The areas to be considered are intellectual property, privacy, information access, freedom of speech, and virtual communities. This module will expand upon what is usually addressed regarding these issues in a computer ethics course.

3.5 Computer Science Education in Asia

Enriching our knowledge of computer science education elsewhere in the world can inform development of U.S. curricula. Very little has been written about computer science education in the Pacific Rim. Together with our Asian partners, we are writing articles on CS Education in the Pacific Rim: China, Japan, Korea, the Philippines, and Vietnam.

As an example, we give some highlights from our SIGCSE 2010 paper on *Undergraduate Computer Science Education in China.*[4]

Established in 1956, China's flagship discipline, Computer Science and Technology, has become the largest undergraduate major in China with almost 800 departments nationwide enrolling over 430,000 undergraduate majors. While Chinese computer science education follows the ACM Computing Curricula 1991 guidelines, this model does not completely meet the economic needs nor the scale of the Chinese educational system. This need has been intensified as China moves from an elite education model to a mass education model. In order to address these challenges, the Chinese Ministry of Education has adopted a pyramid model of computing education that identifies three basic models for training the nation's high tech workforce: science-based education which prepares China's elite scientific talent pool for research-oriented careers; engineering-oriented education to train students in engineering design and implementation; and technology-oriented education focused on preparing a large workforce to produce applied systems to meet customers' needs. In addition, China is pursuing forums for dialog with international colleagues on advances in computer science education. In 2008, the first ACM Summit on Computing Education in China took place in Beijing; in October 2009, the Ministry of Education convened the 5th University Course Forum of Computer Science with keynote speakers Richard LeBlanc and Barbara Owens-Boucher, both leaders in the U.S. computer science education community. The next decade will be a time in China for innovation, international collaboration, and broader expansion of programs, as China evaluates the outcomes of recent educational initiatives and explores the future of computer science education in China and its role throughout the world.

4. INTERNATIONAL SUMMER SCHOOLS

In order to offer computer science students with immersive international experiences that fit into their heavy aca-

[4]by M. Zhang, Peking University and V. Lo, University of Oregon, *in press.*

demic schedules, we plan to establish an international summer school program: the *Pacific Rim Summer School in Global Software Development and Computer Science*. The summer school will provide a venue for faculty to implement new curricula in globally software development, multicultural communications, cross-cultural HCI, international computer ethics (as described in Section 3), and will provide students with the opportunity to work in cross-cultural teams and to take classes with students from around the world, in an intensive immersion-style experience. Our summer schools will bring students from both sides of the Pacific Rim to develop the hard and soft computer science skills that are needed to prepare them to work in an international context.

The anchor of our summer school will be courses with cross cultural content. These course modules are designed to be short (approx. 6 hours each) so that they fit into a one or two week summer school program. Students and faculty participating in inter-institutional global distributed software engineering projects during the academic year, will have a face-to-face meeting at the Summer School. In addition, participating faculty and industry representatives will offer courses and seminars in their own areas of expertise.

The first summer school is tentatively planned for July 2010 at Peking University's Wuxi Campus of the School of Software and Microelectronics. Located less than one hour from Shanghai, the campus covers an area of 500 Chinese acres and houses classrooms, research and development laboratories, dormitories, and faculty apartments. Dean Zhong Chen, Peking University, and Professor Andrzej Proskurowki, University of Oregon, head the Summer School Advisory Board which includes faculty and industry partners from the CPATHi18n Pacific Rim Community. For the first year, the Summer School will be limited primarily to CPATHi18n partner institutions. In subsequent years, we hope to make this opportunity available to a wider range of universities throughout the world.

In July 2009, we hosted the *International Summer School of Network Design and Operations*, on the campus of the University of Oregon, as a warm up to next summer's activities. This intensive hands-on course was attended by an international group of students from Africa, South Asia, China, and Oregon. The all-day classes were taught by staff from the NSRC (www.nsrc.org) and UO Information Services as part of the NSRC's mission to help develop and deploy networking technology to under-served parts of the world. After the week-long class, CPATHi18n students, who came from Tsinghua University and Peking University in China, took a four day trip with U. of Oregon students and faculty to visit some of our CPATHi18n partners in Oregon and Washington (Intel, Microsoft, Google, and the University of Washington).

5. SUMMARY AND FUTURE PLANS

We plan to synthesize the results of our efforts by developing a model *i18n* curriculum as a pathway through the computer science major. We will draft of a white paper recommending the addition of *i18n* topics to the IEEE/ACM Curriculum 2001 for the B.S. degree in Computer Science. This will amplify the recommendations of the IEEE/ACM Computer Science Curriculum Review Taskforce in July 2008.

We chose international collaboration in the Pacific Rim because of the growing importance of this region in the high tech industry and because our institutions have developed exceptionally strong Pacific Rim ties and expertise. We have worked within our regional context, but our outcomes should be globally relevant and long-lasting. The core of our developmental activities is a series of community building workshops involving a diverse group of academic and industrial partners across the Pacific Rim. The workshops addressed four key topics: assessing the needs, benefits and barriers to internationalization; cultural impacts on computer science courses and pedagogy; cultural awareness through international experiences; and community sustainability.

We are in the process of developing a globally available online resource repository for internationalization of computer science education[5]. This repository collects the results from our workshop series: seed ideas and recommendations for programmatic change, proposals for curricular innovation, new technologies for international pedagogy and collaboration, a database of international programs, key contacts, and bibliographic references.

We believe that we are well on the way towards effectuating the concept of internationalization of computer science education using the Pacific Rim as a model community. We have now a better understanding of the nature, challenges, and successful approaches for this transformation to be truly international in scope. Our projects contribute to a national discourse in this important arena.

The long term impacts of our Pacific Rim community-building project will be to give students at the participating institutions a competitive advantage in a global world, whether in research or industry. Internationalization of computer science education will help attract the best and brightest students and broaden the appeal of computer science to a much more diverse population. Computer science will be seen as a pathway to a career not in an isolated cubicle but in the wide-open world. Because scientific discovery is driven to a considerable degree by advances in computer science, students with global understanding of computer science will become better scientists, as well. Finally, internationalization will move our discipline towards the maturity and recognition it deserves, as more computer scientists move into leadership positions in commerce, education, and government.

6. REFERENCES

[1] Carmel, E., *Global software teams: collaborating across borders and time zones* Prentice Hall (1999), chptr. 5

[2] Geert Hofstede, http://www.geert-hofstede.com/

[3] Computer Science Curriculum 2008: An Interim Revision of CS 2001December 2008, ACM/IEEE.

[4] Wing, J. M., *Computational thinking*, Commun. ACM 49,3 (2006) 33-35.

[5] Conway, M. E., *How do committees invent?*, Datamation 14,4 (1968) 28-31.

[6] Brooks, F.P., *The Mythical Man-Month*, Addison-Wesley 2nd ed. (1995)

[7] Parnas, D.L., *On the Criteria to be Used in Decomposing Systems into Modules*, Communications of the ACM, 15,12, (1972) 1053-1058

[8] Parnas, D.L., *On the modular structure of complex systems*, in Proceedings of the 7th international Conference on Software Engineering, (1984) 408 -417

[5]http://www.cpathi18n.org

Empirical Evidence for the Existence and Uses of Metacognition in Computer Science Problem Solving

Jennifer Parham
Clemson University
School of Computing
Clemson, SC 29634
+1 864 245 4177
jparham@g.clemson.edu

Leo Gugerty
Clemson University
Department of Psychology
Clemson, SC 29634
+1 864 656 4467
gugerty@clemson.edu

D. E. Stevenson
Clemson University
School of Computing
Clemson, SC 29634
+1 864 656 5880
steve@cs.clemson.edu

ABSTRACT

We describe the second phase of an ongoing study whose aims are to explore how computer science students solve problems and to understand the relationship between metacognition and schemata. This research uses verbal protocols from computer science students, and based on the analysis of their transcripts, empirical evidence supports metacognition as a significant role in computer science problem solving. For the problem solved in this research, the students reveal a pattern in their interactions between metacognitive processes and the domain-specific strategies used to develop a program.

Categories and Subject Descriptors

K.3.2 [**Computers and Education**]: Computer and Information Science Education: *Computer science education.* E.1 [**Data Structures**]: arrays.

General Terms

Human Factors.

Keywords

computer science education, problem solving, metacognition, schemata, cognitive processing.

1. INTRODUCTION

Previous research using verbal protocols from students' solving a complex data structures problem determined that solving problems in computer science is a dynamic process, that there are significant differences in the cognitive processes used by students, and that a domain-specific vocabulary needs to be developed to determine specific cognitive processes influencing problem solving in computer science [11]. This research establishes a taxonomy of schemata and metacognitive processes, which are used to control and monitor cognition, and investigates the interactions between these processes and domain-specific strategies while solving a computer science problem. To support the existence of these metacognitive processes in computer science and explain their relationship with schemata, this research used the verbal protocol method presented in Ericsson and Simon's book [4], *Protocol Analysis.* The taxonomy was developed using the foundations of metacognition from psychology and the current software development strategies from computer science to determine differences among students' metacognitive processing and schemata for writing a simple program. This is the second phase from the authors' continuous research on how people store, retrieve, and manipulate knowledge while solving problems in computer science, thereby impacting pedagogy, learning, and testing strategies at the university level.

SIGCSE'10, March 10–13, 2010, Milwaukee, Wisconsin,, USA.

2. RELATED WORK

To address the issue of retrieving and storing information while solving computer science problems, this study uses verbal protocols from first-year and second-year computer science students as they solve a problem requiring prior content knowledge about one-dimensional arrays, looping, and other basic first-year concepts used to write a computer program. Verbal protocols include all methods for obtaining oral and/or written reports of thinking, such as interviews, thinking aloud while solving a problem, categorizing problems, reflective thinking about solutions or problem statements, and asking participants to describe or explain their verbalizations. As computer science researchers have begun to recognize the importance of verbal protocols [1, 3, 11], they have adapted Ericsson and Simon's guidelines for producing and analyzing verbalizations in *Protocol Analysis.* After comparing various methods, verbal protocols were determined to be an appropriate methodology for yielding details about the relationship between metacognition and schemata used in computer science problem solving, and the research presented here is based on Ericsson and Simon's protocol for explaining the details of cognitive processes.

Metacognition is an integral part of the problem-solving process, and the term, metacognition, has a directing or monitoring connotation depending on the context in which it is used. According to Flavell, metacognition is the control one has over their own cognition and learning [5]; whereas, J. T. Hart defines metacognition as the processes that allow an individual to observe, to reflect on, or to experience his/her own cognitive processes [7]. In the mid-1980's, Robert Sternberg combined these two definitions in his triarchic theory of human intelligence, and in his theory, he addresses the metacomponents of metacognition [13]. Sternberg defines metacognition as the higher-order, executive processes used to direct and monitor cognition, and the metacomponents decide what to do, monitor what is being done, evaluate what is done, and interact with the performance components used to execute a task and the knowledge acquisition components used to learn how to perform a task. Even though the existence of metacognition has been supported in the problem-solving literature, the interactions between metacognition and schemata have not been studied.

Moores et al. measured the relationship between metacognition and student performance on a test covering data-flow and entity-relationship diagrams [9], and these authors discovered that metacognition is related to procedural knowledge, that the relationship is based on problem complexity, and that future studies need to clarify this relationship. Other computer science research investigated metacognition as a means for evaluating students' data structure knowledge, their perception of task difficulty, their game-based learning, their comprehension of programs, and intelligent tutoring [10, 8, 12, 2].

3. METHOD

To investigate students' metacognition and schemata more accurately, this research collected verbalizations from participants using a combination of thinking aloud while solving a problem, providing participants with information when asked, and conducting off-line interviews after the participant reached a solution. At this time, this research is concerned only with conscious thoughts; however, it recognizes unconscious thoughts and does not dismiss the possibility of their being a part of the explanation for the results during periods of silence.

3.1 Data Collection

The participants included students enrolled in either Computer Science II or Data Structures and Algorithms volunteering one hour of their time in exchange for ten dollars, under IRB consent, to participate in this research study yielding a sample size of 11. After volunteering to participate in this study, participants received a demographics sheet to minimize confounding variables such as years of professional programming experience versus university programming experience. The physical, mental, and emotional state of the participant was ignored. However, future studies can capture this information on the demographics sheet to establish the differences in metacognition and schema use under different conditions due to external variables such as caffeine, sleep deprivation, empty stomach, and stress.

3.2 The Research Study

A pilot study was conducted to ensure analyzable data based on the initial demographic sheet and the problem selected. For example, the first participant was given the original demographics sheet, but after completing the verbal protocol, the demographics sheet was updated to include the number of English speaking years for accuracy in transcription and analysis. After informing the participants that they could ask a question at any time, the researcher supplied every participant with a computer capable of browsing the web, accessing old programs, and writing new programs as well as a blank piece of paper, pencils, pens, textbooks on Java, C, and C++ languages, and a paper-copy of the problem statement.

In addition to good audio quality needed to capture the details of metacognition and schemata in the transcript, piloting the selected problem was important. A problem too simple or too hard will not yield as much verbalization as a problem complex enough to stimulate thought [4]. Before the students were instructed to begin working on the problem, the experimenter read the following version of Chapter 8 Programming Project 1 from *Problem Solving and Program Design in C* [6]:

> "Write a program to take two numerical lists of the same length ended by a sentinel value and store the lists in arrays x and y, each of which can hold a maximum number of 10 elements, and populate both lists by entering the actual data values from within the program. Let n represent the actual number of data values in each list. For example, x and y can hold up to 10 elements, but the two arrays may only contain 5 actual data values, i.e. n=5. Store the product of corresponding elements of x and y in a third array z, also of maximum size 10. Print the contents of the arrays x, y, and z. Then compute and print the square root of the sum of the items in z."

This problem was given to the initial five students with various backgrounds, and the resulting data contained enough detail among these participants to continue using the problem throughout the research study.

As in the pilot study, every participant received a demographics sheet, and the verbal protocols were recorded on a desktop computer in the room using Morae software and a microphone. Morae software records a person's voice and computer actions, resulting in a video of the participant writing computer code and talking aloud simultaneously while solving a computer science problem. Due to the absence of a video camera and eye tracking software, participants were instructed to verbalize their actions performed off the computer such as designing, reading the problem statement, and using textbooks. The interviewer answered questions and provided hints only when the student specifically asked the interviewer for help or appeared to be struggling on the same thought for longer than 5 minutes, and participants were reminded to think aloud if silent for more than 10 seconds to increase the number of thoughts captured.

3.3 Transcription of the Data

The recorded data from the 11 participants consisted of 298 minutes of audio and video, but due to the inability to understand the first participant, this verbal protocol was not transcribed or analyzed. This yielded 241 minutes and 32 seconds of audio/video to transcribe and analyze. For the 10 remaining participants, excel spreadsheets were created to capture the details about their computer actions and keystrokes, and their verbal statements were manually transcribed into text, while viewing and listening to the movie file. The transcripts from the 10 participants resulted in 200 pages of data to analyze and code. Even though transcription and analysis might take less time using only computer actions, the verbal transcript is needed to capture the metacognitive processes.

3.4 Establishing Reliability for Analysis

After transcribing the 10 participants, a process of joint and individual coding of transcripts by psychology and computer science researchers established the reliability for the vocabulary and transcript analysis. Initially, the researchers analyzed the transcripts for general commonalities using the experimenter's raw observations after each verbal protocol to develop the initial vocabulary for coding metacognitive processes and schemata. The final vocabulary was a result of 7 versions of joint and individual coding/recoding over 4 months to reach an acceptable inter-rater reliability greater than 80% on the metacognitive processes and programming schemata.

The first two months consisted of 150 hours spent on reaching a joint agreement on the terms and definitions to use for analyzing the participants' verbal protocols. The next two months consisted of the researchers individually coding two students to reach an acceptable inter-rater reliability on the coding scheme for the metacognition and the schemata. Using the first coding scheme, the raters reached a 71% agreement on 60 codes from half a transcript. This inter-rater reliability is lower than the accepted 80% or higher in psychology leading to the development of a new code capturing participants' diagnosing errors before fixing them and to the improvement of definitions. The next inter-rater reliability was 60%, which was lower than the initial reliability, on 120 codes from a different transcript. Perhaps, this 11% drop in agreement is because of the addition of codes without clear definitions and/or a longer transcript with twice as many codes. Based on the disagreements, subcodes were added to the diagnose code to capture the different diagnosing strategies such as recognition, elimination, and backtracking and to the planning code to include general scheduling of activities. This sixth version of the taxonomy was individually re-applied to another participant, and the raters agreed on 64 out of 96 codes, improving the inter-rater reliability of the coding document to 67%. Most of the disagreements in this third inter-rater reliability coding were due to subcodes rather than the high-level codes. Therefore, the coding document was simplified by combining and removing the subcodes, and recoding the 96 codes with this final version resulted in an 85% reliability for the taxonomy of metacognitive processes and schemata identified in Table 2.

4. OBSERVATIONS

As a result of reaching an agreeable inter-rater reliability, a vocabulary for metacognitive processes and schemata was established to determine students' cognitive behavior. Provided in Table 2 is the resulting taxonomy with a brief definition and an example of the 6 metacognitive processes and 6 schemata. The schemata include design, write code, compile, execute, diagnose, and fix code, which are high-level schemata representing domain-specific strategies used to develop a program and were derived from the waterfall and iterative methods for software development, i.e. requirements/plan, design, implementation, testing, evaluation, and maintenance. Whereas, the broad metacognitive processes, start/revisit goals, understand the problem/plan, verbalize having low knowledge, read/consider a design, inspect the solution, and compare the solution to the problem statement, were identified from the psychology literature. At this time, the results address the existence of these 6 schemata and their interactions with one another and with the 6 metacognitive processes in the taxonomy. Future studies can determine how these high-level schemata interact with other metacognitive processes and the low-level schemata representing conceptual and procedural knowledge.

4.1 The Existence of Metacognition and Schemata

In order to support the need for metacognition and schemata in computer science problem solving, the taxonomy was applied to the verbal statements and computer actions in the 10 transcripts, and the sums of visits to each process, strategy, and external source were calculated. Based on individual participants, Table 1 addresses the total uses of the 6 metacognitive processes and 6 domain-specific schemata as well as external sources. Table 1 supports the existence of metacognition and schemata, as well as the use of external sources, in computer science problem solving. On average, the participants in this study used metacognition 44% of their total mental processes to write a program, supporting metacognition as a tool for solving problems in computer science, and 90% of the participants needed to use an external source, which included as many as 25, in order to solve the problem.

Table 1 Total uses of metacognition, schemata, and external sources of information per participant.

Processes Visited	Participant									
	2	3	4	5	6	7	8	9	10	11
Metacognition	86	110	70	52	63	32	49	71	93	85
Start/Revisit Goals	28	32	15	24	17	14	16	14	24	26
Understand Problem/Plan	10	22	28	11	18	5	11	19	8	12
Read/Consider Design	0	0	0	0	0	0	0	0	0	0
Verbalize Low Knowledge	15	3	4	4	8	5	1	10	5	4
Inspect	33	50	23	11	13	7	21	26	56	42
Compare	0	3	0	2	7	1	0	2	0	1
Schemata	98	133	60	76	85	87	61	86	101	87
Design	0	1	0	0	0	0	0	0	0	0
Write Code	36	72	34	41	39	31	38	49	44	34
Compile	18	9	6	8	9	13	4	9	5	8
Execute	3	4	6	5	5	8	3	10	3	3
Diagnose	24	17	6	12	17	15	7	9	24	20
Fix Code	17	30	8	10	15	20	9	9	25	22
External Source	25	3	1	14	3	7	0	10	2	10

Even though participants used schemata more than metacognition or external sources, two metacognitive processes were more widely used than all programming schemata besides *write code*. In more detail, the participants used the *write code* strategy the most, averaging 27% of their total mental processes, and the *start/revisit goals* and *inspect* metacognitive processes respectively averaged 13% and 17% (see Figure 1). The participants used the metacognitive process *understand problem/plan* as much as the *diagnose* strategy, averaging 9%. The average uses of the *fix code* strategy exceeded the uses of *diagnose* by 1% due to participants' lack of a diagnosis. The *compile* and *execute* domain-specific strategies for checking and detecting errors averaged only 6% and 3% of their mental processes implying that syntax errors were the majority, but 4% of the participants' syntax errors were detected using metacognition for inspecting their solution.

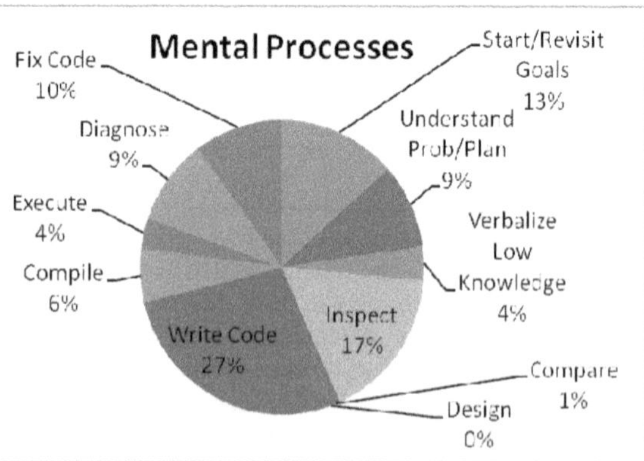

Figure 1 Average uses of metacognitive processes and domain-specific schemata.

Table 2 A taxonomy for the metacognitive and schematic processes used by the participants in this research.

Processes/Strategies	Brief Definition	Example
Start/Revisit Goals	Explicitly or implicitly begin or return to tasks/subtasks in the problem statement	"Ok, now I need to go back to the loop I was working on."
Understand Problem/Plan	Think about the problem statement, read/reread the problem, or schedule time/activities.	"First I have to sum the elements in z, then I can take the square root."
Read/Consider Design	Read design, drawings, and/or notes from the piece of paper	"Let me look at my design to see if I'm right."
Verbalize: Low Prior Knowledge	Explicitly state needing to learn or find out more information, make a low confidence statement, mention the difficulty of a task, or guess computer syntax	"I know I should use a for loop, but I'm not good at for loops."
Inspect	Check code via visual/mental inspection and compare it to own knowledge and/or use own knowledge to execute existing code	"That equals one, then that will go to the second thing in the list equals one, and then…"
Compare	Comparing computer code or knowledge to the problem statement	"Yep, I took the square root then printed it."
Design	Draw, design, and/or take notes on the blank piece of paper.	"Let me put these ideas on paper before I begin"
Write Code: High/ Low Prior Knowledge	Type correct or incorrect computer program statements or mentions wanting to write a program/code	"z sub i equals x sub i plus y sub i."
Compile	Tests code via compiling it and inspecting the compiler messages	"I'm going to compile and check for errors."
Execute	Test code via executing a compiled program and compare the actual and expected output or use test-write statements or a debugging application to inspect internal program data	"Good, ok, just what I wanted it to output."
Diagnose	Use reasoning strategies to identify the cause of incorrect output/error or use statements to indentify the cause of an error	"The x and y variables have the correct value, so it must be the z variable causing problems."
Fix Code	Changing code after detecting and diagnosing an error	"Ah man, I have to go fix all the loop counters."

As seen in Figure 1, participants' used their metacognition to *verbalize low knowledge* more than using *execute* and *design* strategies. Two metacognitive processes, *compare* and *read/consider design,* were not used by all participants. On average, participants used the metacognitive process *compare* only 1% of their mental processing; yet, 60% of the participants used the process at least once, usually before finishing a goal. However, none of the participants used *read/consider design*, which might be attributed to 90% of the participants never using the *design* strategy.

4.2 The Relationship between Metacognition and Schemata

The empirical evidence of metacognition and schemata in computer science problem solving allows for the analysis of the interactions among them. *Inspect* and *compare* processes from metacognition, as well as the *compile* and *execute* strategies from schemata, were combined into processes and strategies for checking and detecting errors. In order to analyze the interactions among specific metacognitive processes and schemata, the transitions between codes were counted to create a transition frequency matrix for individual participants. Even though the *design* strategy was used only once, the participant appeared to go from *understand problem/plan* to *design*, go from *design* to *start/revisit goals,* and never return to *read/consider design.* These participants show no interactions between one *start/revisit goals* and another *start/revisit goals*; whereas, all other mental processes appear to have interactions.

None of the participants appeared to move from *start/revisit goals* directly to *compile* and *execute* strategies for checking and detecting errors; whereas, 12% of the participant uses of metacognitive processes for checking and detecting errors were directly after *start/revisit goals.* However, both of the metacognitive processes and the schemata for checking and detecting errors each averaged 12% of the uses leading to *start/revisit goals.* There was no evidence of participants using *write code* directly before diagnosing an error without using metacognition or schemata for checking and detecting the error. In addition, there was no evidence of the participants using the *compile* or *execute* strategies before fixing an error without using *diagnose.*

The use of the *diagnose* strategy before fixing an error was the only interaction with an average greater than 50%, and 30% of the other uses of *diagnose* led to *start/revisit goals* implying that the participants diagnosed an error outside their current goal requiring the participant to switch to a prior goal before fixing the error. This interaction between *diagnose* and *start/revisit goals* explains why 24% of the visits to goals were directly before fixing an error, but the majority, 47%, of the visits to goals resulted in writing code. Even though processes from metacognition can be followed by another metacognitive process, most had interactions with schemata. The metacognitive processes used to check and detect errors versus the *understand problem/plan* metacognitive process averaged more interactions with schemata due to 29% of participant uses of *understand problem/plan* before *start/revisit goals*, and 29% of their uses of the metacognitive processes for checking and detecting errors were before diagnosing an error. On average, 33% of participant uses of *write code* led to *inspect* and *compare* metacognitive processes, and 25-26% of the *inspect*, *compare*, and *understand problem/plan* metacognitive processes led back *write code*, totaling 51% of all uses of *write code.* Only 2% of the uses of *write code* were after using the compiler or executing the program, also showing that participants in this study rarely had successful compilations or executions and had successful ones after completing all goals. After fixing errors, participants used either a metacognitive process or schema for evaluating their fix and checking/detecting more errors; each averaging 33% and 30% of the uses after fixing an error.

The analysis of these ten participants' interactions between schemata and metacognitive processes reveal a trend of how students move through the software development process using metacognition to solve a problem. On average, participants in this study did not use the *design* strategy to develop their software; therefore, showing no interactions between one of the initial software development strategies and writing code. However, students did appear to use their metacognitive process for understanding the problem/planning before writing code. The sixth taxonomy had a requirements strategy as part of its vocabulary, but the strategy was dropped due to its confusion with metacognitive planning. Figure 2 illustrates the appearance of these significant relationships between metacognition and software development strategies occurring greater than 3%.

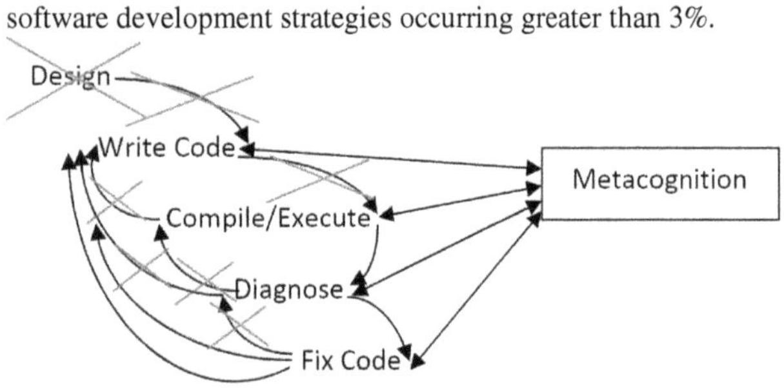

Figure 2 Overall interactions between domain-specific strategies derived from software development methods and metacognition.

As seen in Figure 2, the participants do not go from *write code* to the *compile* and *execute* strategies, but rather, they appear to use metacognition before compiling or executing. In addition, these students' *write code* strategy had an inverse relationship with fixing code, where an average of 12% of the uses of *fix code* returned to *write code*, and 30% of the uses returned to the *compile* and *execute* strategies. Even though these participants appeared to have few transitions from writing code to compiling/executing, they did move from the *compile* and *execute* strategies to *diagnose* and from *diagnose* to *fix code* without skipping the *diagnose* strategy. However, every strategy during their software development appeared to have a relationship with metacognition, and these participants used their metacognition to return to domain-specific strategies, except when returning to *write code*, *compile*, or *execute* from fixing an error.

5. CONCLUSION

This experimental research continues to provide insight on how people solve computer science problems leading to advancements in pedagogy and assessment. Out of all the mental processes used by these participants to solve the problem in this research study, the strategy *write code* averaged the most uses, but two metacognitive processes, *inspect* and *start/revisit goals* averaged more combined uses than any other mental process. This research supports metacognition as a significant role in writing a program, and this analysis provides insight into the types of metacognitive processes and schemata used by students to solve a computer science problem. Future studies can determine the impact of these processes on problem-solving performance and the differences between experts and novices solving computer science problems.

6. REFERENCES

[1] Almstrum, V. L., Henderson, P. B., Harvey, V., Heeren, C., Marion, W., Riedesel, C., Soh, L. and Tew, A. E. 2006. "Concept inventories in computer science for the topic discrete mathematics." *SIGCSE Bull.*, 38(4), 132-145.

[2] Anderson, M. L. and Oates, T. (Eds.). 2005. Metacognition in Computation: Papers from the 2005 AAAI Spring Symposium. Menlo Park, CA: AAAI Press.

[3] Chinn, D., Spencer, C., and Martin, K. 2007. Problem solving and student performance in data structures and algorithms. *Proceedings of the 12th Annual SIGCSE Conference on Innovation and Technology in Computer Science Education* (June 2007), 241-245.

[4] Ericsson, K. A. and Simon, H. A. 1993. Protocol Analysis: Verbal Reports as Data. MIT Press, Cambridge, MA.

[5] Flavell, J. H. 1979. Metacognition and cognitive monitoring: A new area of cognitive-developmental inquiry. *American Psychologist* 34, 10 (Oct. 1979), 906-911.

[6] Hanly, Jeri R. and Koffman, Elliot B. 2006. Problem Solving and Program Design in C, 5th ed. Addison Wesley.

[7] Hart, J. T. 1965. Memory and the feeling-of-knowing experience. *Journal of Educational Psychology* 56, 4 (1965), 208-216.

[8] Kim, B., Park, H., and Baek, Y. 2009. Not just fun, but serious strategies: Using meta-cognitive strategies in game-based learning. *Computers & Education* 52(4) , 800-810.

[9] Moores, T. T., Chang, J. C., and Smith, D. K. 2006. Clarifying the role of self-efficacy and metacognition as predictors of performance: construct development and test. *SIGMIS Database* 37, 2-3 (Sep. 2006), 125-132.

[10] Murphy, L. and Tenenberg, J. 2005. Do computer science students know what they know?: a calibration study of data structure knowledge. In *Proceedings of the 10th Annual SIGCSE Conference on innovation and Technology in Computer Science Education* (June 2005), 148-152.

[11] Parham, J., Chinn, D., and Stevenson, D. E. 2009. Using Bloom's taxonomy to code verbal protocols of students solving a data structure problem. In *Proceedings of the 47th Annual Southeast Regional Conference* (March 2009), 1-6.

[12] Shaft, T. M. 1995. Helping programmers understand computer programs: the use of metacognition. *SIGMIS Database* 26, 4 (Nov. 1995), 25-46.

[13] Sternberg, R. J. 1985. Beyond IQ: A triarchic theory of human intelligence. Cambridge University Press.

PeerWise: Replication Study of a Student-Collaborative Self-Testing Web Service in a U.S. Setting

Paul Denny
Dept. of Computer Science
The University of Auckland
Auckland, NZ
paul@cs.auckland.ac.nz

Brian Hanks
Computer Science Info Sys.
Fort Lewis College
Durango, CO USA
hanks_b@fortlewis.edu

Beth Simon
Computer Science and Engr. Dept.
University of California, San Diego
La Jolla, CA USA
bsimon@cs.ucsd.edu

ABSTRACT
PeerWise is a collaborative web-based system that engages students in the creation and evaluation of a test bank of multiple-choice questions. Previous studies involving two large CS1 courses in New Zealand have provided preliminary evidence that PeerWise usage is positively correlated with exam performance. In addition, it was reported that the student generated assessment questions were mostly free from errors and were clearly written, and the students appeared to positively value the system. Here we report on the first use of PeerWise in a CS1.5 course (second programming course) in the United States. Although the usage model was modified slightly to accommodate pedagogical factors, we highlight similar positive outcomes to those observed in New Zealand. Of particular note, students who were most active using PeerWise improved their rank in class relative to their peers who were less active.

Categories and Subject Descriptors
K.3.2 [**Computer Science Education**]: Introductory Programming – *abstract programming concepts*

General Terms
Algorithms, Human Factors

Keywords
CS1, MCQ, multiple choice question, peer assessment, educational technology, collaborative systems.

1. INTRODUCTION
Traditionally, multiple-choice questions (MCQs) have been created by instructors and used for summative assessment. PeerWise is a web-based tool that provides a framework for students to work collaboratively with their classmates to create a large repository of MCQs [3]. By creating the question bank, rather than just accessing an existing one, students are transformed from passive recipients to active learners.

The process of creating a question engages a student in reflecting on the learning outcomes of the course, and requires they express their question clearly and consider misconceptions when proposing distracters (plausible, yet incorrect, answer options). Students are also encouraged to justify their understanding by explaining the answer to their question in their own words. The process of self-explanation promotes deeper conceptual understanding, as shown by Aleven and Koedinger [1] in a study of mathematics students.

Once questions have been submitted, students can answer them as a self-assessment activity and several opportunities for peer-comparison arise. Upon selecting an answer, a student is shown the question author's answer and the most popular answer of their peers. The explanation for the question is also displayed, and students are able to read and contribute to the discussion threads associated with each question. Students are encouraged to evaluate the quality of the questions and explanations, a process that requires behaviors at the highest level in Bloom's taxonomy of the cognitive domain [2].

PeerWise provides regular opportunities for students to test their knowledge with questions aligned with course learning outcomes. Roediger et al. [8] showed that repeated testing, where students are regularly required to recall and apply their knowledge, is better than repeated studying at improving students' long term retention of information. He asserts "incorporating more frequent testing into a course may improve students' learning and promote retention of material long after a course has ended".

Murphy and Tenenberg [7] empirically investigated the extent of Computer Science students' knowledge of their own learning, and concluded that, "students should be provided with regular opportunities for empirical validation of their knowledge as well as being taught the metacognitive skills of regular self-testing". As an instructional strategy, PeerWise may indeed go some way towards addressing this call, by providing students with regular opportunities for self-testing and reflection.

The use of PeerWise has been evaluated previously in two CS1 courses taught at the University of Auckland. The driving force behind this prior work was a desire to address three common concerns expressed by instructors interested in using the tool in their own courses.

1. **Repository quality.** Instructors were unsure of the ability of students to write good questions that would form a useful learning resource.
2. **Learning benefits.** As an always-available online resource, another instructor concern was whether students who became actively engaged using the tool were spending their time wisely. Does PeerWise appear to offer any measurable learning benefits to those students who become most involved with it?

SIGCSE'10, March 10–13, 2010, Milwaukee, Wisconsin, USA.

3. **Student perceptions of activity value.** Given that PeerWise is entirely student driven, it places virtually no burden on the course instructor. Instructors were interested in whether students would perceive it simply as an increase in their workload or whether they would enjoy the activity. In particular, voluntary student contributions to PeerWise would be a good sign that they value the peer-generated resource.

In this paper we report on the first use of PeerWise in the United States. This study examines data from two independent terms (Winter 2009 and Spring 2009) of a CS1.5 course taught at the University of California, San Diego (UCSD). We performed the study to investigate whether cultural and logistical differences have an impact on the effectiveness of this tool. We highlight the differences from its use in New Zealand, and compare our results to several of those from earlier work.

2. RELATED WORK

Previous studies have reported on the use of PeerWise in two CS1 courses taught by the system creator (Denny) at the University of Auckland. In this section, we reflect on these earlier results to set the scene for our study.

Repository quality. In 2008, a repository of 617 questions was developed by a class of 407 CS1 students [6]. A sample of 10% of the questions was examined and categorized, and it was found that 93% of the questions were clearly worded and 87% had a full set of feasible distracters. The majority of the questions were free from errors, with 80% having no errors in either the question stem or any included source code, and the correct answer was indicated by the question author in 89% of the cases. In every case examined where the answer was not correctly specified by the question author, this was detected and corrected by other students in the question discussion area.

After answering a question, students were given the opportunity to rate the quality of the question on a 6-point scale (0-5). The questions in the repository could be sorted by the average rating assigned. While the repository contained a number of low quality questions, students used the ratings of their peers to answer the high quality questions more frequently than the low quality questions [6].

Learning benefits. A quantitative analysis of a 460 student CS1 course taught in 2007 suggested that students who used PeerWise actively performed better in final examinations than their peers of similar initial abilities, but who were not as active [5]. The initial abilities of students were measured by their performance on a mid-term test, administered approximately half-way into the course, before PeerWise was introduced. While significant differences in final exam performance were found between the most and least active students within all achievement quartiles based on mid-term test performance, the greatest differences were found amongst students in the lowest quartile.

Student perceptions of activity value. Surveys showed that students enjoyed using the tool [4], quoting its value as a useful exam review resource as its biggest benefit. Although the amount of course credit offered to students for their participation was small (only 2%), students used PeerWise more often than was required. In 2007, students answered more than double the number of questions necessary to receive course credit, and 44% of the class used PeerWise voluntarily for exam review after the participation deadline [3].

3. METHODOLOGY

PeerWise was used in two second-quarter programming courses (CS1.5) at UCSD in 2009. We will refer to these two courses as Winter and Spring, corresponding to the terms in which they were taught. We examined repository quality, learning benefits, and student perceptions of activity value by replicating several of the analyses of previous studies.

In the case of repository quality, we have not replicated the expert analysis of question content, but instead we acknowledge that in a student generated repository there will be a range of questions of varying qualities. We focus on whether students can effectively find high quality questions at appropriate levels of difficulty based on ratings assigned to the questions by their peers.

For our analysis of learning benefits, the small number of students in our UCSD classes precludes direct replication of the analysis by quartile in [5]. In this study, PeerWise was used over the entire term (not just the second half of the term), so we use the final course grade in the prerequisite CS1 class as a baseline performance indicator. This allows us to examine the change in class rank of each student based on their level of activity.

Student perceptions of the value of the PeerWise activity are examined by considering the levels of voluntary usage of PeerWise in the Winter and Spring classes and by student survey.

3.1 CS1 in New Zealand

CS1 at the University of Auckland in New Zealand is a 12-week introductory programming course in Java. It is taken by both majors and non-majors and enrollment typically ranges between 400-500 students. Approximately 30% of students who originally enroll in the course either fail or withdraw.

In 2007 and 2008, when the previous studies were conducted, PeerWise was introduced to students half-way through the course, immediately after a mid-term test was conducted. Students were required to contribute two questions and to answer ten questions in the 6 weeks before the end of the term, for 2% of their course grade. The system remained available for voluntary use after the end of lectures and before the final exam (a period of two weeks).

3.2 CS1.5 in the U.S.

CS1.5 at the University of California, San Diego is a 10-week second programming course using Java. In this study, both the Winter and Spring CS1.5 courses, as well as both prerequisite CS1 courses, were taught by the same instructor (Simon). Failure rates (WDF) for the Winter and Spring CS1.5 courses were 6% and 12% respectively. The course is taken primarily by majors, with 84% majors in Winter and 54% majors in Spring.

The classes were considerably smaller than in Auckland, with 79 students in Winter and 63 in Spring. However, in order to have a consistent baseline performance measure (final grade in CS1 the previous term) we report on only 73 (Winter) and 53 (Spring) students who met that criterion. This allowed us to have students use PeerWise throughout each term, unlike in previous studies where the introduction of PeerWise was delayed in order to conduct a test to measure student abilities.

The requirements for students to use PeerWise differed between the Winter and Spring terms of CS1.5. In both, students used PeerWise on alternate weeks (when in-class quizzes were not given). In Winter this was 6 weeks – each week, half of the class contributed 1 question by Monday and the other half of the class answered 3 questions by Tuesday. This meant that the minimum required contribution per student involved writing 3 questions and answering 9 questions over the term for 4% of the course grade. The instructor did not spend class time promoting the system, other than to say that it served as a self-assessment mechanism for the weeks where a formal quiz was not given. The instructor did not view student questions or responses during the term. Students in the Winter course created a repository of 202 questions.

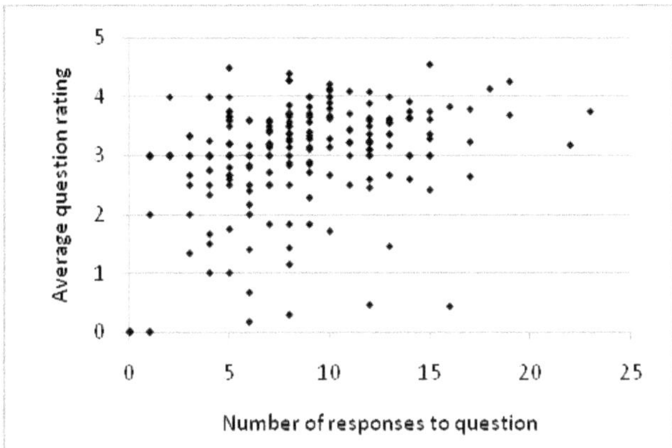

Figure 1: Question popularity vs. rating (Winter)

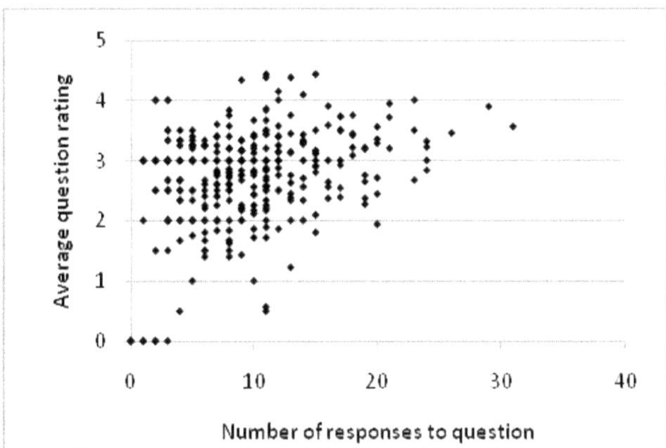

Figure 2: Question popularity vs. rating (Spring)

In the Spring term, students used PeerWise a total of 5 weeks – each week writing 1 question and answering 3 questions earning 4% of the course grade. This increased the minimum required contribution per student to writing 5 questions and answering 15 over the term (and made for an assignment that was simpler to remember). The instructor was considerably more active in the Spring term promoting the use of PeerWise to students, and every week identified interesting questions to present in class. She discussed her rationale for why certain questions were useful, and gave suggestions for those that could be improved. She once awarded small prizes for good questions. At the end of the term, she presented research on the benefits of repeated testing and effortful recall [8], and emphasized the opportunities for such practice that PeerWise provides. Students in the Spring course created a repository of 297 questions.

4. RESULTS

In this section, we present the results of our examination of repository quality, learning benefits, and student perceptions of activity value for both the Winter and Spring classes, and make comparisons to earlier studies where appropriate.

4.1 Repository Quality

In [6], it was reported that questions rated highly for quality received a greater number of responses than poorly rated questions. It was also shown that student assigned quality ratings were well correlated with instructor ratings of the same questions. Figures 1 and 2 show the number of responses each question received in the Winter and Spring classes, against the average quality rating of that question. It is clear from these figures that poorly rated questions generally did not receive a large number of responses, consistent with the results in the New Zealand courses. This indicates that while the quality of the questions in the repository naturally varies, students do use the ratings assigned to the questions by their peers to help them determine which questions to spend their time answering.

Table 1 presents the correlations between question quality and question popularity for both the Winter and Spring courses, as well as for the New Zealand course reported in [6]. All correlation values are very similar, and above 0.3.

Table 1. Student rating (quality) correlated with number of responses (popularity)

Course	NZ	Winter	Spring
Correlation (R)	0.34	0.35	0.31

In addition to quality ratings, students are also given an opportunity to rate the difficulty of questions they answer on a 3-point scale (0-2). Like the quality ratings, these difficulty ratings are shared and can be used by students to answer questions at a difficulty level they are comfortable with. We are able to measure the accuracy of these difficulty ratings by comparing them with an objective measure of difficulty – the percentage of responses to a question that are correct. Table 2 summarizes the correlation between student assigned difficulty ratings and the percentage of correct responses. There are strong negative correlations in both the Winter and Spring courses (showing that questions rated more difficult by students have fewer correct responses). Although not previously reported in the New Zealand studies, data from the 2008 course yields a correlation of -0.56.

Table 2. Difficulty rating correlated with percent of correct responses

Course	NZ (2008)	Winter	Spring
Correlation (R)	-0.56	-0.58	-0.60

4.2 Learning benefits

Previous studies have shown that students who are most active using PeerWise, particularly when measured by the number of questions answered, outperform their less active peers in formal examinations.

In the New Zealand study, the midterm test grades were used to establish a performance baseline, which was used to assess the impact of PeerWise use on student performance. In our study, each student's final course grade in their CS1 course was used to give them an initial class rank in the CS1.5 course. At the end of the Winter and Spring courses, the student rank was again computed. Every student therefore had a change in rank depending on whether their position in class improved or declined relative to their peers. Figures 3 and 4 show the average change in class rank when the students are divided into quartiles based on the number of PeerWise questions they answered, where Q1 is comprised of the most active PeerWise users (the values in parentheses in each of these figures are the mean number of questions answered by students in the corresponding quartile). These figures clearly show that the more questions a student answered when using PeerWise, the greater the improvement in their class rank. In fact, the most active students were improving their class rank by an average of 8 places in a class of 73 (Winter) and by an average of nearly 6 places in a class of 53 (Spring). A one-way ANOVA on the Winter data showed that significant differences existed between the quartiles, and a Bonferroni corrected pairwise t-test showed that the difference between the rank changes in the most active (Q1) and least active (Q4) group was highly significant (p=0.004). While a one-way ANOVA on the Spring data showed that the differences were not significant (although very close, p=0.060), the probability of both charts exhibiting a monotonic trend by chance is less than 0.7%. The fact that in both cases the trend is monotonically decreasing is very strong evidence of a positive relationship between student activity and improvement in class rank.

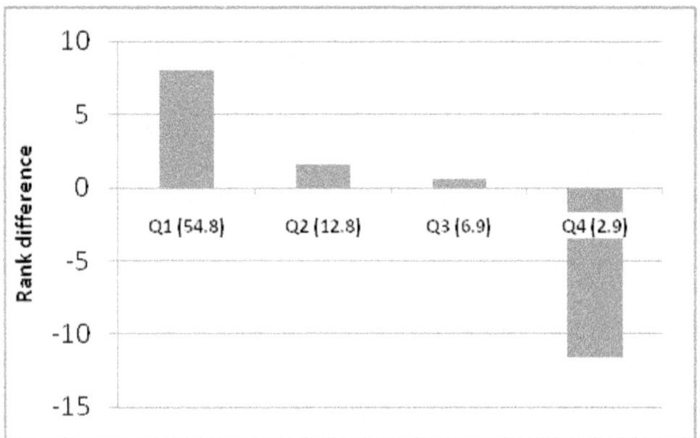

Figure 3. Average change in class rank per quartile based on number of PeerWise questions answered (Winter)

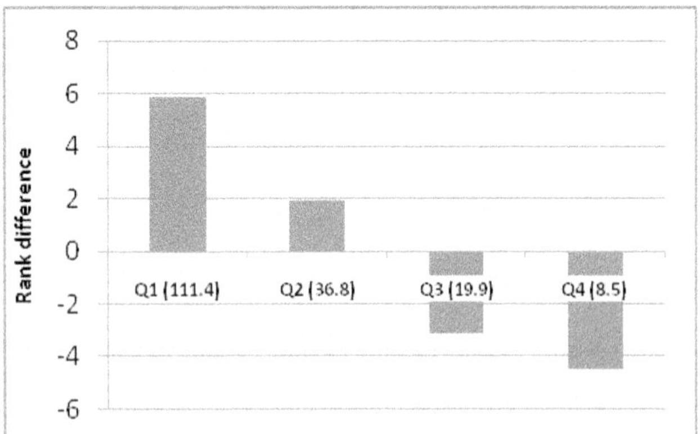

Figure 4. Average change in class rank per quartile based on number of PeerWise questions answered (Spring)

When we examined the data over the entire class, there was a positive relationship between the number of questions answered and the improvement in class rank. Figure 5 shows the change in class rank against the log of the number of questions answered for the Winter course (we have used the log as a few students answered a very large number of questions). This relationship is statistically significant (ANOVA: $p < 0.001$, adjusted $R^2 = 0.135$). A similar response pattern was found for the Spring course which was marginally significant for log data ($p = 0.068$, adjusted $R^2 = 0.046$) and statistically significant for raw data ($p = 0.030$, adjusted $R^2 = 0.071$). Although the relationship is not strong, the data shows that there is a positive relationship between increased PeerWise activity in terms of questions answered and change in class rank. Students who used PeerWise more tended to improve their class rank compared with their peers.

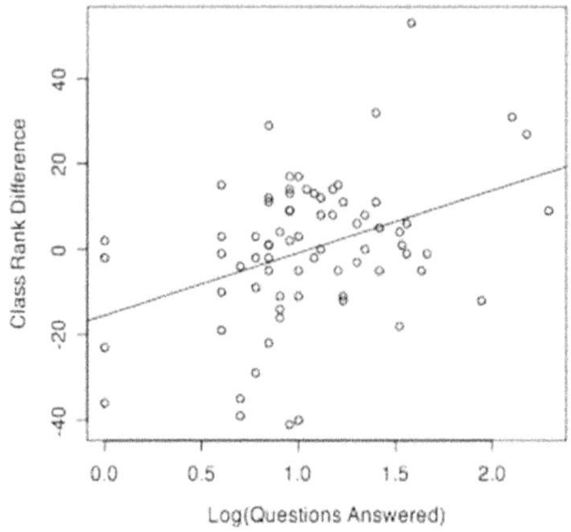

Figure 5. Rank change vs. log of questions answered (Winter)

We'd like to highlight that the relationship between PeerWise use and change in class rank was similar in both courses, even though the pattern of PeerWise use in the two courses differed markedly. In Winter, those students who were the highest performing in the prerequisite CS1 course tended to be the most active PeerWise users, while in the Spring course it was the lower performing CS1 students who were more active. This suggests that using PeerWise helps all students regardless of their academic standing.

4.3 Student perceptions of activity value

Voluntary usage of PeerWise is a good indicator that students value the peer-generated resource. The total number of questions that students were required to answer in order to be awarded their participation marks was 9 and 15 in the Winter and Spring courses respectively. In Spring, 72% of students answered questions beyond the requirement – a marked increase from 45% who answered more than required in Winter (Table 3). This occurred despite the higher requirement in Spring. This may be attributed to the fact that the instructor spent more time promoting the benefits of the system in this course.

Table 3. Number of students per activity level

Activity level (no. questions answered)	Winter	Spring
0-9	40	5
10-15	10	10
16-19	5	4
20-29	6	12
30-49	8	7
50-99	1	10
>99	3	5

These results are similar to those seen in earlier studies, in which there is clear evidence that many students use the question repository voluntarily, answering questions beyond the requirement for their grade.

Finally, on a survey conducted in the Spring course, student perceptions of the value of PeerWise were generally positive (Table 4), consistent with the earlier results in [4].

Table 4. Survey results (Spring, N=60)

Question	Agree	Neutral	Disagree
Developing new questions helped me learn	47%	37%	17%
Answering other student's questions helped me learn	65%	28%	7%
I would recommend other professors to offer PeerWise in their class	50%	29%	21%

5. DISCUSSION AND FUTURE WORK

Based on our experience using PeerWise in the Winter and Spring courses discussed in this paper, we make the following observations and suggestions for future work.

Repository quality. Accurate student ratings may improve the usefulness of the repository as a review resource. In both Winter and Spring, students made use of the quality ratings to decide which questions to answer, and the difficulty ratings appeared to be very accurate, yielding strong negative correlations with the percentage of correct responses. There may also be options we can explore to better help students find useful questions. Possible options include providing training to students in how to rate questions, rewarding students for accurately rating questions, requiring students to rate more questions (rating questions was voluntary in our studies), and giving greater weighting to instructor, TA, or "top" student ratings.

Learning benefits. Interestingly, the students answering the greatest number of questions in the Winter course tended to be those with a stronger background (based on their CS1 prerequisite mark), whereas in the Spring course it was the students with a weaker background who were more active. We believe this is due to the fact that the instructor promoted the use of PeerWise much more actively in the Spring course. Without repeated instructor encouragement, most use of the tool was made by the already high performing students. However, what is striking is that the relationship between PeerWise use and change in class rank was similar in the Winter and Spring courses (see Figures 3 and 4), indicating that PeerWise may potentially help all students regardless of academic rank. This corroborates previous results [5] that the most active students perform better than the least active students of similar initial abilities.

We also acknowledge that our measure of activity (number of questions answered) is, in some sense, a measure of time on task. However we are pleased to note that this was an entirely student-driven activity, and many students participated to a greater extent than they were required.

Student perceptions of activity value. Students answered significantly more questions than they were required in both courses we studied. This voluntary usage, combined with generally positive survey results, indicates that many students do value both the activity and the peer-created resource.

The numbers alone tell only part of the story. In future work we plan a qualitative exploration of several issues including: is the quality of a student's questions influenced by the number of questions they answer, how do students choose which questions to answer (and does that vary based on whether they are answering voluntarily or to receive course credit), and how do students make their studying choices including investigating how PeerWise use impacts on other forms of studying (reading the textbook, reviewing quizzes, etc.).

6. CONCLUSIONS

In this paper, we reported on the first use of PeerWise in Computer Science courses in the United States. Data collected from two consecutive terms of a CS1.5 course taught at UCSD support results of earlier studies examining CS1 courses taught in New Zealand.

By establishing a learning community that incorporates active learning, peer review, and peer tutoring, we believe PeerWise has the potential to be a powerful teaching tool.

7. REFERENCES

[1] Aleven, V., and Koedinger, K. An effective metacognitive strategy - Learning by doing and explaining with a computer-based cognitive tutor. Cognitive Science, 26, 147-179. 2002.

[2] Anderson, L. W. et al., editor. A taxonomy for learning and teaching and assessing: A revision of Bloom's taxonomy of educational objectives. Addison Wesley Longman, 2001.

[3] Denny, P., Luxton-Reilly, A., and Hamer, J. "The PeerWise system of student contributed assessment questions". In 10th Australasian Computing Education Conference (ACE 2008), CRPIT 78, pgs 69-74, Wollongong, NSW, Australia, 2008. ACS

[4] Denny, P., Luxton-Reilly, A., and Hamer, J. "Student use of the PeerWise system". In 13th Annual SIGCSE Conference on Innovation and Technology in Computer Science (ITiCSE'08), pgs 73-77, Madrid, Spain, 2008. ACM.

[5] Denny, P., Hamer, J., Luxton-Reilly, A., and Purchase, H. "PeerWise: Students sharing their multiple choice questions". In 4th International Computing Education Research Workshop (ICER 2008), pgs 51-58, Sydney, Australia, September 2008.

[6] Denny, P., Luxton-Reilly, A., and Simon, B. "Quality of student contributed questions using PeerWise". In 11th Australasian Computing Education Conference (ACE 2009), CRPIT 95, pgs 45-53, Wellington, New Zealand, 2009. ACS.

[7] Murphy, L. and Tenenberg, J. "Do computer science students know what they know?: a calibration study of data structure knowledge". SIGCSE Bulletin Vol. 37, No. 3, pages 148-152, 2005. ACM.

[8] Roediger, H. L., III, Agarwal, P. K., Kang, S. H. K., and Marsh, E. J "Benefits of Testing Memory: Best Practices and Boundary Conditions." New Frontiers in Applied Memory. Ed. G. M. Davies and D.B. Wright. Psychology Press, Brighton, U.K, in press 2009

How Interactive Multimedia Authoring Transforms Object-Oriented Thinking

Timothy T. Yuen
The University of Texas at San Antonio
One UTSA Circle
San Antonio, TX 78249
timothy.yuen@utsa.edu

Min Liu
The University of Texas at Austin
1 University Station D5700
Austin, TX 78712
mliu@mail.utexas.edu

ABSTRACT
This paper discusses a cognitive study of how interactive multimedia authoring (IMA) affects novice computer science students' conceptual understanding of object-oriented programming (OOP). In this study, interactive multimedia authoring refers to the construction of a role-playing game using a game template developed with Adobe Flash CS3 and ActionScript 2.0. Three cognitive processes of disequilibrium, exploration, and awareness were observed in this study, which aided the transformation of students' understanding of OOP through interactive multimedia authoring.

Categories and Subject Descriptors
K.3.2 [**Computers and Education**]: Computer and Information Science Education – *computer science education, literacy, self-assessment*

General Terms
Human Factors

Keywords
Computer science education, object-oriented programming, Adobe Flash, multimedia authoring, games

1. INTRODUCTION
Object-oriented programming is one of the difficult concepts for students to understand in computer science [5, 6, 11]. OOP requires students to design solutions in an OO-way; that is, decomposing a problem into maintainable and interactive objects.

Visualization tools, such as Alice, Scratch, and LEGOs, have long been used to present OO concepts to students in manageable, familiar, and entertaining contexts [3, 12, 15]. The visual elements provide concrete and real-life scenarios for the OO concepts that complement the textual nature of source code and abstractness of ideas. This study extended the concept of visualization by using interactive multimedia authoring as a way to facilitate and transform students' conceptual understanding of OOP as in the case of cognitive tools [20]. The rationale was that the multimedia components would provide the metaphors in which students can see visual representations of their code, the authoring component provides students the opportunity to exercise their understanding, and the interaction with the game which allows students to experiment with their own implementations.

SIGCSE'10, March 10–13, 2010, Milwaukee, Wisconsin, USA.

2. LEARNING THROUGH INTERACTIVE MULTIMEDIA AUTHORING
Constructivist learning regards learning as an active process of knowledge construction [1]. Thus, higher order thinking and problem solving are skills that are built up over time as learners gain more experiences. Learners' mental models will be refined through multiple revisions and the adaption of new information [21]. Cognitive tools are designed to instigate change and reorganization of these models as a way to guide students towards a more expert way of thinking [20].

Past research in CS education research looked at visualization tools to aid in this knowledge construction. Such tools generally show how each line of code is executed, the flow of logic in the source code, or visualized behaviors of code [4, 10]. The purpose of interactive multimedia authoring in computing is to add different levels of representation through interactive and visual channels to scaffold OOP understanding and learning. Another goal is to provide students with a motivating environment. That is, immersing students in a multimedia environment may play on students' personal experiences and interests in multimedia can be motivating [8]. The specific project of creating a game within an interactive multimedia authoring integrated development environment (IDE) can also play on the continual interests and experiences that younger people have with video games [13].

IMA follows the notion of constructionism in which knowledge construction works alongside the construction of an artifact [19]. In computer science, constructionism is a natural descriptor as students usually write programs as a way to exercise their understanding of a given topic such as a data structure or algorithm. IMA differs from visualization tools in that students are developing multimedia-rich and interactive application themselves. Multimedia is not just an after-thought but also something that students must be involved in creating so as to lead to the construction of better conceptual understanding [2, 18]. The multimedia output and interaction with the output is a direct effect of students' coding and vice versa.

2.1 CSNüb
CSNüb is a template created in Adobe Flash that students use as a basis for creating a role-playing game (RPG). The default game is an underwater RPG named Operation SPLASH and features a

submarine moving around the ocean floor and encountering various life forms and objects. Students are provided basc code, library of graphics, and basic documentation on the overall architecture of the game template. Students use, add, and customize the base code and graphics to create their own games.

3. METHODOLOGY

Since the concern centers on conceptual understandings and how they are formed and changed, a qualitative approach was taken to answer the following research question: How does creating a video game within an interactive multimedia authoring tool affect novices' conceptual understanding of OOP?

3.1 Sample and Participants

Twelve participants (n=12) were recruited from a CS1 and CS2 class at a large university in central Texas in 2007. At this particular university, students may begin with either the CS1 or CS2 course depending on their prior computing experience. In both cases, OOP was not taught until the last third or last half of the semester, respectively. All participants were self-selected. They were all undergraduate males, ranging from ages 18 to 23 with a mean age of 19.25. With the exception of one student who was a Computer Engineering major, all participants were CS majors or had intended to major in CS. Two CS majors were also Math majors.

When asked to rate their programming knowledge on a scale of 0 (needs improvement) to 3 (excellent), participants reported an average score of 1.583. On the same scale, participants reported an average score of 1.667 when asked to rate their knowledge of OOP. Over half of the students reported a score of 1. Only two students reported experience with Adobe Flash.

3.2 Methods

Clinical interviews were used to solicit the participants' cognitive processes and conceptual understanding of OOP. Clinical interviews are generally task-based environments in which the researcher consistently probes students' thinking through questioning and perhaps altering the parameters of the tasks depending on each student's level of development [7]. Process tracing methods were used to structure the researcher interaction with the participants. Process tracing methods involve the observation of behaviors, think-aloud protocols, and retrospective reports [9]. Thus, all behaviors committed by participants, such as compiling the game, opening files, and looking at sample code were recorded into a behavioral log.

3.3 Tasks

Participants were given three tasks to complete during the clinical interviews. Tasks involved implementing a specific feature of the game as well as a concept of OOP. Task 1 asked participants to give hit points (HP), attack points (AP), and defense points (DP) to the submarine and the squid characters. These are standard properties associated with characters in RPGs. It required participants to use variables inherited from a parent class. Tasks 2 and 3 asked participants to implement the interaction between the submarine and an energy barrel and a rock, respectively. In each of these tasks, participants had to write new classes, which should extend from existing classes in the CSNüb template as well as use inherited properties and methods.

These tasks required participants to exercise their understanding of OO systems, class design, inheritance, encapsulation, and object interaction. There was no time limit.

4. ANALYSIS

A microanalysis of the data was conducted through an open coding procedure [17, 22]. Each fragment of the behavioral logs was coded to describe the action and/or theme. Additional data also included field notes, transcripts of the participants' interviews during the tasks, the source code, and the game for the purposes of triangulation [14].

4.1 Cognitive Processes and Factors

Open coding of the data yielded three categories related to how the participants knew and applied their knowledge of OOP. These categories are the cognitive processes of disequilibrium, exploration, and awareness.

4.1.1 Disequilibrium

Disequilibrium is a state of cognitive conflict in which a student's mental model cannot adapt new information received [21]. Disequilibrium occurred when the visual and textual feedback from testing their games was inconsistent with participants' expectations. Though compile time errors also provided conflicts, it is important to emphasize that participants gained most from not just observing the visual feedback, but interacting with their games.

There were two examples of problems that were common among the participants: the never-ending game problem and the *_rotation* problem, both of which placed them in a state of disequilibrium. Each problem can be tied to a discrepancy in the participants' understanding of OOP.

Redundant code was a label given to the ongoing trend in which participants would declare variables or methods that were already inherited from a parent class. Task 1 asked participants to assign specific values for hit points, attack points, and defense points to the submarine and squid characters. Seven participants went to those respective classes and declared new variables and/or methods (e.g., *private var HP:Number;*). When viewing the *Submarine* and *Squid* classes, there is no mention of hit points, attack points, or defense points. However, both classes descend from the *Character* class, which is where they are defined. This represents the problems of narrow perspective or awareness of the entire OO architecture.

Though no compile time error occurred from redundant code, problems did arise during run-time. The most prominent problem that stemmed from redundant code was when the game would not end. In the background, there is a listener that continues to check on the hit points of the submarine (the main character in the game). Should the hit points ever reach the value of zero, the game will end with a lose state, which can be seen on the Game Over screen. Similarly, the listener also checks to see how many enemy life forms (e.g., a squid) and items (e.g., an energy barrel) are remaining. When all of those objects are gone and the submarine has 1 or more hit points remaining, then the game will end with a win state. The feedback from the Game Over scene or lack thereof presented the participants with the conflict.

The *_rotation* problem stems from Task 2, which asked the participants to program the interaction between the submarine (main character) and a rock. The submarine should hit the rock and turn around 180°. Participants were aware that there was a *_rotation* property in the *Submarine* class. So, they simply set the value to 180 (e.g., *this._rotation = 180)*. *_rotation* is a top-level property of Flash's *MovieClip* class, from which all of CSNüb's classes descend. However, participants were unaware that Flash's implementation of an object's *_rotation* is a fixed value. That is, a value of 180 will turn the object facing down no matter its current orientation. Eight participants experienced the *_rotation* problem since they were unaware of its behavior.

Both the issues of the never-ending game and *_rotation* were discovered when playing the games. When in a state of disequilibrium, a learner tries to resolve the situation by making sense of the information. Piaget refers to the processes of assimilation and accommodation; that is, changing the incoming information to conform to one's mental model or changing one's mental model to accept the new information [21]. This paper offers a different take on Piaget's ideas by presenting the cognitive processes of exploration and awareness as methods of adaptation.

4.1.2 Exploration

Exploration was largely the initial method by which participants tried to resolve their moments of disequilibrium during the *_rotation* and never-ending game problems. Exploration was first noted when participants would start opening other files to see what could help them resolve the problems. The interesting part was participants would do this in a methodical manner. That is, they would open other files that were in relationship to the current file they are working with. For example, if participants were working with the *Submarine* class and ran into a problem, they saw that it extended the *Character* class. When they could not find their solution in *Character*, they would see that it extended the *Object* class and opened that file. One participant referred to this as "go[ing] up the chain." Participants also traced out the interactive relationship between classes. In Task 2, one participant noted that the *DisplayPanel* object somehow received information from *Submarine* object and looked in the *DisplayPanel* to see how it was getting the hit points, attack points, and defense points. He noted, "At this point, I'm trying to look what's in the display panel. Because at this point I don't see a display for health. And possibly it would tell me where the health values are set."

Table 1 is a tally of the number of times a participant looked up another file with the explicit purposes of exploring OO relationships between classes. These counts do not include random exploration of files.

Table 1. Look-up counts per task

Task	Min # of Lookups	Max # of Lookups	Mean # of Lookups	Std. Dev.
1	0	5	2.417	2.065
2	1	20	7.833	5.997
3	2	17	7.083	4.999

An increase in Task 2 and Task 3 can be explained by the fact that they required participants to design two new classes (*Rock* and *EnergyBarrel*) that must extend from one of the base class (*Object*) for the purposes of keeping the OO nature of CSNüb. More importantly, the game engine worked under the assumption that all game objects are descended from the top-level *Object* in CSNüb. Task 2 was also the first time that two objects would interact with each other.

Another explanation for the increase in Task 2 over Task 1 is that this is the first task in which participants were asked to implement an interaction between two objects: the submarine and a rock. The role of the game engine is to detect the collision of the two objects and delegate the reaction effects to the submarine. One participant remarked: "I assume there's going to be multiple obstacles in this game and I don't know exactly [what] an obstacle should do yet. So, if I look at the comments and the methods provided in the parent class, I'll know what a rock is supposed to do." This reaction showed the participant trying to understand the behavior of the two classes involved and how to possibly understand the interaction between then.

In Task 1, one participant said, "If I'm going to set the following values, I'm going to find the class of it" while another said "I gotta go find the information for the submarine and both of the squids." These two participants' statements illustrated their initial understanding that the *Submarine* and *Squid* classes were actually part of a larger, interconnected system. It should be noted that not all participants showed this initial understanding, which could also explain why there were fewer look-ups in Task 1 compared to the other three tasks. Thus, exploration is a result of a participant's awareness of the OO system.

4.1.3 Awareness

Awareness is the level at which participants understood the OO architecture of the CSNüb template. The previous discussion exploration showed that participants explored files in a methodical manner with respect to tracing out the hierarchical and interactive relationships between classes. How a participant explored was a reflection of his level of awareness of the OO system. Awareness was best demonstrated in Task 1 when participants wrote redundant code. As evident from the redundant code issue, many of the participants experienced narrowed vision of each class. That is, they did not consider that the Submarine class could have properties and behaviors that are inherited from other classes.

For example, one participant in Task 1 said the variables to represent the HP, AP, and DP "should be at the very top" of the *Submarine* class. He did not see this nor did he notice that *Submarine* extends *Character*, which resulted in the declaration of redundant variables. Another participant noted the variables "should be in the constructor, but there are no instance variables. Do I create those variables?" That is, he was used to seeing variables initialized within the constructor, but participants were provided with an empty constructor. Another participant in the same mindset said, "I'll probably have to define them myself...and then initialize the constructor." He also contemplated writing setter and getter functions for them as well within the *Submarine* class. However, its parent class *Character* already had the variables and the methods. High awareness was demonstrated by the participants that attempted to gain the bigger picture through exploration before writing code. For example, one participant wanted to know how the two objects worked together before any implementation: "If I knew how it was going to use the HP object...how the game is actually going to determine how HP is implemented, it may be useful."

Five participants began Task 1 having a higher-level understanding of OOP. When they were unable to find the variables for the hit points, attack points, and defense points in the *Submarine* class, they knew to explore the parent class. Here is yet another example of how awareness affects exploration. It should be noted that two of these participants were unsuccessful in completing Task 1: they found the variables in the parent class, but copied and pasted the variable declarations into the *Submarine* class which resulted in redundant code.

There was a transition between a narrow awareness to a larger sense of the OO system while participants worked through the tasks in this study. Of the seven participants that showed signs of low awareness, only three were able to resolve the redundant code problem through exploration of files when they encountered the never-ending game problem in subsequent tasks. It gave some participants cause to explore other files.

After an unsuccessful try at Task 2 with redundant code, a participant finally noticed that *Submarine* extended *Character* from the class header. He began to laugh when he saw that the points variables he declared in *Submarine* and *Squid* were already declared in their parent class *Character*, "It seems just what I did. [laughs] I could have been using that for a more efficient solution." He corrected his code to take advantage of the inherited variables after this discovery. Awareness of how objects are related or interact together was changed as participants explored and explicitly traced out such relationships in the code. As in the redundant code issue, it can take cognitive disequilibrium to bring attention to students' inadequacies with regard to awareness.

5. DISCUSSION

Regular programming (e.g., in Java or C++) generally results in numerous occasions in which students experience disequilibrium: bugs in the code, run-time errors, etc. Though these occur in IMA as well, the visual components of the game provide students with multiple representations of the problem: verbal cues from the debugger and source code and the visual components of the game. We want to continually engage the students in moments of disequilibrium—not to further frustrate—but to motivate metacognition and change in students' mental models. Multimedia learning theories contend that feedback is good in that multiple sensory channels are engaged when providing a different representation of the idea [16].

CSNüb is described as a game template and not a game engine. This purposed description is to draw attention to its simplicity whereby students who enter states of disequilibrium can easily sift through the source code and have a general overview of the OO architecture. The data showed that exploration of the source code is the method by which students tried to understand the OO design of the template, especially when they were in the state of disequilibrium.

Such exploration leads to a greater awareness of the OO system and how objects were related and worked together to create the final game. As students designed more complex objects, they saw the results through playing the game. For the students that entered into the activity with a very novice-level or narrow view of programming, they started from a bottom-up approach. The game template put the student in a situation where there was enough support for them to understand the system from a top-down approach.

Interactive multimedia authoring provides cognitive scaffolding on multiple levels. First, the existing source code gives students models. Second, the feedback from the game gives a visual and interactive element in which they can see their code in action. As students construct their better games (e.g., more effective OO design, adding game features, etc.), this should represent a more complex understanding of the OO nature of the game template. This supports the constructionist perspective of learning in that the artifact one creates is a representation of the mental model [19].

6. CONCLUSIONS

The three cognitive processes are not separate entities. In fact, they work together in assisting students with achieving a higher level of thinking and problem solving (See Figure 1). Exploration helps resolve disequilibrium by giving students more information to understand the problem space. Conversely, disequilibrium triggers the exploration process, which was done in a methodical manner according to the OO relationship. The scope of awareness with respect to the OO design of the game template was a major factor in how students explored the classes and other resources. Low awareness resulted in random exploration of files and classes. High awareness resulted in the methodical exploration of classes. When students explored, they found various forms of cognitive scaffolding: through code modeling and multimedia-based feedback from playing the game.

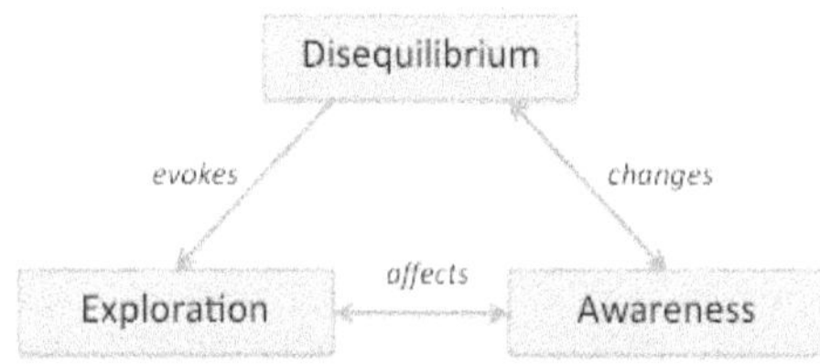

Figure 1. Relationship between disequilibrium, exploration, and awareness during interactive multimedia authoring

The model above illustrates how interactive multimedia authoring can be used to challenge students' thinking of OOP. With further study using a wider range of students, in terms of gender and aptitude at the CS0/CS1/CS2 levels, we can construct a more refined model of how interactive multimedia authoring affects conceptual understanding of OOP or any other topic requiring complex or abstract thinking. It shows a process in which we, as instructional designers, can engage students and positively affect their conceptual understanding, higher-order thinking, and problem solving skills.

7. REFERENCES

[1] J. G. Brooks and M. G. Brooks, *In search of understanding the case for constructivist classrooms*. Alexandria, VA: Association for Supervision and Curriculum Development, 1993.

[2] D. C. A. Bulterman and L. Hardman, "Structured Multimedia Authoring," *ACM Transactions on Multimedia Computing, Communications and Applications,* vol. 1, pp. 89-109, 2005.

[3] S. Cooper, W. Dann, and R. Pausch, "Alice: A 3-D tool for introductory programming concepts," in *CCSC '00: Proceedings of the fifth annual CCSC northeastern conference on The journal of computing in small colleges*, Mahwah, NJ, 2000.

[4] J. H. Cross II, D. Hendrix, J. Jain, and L. A. Barowski, "Dynamic object viewers for data structures," in *SIGCSE 2007 Technical Symposium on Computer Science Education*, Covington, KY, 2007.

[5] N. B. Dale, "Most difficult topics in CS1: Results of an online survey of educators," *inroads - The SIGCSE Bulletin,* vol. 38, pp. 46-53, 2006.

[6] A. Eckerdal, "Novice students' learning of object-oriented programming," in *Department of Information Technology*. vol. Licentiate Theses: Uppsala University, 2006.

[7] H. P. Ginsburg, *Entering the child's mind: The clinical interview in psychological research and practice*. New York, NY: Cambridge University Press, 1997.

[8] M. Guzdial and E. Soloway, "Teaching the Nintendo generation to program," *Communications of the ACM,* vol. 45, pp. 17-21, 2002.

[9] J. R. Hayes and L. S. Flower, "Uncovering cognitive processes in writing: An introduction to protocol analysis," in *Research on writing: principles and methods*, S. A. Walmsley, Ed. New York, NY: Longman, 1983.

[10] S.-C. J. Jehng, S.-H. S. Tung, and C.-T. Chang, "A visualisation approach to learning the concept of recursion," *Journal of Computer Assisted Learning,* vol. 15, 1999.

[11] M. Kölling, "The problem of teaching object-oriented programming, Part 1: Languages," *Journal of Object-Oriented Programming,* vol. 11, pp. 8-15, 1999.

[12] P. B. Lawhead, C. G. Bland, D. J. Barnes, M. E. Duncan, M. Goldweber, R. G. Hollingsworth, and M. Schep, "A road map for teaching introductory programming using LEGO(c) Mindstorms robots," *inroads - The SIGCSE Bulletin,* vol. 35, pp. 191-201, 2003.

[13] A. Lenhart, J. Kahne, E. Middaugh, A. R. Macgill, C. Evans, and J. Vitak, "Teens, video games, and civics: Teens' gaming experiences are diverse and include significant social interaction and civic engagement," Pew Internet & American Life Project, Washington, DC2008.

[14] Y. S. Lincoln and E. G. Guba, *Naturalistic inquiry*. Newbury Park, CA: SAGE Publications, 1985.

[15] D. J. Malan and H. Leitner, "Scratch for budding computer scientists," in *SIGCSE '07*, Covington, KY, 2007, pp. 223-227.

[16] R. E. Mayer, *Multimedia learning*. Cambridge: Cambridge University Press, 2001.

[17] M. B. Miles and A. M. Huberman, *Qualitative Data Analysis*, 2nd ed. Thousand Oaks, CA: SAGE Publications, 1994.

[18] M. Neo and T.-K. Neo, "Engaging students in multimedia-mediated constructivist learning - Students perceptions," *Educational Technology & Society,* vol. 12, pp. 254-266, 2009.

[19] S. Papert, *Mindstorms: Children, Computers, and Powerful Ideas*. New York, NY: BasicBooks, 1993.

[20] R. D. Pea, "Beyond amplification: Using the computer to reorganize mental functioning," *Educational Psychologist,* vol. 20, pp. 167-182, 1985.

[21] J. Piaget, *Psychology of Intelligence*. London, UK: Routledge Classics, 1950.

[22] A. Strauss and J. Corbin, *Basics of qualitative research: Techniques and procedures for developing grounded theory*. Thousand Oaks, CA: SAGE Publications, Inc., 1998.

Manipulating Mindset to Positively Influence Introductory Programming Performance

Quintin Cutts
Dept. of Computing Science
University of Glasgow
Scotland.
quintin@dcs.gla.ac.uk

Emily Cutts
Centre for Confidence & Well-being
Glasgow
Scotland.
emily@centreforconfidence.co.uk

Stephen Draper
Dept. of Psychology
University of Glasgow
Scotland.
s.draper@psy.gla.ac.uk

Patrick O'Donnell
Dept. of Psychology
University of Glasgow
Scotland.
p.odonnell@psy.gla.ac.uk

Peter Saffrey
Dept. of Computing Science
University of Glasgow
Scotland.
pzs@dcs.gla.ac.uk

ABSTRACT

Introductory programming classes are renowned for their high dropout rates. The authors propose that this is because students learn to adopt a *fixed mindset* towards programming. This paper reports on a study carried out with an introductory programming class, based on Dweck's mindset research. Combinations of three interventions were carried out: tutors taught mindset to students; growth mindset feedback messages were given to students on their work; and, when stuck, students were encouraged to use a crib sheet with pathways to solve problems. The study found that the mixture of teaching mindset and giving mindset messages on returned work resulted in a significant change in mindset and a corresponding significant change in test scores – improvements in test scores were found in a class test given immediately after the six-week intervention and at the end-of-year exam. The authors discuss the results and the strengths and weaknesses of the study.

Categories and Subject Descriptors

K.3.2 [Computers & Education]: Computer & Information Science Education—*Computer Science Education*

General Terms

Experimentation, Human Factors

Keywords

Self-theories, growth mindset, CS0, CS1, debugging, programming, Dweck, attitudinal, novice programmers.

1. INTRODUCTION

Some learners behave as though they believe that ability is a fixed commodity and once it has been shown that they cannot do something then they should give up. Dweck has shown that a learner's mindset towards ability levels has a crucial effect on their learning [5]. She identifies two categories of learners, one consisting of those with a *fixed* mindset (the students described above) and the other, those with a *growth* mindset, who act as if persistent effort and attention to data gleaned from failures will lead to the desired learning.

Dweck's work on mindsets highlights a number of ramifications for learning. Each mindset is supported by a motivational framework guiding future thinking and behaviour [3]. Those with a fixed mindset tend to be interested only in *performance* goals – they feel a need to be seen to be achieving well at all times, since this broadcasts their ability to the world. Those with a growth mindset adopt *learning* goals. They are classical deep learners who sacrifice looking good in the eyes of others in order to learn and understand a topic. Those endorsing a growth mindset continue to enjoy learning even after failures and setbacks, compared to those holding a fixed view of their ability [4]. Those with a fixed mindset tend to disregard formative feedback, since the very idea goes against their belief of ability being essentially fixed; someone with a growth mindset will use all the data available in order to help them learn [9]. Negative feedback of any kind is likely to lead the fixed mindset learner to give up, to display a helpless response, or to avoid, because it represents an insurmountable barrier to further progress. Beliefs about effort differ too (e.g, [11]). Those with a fixed mindset believe that if someone has to put effort in then this demonstrates that they do not have what it takes; they lack the ability. Those with a growth mindset view effort as a necessary part of the learning process, and essential for future understanding and success.

Learning to program at university can easily induce a fixed mindset. There are many ways in which a student can get stuck: they do not understand a programming task they have been given, or they understand the task but cannot think of a way of solving it; they do not know the right programming constructs to use; the computer rejects the program because of syntax errors; the program runs but gives the wrong answer; computer science content at university is different from school content which is more about training in computer use; and there are widely differing levels of ability in the class. These are all potential points where a student may get stuck and be susceptible to attributing this to a lack of intellect. Such an attribution

SIGCSE'10, March 10–13, 2010, Milwaukee, Wisconsin, USA.
Copyright 2010 ACM 978-1-60558-885-8/10/03...$10.00.

strengthens a fixed mindset, reducing learning potential and thereby increasing the likelihood of poor performance in tests.

The study presented in this paper addresses whether small changes to an introductory programming course can foster a growth mindset and influence performance. Given that previous studies reveal a relationship between mindset interventions and test scores, this study examines tests scores at three points across the academic year. We describe three interventions, along with the findings from applying these interventions experimentally, and discuss what implications, if any, these have for first year programming students. We conclude with thoughts about the strengths and weaknesses of the design, as well as future research.

2. RELATED WORK

Specific interventions can change mindset and directly influence motivation and performance [1], and have been carried out in subjects similar to computer science such as math [3] and engineering [7].

Computer science seems like the perfect candidate for a mindset intervention. [12] and [14] link the problems faced by new programmers to a fixed mindset detailing the characteristics of the course that may lead to helpless responses in students.

The authors know of only one study that has carried out a mindset intervention with programming students. The intervention did not move the students' beliefs about their ability [14]. The study looked at students' beliefs only and did not measure any changes in student performance. No study, as far as the authors are aware, has examined the impact of a mindset intervention on performance in introductory programming or indeed in any CS course. Though [14] found no change in students' beliefs after their mindset intervention, this does not necessarily mean it doesn't work with this discipline. Dweck uses computer science as an example of a subject that requires a growth mindset [6]. Simon et al. [14] note some flaws in their design, such as less intensive training than other published research, a less personal approach, and not much follow-up.

3. CONTEXT

The course used for this study was a two-semester, 26-week, introductory programming course in Python with around 170 students enrolled. The previous programming experience in the student cohort typically ranges from none at all right up to commercial programming. Students attend two lectures and one 2-hour practical session per week and submit exercises for review by tutors every fortnight. The student cohort for this study was divided into 12 small groups for their practical work, each under the supervision of a tutor. The typical group size is 14 students; in the year of the study, it varied from 9 to 17. The same tutor assists with a student's practical work and marks their work.

The design of the course aims to maximise the frequency and quality of feedback to *all* students in two ways. First, one of the weekly lecture sessions is given over to classwide discussion of issues arising directly from the practical session. Second, the students receive a feedback sheet when their fortnightly submissions are returned that contains extensive feedback on a number of issues arising in the submissions of a representative sample of the class. This level of feedback is far more than can typically be written by hand on each student's printed submission. The tutors can provide high quality feedback cheaply as they simply cross-reference issues in the student's work with the corresponding feedback points on the sheet. Although use of the sheet is not a variable in this study, the design is itself inspired by mindset-related principles: the student's score is at the bottom of the second side, reducing the focus on the summative feedback; the feedback items to which they should particularly pay attention are numbered and noted at the head of the document, accentuating the formative feedback; and there is encouragement to read all points, even if not specifically identified for this student, encouraging learning goals generally.

4. THE THREE INTERVENTIONS

In this study, three different mindset-related teaching interventions were designed in order to gain insight into whether small changes in the course design could effect significant changes in performance. The interventions are described in this section; their experimental application is described in Section 5.

4.1 *Mindset training* intervention (MT)

A series of four 10-15 minute teaching sessions were developed for delivery by tutors at the start of their small-group 2-hr tutorial/lab sessions – to be used over four consecutive weeks early in the semester. The tutors were taught about the material for each of these sessions in the week prior to its delivery. Each session involved the tutor talking about a particular aspect of mindsets and then taking the students through a reflective exercise focusing on their own learning experience and relating it to the mindsets work. Tutors were then encouraged to refer back to this material when working with students encountering problems in the lab environment. The four sessions introduced: fixed and growth mindsets; performance and learning goals; responses to feedback; role models and the neuroscience underpinning mindsets. In addition, a short overview document was created that introduced the fundamental aspects of mindset research.

A survey of the tutors after the third teaching session showed that they had delivered the material in very different ways, with some hardly touching on it at all. It was clear that some tutors were *not* fully on board with the mindsets research, and were themselves displaying a strongly-fixed mindset. Such attitudes in tutors are likely to affect their behaviour towards students to a large extent, according to [6]. These tutors were given access to a range of further research papers and in particular the neuroscience studies that relate to Dweck's work, which they found more engaging than our earlier teaching. Additionally, we developed the overview document covering the main Dweck findings, and asked all tutors to get their students to read this in the final teaching session. In this way, we were sure that all students in the mindset training intervention definitely had knowledge of Dweck's work.

4.2 *Crib-sheet* intervention (C)

Students with a growth mindset tend to have a range of strategies for resolving problems and setbacks in their learning, whereas those with a fixed mindset will keep on trying to fix their problem with a single inappropriate strategy [5]. The collection of 35 ways in which successful computing students get unstuck, reported in [10], is in line with this finding.

In order to assist students to develop these strategies, the course design was extended with a crib sheet containing a list of questions/hints/pointers for what to do when a student gets stuck. Each item on the sheet linked to a wiki entry explaining the item in much more detail and with examples. The aim here was to increase self-efficacy by encouraging the student to see that they could help themselves, any time, whether the tutor was present or not, just by following the questions/steps on the crib sheet. *All* students received a copy of the crib sheet, and half a lecture was spent explaining its purpose.

The crib-sheet intervention (C) required tutors to help students via the crib sheet *only*. The tutor followed the diagnostic questions on the crib sheet during *every* interaction with the student to find their problem. Hence, students in the intervention group were repeatedly (a) reminded by their tutors that they had at their disposal a range of strategies to solve their problems, and (b) taken through the process of picking the appropriate strategy for the current problem.

4.3 *Rubric* intervention (R)

[11] shows that a simple exhortation, based on mindsets research, to make use of the feedback given on assessment tasks improved motivation and performance. For our intervention, the following related script or rubric was added into the text of the feedback sheet attached to the students' fortnightly exercise submissions:

Remember, learning to program can take a surprising amount of time & effort – students may get there at different rates, but almost all students who put in the time & effort get there eventually. Making good use of the feedback on this sheet is an essential part of this process.

The key to this intervention is that students are reminded of their capacity to overcome learning hurdles *precisely at the delivery point* of feedback that can help them do so.

The three interventions were used in a semi-controlled experiment, described in detail in the next section.

5. THE EXPERIMENT

There were 8 different treatment conditions (a 2x2x2 design), giving all possible combinations of the interventions, from none of them to all three. However, it was tutor group, not students, who were assigned to the interventions because the interventions were delivered by tutor.

Tutors were randomly assigned to groups and were told only about the intervention(s) where necessary – tutors in the rubric intervention were not even aware their feedback sheets were different to those of the non-intervention tutors. Students were allocated to tutorial groups by an automated system taking account of their timetable in other subjects, but with no control over their general ability or previous programming experience.

The disadvantages of this assignment by tutorial group not individual student are: a. some doubt about random assignment of students to tutorial group; b. the experiment cannot distinguish between different tutors' skill and different treatment conditions as the causal factor; c. the size of each treatment condition cannot be the same because the number of tutor groups was not a multiple of eight. As will be seen, only interventions MT and R turned out to be of interest, and after further attrition because not all students completed all aspects of the study, the number of students in the two main conditions of interest were:

Total=101	In TM	Not in TM
In R	11	28
Not in R	29	33

The experiment was designed to run for the first six weeks of the first semester, at which point there is a class test in the course. These test scores were used to determine whether the interventions were having any effect. If there were any positive results at the six-week point, those interventions producing it were to be applied to the rest of the class at once, to maintain fairness.

The reason for running the experiment so soon in the academic year was a preventative measure. Students can very quickly get behind in programming classes and this may act to cultivate a fixed mindset. Starting the interventions early provides students with the tools and expectations to get them through the course – in other words, we aimed to foster a mastery approach to learning from the beginning.

As Section 6 shows, there was an effect at the week six checkpoint involving the mindset training and the rubric. All students were then told about the mindset research in lectures and the feedback sheets were standardized for all students to include the rubric. Two further performance measures were used to assess the effect of the experiment on students: a second class test in week 13 and the final examination for the course in week 27.

The students completed two questionnaires, in weeks 1 and 7, to ascertain measures of mindset, self-efficacy and positive and negative affect. The questionnaire in week 7 was completed just after students had received marks and feedback on their class test.

Obvious confounding factors were allowed for. The previous programming experience of the students was measured through a self-report, and gave a hugely significant and sizeable effect when correlated against the students' performance scores. The time of day of the tutorials and their position in the week (and hence in the learning cycle design of the course) were also considered in the allocation of interventions to groups. The existence of statistically significant differences between the treatment groups remained after an attempt to correct for these factors.

A summary of the experimental timeline is as follows:

Wk	Activity
1	1st Questionnaire
2	Crib-sheet distributed to all students
3	MT Session 1 (MT 1), Crib-sheet intervention starts, First Feedback Sheet (FS 1) returned to students
4	MT 2, Crib-sheet continues
5	MT 3, Crib-sheet continues, FS 2 returned to students
6	MT 4, Crib-sheet continues, Class Test 1 (CT1)
7	FS 3 and Class Test 1 returned to students, 2nd questionnaire
9	FS4 – all students now receive the growth mindset rubric
11	FS5 – again, all students receive growth mindset rubric
13	Class Test 2 (CT2)
26	Final Exam (FE)

6. RESULTS

89 students completed questionnaires both in weeks 1 and 7 and so our analysis of the effect on mindset attitude is based on this subset. From the mindset measure taken in the first week, and based on the thresholds set for Dweck's general mindset measure, 19 (21%) of the students displayed a fixed mindset and 38 (43%) a growth mindset. The remainder were between fixed and growth.

Multiple Analysis of Variance (MANOVA) was used to compare the effects of the interventions on mindset and test scores. The results showed no effect due to the crib-sheet intervention.

The students' mindset showed a two-way interaction between the time interval from weeks 1 and 7 and the mindset training intervention ($F(1,75)=4.18$; $p<.044$). Figure 1 shows that, on average, people who were taught about mindsets displayed a shift in their theory of intelligence towards a growth mindset – this is the upper line in the graph. Figure 1 additionally shows that generally those who were not taught about mindset developed a more fixed mindset over time – this is the lower line.

Despite this shift in mindset attitude, the training by itself did not have an impact on any of the test scores.

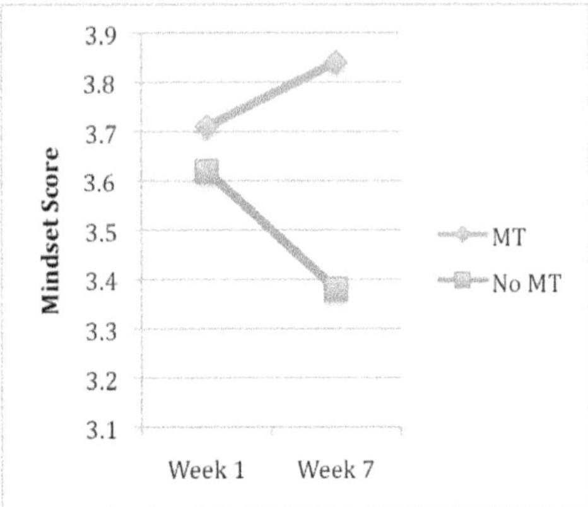

Figure 1. Plot of Means showing shift in mindset between wks 1 & 7 according to mindset training intervention

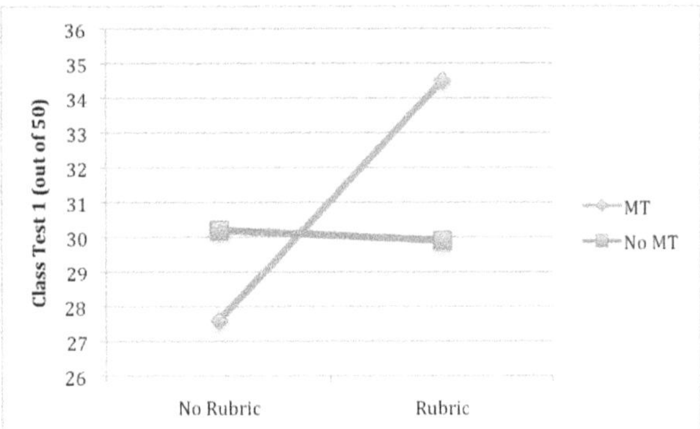

Figure 2. Plot of Means showing first class test performance shift by mindset training and rubric interventions

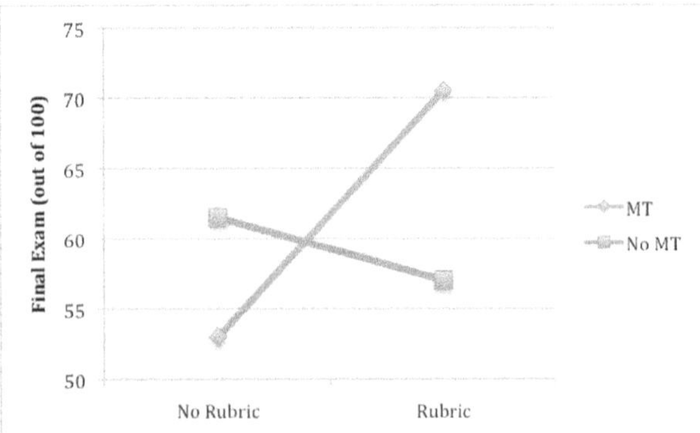

Figure 3. Plot of Means showing final exam performance shift by mindset training and rubric intervention

Of the three test scores, the second (CT2) showed a simple effect for the rubric intervention ($p<.034$).

Figures 2 and 3 show two-way interactions with mindset training and rubric interventions on both the first class test and final exam, respectively ($F(1,91)=4.82$; $p<.031$) and ($F(1,92)=5.43$; $p<.022$).

7. DISCUSSION

In discussing this significant improvement in performance, we first note that the whole course is designed in such a way as to promote a growth mindset approach to learning. Since students can so easily and quickly get stuck when learning to program, it is essential that detailed feedback on progress be provided as early as possible on any student work. We believe the feedback-oriented lecture session and the design of the feedback sheets are a step towards this requirement, given the inevitable constraints of large classes and limited funding. Additionally, students need to develop a range of strategies for getting unstuck if they are to foster a growth mindset, and the crib sheet should help with this.

The interventions described here, to encourage students to focus on the issues raised by mindset research, simply make it more likely that they will make use of the resources that are provided.

Dweck shows repeatedly that teaching mindsets changes a person's belief about their own ability towards the growth mindset (e.g. [5]). Our study supports these findings: students in the mindset training condition became more growth mindset. Other studies (e.g. [2]) have shown that particular scenarios can change a mindset towards fixed. Our study also found that students in the control group became more fixed over time. This fits with our proposition that learning to program may foster a fixed mindset due to the very high number of potential error points. As outlined earlier, students may get stuck at many different stages and could interpret this to mean that they do not have the ability.

Our study found that teaching growth mindset did change mindset but it did not find that this alone transferred to an improvement in test scores. One possible reason for this is that the computer science atmosphere is one where a growth mindset may be challenged repeatedly. Students come up against failure regularly, more than in most other subjects. Hence the mindset message may need to be reinforced regularly. As mentioned earlier, students in the control group became more fixed mindset over time suggesting that the system reinforces a fixed view of ability, despite the course design.

Though a person's mindset may change, the atmosphere within their course may not be conducive to the growth mindset message and may even undermine it. A previous study [8] found than over the course of a 4-year university degree, students moved from endorsing learning goals in 1st year to performance goals in 4th year; linked respectively to a growth, and then a fixed, mindset.

Students in *both* the mindset training and rubric intervention did gain improved scores. The mindset training explicitly taught students about the growth mindset and the consequences that this has on brain and behaviour, providing them with a general schema for approaching their studies. We speculate that the feedback sheet rubric then reinforced this schema, and, as stated earlier, did so at exactly the point where students have received high quality feedback on their learning, enhancing the likelihood of their putting it to good use.

All students received feedback sheets, but only those with both the rubric and mindset training benefitted. This fits with [9] where those with a growth mindset paid attention to formative feedback after failure and did better on future tests.

Educational interventions sometimes do not make themselves apparent until a later date, even years after (e.g. [13]), while others have an immediate impact (e.g. [11]). We found both immediate and long-term gains through mindset interventions.

The crib-sheet intervention did not show any significance on mindset or test scores. This may be because *all* students had the sheet, and if a student has developed a growth-mindset from one of the other interventions, then they would use the sheet whether their tutor encouraged it or not, thereby nullifying the individual effect of this intervention. We could have given the sheet only to those in the intervention; this was not done to avoid students outside the intervention querying why they did not have a sheet.

There are some flaws in the research design. The application of treatment conditions to students could not be truly randomised. It is not clear whether the teaching of mindset, or the reading of the summary sheet, changed mindset. It is also unclear whether we were influencing more significantly the students' or the tutors' minds with both mindset training and the rubric on the feedback sheets – which tutors may have subliminally drawn from as they returned students' work. The effect of previous programming experience was both statistically significant and larger than that due to the interventions, and while the analyses corrected for this in calculating significance, they did not give us a good way of estimating the size of the group effect after subtracting the effect of previous experience because the latter was unevenly distributed between groups. It also remains uncertain whether the effect of the groups was entirely due to the mindset-related interventions or partly to individual tutor skill. We will be re-designing and re-running the experiment with these concerns in mind.

Our difficulty with tutors' adopting the mindset research, noted earlier, is backed up by [14] in which 77% of teaching staff polled disagreed with the statement "Nearly everyone is capable of succeeding in the computer science curriculum if they work at it." It is at least as important that teaching staff have a growth mindset as it is for their students. To effect a really sizeable shift in students with respect to their attitudes towards learning, we may have to instigate a major project to do the same for staff members.

8. CONCLUSIONS

We have designed three interventions for introductory programming based on mindset principles, and applied them in all combinations: tutors taught mindset to students; growth mindset feedback messages were given to students on their work; and, when stuck, students were encouraged to solve problems using a crib sheet with pathways. Performance in a class test and the final exam of the course was better for those students who were taught mindset and who received the mindset message on their feedback sheet.

9. ACKNOWLEDGEMENTS

This work was supported by the Learning and Teaching Development Fund of the University of Glasgow. We acknowledge the on-going support of Carol Craig and Glasgow's Centre for Confidence and Well-being, and finally, we thank the tutors and students who took part in this study.

10. REFERENCES

[1] Aronson, J., Fried, C.B., & Good, C. 'Reducing stereotype threat and boosting academic achievement of African-American students: The role of conceptions of intelligence', *Journal of Experimental Social Psychology,* 38, 113-125, 2002.

[2] Bergen, R. *Beliefs about intelligence and achievement related behaviours*. Unpublished doctoral dissertation, University of Illinois at Urbana- Champaign, 1992.

[3] Blackwell, L.S., Trzesniewski, C.H., Dweck, C.S. Implicit Theories of Intelligence Predict Intelligence across an Adolescent Transition: a Longitudinal Study and an Intervention, *Child Development*, 78(1), 246-263, 2007.

[4] Diener, C.I., & Dweck, C.S. An analysis of learned helplessness: Continuous changes in performance, strategy and achievement cognitions following failure. *Journal of Personality and Social Psychology*, 36, 451-462, 1978.

[5] Dweck, C.S. Self-Theories – Their role in Motivation, Personality and Development. Philadelphia: Taylor and Francis/Psychology Press, 1999.

[6] Heslin, P., Wanderwalle, D. & Latham, G. 'Engagement in employee coaching: The role of managers' implicit person theory', *Personnel Psychology,* 2006.

[7] Heyman, G.D., Martyna, B. and Bhatia, S. Gender and Achievement-related beliefs among engineering students. *Journal of Women and Minorities in Science and Engineering,* 8:41-52, 2002.

[8] Lieberman, D. A., Remedios, R. Do undergraduates' motives for studying change as they progress through their degrees? *British Journal of Educational Psychology*, 77 (2): 379-395, 2007.

[9] Mangels, J.A., Butterfield, B., Lamb, J., Good, C., Dweck, C. S. 'Why do beliefs about intelligence influence learning success? A social cognitive neuroscience model', *Social Cognitive and Affective Neuroscience,* 1 (2): 75-86, 2006.

[10] McCartney, R., Eckerdal, A., Mostrom, J., Sanders, K., Zander, C. 'Successful students strategies for getting unstuck', *ACM SIGCSE Bulletin,* 39(3), 156-160, 2007.

[11] Mueller, C.M. & Dweck, C.S. 'Intelligence praise can undermine motivation and performance', *Journal of Personality and Social Psychology*, 75, 33-52, 1998.

[12] Murphy, L. and Thomas, L. 'Dangers of a fixed mindset: implications of self-theories research for computer science education', *ACM SIGCSE Bulletin*, 40(3), 271-275, 2008.

[13] Shayer, M., Beasley, F. Does Educational Enrichment Work? *British Educational Research Journal.* 13(2): 101-119, 1987.

[14] Simon, B., Hanks, B., Murphy, L., Fitzgerald, S., McCauley, R., Thomas, L. & Zander, C. 'Saying isn't necessarily believing: Influencing self-theories in computing', Proceedings of the 2008 International Computing Education Workshop, 173-184, 2008.

Analyzing Test Items:Using Item Response Theory to Validate Assessments

Leigh Ann Sudol
Computer Science Department
Carnegie Mellon University
Pittsburgh, PA
lsudol@andrew.cmu.edu

Cassandra Studer
Statistics Department
Carnegie Mellon University
Pittsburgh, PA
cstuder@cmu.edu

ABSTRACT

As professional educators we produce a large number of assessments for our students to complete. These assessments or exams are often evaluated informally based upon student feedback and simple measures such as average score on a question. This paper highlights another more rigorous approach to item evaluation, and presents an evaluation of several items from an assessment as examples of the type of information that Item Response Theory can provide.

Categories and Subject Descriptors

L.0.0 [**Science and Technology of Learning**]: Assessment/Evaluation/Measurement—*Assessment and Evaluation*; K.3 [**Computers & Education**]: Computer and Information Sciences Education; I.6 [**Computing Methodologies**]: Simulation and Modeling

General Terms

Item Response Theory

Keywords

Item Response Theory, Assessment

1. INTRODUCTION

There is an increased call for data-driven instruction within educational circles. In the speech that Secretary Arne Duncan gave to the Institute for Education Sciences this past June he called for an increase in research and use of data to direct classroom practices.[1] While there are a number of efforts at the national, regional, and institution level to use data as a tool, even individual teachers and professors can think about using data from within their own classes to improve upon instruction and in doing so improve student learning.

While assessments give us insight into student knowledge and outcomes, they can also be used to help inform us of the alignment between our goals and the instruction provided. On an assessment where a large percentage of students get a particular question incorrect, there could be many reasons why this occurred. The students just did not understand the material, the question was misunderstood, the question was too hard for the population, or perhaps relied upon some other underlying knowledge that wasn't apparent. Statistics, and in particular Item Response Theory can be used to help us determine which of these situations is happening.[2]

In the past 10 years Item Response Theory has been used to validate assessments as well as help researchers understand how question difficulty and student performance interact in order to design better assessments.[3] Within education we are seeing an increase in the use of research designed tools in everyday classrooms. Open source content management systems like Moodle are becoming increasingly more popular in classrooms. As of September 2009 there were almost 38,000 registered sites using the Moodle platform alone.[4] Open source allows for the addition of tools such as item analysis to become available to the educational community. Web environments for data analysis such as the PSLC Data Shop can also be used for the tools they provide.[5]

Previous contributions to the SIGCSE community have advocated the use of Item Response Theory[6] for program level assessment as well as item validation within an instructional tool.[2, 7] This paper offers a case study in the use of Item Response theory to analyze a mid semester assessment with the purpose of improving the assessment for future semesters. In addition to example code from the R statistical package, exemplar graphs and their analysis are included within this paper. The results are shown not to highlight the particular assessment used, but instead to illuminate the process and offer guidance for others who wish to validate their own assessments.

2. WHAT IS IRT?

A student's correct or incorrect response to an exam item is typically a mixture of his proficiency in the area that the exam is covering and the difficulty of the particular item. Item response theory[8] is a method that attempts to enumerate these student and item characteristics in order to calculate the probability that the examinees will answer correctly. Two currently used IRT models are the 1- and 2-parameter logistic (1PL & 2PL) models. Note that we will assume all questions are graded right/ wrong but that the methods can be adapted to account for partial credit scoring without difficulty.

SIGCSE'10, March 10–13,2010, Milwaukee, Wisconsin, USA.

The simplest IRT model is the 1PL or Rasch model. The probability that student i correctly answers item j is modeled as,

$$P_j(\theta_i) = \frac{exp\{\theta_i - b_j\}}{1 + exp\{\theta_i - b_j\}},$$

where θ_i is student i's proficiency and b_j is the difficulty of item j. Higher values of θ indicate higher proficiency and higher values of b indicate more difficult items. In order for a student to have a probability of 0.5 of answering an item correctly, he must have a proficiency equal to the item difficulty, i.e. $\theta_i = b_j$. Student proficiencies are often assumed to have a normal distribution with mean 0 and variance 1. Therefore, values typically fall between -3 and 3. Values outside of this range may indicate a problem with the item.

In addition to problem difficulty, we might want to include information about how well a particular problem differentiates students of varying abilities. We can add a discrimination parameter, a_j, to the model. This model, known as the 2PL, is modeled as,

$$P_j(\theta_i) = \frac{exp\{a_j(\theta_i - b_j)\}}{1 + exp\{a_j(\theta_i - b_j)\}},$$

where θ_i and b_j are the same as the 1PL and a_j is the discrimination of item j. Values of a_j are typically between 0 and 2 with higher values indicating items that better differentiate students. One can note that if $a_j = 1$ for all j, we have the 1PL model. Similar to extreme difficulty parameters, items near the extremes and outside the range of 0 to 2 may indicate problems with the content or wording of the item. Specifically, negative discrimination parameters indicate that students with high proficiency are actually less likely than students with lower proficiency levels to answer correctly. Values near 0 mean that the item may depend on a construct other than the one intended. Discrimination parameters near 2 and above can indicate that an item depends on a "you know it or you don't" trick or fact. These items should be reviewed to make sure they are typical of the type of tasks students should be able to perform.

2.1 Item Characteristic Curves

We can summarize an item's properties by looking at its item characteristic curve (ICC). ICCs represent the probability of correctly answering an item for different values of θ and are logistic curves bounded by 0 and 1. The difficulty of the item can be visualized as the point of inflection on the proficiency (θ) scale. Curves shifted to the left (right) indicate easier (more difficult) items. Alternatively, the discrimination parameter is depicted by the slope of the curve. For reasonable values of a_j, steeper slopes indicate items that are better able to differentiate between students. Negative and flat slopes correspond to negative and low values of a_j, respectively. ICCs that approach a step function indicate particularly high values of a_j.

2.2 Warnings

While IRT is a great method for analyzing the reliability and validity of exam items, it should not be used as a method of assessing students. The estimated proficiency parameters will align identically with the percent correct on the exam. Therefore, a poorly written exam question will effect both a student's grade on the exam and his θ value as well. Also, the proficiency estimate is exactly that, an estimate with a standard deviation. Therefore, one should not be overly dependent on the values. There is little advantage to using θ values in place of exam scores to assess students.

The other warning that we offer is to be aware of the number of students taking the test versus the number of parameters being measured for each item. Trying to estimate too many parameters with too few data points can lead to serious problems of which software designed to perform IRT may not warn. While there is no absolute answer to how many students are needed to ensure valid estimates, there is a general rule of thumb. For teachers who are simply trying to validate their own exams, one can assume that five students are needed for each estimated parameter in the model. This means that ten students are needed to measure the mean and variance of the proficiency distribution and an additional $5 \cdot x \cdot J$ students are needed to estimate the item parameters in the xPL model where we assume the exam has J items. However, more data points will always lead to more precise estimates of the parameters.

3. DATA AND CODE

This example analysis uses a mid semester exam from an introductory computer science course. The main focus of the exam was to assess the students' knowledge of inheritance and interfaces. Although the exam had several parts, only the first part with short answer questions is used for this paper. There are graded response models available, however this paper is focused on the simpler case where we assume questions are marked as either correct or incorrect.

In order to prepare the data for use with the IRT models, it was entered into a spreadsheet. Within the spreadsheet each row corresponds to one student's answers. Each cell is labeled with either a 1(correct) or 0(incorrect) for the student's response to that question. Cell A1 therefore contains the first student's answer to the first question. There are no row or column headers. The file was then saved in .csv format to be imported into the R statistical program.

3.1 R Code

The following are code snippets that can be used in order to import your data and run the IRT models in the statistical package R. Please note that the # sign denotes a comment.

```
#Load the library used for IRT
library(ltm)

#Read your data file into a variable called
#examdata.  You can type the name of the
#file, however the choose command will open
#a standard dialog box.
examdata = read.table(file.choose(),
      header=FALSE, sep=",")

#Verify that the data was entered correctly
#displays the first 10 rows of your data
examdata[1:10,]

#Run the model and store in result variable
result <- ltm(examdata ~ z1)

#display the results (general text output)
summary(result)
```

```
#display the ICCs, the first line sets up
#the window for how many graphs (5 x 3)
par(mfrow = c(5, 3))

#print the graphs
for(i in 1:15)
plot(result, items=i, legend = TRUE,
cx = "bottomright", lwd = 3,cex.main = 1.5,
cex.lab = 1.3, cex = 1.1)
```

The above code for R is merely an example to help you get started. There are various references for R and the ltm package available online.

4. RESULTS

The following section discusses the item characteristic curves that were produced by the two parameter logistic model. This particular exam was chosen for this paper because it produced examples of many of the types of curves that can be encountered. When looking at these graphs the x axis represents the proficiency of the student, θ, and the y axis represents the probability that a student of the given proficiency is able to answer the question correctly. Using figure 1, a student with a mean ability for the class has a 60% chance of getting the item correct.

4.1 Target Curve

Figure 1 represents the desired shape of a valid assessment item. The steep slope indicates that the item does a good job of discriminating between students.

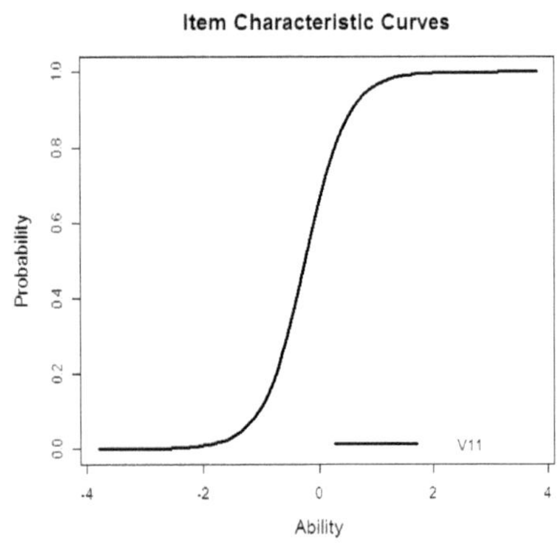

Figure 1: Standard Item Characteristic Curve

The question that corresponds to this graph is:

```
Given the API for the Timestamp and Date objects,
 is the following a valid declaration?

Cloneable c = new Date(...);
```

The steep curve at 0 indicates that the knowledge to answer this question is developing within students of one standard deviation above and below the mean. As an instructor that tells me that the question is best at discriminating among average students. Looking at an entire assessment worth of curves, a good assessment should have curves that discriminate for students of various abilities.

4.2 Guttman Items

Figure 2 also represents a desired shape, and is sometimes referred to as a Guttman Item since it is clear that there is some knowledge construct that is specifically responsible for answering the question correctly. Guttman items are often observed in exams of knowledge recall such as vocabulary tests.

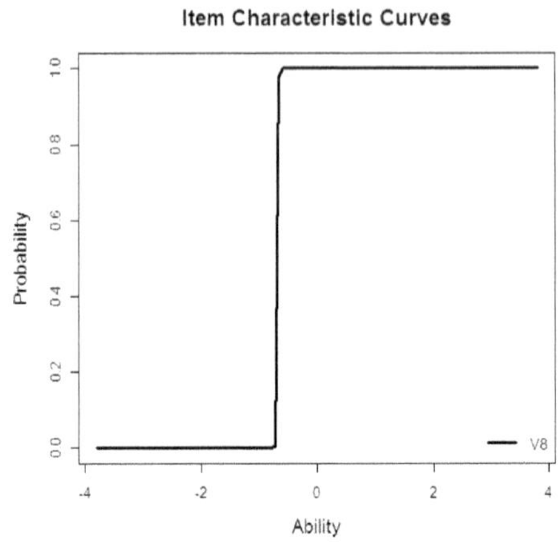

Figure 2: Guttman Item

The question that corresponds to this graph is:

```
Given the API for the Timestamp and Date objects,
 is the following a valid declaration?

Timestamp t = new Cloneable(...);
```

4.3 Easy Questions

Sometimes items are created to be easy and will not discriminate among students within the class. These items are generally represented by curves that exist in the top half of the graph. Figure three contains some easy item examples.

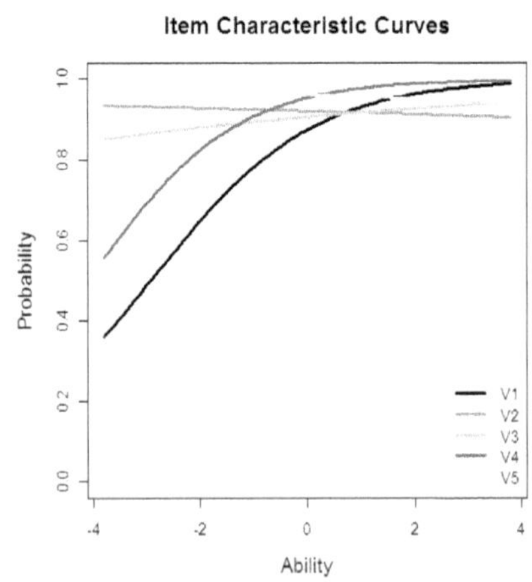

Figure 3: Easy Items

One of the questions that produced this curve was:

```
Fill in the blank.  Date is a ___________
(subclass/superclass) of Timestamp.
```

4.4 Linear Items

Some questions produce Item Characteristic Curves that are linear in shape. These curves indicate that while students with more knowledge are more likely to answer the question correctly, there is something else going on. If the question relied on one, or a few specific skills then you would see the "S" shaped curves from figure 1. These questions should be re-evaluated for what knowledge is required to answer the question correctly.

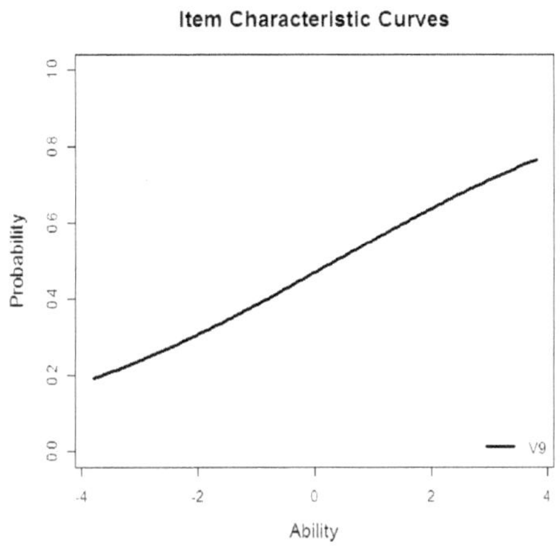

Figure 4: Linear Item

The question that corresponds to this graph is:

```
Given the API for the Timestamp and Date objects,
 is the following a valid declaration?

Cloneable c = new Cloneable(...);
```

In this case we can hypothesize that it is not only a knowledge of inheritance here that is prompting the correct answer, but also the knowledge that you cannot construct an instance of an interface. The combination of those two pieces of knowledge are required to answer the question correctly and so the question is not good at discriminating among students with regards to their knowledge of inheritance, which is what most of the remainder of the exam tests.

4.5 Descending Curves

A descending curve such as figure 5 is a strong warning sign to anyone engaged in this kind of analysis. The descending curve indicates that students who had an better score overall had a smaller probability of answering the item correctly. If this pattern is witnessed then a careful evaluation of the question should be performed in order to determine the cause.

The question that prompted this curve was:

```
Consider the following constructor for the
Timestamp class:

public Timestamp(long time){
//code here
}

Is the following code valid to insert where
```

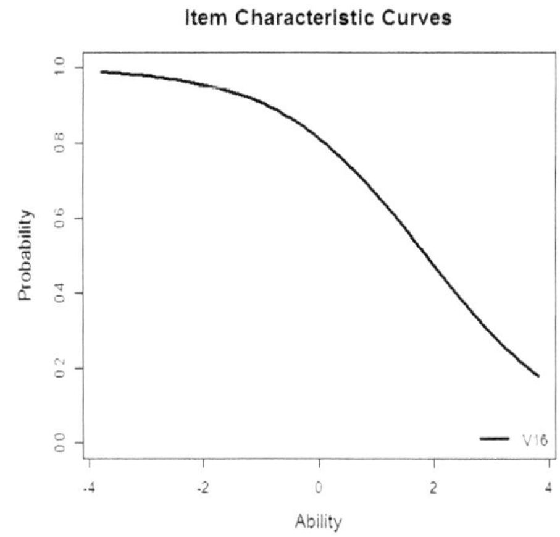

Figure 5: Descending Curve

```
the //code here comment is?
super(2000);
int x = 10;
```

In order to answer this question students needed several concepts. First they needed to identify that the call to super was on the first line, determine that it would call the constructor for the Date class, and then look at the reference for Date (provided) to determine if there was a constructor which accepted the value 2000. There are many reasons why this ICC could be descending including requiring multiple pieces of knowledge to complete the question correctly. As I rewrite this exam for future use, I might ask the question in a different way, or in multiple parts so that it told me exactly what the student misunderstood.

5. GRADED RESPONSE MODEL

The models presented here work with assessment questions that are binary in scoring - ie. correct or incorrect. Additional models are available if the questions are graded with possible partial credit. We anticipate a future paper detailing the graded response models as well as evaluating the results as a data set becomes available.

6. SUMMARY

This paper has presented you with an introduction to Item Response Theory and its potential uses for classroom level assessments. The included code as well as graph analysis is meant to provide the reader with a foundation to build upon as they become more engaged in the practice of assessment evaluation.

There are many other potentially useful tools that assessment validation research can offer such as Item and Test information curves, graded response models, and Knowledge Component models. There are also a number of other possible software tools aside from R that can be used to generate these curves as well. This has been a gentle introduction to a small, but potentially useful part of Item Response Theory that hopefully can be applied in the classroom quickly.

There are two important concepts to keep in mind as educators make use of these tools. First, the Item Characteristic Curves tell you more information about the questions than the students. The x axis is dependent totally upon the student's performance on that assessment and is normalized only for the data it has on the current students. Secondly, while the different shape curves indicate student response patterns, it is up to the instructor to evaluate the questions that generated that pattern and decide what steps to take next.

As data becomes an increasingly larger part of the arsenal that educators weild, so too must we become more sophisticated in the analysis and use of that data. It is the authors' hope that this paper offers a gentle introduction into a powerful topic for the average practitioner.

7. ACKNOWLEDGMENTS

The authors would like to thank Ken Koedinger and Brian Junker for running an item response theory workshop which prompted the idea for this paper. This work was supported through the Program for Interdisciplinary Education Research (PIER) at Carnegie Mellon University. PIER is supported by a grant from the Institute for Education Sciences in the US Department of Education.

8. REFERENCES

[1] Arne Duncan, "Keynote address for ies research conference", June 2009, http://www.ed.gov/news/speeches/2009/06/06082009.html.

[2] Titus Winters and Tom Payne, "What do students know?: an outcomes-based assessment system", in *ICER '05: Proceedings of the first international workshop on Computing education research*, New York, NY, USA, 2005, pp. 165–172, ACM.

[3] Frank B. Baker, *The Basics of Item Response Theory*, Heinemann, 1985.

[4] "Moodle content management system", Website, www.moodle.org.

[5] Pittsburgh Science of Learning Center, "Pslc datashop", Website, http://www.learnlab.org/technologies/datashop/.

[6] Gwen Nugent, Leen-Kiat Soh, Ashok Samal, Suzette Person, and Jeff Lang, "Design, development and validation of a learning object for cs1", in *ITiCSE '05: Proceedings of the 10th annual SIGCSE conference on Innovation and technology in computer science education*, New York, NY USA, 2005, pp. 370–370, ACM.

[7] Titus Winters and Tom Payne, "Closing the loop on test creation: a question assessment mechanism for instructors", in *SIGCSE '06: Proceedings of the 37th SIGCSE technical symposium on Computer science education*, New York, NY, USA, 2006, pp. 169–170, ACM.

[8] Deborah Harris, "Comparison of 1-, 2-, and 3-Parameter IRT Models", *Items: Instructional Topics in Educational Measurement*, pp. 157–163, 1989.

Using Strategies for Assessment of Programming Exercises

Alex Gerdes
School of Computer Science,
Open Universiteit Nederland
alex.gerdes@ou.nl

Johan T. Jeuring
Department of Information and Computing Sciences,
Utrecht University
johanj@cs.uu.nl

Bastiaan J. Heeren
School of Computer Science,
Open Universiteit Nederland
bastiaan.heeren@ou.nl

ABSTRACT

Programming exercise assessment tools alleviate the task of teachers, and increase consistency of markings. Many programming exercise assessment tools are based on testing. A test-based assessment tool for programming exercises cannot ensure that a solution is correct. Moreover, it is difficult to test if a student has used good programming practices. This is unfortunate, because teachers want students to adopt good programming techniques. We propose to use strategies, in combination with program transformations, as a foundation for functional programming exercise assessment. Expert knowledge, in the form of model solutions, can be expressed as programming strategies. Using these strategies we can guarantee that a student program is equivalent to a model solution, and we can report which solution strategy has been used to solve the programming problem.

Categories and Subject Descriptors

K.3.1 [**Computer Uses in Education**]: Computer-assisted instruction (CAI); K.3.2 [**Computer and Information Science Education**]: Computer science education

General Terms

Languages, Human Factors, Measurement

Keywords

Automatic assessment, functional programming, Haskell, strategies

1. INTRODUCTION

Every computer science curriculum offers courses in which beginners learn to program, and every year, thousands of students take such courses. To support learning programming, it is important to assess the students' progress and provide timely feedback. Traditionally, a teacher or an assistant assesses a student's abilities and progress. However, in the case of large class sizes, providing timely feedback is not always possible. Furthermore, repeatedly assessing student exercises is tedious, time consuming, and error prone. It is difficult to keep judgements consistent and fair. To assist teachers in assessing programming assignments, many assessment tools have been developed.

Most automated assessment tools for programming languages are based on some form of testing [1]. Test-based assessment tools try to determine correctness by comparing the output of a student program to the expected results on test data. Using testing for assessment has a number of problems. First, an inherent problem of testing is coverage: how do you know you have tested enough? Testing does not ensure that the student program is correct. Second, assessing design features, such as the use of good programming techniques or the absence of imperfections, is hard if not impossible with testing. Consider the following function that solves the problem of converting a list of binary numbers to its decimal representation:

$$
\begin{aligned}
&\mathit{fromBin} :: [\mathit{Int}] \rightarrow \mathit{Int}\\
&\mathit{fromBin} = \mathit{fromBin'}\ 2\\
&\mathit{fromBin'}\ n\ [\,] \qquad\quad = 0\\
&\mathit{fromBin'}\ n\ (x : xs) = x * n\,\hat{}\,(\mathit{length}\ (x : xs) - 1)\\
&\qquad\qquad\qquad\qquad + \mathit{fromBin'}\ n\ xs
\end{aligned}
$$

This function returns correct results, hence test-based assessment tools will most likely accept this as a good solution. However, this implementation contains at least one imperfection: the length calculation is inefficient (an element is added to the list and then the length of the list is subtracted by one). We found this imperfection frequently in a set of student solutions. It would certainly help if we had means to report and explain such inefficient or imperfect solutions. Third, testing cannot reveal which algorithm has been used. For instance, when asked to implement quicksort, it is difficult to discriminate between bubblesort and quicksort. Fourth, testing is a dynamic process and is therefore vulnerable to bugs, and even malicious features, that may be present in solutions.

strategy language [3]. We use this language to capture expert knowledge about how to solve an exercise. The framework can handle exercises from multiple domains, such as proposition logic, linear algebra, etc. Recently, we have extended our framework with the ability to reason about programming exercises [2]. We use this framework, in combination with program transformations, based on the lambda calculus, to assess functional programming exercises. Our approach is rather different from testing: we can *guaran-*

tee that the submitted student program is equivalent to a model program. We can recognise many different equivalent solutions from a model solution. For example, the following student solution:

$$\begin{array}{l} \mathit{fromBin} = \mathit{fromBaseN}\ 2 \\ \mathit{fromBaseN}\ b\ n = \mathit{fromBaseN'}\ b\ (\mathit{reverse}\ n) \\ \quad \textbf{where} \\ \qquad \mathit{fromBaseN'}\ \_\ [\,] \qquad\quad = 0 \\ \qquad \mathit{fromBaseN'}\ b'\ (c : cs) = c + b' * (\mathit{fromBaseN'}\ b'\ cs) \end{array}$$

is recognised from this model solution:

$$\mathit{fromBin} = \mathit{foldl}\ ((+) \circ (2*))\ 0$$

Despite the fact that this solution appears very different from the model solution, it will be recognised as equivalent. The two solutions are essentially the same. The *foldl* function can be defined as a *foldr*:

$$\mathit{foldl}\ \mathit{op}\ b = \mathit{foldr}\ (\mathit{flip}\ \mathit{op})\ b \circ \mathit{reverse}$$

The first solution makes use of this equivalence. It uses, however, the the explicit recursive definition of *foldr*.

In this paper we show how programming strategies and program transformations can be used to assess functional programming exercises. Using strategies for assessing student programs solves the four problems of using testing for assessment described above: if a program is determined to be equivalent, it is guaranteed to be correct; we can recognise and report imperfections; we can determine which algorithm has been implemented; and strategy-based assessment is carried out *statically*. In contrast with our approach, test-based assessment tools can give a judgement of all programs including incorrect ones. Test-based assessment tools can prove a program to be incorrect by providing a counter-example. However, finding a counter-example also suffers from the coverage problem.

We use the functional programming language Haskell as our object language. We have integrated the Haskell compiler Helium [4] into our assessment tool. We believe, however, that our approach is equally well applicable to other programming languages and programming paradigms.

This paper has the following contributions:

- We automatically assess student programs based on a set of model solutions using programming strategies, and program transformations (sections 2 and 3).
- We show the results of applying our assessment tool to 94 student solutions of a typical functional programming exercise (Section 4).

2. STRATEGY BASED ASSESSMENT

The most important features we want to assess in a student program are:

- Correctness: does the program implement the requirements?
- Design: has the program been implemented following good programming practices?

A model solution is a preferred way to solve a problem. Model solutions use good programming techniques, and we want our students to use these techniques. Model solutions can be transformed to model strategies automatically. These programming strategies are defined in the strategy language mentioned above.

We propose to use programming strategies as a foundation for assessment of programming exercises. We generate a set of solutions equivalent to the model solution(s) described by a programming strategy. A student solution is correct if it is an element of the generated set. Usually, however, strategies do not generate all solutions that are in essence equivalent to the model solution described. For example, a student should be free in choosing the identifiers in a program, and for this we incorporate α-renaming in our framework. To increase the number of accepted correct student programs, we *normalise* the generated set of model solutions and the student program using meaning preserving program transformations from the lambda calculus, such as β- and η-reduction. After normalising we syntactically check if the program is an element of the set of normalised model solutions.

A strategy is a well-defined plan or a sequence of steps for solving a particular problem. It represents expert knowledge for problem solving. Strategies are also known as procedural skills. We have implemented a programming strategy as a *context free grammar* with refinement rules as symbols. A refinement rule refines an undefined part (a hole) of an incomplete program. Examples of refinement rules are: introducing a variable, and distinguishing the empty list case from the non-empty list case. A programming strategy describes a sequence of refinement steps necessary for constructing a program.

We have developed a library with an embedded domain-specific language for specifying strategies for exercises. The language can be used for many domains, provided that the domains are based upon rewrite rules or refinement rules. The strategy language consists of a set of strategy combinators. These combinators are very similar to parser combinators [6] and are used to define strategies that consist of several substrategies. Examples of strategy combinators are: a sequence combinator that applies its argument strategies one after another, and a choice combinator that offers the possibility to choose between two strategies.

Strategies can also be used to detect common mistakes. These are called *buggy strategies*. For example, a common mistake we detected in a set of student solutions is the inefficient way of calculating the length of a list described in the introduction of this paper. Using buggy strategies we can report to the student that a common mistake was detected, and provide detailed feedback by explaining what is wrong, and how this should be corrected.

Programming strategies can be automatically derived from model solutions. To use our assessment tool, a teacher merely needs to specify one or more model solution. A teacher does not have to learn a formalism for specifying strategies.

2.1 Standard strategies

Using strategy combinators we have defined a set of standard programming strategies. These standard strategies are strategies for the functions in the standard library, and for the basic language constructs of Haskell. The standard library (the Haskell Prelude) defines common basic functions, such as addition and concatenation. Examples of Haskell language constructs are lambda expressions and *where* clauses. The standard strategies generate many syntactically different solutions from a single model solution. The automatically derived programming strategies are defined in terms of these standard strategies. For example, using the strategy for function composition ($f \circ g = \lambda x \rightarrow f\ (g\ x)$), we can recognise both composition itself, and composition expressed in terms of the lambda expression from its definition. This is used, amongst others, to check that the following two programs are equivalent:

$$\begin{aligned} &\mathit{fromBin} = \mathit{foldl}\ ((+) \circ (2*))\ 0 \\ &\mathit{fromBin} = \mathit{foldl}\ (\lambda x\ y \rightarrow 2 * x + y)\ 0 \end{aligned}$$

3. PROGRAM TRANSFORMATIONS

One of the advantages of assessing programming exercises using strategies is that an accepted program is guaranteed to be equivalent to a model solution. However, most basic strategies are rather strict, and might reject programs that are equivalent but have some differences. Not all of these differences can or should be captured in a strategy, because they are standard transformations of a program, independent of a particular strategy. For example, inlining a helper-function should be considered correct in any strategy. We use program transformations to transform a program to a normal form[1]. We are not so much interested in the exact normal form, as long as it can be used to efficiently compare two terms for equality.

Our program transformations are based on the *lambda calculus*. The lambda calculus is at the core of our functional programming language, and its reduction rules form the heart of the evaluation machinery. In particular, we use η- and β-reduction, and α-conversion. In general, comparing two lambda terms for equality is undecidable. However, we can decide equivalence for many terms using program transformations. Our equivalence checker may reject equivalent programs and hence we may have false-negatives. Until now we have not found this to be a problem in practice. If programs are found to be equivalent, they are semantically equivalent, so we do not obtain false-positives.

3.1 Preprocessing

In addition to the reduction rules of the lambda calculus, which we will discuss in the next subsection, we apply a number of preprocessing transformation steps. These steps are either for removing syntactic sugar or superficial syntax, or to trigger other transformations steps. We give a brief description of the most interesting transformation steps.

Constant arguments. Wherever possible we try to detect constant arguments. A couple of student solutions of the *fromBin* problem introduced in Section 1 use a constant argument:

```
fromBin = fromBaseN 2
fromBaseN b n = fromBaseN' b (reverse n)
  where
    fromBaseN' _ []       = 0
    fromBaseN' b' (c : cs) = c + b' * (fromBaseN' b' cs)
```

Here the argument b' is constant. A technique often used in compilers is to optimise such constant arguments away:

```
fromBin = fromBaseN 2
fromBaseN b n = fromBaseN' b (reverse n)
  where
    fromBaseN' b' =
      let fromBaseN'' []       = 0
          fromBaseN'' (c : cs) = c + b' * (fromBaseN'' cs)
      in fromBaseN''
```

[1]We consider a program in normal form if it cannot be transformed by any of our rules anymore.

The reason to transform constant arguments away is to enable the inlining and β-reduction steps.

Inlining. Inlining replaces an expression by its definition. After inlining a lambda expression, we can often perform a β-reduction. Inlining is rather tricky: scope and binding play an important role. Before inlining a few other preprocessing steps have to be performed, such as rewriting *where* clauses to *let* expressions. The following definition shows the result of applying these preprocessing steps (including inlining) to the *fromBin* solution given above:

```
fromBin =
  ( let fromBaseN' b' =
      let fromBaseN'' []       = 0
          fromBaseN'' (c : cs) = c + b' * (fromBaseN'' cs)
      in fromBaseN''
    in λb n → fromBaseN' b (reverse n)
  ) 2
```

Prefix notation. Operators may be used in infix or prefix position both when they are defined and used. For example, both $f\ x\ y = x + y$ and $f\ x\ y = (+)\ x\ y$ may be used. We have chosen to use the prefix notation in our abstract syntax trees, and transform every infix application to the equivalent prefix application.

3.2 α-conversion, η,β-reduction

α-conversion renames bound variables. To check that a program is syntactically equivalent to a model solution, we need to α-convert both the submitted student program as well as the model solution. α-conversion ensures that all variable names are unique, and this simplifies other transformation steps, such as β-reduction. α-conversion is included in the preprocessing step.

Previous transformation steps have been illustrated with a student solution for *fromBin*, using the names from the student program. After α-conversion this program looks as follows:

```
fromBin =
  (let x5 x6 =
      let x5 []        = 0
          x5 (x7 : x8) = (+) x7 ((*) x6 (x5 x8))
      in x5
   in  λx3 x4 → x5 x3 (reverse x4)
  ) 2
```

η-reduction replaces $\lambda x.f x$ by f if x does not appear free in f. We η-reduce the abstract syntax tree at all possible locations. Function bindings are η-reduced as well, so $f\ x = \mathit{not}\ x$ is replaced by $f = \mathit{not}$.

In lambda calculus, β-reduction is used when applying a function. β-reduction is defined using substitution: $(\lambda x \rightarrow \mathit{expr})\ y \Rightarrow_\beta \mathit{expr}[x := y]$. The substitution $[x := y]$ replaces all free occurrences of the variable x by the expression y. We don't expect a student to write a program containing a β-redex, but in practice this happens. The main reason we need β-reduction is to inline helper-functions.

After applying all transformations, including β-reduction, the *fromBin* function looks as follows:

$$\begin{aligned}
&\mathit{fromBin} = \lambda x_2 \rightarrow \\
&\quad \textbf{let } x_3\ [\,] \quad\quad\quad = 0 \\
&\quad\quad\quad x_3\ (x_4 : x_5) = (+)\ ((*)\ 2\ (x_3\ x_5))\ x_4 \\
&\quad \textbf{in } x_3\ (\mathit{reverse}\ x_2)
\end{aligned}$$

4. USING OUR ASSESSMENT TOOL

We have applied our assessment tool to student solutions that were obtained from a lab assignment in a first-year functional programming course at Utrecht University (2008). We were not involved in any aspect of the assignment, and received the solutions after they had been graded ('by hand') by the teaching assistants. In total we received 94 student solutions.

The students had to implement the *fromBin* function introduced in Section 1. This function should convert a list of bits to a decimal number. For example, applying *fromBin* to $[1,0,1,0,1,0]$ should return 42. This is a small exercise, typical for learning how to program in Haskell. The *fromBin* exercise can be solved in various ways, using different kinds of higher-order functions. There are a number of model solutions, which differ quite a bit from one another. All of them use recommended programming techniques.

The first of our model solutions uses a *foldl*, which is a higher-order function that processes a list from left to right and constructs a return value.

$$\mathit{fromBin} = \mathit{foldl}\ ((+) \circ (2*))\ 0$$

Tupling is a well-known programming technique that groups results in a tuple, which is passed around in a recursive function. The second model solution uses this technique. The tuple is passed in the form of multiple function arguments.

$$\begin{aligned}
&\mathit{fromBin}\ xs = \mathit{fromBin}'\ (\mathit{length}\ xs - 1)\ xs \\
&\quad \textbf{where} \\
&\quad\quad \mathit{fromBin}'\ _\ [\,] \quad\quad\ = 0 \\
&\quad\quad \mathit{fromBin}'\ l\ \ (x : xs) = x * 2^\wedge l + \mathit{fromBin}'\ (l - 1)\ xs
\end{aligned}$$

The third solution reverses the input list, and then computes the inner product of this list and a list of powers of two.

$$\mathit{fromBin} = \mathit{sum} \circ \mathit{zipWith}\ (*)\ (\mathit{iterate}\ (*2)\ 1) \circ \mathit{reverse}$$

The above model solutions are both elegant and efficient. The fourth (and last) model solution we consider is simple, but inefficient:

$$\begin{aligned}
&\mathit{fromBin}\ [\,] \quad\quad\ = 0 \\
&\mathit{fromBin}\ (x : xs) = x * 2^\wedge \mathit{length}\ xs + \mathit{fromBin}\ xs
\end{aligned}$$

Because the length of the list is calculated in each recursive call, this definition takes time quadratic in the size of the input list to calculate its result. The other model solutions are all linear. It is up to the teacher to decide to either accept or reject solutions based on this model. This flexibility is one of the advantages of our approach. It is also possible to turn this solution into a buggy strategy and report to the student why their solution is rejected (or accepted with reservations).

4.1 Categories

We have partitioned the set of student programs into four categories by hand:

Good. A good program is a proper solution with respect to the features we assess (correctness and design). It should ideally be equivalent to one of the model solutions.

Good with modifications. Some students have augmented their solution with sanity checks. For example, they check that the input is a list of zeroes and ones. Since the exercise assumes the input has the correct form, we have not incorporated such checks in the model solutions. Furthermore, the transformation machinery is not yet capable of removing these checks. We have removed the checks by hand.

Imperfect. An imperfect program is a program that is rejected because we want to report the imperfection. The solution to *fromBin* given in Section 1 is an example of an imperfect solution. Another common imperfection we found is the use of a superfluous case:

$$\begin{aligned}
&\mathit{fromBin}\ [\,] \quad\quad\quad = 0 \\
&\mathit{fromBin}\ (x : [\,]) = x \\
&\mathit{fromBin}\ (x : xs) = (x * 2^\wedge \mathit{length}\ xs) + \mathit{fromBin}\ xs
\end{aligned}$$

In this student example, the second case is unnecessary.

Incorrect. A few student programs were incorrect. They all contained the same error: no definition for the empty list.

4.2 Results

From the 94 student programs, 64 programs fall into the good category and 8 fall into the good with modifications category. From these, our assessment tool recognises 64 programs (89%). Another, and perhaps better, way of looking at these figures is that 64 student solutions are accepted based on just four model solutions. The acceptance rate can be increased by adding more model solutions. Using our tool a teacher merely needs to assess the remaining student solutions. These remaining student solutions can be either correct or incorrect, our tool can not tell.

All of the incorrect and imperfect programs were rejected in the test. Some of these incorrect programs were not noticed by the teaching assistants that corrected these programs.

It might happen that a student solution does not correspond to a model solution, although it is correct. In such a case a teacher might add the solution to the set of model solutions. It is likely that some student solutions do not qualify as a model solution, although they cannot be considered imperfect or wrong as well. For example, the following student solution uses the tupling technique:

$$\begin{aligned}
&\mathit{fromBin}\ [\,] \quad\quad\quad\quad = 0 \\
&\mathit{fromBin}\ [s] \quad\quad\quad\ = s \\
&\mathit{fromBin}\ (s : t : \mathit{rest}) = \mathit{fromBin}\ ((2 * s + t) : \mathit{rest})
\end{aligned}$$

Instead of using a tuple or an extra argument, this solution 'misuses' the head of the list to store the result.

By checking all model solutions independently, we can tell which model solution, or strategy, a student has used to solve the exercise. Our test showed that 18 students used the *foldl* model solution, 2 used tupling, 2 the inner product solution, and 40 solutions were based on the last model solution with explicit recursion.

It is unlikely that a solution is accepted by more than one model solution. In our test all solutions were accepted by a single model solution. If model solutions are very similar, it is probably possible to adapt one of the standard strategies to recognise both from a single model solution.

A second assessment shows similar results as the one discussed in this paper.

5. RELATED AND FUTURE WORK

The survey of automated programming assessment by Ala-Mutka [1] shows that many assessment tools are based on dynamic testing. In contrast, our assessment tool statically checks for correctness. The survey provides many pointers to related work. We describe the three closest approaches.

The PASS system, developed by Thorburn and Rowe [7], assesses C programs by evaluating whether a student program conforms to a predefined solution plan. A drawback of the system is that it needs testing for this evaluation. Moreover, a solution plan is much more strict compared to a strategy. For example, the system considers the definition of any helper-function incorrect. Our approach allows a higher degree of freedom by means of standard strategies and program transformations.

The approach of Truong et al. [8] is also based on model solutions and abstract syntax tree inspections. However, their primary use is to assess software quality and not so much correctness. In addition to similarity checks, their system also calculates software metrics, which are used to give feedback to a student. A drawback of their approach is that it does not take the different syntactic forms of a model solution into account. Moreover, the similarity check considers only the outline of a solution and not its details.

Xu and Chee [10] show how to diagnose Smalltalk programs using program transformations. Our work is quite similar to theirs. For a functional programming language the set of transformations is much smaller and simpler. We would like to implement their advanced method for locating errors in student programs.

Program verification tools are used to prove programs correct with respect to some specification [5]. Automatic program verification tools provide as much support as possible in constructing this proof. However, users will always have to give hints or proof steps to complete proofs for non-trivial programs, such as *fromBin*. We expect it is easier both for teachers and students, to check student solutions against model solutions.

Future work. In addition to assessing programming exercises, we also want to use programming strategies to generate semantically rich feedback when a student develops a program step-wise. However, as soon as we use program transformations it is hard to relate the student program to a model solution: the program transformations changes the student program in an unrecognisable way. Therefore, we would like to investigate how we can retain the relation with the student steps as long as possible.

The approach we presented in this paper is focussed on functional programming languages, in particular Haskell. We believe that our approach is also applicable to other programming languages and to other programming paradigms. Our method is not tied to a particular programming language. The concepts on which our approach is based, such as strategies, refinement rules, and program transformations, are applicable to every programming language. We plan to investigate how well our approach works for developing programs in a programming language such as Java.

Our approach can guarantee that a program is correct. Test-based approaches can guarantee that a program is incorrect. We plan to investigate how we can extend our approach with testing, property checking, or static contract checking [9].

6. CONCLUSIONS

We have shown that strategies can be successfully used for programming exercise assessment. Our approach differs from test based assessment tools in that we can *guarantee* a student solution to be equivalent to a model solution. Strategies in combination with programming transformations are able to recognise many different student programs from a limited set of model solutions. In a test we performed on almost 100 student programs we managed to recognise and characterise 89% of the correct solutions, and we found several programs that had been incorrectly graded as correct by student assistants. Programming strategies can be specified in a convenient way and are very flexible.

7. ACKNOWLEDGEMENTS

The authors would like to thank Stefan Holdermans of Utrecht University for providing a set of suitable programming exercises, accompanied with a large amount of corrected student solutions.

8. REFERENCES

[1] K. Ala-Mutka. A survey of automated assessment approaches for programming assignments. *Computer Science Education*, 15(2):83–102, 2005.

[2] A. Gerdes, B. Heeren, and J. Jeuring. Constructing Strategies for Programming. In J. Cordeiro et al., editor, *Proceedings of the First International Conference on Computer Supported Education*, pages 65–72. INSTICC Press, March 2009.

[3] B. Heeren, J. Jeuring, A. v. Leeuwen, and A. Gerdes. Specifying strategies for exercises. In *MKM 2008: Mathematical Knowledge management*, volume 5144 of *LNAI*, pages 430–445. Springer-Verlag, 2008.

[4] B. Heeren, D. Leijen, and A. v. IJzendoorn. Helium, for learning Haskell. In *Haskell 2003*, pages 62–71. ACM, 2003.

[5] M. d. Mol, M. v. Eekelen, and R. Plasmeijer. Theorem proving for functional programmers - Sparkle: a functional theorem prover. In *IFL 2001, Selected Papers, volume 2312 of LNCS*, pages 55–72. Springer, 2002.

[6] S. D. Swierstra and L. Duponcheel. Deterministic, error-correcting combinator parsers. In J. Launchbury et al., editor, *AFP*, volume 1129 of *LNCS*, pages 184–207. Springer-Verlag, 1996.

[7] G. Thorburn and G. Rowe. Pass: an automated system for program assessment. *Computers & Education*, 29(4):195–206, 1997.

[8] N. Truong, P. Roe, and P. Bancroft. Static analysis of students' Java programs. In *ACE '04: Proceedings of the sixth conference on Australasian computing education*, pages 317–325, Darlinghurst, Australia, Australia, 2004. Australian Computer Society, Inc.

[9] D. N. Xu. *Static Contract Checking for Haskell.* PhD thesis, Cambridge University, 2008.

[10] S. Xu and Y. S. Chee. Transformation-based diagnosis of student programs for programming tutoring systems. *IEEE Transansactions on Software Engineering*, 29(4):360–384, 2003.

Measuring High School Students' Attitudes Toward Computing

Daniel Heersink
Colorado School of Mines
Mathematical and Computer Science, 1500 Illinois St.
Golden, Co 80439
1-303-273-3860
daniel.heersink@gmail.com

Barbara M. Moskal
Colorado School of Mines
Mathematical and Computer Science, 1500 Illinois St.
Golden, Co 80439
1-303-273-3867
bmoskal@mines.edu

ABSTRACT

Many projects throughout the United States are underway that seek to increase the appeal of technology as a field of study. To better understand the impacts of such projects, validated instruments are needed which measure students' attitudes and beliefs in both computer science and information technology. This paper describes the development and validation of two assessment instruments. One measures attitudes and beliefs about computer science; the other measures attitudes and beliefs about information technology. The questions that comprise these instruments are identical with the exception of the use of the terms "computer science" and "information technology". Both instruments sought to measure five constructs: confidence, interest, gender, usefulness, and professional. Based on the results of factor analyses, high school students are able to distinguish among these constructs in computer science but not in information technology. This raises questions as to what high school students understand about field of information technology.

Categories and Subject Descriptors

Research Studies

General Terms

Measurement, Human Factors

Keywords

Assessment, outreach, high school computing

1. INTRODUCTION

As the employment demand for science and technology majors increases, the number of students enrolling in computing degrees in the United States is declining [21]. Enrollment in introductory programming courses and in computer science and information technology degree programs has decreased over the last eight years. Studies [17,24,26,28] have been conducted that seek to better understand the attitudes and beliefs of students that contribute to this decline. Most of these studies use qualitative research techniques and many have focused on female students.

Women are severely underrepresented in computing [29], representing only 20% of computer science bachelor's degrees awarded across the nation in 2006 [19]. Studies have examined gender differences that influence enrollment in computing related degree programs [3,4,24]. High school girls, in particular, have identified the following reasons for their lack of interest in computing: i.) lack of female role models, ii.) limited or no knowledge of the applications of computing, iii.) interest in things other than computers, and iv.) negative perceptions of computing as "nerdy" [15]. The broader population of students has expanded this list to include: i.) a perception that the number of jobs in computing is decreasing, ii.) a lack of familiarity with computing fields and iii.) incorrect perceptions that computing professionals spend the majority of their time programming and rarely use computing in problem solving [5].

Today's students grew up with technology and video games. Through these experiences, they have come to view technology as fast-paced and exciting. Yet, their first programming experiences are tedious and boring [2,16,22]. Studies have further shown that many students lack confidence in their basic programming skills [9]. The dot.com bust has also had a negative impact on students' perceptions of the field and of professionals in the field, especially the perceptions held by young women as to the field [7,25].

One method of reversing the damaging trend of decreasing numbers of students pursuing computing degrees is to change students' perceptions of computing fields. Many studies that have sought to reverse this trend have relied on qualitative methods to measure students' attitudes and beliefs with respect to computing [8,10,13,14]. Qualitative methods provide detailed information concerning the participating group; however, they are limited as to the extent to which they can be generalized beyond that group.

Some studies have sought to address this limitation by developing surveys that measure students' attitudes toward computer science. For example, Wiebe, Williams, Yang and Miller [27] created a survey that seeks to measure attitudes in computer science based on an instrument which was originally designed to measure students' attitudes in mathematics [10]. A major assumption of their work is that the same factors that discourage participation in mathematics also discourage participation in computer science; no evidence is presented by these authors to support the accuracy of this assumption. Other instruments [20] have also been developed to examine students' attitudes with respect to computer science once students have enrolled in a computer science course. These instruments are limited in that a major obstacle is getting students to enroll in that first computer science experience.

The study presented here introduces two surveys that are designed to measure students' beliefs and attitudes with respect to computing with respect to five constructs. These five constructs were selected based on the qualitative research in computing concerning factors that discourage student participation. The first instrument is designed for computer science and the second for information technology. Factor analyses were used to examine the effectiveness of each instrument in measuring the following constructs on a high school population:

Confidence Construct (C):	students' confidence in their own ability to learn computing skills;
Interest Construct (I):	students' interests in computing;
Gender Construct (G):	students' perceptions of computing as a male field;
Usefulness Construct (U):	students' beliefs in the usefulness of learning computing; and
Professional Construct (P):	students' beliefs about professionals in computing.

The primary difference between the two instruments is the replacement of "computer science" in the computer science instrument with "information technology" in the information technology instrument. The computer science instrument was originally designed for a first year college population [11, 18] and this study represents the first effort to validate the instrument on a high school population. Representative questions from each construct can be found in Table 1 and the full surveys are available through requests from the authors. High school was selected as the target population for this investigation because this is a period in which students form opinions about future majors and careers.

Table 1. Representative questions from each construct

Confidence:	C4. I can learn to understand computing concepts. C8. I am uncertain that I can achieve good grades (C or better) in computing courses.
Interest:	I5. I like to use computer science to solve problems. I9. I think computer science is interesting.
Gender:	G1. I doubt that a woman could excel in computing courses. G15. Men and women can both excel in computing courses.
Usefulness:	U6. Knowledge of computing skills will not help me secure a good job. U7. I do not use computing skills in my daily life.
Professional:	P1. Doing well in computer science does not require a student to spend most of his/her time at a computer. P2. A student who performs well in computer science will probably not have a life outside of computers.

The study presented here was partially support by the National Science Foundation (NSF) DUE-0512064 and was in collaboration with NSF DRL-0623808 and NSF DRL- 0737679. The latter two projects required validated assessment instruments to support the measurement of students' attitudinal changes as a result of interventions in computer science and information technology, respectively; the former project supports the validation of these instruments. The ideas and opinions expressed are that of the authors and are not necessarily reflective of that of the NSF or of the investigators of the collaborative projects.

2. RESEARCH QUESTION

The research questions that guided this investigation are:

1. Based on a factor analysis, is there evidence to support that the computer science and information technology surveys measure the five intended constructs when used with a high school population?
2. Are the two instruments equally effective for measuring students' attitudes and beliefs within the two fields (i.e., computer science and information technology)?

3. METHODS

This section begins with a description of the two assessment instruments. This is followed by a description of the participating student population, administrative procedure and analysis process.

3.1 Instrument

Both instruments, the computer science and information technology survey, were originally designed with 52 statements in Likert format (Strongly Agree, Agree, Disagree, Strongly Disagree). A neutral option was not included in order to force a decision between agree or disagree. The only difference between the computer science instrument and the information technology instrument was the replacement of the phrase "computer science" with "information technology." As a result of an initial factor analysis and Cronbach's Alpha on an undergraduate student population, the computer science survey was reduced to 38 statements prior to the current administration [11,18]. The information technology instrument was tested in this study for the first time, and therefore was in original 52 statement format.

3.2 Subjects

The data reported here is restricted to the students whose parents or legal guardians signed consent to participate in NSF DRL-0623808 or DRL- 0737679. No information is available on students whose parents did not provide consent. All subjects self-selected to enroll in the summer enrichment programs.

The computer science version of the attitudes survey was administered to 77 high school students who participated in one of four workshops offered during the summer of 2008 in the following states: North Carolina, South Carolina, Mississippi, and California. Attending students ranged in grade level from high school freshman to high school seniors.

The information technology version of the attitudes survey was administered to 63 high school students who participated in a workshop during the summer of 2008 in Indiana. Attending students ranged in grade level from high school freshman to high school seniors.

3.3 Administrative Process

The attitude survey was administered to each of the participating groups in a pre and post format. The pretest occurred prior to workshop instruction; the posttest immediately following the workshop instruction. However, for the purpose of this investigation, the goal was to confirm that the survey was measuring students' attitudes with respect to computer science or information technology without intervention. Therefore, this analysis examines pretest results only.

3.4 Analysis Methods

Responses to each survey were converted to numerical scores. For positively phrased questions, "Strongly Agree" was coded as a "4", "Agree" as a "3", "Disagree" as a "2" and "Strongly Disagree" as a "1". Negatively phrased questions were coded in reverse order such that a positive response always corresponded to a higher numerical value. For the gender questions, a gender neutral attitude reflected a higher numerical score.

A confirmatory factor analysis using a promax [1] rotation was performed on the number-valued survey responses. The promax rotation is oblique as opposed to the traditional orthogonal rotation. Oblique rotations allow for correlations between the different factors, and in a survey such as this, the five constructs are designed to be correlated. Also, using oblique rotations will result in factor loadings that are very close to the orthogonal rotation when the factors are only minimally correlated or uncorrelated. Thus, the oblique rotation is the preferable method of analysis when it is anticipated that across constructs the factors will correlate [6].

4. RESULTS

This section begins with a description of the participating student population. This is followed by a discussion of the results of the factor analysis on the computer science and information technology instruments.

4.1 Descriptions

Both surveys included three demographic questions at the end of the survey. The first question asked for gender. The second question asked for grade level with the four options being ninth, tenth, eleventh or twelfth grade. The final demographics question asked for ethnicity with the following possible choices: i) American Indian; ii) Asian; iii) Black or African American; iv) Hispanic; v) White; vi) Multi-Racial; vii) Other, Please Specify; and viii) Choose not to Respond.

Forty-five percent of respondents to the computer science instrument were female. Forty percent of the computer science survey respondents were in ninth grade, twenty-four in the tenth grade, twenty-four in the eleventh grade and twelve in the twelfth grade. Approximately half (48%) self-identified as White, twenty six percent as Black or African American, twelve percent as Asian, six percent as Other, with the remaining eight percent (representing two students) being American Indian, Hispanic, Multi-Racial, and Choose not to Respond. Their exact responses are not identified here to ensure the confidentiality of this smaller segment of the student population.

Of the students that responded to the information technology survey, sixty-six percent of respondents were female. The respondents were distributed as follows among the four grade levels with nineteen percent in ninth grade, thirty-seven percent in tenth grade, thirty percent in the eleventh grade and fourteen percent in the twelfth grade. The majority of the respondents self-selected as White (65%). Twelve percent self-selected as Black or African American, nine percent as Multi-Racial, seven percent as Asian and six percent as Hispanic. One person or 1% of respondents chose not to respond.

4.2 Computer Science

This section addresses the results of the factor analysis on the computer science instrument. The results of the promax rotation factor analysis indicated that question P1, "A student who performs well in computer science will probably NOT have a life outside of computers", factored into the usefulness construct instead of the professional construct. This may indicate that the responding students viewed this statement as a reflection of the extent to which computer science is useful to his/her own life rather than as a stereotype concerning computer science as a profession. Also, question U6, "I do NOT use computing skills in my daily life", factored into the confidence construct instead of the anticipated usefulness construct. Students may not use computing skills in their own life because they are not confident in their skills.

A common practice in factor analysis is to set a cutoff for the acceptable factor loadings between 0.3–0.4. Loadings within this range or higher are considered significant and factor loadings less than this range are examined individually to determine their significance [6]. In this study, a cutoff of 0.35 was used.

Question P1 was removed and the factor analysis was performed on the remaining 37 questions. This analysis resulted in all questions factoring into the intended factors with the exception of question U6. This question continued to load highly on the confidence construct, but also loaded on the intended, usefulness construct. Also, question P2, "A student who performs well in computer science will probably not have a life outside of computers" was below the 0.35 cutoff established for this study. This question continued to load highest on the intended construct though, so the question was not removed. A third factor analysis was conducted after removing the problematic question U6. This negatively impacted the loading of other statements, resulting in the decision to maintain U6 in the analysis but as a measure of confidence rather than usefulness.

4.3 Information Technology

As was the case for the computer science version of the instrument, a promax rotation factor analysis was completed on the collected data. Only the gender construct loaded as expected and none of the statements from the professional construct were loading on a single factor. This may be an indication that high school students do not know what it means to be a professional in information technology. The professional construct statements were eliminated from the data and a secondary factor analysis was completed. Results of this second factor analysis indicated the existence of only two factors – a gender construct and a second construct comprising usefulness, confidence and interest in information technology. Based on this analysis, it appears that with respect to information technology, the constructs under investigation are ill-defined for a high school population.

Based on this analysis, the information technology survey has been shortened to include only twenty questions, ten for each of two factors. The questions that were selected for this revised instrument were those that loaded highest with regard to each factor. Additional data will be collected to validate this revised instrument.

5. DISCUSSION

This article reports on the research efforts that have been used in the ongoing validation of a computer science attitudes survey and the initial efforts to develop an information technology attitudes survey. Both instruments were administered during summer workshops to self-selected high school students and both were analyzed using factor analysis. With the removal of one question from the computer science instrument and the redefinition of another question to a new category, the factor analysis provided support that the instrument was measuring the five intended constructs for a high school population.

Based on the factor analysis, the information technology instrument was only measuring two factors: gender and a general factor collectively addressing students' interest, confidence, and perceived usefulness of information technology. It is possible that interest, confidence and usefulness were reflected through the responses but that the various factors were so highly correlated that they became indistinguishable through the analysis process. Another interpretation is that high school students were unable to distinguish their attitudes and beliefs, because they do not know what information technology is. The later interpretation is of greater concern to the computing community and warrants future investigation. This may indicate that students are unaware that there are options in computing outside of computer science and this limits the potential growth of information technology.

The results do provide strong evidence that the computer science survey is measuring students' attitudes and beliefs with respect to computer science for the five intended constructs, or the first component of research question 1. The five constructs measured through this instrument and the statements that comprise each construct resulted from a review of the literature and expert feedback [18]. The factor analysis indicates that the questions that comprise these constructs are correlated. The results are less promising with respect to the information technology survey. Based on the factor analysis, only the gender construct appears to be effectively measured through this instrument. In response to the second half of research question 1, the evidence does not support that the information technology survey is measuring the five intended constructs. Three of the constructs, however, can be measured as a general construct.

These results also raise concerns as to the common practice of altering validated surveys to fit the needs of new programs, without additional validation. In this case, the term "computer science" was changed to "information technology". The factor analysis of the first instrument provides evidence to support its validity; the factor analysis of the second instrument provides evidence to challenge its validity in the original survey form. What appeared to be a minor language alteration significantly impacted the instrument's capability of providing accurate and interpretable measurements. Unfortunately, the same methods that were used in the development of the computer science survey instrument, a literature review and expert review, cannot be used for the information technology survey. Much of the research that is available does not distinguish between the two fields. Additionally, many computer science instructors also act as information technology instructors, blurring the professional distinction between the fields.

Based on this analysis, the information technology instrument is not yet ready for general use. Additional research and validation is needed. As a result of the current investigation, this instrument has been rewritten with only two constructs, a gender construct and a general interest construct, and has also been shortened to 20 questions. An open-ended question has been added which asks students to define the term "information technology". This instrument was pilot tested in the summer of 2009 and an analysis is underway. In response to the second research question, only the computer science instrument is ready for general use in the measurement of students' attitudes and beliefs with respect to the five intended constructs.

The study presented here has three known limitations. First, factor analyses do not define constructs; rather they provide statistical evidence as to correlations. In this investigation, expert review was used to define and confirm the five factors. Second, different populations of students were used in the study of each instrument. Variations among these groups may have had unexpected impacts on the reported results. Third, all of the participating students where self-selected. Students who self-select to participate in a summer workshop may respond in a manner that is different from those that do not select to participate in such programs.

6. ACKNOWLEDGEMENTS

The authors would like to thank the NSF for their support of this research effort (NSF DUE-0512064) as well as the collaborating projects (NSF DRL-0623808; NSF DRL- 0737679). The authors acknowledge the contributions of Wanda Dann, Carnegie Mellon University, Steven Cooper, Purdue University, and Mark Guzdial, Georgia Tech, in the development of the original 52 question version of the computer science survey and Alka Herriger, Purdue University, in the instrument's conversion to an information technology survey. Wanda, Steven and Alka further supported the validation of these instruments with a high school population through collaborative projects (NSF DRL-0623808; NSF DRL-0737679). Ashlyn Munson, Andy Hoegh and Nathan Behrens each participated as graduate research assistants during various components of the survey development process. The late Randy Pausch, Carnegie Mellon, developed the Alice software which inspired the need for the original computer science survey.

7. REFERENCES

[1] Abdi, H. 2003. FactorRotations in Factor Analyses. In: Lewis-Beck, M. Bryman, A., Futing T. (eds.): Encyclopedia for Research Methods for the Social Sciences. Sage: Thousand Oaks, CA, 792-795.

[2] Bailey, M. W., Coleman, C. L., and Davidson, J. W. 2008. Defense against the dark arts. In Proceedings of the 39th SIGCSE Technical Symposium on Computer Science Education (Portland, OR, USA, March 12 - 15, 2008). SIGCSE '08. ACM, New York, NY, 315-319.

[3] Beyer, S., DeKeuster, M., Walter, K., Colar, M., and Holcomb, C. 2005. Changes in CS students' attitudes towards CS over time: an examination of gender differences. In Proceedings of the 36th SIGCSE Technical Symposium on Computer Science Education (St. Louis, Missouri, USA, February 23 - 27, 2005). SIGCSE '05. ACM, New York, NY, 392-396.

[4] Beyer, S., Rynes, K., Perrault, J., Hay, K., and Haller, S. 2003. Gender differences in computer science students. In

Proceedings of the 34th SIGCSE Technical Symposium on Computer Science Education (Reno, Nevada, USA, February 19 - 23, 2003). SIGCSE '03. ACM, New York, NY, 49-53.

[5] Carter, L. 2006. Why students with an apparent aptitude for computer science don't choose to major in computer science. In Proceedings of the 37th SIGCSE Technical Symposium on Computer Science Education (Houston, Texas, USA, March 03 - 05, 2006). SIGCSE '06. ACM, New York, NY, 27-31.

[6] Costello, Anna B. & Jason Osborne 2005. Best practices in exploratory factor analysis: four recommendations for getting the most from your analysis. Practical Assessment Research & Evaluation, 10, 7.

[7] Craig, A., Paradis, R., and Turner, E. 2002. A gendered view of computer professionals: preliminary results of a survey .SIGCSE Bull. 34, 2 (Jun. 2002), 101-104.

[8] Dewitt, P. 2007. "Effectiveness of Alice in computer science education." Master's Thesis, Colorado School of Mines.

[9] D'Souza, D., Hamilton, M., Harland, J., Muir, P., Thevathayan, C., and Walker, C. 2008. Transforming learning of programming: a mentoring project. In Proceedings of the Tenth Conference on Australasian Computing Education - Volume 78 (Wollongong, NSW, Australia, January 01 - 01, 2008). S. Hamilton and M. Hamilton, Eds. Conferences in Research and Practice in Information Technology Series, vol. 315. Australian Computer Society, Darlinghurst, Australia, 75-84.

[10] Fennema, E., and Sherman, J.A. (1976). "Fennema-Sherman mathematics scales", JSAS: Catalog of Selected Documents in Psychology, 6, 31.

[11] Hoegh, A. and Moskal, B. 2009. "Examining Science and Engineering Students' Attitudes Toward Computer Science." Paper in the proceeding of the Frontiers in Education Conference, San Antonio, Texas.

[12] Hutchinson, A. 2005. "A statistical analysis of outcomes in an educational assessment: Impact of the Alice curriculum on male and female performances and attitudes at community colleges." Master's Thesis, Colorado School of Mines.

[13] Hutchinson, A., Moskal, B., Dann, W. & Cooper, S. 2008. "Impact of the Alice curriculum on community college students' attitudes and learning with respect to computer science." Paper appears in the proceedings of the annual meeting of the American Society for Engineering Education, Pittsburgh, PA .

[14] Hutchinson, A., Moskal, B., Dann, W., Cooper, S., & Navidi, W. 2008. "The Alice curricular approach: A community college intervention in introductory programming courses." Innovations 2008: International Network for Engineering Education Research. Begell House Publishing, Chapter 15, ISBN, 978-0-9741252-8-2 (p. 157-176).

[15] Jepson, A. and Perl, T. 2002. Priming the pipeline. SIGCSE Bull. 34, 2 (Jun. 2002), 36-39.

[16] Ladd, B. C. 2006. The curse of Monkey Island: holding the attention of students weaned on computer games. J. Comput. Small Coll. 21, 6 (Jun. 2006), 162-174.

[17] Lewis, C. 2007. Attitudes and beliefs about computer science among students and faculty. SIGCSE Bull. 39, 2 (Jun. 2007), 37-41.

[18] Moskal, B., Behrens, N., Guzdial, M., Tew, A., Dann, W. and Cooper, S. 2007. "Computer science assessment instrument development: Evaluating attitudes and outcomes." Paper in the proceedings of the National STEM Assessment Conference, Washington DC, pp. 194-201.

[19] National Science Foundation. 2006. Table C-14 Bachelor's Bachelor's degrees, by race/ethnicity, citizenship, sex, and field: 2006.

[20] Palaigeorgiou, G., E., Siozos, P.D., Konstantakis, N.I., & Tsoukalas, I. A. 2005. "A computer attitudes scale for computer science freshman and its educational implications", J. of Computer Assisted Learning, 21, 5, 330-342.

[21] Patterson, D. A. 2005. Restoring the popularity of computer science. Commun. ACM 48, 9 (Sep. 2005), 25-28.

[22] Rankin, Y., Gooch, A., and Gooch, B. 2008. The impact of game design on students' interest in CS. In Proceedings of the 3rd international Conference on Game Development in Computer Science Education (Miami, Florida, February 27 - March 03, 2008). GDCSE '08. ACM, New York, NY, 31-35.

[23] Reges, S. 2006. Back to basics in CS1 and CS2. In Proceedings of the 37th SIGCSE Technical Symposium on Computer Science Education (Houston, Texas, USA, March 03 - 05, 2006). SIGCSE '06. ACM, New York, NY, 293-297.

[24] Rowell, G. H., Perhac, D. G., Hankins, J. A., Parker, B. C., Pettey, C. C., and Iriarte-Gross, J. M. 2003. Computer-related gender differences. In Proceedings of the 34th SIGCSE Technical Symposium on Computer Science Education (Reno, Nevada, USA, February 19 - 23, 2003). SIGCSE '03. ACM, New York, NY, 54-58.

[25] Schulte, C. and Knobelsdorf, M. 2007. Attitudes towards computer science-computing experiences as a starting point and barrier to computer science. In Proceedings of the Third international Workshop on Computing Education Research (Atlanta, Georgia, USA, September 15 - 16, 2007). ICER '07. ACM, New York, NY, 27-38.

[26] Schulte, C. and Magenheim, J. 2005. Novices' expectations and prior knowledge of software development: results of a study with high school students. In Proceedings of the First international Workshop on Computing Education Research (Seattle, WA, USA, October 01 - 02, 2005). ICER '05. ACM, New York, NY, 143-153.

[27] Wiebe, E., Williams, L., Yang, K. & Miller, C. 2003. "Computer Science Attitude Survey", Technical Report, Department of Computer Science, NC State University, Raleigh, NC, TR-2003-01.

[28] Wiedenbeck, S. 2005. Factors affecting the success of non-majors in learning to program. In Proceedings of the First international Workshop on Computing Education Research (Seattle, WA, USA, October 01 - 02, 2005). ICER '05. ACM, New York, NY, 13-24.

An Advanced Assessment Tool and Process

Legand L. Burge Ronald J. Leach
Howard University
(blegand, rjl)@scs.howard.edu

ABSTRACT

In this paper we describe a tool developed as part of the assessment process used at our university. The tool allows the automatic determination of the degree to which individual students meet the learning objectives that indicate how well students meet both course objectives and program directives. We also describe a portion of our assessment process that helps us perform the difficult step of "closing the loop" to make sure that the results of our data analysis are used to insure continuous program improvement.

Categories and Subject Descriptors
K.3.2 [Computer and Information Science Education]: Accreditation

General Terms: Measurement

Keywords: ABET, assessment

1. INTRODUCTION

In the Computer Science and engineering communities, the term "assessment" is often used to describe the evaluation of educational programs. We have developed some new evaluation techniques that will serve the Computer Science field, and perhaps the larger engineering field, well.

ABET accredits many undergraduate programs; Computer Science accreditation is done under a sub-organization known as the Computer Accreditation Commission, or CAC [1]. Many programs, especially at smaller colleges and universities are struggling under the load of the assessment process. It appears that a major factor in this difficulty is the lack of automated tools to help with the data collection and analysis process. The ABET accreditation process has become increasingly complex because it is heavily based on the creation of goals and objectives for programs. The assessment of these goals and objectives is often a time-consuming process [2, 3, 4, 5].

Our department has developed a process for assessment that includes the creation of automated software tools to help with the very difficult task of collecting and coordinating assessment data in a way that makes meaningful analysis feasible.

How effective is our process? During an ABET accreditation visit last year, preliminary discussions were begun between the department and ABET with the goal of partnership to extend our software to all ABET schools. ABET currently has no tools that provide the aggregation capability of our assessment tools. The faculty reflections process (discussed in section 2) is being considered by ABET for being promulgated as a "best practice."

SIGCSE'10, March 10-13, 2010, Milwaukee, Wisconsin, USA.

2. ASSESSMENT

The assessment process begins with the setting of desirable program outcomes, and the setting of learning objectives for each course. The department as a whole, set the program outcomes, and developed a mapping of the department's program outcomes to the ABET requirements commonly known as "A through K." With the special input of its curriculum committee, the individual instructors set the learning objectives for each course.

We also developed a rubric for retrospective analysis of their courses by the faculty who have taught them. (This rubric is in addition to some other standard rubrics that have been obtained from other universities for the purposes of measuring student's performance in written and verbal communications, as a member of a project team, and on design projects.) These retrospective reflections of faculty members provide considerable guidance to other faculty members teaching the course in subsequent years.

It should be noted that, as in most colleges and universities, the development and alignment of program outcomes is heavily affected by inputs from the major stakeholders: students alumni, recruiters, advisory board, etc., as well as external inputs from the mission, vision, and core values statements and policies of the encompassing college and the university itself.
Reflections of the faculty in the most recent self-study included the following:

- Reduce or eliminate the coverage of parsing and grammar issues in a computer languages course, especially since it was covered elsewhere in the theory of computation course.
- Spend additional time in the fundamentals of algorithms course to reflect the apparent weakness of the students in their entering knowledge of statistics.
- Include more project management and estimation in the software engineering course.

The ABET accreditation visiting team was so impressed by the department's process of using faculty reflections for course improvement that they recommended that the faculty reflections process be considered as a "Best Practice" by ABET.

B42 9. Deliver the program.

	A	B
1	**LEARNING OBJECTIVES**	
2		
3	**Learning Objective**	**Description**
4	**1**	1. Define the term "software engineering" and some related terms.
5	**1a**	a. Describe the typical phases of a software engineering project: systems engineering, requirements, design, code, integration, test, maintenance.
6	**1b**	b. Describe software reuse, COTS, and software reliability.
7	**2**	2. Describe several software life cycle models, including the waterfall model, prototyping model, and spiral model.
8	**2a**	a. Determine which software life cycle model is best suited to your particular software problem.
9	**3**	3. Understand and apply the ACM and IEEE Code of Ethics and other ethical issues to a software engineering project.
10	**4**	4. Understand the basic issues in process management.
11	**4a**	a. Participate effectively in a team.
12	**4b**	b. Develop a plan, including schedule.
13	**4c**	c. Allocate resources, both human and computing.
14	**4d**	d. Manage the project.
15	**4e**	e. Measure project status.
16	**4f**	f. Create written progress reports as required by the customer.
17	**4g**	g. Report project status orally.
18	**4h**	h. Keep personnel and the project on track by assessment metrics.
19	**5**	5. Understand the requirements process
20	**5a**	a. Elicit requirements from a customer.

Instructions | **Learning Objectives** | Program Outcomes | 1 | 1a | 1b | 2 | 2a | 3 | 4 | 4a | 4b | 4c | 4d | 4e | 4f | 4g | 4h | 5 | 5a | 5b | 5c

Figure 1. A course's learning objectives.

A4 1a,1b,2c,4a,5b,6a,6b,8

	A	B	C
1	**PROGRAM OUTCOMES**		
2			
3	**Learning Objectives**	**Program Outcomes**	**Description**
4	**1a,1b,2c,4a,5b,6a,6b,8**	**A**	An ability to apply knowledge of computing and mathematics appropriate to the discipline.
5	**1a,1b,2a,2b,2c,3c,5b,6a,7a,7c,9**	**B**	An ability to analyze a problem, and identify and define the computing requirements appropriate to its solution.
6	**1a,1b,2a,2b,2c,3d,3e,4a,5b,7b,8, 9**	**C**	An ability to design, implement, and evaluate a computer-based system, process, component, or program to meet desire
7	**2c,7b,10a**	**D**	An ability to function effectively on teams to accomplish a common goal.
8	**7a,7c,11**	**E**	An understanding of professional, ethical, legal, security and social issues and responsibilities.
9	**3a,3b,3c,3d,3e**	**F**	An ability to communicate effectively with a range of audiences.
10	**7a,11**	**G**	An ability to analyze the local and global impact of computing on individuals, organizations, and society.
11		**H**	Recognition of the need for and an ability to engage in continuing professional development.
12		**I**	An ability to use current techniques, skills, and tools necessary for computing practice.
13	**1a,1b,2c,4a,5c,6a,6b,7b,8**	**J**	An ability to apply mathematical foundations, algorithmic principles, and computer science theory in the modeling an
14		**K**	An ability to apply design and development principles in the construction of software systems of varying complexity.

Instructions | Learning Objectives | **Program Outcomes** | GradeSheet Broken Down by Prob

Figure 2. Mapping a course's learning objectives to program outcomes.

3. THE ASSESSMENT TOOL

The initial deployed version of the assessment tool is a set of macros in Microsoft Excel to facilitate the measurement of the success of each course in achieving a course's learning objectives, which are then used to measure the effect on the entire program's outcomes. The common set of macros is used for every course.

A Microsoft Excel spreadsheet with a portion of the course learning objectives for a junior-level software engineering course is shown in Figure 1. All figures have been cropped.

The learning objectives for each course must be created in the context of the program's overall objectives. Mapping of this particular course's learning objectives to the overall program outcomes is shown in Figure 2.

The small subset of learning objectives shown in Figure 1 exemplifies the course's coverage. The bottom row of Figure 1 lists some of the individual sheets in this spreadsheet using separate tabs. Clicking on any of these tabs brings up a sheet showing the particular learning objective and the student's performance on this particular learning objective.

Entering the data for each learning objective on a separate sheet is far too time-demanding to be useful for faculty to use it willingly. Faculty members use a special sheet named "Grade Sheet Broken Down by Problem" (shown in Figure 3) in which each assessed item is listed, together with the total number of points for it.

H21 | fx 5

	A	B	C	D	E	F	G	H
10	HW 3	Prob 1	5,5a,5c,5d,5e	25	25	25	20	20
11	HW 3	Prob 1	sum	25	25	25	20	20
12	HW 4	Prob 1	5,5a,5c,5d,5e	20	18	18	18	18
13	HW 4	Prob 1	sum	20	18	18	18	18
14	EXAM 1	Prob 1	1,1d	10	10	10	10	10
15	EXAM 1	Prob 2	1a	10	5	5	5	8
16	EXAM 1	Prob 3	2	10	10	10	8	5
17	EXAM 1	Prob 4	4h	5	5	5	5	5
18	EXAM 1	Prob 5	2a	10	8	8.5	15	0
19	EXAM 1	Prob 6	5b	15	15	13	10	15
20	EXAM 1	Prob 7	5	10	5	5	10	5
21	EXAM 1	Prob 8	6,6a	5	5	5	5	5
22	EXAM 1	Prob 9	5,6b,6c	30	30	30	30	25
23	EXAM 1		sum	105	93	91.5	98	78
24	ORAL 1	Prob 1	5,5a,5b,5c	25	25	25	25	25
25	ORAL 1	Prob 1	sum	0	0	0	25	25
26	ORAL 2	Prob 1	5c,5d	25	20	20	20	20
27	ORAL 2	Prob 1	sum	25	20	20	20	20
28	ORAL 3	Prob 1	6,6a,6d	25	25	25	25	25
29	ORAL 3	Prob 1	sum	25	25	25	25	25
30	ORAL 4	Prob 1	4&9g	25	20	20	20	20

8e / 8f / 9 / 9a / 9b / 9c / 9d / 9e / 9f / 9g / 10 / 10a / 10b / Grade Sheet Sun

Figure 3. A "Grade Sheet Broken Down by Problem" data sheet showing recording of learning objectives.

C4 | fx

	A	B	C	D	E	F	G	H	I	J	K	L
4	LO											
5	1			2	4	4	1	4	1	4	4	
6	2			1	4	5	1	4	1	5	4	
7	3			1	3	5	1	3	1	4	4	
8	4			2	3	5	1	2	3	3	5	
9	5			1	4	4	1	4	1	4	4	
10	6			3	3	4	1	4	1	4	4	
11	7			2	4	4	1	3	5	4	4	
12	8			4	4	4	1	4	5	4	4	
13	9			5	5	5	4	5	4	5	5	
14	10			3	3	5	1	3	1	4	5	
15	11			3	3	4	1	3	1	4	5	
16	12			3	3	4	1	3	1	4	5	
17												
18	Student Average Score			2.5	3.583333	4.416667	1.25	3.5	2.083333	4.083333	4.416667	
19												
20												
21												
22												
23												

Grade Sheet Summary / Graph / **Course Outcomes Summary** / Prog Outcomes Summary / GradeSheet Broken Do\

Figure 4. A "Course Outcomes Summary" data sheet for all learning objectives in a course.

Items such as examinations will ordinarily have several questions; each question will have one or more associated learning objectives with it, as shown in Figure 3. Faculty members make sure that the learning objectives for the course are all in place in the spreadsheet, and must enter the data. Once the spreadsheet is created, the effort to record grades is only slightly greater than simply entering grades into a spreadsheet or commercial grade book software package.

A "Calculate" button (not shown) on this sheet enables a large set of macros to run. These macros create and fill out individual sheets for each of the learning objectives in the course as well as summary data that can easily be aggregated across the entire curriculum. The following sheets are created using the macros:

- Assessment sheets (not shown) for each item evaluating a specific learning objective.
- A grade sheet summary (not shown) that includes means and standard deviations of the grades.
- A graph (not shown) of the course overall grade totals.
- A summary of course outcomes (shown in Figure 4) in the form of measurements of the performance of the students on the specific learning objectives.
- A summary of performance on the program outcomes. This is shown in Figure 5 below for another, small class.
- Suggested grades for the class and a grade distribution (not shown).

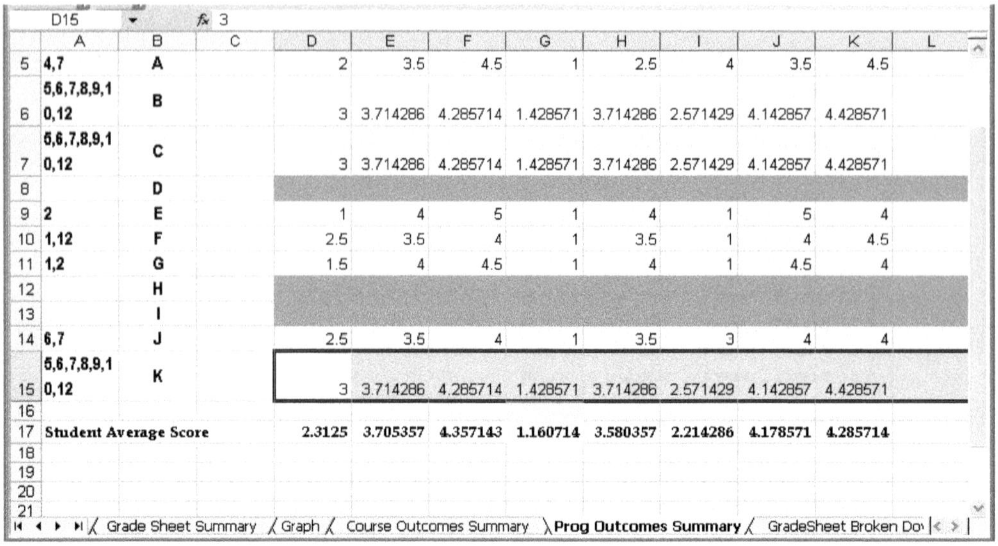

D15 fx 3

	A	B	C	D	E	F	G	H	I	J	K	L
5	4,7	A		2	3.5	4.5	1	2.5	4	3.5	4.5	
6	5,6,7,8,9,10,12	B		3	3.714286	4.285714	1.428571	3.714286	2.571429	4.142857	4.428571	
7	5,6,7,8,9,10,12	C		3	3.714286	4.285714	1.428571	3.714286	2.571429	4.142857	4.428571	
8		D										
9	2	E		1	4	5	1	4	1	5	4	
10	1,12	F		2.5	3.5	4	1	3.5	1	4	4.5	
11	1,2	G		1.5	4	4.5	1	4	1	4.5	4	
12		H										
13		I										
14	6,7	J		2.5	3.5	4	1	3.5	3	4	4	
15	5,6,7,8,9,10,12	K		3	3.714286	4.285714	1.428571	3.714286	2.571429	4.142857	4.428571	
16												
17	**Student Average Score**			**2.3125**	**3.705357**	**4.357143**	**1.160714**	**3.580357**	**2.214286**	**4.178571**	**4.285714**	
18												
19												
20												
21												

Grade Sheet Summary / Graph / Course Outcomes Summary / **Prog Outcomes Summary** / GradeSheet Broken Do

Figure 5. A "Program Outcomes Summary" data sheet showing how particular learning objectives are met.

It is easy to see from these and other sheets when students are in need of additional assistance.

In Figure 4, the light gray background color (yellow on the original spreadsheet) in cell G18 indicates that a student did not perform at a satisfactory level on the learning objectives for this course. A row entirely in yellow would indicate that the entire class performance was below preset criteria for learning, thus helping to close the loop in the assessment process.

Student performance on program outcomes as measured for this particular course is shown in Figure 5. This information is similar, but not identical, to the results indicated in Figure 4, where we showed the "Course Outcomes Summary" sheet displaying this particular course's learning objectives.

The darkest background color (red on the original) in Figure 5 indicates that some of this particular course's learning objectives did not address particular program outcomes as defined by the department. (This information could have been seen by a previously discussed sheet that described the mapping of the course objectives to program outcomes.) Note that several different course learning objectives may be aggregated into a single program outcome. As was the case with Figure 4, a yellow background color (cell G17 in Figure 5) indicated that student performance was below preset criteria.

The entire collection of "Course Outcomes Summary" and "Program Outcomes Summary" sheets from the individual courses can be aggregated into a single sheet (not shown here) to provide a complete assessment of the department's effectiveness in meeting its educational objectives. This information can, in turn, be used to improve the curriculum and the rest of the department's education process, using our assessment process, much in the same manner that the CMM and CMMI models are intended to improve the software development process [6, 7].

4. FUTURE WORK

The first generation of this copyrighted tool, which produces accurate results, will be revised to improve the user interface, and provide stress testing to make sure that our software can handle larger class sizes than we currently have. We will also improve our overall system by interfacing the spreadsheets with a database.

Since the department's undergraduate programs had to undergo the ABET assessment process, and the entire collection of graduate programs at our university will be undergoing a university-wide graduate program review, we have decided to use our tools for the assessment of its beginning graduate courses. We expect this approach will strengthen the department's course offerings and allow greater continuity when different instructors teach these beginning graduate courses.

ACKNOWLEDGEMENT

This research was partially funded by the National Science Foundation under grant number 0324818. Any opinions, findings and conclusions or recommendations expressed in this material are those of the author and do not necessarily reflect the views of the United States government.

REFERENCES

[1] Criteria for the Accreditation of Computing Programs, ABET, document available on-line at abet.org/forms.shtml#For_Computing_Programs_Only

[2] Dunning, Scott, available on-line at www.eece.maine.edu/EET/SCOTT/main_files/VITApub.htm

[3] John, Vijay, document available on-line at cbe.tulane.edu/news/documents/ChEWave_SF_02.pdf

[4] Leach, Ronald J., "Analysis of ABET Accreditation as a Software Process," *ITiCSE*, June 27-30, 2008, Madrid, Spain

[5] Smith, Gary, document available on-line at www.ndsu.edu/ndsu/cea/2005_source.pdf.

[6] Capability Maturity Model, version 1.0, *Software Engineering Institute*, Carnegie Mellon University, Pittsburgh, Pennsylvania, 1991.

[7] CMMI Product Team, "CMMI for Development, Version 1.2," Technical Report CMU/SEI-2006-TR-008, *Software Engineering Institute*, Carnegie Mellon University, Pittsburgh, Pennsylvania, 2006.

24/7 Lectures as an Exam Review Technique

James B. Fenwick Jr. and Cindy Norris
Computer Science Dept.
Appalachian State University
Boone, North Carolina, USA
{fenwickjb,norrisca}@appstate.edu

Andrew R. Dalton and William Kreahling
Mathematics and Computer Science Dept.
Western Carolina University
Cullowhee, North Carolina, USA
{adalton,wkreahling}@email.wcu.edu

ABSTRACT

Assessment of student learning through tests, or examinations, is one of those necessary evils. No one seems to enjoy it, but everyone admits the necessity of it. Reducing student anxiety and frustration is an important activity to obtain a meaningful assessment of their learning. A common way for teachers to help students prepare is with a review session. This paper describes a structured review technique that actively engages every student in a multisensory way, requires little work on the part of the instructor, and is both entertaining and fun. Most important, this paper describes an empirical study that demonstrates the dramatic efficacy of the technique.

Categories and Subject Descriptors

K.3.2 [**Computers and Education**]: Computer and Information Science Education—*Computer science education*

General Terms

Performance, Human factors, Experimentation

Keywords

Pedagogy

1. INTRODUCTION

An ample supply of education research exists indicating the important role feedback plays in student learning. As early as 1923, Jones determined that administering practice tests immediately after lectures led to improved retention of material among students [7]. In his seminal teaching handbook "Teaching Tips", McKeachie suggests a non-graded practice test as a method of reducing student anxiety and improving test performance [11]. Lowman suggests short practice exams that are graded and returned but not recorded [10]. Addison notes in a study of two courses that students who missed one or more post-exam review sessions performed significantly worse on the final than students with no absences [1]. Furthermore, Balch reports that practice exams are more effective than reviewing exams and the increased scores are irrespective of student academic ability [2].

Another form of test preparation is the use of review sessions that are held before tests or finals. Unstructured review sessions in which instructors prepare review material and answer student questions are one option. Unfortunately, instructors find the lack of student participation in such review sessions frustrating [10]. Students often do not prepare questions and some attend only to avoid missing anything – they do not wish to actively participate. Instructors can improve student attendance by using a regular class session, but at the cost of losing class time that could be spent on new material.

Lowman suggests a better review session method is one that is structured. For example, all students answer practice questions, compare responses with other students, and discuss answers provided by the instructor. Another way to structure a review session is to model the activity after popular games or television shows. Kaupins describes variations of "Who Wants to Be a Millionaire", "Family Feud", "Boggle", "Outburst", and "The Amazing Race" that function as exam review sessions [8]. Keck describes a similar strategy based on the "Jeopardy" game show [9]. These types of reviews can be fun and entertaining, properties that can serve to engage student participation. Deeter uses another structured review session in which students help her develop many of the exam questions [3]. Beginning with lists of content, she challenges students to generate questions that would assess their understanding of these concepts. A part of this process includes discussion of the correct answers.

A drawback of these types of review techniques is that the onus for preparation is placed upon the instructor. In addition, these techniques tend to be quite time-consuming to conduct, possibly causing the instructor to decide to hold the session outside of class and risk students being unable or unwilling to participate. In this paper, we discuss the use of a simple review technique based upon the 24/7 Lectures presented in the Ig Nobel Award ceremony. Our 24/7 review technique requires a minimum amount of effort on the part of the instructor, yet engages the student in a multisensory manner. The technique can be structured to take less than a regular session if instructional time is limited. In addition, an analysis of exam results indicates that students, in general, perform better on those questions related to their 24/7 Lecture. We believe that with a little "tweaking" of our 24/7 review technique, student performance will increase even more.

2. 24/7 LECTURES

Improbable Research is an organization focusing on research that makes people laugh and then think. For example, a classic article in the Annals of Improbable Research titled "Does it Rain More Often on Weekends?" uses valid weather data to arrive at an answer to this quirky question. In addition to the magazine, the organization sponsors a website and the annual "Ig Nobel Prizes" awards ceremony. The Ig Nobel Prizes are a frequent topic of a fall episode of NPR's Science Friday. Part of this ceremony is the 24/7 Lectures in which top thinkers explain their subject twice: first is a complete, technical description in 24 seconds, and second is a clear summary that anyone can understand in 7 words.

The lectures are entertaining and informative. As an example, below is the 2006 24/7 Lecture on History by Jill Lepore of Harvard University [12, 6]. (Note that to ensure they finish within the time limit, many lecturers speak very fast resulting in some difficulty in transcription.)

> *History is in an enduring travel to an archive repository or a library, bring in pencil, fill out little (unintelligible); be the chicken scratch of letters, diaries, love notes, speeches, scrapbooks, (unintelligible), unopened mails, stranger and wondrous people you've never met and never will but you probably should could have. Find out everything you can about how they understood why hens lay eggs. Think about it. Think about it some more, and then make up some cock-and-bull story.*
>
> The 7 word summary was, **History is the study of dead people.**

In the fall of 2007, one of the authors just happened to tune into the NPR Science Friday show that presented the Ig Nobel Prizes and realized that the 24/7 Lecture format might be a way to actively involve students in their learning. The following semester the author had students prepare lectures on various sections of textbook chapters and deliver them to the class. The results were disappointing. Upon reflection, it was determined that what makes the 24/7 Lectures humorous and informative is that the audience has a high level of familiarity with the subject matter. However in this particular case, students only read their assigned section and so were not familiar enough with other students' textbook subject material. The thought was then to use the 24/7 Lecture as a review mechanism on course material that all students were previously exposed to during the term. In the spring of 2008, the author retried the 24/7 Lectures this new way with great success. The exam review session was fun, students expressed genuine interest even asking for a second session, and many of the lectures were quite good and useful. After collaborating with the other authors, it was decided to attempt a more rigorous study of the efficacy of the technique.

3. THE EXPERIMENTAL SETUP

The goal of the experiment was to measure the effectiveness of using the 24/7 Lecture as a means to structure an exam review session. Students prepare one or more 24/7 Lectures on various topics related to the course and provide written versions on a class wiki so that all students would be able to use them when studying. In addition, during the exam review session each student delivers orally their own 24/7 Lecture.

Four instructors at two different schools teaching six different courses across all levels of students (freshman through senior) participated. The 24/7 Lecture format introduces constraints on the students. We modified the constraints slightly to investigate any affects. Two instructors used the classic 24/7 format of 24 seconds with a 7 word summary. Students were told they could not be over (a very loud buzzer would sound) or be too far under the 24 second clock. The other instructors used a modified format of 24 words with a 7 word summary. Table 1 shows some of the course parameters.

Some of the instructors assigned review lecture topics and some did not. One class used the technique for a test and the rest for the final exam. Some of the student lectures were deemed "unusable" for the study. This could occur when a student selected a topic that was too easy (e.g., one Data Structures student lectured on sequential search) and thus this lecture was not covered by any exam question. Some students presented a lecture during the review session (so they prepared), but did not post to the wiki and so our ability to map their lecture topic to exam question(s) was impaired.

A short eight question survey was developed to attempt to measure student perceptions about the technique on a 5-point Likert scale. One instructor had student evaluations be optionally completed outside of class and returned, and the others provided a small amount of class time for student evaluations.

4. EXPERIMENT EVALUATION

Three forms of evaluation are presented, an objective measure of student performance, a subjective measure of student perceptions, and a subjective measure of instructor attitudes.

4.1 Student Performance

The objective measurement relates student exam performance to student preparation of a 24/7 Lecture. Exams were graded by the instructors, but in the usual way with no conscious predisposition to lecture topics or exam questions. Exams were generally administered several days after the review session and graded several days after the administration. Later, instructors correlated lecture topics to exam questions. Some lecture topics were not covered by any exam question and some exam questions assessed course material not covered by any student lecture. However, there were 70 instances of student lectures that did map directly to examination question(s).

For each topic, the number of exam points was calculated. Some topics were covered by more than one question. For each student, their score on those questions was computed. All scores are normalized to 100. This results in a table similar to the one shown in Table 2.

The asterisks denote that the student prepared a lecture topic; thus, student 2 prepared a 24/7 Lecture on AVL trees. Generally, half of a class will score above the average and half below. Thus, we hope that students consistently score

Table 1: Some experimental parameters

Course	# Students	# Usable Lectures	24/7 Format
Machine Organization	17	11	24 seconds, 7 words
Data Structures	27	31	24 seconds, 7 words
CS2	20	9	24 words, 7 words
Operating Systems	13	7	24 words, 7 words
CS1	13	7	24 words, 7 words
Graphics	10	5	24 words, 7 words
Totals	100	70	

Table 2: Sample data collection

Student	Heaps	AVL trees	Iterators
1	62	*100	50
2	71	*33	75
3	76	*78	*63
4	95	100	*88
5	*95	78	100
...	...	...	...
N	100	100	*100
Averages	67	51	72

above the average on questions that they specifically reviewed through their 24/7 Lecture. In Table 2, we can see that students 1 and 3 did score above the class average on the AVL trees questions; however, student 2 scored below the average. Only student 5 delivered a lecture on heaps, scoring above the average.

Across all 6 courses we have 70 instances of correlated topics and questions (i.e., asterisk entries). In these cases, 71% of the time students scored at or above the class average on topics on which they had prepared a 24/7 Lecture. Breaking out the differences in the lecture formats results in 67% for the classic 24/7 format and 79% for the modified format in which student lectures consisted of exactly 24 words. Thus, having students prepare a 24/7 Lecture does indeed seem to improve student exam performance.

We expect that very good students would be scoring above the average anyway and likely contributed usable lectures. We wanted to consider the results by eliminating this "upward pulling" effect. We examined the data again focusing on only those students whose overall examination score placed into the lowest third of the course. These students are generally scoring below the average. Yet, for those questions that these students prepared a 24/7 Lecture, they scored above the entire class average 59% of the time. Breaking out the differences in the lecture formats results in 57% for the classic 24/7 format and 63% for the modified format. This indicates that the 24/7 Lecture exam review technique is indeed helping those students who need the most help.

The next question to consider is the effect 24/7 Lectures have on other students. That is, does student A's 24/7 Lecture help student B and student C do better too? To answer this question the data was examined comparing student performance on all the questions covered by any student's 24/7 Lecture to student performance on the exam as a whole. We found that 54% of the students scored higher than their overall exam grade on those questions that were covered by some 24/7 Lecture. In addition, the average score (normalized out of 100 points) was 2 points higher on that portion of the exam that related to the 24/7 Lectures than the average score of the entire exam. This is a mild indicator that even just hearing another student's review lecture can be beneficial.

4.2 Student Perceptions

Students were asked to complete a survey to gauge their perceptions of the 24/7 Lecture exam review technique. Responses were received from 84 students with results shown in Figure 1. We surveyed students after the review session and before administration of the final exam.

Questions 2 and 3 indicate that students do not feel overwhelmed by the activities required on their part for this review technique. Questions 4 and 5 reveal that most students agree or strongly agree that the technique is beneficial to them. Question 1 shows that about a third of students are uncomfortable presenting in front of class; however, when asked in question 7 about presenting their 24/7 Lecture only about 20% expressed an uncomfortableness. Thus, for a number of students the fun aspect of the activity won out over their normal predisposed fears. Generally, most students found the review technique an experience worthwhile enough to recommend to others. There were, however, a small group of students that were not satisfied with the experience as indicated by several survey results in which students consistently selected the more negative response.

4.3 Instructor Attitudes

The instructors believe that the 24/7 Lectures were an effective review technique for their students. Given that the results were not substantially different for the two forms of lectures we used, we believe that the real learning is occurring for three reasons. First, the format demands a repeated engagement with the material. In the case of the classic 24 second format, students must develop their initial lecture and then practice delivering it. Likely they will need to make some adjustments – it might be a little too long or a little too short. They must then return to the writing and practice again. In the case of the modified 24 word format, they would likely need to rephrase wordings several times to end up with 24 words. It is interesting that it does not seem to matter what the constraint actually is so much as there is some constraint that forces this repeated engagement. The second reason we believe it was successful is the multisensory nature of the experience. Students are engaging with the material visually by seeing their own writing, tactilely by doing the writing, and aurally by hearing themselves speak. Finally, the 24/7 Lecture is an application of the pedagogical pattern "Explain It Yourself" based upon the insight that individuals understand concepts better when they can explain them in their own words [4].

The 24/7 Lecture review technique requires very low ef-

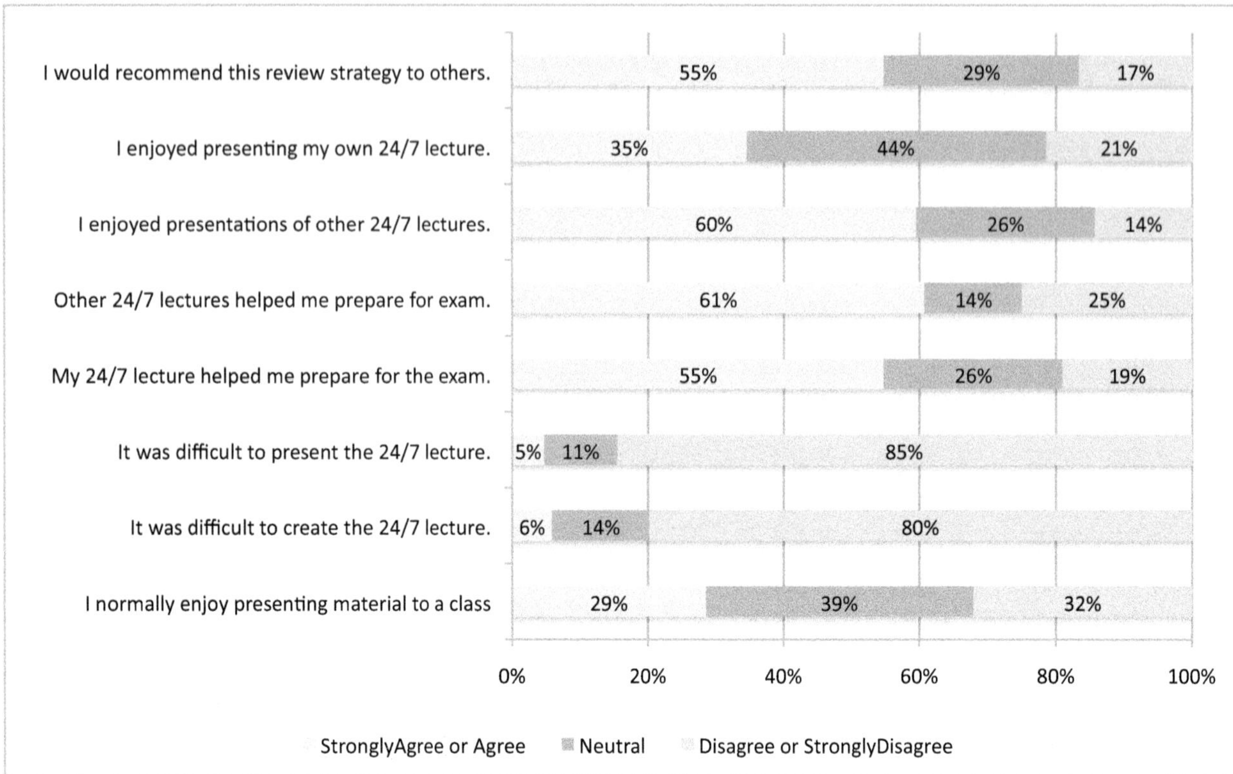

Figure 1: Student perception survey results

fort on the part of the instructor. Some instructors chose to come up with categories of questions, but these are more-or-less aligned with course goals and objectives and is thus not a difficult task. Some of the instructors spent some effort to keep the review wiki page formatted nicely and sensibly (some students just cut/paste their wiki lecture entry anywhere!).

The instructors are excited about continuing to use the review activity with perhaps a few slight modifications (see the next subsection). In addition to the fun of the activity and improved exam scores, students are provided with an opportunity to improve public speaking skills. As the students indicated in the survey, they do not generally feel comfortable speaking in front of a class. Yet, it has long been recognized that strong communication skills are crucial for CS majors [5]. Small, well-structured opportunities for public speaking, like this review technique, can be an important part of this skill development.

Some of the lectures were not of a high quality, but many of these students would probably be minimally engaged in any review activity. Yet, overall, we were impressed with the lectures. The first sample below is taken from the set of 24/7 Lectures created for a *Data Structures* class. The second lecture is taken from the sest created for *Assembly Language and Machine Organization.*

> *An AVL tree is a balanced binary tree because it keeps the entries balanced around the root. To keep the balance the tree performs a rotate left or rotate right depending on where the new node was placed. These can come as a single rotate or a double rotate. A double rotate is just a combination of both single rotates, just in a specific order. Double rotates are caused by inner grandchildren, while single rotates are outer grandchildren.*
> Summary (referencing the movie The Karate Kid): **A rotate right looks like wax on.**

> *With the n-thpe if it is given 2.9 Volts than it's gate link will be closed, but if the n-type is given 0 Volts then it's gate will be open. The p-type is the exact opposite. So basically for an inverter if the input is a 1 then n-type will cause the output to be a 0, but if the input is a 0 then the n-type can't run the power out and the p-type will cause the output to be a 1.*
> Summary: **n is zero so p is hero.**

4.4 What might we try different?

We are excited by the success of the technique and intend on using it again in the fall 2009 term. Based on our experiences, here are a few ways we could "tweak" the approach.

Letting students choose their own 24/7 Lecture topic can be a weakness. There were definitely a number of lectures submitted that were on subject matter not deemed all that important by the instructor. For example, in the Data Structures course, the unit on Big-Oh complexity analysis begins with a simple O(n) sequential search to lay the groundwork. This is followed by the more interesting and important binary search and the various sorting algorithms. However, one student chose sequential search as their lecture topic. To address this, we will likely provide students with a list of review topics to ensure a decrease in lectures on topics that are not covered by questions on the exam.

Delivery of an individual 24/7 Lecture takes very little time so the technique could be incorporated into class sessions other than an exam review session. It might be beneficial for students to consistently be developing 24/7 Lectures during the term. Periodically, the instructor could use 5 minutes of class time for randomly selected students to deliver their lectures. By the time of the final exam review session, students would have developed a portfolio of course 24/7 Lectures. A final exam review session might not even be needed, since it essentially has been distributed throughout the course. However, a fun review session could involve voting for the most clever lectures of the year and reprising those during the review session.

As was described previously, we attempted a modified format that used 24 words rather than 24 seconds. Interestingly, the results are not that different between the formats. We believe the key to the improved student learning that is occurring with both formats is the presence of the constraint (24 words or 24 seconds). So, modifying the constraint in various ways could still serve the purpose of increased student learning. One idea is to provide a third level. Allow a student to write an "unlimited" lecture (or provide a high cap of 250 words for instance). Then require them to also provide a version of the same lecture that is pared down to say 50 words. Lastly, require a third version that is pared down to the seven word summary. This approach teaches valuable skills including abstraction and stepwise refinement.

5. CONCLUSIONS

This paper presented a review technique based upon the entertaining 24/7 Lectures presented at the Ig Nobel Award ceremony. An analysis of the exam results indicated that 71% of the time students scored at or above the class average on exam problems related to their 24/7 Lecture. 54% of the students scored better on those portions of the exam related to the 24/7 Lectures presented by the class than they scored on the exam overall. In addition, the average student score for students on the portion of the exam related to the 24/7 Lectures was 2 points higher than the average score on the exams overall. The technique requires little effort on the part of the instructor yet engages students in a fun and multisensory way.

6. REFERENCES

[1] W. Addison. Consequences of missing postexam review sessions. *Teaching of Psychology*, 22(2):121–123, April 1998.

[2] W. Balch. Practice versus review exams and final exam performance. *Teaching of Psychology*, 25(3):181–185, 1998.

[3] L. Deeter. Incorporating student centered learning techniques into an introductory plant identification course. *NACTA*, 47(2), June 2003.

[4] J. Eckstein, J. Bergin, and H. Sharp. Feedback patterns. In *EuroPLoP '01: Proceedings of the 2001 European conference on Pattern Languages of Programs*, 2001.

[5] E. Giangrande, Jr. Communication skills in the cs curriculum. *J. Comput. Small Coll.*, 24(4):74–79, 2009.

[6] Improbable Research. Improbable research collection #106: Superior shot, history 24/7. http://www.youtube.com/watch?v=G-j3y7cID5c.

[7] H. Jones. Experimental studies of college teaching. *Archives of Psychology*, 10:5–70, 1923.

[8] G. Kaupins. Using popular game and reality show formats to review for exams. *The Teaching Professor*, 19(1):5–6, January 2005.

[9] M. Keck. A final eam review activity based on the jeopardy format. *Journal of Chemical Education*, 77:483–+, April 2000.

[10] J. Lowman. *Mastering the Techniques of Teaching.* Jossey-Bass, 1995.

[11] W. McKeachie and M. Svinicki. *Teaching Tips: Strategies, Research, and Theory for College and University Teachers.* Wadsworth Publishing, 2005.

[12] NPR. *Highlights from the ig nobel awards.* http://www.npr.org/templates/transcript/transcript.php?storyId=16576776.

Principles of Asking Effective Questions During Student Problem Solving

Kristy Elizabeth Boyer, William Lahti, Robert Phillips*, Michael D. Wallis*, Mladen A. Vouk, James C. Lester

Department of Computer Science, North Carolina State University, Raleigh, NC

*Dual affiliation with Applied Research Associates Inc., Raleigh, NC

{keboyer, wjlahti, rphilli, mdwallis, vouk, lester}@ncsu.edu

ABSTRACT

Using effective teaching practices is a high priority for educators. One important pedagogical skill for computer science instructors is asking effective questions. This paper presents a set of instructional principles for effective question asking during guided problem solving. We illustrate these principles with results from classifying the questions that untrained human tutors asked while working with students solving an introductory programming problem. We contextualize the findings from the question classification study with principles found within the relevant literature. The results highlight ways that instructors can ask questions to 1) facilitate students' comprehension and decomposition of a problem, 2) encourage planning a solution before implementation, 3) promote self-explanations, and 4) reveal gaps or misconceptions in knowledge. These principles can help computer science educators ask more effective questions in a variety of instructional settings.

Categories and Subject Descriptors

K.3.2 [**Computer and Information Science Education**]: *Computer Science Education*

General Terms

Design, Human factors

Keywords

Computer science education research, instructional discourse, question-asking, tutoring

1. INTRODUCTION

Instructional discourse and dialogue are ubiquitous in computer science education. Channels for this discourse include formal lecture classes [11, 17], office hour help sessions, online message boards [20], email, blogs and Twitter channels. In each of these situations, instructors have the opportunity to increase the efficacy of classroom time and homework exercises by facilitating students' learning. An instructor's choices during instructional discourse and dialogue can profoundly affect the experience of the students [1]. In particular, carefully formulated questions can encourage students to self-explain [6], promote comprehension of requirements and effective planning of solutions [14], and reveal important gaps in student knowledge [22]. Yet, instructors' natural tendencies may not be to pose these questions, possibly because other approaches seem more direct [9, 18].

The objective of the current work is to identify question-asking principles that promote deep student learning through instructional dialogue. We examine the natural question-asking tendencies of untrained instructors and compare these approaches to principles of effective question asking from the relevant cognitive science, psychology, and computer science education literature. The empirical basis for this research is a collection of dialogues between human tutors and novice computing students working to implement the solution to a programming exercise. We have developed a novel question classification scheme and applied it to the questions that occur in the dialogues. The results of the question classification study, when contextualized with the relevant literature, highlight several patterns of "what not to do" for question asking during guided problem solving. The principles of effective question asking described here have direct, practical implications for computer science educators.

2. RELATED WORK

Several lines of research have investigated *student* questions in the context of computer science education. For example, pair programming students ask higher-level questions of the instructors than solo programming students [15]. Intelligent agents that monitor collaborative group activity may encourage students to produce higher quality questions [21]. The instructional setting also influences the nature and topic of student questions. For example, students ask different types of questions in online discussions than they do in class lectures [17].

Studying *student* questions can yield valuable insights into how people come to understand computing. In a complementary vein, investigating the impact of *instructor* questions can lead to more effective question-asking practices on the part of educators. Asking effective questions prompts students to engage in valuable learning behaviors they might not otherwise have undertaken. For example, one important role of questions is to encourage students to self-explain, which has been shown to be highly beneficial for learning [6], a possible source of the effectiveness of Socratic dialogue [12]. With novice computer scientists, asking effective questions during the early phases of planning a solution can support the students' comprehension and decomposition of the problem at hand [14]. Asking targeted, specific questions is useful for revealing knowledge gaps with novices, who are often unable to articulate their questions [22].

SIGCSE'10, March 10–13, 2010, Milwaukee, Wisconsin, USA.

Gaining confidence in asking effective questions is an important step toward developing pedagogical expertise. Research in one-on-one tutoring indicates that novice tutors ask far fewer questions than expert tutors [9]. In addition to asking more questions, skilled instructors recognize that the type of question has important implications for student responses. For example, in software engineering, open-ended questions have been found to elicit a wide range of student responses that are valuable in classroom discussion [19].

This paper builds on the related work noted above by examining the types of questions present in a body of tutorial dialogue for introductory computer science. The results illustrate specific ways in which instructors can improve their question-asking approaches to facilitate student learning.

3. METHODOLOGY

One-on-one tutoring is a valuable arena for conducting research on instructional approaches [18]. The empirical results presented in this paper are based on classifying the questions that occurred naturally in tutoring dialogues between untrained tutors and novice computer science students.

3.1 Tutoring Study Participants

The data consist of instructional dialogues that were recorded during the course of two tutoring studies. Participants were 78 students enrolled in a university introductory computer science class who participated in the study in exchange for a small amount of class credit. The 17 tutors were graduate and upper-division undergraduate students, all with research interests in computer science education and varying degrees of experience in peer tutoring. None of the tutors received formal training in tutoring.

3.2 Tutoring Session Format

Students and tutors reported to separate rooms to ensure anonymity and complete capture of the instructional interaction. They interacted through an Eclipse plug-in that facilitates real-time remote collaboration with textual dialogue [3]. The tutor's interface featured a synchronized view of the students' programming window, and the students and tutors engaged in typed dialogue through a textual dialogue pane. All dialogue and programming actions were recorded in a database.

The tutoring studies were conducted during weeks eight and nine of a twelve-week semester. In both studies, the programming exercise involved applying array data structures and *for* loops to solve a programming problem using Java. Additional details about the participants, programming problems, data collection, and learning outcomes for the two studies are reported in [2, 4].

3.3 Data

The 78 tutoring sessions produced a data set of 10,179 textual dialogue messages. Tutors account for 6,558, or 64.4%, of these messages. This proportion of tutor and student dialogue turns is consistent with data sets from other technical domains such as physics [8]. Our previous research classified all the dialogue messages as statements or questions. Of all the tutor dialogue messages, 714 were classified as questions that were on-topic (off-topic questions include "Is it hot in your room?" or "How are you today?") [2, 4]. This paper reports on the further classification of these 714 questions according to a two-level classification scheme that is intended to capture 1) the *instructional goal* that motivated the question, and 2) the realized *question type*.

3.4 Question Classification

Existing literature on question asking has produced several question classification schemes that have been applied to instructional discourse in a variety of domains [10, 16]. We adapted these taxonomies for application to the computer science dialogues by adding several categories that facilitate classifying problem-based and interactive dialogue questions. The iterative process of creating the final question classification scheme proceeded as follows. First, two researchers independently classified the question goals and types in a training subset of the data. Next, all questions that could not be adequately classified with the existing categories were clustered to create new categories. Finally, the revised scheme was tested on a previously unseen subset of the data. This training and refinement loop concluded when the two researchers classified the questions in a training set with an acceptable level of inter-rater reliability [13], indicating that the taxonomy was sufficiently reliable for the data at hand. Table 1 displays the top level in the hierarchy, the instructional goals. Each of these goals can be instantiated as more than one question type. Table 2 displays these types, which constitute the bottom level of the hierarchy.

Table 1. Instructional Goals for Question Asking

Plan: Establish a problem-solving plan. Ascertain what the student wants, prefers, or intends to do.
Ascertain Student's Knowledge: Find out whether the student knows a particular factual or procedural concept.
Hint: Scaffold the student's problem-solving effort.
Repair Communication: Disambiguate or correct a previous statement or question.
Confirm Understanding: Confirm the student understands a previous problem-solving step or previous tutor statement.
Engage Student: Elicit a response from the student either at the beginning of the tutoring session or after prolonged silence.
Remind/Focus: Direct the student's attention toward a previous statement or problem-solving step.

When the classification scheme had been finalized, an inter-annotator agreement study was conducted. For both levels of the classification scheme, one researcher classified the entire set of 714 tutor questions and a second researcher classified a subset of approximately 17% that had not been used during the training and refinement phase. The Kappa statistic for inter-rater agreement was 0.85 for the question goal classification and 0.84, indicating "very good" reliability [13].

4. RESULTS AND DISCUSSION

The results from classifying tutor questions according to the above taxonomy suggest that the untrained tutors engaged in notable examples of "what not to do" in their question-asking approaches. We begin by examining the frequencies of question types that occurred, and then consider excerpts from the dialogues that illustrate the importance of some question-asking principles.

Table 2. Instructional Question types (* denotes category not found in classification schemes of [10, 16])

Question Type	Example
Assessment*	Do you think we're done?
Backchannel*	Right?
Calculation	What is 13 % 10?
Causal Antecedent	Why are we getting that error?
Causal Consequence	What if the digit is 10?
Clarification*	What do you mean?
Confirmation*	Does that make sense?
Feature/Concept Completion	What do we want to put in digits[0]?
Definition	What does that mean?
Enablement	How are the digits represented as bar codes?
Focus*	See where the array is declared?
Free Creation	What shall we call it?
Free Option	Should the array be in this method or should it be declared up with the other private variables?
Goal Orientation	Did you intend to declare a variable there?
Hint*	We didn't declare it; should we do it now?
Improvement	Can you see what we could do to fix that?
Judgment	Would you prefer to use math or strings?
Justification	Why are we getting that error?
Knowledge*	Have you ever learned about arrays?
Plan	What should we do next?
Procedural	How do we get the ith element?
Quantification	How many times will this loop repeat?
Status*	Do you have any questions?

4.1 Question Type Frequencies

All of the questions from the introductory computer science dialogues were classified according to the question's *goal* and the question *type*.

As depicted in Figure 1, the most common instructional goal was to ascertain the student's knowledge; this goal accounts for just over one-third of the questions. Giving a hint to the student through a question, which is likely an example of an indirect and polite conversational strategy [5], also occurred frequently. This instructional goal accounted for nearly one-fifth of the tutors' questions.

Figure 2 displays the frequency of each question type. *Hint* questions and *procedural* questions are the most common question types, each accounting for nearly one-fifth of the tutors' questions. The second most common questions are *feature/concept completion* and *knowledge* questions. These question types are both intended to gauge student knowledge, with the former being a question directly about the subject matter, while the latter asks whether the student believes he knows or understands a topic.

Some types of questions are known to occur in tutoring from other domains [10, 16], yet these question types are absent from the introductory computer programming dialogues presented here. Some examples of such questions include *composition* questions that ask about the components of an item, *comparison* questions that ask the student to compare items, *example* questions that ask the student to give or interpret an example, and *interpretation* questions that ask for a subjective viewpoint. The absence of these questions may be due in part to the subject matter of the instructional discourse. For example, relatively few introductory computing questions would involve subjective interpretation. On the other hand, some types of questions, such as examples, might be effective in the computing context but were not utilized by the untrained tutors in these studies.

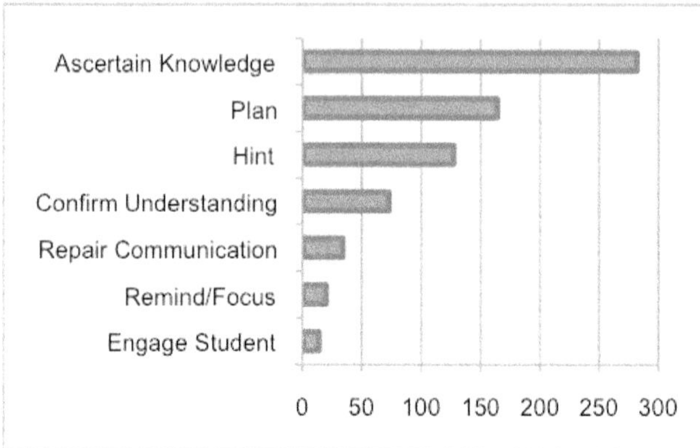

Figure 1. Instructional Goal Frequencies ($n_{questions}$=714)

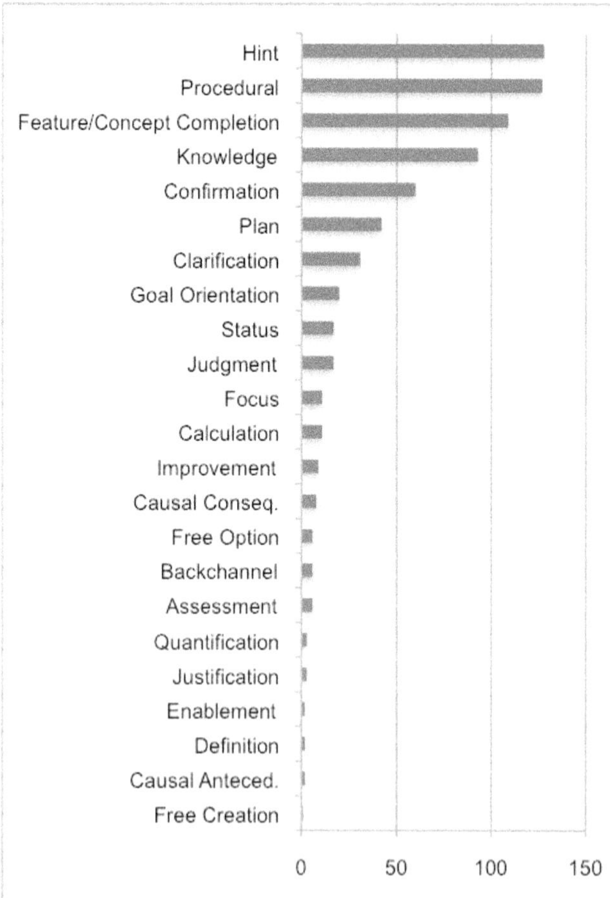

Figure 2. Question Type Frequencies ($n_{questions}$=714)

A small percentage, only 11% of the 6,558 tutor dialogue messages, were questions. This ratio of tutor questions is consistent with findings that untrained instructors, such as the novice tutors used in these studies, tend to ask fewer questions than more highly trained expert instructors [9]. This discrepancy between expert and novice instructors highlights the importance of research on question-asking techniques: effective approaches may not come naturally, yet they hold the potential to improve teaching effectiveness.

The remainder of this section presents excerpts from the data to illustrate the tutors' question asking in context as the student worked to solve the introductory programming problem. For each excerpt, we compare the untrained tutors' question-asking approaches with principles from the literature and discuss how applying these principles may have improved the instructional dialogue.

4.2 Encouraging Comprehension and Decomposition of the Problem

Experienced computer scientists recognize the importance of thoroughly understanding a problem before beginning to construct a solution [14]. In contrast, novices may be more likely to begin implementing a solution without an adequate understanding of the requirements [7]. Figure 3 presents an excerpt that illustrates this phenomenon. The instructional approach illustrated in this excerpt does not encourage the student to think deeply about the problem at hand before beginning to work on the solution; in fact, the tutor encourages the student to move forward with implementation by asking, "Where would you like to start?"

[Tutor and student greet each other]

Tutor 1: Ok, let me know when you're ready to start.

Student 1: I think I'm ready.

Tutor 1: Ok.

Tutor 1: Where would you like to start?

[Goal: Plan, Type: Plan]

Student 1: I guess with the *extractDigits* method.

Tutor 1: Sounds good.

Student 1: I'm already confused.

Figure 3. Not Encouraging Comprehension and Decomposition of the Problem

Because the student had only just finished reading the problem description and had likely not yet fully understood it, questioning the student directly about a plan might have been premature. This possibility is confirmed by what seems like a guess on the part of the student, followed by immediate admission of confusion.

The tutor's goal of establishing a problem-solving plan might have been instantiated more productively as a different question type. For example, a *feature/concept completion* question, (*e.g*, "What are the main steps in completing this assignment?") could have encouraged the student to reflect on and discuss the assignment first. In this context, a useful instructional principle is that *asking specific questions about a problem description can facilitate a student's thorough comprehension of the problem at hand.*

4.3 Eliciting Self-Explanations

At many junctures in instructional discourse, an instructor can choose whether to tell a piece of information to the student or whether to elicit that information by asking a question or a series of questions. Research has shown that self-explaining, in which a student express her own understanding, improves learning [6]. Despite the demonstrated effectiveness of active approaches such as self-explanation, a natural tendency of instructors, especially those with less pedagogical expertise, is to tell the student information that is intended to fill gaps or correct misconceptions in the student's knowledge. Figure 4 illustrates this tendency in an excerpt from the introductory programming dialogues.

Student 2: Ok so *String z = "" + zipcode?*
Tutor 2: Yeah.
Student 2: Then what?
Tutor 2: Ok so now we need somewhere to keep the individual digits.

Figure 4. Tutor "Tells" Rather than Eliciting Student's Explanation

This tutoring session's history has included the tutor giving numerous hints to scaffold the student's problem-solving efforts, and this excerpt represents a transition point at which the tutor could have chosen to ask the student to describe the most reasonable next step (*e.g.*, "Well, given what we've accomplished, what do you think makes sense?"). Instead, the tutor chooses to tell the student what to do next. This illustration of a natural instructional tendency reminds us of the following principle: *Rather than telling the student, asking questions that prompt student self-explanations can improve the student's learning.*

4.4 Asking Targeted Questions

The specificity of questions should be appropriate for the context, which includes the student's knowledge level. Novices often believe they understand when in fact their knowledge is incomplete or incorrect [22]. Figure 5 illustrates an excerpt in which a tutor asks the student whether he has any questions, and the student responds "No." However, after reading a two-page problem description whose solution will constitute his first application of arrays and *for* loops, it is likely that the student has significant knowledge gaps about the problem at hand. The student's lack of experience may render him unable to articulate the questions he has, or he may prefer to begin implementing the solution rather than to discuss his questions.

Tutor 3: Did you have any questions about what the lab wants you to do?

[Goal: Knowledge, Type: Status]

Student 3: No.

Tutor 3: Ok, what method do you want to start with?

[Goal: Plan, Type: Judgment]

Figure 5. Tutor Asks a Vague Question

In this situation, the tutor could have asked the student to explain a key component of the problem description, especially a point that is a known trouble spot for students. For example, an *enablement* question about mechanisms that allow certain behaviors to occur could have been used to illuminate details of the student's understanding (*e.g.*, "How do you think loops will be used to solve this problem?"). *Asking a specific content question can reveal a student's incomplete or incorrect knowledge so that the instruction can proceed productively.*

5. CONCLUSIONS AND FUTURE WORK

Asking effective questions is an important component of pedagogical expertise. By examining tutorial dialogue exchanged between untrained tutors and novice computer science students, we have investigated some types of questions that untrained instructors naturally ask. All of the tutors' questions were classified according to a two-level hierarchical question taxonomy that was based on existing classification schemes enhanced to capture the nuances of the instructional context. The results of this question classification study revealed that the instructors' question-asking approaches could have been improved by applying principles from the relevant literature. We discussed excerpts of tutorial dialogue that lack sophisticated question-asking approaches. The findings illustrate the following principles: 1) *Facilitate comprehension and decomposition.* In problem-solving contexts such as software engineering and programming, asking targeted questions can encourage students to think deeply about the problem at hand. 2) *Prompt for self-explanation.* Periodically asking students to explain their reasoning or understanding results in self-explanation, which has been shown to benefit student learning [6]. 3) *Ask targeted questions.* Content-specific questions, especially questions that focus on known problem areas in the material, are an excellent means for identifying incorrect or incomplete student knowledge. 4) *Ask questions frequently.* Good questions stimulate students to think deeply, explain themselves, and reveal gaps or misconceptions in knowledge. An important component of pedagogical expertise is to ask questions frequently [9].

The work presented here is based on data from tutoring studies. Future work should include experiments designed to assess the effectiveness of specific question-asking approaches. Such experiments would be valuable for confirming the cross-domain applicability of the question-asking principles presented here. Additionally, targeted experiments can shed light on the differences between question-asking approaches for various instructional contexts.

6. ACKNOWLEDGEMENTS

The authors thank Andy Meneely for feedback on this manuscript. This work is supported in part by the NCSU Department of Computer Science along with the National Science Foundation through Grants REC-0632450 and IIS-0812291, a Graduate Research Fellowship, and the STARS Alliance Grant CNS-0540523. Any opinions, findings, conclusions, or recommendations expressed in this report are those of the participants, and do not necessarily represent the official views, opinions, or policy of the National Science Foundation.

7. REFERENCES

[1] Barker, L. J. and Garvin-Doxas, K. Making Visible the Behaviors that Influence Learning Environment: A Qualitative Exploration of Computer Science Classrooms. *Computer Science Education*, 14, 2 (2004), 119-145.

[2] Boyer, K. E., Phillips, R., Wallis, M. D., Vouk, M. A. and Lester, J. C. Balancing Cognitive and Motivational Scaffolding in Tutorial Dialogue. In *Proceedings of the 9th International Conference on Intelligent Tutoring Systems*, 2008, 239-249.

[3] Boyer, K. E., Dwight, A. A., Fondren, R. T., Vouk, M. A. and Lester, J. C. A Development Environment for Distributed Synchronous Collaborative Programming. In *Proceedings of the 13th Annual Conference on Innovation and Technology in Computer Science Education*, 2008, 158-162.

[4] Boyer, K. E., Vouk, M. A. and Lester, J. C. The Influence of Learner Characteristics on Task-Oriented Tutorial Dialogue. In *Proceedings of the 13th International Conference on Artificial Intelligence in Education*, 2007, 365-372.

[5] Brown, P. and Levinson, S. *Politeness: Some Universals in Language Usage*. Cambridge University Press, 1987.

[6] Chi, M. T. H., Leeuw, N., Chiu, M. H. and LaVancher, C. Eliciting Self-Explanations Improves Understanding. *Cognitive Science*, 18, 3 (1994), 439-477.

[7] Ehrlich, K. and Soloway, E. M. An Empirical Investigation of the Tacit Plan Knowledge in Programming. In Thomas, J. and Schneider, M. L. eds. *Human Factors in Computer Systems*. Ablex, 1983.

[8] Forbes-Riley, K., Litman, D., Huettner, A. and Ward, A. Dialogue-Learning Correlations in Spoken Dialogue Tutoring. In *Proceedings of the 12th International Conference on Artificial Intelligence in Education*, 2005, 225-232.

[9] Glass, M., Kim, J. H., Evens, M. W., Michael, J. A. and Rovick, A. A. Novice vs. Expert Tutors: A Comparison of Style. In *the 10th Midwest Artificial Intelligence and Cognitive Science Conference*, 1999, 43-49.

[10] Graesser, A. C., McMahen, C. L. and Johnson, B. K. Question Asking and Answering. In Gernsbacher, M. A. ed. *Handbook of Psycholinguistics*. Academic Press, San Diego, CA, 1994, 517-523.

[11] Graesser, A. C. and Person, N. K. Question Asking During Tutoring. *American Educational Research Journal*, 31, 1 (1994), 104.

[12] Jones, J. S. Participatory Teaching Methods in Computer Science. *SIGCSE Bulletin*, 19, 1 (1987), 155-160.

[13] Landis, J. R. and Koch, G. The Measurement of Observer Agreement for Categorical Data. *Biometrics*, 33, 1 (1977), 159-174.

[14] Lane, H. C. and VanLehn, K. Teaching the Tacit Knowledge of Programming to Novices with Natural Language Tutoring. *Computer Science Education*, 15, 3 (2005), 183-201.

[15] Nagappan, N., Williams, L., Ferzli, M., Wiebe, E., Yang, K., Miller, C. and Balik, S. Improving the CS1 Experience with Pair Programming. In *Proceedings of the 34th SIGCSE Technical Symposium on Computer Science Education*, 2003, 359-362.

[16] Nielsen, R., Buckingham, J., Knoll, G., Marsh, B. and Palen, L. A Taxonomy of Questions for Question Generation. In *Proceedings of the 1st Workshop on Question Generation*, 2008.

[17] Postner, L. and Stevens, R. What Resources do CS1 Students Use and How do They Use Them? *Computer Science Education*, 15, 3 (2005), 165-182.

[18] Ragonis, N. and Hazzan, O. Tutoring Model for Promoting Teaching Skills of Computer Science Prospective Teachers. In *Proceedings of the 13th Annual Conference on Innovation and Technology in Computer Science Education*, 2008, 276-280.

[19] Razmov, V. and Anderson, R. Pedagogical Techniques Supported by the use of Student Devices in Teaching Software Engineering. In *Proceedings of the 37th SIGCSE Technical Symposium on Computer Science Education*, 344-348.

[20] Sheard, J. Electronic Learning Communities: Strategies for Establishment and Management. *SIGCSE Bulletin*, 36, 3 (2004), 37-41.

[21] Soh, L. K., Jiang, H. and Ansorge, C. Agent-Based Cooperative Learning: A Proof-of-Concept Experiment. In *Proceedings of the 35th SIGCSE Technical Symposium on Computer Science Education*, 2004, 368-372.

[22] Tenenberg, J. and Murphy, L. Knowing What I Know: An Investigation of Undergraduate Knowledge and Self-Knowledge of Data Structures. *Computer Science Education*, 15, 4 (2005), 297-315.

Computer Science Illustrated: Engaging Visual Aids For Computer Science Education

Ketrina Yim
EECS Department
University of California, Berkeley
kyim@berkeley.edu

Daniel D. Garcia
EECS Department
University of California, Berkeley
777 Soda Hall
Berkeley, CA 94720-1776
+1 510-642-9595
ddgarcia@cs.berkeley.edu

Sally Ahn
CS Department
University of California, Berkeley
sallyahn@berkeley.edu

ABSTRACT

Computer Science Illustrated[1] is an endeavor to help visual learners comprehend computer science topics through a series of resolution-independent illustrations, which are made available online for use as handouts in class and posters in the computer labs. These illustrations are designed to present concepts as engaging and memorable visual metaphors combined with concise explanations or short narratives, intended to maintain the students' interest and facilitate retention. An additional goal of the project is to make learning the concepts an entertaining experience through the use of colorful and whimsical characters in the illustrations. In producing our twenty-seven illustrations, we determined which topics were most difficult for students to understand in our university's introductory computer science courses and followed a step-by-step process of design, redesign, and revision to generate our illustrations. We also assessed the effectiveness of our creations, using both subjective and objective measures.

Categories and Subject Descriptors

K.3.2 [**Computers and Education**]: Computer and Information Science Education – *Computer Science Education.*

General Terms

Algorithms, Measurement, Human Factors, Standardization, Performance, Languages.

Keywords

Introductory curriculum, illustration, visual learning, cartoon, learning style.

[1] `http://csillustrated.berkeley.edu/`

SIGCSE'10, March 10–13, 2010, Milwaukee, Wisconsin, USA.

1. INTRODUCTION

The relationship between a student's learning style and performance in computer science courses is a topic of considerable interest in computer science education research. Felder has shown that students have preferred modes of learning that can be categorized using the Index of Learning Styles, forty-four questions designed to determine a student's learning preferences, and Chamillard's work revealed the correlation between learning styles and course performance, regardless of the instructor teaching the course [4, 2]. More specifically, a study conducted by Thomas et al. showed that verbal learners perform significantly better than visual learners in introductory programming courses [8]. The implication is that current methods of teaching computer science present an advantage to students who learn verbally rather than visually. Students who learn visually frequently have difficulty understanding computer science topics because the lectures often lack images, charts, diagrams, and animations due to the time and skill required to produce them and the abstract nature of most concepts. Thus, the primary goal of this project is to assist visual learners by providing illustrations that convey the concepts. However, all students can benefit from this work, because it allows them to see the material presented in a fun and different way.

Constructivism also plays a role in a student's understanding of computer science subjects. According to the constructivist theory, students create knowledge structures by mentally selecting and organizing visual and verbal material and subsequently integrating it with prior knowledge they have on the subject [7]. These structures can be fallible, due to gaps in understanding. If the gaps go unnoticed, some students create mental models based on incorrect prior knowledge and require guidance to reconstruct them. At the same time, other students may enter a computer science course with no prior model of the concepts and may require guidance to prevent faulty constructions. Thus, this work also serves a purpose in constructivist learning by helping students with their mental models.

2. RELATED WORK

Incorporating visuals into computer science education is not novel. Diagrams, graphs, and data tables are often found sandwiched between text blocks in computer science books, but some authors let images play a larger role. One notable example is Larry Gonick's wonderful *Cartoon Guide to Computer Science*, a book describing the basics and history of computer science through hand-drawn diagrams and an assortment of characters [5].

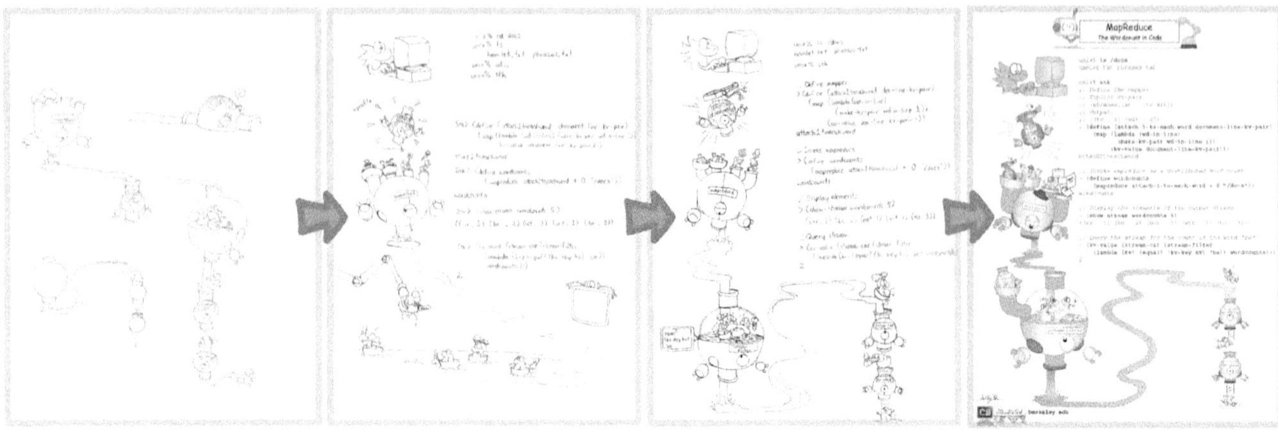

Figure 1. The production process (left to right): initial sketch, first and revised prototypes, and final digital illustration

These comical pictures help readers remember ideas by associating concrete objects with the abstract concepts, while at the same time offering a friendly introduction to basic computer science concepts. Another example is the *Teach Yourself Visually* series of texts by IDG Books. In addition to a variety of other subjects, *Teach Yourself Visually* conveys computer-related topics through step-by-step illustrations to reach out to visual learners.

In the space of computer science education research, attempts have been made to develop learning tools benefiting visual learners. Some incorporate visual elements into programming languages, such as Wally Feurzeig's LOGO. Through the use of turtle graphics, LOGO helps students learn programming as they procedurally generate line drawings. Scratch is another language that relies on visuals, allowing the creation of applications with graphical code blocks.

Most other approaches fall into the category of algorithm visualizations. Attempts have also been made to present visualizations of algorithms at various levels of abstraction, such as Müldner's Algorithm Explanation [6]. Animation is another option considered in algorithm visualization, since seeing the algorithm in action often helps with the understanding of its inner workings. Sorting algorithms are commonly explained through animated visualizations, as seen in Baecker's *Sorting Out Sorting*, a video explaining nine sorting methods [1]. While these visualizations have proven to be effective education tools, they are limited by three ways. First, their main purpose is to teach how algorithms work, so the methods used do not necessarily extend to all computer science concepts. Second, many algorithm visualizations, particularly animations, are presented through the computer and thus cannot be used as offline resources. Third, the visualizations commonly rely on abstract lines and shapes, which can convey actions without visual distraction but make it difficult to form memorable mental pictures of concepts.

Our approach can be considered a complement to algorithm visualization. It covers essential concepts as well as algorithms, and the illustrations are printable, which makes them accessible away from the computer. We also make use of visual metaphors to connect computer science concepts with concrete characters and objects, which students can more easily relate to than lines, shapes, and numbered nodes. This can help students when they attempt to formulate mental images.

3. PRODUCTION PROCESS

3.1 Development

The process of producing one of our illustrations follows the standard design process between artists and clients, beginning with determining which concept should be visualized. Topics are typically chosen from the set of subjects students most often have difficulty grasping within the courses. Occasionally, faculty will directly suggest a topic to illustrate.

Once a suitable topic has been selected, we plan out the illustration, discussing which aspects should be represented by images and which should be included as accompanying text. While the pictures are designed to convey as much of the information as possible, the inclusion of text is sometimes unavoidable, such as when code fragments or narrative segments form an integral part of the illustration. The product of these meetings is a set of sketches plotting out the basic structure of the illustration and rough ideas for the characters and objects that will be used as visual metaphors of the concept.

In the next step, we design the visual metaphors that will illustrate the concept and begin to consider factors such as how understandable, memorable, and aesthetically appealing the metaphors are. The illustrations often contain multiple metaphors, new and old, interacting with each other, so consistency with prior metaphors is essential in preventing confusion among students. Developing the visual metaphors is both the most important and the most difficult aspect of production.

After prototyping the illustration, setting the layout, and refining the visual metaphors' appearance, we start the revision process. In addition to inspecting the illustration ourselves, we present the prototypes to the teaching faculty and other members of the course staff and ask for feedback regarding accuracy, consistency, and clarity. Aside from corrections and suggestions for improvement, responses from the previewing audience can also include different opinions on how to present the concept and advice involving possible alternative visual metaphors. These responses can sometimes significantly alter the appearance of the final product, as well as increase the iterations of revision needed. An illustration may undergo numerous revisions before being considered ready for distribution, but at some point it must be considered "done" so that the next topic can be tackled. We have developed a checklist to know when we've finished:

1. All typographical and visual errors have been corrected.
2. The meaning of the text is clear.
3. The visual metaphors used are understandable.
4. For code segments, the code is free of syntax errors and the output is consistent with the input.
5. If the illustration contains aspects common to multiple illustrations, the visual metaphors used for those aspects are consistent.

On occasion, a revision in one aspect necessitates revision in the rest of the illustration. Thus the guidelines must be consulted at every revision step. Once the illustration satisfies all of the guidelines, it is added to the collection for distribution.

The final step is to draw the illustrations digitally [Fig. 1], allowing for online distribution of the illustrations and flexibility in printing. We convert the paper prototype into vector graphics and text in Adobe Illustrator, the industry standard for creating and editing vector illustrations. We use vectors instead of rasterized images for the digital illustration because vector graphics are infinitely scalable without loss of quality, which allows the illustration to be printed in arbitrary sizes. The conversion phase is also the point at which we add color and further detail to the illustrations. Details are added to the illustrations to make them professional, and include gradients for shading, grounding shadows, and variations in character poses to prevent a "cut-and-paste" appearance. All of the work is done on drawing tablets, the standard tool of graphic designers and illustrators in industry. To make the most efficient use of time, this conversion can take place in parallel with the revision step. The final output is a Portable Document Format (PDF) file.

The production process for one illustration requires two weeks, working six to ten hours per week, on average. Planning and revision occupies the bulk of the two-week span. However, revision of one illustration often occurs concurrently with the planning and drawing of another illustration, though one artist will usually work on no more than two at any given time.

3.2 Challenges

Through several iterations of the production process, we have identified four main challenges that we must address: what to illustrate, what metaphors to use, level of detail, and keeping consistent.

For the first challenge, we typically choose to illustrate topics students consider to be difficult. We gather sets of topics from the course staff, because instructors and teaching assistants can often identify problematic areas from interactions with students during office hours and discussion, as well as from the portions of assignments and tests where students are weakest. In addition, we must determine the reasons why students find a topic difficult to understand. Identifying the problem areas allows us to decide what aspects of the topic to visualize and guides the creation of visual metaphors.

The second challenge is ensuring the effectiveness of the metaphors used to convey the concepts. To allow students to quickly and easily make the connection between what occurs in the illustrations and the ideas they represent, the imagery must be simple, clear, and memorable. The additional factor of aesthetic appeal enhances retention and recall of the metaphor and its corresponding idea. However, many aesthetically appealing designs are not simple or easy to memorize, while the simplest or clearest representation may not be the most attractive. In designing a metaphor, we seek to achieve a balance among the four competing factors, a task depending heavily upon the knowledge, skill, and creativity of the illustrators.

Often metaphor generation involves producing a design that encapsulates the most important aspects of the represented concept or element. For instance, in Scheme lists, the characteristics to emphasize are the groupings established by the lists' parentheses and the fact that list elements are ordered. Thus lists are symbolized by ordered rows of values occupying rectangular buckets marked with parentheses [Fig. 2].

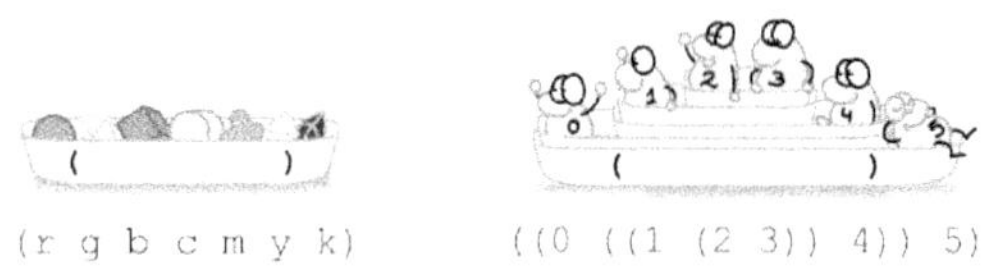

Figure 2. Visual metaphors for a simple Scheme list (left) and a nested Scheme list (right). The nesting of buckets makes the nesting of parentheses more apparent.

Embodying the key aspects of the concept or element allows students who already have a working knowledge of what the illustrations represent to follow along when the metaphors are used to teach something they are less familiar with.

Compromises must be also made regarding the level of detail provided by each illustration. Insufficient detail can contribute to confusion and reduce the illustration's usefulness, but covering too many points at once can overwhelm the viewer.

Consistency among visual metaphors in illustrations, and among the illustrations themselves, is essential to the project. The visual metaphors are designed to help students establish a mental image of computer science concepts. Sudden changes in representations can cause confusion and misunderstanding, so a metaphor must remain an effective representation of an aspect, whether it is alone or combined with another metaphor. There are two main cases where consistency must be ensured: between subtopic illustrations and among different topics within the course. For example, representations of different Scheme functions share a common appearance, regardless of the number or type of arguments they take [Fig. 3]. Unnecessary visual variations here could lead students to false conclusions, such as one saying functions are different datatypes.

Figure 3. All Scheme functions are given the appearance of an input-output machine.

Since illustrations can use multiple metaphors interacting with each other to convey information, old and new metaphors often interact. For example, the docking station found on higher-order function machines was developed to maintain the consistency of list and sentence input as boats. If the characters' or objects' modes of interaction are not compatible, inconsistencies will emerge during the narratives.

4. DISTRIBUTION

Once an illustration is produced, there are three main methods that it can be put to use in a computer science course. Online distribution is one avenue we have established. The illustrations that we have created so far are available in PDF on a publicly accessible website, along with brief descriptions of the project, the illustrators, and recurring characters in the illustrations.

The second use we intend for the illustrations is as course handouts, supplementing the lecture or discussion sections. We foresaw the possibility of printing illustrations as handouts, so all those currently produced are designed to fit the standard 8.5"x11" paper size. Finally, the resolution-independence of our graphics also allows larger scale printing, allowing faculty to print them as computer lab posters [Fig 4].

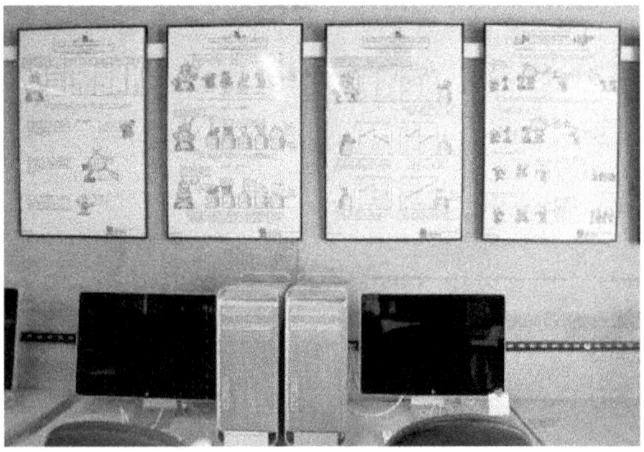

Figure 4. Illustrations proudly on display in one of our labs.

With these distribution options, particularly online availability, the matter of intellectual property becomes a concern. We chose to release our work under the *Creative Commons Attribution-Noncommercial-Share Alike 3.0* license to enable non-commercial use of the illustrations and the creation of derivative works based on them [3].

5. RESULTS

To quantitatively measure the effectiveness of Computer Science Illustrated, we conducted experimental assessments and a survey on the students of the introductory computer science courses. In particular, we selected the introduction to programming course and the machine structures course for our assessments. We chose these two courses because their lab sections were presented through UCWISE, a platform for displaying lessons, activities, and student assessments online [9].

For the study conducted on the introduction to programming course, the lab sections of the course were randomly divided into two groups: the control group and experimental group. The students were not informed of this division, and all received the same instruction in lecture. During the lab sessions, both groups received a seven-question Scheme quiz. The experimental group was allowed to view three illustrations relevant to the quiz topics beforehand. To ensure fairness, in case the illustrations offered a significant advantage, every student received the illustrations at some point; the control group was allowed to view them after completing the quiz. The quiz scores collected were then analyzed to gauge whether the illustrations were helpful for the students' understanding of the concepts.

This first study suggested that student understanding of concepts improved when the lessons were supplemented with the illustrations. On average, the group of students who received the illustrations scored higher on the quiz than the control group. The average score experimental group was 6.053, while the control group had an average score of 4.771. Both scores were out of seven points.

Despite the outcome, a couple of concerns emerged. The first was the possibility that the experimental group had an obvious advantage, since the control group had no supplements. Another issue was that providing the illustrations to the experimental group minutes before the quizzes may not allow time for students to fully comprehend the metaphors and remember the ideas. Therefore, we structured the study conducted on students of the machine structures course differently. This time the illustrations, covering caching, were presented a week prior to the quiz. This gave the students of the experimental group more time to study the illustrations and us the chance to determine if any deep learning was taking place. Additionally, the control group received text-only equivalents of the illustrations, so that the assessment would be a direct comparison between illustrated lessons and text-based lessons. The quiz consisted of three questions about caching and cache misses in general. Again, to maintain fairness, both groups received the text supplements and illustrations after the quiz.

Despite considering these additional factors, the study conducted on the machine structures course produced inconclusive results. There was no significant difference between the average quiz scores of the control and experimental groups, which were 2.429 and 2.433 respectively. These quiz scores were out of three points, so it may be that the quiz was too short or the questions too general to determine the students' understanding of the concepts. Perhaps the supplements improved comprehension, regardless of whether they were purely text or illustrations. It is also possible that by giving both groups a week to absorb the information, the students consulted other resources and achieved nearly equal levels of understanding. The lessons learned from both experiments will serve to improve future assessments and create better gauges of the illustrations' effectiveness.

The responses from the subjective survey revealed that the students' reception of the illustrations was very positive overall [Fig. 5]. The average rating, a score between 1 (poor) and 7 (excellent), students gave the illustrations was 5.12, with a mode of 6. When asked if they wanted to see illustrations offered in other computer science courses, more than half the students agreed. As for how they used the illustrations, most students used them as introductions and to create mental models of the concepts. In the open-ended responses, most of the students who used the illustrations stated that they were "helpful in visualizing what some of the functions did," "easy to read and understand," "a cool way to teach CS to beginners," "amusing", and "cute." Among the small minority of students who did not find the illustrations helpful, the most common comment was that the textbook and other course material were adequate for their understanding, suggesting these students already had a good grasp of the concepts prior to viewing the illustrations.

6. SUMMARY

We have presented an approach to facilitate computer science education through the use of visually engaging and informative illustrations made available to students as course handouts, as an online resource, and as large posters to view in the computer labs. The detailed process we go through and the challenges we must address for every illustration ensures the visual metaphors encapsulating the concepts are understandable, memorable, and consistent within the groups they are used.

The assessments we conducted to evaluate the effectiveness of the illustrations seem to suggest that they are useful as supplements to the lessons taught in class, though further studies will be necessary to arrive at a more solid conclusion. Surveys have also shown that students are highly in favor of using the illustrations as entertaining introductions to the concepts, as well as guides to forming mental models.

7. ACKNOWLEDGMENTS

We wish to thank Michael Clancy for his encouragement, and providing assistance during the assessments. We would also like to thank Nate Titterton and Colleen Lewis for helping out with the UCWISE assessments. This work was funded by the Weiner Foundation and the UC Berkeley Office of Educational Development.

8. REFERENCES

[1] Baecker, R., *Sorting Out Sorting*. Videotape, 1981.

[2] Chamillard, A. & Karolick, D. Using Learning Style Data in an Introductory Computer Science Course. *ACM SIGCSE Bulletin*, Vol. 31 No. 1 (Mar 1999) 291-295.

[3] Creative Commons. *Attribution-Noncommercial-Share Alike 3.0*. http://creativecommons.org/licenses/by-nc-sa/3.0

[4] Felder, R. & Spurlin. J., Applications, Reliability, and Validity of the Index of Learning Styles. *International Journal of Engineering Education*, Vol. 21 No. 1 (2005) 103-112.

[5] Gonick, L., *The Cartoon Guide to Computer Science*. New York: Harper & Row, Publishers, Inc., (1983).

[6] Müldner, T. & Shakshuki, E., A New Approach to Learning Algorithms. Proceedings of the International Conference on Information Technology: Coding and Computing; 2004 Apr 5-7; Las Vegas, NV. Los Alamitos: IEEE Computer Society; (c2004).

[7] Otero, J. et al., *The Psychology of Science Text Comprehension*. Mahwah: L.Erlbaum Associates, (2002).

[8] Thomas, L. et al. Learning Styles and Performance in the Introductory Programming Sequence. Inroads, Vol. 34 No. 1, (Mar 2002) 33-37.

[9] UCWISE. *Home page*. http://www.ucwise.org/

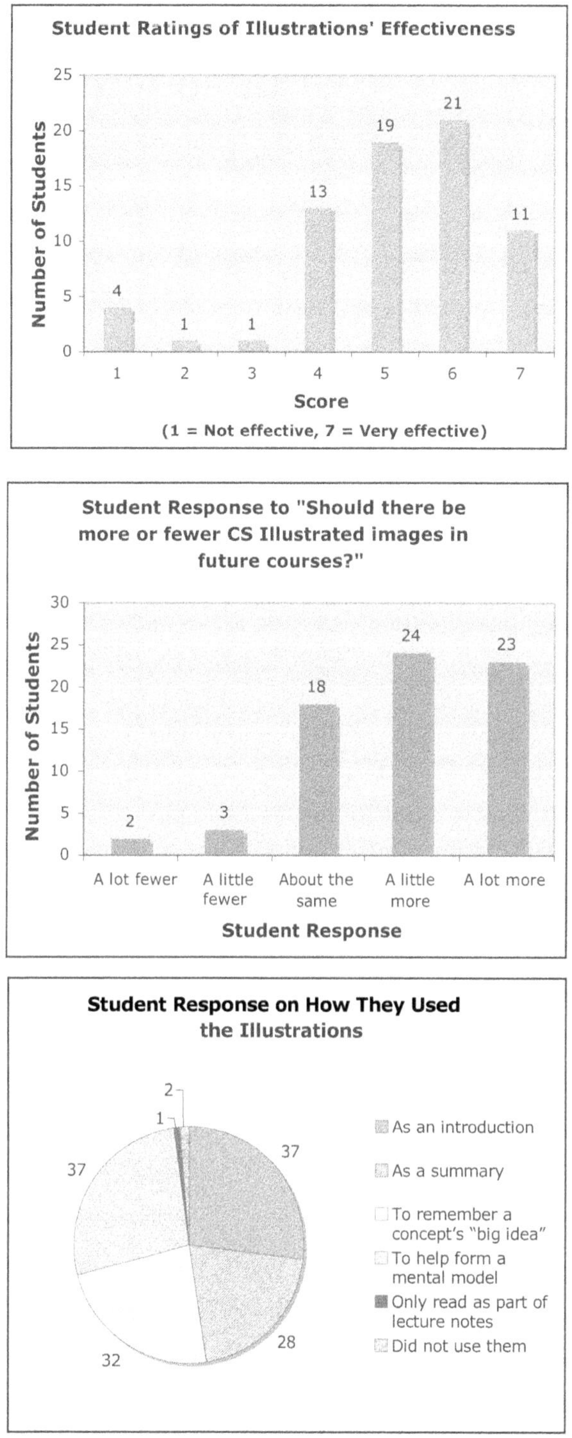

Figure 5. Results from student surveys regarding the effectiveness, future, and uses of CS Illustrated.

Using YouTube to Enhance Student Class Preparation in an Introductory Java Course

Martin C. Carlisle, *Distinguished Educator*
United States Air Force Academy
2354 Fairchild Dr, Suite 6G101
USAFA, CO 80840-6234
+1-719-333-3590
carlislem@acm.org

ABSTRACT
We provided 21 short YouTube videos for an *Introduction to Programming in Java* course. Students were surveyed on how often they watched the videos and did the readings, and how much these activites contributed to their learning. When professors reduced lecture time and increased lab time, students watched videos and read significantly more. Their test scores were at least as high and they indicated they would prefer to not have more lecture. The YouTube videos also provided a source of outreach for the university, drawing a large number of views, including the 13-17 year-old demographic.

Categories and Subject Descriptors
K.3.2 [**Computers and Education**]: Computer and Information Science Education, H.5.1 [**Information Interfaces and** Presentations]: Multimedia Information Systems – *video,* D.3.3 [**Programming Languages**]: Language Constructs and Features.

General Terms
Languages.

Keywords
YouTube, Java, videos.

1. INTRODUCTION
There seems to be a Catch-22 in teaching computer science. Ideally, we would like to spend class time helping students engage with the material and not simply lecturing; however, this requires students to have some knowledge of the material before class. So we assign readings, but repeated studies have shown that only 20-30% of our students will have read before class starts [1]. As a result, we often spend a significant amount of class time summarizing and presenting the readings, but this simply reinforces to students that they don't need to prepare for class [2]. The internet has also changed the dynamic for teaching. More and more lectures from prestigious universities are available online (see, e.g. [3,4]). If we end up mostly lecturing with students as passive learners in the classroom, why should they choose to come to our classes, instead of watching lectures on the same topics online?

SIGCSE'10, March 10-13, 2010, Milwaukee, Wisconsin, USA.
ACM 978-1-60558-885-8/10/03.

A significant amount of ink has been spilled trying to figure out how to get students to read more before class (e.g. [1,2,5,6]). Generally, the ideas rely on negative motivation—you should design your course so that students will not succeed if they don't read. This is accomplished by quizzing, random questioning and monitoring compliance. There are, however, positive suggestions on motivating the readings, selecting them more purposefully and assigning readings closer to the due date.

The question left unasked, though, is "Is reading the best way for students to prepare for class?" Since between 75% and 83% of students are visual learners instead of verbal learners [7,8], readings are not playing to their strengths. Additionally, some faculty may even feel a bit hypocritical pushing student reading so much when they managed to be very successful in academia without reading before class, or sometimes even purchasing the textbook.

After asking this question, and considering both the prevalent learning style of our students and the fact that college students on average have spent almost four hours a day watching videos and less than an hour a day reading [9], we started exploring the idea that videos might be a better way to get students to prepare for class. We first asked a number of students, "if we asked you to watch a short YouTube video before each class, would you do it?" Unanimously, the students all said this would be a great idea.

Of course, saying you will do something is different than actually doing it, but the positive response was sufficiently motivational to put the effort in to make videos for our introductory Java course. To make sure students would stay motivated and focused, our goal for each video was to be less than five minutes in length. We ended up averaging four minutes per video, with a median time of three and a half minutes, and only two videos exceeding six minutes. YouTube imposes a maximum length of 10 minutes, which ensured even the longest video did not become exceedingly long.

As it turned out, students did end up watching the videos, and we capture some of their feedback in Section 4. Section 3 gives more details on how we made the videos and their content. Work by others on "inverted classrooms" and "hybrid classrooms" are described in Section 2. At the end, Section 5 describes possibilities for future work.

2. RELATED WORK
Using media outside the classroom to free classroom time for discussion, experiments and labs is not a new idea. The "inverted classroom" [10] basically swaps what are traditionally in-class

activities (lectures) with what are traditionally outside of class activities (homework assignments). Lage, Platt and Tregalia used this in an economics course. Students were supposed to watch a recorded lecture before coming to class. The instructors began each 75 minute class by answering student questions on the videotaped lectures, then used a hands-on activity to demonstrate the concept, followed by worksheets and review questions. They reported that generally students liked this format. (Only two of their 189 students requested a change to a lecture-oriented class, and the students' response to "I believe I learned more economics with this classroom format" was 3.9 on a 5 point scale).

Kaner and Fiedler [11, 12] use the term "blended learning" to describe their makeover of a course on software testing to move lecture outside the classroom as videos. They describe how they adapted their course (providing information on hardware and software used, totaling $8000, and also the amount of work involved—35 hours per each hour of videotaped lecture). They do not provide detailed student feedback.

Day and Foley [13] ran an experiment with two sections of a human-computer interaction course at Georgia Tech. In the experimental section, classroom lecture time was replaced with hands-on learning activities. Students watched 27 web lectures (totaling 9 hours) to learn this content. Day and Foley made strong efforts to control as many variables as possible in what they called a "quasi-experiment" and found that students who were in the experimental (web video) section (on average) performed better on every course assignment.

Gannod, Burge and Helmick [14] applied these principles to a software engineering curriculum at Miami University. They provide the results of student surveys in a special topics course on service-oriented architecture. In that course, they made 65 podcasts available to students (ranging in length from a few minutes to 50 minutes). During the course meeting time, instructors answered questions on the podcasts and then students worked on assignments. Their results with this model were mixed. 100% of students indicated that "podcast lectures are helpful...and allow class time for assignments." 86% agreed that "we like the inverted class structure." On the other hand, 92% agreed that "the class shouldn't rely so heavily on podcasts" and 56% agreed that the instructors should "use podcasts to supplement class lectures instead of replacing them."

Hybrid classes (a combination of distance learning and classroom learning) also use videotaped lectures combined with in-class activities [15]. Linsday [16] describes this as the "best of both worlds", but Reasons, Valadares and Slavkin [17] ran an experiment where students in a hybrid class did worse than both traditional and distance learners.

In each of these cases, the principle is to provide more time for student interaction in the classroom by having students spend a significant amount of time watching videotaped lectures before coming to class. While we have a similar goal (making the classroom more interactive), our approach is different. Rather than having students watch a full lecture before coming to class, we instead provide very short videos that give the highlights and introduce students to the material. By keeping the videos short, we hope to maintain a high level of motivation and viewing. This was the first question students always asked when we were sounding out the idea—"how long will they be?"

3. THE VIDEOS

We began the process of creating the videos by looking through the syllabus for the introductory Java class and identifying 21 topics for which we would make videos. Eighteen of these were language topics not specific to an Integrated Development Environment (IDE). Those topics are:

1. Hello World	10. Reading a Text File
2. Basic Types and Objects	11. Writing a Text File
3. If Else Statements	12. Arrays
4. While Loops	13. 2D Arrays
5. For Loops	14. ArrayLists
6. Exceptions and Input	15. Creating a Class
7. Drawing a Picture	16. Java Constructors
8. Static Methods & Constants	17. Equality
9. Animation	18. Inheritance

For the drawing lessons, we used a variant of the DrawingPanel class provided by Reges and Stepp [18]. We added mouse and keyboard input, double-buffering and Javadoc style documentation to the DrawingPanel class.

Three videos were specific to the NetBeans environment:

1. Getting Started with NetBeans
2. Using the NetBeans Debugger
3. Making a GUI in NetBeans

For each video, we began by writing a script. The script consisted of the words that would be spoken by the narrator, the Java source code for all the programs that would be discussed, and, for some videos, animations done in PowerPoint.

The narrator never appears in the videos. We did not think being able to see the narrator added value, and it also simplified the creation of the video. We did not need to go to the expense of purchasing a video camera, and the mechanics of making videos via screen-capture is simpler than using a video camera.

For each video, we first recorded the audio. Getting quality digital audio was the most difficult part of the project, especially as we did not have much money to allocate to purchasing hardware or software. We tried several different microphone and software configurations. The built-in microphone in our Fujitsu T series laptop generated audio files with too much background noise. A Cyber Acoustics AC-102b headset (~$15) with microphone did much better; however, there was still a certain amount of audible buzzing. An RCA Digital Voice Recorder VR5220 (~$40) had the least noise, but had the unfortunate side-effect that it gave the narrator's voice a pronounced lisp, even using the highest quality setting on the recorder. After more research, we purchased a Plantronics Audio 655 USB headset (~$31) to avoid going through the microphone jack on the laptop. This produced the best quality sound, but still required cleaning up the audio with Audacity [19] using its "noise removal" feature at a very low setting.

Getting high-quality video was much easier. We recorded the video using a free screen capture program, VidShot Capturer [20].

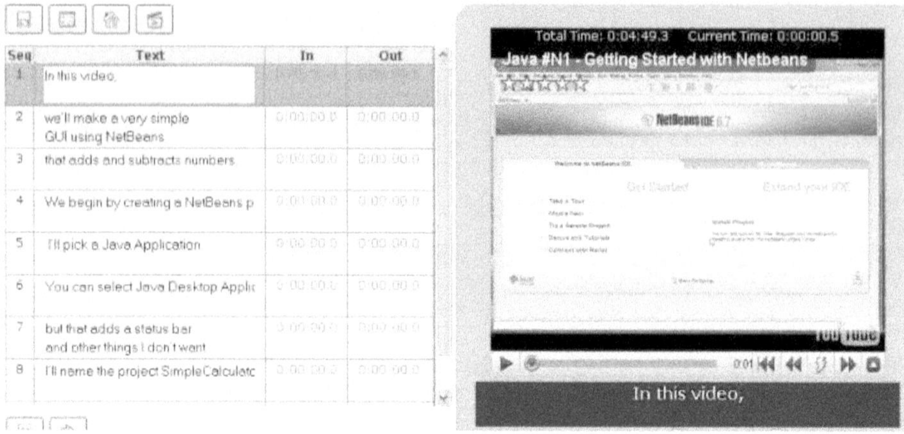

Figure 1: YouTube Subtitler.

While listening to the audio, the narrator used the mouse and keyboard to highlight text, progress through a PowerPoint animation or run the programs. We did experiment with recording the video and audio simultaneously, but found that this generated more out-takes. Also, we determined it was easier for us perform the actions in the video in time with pre-recorded audio than it was to try to make the audio match with pre-recorded video. Since there isn't constant action in the video, it was hard for the narrator to gauge the pace at which to read. When arriving at the next action, there might be an awkward pause if read too fast, or the narrator would suddenly realize he was a sentence or two behind.

Windows Movie Maker [21], available as a free download, enabled us to combine the video and audio files into a movie suitable for uploading to YouTube. Additionally, we used it for adding some captions in the videos and putting a title at the end.

We elected to use YouTube for hosting the videos because it was simple and free. One unanticipated benefit was that a large number of people from around the world have discovered and viewed the videos. The video on Making a GUI in NetBeans is the most popular, and averages 500 views a month from users around the world. Thirty percent of these viewers are 13-17, and 55% are above 24 years old.

Although we do not have any hearing-impaired students in our program, we do make the videos available to the world on YouTube, so we added closed-captioning. YouTube Subtitler [22] made this very easy. The first step is to split the script into short lines or pairs of lines (40 characters or less) separated by blank lines. You then paste this into the text window and push synchronize.

As shown in Figure 1, you can now watch the movie while advancing through the subtitles. Underneath the video on the right is a lightning button. Simply push the button when a subtitle should appear and release when it should leave. After working through the whole video, you can download a text file with the timings, or simply click a link to upload the subtitles directly to the YouTube video (assuming you are already logged into YouTube). Adding subtitles not only makes your videos available to a wider audience, but also provides additional information to Google about the content of the video, which can make it more likely to be a search result.

For the content of the videos, we provide one or more Java programs that are concrete examples of the concept being introduced. Source code for the videos can be downloaded from http://java.martincarlisle.com. The first video, "Hello World", simply walks through a Java program that prints "hello!" to the screen, explaining each word that appears. Some introductions to Java treat this as a "magical incantation" [18], delaying explanation to later, but we have found that freshman and sophomore college students are extremely uncomfortable with that much abstraction right away, and need time before they can reason about programs without having some idea of how each part works.

Later videos walk through small Java programs that perform tasks like printing the numbers from one to five, converting liters to gallons, counting the number of words in a file, or sorting a set of numbers. Each program is designed to demonstrate a particular feature of the language (for loops, static methods, Scanners, ArrayLists).

4. RESULTS

We used the set of videos in an Introduction to Programming in Java course at the United States Air Force Academy. The Air Force Academy is an undergraduate institution with an enrollment of approximately 4,400 students. All of the students are traditional students, live on campus, and are between 17 and 27 years old. The Introduction to Programming course is taken by approximately 60 sophomores and juniors each year who are majoring in computer science, computer engineering, or information systems. The course is offered as a double-period lab (i.e., there is a one hour lab period immediately following each lecture hour in the same classroom). This is the first course in the computer science major (during the freshman year students take only core requirements). The videos were given to the students as links to YouTube from the syllabus on the course web site.The course had four offering times taught by 3 different professors. All three professors have over ten years of experience as full-time faculty members. Each of the four offerings used the same syllabus and graded events. Professor 1 created and narrated the videos. His course offering was first, and both Professor 2 and Professor 3 observed his lectures before teaching theirs.

Professor 1 spent the least amount of time lecturing. He began each class by highlighting both correct and incorrect examples from student submissions on the previous labs. (Incorrect examples were anonymized). He would answer questions, and show very briefly the new concept. After this, he had the students work on the day's lab, and remained in the classroom to answer questions.

Professor 2 gave the longest lectures. He presented each concept in detail in the classroom before starting the labs. He taught two of the four offerings. Professor 3's style was somewhere between that of Professor 1 and Professor 2. He did prepare PowerPoint slides and gave a lecture at the beginning of each class, but it was shorter than that of Professor 2.

Fifty-seven students across the four offerings completed a survey providing feedback on the videos, the readings (from [18]) and the lab activities. Students were asked how often they watched the videos and read before class. For the videos, readings and labs, they were asked on a five point Likert scale if each helped them understand the material and if they were enjoyable. They were also asked if they would like more lecture, and had open responses for comments on the videos, readings and labs.

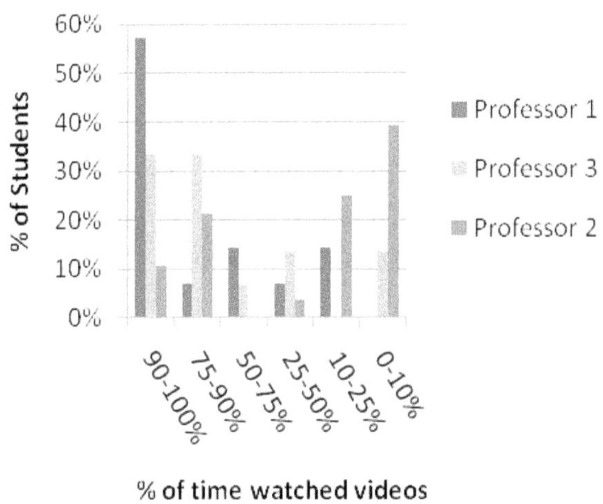

Figure 3: How often students watch videos before class

Figures 3 and 4 show how often students watched videos and read before coming to class. Assuming the midpoints of the ranges, Professor 1's students watched videos most often—74% of the time, compared to 34% for Professor 2 and 68% for Professor 3. Professor 1's students agreed more that the videos helped them understand the material—4 vs. 3.56 and 3.57. They also reported enjoying them more—3.5 vs. 2.84 and 3.35. Half of Professor 1's students reported watching videos more often than reading, and half the same.

Professor 3's students read most—71% of the time, vs. 59% for Professor 1 and 39% for Professor 2. His students reported that the readings helped their learning most—3.9 vs. 3.6 and 3.6. Four students reported reading more than watching videos, five watched videos more and five reported the same. Eight reported the readings helped them understand the material more than the videos (including two who watched videos more than they read). Four reported the videos were more helpful.

Professor 2's students prepared for class the least. 13 of 28 students reported they both watched videos and read less than 25% of the time. Eight read more than they watched videos, five watched videos more and 15 were the same. Seven said videos helped them understand more and five said the readings were more helpful.

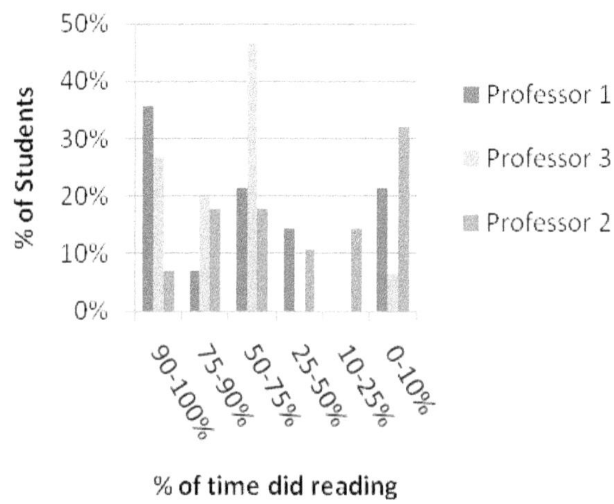

Figure 4: How often students read before class

Common to all three professors was that the students did not want more lecture. Only one student each for both Professors 1 and 3 agreed that they "would prefer more lecture time." (Four of Professor 2's students agreed with this statement, which was a bit surprising, as his lectures were the longest. He did have 8 strongly disagree, a rate four times that of the other two professors). Also, all four sections rated the labs as most helpful (4.5, 4.1 and 4.9 respectively).

One surprising result was that Professor 1's students were more positive about the videos than the others. Eight of fourteen students reported watching the videos 90-100% of the time and their written feedback was the most enthusiastic—"I wish every class did this" and "videos are better than reading." We believe this is because Professor 1 narrated the videos and the students felt more connected to his voice. Professor 1 did not advertise the videos any more than his colleagues. One suggestive comment from a student in a different class was that they wanted to "see who is talking," which obviously doesn't affect the content.

Professor 1's students also scored highest on a programming test (averaging 82.9%). Professor 3's students averaged 78.5% and Professor 2's students averaged 73.0%. The entering GPAs were 2.95 for Professor 1, 2.91 for Professor 2 and 2.89 for Professor 3. Since the class sizes were so small, the two-tailed t-test did not allow us to reject the null hypothesis that the means were equal. Nonetheless, the fact that Professor 2's students did worse than Professor 3's despite having a higher incoming GPA is suggestive that this might be related to the fact that they spent so much less time preparing for class.

5. CONCLUSIONS AND FUTURE WORK

Creating short videos can be a positive way to get students to engage with the material before coming to class. Students indicated the videos helped them learn the material. The professors who reduced their lecture time found that students prepared more for class not only in watching videos, but also in doing the reading. These students preferred the shorter lectures and having more time to work on programming in class. They also performed better on the test (though the sample size was not sufficient for this to be statistically significant). The videos are not only helpful for an on-campus course, but placing them on YouTube can be a simple outreach for your university (we had a large number of views from 13-17 year olds).

One possible future experiment is having multiple different narrators for the same videos. This would allow us to test how important it is for students to have a connection to the narrator. Another useful experiment would be to create videos for a larger course, which would provide bigger sample sizes for the statistical analysis.

6. REFERENCES

[1] Hobson, E. H. (2004). "Getting Students to Read: Fourteen Tips." IDEA PAPER #40, Online [August 13, 2009]. Available at http://www.theideacenter.org/sites/default/files/Idea_Paper_40.pdf.

[2] Brost, B. and Bradley, K. Student Compliance with Assigned Reading: A Case Study. *Journal of Scholarship of Teaching and Learning* 6,2 (Oct. 2006), 101-111.

[3] *Stanford Engineering Everywhere.* Online [August 13, 2009]. Available at: http://see.stanford.edu.

[4] *MIT Open Courseware.* Online [August 13, 2009]. Available at: http://ocw.mit.edu.

[5] Office of Support for Effective Teaching-The University of New Mexico (2009). "How Do I Get My Students to Complete Reading Assignments?" Online [August 13, 2009]. Available at: http://www.unm.edu/~oset/SupportingDocuments/Getting%20students%20to%20read.pdf

[6] Weimer, M. "Getting Students to Read." Online [August 13, 2009]. Available at: http://www.teachingprofessor.com/articles/teaching-and-learning/getting-students-to-read.

[7] Fowler, L., Allen, M., Armarego, J., and Mackenzie, J. Learning styles and CASE tools in Software Engineering. In A. Herrmann and M.M. Kulski (eds), Flexible Futures in Tertiary Teaching. Proceedings of the 9th Annual Teaching Learning Forum, February 2000.

[8] Thomas, L., Ratcliffe, M., Woodbury, J. and Jarman, E. Learning Styles and Performance in the Introductory Programming Sequence. Proceedings of the 33rd SIGCSE Symposium (March 2002), 33-42.

[9] Kaiser Family Foundation (2005). "Generation M: Media in the Lives of 8-18 Year-olds." Online [August 13, 2009]. Available at: http://www.kff.org/entmedia/entmedia030905pkg.cfm

[10] Lage, M., Platt, G., and Treglia, M. Inverting the Classroom: A Gateway to Creating an Inclusive Learning Environment. *Journal of Economic Education* 31,1 (Winter 2000), 30-43.

[11] Kaner, C. and Fiedler R. Inside Out: A Computer Science Course Gets a Makeover. In *Proceedings of the Association for Educational Communication and Technology International Conference*, Orlando FL, October 2005.

[12] Kaner, C. and Fiedler, R. Blended Learning: A Software Testing Course Makeover. In *Proceedings of the 11th Sloan-C International Conference on Asynchronous Learning Networks*, Orlando FL, November 2005.

[13] Day, J. and Foley, J. Evaluating a Web Lecture Intervention in a Human-Computer Interaction Course. *IEEE Transactions on Education*, 49,4, (November 2006), 420-431.

[14] Gannod, G. C., Burge, J. E., and Helmick, M. T. 2008. Using the Inverted Classroom to Teach Software Engineering. In *Proceedings of the 30th international Conference on Software Engineering*, Leipzig, Germany, May 2008, 777-786.

[15] Hensley, G. Creating a Hybrid College Course: Instructional Design Notes and Recommendations for Beginners. *Journal of Online Learning and Teaching*, 1,2 (December 2005).

[16] Lindsay, E. The Best of Both Worlds: Teaching a Hybrid Course. *Academic Exchange Quarterly*, 8,4 (Winter 2004), 16-19.

[17] Reasons, S., Valadares, K. and Slavkin, M. Questioning the Hybrid Model: Student Outcomes in Different Course Formats. *Journal for Asynchronous Learning Networks*, 9,1 (March 2005).

[18] Reges, S. and Stepp, M. *Building Java Programs: A Back to Basics Approach.* Pearson Education, Boston, MA, 2008.

[19] *Audacity.* Online [August 24, 2009]. Available at: http://audacity.sourceforge.net.

[20] *VidShot Capturer.* Online [August 21, 2009]. Available at: http://www.geovid.com/VidShot_Capturer/.

[21] *Windows Movie Maker.* Online [August 24, 2009]. Available at: http://www.microsoft.com/windowsxp/downloads/updates/moviemaker2.mspx.

[22] *YouTube Subtitler.* Online [August 24, 2009]. Available at: http://yt-subs.appspot.com/.

Building an Online Educational Community for Algorithm Visualization

Clifford A. Shaffer
Dept. of Computer Science
Virginia Tech
shaffer@cs.vt.edu

Thomas L. Naps
Dept. of Computer Science
U. of Wisconsin, Oshkosh
naps@uwosh.edu

Susan H. Rodger
Dept. of Computer Science
Duke University
rodger@cs.duke.edu

Stephen H. Edwards
Dept. of Computer Science
Virginia Tech
edwards@cs.vt.edu

Categories and Subject Descriptors

E.1 [**Data Structures**]; K.3.2 [**Computers and Education**]: Computer and Information Science Education

General Terms

Algorithms

Keywords

Algorithm Visualization, Online Educational Community

1. INTRODUCTION

Algorithm visualizations (AVs) are widely viewed as having the potential for improving computer science education, yet the rate of AV use and overall impact has progressed little from the mid 1990s. Surveys of CS faculty [1] show that the impediments to successful use of AVs are related to difficulties in first finding good materials, and then difficulties in effectively deploying them in classes. Fortunately, much progress has been made in recent years. There are many high-quality AVs available (though there are enough poor quality AVs that sorting out the good ones can be time consuming) [2]. There is a growing body of research on how to effectively use AVs in the classroom (though getting up to speed on this information is again time consuming). These impediments could be overcome with adequate dissemination of information about which AVs are of good quality and how they can best be used. From the developers' side, more information about what makes for an effective AV, as well as information about which topics are of greatest need, could lead to more effective AVs being produced.

Thus, we find that information and dissemination of best practice plays a key role in the successful deployment of AVs into the classroom. Given that much of the needed information has to do with rating of educational material and experiences with use of this material in the field, the most effective way to improve instruction is through an active community of AV users and developers interacting to provide the necessary information.

SIGCSE'10, March 10–13, 2010, Milwaukee, Wisconsin, USA.
ACM 978-1-60558-885-8/10/03.

The purpose of this session is to facilitate ongoing efforts to develop an online educational community to promote the use of AVs in the classroom. A major part of such a community is likely to come through a central online community presence. The NSF-supported AlgoViz project (`http://algoviz.org`) seeks to provide this presence. Our session will discuss ways that audience members can participate in the online community, and ways to generate ideas for growing the community.

2. OVERALL OBJECTIVE

The objective of the session is to introduce SIGCSE attendees to ideas for building an online educational community whose goal is to increase the use of AVs in the classroom. Techniques for community building, and lowering the barriers to participation, will be an important focus for the discussion. Our analogy is to Amazon.com. While the backbone of Amazon is their catalog and purchasing infrastructure, Amazon is much more than this from a community standpoint. An important component to Amazon's success is the community-generated ratings and reviews. In the context of digital libraries, a successful online educational community is much more than just a collection of information. It must also include community-added content that raises the value of the information beyond that of a traditional digital library. This includes dicussion of best practice, and user evaluation for the items in the library.

Due to the size of its user base, Amazon is successful even with only a small fraction of one percent of their customers provide ratings or reviews. An online educational community for a topic such as AV use has an additional burden, since it must get a much higher percentage of the potential "market" to actively engage, probably between 1 and 10% of the membership, depending on how that is defined. Fortunately, members of that "market" also have a greater incentive to become active participants.

We will describe our own community-building efforts, and ways in which the audience can participate in the AV community at the AlgoViz Portal (referred to as AlgoViz.org). A number of existing mechanisms are available at AlgoViz.org. These include forums, field reports, ratings, catalog submissions, and contributing to the OpenAlgoViz AV software repository. Field reports in particular are the equivalent of

Amazon "reviews" in that they are descriptions of how individual instructors used specific AVs in their courses.

Since a relatively high percentage of the community must actively engage to reach the needed critical mass, our research work focuses on ways to lower the barriers to participation. This includes technology to support easy/automatic login from allied sites (to avoid additional registration or login overhead), a robust notification system to inform users when new information of interest has been provided at the site, and mechanisms to solicit ratings information. Notification systems let users know when something of interest has occurred, motivating them to return to the site and participate. Active solicitation of ratings also encourages users to become active participants.

An important aspect of this special session is letting the community interact in a face-to-face setting with an open discussion. This helps people better know each other. The discussion session also gives the audience a good opportunity to provide the AlgoViz project developers with valuable feedback about the site.

We will conclude by showcasing a small collection of high-quality AVs, the winners of the AlgoViz Awards. The AlgoViz Awards voting began at the end of August, 2009, and will conclude in January 2010. AlgoViz Award winners are selected by the community since all those who register at the AlgoViz Portal are eligible to rate AVs for the competition.

3. OUTLINE OF THE SESSION

The presenters are all members of the AlgoViz Project Steering Committee (made up of roughly twenty active members of the AV research community). They are all well known within the community. Here follows an outline of the major topics for the session.

1. Building an AV community: overview. 10 minutes
   - Goals of the AV community
   - How an online AV community can impact education
   - How to lower barriers to participation: changing the digital library model
2. Overview of algoviz.org and OpenAlgoViz. 15 minutes
   - Collections and resources
   - The role of community-added material, including ratings, reviews, discussions
   - Field reports
3. Open discussion. 30 minutes
4. Announcement of AlgoViz Award winners. 20 minutes, including a brief showcasing of winning AVs.

A key part of the session is the open discussion phase. Attendees will have the opportunity to comment on what impediments they have faced in choosing whether to use AVs in their courses or not, and whether the AlgoViz project does or can address those impediments. This special session is intended not only to "get the word out" about AlgoViz.org. It is also intended to get the community to interact in a physical (as opposed to online) forum, and to provide clear feedback from the community on whether the project is on course.

4. EXPECTATIONS

Attendees should come out of the session knowing about the goals of the AV community and how their participation can help to achieve those goals. They should understand some methods for lowering the barriers to participation, and will have provided feedback to us on how we can increase participation rates. Attendees will get an overview of the AlgoViz project, what the major assets of AlgoViz.org are and how they are of use, and some idea of what makes for a high-quality AV. Attendees will hopefully come out of the session with an interest in contributing, whether through ratings of AVs, sharing their classroom experiences through field reports, or contributing AV source code to the OpenAlgoViz repository. Attendees will also have been exposed to a collection of award-winning AVs, selected by the community.

5. SUITABILITY FOR SPECIAL SESSION

We believe that an online educational community can have a significant impact on CS Education. The key difficulty is jump starting an active community, and that involves outreach and interaction with potential contributors at venues like SIGCSE. A paper presentation does not seem appropriate for this activity, since describing the project and the opportunities for community involvement is not a likely topic for a research paper, especially at this early stage of the project. Even if we were in a position to present a compelling research paper, the standard paper presentation length and format would not be sufficient to accomplish our goals at this stage. In particular, we need a sufficient block of time to inform attendees about the project and what we have to provide, and far more time for their feedback than a paper session provides. Nor is this appropriate for a panel discussion (though we may have several presenters from our Steering Committee involved in the session) since it is not the sort of thing where several people with differing viewpoints stake out a position.

Presentation of the AlgoViz Awards should be an interesting activity in its own right. CS Faculty are likely to be curious about what are considered to be high-quality AVs, and people are generally interested in the outcome of any competition. We will provide a brief showcase of the winning AVs, which should be visually interesting to the audience.

6. REFERENCES

[1] Thomas L. Naps, Guido Rössling, and nine other authors. Exploring the role of visualization and engagement in computer science education. In *ITiCSE-WGR '02: Working Group Reports from ITiCSE on Innovation and Technology in Computer Science Education*, pages 131–152, New York, NY, USA, 2002.

[2] C.A. Shaffer, M.L. Cooper, and S.H. Edwards. Algorithm visualization: a report on the state of the field. In *SIGCSE '07: Proceedings of the 38th SIGCSE Technical Symposium on Computer Science Education*, pages 150–154, March 2007.

The Development and use of Scoring Rubrics*

*or how to grade thousands of exams without losing your mind

Karen Donathan
AP CS Development Committee Member
George Washington High School
Charleston, West Virginia
+1.304.348.7729
kdonathan@suddenlink.net

Paul Tymann
AP CS Development Committee Member
Rochester Institute of Technology
Rochester, NY
+1.585.475.7908
ptt@cs.rit.edu

Summary

Every year, for the past 10 years, more than 10,000 students have taken the Advanced Placement Computer Science exam (AP CS). The free response section of the AP CS exam is manually scored by a group of about 100-150 high school and college faculty referred to as *readers*. The exams are scored accurately and consistently even though thousands of exams are being scored by dozens of readers. This accuracy is due in large part to the rubrics that are developed to score the exams. Rubrics not only improve the consistency and speed at which exams can be scored, they also can be used to communicate expectations to students. This special session will discuss how to develop a rubric, show how they are used in the AP CS scoring process and illustrate how rubrics can be used to convey expectations to students.

Categories and Subject Descriptors

K.3.2 [**Computers and Education**]: Computer and Information Science Education – *assessment, scoring rubric.*

General Terms

Measurement.

Keywords

Assessment, rubric, scoring techniques.

1. INTRODUCTION

The Advanced Placement Computer Science exam consists of two parts. The first part consists of 40 multiple choice questions, and the second part consists of four free response questions. Every year, for the past 10 years, more than 10,000 of these exams have been administered. The multiple choice section of the exam is scored mechanically, and the free response section is scored by hand. Every year at the AP reading approximately 150 high school and college faculty referred to as *readers*. The exams are scored accurately and consistently throughout the seven day reading.

A key to the consistent grading of the free response questions is the development of a rubric that guides the grading process. Each question is scored using a 0-9 point scale, and the rubric indicates how the points should be awarded based on the concepts that are being assessed. The question and the rubric are developed in tandem. At the start of the reading, readers are introduced to the rubric and trained on its application. While the primary purpose of the rubric is to maintain consistency during the reading process, it also cuts down on the amount of time required to score the questions.

The use of rubrics by individual faculty members has many advantages. Rubrics help an instructor to consistently grade work submitted by students. Secondly, they can reduce the amount of time required to grade assignments submitted by students. Finally rubrics provide a way of effectively communicating expectations to the students.

2. OBJECTIVE

The objective of this special session is to introduce faculty, to the use of rubrics in a class. Participants will be shown how to develop a rubric and illustrate how they are used as part of the AP reading process. The goal of the session is to introduce rubrics as a way to improve the scoring process and as a means of communicating instructor expectations to students.

3. OUTLINE

The session will begin with a discussion of how to develop a rubric. During this part of the workshop participants will be shown free response questions that have been given on past AP CS exams and the rubrics that were developed to score them. This portion of the presentation will end with an exercise in which participants will develop a rubric in small groups. The resulting rubrics will be presented and compared to a rubric developed by the session leaders.

In the second portion of the special session, participants will be given a rubric for a free response question and will apply that rubric to actual solutions submitted by students. Participants will work in small groups that will be lead by an individual who has served as a reader.

4. EXPECTATIONS

Faculty, at either the high school or college level, will benefit from this special session. By attending the special session participants will have seen techniques that will improve their grading and reduce the amount of time spent scoring student work.

5. SUITABILITY

Given the interactive nature of this session we believe that it is best done as a special session. There is not enough material to warrant offering this presentation as a workshop.

SIGCSE'10, March 10–13, 2010, Milwaukee, Wisconsin, USA.
ACM 978-1-60558-885-8/10/03.

Nifty Assignments

Nick Parlante, Julie Zelenski
(moderators)
Stanford University
nick.parlante@cs.stanford.edu
zelenski@cs.stanford.edu

David J. Malan
Harvard University
malan@post.harvard.edu

Mark Sherriff
University of Virginia
sherriff@virginia.edu

Zachary Dodds,
Wynn Vonnegut
Harvey Mudd College
dodds@cs.hmc.edu
wvonnegut@hmc.edu

Thomas P. Murtagh
Williams College
tom@cs.williams.edu

Daniel Zingaro
University of Toronto
daniel.zingaro@utoronto.ca

Todd W. Neller
Gettysburg College
tneller@gettysburg.edu

Categories and Subject Descriptors
K.3.0 [**Computers and Education**]: General.

General Terms
Algorithms, Design, Languages.

Keywords
Education, assignment, homework, project, repository, library, nifty, object oriented programming.

Introduction
Though we dream of awesome lectures, much of what students actually take away from a course are due to the assignments. Unfortunately, creating successful assignments is time consuming and error prone. With that in mind, the Nifty Assignments session is about promoting and sharing successful assignment ideas, and more importantly, making the materials available on the web.

Each presenter will introduce their assignment, give a quick demo, and describe its niche in the curriculum and its strengths and weaknesses. The presentations (and the descriptions below) introduce each assignment. The Nifty Assignments home page, **http://nifty.stanford.edu** provides more information for each assignment, with handouts, data files, starter code, etc. Nick's running ACM editorial: given its mission to promote CS, the ACM should distribute all its materials freely on the web.

If you have an assignment that works well and would be of interest to the CSE community, please consider applying to present at Nifty Assignments at: **http://nifty.stanford.edu**

Picobot: CS 1, Assignment 1, Problem 1 - (CS1) Zachary Dodds, Wynn Vonnegut
YAK!? That is, Yet-Another-Karel!? Surely such a thing is redundant in 2010. This assignment is why we don't think so. Picobot is a Karel-like assignment suitable for the first problem of the first assignment of a first CS course. We have used it that way for the past five years. We have also used it as a hands-on introduction to "What is CS?" for visiting applicants, orientation participants, and in high-school outreach. Beyond the accessibility that all Karel-like assignments boast, Picobot has idiosyncrasies that suit its position as CS1-Hw1-Problem1 well:

- It is conceptually small and self-contained, needing no software beyond a browser.
- It is language-independent: it does not use Python, C, C++, Java, Scheme, or any other language.
- Because of this language-independence, Picobot is background-independent: every student successfully completes the first environment, and no student has completed the most difficult environment.
- Because of this background-independence, it reduces the "show-off" factor that we have found can creep into early CS 1 lectures among certain students.
- It asks students to program, but also concretely motivates CS beyond programming:

  Applications: It is a discretized version of the environmental coverage problem in robotics and path planning.

  Complexity: The number of Picobot rules and states are tangible examples of computational complexity, and we challenge students to create maximally efficient solutions.

  Computability: Not all environments are computable! We need not look elsewhere to motivate fundamental issues of (un)computability.
- Perhaps most importantly, Picobot is simple enough that we can assign it as a final project in CS 1. With that project, students realize they can now *build* the simulator that had introduced them to CS at the start of the term!

The Game of Pig - (CS1) Todd Neller
The Game of Pig is a folk jeopardy dice game that offers one of the best fun-to-SLOC (source lines of code) ratios of any game. One would be hard pressed to find another game with such simple rules that engages and leaves one on the knife-edge of indecision.

SIGCSE'10, March 10-13, 2010, Milwaukee, Wisconsin, USA.
ACM 978-1-60558-885-8/10/03.

As such, it is a teaching treasure. Mathematics instructors have long used this game to teach concepts of probability. We here offer a rich collection of CS1 Pig exercises that illustrate bottom-up development, Monte Carlo simulation, object-oriented design, and simple GUI design.

The rules of Pig are simple: Two players race to reach 100 points. Each turn, a player repeatedly rolls a die until either a 1 ("pig") is rolled or the player *holds* and scores the sum of the rolls (i.e. the *turn total*). At any time during a player's turn, the player is faced with two decisions:

- *roll* - If the player rolls a

  1: the player scores nothing and it becomes the opponent's turn.

  2 - 6: the roll is added to the player's turn total and the player's turn continues.

- *hold* - The turn total is added to the player's score and it becomes the opponent's turn.

Sounding Off: Digital Sound Processing (CS1) - Daniel Zingaro

The yearly SIGCSE Nifty Assignments session almost invariably includes assignments based on images or animations. To give more non-visual learners the opportunity to exhibit their strengths, I propose a CS1 assignment that focuses on digital sound rather than digital images.

In this assignment, students begin by implementing simple filters on sounds: reversing sounds, adding echo, mixing sounds together, and changing volumes. These filters can each be written in ten or fifteen lines of code, using objects that represent sounds and their samples. Students experiment with the filters on standard wav files, helping them appreciate the assignment's practical context of digital sound processing. With this emerging understanding, students use their filters in a program that generates songs from "notestrings" — strings of data representing the sequencing of notes. Notestrings encode features such as note length, volume, octaves, and the ability for multiple "hands" to play simultaneously. I provide sample notestrings of varying complexity so that the students hear recognizable tunes when they have properly generated the corresponding songs.

The assignment gives students practice with loops, array/list processing, string manipulation, and function composition. It can be extended by encouraging students to implement more filters or more notestring features. Finally, though it appeals to a domain with which most students are familiar, it particularly engages musically-inclined students who may generate notestrings to share with the class.

CSI: Computer Science Investigation - (CS0-CS2) David J. Malan

Each semester, I somehow manage "accidentally" to format my digital camera's CompactFlash (CF) card on which are (were!) some terribly important photographs. And so I make for our students a "forensic image" of that CF card (using a free program called dd) and beg them to recover my photos. They proceed to write a program that iterates over that image's bytes, searching for tell-tale signs of my JPEGs, recovering each photo in turn.

By assignment's end, most students are amazed that such an important process reduces to some file I/O, one or two loops, and familiarity with hex. We daresay that students are excited that, with just a few weeks of CS under their belt, they can actually tackle an actual, real-world problem (that may have even happened to them).

We assume for this problem set familiarity only with loops. File I/O and hexadecimal notation are introduced in the problem set's own narrative.

Upon recovering my photos, students learn that each is of some "non-obvious but identifiable" location on campus. They are then challenged to find and photograph themselves in front of each of those spots in exchange for what we promise will be an amazing prize.

Encryption Chase (CS1-CS2) - Mark Sherriff

Do you or your students enjoy scavenger or puzzle hunts? The Encryption Chase gets CS1 or CS2 students working through the basics of encryption in an active-learning environment through a puzzle hunt where the puzzles are all based around various encryption schemes. Students work through clues around your building or around campus using Caesar ciphers, Vigenere ciphers, RSA, and other encryption schemes. The chase can be as rigorous as you want, based on the difficulty of the clues you present. There can be as little or as much programming involved as you like, so it's possible to tailor this assignment for both CS1 and CS2 students. After a successful chase, students come back with an appreciation of the various forms of encryption that have been used throughout history. An example chase will be presented with some tips and tricks on how to write your own custom chase for you students. Come to hear about the assignment yourself, and you may find yourself in the middle of your own chase!

Chatting AIM-lessly: Implementing an IM Client (CS1-CS2) - Thomas P. Murtagh

Our students spend much of their time (including class time!) texting, tweeting, or chatting using AOL or Google. Why not take advantage of this enthusiasm for short strings?

In this assignment, students construct a program that can be used to chat using AOL's IM messaging system. The completed program allows its user to conduct simultaneous chats in separate windows with several individuals and to keep track of which of their friends are online. The assignment only requires support for plain text messages, but enthusiastic students have often implemented extensions for emoticons, fancy fonts, etc. Their enthusiasm is partly inspired by the fact that they can use their own programs to chat with others who are using *real* IM clients.

The assignment is designed to be used about half way through a CS1 course. It is divided into two one-week exercises. The primary goals during the first week are to give students experience writing loops and manipulating strings. The goal of the second week is to introduce the use of multiple classes. An instructor could choose to either use the complete assignment or just the first week. The program completed in the first week is fully functional, but all chats are displayed together in a single window.

The assignment was designed for a course that uses Java and depends on a supplied class that provides simple mechanisms for exchanging packets with AOL's TOC server.

Teaching Operating Systems Using Virtual Appliances and Distributed Version Control

Oren Laadan
Dept of Computer Science
Columbia University
New York, NY 10027
orenl@cs.columbia.edu

Jason Nieh
Dept of Computer Science
Columbia University
New York, NY 10027
nieh@cs.columbia.edu

Nicolas Viennot
Dept of Computer Science
Columbia University
New York, NY 10027
nviennot@cs.columbia.edu

ABSTRACT

Students learn more through hands-on project experience for computer science courses such as operating systems, but providing the infrastructure support for a large class to learn by doing can be hard. To address this issue, we introduce a new approach to managing and grading operating system homework assignments based on virtual appliances, a distributed version control system, and live demonstrations. Our solution is easy to deploy and use with students' personal computers, and obviates the need to provide a computer laboratory for teaching purposes. It supports the most demanding course projects, such as those that involve operating system kernel development, and can be used by both on-campus and remote distance learning students even with intermittent network connectivity. Our experiences deploying and using this solution to teach operating systems at Columbia University show that it is easier to use, more flexible, and more pedagogically effective than other approaches.

Categories and Subject Descriptors

D.4.0 [**Operating Systems**]: General; K.3.1 [**Computers and Education**]: Computer Uses in Education—*distance learning*; K.3.2 [**Computers and Education**]: Computer and Information Science Education—*computer science education*

General Terms

Design, Experimentation, Human Factors

Keywords

Operating systems, computer science education, virtualization, virtual machines, open-source software, version control

1. INTRODUCTION

Programming projects are an important aspect of learning about many computer science subjects, especially operating systems. Hands-on experience with operating system code development, debugging, and testing is crucial for helping students to understand how operating system concepts really work in practice. Many approaches have been developed for providing such programming experience, including systems programming projects, operating system simulation environments, pedagogical operating systems, and kernel development in commercial operating systems. All of these approaches share a common need. Students need to be provided with some common software code base to start from to do their programming projects, and they need to be provided with a consistent computing environment with the right versions of development tools so that their programming projects can be accomplished successfully and evaluated correctly.

Many universities provide computer laboratory facilities to support these computing needs. Instructors work with computer support staff to ensure that the facilities provide the necessary development tools, access to required software code bases, and the correct versions of everything to make all the software work together correctly. These facilities typically provide reliable storage space that is backed up, minimizing the impact of hardware failures on students' work in these facilities. Virtualization software is increasingly being made available on these shared computer facilities to support kernel-level programming projects for operating system courses. A student can be given root and dedicated access to a virtual machine so that the kernel development cycle of plan-implement-reboot-test-debug can be done without inconveniencing other users of the laboratory facilities.

Unfortunately, providing and maintaining these computer laboratory facilities for teaching purposes is often difficult. If facilities do not yet exist, just finding the space for such a laboratory can be hard at many sites, especially those in urban environments with more constrained space availability. This can be ameliorated in part by using space-efficient racks of remotely accessible servers in lieu of laboratories where students can sit, but this requires machine room space with suitable power and cooling which can also be quite limited in availability. Even if computer laboratory facilities already exist, they require computer support staff to maintain the facilities, upgrade and repair machines, and install and maintain software required by instructors for teaching purposes. Because computer support staff can be expensive, they are often in limited supply in a university setting, making it more difficult to complete these tasks in a timely fashion. Computer hardware becomes quickly out of date, and finding funds to periodically upgrade computer laboratory facilities, especially those used primarily for teaching

SIGCSE'10, March 10–13, 2010, Milwaukee, Wisconsin, USA.

purposes, can be problematic. As a result, such facilities are often underprovisioned for the number of students that need to use the hardware, resulting in overloaded machines especially just before homework assignments are due.

These problems are only exacerbated when it comes to computing support for teaching operating systems. Virtual machines are often used in this context, along with large software code bases such as that for an entire commodity operating system such as Linux. Running virtual machines and frequently building entire operating system kernel trees can tax machine resources much more than running regular applications. They impose higher CPU and memory requirements on already overloaded machines. Students may frequently snapshot their virtual machines so that they can easily revert to an uncorrupted system when a kernel crash takes out the system. While virtual machines already incur high disk space requirements, frequent snapshots by many students can easily use up all available disk space, bringing everything to a grinding halt at the most inopportune times when homework assignments are due. Since students doing operating system kernel projects need root privileges inside the virtual machines and can install anything they want, there are increased security risks associated with the virtual machines. To minimize these risks, computer support staff often limit network access to the virtual machines, which can make it more difficult for students to use them to complete their homework assignments.

A benefit of providing shared computer laboratory facilities for running virtual machines is that both students and instructional staff can access them. This can make grading programming projects easier as instructional staff can just log on to the respective students' virtual machines to evaluate their projects. However, this has its own problems as instructional staff need to schedule time with students when their virtual machines are unavailable, and instructional staff must face the risks of using untrusted virtual machines managed by students that may have keyboard loggers and other malicious software installed inside them.

To address these problems, we observe and leverage three recent trends in computing. First, laptop computers have become inexpensive enough and indispensable for education that all computer science students own one. Second, laptop computers have become powerful enough that they can run almost any software that is needed for gaining hands-on experience in programming projects for courses. Third, virtualization technology has become ubiquitously available at little if any cost to students. For example, VMware has products that are freely available to everyone to run virtual machines, and has agreements with many universities that make all products freely available for academic purposes.

Building on these trends, we introduce a new approach to teaching operating systems based on virtual appliances, a distributed version control system, and live demonstrations. We create a virtual appliance for doing operating system homework assignments which can be easily deployed and run on students' personal computers in virtual machines without interfering with any existing software on the their computers. We combine virtual appliances with a distributed version control system to provide reliable storage for students' homework assignments, support students working together on group homework assignments, and manage the submission and grading of homework assignments. We leverage virtual appliances and the version control system to enable students to do live demonstrations of their work as part of grading their assignments to simplify grading, providing better feedback to students and greater interaction between instructional staff and students to facilitate learning.

Our solution is easy to deploy and use with students' personal computers, and obviates the need to provide a computer laboratory for teaching purposes. It supports the most demanding course projects, such as those that involve operating system kernel development, and can be used by both on-campus and remote distance learning students even with intermittent network connectivity. Our experiences deploying and using this solution to teach operating systems at Columbia University show that it is easier to use, more flexible, and more pedagogically effective than other approaches.

2. VIRTUAL APPLIANCES

Students already have their own computers, but they come in diverse software and hardware configurations. Linux serves as an excellent basis for teaching courses such as operating systems, but most students do not run Linux on their computers. Students would be loathed to install Linux natively on their computers just to take a course, given the risks of adversely affecting their existing software configurations and other already installed applications. Instructional staff would face almost insurmountable hurdles to get Linux installed on all students' computers given the diversity of software and hardware configurations in use.

Virtualization solves this problem by making it easy to run Linux operating system instances in virtual machines without affecting existing software already installed on a student's computer. VMware provides commercial virtualization software products on all major operating systems, and their products are as easy to install and use as other regular applications. We use VMware Workstation 6.5 for Windows, VMware Workstation 6.5 for Linux, and VMware Fusion 2.0 for Mac since these products provide excellent support for software development and are freely available to our students through academic licensing agreements.

Using VMware allows us to introduce virtual appliances to provide all the necessary software we need for teaching operating systems. A virtual appliance is a pre-built software bundle that can be downloaded and run locally inside a virtual machine. Unlike generic virtual machines, a virtual appliance need not be installed and configured. It is readily deployable—students just download and use it, avoiding any installation issues. Instructional staff create a Linux virtual appliance for doing operating system programming projects, with the operating system, development tools, version control software, and all other necessary software already configured and bundled together. Once it is working, the files representing the virtual appliance are turned into a compressed archive and made available for download from the class Web site.

To use the virtual appliance, students install VMware Workstation for Windows or Linux, or VMware Fusion for Mac. Students then download the virtual appliance, uncompress the archive, and just launch it in VMware to start running the appliance. VMware virtualization software ensures that the virtual appliance is completely isolated from the rest of the student's computer, and enables the appliance to run a completely different operating system while coexisting with the one already installed on the student's computer. Since students all use the same virtual appliance, everyone is ensured of running the exact same environment, avoiding discrepancies that can arise when a program is developed and tested with different compilers and operating system versions. Students are free to change the software and hardware configuration of their virtual appliances. They can always get a clean, unmodified version of the appliance by just downloading it again.

Virtual appliances provide a number of important benefits. First, since they run on students' computers, they obviate the need to provide computer laboratory facilities for teaching purposes, and avoid all the related difficulties. There is no need for the associated hardware costs and computer support staff costs for running such a lab. There are no more concerns about network security for a lab. Second, they provide complete isolation from other software running on the students' computers, ensuring that courseware does not interfere with other software and allowing courseware developed for just one operating system to be used portably across many different operating systems and software configurations without additional development cost. Third, since virtual appliances are pre-configured by the instructional staff, they avoid the installation problems and complications that can be associated with directly installing non-commercial grade courseware on students' computers. Fourth, since students control the hardware that runs the virtual appliance, students have the power and flexibility to allocate resources to the virtual appliance as they see fit. They can allocate more CPU or memory, run more copies of the virtual appliance, and enable full network access to make it easier to access network resources. Finally, since virtual appliances are run locally on students' computers, they make it easy to support remote distance learning students as well as on-campus students. Distance learning students do not need to access a campus computing facilities to work, and can work in their virtual appliances even in the absence of network connectivity.

To teach operating systems, we assigned various programming homework assignments that involved modifications to the Linux kernel. This approach provided the advantages of gaining hands-on experience doing kernel-level software development, learning from examples in a real commercial operating system and how to manage the complexity of a large system, and acquiring skill with a widely used commercial operating system that can be used for future employment. For students to do these homework assignments, we configured a Linux virtual appliance with a small footprint on disk and that boots quickly. The small footprint allows it to be quickly downloaded and consume only a modest amount of disk space. Quick downloads make it easier to retrieve clean copies of the virtual appliance to start over if needed. The fast boot allows faster kernel testing and debugging.

We used the Gentoo Linux distribution, which can be automatically optimized and customized to provide the desired small footprint and fast boot times. We customized our installation for kernel testing and debugging. For this purpose, we do not need all the services typically provided by a full Linux distribution and installed a bare minimum base system. For example, we did not install mail, the cron server, syslog daemon, HAL, D-Bus and ALSA utilities, Bluetooth or WiFi capabilities, or ACPI utilities. Since Gentoo is a source-based distribution, it already contains the toolchain for Linux kernel development. A DHCP client, text editors, and Git, for version control, were installed on top of the base system. We did not need a graphical interface for the virtual appliance for our purposes, though we could install one if desired. Once the system was installed and configured in a virtual machine, we cleaned up the system by removing downloaded sources and removing SSH server keys. To make the appliance available for download, we shrank the disk file by wiping the free space on the drive (`dd if=/dev/zero of=tmp; sync; rm tmp`) and shrinking the disk with the vmware-vdiskmanager command. The size of the bzip2 compressed virtual appliance was only 240 MB, which downloads in only a few minutes for most network connections.

3. DISTRIBUTED VERSION CONTROL

Two important issues in using virtual appliances on students' computers are that instructional staff no longer have easy access to the students' virtual machines and students' computers are often not backed up. We need to provide a way for instructional staff to help students, test and grade homework assignments done in the virtual appliances, and limit the damage caused by students' computer failure.

We combine virtual appliances with a distributed version control system to provide reliable storage for students' homework assignments and manage the submission and grading of homework assignments. We use Git, the version control system used for many commercial open source software projects, including the Linux kernel. Git provides several advantages. First, it enables students to learn how to use a production version control system. Second, unlike systems such as CVS, it is designed from the ground up to support distributed version control for facilitating collaborative work among users that may be loosely connected in their work, which is particularly helpful for supporting distance learning students. There is no problem with offline work since each repository is self-contained and independent.

We provide a Git server for check ins and submissions. The system has modest computing and storage requirements, and can be used with any backed up machine as a server, including a virtual machine installed on an instructor's desktop computer. Students simply check in code to reliable storage, and do not need to back up their own computers for this purpose. The version control repository also enables multiple students to work together on group homework projects. We ask students to check in early and often. This helps the instructional staff to see who is doing the work in group programming assignments, and identify problems that students may be having well before the homework submission deadline so that we can help. We use the same system for submitting homework assignments, guaranteeing that students cannot tamper with submission dates and times. We also use the same system for returning graded homework assignments, whereby instructional staff can check in comments directly into students' code to provide better feedback to students. For our operating system assignments, students write C code. Our convention is to have students comment their code using `/* */` syntax to easily distinguish from instructional staff comments using `//` syntax.

We set up the Git server by providing each student a UNIX account on the machine using their university ID, but with only access to a specialized Git shell for running Git commands, namely `/usr/bin/git-shell`. Students connect to the server using SSH keys, which is secure and convenient. Each student repository is a clone from a template repository, where we provide the base file structure like the kernel sources, or empty files to fill up. We optimize how repositories are stored since almost all programming assignments involve modifications to the Linux kernel tree, which can be large. By leveraging Git clone hardlink capability, the actual data is stored only once on the physical layer although each repository contains the kernel tree. Each repository stores only diffs from the template. Permission on repository is made with standard UNIX permissions. Each repository is `chmod 740`. Only the respective student and the instructional staff can access the repository. Repository corruption cannot happen since students have no access on the file system, and Git itself will not corrupt itself.

To guarantee that students cannot tamper with submission dates and times, we log all the pushes on the server, which contains the date of the push, the username, and the object hashes. This allows us to know who did what and when. In addition to logging, when students push their commits, they see in their console how much time is left until the homework submission deadline. Pushes after the deadline are rejected. We do not trust the timestamps in their commits, which can be manipulated since they simply reflect the timestamps of the students' computers.

4. LIVE DEMONSTRATIONS

Since instructional staff did not have easy access to students' virtual appliances, we could not test students' work directly in their virtual appliances. Having students check in their appliances instead of source code would incur too much storage overhead. We could build their programs and install, reboot, and test them in our own virtual appliances, but that would be time consuming for a large class.

We instead decided to require students to do live demonstrations of their kernel programming homework assignments. Students were assigned different 20 minute time slots during office hours to do their demonstrations. We automated the build process for the submitted code to generate a bootable kernel image for each homework submission. Students were given a clean virtual appliance and asked to install, reboot, and demonstrate the functionality of their kernel images. By starting with the submitted code, we ensured that the kernel images generated were based on the actual homework submissions. By having students demonstrate their submissions, we made grading those submissions easier since instructional staff did not have to manually perform the time consuming install, reboot, and testing for each submission.

More importantly, the live demonstrations provided a good opportunity for students to interact with the instructional staff and gain a better understanding of what they did right and what they did wrong in their programming assignments. Instructional staff could identify which students knew the material and which did not, and also which students really did the work and understood the material.

5. EXPERIENCES

We have taught operating systems at Columbia University for almost ten years using various forms of virtualization to support students working in groups of two or three to gain hands-on experience with Linux kernel development. We have used three methods for teaching and discuss and compare our experiences with each of them.

We started out using a shared computer laboratory with Linux desktop machines running VMware Workstation to support virtual machines. There was no shared storage infrastructure available to store the virtual machines, so they were stored locally on each desktop and statically assigned to students. Each time the course was taught, a computer support staff had to install the right version of VMware, create and distribute the virtual machines to each desktop, and deal with hardware failures and other issues as the desktop machines became out of date. While students learned a tremendous amount about operating systems, it was at times hard for students to work with the laboratory infrastructure. Even though we provided students with backup virtual machines allocated on other desktops, a desktop machine failure could cause a group of students to lose all their work on the virtual machines assigned to that desktop. Students lacked administrative privileges on the machines, and so could not fix the problems even if they knew how, instead having to wait until normal business hours before a support staff addressed the issue. This problem also occurred at times when students corrupted their virtual machine and lacked the access rights to install a clean virtual machine so they could start over. Finding funds to replace old or dead machines was often an issue. We did not use a version control mechanism at the time and relied on university submission tools, which were painful to use for both students and instructional staff. In particular, there was no way for students to verify the completeness of their submissions.

We have also used a server cluster consisting of a set of powerful multi-core servers and a dedicated SAN infrastructure for running VMware ESX server to support virtual machines. This infrastructure made it much easier to manage virtual machines, assign them to students, and dynamically allocate resources among virtual machines, but had some other problems. The more centralized infrastructure was easier to manage, but a configuration mistake or a hardware malfunction could bring down all of the virtual machines. The shared infrastructure became noticeably slow right before homework assignments were due when it was being used by everyone intensively at the same time. VMware snapshot functionality was very useful for reverting a corrupted virtual machine to a good state, but some students took so many snapshots that they filled up the entire multi-TB SAN. Computer support staff limited network access to the infrastructure for security reasons, making it more difficult for students to use their virtual machines.

Most recently, we have been using our virtual appliance and distributed version control solution to teach operating systems for the last year. The experiences of both students and instructors with this approach to teaching operating systems have been very positive. Students like running virtual appliances on their own computers, as they have full control over how resources are used, eliminating previous complaints about the hardware used to support the virtual machine infrastructure. Students also like no longer having to pay fees associated with using university computer facilities. The Git version control system provides experience with real-world software development tools and makes homework assignments much easier to manage. Students can check out what they submitted to make sure the submission works properly. Instructional staff can view check in logs and see how students are progressing, which students are contributing to group homework assignments and which ones are not, and can add comments to students' code bases directly to provide helpful feedback as part of the homework grading process. Students like the increased interactions with instructional staff provided by having live demonstrations and code review of kernel programming assignments. Instructional staff find it easier to grade the assignments by relying on students to demonstrate their work instead of having to install, reboot, and test students' kernel programming submissions themselves. Our experience has been that the combination of virtual appliances, distributed version control, and live demonstrations has been a powerful pedagogical tool for teaching operating systems.

6. RELATED WORK

Many approaches have been explored for providing programming experience in operating system courses. Courses with user-level projects require only developing code designed to run in unprivileged mode. Examples of such projects include writing modules for a user-level simulator such as Nachos [2], user-level threads programming, or systems programming with a production operating system such as Linux, Solaris or Windows XP. While user-level projects do provide students with some hands-on experience with operating systems, they do not provide direct kernel-level development experience. As a result, user-level projects do not effectively address important issues such as bootstrapping, handling interrupts, the kernel-level development and debugging process, or understanding the kernel internals of a full-featured operating system.

Courses with kernel-level projects require writing or modifying code designed to run in supervisor mode. Kernel-level projects can provide a better pedagogical vehicle for learning about real-world operating system design and implementation. Some are based on a small pedagogical operating system like MINIX [8] or Pintos [6], or involve a pedagogical operating system to be used only in a simulated environment [3]. Pedagogical operating systems are smaller than production operating systems and do not expose students to many of the real-world issues that arise in practice. Because pedagogical operating systems are not used in practice, keeping them from becoming dated can require substantial effort and they may have more limited lifetimes due to changes in technology and operating system practice [3].

Other courses involve kernel-level projects with production operating systems. One of the authors developed the first course to leverage virtual machines for teaching operating systems with Linux kernel projects [4], an approach which has since been widely adopted. This work was initially done using a shared computer laboratory [5]. Others have built on this work by also using a server cluster [1]. We build on our prior work to provide a solution that does not require providing or maintaining significant computing infrastructure, and introduces course management techniques based on distributed version control and live demonstrations to improve the pedagogical value of the course.

Production version control systems such as CVS have been used in operating system courses [3] for supporting source code development, but not for managing homework submissions and facilitating grading. CVS has also been used for homework submissions in lieu of homebrew university submission tools [7], but required use of university computer laboratory facilities, did not provide effective safeguards against repository corruption, and did not support the requirements of operating system courses with kernel-level programming projects. Unlike these approaches, we use Git to provide distributed version control management and reliable storage without using and maintaining university computer laboratory facilities. Git provides a better, more scalable model than CVS for reliable and consistency check ins for kernel development, resulting in its adoption by the Linux kernel developer community. We also show how Git and live demonstrations can be used to provide better grading mechanisms for homework assignments and improved feedback to students to enhance their learning.

7. CONCLUSIONS

We have developed a new approach for teaching operating systems that provides hands-on kernel-level project experience without the need for computer laboratory facilities for teaching purposes. Our solution creates a virtual appliance for doing operating system homework assignments which can be easily deployed and run on students' personal computers in virtual machines without interfering with any existing software already on the students' computers. We combine virtual appliances with a distributed version control system to provide reliable storage for students' homework assignments, support students working together on group homework assignments, and manage the submission and grading of homework assignments. Live demonstrations are also used to simplify grading and provide better feedback to students. We have used this approach to teach operating systems to both undergraduate and graduate students, and both on-campus and remote distance learning students. Our experiences demonstrate that this solution is cost-effective, easy to deploy and use, and improves the educational experience of students in learning about operating systems.

8. ACKNOWLEDGMENTS

This work was supported in part by VMware and NSF grants CNS-0426623, CNS-0717544, and CNS-0914845.

9. REFERENCES

[1] J. C. Adams and W. D. Laverell. Configuring a Multicourse Lab for System-Level Projects. In *Proceedings of SIGCSE 2005*, St. Louis, MO, Feb. 2005.

[2] W. Christopher, S. Proctor, and T. Anderson. The Nachos Instructional Operating System. `http://cs.berkeley.edu/~tea/nachos/nachos.ps`.

[3] D. A. Holland, A. T. Lim, and M. I. Seltzer. A New Instructional Operating System. In *Proceedings of SIGCSE 2002*, pages 111–115, Feb. 2002.

[4] J. Nieh and Özgür Can Leonard. Examining VMware. *Dr. Dobb's Journal*, pages 70–76, Aug. 2000.

[5] J. Nieh and C. Vaill. Experiences Teaching Operating Systems Using Virtual Platforms and Linux. In *Proceedings of SIGCSE 2005*, St. Louis, MO, Feb. 2005.

[6] B. Pfaff, A. Romano, and G. Back. The Pintos Instructional Operating System Kernel. In *Proceedings of SIGCSE 2009*, Chattanooga, TN, Mar. 2009.

[7] K. L. Reid and G. V. Wilson. Learning by Doing: Introducing Version Control as a Way to Manage Student Assignments. In *Proceedings of SIGCSE 2005*, St. Louis, MO, Feb. 2005.

[8] A. Tanenbaum. A UNIX Clone with Source Code for Operating Systems Courses. *Operating Systems Review*, 21(1):20–29, Jan. 1987.

Linux Kernel Projects for an Undergraduate Operating Systems Course

Rob Hess and Paul Paulson
School of Electrical Engineering and Computer Science
Oregon State University
Corvallis, OR 97331, USA
{hess,paulson}@eecs.oregonstate.edu

ABSTRACT

In this paper, we present a series of programming projects based on the Linux kernel for students in a senior-level undergraduate operating systems course. The projects we describe cover several key operating systems concepts, including process scheduling, I/O scheduling, memory management, and device drivers. In addition, we assess these projects along several dimensions, from their difficulty to their capacity to help students understand operating systems concepts, based on six terms (three years) of detailed student exit surveys along with observations and anecdotal evidence. Through this assessment, we conclude that our Linux-based projects are an effective means by which to teach operating systems concepts and, additionally, that students' response to these projects is overwhelmingly positive.

Categories and Subject Descriptors

K.3.2 [**Computers and Education**]: Computer and Information Science Education; D.4.7 [**Operating Systems**]: Organization and Design

General Terms

Human Factors, Design, Experimentation

Keywords

Linux, Kernel, Operating Systems, Projects, Open Source

1. INTRODUCTION

Effectively teaching operating systems requires providing students with a good balance of theory and practice. How to teach operating systems *theory* is fairly well established, and a number of good textbooks exist for this purpose. How to teach operating systems *practice*, however, is a topic that still receives a great deal of attention in the literature.

The most basic approach to teaching operating systems practice is to have students implement solutions to hypothetical problems that are analogously related to operating systems concepts. Examples of such problems include the dining philosophers problem, which illustrates concurrency issues, or the elevator problem, which illustrates issues related to disk I/O. These problems and their solutions, however, really skirt the issue of operating systems practice by sidestepping most of the important details that lie at the heart of a functional operating system, and, in the end, they really only reinforce operating systems theory rather than teaching operating systems practice.

An alternative approach has students program within an instructional operating system such as Nachos [4] or Minix [12]. Anderson and Nguyen [2] provide an excellent survey of the many existing such systems. The motivation behind the use of these instructional systems is to expose students to some of the issues involved in making an operating system "work" while, at the same time, protecting them from as many as possible of the more formidable, nuts-and-bolts aspects of a real production operating system.

In this paper, we argue that protecting senior-level students completely from the details of a production operating system is not necessary and, further, that exposing them to some of these details can, in fact, prove to be beneficial.

Many educators have already documented their success in having students work on production software in other domains [7, 3, 6, 11, 1]. Some of the benefits of classroom production programming described by these educators include teaching students that most real programming projects are not started and finished by a single programmer alone, but are rather the collaborative effort of many; teaching them how to break down, understand and contribute to very large pieces of software written by other people; introducing them to programming environments similar to those they will use later in their careers; teaching them the importance of good documentation and well-written, self-documenting code; increasing their interest in programming and hence their motivation to program; and, most importantly, giving them a sense of achievement and pride in their work.

In fact, some educators have already begun having students do production programming in their operating systems courses. Indeed, as of 2005, an almost surprising 14% of the top 100 computer science schools reported using the Linux kernel in some form in their undergraduate operating systems course [2]. In the literature, Nieh and Vaill [10], like us, describe several projects that involve students programming directly within the Linux kernel. Similarly, Lawson and Barnett [8] describe having students modify a custom Linux kernel designed to run on the iPod. In both of these cases, the authors report not only that their students were able to successfully program within a complex production operating system, but that they did so with tremendous enthusiasm.

The goal of this paper is thus not to introduce Linux programming in an operating systems course as a novel practice, but rather to present a set of Linux kernel-based operating systems projects which can be seen as complimentary to the ones already described in the literature. Specifically, we describe five projects that cover system calls, process scheduling, memory allocation, I/O scheduling, and device drivers. Each of these projects (with the exception of the process scheduler, for which we provide students with virtual machine and skeleton scheduler code derived from the Linux process scheduler) is implemented directly within the Linux kernel and involves understanding and modifying existing Linux code to create new functionality.

We have run our senior-level operating systems course for six terms (three years) using these Linux-based projects, and like previous authors, we too have seen a great deal of enthusiasm in our students as they complete these projects. Our previous experience using an instructional operating system in the same course suggests that it is far more difficult for students to achieve the same level of enthusiasm using an instructional operating system as we have seen them achieve when programming in the Linux kernel.

We have seen other benefits to having students do Linux programming in our course, as well. The foremost of these is the exposure it gives them to the type of programming many of them will perform later in their careers, involving understanding and modifying a large, complex piece of software written by someone else. After doing this type of programming, many students demonstrate noticeably improved self-confidence in their own computer science abilities. Again, this is markedly different from our experience using an instructional operating system in the same course.

After outlining our set of Linux-based projects, we more fully assess their effectiveness in an analysis based on data from exit surveys distributed in each of the six terms we used our Linux-based projects. Through this analysis we show that students find the difficulty of our Linux-based projects to be appropriate for a senior-level course and, moreover, that students find these projects to be an effective way to learn operating systems concepts in practice. In addition, we combine our survey results along with personal observation and anecdotal evidence to demonstrate the level of enthusiasm our course generates and, further, to describe some of the benefits students see as a result of having completed our Linux kernel development-based projects.

2. COURSE DESCRIPTION

Our work is set in a one-quarter, senior-level course on the principles of operating systems. The course's learning objectives include concepts related to concurrency, process management, CPU scheduling, synchronization, deadlock, memory management, disk management, I/O scheduling, etc. We address the theoretical aspects of these concepts in our lectures. However, another primary course objective is to have students design, implement and test functions related to these concepts within a large, complex code base.

For many years, we used the Java-based Nachos instructional operating system [4] as our code base for student development, but, while this package included a virtual machine and a small set of projects with auto-graders which made it fairly easy to use, we found that it was poorly documented and poorly maintained. In addition, because we had assigned the projects for several years, students were beginning to reference other students' solutions from previous offerings of the course. Students also commonly complained that the projects had no relevance to the theoretical topics discussed in the course, and exit surveys showed that they would prefer more realistic projects.

Instead of developing new projects for a system we felt was too limited, we decided to choose a new system, but using another instructional operating system seemed like only a partial solution to our problems. Linux was attractive to us because it is both a real operating system and an open-source project with which students are familiar. This latter point was important to us because we felt it would help students approach our operating systems course enthusiastically, knowing that part of our course would involve them modifying a well-known and well-respected piece of software.

2.1 Development Environment

In the six terms we have run our course using Linux, we have evolved a development environment similar to the one described by Nieh and Vaill in [10]. Specifically, students work in teams of three to four members, and each team is provided with a virtual machine (VM) for testing their kernel code. Our VMs are hosted using VMware Server (freely available at `www.vmware.com`). This setup allows students to access their VMs from anywhere on or off campus, and it provides an inexpensive and less risky alternative to supplying each team with its own physical testing machine.

Each student team is also provided with a Subversion repository for revision control of the code they develop. This is useful, as it permits different team members to easily work on separate parts of their code in parallel. More importantly, using Subversion helps us to simulate a real production development environment where some form of version control software is generally employed.

To help students browse the Linux source code and easily track down function, structure and variable definitions, we refer them to an indexed, cross-referenced version of the Linux source, available online at `lxr.linux.no`. This has proved to be an invaluable resource for students, as has a course email list, over which we permit a certain degree of collaboration among student teams.

3. LINUX KERNEL-BASED OS PROJECTS

Below we describe our set of five Linux-based projects[1]. Following that, we discuss several ideas for projects that are under development. As a compliment to these projects, we recommend using a good Linux kernel reference, such as the excellent book by Love [9]. Note that, because the projects we describe here involve low-level Linux kernel programming, familiarity with C or a similar language is a prerequisite. Also, note that the descriptions below are based on version 2.6.23 of the Linux kernel, though they likely apply to other versions as well.

3.1 Simple System Call

Our first programming project is designed to help students set up and acclimate themselves to our Linux kernel development environment and to help them overcome any initial

[1]Full project descriptions and the virtual machine and skeleton code for our process scheduling project can be found online at `http://eecs.oregonstate.edu/~hess/cs411.html`.

apprehension they might have about modifying Linux kernel code. In this project, each student team must download and initialize their Subversion repository with a copy of a recent stable version of the Linux kernel source code and then compile and install that version of the kernel. Once they have successfully done this, they must create a new branch in their repository, and within this branch, they must write a simple system call and register it with the kernel. To test their work, they must compile and install their modified version of the kernel and write a simple C program to invoke their system call. This project is very straightforward, and we generally allot one week for students to complete it.

3.2 Process Scheduler

The process scheduler is one of the most important parts of an operating system, and it is thus something we feel students should gain practical experience with in an operating systems course. However, the Linux process scheduler is one area of the kernel that does not lend itself well to student modification, as the fact that it must deal with issues like symmetric multi-processing, kernel preemption, and atomic execution makes it an incredibly complex piece of code.

For this reason, we have developed a simplified version of the Linux process scheduler, which does not deal with such complicating issues as the ones mentioned above but still retains the basic structure and functionality of the original Linux process scheduler. This scheduler runs on a simple virtual machine, which we also developed.

In our process scheduler project, we provide students with a skeleton version of our simplified Linux scheduler, which they must modify to implement a round-robin scheduler. Specifically, processes which are created by the virtual machine are submitted to the scheduler in the same manner as processes are submitted in the Linux kernel. Students must design a scheduler that assigns a time-slice to each of these processes and cycles through processes as their time-slices expire. Students' schedulers must also account for issues such as processes sleeping while waiting for I/O.

Our simplified process scheduler is designed to be as similar as possible to the real Linux scheduler. Thus, to complete this project, students must still use most of the original structures and functions from the Linux process scheduler. For example, in this project, students are introduced to Linux's rather elegant linked list implementation (located in the Linux kernel tree at `include/linux/list.h`).

This project is fairly extensible, in that the skeleton we provide to students can be filled out to implement any number of different process scheduling algorithms. For example, it would be straightforward to have students implement Linux's constant time scheduler. In addition, our virtual machine operates on process "profiles" which can be hand designed and produce a deterministic process ordering for a given scheduling algorithm with fixed parameters. This makes testing students' schedulers for correctness very easy.

Because this project does not involve the full kernel development process, which includes kernel compilation, installation, and debugging, it helps students begin to get comfortable accomplishing tasks within an existing piece of Linux kernel-like code. For this reason, we assign this project second, before projects that involve going deeper into the machinery of the Linux kernel. This project is moderately challenging and we typically allot two weeks for it.

3.3 Memory Allocator

The Linux kernel is equipped with three memory allocators: SLAB and SLUB, which are complex frameworks designed for use in resource-rich systems to reduce internal fragmentation of memory and to permit efficient reuse of freed memory; and SLOB, which is a lightweight, efficient framework designed for use in embedded systems and other systems with limited resources.

The SLOB (Simple List Of Blocks) allocator, located in the Linux kernel tree at `mm/slob.c`, is a piece of the kernel that, unlike the process scheduler, can easily be extended by students. It works by maintaining a linked list of available blocks of contiguous memory called the free list, and, when a request for memory is made, it is serviced from the free list in first-fit fashion. If there are no available blocks large enough to service a given request, a new page of memory is allocated and prepended to the free list. Requests larger than one page are serviced separately.

As a project, we have students modify the SLOB allocator to service requests from the free list in either best-fit or worst-fit fashion, both of which are classical allocation strategies discussed in most operating systems textbooks. To verify that their implementation works, students use configuration scripts to select their allocator and then compile and install the modified kernel. A defective implementation will typically not survive a small amount of normal usage.

To test the correctness of their implementation, we also have students write system calls to compute the total amount of memory on the free list as well as the total amount claimed by the SLOB allocator for allocations less than one page (i.e. memory that is either on the free list or has been allocated off the free list and not released). The values returned by these functions can be used to compute a rough measure of internal fragmentation, and students can use these values to compare the amount of fragmentation that results from using different allocation strategies in the SLOB allocator (typically, the best-fit and worst-fit strategies will suffer less from fragmentation than does the first-fit strategy).

This project is also straightforward and does not require a great amount of coding, but it begins to bring students into the inner workings of the Linux kernel and requires them to understand the code they are modifying before they start hacking. We typically allot two weeks for this project.

3.4 I/O Scheduler

Another piece of the Linux kernel that is simple and easily extensible by students is the no-op I/O scheduler, located at `block/noop-iosched.c` in the kernel tree. This scheduler services I/O requests in first-in, first-out (FIFO) order and is designed to be used with devices such as flash drives, where disk access time is constant and independent of physical location on the disk. To determine the FIFO ordering of requests, the no-op scheduler maintains a request queue using the Linux kernel's linked list implementation.

As a project, we have students extend the no-op scheduler to implement the shortest seek time first algorithm (SSTF), which services I/O requests in order of increasing distance from the current location of the disk head. This is another classical algorithm discussed in most operating system textbooks. Extending the no-op scheduler to implement SSTF can be achieved in several ways. The most straightforward of these involves sorting the list of pending requests by their physical location on the disk and selecting the one closest to the current location of the disk head whenever the kernel signals that a request should be serviced.

This project is quite versatile. For example, it can be changed from term to term by having students implement a different classical scheduling algorithm, such as SCAN or LOOK. In addition, it can be made more challenging by having students implement the sorted request list using the Linux kernel's red-black tree implementation (`include/linux/rbtree.h` and `lib/rbtree.c`); by having them include additional features, like request aging; or by having them implement various optimization features available in Linux's I/O scheduler API, such as request merging.

To verify the correctness of their implementation, we find it easiest to have students print to a log file the order in which requests are submitted to their scheduler and the order in which they are serviced. A quick examination of this file should suffice to show that requests are serviced in proper order. Alternative—though perhaps more complicated—methods for testing the I/O scheduler are available, such as the `blktrace` functionality built in to the kernel.

This project is more challenging than the previous two, as it requires significantly more design and coding, and we typically give students three weeks to finish it.

3.5 Device Driver

A common boast among Linux kernel developers is that Linux supports more devices than any other operating system in history. Indeed, device drivers account for more than half of the code in the Linux kernel. However, many devices exist that are still unsupported by Linux, and one of the best ways for a developer to get his or her code into the Linux kernel is by writing a driver for one of these. Writing a driver is also one of the most common tasks initially assigned to those hired by a company to do Linux kernel development. For these reasons, students find it particularly interesting to write a device driver as a project.

Unfortunately, since our development environment involves VMs hosted on a remote server and because we are constrained to work within a ten-week quarter, it is difficult to find real devices for which students can easily write drivers. Moreover, providing devices to students might be financially infeasible, even if an appropriate device could be found. We have thus found it easiest for students to write a driver for a virtual device. Specifically, we have them implement a RAM disk driver, which allocates a large block of memory and presents it in the form of a block device (i.e. a disk).

Chapter 16 of Corbet *et al.*'s book on Linux device drivers [5] provides a nice step-by-step tutorial on writing a RAM disk driver, and we have students follow this tutorial to produce a basic, working RAM disk. We typically have students extend their basic driver, for example, by using the Linux kernel's built-in cryptography API to encrypt their disk or by having them add additional functionality, such as an "eject" function, which can be implemented as an `ioctl` command. Validating a RAM disk driver implementation involves mounting the disk, creating a filesystem on it, and then using that filesystem and observing whether data is correctly stored to and retrieved from the disk.

This project serves not only to have students write a real Linux device driver; it also introduces them to several key kernel APIs, such as the block device API and the cryptography API. Because this project does not deal directly with any of the theoretical material we cover in lecture, because students find it more interesting than other projects, and because they are allowed to follow the RAM disk driver tutorial in [5], we typically assign this project last, at a time when students are generally busy with final projects for other classes and studying for final exams. Two weeks are usually sufficient for students to complete this project.

3.6 Projects Under Development

Our course is under continual development, and there are a number of projects we are developing that we have not yet assigned to students or which we decided to develop further due to poor outcomes. Here, we discuss some of these.

Filesystem. Filesystems are another important part of the operating system, so we are working to develop a filesystem project. We are specifically considering one in which students modify the RAM filesystem (located at `fs/ramfs/`) to support version control functionality. As an alternative, we are also considering a project in which students would implement a filesystem in userspace using FUSE, an open-source Linux kernel module that allows users to develop filesystems outside of the kernel (available at `fuse.sf.net`).

Process Synchronization. Process synchronization is also an important part of an operating system, and we would like to develop a project in which students implement a process synchronization method and replace calls to existing synchronization methods in Linux with calls to their own. Nieh and Vaill describe a project along these lines [10].

More Device Drivers. Although the RAM disk driver project is one of our more popular ones, it does not give students the satisfaction of writing a driver for a real, physical device and seeing that device function properly when the driver is finished. Virtual machine-related issues aside, to have students write a driver for a real, physical device would require finding an inexpensive device that was enough and that came with a clear set of hardware specifications so that students could be reasonably expected to write a driver for it as a two- to four-week project. We do believe, though, that such a device exists, and we are considering options such as a simple USB device, like a thermometer, or a simple serial port device. Recently, our department also instituted an initiative in which students complete various course-related projects on their own Linux-based handheld devices as they progress through the Computer Science curriculum, and we are now working to develop driver projects for these devices.

4. COURSE ASSESSMENT

In every term we taught our course using the Linux kernel development-based projects, we conducted a detailed, open-ended exit survey of all of the students. In all, we received 243 responses to these surveys over six terms. While our surveys were designed to gather information of our own interest rather than as the basis for a formal research study, they still provide a great deal of information that is both useful and relevant to this paper.

Here, we use these surveys to answer three main questions:

1. *Are our projects appropriately difficult for a senior-level undergraduate course?*
2. *From our students' perspective, are our projects an effective means by which to teach operating systems concepts in practice?*
3. *What degree of interest and enthusiasm do our projects engender in our students?*

The first two of these questions we ask students directly in the surveys. To answer the third, we use the following question as a proxy:

3′. *Have the projects increased your interest in doing work on the Linux kernel or on other open-source projects?*

Our rationale here is that students who are enthusiastic about the work they do in our course will be interested to continue doing that work after the course has ended.

Difficulty. To gauge whether our projects are appropriately difficult, we classified each student's responses to question 1 as indicating that the projects were either appropriately difficult, too difficult, or too easy. In this way we determined that 66% of the 243 responding students found our projects to be appropriately difficult, and 7% found them to be too easy, while only 24% found them to be too difficult. These numbers suggest fairly conclusively that our projects are appropriately difficult for senior-level undergraduates.

One student's answer to this question sums up students' general attitude about our projects' difficulty: "kernel programming... isn't the black magic I used to think it to be."

Effectiveness. To determine whether students felt that our projects were an effective means through which to learn operating systems concepts, we similarly classified students' responses to question 2. Through this classification, we determined that 74% of the 243 responding students did feel the Linux-based projects were a good way to learn operating systems concepts, while only 23% felt they were not.

Again, we consider these numbers to be fairly conclusive proof of our students' satisfaction with these projects. However, it is also informative to read some of what they wrote in this regard. For example, one student writes, "this was a great way to teach operating system concepts, just because it's so practical, which makes us want to really understand what we're doing." Another writes, "I've always had a conceptual idea of how an OS works, but diving in like this made it very clear."

Enthusiasm. We analyzed question 3′ in the same manner as we did questions 1 and 2, and found that 48% of students described an increased interest in open-source programming or Linux kernel development in particular, while 52% did not. Note, however, that this question, unlike questions 1 and 2, is not a zero-sum question. In other words, here, we are looking not for a majority opinion of the students surveyed but, rather, for the total number of students who reported increased interest. Indeed, we find it quite compelling that nearly half of our students have wanted to continue working on Linux or another open-source project after completing our course.

Again, it is informative to read some of what students wrote here. For example, one writes, "thanks to this class, I can follow my interest in developing device drivers for the kernel." Another writes, "I've been interested in kernel development, but afraid to try. This course has given me a whole new perspective."

Self-confidence. The last quote above also touches on a benefit of our projects that we didn't try to measure formally through our surveys. Specifically, after completing our projects, many students appear to gain a good deal of self-confidence in their computer science abilities. Many of them speak to this in their survey responses. One student writes, for example that our projects "gave [him] confidence that [he] could do this as a career." The following quote, however, epitomizes the attitude with which we believe many students leave our course.

> *I was always so scared of the Linux kernel and now I feel like most operating systems have similar concepts, and I don't have to be scared [of] those either... The transitive property of working on the Linux kernel has given me confidence for other systems as well.*

Hirability. Finally, we note that many students see increased hirability as a benefit of their work on our Linux kernel-based projects. Many students who have graduated since taking our course have described to us how their work on our projects helped them earn a job. Some students, such as this one, even discuss this in their surveys: "I will be working on and contributing to another open source project... during an internship at Intel, and telling them about what we've done in this class helped me get the job." Others have told us informally that the Linux programming environment they used in our class prepared them well for the build environments they work with in industry.

5. CONCLUSIONS AND FUTURE WORK

In this paper, we described a set of Linux kernel-based projects for a senior-level undergraduate operating systems course, and we assessed those projects along several dimensions, both formally and informally. There are many directions for future work, most notably in developing new projects, but also, for example, in devising better methods to grade our current projects.

6. ACKNOWLEDGMENTS

Much of our students' enthusiasm is attributed to guest-lectures by Linux kernel maintainer Greg Kroah-Hartman, to whom we are extremely grateful. We are also indebted to Mike Marineau, Yunrim Park, and Ian Oberst for their hard work to help develop and run our course. We would also like to thank Google for their financial support.

7. REFERENCES

[1] E. Allen, R. Cartwright, and C. Reis. Production programming in the classroom. In *Proc. SIGCSE*, 2003.

[2] C. Anderson and M. Nguyen. A survey of contemporary instructional operating systems for use in undergraduate courses. *JCSC*, 21(1), 2005.

[3] D. Carrington and S.-K. Kim. Teaching software design with open source software. In *Proc. FIE*, 2003.

[4] W. A. Christopher, S. J. Proctor, and T. E. Anderson. The Nachos instructional operating system. Technical Report CSD-93-739, University of California, Berkeley, 1993.

[5] J. Corbet, A. Rubini, and G. Kroah-Hartman. *Linux Device Drivers*. O'Reilly Media, 3rd edition, 2005. Freely available at `http://lwn.net/Kernel/LDD3/`.

[6] H. J. C. Ellis, R. A. Morelli, T. R. de Lanerolle, J. Damon, and J. Raye. Can humanitarian open-source software development draw new students to CS? In *Proc. SIGCSE*, 2007.

[7] C. P. Fuhrman. Appreciation of software design concerns via open-source tools and projects. In *Proc. ECOOP*, 2006.

[8] B. Lawson and L. Barnett. Using iPodLinux in an introductory OS course. In *Proc. SIGCSE*, 2008.

[9] R. Love. *Linux Kernel Development*. Novell, 2nd edition, 2005.

[10] J. Nieh and C. Vaill. Experiences teaching operating systems using virtual platforms and Linux. In *Proc. SIGCSE*, 2005.

[11] M. Pedroni, T. Bay, M. Oriol, and A. Pedroni. Open source projects in programming courses. In *Proc. SIGCSE*, 2007.

[12] A. S. Tannenbaum. A UNIX clone with source code for operating systems courses. *SIGOPS OSR*, 21(1), 1987.

Teaching Operating Systems – Windows Kernel Projects

Alexander Schmidt
Hasso Plattner Institute at University of Potsdam
Operating Systems and Middleware
Prof.-Dr.-Helmert-Str. 2-3
14482 Potsdam, Germany
alexander.schmidt@hpi.uni-potsdam.de

Andreas Polze
Hasso Plattner Institute at University of Potsdam
Operating Systems and Middleware
Prof.-Dr.-Helmert-Str. 2-3
14482 Potsdam, Germany
andreas.polze@hpi.uni-potsdam.de

Dave Probert
Windows Kernel Architecture
Microsoft Corporation
One Microsoft Way
Redmond, WA 98052, USA
dave.probert@microsoft.com

ABSTRACT

When studying operating systems, students need to understand **u**ser-mode system interfaces (U), they need to learn about tools to monitor and **m**easure OS behavior (M), and they finally should understand central implementation details of the OS **k**ernel (K). Following the *UMK approach*, even complex projects such as modifying the memory management inside the Windows kernel can be carried out in an undergraduate OS curriculum.

Here we concentrate on the kernel- and measurement part and present the Abstract Memory Management (AMM) project. AMM provides a framework for modifying the working set management in Windows while still hiding many implementation details of the kernel. AMM has been used in OS courses at U of Washington Bothell and HPI/U of Potsdam, Germany, with very good results.

The AMM lab – together with other labs – is based on the Windows Research Kernel (WRK) as available in source from Microsoft. These labs complement our previously developed Curriculum Resource Kit (CRK) and are available for download.

Categories and Subject Descriptors

D.4.0 [**Operating Systems**]: General—*Microsoft Windows NT*; D.4.2 [**Operating Systems**]: Storage Management—*Virtual Memory*; K.3.2 [**Computers and Education**]: Computer and Information Science Education—*Computer Science Education*

General Terms

Algorithms, Experimentation, Human Factors

Keywords

Operating Systems, Windows Sources, Memory Management, Windows Research Kernel

SIGCSE'10, March 10–13, 2010, Milwaukee, Wisconsin, USA.

1. INTRODUCTION

The roots of Windows reach back to the late 1980s. Back then, many interesting things were happening in the operating system design space – including SVR4, the Mach microkernel, innovations in networking and windowing systems, and many research projects on OS fundamentals. The desire to gain in-depth knowledge of these exciting developments motivated many CS students to study operating systems back then. With our OS projects we want help to re-spark interest in operating systems again.

Within this paper, we advocate a hands-on approach towards teaching (and learning) OS concepts. We present our experiences from teaching Windows-based OS courses during the last ten years. We suggest a three-phase scheme, where students first learn to master **u**ser-mode system interfaces (U) – often referred to as "system programming". Secondly, they need to master principles and tools to monitor and **m**easure OS behavior (M). And third, students should be presented with central implementation details of the OS **k**ernel (K). Following the *UMK Approach*, even complex projects such as the modifying the implementation of memory management inside the Windows kernel can be carried out in an undergraduate OS curriculum. Undertakings, such as the Abstract Memory Management (AMM) project, integrate well with our previously developed courseware – the Microsoft Windows Internals Curriculum Resource Kit (CRK) [6, 2].

Microsoft made the Windows kernel sources widely available to academia in 2006 [3], replacing the earlier limited distribution that was available only to select universities. Since then, we have expanded our earlier use of Windows in OS courses by developing a number of projects and labs that rely on modifying the Windows kernel. These projects focus on topics such as scheduling/dispatching, synchronization, and memory management. Within this paper, we present the Abstract Memory Management (AMM) experiment which is comprised of a U section, where students practice relevant system APIs (such as Windows API function `VirtualAllocEx()`), an M section, where we ask students to familiarize themselves with measurement techniques and tools (such as the Windows performance monitor – *perfmon.exe*), and a K section where students need to modify source code (e.g.; ntos/mm/wsmanage.c), compile, and run their own version of Windows. During the course, projects are assigned to groups of three students.

In the remainder of the paper, we first present an overview

about the projects we created for the WRK. Then, we present the kernel (K) and the measurement (M) part of the AMM project. (We have omitted the user-mode (U) part due to space limitations.) Instead we present feedback from students who took our course. Finally, we conclude the paper with an outlook on future UMK projects.

2. WRK PROJECTS

The Windows Research Kernel (WRK) is based on the x86/x64 source code of the Windows Server 2003 operating system kernel with Service Pack 1. Figure 1 gives a brief overview of the source code components that are shipped with the WRK. Gray, rectangular boxes denote modules that are available as source code, while the white rectangular boxes denote components that are either provided as static library, like the power management module, or not at all, like device drivers and all user mode components.

Our operating system projects – such as the AMM lab – are structured in such a way that they align well with the Curriculum Resource Kit (CRK) and the IEEE/ACM Computer Science Body of Knowledge (CSBOK) for operating systems. An introductory project helps students to familiarize themselves with the WRK build-process. This project just presents how to modify the kernel sources, rebuild the WRK, deploy the kernel on a test system and show some debugging output. This preliminary project is denoted as P1 in Figure 1. In physics, and other natural sciences, experiments are the fundamental approach to obtaining new insights into the subject material and to cement the knowledge gained from the classroom [1]. Experiments are used to test a theory against the physical world, to gain experimental proof, or to investigate natural phenomena in order to postulate a theory. We believe the former approach to be appropriate for teaching operating systems as well. While the lecture formulates some sort of model, or principle, experiments should be used to test this model against the physical world, in our case the behavior of the computer system.

All of our experiments are structured in the same way: we re-iterate important principles of the respective CRK or CSBOK-OS section, we propose a programming task that must be accomplished in user-mode (U) by facilitating existing programming interfaces (API) and in kernel-mode (K) by extending or modifying operating system source code. We provide a test framework that allows our students to measure (M) benefits and disadvantages of either implementation.

By using this two level approach, we believe we achieve two things: (1) increasing the students' system-programming abilities and (2) improving their understanding of OS design and implementation principles. In the following sections, we concentrate particularly on the kernel mode implementation of the AMM experiment, as we want to report on the challenges we dealt with when running these experiments. We also present the overall goal of the experiment and the respective CRK section of the experiment.

2.1 System Service Call Implementation

This project is designed as an experiment for CRK section OS2: Operating System Principles. System services, encapsulated in application programming interfaces (APIs), are the fundamental abstraction for operating systems to provide functionality to applications. Our experiment addresses the transition from user mode to kernel mode and vice versa. It discusses how parameters are passed from the user space into kernel space on Windows, and how system service calls are dispatched. Therefore, we ask our students to write a simple system call that can alter visibility properties of system resources like processes.

Listing 1: Sample implementation for unlinking a process (`ProcessId`) from the `FromList` and linking it to the `ToList`. Depending on how the function is called, `ToList` may be either the active list of processes or the internal list to keep track of invisible processes. The same holds for the `FromList` parameter.

```
NTSTATUS WrkRemoveAndAppendProcess(
  HANDLE ProcessId, PLIST_ENTRY FromList,
  PLIST_ENTRY ToList)
{
  NTSTATUS Status =
    STATUS_OBJECT_NAME_NOT_FOUND;
  PETHREAD CurrentThread =
    PsGetCurrentThread();
  PLIST_ENTRY LoopEntry;
  PEPROCESS Process;

  PspLockProcessList(CurrentThread);

  for (LoopEntry = FromList->Flink;
      LoopEntry != FromList;
      LoopEntry = LoopEntry->Flink)
  {
    Process = CONTAINING_RECORD(
      LoopEntry, EPROCESS,
      ActiveProcessLinks);

    if (Process->UniqueProcessId ==
        ProcessId)
    {
      Status = STATUS_SUCCESS;
      break;
    }

  }

  if (!NT_SUCCESS(Status))
  {
    PspUnlockProcessList(CurrentThread);
    return Status;
  }

  RemoveEntryList(LoopEntry);
  InsertHeadList(ToList, LoopEntry);
  PspUnlockProcessList(CurrentThread);
  return Status;
}
```

The basic idea in this particular project is to unlink a process's control structure, an `EPROCESS` block, from the OS maintained list of active processes. To restore the process's visibility, it is simply reattached to the process list. Listing 1 shows a sample implementation.

The test application we provide performs a process enumeration on the running system. The user mode implementation simply hides a process from that enumeration and is implemented as a library. Now, when executing the kernel mode implementation, two things should become clear: (1) the implementation difference between normal library calls and system service calls and (2) system service calls usually cost more time than simple function calls. This experiment also forms the basis for several other experiments, as system service calls are the simplest way to extend kernel functionality.

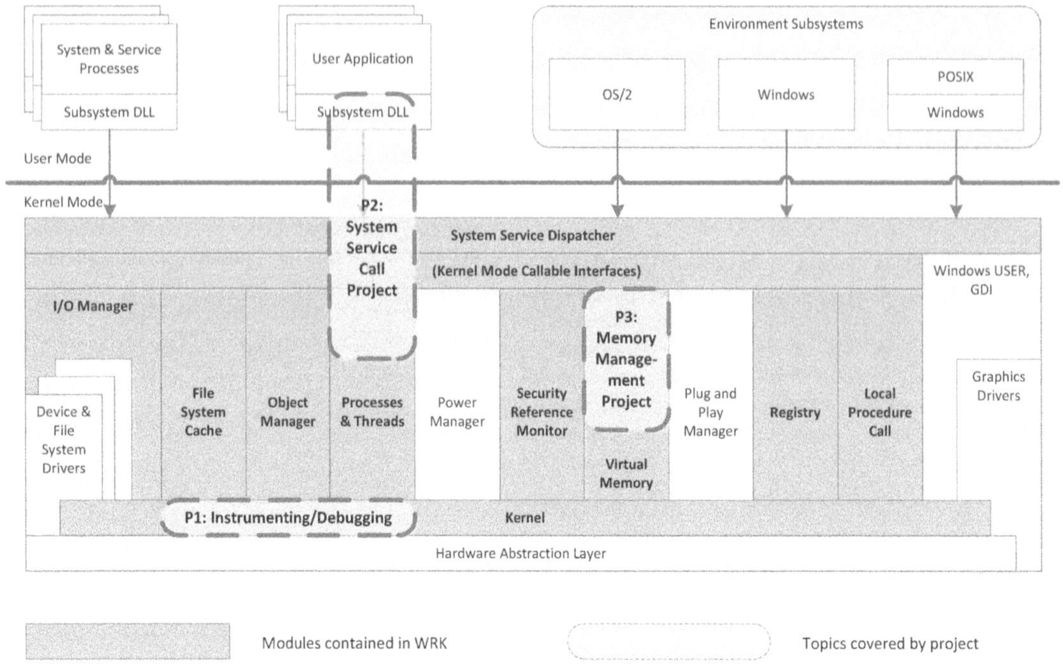

Figure 1: Contents of the WRK. Shaded rectangles denote modules for which sources are available through WRK. White shaded boxes denote modules that are shipped as static libraries. Dashed boxes denote those modules that are covered by the projects presented herein.

2.2 Page Replacement

Besides CPU scheduling, memory management is the most fundamental responsibility of an operating system. Changes within memory management algorithms may have a huge impact on the overall performance of the OS and its applications. Within this experiment we only focus on a small subproblem of memory management: page replacement strategies for working sets.

A process' working set is comprised of all pages in memory that are accessible to the process without incurring a page fault. Therefore we start with designing a suitable data structure to keep track of what pages are currently mapped into physical memory for a particular process – the *working set*. We then proceed to problems associated with that: given a fixed working set size, *i.e.*, the number of pages that can be mapped into physical memory remains constant, replacing pages becomes necessary once the working set is full.

There are several well-known approaches to dealing with that issue, like Second Chance or Aging [8, 9, 10]. However, each page replacement strategy has its advantages and disadvantages, which will be highlighted by our test framework. Also, implementing the working set management as well as a page replacement strategy, in our opinion, helps students to reinforce their understanding and knowledge of virtual memory, working sets, efficient data structures, and finally how all of those may affect the operating system performance.

To accomplish those goals, we had to overcome several challenges encountered during our preparation phase:

- To fully understand the memory management system in general and the page replacement implementation of the WRK in particular is, although inspiring, a difficult and time-consuming task for undergraduate students.

- Making mistakes is just human nature. Doing so in memory management source code, however, complicates matters, as debugging might not be an option. And even with the chance of debugging, finding the cause for an error is still a sophisticated task given the complexity of the virtual memory management system in Windows.

- It may be beneficial to preserve the original implementation, *i.e.*, allowing the students' implementation and the original WRK implementation to co-exist at the same time for the purposes of side-by-side comparison.

Because of these issues, we decided to build an abstraction layer on top of the WRK virtual memory management system, which we henceforth denote as *abstract memory management* (AMM) system and which is basically a framework that provides a simple interface to the WRK Memory Manager. This interface allows students to remove pages from physical memory, to query usage statistics (*e.g.*, whether the page has recently been accessed or modified), and to transparently enable abstract memory management only for specific processes and specific address ranges. In order to modify the memory management system, students have to implement a set of simple function callbacks that are invoked

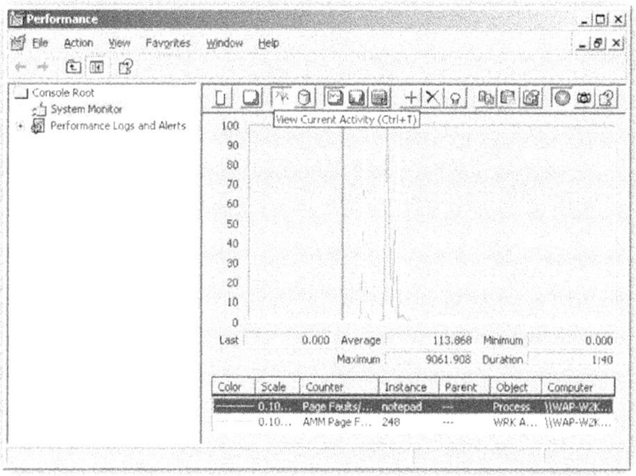

Figure 2: **A screenshot showing the WRK page fault performance counter and the AMM page fault performance counter for comparison.**

by the AMM system as appropriate, *e.g.*, when a page fault occurs.

The framework is provided as a Visual Studio solution file, mainly for convenience. We decided to use this integrated development environment (IDE) as it allows us to point out those files that need to be modified. IDEs typically provide syntax highlighting, and usually provide an auto-completion feature that assists in handling function names and structure definitions. Additionally, we provide two measurement programs that must be executed on the WRK to test the students' AMM implementation. The results of these measurements are used for evaluating the experiment.

In order to master the AMM lab, students are asked to implement two different page replacement strategies. While our students are free to choose an algorithm, we suggest implementing the FIFO algorithm and the Second Chance algorithm. The measurement part of the experiment then consists of executing test applications, once for each page replacement strategy.

The first test application aims at understanding the implemented approach. We give our students a sequence of page accesses and a number of working set entries, for which they have to first manually calculate when which page resides in what working set entry. For the sake of brevity, we assume here that the working set entry position reflects the position in memory. Having calculated the working set for each discrete access time, our students need to verify that their implementation adheres to the scheme and if not they must find the reason for the discrepancy.

The second test program aims at direct competition between the original page replacement strategy and the AMM implementation. The test program therefore adds some Windows performance counters that retrieve the page fault rate of both the WRK memory management and the AMM. These values are displayed using the Windows performance monitor (perfmon.exe, see Figure 2) to analyze the page fault rate over time. Again, students have to discuss why one implementation performs differently than the other. This experiment is executed under supervision of a tutor and discussed with the lab supervisor right afterwards.

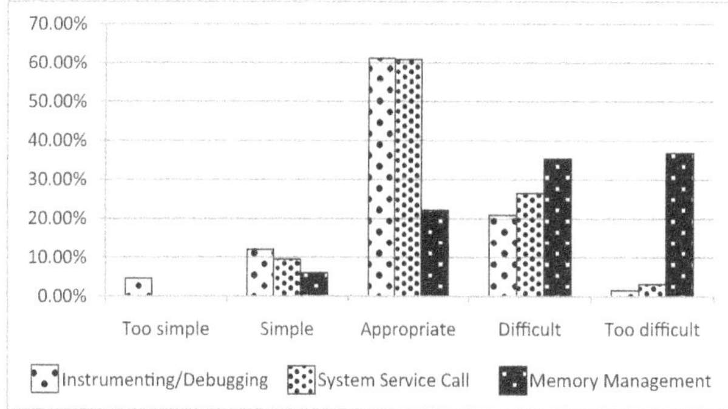

Figure 3: Level of difficulty as perceived by our students.

3. EVALUATION

After the semester, we have conducted a survey on our students to get some feedback on the exercises. In total 69 students participated in the survey. We have asked for feedback in two categories. First, we asked questions about the course in general, in the second part, we wanted to get feedback about the particular exercises that dealt with the Windows Research Kernel.

3.1 General Course Feedback

Within this set of questions, we wanted to know, how the students liked the idea of using the WRK (instead of a purely instructional OS [5, 6]), whether it was easier to do exercises by providing a fully functional IDE, and whether the exercises were understandable. 79% of our students liked using the WRK, and more satisfyingly, 80% considered the WRK as a helpful resource in comprehending OS principles. The survey results also demonstrated that students are well aware that there is no black and white when it comes to operating systems: 56% were interested in also using different operating systems, *e.g.*, MacOS, or UNIX (which they know we cover in our advanced OS course). When it comes to the WRK, providing a fully functional IDE helps lowering the bar for student OS experiments: 67% of our students could work more easily with the WRK when being equipped with a Visual Studio-like build environment. Please note that the WRK is shipped just with a makefile build environment that works perfectly well, if you are used to command line enviroments.

3.2 Exercise Related Feedback

In the second part of our feedback questionnaire we wanted to know more about specific projects. The graphs shown here aggregate the answers specific to our three WRK projects: The simple and introductory debugging task, the system service call task, and the memory management task that was introduced in the previous section.

The first thing we wanted to know was how difficult it was, from our students perspective, to solve a particular task. Figure 3 shows the summary. Given the normal distribution of skills in the audience of a course, *i.e.*, few students have exceptional skills, and few students have skills below average, the Figure shows that our first two experiments were appropriate for the majority of the course. That is,

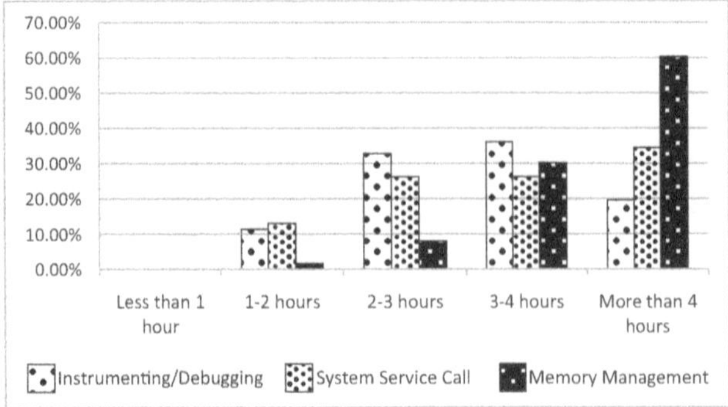

Figure 4: Average time spent to accomplish particular exercise.

the perceived difficulty level reflects the Gaussian distribution of student abilities.

However, the memory management project was different. More than 60% indicated that the exercise was difficult or, even worse, too difficult.

Figure 4 reflects those observations on a timely basis. We asked our students about how long they spend for solving a particular task. As we give out exercises on a bi-weekly basis, we considered it appropriate for students to spend up to 4 hours on these assignments. Again, for the first two tasks, the majority of the course was well in the estimated time range. The memory management project, however, being the most challenging one, took most of our students more than 4 hours of time.

Although being the toughest of all projects, informal question and answer sessions showed us that our students received the most benefit out from this project as they had to relate theoretical knowledge with implementation details as well as coding skills. Mastering the exercise was therefore a big success and huge gain in their abilities as software engineers. However, we want to address the issue by refining our documentation and also the provided framework in order to reduce the fraction of students who may not have a positive experience with the project.

4. CONCLUSION

When studying operating systems, students need to understand user-mode system interfaces (U), they need to learn about tools to monitor and measure OS behavior (M), and they finally should understand central implementation details of the OS kernel (K). Prior to the Windows Research Kernel (WRK), OS experiments in the Windows domain were limited to the system programming level [4].

Using the Abstract Memory Management (AMM) project as an example, we have briefly discussed our approach to teaching operating system concepts based on Windows and the WRK in particular. The authors have used the WRK in undergraduate courses taught at Hasso Plattner Institute, University of Potsdam in Germany, University of Washington Bothell, and Blekinge Institute of Technology in Ronneby, Sweden. Both WRK and the accompanying Curriculum Resource Kit (CRK) are available for faculty to download through Microsoft's Faculty Connection website or by contacting Microsoft at Compsci@Microsoft.com.

The AMM project is part of a forthcoming book on experimenting with the Windows kernel. Additional experiments will focus on topics such as concurrency and synchronization, the Windows object manager, thread scheduling and dispatching, and the input/output-system. The authors maintain a WRK-related blog that provides help and additional information for using the Windows kernel as a teaching vehicle [7].

Operating systems are exciting, complex software systems. However, today most users do not even distinguish the computer and its operating system. Students often do not see the need to understand the internals of the OS they use. With our OS projects, based on the operating system most students are likely to use upon graduation, we are attempting to re-spark interest in operating systems again. Student feedback has been very promising, but still much pedagogical work remains.

Acknowledgements

We would like to thank Bernhard Rabe and Michael Schöbel for their valuable feedback and fruitful discussions.

5. REFERENCES

[1] A. Franklin. Experiment in physics. In *Stanford Encyclopedia of Philosophy*. Stanford University, January 2009.

[2] Microsoft. Windows Operating System Internals Curriculum Resource Kit. http://www.microsoft.com/resources/shared-source/windowsacademic/curriculumresourcekit.mspx.

[3] Microsoft. Windows Research Kernel. http://www.microsoft.com/resources/sharedsource/Licensing/researchkernel.mspx, 2006.

[4] G. J. Nutt. *Operating System Projects Using Windows NT*. Addison Wesley Publishing Company, January 1999.

[5] B. Pfaff, A. Romano, and G. Back. The pintos instructional operating system kernel. In *SIGCSE '09: Proceedings of the 40th ACM technical symposium on Computer science education*, pages 453–457, New York, NY, USA, 2009. ACM.

[6] A. Polze and D. Probert. Teaching operating systems: the Windows case. In *SIGCSE '06: Proceedings of the 37th SIGCSE technical symposium on Computer science education*, pages 298–302, New York, NY, USA, 2006. ACM Press.

[7] M. Schöbel and A. Schmidt. Windows research kernel @ hpi. http://www.dcl.hpi.uni-potsdam.de/research/WRK, May 2007.

[8] A. Silberschatz, P. B. Galvin, and G. Gagne. *Operating System Concepts*. Wiley, 8th edition, July 2008.

[9] W. Stallings. *Operating Systems: Internals and Design Principles*. Prentice Hall, 6th edition, April 2008.

[10] A. S. Tanenbaum. *Modern Operating Systems*. Prentice Hall, 3rd edition, 2007.

Evaluating the Impact of PBL and Tablet PCs in an Algorithms and Computer Programming Course*

Ana Paula L. Ambrósio and Fábio M. Costa
Institute of Informatics
Federal University of Goiás (UFG)
Goiânia-GO - Brazil
(apaula|fmc)@inf.ufg.br

ABSTRACT

The introductory undergraduate course on Algorithms and Computer Programming, commonly known as CS1, has always presented a challenge when considering student failure and drop out rates. Despite this, it is acknowledged that this is a foundational course for a large part of the CS curriculum. In this paper we present the results of a project that combines the use of mobile, pen-based, computing technology and Problem-Based Learning in the redesign of an introductory computer programming course. The course redesign focused on the integrated use of tablet PCs to assist in the several activities involved in the use of the PBL method in the classroom. The results show a promising future for the methodology, also pointing to the need for some important adaptations in order to make its use more effective to teach and learn this particular discipline.

Categories and Subject Descriptors

K.3.2 [**Computers and Education**]: Computer and Information Science Education—*Computer Science Education*

General Terms

Algorithms

Keywords

Algorithm teaching, Problem-based learning, Pen-based computing

1. INTRODUCTION

Traditionally, Computer Programming courses are taught as a sequence of topics, covering basic to advanced-level techniques, including flow control and program modularization. Concepts are exposed first, followed by previously prepared examples of their application and, finally, by specific problems for which students have to reproduce and extend learned solutions. With this methodology, few students in each class show adequate levels of success, while others seem not to grasp key concepts, their relationships and applications.

It has been argued that the problem lies in the students' (lack of) ability to perform abstract thinking [8]. Some advocate a more natural way of learning, where a typical scenario is to face the problem first, working out a solution from an analysis of the problem and from previous experience [13]. Others believe that students lack motivation because the course is usually dull, taught without the interest of the students in mind [5]. Others still, believe developing collaborative skills is vital in programming education [10].

In fact, teaching Algorithms and Computer Programming is a complex matter, and, in different degrees, all of the above aspects contribute to the problem. We are currently investigating the use of problem-based learning (PBL) and mobile computing technologies to enhance teaching in an introductory course on this discipline.

Problem-based learning (PBL) is "an instructional method characterized by the use of 'real world' problems as the context within which students learn critical thinking and problem solving skills, and acquire knowledge of the essential concepts of the course. Using PBL, students acquire lifelong learning skills which include the ability to find and use appropriate learning resources" [4]. Even though the use of PBL does not necessarily mean an increase in grades, it has been verified that it fosters knowledge retention and enhances intrinsic interest in the subject matter [11]. Furthermore, it has led to recognized improvements in student programming skills related to abstraction and problem solving, and also in communication and argumentation skills, as well as responsibility and peer support [13].

Mobile technology, in our case based on tablet PCs, enables a much more flexible classroom environment, where both students and tutors are free to move around, if needed, while carrying their always-connected devices. This is similar to previous initiatives involving the use of handheld devices in education, such as in [12], and is key to facilitate classroom rearrangement, interaction, experimentation, and access to external resources. In addition, ink-based computing presents students with a powerful tool for note taking and for expressing their creativity when working in the abstract reasoning associated with algorithmic thinking. Furthermore, the simple use of tablets is a stimulating factor, attracting attention to the course, and contributing to engage students. It gives students more possibilities to collaborate

*Work partly funded by the HP Technology for Teaching Higher Education Grant'2007 and by CAPES-Brazil.

SIGCSE'10, March 10–13, 2010, Milwaukee, Wisconsin, USA.

with each other, exchanging, evaluating and complementing each other's solutions to problems. Tablets also facilitate the implementation of the PBL method by giving students access to on-line information "at the tip of the pen", instrumenting the search for solutions and helping increase their proactivity and content retention. Thus, teachers move from an information providing position to a guiding position, focusing on teaching students how to think for themselves, stimulating logical reasoning and independence.

Redesign of the whole classroom experience towards a more interactive, collaborative, and group-based model, is the aim of a two-year research project that we initiated in January 2008. The project involves both the methodological and technological aspects related to the learning of Algorithms and Computer Programming. It includes the analysis, application and development of methodologies and software that may facilitate and enhance the learning experience with the use of tablet PCs and PBL. During this time we have worked with students in courses from Computer Science, Information Systems, Agricultural Science and Mathematics. The current methodology in use, described in the next section, is the result of improvements to our initial attempts, which have helped increase the learning efficiency and also the acceptance by the students. An evaluation of this experience is presented in Section 4.

2. METHODOLOGY

The proposed methodology aims to develop student's algorithmic reasoning by offering a collaborative and motivating environment where students work on problems that simulate real world situations. In this environment, students are encouraged to solve the problems by applying abstract thinking. They must first focus on building an algorithm that provides a solution to the problem before implementing the algorithm in a programming language.

To create this environment, the use of tablet PCs plays an important role. Motivating students from the beginning causes a positive impact on their approach to problem solving, making the learning process more beneficial and fun [17]. The use of digital ink in the classroom not only stimulates interest because it represents state-of-the-art technology, but also because it allows for different types of expression that include, but are not limited to, diagrams, sketches, free-hand drawings, and mathematical formulas. This freedom of expression allows students to bring forth their creativity and communicate in a more natural way.

In addition to the motivation aspect of tablet PCs, the ability to use them as collaboration tools is also important. Collaborative learning is based on the mutual exchange of knowledge among students and between students and teachers, and is founded in the work developed by Vygotsky. For him, collaboration between students helps develop general strategies and abilities for problem solving through the implicit cognitive processes contained in interaction and communication [18]. Collaborative learning can be seen as a combination of communication, coordination and cooperation, where communication is related to the exchange of messages and information between people, coordination is related to people, activity and resource administration, and cooperation is related to the production that occurs in a shared environment [6]. Research in this domain demonstrates that this dialog among students and between students and teachers helps in the learning process [7].

In this environment, we use the PBL method [16] to introduce the concepts in the course syllabus as a series of open-ended problems. We employ an adaptation of the method described in [13], as follows. In the beginning of the semester, students are arranged into four groups of 5 members each. For each problem, each group is encouraged to collaboratively seek the solution through a series of steps, usually in two consecutive meetings. They start the first meeting by reading the problem description in order to identify its main elements. This usually takes around 20 minutes. Secondly, the group carries out a 40-60 minute brainstorming session in order to identify and relate the concepts they already know and the open issues they don't know how to solve yet. Based on these open issues, each student has to write up a short report pointing to the learning objectives for the problem. These learning objectives are then pursued by each group member independently (as homework). In a second meeting the group comes together to discuss what each member has learned and use this new group knowledge to devise a solution for the problem. During both meetings, the instructors (usually two for a class of 20 students) act as tutors, inducing the discussions in the groups and preventing them from drifting from the learning goals.

The use of PBL is complemented with mini-lectures using ink-annotated slides, as well as individual programming exercises to consolidate the knowledge acquired during problem solving. This set of lecture notes and exercises is managed using the Moodle course management system. Individual programming assignments have also been included to verify that all students have grasped the course concepts. In addition, two traditional exams (at the middle and end of semester) are used to permit a closer comparison with pre-PBL editions of the course.

2.1 Programming Environments

To contribute in this process, a mix of programming-related tools have been used to help students think the problems abstractly and collaboratively. To help students exercise their algorithmic solution, we adopt a similar approach as in [14]. In the beginning of the course, we introduce a visual programming environment, which enables students to focus on the semantic aspects (logic) of the problem instead of worrying about syntax. For this, in different instances of the course we have used Alice 3D [3] and Scratch [19]. These tools have an interactive interface, where students manipulate graphic tiles representing control and data structures in order to create a running program. This enables students to more easily understand the relationship between the programming statements and the program's behavior. Visual programming environments have proven to be valuable tools to introduce the basic concepts of computer programming while maintaining students focused on the abstract solution for the problems. In these environments, problems are mainly related to graphics animation and storytelling.

Later on, we introduce a more traditional programming language. In our first iteration we used Java and the NetBeans IDE. In the iterations that followed, we have used C with DevC++, in order not to confuse students with object-oriented concepts (which are not part of the course syllabus). The basic concepts of programming are then revisited in this new environment, along with new concepts such as one- and n-dimensional arrays, functions and recursion. Problem-based methodology is maintained, now through the definition of strictly algorithmic problems, closer to the programming activities typically related to the Computer Science profession. Examples of problems at this stage include the implementation of a naval battle game and a bank password system. Even though part of the course syllabus (already covered with the visual programming environments) is repeated, we are able to cover the whole syllabus well ahead of schedule, leaving plenty of time to focus on exercises to consolidate learning.

In the Java/C programming language environment, students usually have a tendency to jump directly from problem definition to implementation, skipping the abstraction/ algorithmic problem-solving phase. This jump is strongly discouraged because it leads to poor programming habits that will be hard to change in the future. We emphasize the importance of defining an abstract solution, reminding students that most of the programming errors originate in the requirements analysis phase. To stimulate problem abstraction, students are thus required to define a flowchart diagram describing the proposed solution before proceeding to implementation.

3. TECHNOLOGY ASPECTS

Tablet PCs on their own right are valuable tools in the process. Having one tablet per student in the classroom is an important factor contributing to the success of this initiative. Students feel motivated by having access to a state-of-the-art tool that not only serves the usual functions of a connected computer, but can also be used to replace pen-and-paper with great advantage and to augment face-to-face interaction.

We believe the key to take full advantage of tablet PCs is to explore the capabilities of digital ink. At a minimum, we strongly encouraged students to develop the habit of note taking using handwriting on the tablet. This was performed in two ways. First, during the PBL sessions, students use a simple note taking tool, such as Windows Journal, in order to document their discussions. The exception was on the first instance of the course (2008/1), when we strongly encouraged students to use collaborative note taking tools. For that purpose, we used Jarnal, which allows the coordinated sharing of a virtual sheet of paper among a group's tablets [9], and Group Scribles [15], which enables the creation and sharing of small notes in the form of virtual stickers. The choice of which of these tools to use, however, is left to each group. In any case, at the end of class, students have to submit (via Moodle) the product of this note taking activity.

Experience has shown that most students prefer to use a mix of written notes and freehand sketches, allowing them greater expressiveness. However, we observed that they usually prefer more informal exchanges, rather than the more prescriptive forms of interaction imposed by some collaboration tools.

Second, during the mini-lectures, we use Classroom Presenter [2], which instantly communicates slides and ink annotations drawn by the instructor to the students' tablets, who in turn can do their own annotations on them. We also encouraged students to use Presenter as an extra form of interaction with the instructor, by submitting questions and answers to quick exercises during lectures.

We have also developed a Digital Ink Wiki [1] that allows students to continue problem discussion asynchronously after class. This environment allows students to collectively construct a solution through a wiki that offers ink manipulation capabilities along with traditional text manipulation. This is a valuable tool in the independent study phase of the PBL method.

With respect to programming-related activities, the use of the tablet is still considered an aspect to be further developed. While the use of the pen to conveniently drag and drop program statements in visual programming environments is an interesting feature, we acknowledge that there is more to it. In particular, when we moved on to a traditional programming language, most students preferred the use of the tablet as a notebook (we used a convertible tablet model, the Compaq 2710p from HP), mostly because the keyboard was considered a more agile input method for writing programs. Although this dependence on the keyboard seems to be inherent to the current practice of computer programming, we feel there are other ways to explore the use of digital ink in this context, an aspect that deserves further research.

4. EVALUATION

We evaluated our approach mainly by means of observations and surveys answered by students at different moments during the course of the semester. This evaluation took place in two classes of undergraduate CS students, totaling about 80 students. These students took the introductory computer programming course, respectively, in the first semester of 2008 (2008/1) and in the first semester of 2009 (2009/1). In this section, we present the major findings, which enable us to draw conclusions about the respective roles of PBL, tablet PCs and group work.

Regarding the role of PBL, Figure 1 shows students' perceptions for the 2008/1 class in three different moments: early in the semester, at the end of the semester and at the end of the following semester, when they finished taking a more advanced programming course. In this and in the following charts, a rating of 1 means a very negative opinion, while 5 means a very positive one.

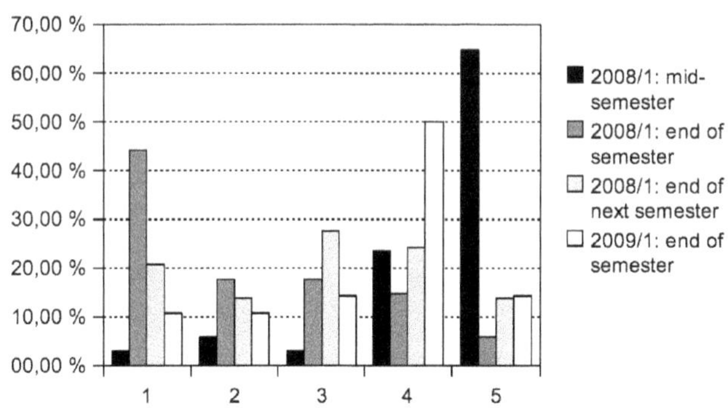

Figure 1: Students' evaluation of the role of PBL.

As we can see, they started with great enthusiasm but as the semester approached its end, opinions were much less positive. However, at the end of the advanced programming course, as they compared PBL with a more traditional approach to teaching (and learning), nearly 65% of the students rated the role of PBL as being either regular (3) or positive (4 and 5). Students' early perceptions may have been influenced by comparisons with other courses they were taking at the same time (which used more traditional methodologies), especially considering that PBL demanded more active participation and effort than they were used to. In 2009/1, as we introduced changes to the way PBL was employed, mainly by offering students a compact set of study materials, and by systematically giving mini-lectures to consolidate learning after each problem, students had a much more positive opinion at the end of the semester.

Regarding the use of tablet PCs, students' opinions in the end-of-semester survey (in both classes) were somewhat more consistent, as seen in Figure 2. The 2009/1 class, however, had a much more positive evaluation (nearly 80%). We believe this was due to the less prescriptive approach we adopted for the use of the tablet from 2009. In particular, we chose to stop using collaboration software in the classroom. The systematic use of such tools seemed to limit the possibilities of face-to-face interaction, sometimes making group work somewhat frustrating as students knew what to do but couldn't do it properly using the tools. We believe further work towards maturing classroom-based collaboration software can help overcome this drawback. We are currently carrying out investigations on this subject. In addition to that, we observed that the main feature in favor of the tablets was their inherent mobility, as well as the possibilities allowed by ink-based applications, especially for drawing sketches of flowcharts and for annotations.

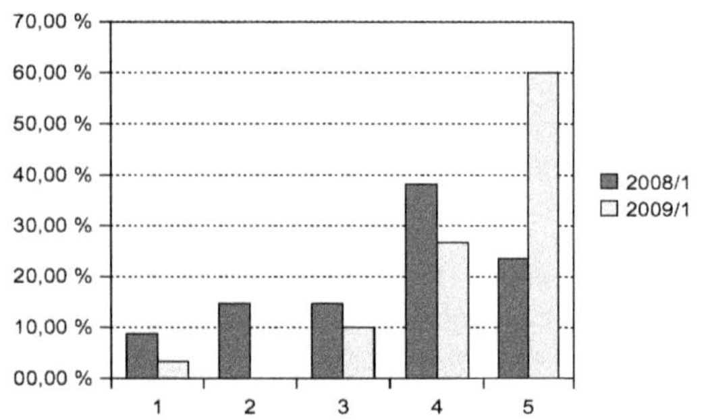

Figure 2: Students' evaluation of the role of tablets.

With respect to the role of group work, which is a central piece of the PBL method [16], Figure 3 shows a similar situation, with the majority of students (in the end-of-semester survey carried out in both classes) agreeing on its importance. Interestingly, at the end of the following semester, the majority of the 2008/1 students answered "yes" when asked whether or not this aspect of the methodology helped them develop collaborative abilities (62%) and proactiveness (75%). We consider this as one of the most important results we achieved as it will certainly impact students throughout their careers. In addition, when asked about the contribution of tablet PCs for collaborative work (in the end-of-semester survey), the majority of students had positive opinions, as shown in Figure 4, with the 2009/1 class showing a similar trend as observed above.

Importantly, it is worth considering the role of collaboration and the socialization phenomenon that arose from it. We observed a high level of spontaneous interaction among students, especially outside classroom, using the on-line forum that was set up for the course. Students were keen to use the forum to discuss issues raised during the independent study step of PBL. Initially, the instructors had to post

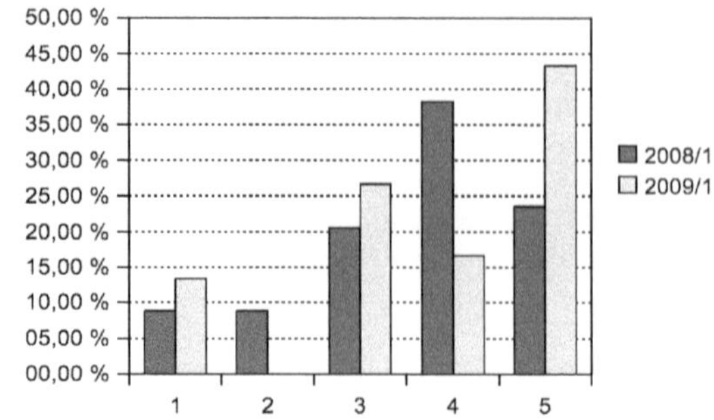

Figure 3: Students' evaluation of group work.

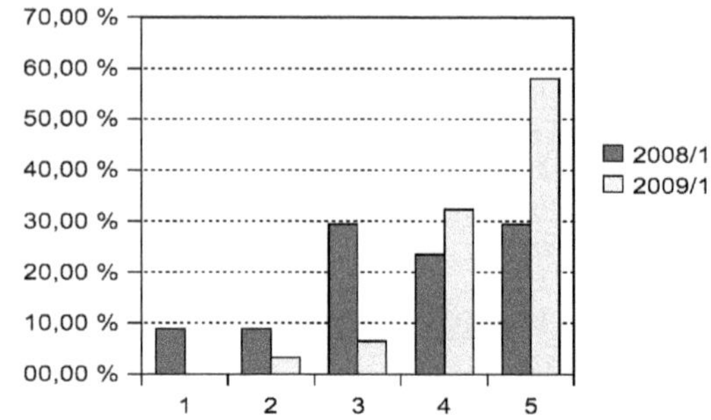

Figure 4: Students' evaluation of the contribution of tablet PCs for group work.

answers to their questions. However, as time progressed, students became responsible for most of the answers, and the instructors limited themselves to monitoring the forum. As a result, a rich environment for the exchange of experiences was created, where those students who had successfully solved some aspect of the problems felt encouraged to share descriptions of their solutions with others, getting further comments and suggestions from their peers. We believe this kind of experience is unique to teaching methods that encourage proactivity and self-learning, such as PBL. This is evidenced by the survey carried out with the 2008/1 students at the end of the advanced programming course, when more than 70% of them confirmed that they were more active forum users during the introductory programming course. We nevertheless believe that this experience has contributed for them to develop a lifelong ability to socialize knowledge.

Finally, we also performed an evaluation of our PBL-based classes, with respect to student grades, comparing them with pre-PBL classes (as in previous years, written assignments were the major means for student evaluation). Out of the 38 students from 2008/1, one dropped out and 4 failed the course with an average grade of 4.4 (5.0 was the minimum to pass). The class' overall average grade was 6.3, with 9.7 as the highest grade and 1.2 as the lowest. In the 2009/1 class, in turn, out of 40 students, 4 dropped out and 8 failed the course with an average grade of 4.0. The class' overall average was 6.2, with 10.0 as the highest and 0.0 as the lowest grade. This represents an 86% approval rate in 2008/1 and a 70% approval rate in 2009/1, against a 55% approval rate average verified in the pre-PBL classes. With respect to grades and drop-out rates, the comparison also favors the PBL-based approach, as the pre-PBL average grade was 5.4, while the drop-out rate was above 20%.

5. CONCLUSIONS

Introductory courses on algorithms and computer programming have always posed a challenge for both teachers and students. This paper presents results of a two-year project that blends mobile computing and digital ink technology with active learning through the use of Problem-Based Methodology, in order to transform a CS1 course into a stimulating and challenging experience for students. The proposed methodology targets the development of algorithmic/abstract reasoning by offering a collaborative and motivating environment where students focus on the solution to problems that simulate real life cases. Our use of PBL is based on group interaction and individual study to firstly obtain abstract solutions to the proposed problems, which are then implemented on a given programming language. The need to search for information that will help in the solution promotes students' proactivity and the necessary group interaction helps develop communication and collaboration skills. Tablet PCs represent a valuable tool, not only for motivating students due to the innovative technology, but also due to their flexibility for collaboration and the sharing of ideas when compared to desktop and laptop computers.

The use of PBL was criticized by students due to the workload it imposed, but believed by the great majority as a positive contribution to their learning process. It must be observed that the proposed methodology attained its objective to be motivating and stimulating from the start, engaging students and achieving lower drop out rates. Even though students did not obtain significantly higher grades in the written exams, the average overall failure rate (including drop outs and grade failures) was around 21%, as opposed to nearly 45% in previous years. We believe this was mainly due to the emphasis on developing the students' ability for problem solving. Nevertheless, we acknowledge the need for further improvements on the methodology, targeting lower failure rates.

Overall, we believe the new methodology has had a positive influence on students, not only from the academic/learning perspective but also from a personal perspective, making them more independent, proactive, responsible and prepared to work with peers. We hope to verify the long lasting effects of the methodology by accompanying this group of students along their undergraduate program, in terms of their achievements in other programming-related courses.

Acknowledgments

We would like to thank our research students for their valuable contributions to this work. In alphabetic order: Bruno Souza, Charles Gomes, Halley Gondim, Lucas Provensi, and Luciana Oliveira.

6. REFERENCES

[1] C. G. Almeida, A. P. L. Ambrósio, and F. M. Costa. Digital Ink Wiki. In *7th Intl. Information and Telecommunication Technologies Symposium*, 2008.

[2] R. Anderson, R. Anderson, P. Davis, N. Linnell, C. Prince, V. Razmov, and F. Videon. Classroom Presenter: Enhancing interactive education with digital ink. *Computer*, 40(9):56–61, 2007.

[3] M. Conway, S. Audia, T. Burnette, D. Cosgrove, and K. Christiansen. Alice: lessons learned from building a 3D system for novices. In *CHI '00: Proceedings of the SIGCHI conference on Human factors in computing systems*, pages 486–493, New York, NY, USA, 2000. ACM.

[4] B. J. Duch. What is problem-based learning? *About Teaching*, 1995(47), January 1995.

[5] M. Feldgen and O. Clua. New motivations are required for freshman introductory programming. *ASEE/IEEE Frontiers in Education Conference*, 1:T3C–T24, 2003.

[6] H. Fuks, A. B. Raposo, M. A. Gerosa, and C. J. P. de Lucena. Applying the 3C model to groupware development. *Intl. J. Cooperative Inf. Syst.*, 14(2-3):299–328, 2005.

[7] M. Guzdial and K. Carroll. Exploring the lack of dialogue in computer-supported collaborative learning. In *Proceedings of the Computer Supported Collaborative Learning 2002. Mahwah, NJ: Lawrence Erlbaum Associates*, pages 418–424, 2002.

[8] J. Kramer. Is abstraction the key to computing? *Commun. ACM*, 50(4):36–42, 2007.

[9] D. K. Levine and G. Teege and G. Hagerer. Jarnal Home Page - Java Notetaker and PDF Annotator. Project website: http://www.dklevine.com/general/software/tc1000/jarnal.htm, 2007 (access: Dec/2009).

[10] L. Ma, J. D. Ferguson, M. Roper, M. Wood, and J. Wilson. A collaborative approach to learning programming: A hybrid learning model. In *6th Annual Higher Education Academy Subject Network for Information Computer Science conference*, 2005.

[11] G. R. Norman and H. G. Schmidt. The psychological basis of problem-based learning: A review of the evidence. *Academic Medicine*, 67(9):557–565, 1992.

[12] C. Norris and E. Soloway. Envisioning the handheld-centric classroom. *Journal of Educational Computing Research*, 30(4):281–294, 2004.

[13] E. Nuutila, S. Törmä, and L. Malmi. PBL and Computer Programming – The Seven Steps Method with Adaptations. *Computer Science Education*, 15(2):123–142, June 2005.

[14] K. Powers, S. Ecott, and L. M. Hirshfield. Through the looking glass: teaching CS0 with Alice. In *SIGCSE '07: Proceedings of the 38th Technical Symposium on Computer Science Education*, pages 213–217, New York, NY, USA, 2007. ACM.

[15] J. Roschelle, D. Tatar, S. R. Chaudhury, Y. Dimitriadis, C. Patton, and C. DiGiano. Ink, improvisation, and interactive engagement: Learning with tablets. *Computer*, 40(9):42–48, 2007.

[16] H. G. Schmidt. Problem-based learning: Rational and description. *Medical Education*, 17:11–16, 1983.

[17] S. Turner, K. Kim, M. A. Perez-Quinones, and S. H. Edwards. Note taking and the tablet PC. In *First Workshop on the Impact of Pen-based Technology on Education*, April 2006.

[18] L. S. Vygotsky. *Mind in Society: The Development of Higher Psychological Processes*. Harvard University Press, November 1980.

[19] U. Wolz, H. H. Leitner, D. J. Malan, and J. Maloney. Starting with scratch in CS1. In *SIGCSE '09: Proceedings of the 40th ACM Technical Symposium on Computer Science Education*, pages 2–3, New York, NY, USA, 2009. ACM.

Does Studio-Based Instruction Work in CS 1? An Empirical Comparison with a Traditional Approach

Christopher Hundhausen*, Anukrati Agrawal*, Dana Fairbrother[†], and Michael Trevisan[†]
*School of Electrical Engineering and Computer Science
[†]College of Education
Washington State University
Pullman, WA 99164
+1 509-335-4590

hundhaus@wsu.edu, aagrawal@eecs.wsu.edu, danafairbrother@wsu.edu, trevisan@wsu.edu

ABSTRACT
Given the increasing importance of communication, teamwork, and critical thinking skills in the computing profession, we believe there is good reason to provide students with increased opportunities to learn and practice those skills in undergraduate computing courses. Toward that end, we have been exploring *studio-based* instructional methods, which have been successfully employed in architecture and fine arts education for over a century. We have developed an adaptation of studio-based instruction for computing education called the *pedagogical code review*, which is modeled after the code inspection process used in the software industry. To evaluate its effectiveness, we carried out a quasi-experimental comparison of a "studio-based" CS 1 course with pedagogical code reviews and an identical "traditional" CS 1 course without pedagogical code reviews. We found no learning outcome differences between the two courses; however, we did observe two interesting attitudinal trends: (a) self-efficacy decreased more in the traditional course than in the studio-based course; and (b) peer learning decreased in the traditional course, but increased in the studio-based course. Additional questionnaire and interview data provide further evidence of the positive impact of studio-based instruction.

Categories and Subject Descriptors
K.3.2 [**Computer and Information Science Education**]: *Computer science education, Curriculum.*

General Terms
Design, Experimentation, Human Factors.

Keywords
Studio-based learning and instruction, pedagogical code review, code inspection, peer review, CS1

1. INTRODUCTION
Computer science instruction has traditionally emphasized individual problem solving and programming skills, especially at the introductory level. We believe that this traditional approach is deficient, because it may not adequately prepare students for jobs in the computing profession, which are increasingly requiring communication, collaboration and critical thinking skills in addition to programming skills.

To address this deficiency, we have been exploring *studio-based instruction* as a means of providing students with increased opportunities to learn communication, collaboration, and critical thinking skills in core computing courses [9]. Adapted from architectural and fine arts education, our general studio-based approach includes four key steps:

1. Students are given complex and meaningful problems for which they have to construct computational solutions.
2. Students present their solutions and justifications to the entire class for discussion and feedback.
3. Their peers critique the solutions and provide comments.
4. Students are given the opportunity to respond to comments and criticisms, and modify their solutions appropriately.

How might this approach be adapted for lower-division computing courses, which traditionally revolve around a series of individual programming assignments? Based upon the formal code inspection process used in industry (see, e.g., [7]), we have developed the *pedagogical code review (PCR)* [8], in which students first review each other's code solutions individually, and then come together in teams to identify, discuss and log issues with the code (defects and improvements). Students are then given the opportunity to resubmit their code solutions based on the feedback they receive in the reviews. In addition to including the four key steps of our general studio-based approach, the PCR process provides students with opportunities to develop a variety of skills that are important in the computing profession, including computer programming, communication, collaboration, and critical thinking.

In a previous empirical study [8], we gathered preliminary evidence that PCRs can positively influence the quality of students' code solutions, engage them in meaningful discussions, and promote a sense of community. In this paper, we present a more rigorous empirical evaluation of the educational effectiveness of PCRs. Our quasi-experimental study compared student learning outcomes and attitudes in two CS 1 courses: a "studio-based" course that implemented PCRs, and an identical "traditional" course without PCRs. While we found no learning outcome differences between the two courses, we did observe two interesting trends in our attitudinal data: (a) students' self-efficacy decreased more in the traditional course than in the studio-based course; and (b) students' peer learning decreased in the traditional course, but increased in the

SIGCSE '10, March 10–13, 2010, Milwaukee, Wisconsin, USA.

studio-based course. We speculate why this might have been the case, and identify directions for future research into studio-based instruction for computing education.

2. BACKGROUND AND RELATED WORK

Studio-based instructional approaches evolved out of the master-apprentice educational system of the Middle Ages [10]. Architecture and fine arts educators adapted this approach in the form of the *design studio*: a shared space where students work iteratively on assigned design projects, periodically presenting their work to their peers and instructor for critical review and feedback in so-called *design crits* (design critiques).

Studio-based approaches have been successfully integrated into science and math instruction at both the high school [4] and undergraduate (e.g., [11]) levels. Several computing educators have explored the use of studio-based learning in their courses (see, e.g., [14,17]). There are even entire computing degree programs built upon the studio model (see, e.g., [3,12]).

In a similar vein, as part of a multi-institutional research project to adapt studio-based instruction for core computing courses [9], we have developed the *pedagogical code review* (PCR) [8], a form of studio-based instruction rooted in peer reviews of students' code solutions. Recognizing the pedagogical value of peer reviews in promoting critical thinking, collaboration, and teamwork skills (e.g., [1,6,19]), several computing educators have explored the use of peer reviews in both introductory (e.g., [19]) and upper-division (e.g., [1]) computing courses. In addition, several web-based systems have been developed to support asynchronous online peer reviews (e.g., [5,16,18]).

While several computing educators have gathered anecdotal evidence of the effectiveness of their studio-based approaches, few have evaluated their approaches empirically. Moreover, only one study (to our knowledge) actually compares the learning outcomes of students who participate in studio-based learning against students who do not [16]. The study presented here contributes to this line of research by providing a rigorous quasi-experimental comparison of a studio-based and a traditional course based on both learning and attitudinal outcomes.

3. QUASI-EXPERIMENTAL STUDY

We hypothesized that the process of participating in PCRs would be educationally beneficial in two respects:

H1:	Students who participate in PCRs will learn computer programming significantly better than students who do not.

H2:	Students who participate in PCRs will experience positive shifts in their attitudes toward learning that are significantly higher than those who do not.

To test these hypotheses, we conducted a between-subjects quasi-experimental study with two treatments: *Traditional* and *Studio*. In the Traditional treatment, which corresponded with the Fall, 2008 offering of the CS 1 course at Washington State University, students participated in a traditional CS 1 curriculum that focused on the C programming language. The course included a weekly 170-minute lab in which students worked together on programming problems under a teaching assistant's supervision. In contrast, in the Studio treatment, which corresponded with the Spring 2009 offering of the same CS 1 course at Washington State University, students participated in PCRs instead of regular lab activities for three of the labs: those that took place in weeks 8, 11, and 13 of the fifteen-week semester.

The courses that defined each treatment were identical in nearly every respect except for the presence or absence of PCRs. The same instructor (not involved in this research) taught both courses. Moreover, the same textbook, lecture slides, assignments, and labs were used in both courses. Only the weekly quizzes, along with two midterm exams and one final exam, differed slightly—the instructor's modest attempt to make cheating more difficult.

Participants' learning outcomes were measured using pre-test to post-test improvement on a test of target programming knowledge. Participants' attitudinal changes were measured using pre-survey to post-survey differences. In addition, we gathered qualitative data on student attitudes by conducting exit interviews with a small sample of students in each treatment, and we gathered qualitative data on students' perceptions of the PCRs in the Studio treatment by administering exit questionnaires at the end of each of the three PCR sessions.

3.1 Participants

The fall, 2008 offering of the CS 1 course at Washington State University (the Traditional treatment) enrolled 89 students, whereas the spring, 2009 offering (the Studio treatment) enrolled 87 students. In both treatments, the pre-test and post-test were a required part of the course. In the Studio Treatment, students were also required to participate in the PCRs and fill out the PCR exit questionnaires. Students were given the option of signing an informed consent form to release their data from these required parts of the course for analysis in the study.

In contrast, participation in the pre- and post-surveys and exit interviews were optional course activities. Students could agree to engage in these activities, for which they received course extra credit, by signing the informed consent form. Because not all students signed the informed consent form, the sample sizes considered in this study were smaller than the enrollments in each course. Moreover, because not all consenting students actually completed both the pre- and post-survey and exit interview, and because we chose to interview only a small number of consenting participants, our sample sizes within each treatment differed across our study measures (see Table 1).

In addition to the students who participated in this study, we hired six computer science graduate and upper-division undergraduate students to serve as moderators for the PCR teams in the Studio treatment. We required the moderators to attend a one hour training session prior to the first PCR. We paid moderators $40 for each PCR lab in which they worked.

3.2 Materials and Procedure

The course that defined each treatment took place during a fifteen-week semester.

Table 1. Sample sizes of the two treatments by measure

Measure	Traditional	Studio
Pre-/Post-Test	26	63
Pre-/Post-Survey	23	19
PCR Questionnaire	—	65
Exit Interview	8	4

In the first and last week of the semester, study participants took a survey that included both the 83-question Motivated Strategies for Learning Questionnaire (MSLQ) [15], and the Sense of Community Questionnaire (SCQ) [13]. Participants were given one week to complete the survey, and could save partial progress and come back to the survey as often as they wished within that week. Both these questionnaires were designed to get at students' attitudes regarding their own learning, motivation, and sense of community.

Likewise, during the first week of the course, and again as part of the course final exam, students were required to complete a 30-question test of the programming knowledge covered in the course. The test included (a) 20 multiple-choice questions that required students to trace and identify the elements of code snippets of at most 20 lines; and (b) 10 short-answer questions that required students to trace code snippets and write short pieces of code. Students were given up to 45 minutes to answer the pre-test questions, and two hours to complete the comprehensive final exam in which the same post-test questions were embedded.

During the final week of both courses in the study, we interviewed a small sample of students in each course. To select students to interview, we partitioned the study participants in each course into three groups (low, medium, and high) based on their course performance thus far. We then randomly chose one to two students from each group for a 15 to 30 minute interview. Interviews consisted of 16 open-ended questions that focused on three broad issues: (a) students' sense of community and the extent to which they interacted with others in the course; (b) the perceived impact of various course features, including studio-based activities in the studio course, on students' learning; and (c) students' intention to persist in computer science.

Recall that the course activity that differentiated the two treatments was the presence or absence of PCRs. In the Traditional treatment, students were given a series of programming problems to solve in each lab. They were asked to work through the problems during the lab with a partner. A graduate teaching assistant was present both to answer questions, and to ensure that students made progress on the tasks.

In contrast, in the Studio treatment, PCRs were substituted for the regular labs in weeks 8, 11, and 13 of the semester. The PCRs focused on three of the eight course assignments. The first assignment required students to perform computations on a file of numbers, and to solve equations in different forms; its solution required roughly 150 lines of code. The second assignment, the longest and most complex (over 500 lines of code), had students implement the game of battleship. The final assignment required students to implement a nine-function string library; it required roughly 250 lines of code.

Five days after each assignment was due, students in the Studio treatment came together for the PCRs, in which teams of three to four students, led by a trained moderator, reviewed their members' code against an established checklist of coding best practices [20] augmented with a list of requirements for the specific programming solution being reviewed. The checklists included questions in seven general categories, including "structure and design," "loops and branches," and "defensive programming." Each individual code review was limited to 30 minutes, and followed a well-defined procedure we have detailed elsewhere [8]. At the conclusion of each PCR session, students filled out an exit questionnaire that elicited their perceptions of the activity.

3.3 Results

We organize the presentation of our results around the study's four dependent measures: attitude surveys, programming knowledge tests, PCR exit questionnaires, and exit interviews.

3.3.1 Attitude Survey Results

Items on the MSLQ were scored using a seven point Likert-type scale with 1 being "not at all true of me" and 7 being "very true of me." The MSLQ defined seven scales of interest to our study: *intrinsic motivation*, *extrinsic motivation*, *self efficacy*, *critical thinking*, *self-regulation*, and *peer learning*. In contrast, items on the SCQ, which gave us a measure of sense of community, were scored on a five point Likert-type scale with 1 being "strongly agree" and 5 being "strongly disagree." Thus, the scale of the SCQ was the opposite of that of the MSLQ: lower scores indicated a higher scale level.

Table 2 presents the pre- and post-survey means by treatment. We used a repeated measures analysis of variance (ANOVA) to assess differences in levels of the seven scales from pre-survey to post-survey by treatment. Given the field-based nature of our study and its use of quasi-experimental design, we set the alpha level at 0.10. In order to correct for Type I error, we then divided it by 7, giving us a threshold p-value of 0.014. We found no statistically significant within-subjects differences, although we can note one difference that trended toward significance: in the Traditional treatment, self-efficacy decreased from pre-survey to post-survey ($df = 1$, $F = 5.68$, $p = 0.0262$). No such significant decrease occurred in the Studio treatment ($df = 1$, $F = 0.72$, $p = 0.4065$).

To measure differences in survey gains between students enrolled in the Traditional and Studio treatments, we employed a between-subjects ANOVA. Again, to correct for Type I error, we divided the alpha level by 7 to obtain a threshold p-value of 0.014. Although we were unable to detect any significant between-subjects differences, we can report one notable observation: Students in the Studio treatment made a gain in peer learning, as compared to students in Traditional treatment, that trended toward significance ($df = 1$, $F = 3.78$, p = 0.059). It was also notable that students in the Studio treatment had a significantly higher mean post-survey peer learning score ($df = 1$, $F = 10.38$, $p = 0.0025$).

Table 2. Pre- and post-survey means by treatment (std. dev. in parentheses)

	Traditional		Studio	
Scale	**Pre**	**Post**	**Pre**	**Post**
Intrinsic Motivation	5.25 (1.06)	4.84 (1.16)	4.96 (0.98)	4.65 (1.10)
Extrinsic Motivation	4.97 (1.38)	5.01 (1.05)	5.15 (1.16)	5.10 (0.86)
Self Efficacy	5.78 (0.66)	5.26 (1.06)	5.42 (1.11)	5.19 (1.25)
Critical Thinking	3.72 (0.98)	3.68 (1.43)	3.84 (0.91)	3.88 (1.10)
Self Regulation	3.90 (0.44)	3.91 (0.54)	4.21 (0.68)	4.13 (0.80)
Peer Learning	2.72 (1.17)	2.52 (0.98)	3.08 (1.16)	3.64 (1.28)
Sense of Community	2.81 (0.49)	2.78 (0.63)	2.92 (0.55)	2.95 (0.73)

3.3.2 Programming Knowledge Test Results

A total of 68 points were possible on the programming knowledge test. Table 3 presents the mean pre- and post-test scores by treatment. Both treatments experienced a significant gain in test performance from pre-test to post-test (Traditional: $df = 1$, $F = 203.69$, $p < 0.0001$; Studio: $df = 1$; $F = 613.83$; $p < 0.0001$). However, there was no significant difference in the pre-test- to post-test improvement of the two treatments ($df = 1$, $F = 1.02$, $p = 0.3162$).

3.3.3 PCR Exit Questionnaire Results

The first question on the PCR exit questionnaire asked students whether they found the code review of their own assignment solution to be helpful. Answers to this question were generally positive, with 77 percent of the responses expressing that the reviews were helpful, and another 8 percent expressing that the reviews were somewhat helpful. For example, one student said that "I found the code review of my assignment solution helpful because it was much easier to identify errors in the group," while another student said that "it was a good way to go over everyone else's code and help each other out, [as] others might see an error that I overlooked."

In response to the second question, which asked students about the lessons they learned from the review of their own code, one student stated that "having someone else read my code out loud showed me some simple problems I didn't notice." Another student remarked that "I learned to appreciate criticism."

Students also appreciated the opportunity to review other students' code. Eighty-one percent of responses to the question "Did you find the code review of your team members' assignment solutions helpful?" were in the affirmative, with another 6.5 percent expressing that reviews of peers' code were somewhat helpful. For instance, one student remarked that "getting different perspectives on code gave me different ideas on how to go about this program next time." Another student stated that "it's better to get help from someone than to give up [on] the assignment." A third student saw the value of working with others, stating that "I learned that it will help to work with other people."

Finally, in response to a series of questions that asked students about their experiences working on their PCR team, a vast majority of respondents thought that their team functioned well (90 percent) or fairly well (5 percent). Ninety-six percent of the respondents had the sense that they were part of the team. Likewise, 96 percent of respondents said that they would consider working with a member of their review team on a future assignment. For example, one student said that his team "understood where each other is coming from and didn't take offense to the critique of each other's programs." This comment was echoed by a student who said that all team members "talked openly, giving suggestions and taking criticism." Another student felt that his "voice was heard, and was able to listen to and appreciate others' opinions."

Table 3. Pretest, posttest, and pre- to post-test improvement means by treatment (std. dev. in parentheses)

Treatment	Pre	Post	Improvement
Traditional	14.3 (8.0)	38.3 (8.7)	24.1 (8.6)
Studio	9.9 (7.6)	35.8 (7.9)	26.1 (8.4)

3.3.4 Exit Interview Results

For several of the interview questions, student responses were remarkably similar, regardless of whether they were enrolled in the studio or traditional offering of the course. For example, nearly all students cited the instructor as having had a positive influence on their learning. (The same instructor taught both the traditional and studio versions of the course.) Perhaps based upon this positive perception of the instructor, all but one of the students we interviewed said that they would recommend the course to others, with the caveat that the course is difficult and only suitable for those who are genuinely interested in learning computer programming and problem solving. In addition, students in both treatments generally agreed that completing programming assignments was a valuable learning activity.

With respect to the questions that focused on students' sense of community and interaction with others, we can identify some key differences in the way in which students in the Traditional and Studio treatments responded. One question asked students whether they had received helpful feedback on their programming assignments. The students in the Studio treatment responded nearly uniformly that they had received helpful feedback from the moderators in their PCRs, and, to a lesser extent, from the students on their PCR team. In contrast, five of the eight students in the traditional section said that they had received helpful feedback from the TA in writing; however, the other three students said they had not received helpful feedback at all. Likewise, in response to a question that asked whether students had a sense of shared experience with others in the course, all four students in the Studio treatment said that they had a sense of shared experience, whereas only half of the students in the Traditional treatment said so. Finally, in response to a question that asked students whether their experiences in the course had helped them feel more comfortable with interacting with others about computer programming, all students in the Studio course answered "yes," whereas students in the traditional course seemed less sure, with only five of the eight students answering "yes."

4. DISCUSSION AND FUTURE WORK

Our study results would appear to furnish limited empirical evidence for one of our two hypotheses. While we found no evidence that PCRs improved student learning outcomes as compared to traditional course activities (H1), we did find two pieces of evidence that PCRs may have positively influenced student attitudes about their own learning (H2).

The first piece of evidence relates to students' self efficacy, which can be seen as a measure of their self-confidence in computer programming. While self efficacy diminished in the Traditional treatment at a level that approached significance, it did not decrease significantly in the Studio treatment. Why might this have been the case? Bandura's theory of self efficacy [2] holds that *enactive experiences*, in which learners have opportunities to assess their self efficacy accurately, have the most influence on their perception of self efficacy. We speculate that PCRs were powerful enactive experiences in the Studio treatment. In PCRs, students received feedback from other students on their own progress, and also provided feedback to others on their progress. Thus, PCRs provided students with powerful resources for judging their own progress relative to others in the course. Perhaps when students saw that their peers, too, struggled with the same things they did, computer programming seemed less intimidating, and their self efficacy did not decrease as much as it might otherwise have without PCRs.

The second piece of evidence relates to students' attitudes toward peer learning—a measure of students' ability to use each other effectively as learning resources. We found a statistical trend in favor of the Studio treatment with respect to its gain in peer learning. In addition, the Studio treatment had a significantly higher post-survey peer learning value. To explain this, we first note that PCRs are clearly a form of peer learning; they provide students with opportunities to improve their assignment solutions based on the feedback of their peers. As our PCR exit questionnaire data suggest, PCRs may have had positive effects beyond the three PCR sessions. Indeed, 96 percent of students said that they would consider working with another student on a future assignment. Thus, it appears that PCRs instilled in students a positive attitude toward peer learning. The Traditional treatment provided fewer opportunities for peer learning, and hence did not promote such a large shift in attitudes toward peer learning.

In interpreting our results, we believe it is important to keep in mind that, in the Studio treatment, PCRs constituted a relatively small part of the course. Indeed, students reviewed each other's code for only three of the eight programming assignments in the course. We wonder whether a fuller implementation of studio-based instruction—for example, one that required students to engage in PCRs for *all* course assignments—might have had a more profound impact on both student learning outcomes and attitudinal changes. In future work, we will implement studio-based instruction more fully in a CS 1 course by requiring nearly every assignment to be peer reviewed. By collecting the same data as in the study presented here, we will be able to determine whether more studio work really is better.

In addition, in future work funded by a new multi-institutional NSF CPATH Class II Award, we will develop studio-based instructional methods for a greater variety of courses, and study the impact of studio-based instruction across many courses and institutions. Presently, more than 15 colleges and universities have committed to participating in this new line of research. We invite interested readers to contact the first author if they are interested in collaborating with us in this research.

5. ACKNOWLEDGMENTS

We are grateful to the anonymous instructor who allowed us to carry out this study in two of his courses. This project is funded by a National Science Foundation CPATH Award (CNS-0721927). Contributions to this work by other members of the research team—N. Hari Narayanan, Martha Crosby, Margaret Ross, and Rita Vick—are gratefully acknowledged.

6. REFERENCES

[1] Anewalt, K. Using peer review as a vehicle for communication skill development and active learning. *Journal of Computing Sciences in Colleges 21*, 2 (2005), 148-155.

[2] Bandura, A. *Self-efficacy: the exercise of control*. Worth, New York.

[3] Docherty, M., Sutton, P., Brereton, M., and Kaplan, S. An innovative design and studio-based CS degree. In *Proc. 32nd SIGCSE Technical Symposium on Computer Science Education*. ACM, New York, 2001, 233-237.

[4] Faro, S. and Swan, K. An investigation of the efficacy of the studio model at the high school level. *Journal of Educational Computing Research 35*, 1 (2006), 45-59.

[5] Gehringer, E. Electronic peer review and peer grading in computer science courses. In *Proc. 32nd SIGCSE Technical Symposium on Computer Science Education*. ACM Press, New York, 2001, 139-143.

[6] Gehringer, E., Chinn, D., MArdis, M., and Perez-Quinones, M. Panel: Using peer review in teaching computing. In *Proc. 36th SIGCSE Technical Symposium on Computer Science Education*. ACM Press, New York, 2005, 321-322.

[7] Gilb, T. and Graham, D. *Software Inspection*. Addison-Wesley, Menlo Park, CA, 1993.

[8] Hundhausen, C., Agrawal, A., Fairbrother, D., and Trevisan, M. Integrating pedagogical code reviews into a CS 1 course: an empirical study. In *Proc. 40th ACM Technical Symposium on Computer Science Education*. ACM, New York, 2009, 291-295.

[9] Hundhausen, C., Narayanan, N., and Crosby, M. Exploring studio-based instructional models for computing education. In *Proc. 39th SIGCSE Technical Symposium on Computer Science Education*. ACM Press, New York, 2008, 392-396.

[10] Lackney, J. A History of the Studio-based Learning Model. 1999. http://www.edi.msstate.edu/studio.htm.

[11] Lister, B. Next generation studio: A new model for interactive learning. 2001. http://www.ciue.rpi.edu/pdfs/nextGenStudio.pdf.

[12] Lynch, K., Carbone, A., Jamieson, P., and Arnott, D. Adopting a studio-based education approach into information technology (poster session). *Proc. Australasian conference on computing education*, ACM New York, 2000, 254.

[13] McKinney, J., McKinney, K., Franiuk, R., and Schweitzer, J. The college classroom as a community: Impact on student attitudes and learning. *College Teaching 54*, , 281-284.

[14] Myneni, L., Ross, M., Hendrix, D., and Narayanan, N. Studio-based learning in CS2: An experience report. In *Proc. 46th ACM southeast conference (ACM-SE 2008)*. ACM Press, New York, 2008, 253-255.

[15] Pintrich, D., Smith, D., Garcia, T., and McKeachie, W. *A manual for the use of the motivated strategies for learning questionnaire*. National Center for Research to Improve Postsecondary Teaching and Learning, Ann Arbor, MI, 1991.

[16] Reily, K., Finnerty, P.L., and Terveen, L. Two peers are better than one: aggregating peer reviews for computing assignments is surprisingly accurate. *Proc. ACM 2009 International Conference on Supporting Group Work*, ACM, New York, 2009, 115-124.

[17] Reimer, Y. and Douglas, S. Teaching HCI design with the studio approach. *Computer Science Education 13*, 3 (2003), 191-205.

[18] Trivedi, A., Kar, D., and Patterson-McNeill, H. Automatic assignment management and peer evaluation. *Journal of Computing Sciences in Colleges 18*, 4 (2003), 30-37.

[19] Trytten, D. A design for team peer code review. In *Proc. 36th SIGCSE Technical Symposium on Computer Science Education*. ACM Press, New York, 2005, 455-459.

[20] Wiegers, K. Improving quality with software inspections. *Software Development 3*, 4 (1995), 55-64.

Implementing Studio-Based Learning in CS2

Dean Hendrix, Lakshman Myneni, Hari Narayanan, and Margaret Ross*

Computer Science and Software Engineering

Educational Foundations, Leadership and Technology*

Auburn University

Auburn, AL 36849

{hendrtd | mynenls | naraynh | rossma1} @auburn.edu

ABSTRACT

This paper presents an experience in designing, implementing, and evaluating a studio-based learning model for CS2. Adapted from architecture and art education, as well as from collaborative problem-solving pedagogies, studio-based learning has shown great promise for computing education. Key elements of studio-based learning include exploring multiple solutions to a problem, justifying the choice of one solution, and being subject to, as well as providing, peer reviews. We describe the design, implementation, and revision of a studio model for CS2, and then present the results of an evaluation of the model when compared to traditional instruction in CS2.

Categories and Subject Descriptors

K.3.2 [**Computer and Information Science Education**]: *Computer science education, Curriculum.*

General Terms

Design, Experimentation.

Keywords

Studio-based learning, CS2, computer science education research, peer review, design critiques, pedagogy.

1. INTRODUCTION

Studio-based learning is an instructional technique that emphasizes collaborative, design-oriented learning [10]. The pedagogy itself is not new; its roots extend as far back as Platonism and it is fully realized in modern architectural and industrial design education [8]. Proponents of studio-based learning argue that its learn-by-doing approach and its high degree of interaction, collaboration, and feedback offer many advantages to the student [2, 12].

While there is a notable example of a full-scale implementation of studio-based learning in a computing curriculum [5], adoption of the pedagogy by the computing education community has not been common [10]. Only recently has the literature evidenced a renewed interest in studio-based learning for computing programs. In the face of declining enrollments, the computing community has gone through a healthy self-examination and concluded that it is critically important to increase student enjoyment in problem solving and raise student motivation levels and their interest in computer science. In short, new approaches to computing education are needed; approaches that engage and excite students yet at the same time effectively facilitate learning. Prior work has shown that studio-based learning can be effective in meeting these goals [9, 10, 13].

While the studio-based learning paradigm is somewhat standardized and uniform in classic design fields such as architecture, art, and industrial design, its implementation in computing education can vary widely. In particular, design activities adapted to early courses in computing tend to be small-scale software design and programming, which are narrower in design scope than the corresponding activities found in domains such as architecture. However, recent research (e.g, [1]) suggests that the design perspective and the studio-based instructional approach are still valuable to consider for early computing courses such as CS2.

Previous work has identified two learning activities as being fundamental to studio-based learning [10]: (1) Students construct their own artifacts (e.g., design, source code, visual description, etc.) as appropriate to the problem at hand. (2) Students present their artifacts for review in sessions commonly called design critiques or design crits. It is this second activity in particular that differentiates studio-based learning from other pedagogical approaches. Indeed, the design critique is considered the centerpiece of the model and forms the basis of a particular way of thinking and learning [12].

We can expand these two core principles into specific course activities as follows [13]: (a) Students are given non-trivial problems for which they have to design and implement computational solutions individually or in groups. (b) These problems are amenable to multiple solution strategies. Thus, students have to consider alternate solutions and their tradeoffs in terms of efficiency and software engineering considerations, choose the best, and justify their choice. (c) Students must articulate their solutions and justifications to other students for peer review, feedback, and discussion. This can be done orally, in writing, or both. (d) Their peers and the course instructor must provide comments and criticisms, again in writing, orally, or both. (e) Students are given the opportunity to respond to this feedback and modify their solutions appropriately.

It is the expectation that by reflecting on and learning from these design exercises over the course of a semester, students will become more proficient in computational problem solving and more engaged in the learning process.

This paper reports on our experience in adapting studio-based learning to the CS2 (data structures) course at Auburn University. We completed the course design and adaptation over a two-semester period (fall 2007, spring 2008), with the first semester being a pilot and the second being a full studio implementation. We used a formative evaluation based on both formal and informal data to guide our decisions and shape the ultimate form of the studios [19]. At the end of this two-semester period, we had developed a robust studio-based learning model for CS2.

To measure the efficacy of our SBL model in CS2, we used the subsequent two semesters (fall 2008, spring 2009) to compare our studio-based learning model to a traditional, non-studio offering of the course. The CS2 course was offered in studio format during fall 2008 and in a traditional, non-studio format in spring 2009. Data was collected that allowed us to compare the difference in both student learning and student motivation and attitudes between studio-based instruction and traditional instruction.

We have organized the paper as follows. Section 2 provides a brief overview of related work, while Section 3 describes our particular approach in detail. Section 3 also provides a discussion of our two-semester implementation and revision of the studio model, including the results from our initial formative evaluation. Section 4 discusses the initial results from our experimental comparison of a studio-based offering of CS2 to a traditional offering of the same course, and draws conclusions from the resulting data analysis. Section 5 concludes the paper with a brief summary of our work and results.

2. RELATED WORK

One of the most extensive implementations of studio-based learning in computing education is the Bachelor of Information Environments degree at the University of Queensland. This program combines core computer science content with courses on design and immersive design studios fashioned after the architectural studio model [5]. The Bachelor of Information Management and Systems (BIMS) degree at Monash University is another example of an extensive implementation of the studio model in computing education. The BIMS degree uses an architecture-like studio model that incorporates not only a studio-based approach to teaching, but also a studio-centric physical layout of facilities and lab space [3].

Other reports of studio-based learning activities in the computing education literature tend to be focused on a small number of higher-level courses like software engineering [6] and human-computer interaction [14], or they tend to be focused on a particular learning style such as experiential learning [7] or active learning [1, 11]. We are unaware of any other work that articulates and evaluates the particular model of studio-based learning that we have implemented.

3. IMPLEMENTING SBL IN CS2

The CS2 course at Auburn University is typical in content, focusing on data structures and associated algorithms from an object-oriented perspective. The instructional language is Java and the instructional IDE is jGRASP (jgrasp.org). CS2 is a 4 credit hour course and meets for 2.5 clock hours of lecture per week and 2.5 clock hours of lab per week. All students meet together for the same lecture, but they meet separately in small, 75-minute lab sessions twice weekly. Each lab session has no more than 23 students, and the total course enrollment is typically between 60 and 70 students per semester.

3.1 Pilot Semester

We began the implementation of a studio-based learning model for CS2 in the Fall 2007 semester. This was treated as a pilot semester to give us a chance to try things out and learn from our mistakes. Data was collected for formal analysis, but we made many adjustments as the semester went along based on an intuitive sense of what seemed to be working and what seemed to need improvement.

There were five programming assignments during the pilot semester, and we used a studio-based learning model for the last four. Each of those assignments was approximately 2 to 2.5 weeks in duration. The assignments were at a level of complexity similar to many of the Nifty Assignments traditionally presented at SIGCSE conferences (http://nifty.stanford.edu). An assignment presented a problem with multiple possible solution strategies, and students were required to develop both a "design" and an implementation. The "design" consisted of a high-level description of at least two possible solutions, a visualization of each solution being applied to a sample instance of the problem, and a justification of the choice that the student made in choosing a strategy to implement. The implementation consisted of the Java source code files that expressed their chosen strategy. The design and implementation were due at the same time.

After the assignment deadline had passed, the course TAs uploaded all the submissions to a website and assigned each student up to five other students' work to review. This peer review required the students to read and evaluate each other's work and make meaningful comments regarding its correctness, efficiency, creativity, etc. Students were assigned "posting codes" at the beginning of the semester and were instructed to use these codes in place of their names in identifying their work. Thus, the peer reviews were performed anonymously.

Students were given three days to perform their assigned peer reviews using an online review system. During the lab session immediately following the peer review deadline, students were allowed to orally respond to the reviews that their work had received. All students who discussed their reviews in lab were given three extra points on the assignment.

The pilot semester went generally well, and it allowed us to make small adjustments during the semester as well as plan larger changes for the next semester. The major adjustment that we made several times through the pilot semester was changing the point distribution for the various components of a lab assignment. We were accustomed to grading only source code and were hesitant to award substantial points to any other component. It became apparent, however, that unless there were significant point values associated the design, peer reviews, and oral response, students wouldn't put as much effort into those components as we would like.

Once the pilot semester ended we held a "lessons learned" planning session for the next semester. The overall sense was definitely positive, and we were convinced that the studio-based pedagogy held much promise for CS2 (see [13]).

We identified four major changes to implement during the next semester. First, students had performed the peer reviews while they were working on the next assignment. Although very few students actually complained about this, we felt that this overlap was a distraction for students and that it would be better if the peer reviews occurred after one assignment is submitted and before the next is assigned. We also decreased the number of reviews that each student had to perform to three (instead of five) to allow more effort to be expended on each one. Second, the post-mortem nature of the peer reviews didn't give students a real chance for the give-and-take that we wanted to see during the labs. Students were reviewing and commenting on things that were already completed and couldn't be changed, and the authors had little opportunity to present their work and respond to questions. We felt that there would be value in introducing a *charrette* component [4] to the labs, where students would present their works-in-progress to classmates and receive feedback that could be incorporated into their solution. Third, due to enrollment numbers and the length of the lab sessions, we planned to have students work in pairs on assignments in order to accommodate the charrette. Finally, we decided that the assignments should include more architectural issues rather than focusing more closely on the algorithmic level. Thus, designing appropriate interfaces, classes, and their associations was given more weight in the assignments.

3.2 Full Studio Semester

Spring 2008 was the first "full studio" semester, having incorporated the lessons learned from the pilot offering of CS2. By this point, we had distilled the following five student activities as being fundamental to our implementation of the studio-based learning model: (1) Develop multiple solution strategies. (2) Justify the choice of one solution strategy. (3) Present work-in-progress to peers and respond to comments. (4) Submit final work to peers for review. (5) Review the work of others

All five lab assignments were studio-based. Each assignment was completed in teams of two, chosen by the instructor on a per-assignment basis. Six lab sessions were allocated to each assignment. The first two labs were work sessions during which team members worked together to complete their design and begin their solution in source code. The next two lab sessions were "studio labs" during which each team presented their design to the class and received feedback from other students (the charrette). The final two lab sessions were additional work sessions in which the teams could finalize their designs and implementations, possibly based on feedback from the studios. The assignment was due at the end of the sixth lab day.

Requirements for the design submission were kept the same. The design consisted of a high-level description of at least two possible solutions to the problem, a visualization of each solution being applied to a sample instance of the problem, and a justification of the choice that the student made in selecting a strategy to implement. However, the specific content of students' designs changed slightly since there were more architectural issues to address than before. The design was due the night before the first studio lab, and each team presented their design during one of the studio labs for that assignment. The studio labs were designed to encourage input and a free exchange of ideas among the students. Teams were informed that they could change any element of their proposed solution based on the feedback they received in the studio. Figures 1 and 2 show excerpts from sample design presentations done during studios.

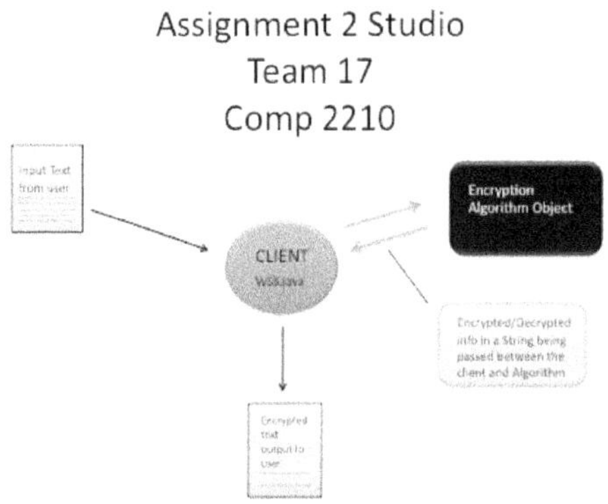

Figure 1. Excerpt from a studio presentation, architectural level.

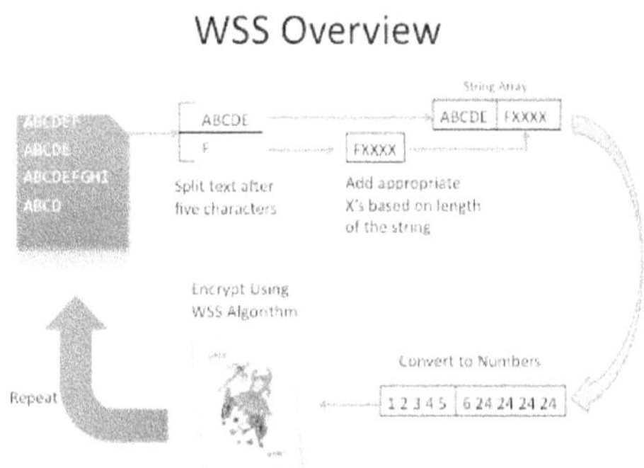

Figure 2. Excerpt from a studio presentation, algorithmic level.

The implementation consisted of the Java source code files that expressed their chosen strategy and it was due one week after the studio labs. Students had to turn in their design (possibly revised) along with their implementation. After the assignment deadline had passed, the submissions were uploaded to the online review system. Students had approximately four days to complete the review of up to three other students' work. The next assignment was posted after the review deadline had passed.

3.3 Formative Evaluation

The formative evaluation of our studio-based learning model for CS2 addressed student performance, attitudes, and motivation. A pre/post content test along with graded items from the course were used to measure student performance, and the Motivated Strategies for Learning Questionnaire (MSLQ) from the National Center for Research to Improve Postsecondary Teaching and Learning was used to assess student attitudes and learning motivation.

We developed a pre/post content test that covers most of the major "core" topics in the CS2 course. The pre-test is designed to be a minimalist content test for a typical CS2, and it was developed in concert with two other universities [13]. The pre-test was administered to the students during the first week of class during both semesters. The post-test, which contained the same questions as the pre-test, was administered as a subset of the comprehensive final exam for the course during each semester. The post-test questions were not labeled, separated from other questions, or identified in any way to the student. From a student's perspective, there was no "post-test" per se for the course, only a final exam.

In the pilot semester ($n = 49$), the average pre-test score was 27.46 and the average post-test score was 55.06, for a 27.60-point improvement from pre-test to post-test. In the full studio semester ($n = 55$), the average pre-test score was 16.65 and the average post-test score was 57.00, for a 40.35-point improvement from pre-test to post-test. Certainly these results tell us that the students increased their mastery of CS2 content in both course offerings (as expected). But the results also suggest the possibility that the changes we made from the pilot semester to the full studio semester were effective. Indeed, the "learning curve" difference between the pilot semester and the full studio semester suggests that the full SBL model offered learning advantages to the students.

The difference between average pre-test scores for the two course offerings suggests that students in the pilot semester were, as a whole, at a significantly higher achievement level coming into the course than the students in the full studio offering. The difference between the two groups' post-test scores, however, was not statistically significant. That is, by the end of each course offering both groups were at essentially the same achievement level. This suggests the possibility that the full SBL model facilitated a greater net gain in student performance.

A comparison of the lab assignment averages from the pilot semester and the full studio semester reveals another improvement. The pilot semester lab assignment average was 68.6 while the full studio semester lab assignment average was 89.1, which is a statistically significant difference of 20.5 points ($p < 0.001$). This indicated that the full studio approach offered definite, measurable improvements over our initial pilot implementation.

To assess student attitudes and motivation we focused on the following MSLQ subscales: intrinsic motivation, extrinsic motivation, self-efficacy, peer learning, critical thinking, self-regulation, and sense of community. For the pilot semester, all scales showed improvement from pre-survey to post-survey, with statistically significant gains shown by t-tests (alpha=0.05) in intrinsic motivation (pre-survey mean: 5.00, post-survey mean: 6.01, $p<0.001$) self-efficacy (pre: 4.67, post: 5.46, $p<0.001$), critical thinking (pre: 4.32, post: 4.85, $p<0.001$), and self-regulation (pre: 4.28, post: 4.60, $p<0.019$). The full studio semester saw significant increases in intrinsic motivation (pre: 5.06, post: 5.57, $p<0.001$), extrinsic motivation (pre: 5.16, post: 5.54, $p<0.036$), self-efficacy (pre: 5.11, post: 5.92, $p<0.001$), peer learning (pre: 3.06, post: 3.89, $p<0.001$), self-regulation (pre: 4.47, post: 5.26, $p<0.001$), and sense of community (pre: 2.05, post: 2.82, $p<0.001$; note that for this subscale lower values indicate higher sense of community). Increase in the critical thinking subscale (pre: 4.11, post: 4.16) did not reach significance. We also saw significant gains in extrinsic motivation (pilot: 5.16, full: 5.54, $p<0.028$), self-efficacy (pilot: 5.23, full: 5.92, $p<0.001$), and self-regulation (pilot: 4.60, full: 5.26, $p<0.001$) from the pilot semester to the full studio semester when comparing post-surveys.

4. COMPARISON OF STUDIO-BASED AND TRADITIONAL INSTRUCTION

After our two-semester implementation and refinement process, we were confident that we had arrived at a workable, effective model of studio-based learning appropriate for a CS2 course. Indeed, the year-long development and formative evaluation of our studio-based learning model showed that students were learning and were improving in key measures of attitudes and learning motivation. To truly assess the effectiveness of this model, however, a studio-based offering of CS2 must be empirically compared to a traditional (non-studio) offering of the same course. To facilitate a rigorous experimental comparison, we offered the CS2 course in the studio format during the fall 2008 semester and in the traditional (non-studio) format during the spring 2009 semester.

Data collected from both semesters include the following: Pre/Post course content tests, Pre/Post attitude and sense of community surveys, video recording of studio sessions, all graded items from the course, and exit interviews of selected students from the top, middle, and bottom of the class. This is a rich set of data and it will ultimately allow us to compare the difference in both student learning and student motivation and attitudes between studio-based instruction and traditional instruction. The full analysis of this data is not yet complete, and for this paper we will focus only on the evaluation of student performance.

The particular performance measures that we used as the basis of our evaluation were student scores on the pre-test and post-test, and their average scores on the exams and programming assignments. This data is summarized in Figure 3.

Comparing the improvement in pre-test to post-test scores for both semesters tells us that student learning increased in both the studio and traditional offerings of the course (as expected). The mean pre-test score from the studio offering was higher by 4.29 points than the mean pre-test score from the traditional offering. The mean post-test score from the studio offering was similarly higher by 3.83 points than the mean post-test score from the traditional offering. There is not a statistically significant difference between the two post-test means. So we can conclude that both groups ended the course at essentially the same level of mastery of the content covered by the pre/post-test questions. However, recall that the pre/post-test is a minimalist content test and is not a comprehensive metric of student learning and performance. Therefore, we conducted comparisons of student performance in programming labs and exams of the course, and these are described below. Furthermore, though there was a statistically significant difference between the pre-test means of the studio and traditional offerings, we do not believe that this is indicative of the students of the studio offering entering the course with more prior knowledge. We gave students explicit instruction about not guessing the answers to the pre-test questions in the Spring 2009 semester (the traditional offering) after noticing the possibility that this might have been happening before. Such explicit instruction was not given for the pre-tests in prior semesters including the Spring 2008 semester (the first studio offering). We subsequently found that pre-test means from the three semesters prior to Spring 2009 were higher than the Spring 2009 pre-test mean. Therefore, we should be cautious about drawing conclusions about prior knowledge based on pre-test comparisons.

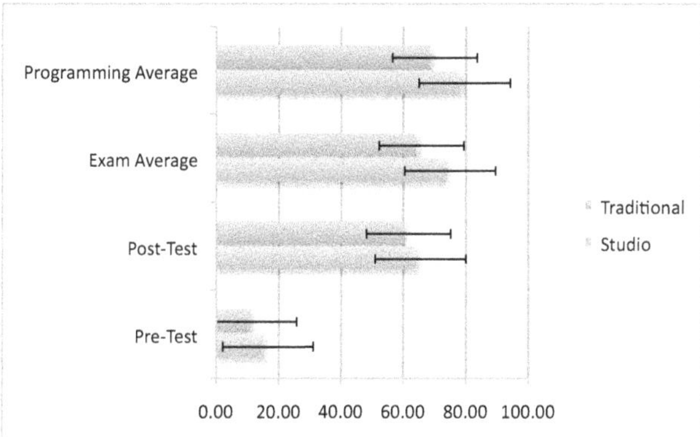

	Studio N = 56 (Means)	Traditional N = 64 (Means)
Programs	79.64	70.06
Exams	74.99	65.74
Post-Test	65.47	61.64
Pre-Test	16.51	12.22

Figure 3. Summary of student performance measures.

When we examined the graded items from the course (exams and programming assignments), we saw significantly higher performance from students who took the studio offering. The average exam score in the studio semester was 74.99, while the average exam score in the traditional semester was only 65.74. This difference of 9.25 percentage points is statistically significant ($p < 0.001$) and suggests that students in the studio offering were able to perform at a higher level on exams than the students in the traditional offering of the course. Students in the studio offering also exhibited significantly better performance in programming tasks as well. The average programming assignment score in the studio semester was 79.64, compared to 70.06 in the traditional semester. This difference of 9.58 percentage points is again statistically significant ($p < 0.01$) and suggests that students in the studio offering were able to develop better programs than the students in the traditional offering.

5. SUMMARY

We have adapted a studio-based learning model for a typical CS2 course and evaluated its effectiveness. In our model of studio-based learning, students get experience in: (1) individually and collaboratively solving computational problems, (2) evaluating and selecting among competing solutions based on engineering design issues, (3) explaining their solutions to others in writing and through oral presentations, (4) critically analyzing each other's solutions in peer reviews, and (5) reflecting on and learning from these studio sessions over the course of a semester. A formal evaluation in which the studio-based learning model was compared to a traditional offering of a CS2 course revealed that the studio-based learning model offered significant benefits to students in terms of both course content mastery and programming achievement. We are quite optimistic that the studio-based learning model will prove to be an effective approach to reinvigorating computing education.

6. ACKNOWLEDGMENTS

This paper is based on work done at Auburn University as part of a multi-university research project in which researchers from Auburn, the University of Hawaii, and Washington State University (A. Agrawal, M. Crosby, D. Hendrix, C. Hundhausen, S. Myneni, H. Narayanan, M. Ross, M. Trevisan, and R. Vick) are participating. This work is supported by the National Science Foundation under CPATH Grant No. CNS-0721927.

7. REFERENCES

[1] Barak, M., Harward, J., and Lerman, S. 2007. Studio-based learning via wireless notebooks: A case of a Java programming course. *Intnl. Jrnl. Mobile Learning and Org.*, Vol. 1, No. 1, 2007, pp. 15-29.

[2] Boyer, E. L., and Mitgang, L. D. 1996. *Building Community: A New Future for Architecture Education and Practice*. Princeton, NJ: The Carnegie Foundation for the Advancement of Teaching.

[3] Carbone, A., and Sheard, J. 2002. A studio-based teaching and learning model in IT: what do first year students think? *Proc. ITiCSE 2002 Science Education*, pp. 213-217.

[4] Denning, P. J., and Yaholkovsky, P. 2008. Getting to "we." *Comm. ACM*, Vol. 51, No. 4, April 2008, pp. 19-24.

[5] Docherty, M., Sutton, P., Brereton, M., and Kaplan, S. 2001. An innovative design and studio-based CS degree. *ACM SIGCSE Bulletin*, Vol. 33, Issue 1, March 2001, pp. 233-237.

[6] Gannod, G. C., Burge, J. E., and Helmick, M. T. 2008. Using the inverted classroom to teach software engineering. *Proc. ICSE 2008*, pp. 777-786.

[7] Gonsalvez, C., and Atchison, M. 2000. Impl. studios for experiential learning. *Proc. ACE 2000*, pp. 116-123.

[8] Green, L. N., and Bonollo, E. 2003. Studio-based teaching: history and advantages in the teaching of design. *World Transactions on Eng. and Tech. Edu.*, Vol. 2, No. 2, pp. 269-272.

[9] Hundhausen, C. D., and Brown, J. L. 2004. Personalizing and discussing algorithms within CS1 studio experiences: an observational study. *Proc. ICER 2005*, pp. 45-56.

[10] Hundhausen, C. D., Narayanan, N. H., and Crosby, M. E. 2008. Exploring studio-based instructional models for computing education. *Proc. SIGCSE 2008*, pp. 392-396.

[11] Ludi, S., Natarajan, S., and Reichlmayr, T. 2005. An introductory software engineering course that facilitates active learning. *Proc. SIGCSE 2005*, pp. 302-306.

[12] Maitland, B. M. 1991. Problem-based learning for an architecture degree. In: *The Challenge of Problem-based Learning*, Boud and Feletti (Eds.).

[13] Myneni, L., Ross, M., Hendrix, D., and Narayanan N. 2008. Studio-based learning in CS2: An Experience Report. *Proc. ACM-SE 2008*, pp. 253-255.

[14] Ungar, J. M., and White, J. A. 2008. Agile user-centered design: enter the design studio – a case study. *Proc. CHI 2008*, pp. 2167-2177.

Using Contour Diagrams and JIVE to Illustrate Object-Oriented Semantics in the Java Programming Language

James T. Streib
Department of Computer Science
Illinois College
Jacksonville, IL 62650 USA
jtstreib@ic.edu

Takako Soma
Department of Computer Science
Illinois College
Jacksonville, IL 62650 USA
tsoma@ic.edu

ABSTRACT

Organick, Forsythe, and Plummer extensively used contour diagrams to illustrate the semantics of procedural and functional programming languages. However, many of the benefits of contour diagrams can still be utilized in explaining the semantics of object-oriented languages and is evident in the software JIVE created by Gestwicki and Jayaraman. This paper illustrates the use of both contour diagrams and JIVE to help students understand passing objects via parameters, returning objects from methods, comparing objects, and using inheritance in the Java programming language. The results from a small informal survey are included. This paper is useful to those teaching Java in a first-year computer science sequence.

Categories and Subject Descriptors

K.3.2 [**Computers and Education**]: Computer and Information Science Education – *Computer Science Education.*

General Terms

Design, Languages.

Keywords

Contour Diagrams, JIVE, Object-Oriented Semantics, Java.

1. INTRODUCTION

As colleges have shifted from teaching procedural languages to object-oriented languages in the first-year computer science course sequence, there are a number of object-oriented concepts that are now introduced much earlier than they might have been previously. These concepts are sometimes very difficult for first-year students to comprehend and this is especially true when students are just examining code and only have verbal descriptions to supplement the code.

Although UML diagrams are useful in understanding the overall design of an object-oriented program, sometimes students have difficulty understanding the semantics of object-oriented code. In various attempts to help with this understanding, textbook authors such as Malik and Nair use diagrams to help distinguish between reference variables and objects [4]. In Wu's textbook, he expands the notion of a UML diagram into "state of memory diagrams" to assist students in understand passing and returning objects to and from methods and the concept of inheritance [6].

Although these attempts are very good and have been used by the authors of this paper in their classrooms, there is a supplemental method used by the authors to help students with the understanding of the semantics of Java programs.

SIGCSE'10, March 10–13, 2010, Milwaukee, Wisconsin, USA.

2. CONTOUR DIAGRAMS AND JIVE

Organick, Forsythe, and Plummer used the idea of snapshots utilizing contour diagrams in their text *Programming Language Structures* to illustrate how sub-programs work, how various types of parameter mechanisms transfer data to and/or from sub-programs, and how recursion can be modeled [5]. At the time their book was published (1978), the mainstay of programming involved procedural languages and they also included sections on functional languages. They pointed out that the original designer of the Contour Model was Johnston [2]. Others to follow Organick, et al, included MacLennan in his programming languages text [3].

Although contour diagrams do not seem to be used as frequently in texts today, the authors of this paper have found the basic model has remained quite durable and modifiable to help in presenting many object-oriented concepts. The authors of this paper use modified versions of contour diagrams to help students understand many of these fundamental concepts and have also found Gestwicki and Jayaraman's JIVE (Java Interactive Visualization Environment) software [1] useful to help facilitate visual learning of advanced object-oriented concepts and help correct various student misconceptions. Although there are a number of features in the original model that are helpful to students in the classroom, some have been changed here to help save time and space in this paper. The first example uses contour diagrams and the second example uses the JIVE software.

3. PASSING AND RETURNING OBJECTS USING CONTOUR DIAGRAMS

The passing, comparing, and returning objects can be difficult concepts to grasp, especially in a first-year sequence in Java programming. The following example program illustrates the passing of an object from one method to another as well as returning an object from one method to another. In actual classroom discussion, homework, quizzes, or exams, these concepts could be separated into different examples to help students understand the concepts individually, but they are combined here for efficiency. Also a number of contours have been omitted here to save space, where the omitted contours can be added at the discretion of the instructor based on the needs of the students.

```
public class Geometry1 {                          // Line 1
  public static void main(String[] args) {        // Line 2
    double radius1, radius2;                      // Line 3
    Circle circle1, circle2;                      // Line 4
    circle1 = new Circle(1.0);                    // Line 5
    circle2 = circle1.makeObj();                  // Line 6
    circle2.copyRadius(circle1);                  // Line 7
    radius1 = circle1.getRadius();                // Line 8
    radius2 = circle2.getRadius();                // Line 9
  }                                               // Line 10
}                                                 // Line 11
public class Circle {                             // Line 12
  protected double radius;                        // Line 13
  public Circle() {                               // Line 14
    radius = 0.0;                                 // Line 15
  }                                               // Line 16
  public Circle(double r) {                       // Line 17
    radius = r;                                   // Line 18
  }                                               // Line 19
  public double getRadius() {                     // Line 20
    return radius;                                // Line 21
  }                                               // Line 22
  public Circle makeObj() {                       // Line 23
    Circle temp;                                  // Line 24
    temp = new Circle();                          // Line 25
    return temp;                                  // Line 26
  }                                               // Line 27
  public void copyRadius(Circle c) {              // Line 28
    radius = c.radius;                            // Line 29
  }                                               // Line 30
}                                                 // Line 31
```

It should be noted that both classes and methods are drawn as contours, except the main method in order to save space. When a contour is nested, it has access to all the variables that encompass it, but does not have access to any other contours. Further, in the original model, superscripts were used on contours of subprograms to help illustrate recursion, however since recursion is not being used here, superscripts are used only to indicate instances of objects. Also, note that the name of a variable is in the first column, the type is in the second column, and the contents are in the third column, where a blank cell indicates an uninitialized variable. The original model included a return value cell (retval) for returning values from functions, and a return label (retlab) cell to indicate which line and method to return to, however these too are omitted here to save space, but can be included in classroom examples.

First, when the constructor is invoked from line 5, the contour for both the object circle and a corresponding nested contour for the constructor are created, where the argument 1.0 is passed to the parameter r and then assigned to the variable radius. The arrow is used to show that the variable circle1 contains a reference to an instance of the Circle class, and demonstrates to students that the **new** method not only created a new instance of the class Circle, but that upon return from the **new** method, a reference to the new instance of the class Circle is returned and then assigned to the variable cricle1 by the assignment symbol in line 5. After a contour is shaded, such as the constructor Circle(r) below, it no longer needs to be shown in subsequent figures in order to save space. However, it can also be retained to allow one to refer back to previous logic or for the purposes of grading an assignment, quiz, or exam. The contour below shows the state of execution just prior to the execution of line 6 in the main program (fig. 1).

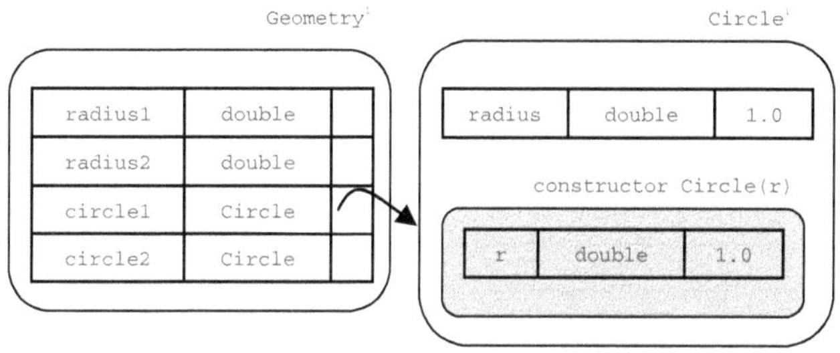

Figure 1: Contour Diagram prior to Line 6

After starting line 6, the contour for the value returning method makeObj is created in Circle[1] below. After invoking the **new** method in line 25, and the execution of line 15 in the constructor Circle(), note that memory cells are not allocated for local variables or parameters. After line 15 in the constructor and the completion of the statement in line 25, just prior the return statement in line 26, the variable radius has the value 0.0 stored in it and the constructor is again shaded. This helps illustrate to students that the reference to this new instance of the class Circle, indicated via an arrow to Circle[2], is assigned to the memory location temp in Circle[1] and not to a variable in the main program.

The following drawing (fig. 2) then shows the state of execution after the return statement in line 26 has been executed, and just prior to the execution of line 7 in the main program. As with the constructors previously, note that both the constructor and the value returning method makeObj are shaded to indicate that they are deallocated. Also, a copy of the reference to the second instance of the Circle class has been returned to the main program and then assigned to the variable circle2 as an arrow. The previous reference is optionally shown as a dotted arrow to illustrate that it too has been deallocated along with the method.

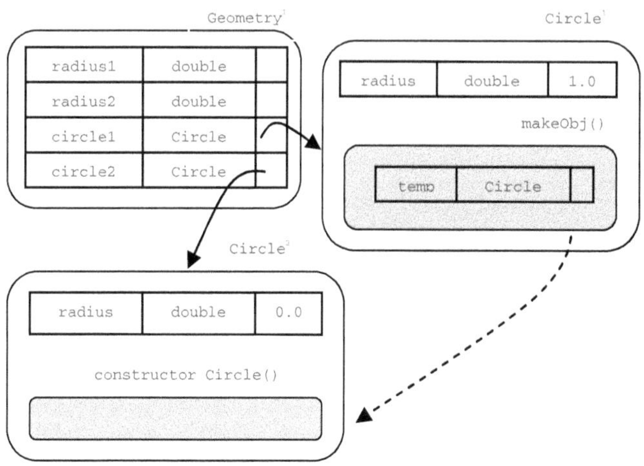

Figure 2: Contour Diagram prior to Line 7

After starting execution of line 7 and just prior to line 29 in copyRadius method, a copy of the argument circle1 from the main program appears in the parameter c of type Circle in the method, copyRadius. Then after executing line 29, the radius, 1.0, of the object c pointing to circle[1] is assigned to the variable radius in the current instance of Circle, circle[2], illustrating to students how values can be copied from one object to another. After the assignment statement is complete, the control returns back to line 8 in the main program and the copyRadius contour is deallocated and shaded, and the reference shown as a dashed arrow (fig. 3).

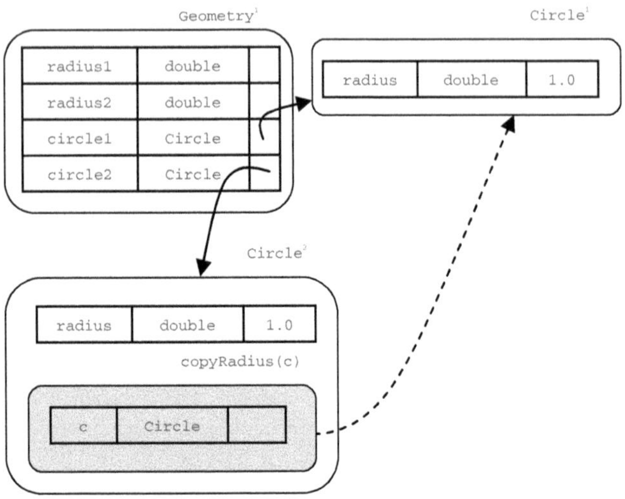

Figure 3: Contour Diagram prior to Line 8

Another source of confusion to beginning students, is when they try to compare two different instances of a class. Sometimes they try something like, "if(circle1 == circle2)" and are confused that "1.0 == 1.0" is false. The advantage of a contour example such as the one above is that the student can see what they are in fact comparing is not the contents of radius, but rather the references to each object, where the references represented by the arrows are not equal. The result is that the student should see that a method is necessary to gain access to the private data members within each instance and be able to correctly write the necessary code.

4. ILLUSTRATING INHERITENCE USING JIVE

This second example is more in depth than the first example and shows a number of complicated features of object-oriented programming in Java such as typecasting and the methods **this** and **super**. As with the first example, these features can be broken up into simpler examples for classroom presentation but are combined here to save space. Further, as was done toward the end of the previous example, various steps are skipped and can also be omitted in the classroom, however they can be reintroduced if necessary to review key concepts.

```
public class Geometry2 {                                   // Line 1
  public static void main(String[] args) {                 // Line 2
    Circle shape1, shape2;                                 // Line 3
    double area1, area2;                                   // Line 4
    shape1 = new Cylinder(2.5, 5.7);                       // Line 5
    shape2 = new Cylinder((Cylinder)shape1);               // Line 6
    area1 = shape1.area();                                 // Line 7
    area2 = shape2.area();                                 // Line 8
  }                                                        // Line 9
}                                                          // Line 10
public class Circle {                                      // Line 11
  protected double radius;                                 // Line 12
  public Circle(double r) {                                // Line 13
    radius = r;                                            // Line 14
  }                                                        // Line 15
  public double area() {                                   // Line 16
    return Math.PI * radius * radius;                      // Line 17
  }                                                        // Line 18
  public double circumference() {                          // Line 19
    return 2*Math.PI * radius;                             // Line 20
  }                                                        // Line 21
}                                                          // Line 22
public class Cylinder extends Circle {                     // Line 23
  protected double height;                                 // Line 24
  public Cylinder(double r, double h) {                    // Line 25
    super(r);     // radius = r;                           // Line 26
    height = h;                                            // Line 27
  }                                                        // Line 28
  public Cylinder(Cylinder c) {                            // Line 29
    this(c.radius, c.height);                              // Line 30
  }                                                        // Line 31
  public double area() {                                   // Line 32
    return 2*super.area()+height*circumference(); //        Line
                                                           33
  }                                                        // Line 34
}                                                          // Line 35
```

Obviously similar to the hand written contours, the JIVE contours sometimes have more information than needed and use a slightly different notation, however after students have mastered the hand written contours, the transition to the JIVE model is relatively easy. Some of the obvious differences are that JIVE uses "rpdl" and a light gray arrow for the return label, constructors are labeled as "<init>" and it can be determined which one is which by their nested location, and references to other objects are referred to as "instance of…", which can be a little confusing.

When line 5 in the main program is executed, the constructor Cylinder is allocated as a subclass and it invokes the corresponding constructor in the superclass Circle via **super**(r) in line 26. The following figure (fig. 4) shows the state of execution after line 14 in the Circle constructor, but prior to the execution of line 27 back in the Cylinder constructor. The Circle constructor is shown inside the contour for Circle because, that is where it is defined and this helps illustrate to students what variables are accessible, such as radius in Circle, but not height in Cylinder.

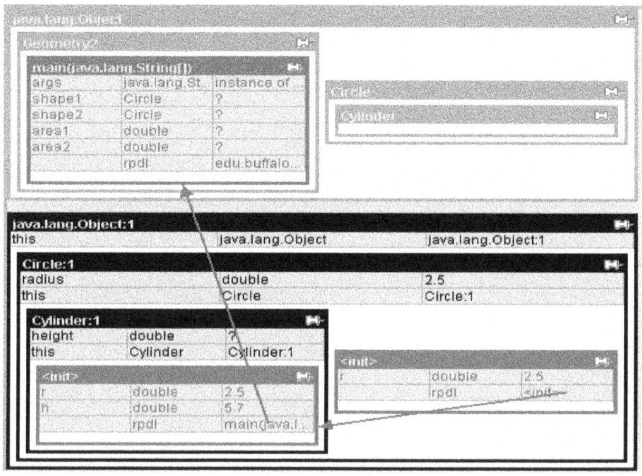

Figure 4: JIVE Screenshot prior to Line 27

After the execution of line 14, the Circle constructor is deallocated. Then the following figure (fig. 5) shows the state of execution just prior to the execution of line 6, where the Cylinder constructor has also been deallocated and the value in h has been copied to the variable height. Further, it should be noted that the **new** method has returned a reference to an object of type Cylinder and that reference has been placed in the memory location of shape1 of type Circle. At first this might bother some students, but a reminder at this time is usually helpful that the class Cylinder is a subclass of the Circle class and the assignment is perfectly legal.

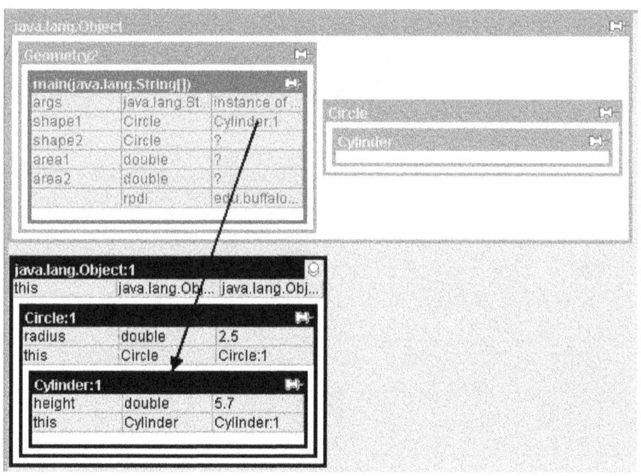

Figure 5: JIVE Screenshot prior to Line 6

The next figure (fig. 6) shows the state of execution as line 6 has begun and just prior to the execution of line 30 in the copy constructor. As before, first the contours for Cylinder and Circle are drawn where the variables for height and radius are declared, respectively. Then, the contour for the copy constructor **public** Cylinder(Cylinder c) is created where the memory cell for the parameter c is given as type Cylinder. However, shape1 in the main program is of type Circle, where Circle is the superclass and Cylinder is the subclass, which is essentially the exact opposite of what happened in the previous figure. Here, a helpful reminder to students is that unlike the previous figure, a reference to a superclass cannot be placed into a memory cell of the type of the subclass. As a result, the use of a typecast operator is required in the argument in line 6. The parameter c now also has a copy of the reference to the same cylinder object as referenced in shape1.

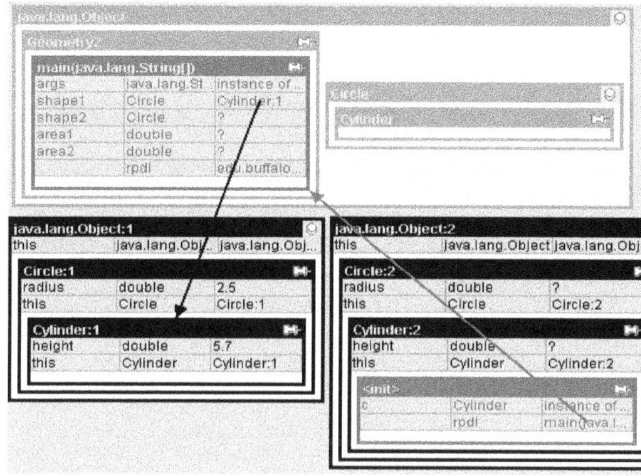

Figure 6: JIVE Screenshot prior to Line 30

Although the copy constructor could have been written similar to the other constructor, as written it allows the opportunity to illustrate the use of **this**, where the following figure (fig. 7) shows the state of execution after line 30, just prior to the execution of line 7. When line 30 is executed the contents of the arguments c.radius and c.height are sent to the constructor on line 25 and the parameters r and h contain the corresponding values. Then as before, the constructor for Circle is executed via **super**(r), where the argument r is sent to the corresponding parameter r, and then the value for r is copied to the data member, radius.

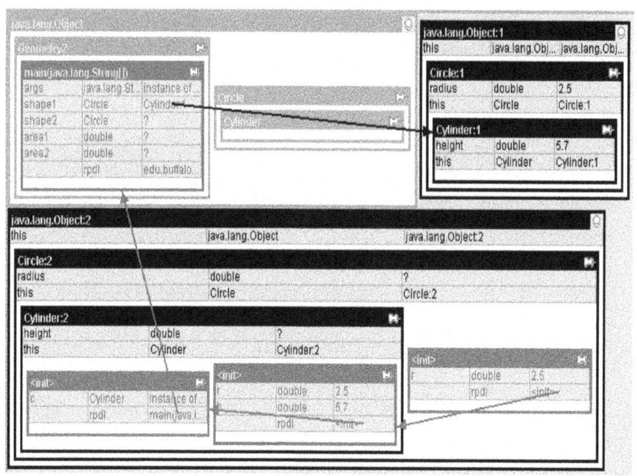

Figure 7: JIVE Screenshot prior to Line 27

After the value for r is copied, the Circle constructor is deallocated, and after assigning the value of the parameter h to the variable height in line 27, control is returned to the copy constructor after line 30, where the Cylinder constructor is deallocated. From there, control is transferred back to the main program, where the copy constructor dealloacted as well. Then back at line 6, the reference to the newly created Cylinder is placed in shape2, where the following figure (fig. 8) shows the state of execution just prior to line 7 back in the main program.

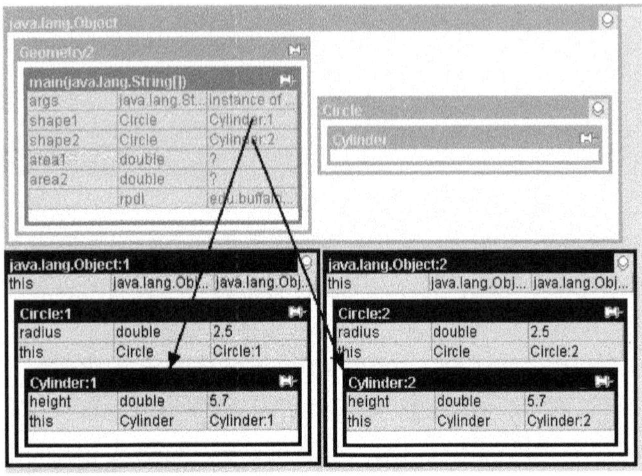

Figure 8: JIVE Screenshot prior to Line 8

5. COMPARISON OF CONTOURS AND JIVE

As can be seen in both of the above examples, the use of contour diagrams and JIVE have the potential to help demonstrate and clarify various semantics in object-oriented programming. In a informal survey of a small second semester CS 2 class of nine students at a small liberal arts college, four questions asked of the students were whether the use of each of the following listed below helped in their understanding of objects in Java. The responses were on a scale of 1 to 5, where 1 represents it did not help, 3 represents that it helped somewhat, and 5 represents that it helped a lot. The average for each appears below:

Contour diagrams in the classroom:	3.78
Contour diagrams in your homework:	3.33
JIVE in the classroom:	3.56
JIVE in your homework:	3.11

The results in all four cases were between 3 and 4, which indicates a positive result, but is a little less than what was expected. However, the specific responses for the first category with a 3.78 average was that two responded with a 5, five with a 4, one with a 3, and one with a 1, where the one low response significantly pulled down the average given the small sample size.

Another aspect of the data that seems somewhat contradictory is that the use of hand-written contour diagrams scored correspondingly higher than the use of the software JIVE, where two or three of the responses were either a 1 or a 2 and brought down the JIVE average. One reason why that might have happened is that a couple of students appear to have missed a key lecture on how to use the software. As a result, they might not have adequately learned how to use the software correctly and thus the software might not have been as helpful to them.

Lastly, the students indicated that the use of contour diagrams and JIVE in the classroom helped them more than using either in their homework. At first, this seems somewhat counterintuitive, where it would seem that active learning on homework should provide more understanding than passive learning in the classroom. However, the reason for this might be similar to when a student thinks they understand how to solve a mathematical problem by observing an example on the board in the classroom, but they subsequently have difficulty when they attempt to actually solve a similar problem in the exercises in the back of the textbook. The result is that when working on the homework it might appear that one doesn't have as much understanding, but in reality it is the homework that actually helps one gain real understanding.

6. SUMMARY AND CONCLUSIONS

Which of the two methods should be used (drawing contours by hand or using JIVE) is largely a matter of preference or need by the instructor and/or students. The disadvantage of drawing is that it can be slow and tedious, which is a real advantage for using JIVE. However, using an automated system of JIVE has the disadvantage that a student might just passively point and click their way through the contours without actually thinking much about the process, whereas when students are drawing the contours, they are forced to think about the next step and draw it accordingly.

The authors of this paper actually use both methods. The drawing of contours can help pinpoint students' misconceptions when working with the instructor or a tutor. Not erasing deallocated contours can also be helpful to assess the students' understanding of the material early on in homework prior to the introduction of JIVE, and especially on quizzes and exams, where they do not have access to JIVE. On some medium-sized programs, the authors previously used prepared overhead transparencies with the contours already drawn, where the instructor could then quickly write in the necessary values and references in the pre-drawn spaces for the variables. With more complex programs the hand drawn method becomes untenable, however with the advent of JIVE, both medium-sized and more complex programs can be demonstrated easily due to JIVE's convenience, speed, and the ability to move forward and backward through the contours, at will. In the end, both contours and JIVE appear to have made a difference in students' understanding of various object-oriented concepts. It is expected that with further experience using both of these tools by the authors, that students should gain an even better understanding of object-oriented semantics in the future.

7. REFERENCES

[1] Gestwicki, P. V., and Jayaraman, B. 2005 Methodology and Architecture of JIVE, In Proceedings of the ACM Symposium on Software Visualization (SOFTVIS), (Oct. 2005), 95–104.

[2] Johnston, J. B. 1971 The Contour Model of Block Structured Processes, SIGPLAN Notices, 6, 2 (Feb. 1971), 55-72.

[3] MacLennan, B. J. 1987 *Principle of Programming Languages: Design, Evaluation, and Implementation*, Second Edition, Hotl, Rinehart & Winston.

[4] Malik, D. S., and Nair, P. S. 2003 *Data Structures Using Java*, Thomson Course Technology.

[5] Organick, E. I., ForSythe, A. I., and Plummer, R. P. 1978 *Programming Language Structures*, Academic Press.

[6] Wu, C. T. 2007 *A Comprehensive Introduction to Object-Oriented Programming with Java*, McGraw-Hill.

Interfaces First (and Foremost) With Java

Paolo A. G. Sivilotti
Computer Science and Engineering
The Ohio State University
Columbus, OH 43210
paolo@cse.ohio-state.edu

Matthew Lang
Mathematics and Computer Science
Moravian College
Bethlehem, PA 18018
lang@cs.moravian.edu

ABSTRACT

Abstraction is a critical concept that underlies many topics in computing science. For example, in software engineering, the distinction between a component's behavior and its implementation is fundamental. Java provides two constructs that correspond to precisely this distinction: A Java interface is a client's abstract view of a component's behavior, while a class is a concrete implementation of that same component. We have developed a course that introduces Java while following a discipline of diligently decomposing *every* component into these two separate linguistic elements. In this course, interfaces are given the same prominence as classes since both are needed for a complete component. This approach is helpful to students by providing: (i) a clear manifestation of the role of abstraction in software systems, and (ii) a framework that naturally motivates many good coding practices adopted by professional programmers.

Categories and Subject Descriptors

K.3.2 [**Computers and Education**]: Computer and Information Science Education—*computer science education*

General Terms

Design, Languages

Keywords

abstraction, concrete state, behavioral specification

1. INTRODUCTION

Abstraction is a key concept in computing science and software engineering [3,5–7]. Students encounter it, in some form, in practically every major topic including architecture, operating systems, complexity, data structures, and programming languages. Indeed, the ACM 2001 Computing Curricula recognizes the importance of abstraction at the pedagogical core of our discipline [22]. As one of its guiding principles, the Computer Science volume states (p. 12):

> All computing science students must learn to integrate theory and practice, to recognize the importance of abstraction, and to appreciate the value of good engineering design.

Ironically, the ubiquity of abstraction may actually be a barrier to its recognition and appreciation by students. It is such a common theme that educators may use it casually, without explicitly drawing attention to it.

We have developed an introduction to Java course based on the principle of deliberate and explicit application of behavioral abstraction. Although it is a first course in Java, it is not designed as a first course in programming. Students have completed an introductory sequence (using C++) before taking this course. Beyond teaching students about abstraction, this approach has the additional benefit of motivating and explaining several important (but subtle) concepts and professional best practices in Java.

From the beginning, and throughout the course, students think about components as having two distinct parts: an abstract client-side view and one or more concrete implementations. The two views are segregated in distinct program artifacts: the client-side view is given by a Java interface while each concrete realization is given by a Java class that implements the interface.

Of course, these are exactly the intended roles of these two language constructs. What is unique about our approach is our insistence that *all* components be decomposed into these two parts. Interfaces are used early, they are used throughout, and they are used prominently. This approach does not require special frameworks or IDEs. It simply leverages existing Java constructs.

This discipline of component decomposition enforces a clear separation of concerns. It creates an explicit scaffolding, supported by Java language constructs, for distinguishing behavioral abstraction from concrete implementation. This scaffolding can then buttress and augment students' understanding of abstraction and modularity.

The rest of the paper is organized as follows. Section 2 compares our work with similar curricular structures. Section 3 describes the separation discipline and its implications on documentation and testing. Section 4 sketches some exemplar homework assignments from this course. Section 5 lists many good coding practices that follow or are related to this discipline, while Section 6 outlines some difficulties in adopting the discipline in full. Finally, Sections 7 and 8 evaluate this curricular structure and conclude.

SIGCSE'10, March 10–13, 2010, Milwaukee, Wisconsin, USA.
Copyright 2010 ACM 978-1-60558-885-8/10/03 ...$10.00.

2. RELATED WORK

The order of topics in a first Java course has been a matter of considerable debate within the SIGCSE community. One popular structure is to introduce objects early, even as soon as day 1. This technique, known as "objects first", is exemplified by the BlueJ IDE which allows students to easily interact with objects and observe object state with minimal syntactic scaffolding [1, 12]. Although such structures can help build up student intuitions about object-oriented systems, they can mingle abstract and concrete state, blurring for students the distinction between the two.

An alternative structure, termed "components-first", emphasizes the separation of client-side view and implementer's view of components. Students begin by learning how to be clients of components, or APIs, or libraries. They subsequently learn how to implement these components. Examples of this approach include [11, 16, 18]. All of these approaches are similar to ours in philosophy in that they recognize the importance of distinguishing between the two views of a component. The differences are that our design leverages standard Java constructs and that the decomposition is applied consistently throughout the course.

The separation of abstract and concrete states for specification purposes is a well-known technique from abstract data types. Serious Java-based specification notations all support this separation. For example, Liskov & Guttag's book [14], JML [13], and the "Laboratory in Software Engineering" course at MIT, number 6.170 [17], all use specification fields in the documentation of a class to define object state and method behavior. These strategies rely on a documentation discipline of declaring specification variables, then writing pre and postconditions in terms of these variables, rather than fields in the implementation. Such disciplines, however, are difficult to strictly enforce and students may see the declaration of specification variables that closely match fields in the concrete implementation as an unnecessary extra step.

Perhaps the closest work to our own is [20], where the case is made for teaching interfaces *before* inheritance. This ordering is reflected in one popular introductory textbook [9] where interfaces and polymorphism come before inheritance. We agree with this ordering, but this is just one example of placing interfaces earlier in the curriculum and giving them greater prominence. Our approach advocates consistently decomposing components into interfaces and classes. For example, we present the Collections Framework entirely in terms of interfaces (List, Queue, Deque, Set, SortedSet). Iterators (and ListIterators) over these collections are interfaces as well, so the presentation can be quite sophisticated before the implementing classes are even discussed.

3. SEPARATION OF CONCERNS

One way to motivate the interface construct is simply as a mechanism for overcoming Java's single-inheritance restriction. Another option is to present the interface construct as simply a variant of the class construct, much like an abstract class, but with further restrictions (*e.g.*, it can contain only public members, no constructors, and no static methods). Such characterizations, as exemplified in [19], are common in introductory Java courses and serve to relegate the interface construct to secondary standing. In [19], interfaces are not even mentioned until p. 694, where they are covered in half a chapter. This treatment is similar to other popular introductory Java textbooks. While this treatment may reflect the use of Java interfaces in practice, it misses an opportunity to accomplish a larger pedagogical goal: teaching students about abstraction.

Our curricular approach, on the other hand, sets interfaces and classes on equal footing. Every software component is decomposed into two distinct artifacts: (i) a Java interface which is the (abstract) client-side view of the component, and (ii) a Java class which is the (concrete) implementation. Thus, the interface construct is present early and often. Both an interface and a class, together, are required for a complete component.

The notion of separating abstract and concrete state is a classic idea of abstract data types. Specification notations such as JML permit exactly this separation (through model or specification fields). What characterizes our "interfaces first and foremost" approach is the *requirement* of creating a Java interface; separation of abstraction from realization follows as a consequence. Since the interface is a distinct lexical scope from any implementing classes, students see the need for a clear and thorough description of the behavioral cover story in an implementation-neutral manner.

3.1 Documentation with Javadoc

In addition to all the standard Javadoc tags, interfaces and classes are documented in accordance with the distinct roles they serve in defining a component. Custom tags are used to further structure this information.

For interfaces, the documentation defines both the abstract state of the component and the behavior of each (public) method in terms of its effect on that abstract state. That is, the interface documentation must present a cover story that is understandable to a client with absolutely no knowledge of the component implementation (*i.e.*, class).

The cover story can be given with various degrees of formal rigor. We use a collection of custom tags as hooks for telling the client-side cover story:

`@mathmodel`: abstract fields whose types are mathematical concepts such as integers, sets, and strings

`@mathdef`: derived abstract fields that serve as convenient shorthands

`@constraint`: invariants on state

`@initially`: guarantees on the initial state

`@requires, @alters, @ensures`: classic behavioral descriptions of each method

The tag arguments can be written as formal mathematical expressions or informal prose. Either way, the cover story is isolated in a construct with no lexical connection to any underlying implementation. Thus, invariants, preconditions, and postconditions must perforce be written in terms of abstract state. This explicit separation reinforces for students the mental model of distinguishing the abstraction from the realization.

Classes are also carefully documented with Javadoc. In this case, however, the documentation is written in terms of concrete state (*i.e.*, private fields). Custom tags for class documentation include:

`@convention`: invariants on (concrete) state

`@correspondence`: the abstraction relation [21] for mapping (concrete) state to abstract fields

Behavior descriptions (requires and ensures clauses) of public methods are *not* written because this (client-side)

```
public abstract class BigNaturalTest {
  private BigNatural b;
  protected abstract
    BigNatural create(int value);

  @Test
  public void smallInitialization() {
    b = create(34);
    assertEquals("Two-digit initialization",
                 "34", b.toString());
  }

  //more test cases
}
```

Listing 1: Abstract test class with test cases

```
public class SlowBigNaturalTest
  extends BigNaturalTest {

  @Override
  protected BigNatural create(int value) {
      return new SlowBigNatural(value);
    }
}
```

Listing 2: Derived test class provides factory

documentation is already in the interface. On the other hand, private (helper) methods, which exist only in the class, are documented with `@requires`, `@alters`, `@ensures` tags as above. An important difference is that these descriptions are written in terms of concrete state. Again, this practice is easy for students to adopt because of the lexical scoping provided by the Java interface and class constructs.

3.2 Testing with JUnit

The use of JUnit to test software components can further leverage and reinforce the explicit separation of client-side view and implementation.

Black-box test cases are written in a standard JUnit test class using *only* the interface of the component under test. The test class includes one or more abstract factory methods that serve to generate instances for test cases to exercise. Each test case begins by calling these factory methods. Thus, the test class is completely independent of any particular implementation. Listing 1 illustrates part of a test class written in this manner, where `BigNatural` is an interface type.

The test class is an abstract class since it includes an abstract method. In order to execute tests, this class is extended and an implementation for the factory provided (see Listing 2). The derived test class does not provide any new test cases.[1] Of course, this style of test case coding is not new. The point is for students to observe and carefully respect the division achieved by separating abstraction from realization.

In summary, each component consists of an interface/class pair related by implementation. To test this component, a pair of test classes related by inheritance is used.

[1]Implementation-specific test cases could be provide in the derived test class, but this is the exception rather than the rule.

4. CANONICAL SAMPLE ASSIGNMENTS

A good early assignment is to develop an unbounded natural number component. The requirements are simple: A natural number can be initialized, incremented without bound, decremented when it is positive, and its value displayed as a string. The abstraction is clean. The implementation, however, is more complicated since it must account for an unbounded growth. Students quickly see that many design choices for implementing the concrete state exist, including an array of bytes and a string of characters. Furthermore, these design choices involve trade-offs in performance and complexity for implementing the small set of required behaviors.

A simple component such as this one is then refined over the subsequent assignments to illustrate concepts as covered in lectures, including documentation, testing, exceptions, comparability, and immutability. Comparing the (abstract) view of an unbounded natural number with Java's BigInteger is also a nice hook for introducing the subtleties of behavioral subtyping.

For an assignment related to subtyping, we have used a set of three components: Person, Student, and Faculty. All three can contribute to a university's scholarship fund and all three can enter a lottery for football tickets. Only the Java interface is given for each of these components. The components differ in how much prior contribution is required for eligibility in the ticket lottery and in the quality of seats the nondeterministic lottery might yield. Students are asked to identify subtyping relationships and to modify interface descriptions so new subtyping relationships exist. Again, the discipline of decomposing components into both an interface and a class clarifies for students the distinction between subtyping and inheritance [4].

5. GOOD CODING PRACTICES FOR JAVA

Beyond language syntax and structures, students should also learn effective idioms and strategies that support writing good code. There are many such strategies [2], some of which are quite subtle. Using an "interfaces first and foremost" approach clarifies the motivation and key concepts behind many of these strategies, making them easier for students to understand, remember, and appreciate.

Code to the interface.

Recommended practice is to prefer the use of interface types (over class types) for all declared types (*i.e.*, local variables, fields, parameters, and return types). The advantage of this practice is the resulting generality and loose-coupling of the code.

This good practice follows directly from our decomposition discipline. Clients, as far as possible, work only with interfaces.

Document the contract.

Recommended practice is to document method *behaviors* rather than implementations with Javadoc. This practice is sensible given the role Javadoc plays as client-side documentation for a class. Unfortunately, an uncomfortable tension exists between this ideal and the pragmatic observation that Javadoc, as a universally understood documentation notation, can also effectively be used to describe matters of interest to the implementer and future maintainers of an implementation. Indeed, a single command-line flag instructs Javadoc to produce documentation for all private members of a class too.

By decomposing every component into an interface and a class, students do not encounter this tension. They use Javadoc to produce all possible documentation for the interface and all possible documentation for the class, including private members. The former is for the client's consumption and the latter is for the implementer and maintainer.

Design getters/setters properly.

Using public methods to read and write private fields is certainly better than making the fields themselves public. Tools such as Eclipse can even generate these methods automatically for a class with private fields. The problem, however, with this style is that the concrete state drives the abstract behavior instead of the other way around [8].

When students work with an interface and class-based decomposition, however, they recognize the role of getters/setters as readers and writers of abstract state. Facilitating the implementation of these methods is just one factor in the design of a class's concrete state.

Make defensive copies.

Given the ubiquity of references in Java, it is easy for dangerous aliases to a class's concrete state to exist. For example, if a constructor assigns a private field `x` to an argument `y`, both the caller of the constructor and the object itself have references (through `y` and `x` respectively) to the same thing. This is dangerous since the caller of the constructor can make changes to the concrete state of the constructed object directly without going through its public interface.

The separation of interface and implementation does not, itself, mitigate the dangers of aliasing in Java. It does, however, simplify the presentation of these dangers. If students are comfortable with simultaneously considering both the abstract and concrete state, and with maintaining the correspondence between the two, the dangers of aliasing are easily illustrated and quickly appreciated.

Use exceptions properly.

The proper use of exceptions is a matter of much debate, even amongst seasoned Java developers. The choice of whether exceptions should be checked or unchecked, and what kind of exception should be used is often a subtle design choice involving many trade-offs.

Some aspects of exception design, however, follow directly from the disciplined decomposition of our approach. For example, the need to catch an exception and then re-throw it as a *new* exception, possibly of a different type, is clear. The method signatures, including checked exceptions, that appear in the interface must make sense to the client in terms of the abstract cover story. Students recognize when an exception reveals aspects specific to a particular implementation.

As for when to use exceptions, advice is often generic and even circular, for example: Use exceptions for exceptional situations. A better guide is to clearly characterize situations where exceptions are useful. For example, if the client can not unilaterally guarantee the precondition of a method, exceptions are appropriate. A classic example is the existence of a file. Because the code runs concurrently with a real file system in which files may be created and deleted, a client can not know whether the file exists when the method it calls actually starts to execute. Appreciating this lesson is easier if the students are comfortable with behavioral specifications.

Respect behavioral subtyping.

Behavioral subtypes can be dynamically substituted for their supertypes without affecting the correctness of client code [15]. This substitution is sound only when the subtype's invariant and ensures clauses are covariant, while its requirements are contravariant. Since class inheritance involves coupling of concrete implementations, subtyping is best modeled in Java as a relationship between interfaces. A discipline of always declaring Java interfaces is therefore helpful in creating a context for presenting subtyping and its implications.

6. CHALLENGES

In Java, the interface construct corresponds most closely to a purely abstract, client-side view of a component. A Java interface, however, can not include a constructor. That is, an interface is actually the client-side view of an *instance* of a component, and the creation of (other) instances is not generally part of that behavior. On the other hand, some clients do need to create instances. Ideally, such clients would only need the name of the implementing class, nothing else. Unfortunately, without a constructor in the interface, the implementing class must be consulted to confirm the existence of a constructor with the proper signature.

There are several ways to circumvent this difficulty. One is to use a creation pattern in which a separate component serves as a factory. The interface of that factory component defines the valid signatures for instantiating the original component. Apart from leaving a bootstrapping problem (how does the client know how to create a factory?), this solution is somewhat cumbersome since it requires components to consist of 4 artifacts: an interface/class pair for the core component and an interface/class pair for the factory.

Another approach is to require all classes to have a zero-argument constructor. This strategy, however, is limited when it comes to immutable types (which typically do not have zero-argument constructors). Our compromise is to document in the interface the signatures of constructors that implementing classes are expected to have.

7. EVALUATION

The "interfaces first and foremost" approach described here has been the basis for a course that has been offered 5 times, with a total enrollment of 156 students. Survey results indicate the course was well-received by students. The course has averaged 4.7 for "overall rating" (on a Likert-type response scale with 5 being the highest) and 4.2 for "relative ranking compared to other courses in computer science".

Beyond student reaction, however, a better measure for the success of such an approach is the degree to which it transforms students' thinking and instills sound principles of the discipline. To this end, we have followed the cohort of students from our early pilot offerings that subsequently enrolled in the "programming in the large" software engineering course (an existing course that entails significant software design, development, testing, and documentation all done as part of a team). In that second course, students are free to use whatever language they prefer and most choose C++ (the language used in the introductory sequence).

The followed cohort consisted of 85 CS majors. Their work was qualitatively different than that of their peers, according to the instructors for that subsequent course. The recognition and clear application of separation between abstract behavior and concrete representation was present in all of their work (and not their peers). This separation was manifested in their design, documentation, and testing. On surveys, they reported feeling better prepared for a significant software development project than their peers.

8. CONCLUSIONS

In the "real world", Java programmers do not define an interface for every class. While the benefit of encapsulation and information hiding offered by OO are widely recognized, the effort of defining two separate structures for each type is usually too onerous in a deadline-driven environment. Thus, professional programmers often work with just a class and intermingle the realization with its abstraction. As a mental model, the two are hopefully kept somewhat distinct, but this distinction is usually not directly reflected in the code (beyond visibility modifiers such as private and public).

For students of computing science, however, this intermingling should be avoided. Not only does a clear separation help to motivate a wide variety of good coding practices, it also provides an exemplar for the general notion of abstraction, which plays such a fundamental and cross-cutting role in our discipline.

We have used this strategy in the development of a new class that follows an introductory course sequence. Students come to the class knowing imperative programming but not Java. We are optimistic that this strategy could also be adopted for the intro level, especially given the success reported from other efforts in that direction [10,11,18,20]. For example, the materials for this course have been adopted at Clemson and initial reaction there has been positive.

9. ACKNOWLEDGMENTS

This material is based upon work supported in part by the National Science Foundation under Grant No. 0931669.

10. REFERENCES

[1] D. J. Barnes and M. Kölling. *Objects First with Java: A Practical Introduction Using BlueJ.* Prentice Hall, 2002.

[2] J. Bloch. *Effective Java.* Prentice Hall, 2nd edition, 2008.

[3] T. Colburn and G. Shute. Abstraction in computer science. *Minds Mach.*, 17(2):169–184, 2007.

[4] W. R. Cook, W. Hill, and P. S. Canning. Inheritance is not subtyping. In *POPL '90: Proceedings of the 17th ACM SIGPLAN-SIGACT symposium on Principles of programming languages*, pages 125–135, New York, NY, USA, 1990. ACM.

[5] D. Gries. A principled approach to teaching OO first. In *SIGCSE '08: Proceedings of the 39th SIGCSE technical symposium on Computer science education*, pages 31–35, New York, NY, USA, 2008. ACM.

[6] O. Hazzan and J. Kramer. The role of abstraction in software engineering. In *ICSE Companion '08: Companion of the 30th international conference on Software engineering*, pages 1045–1046, New York, NY, USA, 2008. ACM.

[7] P. B. Henderson, D. Baldwin, V. Dasigi, M. Dupras, J. Fritz, D. Ginat, D. Goelman, J. Hamer, L. Hitchner, W. Lloyd, J. Bill Marion, C. Riedesel, and H. Walker. Striving for mathematical thinking. *SIGCSE Bull.*, 33(4):114–124, 2001.

[8] A. Holub. Why getter and setter methods are evil. http://www.javaworld.com/javaworld/jw-09-2003/jw-0905-toolbox.html, September 2003.

[9] C. Horstmann. *Big Java.* John Wiley & Sons, 3rd edition, 2008.

[10] E. Howe, M. Thornton, and B. W. Weide. Components-first approaches to CS1/CS2: Principles and practice. In *SIGCSE '04: Proceedings of the 35th SIGCSE technical symposium on Computer science education*, pages 291–295, New York, NY, 2004. ACM.

[11] A. Koenig and B. E. Moo. *Accelerated C++: Practical Programming by Example.* C++ In-Depth Series. Addison-Wesley, 2000.

[12] M. Kölling, B. Quig, A. Patterson, and J. Rosenberg. The BlueJ system and its pedagogy. *Journal of Computer Science Education*, 13(4):249–268, December 2003.

[13] G. T. Leavens, K. R. M. Leino, E. Poll, C. Ruby, and B. Jacobs. JML: notations and tools supporting detailed design in Java. Technical Report TR #00-15, Iowa State University, August 2000.

[14] B. Liskov and J. Guttag. *Program Development in Java: Abstraction, Specification, and Object-Oriented Design.* Addison-Wesley Longman Publishing Co., Inc., Boston, MA, USA, 2000.

[15] B. H. Liskov and J. M. Wing. A behavioral notion of subtyping. *ACM Trans. Program. Lang. Syst.*, 16(6):1811–1841, 1994.

[16] T. J. Long, B. W. Weide, P. Bucci, D. S. Gibson, J. Hollingsworth, M. Sitaraman, and S. Edwards. Providing intellectual focus to CS1/CS2. *SIGCSE Bull.*, 30(1):252–256, 1998.

[17] Massachusetts Institute of Technology. 6.170: Lab in software engineering. Course notes on web, Fall 2007. http://www.mit.edu/~6.170/.

[18] H. Roumani. Practice what you preach: Full separation of concerns in CS1/CS2. *SIGCSE Bull.*, 38(1):491–494, 2006.

[19] W. Savitch. *Absolute Java.* Pearson Education, 3rd edition, 2008.

[20] A. Schmolitzky. "Objects first, interfaces next" or interfaces before inheritance. In *OOPSLA '04: Companion to the 19th annual ACM SIGPLAN conference on Object-oriented programming systems, languages, and applications*, pages 64–67, New York, NY, USA, 2004. ACM.

[21] M. Sitaraman, B. W. Weide, and W. F. Ogden. On the practical need for abstraction relations to verify abstract data type representations. *IEEE Trans. Softw. Eng.*, 23(3):157–170, 1997.

[22] The Joint Task Force on Computing Curricula. Computing curricula 2001. *Journal on Educational Resources in Computing (JERIC)*, 1(3es):1–240, 2001.

Performance of Python CS1 Students in Mid-level non-Python CS Courses

Richard J. Enbody and William F. Punch
Department of Computer Science and Engineering
Michigan State University
East Lansing, Michigan
[enbody,punch]@cse.msu.edu

ABSTRACT

If you change the CS1 language to Python, what is the impact on the rest of the curriculum? In earlier work we examined the impact of changing CS1 from C++ to Python while leaving CS2 in C++. We found that Python-prepared CS1 students fared no differently in CS2 than students whose CS1 course was in C++, even though CS2 was taught in C++ and covered the same topics as in previous years. Was that an anomaly? What happens in the next tier of courses? When our CS1 was first changed to Python there were many students who had taken CS1 in C++ still in the system. The result is that there is a cadre of students with either CS1 in Python or CS1 in C++ moving together through our curriculum. This one-time occurrence is an opportunity to study the students with many variables fixed. Our next tier of courses is a C-based computer organization course, a C++ based object-oriented software design course, and a data structures course. We found that the students who started with Python fared as well as the CS1 C++ students. As before, the best predictor of performance was their college GPA. Python versus C++ CS1 preparation was not a predictor of performance in any course. We conclude again that in our C++ based curriculum changing CS1 to Python had no negative impact on student performance and did not require any significant change in those subsequent courses.

Categories and Subject Descriptors

K.3.2 [**Computers and Education**]: Computer and Information Science Education—*computer science education, curriculum*

General Terms

Measurement, Experimentation

Keywords

CS1, Python, curriculum, intro. to programming

1. INTRODUCTION

If you want to start a vigorous debate (fight) in the field of computer science, ask "What is the best first programming language?" Not only does the question generate passionate debate, but it is also a recurring question on the Internet. For example, during the summer of 2009 there were at least four discussions on Slashdot[1], a popular website for computer folk, that started or devolved to that topic.

As teachers of first-time programmers, it is both confusing and understandable as to why this debate persists. Confusing because the programming language is typically not the biggest problem the first-time programmer faces. Rather, most first-time programmers struggle with problem solving, turning a problem into a series of steps to effectively solve it. Understandable because the obvious, novel element of a first programming class is the learning of a new topic, a programming language.

The question before us here is: what is the impact on the curriculum of changing the language in the first programming course? In particular, what effect(s) does it have on the students and what changes must be made in subsequent courses, if any?

2. IT'S PROBLEM SOLVING

We embarked on this path because we believe that an important goal of a first course in computer science should be the ability to use programming as a useful problem-solving tool. After much discussion, we have decided that our goal can be rather simply stated. We hope that, subsequent to our course, a student would have the following thought: *"Hey, I'll just write a program to solve that!"* That is, after completing an introductory course a student should have a new tool in their kit, and one that they will actually use in school and later.

After fifteen years of teaching C++ in CS1 it was apparent to us that one semester of C++ does **not** provide students with that kind of problem solving tool, one which would foster the above thought. C++ requires more exposure than a single semester to be effective in this way. This need for effectiveness in a single semester becomes more important given that we have seen non-majors become the majority in our CS1 course. A typical CS1 class at MSU has about 25% CS majors, and about 20% other engineering students leaving more than 55% as majors from all walks of the university. As we have not been able to define course outcomes, that would be different for non-majors, we have resisted splitting

[1]http://www.slashdot.org

the class. In addition, since most non-majors only want one course in programming we would serve them best by providing them with a useful tool when they were done. Wouldn't that also be good for majors?

Redefining course goals in this way opens up a variety of possibilities for the first language. However, the question is: what is the impact of changing the CS1 language on the rest of the CS curriculum? In our case, the curriculum has been C++ based for fifteen years.

We had multiple goals:

- Students should have a useful tool after one semester (and actually use it outside of this class).
- CS majors should be prepared for a C++ based curriculum.

In our SIGCSE 2009 paper [2], we showed that the Python-prepared students did as well as the non-Python prepared students in a C++ based CS2 course. What happens after that? Oldham [5] noted that, after adopting Python in CS1, they observed no difference in ETS exam scores in their graduates, but provided no measurements. Here we present objective measures to the question: what happens next?

3. USEFUL TOOL?

Because we raised the point, let's briefly digress to look at the first goal: students should have a useful tool. We have not yet found a hard and fast measure for this goal. However, anecdotal evidence indicates that it is being met to some extent. In fifteen years of teaching CS1 with C++ neither of us ever had a non-major ask for help in applying programming to some problem they were solving outside of class. In the two years of teaching Python in CS1 there have been many such requests. Here are a few from the most recent semester:

- wrote a slot-machine game.
- wrote a program to calculate and keep track of his golf handicap.
- wrote a program for a science lab.
- wrote a program to rearrange a spreadsheet for work. Someone had made a spreadsheet with one column, 3600 rows, and each cell had 37 (!) pieces of information. She wrote a program to split the data into columns.

In each case, the student came by for some guidance. In the spreadsheet example, the student was having difficulty with the CSV file. She had found Python's csv module, but forgot the "U" option when opening the Excel-generated CSV file.

Each semester has brought students to us who had the problem mostly solved, but needed a little help. Of course, we didn't hear from students who did not need help. Maybe the students with C++ never needed any help, but that doesn't seem to be a reasonable explanation for what we are seeing.

3.1 Python

What about Python helps students have a useful tool after one semester of study? We believe that Python has lower "cognitive load." By this, we mean that the features made available by Python tend to directly help in solving common problems. Furthermore, the focus of Python is typically "One way to do it," avoiding overload of the introductory student with too many options. With a lower load for learning the language, students can focus more on problem solving. We cannot yet prove that is the case, but that is what we have observed.

For example, in Python you can iterate through nearly every data structure, either built-in or downloaded, using a **for** statement. We introduce strings early as a first data structure and instruct the students on how **for** iterates through each element of a string, that is, each character. When later faced with new data structures such as lists, tuples, dictionaries, and sets, the students already know how to examine all the elements in that structure: they use the **for** as before. The concept even extends beyond traditional data structures. A file can be iterated through in the same way, by default grabbing a line at at time using the **for** iterator. Learning "one thing" that applies so broadly makes the student's job easier, focusing less on new language issues for every problem and focusing more on applying what they already know to a new problem.

Another aspect is the direct availability of useful data structures and their associated methods such as dictionaries, lists, and sets. These are not "advanced" topics to be taught later, but are integral to Python's approach and, as such, allow one to crack difficult problems earlier. Python's string handling facilities are one example. They allow one to process text easily, especially text files. With tools like these, it is easier to tackle problems early on using real world data from publicly available sources.

In the tone of [3] we've had students work with real data such as stock market data analysis, building a classifier for breast cancer data, digging through sports data to figure out who was the "best" player, "six degrees of Kevin Bacon," etc. In addition, Python provides powerful tools for both drawing and graphing.

And we can do all that in one semester using Python!

We have summarized our experience by writing a CS1 textbook using Python [7].

3.1.1 Other benefits for CS majors

Obviously, one benefit of Python in CS1 is that CS majors get experience in a second programming language—something that is generally agreed to be good [4, 1]. In that tenor, Python's ability to work as a high-level scripting language can be useful in subsequent courses, especially in how well it plays with operating systems (e.g. using the os module) and with other languages.

4. IMPACT ON CURRICULUM

How do CS majors fare, especially in subsequent courses?

The sequence in our CS curriculum begins with CS1 and CS2—the courses we considered in our earlier study. The third course is discrete structures, but that is unrelated to programming so we have not included it. The next three courses: computer organization, object-oriented software design, and algorithms & data structures complete the six-course core of our curriculum. Here are their official descriptions:

	CSE 320	CSE 331	CSE 335	Total
Count	20 (18)	17 (10)	30(9)	51(23)
Mean Grade	2.75(2.94)	2.77(2.85)	3.15(3.06)	
Mean GPA	3.24(3.31)	3.26 (3.30)	3.31 (3.29)	

Table 1: Results by course. Python students are shown in parentheses, non-Python students without parentheses.

CSE 320 Computer Organization and Architecture Boolean algebra and digital logic. Combinational and sequential circuits. Representations of data and instructions. Architecture and major components of computer systems. Assembly language programming and interfacing to high level languages. Assembler and linker processing.

CSE 331 Algorithms and Data Structures Linear data structures, trees, graphs and algorithms which operate on them. Fundamental algorithms for searching, sorting, string matching, graph problems. Design and analysis of algorithms.

CSE 335 Object-oriented Software Design Development of large software products, libraries, and product families. Object-oriented programming using inheritance and polymorphism. Design methods. Specification and the use of contracts to design reliable software. Configuration management and life-cycle issues.

These courses are appropriate for our study for the following reasons:

CSE 320 Computer Organization The medium for interfacing with and studying assembly language is C. Part of this course looks at how various data structures are handled in assembly, and how function calls and operating system calls are handled in assembly. The result is quite a bit of C programming.

CSE 331 Alg & Data Structures While the theoretical analysis is language independent, it can be useful to also consider the algorithms and data structures in some language. In this case, the language used is C++, so homework that involves implementation is coded in C++.

CSE 335 OOP Design While design is a critical component of this course, there is also intensive C++ programming to get a sense of programming in the large.

4.1 Analysis

To answer the question of how Python-prepared students fared in subsequent courses we collected data on the students. We got approval for the study of students from our Institutional Review Board (IRB), and using the approved process we received permission from 74 students who represented most of the 98 individuals across the three courses. There were 23 students who took CS1 with Python and 51 other students, most of whom took CS1 with C++, but a couple transferred in CS1 courses based on Java. The breakdown is shown in Table 1 with the number of participants in each course and their associated mean course grade (four-point scale), with the value in parentheses used to indicate the Python group. Many of the students were enrolled in more than one course so the total's column is not the sum of the individual courses. The semester was Fall 2008—when the students from the Fall 2007 Python-based CS1 course reached that level.

The question we wished to ask was whether the difference in course grade mean was significant between the two populations in the three courses.

Mean Tested	CSE 320	CSE 331	CSE 335
p for course-grade mean	0.57	0.83	0.82
p for GPA mean	0.56	0.85	0.88

Table 2: p values for the indicated means for the Python versus the non-Python samples.

4.2 t-test

For the analysis we used the *R* statistical language [6]. By default, the *R* two-sample t-test uses the null hypothesis that the means of the two populations are equal. We look for a p value at the level of 0.05 or less to reject that hypothesis and accept the alternate hypothesis that there is a difference in the means. The results are shown below for the three classes:

1. A significant difference of the mean course grade for students who took Python in CS1 versus students who did not take Python in CS1.

2. A significant difference of the mean student GPA for students who took Python in CS1 versus students who did not take Python in CS1.

Table 2 lists the p values. Because the p values are greater than 0.05 for all three grade means and GPA means, we do not reject the hypothesis that the means are different, so we conclude that the means of Python students and non-Python students are not significantly different.

Therefore, the t-test indicates that there was no significant difference in the mean grades of Python versus non-Python students in any of the three courses. Maybe the Python students were smarter. However, there was also no significant difference in the mean GPAs associated with Python versus non-Python students, meaning that (measured by GPA, at least) the Python students were not "smarter" than the other students.

4.3 Linear regression analysis

We continued with our statistical analysis of the three groups. Using *R*, we wanted to see if any of the following factors were useful as a linear predictor of performance for the class grade:

1. ACT-Math score

2. GPA

3. Python in CS1 vs. non-Python in CS1

Factor	CSE 320	CSE 331	CSE 335
ACT-Math	0.31	0.44	0.09
Python	0.60	0.99	0.60
GPA	0.00	0.00	0.00

Table 3: p values for the three β factors in each of the three courses.

Using the linear modeling package *lm*, we created the following linear model used R to approximate the shown β factors:

$$CourseGrade = \beta_0 + \beta_1 ACT\_Math + \beta_2 GPA + \beta_3 Python\_vs\_nonPython$$

What the linear model results report are the β factor approximations, plus a p value for each factor. The p values are again used to reject the null hypothesis, which in this case is that the particular β value is 0. The p value results are listed in Table 3. For the ACT_Math and Python factors, the p values are all greater than 0.05 so we do not reject the hypothesis that they are 0. That is, we conclude that they are 0, so they do not contribute significantly to the course grade. However, for the GPA factor the p values are all less than 0.05 so we reject the hypothesis that they are 0. That is, we conclude that they are different than 0 so they contribute significantly to the course grade.

Therefore, the linear regression analysis listed in Table 3 indicates that only GPA was a significant predictor of course performance. The other factors, Python vs. non-Python and ACT_Math, were not deemed significantly different from 0, meaning that they were not useful for predication.

5. CONCLUSION

When we proposed replacing C++ with Python in CS1, the question was raised about the impact of that change on the rest of the curriculum. Because students with C++ CS1 preparation remained in the system, this moment provided an opportunity to compare the Python vs. non-Python students. In our previous work we looked at their performance in a C++ CS2 course and found no difference. In this study we looked at the next level of courses, and found again that the Python-prepared students performed as well as the non-Python students in spite of the fact that these courses were based on C and C++.

We conclude that starting students with Python has not had a negative impact within a C++ based curriculum. It would have been nice to conclude that the Python students did better in these courses, but the evidence does not appear to support that hypothesis.

6. REFERENCES

[1] ABET. Criteria for accrediting computing programs: 2010-2011 cycles. http://www.abet.org, 2009.

[2] R. J. Enbody, W. F. Punch, and M. McCullen. Python cs1 as preparation for c++ cs2. In *SIGCSE '09: Proceedings of the 40th ACM technical symposium on Computer science education*, pages 116–120, New York, NY, USA, 2009. ACM.

[3] N. Jukic and P. Gray. Using real data to invigorate student learning. *SIGCSE Bull.*, 40(2):6–10, 2008.

[4] R. P. Loui. In praise of scripting: Real programming pragmatism. *IEEE Computer*, 41(7):22–26, July 2008.

[5] J. D. Oldham. What happens after python in cs1? *J. Comput. Small Coll.*, 20(6):7–13, 2005.

[6] G. project. R statistical language.

[7] W. F. Punch and R. J. Enbody. *The Practice of Computing Using Python*. Pearson: Addison-Wesley, New York, 2010.

Integrating Sustainability Into Undergraduate Computing Education

Yu Cai
Michigan Technological University
Houghton, MI, USA
cai@mtu.edu

ABSTRACT

In the past few years sustainability and green computing have received tremendous interest across the world. Computing plays a critical role in our society, thus it has a special responsibility for sustainability and green movement. In this paper, we advocate sustainability integration into undergraduate computing education. We present three sustainability integration strategies, our efforts to develop a green computing course and learning modules, and course evaluation. We believe that sustainability integration will help prepare our graduates with computing competencies, multi-disciplinary knowledge, and computational thinking to create a sustainable future.

Categories and Subject Descriptors

K.3.2 [**Computers and Education**]: Computer and Information Science Education

General Terms

Human Factors

1. INTRODUCTION

"*To me, going green is the great challenge - and opportunity - of the 21st century*", said by columnist and best-selling author, Thomas L. Friedman [7]. President Obama's economic stimulus plan also has a strong green hue. The plan would put half a million Americans to work on energy projects and push America toward a green and sustainable future [19].

People around the world are increasingly aware of and concerned about sustainability and green movement. Computing plays a critical role in our society, thus it has a special responsibility for social development and welfare of human beings - not only for this generation but also for future generations. Despite the continuous efforts in the computing community, today's undergraduate computing education often fails to address our social and environmental responsibility [12].

In this paper, we present our efforts to revitalize undergraduate computing education by understanding, advocating, integrating, and assessing the study of sustainability in computing education; by doing so, we will better prepare our graduates with computing competencies, multi-disciplinary knowledge, and computational thinking to create a sustainable future.

2. WHAT IS SUSTAINABILITY?

In the past few decades sustainability has received tremendous interest across the world. Sustainability is often defined as "meeting the needs of the current generation without compromising the ability of future generations to meet their own needs" [18]. The term is often used in reference to the potential longevity of environmental and human ecological systems, such as climate, agriculture, forestry, and human communities in general.

The widespread adoption of Information Technology(IT) has thrown the spotlight on the environmental and social impact of computing systems and IT infrastructure. For example, the power consumption of data centers in the U.S. doubled between 2000 and 2005, and will likely triple again soon [25]. In 2006, the U.S. Congress passed bills to raise the IT industry's role in energy and environmental policy to the national level [2].

Green computing is the study and practice of using computing resources in an energy efficient and eco-friendly manner [11, 17]. It is a holistic approach that stretches from power, to waste, to application, to education. Green computing represents a dramatic change in the priority of IT industry from the traditional economic cost/benefit model to the new sustainable model by mutually advancing economic, environmental, and social goals.

3. WHY STUDY SUSTAINABILITY?

Sustainability is and will continue to be an important issue for the next few decades. Many professional groups including the Royal Academy of Engineering and the National Academy of Engineering have already addressed sustainability through their professional guidelines and codes [21, 22]. The Accreditation Board for Engineering and Technology (ABET) also called a shift towards sustainability education in engineering disciplines [6]. As educators in the computing discipline, now it is our responsibility to integrate sustainability into undergraduate computing education.

SIGCSE'10, March 10–13, 2010, Milwaukee, Wisconsin, USA.
Copyright 2010 ACM 978-1-60558-885-8/10/03 ...$10.00.

Unfortunately, despite the clear calls, today's computing education acts slow to such a shift towards sustainability education [10]. In Association for Computing Machinery (ACM) computing curricula [4], there is no mention of sustainability or similar terms until the latest update in 2008. Researchers have identified barriers and challenges in sustainability development in computing education [12]. Some of the barriers include: a fundamental lack of interest, a lack of staff training, a lack of tradition, and a lack of priority.

We argue that sustainability and green computing study in computing is not only critical and imminent for the long term benefit of human beings, but also has the potential to attract more students to computing, increase workforce diversity, and improve the retention rate of computing students.

One of the major challenges faced by the engineering education community is the declining proportion of students choosing engineering as a profession. From 1994 to 2004, enrollment in U.S. higher education institutions increased by 20%, however the number of engineering degrees conferred remained relatively flat [5], with little diversity overall [20].

Computing education faces an even more serious enrollment problem. The percentage of incoming undergraduates who indicated they would major in computer science declined by 70% between 2000 and 2005 among all U.S. higher education institutions [26]. Research [13] indicates that it is partly attributed to students' perceptions that computing is boring, geeky and asocial.

According to a survey of 3,000 teens, the 14-18 year olds are committed to equality, and prefer companies that act responsibly for a clean environment [23]. According to the Women's Experiences in College Engineering Project, women leave engineering programs not because of poor academic performance, but because of a lack of connection to their goals of helping society [8]. These studies suggest that young people don't choose engineering in part because this profession is perceived to have little connection to improve the world around them.

Recent research indicates that sustainability is attracting the attention of students around the world. Some studies suggest that sustainability curricula may increase the recruitment and retention of women and minority in engineering [27]. Successful examples of sustainability integration include chemistry [27], civil engineering [16], environmental engineering [14] and mechanical engineering [9].

The authors in [12] examine the status of education for sustainability in computing. Despite the importance of this topic, it seems that there is little room left for sustainability study in the over-crowded computing curricula [15]. The existing work on this topic is limited and isolated. For example, several computing courses with sustainability integration are described in [3, 10]. A software engineering course using a sustainable approach is introduced in [28]. A sustainability infused Computer-Human Interaction(CHI) activity is described in [1].

Although there is no direct evidence to support sustainability integration in computing, the literature review indicates that there is sufficient evidence to show the positive impacts of sustainability integration in non-computing engineering disciplines.

It is our contention that by adding sustainability to computing education will escalate interest in computing among those socially-minded young adults, both male and female. Sustainability studies will help students realize their social and environmental responsibility, motivate them to serve the community, and make the world a better place to live. By being rewarded with a feeling of accomplishment and making differences, more students, including women and minorities, will be attracted to computing, and the retention rate of college students may also be improved.

4. CURRICULUM DEVELOPMENT

4.1 Barriers and challenges

We list a group of barriers for sustainability integration into computing education (identified by [24]) along with our comments.

• A fundamental lack of interest. IT industry has a poor track record in term of environmental protection and sustainability development, so does computing education. However, the sharp rising cost of energy in the past few years has forced people to re-think their IT investment strategy and adopt energy-efficient computing. Principles such as economic viability, social responsibility, and environmental impact must be taken into account as a whole when designing, implementing and managing computing systems.

• Staff training. Lack of training and expertise is indeed a major obstacle. However, sustainability is an on-going research/education topic in many other engineering disciplines. Through true collaboration, computing professionals can borrow expertise, lesson learned, and good practice from other fields. Professional workshops, seminars and online tools will also bring people from different disciplines together and introduce sustainability to computing professionals.

• A lack of tradition. Indeed this should not be a barrier since computing itself is a young and fast-growing discipline. The question that the computing education community should ask is: how can we take the lead in the shift from traditional cost/benefit model to the new sustainable model instead of being left behind?

• A lack of priority. There are many important issues in computing education. It seems not too much space left for a "buzz" word like sustainability. However, we hope that this paper may help people realize that sustainability has the potential to revitalize computing education. This will move sustainability to the top priority list in computing education.

4.2 Solutions and strategies

Admittedly, some arguments against sustainability study in computing are legitimate and based on reality, for example, lack of funding and support, over crowded computing curricula. In this paper, we propose three approaches for sustainability integration in computing (Figure 1).

The first option is probably the most straight-forward approach, by developing a new course named "green computing". The new course will cover selected sustainability and green computing topics.

The second option is a low-cost, modular, progressive approach. We will design and develop independent green computing learning modules and projects. These modules and projects can be easily plugged into the existing computer courses with little or no cost. This approach is ideal for sustainability topics which don't require transformative changes in computing courses.

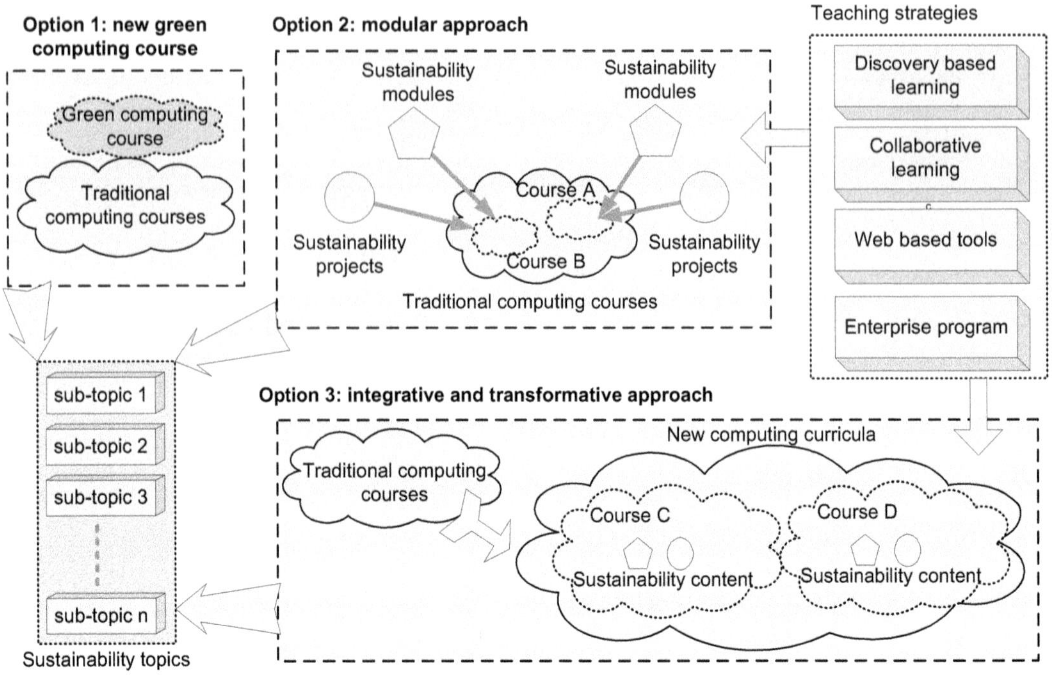

Figure 1: Options and strategies for sustainability integration in computing.

The third option is an integrative and transformative approach. We hope to be able to completely re-design some computing courses with sustainability as one of the top priorities. For example, there exists a significant body of research/education work on computer architecture, operating system, database system, and resource management which largely focus on pure performance or cost. By promoting energy to a first-class resource, people will gain new insights and findings on how to achieve energy saving in the current IT systems.

4.3 Development of a green computing course

An undergraduate course SAT4541 - Green Computing & Network Services was developed by the author, Dr. Yu Cai at Michigan Technological University.

The SAT4541 course covered the following green computing topics:
1) General concepts and principles of sustainability and green computing.
2) Background and motivation for green computing.
3) Server virtualization technology, including what is virtualization, how virtualization works, typical products like VMware and Xen, how to use virtualization to save energy.
4) Green data center, including why saving energy is important to data centers, common energy saving practices in data centers.
5) Power-aware computing, including energy-efficient hardware innovation, energy-efficient software innovation, memory and disk management, benchmarking and assessment.
6) Energy information system and smart power management.
7) Electronic waste disposal and recycle,
8) Regulatory compliance

The new SAT4541 course was designed to piggyback on an existing 3-credit network service course. The 1st half of the semester is on advanced network topics (such as directory services), and the 2nd half of the semester is on green computing. This design allows us to infuse green computing in the overly-crowded computing curriculum.

The new SAT4541 course was taught in Fall 2008 (35 students), Summer 2009 (7 students), and will be taught again in Fall 2009 (estimated 37 students). Most students are seniors majored in Computer Network and System Administration (CNSA) at Michigan Technological University. A small portion of the students are from CS, ECE and bioinformatics.

4.4 Development of green computing course modules

We developed the following green computing modules that can be used independently in other computing courses.

1) Green computing introductory module: including general concepts and principles of sustainability and green computing, background and motivation for green computing, electronic waste disposal and recycle, and regulatory compliance. This module can be used in a CS introductory course or a CS ethical course.

2) Server virtualization module: including what is virtualization, how virtualization works, typical products, and how to use virtualization to save energy. This module can be used in an operating system course or other related courses.

The server virtualization module was used in SAT4600 - Advanced Internet Technology in Spring 2009 (45 students). More course modules will be developed and tested in the future.

4.5 Development of green computing senior design projects.

The following green computing senior design projects have been developed:

1) Solar Powered Computer: this project is to design and build a prototype to use solar energy as power supply for a laptop computer. The system includes a solar panel, a battery, and interface to a laptop. Solar technology is still an expensive technology today, and the purpose of the project is to build a proof of concept prototype.

2) Measurement of energy consumption curves in computing systems. This project is to study the energy consumption curves of real world computer systems. The team also developed a prototype of wireless watts meters which can collect energy consumption data wirelessly from multiple sources.

Table 1: Exit survey questions and the average responses in SAT4541 green computing course

Section 1. As a result of your work in this class, how well do you think that you now understand each of the following?	
1. What is green computing?	4.3
2. What is sustainability?	4.6
3. How to set up virtual machines and optimize their performance?	4.6
4. What is energy information system?	4.2
5. What are the best practices to build energy efficient data centers?	3.7
6. How to optimize power management?	3.7
7. How to save energy in computing hardware?	3.9
8. What is power-aware computing?	3.8
9. How to recycle e-waste?	3.1
10. How to ensure regulatory compliance?	3.2
Section 2. How much of the following do you think you will remember and carry with you into other classes or aspects of your life?	
1. Understanding the concepts of sustainability and green computing	3.7
2. Feeling comfortable with virtual machines	4.4
3. Feeling comfortable with other major techniques in green computing	3.9
4. Understanding how green computing may be applied to other fields	3.7
5. Feeling comfortable to use computational thinking	3.9
6. I have strong enthusiasm in green computing	4.4
7. I am confidence in my ability to do computing	4.3
8. I want to work for a company who really cares about green movement	3.4
9. I want to help improving the world around me with green techniques	3.6
10. I want to learn more green technologies	3.6

5. COURSE ASSESSMENT

Students who took the SAT4541 green computing course completed an exit survey to measure changes on content knowledge, attitude, and behavior on a voluntary base. Preliminary survey data was collected and analyzed. The response ratio is 83% (35 responses out of 42 students who took SAT4541 in Fall 2008 and Summer 2009).

There are more than 60 questions in the SAT4541 exit survey. To save space, only selected questions and average response results are showed in the following table 1.

For each survey question, there are five scales: 1- No help, 2- A little help, 3- Moderate help, 4- Much help, 5- Very much help. Students check one value for each question on each scale. If the question is not applicable, check "0 - N/A". Students may add a comment for any item in the text box at the end of the survey.

The official course rating of SAT4541 is 4.7 (on a 1 to 5 scale), which is among the top 10% of all the course ratings at Michigan Tech. Most students think the course help them learn green computing technologies. The students understood green computing concepts and techniques well (from section 1 in the survey). The students also maintained high confidence and enthusiasm in green computing (from section 2). However, the impact of a single course on students' future decisions seems less significant (from section 2).

6. CONCLUSION

In this paper, we advocate sustainability integration into undergraduate computing education. We present three sustainability integration strategies, efforts to develop a green computing course and modules, and course evaluation. Our work is still in the development stage and there are many challenges and questions not answered. It is our hope that the research results can increase the awareness of green computing movement, produce a valuable sustainability education model that can be used elsewhere, and provide insights for further sustainability and green computing education.

Acknowledgments

We would like to thank Linda Ott and Kedmon Hungwe for their valuable insights and pointers and the anonymous reviewers for their suggestions. This research work was supported in part by National Science Foundation (NSF) under grant number CNS-0829619.

7. REFERENCES

[1] E. Blevis. Sustainable interaction design: invention & disposal, renewal & reuse. In *Proc. of SIGCHI conference on Human factors in computing systems*, 2007.

[2] US Congress. House bill 5646. To study and promote the use of energy efficient computer servers in the united states. http://www.govtrack.us/congress/bill.xpd?bill=h109-5646. Retrieved: 02-14-2008.

[3] L. Down. Addressing the challenges of mainstreaming education for sustainable development in higher education. *International Journal of Sustainability in higher Education*, 7(4):390, 2006.

[4] Association for Computing Machinery (ACM). Computing curricula recommendations. *http://www.acm.org/education/curricula.html.*

[5] National Center for Education Statistics. Integrated post-secondary education data system completions survey. *Survey report*, 2007.

[6] Accreditation Board for Engineering and Technology (ABET). Engineering accreditation criteria: For engineering programs. *http://www.abet.org/forms.shtml.*

[7] Thomas L. Friedman. *Hot, Flat, and Crowded: Why We Need a Green Revolution–and How It Can Renew America* . Farrar, Straus and Giroux; 1 edition, 2008.

[8] I.F. Goodman and et. al. Final report of women's experiences in college engineering project. *Report of Goodman Research Group*, 2002.

[9] V. Kumar and et. al. Infusing sustainability principles into manufacturing/mechanical engineering curricula. *Journal of manufacturing systems*, 24(3):215–225, 2005.

[10] A. Kurkovsky. Educational aspects of sustainable development analysis: computational models and software. *Journal of Computing Sciences in Colleges*, 21(4):24–31, 2006.

[11] C.E. Landwehr. Green computing. *IEEE Security & Privacy Magazine*, 3(6):3–3, 2005.

[12] S. Mann and L. Smith. Computing education for sustainability. In *Proc. of Annual Conference of the National Advisory Committee on Computing Qualifications*, 2007.

[13] J. Margolis and A. Fisher. *Unlocking the Clubhouse: Women in Computing.* MIT Press, Cambridge, MA, 2002.

[14] W. McDonough, M. Braungart, P.T. Anastas, and J.B. Zimmerman. Applying the principles of green engineering to cradle-to-cradle design. *Environmental Science and Technology*, 37(23):434A–441A, 2003.

[15] A. Mcgettrick, R. Boyle, R. Ibbett, J. Lloyd, G. Lovegrove, and K. Mander. Grand challenges in computing: Education - a summary. *The Computer Journal*, 48(1):42–48, 2005.

[16] J.R. Mihelcic and D.R. Hokanson. Educational solutions: For a more sustainable future. *Environmental Solutions, Elsevier*, 2005.

[17] S. Murugesan. Harnessing Green IT: Principles and Practices. *IEEE IT Professional*, 10(1):24–33, 2008.

[18] United Nations. Report of the world commission on environment and development. In *General Assembly Resolution 42/187*, 1987.

[19] NPR news: Green Energy Scores Big In Obama's Stimulus Plan. http://www.npr.org/templates/story/story.php?storyId=99895320.

[20] NSF/SRS. Science and engineering degrees, by race/ethnicity of recipients. *Survey report*, 2002.

[21] National Academy of Engineering. *The Engineer of 2020: Visions of Engineering in the New Century.* The National Academies Press, 2004.

[22] Royal Academy of Engineering. *Engineering for Sustainable Development: Guiding Principles.* Published by the Royal Academy of Engineering, 2005.

[23] A. States. Get ready for a pickier workforce: Today's teens say employers without a social conscience need not apply. *Business Week*, page 82, 2006.

[24] I. Thomas. Where is the green curricula, or sustainability education in australian universities. *Eingana*, 27(1):17–18, 2004.

[25] U.S. Environmental Protection Agency. Report to Congress on Server and Data Center Energy Efficiency. August 2007.

[26] J. Vegso. Continued drop in CS bachelor's degree production and enrollments as the number of new majors stabilizes. *Computing Research News*, 19(2), 2007.

[27] J.B. Zimmerman and J. Vanegas. Using sustainability education to enable the increase of diversity in science, engineering, and technology related disciplines. *International Journal of Engineering Education*, 2006.

[28] T.E. Zorn and E. Collins. Green is the new black: Are csr and sustainable business just fads? In *Proc. of Australia-New Zealand Academy of Management Conference*, 2006.

An Approach to Integrating ICTD Projects into an Undergraduate Curriculum

Richard J. Anderson, Ruth E. Anderson, Gaetano Borriello
Dept. of Computer Science & Engineering
University of Washington
Seattle, WA, USA
{anderson, rea, gaetano}@cs.washington.edu

Joyojeet Pal
Technology & Social Change Group
University of Washington
Seattle, WA, USA
joyojeet@u.washington.edu

ABSTRACT
Applying information and communication technologies to development (ICTD) is emerging as an interesting and motivating research area in computer science and engineering. It spans application areas from healthcare to transportation, and requires the use of computing skills from networking to user interface design. Addressing problems of developing regions and under-served communities lets students explore a different part of the ICT design space, leading to new implementation and research questions. ICTD is also an area that has the potential to excite students about the CSE field more generally, with its emphasis on enabling social benefits with technology, and is rich in possibilities for interesting student projects. In this paper we report on two offerings of a course at the University of Washington that introduce students to the field by way of 1) reading papers from literature in the area to gain exposure to this very different design mindset and 2) doing practical projects that engage students in engineering problems under unique design constraints. Our hope is that CSE educators may find our experiences useful in identifying an approach to integrating the field of ICTD into their curricula.

Categories and Subject Descriptors
K.3.2. [**Computers and Education**]: Computer and Information Science Education – *Computer Science Education, Curriculum.*

General Terms
Human Factors.

Keywords
Capstone courses, service learning, socially-relevant projects, information and communication technologies for development

1. INTRODUCTION
Information and Communication Technologies for Development (ICTD) is emerging as an active area of research that showcases the connections between computing and the future of billions of citizens of our planet [4, 11]. The third IEEE/ACM sponsored conference on ICTD was held in April 2009 [14]. Projects currently exist in many computer science departments and emphasize the importance of collaboration with fields such as public health, education, agriculture, and business. Examples of projects in this area include flood detection, HIV/AIDS tracking, making crop prices available to farmers, microfinance, transportation coordination, and governance.

At the same time, research on attracting and retaining students suggests that educators should portray computing as a field through which one can contribute to the social good. ABET asks that by time of graduation, we provide our students with [1] "an ability to analyze the local and global impact of computing on individuals, organizations, and society." Exposing students to ways that computing is having an impact in low-income regions and the developing world is one mechanism for making the field relevant and showing its power to impact the world positively.

In this paper, we describe our experiences teaching two offerings of a year-long undergraduate capstone design course on computing in the developing world, consisting of a one-quarter reading seminar followed by two quarters of design and implementation. We found that students were able to comprehend and be motivated by papers from the ICTD literature. Student groups implemented a variety of interesting ICTD-related projects that forced them to consider design challenges not encountered in their previous CSE courses. These challenges included creating low-cost technology solutions suitable for environments with intermittent power and low Internet connectivity, and designing interfaces appropriate for users who were illiterate or had a lack of comfort with technology.

2. RELATED WORK
There is a long history of interest in incorporating projects that have a positive impact on society into computing courses via service learning [5, 12, 18, 22]. Benefits of service learning include providing opportunities to build stronger relationships between the university and the community and to attract students to the field through the context of projects that have a positive impact on society. While not all projects in our courses went on to be directly deployed in the communities for which they were designed, we still saw students driven by a similar interest in using their technology skills to enable social benefits.

There has also been much recent interest in socially relevant computing (defined as the use of computation to solve problems of societal and interpersonal relevance) [7]. Examples include the incorporation of open-source humanitarian projects [17] and assistive technologies [6] into senior capstone design courses or as independent study projects. Layman et al. discuss the importance of designing individual assignments to demonstrate how computer science can be used to aid society or to have some practical value [15]. Socially relevant projects are seen as a good fit for the altruistic leanings of this generation of students [19].

Our course builds on the motivation and success of the work mentioned above in that it focuses on projects that have the potential to impact society in a positive way—in our case, in the context of low-income and developing regions. A few universities are beginning to integrate the topic of ICTD into their undergraduate curricula [8, 24] although most such courses are at the graduate level, are housed in departments other than computer science, or do not involve implementation projects.

3. OUR COURSE

All computer engineering majors (and many computer science majors) at the University of Washington take a one-quarter capstone design course. These courses are mandated by ABET and are offered on a variety of traditional topics, ranging from computer animation to embedded systems, and give students the opportunity to design and implement substantial group projects. In addition, students gain experience presenting their work and justifying their design decisions.

In the 2007–08 and 2008–09 academic years, a new capstone design experience on the topic of technology for low-income and developing regions was offered [26]. The traditional, one-quarter capstone course was expanded to include two preliminary quarters of background and discussion in the area of ICTD. The reason for doing this, is that unlike the case for the more traditional capstone topics, students had not had much previous exposure to ICTD topics except, possibly, in the popular press. Furthermore, it was felt that having more time to iterate with potential users and/or ICTD experts would provide a richer experience and make the point that technology, to be meaningfully applied, has to involve stakeholders in its design from the very beginning.

3.1 Reading Seminar

The first quarter took the form of a one-credit literature review, in which students familiarized themselves with some of the challenges faced by residents of low-income regions. The course met an hour each week, and a different application area or design constraint was discussed at each meeting. Sample topics include education[21], transportation[25], non-literate user interfaces[16], microfinance[20], healthcare[10], and agriculture[13]. Reading lists can be found on the course web pages [26]. Our approach was to bias the paper selection toward papers written by technologists working in ICTD so that the students could more easily relate to the experiences they read about.

3.2 Project Design and Implementation

For the second quarter, in a two-credit design studio class, students were asked to organize themselves into groups of 4 to 6 based on their common interests and asked to come up with design ideas and implementation plans. In 2007-08, there were six project groups, in 2008-09 there were four. Throughout the quarter, students were continually asked to present their design ideas to the class and outside experts for feedback. We asked representatives of local NGOs working in ICTD, engineers of major companies in the local area working on applications for emerging markets, and other UW faculty familiar with the field to listen to student presentation and press on their reasoning both in terms of application space and design decisions. Again, the objective was to provide a realistic team design experience where decisions must be rationalized and explained to a wider audience.

The final quarter followed the more traditional form of other 5-credit capstone courses, although the focus here was primarily on implementation rather than design and implementation. Throughout the last two quarters, student groups were frequently required to present their ideas to the class and to panels of experts in formal presentations, poster sessions, and written reports.

4. EXAMPLE PROJECTS

In this section, we describe three of the course projects in greater detail. Other student projects from our two offerings of the course covered a variety of areas and technologies: writing educational games that allow several students to share a single computer via cheap USB keyboards, creating an educational application for the OLPC (One Laptop Per Child) platform, helping community health workers in Tanzania manage patient care using cell phones, empowering women in Kenya via community radio, making agricultural outreach video presentations more interactive via technology, and building a device that permits the safe and efficient recharging of batteries.

4.1 Improving Transportation in Kyrgyzstan

The goal of the *bus ("star-bus") project was to provide reliable transportation information to bus riders in Kyrgyzstan via GPS tracking devices and text messages. Currently, buses in Kyrgyzstan have set routes but no set stops or schedules. Riders must wave down a bus when they see one and have no idea when a bus will arrive. This leads to wasted time, and money (if a more expensive taxi must be taken instead), and can be a safety issue for riders waiting alone at night when service is less frequent.

In many places in the developed world bus riders have access to real-time transit information via electronic signs posted at stations or via the web – which they may have access to from a personal web-enabled phone. Students with GPS-enabled phones with Internet access may even be accustomed to keeping track of the location of their friends possessing similar technology.

In designing a transportation information system for Kyrgyzstan, students were forced to work within the constraints of a dramatically different landscape. While cell phones are owned by over 70% of the population, less than 15% own a computer or use the Internet (compared to 85% Internet use in the US) [25].

Students took this knowledge of technology use patterns in Kyrgyzstan into account, and designed an information system that fit well with a method of communication seen as common and affordable – SMS (a.k.a. text messages). Students wrote a server that runs on a computer with intentionally minimal requirements – a cheap laptop connected to a cell phone (no Internet access was required by the server). In the designed system, riders send text messages to the server inquiring about the arrival of their bus. The server sends its response back to the rider via SMS.

For their project, students also devised a mechanism for collecting information about the location of buses. Students built a hardware prototype device containing a GPS module that could be installed on buses being tracked by the system. These *box devices would then relay their location information over SMS to the server. The *box was intentionally designed to have a non-threatening appearance, low power requirements, and minimal street value to discourage theft (instead of equipping buses with GPS-enabled phones). An SMS interface to the tracking devices was also developed so that administrators could access them remotely and drivers would not be required to interact with them extensively.

The project is an example of one that was posed to the class by a colleague from another department, who identified the problem after years of experience in Kyrgyzstan. At the end of the course, some students from the project joined forces with another project group that had developed a system for supporting SMS-based applications. The newly formed group continued iteration on the project and eventually visited Kyrgyzstan to deploy their system, resulting in a senior thesis and research publications.

4.2 Marketing Native Crafts

The Empowering Artists group teamed up with business students at Heritage University in rural Washington state to allow artisans in remote regions to sell their art to the world. The group at Heritage had connections with local Native Americans and, by way of students at other universities, with Huichol artisans in villages in remote parts of Mexico that were interested in marketing their work. Although web sites such as eBay allow the sale of items directly from artist to consumer, most artists in these communities did not have either sufficient access or facility with technology to make use of these options. In addition, they did not want to compete directly with mass-manufactured replicas or culturally irrelevant goods, instead expressing a desire to preserve and accurately portray their cultural skills and values.

In investigating a possible solution, the UW computing students collaborated with their partners at Heritage to understand the problem constraints. It was eye-opening for the computing students to encounter the levels of mistrust of technology and outsiders expressed by some of the artists. To address this problem, the students proposed using the university students as both art documenters and trusted transaction intermediaries who would access technology on their behalf. This human-computer solution allowed students to recognize that technology alone rarely provides the entire solution.

While university students in both locales had reasonable Internet connectivity and computer skills, the CSE students still needed to create an easy-to use web-based back end for uploading content and keeping track of inventory that could be available in (at least) English and Spanish. In addition, they created a front end website that presented goods for sale in a way that would be acceptable to a wide variety of artists. Throughout the process, students were made aware of cultural sensitivity. For example, when one CSE student suggested using a Yakama language word to brand the project, Heritage students explained that many Native American tribes, including Yakama, did not want their languages used by outsiders. When the CSE students suggested enhancing the web site to support commissioning of artwork, they learned how the majority of Huicholes produce art sporadically and rarely by request.

4.3 Radio Craiglist

The CellPost project (a.k.a. Radio Craigslist) created a low-cost mechanism for advertisement of goods and services, employment opportunities, community announcements, lectures, and healthcare information. Students were inspired by reading about the use of community radio in the AIR [23] project, where it gave women a voice in communities in Africa. They were interested in using low cost technology to bring services such as those available on Craigslist [9] to people in remote communities.

To address this problem they combined two relatively cheap and available technologies: cell phones and community radio. Users with cell phones would call a server to leave messages (such as an advertisement of an item for sale or a job opportunity) that they wanted broadcast. The server was responsible for determining a schedule for broadcasting messages and was connected to an FM transmitter to allow local broadcast over a range of several miles. For their project, students selected and assembled a functioning suite of hardware (FM transmitter, antenna, cell phone, and low-cost laptop) and created the server software.

The students found several software packages available to help them construct the system. Asterisk [3], an open source telephony engine, was used to connect a cell phone (for handling incoming calls) to the server via Bluetooth. Voice menus were created to guide users to place their messages in the correct category and to allow administrators to remove inappropriate content. The use of voice as the mechanism for placing ads allows the system to be used by illiterate users. Similarly, the broadcast of content in audio form to radios (a low cost technology that is easily shared) makes the system available to a wide range of users.

A web GUI was designed so that (if the server was connected to the Internet) a remote user could upload content such as audio books, farming lectures, or English lessons from anywhere in the world for broadcast on the local station. The success of a similar system VoiKiosk [2] makes the students' solution look promising for actual deployment.

5. LESSONS LEARNED

5.1 Success of Course Structure

Our year-long model for the course, (1) a reading seminar followed by (2) a design studio and then (3) an intensive implementation push, worked well and spread the project effort nicely across the three quarters. The papers in the reading seminar were accessible to undergraduates to the point that they were capable of both leading and summarizing the discussion each week. We believe that the reading seminar could stand on its own as a course that would be relatively easy for instructors at other institutions to implement. Individual papers from the seminar could also be used as interesting supplements to courses such as human-computer interaction, operating systems, or networking.

We expect that it would be difficult to do ICTD-related projects similar in scope to the ones our students accomplished in a single quarter or semester. In our experience, students need time both to absorb content from the reading seminar and to appreciate the unique design constraints of their projects. Furthermore, having ample opportunity to present their ideas to a range of practitioners was immensely educational and reinforced the design concepts presented in the classes. Our model of gearing up in level of commitment and intensity from quarter to quarter also seemed to work well. Several students dropped after the first quarter, and we did have a couple that joined in the last two quarters, but, given the small numbers, this did not pose a significant problem.

5.2 Resource-Constrained Design

Typical capstone course projects are in domains at least somewhat known to students (games, animated films, social networking, education, shopping, trip planning) and are meant to be used in a context they are familiar with (e.g., by students like themselves or professionals living in a city similar to their own). These projects require students to design a solution to the given problem within a set of constraints (time, skills of group, hardware or software needed), and students inevitably wrestle with difficulties such as dealing with poorly documented software, hardware that does not work as advertised, and all the challenges inherent to group work.

One of the benefits of having students do projects in the area of ICTD is that it exposes them to a set of design constraints that they are unlikely to have encountered in any previous CSE course. Design constraints our students had to consider included:

- **Very Low cost** – Cost obviously takes on a new meaning in scenarios where people live on less than $2 a day. Expensive computing devices are at risk of theft or can even put their owners in personal danger. The *appearance* of low cost can be equally important to the actual cost.
- **Low power** – Although students will probably be familiar with the idea of conserving power for environmental reasons or to extend portability of devices, they are not likely to have designed for an environment where power is intermittent or relatively expensive or both.
- **Low connectivity** – While cell phone coverage is becoming more and more available worldwide, Internet coverage is still far from universal, and continues to be expensive. We simply can not rely on partitioning of tasks between mobile devices and servers, for example.
- **User interface challenges** – Several of our student projects had to design user interfaces that would be accessible not only to people of different languages and cultures but also to those who were illiterate or who had a fear or distrust of technology. Cultural sensitivities add another dimension.
- **Ease of maintenance** – Solutions that are deployed in remote areas or that must be maintained by inexperienced users pose an extra challenge. Hardware and software should be robust to the elements and designing a system so that experts can access it remotely can be invaluable.

The fact that design in ICTD inherently relies on the use of low-cost technology can be a benefit when trying to secure resources for student projects. Wide coverage and growing access has led the cell phone to become a much-used computing platform in the developing world. While voice connections can still be expensive and of varying quality, SMS (text messages) has proved useful for many applications. Low cost laptops like the OLPC and the new generation of netbooks are also starting to be deployed and present an interesting design point between phones and full-featured laptops. Community Radio is another technology that provides low cost broadcast communication.

5.3 Impact on Students

Overall course evaluations have been very positive. On evaluations, several students mentioned the value of thinking in a new way ("Very different view to develop technology for developing regions", "Thinking outside the box is really good for all engineering disciplines"). Several students mentioned the real-world and altruistic nature of projects as appealing ("Gave students an opportunity to help people…", "I had been looking for a class like this for some time. There should be more classes that offer a focus for the technology instead of just the technology."). They also frequently spoke positively about the year long nature of the course ("For developing world capstones, definitely keep the leading two quarters of introduction and design. The insight gained from studying previous work was crucial to developing a relevant capstone project.").

Despite most course projects only being prototypes, we had several students continue work on their projects well into the summer or the following year. Several of these took on lives as research projects, often leading to publications or senior theses. In a few cases, funding was found to allow students to travel to the region for deployment or usability testing of their project. Several students from the course are planning to continue work in ICTD in graduate school, another accepted an ICTD-related internship.

6. ADVICE TO INSTRUCTORS

Although several of our projects evolved from existing connections with other researchers, we believe you would not need to be an expert in the field or to have such connections to teach an ICTD-inspired project course. Instructors can use the background provided in the reading seminar to provide a motivating context for projects in low resource environments both close to home and abroad. Here we give suggestions for instructors interested in teaching similar courses.

- **Students need the background seminar in order to understand the human side of project goals and the source of unique design constraints.**

  Although in our experience this background proved to be eye-opening and created excitement for the majority of students, not all students may appreciate the broader implications of technological solutions or be motivated by projects in ICTD.

- **Instructors need to provide greater guidance in project selection.**

  Excitement about the potential humanitarian impact of their solutions coupled with a lack of deep understanding of an unfamiliar context can lead students to be overly ambitious when selecting projects. In our experience, instructors need to be particularly careful to reign in elaborate plans students may first propose when working in this new area and ensure that projects include a reasonable technical component whose implementation can be achieved in the time available (including experiments and contingency plans).

- **Instructors may need to provide more guidance during projects.**

  We found that while some student projects were self-directed, others needed significantly more guidance along the way. We suspect that this could be due to students' lack of certainly when working in this unfamiliar area. Besides a lack of direct experience with the domain (healthcare, agriculture), geographic region (sub-Saharan Africa, Kyrgyzstan), or culture, they may also have more difficulty finding answers to questions than they might with projects where information is more readily found on the Internet or from a local pool of potential users.

- **Keep in mind that projects are only prototypes.**

  The overall goal of student projects should be to prototype a solution with these unique design constraints, and to gain some understanding of the domain. While it is useful to hold students to reasonable reality checks (e.g., constant Internet connectivity is expensive and unlikely to be available), at the same time, an instructor can allow some flexibility in meeting these design constraints for the purpose of proof-of-concept and validation of the project's core idea (e.g., students might build specialized hardware to allow for the exploration of a design space, while at the same time calculating that larger quantities could be produced much more cheaply or that less-costly, off-the-shelf options could be used). For projects that lived on beyond the course, re-engineering parts of the system was often required.

- **Look locally for possible projects.**

  You may find low-resource communities in urban or rural environments in close physical proximity that allow students to pursue projects similar to those they read about in the ICTD literature. Reading the ICTD literature will help students be sensitive to issues that apply locally as well. Physical proximity may also allow visiting the site – which proved invaluable in our experience. We also found it useful to explore project ideas posed by colleagues in other departments that had significantly more experience with the context (e.g., transportation in Kyrgyzstan).

- **Consider having students do projects that are part of a larger effort.**

  The HFOSS project [17] allows students to contribute to open-source humanitarian projects, several of which have roots in the developing world (e.g., OpenMRS, Sahana disaster-management system). Participating in projects like HFOSS where students develop modules for existing projects allows students to leverage resources of a larger development community and more easily deploy their solutions in the field. Developing applications for a platform like the OLPC can have similar benefits.

Overall, we found that the course topic of computing for low-income regions and the developing world inspired many successful projects, while being motivating and eye-opening for students. The course has been offered twice so far and will be offered again in the coming year. A video about the course has been created for use as a recruiting tool [27].

7. REFERENCES

[1] ABET 2008-2009 Computing Accreditation Criteria http://www.abet.org/

[2] Agarwal, S., Kumar, A., Nanavati, A. and Rajput, N., "VoiKiosk: Content Creation and Dissemination by-and-for Users in Rural Areas," ICTD 2009.

[3] Asterisk :: The Open Source PBX & Telephony Platform. http://www.asterisk.org/

[4] Brewer, E. et al., "The Case for Technology in Developing Regions," *IEEE Computer*, 38(6), June 2005, pp. 25-38.

[5] Brooks, C., "Community Connections: Lessons Learned Developing and Maintaining a Computer Science Service-Learning Program," SIGCSE 2008, pp. 352-356.

[6] Buckley, M., Kershner, H., Schindler, K., Alphonce, C. and Braswell, J. "Benefits of using socially-relevant projects in computer science and engineering education," SIGCSE 2004, pp. 482-486.

[7] Buckley, M., Nordlinger, J. and Subramanian, D., "Socially relevant computing," SIGCSE 2008, pp. 347-351.

[8] Carnegie Mellon TechBridgeWorld http://www.techbridgeworld.org/courses/

[9] Craigslist. http://www.craigslist.org

[10] DeRenzi, B. et al., "e-IMCI: Improving Pediatric Health Care in Low-Income Countries," CHI 2008, pp. 753-762.

[11] Dias, M. and Brewer, E., "How Computer Science Serves the Developing World," *CACM* 52(6), June 2009, pp. 74-80.

[12] EPICS: Engineering Projects In Community Service. https://engineering.purdue.edu/EPICS

[13] Gandhi, R., Veeraraghavan, R. Toyama, K. and Ramprasad, V. "Digital Green: Participatory Video for Agricultural Extension," ICTD 2007, pp.21-30.

[14] International Conference on Information and Communication Technologies and Development (ICTD 2009), http://www.ictd2009.org/

[15] Layman, L., Williams, L. and Slaten, K., "Note to self: make assignments meaningful," SIGCSE 2007, pp. 459-463.

[16] Medhi, I., Sagar, A. and Toyama, K. "Text-Free User Interfaces for Illiterate and Semi-Literate Users," ICTD 2006, pp. 72-82.

[17] Morelli, R.A. et al, "Revitalizing Computing Education by Building Free and Open Source Software for Humanity," *CACM* 52(8), August 2009, pp. 67-75.

[18] Oakes, W. et al., "Service-Learning in Engineering," ASEE/IEEE Frontiers in Education (FIE) 2002.

[19] Oblinger, D. and Oblinger, J. "Educating the Net Generation." Boulder, CO: Educause, 2005.

[20] Parikh, T., Javid, P., K., Sasikumar, Ghosh, K. and Toyama, K., "Mobile phones and paper documents: evaluating a new approach for capturing microfinance data in rural India," CHI 2006, pp. 551-560.

[21] Pawar, U., Pal, J. and Toyama, K., "Multiple Mice for Computers in Education in Developing Countries," ICTD 2006, pp. 64-71.

[22] Rosmaita, B., "Making service learning accessible to computer scientists," SIGCSE 2007, pp.541-545.

[23] Sterling, S. R., O'Brien, J. and Bennett, J. "Advancement through Interactive Radio," ICTD 2007, pp. 68-75.

[24] University of London, http://www.ict4d.org.uk/

[25] Anderson, R. E. et al., "Building a Transportation Information System Using Only GPS and Basic SMS Infrastructure," ICTD 2009.

[26] Course web pages, 2007-08, http://www.cs.washington.edu/education/courses/cse477/

[27] Course video, http://www.cs.washington.edu/info/videos/asx/CSE477_08sp_2083k_850x480.asx

In Their Words: Student Feedback on an International Project Collaboration

Archana Chidanandan
Computer Science and Software Engineering
Rose-Hulman Institute of Technology
Terre Haute, IN, USA
+1 812 877 8358
chidanan@rose-hulman.edu

Lori Russell-Dag
Computer and Instructional Technology Teacher Education
Bilkent University, Ankara, Turkey
+90 312 290 33 56
russell@bilkent.edu.tr

Cary Laxer
Computer Science and Software Engineering
Rose-Hulman Institute of Technology
Terre Haute, IN, USA
+1 812 877 8429
laxer@rose-hulman.edu

Reyyan Ayfer
Computer and Instructional Technology Teacher Education
Bilkent University, Ankara, Turkey
+90 312 290 50 65
ayfer@bilkent.edu.tr

ABSTRACT

In this paper, we describe a collaborative course experience between students from universities in the USA and Turkey. Student teams worked together on a software engineering project for a non-profit organization based in Turkey. The students learned valuable skills in team-work, collaboration-facilitating software tools and working with peers from a different culture and a different time-zone. At the end of the course, in a focus group, students were asked for feedback regarding the course and its outcomes. In this paper, we describe the course from the student perspective. From this, and the instructor's experiences we provide a list of guidelines.

Categories and Subject Descriptors

K.3.2 [**Computers and Education**]: Computer and Information Science Education – *Computer science education, Curriculum.*

General Terms: Experimentation

Keywords

International collaboration, software engineering, teamwork

1. INTRODUCTION

Software Engineering is a field where international collaborations are now the norm. Software teams can be spread around the world and work across time-zones and language barriers. Students entering the current workforce need to be comfortable with the challenges that arise in these situations.

In [5], different mechanisms to provide an international dimension to the Computer Science curriculum internships, study abroad programs, short courses abroad, and student and faculty exchanges. One idea that is described is a collaborative project between student teams that are situated in different countries. This provides students with an opportunity to experience the challenges and benefits of international collaborations.

In 2009, a collaborative project course was offered by Rose-Hulman Institute of Technology(RHIT) in the United States and Bilkent University(BU) in Turkey. In this work, we will describe the collaboration between the two departments, and the feedback received from the students regarding the challenges and successes of the course. Using this feedback, and the instructors' experience, we will provide guidelines for similar projects.

Reviewing reports on similar collaborations, we see that authors have looked at various aspects of such collaborations. In [4], the authors study the role of collaborative technologies and culture how it affects students' perceptions of their collaborations. In [8], the authors describe the Global Studio Project. The authors describe how learning to improvise in a rapidly changing real-world project is an important skill that students need to learn and that collaborative projects with real clients can provide a learning opportunity. In [6], the authors describe the creation and progress of a collaborative project course between student team from RHIT and Uppsala University in Sweden. The course that we describe in this paper is an offering of the course described in the paper, where the collaboration is now between RHIT and BU. In this paper, we describe the collaborative course and the experience from the student perspective. We used feedback obtained from the students through focus groups and several informal conversations with the students.

In section 2, we will describe how the course was organized. In section 3, we will talk about the challenges faced by the students and how these were handled by the students and instructors. In conclusion, we will provide our guidelines.

2. THE COLLABORATION

2.1 The schools

BU is a private nonprofit university in Turkey. The Department of Computer and Instructional Technology Teacher Education (CTE) is an undergraduate program which provides students with a strong computer science and technology background from an educational perspective. Students graduate as qualified teachers.

RHIT is a private engineering school in the United States. The Computer Science and Software Engineering department offers undergraduate programs in Computer Science and Software Engineering.

2.2 The course

RHIT's Computing in a Global Society course which is an elective for Computer Science and Software Engineering majors has the following outcomes:

SIGCSE'10, March 10–13, 2010, Milwaukee, Wisconsin, USA.

1. Explain the importance and relevance of globalization, in particular as it relates to computer science and software engineering.
2. Effectively communicate with teams from other countries and cultures.
3. Effectively work with teams from other countries and cultures to complete a project.

In order to meet outcomes 2 and 3 effectively, students would collaborate with students at BU.

As part of the CTE curriculum at BU, students complete a required project development course. During the spring 2009 semester students were given the option of opting for this new collaborative course.

Since the CTE course had to satisfy the outcomes

1. To understand and apply modern principles of software requirements analysis and software design to develop a software project with a fixed deadline.
2. To work as a part of a team to develop a software project by applying strong interpersonal communication, and problem resolution skills.

it was decided by the instructors that the collaborative course would closely mirror the original CTE course. In total, there were eleven students registered to the course, three from RHIT and 8 from Bilkent. BU's spring term begins about three weeks before RHIT's and therefore the BU students began work on the project at least three weeks before the RHIT students.

2.3 The client

The client was the International Children's Centre (ICC) Child Right's Programme. It is a non profit, non-governmental organization based in Ankara, Turkey. It has activities and projects that focus on child and youth advocacy and awareness. Two ICC employees served as liaisons between the students and the ICC itself. Since the ICC was based in Ankara, BU students had more direct contact with the ICC contacts. It was clear that the project would be centered on children's rights to serve the purpose of the organization, but that was the most the client was sure of. Because of the youth centered focus of the organization, the client was eager to have as much input and direction from the students as possible. Therefore, the first challenge for the students was to determine what the needs of the ICC were and how the students could help with these needs.

2.4 Collaborative tools

Since a large portion of the work done by the students is intended to be done when they are in their respective schools, online collaborative tools play a key role in facilitating group work. Many tools have been advocated by other teams that have dealt with a similar course such as a combined e-mail lists and Microsoft NetMeeting in [7], websites and Skype in [3], and Wikis in [9].

Our students used a range of collaborative tools. For weekly meetings, Skype was used for videoconferencing. For other communication they used: Moodle CMS page and forums, and an e-mail list with all the students and instructors. SVN repositories were created for the student teams to maintain and share documentation and code for the project. Students were required to submit all their deliverables in designated folders in the SVN repositories. Students also used Google Docs before they had access to the SVN repositories. In [1], students describe their experiences with various collaborative tools.

3. COURSE ORGANIZATION: CHALLENGES AND SOLUTIONS

The project and hence the course was divided into three stages. The three stages were Planning and Analysis, Design, and Implementation. Prior to the Planning and Analysis stage, the BU students also conducted a preliminary investigation.

4.1 Preliminary Investigative Stage

Because the BU students' semester began earlier than their international colleagues, during the first three weeks of their course they completed a preliminary investigation. Students from BU met with the client and the client educated them on the UNICEF convention on the rights of the child, and some of the work that is being done to spread awareness. Students used this opportunity to formulate possible projects for the client. Information from these meetings and workshops were communicated to all team members using the online course environment. Prior to the arrival of the RHIT students an introductory meeting was organized via Skype where all students and instructors had a chance to meet and discuss what they had learned, potential projects and visit related details.

4.2 Planning and Analysis

At this stage, RHIT students joined the project. The students visited BU and the entire team was able to interact directly with each other. This was an important first step for the students. They met their peers and got to understand each other's technical backgrounds and to some extent their cultural backgrounds. The RHIT students learned from the BU students what information had been gathered in the initial phase with the client. During the analysis week, students worked together to determine the problem statement. From this, two projects were selected. The first project involved building an interactive web site, in both Turkish and English, designed to teach children about their rights. The web site would be designed with a child-friendly interface, and was to include interactive games, videos, and stories from children around the world. The second project was designed for use by ICC staff to provide a tool for collecting and browsing news items centered around children's rights. The implementation was a Google-supported map where staff could add and browse interesting news items. Students then divided into three teams – one to design and implement the web site, a second to design and implement educational web games, and the third to design and implement the Google-based mapping tool. At the end of the visit, students presented their proposal to the client, instructors and other students. Following the visit, each team had to submit an analysis report.

4.3.1 Challenges faced during Analysis Phase

There were two major complaints from students at this stage. RHIT students were frustrated by the apparent lack of a clearly defined project and did not understand decisions that had been made before they arrived.

According to a student:
"One of the problems early on was that the client did not have firm idea about what they wanted and there was no set problem were went to solve, It was us giving a solution to a problem that we were guessing they had."

To address this challenge, a student recommended:
"Having a set problem, [it was frustrating to] go to the client and figure out what their problem was. This [project] was us trying to figure out problems and solutions."

BU students, on the other hand, had spent considerable time working with the client. The students did attempt to communicate the information from the client via the online course environment, however because the RHIT students were at the end of their previous term, they were not able to be as involved in the project as the BU students who were just starting a new term. Based on discussions with the client the BU students then decided on a project they felt was most interesting to them. They were frustrated when the project changed during the visit week.

Again, the responses received from the students:
"[RHIT students] started the project after 3 weeks, after we started, we planned, we analyzed and then they changed our analysis plan."

"There was a lot of interfacing with a client, that [RHIT students] probably never got the full feedback on because we were out of the loop as far as communication goes."

Also,
"It would be nice if the schedules matched better. They had 3 weeks of classes before our semester started, so they worked for 3 weeks and then they had to explain what has been happening for the past 3 weeks, then when we started everything changed."

However, during the visit week, students felt that the face-to-face interactions were helpful in improving communication, and building personal bonds which made them feel more like members of a team.

According to a student:
"What would take hours/days to do emailing, [during the visit] we get done very quickly. Also it helps to create personal bonds between the team members, a better feel and better interactions with team as a whole."

4.3 Design Phase

In this phase, students worked from their respective campus locations. They were required to attend a weekly meeting where the students used Skype to communicate. The meetings provided students with an opportunity to interact with all the teams and get feedback from both instructors. Although it was not a formal requirement, generally students established weekly meeting times where they could meet with their sub-team members. Students had to submit a design report at the end of this phase.

4.3.1 Challenges faced during the Design Phase

This was perhaps the most challenging phase for the students, since they had no direct interactions with each other. It required them to plan carefully and co-ordinate well. This is perhaps where most of the learning took place for the students in terms of learning to interact with peers from a different location. Students found remote communication difficult due to busy schedules, time differences, and the resulting delay in feedback First, there were the logistical challenges, such as arranging common meetings, and establishing regular communication:

"Because of the time difference we sometimes missed a meeting. [Remote communication] wasn't really effective."

"[in other project]a lot of times the meetings are less formal, but this needs more formality because you have to organize across time zones, reserve rooms get on the web cam."

"there is a time difference, it is hard to find [international teammates]. If I took a domestic term project, I can reach my friends anytime I want because they are close to me."

"Normally I know if [a teammate] reads my email because I can ask to check it but here we just communicate by email or by Skype once a week, I think it is hard"

"we have a class on [the meeting day] in the morning and then we have to we wait all day for the Skype meeting."

As well, the differences in the courses (outcomes, required vs. elective) at both institutions lead some student to believe that not all students were fully invested in the course, and that the project related deliverables(and resulting grades) were more important to some students than to others.

"There were problems because of different aims of course. The course is important for CTE students, their course is a globalization course. Sometimes they do not care about the project. They should be the same."

Contributing to this problem was that students had many commitments outside the course, so much of the work was left until the last minute.

"We were very busy this semester, had many projects... It was hard for me because I had very little time. The design part was very long, implementation was too short. I think it was a problem. The structure of the project should be revised."

This meant that they may not have communicated as regularly during the weeks leading up to the deadline as they needed, and as a result there was not enough time to work together to complete the deliverable, due to conflicting schedules and time differences

While they definitely faced many challenges during the design phase, they managed to produce detailed design documents for each of the three modules. In doing so, they were able to leverage their varied backgrounds quite effectively. For example, the web site group at BU interacted with a graphic designer from outside BU to determine the aesthetics of the web site. Students from RHIT were able to use their experience with open-source software to understand and apply Google's API for the mapping tool.

4.4 Implementation Phase

This phase had two milestones. The first milestone required students to produce a prototype for the client. The client would then provide some feedback. Students would then complete the second phase, which was the finalized implementation and user manuals. The second phase included the final visit by the RHIT students to BU which coincided with the end of the project. At the end of the visit, students had to present their work to the client, BU faculty and students and their instructors.

This final phase concluded a week after the last exams for both sets of students, as this was the only time a visit could be coordinated.

4.4.1 Challenges faced during the Implementation Phase

While there were a couple of issues with students having to delay the start of their internships, most issues were quickly resolved. In spite of the long flights and having to work immediately after their final exams, both student teams relished the opportunity to work with each other face-to-face and finish the implementation. As in the initial visit, students felt that the final visit was important to the project as any problems in communication experienced during the semester were quickly overcome with in person interaction.

Some comments about the final visit week:

"[the visit] was the best part of the project. We all came together and had a chance to work on the project all together. Because our colleagues were far away, it was hard to come together to finish something."

"Technology is really cool these days as far as global computing but it's still hard to beat face to face interaction."

The client's response to the final project deliverables and the presentation was that the students' work had far exceeded his expectations.

4. General Observations and Analysis

We used two focus groups to obtain students feedback – one for the BU students and one for the RHIT students. The mediators and recorders were people unconnected to the course and were provided with a set of questions by us. Topics other than those on the provided list were also discussed.

During the focus groups, students were also asked to provide some general observations regarding the course and its outcomes. Based on the responses we obtained from the focus groups and other informal feedback, we make the following observations:

Students would like reciprocal visits. This was a recurring theme throughout the semester, and there were several reasons for this. Some felt that it would give the Turkish students a chance to learn more about the American culture, and also act as an incentive.

"There should be a trip from Turkey to the US to understand their culture...and to be motivated. We always discuss this...because they are coming, traveling and of course they are working, we are just working, working, no traveling."

"we tried to teach our culture, but we don't think we learned much."

"I would have them come to the US, with the one way collaboration we get a lot of their culture and they do not get much of ours. Definitely [a US visit] could be useful."

Also, some RHIT students appreciated learning about another culture, and felt that it was one of the most important aspects of the trip:

"You get to experience the culture differently when you have friends here and they can show you around. I didn't know much about Turkey before... it was cool to learn about the history. The cultural aspect was my favorite."

Students had difficulties with the language barrier, but believed they improved their verbal communication skills. Some responses from the RHIT students regarding communication difficulties:

"I have worked with [others] from time to time, and [who are] not a native English speakers, but [their] English is very good. It's really nothing compared to working with extremely non-native English speakers. It has definitely improved my ability to communicate visually or to use other means of communication to get around that."

"[Over Skype], sometimes when they said something, they didn't pronounce it correctly, and there was signal/noise. ...when they type in English the way I interpreted is not what they meant. That was the greatest challenge."

"At various points I would try to communicate an idea, sometimes even if they did not understand/were not clear, there was miscommunication, and we both did different/unexpected things different than intended. Communicating visually more would have helped more, text conversations didn't convey a misunderstanding."

The BU students also had difficulties with communication, such as:

"Because we have no non-verbal cues, it is really hard [to communicate] on instant messaging"

"Not understanding the difficulties of a second language. They always talk fast, they don't know."

"It is very frustrating, when we are trying to complete our sentence, it is hard for us. When we finish our sentence, sometimes their response is 'huh?'. When I try to repeat the sentence, they say forget about it."

But because of these difficulties, they did feel that they improved their communication skills:

"[The project] improved our English. Both verbal and in writing. Sometimes in messaging we misunderstood each other because the [difficulty], how to write an email in order to communicate. And I think it helped me a lot with communication."

Students would prefer to have the same assessment criteria for the course grade. Since the courses have different outcomes, each instructor had different assessment tools. While every member of the team got the same grade for a particular phase of the project, the overall grade was different. For example, the RHIT students had to perform some research and make a presentation to meet outcome 2. BU students had to complete a preliminary analysis report at the beginning, and completed weekly peer assessments that included an assessment of weekly participation (meeting attendance, meeting performance, contribution to the team).

Students wished for a closer match between their skill sets. While students may consider this a drawback, this is exactly what they will encounter in the workplace and honing the ability to leverage these differences, in the authors' opinions is a goal of these types of projects.

"We're computer science majors and here it's based on computer education which is different ways of viewing the world teaching that aspect and we just do it for the research and applications aspects. There were a bit of differences as far as expertise goes in that way"

"in a domestic group, because we all went through the same curriculum, we have used the same tools, we all use subversion, and we've used eclipse from our first freshman year classes. Everyone having that same knowledge, especially with subversion...in [other projects] we relied on it like a crutch here it

is a bit of a change…and we had to change based on those assumptions."

5. Conclusion

Using the student feedback as a guide, and looking at assessments in [2], [5], [6], and [10], the following is a list of lessons learned from the course:

o Choose a project that can draw from the strengths of both groups of students. Because they are from different backgrounds, their skill sets will never be the same, however the project should be selected in a way that all students can feel they have an equal contribution and are adequately challenged.

o Have a limited number of clearly defined project ideas from the client which are communicated to all team members in the same way from the start.

o Have all students begin work on the project together, during the initial visit week, and not before. This would mean that the BU course be restructured, rather than completing a preliminary investigation and starting work on the project early, students may focus their time on learning and setting up collaboration tools to be used during the course, and readings to better understand the aims and outcomes of the course.

o Synchronize meeting times, project deliverables from the outset, according to academic calendars, time changes, etc. We had a tentative meeting time scheduled when students were signing up for the respective courses. However, eventually the meeting was changed to a different time, which resulted in one student being able to attend only part of the meetings.

o Synchronize the weights of the project deliverables for both groups, but also allow for other assessments for differing course outcomes, and communicate this to the students.

o Choose courses from both where students are equally motivated,Participation in the project should be elective. With all the challenges that come with long-distance collaboration, having one group of students less motivated than the other can result in a lot of frustration

o Expect language to be a barrier. If English is not the native language for any one group of students, it can lead to misunderstandings and stalled work. [2] proposed a solution to limit language barriers, which was to use English as the common language, and ensure students spoke it at least moderately well. In our experience, although this was true of the BU students, language barriers still arose. Even with a moderate ability in English, students still had trouble expressing or asserting themselves in a non-native language, and although they may understand what is being said, the perceived language barrier influences how they interpret its meaning.

o Require students to take responsibility for managing meetings. They should be encouraged to post an agenda in advance, take minutes, and so on.

o Do not expect remote communication among team members to be automatic to the students. As stated in [2], it is important to be clear as to what level of interaction is required. Students should schedule weekly sub-team meetings to discuss details of the project, in addition to weekly team video-conference, and update all team members of the progress during the video-conference.

o Do not expect that students will work at the same/consistent pace. To facilitate continuous work, and to give students incentive to work consistently during each phase (rather than leaving all work until the end), include deliverables such as Gantt charts, so all team members are aware of the work that needs to be done and have multiple document revisions to allow for feedback.

Despite the challenges, students enjoyed many aspects of the course. When asked if the course should be offered again, the following student response nicely summarizes the goals of this experience:

"[Student would] Definitely recommend [the course] to people who are interested in knowing how people from other cultures think and also if the country is relevant to their future career it is definitely worth going. We are also working for an organization local to the country. See how a project is handled and collaborated from a different point of view."

6. ACKNOWLEDGMENTS

We would like to thank Ipek Sozen and our client representatives Adem Arkadas and Gulgun Muftu and the International Children's Center for their support of this work. We would also like to thank our students for their participation in the focus groups.

7. REFERENCES

[1] Altin, R., et. al., "Use of Intuitive Tools to Enhance Student Learning and User Experience," Proc. Annual Conference on Innovation and Technology in Computer Science Education, 2009, Paris, France.

[2] Azadegan, A. and Lu, C. , "An International Common Project: Implementation Phase," Proc. Annual Conference on Innovation and Technology in Computer Science Education, 2001, Canterbury, UK

[3] Chan, A., Frydenberg, M., and Lee, M. "Facilitating Cross-Cultural Learning through Collaborative Skypecasting," Proc. ACM SIGITE Conference on Information Technology Education, 2007, Sandestin, FL

[4] Diamant, E., Fussell, S, and Lo, F., "Where Did We Turn Wrong? Unpacking the Effects of Culture and Technology on Attributions of Team Performance." Proc. ACM Conference on Computer Supported Cooperative Work, 2008, San Diego, CA

[5] Fuller, U., et. al., "Facilitating student learning through student abroad and international projects," Proc. Annual Conference on Innovation and Technology in Computer Science Education, 2007, Lisbon, Portugal

[6] Laxer, C. et al. "Evolution of an International Collaborative Student Project," in the proceedings of Australasian Computing Education Conference, 2009, Wellington, New Zealand.

[7] Macek, T., et. al., "Global Cooperation Project in Computer Programming Course," Proc. ACM Technical Symposium on Computer Science Education, 1999, New Orleans, LA

[8] Richardson, I. et al. "Distributed Development – an Education Perspective on the Global Studio Project." Proc. the International Conference on Software Engineering, 2006, Shanghai, China

[9] Schadewitz, N. and Zakaria, N. "Cross-cultural Collaboration Wiki – Evolving Knowledge about International Teamwork." Proc. International Workshop on Intercultural Collaboration, 2009, Palo Alto, CA

[10] Tabrizi, M., Collins,C. and Kalamkar, V. "An International Collaboration in Software Engineering." Proc. ACM Technical Symposium on Computer Science Education, 2009, Portland, OR

Closed Labs in *Computer Science I* Revisited in the Context of Online Testing

Amruth N. Kumar
Ramapo College of New Jersey
505 Ramapo Valley Road
Mahwah, NJ 07430
1 201 684 7712
amruth@ramapo.edu

ABSTRACT

The majority of earlier studies have found no positive effect of closed labs on student performance or retention in *Computer Science I*. Since these studies used written tests to assess student performance, their results may have been affected by a mismatch between what was taught in closed labs and what was assessed in the written test. On the other hand, online tests that involve writing and debugging programs assess the very knowledge and skills taught in closed labs. So, we conducted a study to evaluate the effect of closed labs on student performance and retention when they are combined with online testing in the course.

We found that even with online testing, closed labs did not significantly affect either the total score of the students in the course or retention in the course. On the other hand, students with closed or even optional labs scored significantly better on their online first test than students with open labs scored on their written first test. Since this is in spite of the fact that online tests are more stressful to students than written tests, closed labs helped students prepare for online tests. Closed labs, when combined with online testing, helped significantly improve the course performance of above-average students. Finally, there was significant and large correlation between Math SAT score and student performance in *Computer Science I*.

Categories and Subject Descriptors

K.3.2 [Computing Milieux]: Computer and Information Science Education

General Terms

Measurement, Experimentation

Keywords

Closed Lab, Online Testing, Computer Science I, Retention.

1. INTRODUCTION

Closed labs are defined as laboratory sessions of fixed duration when students work on programming assignments under supervision [19]. These sessions are in addition to the programming projects that students carry out on their own time. Closed labs with a protocol are called **structured labs** - the protocol may be fashioned after labs in natural sciences and involve steps, such as description of declarative concepts, explanation of procedural/programming techniques, programming assignment(s) and a laboratory report, or they may be fashioned after engineering design lab model and involve pre-lab, in-lab and post-lab activities. In contrast to closed labs and structured labs, **open labs** are simply programming assignments that students attempt on their own time and turn in to be graded. Open labs have also been referred to as informal labs and closed labs have been referred to as formal labs in literature.

The pedagogical benefits of incorporating closed labs in *Computer Science I* have been well cataloged, but so have the factors that constrain the use of closed labs and ways to overcome those constraints [18]. The effect of using closed labs in *Computer Science I* on student learning and retention has been investigated with mixed results.

In one of the few studies that showed a positive effect of closed labs on student scores [17], researchers found that students in closed lab sections had significantly higher scores than those in open lab sections on the final comprehensive written exam, which consisted of short answer, multiple choice and subjective questions. However, there was no significant difference in the retention of the two groups.

In almost all the other studies, researchers found no positive effect of closed labs on student performance or retention. In one of the earliest studies [15], researchers found no significant difference between the test scores of open and closed lab students. Instead, attendance was highly correlated with scores on the programs submitted in the course.

In another study on the effects of closed labs in *Computer Science II* [2], researchers found no significant difference in the comprehension of concepts or the perception of effectiveness of the course between open and closed lab groups, even among the students identified as less likely to succeed in the two groups.

Similarly, in a study conducted a few years later in *Computer Science I* [7], researchers compared the effect of open and closed labs and found that open labs were just as effective on student achievement and attitudes as closed labs. The only significant factor influencing student achievement in *Computer Science I* was the math background of students: those who had a background at the level of *Calculus I* or higher had significantly greater achievement than those whose background was at a level lower than *Calculus I.*

We conducted a preliminary study [9] comparing open-lab version of *Computer Science I* against a version with *optional* closed lab, i.e., closed lab experience offered to students as optional extension of the regular lecture class. We found that optional closed lab did not help improve retention or project completion rates, but resulted in a qualitative improvement in student learning.

Finally, in another recent study [16], researchers found that student performance in the closed lab correlated with their performance on written course exams and programming assignments. However, closed labs did not increase student motivation and therefore, their performance or retention.

There have been subsequent studies about different closed lab options in *Computer Science I* – e.g., closed lab where students work individually and hands-on versus one in which they work in an interactive group [5]; using the same instructor for both lecture and lab versus using different instructors for lecture and lab [14]; and using different types of closed laboratories - those with only a help session, those where timed programming quizzes are administered, and those with timed quizzes as well as programming experiments [12]. But, given the implications on course credit, laboratory and personnel cost of incorporating closed labs in *Computer Science I*, it is both surprising and disappointing that the majority of the studies did not find any positive effect of using closed labs on student learning or retention in the course.

The lack of positive results could be due to mismatch between what is taught in closed labs and what is assessed in *Computer Science I*. The majority of the studies listed above used written tests to assess student learning in the course. Written tests do not adequately assess the student's ability to write and debug programs, two of the primary objectives of closed labs in *Computer Science I*, since these are hands-on activities. An online test that involves problem-solving and hands-on programming during the test will provide a better assessment of student learning in a *Computer Science I* course with closed lab. *With inclusion of online testing in the course, closed labs may have a significant and provable effect on student learning and retention in Computer Science I* – this was the hypothesis we set out to test in the study reported in this paper.

2. ONLINE TESTING

Online tests have been proposed for *Computer Science I*, both as a supplement to traditional written tests (e.g., [3, 4]), and as replacement for traditional tests (e.g., [13]). Our use of online tests in *Computer Science I* is in lieu of traditional written tests – students take two online tests during the semester, followed by an online final at the end of the semester. The course grade is based entirely on these three online tests.

Online tests as reported in literature could include multiple-choice questions, short free-text questions, as well as programming problems (e.g., [6]). In our case, the online tests consisted solely of programming problems. Each of our on-line tests consists of two questions:

1. Students are given a problem, and asked to write a program to solve it, compile the program and debug it. Students are given sample inputs and the expected outputs.
2. Students are asked to debug a program that contains a specified number of bugs. Both syntax and logic errors are included, and logic errors are given greater weight than syntax errors. Once again, a description of the problem being solved, sample inputs and expected outputs of the correct program are provided.

The primary activities in which students engage during the online test are solving a problem, writing a program and debugging a program. These activities assess the very knowledge and skills taught in closed labs in our *Computer Science I* course. Therefore, there is congruence between what is taught and what is assessed in the course, making the course an ideal test-bed for evaluating the effect of closed lab on student performance and retention in *Computer Science I.*

We do not use automated graders to grade the test programs, as some educators have reported in literature (e.g., [6]). Instead, the instructor reads every program, and assigns credit for each step correctly completed by the student, e.g., 3 points for validating input, 4 points for handling nested selection, etc. In other words, students can qualify for partial credit even if their program does not even compile. In order to reward completion of the program, 5% of the total grade is set aside for successful compilation, and another 10% for correct execution. Students are apprised of this partial credit scheme at the start of the test.

During the test, students are given the opportunity to ask the instructor for hint(s), on the condition that they will forfeit the points for the step to which the hint(s) pertains. This provision is meant to prevent students from failing the entire test if they get stuck on one small step. Provision of partial credit for incomplete programs and provision of hints during the test go a long way to alleviate the stress that researchers have associated with students taking online tests [3, 6, 20].

Finally, the tests are open-book, open-notes. Each student works at a separate computer. No collaboration or communication is allowed among students during the test. Students submit their programs and sample runs by email at the end of the test.

In an evaluation of online tests as replacement of traditional (written) tests, researchers found that online tests can result in increased student motivation and programming efficacy [20], and that both students and instructors agree that online tests provide a more accurate measure of student efficacy.

In our own prior evaluations of online testing in *Computer Science I*, we have found that students who do well on written tests do at least as well on online tests; and that online testing rewards better problem-solving skills [10]. We have also found that online tests do not increase attrition in the course; the class average does not suffer even when online tests are harder than written tests; and that there is a correlation between the number of projects completed and the score on online tests [11].

Both our evaluations were conducted in open lab versions of *Computer Science I*, when we had just introduced online testing into the course. Since then, we have taught the course first with optional closed lab, and later, with integral closed lab. All along, we have been administering online tests in the course. We will use data from these semesters to evaluate the effectiveness of closed labs in *Computer Science I* in the context of online testing.

3. METHODOLOGY

For this study, we considered data from three versions of our *Computer Science I* course - open-lab, optional lab and closed lab:

- Open lab version: This was a 3-credit course taught lecture-style in a lecture hall. The first test was written, but the second test and final exam were online. Data was collected from 3 sections of the course in fall 1998.
- Optional lab version: This was a 3-credit course. The class met in a lecture hall, but adjourned to a computer lab for the last 45 minutes of the class. The lab session continued for an additional 45 minutes after class. The first 45 minutes of the lab was treated as required part of the course. Students were not required to stay for the second 45 minutes of the lab, but were strongly urged to do so. During the lab, students were given programming assignments to complete online. The assignments were not graded. All three tests in the course were online. Data was collected from two sections in spring and fall 2001. This was the data used for our preliminary study [9].
- Closed lab version: This was a 4-credit course taught in a computer laboratory with one computer per student. After each programming construct was introduced, students were asked to write a program in class using the construct. The programs were not graded. All three tests in the course were online. Data was collected from 8 sections taught between 2002 and 2008.

All three versions of the course had the same instructor, used the same programming language (C++), same text-book/edition, and required similar after-class programming projects. Final grades in all three versions of the course were based solely on the three open-book tests in the course. The course satisfies General Education Science requirement. So, it was taken by majors as well as non-majors, students with widely varying computing backgrounds.

4. ANALYSIS AND RESULTS

Since earlier research had shown math background as a significant factor influencing student achievement in *Computer Science I* [7], we used Math SAT score as the basis for comparing cohorts from different semesters. Since SAT score was not available for the students who had transferred to the institution (as opposed to those who had registered as first-year students), their data was not included in the analysis. The populations for the various versions of *Computer Science I*, henceforth referred to as treatments, were: 24 for open labs, 22 for optional labs and 98 for closed labs. A one-way ANOVA analysis of the Math SAT score showed no significant main effect for the semester: [$F(9,143) = 1.005$, $p = 0.439$] or the type of treatment [$F(2,143) = 2.152$, $p = 0.12$]. So, the groups for the three different treatments were comparable.

4.1 Effect on Total Score in the Course

First, we considered the effect of treatment on the total score in the course, calculated as a weighted average of the scores on the three tests. The total score was normalized to the range 0 → 1. One-way ANOVA with the total score as the dependent variable and treatment as the independent variable showed no significant main effect for treatment [$F(2,143) = 1.677$, $p = 0.191$]. This remained the case even when we conducted one-way ANCOVA with Math SAT score as the co-variant [$F(2,143) = 0.213$, $p = 0.808$]. *In other words, the various treatments did not affect the total score of the students in the course even with online testing.*

4.2 Correlation with Math SAT Score

When we analyzed the total score using one-way ANCOVA, with Math SAT score as the covariant, even though we did not find any significant main effect for treatment, the ANCOVA model itself was significant [$F(3,143) = 38.736$, $p < 0.001$], and Math SAT score accounted for it [$F(1,143) = 110.256$, $p < 0.001$]. We plotted the average of the total scores of students with each Math SAT score against Math SAT score, as shown in Figure 1. We found polynomial correlation between total score in the course and Math SAT score, with a correlation coefficient of 0.9356. *So, the correlation between Math SAT score and performance in Computer Science I was both significant and large.* This result is in keeping with earlier work, wherein, SAT score was found to be one of the factors predicting the level of achievement in *Computer Science I* (e.g., [1, 8]).

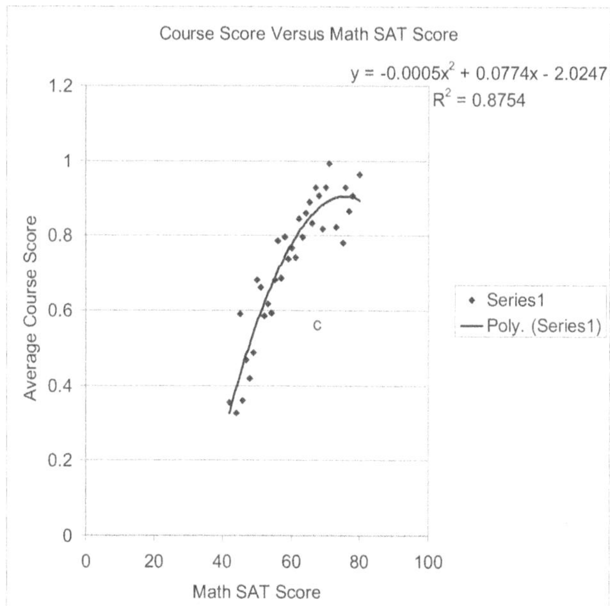

Figure 1. Polynomial correlation was found between total course score and Math SAT score

4.3 Effect on the First Test

In earlier studies, researchers found that students tend to do poorly on the first online test [3, 6, 20] – so much so that researchers in these studies strongly recommended that multiple online tests be conducted in order to eliminate the stress associated with online testing. We wanted to find out whether the treatment, and in particular, closed labs, had any effect on the first test.

One-way ANOVA with the first test score as the dependent variable and treatment as the independent variable showed significant main effect for treatment [$F(2,143) = 4.565$, $p = 0.012$]. The main effect of treatment remained marginally significant in one-way ANCOVA analysis with Math SAT score as the co-variant [$F(2,143) = 2.502$, $p = 0.086$]. The estimated marginal means or un-weighted means that controlled for the confounding effect of Math SAT scores were 0.813 for closed lab, 0.869 for optional lab and 0.764 for open lab.

So, students with closed or even optional lab scored better on online first test than students with open lab scored on written first test. This could be attributed to the fact that closed lab mitigates the stress of writing and debugging programs in real-time during tests by introducing students to similar working conditions before they get to the first test. In other words, *closed labs prepared students for online testing in Computer Science I.*

We did not find a similar main effect of treatment on the second test score [$F(2,143) = 0.576$, $p = 0.564$] or the final exam score [$F(2,143) = 1.333$, $p = 0.267$]. *So, the beneficial effect of closed labs was limited to the first third of the course even with online testing.*

4.4 Effect on Course Grade Distribution

Figure 2 shows the un-weighted average of the percentage of the class that scored grades A-F or withdrew from the course (W) for each treatment. For this analysis, we considered data of all the students, not just those whose Math SAT scores were available. So, the population sizes were 154 students over 8 sections for closed lab, 49 students over 2 sections for optional lab and 69 students over 3 sections for open lab. We found no significant main effect for treatment in one-way ANOVA analysis with letter grade as the dependent variable and treatment as the independent variable [$F(2,271) = 0.298$, $p = 0.743$]. In particular, note that the number of withdrawals is the same percentage of the class, regardless of the treatment. So, *closed lab did not significantly affect retention in the course even when online testing was used in the course*.

It is also clear from the figure that the percentage of the class earning Cs, Ds and Fs is around the same regardless of the treatment. The only difference seems to be in the number of A and B grades earned – about 10-15% of the class that would have earned a B with open lab manages to earn an A with closed or optional lab. This difference in A and B grades was statistically significant – we found a significant main effect for treatment in one-way ANOVA analysis with letter grades restricted to A and B as the dependent variable, and treatment as the independent variable [$F(2,129) = 3.299$, $p = 0.04$]. So, *closed labs, when combined with online testing, helped significantly improve the performance of above-average students, i.e., students who scored better than a C.*

5. DISCUSSION

The majority of the earlier studies had reported no significant effect of closed labs on student performance. Even with online testing, we found this to be true for the second test, final exam and total score in the course. But, we found two positive effects of closed labs when combined with online testing:

- Students with closed or even optional labs scored better on their online first test than students with open labs scored on their written first test. This can be interpreted as that closed labs prepare students for online testing, which has been identified in literature as a source of stress for students [3, 6, 20].
- Closed labs, combined with online testing helped significantly improve the course performance of above-average students, i.e., students who scored better than a C. Given the hands-on experience and one-on-one attention in closed labs, we are surprised that the beneficiaries of closed labs are not so much the weaker students as the above-average students.

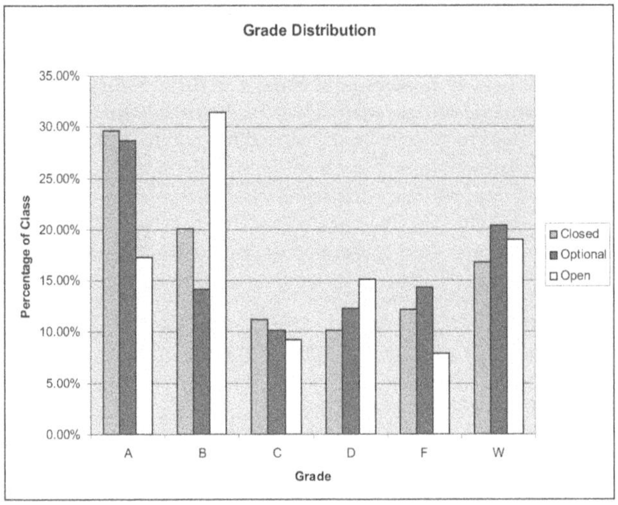

Figure 2. The grade earned by the largest group with closed or optional lab is A, and that with open lab is B.

Similarly, the majority of the earlier studies had reported no significant effect of closed labs on retention in the course. Surprisingly, even with the obvious congruence of the learning objectives of closed labs and the assessment objectives of online testing, we found no significant effect of closed labs on retention.

An earlier study [7] had found the math background of students at the level of Calculus I to be a significant factor influencing their achievement in *Computer Science I.* Other studies had found that SAT score was one of the factors predicting the level of achievement in *Computer Science I* (e.g., [1, 8]). We found a significant and large correlation between Math SAT score and performance in *Computer Science I.*

This was an *in-vivo* study, with some confounding factors such as unavailability of SAT scores for the entire population, and fluctuating enrollment in the course over the years. Yet, our results are in agreement with most of the results from earlier research on the use of closed labs in *Computer Science I*, although in the context of online testing. This study has shed some additional light on who benefits from closed labs when testing is online, and when they benefit from closed labs.

6. REFERENCES

[1] Braught, G., L.M. Eby, and T. Wahls. The effects of pair-programming on individual programming skill. in SIGCSE Technical Symposium. 2008. Portland, OR: ACM. p. 200-204.

[2] Burton, D.L., The effect of closed laboratory activities on the comprehension of five concepts and the perception of effectiveness of the course in a second semester computer science course, in Department of Computer Science. 1992, The University of Texas at Austin: Austin, TX.

[3] Califf, M.E. and M. Goodwin. Testing skills and knowledge: introducing a laboratory exam in CS1. in SIGCSE Technical Symposium. 2002. Covington, KY. p. 217-221.

[4] Chamillard, A.T. and J.K. Joiner. Using lab practica to evaluate programming ability. in SIGCSE Technical Symposium. 2001. Charlotte, NC. p. 159-163.

[5] Corritore, C., et al., A Comparison of Two Laboratory-based Approaches for Teaching Introductory Computer Science. Innovations in Education and Teaching International, 1999. 36(4): p. 292-301.

[6] English, J. Experience with a computer-assisted formal programming examination. in Innovation and Technology in Computer Science Education. 2002. Aarhus, Denmark. p. 51-54.

[7] Henderson, J.F., Restructuring the CS 1 classroom: examining the effect of open laboratory-based classes vs. closed laboratory-based classes on computer science 1 students' achievement and attitudes toward computers and computer courses. 2007, Florida Institute of Technology: Melbourne, FL. p. 328.

[8] Katz, S., et al., Gender, achievement, and persistence in an undergraduate computer science program. ACM SIGMIS Database 2006. 37(4): p. 42-57.

[9] Kumar, A.N., The Effect of Closed Labs in Computer Science I: An Assessment. The Journal of Computing Sciences in Colleges, 2003. 18(5): p. 40-48.

[10] Kumar, A.N., The Design of On-line Tests for Computer Science I and their Effectiveness, in Frontiers in Education Conference (FIE 99). 1999: San Juan, Puerto Rico. p. 13b3, 1-5.

[11] Kumar, A., On Changing from Written to On-line Tests in Computer Science I: An Assessment, in Innovation and Technology in Computer Science Education. 1999: Cracow, Poland. p. 25-28.

[12] Lang, J.E. and S. B.A., Scheduled Supervised Laboratories in CS I: A Comparative Analysis, in 24th Technical Symposium on Computer Science Education (SIGCSE 94). 1994: Indianapolis, IN. p. 185-188.

[13] Mason, D.V. and D.M. Woit. Integrating Technology into Computer Science Examinations. in SIGCSE Technical Symposium. 1998. Atlanta, GA. p. 140-144.

[14] McCauley, R., et al., Is CS1 Better with the Same Lecture and Lab Instructor?, in inroads – The SIGCSE Bulletin. 2006. p. 54-60.

[15] Peterson, C.G. and N.E. Miller. Open lab vs. closed lab: Computer Programming I at Mississippi State University. In SIGCSE Technical Symposium. 1985. New Orleans, LA. p. 78-81.

[16] Soh, L.-K., et al. Analyzing Relationships between Closed Labs and Course Activities in CS1. in SIGCSE Technical Symposium. 2005. St. Louis, MO. p. 183-187.

[17] Thweatt, M. CS1 Closed Lab vs. Open Lab Experiment. in SIGCSE Technical Symposium. 1994. Phoenix, AZ. p. 80-82.

[18] Titterton, N. and M.J. Clancy. Adding some lab time is good, adding more must be better: The benefits and barriers to lab-centric courses. in International Conference on Frontiers in Education: Computer Science & Computer Engineering (FECS 2007). 2007. Athens, GA: CSREA Press. p. 363-367.

[19] Tucker, A. and A. Turner, Computing Curricula 1991: Summary of the Joint Curriculum Task Force Report, in Communications of the ACM. 1991.

[20] Woit, D. and D. Mason. Effectiveness of online assessment. in SIGCSE Technical Symposium. 2003. Reno, NV. p. 137-141.

How Do Computing Faculty Adopt Curriculum Innovations? The Story from Instructors

Lijun Ni
School of Interactive Computing
Georgia Institute of Technology
Atlanta, GA, 30332-0760
lijun@cc.gatech.edu

Tom McKlin
The Findings Group
1031 North Hills Drive
Atlanta, GA, 30033
tom@thefindingsgroup.com

Mark Guzdial
School of Interactive Computing
Georgia Institute of Technology
Atlanta, GA, 30332-0760
guzdial@cc.gatech.edu

ABSTRACT
This paper presents the findings of an exploratory, qualitative study revealing computing instructors' experience in adopting curriculum innovations. We interviewed eight instructors a year after they attended workshops on several innovative introductory Computer Science (intro CS) courses at undergraduate level. The interview was designed to elicit the extent to which instructors had adopted or adapted what they learned from the workshops, and what drove or prevented their efforts to make curriculum change. The results of this study reveal that the adoption and adaptation of computing curriculum innovations in new situations may involve systemic change affecting instructors, departments and institutions as a whole. The findings of this study suggest a list of questions that a computing instructor might ask before committing to a new innovation. We also consider implications of this study for disseminating computing education innovations.

Categories and Subject Descriptors
K.3.2 [**Computers and Education**]: Computer and Information Science Education–*computer science education.*

General Terms
Design, Experimentation, Theory.

Keywords
Computing Instructors, Adoption, Change

1. INTRODUCTION
Due to the relative young and evolving nature of the computing discipline, the Computing Education community is faced with frequent changes to technologies they are teaching and teaching with. Innovative approaches to teach computing are being created to address the challenges we are facing in computing education (e.g., the evolving computing knowledge, the declining enrollment and interest in CS) [11] , as well as to improve the quality of computing education. These innovations include new pedagogical approaches, curriculum and educational software aimed at promoting learning and teaching in computing.

To make those innovations or best practices have real impact on teaching practices, we eventually need computing instructors to adopt those innovations and integrate them into their own classrooms. Therefore, it is critical to understand how instructors actually adopt, adapt and implement computing education innovations in the contexts of their departments and courses.

Meanwhile, one major channel to disseminate educational innovations is through offering professional development (PD) opportunities for teachers [5, 9]. Related research indicates that faculty development participation has strong, statistically significant impact on faculty's adoption of innovative teaching practices [6]. Therefore, in particular, we are interested in exploring, how a computing instructor actually adopts (or fails to adopt) a curriculum innovation into the local school context after attending PD activities related to that innovation.

We interviewed eight CS faculty members from different universities about a year after they attended workshops on several innovative intro CS courses. This interview was designed to elicit the extent to which those instructors had adopted or adapted what they learned from the workshops. Furthermore, we attempted to understand what contributed to instructors' actual decisions on whether to make change within their local contexts.

In the following section, we introduce our methods, present the findings from this study, and discuss the implications of these findings for disseminating computing education innovations.

2. INTERVIEW STUDY
As Seidman [8] recommended, interviewing is a basic mode of inquiry into people's experience, which provides access to the context of people's behavior and thereby provides a way for researchers to understand the meaning of their action. In this study, we use interviewing as our method to start exploring computing instructors' curriculum change experience. We conducted semi-structured interviews with eight CS faculty members who had attended at least one summer workshop on several innovative intro CS courses for undergraduates.

2.1 Interview Population
The instructors attended at least one of the three workshops offered in summer 2007. These workshops introduced several contextualized computing courses offered for undergraduates to encourage diversity and to improve the enrollment and retention of students in CS [3, 4]. These courses emphasize the use of a specific context or theme (e.g. media manipulation or robotics) throughout the whole course, which students recognize as being authentic and relevant for computing [4].

The workshops were organized into 4-5 sections each day, around example lectures, follow-up exercises and discussions on how instructors could implement them into local school contexts. During the workshops, the workshop lecturer presented related research results, providing evidence that these contextualized curricula contributed to improvement on student motivation and retention [1, 10]. In order to help the instructors build confidence about using the contextualized approach, we encouraged them to work on learning tasks proposed in each course, e.g. creating an image collage computationally.

Interview participants were selected based on an adoption survey administered to collect participants' adoption decisions several months after the workshops [7]. From 24 instructors who reported adoption decisions, we randomly picked up eight instructors (four *adopters* and four *non-adopters),* who were willing to be interviewed. All of them were CS faculty members from different four-year universities, with experiences in teaching computing courses from 2 years to over 15 years. To improve the reliability of the interviews, we asked the second author to conduct the interviews, who was the external evaluator of this project.

2.2 Interview Questions

We used a semi-structured interview protocol to elicit the extent to which the instructors had adopted or adapted the contextualized computing courses and what were the influencing factors. The interview protocol was designed based on Guskey's [2] five levels of professional learning. Specifically, the participants were asked what content and pedagogical techniques they recalled from the workshop and how they applied those techniques. They were then asked what action they had taken as a result of their workshop participation, whether their participation resulted in any organizational change to their department, curriculum, instruction, etc. They were also asked to describe any student success they had observed related to using those innovations. Finally, they were asked about their future plans to adopt those courses. Throughout the interview, the participants were explicitly asked to reflect on what contributed to their actual adoption decisions.

2.3 Interview Analysis

Each interview was recorded and transcribed. We then performed a multistep analysis to increase coding reliability and fidelity. First, two authors examined four separate interview transcripts each to obtain an initial understanding of how computing instructors adopt curriculum innovations in their local school contexts. The individual transcripts were read several times. The portions of the transcripts directly related to instructors' change experience (e.g., adoption status, adoption factor, etc) were extracted for each transcript. Each researcher separately came up with themes or codes to categorize the extracts. The authors then came together to review the variations of computing instructors' adoption experiences. The authors then created a *code book*, a list of codes with a definition and an example of each code. Using this code book, one author then reviewed and coded all eight transcripts. During this process, categories of description were formed and reformed to capture the variation of the eight instructors' change experience. In the end, the authors reviewed and discussed the final coding results. The main results of this analysis are presented in next section.

3. RESULTS

In this section, we outline how the participants actually made or did not make any changes, based on what we found from the interviews. First, we summarize participants' reasons for considering curricular and pedagogical changes to teaching computing. We then describe their most pressing concern: making the innovation fit and work in a local department with multiple competing needs. We present the competing needs in terms of what prevents or facilitates instructors' change. Finally, we derive a set of questions from the interview transcripts that instructors contemplating a computing education innovation may consider.

3.1 Reasons for Considering Change

The major motivation for the instructors to look for curriculum innovations came from a need to change the current situation: lackluster student motivation, declining enrollment and retention of students in CS, and shrinking participation among women and under-represented minorities. The illustrative extracts below are what the faculty told us about what drove their intent to adopt the curriculum innovations from the workshops.

> P1: Enrollment really dropped. That is one reason why we tried to look at other ways and make changes in intro classes. The retention rate is also bad. We have a retention rate of like 30% in the school, and in our department, it was like 10%. There're serious problems. We had to think about what was wrong and the main problem was the intro class. So we tried to make it more interesting to get them to stay in the program.

> P3: The enrollment of women in CS has fallen off precipitously. That started 20 years ago, but now, it's a rather low percentage. I have about one woman in one of my senior classes. And that's not very many at all.

3.2 Adoption Status

While the faculty we interviewed were motivated to make changes and interested in adopting the curriculum innovations, all faced roadblocks to making the changes actually occur. The extent and nature of the roadblocks *determined* the status of their adoption.

- One participant can be described as a full adopter. He has adopted one Intro to Media Computation course *successfully* for two semesters, and then his department has decided to adopt it in the whole department in the coming semester.
- Another participant tried one Media Computation course in 2007. He has decided to teach it again this coming Fall when will be his turn to teach the CS1 course in his department.
- Another participant has chosen to adopt one element of the workshop, a new IDE, into his CS1 course. Now he and his colleagues who also teach that course are using this new IDE.
- One participant is hoping to adopt in the near future. She is waiting for a textbook for the new Media Computation Data Structures course to be available.
- The remaining four participants has expressed interest in adopting in the future; none has said that they has given up hope of adopting the innovation altogether.

3.3 Changing Organizations

The analysis of the interview transcripts also reveals that the adoption of computing curriculum innovations by individual instructor may involve organizational change beyond one individual instructor. Here, the code "organizational change" is used to describe the process of getting members of the computing department to support or conduct an innovation. Most of the conversations on the topic of organizational change occurred among the non-adopters. Although many instructors described the flexibility they enjoyed in changing their own teaching strategies, a majority of these comments focused on the difficulty of getting one other person in the department to change in order to introduce both the content and teaching strategies inherent in the innovation.

> P8: There are four of us that are willing to try things and there is one of us that absolutely would not. I don't think you are going to get a whole departmental change to embrace Media Computation at this point.

> P7: I think it has possibilities for our CS0 course, but we haven't acted on that yet because the person in charge of that course did not leave. We were thinking of changing this if we took over that course or if we had responsibility for hiring somebody else.

While many claimed that the root of their adoption issues lied in getting one other person in the department to change, the real issue might not lie with that one person but with the organizational system supporting that one person's behavior. This coding category describes barriers that prevent the original adopter from introducing an innovation to a local computing department. Interestingly, this coding category was used more often than any other coding category.

3.4 Barriers to Change

The implementation of an innovation will face numerous barriers. These barriers can either slow down or completely stall a change that an individual instructor wants to create, despite the overwhelming need to try something different. Below, we outline some of the common barriers from the transcripts.

3.4.1 Little Freedom for Content Change

Many respondents said that they enjoyed the freedom to teach CS content in whatever way they wished, provided that the material was covered, the learning objectives were met, and the students were well-prepared for the next level. However, that freedom did not extend to changing what content was covered. Respondents felt that the new approach required a change to the content.

> P3: You know, the course content is already designed, and I think [the new] approach is very interesting. But, I don't have that flexibility to change the content. There are other faculty members teaching the course, so I have to use the course that is already developed.

3.4.2 Demand for Faculty Development

Adopting a curriculum innovation may require instructors to take time to learn something new, which competes with other faculty demands. In the following examples, the participants expressed the concern that adopting the innovation required training other instructors, a commitment that might over-burden stressed faculty.

> P7: Some other issues that are important are about faculty development. I have been to these workshops. I am familiar with the [innovations]... How are we going to do the faculty development? We made some changes before when moving to an object-oriented approach for our first course, and that was a lengthy transition.

> P4: The entire faculty is really overloaded with trying to meet teaching loads, advising loads and committee loads. So for the younger faculty members, that is going to be a real issue.

3.4.3 Poor Ability and Background of Students

Instructors might perceive that the change simply would not work within their own schools. For example, some participants felt their students' ability and background was a bad match with the innovation. They perceived that the students at the innovating institute might handle the innovation more easily.

> P5: This is too difficult for our kind of students. It might work well for students at [the university that developed these courses], but our students are a little different. Usually they are weak in foundations even if they went to CS0, CS1 and CS2. When they come into my class, some of them have a hard time to write even just simple programs or read programs. One really can't expect they already have any major math skills to learn programming. I don't think I would be able to incorporate that, at least for the data structures class.

3.4.4 Different Focuses on Learning Outcomes

New curricula may have different emphasis on learning outcomes. Faculty may disagree with this change. Some participants explicitly questioned the innovation because it strayed from a traditional approach and traditional values in teaching intro CS.

> P5: I think myself have some disagreement with the department that a lot of things that would go a little bit away from hardcore programming and still Media Computation requires a low level programming. There is a lot of programming in our program. Generally, some people want to push for less programming and others want to keep the status quo. So, there is disagreement in which way to go.

By changing the priority of learning outcomes, a new approach might attract students who prefer the new values. Faculty may not want those new students in their program. Another participant worried that a non-traditional approach might attract the *wrong* students and possibly set them up for failure later in the major.

> P8: I guess [Media Computation] is very visual, highly interactive, but there are other pieces to CS. There is a lot of it that is related to applied mathematics: computer theory, assembly language and machine organization, and all these kinds of components aren't going to be drawing pretty pictures and highly visual. In fact the [content] is going to be rigorous and very formal, requiring analytical skills that some people don't want to bother with. So I am not sure if it would attract the right people for the right reasons.

3.4.5 Near and Far Ripple Effect of Change

The participants also mentioned that change to first courses would result in cascading and possibly unexpected changes, both to the courses in which the innovation was adopted and to courses later in the sequence. They reflected on what they currently valued in a course, and the affect of the innovation on subsequent courses.

> P6: The new course really requires rethinking of two things: 1) How do we teach fundamentally the same material? 2) What's important? What are the really important concepts here? If we change, it means that some of what we used to do, we no longer do, and some of what we are doing now we probably will be deemphasizing if we take the new approach. Is that good? Is that bad? It takes discussions and different faculty will react differently to this.

> P5: It does have an effect not only in the beginning courses. What can we assume that the students already know in subsequent courses? So there is a ripple effect throughout several courses in the curriculum.

3.5 Accelerators to Change

Just as there are barriers to adopting an innovation, we also see systemic conditions that not only motivate the innovation but might increase the rate at which that innovation may be adopted. We call the latter "accelerators."

3.5.1 Sense of Urgency

One accelerator was a strong sense of urgency about issues outlined in the section above, "Reasons for Considering Change." All participants were troubled by the declining enrollments in the department, low retention rates in CS, and homogenous student body. Some participants perceived this as a reason enough to try an innovation, whereas others might not be as affected by these trends and might be less likely to adopt. One participant summed it up by saying, "I think what we're finding here is that having a real traditional CS curriculum is not working."

3.5.2 Perceived Benefits for Students

The adopters among our interview group believed that motivating students was essential for increasing enrollment and retention, and the new approach would help to motivate their students.

> P4: I think students would enjoy Media Computation, and I think it would be valuable for them. It would help them understand computing a little bit, and it would be an interesting introduction for that purpose. Students seem to be more interested because they have a sense of ownership to the objects they are manipulating.

Faculty members were willing to invest efforts to change when they believe their change would help their students.

> P2: I really do believe students can learn this material and I do want them to learn it. And it's a way to bring more people into computing. Already, I've seen at least two people that have come over in our department and they have told me it's because of my class. So, I feel like I am making that type of positive impact. It's probably for their best interest and partly mine to make sure I am keen on those things that really help them.

3.5.3 Successful Experiment

One participant actually conducted an experiment comparing two courses, one using the new approach and the other taught in a traditional way. The *successful* initial adoption convinced him to further adopt this innovative course, even drove a full adoption in the whole department later on.

> P1: We did an experiment this year. I was teaching the course using Media Computation and my colleague was teaching the course in the way we've always been teaching it. We have discovered that the students seem to be responding better and they are more excited about the new course. The performance of students taking the new CS1 course in the next course (CS2) is on a par with the students who are coming out of the other courses. The plus side of all this is we've got more students finishing the new CS1 course successfully than in the traditional course. I think I've won over my colleagues and everybody in the department will be using Media Computation in the coming Fall.

3.5.4 Recommending Pedagogy

The participants mentioned earlier that they usually did not have the flexibility to change course content, which prevented their adoption. The courses presented at the workshops included change to pedagogy, suggesting particular ways of presenting CS concepts and new kind of student assignments. These were sometimes seen as a kind of *restrictions* for the faculty. However, some instructors perceived these *restrictions* as a positive step.

> P1: Traditionally, we've been able to teach what we want, just in the constraints of language that we're using. Now you are telling us how we are going to teach the course. And that is a shift in the way we have done things. But this was the right thing to do. When we switched from C++ to Java a couple years back, there was no discussion about how to teach the course, just "here is a different language to teach it". So the faculty members still pretty much designed their own approach to teaching. With [the new approach], there is a little bit more constraint. There is more focus on the types of assignments students will do even though there is latitude in picking the exact assignments.

Faculty might enjoy the freedom to choose the way to teach as long as the material is covered. However, under this situation, they may be inclined to focus more on covering the required material than on determining whether the students have learned the material. Otherwise, when an innovation brings corresponding pedagogy as well, faculty would likely implement a wholly change involving pedagogical innovations.

3.6 Critical Issues in Making Change

We derived a set of questions from the interview transcripts that a potential adopter may ask or consider before committing to an innovation. These questions were harvested from all interviews and reflected questions that were most asked by the faculty while considering adoption. These questions are:

- What is the important material or content for the course, and how will the innovation highlight the important content?

- What actual changes will I have to make to implement the innovation?
- How will we ensure that students learn the most important concepts and gain the same skills with the new approach?
- How might current and incoming students respond to the innovation?
- How will the innovation motivate students to enroll and persist in computing major?
- How will the innovation help us maintain the quality (of the computing course and thereby the quality of students)?
- How will the innovation assure us that students are well-prepared for upper-level computing courses?
- How will this change affect other stakeholders in our computing department?

Some stakeholders could be lab instructors, teaching assistants, instructors teaching the same course or upper-level courses, and instructors in other departments participating in a joined program. For example, a computing faculty might consider how the change might influence upper-level instructors: How will this curricular change prepare students for upper-level courses? Will upper-level instructors have to cover material that is not learned earlier?

These questions indicate different types and stages of adoption concerns from instructor who are considering and experiencing change: *personal concerns* about how change will affect themselves, *task concerns* about how to manage the new practice, and finally *impact concerns* about how the new practice will affect students and other stakeholders [5, 9]. In general, early concerns are more self-oriented, e.g. what is the innovation? How will it affect me? Our participants reported mainly the latter two concerns. One possible explanation might be: participating in related PD program helped to solve their early concerns. In other words, they had gained some knowledge about the innovation from the workshop, which helped to answer their early concerns.

4. DISCUSSION

This study provides an initial source of empirical data to explore how computing instructors adopt curriculum innovations. First, the results of this study indicate that one pressing concern for instructors (who want to adopt a curriculum innovation) is making the innovation fit and work in a local department. Adopting a new curriculum might become a major change involving systemic change affecting instructors, departments and sometimes other departments or even the institution as a whole. In addition to macro-level organizational change, successful adoption might also require micro-level change or agreement in terms of instructors' perceptions about the field and the learning goals to achieve. For example, in section 3.4.4, some interviewees *blamed* the new approach in distorting the image of CS. What underlies that disagreement is not just about different approaches, but more about different perceptions on what is CS and what is the most important to teach in intro CS courses.

Second, the findings of this study are consistent with an earlier study surveying CS teachers' adoption concerns in the end of the workshops [7]. Our results also indicate the complexity of implementing change in new contexts. Although the instructors we studied wanted to create change (had a strong motivation already), and had attended helpful PD activities, they still experienced a variety of challenges when making actual adoption. Meanwhile, our findings are actually based on what the instructors believed as necessary to make change and the barriers they had encountered. It's fair to say that what instructors say are not necessarily the most critical issues for curriculum change. However, since instructors are the ones who actually implement the innovations in classrooms, it is critical to take into account their perceptions in order to effectively disseminate and implement curriculum innovations. For example, researchers and innovative curriculum developers might want to provide pedagogical recommendations and lecture examples within a new curriculum for easier adoption. Professional developers and facilitators need to understand what concerns PD participants face, and try to address those issues (example questions are listed in section 3.6). Particularly, when designing and organizing PD activities to disseminate innovations, PD developers and facilitators should consider how the PD could help motivate instructors to change and solve early stages of concerns [5].

5. ACKNOWLEDGMENTS

We would like to thank all the instructors participating in our study. This work is supported by the National Science Foundation under Grant Nos. 0618674 and 0634629. Any opinions, findings, and conclusions or recommendations expressed in this material are those of the author(s) and do not necessarily reflect the views of the National Science Foundation.

6. REFERENCES

[1] Forte, A. and Guzdial, M. Computers for communication, not calculation: media as a motivation and context for learning. in *Proceedings of the 37th Annual Hawaii International Conference on System Sciences*, IEEE Computer Society, Washington, 2004, Track 4, 40096.1.

[2] Guskey, T.R. and Sparks, D. *Evaluating Professional Development*. Corwin Press, 2000.

[3] Guzdial, M., & Forte, A. Design Process for a Non-majors Computing Course. in *Proceedings of SIGCSE 2005*, St. Louis, Missouri, USA, 2005, 361 - 365.

[4] Guzdial, M. and Tew, A.E. Imagineering inauthentic legitimate peripheral participation: an instructional design approach for motivating computing education. in *Proceedings of ICER 2006*, ACM Press, 2006, 51-58.

[5] Hall, G.E. and Hord, S.M. *Implementing Change: Patterns, Principles, and Potholes*. Allyn and Bacon, Boston, 2001.

[6] Matney, M. *Institutional and departmental factors influencing faculty adoption of innovative teaching practices*. School of Education, University of Michigan, 2001.

[7] Ni, L. What makes CS teachers change? Factors influencing CS teachers' adoption of curriculum innovations. in *Proceedings of SIGCSE 2009*, 544-548.

[8] Seidman, I. *Interviewing as Qualitative Research: A Guide for Researchers in Education and the Social Sciences*. Teachers College Press, 2005.

[9] Smith, C. and Gillespie, M. Research on professional development and teacher change: implications for adult basic education, NCSALL, 2007, 226-234.

[10] Tew, A.E., Fowler, C. and Guzdial, M. Tracking an innovation in introductory CS education from a research university to a two-year college in *Proceedings of SIGCSE 2005*. ACM Press, 2005, 416-420.

[11] Vegso, J. Interest in CS as a major drop among incoming freshmen. *Computing Research News, 17* (3).

CS1, Arcade Games and the Free Java Book

Daniel L. Schuster
MCIS Dept
Western State College
Gunnison, CO 81231
970-943-2999
dschuster@western.edu

ABSTRACT

Computer game programming has been adopted by some instructors and schools in an effort to motivate students and make the learning more relevant to the student's world than the console programs many of their instructors learned with. This paper describes the author's experience teaching CS1 using the ACM Java library to write arcade game programs. An online book, the Free Java Book, has been written to support this approach. Experience over the last two years teaching with this approach will be shared and the book will be described.

Categories and Subject Descriptors

K.3.2 [**Computers and Education**]: Computer and Information Science Education—computer science education, curriculum.

General Terms

Design, Human Factors

Keywords

CSI, Games, ACM Java, Free Java Book

1. INTRODUCTION

About eight years ago the author began to struggle with what he felt was an increasing lack of relevance in the CS1 course. The work done in CS1 looked nothing like the computer applications the student grew up with. Many students appeared bored, and certainly the author was bored. Alternatives were explored but all were thought to be lacking in one way or another.

In August of 2006 the ACM Java Task Force released the first version of the ACM Java Library. This library includes a wealth of tools that bring more advanced Java subjects to the introductory level. In particular, the graphics library makes simple graphics and animation accessible at the very beginning of the introductory course. An updated version of the library was released in 2008.

Games are a well known motivator for students learning to program [1]. Studies have indicated that generally students prefer game assignments to non-games [2]. Game programming assignments allow the students to work in a visual, interactive domain that is perhaps more interesting and more real than the console based environment that some other approaches use. Schools have reported success with a gaming approach [1,2,3,4] and some have tried gaming to introduce more advanced topics [5].

The author began teaching with the ACM Java Library in the spring of 2007, and each semester has included more elements of animation and gaming in the CS1 course. Currently CS1 at Western State College of Colorado uses graphics and game programming for about 95% of the course, the remainder being console programming. Note also that at Western essentially all students enter CS1 with no programming experience and sometimes little idea of what programming is, so CS1 must begin at the very beginning.

A textbook has been written to support this approach. The Free Java Book (FJB) is available online at www.freejavabook.org and is available at no charge to educational institutions.

It is important to recognize that it is not the purpose of this CS1 course to teach game programming or the ACM Java library. They are merely a means to an end. The purpose of the course is to teach the usual CS1 topics—loops, decisions, modularity, objects, problem analysis, etc. Game programming provides an interesting application domain and the ACM Java Library provides a thin layer that makes this domain accessible to the beginner.

2. THE ACM JAVA LIBRARY

The ACM Java Library provides several fundamental classes that are the foundation of the arcade game approach.

The GraphicsProgram class and the GObject class provide an application window and a variety of visual shapes to work with. These include rectangles, ovals, lines and labels. These shapes can be collected into a compound object with its own constructors and methods.

The ConsoleProgram class provides simplified input and output for console programs, which are helpful for illustrating some very basic concepts.

A useful random generation capability is also provided by the ACM library.

Standard Java provides the necessary mouse and keyboard interactivity.

All programs run as Java applets, but this is invisible to the student.

The current website for the latest version of the ACM Java Library is www-cs-faculty.stanford.edu/~eroberts/jtf.

SIGCSE'10, March 10–13, 2010, Milwaukee, Wisconsin, USA.

3. THE FREE JAVA BOOK

CS1 as taught at Western State College has transitioned from Pascal to C to C++ and most recently Java. For two and a half years the course has been taught increasingly in the arcade game domain.

As is sometimes the case, handouts became more extensive notes which became crude chapters which grew and eventually became the FJB. As of this writing, the FJB is incomplete. Eleven chapters are ready or almost ready for release, with the remainder to written as time allows.

Twenty years of teaching CS1 and five semesters of experience with this approach have led the author to the following topic ordering and general content:

1) Fundamentals – a quick introduction to programming and the basics of the ACM Java library. The student is able to write simple console programs and draw simple static graphic images.

2) ACM Java Graphics – a detailed look at some of the components of the ACM Java Library including rectangles, ovals, lines, labels, graphic images, and the application window. The student is able to characterize the application window, manipulate graphic objects and create simple animations.

3) Making Decisions – logical expressions, the boolean data type, and conditionals are covered in detail. The student is able to write animations with changeable behavior.

4) Loops – for and while loops and the game loop are covered. The student can write more complex animations and learns some loop related algorithms.

5) Methods and Objects I – covers void methods, passing primitive data types as arguments and simple programmer defined objects. Basic UML for objects is introduced. The student can decompose elementary problems into methods and objects.

6) Game Programming I – introduces standard Java applet components, elements of simple games such as object collision, some mouse and keyboard interactivity, and random integers. The student is able to write simple but real games such as Pong, keep score, provide instruction screens and levels of play.

7) Useful Java Objects – covers Java chars, the Character and String classes, the Math library and the ACM Random class. The student can write String based activities (Talk Like a Pirate translations for example) and add significantly to game character with more sophisticated mathematically controlled behaviors and additional random characteristics.

8) Arrays and ArrayLists I – cover the fundamentals of these objects so that the student can conveniently work with large numbers of game elements.

9) Methods II – more about methods, arguments and returned values. The student learns more techniques for dealing with complexity.

10) Objects II – more complete coverage of objects including accessors and mutators, the toString method, etc. UML is revisited. The student can create more fully featured objects.

11) Game Programming II – more sophisticated mouse and keyboard interaction, time dependant object behavior, more complex gaming. The student can write more sophisticated games with more complex interaction and object behaviors.

12) Arrays and ArrayLists II – more about arrays and ArrayLists, searching and sorting algorithms.

Additional coverage on Text Files, Multi-dimension Arrays and ArrayLists may be required for courses at some schools and is planned.

Quick Reference and Setting Up Your Computer appendices have been written. Additional appendices on compilation errors and the standard Java language are planned. A support forum exists.

The Free Java Book has some characteristics that are beneficial to the beginning student.

- language focus – there is no attempt to cover a large subset of the Java language with a massive book. Instead focus is only on those elements that form a foundation for arcade game programming and further study as a CS student.
- application domain focus – the application domain is almost completely restricted to arcade game programming. The student works constantly on animation and games, while remaining in Java.

The result is that the student is surrounded and immersed in what they need, but distractions and possibly extraneous material are removed from their environment.

4. SAMPLE ASSIGNMENTS

The arcade game application domain provides a wealth of assignments at every point in the curriculum and every level of difficulty. A few representative problems are described.

Robot Assignment – the student produces a robot.

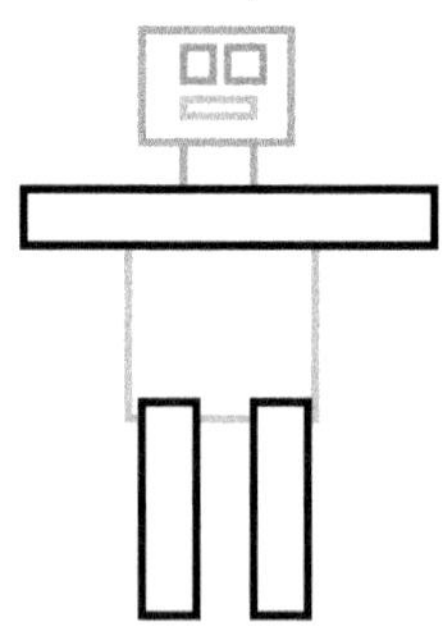

Figure 1. Robot

The assignment teaches sequence, familiarity with the coordinate system and working with objects from the ACM Library.

Drop And Roll assignment – the student produces an animation of a ball falling off and rolling away from a block, snapshots of which are shown below.

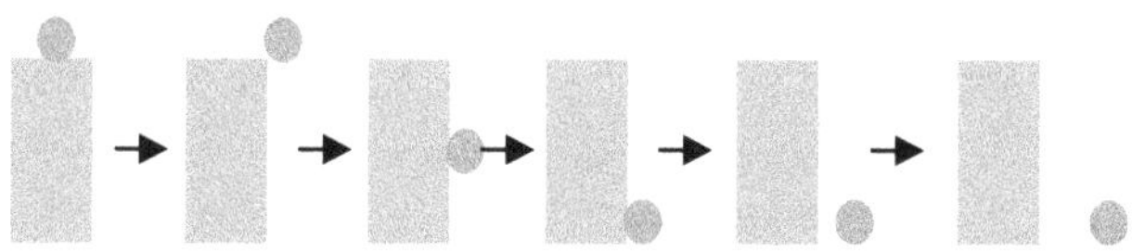

Figure 2. Rolling Ball

The assignment teaches boolean expressions, loops and animation basics.

Crash assignment – the student flies a UFO across the application window, with a flickering exhaust or flashing lights. When the UFO hits a space mine it blows up into several pieces but the alien parachutes to the ground. The program concludes with the message *The End* which scrolls right to left, starting at the right side.

In this assignment the student works with multiple objects, multiple loops, detects collision by comparing coordinates and produces differentiated movement of objects. Some students have produced elaborate versions with more action.

This assignment was inspired by a student who took a simpler version of it and added the parachuting alien.

You Choose 1 assignment – the student creates an interactive game of their choice, with the instructor's approval.

Allowing the student to select their own task increases their engagement. The instructor's approval is required to insure that they are taking on a task they can handle at this point in the course, and that the assignment requires enough of the student.

Students have produced good, straightforward versions of Pong, Helicopter in a Cave, Dodgeball, various shooting/clicking games, a juggling game, BreakOut, Lunar Lander and Frogger as seen in Figure 3.

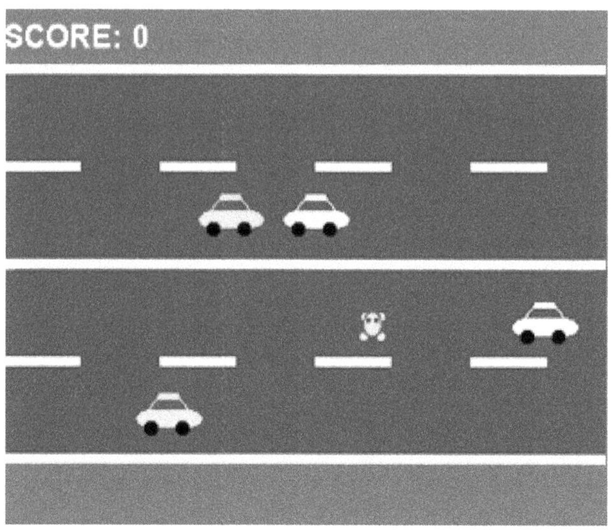

Figure 3. Frogger by Curtis Prock

The assignment requires programmer created objects and methods, mouse or keyboard control, scoring and levels.

BugBot assignment – the student creates a bug robot that wanders a playing field, bumps into objects and searches for a goal. The assignment does not require interactivity but makes significant use of methods and objects.

Asteroid Escape assignment – the student creates a version of the classic Asteroids game. The game features user created objects for the asteroids, the spaceship, black holes, etc. The spaceship is a complex object with several mutators and accessors. The keyboard is used to control the spaceship. Instructions are displayed, current spaceship status (fuel, etc.) are displayed, scoring is kept and there are multiple levels.

The student works with more sophisticated objects and significant additional complexity.

You Choose 2 assignment – the student creates an interactive game of their choice, with the instructor's approval. Suggested games include Missile Command, Helicopter Rescue or various puzzles. Students have also turned in excellent versions of Frogger, Asteroids and shoot-em-ups.

At Western State College, this assignment is the final project of the CS1 course. The student builds on their existing tools and skills and adds the capability to handle large amounts of data and implement more sophisticated behavior. It is expected that resultant game (or activity, because some students opt for puzzles, etc.) will be at least reasonably professional. And some of them are. Figure 4 is a screen capture from an elaborate version of Asteroids written by a student with little previous programming experience.

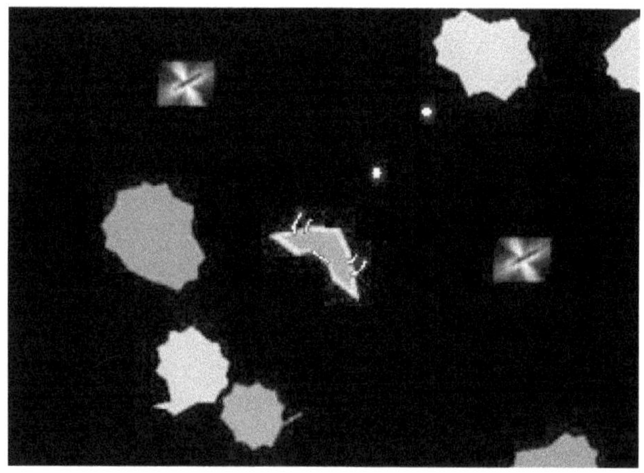

Figure 4. Asteroids by Peter Lewis

5. COMMENTS ABOUT THIS APPROACH

Most topics of the ACM library are taught as "black magic", with as little explanation as possible. The student learns about the ACM objects and methods as tools, not as interesting in themselves. For the sake of brevity, some obvious topics such as GPolygons are simply left out. The author's experience is that some more advanced students will ask for more powerful tools and a reference to online documentation on GPolygons has been sufficient.

Much of the course is taught Just In Time (JIT). Thus a topic is taught when it is needed and when the student is likely to be ready for it, and not before.

Consider the introduction to objects. At this point in the course students are writing programs of perhaps 200 lines of code, with a fair amount of this being repeated code. Void methods have been introduced to encapsulate tasks such as displaying instructions.

Students are also writing programs that move a multi-part graphic object, perhaps 3-component UFO as seen in Figure 5.

Figure 5. UFO

To move this UFO using what the student already knows at this point requires moving each of the three components. The student realizes, as one of mine said, "there must be a better way." And there is—objects. Gathering these three components into one object makes the student's work simpler. The student learns the default and non-default constructors. Objects are embraced by the students because they are easy to grasp and they are necessary. Later in the course, when the student's increasing sophistication demands more powerful objects, more thorough coverage is appropriate.

In this approach game playing is also introduced JIT. The student learns basic mouse and keyboard interactivity, object collision, randomizing the action, how to keep time and score and play levels early in the course. This allows them to write good, basic, playable games just a few weeks into the course. More sophisticated interactivity and time dependant object behavior should be delayed until the student is ready for it.

The majority of students will turn in simple but playable and fun games. These students will have accomplished the goals of a CS1 course, but not created works of the gaming art. They might produce little better than a good version of Space Invaders or Break Out. On the other hand a few will produce stunningly good programs. Students in this course have written wonderful, colorful, complex versions of Missile Command and Asteroids and other games created with this course as their only programming experience. They've been challenged, had a lot of fun and learned what they needed to learn.

6. OTHER APPROACHES WITH GAMING

The ACM Library provides a thin layer over standard Java and might be viewed as the *minimal* toolkit needed to accomplish graphics game programming at the CS1 level, while still keeping the student immersed in Java. The ACM Library works with any programming editor capable of working with Java. Thus this approach involves as much standard Java and standard tools as possible.

Greenfoot is, to the author's understanding, a thicker layer above standard Java that allows more sophisticated simulation and game creation. The student writes Java code that runs in the Greenfoot framework. Development takes place in the Greenfoot application, with significant tools for abstraction and visualization [6].

Alice is another level (or several) up the abstraction ladder, with the student creating a program using a drag-and-drop interface, with visual elements corresponding to standard programming language statements. Developers work within the Alice application [7].

7. PROS AND CONS OF THIS APPROACH

In five semesters of increased reliance on the arcade game approach, including three that use essentially only gaming, the author has perceived several important advantages of an arcade gaming approach:

- **increased motivation and interest** – it is very clear that students are far more interested. Students ask more questions in class, come in for more help, take on more extra challenges. A problem that could be solved in 200 lines of code is likely to have an extra 300 lines because of extra features that students has added.
- **real java programming** – the ACM Java Library is a thin layer, so the student is writing real Java programs from the beginning.
- **various student levels are easy to accommodate** – the nature of games allow the more advanced student to add extra features. Some choose to add extra characteristics for more visually interesting game elements. Others add more elaborate play such as a BugBot with more intelligence or an Asteroids game where the spaceship has shields. Not all of these innovations are successful however.
- **minimal knowledge of specialized techniques** – time dependant object behavior is the only game specific technique used in this approach. The student is always learning real and useful Java.
- **natural progression to objects** – there's no question of objects early or objects later. They are introduced when needed and further developed when required.
- **enhanced opportunities for artistic expression and creativity** – many students will create only very basic visual objects, but some will go to considerable trouble to produce attractive, accurate or complicated game elements and backgrounds.
- **flexible problem domain** – the approach builds non game activities such as slide show software or puzzles easily.
- **infinite number of varying assignments** – almost any arcade game or puzzle is a candidate for an assignment. However care is required to be sure that the student has the appropriate skills at the time of assignment.
- **minimal set up and cost** – the student need only download the acm.jar file containing the library, configure the IDE to find it, and they are ready to go. The games run successfully on older computers and the ACM library is available at no cost. No special IDE is required—the author has used both TextPad and Dr. Java.
- **reliability of the ACM Java Library** – the author experienced very few problems, odd behaviors or unexplained crashes.

In the author's experience, there is one minor downside to the gaming approach. Some learning overhead is required—the student has to become moderately fluent with a subset of the ACM Java library, and some very basic gaming techniques. The trade-off is well worth it though.

There is also one considerable downside—the lack of support materials. The Free Java Book is the author's attempt to overcome this problem.

8. TRANSITIONING TO STANDARD JAVA

The transition to pure standard Java is painless, and is handled by one example program that covers the structure of a standard program and console input and output, with perhaps some assigned reading.

9. CONCLUSIONS

The ACM Java library successfully brings graphics into a Java based CS1 class. Creating, modifying and moving graphic objects is very simple. Working with programmer defined graphic objects is naturally more complex, but still easily accessible. Interactions between objects is available to the beginning student. The ACM library, combined with standard Java, provides all the tools needed for the beginning student to work in the arcade game application domain.

Using the ACM library as a starting point the beginning student is able to write basic interactive arcade games within a few weeks, and much more refined games as the course progresses. At the end of the course strong students are able to write excellent arcade games that fully explore the topics, skills and techniques that a CS1 course should cover.

The arcade game application domain is suitable for CS1 and provides a wealth of possible assignments. Students enjoy creating animations and games, and student enthusiasm is notable.

The Free Java Book provides support for instructors wishing to undertake this approach to the CS1 course.

10. REFERENCES

[1] deLact, M., Kuffner, J., Slattery, M., and Sweedyk, E. Panel Session:Computer Games and CS Education: Why and How. In *Proceedings of the Thirty-Sixth SIGCSE Technical Symposium on Computer Science Education (SIGCSE 2005)*, February 23-27, St. Louis, Missouri, 2005, 256-257.

[2] Cliburn, D. The Effectiveness of Games as Assignments in an Introductory Programming Course. In *Proceedings of the Thirty-Sixth ASEE/IEEE Frontiers in Education Conference (FIE 2006)*, October 28-31, San Diego, California, 2006.

[3] Bayliss, J. Using Games in Introductory Courses: Tips from the Trenches. In *Proceedings of the Fortieth SIGCSE Technical Symposium on Computer Science Education (SIGCSE 2009)*, March 4-7, Chattanooga, Tennessee, 337-341, 2009.

[4] Morrison, B. Engagement: Gaming throughout the Curriculum. In *Proceedings of the Fortieth SIGCSE Technical Symposium on Computer Science Education (SIGCSE 2009)*, March 4-7, Chattanooga, Tennessee, 342-346, 2009.

[5] Kote, L., Anderson, S., Good, J., Pain, H. Learning by Game-Building. In *Conference Proceedings of the 12th SIGCSE Annual Conference on Innovation and Technology in Computer Science Education (ITCSE 2007)*, June 25-27, Dundee, Scotland, UK, 2007

[6] Henriksend, P., Kölling, M. Greenfoot Invent – Program – Share, http://www.greenfoot.org

[7] Carnegie Mellon University, Alice An Education Software that teaches students computer programming in a 3D environment, http://www.alice.org

Consultants on Systemic Reform for Gender Balance

J. McGrath Cohoon (Moderator)
National Center for Women & IT (NCWIT)
University of Virginia
1.434.243.2143
jmcohoon@virginia.edu

Leisa D. Thompson
NCWIT
University of Virginia
Charlottesville VA
1-210-883-6204
thompson@ncwit.org

Jennifer Goodall
NCWIT
University at Albany
Albany NY
1.646.388.0327
jennifer.goodall@ncwit.org

Rebecca Dohrman
NCWIT
Purdue University
Lafayette, IN
1-618-806-2315
dohrman@ncwit.org

Elizabeth Litzler
Center for Workforce Development
University of Washington
1.206.543.4810
elitzler@u.washington.edu

SUMMARY

Despite concern over gender imbalance in computing, very few undergraduate programs have succeeded in their efforts to improve women's representation. This panel will describe the process followed and value added by trained consultants providing free customized services to "client" departments seeking to recruit and retain more women students. These professional services are provided at no charge by the National Center for Women & IT (NCWIT) Extension Services for Undergraduate Programs (ES-UP), with support from the National Science Foundation.

Increasing participation of women in undergraduate programs requires a multi-pronged, systemic approach that includes:

- Improved recruitment
- Inclusive pedagogy
- Meaningful curriculum
- Support for students from faculty and other students
- High-level institutional support and appropriate policies
- Ongoing assessment of initiatives and progress

Expert assistance helps academic departments with the complex undertaking of addressing the entire system that affects undergraduate students' experience as computing majors. The research-based ES-UP process for providing this confidential assistance is illustrated in Figure 1. [Sources employed for developing the ES-UP model include 4, 5, and 6.]

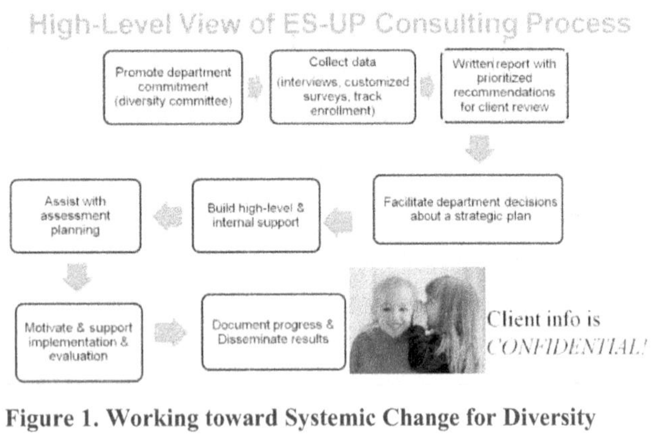

Figure 1. Working toward Systemic Change for Diversity

At this time, ES-UP serves 36 departments and is operating at full capacity. Early clients have reported substantial success [1, 2, 3], and several other clients have used Baseline Reports to obtain financial support for implementing initiatives. Additional funding is being sought to meet further demand from potential ES-UP clients.

SIGCSE'10, March 10-13, 2010, Milwaukee, Wisconsin, USA.
ACM 978-1-60558-885-8/10/03.

Categories and Subject Descriptors

K.3.2. Computers and Education. Computer and Information Science Education.

General Terms

Human Factors

Keywords

Gender, Women, Diversity, Systemic Change.

1. J. McGRATH COHOON

As co-PI for this project, Dr. Cohoon will briefly describe its motivation and process design. She will also introduce the other panelists.

2. REBECCA DOHRMAN

Campus visits are the heart of the information-gathering process, a crucial early step in the ES-UP service. As a new Extension Services Consultant, Ms. Dohrman will describe preparations for this important task, so that audience members might perform investigations for their own departments. She will use the results from a recent visit with her client department to illustrate both the process and the valuable results it produces.

3. JENNIFER GOODALL

Dr. Goodall is one of only two Extension Services Consultants who are also representatives of client departments. Speaking as her school's Diversity Coordinator, she will describe both her experiences as a client pulling together data from official university records to track gender balance in enrollment and retention, and faculty reaction to their Baseline Report.

4. LEISA D. THOMPSON

As Director of Research and Consultation for ES-UP, Dr. Thompson has a high-level view across all the consultants and clients. She will describe the similarities and differences in client departments related to enrollment trends, retention rates, and institutional support for diversity efforts.

5. ELIZABETH LITZLER

As external project evaluator, Ms. Litzler has valuable observations about the time it typically takes for undertaking systemic change and what departments might do when they do not have the benefit of an Extension Services Consultant, including the process of creating buy-in for systemic change efforts.

6. ACKNOWLEDGMENTS

This material is based upon work supported by the National Center for Women and Information Technology with funding from the National Science Foundation under grant number HRD-0533565. Any opinions, findings, and conclusions or recommendations expressed in this material are those of the authors and do not necessarily reflect the views of the National Science Foundation or other supporting organizations.

7. REFERENCES

[1] Cohoon, J. P. 2007. An introductory course format for promoting diversity and retention. In *Proceedings of the 38th SIGCSE Technical Symposium on Computer Science Education* (Covington, Kentucky, USA, March 07 - 11, 2007). SIGCSE '07. ACM, New York, NY, 395-399. DOI= http://doi.acm.org/10.1145/1227310.1227450

[2] Jacobson, N. and Schaefer, S. K. 2008. Pair programming in CS1: overcoming objections to its adoption. SIGCSE Bull. 40, 2 (Jun. 2008), 93-96. DOI= http://doi.acm.org/10.1145/1383602.1383643

[3] Ely, D. (1990). Conditions that facilitate the implementation of educational technology innovations. Journal of Research on Computing in Education, 23(2), 298-305.

[4] National School Board Association "What is systemic change?" Information and tools for systemic change in education: http://www.nsba.org/sbot/toolkit/edsctls.html Armenakis, A. A., Harris, S. G., & Mossholder, K. W. (1993). Creating readiness for organizational change. Human Relations, 46(6), 681-703.

[5] Conger, J.A. (1998) The Necessary Art of Persuasion. Harvard Business Review.

[6] Fernandez, S. and Rainey, H.G. (2006) Managing Successful Organizational Change in the Public Sector. Public Administration Review. 66(2), p 168-176.

Interdisciplinary Computing Education for the Challenges of the Future

Guy-Alain Amoussou
National Science Foundation
4201 Wilson Boulevard
Arlington, VA 22230
1-703-292-4645
gamousso@nsf.gov

Myles Boylan
National Science Foundation
4201 Wilson Boulevard
Arlington, VA 22230
1-703-292-4617
mboylan@nsf.gov

Joan Peckham
National Science Foundation
4201 Wilson Boulevard
Arlington, VA 22230
1-703-292-7344
jpeckham@nsf.gov

SUMMARY

This session will be conducted by panelists who have carried out funded interdisciplinary research and education, and who have funded and managed interdisciplinary programs. They will provide an opportunity for computing educators to engage in a conversation to assess what is needed to better educate the next generation of students to participate and contribute actively in resolving emerging and future interdisciplinary challenges. Many of the computing education discussions have recently been around "computational thinking" and how this might prepare students in all disciplines, including computing, to formulate and solve problems with other disciplinary partners. The difficult question is how to prepare students to engage in these activities without eroding the depth that is also needed to tackle the deepest and most difficult problems.

Categories and Subject Descriptors

K.3.2 Computer and Information Science Education

General Terms

Documentation, Design, Experimentation

Keywords

Multidisciplinary, Interdisciplinary, Computing, Education, Research, future challenges

1. INTRODUCTION

During the 21st century we will face challenges in various disciplines that will require computing skills, knowledge and power to be resolved. Students must be educated well in their own disciplines and at the same time be prepared to engage in interdisciplinary teams because many of the most pressing problems of the day are best solved using interdisciplinary approaches [1]. Some disciplines are interdisciplinary by their very nature. For example students of oceanography [2] typically are trained in the traditional science and social science disciplines before entering graduate programs in oceanography where they are mentored to function in interdisciplinary teams. The biologists of today are compelled to employ chemical, physical, engineering and computational approaches to solve the most challenging problems. The same trend of using computational tools is prevalent in weather forecast and the prediction of extreme events [3]. Today virtually all disciplines, scientific and non scientific benefit from the support of computer software to aid their investigations and to convey the results broadly. Measuring the success of interdisciplinary education and research initiative is not a trivial endeavor [4, 5]. However, many are just beginning to engage "computational thinking" experts to formulate and solve the most fundamental problems. This argues for better education of computing and non-computing majors to provide the appropriate depth of computational thinking alongside the collaborative skills needed to be successful.

SIGCSE'10, March 10-13, 2010, Milwaukee, Wisconsin, USA.
ACM 978-1-60558-885-8/10/03.

2. CURRENT CHALLENGES IN VARIOUS DISCIPLINES

A quick survey of selected program officers in the division of undergraduate education at the National Science foundation has identified a few challenges. The intention here is not to be complete, but instead, to provide a snapshot of challenges we are or will be facing within the century. Here are a few quotes:

"when I think of challenges in computing, in biology, I think of proteomics, bioinformatics and genomics as well as biodiversity, namely all the challenges we have in handling large data bases (assembling, analyzing, updating, collating with other large databases, modeling) and in converting raw data into mega-information concerning molecular shape, cell interactions, interaction between life forms and the environment, metabolic interactions, organ function including brain function."

"In the discipline of economics, the role of computer science is to facilitate further developments in economic game theory, generally by modeling increasing sophistication, including stochastic elements. In economics, game theory, also known by the name "experimental economics," is used both for research and for education. It involves elaborate simulations of economic scenarios where live players interact over a period of time - much the way some video games are played."

In Chemistry, the National Research Council of the National Academies in its report "Beyond the Molecular Frontier" [6] does spell out the need for predictive computational modeling of molecular motions using large-scale parallel processing arrays. The chapter 6 of the report focuses on Chemical Theory and Computer Modeling: From Computation Chemistry to process systems engineering.

The last examples are provided by the National Academy of Engineering Committee on Engineering's Grand Challenges that indentified 14 areas including: Make solar energy economical, Provide energy from fusion, Provide access to clean water, Reverse-engineer the brain, Advance personalized learning, Develop carbon sequestration methods, Engineer the tools of scientific discovery, Restore and improve urban infrastructure, Advance health informatics, Prevent nuclear terror, Engineer better medicines, Enhance virtual reality, Manage the nitrogen cycle, Secure cyberspace [7]. There are many more challenges in various disciplines that could have been listed here. Considering this landscape of sample challenges to be faced in the next century, the next section presents a rational for the proposed session.

3. WHY THIS SESSION?

The goal of this session is to provide as much time as possible for the audience to engage openly with each other as well as the panel to identify the top challenges and potential solutions to the problem of educating students to develop interdisciplinary computing skills. This includes a computing perspective to interdisciplinary problems that enables us to think deeply about difficult problems and at the same time engage well under differing disciplinary perspectives.

This special session will start to engage the computing education community in assessing for the next decades the need for educating the next generation of computer scientists who are prepared and capable to contribute to and resolve these challenges from an interdisciplinary perspective.

4. PLAN AND ORGANIZATION OF THE SESSION

The session will be organized in two phases:

The first phase will consist of gathering from the community and conference participants some answers to the question proposed in the next section. We plan to have a whiteboard available near the NSF showcase, to allow the collection of answers and input.

The second phase will be the session itself. It will include the following:

1- Short introductory comments by the panelists that will include a summary of the information collected in the first phase.

2- Facilitated discussion of the questions by the panel moderator (with active participation by the audience)

3- Proposed action plan to continue the conversation.

5. QUESTIONS TO BE DISCUSSED

The following sample questions are proposed for the conversation.

What are the best scientific challenges that beg for computational thinkers on the research teams?

What goals and strategies are needed for interdisciplinary computing education and research?

How interdisciplinary computing education and research is measured against the goals we set?

What tensions exist between preparing students deeply and teaching them to engage in interdisciplinary research?

What partnerships should we form to better prepare students?

What programs and curriculum will contribute to a necessary transformation of computing science education, both in the major and in the general education of everyone?

What other questions we should be asking ourselves in this need assessment?

6. CONCLUSION

Few would argue with the notion that the scientific world is changing at a rapid pace with deep and difficult research problems emerging at a breath-taking rate. Many of these problems are interdisciplinary by their very nature, and many others will yield to unexpected interdisciplinary approaches and perspectives. Historically, we have created disciplinary silos of expertise needed to solve problems that are deep and highly focused. Now also needed is a nudge toward educational practices that prepare students for interdisciplinary challenges. This discussion between panelists and the audience is intended to uncover potential solutions and pitfalls, and to encourage educators to think deeply about how to better prepare the next generation of students.

The expected outcome of this conversation is to initiate and continue the conversation about what is needed for an effective interdisciplinary / multidisciplinary computing science education and research what are the expected outcomes of this conversation

7. REFERENCES

[1] National Academy of Sciences, National Academy of Engineering, Institute of Medicine, Facilitating Interdisciplinary Research, ISBN: 0-309-54727-X, 2004

[2] Powell, Thomas, The Rise of Interdisciplinary Oceanography, Oceanography, Volume 21, # 3, Sept. 2008 http://www.tos.org/oceanography/issues/issue_archive/issue_pdfs/21_3/21.3_powell.pdf

[3] Predicting weather, climate, and extreme events, The Journal of Computational Physics, Volume 227, Issue 7

[4] Rhoten, Diana, The NSF's 'cool' project: a charrette assesses interdisciplinary graduate education, with surprising results. http://globalhighered.wordpress.com

[5] Jacobs, Jerry and Frickel, Scott, Interdisciplinary: A Critical Assessment, Annual Review of Sociology, Volume 35: 43-65, August 2009 http://arjournals.annualreviews.org

[6] National Research Council of the National Academies in its report http://www.nap.edu/openbook.php?isbn=0309084776

[7] National Academy of Engineering Committee on Engineering's http://www.engineeringchallenges.org/

It Seemed Like a Good Idea at the Time

Jonas Boustedt
Dept. of Mathematics, Natural and Computer Science
Univ. of Gävle, Sweden
jbt@hig.se

Robert McCartney (moderator)
Dept. of Computer Science and Engineering
Univ. of Connecticut
robert@engr.uconn.edu

Josh Tenenberg
Computing and Software Systems
Univ. of Washington, Tacoma
jtenenbg@uw.edu

Edward F. Gehringer
Dept. of Computer Science
North Carolina State University
efg@ncsu.edu

Raymond Lister
Faculty of Information Technology
University of Technology, Sydney
raymond@it.uts.edu.au

Dave Musicant
Dept. of Computer Science
Carleton College
dmusican@carleton.edu

The Mystery Presenter
??
??

Categories and Subject Descriptors

K.3.2 [**Computer and Information Science Education**]: self-assessment; K.4.2 [**Social Issues**]: employment

General Terms

Design, Experimentation, Human Factors, Measurement, Performance, Verification

Keywords

fiasco, disaster, breakdown, failure, humiliation, doom, gloom, termination

SUMMARY

We often learn of successful pedagogical experiments, but we seldom hear of the the ones that failed. For this special session we solicited submissions from the SIGCSE membership, selected the best from among these, and will have presentations at the session by the selected authors. Our contributions describe pedagogical approaches that seemed to be good ideas but turned out as failures. Contributors will describe their pedagogical experiment, the rationale for the experiment, evidence of failure, and lessons learned.

1. OVERVIEW

Educators are always tinkering with their methods, their materials, and their interactions with students to better fit teaching to student needs and the local setting; we are all *bricoleurs* [4], using the material at hand to craft a response to the daily demands of the classroom. As in most academic disciplines, what gets published in computing education are the success stories, the examples to follow. Rarely do we hear about the failures and errors, things we might discuss only behind closed doors with trusted colleagues. Given that negative results can be as valid as positive results, it seems natural that there should be a public forum for the discussion of the negative experiences in CS Education.

This session, "It Seemed Like a Good Idea at the Time", provides a forum for discussion of the failures we have all had, with the hope that others can avoid the paths that led to these unanticipated results. This session is structured like Parlante's "Nifty Assignments" sessions: a set of presenters selected from submissions solicited by a general CFP to the SIGCSE community. It follows in the footsteps of similar sessions at SIGCSE 2007-2009 [3, 2, 1] which were wildly successful. See http://depts.washington.edu/goodidea/ for more details.

2. OVERALL OBJECTIVE

Much like Tolstoy's happy families, successful experiments are all similar but failed experiments all fail in their own way. However, not all failures are interesting or would make for a good discussion. We selected teaching interventions for which there was reasonable expectation of success, for example those based on previously published work. We also selected for reports that provided evidence of failure – or at least significant deviations from expected outcomes, reasons for the failure, and implications for practice for other CS teachers.

By presenting these experiences, the authors provide cautionary tales (and some entertainment) to other instructors. By providing a forum for the failed experiment, we hope to encourage risk taking in the classroom, and by focusing on evidence we hope to foster a community with a greater eye for documenting our classroom experiments.

The audience *might* learn some particular facts, but more likely they will see their own experiences in the experiences of the presenters. The session will encourage audience discussion at the session and ongoing conversations for the rest of the conference.

SIGCSE'10, March 10–13, 2010, Milwaukee, Wisconsin, USA.
ACM 978-1-60558-885-8/10/03.

3. THE GOOD IDEAS

Too Much Research in One Semester, or, How I Got the Worst Course Evaluations of My Life (Ed Gehringer)

It is usually a good idea to do research during programming classes. Not only can one investigate teaching strategies, but the classroom also offers an ideal environment to compare approaches and tools for programming. But danger lurks for those whose goals are ambitious and interlocking. In Fall 2006, I tried to do two simultaneous experiments in an o-o design class: one on refactoring open-source code, and one on a visual distributed pair-programming environment. The visual DPP environment could not be made to work, due to forces beyond our control, and it led to false starts and long delays in the refactoring experiment. The consequences included two abandoned masters theses, homework compressed into the last half of the semester, and the worst course evaluations of my life.

Abstraction and Memorization (Raymond Lister)

All I wanted to do was pass more of my CS1 students. So I thought I'd decrease the emphasis in the final exam on writing new code and increase the emphasis on recognizing old code. About one quarter of the multiple choice questions in the final exam were changed to be about algorithms we'd studied during semester. In each question, I'd present the code we'd studied, with one or two lines missing, and the students had to identify from the four options the missing lines of code.

The students did not have to memorize the algorithms. At the back of the exam paper, I attached ALL the PowerPoint lecture notes that described, not in code but in diagrammatic form, every algorithm we'd studied in the semester (101 diagrams, 6 to a page – longer than the exam paper itself). But wait! There's more! The students had already seen the multiple-choice questions. Weeks prior to the exam, the students were provided with a pool of questions, and they were told that about a quarter of those questions would appear in the final exam. For the exam itself, I did not even bother to reorder the four options in each question.

As it turned out, the students did WORSE on these questions than on other multiple-choice questions about code they had never seen before! Having set out to pass more students, it turned out I had to flunk more students than ever before (because you can't give "pity marks" on a multiple choice question).

For many of my students, there was no point to having the diagrammatic PowerPoint slides attached to the exam, because those diagrams were an abstraction that they had not yet learned to use. Indeed, one might argue (and many have) that learning to program is all about learning to work with abstractions.

Computers in Modern Society – Special Edition (Robert McCartney)

In the semester before I was to be evaluated for tenure, I designed and offered a new version of our general-education computing course. Instead of trying to survey all of computing, augmented by training in word processing and spreadsheet software, the new course would emphasize "fundamental issues", with the stated goal that the students leave with "an understanding of the range of the field and some of the underlying culture of the computing community." The issues included algorithm design and analysis, complexity and computability, and legal and ethical considerations. Additionally, to gain an appreciation of programming, the students would learn to program in SCHEME, chosen for its small size, clean syntax and semantics, and free availability. The teaching assistants were experienced and enthusiastic.

The result was that the course reached unprecedented levels of student discontent. Half the class dropped even though the course was a graduation requirement. The department chair received complaints via the deans of three schools (not engineering, as there were no engineering students in the course). There was exactly one positive course evaluation from the 44 students who stuck it out.

In retrospect, there was a disconnect between the students' goals and expectations (i.e. fulfill a degree requirement, in a non-demanding course) and mine (i.e. present awesome things from CS, and students find it exciting).

Improving The Quality Of Student Presentations: Or Failing To Do So... (Dave Musicant)

Edward Tufte is a writer and a speaker who has built his career on explaining how to present technical information. In particular, he is a vocal opponent of bulleted presentation tools (e.g. PowerPoint, Keynote, etc.), and delivers compelling arguments as to how their use degrades the quality of presentations. I decided to try to bring his ideas into my classroom. In a course that I teach annually where students deliver short presentations throughout the term, I encouraged my students to avoid bulleted slides and to focus instead on handouts and discussions (as well as other projected visual aids) that allowed a more detailed examination of the technical subject at hand. My advice resulted in the worst student presentations I've seen. My key flaw, so clear in hindsight, was not realizing that these sorts of ideas were relevant only for strong speakers. The opposite may be true for inexperienced speakers.

Title witheld to maintain anonymity (The Mystery Presenter)

Note: in the 2009 "It Seemed Like a Good Idea at the Time" session it was necessary that one presenter remain anonymous. Remarkably, this has happened again, so this presenter, topic, and description must remain secret for now.

4. REFERENCES

[1] J. Boustedt, R. McCartney, K. Deibel, J. Huggins, B. Simon, S. Westbrook, and T. M. Presenter. It seemed like a good idea at the time. In *SIGCSE '09 Proceedings*, pages 265–266, 2009.

[2] J. Boustedt, R. McCartney, J. Tenenberg, S. D. Anderson, C. M. Eastman, D. D. Garcia, P. V. Gestwicki, and M. S. Menzin. It seemed like a good idea at the time. In *SIGCSE '08 Proceedings*, pages 528–529, 2008.

[3] J. Boustedt, R. McCartney, J. Tenenberg, T. Winters, S. Edwards, B. B. Morrison, D. R. Musicant, I. Utting, and C. Zander. It seemed like a good idea at the time. In *SIGCSE '07 Proceedings*, pages 346–347, 2007.

[4] C. Lévi-Strauss. *The savage mind.* University of Chicago Press, 1966.

Keynote Talk

Suddenly, All Computing Is Parallel: Seizing Opportunity Amid the Clamor

Michael Wrinn
Manager, Innovative Software Education
Intel Corporation
Hillsboro, Oregon USA
michael.wrinn@intel.com

Abstract

The shift in computing hardware to parallel systems is well underway. Sequential chips are no longer designed, and the proud era of von Neumann architecture passes into history.

Foundational change of this magnitude will disrupt traditional habits throughout the discipline, especially how students are to be introduced to and prepared for new challenges. But prepared how, and for what, exactly?

With parallel programming models evolving, and a variety of approaches being tried in academia and industry, flexibility is vital. Customary time lags between research findings and classroom experience will have to be shortened, and industrial best practices find a new level of academic pertinence, quickening the pace of adoption for parallel education. In this talk, we'll look at some of these university/industry collaborations now underway.

Categories & Subject Descriptors: K.0 [Computing Milieux]: General; K.3.2 [Computers and Education]: Computer and Information Science Education – computer science education

General Terms: Human Factors

Bio

Michael Wrinn manages Intel's Innovative Software Education team, which collaborates with universities to bring parallel computing to the mainstream of undergraduate education. He also works with the ACM Education Council to bring industrial perspective to curriculum evolution. Prior Intel roles include managing Intel's software engineering lab in Shanghai, and directing research on human interface technology. He was Intel's representative for the original OpenMP specification, and remains active in the parallel computing community. Before joining Intel, Michael worked at Accelrys, implementing commercial and research simulation codes on a wide variety of parallel/HPC systems. He holds a B.Sc. and Ph.D. (in quantum mechanics) from McGill University.

SIGCSE'10, March 10–13, 2010, Milwaukee, Wisconsin, USA.
ACM 978-1-60558-885-8/10/03.

SIGCSE 2010 Workshops

Wednesday Workshops, 7:00 p.m. to 10:00 p.m.

1. Teaching about Computer Ethics and Professional Conduct within the Computer Science Curriculum

Don Gotterbarn, *East Tennessee State University*
Keith W. Miller, *University of Illinois Springfield*

To help interested faculty provide students with tools to better understand and resolve the ethical challenges in their professional lives we will present well developed examples and modules which can be used to engage students in the study of applied ethics. We will present materials to be used in a complete computer ethics course and examples that can be used as examples and exercises in specific technical courses. We will review computer ethics course syllabi and textbooks, describing advantages and disadvantages. We will introduce some examples of realistic, ethically-charged decisions that computing professionals face, and explore techniques that can be used by the practicing professional to make wise and creative decisions. The intended audience is CS and IT educators who teach or will teach computer ethics issues in technical classes or in a standalone computer ethics class. **Laptop optional.**

2. Hands-On Experience with GLSL Shaders

Mike Bailey, *Oregon State University*
Steve Cunningham, *Brown Cunningham Associates*

Programmable shaders are important for high-performance graphics and because OpenGL 3.0 replaces fixed-function operations with shaders. This workshop gives hands-on experience with vertex, fragment, and geometry shaders, including shader theory and the GLSL shader language. Participants will examine, modify, and create examples of each shader class. We will use the glman tool to work with shaders separately from applications, and will integrate shaders with applications using the GLSL API. The workshop will be valuable for anyone who teaches or develops computer graphics. **Participants must have OpenGL experience and bring a shader-capable Windows or Linux laptop with C or C++ compiler.**

3. Developing Objectives and Outcomes for a Student Based Outcomes Assessment Program

Donald Sanderson, *East Tennessee State University*

New approaches to student assessment require programs to define both student outcomes and objectives. This workshop will focus on the techniques needed to create appropriate, practical, measurable outcomes and objectives for a program. Specific areas addressed:

1. Where do these fit in an overall assessment program
2. How to differentiate between outcomes and objectives
3. How to link them.
4. Techniques for building them top down, bottom up, and from existing programs
5. Methods for minimizing the time needed to develop them

The workshop is aimed at faculty tasked with creating or updating their departmental assessment program. Participants will leave with the tools they need to effectively and efficiently determine their programs objectives and outcomes. **Laptop optional.**

4. Peer Led Team Learning in Introductory Computer Science

Susan Rodger, *Duke University*
Susan Horwitz, *University of Wisconsin – Madison*

This workshop is for those interested in learning about and implementing Peer-Led Team Learning (PLTL) in an introductory computer science course. PLTL students take the regular introductory course and also meet weekly in small groups run by an undergraduate peer leader to work together on exercises designed to cement understanding of course material. We discuss how to start and run a PLTL program, and the benefits it provides to both students in the course and the peer leaders. Workshop participants will experience hands-on sample PLTL sessions based on programs we have run for over four years. Other topics include training of peer leaders, recruiting strategies, our database of PLTL materials, results from our four-year study, and other implementation details. Current student peer leaders will present their experiences. **Laptop optional.**

5. Writing More Effective NSF Proposals

Victor Piotrowski, *National Science Foundation*
Guy-Alain Amoussou, *National Science Foundation*
Scott Grissom, *National Science Foundation*

This workshop will focus on writing effective education NSF proposals. The workshop will cover the following topic areas: writing effective goals, objectives and outcomes; writing a convincing rationale; preparing a responsive evaluation plan; preparing an effective and believable dissemination plan; and dealing with the realities of the review process. The workshop will use a structured guided-interactive methodology that leads participants through each of these topics by introducing the issues related to the topic, engaging participants in group exercises designed to explore and share their understanding of these issues, and then providing some "expert" opinion on these issues. **Laptop not needed.**

6. An Audacious iPhone Workshop

Michael P. Rogers, *Northwest Missouri State University*

While the iPhone may be a useful means of attracting students to Computer Science — the coolness factor is phenomenal —it does require that faculty grasp the underlying technology. This workshop will help, by providing a fast-paced introduction to the languages, IDEs, and frameworks that make iPhone apps possible. Participants, using Macintosh computers and the iPhone SDK, will be guided through the construction of several modest, proof-of-concept apps. By the conclusion of the workshop, they will have gained a deeper appreciation of what is required to create iPhone apps, and how they might employ the technology in their own classrooms/curricula. All workshop activities will be conducted on Macs using a simulator; iPhones are not required. **Participants may choose to simply observe, but for a more active experience, please bring an Intel-based Macintosh laptop, preloaded with the latest version of the iPhone SDK (available at developer.apple.com).**

7. Develop Game-Themed Examples for CS1/2 Without Background in Graphics or Games

Kelvin Sung, *University of Washington, Bothell*
Michael Panitz, *Cascadia Community College*
John Nordlinger, *Microsoft External Research*

The recent development and success of computer gaming classes and gaming-themed curricula are exciting and have demonstrated interesting potential. However, for faculty members with no computer gaming or graphics background the prospect of adopting or developing games-related courseware materials may seem daunting. This workshop is designed specifically for these faculty members. Based on the Microsoft XNA framework, we have developed an extremely simple game engine with 3 predefined classes and a handful of utility functions. Simple and effective game-themed courseware materials have been developed based on this simple game engine. For example, a Pong game like framework suitable for teaching conditional statements can be constructed in less than 30-lines of C# code. This workshop will present our simple game engine and guide participants in developing a complete Pong game. The workshop will also present examples of existing game-themed instructional modules and assignments. **Laptop required.**

8. Web Development with Python and Django

Ariel Ortiz, Tecnológico de Monterrey, *Campus Estado de México*

Many instructors have already discovered the joy of teaching programming using Python. Now it's time to take Python to the next level. This workshop will introduce Django, an open source Python web framework that saves you time and makes web development fun. It's aimed at CS instructors who want to teach how to build elegant server-side web applications with minimal fuss. Django is Python's equivalent to the popular Ruby on Rails framework, and it runs on Windows, Linux and Mac. Topics that will be covered include: setup and configuration, template language, and database integration through object-relational mapping. Participants should have some familiarity with HTML and Python. Please check the following link to get more information: http://django.arielortiz.com/ **Laptop required.**

9. OpenMP in the Classroom

Hui Yang, *San Francisco State University*
Michael Wrinn, *Intel Corporation*

OpenMP is one of the most straightforward language extensions for writing parallel programs; the simple syntax makes it suitable for introducing college students to parallel computing. OpenMP has evolved from its data-parallel roots to the point where it can illustrate a wide range of concurrent software issues. This workshop covers traditional OpenMP capabilities (loop-level parallel, numeric applications) and its expansion to fundamental areas such as searches and linked lists. We review in (hands-on) detail the programming labs which were assigned to students in the course, Fundamentals of Computer Science (C++), covering the relevant syntax as well as challenges encountered by students. **Laptop with dual core (or more) required.**

10. Teaching With Embedded Xinu

Dennis Brylow, *Marquette University*
Paul Ruth, *University of Mississippi*

The Nexos Project is an NSF-funded effort to develop inexpensive, hands-on, embedded system laboratory experiences with a high "wow factor" at multiple levels of the college computer science curriculum. This workshop will share ready-made curriculum resources that have been used successfully to teach hardware systems, operating systems, realtime/embedded systems, networking, and compilers with the Embedded Xinu platform at several colleges/universities. Commodity wireless router hardware or equivalent virtual machines, combined with freely-available software and tools, make for a powerful and flexible learning platform without having to fake any components. Come see what Nexos has to offer for your program. **Laptop recommended.**

11. Developing Portable and Hands-On Laptop-Based Networked Instructional Workshops and Exercises

Paul J. Wagner, *University of Wisconsin – Eau Claire*
Thomas Paine, *University of Wisconsin – Eau Claire*
Daren Bauer, *University of Wisconsin – Eau Claire*
Jamison Schmidt, *University of Wisconsin – Eau Claire*
Jason Wudi, *JAMF Software, Minneapolis, MN*

This workshop is intended for educators seeking to develop hands-on education in a wireless laptop environment, which could include developing workshops for conferences like SIGCSE, or developing portable laptop laboratory exercises for computer science curricula. We will look at the structure of the MOBILE portable laptop-based wireless instructional environment we have developed, examine example domains to show what can be accomplished within this environment, and discuss how participants can create their own portable instructional workshops or laboratory exercises. Participants will receive a prototype version of the MOBILE system, with instructions on how to develop their own ad-hoc laptop-based workshops with this system. **Laptop required.**

12. Threaded Programming Methodology

Clay Breshears, *Intel*

This workshop illustrates the process of migrating a serial program to a parallel (threaded) equivalent using the OpenMP model and appropriate software tools. The overarching framework for this process is a four step Threading Methodology: Analysis, Design & Implementation, Debugging, and Tuning. There are several hands-on lab activities in the workshop to give participants the chance to practice concepts demonstrated in the lecture. The lab sequence will take a simple serial code and transform it into an efficient parallel version via the Threading Methodology. Several correctness and performance issues of parallel programs will be encountered and solved during the labs. The material presented in this workshop can stand alone, be used as the sole threading session in a more general course, or as part of an overall threading course. **Laptop recommended.**

13. Test-First Design Pedagogy and Support for Introductory OO Programming

Viera K. Proulx, *Northeastern University*

Typical introductory programming courses do not require that students design a comprehensive test suite for their programs. Our Java *tester* library supports the design of tests by a novice programmer — without any new syntax or the need to override the 'equals' method. It displays for each failed test both the actual and the expected value, with a link to the source of the test. (http://www.ccs.neu.edu/javalib) This workshop illustrates hands-on the benefits of test-first pedagogy on a series of typical introductory programming assignments. It prepares the participants to adopt test-first design approach in their introductory (and advanced) courses. **Laptop required.**

14. Moving Your Course into the Cloud

David J. Malan, *Harvard University*

This workshop will introduce participants to cloud computing in general and to Amazon Elastic Compute Cloud (EC2) specifically. Participants will learn what other educators are using EC2 for and what it can and cannot do for their own classes. Participants will learn how to launch and manage virtual machines (VMs) running both Linux and Windows, how their students can connect to those VMs, and how they can use those VMs for classes and projects. Participants will receive $100 vouchers with which to experiment with EC2 during and after the workshop. Workshop itself will be entirely hands-on. **Laptop required.**

Friday Workshops, 7:00 p.m. to 10:00 p.m.

15. JavaFX: Fast Track to GUI Development

Barry Burd, *Drew University*

What's better than a good windowing API? How about a language that streamlines all aspects of GUI program development? Instead of writing code in a general purpose language, use a no-nonsense declarative language — a language whose purpose is to create cool GUI applications. JavaFX compiles to the Java virtual machine, and is compatible with other Java technologies. The traditional Java libraries are available in JavaFX. For students whose first language is Java, JavaFX provides a smooth learning path. Coding in JavaFX is quick and intuitive, with support for everything from simple "Hello GUI" programs to eye-catching media demos. **Laptop recommended.**

16. Using Networking Examples for Labs and Enrichment in Introductory Courses

Thomas P. Murtagh, *Williams College*

Our students depend on IM, email, Facebook, YouTube, etc. every day. Programming assignments involving network applications can therefore be very motivating. This workshop will provide instructors teaching introductory programming courses with 1) techniques for making networking projects accessible to their students 2) strategies for using programming examples involving network applications to introduce and reinforce fundamental programming skills, 3) an understanding of several protocols, including mail and IM protocols, sufficient to design network-based laboratories, 4) examples of labs that have been successfully used in a Java-based CS1, and 5) strategies for enriching introductory courses by exploring networking technology. **A laptop is recommended for hands-on activities.**

17. Scala in the Computer Science Curriculum

Cay Horstmann, *San Jose State University*

The Scala programming language is a multi-paradigm programming language for the Java and .NET virtual machines that blends object-oriented and functional programming. In this workshop, you will experience how Scala lends itself to exploratory programming in a CS1, data structures, or programming languages course. You will gain an understanding of the advantages and pitfalls of using Scala instead of Java, and you will become familiar with the tools landscape for Scala. This workshop is intended for CS educators who are very familiar with Java and who are interested in bringing a more modern language to their students. For more information, please see http://horstmann.com/scala-workshop. **Laptop required.**

18. Using Drupal for Educational Web Site Development

Lillian Cassel, *Villanova University*
Robert Siegfried, *Villanova University*
Sridhara Potluri, *Villanova University*

Drupal is an open source content management system that allows users and content experts to focus on what they want a web site to do, rather than how to make it work. Drupal is both a stand-alone web presence with many optional modules and a suitable front end to other types of web environments. This workshop will explore use of Drupal to support computing education: to provide a powerful web presence for faculty, a support for collaborative activity, and as the public face of the Ensemble computing community within the National Science Foundation National STEM Digital Library (NSDL). **Laptop recommended.**

19. Alice 3 and Java for CS1 & AP CS

Wanda Dann, *Carnegie Mellon University*
Stephen Cooper, *Purdue University*
Don Slater, *Carnegie Mellon University*

This workshop, designed for instructors of CS1/AP, introduces Alice3 with built-in transition from Alice to Java. The workshop offers hands-on experience programming with Alice3 and integrating a transition to Java IDE, e.g. NetBeans. Alice3 builds on Alice2's powerful program visualization technique, enabling students to "see" objects and work with object-oriented programming. Participants will learn how to use Alice3 to build virtual worlds and how to use this approach in CS1 courses (introductory programming for majors and non-majors and AP CS). Participants will receive a thumb-drive containing the latest version of Alice3 and sample virtual worlds developed as part of NSF-0736552. **Laptop required (PC, Mac, or Linux).**

20. Teaching a Hands-on Undergraduate Grid Computing Course

Barry Wilkinson, *University of North Carolina Charlotte*
Clayton Ferner, *University of North Carolina Wilmington*

This workshop is intended for CS educators with no practical experience of Grid computing to gain hands-on experience for designing an undergraduate Grid computing course. Participants will access a Grid computing platform consisting of computer systems at University of North Carolina Charlotte and University of North Carolina Wilmington through a production-style portal, the command line, and through the GridNexus graphical workflow editor. Each participant will receive a copy of a new Grid computing course textbook. Comprehensive additional materials for your own course are provided at http://www.cs.uncc.edu/~abw/gridcourse/index.html. **Laptop required with Java 1.5+. Additional software will be installed during the workshop.**

21. Introduction to Parallel Computing using MPI for Computer Science Educators

Charles Peck, *Earlham College*
Daniel Ernst, *University of Wisconsin – Eau Claire*
Thomas Murphy, *Contra Costa College*

With parallel hardware becoming commonplace, are your students asking how to make use of their multi-processor resources? This workshop is intended to introduce participants to common distributed-memory parallel programming techniques using MPI. The workshop proceeds in an iterative faction, where portions of MPI are taught and then practiced using working lab examples designed to reinforce the material while at the same time modeling how it can be used to teach an undergraduate audience. Finally, the workshop will take time for a discussion of the role this material can play in a variety of computer science courses. **Laptop required.**

22. Creating Mobile Phone Applications with App Inventor for Android

Ellen Spertus, *Mills College*
Hal Abelson, *Massachusetts Institute of Technology*
Jill Dimond, *Georgia Tech*
Franklyn Turbak, *Wellesley College*

App Inventor for Android (AIA) is a new visual programming environment created by Google to enable non-programmers to easily create mobile phone applications without needing to learn traditional text-based programming languages. It was used in introductory computer science courses at twelve different colleges and universities in Fall 2009. This workshop will provide (1) hands-on experience in using AIA, (2) examples of actual and potential student projects, and (3) demonstrations of effective teaching techniques in order to help attendees decide whether and how to offer similar courses. Attendees will be able to write AIA applications during the session and test them on phones that will be provided. Intended audience: Faculty teaching introductory computer science courses at the college or high-school levels. **Laptop required. Attendees' laptops can run any operating system, as long as they have a supported browser (Firefox 3 or higher) and version 1.6 or higher of the Java Runtime Environment.**

23. Starting from Scratch (literally) in CS 1

Ursula Wolz , *The College of New Jersey*
Henry H. Leitner, *Harvard University*
David J. Malan, *Harvard University*
John Maloney, *Massachusetts Institute of Technology*

Scratch is proving to be a powerful vehicle for introducing programming. The ease with which interactive graphical programs are created, combined with freedom from syntax errors and a fluid development process, result in high levels of student engagement. This workshop demonstrates how to use Scratch in the first weeks of a rigorous introduction to computer science. We present our pedagogy and show how we transition to C++, Java, or Processing in a single semester. This workshop is for those teaching introductory computer science at the high school or undergraduate levels. For further information, see http://www.tcnj.edu/~ijims/SIGCSE_ScratchWorkshop2010. **Laptop required.**

24. Greenfoot — Introducing Java With Games And Simulations

Michael Kölling, *University of Kent*

Greenfoot is a programming environment, developed by the creators of BlueJ, that allows teaching of object-oriented programming concepts – using Java – in a highly motivating context. Built to be highly interactive and graphical, Greenfoot offers a more stimulating and experimental experience than previous systems. Building widely differing scenarios, such as simulations or games, is easy and quick. This workshop is aimed at teachers of introductory Java programming courses (high schools and universities). Activities are practically oriented and allow participants to use Greenfoot in their classroom immediately. **Laptop recommended for hands-on exercises. Participants without laptops will be paired with laptop owners.**

25. Active and Cooperative Learning Techniques for Computer Science Education

Jeffrey J. McConnell, *Canisius College*

Active and cooperative learning (ACL) provides a powerful mechanism to enhance depth of learning and increase material retention. ACL gets students involved with the material rather than passively listening to a lecture. This workshop uses introductory material on ACL for a number of activities that gives participants direct experience with and the chance to observe these techniques in action. There are also opportunities for open discussion of situations that participants may have already encountered and for the development of new activities for the classroom. Intended for faculty wanting to create a more student-centered classroom. **No laptop needed.**

26. Leveraging Commonsense Computing

Tammy VanDeGrift, *University of Portland*
Dennis Bouvier , *Southern Illinois University Edwardsville*
Tzu-Yi Chen, *Pomona College*
Robert McCartney, *University of Connecticut*
Kate Sanders, *Rhode Island College*
Beth Simon , *University of California San Diego*

Attendees will learn how to use the Commonsense Computing activities (sorting, debugging, concurrency, logic, algorithm analysis) in their courses to gain information on student preconceptions and leverage them to enhance instruction. The workshop will consist of two parts: (1) participants will learn how to use the commonsense activities in their own classrooms; (2) participants will receive training in how to prepare commonsense studies. We will provide kits based on our studies, show you how to use the activities in your classroom, and help you develop activities particular to your course and students. The intended audience includes educators who want to use the commonsense activities in their courses and/or educators who want to learn more about exploring this type of research. No special hardware or software is required for workshop attendees. **Laptop optional.**

27. Computer Science Unplugged and Outreach Activities

Tim Bell, *University of Canterbury*
Bengt Aspval, *Blekinge Institute of Technology*
Daniela Marghitu, *Auburn University*

You've been asked to talk to an elementary or high school class about Computer Science, but how can you ensure that the talk is engaging? Or perhaps you're trying to introduce a concept from Computer Science to a school group, but you want a fun way to get the class engaged. This workshop introduces Computer Science Unplugged (www.csunplugged.org), a widely used set of kinesthetic, fun activities that cover many core areas of computer science without using high technology. We will explore how to use the activities in a variety of situations (including with special needs students), show some novel applications, and discuss ways that they can be combined with "plugged-in" activities. Attendees will receive a copy of a handbook for teachers. This workshop is for K-12 teachers, faculty involved in outreach, and those interested in novel/fun ways to teach CS classes. **Laptop optional.**

Saturday Workshops, 2:15 p.m. to 5:15 p.m.

28. Preparing Students for IPv6

James Early, *SUNY Oswego*

This workshop presents an introduction to the Internet Protocol version 6 (IPv6). IPv6 has emerged as the foundational protocol for the Internet as the IPv4 address space nears exhaustion. Yet many students and teachers are unfamiliar with IPv6 and the new paradigms it brings. Presentation topics include IPv6 Addressing, Neighbor Discovery, and Security enhancements. We will also present a series of hands-on exercises to help educators bring these important ideas to their classrooms. The workshop is intended for secondary and post-secondary educators who teach courses in networking. **Laptop required.**

29. Developing Learning Activities Based on Open Source Software

Heidi Ellis, *Western New England College*
Greg Hislop, *Drexel University*

This workshop will help you tap the instructional potential of Free and Open Source Software (FOSS). In it you will learn about use of FOSS in the classroom including how to have your students become active contributors to FOSS projects. During the workshop, we will develop and exchange ideas and particular exercises to involve students in FOSS. Topics will include sources of FOSS information for instructors, examples of FOSS use in courses, approaches to getting students started in FOSS projects, road blocks and challenges in instructional FOSS use, student FOSS activities beyond code creation, and FOSS for non-majors and introductory students. This workshop is intended for instructors in any of the computing disciplines. **Laptop recommended.**

30. Teaching Probability Theory to Computer Scientists

Mehran Sahami, *Stanford University*

The last decade has seen a significant increase in the use of probability theory in computer science. This workshop focuses on effectively teaching probability theory to computer science students. We provide a very brief review of concepts in probability theory, and then focus on teaching several common probabilistic models in the context of computer science applications. We present examples of the use of probability in the analysis of algorithms and data structures as well as in the measurement of robustness in distributed systems. We also examine probabilistic methods for data analysis and machine learning in applications such as email spam filtering. Handouts are provided covering the material presented in the workshop and more. Hands-on demonstrations of probability suitable for in-class use will also be shown. The intended audience is potential teachers of discrete math/probability or anyone interested in learning more about this quickly growing area. **Laptop optional.**

31. Reinvigorating CS1 with Creative Web 2.0 Programming

Stephen Edwards, *Virginia Tech*
Godmar Back, *Virginia Tech*

Improving recruitment and retention depends on linking activities to real-world contexts that illustrate the social and societal impact of computer science. The sleek interaction and underlying technologies that define Web 2.0 applications offer a unique opportunity to teach CS concepts in a real-world context. Learn how students can create engaging Web 2.0 applications using simple Java programming and basic XHTML, *without* learning JavaScript or AJAX. See a full set of CS1 assignments leveraging this strategy. See how students can write a personal "Facebook-lite" they can show to friends. Play with live demos yourself. Leave with new assignment ideas. **No laptop needed.**

32. Multimedia Projects in Python for Introductory CS Courses

Pamela Cutter, *Kalamazoo College*
Nathan Sprague, *Kalamazoo College*

Construction and manipulation of images and sounds is a motivating context for majors and non-majors in introductory computing classes or summer camps. The algorithms to create interesting multimedia effects provide concrete and interesting results, and easily fit within the constraints of introductory courses' curricula. The visual and audible feedback provides students an immediate measure of their success, as well as a "cool" factor. This workshop will introduce a series of multimedia examples and assignments that are appropriate for beginning students, using the Python language. Intended for educators at the high school and lower-division undergraduate levels. **Laptop strongly recommended.**

33. Game Design and Development 101

Scott Leutenegger, *University of Denver*
Rafael Fajardo, *University of Denver*

You have attended or heard about the game talks at SIGCSE, you know inside that there is something there, your students want to make games, but, you have no clue how to go about designing and creating a game. You can write/teach the code to move objects around and detect collisions between objects, but how the heck do you design the game? In this workshop we will teach participants how to create a simple 2D Scratch game using their ideas. Participants will be given grid paper, some tokens, and a set of design constraints that will allow participants to quickly design their own single-player computer game. Intended Audience: Any CS instructor wishing to use game creation as an assignment but who is uncomfortable/unknowledgeable about how to design and create a simple game. **Laptop required: Windows or Mac. Please install Scratch (www.scratch.mit.edu) before the workshop.**

34. Haskell: Functional Programming without Compromise

Barry Burd, *Drew University*

Functional thinking can be very powerful. A single idea – the notion of a function – can form a basis for both mathematics and computer programming. Pure functional programming doesn't have assignment statements. Multi-threading is simpler because a thread can't interfere with another thread's assignments. But it's not all roses. Important tasks, including input and output, aren't easily described as functions. That's why many languages mix functional and non-functional features together. But Haskell forces the programmer to think functionally. Haskell uses functions for every corner of a programming problem, and provides a proof of concept for the purely functional programming paradigm. **Laptop recommended.**

35. BotWord, an Objects-First, Algorithms-Early Java Microworld

Jean Griffin, *University of Pennsylvania*
Ryan Menezes, *University of Pennsylvania*
Diana Palsetia, *University of Pennsylvania*

(See http://www.seas.upenn.edu/~botworld) This workshop introduces BotWorld, a lightweight, Java- based, PacMan-like microworld that provides a friendly introduction to object oriented programming and an early introduction to algorithmic thinking. Students with no prior programming experience can complete the first activity and gain an understanding of objects, methods, and navigating Javadocs. Workshop participants will try two introductory projects and explore a third project of their choice. They will be given six projects (including solutions and grading software) to take home. Presenters will relay how teachers and students can create their own projects/games/simulations. BotWorld was developed at the University of Pennsylvania and has received favorable reviews from students who have used it since 2005. Intended audience: Teachers of college or high school introductory computer science courses that use Java. **Laptop required.**

36. Exploring Wonderland: Teaching with Alice and Media Computation.

Barbara Ericson , *Georgia Institute of Technology*
Wanda Dann, *Carnegie Mellon University*
Stephen Cooper , *Purdue University*

This workshop is designed for instructors who are interested in teaching a course combining Alice and Media Computation in Java. The goal of this approach is to provide a complete CS1 that uses Alice to reduce syntax frustration while beginners are learning computing concepts and then uses Media Computation to reinforce the same concepts in Java. We will describe how to assist students in transferring knowledge from Alice to Java. Participants will create some combined Alice and Media Computation projects. For example they will use chromakey to change the background of an Alice movie. See http://home.cc.gatech.edu/TeaParty for more information on Alice and Media Computation. **Laptop required.**

37. Introducing and Teaching Smartphone Application Development

Qusay H. Mahmoud, *Centre for Mobile Education and Research*

The diversity of mobile hardware and software platforms is one of the major challenges in designing and developing applications for smartphones. Such applications are developed on one platform like MS Windows or Linux and deployed on a totally different platform such as a mobile phone or a BlackBerry device. Integrating mobile devices into computing education can raise the level of excitement and satisfaction among students; see http://cmer.cis.uoguelph.ca. This workshop will help participants understand the opportunities, challenges, and the different technologies that can be used to develop applications for smartphones, with a particular focus on using the Java platform, Micro Edition (Java ME) and the BlackBerry smartphone. This workshop will be of particular interest to faculty interested in integrating smartphones into their CS/IT/Engineering Curricula. **Laptop optional.**

38. The New Wave of Parallelism, Part I: Teaching Map-Reduce at Multiple Levels in the CS Curriculum

Richard Brown, *St. Olaf College*
Libby Shoop, *Macalester College*

As summarized in www.cs.stolaf.edu/manycore.html, emerging changes in hardware will demand more and more parallelism in software. Map-reduce, the cornerstone of Google- and Yahoo!-style computing, has star appeal to draw students to the study of parallelism. Workshop participants will carry out exercises that introduce data-parallel processing concepts, using Yahoo!'s open-source Hadoop map-reduce programming environment. The exercises, at the CS1, intermediate, and advanced curricular levels, offer choices of programming languages for various courses and institutions. CS1 exercises use a simplified interface developed by the presenters for Hadoop programming by introductory students, using Java, Python, Scheme, or other languages. Intermediate and advanced exercises use standard Hadoop programming in Java or C++. Expository materials and portable software infrastructure provided to participants. Intended audience: CS instructors. **Laptop required (Windows, Mac, Linux).**

39. Cooperative Learning for CS1 and Beyond: Making It Work for You

Leland L. Beck, *San Diego State University*
Alexander W. Chizhik, *San Diego State University*

Would you like to bring the benefits of cooperative learning into your classroom, but have questions about how to do it? If so, this workshop is for you. After a brief overview of cooperative learning principles and research, we will work together to focus on practical issues, such as course planning, classroom management, and methods for guiding group processes. You will be able to experience a cooperative learning process yourself, and also share ideas and experiences with other participants. The principles and activities in the workshop will be applicable throughout the computer science curriculum. In addition, you will receive a complete set of class-tested cooperative learning activities that have raised test scores in CS1 by 25% at our institution. No prior experience with cooperative learning is necessary. **No laptop needed.**

SIGCSE 2010 Birds of a Feather

The following Birds-of-a-Feather sessions were organized for attendees of the SIGCSE 2010 symposium.

Accessibility of Educational Technology in Computer Science Courses

Daniel Zingaro, *University of Toronto*
Salvador Garcia-Martinez, *Concordia University*

Among Computer Science (CS) faculty, there is no shortage of novel classroom uses of technology. For example, faculties are communicating "digital ink" annotations to students using tablet PCs, and mobile phones are being used as program development environments. Ideally, every student should have access to this technology; however, many times, this is not the case. Students with disabilities are often isolated in a regular classroom. What are the accessibility-related ramifications of these rapidly evolving technologies? Are our innovative uses of technologies contributing to the exclusion of students with disabilities from the classroom? We would like to discuss experiences and concerns related to accessibility in technology-centric CS courses.

Best Practices for HS Teachers and the Introductory CS Course

Ria Galanos, *Centennial High School*

Many high school computer science teachers find themselves teaching in isolation as they are often the only programming teacher in their school. This BOF will provide a platform for sharing teaching methods, fun ways to introduce computer science topics, and ideas for hands-on activities that illustrate a variety of introductory computer science topics. In addition, the beginnings of a community can be formed by exchanging names and contact information.

BlueJ Users Forum

Ian Utting, *University of Kent*
Michael Kolling, *University of Kent*
John Rosenberg, *La Trobe University*

A forum for teachers using the BlueJ IDE to make contact with each other and with members of the BlueJ team, and to discuss their use of the system along with recent and future developments.

Building Sustainable K-12/Post Secondary Partnerships

Chris Stephenson, *Computer Science Teachers Association*
Mindy Hart, *Purdue University*
Deborah Klipp, *Mainland Regional High School*
Bill Hogan, *Max Planck Institute*

The enrollment crisis has prompted many post-secondary computer science and engineering departments to launch or enhance their K-12 outreach programs but these efforts are often hampered by a lack of familiarity and differing objectives. This BOF is intended to promote discussion on the challenges faced on both sides of the K-12/post secondary partnership and to share strategies and best practices for ensuring the success of outreach programs. The session will solicit the experiences and opinions of audience members with regard to the benefits, challenges, and proven best practices for conducting outreach programs and building long-term relationships between K-12 and post-secondary educators.

Computer Science Activism in Under-Resourced Communities

Douglas Turnbull, *Swarthmore College*
Tarsem S. Purewal, Jr, *University of Tennessee at Chattanooga*

There are many under-resourced communities in the United States where people a) do not have access to computers, and b) do not know how to use computers. As a result, an important part of our population is excluded from social, political and financial opportunities. Most computer science students, on the other hand, have had access to computers from a very early age and are highly capable technology consultants. In this BOF session, we will discuss how we can inspire and enable our student to get involved in "tech activism." This might involve revitalizing donated computers and placing them into low-income homes, building community computer labs, and teaching people how to use computers. Some topics we plan to discuss are service-based CS learning courses, university-sponsored student organizations, and grassroots social entrepreneurship.

Connecting Computer Science Education and Music

Bill Manaris, *College of Charleston*
Jesse Heines, *University of Massachusetts Lowell*
Douglas Turnbull, *Swarthmore College*

This BOF will focus on leveraging the connection between music and computer science education to increase student retention, motivation, learning and satisfaction. Among many possibilities, this exploration can (a) provide inspiration for engaging CS1/2 assignments; (b) lead to a two-course sequence covering all the CS1/CS2 material; (c) inform existing courses, such as HCI and AI; (d) help create new courses at the junior/senior level (e.g., Music Information Retrieval), and (e) lead to innovative research (e.g., generative music). This BOF may lead to the creation of collaborative teams that span disciplines and bring CS students together with students in the Arts.

Could Scratch Be the Only Language in an Introductory Computer Science Course?

John Maloney, *Massachusetts Institute of Technology*
Ursula Wolz, *The College of New Jersey*
David Malan, *Harvard University*
Brian Harvey, *University of California, Berkeley*

Scratch has proven an effective way to introduce programming in college level introductory computer science classes for both majors and non-majors. Scratch's interactive nature and lack of syntax allows students to get results quickly, while focusing on problem solving and learning transferable programming concepts. Typically, Scratch is used only for a short while before switching to a text-based language such as C, Java, or Processing. But could Scratch -- or some variant of it -- be used to teach a full-length, programming-heavy computer science course? If so, for what type of classes is it best suited (CS0, CS1, ...)? If not, what's missing? When should students transition to another language, and can that transition be made smoothly?

The Current State of the Advanced Placement Computer Science Program

Paul Tymann, *Rochester Institute of Technology*

The purpose of the session is to provide high school and college faculty who are involved with the APCS program with an opportunity to interact with members of the APCS development committee. Participants will obtain updated information on the APCS curriculum and exam. Members of the APCS development committee will facilitate discussions based on the following topics: the latest news from the College Board, results of the 2009 AP exam, changes in the APCS curriculum, new types of questions on the exam, teaching tips and techniques.

Curricula in Concurrency and Parallelism

Jens Mache, *Lewis & Clark College*
Kim B. Bruce, *Pomona College*
David P. Bunde, *Knox College*
Curtis Clifton, *Rose-Hulman Institute of Technology*
Daniel Ernst, *University of Wisconsin - Eau Claire*
Vijay Saraswat, *IBM*

Multicore, multiprocessor, and clustered platforms are becoming the standard computing platforms available for executing programs. Thus, Computer Science education increasingly entails education in parallel and concurrent programming. This BOF is designed to gather colleagues to exchange ideas and discuss questions such as the following: - What fundamental ideas of concurrency and parallelism should every CS graduate know? - Should concurrency and parallelism be taught top-down (via high-level abstractions such as operations on collections) or bottom-up (with low-level tools such as threads and locks)? - How should concurrency and parallelism be integrated in the curriculum? At what levels and depths? If broad integration is appropriate, what resources are needed to educate the educators?

Distributing Communication Skills Across the Computer Science Curriculum

Gerald Gannod, *Miami University*
Mladen Vouk, *North Carolina State University*
Janet Burge, *Miami University*

Communication skills are critical to success in any profession; the fields of computer science (CS) and software engineering (SE) are no exceptions. Teaching these skills, however, is often relegated to courses outside the discipline. As a result, CS and SE students rarely understand how to apply what they have been taught to courses in their discipline. They often view presentations and documentation as "busy work" rather than a key aspect of their education. Furthermore, the need for communication skills as measurable outcomes of CS and SE programs is demonstrated by their inclusion in the SE2004 model curriculum. This session will provide a forum where like-minded participants from academia and industry can join together to discuss the issues related to teaching communication skills as a discipline integrated into computer science and software engineering.

Education, Computers and Society

Florence Appel, *Saint Xavier University*
Joseph Oldham, *Centre College*

This session is organized by ACM SIGCAS (Computers and Society) for those interested in addressing the social and ethical consequences of computing within their curricula. We will emphasize sharing resources and ideas, and strengthening our network. Discussion items will include best practices and approaches to teaching computer ethics and social impact, developing programs for recruitment and retention of under-represented populations, and implementing service learning course components. We will also address ways in which SIGCAS and SIGCSE can collaborate to support each other's work, including organizing a future pre-SIGCSE conference dedicated to computers and society issues.

Enabling Active, Collaborative, and Other Social Learning

Rebecca Bates, *Minnesota State University, Mankato*
Ryan Campbell, *University of Washington*

Social instruction strategies such as active learning and collaborative learning have long been encouraged but have been slow to be adopted widely in CS. Whether you are just considering incorporating social instruction strategies into your classes or are a seasoned veteran with these techniques, you are invited to share your experiences, concerns, and advice as to how these strategies can be customized and naturally integrated into CS education. Discussion leaders will provide a set of example social instruction scenarios to establish a shared vocabulary and kick off the conversation.

For Me Programming Is: A Call for Large-Scale Study of Attitudinal Student Views

Brian Hanks, *Fort Lewis College*
Beth Simon, *University of California, San Diego*

We propose a simple, widely-deployable survey of introductory programming students to establish a repository of student attitudes toward programming. The proposed survey question is: "Based on my experience in this class, for me programming is…" Participants would select or rank up to five responses from a list of ten choices (such as "fun/cool" or "frustrating"), generated from prior research, which found that students have generally positive attitudes toward programming, although it appears that many other factors affect student attitudes. A wide scale deployment of this simple question would allow the CS education community to answer significant questions about our students. For example, do new teaching approaches result in a more positive attitude among students, thus leading to greater retention? Are student attitudes affected by the choice of introductory programming language? We call on the community to participate in an effort to address these questions.

How Do We Teach Students Effective Practices for Commenting Computer Source Code?

Michael Locasto, *George Mason University*
Peter DePasquale, *TCNJ*

We routinely arm students with strategies for creating complex software systems, but we have little success at getting them to learn good commenting habits. Comments serve as a vital part of the conversation between developers by explaining the logic expressed in the code itself. Typical approaches to evaluating comment quality are manual and subjective. In this BOF, we would like to start a conversation within the SIGCSE community about how to develop strategies for making commenting more rewarding and natural for their students. We aim to facilitate the development of commenting best practices by collecting the experiences and suggestions of the workshop attendees into a concrete list of practices and initiatives, including approaches that consider alternative sequences to developing code first and then documenting it.

Imaging College Educators (ICE)

Matthew Boutell, *Rose-Hulman Institute of Technology*
Jerod Weinman, *Grinnell College*

Within computing, the field of imaging includes computer vision, image understanding, computer graphics, and image processing. While much research and teaching is done at the graduate level, the typical imaging educator at an undergraduate institution is the only specialist in his or her department. This BOF will bring together educators who currently teach imaging courses or may be interested in expanding their curricular offerings. We will emphasize sharing ideas and resources and establishing a network for continued cooperation. Discussion items may include course organization, assignments and projects, and lecture aids such as visualizations. The network will include a mailing list for participants to share ideas about imaging pedagogy and a website to share course materials.

Making Mathematical Reasoning Fun with Tools and Collaborative Learning Methods

Joan Krone, *Denison University*
Murali Sitaraman, *Clemson University*
Jason Hallstrom, *Clemson University*

Can learning mathematical reasoning be made enjoyable? How can we employ collaborative learning activities and reasoning tools to make it both effective and fun? This Birds of a Feather session will bring together computer science educators interested in integrating analytical reasoning principles in the undergraduate curriculum and help share specific ideas, examples, activities, and tools that have worked. The overall goal is to help students understand the connections between mathematics and software and to apply those connections in reasoning rigorously about the software they develop and maintain. the session is motivated in part by discussions that occurred during the past two Math Thinking sessions at SIGCSE, in which participants expressed an interest in such curriculum support, but noted a lack of well-understood techniques and tools for teaching reasoning.

Mathematical Thinking, Computational Thinking and Computation

William Marion, *Valparaiso University*
Doug Baldwin, *SUNY Geneseo*
Murali Sitaraman, *Clemson University*

In the past 4 years discussion has taken place among computer science educators as to how to reorient our way of thinking about our field. Both Jeannette Wing and Peter Denning in Viewpoint columns of the Communications of the ACM [1, 2] have offered their views on how we might describe more broadly what we as computer scientists do, and, hence, rethink what this might mean for our curricula, our research and our collaboration with others. Computational thinking and computation have moved to the forefront of our views of our field. From either perspective mathematical thinking is seen as foundational. In this session we will discuss what effect this reorientation might have on the "mathematical content" of introductory courses in computer science and discrete mathematics and the role mathematical reasoning must play.[1] Denning, P., 2009, The Profession of IT Beyond Computational Thinking, Comm. of ACM, 52(6):28-30 [2] Wing, J., 2006, Computational Thinking, Comm. of ACM, 49(3):33-5

Online Exams

Ed Gehringer, *North Carolina State University*

In today's world, tests and exams are given in an environment that is increasingly artificial. Most technical work is done with computers. Few people would attempt to write a computer program, analyze forces on a building, or even write a piece of prose without the aid of a computer. But that's just the kind of environment we place our students in when they take an exam on paper. All of the major learning-management systems and textbook publishers have online testing modules that can be used to deliver quizzes or exams. When you use these to examine your students, a new set of challenges appear. Attend this BOF to find out what they are, and to discuss them.

Opportunities for Collaboration with Colleagues in China

Richard LeBlanc, *Seattle University*
Ming Zhang, *Peking University*
Virginia Lo, *University of Oregon*
Andrzej Proskurowski, *University of Oregon*

The large computer science education community in China offers a variety of opportunities for collaboration. Computer science educators in China face some unique challenges, but also many that are familiar to all CS educators. Interaction with the well-organized Chinese CS education community offers possibilities for enriching experiences for educators from outside of China and a path to including meaningful international experiences as part of computer science programs everywhere.

Professional Certificates vs. Degree Programs, Which Are the Best Career Entry Credentials?

Soon Park, *Governors State University*
Karen D'Arcy, *Governors State Univerisity*
Ram Raghuraman, *Joliet Junior College*
Linda Washington, *Argonne National Laboraotry*
Clare Tang, *Governors State University*
Gretchen Koch, *compTIA*

Entry level jobs in the IT sector often emphasize experience and certifications as recommended preparation, rather than college degrees. Computer science students are often curious about certifications as they begin their studies. Community Colleges in Illinois provide opportunities for students to earn associate degrees as well as certifications. What is the best advice for students as they enter college to prepare themselves for a career in IT? This BOF will compare professional certificate programs with degree programs, exploring the pros and cons of each in the context of education and job appeal to the IT industry. Our discussions are informed by employer information gathered during a recent NSF CPATH grant. NSF CPATH grant number 0722301 supported this work.

Promoting Engagement and Retention Through Sense of Belonging

Ken Yasuhara, *University of Washington*
Nanette Veilleux, *Simmons College*

Research has identified a wide variety of factors affecting student engagement, which in turn affects key outcomes including academic achievement and retention. Feeling connected to a community and sense of belonging can substantially influence student engagement, particularly for members of underrepresented groups who are more likely to feel isolated. This BOF will open with a brief discussion to establish a common understanding and vocabulary for the concept of sense of belonging. Then, the group will discuss ways in which computer science educators can enhance student sense of belonging. This will include the sharing of best practices (e.g., related to mentoring, classroom climate, extracurricular activities), but we also hope that discussion will help educators recognize and become more intentional about decisions they make that are likely to affect sense of belonging.

Security in the CS Curriculum

Blair Taylor, *Towson University*
Bill Chu, *University of North Carolina, Charlotte*
Maureen Doyle, *Northern Kentucky University*
Kevin Du, *Syracuse University*
Siddharth Kaza, *Towson University*
Carol Taylor, *East Washington University*

Security remains a vital concern in the computer industry. Despite its importance, security education remains the poor stepchild of undergraduate computing curricula and exists primarily in the form of specialized tracks and upper-level elective courses. In order to better prepare our graduates to address tomorrow's security challenges, we wish to examine the following questions: • Does security have a place in CS1, CS2, and Data Structures? • How can we better include security in upper level courses such as Database Management, Operating Systems, and Web Programming? • Are security tracks enough? • How do you include security in your classes?

Teaching Social and Ethical Issues in CS0 and Beyond

Marge Coahran, *Grinnell College*
Jerod Weinman, *Grinnell College*

CS0 courses frequently address social and ethical issues in addition to technical aspects of computing. Yet CS instructors may feel less comfortable with these topics and may have less experience with classroom activities that are well suited to these topics (eg, discussion sessions, debates, mock trials). The purpose of this BOF is to gather CS educators who teach or are considering teaching about the ethical and social aspects of computing in CS0 or in other CS courses. It will provide an opportunity to share strategies and experiences, to seek advice on difficulties encountered, to vet nascent ideas, and to learn about new ideas. Questions that might arise include: how do we balance and integrate the social with the technical in CS0, what classroom activities have we tried and how successful have they been, what classroom management techniques are helpful during these activities, and how do we assess student participation in them?

Teaching Track Faculty in CS

Donald Slater, *Carnegie Mellon University*
Susan Rodger, *Duke University*

A panel at SIGCSE 2004 illustrated the trend in computer science departments to hire faculty to teach in a teaching-track position that parallels the standard tenure-track position, providing the possibility of promotion, longer-term contracts, and higher pay for excellence in teaching and service. This birds-of-a-feather is designed to gather educators who are currently in such a position to share their experiences as members of the faculty of their departments and schools, and to provide opportunities for schools considering such positions to gather information.

Teaching Using Virtualization

William Thomas, *Juniata College*
Paul Wagner, *University of Wisconsin Eau Claire*
Alex Seazzu, *University of New Mexico*

Virtualization is being widely used in industry as an alternative to server farms. It is heralded as a green technology; allows much easier system management and produces the lowest total cost of ownership (TCO). Virtualization also has important uses in the classroom especially in a lab environment serving multiple classes. Virtualization can be used to give students the experience of installing and configuring an operating system. Virtualization is well suited to teaching computer security. This BOF session is an opportunity to discuss and explore the ways faculty have used virtualization in the classroom. Attend this BOF to share your own uses of virtualization and learn from your colleagues.

Teaching Web Programming

Marty Stepp, *University of Washington*
Jessica Miller, *University of Washington*

For the last two years we have held BOF sessions about teaching web programming at the college level. Our feedback indicates that the most valuable aspect of the past sessions was simply to get everyone together for an exchange of ideas and information, so this will be the focus of the session this year. We'd like to put emphasis on bringing together two main groups of web programming instructors: Newcomers who have not yet taught this material before (or are just starting) and want to soak up information, and veterans who have now taught it and have insights to share with the group. Newcomers can ask questions about materials, languages and technologies to use, what works and what doesn't, and so on. Veterans can share tips from the classroom and helpful resources. We can also discuss the latest web technologies such as HTML 5, ECMAScript 3.5, Flash, JavaFX, Google Wave, iPhone/Android, and web application frameworks such as Django, JSP, .NET, and Rails.

Teaching With Alice

Donald Slater, *Carnegie Mellon University*
Wanda Dann, *Carnegie Mellon University*
Stephen Cooper, *Purdue University*

This session is for anyone currently using Alice, or exploring the possibility of using Alice in their curriculum. The discussion leaders and experienced Alice instructors will share teaching strategies, tips, and tricks with each other and those new to Alice. The session provides an arena for sharing Alice instructional materials and ideas for courses at all educational levels. This is an opportunity to share assignments and pointers to web sites where collections of instructional materials, such as syllabi, student projects, exams, and other resources are available. In addition, Alice 3 (the latest version) will be a topic of discussion.

Teaching Your Computer Science Course in Context

Steve Cunningham, *Brown Cunningham Associates*
Steve Cooper, *Purdue University*

Computer science instructors have used a number of techniques, from Alice and media computation in the beginning source to computational science in more advanced courses, to engage students in the computer science and to ground the subject in ways the students can identify with. These techniques all fall under the general concept of teaching computer science topics in a context outside the field. This BOF will let attendees share their experiences and will help us identify the breadth of contexts that people have used and their reflections on whether the context was effective and/or how to make the use of a context more effective in teaching computer science content.

TeachScheme/ReachJava

Viera K Proulx, *Northeastern University*

TeachScheme/ReachJava is an unconventional introductory computing curriculum that introduces both functional programming and the object-oriented program design in a systematic design-driven style. The design recipes for designing data, designing functions/methods, and designing abstractions empower both the student and the instructor. The design recipe for designing functions/methods enforces the test-first design from the beginning. The ReachJava part focuses on understanding data design and adds Java language features only when needed. Instructors experienced in using TeachScheme/ReachJava curriculum will be invited to share their experiences and course materials with each other. Those interested in learning about TeachScheme/ReachJava will have the opportunity to ask questions, see examples of student work, and learn more about the TeachScheme/ReachJava pedagogy.

Technology that Educators of Computing Hail (TECH)

Daniel Garcia, *UC Berkeley*
Don Bailes, *East Tennessee State University*
Sally Fincher, *University of Kent*

The judicious use of technology in computing education (in and out of the classroom) can be empowering and transformative. However, it is very difficult to discover what tools are available and how effective they have been. The ACM Education Council hopes to address this with a new website, "Technology that Educators of Computing Hail (TECH)", that will serve to provide a central, organized collection of links to teaching resources. It will feature search, rating, tagging and commentary. The goal of this BOF is to collect "experience reports" from educators who have used technology for teaching computing – with success or not!

A Town Meeting: SIGCSE Committee on Expanding the Women-in-Computing Community

Gloria Townsend, *DePauw University*

In January 2004, we organized the second SIGCSE Committee ("Expanding the Women-in-Computing Community"). Our annual Town Meeting provides dissemination of information concerning successful gender issues projects, along with group discussion and brainstorming, in order to create committee goals for the coming year. We select projects to highlight through listserv communication and through our connections with NCWIT, ACM-W, etc. This year we anticipate project information from the Coalition to Diversify Computing and from the Empowering Leadership Alliance and other major organizations dedicated to expanding the community of women and minorities in computing.

SIGCSE 2010 Poster Sessions

Posters present work-in-progress and other topics for which dialog with Symposium attendees is particularly appropriate. Posters are on display Friday morning and afternoon, and authors will be available for discussion during these sessions.

Session I: Friday, March 12, 10:00 – 12:00, Exhibit Hall 301A

COMTOR: A Source Code Comment Mentoring System

Peter DePasquale, *The College of New Jersey*
Michael Locasto, *George Mason University*

By the Numbers: The Status of Women in Information Technology

Wendy DuBow, *National Center for Women and Information Technology*
Lecia Barker, *University of Texas at Austin*

An Undergraduate Data Mining Course Integrated with Research and Industry Projects

Ping Chen, *University of Houston-Downtown*
Irene Chen, *University of Houston-Downtown*
Rakesh Verma, *University of Houston*

Measuring Perceptions of Parallelism in the CS1 Classroom

Brian Rague, *Weber State University*

Teaching and Learning via Original Historical Sources

Inna Pivkina, *New Mexico State University*

Interactively Exploring Functional Multimedia with Escalator

Brian Howard, *DePauw University*
Jeremy Kings, *Illinois Wesleyan University*
Christopher Monsanto, *Transylvania University*

Computing for Poets

Mark LeBlanc, *Wheaton College*

Becker's++: A Fun and Effective Way to Learn Programming

Samreen Anjum, *Carnegie Mellon University - Qatar*
Rishav Bhowmick, *Carnegie Mellon University - Qatar*
Hoda Fahmy, *Carnegie Mellon University - Qatar*
Saquib Razak, *Carnegie Mellon University - Qatar*

An Approach To Teaching Cryptology At All Levels

Rong Yang, *Western Kentucky University*
Layne Wallace, *University of North Florida*

MessageGrid ReplayInk: Understanding How Students Solve Problems

Roy Pargas, *Clemson University*
Eric Anderson, *Clemson University*
Samuel Bryfczynski, *Clemson University*

A Comparison of Existing Game Curriculum Literature to the Literature in the Related Fields of Art and Computer Science

Monica McGill, *Bradley University*

Publishing Undergraduate Research

Jacob Furst, *DePaul University*
Daniela Raicu, *DePaul University*

Video Game Programming, A High School Curricular Initiative

David Ruth, *Niles North High School*

Practice Makes Perfect with CoPractice

Kevin Buffardi, *Virginia Tech*
Dzmitry Churbanau, *Virginia Tech*
Rahul Kanna N. Jayaraman, *Virginia Tech*
Stephen H. Edwards, *Virginia Tech*

Improving Exception Messages with ExceptionDoctor

Michael Woods, *Virginia Tech*
Stephen Edwards, *Virginia Tech*

Creative Computing: A CS4HS workshop for cultivating computational thinking

Karen Brennan, *MIT Media Lab*

CAP Space: An Integrated Tool for Associate-Degree Computing Programs

Robert Campbell, *CUNY Graduate Center*
Elizabeth Hawthorne, *Union County College*
Anita Wright, *Camden County College*

Introducing the CS1 Community Site as part of the NSF/NSDL Ensemble Digital Library for Computing Education

Scott Fletcher, *Portland State University*
Lois Delcambre, *Portland State University*
Payal Agrawal, *Portland State University*

The ACM GUI Testing Framework: Simplifying GUI Unit Testing for Students

Jason Snyder, *Virginia Tech*
Stephen Edwards, *Virginia Tech*

ENSEMBLE: Supporting the Full Range of Computing Education Communities

Monika Akbar, *Virginia Tech*
Edward A. Fox, *Virginia Tech*
Lillian N. Cassel, *Villanova University*
Yinlin Chen, *Virginia Tech*
Stephen Edwards, *Virginia Tech*
Peter L Brusilovsky, *University of Pittsburgh*
Stephen Carpenter, *Texas A&M University*
Lois Delcambre, *Portland State University*
Weiguo Fan, *Virginia Tech*
Richard Furuta, *Texas A&M University*
Frank M Shipman, *Texas A&M University*
Daniel Garcia, *University of California, Berkeley*
Greg Hislop, *Drexel University*
David Maier, *Portland State University*
Manuel Perez-Quinones, *Virginia Tech*
Christine Stephenson, *Villanova University*
Bryant York, *Portland State University*
Haowei Hsieh, *University of Iowa*

Creating a Silver Lining on Dark Clouds: A successful experiment of leveraging fresh graduates waiting for jobs to build community applications on the Microsoft Azure Cloud Computing Platform

Shekhar Sahasrabudhe, *Persistent Systems Limited*
Vikram Rajkondwar, *Microsoft India*
Anand Deshpande, *Persistent Systems Limited*

Stimulating Creative Problem Solving in CS2 Using Video Scenarios

Madalene Spezialetti, *Trinity College*

Adapting Five Key Social Instruction Strategies to the CS Educational Environment

Denise Wilson, *University of Washington*
Rebecca Bates, *Minnesota State University, Mankato*
Ken Yasuhara, *University of Washington*
Ryan Campbell, *University of Washington*
Rachel Sear, *Minnesota State University, Mankato*

Increasing Engagement and Enrollment in Breadth-First Introductory Courses Using Authentic Computing Tasks

Ryan McFall, *Hope College*
Joshua Andrews, *Hope College*

Session II: Friday, March 12, 2:45 – 4:45, Exhibit Hall 301A

Computer Science + Digital Storytelling = More Computer Science Students

Jennifer Polack-Wahl, *University of Mary Washington*
Karen Anewalt, *University of Mary Washington*

A Filtering Approach to Computer-Aided Student Study Group Formation

Kurt O'Hearn, *Grand Valley State University*
Roger Ferguson, *Grand Valley State University*

From Source Code Plagiarism to Social Network

Evandro Luquini, *Universidade Presbiteriana Mackenzie*
Nizam Omar, *Universidade Presbiteriana Mackenzie*

New Trends in Automated Project Grading for Web Programming Classes

Xiang Fu, *Hofstra University*
Kai Qian, *Southern Polytechnic State University*
Boris Peltsverger, *Georgia Southwestern State University*
Kent Palmer, *Wingate University*
Chong-wei Xu, *Kennesaw State University*
Yu Zhang, *Bainbridge College*

Teaching Programming as a Process: Results and Phase 2

Anastasia Tircuit, *Seton Hill University*

An Initial Report on the Impact of Multiple Technical Degree Programs on Undergraduate Recruitment

Amber Settle, *DePaul University*
Liz Friedman, *DePaul University*

Information Security: Audit, Case Study, and Service Learning

Susan Lincke, *University of Wisconsin-Parkside*

Tools and Approach for Teaching Early Introduction to Object Oriented Simulation

Jose Garrido, *Kennesaw State University*

African-American Males in Computer Science - Examining the Pipeline for Clogs

Daryl Stone, *Bowie State University*

So Different Though So Similar?- or Vice Versa? Exploration of Two Paradigms

Bruria Haberman, *Holon Institute of Technology and Davidson Institute of Science Education*
Noa Ragonis, *Beit Berl College and Technion- Israel Institute of Technology*

CFG Experimenter: An Animated Parser-Generator Programming Project for Learning Compiler Algorithms

Curtis Clifton, *Rose-Hulman Institute of Technology*
Brian T. Kelley, *Rose-Hulman Institute of Technology*

Undergraduate Game Degree Programs in the United Kingdom and United States: A Comparison of the Curriculum Planning Process

Monica McGill, *Bradley University*

100P: A Guided Discovery Curriculum for Computer Science

Nicholas A. Kraft, *The University of Alabama*
John C. Lusth, *The University of Alabama*
Xiaoyan Hong, *The University of Alabama*

Cyberspace Meets Brick and Mortar: Finding the Sweet Spot between Cyberlearning and Traditional Instruction

Ashok Basawapatna, *University of Colorado Boulder*
Alexander Repenning, *University of Colorado Boulder*

Lessons Learned From Using a Wiki as a Course Management System

Antonios Saravanos, *Columbia University*
Matthew Curinga, *Columbia University*

The Impact of Creative Achievement on Academic Achievement in Media-Oriented CS1

Paul Gestwicki, *Ball State University*
Khuloud Ahmad, *Ball State University*

An Interdisciplinary Guide for K-8 Computer Science Education

Sarah Carruthers, *University of Victoria*

An Eclipse Plug-in for Enforcing Java Naming Conventions

Matthew Strand, *Chapman University*
Lindsey Hughes, *Chapman University*
Robert Duncan, *University of California, Irvine*
Joseph M. Smith, *Chapman University*
Erik Linstead, *Chapman University*

Teaching Computational Thinking with L-Systems and Turtle Graphics

Bruce Maxwell, *Colby College*

Game Mechanics Without Computer Games: Incentivizing Contributions in Expertiza

Ed Gehringer, *North Carolina State University*

Analysis of a lab-centric instruction in a machine structures course.

Nathaniel Titterton, *University of California, Berkeley*
Colleen Lewis, *University of California, Berkeley*
Michael Clancy, *University of California, Berkeley*

Binary Dungeon: Teaching Search Algorithms through Game Exploration

Acey Boyce, *University of North Carolina at Charlotte*
David Joy, *University of North Carolina at Charlotte*
Daniel McSwain, *University of North Carolina at Charlotte*

Bug Bots: Using Interactive Code Visualization To Teach Debugging In A Game

Andrew Hicks, *University of North Carolina at Charlotte*
Dustin Culler, *University of North Carolina at Charlotte*
Alejandro Rios, *University of North Carolina at Charlotte*
Evan Pittfield, *University of North Carolina at Charlotte*

Student Connections to Community in Computer Science and Engineering Education

Ken Yasuhara, *University of Washington*
Denise Wilson, *University of Washington*
Rebecca Bates, *Minnesota State University, Mankato*
Tamara Floyd-Smith, *Tuskegee University*
Nanette Veilleux, *Simmons College*

SIGCSE 2010 Video Exhibition Abstracts

Image Compression - Making Contact
Tim Bell, *University of Canterbury*; Richard Bell, *Shuriken*

The video ponders how someone from outer space might make contact with us, and picks up Carl Sagan's idea of sending coded images. This moves into a demonstration of students using run-length coding to draw a giant image on the side of a school building. The idea is from the Computer Science Unplugged material, which communicates what Computer Science is without using computers. We find that once teachers have seen the demonstration, they are more motivated to do the activity (available from csunplugged.org) and understand the point a lot better.

Summer Academy for Advancing Deaf & Hard of Hearing in Computing
Richard Ladner, Kay Beck-Benton, Anna Cavender, Pamela Lowell, Robert Roth, *University of Washington*

The Summer Academy for Advancing Deaf & Hard of Hearing in Computing video showcases a program at the University of Washington where deaf and hard of hearing students are encouraged to consider a career in computing. Accepted students are awarded free tuition, transportation, and room and board. Students take a computer programming course for college credit and a certificated class in animation. They also visit companies such as Microsoft and Google where they meet successful deaf and hard of hearing role models already working in computing, as well as others brought in from around the country to speak to students.

Sorting Algorithms (Unplugged)
Tim Bell, *University of Canterbury*; Richard Bell, *Shuriken*

The video shows teachers how they can give their students an idea of the varying performance of sorting algorithms by using balance scales to simulate the comparisons performed by the algorithms. The idea is from the Computer Science Unplugged material, which communicates what Computer Science is without using computers. We find that once teachers have seen the demonstration, they are more motivated to do the activity (available from csunplugged.org) and understand the point a lot better.

Industry Fellows
Josh Tenenberg, *University of Washington, Tacoma*

Describes and illustrates the "Industry Fellows" program at the University of Washington, Tacoma, which pairs a practicing professional with a college professor to teach a course together. Includes footage from the classroom, and interviews with the practitioner, the professor, and the students.

When all the Photoshops Have Turned to Dust: Join the Top of the Software Food Chain
Beth Simon, *University of California, San Diego*

This is an undergraduate student-created video featuring introductory programming students. Join the top of the software food chain. In a post-apoco-something world, we still have technology, but software… well it's not what it was. This video makes rogue heroes of programmers (having studied media computation) who are still capable of manipulating and fixing your digital photos.

Computing as a Career: Deaf & Hard of Hearing Perspectives
Richard Ladner, Kay Beck-Benton, Anna Cavender, Pamela Lowell, Robert Roth, *University of Washington*

Computing as a Career: Deaf & Hard of Hearing Perspectives highlights deaf and hard of hearing professionals in a variety of computing careers within industry and academia reaching out to the intended audience of deaf and hard of hearing students and encouraging them to enter computing. These professionals visited the University of Washington's Summer Academy for Advancing Deaf and Hard of Hearing in Computing, from such companies as Cray, Google, IBM Microsoft, and Oracle, to speak with deaf and hard of hearing students about their careers, the obstacles they faced, and barriers that were non-existent or removed.

Visit Virt-U: We Have Problems

Madalene Spezialetti, *Trinity College*

Come and visit the Virtual Video World of Virt-U, a fictitious university where everyone, including the residents of the near-by city, are having problems. These problems have been captured on video and collected on the Virt-U web site. The videos are designed to encourage computational thinking and creative problem solving, as well as to aid in the development of critical listening and observation skills. The videos are a resource to be used in the classroom and beyond to add a new dimension to the computing education experience.

Undercover Computer Guys

Madalene Spezialetti, *Trinity College*

At a school with an ineffective IT department, a Professor having a printer crisis is aided by students who want to start an undercover enterprise to help people with computer problems. This scenario, which is followed by discussion/design questions, touches on diverse issues including scheduling protocol design and analysis, web design, encoding/decoding and ethics.

Relational Graphs: What Are They?

Sarah Carruthers, *University of Victoria*

What are graphs and how are they used in the world around us? How are they relevant to young students today? Graph theory, like many other theoretical computer science topics, is not taught in elementary classes in much of North America. This video was made as a motivator for the first in a series of Grade Six Graph Theory lessons, developed as part of a larger research study to evaluate graph theory instruction as part of a grade six math class.

Computer Science Buskers? (Error Correction)

Tim Bell, *University of Canterbury*; Michael Bell and Kristin Finnerty, *Orange Studio*

Science Busking is a challenging form of outreach, taking one's teaching into the marketplace to make contact with people in the street – literally! The video takes a humorous approach to the serious question: can we communicate Computer Science concepts to the general public, especially in a situation where we must catch their attention first? The card trick here is from the "Error detection" activity from csunplugged.org, and is deliberately left unexplained, to encourage the viewer to read up about it afterwards.

Issues in Algorithm Visualization

Clifford A. Shaffer, Michael Stewart, Alexander Joel Alon, and Monika Akbar, *Virginia Polytechnic Institute and State University*

While algorithm visualizations (AVs) are viewed as having potential for improving computer science education, the rate of AV use has progressed little from the mid 1990s. CS faculty indicate that impediments to successful use of AVs include: difficulties in finding quality AVs on desired topics; difficulties in adapting AVs to the classroom; and lack of knowledge on their deployment. Many existing AVs are of little pedagogical value, and there is poor distribution of topical coverage. This video illustrates some of these impediments faced by instructors and developers, and introduces the AlgoViz Portal.

SIGCSE 2010 SRC Graduate Student Research Abstracts

Measuring the Impact of App Inventor for Android and Studio-Based Learning in an Introductory Computer Science Course for Non-Majors

Khuloud N. Ahmad, *Ball State University*

In many universities, the CS department is suffering from low enrollment and high attrition rates. Multiple studies have linked these phenomena with introductory CS courses. They are found to lack creativity, relevance, and interest. Students tend to have low motivation, specifically with respect to attitudes towards overtly mathematics-oriented assignments and lecture-oriented pedagogy. This study implements an experimental introductory CS course for non-CS majors that uses a visual blocks programming language for developing mobile applications known as App Inventor for Android (AIA), and Studio-Based Learning (SBL). The purpose is to evaluate their effects on students' motivation, achievement, and attitude towards CS.

"You mean we have to work together!?!": A Study of the Formation and Interaction of Programming Teams in a College Course Setting

David L. Largent, *Ball State University*

This ongoing study is exploring how programming teams form and interact in a college course setting and what a course instructor can do to facilitate this process. The experiences of a college course's teams are compared and contrasted to the theory of Bruce Tuckman's four stages of group development, which he characterized as forming, storming, norming and performing. Recommendations about how educators can incorporate more constructive teaching about teamwork into their courses is offered, along with a set of indicators for which course faculty and/or students can watch to identify a team that is struggling.

A Generic Framework for Detecting Top-k Items from a Stream

Bibudh Lahiri, *Iowa State University*

We propose a generic framework for identifying the k most frequent items from a data stream of length n in a single pass, using $o(n)$ memory words. We fit the Misra-Gries sketch and the count-min sketch into this framework and analyze their space-complexities. With the realistic assumption that the frequencies of the items follow a Zipfian distribution, the Misra-Gries sketch takes only $O(k^{O(1)}/\varepsilon)$ space and guarantees an ε-approximate solution. Under identical input distribution, the top-k algorithm by Charikar *et al* needs $\Omega(\log n)$ space, so our algorithm achieves significant space-reduction; and does not demand any apriori knowledge of n.

Secure Open Source Collaboration: An Empirical Study of Linus' Law

Andrew Meneely, *North Carolina State University*

Open source software is often considered to be secure. Part of this confidence lies in leveraging large developer communities to find security vulnerabilities in code. Eric Raymond declares Linus' Law "Given enough eyeballs, all bugs are shallow." Does Linus' Law hold up ad infinitum? Or, can the multitude of developers become "too many cooks in the kitchen", causing the system's security to suffer as a result? In this project, we performed an empirical case study by examining statistical correlations between the known security vulnerabilities in the open source Red Hat Enterprise Linux 4 kernel and metrics that quantify developer activity.

SIGCSE 2010 SRC Undergraduate Student Research Abstracts

Interactive Curriculum Visualization with CurricVis

Austin Toombs, *Ball State University*

Text-based models for describing curricula need to be replaced with newer models that can elegantly reflect the complex data behind curricula. The proposed solution is to implement a better tool for communicating about curricula via curriculum visualization, the application of information visualization on curricular data. CurricVis is a software system that presents a new, more intuitive way to view curricular data. This research explores the hypotheses that it will help students make tough choices about curricula more confidently, accurately, and quickly.

A Java-based Secure Platform for Parallel Genetic Algorithms in Open Networks

Artem Glebov, *Belarusian State University*

We present a simple platform for parallel genetic algorithms following the master-slave scheme. As an underlying communication technology we employ Java RMI, making use of its dynamic class loading features for running custom code remotely. The platform permits dynamic connection and disconnection of executor nodes and ensures that executors are released when they are no longer used. Additional level of security is brought by introducing Kerberos-based authentication and encryption of messages.

Iris Recognition for Mobile Devices

Tommy Carpenter, *Central Connecticut State University*

Mobile devices such as smart phones often carry confidential information, yet are equipped with the weakest forms of security possible. The objective of this work is to provide a lightweight implementation of an iris recognition system, capable of authenticating users of mobile devices equipped with a camera.

A High-Speed Analog Input/Output Data Acquisition Software Library to Study Bat Echolocation

Peter Lustig, *Fitchburg State College*

The precise mechanisms that permit bats to identify particular prey insects via ultrasonic echolocation remain a mystery. Our work seeks to provide the first binaural, in-flight recordings of bat vocalizations and to analyze echoes generated using these recordings in a controlled environment. This goal necessitated a high-speed, analog input/output (I/O) data acquisition device (DAQ) software library that facilitates reuse of acquired data and synchronized I/O operations. This library was realized through the composition and abstraction of several commercially available libraries. Furthermore, the library provides functionality not present in its constituent libraries and is suitable for all general-purpose data acquisition applications.

Intrusion Detection: Analysis of User Behavior

Stefan Maurer, *Hiram College*

In order to provide continuous authentication during a user's session on an electronic device, we have adapted a version of the Smith-Waterman algorithm to create an intrusion detection system capable of quickly distinguishing the current user's behavior from the user's behavior in the past. The project uses a virtual environment to simulate the user's login, application execution, and logout process while recording the user's behavior. Once the environment gathered a sufficient sample of the user's behavior, initial testing of the algorithm yielded successful differentiation between the legitimate user and an intruder while maintaining the ability to execute in real time.

Get the Picture: Image Comparison and Retrieval

William Mooney, *Hiram College*

As computing power and bandwidth increases, the internet is gaining more multimedia centered sites. Everywhere people browse, there is a new image gallery that is free to use and hosts thousands of files. However, there still seems to be an area that is lacking: searching these galleries. While we can post thousands of images in a gallery online, we are still using basic keyword searches to try and find what we are looking for. We will have users upload a query image, which our system will use to return similar images through the use of percentage based color histograms.

A Network Emulator on Embedded Xinu

Kyle Thurow, *Marquette University*

Network software developers often need a way to test their software's behavior under a variety of network conditions. Although network emulators have been built in the past to fill this void, they often suffer from a few shortcomings. The Embedded Xinu network emulator is designed to avoid shortcomings by providing a solution with lower cost, portability, increased ease of use, and more network interfaces than a typical workstation. It works by letting the developer route traffic through the emulator and setting it to drop, duplicate, corrupt, and/or delay packets. They can observe how well their network software response to problems.

XINU as a Multi-Core Operating System on the PlayStation 3™

Gabriel Van Eyck, *Marquette University*

Teaching classes about operating systems presents several challenges. There are many different operating systems to choose from, however the learning curve is usually rather steep. XINU, an operating system designed for instructional use, helps alleviate some of these issues. With the addition of support for the PlayStation 3 platform for XINU, students also have the ability to explore programming an operating system on a multi-core architecture, a project typically not feasible in many classrooms or curriculums. This research aims to lay the groundwork for a curriculum that aims to include multi-core architectures.

Corona Test Generator: Test Generation Made Easy and Tolerant

Dan Eisemann, *St. Bonaventure University*

To alleviate the tedium of developing JUnit test cases, the Corona Test Generator automates the process of creating JUnit test cases. The generator extracts the logic of creating test cases from the syntax of writing test cases. This allows beginners to learn the practice of testing without being hindered by repeated code and arcane syntax. Unique characteristics include the ability to test any method including the main method; the ability to apply filters to the output; and validation of types for both input and output. Each supports the teaching of introductory programming and the administration of programming competitions.

Programming a Job Accounting and Submission System for IBM's Blue Gene Supercomputers Using Both MySQL and Java

Robert DeMarco, *St. Josephs College*

The research conducted in this particular project was done for Brookhaven National Laboratory, and centers around the topic of databases. At the Laboratory, there are two Blue Gene supercomputer systems, which are used vigorously for computations. My project focused on taking the job accounting data that was output by each machine and develop a central backbone that could be used to store it. In addition, I developed Java applications that would allow users of Blue Gene to have a much more intuitive and friendly job submission site. Finally, these applications also allowed the project managers to view statistics such as node usage, and node hour allocations.

Unsupervised Discovery of Motifs with Amplitude

Eric Drewniak, *Wheaton College*

We introduce an algorithm for unsupervised discovery of frequently occurring patterns in time series databases. Unlike prior approaches that can handle pattern distortion in the time dimension only, our algorithm is robust at finding pattern instances with amplitude shifting and with amplitude scaling. Using an established discretization method, SAX, we augment the existing real-valued time series representation with additional features to capture shifting and scaling. We point toward experimental results on synthetic and real-world data sets that demonstrate our improvement over the state-of-the-art algorithms.

Author Index

NOTES

www.ingramcontent.com/pod-product-compliance
Ingram Content Group UK Ltd.
Pitfield, Milton Keynes, MK11 3LW, UK
UKHW051417290926
15471UKWH00009B/1652

9 781605 588858